# KOBBÉ'S COMPLETE OPERA BOOK

EDITED AND REVISED BY

## THE EARL OF HAREWOOD

PUTNAM

LONDON & NEW YORK

ENGLISH EDITION

*First published October 1922*
*Reprinted May 1924*
*Reprinted June 1925*
*Reprinted June 1926*
*Reprinted August 1927*
*Reprinted March 1929*
*Reprinted July 1930*
*Reprinted October 1933*
*Reprinted May 1935*
*Reprinted March 1937*
*Reprinted September 1949*

*Revised Edition July 1954*
*Reprinted January 1956*
*Reprinted October 1958*


AMERICAN EDITION

*Copyright 1919, 1922, 1924*
*by C. W. Kobbé*

*Made and printed in Great Britain by William Clowes and Sons Ltd*
*London and Beccles*

# CONTENTS

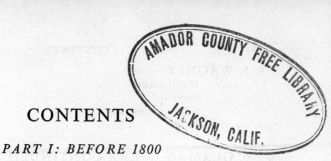

# PLATES

# PREFACE

GUSTAVE KOBBÉ was born in New York in 1857. He received his musical education in that city and at Wiesbaden, in Germany. He began his musical career as co-editor of the *Musical Review*, and in 1882 was sent as correspondent to Bayreuth by the *New York World* for the first performance of *Parsifal*. He contributed many articles on music to the leading American magazines of his day—*The Century, Scribners, The Forum, North American Review*, etc.—and became music critic of the *New York Herald* when that newspaper was owned by James Gordon Bennett, remaining with it for eighteen years. His hobby was sailing, and it was while he was out in the Great South Bay, Long Island, New York, in July 1918, that a seaplane, coming down for a landing, struck his boat and killed him instantly.

At the time he died, Kobbé was on the point of completing the book which was published after his death as *The Complete Opera Book*. Various additions to it were made before publication and also in subsequent editions with a view to fulfilling the claims of the title—although that must always be a virtual impossibility. The present edition has been more drastically revised. Kobbé's original scheme remains—that is to say, the composers are grouped under nationality and century so that some sort of rough historical continuity is preserved; but an attempt has been made to reflect some of the changes which have taken place in the repertory between 1918 and 1954. That such an attempt still cannot hope to achieve anything like a truly 'complete' collection will be only too obvious to the reader.

For this new edition, it soon became apparent that it would be impossible to deal with all the operas that people *might* see or hear; rather one had to include just those that assiduous enough opera-goers are virtually certain of meeting. Inevitably, this leaves gaps, most of all probably in the sphere of contemporary opera—here there seemed no alternative between a vast, comprehensive survey of everything, and the choice of a few of the most eligible works. The need to keep the book to manageable proportions was a potent argument, and we ended by picking only those works that seemed certain to be seen by English-speaking audiences during, say, the next ten or fifteen years.

In this revision, the synopsis of each opera is signed with an initial, 'K' standing for the material left by Mr. Kobbé; 'K. W' for the operas added after Kobbé's death by Katherine Wright, who put together the material left by him; 'F. B.' for Ferruccio Bonavia, who contributed additional material some years later; and 'H' for the present editor. As there has inevitably been some shift in the direction of opinion between 1918 and 1954, there seemed no longer any possibility of keeping contributions by pens other than Kobbé's without personal emphasis of any kind; but his example has been followed in the pattern of each essay and in stressing the inter-relationship of music and story. The lengths of synopses have been governed mainly by the complication of plot or musical structure in the individual operas, and they should not be taken as an indication of anybody's estimate of the relative values of the operas—the fact that Berg's *Wozzeck* has nearly twice as much space as Bellini's *Norma* does not imply that one is nearly twice as good as the other, any more than does a similar comparison between, say, *Otello* and *Götterdämmerung*.

What I have tried to do in those synopses I have added is to supply the reader with exactly the type of thing I looked for (and usually found) in Kobbé when I first started to listen extensively to opera. At school, I heard broadcasts from Covent Garden and Glyndebourne and the Continent, and sometimes did not know the stories of the works I was listening to. Kobbé was invaluable in giving one an idea of what to expect; but I remember my chagrin at finding that, for instance, *La Forza del Destino* had the barest of mentions—and it was small consolation, when this opera was being broadcast almost weekly from Italy, to know that it derived its exclusion from Kobbé to the accident that it was little known in America at the time the book was being written.

In the few instances where I have changed something that Kobbé wrote, that can usually be ascribed to the passage of time since his death. *Elektra* and *Salome*, for instance, are now in effect repertory operas, and can no longer be treated as newly erupted volcanoes. The same sort of thing applies to the oldest operas; works like Monteverdi's *Orfeo* were for all practical purposes unknown at the time of Kobbé's death, but are now recorded for the gramophone, and even to be heard not infrequently in performance by amateurs.

Perhaps this widening of the repertory—in itself a stimulating influence on one's operatic experience—is only a natural corollary of the one really melancholy feature of operatic life in the middle of the twentieth century: the decline of the interest, that was once automatic and widespread, in contemporary works. It is fair to say that this decline applies to music heard outside as well as inside the theatre; but if it is to continue logically, it must gradually eliminate the production of new works, and in the end bring about the extinction of the operatic form through its sheer inability to reproduce itself.

However, there is at present no reason why the opera-lover should despair—he can himself help to remedy this disturbing trend in contemporary musical life simply by interesting himself in new works as well as old. Most of the great operatic organisations emerged from the war of 1939–45 with undiminished vigour and, just as important, with undiminished, even increased, financial support. More and more, under every type of government and behind political curtains of every shade, the principle is accepted that government support in some form or other is essential to the arts in general, and to Opera most of all. It is true that financial stability does not lead to artistic perfection, and performances are ever far from ideal—but then, if history and the memoirs of devotees of the operatic art are to be believed, ever since opera began, the new generation has always been at the disadvantage of not having known the incomparable performances available to its predecessor.

So dismay at the prospect before us is not the keynote of this new edition, any more than it was of the original publication— nor can I believe that Gustave Kobbé would have had it otherwise.

Acknowledgements for the use of musical quotations where the scores are still under copyright are due to:

Messrs Boosey & Hawkes Limited (Rimsky-Korsakov, Strauss, Strawinsky, Prokoviev, Britten, Weinberger, Kodaly); Messrs Chappell & Co. Ltd (Granados); Messrs J. & W. Chester Ltd (Falla); Messrs. Durand & Cie (Ravel, Debussy); Messrs Heugel (Massenet, Charpentier); Novello & Co. Ltd (Rimsky-Korsakov); G. Ricordi & Co. Ltd (Boito, Puccini, Montemezzi,

Zandonai); Messrs Sonzogno (Leoncavallo, Giordano, Cilea, Mascagni); Messrs Stainer & Bell Ltd (Boughton); Messrs Universal Edition (Berg, Janacek); Messrs Joseph Weinberger Ltd (Ravel).

My thanks are due to Mr. Harold Rosenthal, who has provided the details of premières and performances recorded at the head of each opera.

March 1954                                    HAREWOOD

# PART I

# BEFORE 1800

# CHAPTER I

## *Opera Before Gluck*

# CLAUDIO MONTEVERDI

## (1567–1643)

OPERA is usually and conveniently said to have begun in 1600, the date of Peri's *Euridice*, the first surviving opera (his *Daphne*, 1597, has been lost). But before then, there was a good deal of stage music of one sort or another—Miracle plays and Mysteries, Moralities and Sacred Dramas, and, perhaps most important, Masques—and all these played their part in the complicated evolution of opera, a form which is itself to this day in a constant state of evolution.

At the end of the sixteenth century a small group of aristocratic intelligentsia, known collectively to musical history as 'the Camerata', was meeting in Florence. Under the auspices of a certain Count Giovanni Bardi di Vernio, and later of Jacopo Corsi, it included composers such as Vincenzo Galilei (father of the astronomer), Emilio de' Cavalieri, Jacopo Peri, and Giulio Caccini, and the avowed intention was to reproduce as far as possible the combination of words and music which together made up the Greek theatre. With this restorative aim in view, the members laid down that the text must at all times be understood, that the words must be sung with a scrupulously correct and natural declamation, and that above all the music must interpret the spirit of the whole, not concentrate on details of incidents and words or even individual syllables. In a word, taking the Greeks as their authorities, the composers and poets concerned were anxious to end the distortion of the words which was inevitable in polyphonic music; in its place they were instrumental in putting monody (or solo song) in something like the form we know to-day.

Claudio Monteverdi, already highly successful in polyphonic style, was the composer who was able to build on the foundations which had been laid by the Florentine 'Camerata' and his first opera, *Orfeo*, has been described by Professor Westrup as a landmark 'not because it broke new ground but because in it imagination took control of theory'. Opera was perhaps lucky that there should appear so soon a composer whose outlook was essentially dramatic, and certainly Monteverdi's *Orfeo* makes the *Euridice* of

Peri and Caccini (both set Rinuccini's libretto in the same year, 1600) appear pale and monotonous by comparison.

Monteverdi's working career is conveniently divided into two sections: during the first, 1590–1612, he was in the service of the Mantuan court and during the second, 1613–1643, he worked in Venice, as Maestro di Capella of San Marco and as a composer for the theatre. During the first period he wrote three of the twenty-one dramatic (or semi-dramatic) pieces to his credit (*Orfeo* and *Il Ballo delle Ingrate* survive complete, but only a few fragments of *Arianna* exist to-day); of the remaining eighteen, all but four have disappeared (*Tirsi e Clori*, a ballet-opera; *Il Combattimento di Tancredi e Clorinda*, a dramatic cantata; and the operas *Il Ritorno d'Ulisse in Patria* and *L'Incoronazione di Poppea* are the survivors).

The recent tendency is to regard Monteverdi not so much as a great revolutionary but as the culmination of a period of change, as the composer who was thoroughly at home in both the polyphonic and the monodic styles. Professor Westrup has compared him to Purcell as exemplifying the dual nature of the seventeenth-century composer, with his alternation of brilliance and pathos, and has suggested that it was his 'directness of approach' which so powerfully affected the men and women of his time.

## LA FAVOLA D'ORFEO

Opera in a prologue and five acts. Music by Claudio Monteverdi, text by Alessandro Striggio. First produced privately at the Accademia degl' Invaghiti, Mantua, February 1607, with Giovanni Gualberto as Orfeo, and on February 24 of the same year at the Court Theatre, Mantua. In August 1607 the opera was given in Monteverdi's native town of Cremona, and it is likely that there were stage productions in Turin, Florence, and Milan.

*Orfeo* was revived in 1904 in a concert version in Paris (arranged Vincent d'Indy); in 1909 in Milan and other Italian cities (arranged Giacomo Orefice); in 1910 in Brussels. The first modern stage performance was given at the Theatre Réjane, Paris, in 1911, in d'Indy's version.

The opera was first heard in America in concert form at the Metropolitan, New York, in 1912 (arranged Orefice), when Hermann Weil was Orfeo and the cast included Rita Fornia, Anna Case, and Herbert Witherspoon. In 1913 Chicago heard a concert version, conducted by Campanini and with Sammarco in the title role. There was a stage performance in Breslau in 1913 arranged by Erdmann-Guckel, and a new realisation by Carl Orff was heard at Mannheim in 1925. Malipiero's arrangement was first performed in Leningrad in 1929. The first American stage performance took place in 1929 at Northampton, Massachusetts, under the auspices of Smith College (in Malipiero's version) with Charles Kullman as Orfeo and Werner Josten conducting.

In England, the first performance (in concert form, arranged d'Indy) took place under the auspices of the Institut Français in 1924, and a stage version (arranged J. A. Westrup and W. H. Harris) was seen in Oxford in 1925 and in London in 1929. Recent Italian revivals have been at the Rome Opera, 1934 (arranged Benvenuti), with Franci (Orfeo), Gabriella Gatti, Giuseppina Cobelli, and Cloe Elmo, conductor Serafin; at la Scala, Milan, 1935 (arranged Respighi), under Marinuzzi and with Carlo Galeffi (Orfeo), Stignani, Carla Segrera, Palombini; at the Florence Festival, 1949 (arranged Frazzi), with Fedora Barbieri (Orfeo), Rizzieri, Corsi, and conducted Guarnieri. *Orfeo* was produced in Budapest in 1936 (in Respighi's version) and remained in the regular repertory for a number of years.

It is perhaps worth while to give a list [1] of the instruments called for at the beginning of Monteverdi's score of *Orfeo*, and of the additional ones mentioned in the inner pages of the score:

*Fundament instruments* (i.e. chord-playing)
2 clavicembalos
1 double harp (one more needed in performance?)
2 chitarrones (one more called for in score)
2 bass cithers (not listed but mentioned in score)
3 bass gambas
2 organs with wood (flute) pipes (*Organi di Legno*)
1 organ with reed pipes (*Regale*)

*Stringed instruments*
2 small violins (*alla Francese*)
10 viole da braccio (i.e. a string ensemble, possibly 4 violins, 4 violas, 2 violoncellos)
2 contrabass viols

*Wind instruments*
4 trombones (one more called for in score)
2 cornets
1 flautino alla Vigesima seconda (i.e. a high recorder; one more (?) called for in score)
1 high trumpet (*clarino*; possibly referring to use of high range of ordinary trumpet)
3 soft trumpets (*trombe sordine*)

It seems likely that many of the players doubled, and of course not all the instruments were used at once, apart that is to say from the opening *toccata*, some of the *sinfonie*, and the accompaniments of a few of the choruses. Monteverdi indicated what combination of instruments he required, and he used the contrast of orchestral colour for dramatic purposes.

[1] The list is quoted in Donald Grout's *A Short History of Opera* (O.U.P.).

The opera begins with a *toccata* in C major—'shattering', Redlich calls it—played three times by the whole orchestra before the rise of the curtain. The Prologue consists of a recitation by La Musica of her powers; there are five verses, composed on a bass, each introduced by a *ritornello* which is played for the sixth time after the last verse. The same *ritornello* recurs for the seventh and eighth times at the end of Act II and at the beginning of Act V. These *ritornelli* are employed throughout the opera to create appropriate atmosphere for the various scenes.

Act I.    Shepherds and Nymphs are rejoicing over the wedding of Orfeo and Euridice. The two Shepherds and the Nymph have solo verses in between the choruses, and Orfeo himself sings the first of his big solos, 'Rosa del ciel'. This is followed by a stanza for Euridice, and the choruses are repeated. The act ends with a beautiful chorus praying that their happy state may bring no misfortune on the lovers.

Act II is dominated by the great scene for the Messenger, and by Orfeo's lament, but it begins with a long, beautiful pastoral episode. Orfeo sings first, and his short solo is followed by a strophic song for the second Shepherd, and a duet for the two Shepherds; each of these has two verses, and each verse is preceded by its *ritornello*. The Shepherds have a third verse, which is preceded and followed by a different *ritornello*, and the scene is rounded off by a short chorus, in which the Shepherds beg Orfeo to sing. Orfeo sings a strophic song 'Vi ricordo o boschi ombrosi', each of the four verses being preceded by a *ritornello* played by five viole da braccio, one contrabass viol, two clavicembali, and three chitarroni. It is a simple, carefree aria, and perfectly establishes the mood of contentment and happiness which, after the Shepherd has praised Orfeo's song, is so suddenly broken by the advent of the Messenger with the news of Euridice's death. The unclouded happiness and serenity which have seemed to be Orfeo's have aroused the envy of the gods; the chorus is immediately apprehensive of the nature of the Messenger's errand and Orfeo alone is unaware of the approach of tragedy. 'Ahi, caso acerbo' sings the Messenger to a phrase which is later repeated by the Shepherds, and the chorus. The solo is one of great emotional and dramatic import, and the few phrases of dialogue with Orfeo at the beginning, ending with his stunned 'Ohimé', produce an extraordinary intensity by the simplest means. The Messenger's narration over, the first reaction of horror comes (to the words 'Ahi, caso acerbo') from the Shepherds. A moment later Orfeo (as if repeating the last words he heard, suggests Leo Schrade [1]) begins his lament, 'Tu se' morta, se' morta mia vita'. It is short, the feeling is restrained, even classical, but the evocative power of the music is unsurpassed, and the simplicity and passion of the ending 'A dio terra, a dio cielo, e Sole, a Dio', is most moving. The chorus and the Shepherds sing an elaborate threnody to the words 'Ahi, caso acerbo', and mourn the tragedies of Euridice bitten by the Serpent, and of Orfeo transfixed by grief.

Act III. In impressively solemn declamation, Orfeo is confronted by Hope. He resolves to seek Euridice in Hades. The use of trombones is a feature of the orchestration. Caron's sombre utterance is followed by Orfeo's attempt by means of his powers as a singer to gain admission to Hades. The song with its elaborate ornamentation is a great test of virtuosity, and, as if to emphasise this characteristic, each verse and *ritornello* has a different combination of instruments. It is perhaps surprising that Monteverdi should print an alternative and wholly simple version for the use, one supposes, of singers who were not able to do justice to the more elaborate writing. Caron admits that he has listened to the song with intense pleasure, but it is only after Orfeo has renewed his pleading in the simplest recitative that he yields; who could resist the rising semitones of the impassioned 'Rendetemi il mio ben, Tartarei Numi' with which he ends his plea? Preceded and followed by a solemn *sinfonia*, the act ends with a most lovely, madrigalesque chorus of Spirits.

Act IV. Proserpina and Pluto discuss Orfeo's plight, and, prompted by his wife and urged by the captive spirits singly and in chorus, the King of the Underworld agrees to release Euridice to her husband. Orfeo is triumphant but his song of rejoicing is interrupted as he looks back to see if Euridice is following. The spirits lament that her short-lived freedom should be snatched from her by her husband's transgression of Pluto's stipulation.

Act V. Orfeo, wandering on the plains of Thrace, laments his broken heart, and summons nature itself, which has so often benefited from his singing, to join him in his mourning. The *ritornello*, which begins the act, is the same as that used in the Prologue; during the course of the scene, Monteverdi makes use

[1] Leo Schrade: *Monteverdi* (Gollancz).

of an echo device. Apollo, Orfeo's father, descends from Heaven and tells his son that he will be translated to divine immortality, and amongst the stars will be able to see his Euridice again. Father and son ascend to Heaven singing together music full of coloratura ornament. The chorus sings its valediction in a gay 'Moresca'. (It should be noted that Striggio's original libretto brought the legend to an end in accordance with tradition, Orfeo being torn to pieces at a Bacchanalian orgy by the Thracian women, maddened by his unceasing laments for a woman he would not see again.)

'*Orfeo*,' says Professor Westrup,[1] 'is curiously representative of its time. We find in it the new recitative already practised by Peri and Caccini, the rhythmical subtlety of the French *chanson*, the traditional polyphony of motet and madrigal, the conventional practice of embellishing a vocal line with *fioriture*, the chromatic devices of the madrigal transferred to monody. . . . *Orfeo* is hardly an experimental work; it is rather a successful attempt to combine into a single whole the varied methods of musical expression current at the time.'          H.

## ARIANNA

Opera in a prologue and eight scenes, music by Monteverdi, text by Rinuccini. First performed at the Teatro della Corte, Mantua, May 28, 1608, as part of the festivities connected with the wedding of Francesco Gonzaga with Margareta di Savoia. Virginia Andreini was the original Arianna. The score is now lost, apart from the famous lament and a few other fragments, but stage revivals were presented at Karlsruhe in 1926, and in Paris 1931.

*Arianna* seems to have been enormously successful when first performed, and the great lament of Arianna, 'Lasciatemi morire', became immediately the most popular piece of music of the day. It began a long line of *lamenti*, and Monteverdi himself transformed it into a five-part madrigal (in 1610) and into a sacred 'Pianto della Madonna' (published 1640).          H.

[1] In his essay on the composer in *The Heritage of Music*, vol. III (O.U.P.).

## IL COMBATTIMENTO DI TANCREDI E CLORINDA

Dramatic cantata, music by Monteverdi, text by Tasso: verses 52–68 of Canto XII of *Gerusalemme liberata*.

*Il Combattimento* was published in 1638, fourteen years after it was written for performance in the Palazzo of Girolamo Mocenigo. In his introduction to the score, Monteverdi describes the first performance. After some madrigals had been sung as an introduction, Clorinda appeared, armed and on foot, followed by Tancredi, also armed but on a *Cavallo Mariano*. The Narrator began his song, and Clorinda and Tancredi acted, or danced, the story in a way suggested by the words. All details of expression were to be observed by singers, actors, and instrumentalists, and the action, half ballet, half acting, was strictly in time with the words and music. The Narrator is instructed to sing clearly and firmly and to articulate well; only in the stanza to Night can he employ decoration; for the rest, he must narrate *a similitudine delle passioni del' oratione*. At the end, says Monteverdi, the audience was moved to tears and applause at this new sort of entertainment.

Before the action begins, Tancredi, a Christian knight, has fallen in love with Clorinda, a Saracen maiden. She is a brave and skilful warrior and, dressed in man's armour, has assaulted and burnt, with one companion, a Christian fortification. As she is returning from this victory, she is seen and pursued by Tancredi. He thinks her a man and challenges her to mortal combat.

The Narrator (Testo), who remains outside the action but comments upon it, begins by announcing the theme of the story, and straight away we have, in 6/8 time, a representation of the horseback pursuit. Clorinda and Tancredi defy one another, and Tancredi dismounts for the combat. The Narrator begins his description of the phases of the fight, and before the *sinfonia* which introduces the Invocation of Night, we hear for the first time the string *tremolo*, or *stile concitato*, about which more later. The stanza in praise of Night is a beautiful inspiration; it gives way to a graphic account of the battle, whose musical phases change as often as the various stages of the duel. Not only does Monteverdi use the new device of rapidly repeated notes in the orchestra but he makes the Narrator imitate the device by setting some lines at breakneck speed.

In the middle of the battle, the combatants rest, and their exhaustion is faithfully reflected in the music. Tancredi says that whatever the issue he would like to know the name of his opponent, but Clorinda answers proudly that the warrior who opposes him is one of the two responsible for burning the Christian tower. The music is headed 'Guerra' as they return to fight with renewed zeal. Soon Clorinda is beaten and, transfixed by the sword of her opponent, falls dying at his feet. She forgives him, and asks him to mark his forgiveness of her by bestowing Christian baptism on her. He fetches water from a stream which runs nearby, raises her visor and in a moment of horror recognises that his opponent was the Saracen maid he loved so well. He baptises her, and as he does so, she sings a last, rising phrase in which one can feel her soul leaving her earthly body for the heaven which she can see open to receive it: 'S'apre il ciel; io vado in pace.'

In his preface Monteverdi recognises three principal human passions: wrath (*Ira*), temperance (*Temperanza*), and humility or prayer (*Humiltà* or *supplicazione*). Music, he says, has represented the soft, *molle*, and the temperate, but not the *concitato*, the excited. By means of his invention of the string *tremolo* and by applying it to an appropriate text, he hopes to remedy this defect; with the new device is associated for the first time the string *pizzicato*, like the *tremolo* a commonplace to-day.

The opera is scored for quartet of strings (written out in full) supported by contrabass and harpsichord, and it is in Monteverdi's invention for this combination of sound to fit action that the unique quality of this fascinating work lies.                    H.

## IL RITORNO D'ULISSE IN PATRIA

Opera in a prologue and five acts, text by G. Badoaro. First performed in Venice, February 1641. Some doubt has been cast on the authenticity of the ascription to Monteverdi since the score was first published in Vienna in 1923. However, agreement by now seems fairly general that the music is in fact by Monteverdi, and Luigi Dallapiccola, the Italian composer who was responsible for the opera's most recent arrangement (1942), does not hesitate to describe the work as a masterpiece. The opera was revived in concert form in Brussels 1925 (fragments only); in Paris (arranged by d'Indy) in 1925 and 1927; and it was broadcast from London in 1928 (in d'Indy's arrangement, English version by D. Millar Craig). The opera was performed on the stage in Dallapiccola's arrangement Florence Festival, 1942, conducted by Mario

Rossi and with Jolanda Magnoni, Cloe Elmo, Fedora Barbieri, Giovanni Voyer, and Tancredi Pasero; at la Scala, Milan, 1943, with virtually the same cast.

## CHARACTERS

| | | |
|---|---|---|
| Giove | .......................................... | Tenor |
| Nettuno | ............................... | Basso profondo |
| Minerva | ...................................... | Soprano |
| Ulisse | ........................................ | Tenor |
| Penelope, *wife of Ulisse* | ....................... | Contralto |
| Telemaco, *son of Ulisse* | .................. | Mezzo-soprano |
| Antinoo | | ........Basso profondo |
| Pisandro { *Penelope's suitors* } | | ...............Tenor |
| Anfinomo | | ...............Tenor |
| Eurimaco, *lover of Melanto* | ....................... | Tenor |
| Melanto, *Penelope's attendant* | ............ | Mezzo-soprano |
| Eumete, *Ulisse's swineherd* | ...................... | Tenor |
| Iro, *Jester of the suitors* | ..................... | Buffo tenor |
| Ericlea, *Penelope's nurse* | ................. | Mezzo-soprano |

The above distribution is that required for Dallapiccola's arrangement of the score; in d'Indy's version, Ulisse, Eurimaco, and Anfinomo were baritones, Telemaco a tenor, and Penelope herself a soprano. In both versions, Monteverdi's five acts are reduced to three (as they are in the Vienna MS. of the score), and this arrangement is being followed in the description which follows.

Act I. (In Dallapiccola's edition, as in d'Indy's, the prologue, with its allegorical figures—Human Fragility, Time, Fortune, Love—is omitted.) The curtain rises on a room in the royal palace. Penelope, Ulisse's wife, is attended by her nurse, Ericlea, as she bemoans her state of loneliness with her husband still not returned from the war. It is a magnificent lament, proof in its own right that *Ulisse* is by the composer of the *Arianna* lament, say its admirers; 'Torna, torna, deh torna Ulisse' is its poignant refrain. A duet follows between the amorous Melanto and her lover Eurimaco.

The second scene is a discussion between Jove and Neptune on the subject of the gods' punishment of men's sins. The scene changes, and we are with Ulisse on board a Phaeacian ship off the coast of Ithaca. The Phaeacians lay the sleeping Ulisse on the shore. He wakes up, thinks he has been deposited in an unknown land, and laments the fate to whose devices for keeping him from his native country there appears to be no end. Ulisse's lament is not so highly organised as Penelope's in the first scene, but it is one of the most effective moments in the opera. There follows a long scene between Ulisse and Minerva, who appears disguised as a shepherd to comfort Ulisse and spur him on to return home to his wife and his throne. Ulisse eventually recognises Minerva, who tells him that he shall not be recognised by anyone—she will disguise him—but shall return home to rout the suitors who have taken possession of his palace. The scene ends with Ulisse rejoicing at the turn in his fortunes: 'O fortunato Ulisse'.

Act II.     Eumete, Ulisse's old herdsman, is discovered alone. He sings of the contrast between his own contented lot and that of princes, who have possessions but often no happiness. The ridiculous Iro breaks in on his reverie, and smacks his lips over the pampered life *he* leads, contrasting the shepherd's life unfavourably with it. Eumete sends him about his business: 'Corri, corri a mangiar, a crepar' (Haste thee, go and eat, stuff thyself). Ulisse comes in and hears Eumete lament his master's absence; he tells him that Ulisse will not fail his country, and the two go off together, Eumete full of joy at the prospect of Ulisse's return, Ulisse no less happy at having found a guide.

The scene changes to Telemaco's ship, where Telemaco rejoices at the voyage and, joined by Minerva, at the favourable wind. Again there is a change of scene, this time to the grove in which we originally found Eumete. Minerva cautions Telemaco against disregarding her advice now that he is safely landed in his native country. Eumete recognises him and greets him, saying that the old man he has with him (in reality Telemaco's father but not known to either of them) has encouraged him to think Ulisse himself may be on his way to Ithaca. There is a short duet for Ulisse and Eumete on the subject of hope, and Telemaco bids Eumete go to the Queen and warn her that her son has come home to her, and that moreover she should not give up hope of seeing Ulisse himself. No sooner has he gone than Ulisse changes into his own shape and reveals himself to his son. There is a rapturous duet of rejoicing for father and son and the scene ends with Ulisse telling his son to go to Penelope and warn her that Ulisse himself will return before long.

We are in the palace of Penelope, where she is surrounded by her suitors. They beg her, first together then singly, to return their love, but she will have none of them. Into the palace rushes Eumete, bringing the news that Ulisse may be amongst them before long. Penelope leaves the four suitors together, and they agree that come what may they must press their claims on the Queen before it is too late.

Act III.    The Palace. Antinoo mocks the poor beggar (in reality Ulisse), who should, he says, be with Eumete looking after the hogs, not in the palace watching them sup. Iro joins in, stuttering as usual (he is Vasek's forerunner), but is challenged to a wrestling match by Ulisse, and soundly beaten. Penelope compliments the old man on his victory. In a moment the other suitors return to her, and she consents to set them a test: the one who can draw Ulisse's bow shall become her husband. Each in turn fails, but Ulisse asks to be allowed to try his strength; he renounces the prize, and says he is anxious only to join in the trial. He draws the bow, amidst exclamations of surprise from the bystanders; then, to the accompaniment of war-like music, transfixes each of the suitors in turn with an arrow. His triumph is complete.

Iro is found alone. His aria, marked *parte ridicola*, is a masterpiece of parody, with the elevated style Monteverdi had done so much to establish as its object. Even the *ciacona* bass of his own madrigal, 'Zefiro torna', is pressed into service to do justice to the spectacle of Iro lamenting the horror which has come upon him: now that all his patrons are dead, he has an empty belly. He can think of no solution to the difficulty of filling it, and resolves on suicide.

Telemaco and Eumete try to convince Penelope that the old man who successfully drew the bow was Ulisse himself, but even the appearance of her husband in his proper form does not convince her that she is not still the victim of a cruel deception. It is not until Ericlea affirms that she has recognised him by the scar on his shoulder that Penelope allows caution to be replaced by love. Penelope rejoices in an aria before she and Ulisse join in a final duet to celebrate their re-uniting.            H.

# HENRY PURCELL

## (1658–1695)

### DIDO AND AENEAS

O PERA in a prologue and three acts by Henry Purcell, text by Nahum Tate. Première at Mr. Josiah Priest's Boarding School for Girls, Chelsea, London, 1689. Revived by the Royal College of Music under Stanford at the Lyceum Theatre, London, 1895; at the Scala Theatre, London, 1929; at Sadler's Wells, 1931, with Joan Cross, Sumner Austin, and Frances Geraldi; at the Florence Festival, 1940, conducted by Vittorio Gui with Gianna Pederzini, Ettore Parmeggiani, Dolores Ottani, and Edmea Limberti; at Teatro dell' Opera, Rome, 1949, with Giulietta Simionato and Mario Borriello, conducted by Santini and with sets by Clerici. The 1951 Festival of Britain brought three productions in London: at the Lyric Theatre, Hammersmith, by the English Opera Group in Benjamin Britten's new realisation, with Nancy Evans and Bruce Boyce (later Joan Cross and Peter Pears); at Sadler's Wells, with Eleanor Houston and John Probyn; at the Mermaid Theatre, London, with Kirsten Flagstad and Thomas Hemsley. *Dido* is frequently performed in England by amateur operatic societies.

The prologue, which is included in the libretto, appears never to have been set by Purcell, or, at all events, to have been lost.

The overture has the traditional slow and quick sections, and is unmistakably tragic in feeling.

Act I. Dido is discovered surrounded by her court and attended by her lady-in-waiting, Belinda. Belinda's exhortation, 'Shake the cloud from off your brow', is echoed by the chorus, and is in sharp contrast with the grief-laden aria for Dido which follows, 'Ah, Belinda, I am prest with torment'. This is a magnificent expression of sorrow, dignified and restrained as befits the Queen of Carthage, but worthy of the tragedy it foreshadows and at no point belying the conflict implied in its final words: 'Peace and I are strangers grown'. Belinda does not hesitate to diagnose that it is the presence of the 'Trojan guest' which is at the root of the Queen's unhappiness, and the chorus supports her implied suggestion, that a marriage between the two would solve Carthage's troubles. In the dialogue between Dido and Belinda, which ensues, we have a taste of Purcell's extraordinary gift for compressing the most complex emotions into a few bars, and then relieving the tension and crystallising the situation in a set piece for chorus (in this case a *chaconne*) here introduced by a duet for

PLATE I. *L'Incoronazione di Poppea* by Monteverdi, la Scala, Milan 1952. Setting by Gianni Ratto.

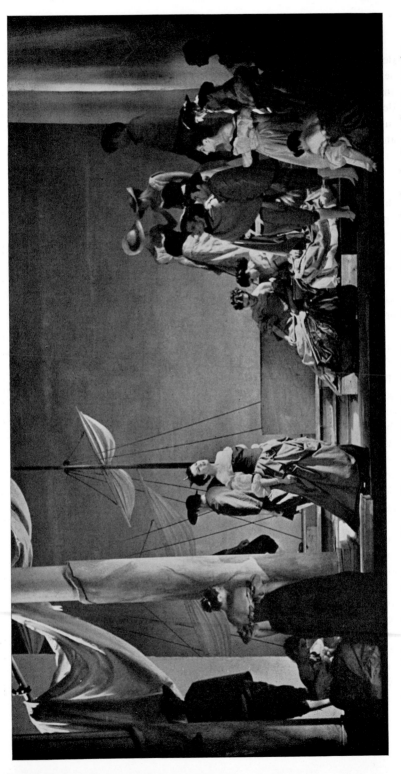

PLATE II. *Dido and Aeneas*: Nancy Evans as Dido, English Opera Group 1951. Production by Joan Cross, sets by Sophie Fedorovitch.

Belinda and an Attendant. Again, her court attempts to encourage her—'the hero loves as well as you'—and, after Aeneas's entrance and Dido's cold reply to his opening sentence, the chorus, then Belinda, and finally the chorus again support his suit in music of surpassing freshness. The scene ends with a Triumphing Dance, and Dido's acceptance of Aeneas is celebrated by the whole court to gay and simple music.

This opening scene is short, but Purcell does not rely on understatement and implication so much as on an extraordinary clarity and economy of expression. He says more in a couple of long meaningful phrases than many a lesser composer in a whole aria, and his compression never for a moment gives the listener the feeling either that the music is over-charged with emotional content or that the issues have been no more than partially stated. Every shade of feeling is there, though it may require more than usual interpretative insight and musical accuracy if it is to be brought out to the full.

The scene changes to a cave, where lives the Sorceress. She invokes her evil companions to join her in plotting the destruction of Dido and of Carthage. The whole scene, with its laughing choruses, its reference (in the strings) to the horn calls of the hunt now in progress, its echo chorus and its echo dance (phrase and echo are differently harmonised), amounts to an illustration of the insidious beauty of movement which can attend the course of evil just as surely as that of good.

Act II. The Grove. Dido and Aeneas, attended by Belinda and their train, pause in the grove in the middle of the hunt. Belinda and the chorus and later the Second Woman sing of the peculiar delights of the spot they have reached, of its attractions for the goddess Diana and of how it was the scene of Actaeon's death, torn to pieces by his own hounds. Meanwhile, the scene is one of activity, a picnic maybe in progress, the attendants moving about, some trophies of the chase carried on, and in the midst of all, Dido and her husband-to-be, Aeneas. The idyll comes to an end as Dido hears the distant thunder, and Belinda, always ready to take a hint from her mistress, warns the company to repair as soon as it can to shelter; 'Haste, haste to town,' she sings to a rapid, decorated tune which will show up any technical deficiencies in the singer of this role. All leave the stage, but Aeneas is stopped by the appearance of the spirit of Mercury—in reality, the Sorceress's 'trusty elf' in disguise. He tells Aeneas that he brings Jove's command that the hero shall put off no longer the task which has been allotted him of founding the new Troy on Latin soil. Aeneas replies in a magnificent recitative—one of the high lights of the score. The decision is easily arrived at—it is the gods' command—but to reconcile himself to leaving Dido is something than which, he says, he 'with more ease could die'.

The published versions of the score make Act II end with this recitative, although the oldest version of the libretto has six further lines after the recitative (for the Sorceress and her Attendants) as well as a dance with which to end the act. When his new realisation of the opera was produced during the Festival of Britain, 1951, Benjamin Britten wrote as follows: 'Anyone who has taken part in, or indeed heard a concert or stage performance, must have been struck by the very peculiar and most unsatisfactory end of this Act II as it stands; Aeneas sings his very beautiful recitative in A minor and disappears without any curtain music or chorus (such as occurs in all the other acts). The drama cries out for some strong dramatic music, and the whole key system of the opera (very carefully adhered to in each of the other scenes) demands a return to the key of the beginning of the act or its relative major (D minor or F major). What is more, the contemporary printed libretto (a copy of which is preserved in the library of the Royal College of Music) has perfectly clear indications for a scene with the Sorceress and her Enchantresses, consisting of six lines of verse, and a dance to end the act. It is my considered opinion that music was certainly composed to this scene and has been lost . . . and so I have supplied other music of Purcell's to fit the six lines of the libretto, and a dance to end in the appropriate key.' A proof of the suitable nature of what he chose was its success in performance during 1951, and there was appropriateness in the added emphasis this threw on Purcell's careful key scheme as a means of obtaining musical unity and contrast for his opera.

Act III.    The scene is set in the harbour of Carthage, with the ships as background. All is preparation for the Trojan fleet's departure, and the orchestra introduces the sailor's song: 'Come away, fellow sailors, come away'. The tune is briskly compelling, the words cynical, as the singer urges his companions to 'take a boozy short leave of your nymphs on the shore'. The chorus repeats the tune after him, and follows it up with a hearty dance. Suddenly, the Sorceress is there with her supernatural band, and the first and second Witches sing a lively duet, whose burden is 'Our plot has took, the Queen's forsook' and which ends with peels of highly organised demoniac laughter. The Sorceress has a short solo in which she plans the destruction of Aeneas as well, and the chorus (whether it consists entirely of supernatural elements or includes some sailors and dockside riff-raff as well is not made clear) underlines her intentions. There is a dance in three sections for the Witches and Sailors, and the stage clears as Dido and Belinda come down to the harbour to look for Aeneas.

Dido is full of foreboding before Aeneas even appears, and his first words confirm her worst fears. With 'Thus on the fatal banks of Nile weeps the deceitful crocodile' she taunts his attempt at explanation, and, when he announces his determination to defy the gods and stay, she will have none of a lover who had once a thought of leaving her. 'Away, away,' she reiterates at the end of their duet; and it is not until his departure that she admits 'Death must come when he is gone'. The chorus sums up the gravity of the situation and prepares the way for Dido's great farewell to life. The recitative is movingly simple, and the aria, 'When I am laid in earth', one of the greatest moments in all opera. Built up on a ground bass,[1] which is first heard as the introduction to the aria after the end of the recitative, this is a piece of controlled vocal writing that is unsurpassed. 'Remember me,' sings the Queen, 'but ah! forget my fate'; and the sense of deep tragedy is increased rather than diminished by the succeeding chorus, 'With drooping wings, ye cupids come, and scatter roses on her tomb'. It is the longest sustained number in the score, and in it Purcell shifts the emphasis of the tragedy from the particular to the universal at the same time as he provides a uniquely beautiful ending to his opera.

Purcell wrote much other music for the stage, but *Dido and Aeneas* must be accounted his only opera proper. *King Arthur* and *The Fairy Queen*, the former with words by Dryden, the latter founded on *A Midsummer Night's Dream*, are included by Dr. Alfred Loewenberg in his monumental *Annals of Opera*; but

---

[1] In each act there is an aria constructed on this principle: Dido's 'Ah, Belinda' in Act I, the Attendant's 'Oft she visits' in Act II, and Dido's lament in Act III.

though they contain magnificent music, this is more in the nature of incidental music to a play than of opera, although the masques in these, and other works (such as *The Tempest*) offered Purcell a chance for writing in more extended forms. As a writer for the voice, Purcell was supreme, and his output includes an enormous quantity of songs, many of them connected with the stage, and all of the greatest beauty. His great mastery is universally admitted, and many of the most gifted of the contemporary English composers are glad to acknowledge their indebtedness to him not only for his inspiration and example but also for the practical lessons they have learned from his music. It is opera's eternal loss that *Dido* should be the only true opera he has left behind him; the feeling for dramatic expression, which it shows to have been his, only emphasises what was removed by his death when he was still less than forty years old.                      H.

# THE BEGGAR'S OPERA

**B**ALLAD opera in three acts; words by John Gay, music collected and arranged by Pepusch. Première, Lincoln's Inn Fields, February 9, 1728, with John Beard as Macheath and Lavinia Fenton (later Duchess of Bolton) as Polly. First performed Covent Garden, 1732; New York, 1750. Revived at Covent Garden in an abridged, two-act version in 1813 with Miss Stephens, Mrs. Davenport, Incledon; 1878, with Sims Reeves as Macheath. In a new version by Frederick Austin, revived Lyric, Hammersmith, 1920, where it ran for 1,463 consecutive nights, with Frederick Ranalow as Macheath, Sylvia Nelis, and Frederick Austin; revived there 1925, 1926, 1928, 1929, 1930; at Criterion Theatre, London, 1935; at Brighton, 1940 (under Glyndebourne auspices), with Mildmay, Michael Redgrave, Roy Henderson. New version by Benjamin Britten produced Cambridge, 1948, and subsequently at Sadler's Wells, with Nancy Evans, Rose Hill, Peter Pears, Otakar Kraus, conductor Britten; Vienna, 1949, with Rohs, Funk, Liewehr, conductor Zallinger; Hamburg, 1950, with Enck, Rothenberger, Schütte, conductor Schmidt-Isserstedt.

## CHARACTERS

| | |
|---|---|
| Beggar | Speaking Role |
| Mrs. Peachum | Mezzo-Soprano |
| Mr. Peachum, *a 'fence'* | Bass |
| Polly, *their daughter* | Soprano |
| Captain Macheath, *a highwayman* | Tenor |
| Filch, *in Peachum's employment* | Tenor |
| Lockit, *the gaoler* | Baritone |
| Lucy Lockit, *his daughter* | Soprano |

| | | |
|---|---|---|
| Mrs. Vixen<br>Suky Tawdry<br>Mrs. Coaxer<br>Dolly Trull<br>Mrs. Slammekin<br>Molly Brazen<br>Jenny Diver<br>Betty Doxy | *ladies of the town* | Sopranos, Mezzos, and Contraltos |
| Harry Paddington<br>Ben Budge<br>Wat Dreary<br>Mat of the Mint<br>Jemmy Twitcher<br>Nimming Ned | *gentlemen of the road* | Tenors, Baritone, and Basses |

| | |
|---|---|
| Mrs. Trapes, *the 'tally woman'* | Mezzo-Soprano |

*Time:* Early Eighteenth Century          *Place:* London

Opera in the early part of the eighteenth century meant, for England as for the rest of Europe, Italian opera. Such works as Clayton's *Rosamond* (with libretto by Addison) were freaks, and more important, failures as well. It was not until 1728 that an English opera that may be said to have been a popular success was written, and then, ironically enough, some of the tunes were taken from Italian-operatic and French sources. *The Beggar's Opera* is a ballad opera—earlier examples of the type were Allan Ramsay's pastoral play *The Gentle Shepherd* (revived at the Edinburgh Festival in 1949), and, according to Burney, Durfey's *Wonders in the Sun*. The music is a compilation of tunes drawn from every imaginable source—contemporary opera, ballads, and folk songs—and arranged so as to form a whole connected by dialogue. The arrangers did the same with 'serious' music as is done to-day by those who collect the music for a Christmas pantomime; everything is laid under contribution, provided only that it is tuneful and popular.

The origin of this particular ballad opera is thought to have been in Swift's often-quoted remark to Gay: 'A Newgate Pastoral might make an odd, pretty sort of thing.' The opera aims partly at satire, partly at parody. Fun is poked at the fashionable opera of the day: '. . . I have a Prison-scene, which the Ladies always reckon charmingly pathetic. As to the parts, I have observed such a nice impartiality to our two Ladies, that it is impossible for either of them to take offence. . . . I hope I may be forgiven, that I have not made my Opera throughout unnatural, like those in vogue; for I have no recitative.' There is also political and social satire, aimed at the Prime Minister, Sir Robert Walpole, and everyone in a position of authority and able to give and to receive bribes. Corruption in all its forms is the stuff out of which the dramatic side of the opera is made.

The success of *The Beggar's Opera* was a serious blow to the prestige and the financial standing of the Italian opera, at whose head was Handel; it also of course made the fortunes of those connected with it. As the wits of the time had it, 'it made Rich gay, and Gay rich' (Rich was the manager of the Lincoln's Inn Fields Theatre and later of Covent Garden). Its success was such that the objects of its political satire were seriously worried at the effect it made, and the sequel, *Polly* (1729), was in fact banned and did not reach the stage until 1777 (although Gay made a good deal of money out of the sale of copies). *The Beggar's Opera* did not lack imitators, quite apart from its author's own sequel, but none of them has succeeded in holding public interest to anything like the extent of the original. This seems to have retained a flavour of its own long after the topical allusions have receded to nothing, and it has inspired composers of the twentieth century to attempt forms of modernisation, working from the assumption that the satire and the tunes are so strong in themselves, that they only need to be dressed in suitable clothing for the audience to react to them as enthusiastically as the original spectators did in 1728.

To a great extent, this contention has been borne out in practice. Austin's arrangement of the tunes (he himself was a well-known singer and played Peachum) took London by storm in 1920 and ran for two and a half years. It concentrated on pointing up the undeniable prettiness of the tunes, and provided them with a pretty framework that was distinctly at odds with the satirical intentions of the eighteenth century. Quite different but no less successful was Kurt Weill's adaptation (*Die Dreigroschenoper*) which appeared in Berlin two hundred years plus a few months after the original had been first heard in London. Weill used hardly any of the old tunes, and his librettist, Bert Brecht, modernised the setting to conform with the jazz idiom of Weill's music. No German who was in Berlin at the end of the nineteen-twenties seems to have escaped the spell of this curious piece, which was hardly less influential than had been Gay's opera in its own day.

The most recent composer to have been inspired by the old ballad opera is Benjamin Britten. He kept more of the original melodies than Austin (sixty-six out of sixty-nine), dispensed with the 'pretty' introductions and postludes, and re-set the tunes with the aim of producing something like the same effect in 1948 as they had done in 1728. He was anxious to rediscover something of the original contrast between the sweetness of the tunes and the bitterness of the words; it was with this in mind that he made his setting, and that the production purposely emphasised the sordid side of the eighteenth century, not its airs and graces. This re-creation is in its way a masterpiece.

There is a Prologue, spoken by a Beggar and a Player, and explaining that the piece is written 'for the celebrating the marriage of James Chaunter and Moll Lay, two most excellent Ballad-Singers'.

Act I.   The curtain goes up to reveal a room in Peachum's house; the owner is sitting at a table, before a book of accounts. He sings 'Through all the employments of life, Each Neighbour abuses his brother'. Filch comes in to report on the fates of various members of Peachum's gang, who are up before the courts. He sings the smoothly-flowing ''Tis Woman that seduces all mankind', before being sent off to deliver Peachum's messages to the various prisoners.

Peachum goes through a register of his gang, commenting on the earning (i.e. pick-pocket) capacities of each. Some, he thinks, he will give up at the next sessions and take the money offered for their apprehension. He reaches the name of Bob Booty, when his wife interrupts to enquire why he should mention that name; women, she admits, are notoriously bad judges of a man, whom they love primarily for his courage: 'If any wench Venus' girdle wear.' They exchange words on the subject of murder, a crime Mrs. Peachum seems to fancy less than her husband, and fall to talking about Captain Macheath. It appears that Polly, their daughter, 'thinks him a very pretty man'. 'If love the virgin's heart invade', sings Mrs. Peachum; if she does not marry, 'she's —what I dare not name'. But Peachum is still worried: '. . . I would indulge the girl as far as prudently we can. In anything, but marriage.' Leaving his wife to take the coronets out of some handkerchiefs, he goes off to 'terrify her from it, by the example of our neighbours'.

Mrs. Peachum is philosophical—'Why must Polly's marriage, contrary to all observations, make her the less followed by other men?'—and she sings 'A maid is like the golden ore'. Filch comes in; Mrs. Peachum owns herself very partial to his company, but questions him on the relations of Captain Macheath and Polly. He seems embarrassed, and she takes him off to tell her more in private.

Enter Polly and her father. She urges her ability to look after herself, 'Virgins are like the fair flower in its lustre'. Peachum utters a stern warning against her marrying, when 'enter Mrs. Peachum, in a very great passion'. She has found out the worst; 'Our Polly is a sad slut' she sings in her fury, and proclaims for all to hear that Polly has got herself married. 'Can Love be con-

trol'd by advice?' asks Polly, but Mrs. Peachum in a delicious
tune objects, 'O Polly, you might have toy'd and kiss'd'. Polly
tries to keep her end up ('I, like a ship in storms, was tossed'),
but is sent off to deal with customers in the front room. When
she has gone, Peachum and his wife plot to turn the whole affair
to their advantage, not forgetting that a lawyer may get his hands
into the business and take all profit out of it: 'A fox may steal
your hens, sir'. Polly returns and is told she must straight away
make plans to become a widow; in a word, Macheath must be
delivered up to the law in time for the next session! 'O ponder
well! be not severe', objects Polly; as a widow, she would cry
her heart out: 'The turtle thus with plaintive crying'.

Polly goes, but hides to hear her parents continue their plot,
which even gets to the stage when the Old Bailey is mentioned.
She is in despair, but the scene changes and she is shown with
Macheath; they sing a love duet:

> 'Pretty Polly, say
> When I was away
> Did your fancy never stray
> To some newer lover?'

Macheath protests his own constancy: 'My heart was so free, It
rov'd like the Bee, 'Till Polly my passion requited', and they
swear mutual adoration in 'Were I laid on Greenland's coast',
with its refrain of 'Over the hills and far away'. But Polly remembers that Macheath's life is not now safe; her father is plotting
against him. 'Oh what pain it is to part' she sings. Their love
scene reaches its climax with 'The miser thus a shilling sees', a
superb and entirely appropriate ending which is unaccountably
omitted from Austin's published score.

The scene changes to a Tavern near Newgate. Macheath's gang
discuss their profession and its hazards, but forget their sorrows

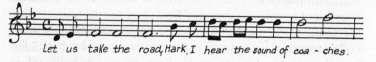

Let us take the road, Hark, I hear the sound of coa - ches.

in a drink: 'Fill every glass'. Macheath comes to tell them that
he cannot go with them that night, owing to his 'difference' with
Peachum. He wishes them luck and they go off singing 'Let

us take the road', to the tune of the march from Handel's *Rinaldo*.

Macheath, alone, muses on the delights to be had from women —he is emphatic about the plural. His romance, 'If the heart of a man', is set to one of the most delicious tunes of the whole score. He does not have to wait long; the women of the town begin to arrive in answer to his invitations previously sent out. He welcomes them and leads them in a dance, 'Youth's the season made for joys'. After some dalliance, Jenny Diver sings suggestively 'Before the Barn-door crowing', and, while the ladies sing 'The gamesters and lawyers are jugglers alike', manages to secure one of his pistols, Suky Tawdry getting hold of the other. They signal to Peachum, who is waiting outside, and he comes in with constables and arrests the Captain. Macheath turns furiously on the women ('At the tree I shall suffer with pleasure'), and is led away, leaving them to dispute about the division of the reward for their work.

The scene changes to Newgate Gaol. Macheath is received by the sinister Lockit, who reminds him that nothing can be had in prison free of charge; 'garnish' is the custom. Macheath is left alone, and reflects that it is Woman that has brought him to his present condition: 'Man may escape from rope and gun'. The tune marvellously combines the lyrical with the dramatic.

Man may escape from rope and gun, nay some have outlived the doctor's pill

Enter Lucy, daughter of Lockit. She loses no time in referring to the 'load of infamy' which she carries, and does not hesitate to blame her pregnancy on Macheath. Revenge is what she is after, she tells him, 'Thus when a good housewife sees a rat'. Macheath pleads with her, and refers to himself as her husband. Lucy is not so quickly taken in ('How cruel are the traitors'), but Macheath works on her to good purpose, and explains away Polly's report of their marriage as mere vanity on her part: 'The first time at the looking-glass'. Lucy takes Macheath off in search of the priest attached to the prison.

Enter Peachum and Lockit, intent on the record of their mutual transactions. Working for the law and at the same time helping to organise crime, they are in a position to make the best of both worlds. Peachum refers openly to the betrayal of friends, and Lockit cautions him to be more careful in his use of words: 'When you censure the age'. Peachum goes further, and questions Lockit's honest dealing. There is a row and the two men are at each other's throats until more moderate counsels prevail, and Peachum eventually leaves with them in seeming agreement.

It is Lucy's turn to have a disagreement with her father; she begs for mercy for Macheath: 'Is then his fate decreed, sir?' Lockit rejoins with rough comfort—be grateful for release, like other widows, 'You'll think ere many days ensue' (Britten combines the two tunes in an effective duet). Macheath rejoins Lucy, and speculates on his chance of bribing his way out of prison: 'If you at an office solicit your due'. Lucy promises to do what she can to help him—but at that moment Polly herself appears and throws herself about Macheath's neck—'my dear husband'. Seeing him thus languishing she makes an ornithological comparison: 'Thus when the swallow seeking prey'.

Macheath's situation seems desperate: 'How happy could I be with either, Were t'other dear charmer away!' he sings in one of the best known airs of the opera. The two 'wives' come back at him with a duet, 'I'm bubbled. I'm bubbled. O how I am troubled'. (Britten follows the air with the duet and combines the two to make a trio.) Things look black for Macheath, but at last the two women begin to take notice of one another. Polly addresses Lucy, 'Cease your funning', and presently they have at one another, 'Why how now, Madam Flirt'. Peachum enters in search of Polly, but she resists his efforts to take her away: 'No power on earth can e'er divide', set to the *Irish Howl*.

No pow'r on earth can e'er di-vide the knot which sa-cred love hath tied.

Peachum eventually prises her away from Macheath, and it is left to Lucy, after comparing herself to a fox's mate ('I like the fox shall grieve'), to release him from his chains and guide him from the prison.

(Both Austin and Britten have omitted the short final scene for Lucy and Macheath, and have taken the eminently suitable tune of 'No power on earth', set it as an ensemble, and used it as a finale.)

Act III takes us again to Newgate, where Lockit is admonishing Lucy for her part in Macheath's escape. She explains that it was not through bribes but from love that she was impelled to help him, and blames Lockit for teaching her to be promiscuous with her kisses—Macheath's naturally tasted so sweet after what she had been through that she lost her heart to him: 'When young at the bar' (the tune is Purcell's). Her mood changes from one of regret for her lost lover to one of recrimination, 'My love is all madness and folly', and Lockit sends her out to repent where he cannot hear her caterwauling. He sums up the whole matter; Peachum is evidently trying to outwit him in the affair of the Captain, and he must at all costs get even with him. 'Of all animals of prey', he reflects, 'Man is the only sociable one.' The aria, 'Thus gamesters united in friendship are found', is bitingly satirical, and in Britten's setting makes a tremendous effect.

The scene changes to a gaming-house, where are assembled ladies and gentlemen, together with Macheath, who there meets Ben Budge and Matt of the Mint, and gives them money. They discuss their affairs, but the scene is dominated by the singing of 'The modes of the court so common are grown', set to the magnificent tune of *Lillibullero*.

Peachum's House. Peachum and Lockit arc again making an attempt to arrive at a settlement of their intricate accounts. They give it up and fall to drinking, agreeing at the same time that it will not be long before Macheath is in their hands again, if they keep a careful watch on Polly: 'What gudgeons are we men'. Mrs. Diana Trapes calls on them, and, before getting down to the business of her visit, toasts them in a fascinating tune, 'In the days of my youth I could bill like a dove'. They join in the refrain. She has come, she says, to see what they have got for her in the way of 'Blacks of any kind. . . . Mantoes—velvet scarfs —petticoats . . . '. In the course of conversation she lets on that she has seen Captain Macheath that very day. Immediately they are all over her, and bid her name her own price for the goods, provided she lead them to the Captain forthwith.

The scene returns to Newgate. Lucy, although still bemoaning her fate ('I'm like a skiff on the ocean tossed'), is planning to even her account with Miss Polly Peachum, whom she is expecting and against whose coming she has the rat's-bane handy. Polly is announced by Filch, and Lucy receives her graciously: 'When a wife's in her pout'. She tries to get her to drink the gin she pours out, but nothing will induce Polly to let a drop pass her lips. They are outwardly all affection: 'A curse attends that woman's love' is not the quarrel the words might suggest, and Polly could not be more affable ('Among the men, coquettes we find') nor Lucy more pressing ('Come sweet lass') as she presses her guest to accept her offer of a drink. The scene is brought to an abrupt conclusion by the precipitate entrance of Macheath, again in chains.

The quarrel is almost forgotten in the duet of commiseration which Lucy and Polly sing together, 'Hither dear husband, turn your eyes', but Macheath seems to take a rather different view of events: 'Which way shall I turn me'. Both Polly and Lucy plead with their respective fathers ('When my hero in court appears', and 'When he holds up his head arraign'd for his life'). Peachum and Lockit remain adamant ('Ourselves like the great'), and order Macheath to prepare himself to be conducted to the Old Bailey. He sings 'The charge is prepared', which, in Britten's version, leads to an extensive ensemble.

The condemned hold. Macheath, in a melancholy posture, laments his fate, and fortifies himself with copious draughts of liquor for the ordeal of hanging. He sings snatches of tune, culminating in an outburst against the injustice of the times, set to the tune of *Greensleeves*. Austin uses only four of the ten tunes specified for this scene, and omits *Greensleeves*. Britten makes it into a scena on the lines of Purcell's 'Mad Scenes'—it is the climax of the opera—and binds it together on a bass derived from *Greensleeves* itself. The result is impressive, and lends real dignity, not only to the figure of Macheath, but to the ideals for which the satire was battling—and satire is mere bitterness unless reared on an ideal and a truth.

Ben Budge and Matt of the Mint come to say farewell to Macheath; his last request is that they should revenge him upon Peachum and Lockit before they themselves come to the sorry pass in which he finds himself. Lucy and Polly appear, protesting that they would gladly take his place: 'Would I might be hanged'. Macheath joins in and the piece takes on the character of a dirge, more particularly when the sound of the passing-bell is heard (Britten uses this with effect). Four more wives appear claiming Macheath as husband, until he protests that he is ready to go with the Sheriff's officers to execution.

Would I might be hanged! And I would so too To be

hanged with you. My dear with you.

At this point, the Player protests to the Beggar that, if Macheath is hanged, the piece will be downright tragedy. The Beggar is persuaded to allow a reprieve, and Macheath returns to lead the finale, 'Thus I stand like the Turk, with his doxies around'.

H.

# GIOVANNI PERGOLESI
## (1710–1736)

### LA SERVA PADRONA

INTERMEZZO in two parts by Giovanni Battista Pergolesi, text by G. A. Federico. First performed August 28, 1733, at the Teatro di S. Bartolomeo in Naples, with Laura Monti and Gioacchino Corrado. The *Intermezzo* was played in between the three acts of Pergolesi's serious opera *Il Prigioniero Superbo*. First performed in London, 1750; in New York, 1858. Revivals: Lyric, Hammersmith, 1919; Mercury Theatre, London, 1939; Metropolitan, New York, 1935, with Editha Fleischer and Louis d'Angelo, and 1942, with Bidu Sayao and Salvatore Baccaloni.

### CHARACTERS

Uberto . . . . . . . . . . . . . . . . . . . . . . . . . . . . . . . . . . . . . . . . . . . . . . . Bass
Serpina, *his servant* . . . . . . . . . . . . . . . . . . . . . . . . . . . . . Soprano
Vespone, *another servant* . . . . . . . . . . . . . . . . . . . . . . . . . . . Mute

Pergolesi was born near Ancona in January 1710, and died near Naples, March 1736. He was a prolific composer of chamber music, sacred music (including the well-known *Stabat Mater*), and operas both serious and comic. *La Serva Padrona* is his only surviving stage work, and the freshness and charm of the music take on added interest when it is remembered that the opera was at the very centre of the famous 'Guerre des Bouffons' in Paris. The production of *La Serva Padrona* by an Italian company in 1752 confirmed the division of all French musicians and intellectuals into two camps, the one favouring Italian opera, the other French. The Nationalists were known as the 'King's Corner' party, their opponents, who included Rousseau and the Encyclopedists, as the 'Queen's Corner' party. The Nationalists admired Lully and the ageing Rameau, the Bouffonists hated what they thought of as the out-moded complexity of French composers. *La Serva Padrona* had one hundred performances at the Opéra before, in 1753, it was transferred to the Comédie Française, where it had ninety-six more.

*La Serva Padrona* is on a small scale, the orchestra consisting only of a quartet of strings. The piece comprises an overture, and two separate *intermezzi*, each of which includes an aria for both characters and a duet. The overture is a gay piece, and the curtain rises to find Uberto dressing to go out and lamenting that he has had to wait three hours for his chocolate, which has still not arrived. His energetic complaints at the time he is kept waiting are expressed in an aria of a less formal type than the others in the score, each of which is in *da capo* form. His complaints are directed more specifically at Serpina his maid in the ensuing recitative. However, when it comes to complaints he is no match for her, and, after she has finished with her master, she turns on Vespone and sends him briskly about his business. Uberto's aria, 'Sempre in contrasti', is a fresh sort of tune, typical of the score, and demanding more than a little agility from the singer. Serpina tells Uberto that it is much too late for him to go out, and lectures him again in her *allegretto* aria, 'Stizzoso, mio stizzoso'. Uberto can bear the tyranny no longer, and asks Vespone to go and find him a wife. An excellent idea, says Serpina: take me! In a duet, she protests her eligibility and he his intention of, if possible, ridding himself of her altogether (but he confesses to himself that the situation looks like becoming too much for him).

The second *Intermezzo* opens with recitative in which Serpina plans a trick to frighten or cajole Uberto into marrying her. Vespone shall help, and she tells Uberto that she has found a husband for herself, a soldier, by name Captain Tempest. She describes his bad temper and his unreasonable nature, and then in a pathetic aria, 'A Serpina penserete', expresses her hope that she will not be entirely forgotten when she has gone. She seems a different woman, but the moment she sees a change come over her employer's face, the tempo of the music changes too, and we see that it is with the same old Serpina that we have to deal. By the end of the aria, Uberto has taken her by the hand, and she feels her plan is working well. Uberto is in a thorough muddle, and does not know what to think. His E flat aria, 'Son imbrogliato io gia', makes it clear that he cannot make up his mind whether he is sorry for Serpina or is in love with her. It is a mixture of *buffo* and mock serious, and its slow refrain, 'Uberto, pensa a te', indicates a very different mood from that we saw at the beginning of the opera. Serpina returns, bringing with her Vespone dressed up as the gallant captain, and looking as though he would blow up at the least provocation but still, as hitherto, without a word to say to anyone. Uberto is horrified by his disagreeable exterior and by his no less alarming behaviour. Is this a suitable husband for Serpina? She says that the Captain demands a substantial dowry; if it is not forthcoming, he will under no circumstances marry her, but he will insist that Uberto himself takes his place. No sooner is the betrothal between master and maid concluded, than Vespone whips off his moustaches and military disguise. Uberto's protests are in vain, and in the concluding duet, he admits that he is in love, and all seems set for the future, with Serpina happily installed as prospective mistress of the house.

H.

# CHAPTER 2

## *Gluck*

# CHRISTOPH WILLIBALD GLUCK
## (1714–1787)

GLUCK is the earliest opera composer regularly represented in the repertory of the modern opera house. *Orfeo
ed Euridice*, produced in 1762, is the oldest work of its kind
on the stage: it is the great-great-grandfather of modern opera.

Its composer combined with the poet and diplomat Calzabigi
in an attempt to reform opera and *Orfeo* was the first product of
the partnership. The libretto of Calzabigi was, for its day, charged
with a vast amount of human interest, passion, and dramatic
intensity, in which particulars, in fact, it was as novel as Gluck's
score. Gluck had been a composer of operas in the florid vocal
style, which sacrificed the dramatic verities to the whims, fancies,
and ambitions of the singers, who sought only to show off their
voices, but he began, with his *Orfeo*, to pay due regard to true
dramatic expression. His great merit is that he accomplished this
without ignoring the beauty and importance of the voice, but by
striking a balance between the vocal and instrumental portions
of the score.

Simple as his operas appear to us to-day, they aroused a strife
comparable only with that which convulsed musical circles during
the progress of Wagner's career. The opposition to his reforms
reached its height in Paris, whither he went in 1772. His opponents
invited Nicola Piccini, at that time famous as a composer of
comic operas in the Neapolitan style, to compete with him. The
two composers seem to have remained entirely unaffected, but
so fierce was the war between their followers that duels were
fought and lives sacrificed over the respective merits of the two
composers.

Gluck retired to Vienna, where he died, November 25, 1787.

## ORFEO ED EURIDICE
### Orpheus and Eurydice

Opera in three acts. Music by Christoph Willibald Gluck; libretto by
Raniero da Calzabigi. Productions and revivals: Vienna, October 5, 1762.

with Guadagni as Orfeo; Paris, as *Orphée et Eurydice*, with Legros, the tenor, as Orphée, 1774; London, 1770. Berlioz's revision of the opera was first heard in 1859 in Paris, with Pauline Viardot-Garcia in the title role; New York, 1863 (in English).

Famous revivals: Covent Garden, 1890, with Giulia and Sofia Ravogli; Metropolitan, New York, 1909, with Homer (later Delna) and Gadski under Toscanini; Covent Garden, 1920, with Clara Butt and Miriam Licette under Beecham; Metropolitan, 1938 and 1941, with Thorborg and Jessner (later Novotna) under Bodanzky (later Walter); Glyndebourne, 1947, with Kathleen Ferrier.

### CHARACTERS

Orfeo ........................................Contralto
Euridice ....................................Soprano
Amor, *God of Love* ..........................Soprano
A Happy Shade ..............................Soprano

Shepherds and Shepherdesses, Furies and Demons,
Heroes and Heroines in Hades

*Time:* Antiquity                    *Place:* Greece : Hades

Following a brief and solemn prelude, the curtain rises on Act I, showing a grotto with the tomb of Euridice. The beautiful bride of Orfeo has died. Her husband and friends are mourning at her tomb. During an affecting aria and chorus ('Chiamo il mio ben cosi') funeral honours are paid to the dead bride. A second orchestra, behind the scenes, echoes, with moving effect, the distracted husband's cries to his bride, until, in answer to the piercing cries of Orfeo, Amor appears. He tells the bereaved husband that Zeus has taken pity on him. He shall have permission to go down into Hades and endeavour to propitiate Pluto and his minions solely through the power of his music. But, should he rescue Euridice, he must on no account look back at her until he has crossed the Styx.

Upon that condition, so difficult to fulfil because of the love of Orfeo for his bride, turns the whole story. For should he, in answer to her pleading, look back, or explain to her why he cannot do so, she will immediately die. But Orfeo, confident in his power of song and in his ability to stand the test imposed by Zeus and bring his beloved Euridice back to earth, receives the message with great joy.

'Fulfil with joy the will of the gods,' sings Amor, and Orfeo, having implored the aid of the deities, departs for the Nether World.

Act II.    Entrance to Hades. When Orfeo appears, he is greeted with threats by the Furies. The scene, beginning with the chorus, 'Chi mai dell' Erebo?' is a masterpiece of dramatic music. The Furies call upon Cerberus, the triple-headed dog monster that guards the entrance to the Nether World, to tear in pieces the mortal who so daringly approaches, and the bark of the monster is reproduced in the score. What lifts the scene to its thrilling climax is the infuriated 'No!' which is hurled at Orfeo by the dwellers at the entrance to Hades, when, having recourse to song, he tells of his love for Euridice and his grief over her death and begs to be allowed to seek her. The sweetness of his music wins the sympathy of the Furies. They allow him to enter the Valley of the Blest, a beautiful spot where the good spirits in Hades find rest, a state that is uniquely expressed in their slow dance with its famous flute solo. Euridice (or a Happy Spirit) [1] and her companions sing of their bliss in the Elysian Fields: 'E quest' asilo ameno e grato' (In this tranquil and lovely abode of the blest). Orfeo comes seeking Euridice. His peaceful aria (with its oboe *obbligato*) 'Che puro ciel' (What pure light) is answered by a chorus of Happy Shades. To him they bring the lovely Euridice. Orfeo, beside himself with joy, but remembering the warning of Amor, takes his bride by the hand and, with averted gaze, leads her from the vale.

Act III.    She cannot understand his action. He seeks to soothe her injured feelings. (Duet: 'Su, e con me vieni, o cara'.) But his efforts are vain; nor can he offer her any explanation, for he has also been forbidden to make known to her the reason for his apparent indifference. She cannot comprehend why he does not even cast a glance upon her and protests in a passionate aria and duet, 'Che fiero momento', that without his love she prefers to die.

Orfeo, no longer able to resist the appeal of his beloved bride, forgets the warning of Amor. He turns and passionately clasps Euridice in his arms. Immediately she dies. It is then that Orfeo intones the lament, 'Che faro senza Euridice' (I have lost my

---

[1] As to whether Euridice or another singer should be entrusted with this aria, Professor Dent has written: 'Managers never realise that Euridice in Act III is a highly sexed person, and wants conjugal rights at once, whereas the Happy Spirit is clearly quite devoid of all human instincts. It is almost impossible to find one singer who can express both these things.'

Euridice), that air in the score which has truly become immortal:

'All forms of language have been exhausted to praise the stupor of grief, the passion, the despair expressed in this sublime number,' says a writer in the Clément and Larousse *Dictionnaire des Opéras*. It is equalled only by the lines of Virgil:

> Vox ipsa et frigida lingua,
> 'Ah! miseram Eurydicen,' anima fugiente, vocabat;
> 'Eurydicen,' toto referabant flumine ripae.
>
> [E'en then his trembling tongue invok'd his bride;
> With his last voice, 'Eurydice,'' he cried,
> 'Eurydice,' the rocks and river banks replied.
>
> DRYDEN]

In fact it is so beautiful that Amor, affected by the grief of Orfeo, appears to him, touches Euridice and restores her to life and to her husband's arms.

The legend of Orpheus and Eurydice as related in Virgil's *Georgics*, from which are the lines just quoted, is one of the classics of antiquity. In *Orfeo ed Euridice* Gluck has preserved the chaste classicism of the original, in spite of the passion and drama which he successfully attempted to get into his music.

The role of Orfeo was written for the celebrated male contralto Guadagni. For the Paris production the composer added three bars to the most famous number of the score, the 'Che faro senza Euridice', illustrated above. These presumably were the three last bars, the concluding phrases of the peroration of the immortal air. He also transposed the part of Orfeo for the tenor Legros, for whom he introduced a vocal number entirely out of keeping with the role—a bravura aria which for a long while was erroneously ascribed to the obscure Italian composer Ferdinando Bertoni. It is believed that the tenor importuned Gluck for something that would show off his voice, whereupon the composer handed him the air. Legros introduced it at the end of the first act, where to this day it remains in the printed score. When the tenor Nourrit sang the role many years later, he substituted the far more appropriate aria, 'O transport, ô désordre extrême' (O transport, O ecstasy extreme), from Gluck's own *Echo et Narcisse*. It may be of interest to note that, for the revival which he conducted at the Metropolitan in 1910, Toscanini introduced the aria 'Divinités du Styx' (from Gluck's *Alceste*) into the scene in Hades.

Some reconciliation between the Vienna and the Paris versions has, to this day, to be made for each and every production, but that the opera, as it came from Gluck's pen, required nothing more, appeared in the notable revival at the Théâtre Lyrique, Paris, November, 1859, under Berlioz's direction, when that distinguished composer restored the role of Orfeo to its original form and for a hundred and fifty nights the celebrated contralto, Pauline Viardot-Garcia, sang it to enthusiastic houses.

The opera has been the object of unstinted praise. Of the second act the same French authority quoted above says that from the first note to the last, it is 'a complete masterpiece and one of the most astonishing productions of the human mind. The chorus of demons in turn questions, becomes wrathful, bursts into a turmoil of threats, gradually becomes tranquil and is hushed, as if subdued and conquered by the music of Orfeo's lyre. What is more moving than the phrase 'Laissez-vous toucher par mes pleurs'? (A thousand griefs, threatening shades.) Seeing a large audience captivated by this mythological subject; an audience mixed, frivolous and unthinking, transported and swayed by this scene, one recognises the real power of music. The composer conquered his hearers as his Orfeo succeeded in subduing the Furies. Nowhere, in no work, is the effect more gripping.'

Gaetano Guadagni, who created the role of Orfeo, was one of the most famous male contralti of the eighteenth century. Handel assigned to him contralto parts in the *Messiah* and *Samson*, and it was Gluck himself who procured his engagement at Vienna. The French production of the opera was preceded by an act of homage, which showed the interest of the French in Gluck's work. Though it had its first performance in Vienna, the score was first printed in Paris and at the expense of Count Durazzo. The success of the Paris production was so great that Gluck's former pupil, Marie Antoinette, granted him a pension of 6,000 francs with an addition of the same sum for every fresh work he should produce on the French stage.

Einstein sums up the work: '*Orfeo ed Euridice* marked an epoch not only in Gluck's work, but in the whole of operatic history. Here for the first time is an opera without *recitativo secco* ... here for the first time was a work so closely grown together into its text that it was unique and could not be composed again. ... An opera at last whose manner of performance required the composer's supervision, the first opera that culminated in the musician's labour!' K.

## ALCESTE

### (Alcestis)

Opera in three acts by Christoph Willibald Gluck, text by Raniero da Calzabigi. Première at the Burgtheater, Vienna, December 26, 1767, with Antonia Bernasconi (Alcestis), Giuseppe Tibaldi (Admetus), Laschi (High Priest and Voice of Apollo). Produced in Paris in a revised version, April 23, 1776, with Mlle. Levasseur as Alcestis, and sung in French. First performance in London, King's Theatre, 1795 (in Italian). Recent revivals include Florence Festival, 1935 (in Italian), under Vittorio Gui, with Gina Cigna, Nicola Rakowski, and Benvenuto Franci; at Covent Garden, 1937, in French, under Philippe Gaubert, with Germaine Lubin, Georges Jouatte, and Martial Singher; at the Metropolitan, New York, 1941 (in French), under Ettore Panizza, with Marjorie Lawrence, René Maison and Leonard Warren, and, in 1952 (in English), with Kirsten Flagstad, Brian Sullivan, and Paul Schöffler conducted by Alberto Erede.

#### CHARACTERS

| | |
|---|---|
| Admetus | Tenor |
| Alcestis | Soprano |
| High Priest | Baritone |
| Hercules | Baritone |
| Evander | Tenor |
| Thanatos | Baritone |
| Voice of Apollo | Baritone |
| Herald | Baritone |
| Leaders of the People | Soprano, Mezzo-soprano, Baritone |
| A Woman | Soprano |

Gluck goes down to history as a reformer, whose battle against the contemporary abuses of opera proved a turning point in the history of the art. Einstein has suggested that the normal eighteenth-century method of reform being by means of satire and parody, and Gluck being constitutionally unfitted to this medium or to that of *opera buffa*, he was obliged to become the first critical creator in opera's history if he was to express his thoughts on the subject; he had no other 'safety valve'. Be that as it may, his preface to *Alceste* is one of the most famous documents in the annals of opera, and it is reproduced here in the translation of Eric Blom (which occurs in his translation of Einstein's biography of Gluck in Dent's 'Master Musicians' Series):

'When I undertook to write the music for *Alceste*, I resolved to divest it entirely of all those abuses, introduced into it either by the mistaken vanity of singers or by the too great complaisance of composers, which have so long disfigured Italian opera and made of the most splendid and most beautiful of spectacles the most ridiculous and wearisome. I have striven to restrict music to its true office of serving poetry by means of expression and by following the situations of the story, without interrupting the action or stifling it with a useless superfluity of ornaments; and I believed that it should do this in the same way as telling colours affect a correct and well-ordered drawing, by a well-assorted contrast of light and shade, which serves to animate the figures without altering their contours. Thus I did not wish to arrest an actor in the greatest heat of dialogue in order to wait for a tiresome *ritornello*, nor to hold him up in the middle of a word on a vowel favourable to his voice, nor to make display of the agility of his fine voice in some long-drawn passage, nor to wait while the orchestra gives him time to recover his breath for a cadenza. I did not think it my duty to pass quickly over the second section of an aria of which the words are perhaps the most impassioned and important, in order to repeat regularly four times over those of the first part, and to finish the aria where its sense may perhaps not end for the convenience of the singer who wishes to show that he can capriciously vary a passage in a number of guises; in short, I have sought to abolish all the abuses against which good sense and reason have long cried out in vain.

'I have felt that the overture ought to appraise the spectators of the nature of the action that is to be represented and to form, so to speak, its argument; that the concerted instruments should be introduced in proportion to the interest and intensity of the words, and not leave that sharp contrast between the aria and the recitative in the dialogue, so as not to break a period unreasonably nor wantonly disturb the force and heat of the action.

'Furthermore, I believed that my greatest labour should be devoted to seeking a beautiful simplicity, and I have avoided making displays of difficulty at the expense of clearness; nor did I judge it desirable to discover novelties if it was not naturally suggested by the situation and the expression; and there is no rule which I have not thought it right to set aside willingly for the sake of an intended effect.

'Such are my principles. By good fortune my designs were wonderfully furthered by the libretto, in which the celebrated author, devising a new dramatic scheme, had substituted for florid descriptions, unnatural paragons and sententious, cold morality, heartfelt language, strong passions, interesting situations and an endlessly varied spectacle. The success of the work justified my maxims, and the universal approbation of so enlightened a city has made it clearly evident that simplicity, truth and naturalness are the great principles of beauty in all artistic manifestations. For all that, in spite of repeated urgings on the part of some most eminent persons to decide upon the publication of this opera of mine in print, I was well aware of all the risk run in combating such firmly and profoundly rooted prejudices, and I thus felt the necessity of fortifying myself with the most powerful patronage of Your Royal Highness, whose August Name I beg you may have the grace to prefix to this my opera, a name which with so much justice enjoys the suffrages of an enlightened Europe. The great protector of the fine arts, who reigns over a nation that had the glory of making them arise again from universal oppression and which itself has produced the greatest models, in a city that was always the first to shake off the yoke of vulgar prejudices in order to clear a path for perfection, may alone undertake the reform of that noble spectacle in which all the fine arts take so great a share. If this should succeed, the glory of having moved the first stone will remain for me, and in this public testimonial of

Your Highness's furtherance of the same, I have the honour
to subscribe myself, with the most humble respect,

'Your Royal Highness's

'Most humble, most devoted and most obliged servant,

'CHRISTOFORO GLUCK.'

Calzabigi has not followed the lines of Euripides's tragedy,
where the role of Admetus is an inglorious one, and the intervention of Hercules due to his desire to vindicate the laws of hospitality, not to any motive of pity for the sorry plight of Alcestis
and Admetus.

Act I.   A magnificently sombre overture fully vindicates
Gluck's avowed intention as set forth in the preface; here indeed
is the argument of the action. The scene represents a great court
in front of the palace of Admetus; at the back can be seen the
temple of Apollo. The people crowd into the courtyard and mourn
the illness of their King, which, the Herald tells them, is likely
to prove fatal. Evander announces the entrance of Alcestis, and
the Queen appears flanked by her two children. She laments the
prospect in front of her children, soon to be fatherless, and bids
the crowd come with her to the temple, there to offer sacrifice to
the gods.

In the temple of Apollo, we hear first a simple tune, designated
'Pantomime' in the score, which may serve as background for a
dance as well as for the entrance of Alcestis. The High Priest and
the chorus call upon the god to avert the fate which is about to
overtake Admetus, and, through him, his wife and his people.
Alcestis adds her prayer, and a sacrifice is prepared, to the music
of another 'Pantomime'. The High Priest, in music that grows
more and more awe-inspiring, invokes the god and commands
the people to be silent to hear the Oracle's judgment. When it
comes, it is more terrible than they had expected: Admetus must
die, unless a friend can be found to die in his stead. The people
lament the harsh pronouncement and rush from the temple in
fear, leaving Alcestis and the High Priest alone. Alcestis awakes
to the reality of the situation and resolves to die for her husband,
without whom she cannot live. 'Non, ce n'est point un sacrifice',
she sings in an aria of noble simplicity. The High Priest tells her
that her prayer is granted and she has the rest of the day to prepare herself for the advent of death.

In an aria which has become the most famous of the opera, Alcestis invokes the gods of the underworld and defies them to do their worst; what dread has she of dying for what she loves best in the world? 'Divinités du Styx' is Gluck at his most intense, justifying his own maxims as regards the situation, but with a result that is no less impressive as music than as drama.

Act II. In a great hall of his palace, Admetus stands to receive the congratulations of his people, headed by Evander, on his apparently miraculous recovery. Dances are performed in his honour. The King enquires what brought about his recovery, and Evander tells him the condition imposed by the Oracle but does not name the victim. The King is horror-stricken and refuses to accept such a sacrifice. Alcestis joins him and shares his joy that they are re-united. The chorus of praise and rejoicing continues, but Alcestis is quite unable to hide the grief she feels as the moment draws near when she must leave her husband and her children for ever. Admetus tries to comfort her in a *da capo* aria of great beauty, 'Bannis la crainte et les alarmes', but to no avail. The Queen avows her love, but finally admits that it is she the gods are taking in place of Admetus. Dramatically, he refuses to accept the sacrifice: 'Non, sans toi, je ne puis vivre'. Alcestis is left alone with the people, and as they mourn for her grief sings 'Ah, malgré moi, mon faible cœur partage vos tendres pleurs'.

Act III. The courtyard of the palace. The people are mourning the deaths of both Alcestis and of Admetus, who has followed her. Hercules arrives, rejoicing that his labours are over, but Evander informs him of the death of his friend Admetus, and of the circumstances surrounding it, and he swears to restore their King and Queen to the people of Greece.

The scene changes to the gates of Hell. Alcestis pleads with the gods of Hell (who remain invisible) that her torment be not prolonged, that she be received at once. Admetus joins her, asking only to be re-united with her in death. He reminds her of her duty to their children, but their duet is interrupted by the voice of Thanatos announcing that the time has come for one of them to offer themselves to Death; the choice is left to Alcestis as to which of the two it shall be. Alcestis will not renounce her right to die for her husband, and the choice appears to have been made, much to the grief of Admetus, when Hercules appears on the scene, determined to deprive the underworld of its prey. He and

Admetus defy Hell and its rulers and fight to rescue Alcestis. At the moment of their success, Apollo appears, and announces to Hercules that his action has won him the right to a place amongst the gods themselves, while Admetus and Alcestis are to be restored to earth, there to serve as a universal example of the power of conjugal love.

The scene changes to the palace court, and Apollo bids the people rejoice that their King and Queen are restored to them. Alcestis, Admetus, and Hercules take part in a trio, and the opera ends in general rejoicing.

More than perhaps any other of the operas of his maturity, *Alceste* illustrates the ideal of 'beautiful simplicity' which Gluck tells us in his preface is his aim. Berlioz's admiration for the temple scene is well known, and Ernest Newman further quotes this composer's detailed objection to the changes made in what we now know as 'Divinités du Styx' when the opera was translated from Italian, changes which ruined the beginning of the aria, according to Berlioz. Ironically, when an Italian soprano now sings this aria, she will use an Italian translation of the French translation of the original Italian, and of course employ the musical form of the French version! It should be noted that the original score included a scene in a gloomy forest near Phera at the beginning of the second act; this is omitted in the French version, which begins with the festivities attending the recovery of Admetus. The third act, while employing much of the music of the original, is entirely altered dramatically, and, says Ernest Newman, distinctly for the worse. Du Rollet's introduction of Hercules has, according to Newman, a vulgarising effect, and only the new scene at the gates of Hell (the entire act originally took place in the courtyard of the palace, where Alceste died, Admetus tried to commit suicide, and a happy ending was provided by the appearance of Apollo) constitutes a worth-while addition to the score as it stood. As with *Orfeo*, a modern performance of *Alceste* entails the preparation of an edition comprising the best elements of the original and the Paris versions.          H.

## IPHIGÉNIE EN AULIDE

Opera in three acts by Christoph Willibald Gluck, text by Raniero da Calzabigi. First performed at the Académie de Musique, Paris, April 19, 1774, with Sophie Arnould (Iphigénie), du Plant (Clytemnestra), Legros (Achilles), Larrivée (Agamemnon).

In 1846 Wagner revised the opera, changing the orchestration, re-writing some of the recitatives, and even introducing a new character, Artemis, into the third act. This version was produced at Dresden in 1847 and was given on many German stages. There was a famous revival under Mahler in Vienna in 1904 with Gutheil-Schoder, Mildenburg, Schmedes and Demuth. The opera was heard in England for the first time as late as 1933 (at Oxford), and was revived in 1937 (in Glasgow). The first American performance occurred in 1935, in Philadelphia, conducted by Alexander Smallens, and sung by Rosa Tentoni (Iphigénie), Cyrena van Gordon (Clytemnestra), Joseph Bentonelli (Achilles), and George Baklanoff (Agamemnon). It was revived at the Florence Festival of 1950 (in the Boboli Gardens), with Guerrini, Nicolai, Penno, and Christoff in the leading roles.

Act I.     Agamemnon, after consulting the oracle, has vowed to sacrifice his daughter, Iphigénie, to Diana in return for a favourable wind to take him and his army safely to Troy. He is persuaded to send for his daughter, on the pretext that her marriage to Achilles shall be solemnised in Aulis. He however secretly sends word to his wife, Clytemnestra, telling her to delay the voyage as the marriage has been postponed. When the opera opens, Agamemnon is seen a prey to agonising remorse, and torn by the conflicting claims of duty and love. The Greeks demand to know the reason of the gods' continued displeasure, and Calchas, the high priest, is filled with sorrow at the thought of the sacrifice that is demanded. He prays to the goddess to find another victim, Agamemnon joins him in prayer, and the Greeks demand the name of the victim that they may immediately make the sacrifice the goddess demands. Calchas assures them that the victim shall be found that very day.

Calchas reasons with Agamemnon in an effort to persuade him to agree to the sacrifice, but the Greek King breaks out into an agonised expression of his overwhelming sorrow. Is it possible that the gods wish him to commit so dreadful a crime? Calchas asks him if his intention is to go against his oath, but Agamemnon replies that he has sworn to sacrifice Iphigénie only if she sets foot on the soil of Aulis. At that very moment, and in the midst of Calchas's denunciation of the King's duplicity, they hear the cries of the Greeks as they welcome Clytemnestra and Iphigénie, newly arrived on the island. As the King and the high priest comment on the possible results of the arrival, the Greeks sing the praises of the Queen and her daughter. Agamemnon secretly informs his wife that Achilles has proved unworthy of Iphigénie and that she and her daughter are therefore to return immediately on their journey. She denounces Achilles to Iphigénie, who is

PLATE III. Kathleen Ferrier as Orfeo in Gluck's opera, Covent Garden 1953.

PLATE IV. *Idomeneo* at Glyndebourne 1951, in Ebert's production; sets by Oliver Messel. *L. to r.* Jurinac, Richard Lewis, Simoneau, Birgit Nilsson.

ready to believe her until Achilles himself appears on the scene, overjoyed at her unexpected arrival. Iphigénie is at first cold and unwelcoming, but explanations follow and the act ends with a duet of reconciliation.

Act II.   In spite of the chorus's attempts at reassurance and congratulation on her forthcoming marriage, Iphigénie is filled with foreboding at the prospect of a meeting between Agamemnon and Achilles who by now knows that his prospective father-in-law was responsible for the rumour of his infidelity to Iphigénie. Clytemnestra bids her daughter rejoice, Achilles, after introducing the warrior Patroclus to her, leads a chorus in her praise, and songs and dances are offered in honour of the happy couple. As Achilles is about to lead his bride to the altar, Arcas, Agamemnon's messenger, intervenes and protests that Agamemnon waits at the altar to sacrifice her in fulfilment of his sacred vow. Clytemnestra begs Achilles to protect his young bride from the consequences of her father's rash action. Achilles impulsively swears to defend her, but Iphigénie reminds him that Agamemnon is her father, and that she loves him in spite of the terrible situation in which fate has placed him.

Agamemnon and Achilles meet, and, in answer to Achilles's reproaches, Agamemnon reminds him that he is supreme commander of the Greek forces and that all owe allegiance to him and obedience to his decisions. Achilles defies him and says that whoever means to lay hands on Iphigénie will have to overcome him first. Agamemnon is left alone with his conscience, and the necessity to decide between his duty to the gods and his love for his daughter. In the end he decides to send Clytemnestra and Iphigénie straight away to Mycenae, and by this means he hopes to avoid the consequences of his oath.

Act III.   The Greeks demand that the vow shall be fulfilled as the only means by which the present wrath of the gods may be turned. Achilles begs Iphigénie to fly with him, but she protests her willingness to die, he insists on his determination to save her. Clytemnestra is left alone with her daughter, and tries every means to save her, but the Greeks are implacable in their demand that the sacrifice shall take place. Clytemnestra calls down the fury of Jove on the cruel hosts of the Greeks.

All is ready for the sacrifice and the Greeks beg for an answer to their prayer which will accompany it. The ceremony is interrupted by the arrival of Achilles at the head of the Thessalians, who fall on the assembled Greek troops. A pitched battle is averted by Calchas, who announces that the gods are appeased and prepared to grant fair weather even though Agamemnon's oath is not fulfilled. Husband and wife, parent and child, lover and beloved are reconciled and re-united and the opera ends with rejoicings as the Greeks prepare to set sail for Troy.

Although *Iphigénie en Aulide* has not quite the unity of style and construction that is so marked a feature of the later *Iphigénie en Tauride*, it is full of remarkable music. The leading figures are strongly characterised. Agamemnon is never less than a heroic figure, and the conflict which is the result of his vow makes him the most interesting character in the drama. His arias are magnificently expressive, that of the first act immediately establishing his commanding stature and essential nobility as well as the appalling dilemma he sees before him, the great scena at the end of the second act (after the scene with Achilles) even more impressively dramatic. Clytemnestra is less positively involved in the drama, but her intense reaction to its events is expressed in wonderfully dramatic music. In her solo scenes, she passes from straightforward fury when she hears from Agamemnon of Achilles's supposed unfaithfulness to Iphigénie, through the extremes of grief when she pleads with Achilles to save her daughter, until in the third act she collapses altogether when her pleas to the Greeks go unheeded. Even nowadays the intensity of her emotions is immediately apparent, and one can imagine that such musical expressiveness must have made an extraordinary effect in Gluck's time. Like Ilia in *Idomeneo*, Iphigénie is the victim rather than the agent of the tragedy, but her resignation and acceptance of her cruel fate gives rise to music of remarkable beauty. Achilles is the ancestor of Radames and a whole line of heroic tenors, uncomplicated as a person and accustomed to express himself vigorously and uncompromisingly, with a wealth of top notes to emphasise his determination. His aria in Act III when he resolves to save Iphigénie by force of arms made an effect at the first performance comparable to that felt by Italian audiences hearing Verdi's music at the time of the Risorgimento. We are told that the gentlemen in the theatre could hardly refrain from drawing their swords and joining him on the stage in his attempt to rescue his Princess.

## IPHIGÉNIE EN TAURIDE

### Iphigenia in Tauris

Opera in four acts by Gluck, words by François Guillard.

Produced at the Académie de Musique, Paris, May 18, 1779, with Levasseur, Legros, Larrivée; London (in da Ponte's Italian translation), 1796; Metropolitan Opera House, New York, November 25, 1916, with Kurt, Weil, Sembach, Braun, and Rappold (in German, arranged Richard Strauss). Revived la Scala, 1937, with Caniglia, Parmeggiani, Armando Borgioli, Maugeri, conducted by de Sabata; Berlin 1941, with Müller, Svanholm, Domgraf-Fassbänder, Ahlersmeyer; Aix 1952, with Neway, Simoneau, Mollet, Massard, conductor Giulini.

#### CHARACTERS

Iphigénie, *Priestess of Diana* .................... Soprano
Oreste, *her Brother* ............................ Baritone
Pylade, *his Friend* .............................. Tenor
Thoas, *King of Scythia* .......................... Bass
Diana ........................................ Soprano

Scythians, Priestesses of Diana, Greeks

*Time:* Antiquity, after the Trojan War          *Place:* Tauris

Iphigénie is the daughter of Agamemnon, King of Mycene. Agamemnon was slain by his wife, Clytemnestra, who, in turn, was killed by her son, Oreste. Iphigénie is ignorant of these happenings. She has become a priestess of Diana on the island of Tauris and has not seen Oreste for many years.

Act I.   Before the atrium of the temple of Diana. To priestesses and Greek maidens, Iphigénie tells of her dream that misfortune has come to her family in the distant country of her birth. Thoas, entering, calls for a human sacrifice to ward off danger that has been foretold to him. Some of his people, hastily coming upon the scene, bring with them as captives Oreste and Pylade, Greek youths who have landed upon the coast. They report that Oreste constantly speaks of having committed a crime and of being pursued by Furies.

Act II.   Temple of Diana. Oreste bewails his fate. Pylade sings of his undying friendship for him. Pylade is separated from Oreste, who temporarily loses his mind. Iphigénie questions him. Oreste, under her influence, becomes calmer, but refrains from disclosing his identity. He tells her, however, that he is from Mycene, that Agamemnon (their father) has been slain by his wife, that Clytemnestra's son, Oreste, has slain her in revenge, and is himself dead. Of the once great family only a daughter, Electra, remains.

Act III.    Iphigénie is struck with the resemblance of the stranger to her brother and, in order to save him from the sacrifice demanded by Thoas, charges him to deliver a letter to Electra. He declines to leave Pylade; nor, until Oreste affirms that he will commit suicide rather than accept freedom at the price of his friend's life, does Pylade agree to take the letter, and then only because he hopes to bring succour to Oreste.

Act IV.    All is ready for the sacrifice. Iphigénie has the knife poised for the fatal thrust, when, through an exclamation uttered by Oreste, she recognises him as her brother. The priestesses offer him obeisance as King. Thoas, however, enters and demands the sacrifice. Iphigénie declares that she will die with her brother. At that moment Pylade at the head of a rescue party enters the temple. A combat ensues in which Thoas is killed. Diana herself appears, pardons Oreste and returns to the Greeks her likeness which the Scythians had stolen and over which they had built the temple.

Gluck was sixty-five when he brought out *Iphigénie en Tauride*. A contemporary remarked that there were many fine passages in the opera. 'There is only one,' said the Abbé Arnaud. 'Which?' —'The entire work.'

The mad scene for Oreste, in the second act, has been called Gluck's greatest single achievement. Mention should also be made of Iphigénie's 'O toi, qui prolongeas', the dances of the Scythians, the air of Thoas, 'De noirs pressentiments mon âme intimidée'; the air of Pylade, 'Unis dès la plus tendre enfance'; Iphigénie's 'O malheureuse Iphigénie', and 'Je t'implore et je tremble'; and the hymn to Diana, 'Chaste fille de Latone' (Chaste daughter of the crescent moon).

Here may be related an incident at the rehearsal of the work, which indicates the dramatic significance Gluck sought to impart to his music. In the second act, while Oreste is singing, 'Le calme rentre dans mon coeur', the orchestral accompaniment continues to express the agitation of his thoughts. During the rehearsal the members of the orchestra, not understanding the passage, came to a stop. 'Go on all the same,' cried Gluck. 'He lies. He has killed his mother!'

Gluck's enemies prevailed upon his rival, Piccini, to write an *Iphigénie en Tauride* in opposition. It was produced in January 1781, met with failure, and put a definite stop to Piccini's rivalry with Gluck. At the performance the prima donna was intoxicated. This caused a spectator to shout: '*Iphigénie en Tauride!* allons donc, c'est *Iphigénie en Champagne!*'

The laugh that followed sealed the doom of the work.

The version used at the Metropolitan was that made by Richard Strauss, which involves changes in the finales of the first and last acts. Ballet music from *Orfeo* and *Armide* was also introduced.

There is much to support the argument that this is Gluck's best opera. Here he comes nearest to a complete reconciliation of his dramatic style with his lyrical, and the extremes represented by *Alceste* and *Armide* are to some extent amalgamated. The dramatic and the sensuous – although this is to characterise them too simply – meet in *Iphigénie en Tauride* to form a whole that is more consistent and more expressive than anything Gluck had previously written. Nowhere else did he achieve such homogeneity of style, with whole scenes dominated by a single idea expressed in music of the greatest power, and seldom before had he displayed such invention in the individual arias.

K., H.

CHAPTER 3

*Mozart*

# WOLFGANG AMADEUS MOZART
## (1756–1791)

### IDOMENEO

OPERA in three acts by Mozart. Text by Abbé Varesco, after a French opera by Campra and Danchet. First performed at Munich, January 29, 1781, with Anton Raaff as Idomeneo, dal Prato as Idamante, Dorothea Wendling as Ilia, Elisabeth Wendling as Electra, Panzacchi as Arbace. Revived at Karlsruhe, 1917; Dresden, 1925; Vienna, 1931 (revised by Strauss, new text by Lothar Wallerstein, and with Maria Nemeth, Elisabeth Schumann, Josef Kalenberg, Eva Hadrabova, Richard Mayr in the cast); Munich, 1931 (revised by Wolf-Ferrari). The first British performance was at Glasgow in 1934, and the first English professional performance at Glyndebourne in 1951, when Fritz Busch conducted a cast including Sena Jurinac (Ilia), Birgit Nilsson (Electra), Richard Lewis (Idomeneo), and Leopold Simoneau (Idamante).

### CHARACTERS

Idomeneo, *King of Crete* .......................... Tenor
Idamante, *his son* ............................. Soprano
Ilia, *a Trojan Princess* ........................ Soprano
Electra, *a Greek Princess* ....................... Soprano
Arbace, *confidant of Idomeneo* ................... Tenor
High Priest of Neptune ......................... Tenor
Voice of Neptune ............................... Bass

People of Crete, Trojan Prisoners, Sailors, Soldiers, Priests
of Neptune, Dancers
The action takes place on the island of Crete

Mozart's third and greatest essay in the form of *opera seria* (his first two, *Mitridate* and *Lucio Silla*, were written respectively ten and nine years earlier) was first performed in 1781 at Munich, for which opera it was commissioned. Revived only once in the composer's lifetime (for a private performance in Vienna in 1786), it was fairly frequently heard in Germany and Austria after his death, but was not performed in Britain until 1934 (at Glasgow in the translation by the Misses M. and E. Radford), and never on the English professional stage until its production at Glyndebourne in 1951. It was not heard in America until 1947 when

performed at the Berkshire Festival, Tanglewood. Why this
neglect? First, by its very nature, *Idomeneo* has never been a
repertory opera. Secondly and more important, it is an example
of an operatic convention whose popularity was nearing its end
at the time of the first performance, and with which we have now
almost no first-hand acquaintance at all. A castrato ('mio molto
amato castrato del Prato', as Mozart called him) was a prominent
member of the original cast, and the opera was conceived during
the period of vocal virtuosity which is associated with that breed.
This is important to an understanding of the whole scheme of
*Idomeneo*, as the composer aimed to give the fullest possible
scope to his singers and the idiom is dependent for its full effect
on singing of considerable stature. But let it not be thought that
the opera is just a series of display pieces and formal movements;
it is far more than that—Einstein in fact describes it as 'one of
those works that even a genius of the highest rank, like Mozart,
could write only once in his life'. He was at the height of his
powers when it was composed, and the arias are superbly expressive, though on a more rarefied plane than the later comedies
have accustomed us to. If drama consists of the interplay of
motives and emotions, and tragedy of the ordering of men's
destinies by a fate their own actions have provoked, *Idomeneo* is
both tragic (in spite of its happy ending) and dramatic. The four
main characters, whose conflict reaches its climax with the great
quartet in the last act, are sharply defined, and what might well
have turned out no more than four stock figures, emerge in the
course of the musical action as personages no less real, if on an
idealised plane, than for instance Susanna or Pamina. In fact we
may take Ilia, with the gradual development of her personality
through the trials she has to undergo, as a sketch, musically
speaking at any rate, for Pamina, Mozart's maturest essay in
what one must think of as his conception of the 'perfect' feminine
type. It is hardly more fanciful to see in Idamante, her lover, the
forerunner of Tamino, even more forceful and generous and
dignified for all that he was originally sung by a castrato.

Act I. Idomeneo, King of Crete, has taken part in the Trojan
war, and it is many years since he left home. Amongst the prisoners
he has sent home is Ilia, daughter of King Priam, who has fallen
in love with Idamante, the son of Idomeneo. The overture immediately establishes the character of an opera whose music,

without exception, never relaxes its intense seriousness throughout its length; from it, without the need of external evidence as to
the conduct of *opera seria*, we may deduce the dignity and stature
of the characters involved. Calmly the drama unfolds. In an aria,
'Padre, germani addio', Ilia reveals that her hatred for the conquerors of her country is as nothing to her love for Idamante.
He enters at its conclusion and in veiled terms states his love for
Ilia, at the same time announcing that, in honour of his father's
imminent return to Crete, the Trojan prisoners are to be set free.
A chorus of rejoicing at this news precedes the entrance of
Arbace to say that Idomeneo's ship has been sunk; the
general consternation is given particular expression by Electra,
who fears that his death will remove all obstacles to the marriage
of Ilia and Idamante, with whom she is herself in love. Seldom if
ever before can passionate fury have been given so illuminating
an expression as in her aria. She leaves the stage and, at the end
of a chorus of intercession, Idomeneo enters with his followers,
whom he dismisses before explaining in an aria the nature of the
vow which secured Neptune's intervention in quieting the storm:
that he will sacrifice the first living creature he meets in return for
deliverance from death. It is, of course, Idamante whom he sees,
and their dialogue is made the more poignant because it is some
time before Idomeneo recognises his son, whom he has not seen
since infancy. In horror, the father orders the son from his
presence, and Idamante laments his father's apparent displeasure
in an aria 'Il padre adorato ritrovo e lo perdo'. The act ends with
a brilliant march and choral *ciaconna* in honour of Neptune and
the returning Cretans.

Act II. The King tells his secret to his counsellor Arbace,
who advises that Idamante be sent to a distant country: let him,
suggests the King, escort Electra back to Greece. The whole
scene, which was originally included to provide an aria for the
tenor Panzacchi, who created the role of Arbace, is usually
omitted in modern performance, the act thus beginning with the
scene between Idomeneo and Ilia whose aria 'Se il padre perdei'
is touchingly beautiful. Idomeneo understands that his vow now
involves not only disaster for himself and Idamante but for Ilia
as well, but he faces the tragedy with courage and dignity in his
great aria 'Fuor del mar ho un mar in seno'. This was written
as a show piece for Raaff, the 65-year-old tenor who created the

title role in Munich; whatever may be thought about his musical taste (he wanted an aria for himself substituted for the Act III quartet), his technique must have been very considerable indeed. As Professor Dent says: 'Coloratura for men has gone out of fashion, thanks to Wagner, and, thanks to the late Madame Patti, coloratura for women has become associated with the frail type of heroine rather than the heroic. In the eighteenth century and especially in the early half of it, the grand period of *opera seria*, coloratura was almost invariably heroic in character. . . . Donizetti's Lucia is paired off with a flute. Handel's heroes compete with a trumpet.' If the reader doubts whether any twentieth-century singer can overcome the difficulties of such music, I would refer him to a record made by Hermann Jadlowker about the time of the 1914–1918 war, in which this aria is sung with extraordinary fluency.

A beautiful, lyrical aria for Electra, whom the prospect of requited love has turned into a happy woman, leads into a march, and thence to the famous barcarolle chorus of embarkation, 'Placido è il mar, andiamo'. Idamante and Electra take leave of Idomeneo in a superb trio 'Pria di partir', but the music quickens and a storm breaks over the harbour heralding Neptune's vengeance at this attempt to evade the consequences of the vow made to him. Idomeneo admits his guilt but accuses the god of injustice, and the act ends as the crowd disperses in terror.

Act III.    Ilia can think only of her love for Idamante, and her expression of it in her soliloquy 'Zefiretti lusinghieri' is one of the most perfect moments of the opera. To her comes Idamante; he is going out to fight the monster Neptune has sent to plague the island, and he may not return. Involuntarily, she confesses her love, which leads to a duet. Idomeneo and Electra interrupt the lovers. Idomeneo still cannot bring himself to explain the exact cause of the disaster which is overtaking them all, and Idamante sadly takes his farewell in the noble quartet 'Andrò ramingo e solo'. Einstein calls it 'the first really great ensemble in the history of the *opera seria*' and Professor Dent does not try to disguise his enthusiasm for it when he describes it as 'perhaps the most beautiful ensemble ever composed for the stage'. In truth, one has no cause to complain that either is exaggerating; it shows Mozart at his noblest and most expressive, and is the moment in the opera when the spirit of tragedy most completely dominates the music. An elaborate recitative and aria for Arbace, which is found here in the score, is usually omitted in performance, and the scene customarily and appropriately ends with the quartet.

After an introduction, the High Priest exhorts the King to confess his sin to Neptune, and the people are duly horrified to hear that the sacrifice of Idamante is the price they and he will have to pay for deliverance from the god's displeasure. The people are gathered in the Temple of Neptune to witness the sacrifice, the priests enter to a march and Idomeneo begins the ceremony with a solemn prayer which is answered by the priests. A shout of triumph is heard outside and Arbace announces that Idamante has met the monster in combat and killed it. However, a moment later Idamante, who by now knows the story of his father's vow, enters and offers himself for sacrifice, and Idomeneo cannot but accept him. The ceremony is about to reach its climax when Ilia interrupts and demands to be sacrificed in Idamante's place. The whole situation is resolved by an oracular pronouncement from Neptune, to the effect that the crime can be expiated, the vow fulfilled, if Idomeneo will renounce the throne in favour of his son. In the general rejoicing, only Electra is left with her worst fears realised; in the most furious of her violent utterances, she gives vent to her despair and rushes from the stage, or, as some versions have it, falls dead or commits suicide.

The atmosphere changes to one of peace and fulfilment as Idomeneo in a last recitative and aria, 'Torna la pace al core', presents Idamante to the people as their new ruler, and takes his farewell of them. At the first performance, this aria had to be cut, much apparently to Mozart's regret, as anyone who hears it nowadays will readily understand. The opera ends with the people celebrating the accession of Idamante in dance and chorus.

When *Idomeneo* was performed privately in Vienna by amateur singers, Mozart added two numbers, transposed the role of Idamante for a tenor, removed most of Arbace's music, and made certain modifications in the rest of the opera. That he gave the role of Idamante to a tenor has been taken by some modern editors to indicate a change of mind as far as the vocal colour of this role was concerned, but this is surely to attach too little importance to the practical conditions of a performance which was after all mostly in the hands of amateur singers; rather few of these would have been likely to have been castrati. In any case, however far the colour of the castrato voice must have been from that of a modern soprano, it is hard to believe that it was nearer to a tenor's.

Arrangers and editors of this score have included the composers Richard Strauss, Wolf-Ferrari, and Hans Gal, but the twin difficulties remain of staging a work conceived in so remote a convention, and of singing music written for another breed of singer. Difficulties of performance, remoteness of convention the work may have, but it is conceived on so noble a level and the rewards would be so infinitely worthwhile if they were overcome, that efforts to achieve a satisfactory modern performance must and no doubt will continue to be made.                H.

## DIE ENTFÜHRUNG AUS DEM SERAIL

Opera in three acts by Mozart. Text by Gottlob Stephanie from a play by Bretzner. First performed at the Burgtheater, Vienna, July 16, 1782, with Caterina Cavalieri (Constanze), Therese Teyber (Blonde), Valentin Ademberger (Belmonte), Ludwig Fischer (Osmin), and conducted by Mozart.

During the first six years of its existence, there were thirty-four performances in Vienna. First performed in London, Covent Garden, 1827, in English, with additional airs by J. B. Cramer, and sung by Madame Vestris, Miss Hughes, Mr. Sapio, Mr. Benson, Mr. Wrenn. The first performance in New York was in 1860. Other performances in London include those at Drury Lane, 1841 (in German), Her Majesty's, 1866 (in Italian, with recitatives by Arditi). Revived Covent Garden, 1927, with Ivogün, Schumann, Erb, Bender, and conducted by Bruno Walter; 1938, with Berger, Beilke, Tauber, Weber, conducted by Beecham. Produced for the first time at Glyndebourne in 1935, with Noel Eadie, Eisinger, Ludwig, Andresen, and Heddle Nash (Pedrillo), conducted by Fritz Busch. The first performance in Italy did not take place until 1935, at the Florence Festival when Bruno Walter conducted a cast consisting of Perras, Schöne, Kullman, and Sterneck; and the opera was first heard at the Metropolitan, New York, in 1946.

## CHARACTERS

Constanze, *a Spanish lady* ..................... Soprano
Blonde, *her English maid* ..................... Soprano
Belmonte, *a Spanish nobleman* ................... Tenor
Pedrillo, *his servant* ........................... Tenor
Pasha Selim ........................... Speaking Part
Osmin, *overseer of his harem* ..................... Bass
Turkish Soldiers, Guards, Turkish women

A curious 'springboard' (as Einstein calls it in his *Mozart; his Character, his Work*) exists for *Die Entführung*. In 1779 Mozart began the music for a *Singspiel*, perhaps in desperation at the small prospects for operatic composition and performance which Salzburg offered. It seems not to have been finished, was only published in 1838 under the title of *Zaïde*, and did not reach the stage until 1866. The reasons are not far to seek: it was conceived on a modest scale—too modest for Mozart's real requirements—and its subject and style were 'Turkish', and very close to those of the opera he undertook a little later, *Die Entführung*, whose story reads like an amplification of *Zaïde*'s. *Zaïde* contains some attractive music, and the aria 'Ruhe sanft, mein holdes Leben' is of the greatest simplicity and beauty.

*Die Entführung* (1782) itself is important amongst Mozart's works not least because of the ambitious and extended view he takes in it of the hitherto modest German *Singspiel*. The drama is carried on almost exclusively in speech and it is only in moments of high emotion that the characters have recourse to song—but on what a sublimated level is that song when it comes! To expect in a *Singspiel* the extended finales that are a characteristic of *opera buffa* is to wish for something which would have been out of character with the convention and which Mozart was not trying to provide. Nevertheless, the music is highly expressive. Constanze and Belmonte, the latter at any rate, are perhaps loftier in their musical aspirations than they are in the field of human behaviour, where they lay themselves open to charges of ingratitude and deception. Blonde and Pedrillo, though entertaining, are little more than stock comedy figures. Osmin, however, is one of the composer's great dramatic creations, genuinely and consistently comic in music as in action, yet no mere figure of fun, and as dangerous as he is laughable.

Act I.   The overture is mainly concerned with establishing the 'Turkish' atmosphere of the piece; Mozart also introduces a reference in the minor to Belmonte's aria, 'Hier soll' ich dich denn sehen, Constanze', which is heard in C major when the curtain goes up. Belmonte is outside the Pasha Selim's house, where he believes his beloved Constanze, who has been carried off by pirates, is a captive. Osmin, in charge of the Pasha's harem and also, it seems, of his garden, appears singing a doleful sort of love song, 'Wer ein Liebchen hat gefunden', one of the delights of the score. He is questioned by Belmonte: is this not the Pasha Selim's house? It is, and he works for the Pasha, but an enquiry for Pedrillo produces an even surlier answer, as this is his *bête noir*, his rival in love for Blondchen; Pedrillo should, he says, without delay, be hanged, drawn, and quartered. He chases Belmonte away, but is immediately confronted with Pedrillo in person, saucier and more impudent than ever. The situation calls for music and he relieves his pent-up feelings with an aria that is a virtuoso expression of rage and also, in good hands, of the comic bass's art.

Belmonte returns to find his former servant; each is delighted at the other's news, Belmonte to hear that Constanze has remained true to him in spite of the Pasha's persuasive powers, Pedrillo that there is a boat waiting to take them all to safety if they can only spirit the women out of the harem. Belmonte sings a song of love for his absent Constanze: 'O wie ängstlich, o wie feurig'. It is filled with a romantic feeling that derives in part, we may suppose, from Mozart's own love for his Constanze, whom he married a few weeks after the production of the opera. The orchestral accompaniment, Mozart tells his father in a letter, represents the throbbing of the lover's heart, the heaving of his breast, his sighs and whispers.

Belmonte leaves the stage as Constanze and the Pasha land from a boat to be greeted in a chorus that is very much in the Turkish style. The Pasha once again assures Constanze of his love and of

his determination to win hers in return. She sings of the love that she knew before her captivity and protests that she will be true to this memory: 'Ach, ich liebte, war so glücklich'. It is a coloratura aria, but full of sadness for her past happiness and of determination to resist temptation. She leaves the stage, and Pedrillo takes this opportunity to introduce Belmonte to the Pasha as an architect of high standing. The Pasha intimates that he will not withhold his favour from him, but after he has gone Osmin remains unimpressed and tries to bar their way. It is only after a lively trio, 'Marsch, marsch, marsch', that they contrive to outmanœuvre him and enter the palace.

Act II.    Osmin is no match for Blonde in a battle of wits, as she demonstrates in her aria, 'Durch Zärtlichkeit und Schmeicheln', and the duet which follows. He knows she will come off best and can do no more than complain at the folly of the English in allowing their women so much liberty (in this story, Blonde is supposed to be English). Constanze unburdens herself to Blonde: 'Traurigkeit ward mir zum Loose'. It is perhaps the most deeply felt number of the score, and one of Mozart's most sublime expressions of grief (like 'Ach, ich fühl's', in the key of G Minor). Blonde retires as the Pasha comes once more to urge his suit.

Constanze is adamant and launches into one of the most considerable arias Mozart ever wrote for soprano voice: 'Martern aller Arten'. Laid out on concerto lines, with four solo instruments and a lengthy orchestral introduction, it is the one moment in the opera where Mozart definitely sacrifices the stage situation—the Pasha and Constanze can do little else but glare at each other during the introduction—to the possibilities inherent in his singers, of whom Caterina Cavalieri, the Constanze, was perhaps the most eminent. But the aria that results is musically such a masterpiece that few people will feel disposed to agree with the purists who maintain that it should be cut in performance (unless, that is to say, the singer is going to make a mess of it).

Blonde is wondering if the empty stage signifies that the entreaties of the Pasha have at last been successful when Pedrillo rushes in to tell her that Belmonte is here and a plan afoot for their escape. Osmin is to be drugged to make way for the double elopement. Blonde's joyful song, 'Welche Wonne, welche Lust', contrasts with Pedrillo's definitely nervous reaction to the prospect of dealing with Osmin single-handed ('Frisch zum Kampfe'). However, he tackles as to the manner born the business of persuading Osmin that the Mohammedan doctrine of teetotalism is better honoured in the breach than in the observance, and he soon has him tippling with the best and praising wine in one of Mozart's most exquisite inspirations, the duet 'Vivat Bacchus'. Osmin sinks into a stupor and Pedrillo is able to drag him out of the way and leave the coast clear for a reunion between Belmonte and Constanze. Belmonte in his aria, 'Wenn der Freude Thränen fliessen', is less passionate than Constanze as she begins the quartet which is to end the act. It is a noble piece in spite of the crisis which is contrived to keep it alive—the men ask to be assured again that their lovers were true during captivity—and the musical integrity is unaffected by the dramatic artificiality.

Act III. With much comic pantomime, Pedrillo organises the disposal of the ladders with the help of the captain of the ship which is to take them to freedom. Belmonte enters and is instructed to sing so that no one will notice that he, Pedrillo, is not serenading his Blonde as usual ('Ich baue ganz auf deine Stärke'). A moment later, Pedrillo is back, and ready to give the signal for escape with his enchanting serenade 'Im Mohrenland gefangen war'.

Romanze

Im Moh-ren-land ge-fan-gen war - - ein Mädchen hübsch und fein

Nothing in the score is more immediately appealing than this graceful piece, which must be the plum of the whole 'second tenor' repertory. Belmonte and Constanze disappear into the darkness, and Pedrillo rushes up the ladder to fetch his Blonde, unaware that his singing has woken up a guard, a mute, who suspects the worst and dashes off to summon Osmin. The latter arrives as the second pair of lovers is on the point of leaving the house, and his suspicions that a double elopement has been planned are confirmed when Constanze and Belmonte are brought back by the guard which has surprised their escape. 'Ha! wie will ich triumphieren' he sings in his joy that at last he is to have the chance of settling a hundred and one old scores with Pedrillo, and several new ones as well with Belmonte. Never has one operatic character gloated so convincingly over the misfortunes of others, and Osmin parades his vengeful notions in an orgy of triumph, touching a top E and sustaining a bottom D in his highly satisfactory efforts to give them adequate musical expression.

The Pasha is informed of the intended escape, and arrives to question the prisoners. Constanze pleads her love for Belmonte as justification for the attempted escape, and her lover assures the Pasha that his father, a rich Spaniard of the name of Lostados, will pay a high ransom for his freedom. Lostados! exclaims the Pasha: you are the son of my greatest enemy, the man who stole from me my love, my career, and my right to live in my native country. Belmonte and Constanze are face to face with death and perhaps torture, and their extensive duet, 'Welch' ein Geschick', reveals a serious approach to their imminent tragedy. The Pasha returns, and announces that he scorns to return evil for evil, that they are free to return to their native Spain whenever they like. The happy couples return thanks in the form of a *vaudeville*, which Belmonte begins, the others singing a verse each and all joining in the refrain:

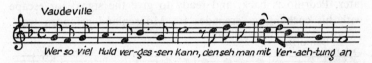

Blonde cannot resist a final dig at the discomfited Osmin, whose rage overcomes him so that he disrupts the harmony of the ensemble with another furious outburst before rushing defeated from the stage, leaving the others to finish on a note of suitable gratitude. They take their leave while the chorus sings the praises of the Pasha and his clemency.                    H.

## LE NOZZE DI FIGARO
### The Marriage of Figaro

*Opera buffa* in four acts by Mozart; text by Lorenzo da Ponte, after Beaumarchais. First performed at the Burgtheater, Vienna, May 1, 1786, with Mme. Laschi (Countess), Storace (Susanna), Bussani (Cherubino), Gottlieb (Barbarina), Mandini (Marcellina), Messrs. Mandini (Count Almaviva), Benucci (Figaro), Kelly (Basilio and Curzio), Bussani (Bartolo and Antonio), and conducted by Mozart. First performed in England (in Italian) at Haymarket Theatre, London, 1812, and (in English) Covent Garden, 1819, with Mrs. Dickens, Miss Stephens, Miss Beaumont, Messrs. Jones, Liston, Isaacs. The first performance in New York took place in 1824. Revived at Old Vic Theatre, London (Professor Dent's translation), 1920; and first performed at Glyndebourne Festival in 1934, conducted by Fritz Busch, produced by Carl Ebert, and with Aulikki Rautawaara, Audrey Mildmay, Luise Helletsgruber, Willi Domgraf-Fassbänder, Roy Henderson, Norman Allin in the cast.

### CHARACTERS

Count Almaviva . . . . . . . . . . . . . . . . . . . . . . . . . . . . . Baritone
Figaro, *his valet* . . . . . . . . . . . . . . . . . . . . . . . . . . . Baritone
Doctor Bartolo . . . . . . . . . . . . . . . . . . . . . . . . . . . . . . Bass
Don Basilio, *a music-master* . . . . . . . . . . . . . . . . . . . . . Tenor
Cherubino, *a page* . . . . . . . . . . . . . . . . . . . . . . . . . . . Soprano
Antonio, *a gardener* . . . . . . . . . . . . . . . . . . . . . . . . . . Bass

Don Curzio, *counsellor at law* ..................... Tenor
Countess Almaviva .......................... Soprano
Susanna, *her personal maid, affianced to Figaro* .... Soprano
Marcellina, *a duenna* ........................ Soprano
Barbarina, *Antonio's niece* ..................... Soprano
*Time:* Eighteenth Century        *Place:* The Count's chateau of
Aguas Frescas, near Seville

Probably the two perfect 'popular' operas are *Figaro* and *Aida* —'popular' in the sense that both are very frequently performed and neither public nor musicians show signs of getting tired of listening to them, 'perfect' in the sense that they combine a sensitivity and delicacy in their musical construction and workmanship with the all-important common touch. It is an easy commonplace—perhaps fatally easy—to pile on superlatives when describing Mozart's operas, and particularly when talking about *Figaro, Don Giovanni, Così fan Tutte,* and *The Magic Flute,* but it is a fault which is very difficult to avoid; the plain fact is that an enormous number of opera-goers would proclaim *Figaro* the most entertaining operatic comedy they had ever heard.

*Figaro* was Mozart's first venture with his most famous librettist, Lorenzo da Ponte (who incidentally provided the libretti for no less than four operas which had their first performance during 1786, the year of *Figaro's* debut). Although he had had no Italian comic opera produced since *La Finta Giardiniera* in 1775, Mozart had in the meanwhile worked on *L'Oca del Cairo* and *Lo Sposo Deluso,* each of which he abandoned. He had also composed the music for *Der Schauspieldirektor,* a slight piece but sufficient evidence of the continuing development of his theatrical and musical craftsmanship. It is surprising in retrospect to note that, in spite of the brilliant libretto and even more brilliant music, *Figaro* made only a moderate success when it was produced in Vienna, where it had to wait until after the triumph in Prague before being received into popular affection. It was incidentally the success of *Figaro* in Prague which led to the commission to compose *Don Giovanni* for that city.

Act I.    The overture is extremely well known, and nothing could make a better prelude to this marriage day of feverish activity than the short *presto* movement. When the curtain rises, Susanna is discovered in front of the looking-glass, and Figaro is measuring out a space on the floor ('Cinque, dieci'). The room, Figaro explains, is to be theirs—'the most convenient room in the castle, just between milord and milady'. (Not all stage designers have been prepared to admit that, in eighteenth-century castle geography, this is likely to have been a box room or a curtained-off portion of a passage, not a grand room with a veranda and a view of the Park.) Susanna astounds him by peremptorily refusing to accept it, but, when he remonstrates ('Se a caso Madama'—Supposing one evening my lady should want you [1]), explains that the position may make it easy for her to go to the Countess, it also makes it easy for the Count to get to her. The Countess rings, and Figaro is left alone to contemplate a situation that is by no means to his liking. In the two movements of his duet with Susanna, the mood has been one of gaiety and light-heartedness, which is hardly interrupted by the hint of intrigue, as Susanna is obviously unperturbed by a situation she feels herself quite capable of dealing with. But 'Se vuol ballare' (If you are after a little amusement) shows Figaro in a state of mind in which determination cannot altogether eliminate apprehension. No sooner has he left the stage than we are shown another aspect of the worry which is to plague him on his wedding-day. Marcellina comes in with Don Bartolo, the pair of them hatching a plot which shall compel Figaro to marry Marcellina as he has defaulted on a debt he owes her. He, Doctor Bartolo, with his legal knowledge will ensure that there is no escape for the rascal ('La vendetta'—Now for vengeance)—a splendid example of what such an aria for *basso buffo* can become in the hands of a composer of genius. As he goes out of one door, Susanna enters the room by another and she and Marcellina meet as they attempt to follow Bartolo; their duet as each offers the other precedence ends in Marcellina's complete discomfiture. Susanna stays behind and is immediately confronted with a disconsolate Cherubino, who wants to enlist her help in getting the Count to reinstate him as the Countess's page. No one takes him seriously except himself. He is just at the wrong age: young enough to be allowed liberties, old enough to take advantage of them (as has happened over his latest exploit with Barbarina, for which he has been dismissed) in a way that cannot be tolerated. He is in love with every woman he comes across, and pours out

---

[1] Dent's translation.

his adolescent aspirations to Susanna in an aria, 'Non so più cosa son, cosa faccio' (Is it pain, is it pleasure that fills me?). No sooner has he finished than voices are heard outside and he has only just time to conceal himself before the Count comes into Susanna's room and starts to protest his affections. It is not her lucky day, as the Count is followed a moment or two later by Basilio; in the scramble for concealment, Cherubino nips into the chair behind which the Count takes refuge. Basilio teases Susanna with gossip about Cherubino and when she will not listen, presses her about the page and the Countess—an intrigue which he says everyone is talking about. The Count can bear it no longer and emerges from his hiding-place to demand that the gossip-mongers shall be found and punished. In the ensuing trio—since 'Non so più cosa son' the action has been carried on in recitative—Susanna faints, but revives in time to plead the cause of the unhappy Cherubino, a mere boy she says. Not so young as you think, says the Count, and describes how he caught him the previous day hiding in Barbarina's room. Suiting the action to the word, he draws the cover from the chair—and there is Cherubino again. Only Cherubino's admission that he had heard what passed between the Count and Susanna ('I did all I could *not* to hear, my lord') stays the penalty that would otherwise be his. Led by Figaro, a band of peasants comes in to sing the Count's praises, and, at its end, the Count yields to the general entreaties, but only to the extent of giving Cherubino a commission in his Regiment, for which he must leave immediately. Figaro speeds him on his way with a spirited description of what his future life has in store for him. Michael Kelly, the Irish tenor who was the Basilio and Curzio in the original production, tells in his memoirs of the splendid sonority with which Benucci, the Figaro, sang the martial air 'Non piu andrai' (Say good-bye now to pastime and play, lad) at the first orchestral rehearsal. Mozart, who was on the stage in a crimson pelisse and cocked hat trimmed with gold lace, kept repeating 'Bravo, bravo, Benucci!' In truth, it is a stirring finale to an act.

Act II. We are introduced to the Countess in a soliloquy, 'Porgi amor' (God of Love). In this aria, whose simplicity makes it one of the most taxing entrances for any soprano, we are made aware of her intense longing for her husband's love and also of the reticence which her breeding makes natural to her. Susanna

explains the situation to her and opens the door to Figaro; his plan is that the Count shall be given an assignation with Susanna, whose place shall be taken by Cherubino, and that at the same time he shall be told in an anonymous letter that the Countess in her turn has made a rendezvous with an unknown man. Cherubino comes in to see if he can be dressed for the part, but first sings the song he has just composed, 'Voi che sapete' (Tell me fair ladies). Not only has Mozart got round the difficulty of introducing a song ('words and music by Cherubino') into a milieu where singing is the natural means of expression, but he has done so in such a way that this piece has become one of the world's most popular tunes. Cherubino tries on the dress to the accompaniment of a song with action, Susanna's 'Venite inginocchiatevi' (Come here and kneel before me now). No sooner is it ended and Cherubino safely buttoned up than a knock is heard at the door. It is the Count. Consternation. Cherubino dashes into the Countess's bedroom and Susanna hides behind a curtain. The Count is suspicious of his wife's all too obvious nervousness, and suspicion that something is being hidden from him becomes certainty when he hears a noise and finds the door of her room locked ('Susanna, or via sortite'—Come out, come out, Susanna). He takes his wife with him as he goes off to get tools to break it down with. While he is away Cherubino slips out of hiding and jumps from the window, leaving Susanna to take his place. The little *allegro assai* duet for Susanna and Cherubino is a comedy interlude of the greatest dexterity amidst the ranting and raging of the Count, which redoubles in fury when the Countess tries to explain that Cherubino is in her room without much on because he was being fitted for a charade. The great finale is begun by the Count in a towering passion: 'Esci omai, garzon malnato' (Out you come, no more concealment). The Countess's pleading seems to be in vain, but both are struck dumb with amazement when, at the height of the storm, Susanna emerges coolly from the inner room. It is one of those incomparable musico-dramatic strokes which no listener who knows the opera ever fails to look forward to, and which comes as an anti-climax only in the worst of performances. The Count rushes in to see if Cherubino is not still there, but, finding he is not, can do nothing but sue for pardon. With Susanna's aid, this is obtained, but with it the Count's suspicions begin to take possession of him again. The anonymous letter? Written by Figaro, delivered by Basilio. He thinks he has found someone he can safely be angry with, but is told he must forgive everyone if he himself is to be forgiven for his jealousy. There is a moment of peace and relaxation which ends as Figaro bounds in to summon his master and mistress to the wedding dance which is about to begin. But the Count sees a chance of getting his own back and questions Figaro about the anonymous

letter. In spite of hints from the Countess and Susanna, Figaro denies all knowledge of it, and has almost turned the Count's suspicions when Antonio, the gardener, bursts in, protesting that his life is a perpetual trial but that to-day they have thrown a man out of the window on to his flower-beds, and that is too much. Figaro says that it was he who jumped out, but Antonio thinks it looked more like the page. Figaro sticks to his story until the Count catechises him about a paper Antonio says was dropped near the flower-bed. Figaro searches his pockets and racks his brains, and in the nick of time the Countess recognises it and whispers to Figaro that it is the page's commission. Why was it left? Again, it is only just in time that the Countess remembers that it had not been sealed. Figaro's triumph is short-lived, as Marcellina comes in, supported by Bartolo and Basilio, to lodge formal complaint before the Count against Figaro for breach of promise. The act comes to an end in pandemonium.

This finale is one of the greatest single sections in all Mozart's operas. For variety of motive, tempo, and texture it is unrivalled; the characterisation is consistent and credible and at no time subordinated to more general musical needs; the level of invention is extremely high; and the whole thing is carried on with resources that make use of the nine principals but involve no chorus or scenic display. It is a marvel of ingenuity, and at the same time a model of simplicity.

Act III.    The Count has not yet given up hope of Susanna, and when she comes to borrow smelling salts for her mistress he seems within reach of his prize. She agrees to meet him that night in the garden. Their duet, 'Crudel, perche finora' (Oh, why are

Andante

Cru-del! per-chè fi -

-no-ra far -- - mi lan-guir cò - sì?

you so cruel), reveals the Count as an ardent lover, Susanna as
an inattentive beloved, but the result is a masterpiece. As Susanna
leaves the room, she meets Figaro and assures him, just a little
too loudly, that he is sure now of winning his case against Marcellina. Sure of winning his case? repeats the Count, and launches
into a superb recitative and aria, 'Vedrò mentr'io sospiro, felice
un servo mio?' (Must I forgo my pleasure, whilst serf of mine
rejoices?)   Professor Dent has observed that the Count, a man of
intense energy, is shown first of all in ensemble, only later in aria,
because, one might almost say, he has not time to sing an aria
until the moment when he has to take stock of his position. It is
an extraordinary piece of self-revelation when it does come, and
takes the Count right out of the category of the unsuccessful
lover and erring husband into something much more sinister.
But the balance is redressed when it is discovered, after he has
given judgment for Marcellina, that that lady is in fact none other
than Figaro's mother. In the great sextet which follows, the
Count is reduced to expressions of impotent fury: what can he
do when confronted with this wholly unexpected development?
The sextet is one of the most satisfactory instances in all opera of

E quel-lo è mio pa-dre che a te lo di - rà, che a te   lo di - rà

pure comedy purveyed in terms of straight-faced music. The
scene is left empty for a moment, and the Countess comes in to
sing the most extended and most moving of her utterances in the
opera. 'Dove sono' (I remember days long departed) consists of
a lengthy recitative followed by a restrained but highly expressive
aria in two sections, *andantino* and later *allegro*. It is her moment
of greatest self-revelation, just as his aria was the Count's; if his
thoughts were of revenge that his desires are not to be satisfied,
hers are of the love he once bore her but which she seems to have
lost. His aria grew out of the situation created by his duet with
Susanna, the Countess's gives audible expression to a situation
which can only be resolved with Susanna's aid and therefore leads
to a duet between the two. Between them they arrange where
Susanna is to meet the Count that evening. The letter duet,
'Che soave zeffiretto' (How delightful 'tis to wander, by the

breath of evening fann'd), is one of the most famous numbers in the score; the mistress dictates a letter to the Count, the maid takes it down, and the voices of both blend as they read it back

together. But the wedding festivities are about to begin and a crowd of village girls presents flowers to the Countess, who is astonished a moment later, when the Count comes in with Antonio, to see one of them unmasked as Cherubino. A tense situation is saved by Barbarina: 'My lord, when you kiss me and tell me you love me, you often say you will give me whatever I want. Give me Cherubino for a husband.' Figaro announces the beginning of the wedding march, the so-called Fandango, the one Spanish element in the score. Like the march in *Idomeneo*

and the minuet in *Don Giovanni* it begins as it were in the middle, and returns to what should properly be the opening section later on. There is a chorus in praise of the generosity and right-mindedness of the Count in having abolished the *droit du seigneur*, and the happy couples—Bartolo and Marcellina as well as Figaro and Susanna—receive their wedding wreaths from the Count and Countess, Susanna taking the opportunity to give the Count the letter she and her mistress have concocted for him. He opens it pricking his finger on the pin—a comedy which is watched all unknowingly by Figaro and commented on with some relish. The Count announces general festivity—song, dance, feasting, and fireworks—and the act ends with a repetition of the chorus in his honour.

Act IV. The last act is mainly devoted to clearing up the various situations which have arisen in the course of Figaro's wedding day, but there is one more complication to be added before the process can begin. The atmosphere is highly charged with an almost sinister feeling of foreboding; more perhaps than can be put down to the fact that it is night by the time the act begins. The action takes place in a part of the garden which contains arbours and sheltered walks. Barbarina begins it with a little half-finished cavatina; she has been given the pin which sealed the letter to return to Susanna, but has lost it. She tells the story to Figaro, who comes in with Marcellina and is overcome with distress at this apparent indication of his wife's unfaithfulness.

Arias for Marcellina and Basilio occur at this point, but both are customarily omitted. Before Basilio's, Figaro watches Barbarina hide in one of the arbours (where she is to meet Cherubino), and tells Bartolo and Basilio that they are to stay near at hand to witness the seduction of his wife by the Count. Now occurs Figaro's recitative and aria, 'Tutto e disposto' (Everything's ready), and 'Aprite un po' quegli occhi' (Yes, fools you are and will be, fools till your eyes are opened), at the same time his most serious moment (the recitative is tragic in the extreme) and his most comic (the horns at the end are surely intended to be illustrative as well as musical). Susanna asks the Countess (they have by now changed clothes) to be allowed to walk a little apart from her, and sings an aria of exquisite sensibility, ostensibly to the lover she is waiting for, but in reality knowing full well that Figaro is listening to her: 'Deh vieni non tardar' (Then come, my heart's delight). The comedy of mistaken identity begins. Cherubino attempts to flirt with what he thinks is Susanna, in reality of course the Countess. Susanna, the Count, and Figaro observe, and the Count interrupts and starts to make

love on his own account to his wife in disguise. Figaro does not
know about the change of clothes and it is his turn to interrupt;
with the stage empty he invokes the names of the gods of antiquity to lend weight to his determination to avenge his honour.
Susanna (still disguised as the Countess) calls to him and he
starts to tell her of the Count's escapade when he recognises that
it is in fact Susanna he is talking to. The dramatic tension which
may lead to tragedy is shattered, and we are once more safely in
comedy. Figaro makes love to her as if she were the Countess,

and then laughs at her attempt to disguise herself from him as much as at her indignation. All is forgiven—Susanna does not mind the joke against herself—and the two combine to make the Count think their extravagant love-making is in reality that of mistress and valet (example, p. 78). The ruse succeeds, the Count summons anyone within hearing to bear witness to the unfaithfulness of his wife, and in succession hauls Cherubino, Barbarina, Marcellina, and the supposed culprit from the arbour in which they have taken refuge. All pleading is in vain, until the voice of the Countess herself is heard behind them all: 'Almeno io per loro perdono ottero?' (May I then for pardon at last intercede?) The dramatic suddenness of her entry combines with the Count's noble phrase of contrition to make this a moment that can be set beside that of the emergence of Susanna from the Countess's room in Act II. The Count begs forgiveness in a swelling phrase, receives it, and the opera ends in general rejoicing, voiced though by the principals alone and unsupported by the chorus.

*Le Nozze di Figaro* is an incomparable masterpiece, one moreover that has been praised throughout its history for a variety of reasons. If it was once the brilliant tunes of the solo songs which attracted audience and performers alike, it would probably nowadays be claimed that the ensembles are the main glories of the work. Nothing, one is inclined to think, could be more perfect than the finale to the second act. Such amazing invention and such dexterity cannot be excelled. Maybe it cannot, but in the last act Mozart has achieved something almost more remarkable in the feeling of anxiety which pervades music and situation alike. It is as though the tapestry of the comedy has been reversed and instead of dazzling with its brilliance, it is shot through with flashes, not of light but of darkness; it is not so much that the garden has a thundercloud hanging over it, but that there is lightning in the air. I know I always have something akin to a feeling of relief when Figaro's little B flat tune arrives to prove that once again we have come through the web of intrigue to the safety and happiness beyond it. At no time does the opera break the bounds of comedy, even in this last act, except in so far as Mozart here, as in *Don Giovanni*, appears to acknowledge no bounds where comedy is concerned.                H.

# DER SCHAUSPIELDIREKTOR
## The Impresario

Another comedy opera, produced 1786, introduces that clever rogue, Schikaneder, at whose entreaty *The Magic Flute* was composed. The other characters include Mozart himself, and Mme. Hofer, his sister-in-law, who was the Queen of the Night in the original cast of *The Magic Flute*. The story deals with the troubles of an impresario due to the jealousy of prima donnas. 'Before they are engaged, opera singers are very engaging, except when they are engaged in singing.' This line is from H. E. Krehbiel's translation of the libretto, produced, with *Bastien and Bastienne* (translated by Alice Matullah, as a 'lyric pastoral'), at the Empire Theatre, New York, October 26, 1916. These charming productions were made by the Society of American Singers with a company including David Bispham (Schikaneder and Colas), Albert Reiss (Mozart and Bastien), Mabel Garrison, and Lucy Gates; the direction that of Mr. Reiss.                                    K.

# DON GIOVANNI

Opera in two acts by Mozart, text by Lorenzo da Ponte. First performed at the National Theatre, Prague, October 29, 1787. The English première took place in London at Her Majesty's Theatre, April 12, 1817, with Mmes. Camporese, Hughes, Fodor, and Messrs. Ambrogetti, Neldi, Crivelli, and Agrisani. The opera was given at Covent Garden (in English) on May 30, 1817, and for the first time in America (as *The Libertine*) in Philadelphia in 1818. It was presented at the Park Theatre, New York, in 1826 with da Ponte present, Manuel Garcia senior as Don Giovanni, Manuel Garcia junior as Leporello, Mme. Garcia as Donna Elvira, and Signorina Maria Garcia (afterwards the famous Malibran) as Zerlina. Recent revivals: Covent Garden, 1926, conducted by Bruno Walter, and with Frida Leider, Lotte Lehmann, Elisabeth Schumann, Mariano Stabile, Fritz Krauss, and Aquistapace in the cast; 1939 in the same theatre with Elisabeth Rethberg, Hilde Konetzni, Mafalda Favero, Ezio Pinza, Richard Tauber, Virgilio Lazzari and conducted by Sir Thomas Beecham. The first performance at Glyndebourne was in 1936, when Ina Souez, Luise Helletsgruber, Audrey Mildmay, John Brownlee, Koloman von Pataky, Salvatore Baccaloni were conducted by Fritz Busch.

The opera has engaged the services of famous artists throughout its history. Faure and Maurel were great Don Giovannis, Jean de Reszke sang the role while he was still a baritone, and Scotti made his debut at the Metropolitan in the role. Renaud appeared as Don Giovanni at the Manhattan Opera House, and recent exponents of the title role have included John Forsell, Mariano Stabile, and Ezio Pinza. Lablache was accounted the greatest of Leporellos, but earlier in his career he had sung Don Giovanni. The role of Don Ottavio has been sung by Rubini, Mario, John McCormack, and Schipa; Lilli Lehmann and Ljuba Welitsch have been renowned in the role

PLATE V. *Le Nozze di Figaro*, Act I, at Aix-en-Provence Festival 1952. The remarkable sets were by Antoni Clavé, and the singers here are Hugues Cuénod (Basilio), Graziella Sciutti (Susanna), and Heinz Rehfuss (the Count).

PLATE VI. *Figaro*, Salzburg 1948, in Casper Neher's sets. Irmgard
Seefried is Susanna, Elisabeth Schwarzkopf the Countess.

of Donna Anna; and Zerlina has been sung by aspiring *prime donne* from Adelina Patti to Geraldine Farrar.

A curious aside in the history of the work was an adaptation by Kalkbrenner which was produced in Paris in 1805. How greatly this differed from the original may be judged from the fact that the trio of the masks was sung by three policemen!

## CHARACTERS

The Commendatore .............................Bass
Donna Anna, *his daughter* .....................Soprano
Don Ottavio, *her betrothed* ......................Tenor
Don Giovanni, *a young nobleman* ..............Baritone
Leporello, *his servant* ...........................Bass
Donna Elvira, *a lady of Burgos* ................Soprano
Zerlina, *a country girl* ........................Soprano
Masetto, *betrothed to Zerlina* ..................Baritone

For years *Don Giovanni* has been, if not the most popular, at all events the most frequently praised of operas. Beethoven is said to have named *The Magic Flute* as his favourite opera, not, as one might have expected, because of the wide range of its ideas and its musical level, but because it contained almost all musical forms, from the fugue to the *lied*. In the same sort of way, perhaps *Don Giovanni* owes part of its success to the almost unique blending of the irresistibly comic and the tragically serious, as much as to the speed of its dramatic and musical action, and to the quality of the music. The other decisive factor in its popularity is the fascinating figure of the Don himself, the libertine and the blasphemer, whose courage endears him to the men and his irresistible reputation to the women.

It has even been asserted that Don Juan Tenorio was a historical personage, but there is little evidence to support this view. His first recorded appearance in literature is in the play *El Burlador de Sevilla*, written by Tirso de Molina (1571–1641). Molière's *Le Festin de Pierre* (1665) has little to do with the Spanish play, but introduces an important character, Donna Elvira; Shadwell's *The Libertine* appeared in England in 1676, by which time the story is described as 'famous all over Spain, Italy and France'; Goldoni in 1736 wrote a verse-play, *Don Giovanni Tenorio o sia Il Dissoluto*; but it was in 1787 that there appeared the most important of the various sources from which da Ponte's libretto derives. This was Bertati's libretto with music by Giuseppe

Gazzaniga. Da Ponte, Professor Dent suggests, may even have proposed the subject to Mozart knowing that he had a convenient source to hand, and certainly he drew copiously on Bertati's book for his own libretto, which is notwithstanding one of his best.

*Don Giovanni* was commissioned for the opera in Prague, where *Figaro* had just been a sensational success. It was performed by the same company, Bondini's, and many of the singers were the same as those who had sung the earlier opera when it was presented in Prague, amongst them Bassi, the 22-year-old Don Giovanni, who had already sung the Count. Besides Bassi, the cast consisted of Teresa Saporiti (Donna Anna), Catarina Micelli (Donna Elvira), Teresa Bondini, wife of the manager (Zerlina), Antonio Baglioni (Don Ottavio), Felice Ponziani (Leporello), and Giuseppe Lolli (the Commendatore and Masetto).

There are many stories about the first performance, few of them supported by any reliable evidence. The overture, for instance, is supposed to have been written almost on the eve of the première (and this may well have been the case). Mozart passed a gay evening with some friends. One of them said to him: 'Tomorrow the first performance of *Don Giovanni* will take place, and you have not yet composed the overture!' Mozart pretended to get nervous about it and withdrew to his room, where he found music-paper, pens, and ink. He began to compose about midnight. Whenever he grew sleepy, his wife, who was by his side, entertained him with stories to keep him awake. It is said that it took him but three hours to produce this overture.

At the first rehearsal, not being satisfied with the way in which Signora Bondini gave Zerlina's cry of terror from behind the scenes when the Don is supposed to attempt her ruin, Mozart left the orchestra and went up on the stage. Ordering the first act finale to be repeated from the minuet on, he concealed himself in the wings. When Zerlina's cue came, he quickly reached out a hand from his place of concealment and pinched her leg. She gave a piercing shriek. 'There! That is how I want it,' he said, emerging from the wings, while Signora Bondini, not knowing whether to laugh or blush, did both.

The overture consists of an *andante* introduction which reproduces the scene of the banquet at which the statue appears. It is followed by an *allegro* which characterises the impetuous, pleasure-seeking Don. Without pause, Mozart links up the overture with the song of Leporello; wrapped in his cloak and seated in the garden of a house in Seville, which Don Giovanni on amorous adventure bent has entered secretly during the night, he is complaining of the fate which makes him a servant to such a restless and dangerous master. 'Notte e giorno faticar' (That's the life a servant leads—who cares when he sleeps or feeds? [1]) runs his song; the music, like all that Leporello subsequently sings, is in the Italian *buffo* tradition, differing in degree of expressiveness but not in kind of expression from that of other contemporary *buffo* creations. Don Giovanni hurriedly issues from the house, pursued by Donna Anna. There follows a trio in which the wrath of the insulted woman, the annoyance of the libertine, and the comments of the watching Leporello are expressed simultaneously. The Commendatore hears the noise, finds his daughter struggling with an unknown man, and draws his sword. In spite of the protests of Don Giovanni, who is reluctant to fight so old an opponent, a duel ensues and in it the Commendatore receives a mortal wound. The trio which follows between Don Giovanni, the dying Commendatore, and Leporello is a unique passage in the history of musical art. The genius of Mozart, tender, profound, pathetic, is revealed in its entirety. Written in a solemn rhythm and in the key of F minor, this trio, which fills only eighteen measures, contains in a restricted outline but in master strokes the seeds of the serious side of the drama, just as the recitative which follows—Don Giovanni makes light of the whole affair—re-establishes the opera on a basis of comedy, only to return to seriousness with Anna's grief over the body of her father. In a duet Don Ottavio, her fiancé, tries to comfort her and swears to avenge the dead man.

The scene changes and Don Giovanni and Leporello are on the prowl again; they perceive a woman—or rather, Don Giovanni does—who appears to be inveighing against a lost lover. It is Donna Elvira, whom they do not recognise as yet, but who has been another of the Don's victims. There are in the tears of this woman not only the grief of one who has been loved and now implores heaven for comfort, but also the indignation of one who has been deserted and betrayed. When she cries with emotion 'Ah, chi mi dice mai quel barbaro dov' e?' (Where shall I find

---

[1] English translation by Edward J. Dent (published by O.U.P.).

the traitor who stole my heart away?) one feels that in spite of her anger, she is ready to forgive, if only a regretful smile shall recall her to the man who was able to charm her. The character of her music is seen straight away in this aria. It is more pliable than Donna Anna's, but perhaps it is the persistent nature it seems to reveal that makes Don Giovanni run quite so fast from her.

As she finishes her outburst, she turns to find that the stranger who is attempting to console her is none other than Don Giovanni himself. Leaving Leporello to explain the reasons why he deserted her, Don Giovanni makes his escape, and Elvira is obliged to listen while the servant runs through a catalogue—grossly exaggerated we may be sure—of his master's conquests. 'Madamina' is a perfect passage of its kind and one of the most famous arias in the repertory of the *basso buffo*. It is an exquisite mixture of grace and finish, of irony and sentiment, of comic declamation and melody, the whole enhanced by the poetry and skill of the accessories. Every word is illustrated by the composer's imagination without his many brilliant sallies injuring the general effect. According to Leporello's catalogue, his master's adventures in love have numbered 2,065—640 in Italy, 231 in Germany, 100 in France, 91 in Turkey, and in Spain no less than 1,003. All sorts and conditions of women have contributed to this formidable total, and it is small wonder that Elvira leaves the stage vowing vengeance upon her betrayer.

The scene changes to the countryside near Don Giovanni's palace not far from Seville. A troop of gay peasants is seen arriving. The young and pretty Zerlina with Masetto, her affianced, and their friends are singing and dancing in honour of their approaching marriage. Don Giovanni and Leporello join this gathering of light-hearted and simple young people. Having cast covetous eyes upon Zerlina, and having aroused her vanity and her spirit of coquetry by polished words of gallantry, the Don orders Leporello to get rid of the jealous Masetto by taking the entire gathering—except, of course, Zerlina—to his château. Leporello complies, but Masetto, while submitting to be removed, makes it clear to Don Giovanni—and to Zerlina as well—that he is not the fool he may look. This aria 'Ho capito, signor si' (You're the master, I'm the man) shows Masetto as a sort of Figaro, duller of wit, and in miniature but an embryonic revolutionary nonetheless. Don Giovanni, left alone with Zerlina, sings a duet with her which is one of the gems not alone of this opera but of opera in general. 'Là ci darem la mano' (You'll lay your hand in mine, dear) provides ample musical evidence, which is later supported by the Serenade, that though the Don may be unsuccessful in each of the love affairs on which he embarks during the course of the opera, his reputation is still well deserved.

As they are going off arm in arm, Donna Elvira reappears and by her denunciation of Don Giovanni—'Ah, fuggi il traditore' (Be warned in time, my child)—makes clear to Zerlina that there can be two opinions concerning the character of her fascinating admirer. She takes Zerlina with her as Donna Anna and Don Ottavio come on to the stage, but no sooner is Don Giovanni in conversation with the two, than Elvira is back again on the scene— a true comedy stroke. In a quartet, she again denounces Don Giovanni as a heartless deceiver, while he for his part says that she is mad; Anna and Ottavio are at a loss to know which to

believe. Elvira goes out, followed a moment later by Don Giovanni, but in the few sentences he speaks Donna Anna recognises the voice of her father's assassin and her own betrayer. Her narrative of the events of that night is a declamatory recitative 'in style as bold and as tragic as the finest recitatives of Gluck'. The aria which follows, 'Or sai chi l'onore' (You know now for certain), is no less grandiose, and its implacable vengefulness (and implacable *tessitura*) presents a problem for the singer entrusted with the role of Donna Anna. Never elsewhere perhaps did

Mozart write music for the soprano voice which is so extremely heavy and taxing.

It is usually at the end of this aria—where it can never fail to come as an anti-climax—that Ottavio's interpolated aria 'Dalla sua pace' (Mine be her burden, bravely to bear it) is sung. No change of scene is indicated, but in the opera house one is often made at this point to allow Don Giovanni to give his orders for the festivity inside his house rather than outside in the garden. However, the exuberant 'Finch' han dal vino' (Song, wine, and women) demands not so much an indoor setting as a baritone with an immaculate technique and sufficient musical sense to sing it as part of the opera and not just as a sample of his vocal dexterity.

Scene 4 takes us to the garden outside Don Giovanni's palace. Masetto reproaches Zerlina for her flirtation, but she begs his forgiveness in an ingratiating air 'Batti, batti, o bel Masetto'. This has always been one of the most popular moments in the opera, and it is true that in the quicker 6/8 section you can almost hear Zerlina twiddling her unfortunate admirer round her little finger. But the aria ended, Masetto's suspicions return when she seems distinctly nervous at the sound of the Don's voice in the distance.

Now begins the finale, one of the great masterpieces of dramatic music. From a hiding place Masetto hears Don Giovanni order his retainers to spare no pains to make the evening a success, and he is able to confront Zerlina and Don Giovanni as the latter attempts to lead her off into an alcove. The situation is well within the Don's compass; he chides Masetto for leaving his bride-to-be alone, and takes them both into the house where the dancing is about to begin. Elvira, Anna, and Ottavio appear, all of them masked. Leporello opens a window to let the fresh evening air into the palace and the violins of a small orchestra within can be heard in the middle of a graceful minuet. He sees the three

maskers, and in accordance with tradition, they are bidden to
enter. After a moment of hesitation, they decide to accept the
invitation, and to carry out their undertaking at all cost and to
whatever end. Before entering the château, they pause on the
threshold and, their souls moved by a holy fear, they address heaven
in one of the most remarkable prayers written by the hand of man.

Trio of the masks:

Inside the ballroom, the festivities are in full swing. Don
Giovanni and Leporello manœuvre to keep Masetto from Zerlina,
but there is a diversion at the entry of the unknown maskers, who
are welcomed by Don Giovanni. The dancing begins with the
minuet we have already heard. Its graceful rhythm is prolonged
indefinitely as a fundamental idea, while in succession two small
orchestras on the stage take up, one a rustic quadrille, the other a
waltz. Only the ladies and gentlemen should engage in the minuet,
the peasants in the quadrille; and before Don Giovanni leads
off Zerlina into an adjoining room he should have taken part
with her in this dance, while Leporello seeks to divert the jealous
Masetto's attention by seizing him in an apparent exuberance of
spirits and insisting on dancing the waltz with him.

Masetto's suspicions, however, are not without justification.
He breaks away from Leporello, who hurries to warn his master.
But just as he has passed through the door, Zerlina's piercing
shriek for help is heard from within. Don Giovanni rushes out,
sword in hand, dragging with him none other than the luckless
Leporello, whom he has opportunely seized in the entrance, and
whom, under pretext that he is the guilty party, he threatens to
kill. But this ruse fails to deceive anyone. Anna, Elvira, and

Ottavio unmask and accuse Don Giovanni of the murder of the Commendatore: 'Tutto, tutto gia si sa' (All your guilt is now made clear). Taken aback at first, Don Giovanni soon recovers himself. Turning at bay, he defies the threatening crowd. A storm sweeps over the orchestra. Thunder growls in the basses, lightning plays on the fiddles. Don Giovanni, cool and intrepid, dashes through the crowd, which falls back in front of him, and makes his escape.

Act II.　A street, with Donna Elvira's house in the background. The beginning of Act II furnishes proof—and proof *is* needed—that *Don Giovanni* is the *dramma giocoso* of its title. The duet with which it opens, 'Eh via, buffone' (Now then, you rascal), is in purest *buffo* style, and it is followed by a trio for Elvira, Don Giovanni, and Leporello which points the moral even more sharply. Donna Elvira, leaning sadly on her balcony, gives voice to her melancholy regrets in a tune of exquisite beaut y In spite of the scene which she has recently witnessed, in spite of the wrongs she herself has endured, she cannot hate Don Giovanni or efface his image from her heart. Her reward is that her recreant lover changes clothes with his servant in the darkness below, and, while Leporello disguised as the Don attracts Donna Elvira into the garden, the Don himself mocks her with exaggerated protestations of love, which she takes at their face value. If the scene is to be taken seriously—and the music of 'Ah, taci, ingiusto core' (Ah, why do I remember) is of a quality to support such an attitude—the way in which sport is made of her pathetic faithfulness would indicate a revolting callousness on the part not only of the man who has loved and left her, but of the composer as well; but if it can be approached by the audience in a spirit of frivolity, of *opera buffa*, this callousness is less in evidence.

Elvira descends, and Don Giovanni sings, to his own mandolin accompaniment (usually played *pizzicato* on a violin), a serenade to Elvira's maid, to whom he has taken a fancy. 'Deh, vieni alla finestra' (Look down from out your window) is one of the most famous numbers of the opera, partly perhaps because of the stress laid on its performance by eminent singers of the title role. Don Giovanni thinks he sees the object of his affections, but, before he can follow up his advantage, round the corner comes Masetto with a band of peasants bent on finding and murdering no less a person than Don Giovanni. They think they are addressing Leporello, and the disguised Don divides them up into parties and sends them off to the four points of the compass in an effective aria, 'Metà di voi quà vadano' (Let half of you go down the road). Masetto, the ringleader, he keeps with him and, having ascertained exactly what weapons he has with him, proceeds to give him a good drubbing and leaves him groaning on the ground. Zerlina, while by no means indifferent to the attentions of the dashing Don, is at heart faithful to Masetto and she comes tripping round the corner when she hears his cries and consoles the poor fellow with the graceful measures of 'Vedrai carino, se sei buonino' (If you will promise not to mistrust me).

The scene changes to the courtyard of a palace in which Elvira and Leporello take refuge. It turns out to be Donna Anna's, and she is on the point of returning home, escorted by the inevitable Don Ottavio and a band of servants bearing torches. Elvira and Leporello make for the door, but are intercepted by Masetto and Zerlina, who are lurking in it. Everyone takes Leporello for his master and demands his death, demands they seem rather reluctant to withdraw when they find out that it is the servant they have caught after all.

The sextet is a fine ensemble, with its variety of action and of musical sections. It is plainly intended, says Professor Dent, as the finale of an act, not as a movement in the middle of one.[1] It was you then who beat Masetto? asks Zerlina; You who so deceived me? continues Elvira. 'Ah, pieta! Signori miei' (Spare me, spare my life I pray), counters Leporello in an aria which dies away while Leporello holds their attention as he creeps to the door and disappears.

Now comes Don Ottavio's famous aria, the solo number which makes the role coveted by tenors the world over, 'Il mio tesoro

intanto' (Speak for me to my lady). Upon this air praise has been exhausted. It has been called the 'pietra di paragone' of tenors—the touchstone, the supreme test of classical song. In spite of its rather obscure dramatic value, its musical beauty is as undeniable as its difficulty of execution. At this point, it is customary to

---

[1] This is on the hypothesis that the opera was intended to be in four acts, but was changed to two in the course of rehearsal.

insert the superb recitative and aria for Elvira, which Mozart
composed for Catarina Cavalieri, who sang the role at the
Viennese première. She had complained to Mozart that the
Viennese public did not appreciate her as did audiences of other
cities and begged him for something which would give her voice
full scope. The result was 'Mi tradì quel alma ingrata' (All my
love on him I lavished). Again its dramatic justification is slight,
and though in it Elvira rises to her full height, it in fact tells us
nothing about her which we could not have gathered from the
rest of her music.

After the escapade of the serenade and the beating of Masetto,
the Don makes off and chances to meet in the churchyard—
which he reaches after some other adventure, we may be sure—
with none other than Leporello, who for his part is thankful to
have got rid of Elvira, Leporello finds it little to his taste that his
master's newest conquest has been someone on whom he—
Leporello—has made an impression. Don Giovanni is prepared
to laugh the whole thing off when he hears a solemn voice which
he is not long in tracing to the statue of the Commendatore,
whose death is laid at his own door:

Leporello is ordered to invite the statue—'O vecchio buffonissimo'
is Don Giovanni's greeting for him—to supper. This he does in a
duet, 'O statua gentilissima', his courage, which fails him at every
sentence, being kept at the sticking point by the vigorous encouragement of his master. The statue's utterances in the recitative
part of the scene are accompanied by trombones, connected in
the opera exclusively with the appearance of the statue and not
used, even in the overture, when it is not visible on the stage.

The scene changes once again, this time to a room in Donna
Anna's house. Ottavio enters, and she reproaches him when he
hints at their forthcoming marriage; at such a time, how could
she think of anything but her murdered father? The scene exists

solely to give Anna another aria to sing, and 'Non mi dir' (Say no more), beautiful and famous though it is, contributes little to the dramatic development of the opera. The coloratura section, which is included in the *allegretto* with which the aria ends, was once adversely criticised—amongst other critics, by Berlioz—as having no place in music written for Donna Anna, but we may agree with Professor Dent who says severely that 'Mozart without coloratura is only a very mutilated Mozart'.

The scene changes to Don Giovanni's palace. During the brilliant introduction, he seats himself at table and sings of the pleasures of life. An orchestra (on the stage in many modern performances, but probably not at the première) plays airs from Vincente Martin's *Una Cosa Rara* and Sarti's *I due Litiganti*, and 'Non piu andrai' from Mozart's own *Figaro*—the last-named selection greeted by Leporello with the observation that it is a bit stale. The music is a wonderful picture of the exuberant and devil-may-care nature of Don Giovanni, and is in the gay, debonair style which has all along been characteristic of his music, not least the recitative. At this point Elvira enters and begs the man who has betrayed her to mend his ways. Her plea falls on deaf ears. She goes to the door, but her shriek is heard from the corridor and she re-enters to flee the palace by another door. Don Giovanni sends Leporello to find out what has frightened her, but he echoes her scream and babbles that the statue is outside. Seizing a candle and drawing his sword, Don Giovanni boldly goes into the corridor. A moment later, he backs into the room, receding before the statue of the Commendatore. The lights go out. All is dark save for the flame of the candle in Don Giovanni's hand. Slowly, with heavy footsteps that re-echo in the orchestra, the statue enters. It speaks.

'Don Giovanni, you did invite me here to supper, so bid me welcome.' Don Giovanni nonchalantly orders Leporello to serve supper. 'Nay, do not go,' commands the statue. 'They who taste of the food of the angels eat no more the corrupt food of mortals . . . Will you come with me to supper?' Don Giovanni accepts and gives his hand to the statue in pledge; it is seized in a grip that is icy cold. 'Think on your sins, repent them'—'No.' A fiery pit opens. Demons seize him, unrepentant to the end, and drag him down. The music of the scene is gripping, yet accomplished without other addition than the trombones to the ordinary orchestra of Mozart's day, without straining after effect, without any means save those commonly to his hand.

In the nineteenth century and in the early years of the twentieth, the curtain used to fall at this point, but there is an epilogue in which the characters moralise upon Don Giovanni's end—an important feature of all the plays dealing with the legend. For the Vienna performance of 1788 Mozart cut it out and this was held by the nineteenth century to justify a tragic or at all events a romantic interpretation of the opera; such a view depends on the convenient forgetting of the ludicrously comic duet for Leporello and Zerlina which Mozart wrote specially for this same performance and which is still printed at the end of the vocal score though never performed. The comedy device of the moralising finale has been used as recently as Strawinsky's *The Rake's Progress*.

Quite apart from the brilliant speed at which the music of *Don Giovanni* proceeds, quite apart from the juxtaposition of stark tragedy and high comedy in the one work, the opera is distinguished by the fascination attached to its central character. He is a brilliant, irresponsible figure, with a dash of philosophy— sometime, somewhere, in the course of his amours, he will discover the perfect woman, from whose lips he will be able to draw the sweetness of all women. He is a villain with a keen sense of humour; inexcusable in real life, possible only in comedy and represented at the first performance, one should not forget, by a youth no more than twenty-two years old! Leporello is a typical *basso buffo*, except that the quality of the music he has to sing is far higher than customary in this type of role. This is not to say that he is not well characterised, only that there is little new in the conception. At the Viennese première, the singer was Benucci, who had created the role of Figaro there. Ottavio very nearly re-creates the function of the confidant of *opera seria*, so little part does he play in the stage proceedings. The musical side of the role of course is a very different matter; in spite of its difficulty, the part is very much sought after, and not uncommonly a tenor with style and a stage personality astonishes the audience with the positive impression he makes in this often negative role.

More interesting than the lesser figures amongst the men are the three female members of the cast. Zerlina is often played as if butter would not melt in her mouth, but for the Vienna performance Mozart added a duet for her and Leporello in which she attacks him with a razor but finally, in spite of her threats, contents herself with tying him up. Elvira, though frequently touching in her faithfulness to the memory of the man who has betrayed her (not least in her resolve in the finale that she will finish her days in a convent), is not without a touch of the scold in her make-up. It is perhaps Anna who is the most diversely interpreted of the three female roles. At one extreme, she has been represented as cold and incapable of love, at the other—notably by the German romantic poet E. T. A. Hoffmann—as consumed with passion for Don Giovanni. Einstein finds another solution to the problem: at the rise of the curtain Don Giovanni has in fact succeeded in seducing her, disguised as Don Ottavio. To support this view, he instances the recitative before 'Or sai chi l'onore', Don Giovanni's indifference to Anna (for the same reason as he is indifferent to Elvira), her insistence that Ottavio should revenge her father's murder himself without recourse to the law, and finally her refusal to marry Ottavio until some length of time has elapsed. Dent, on the other hand, points to the distant, haughty attitude she adopts towards even Ottavio, and suggests that in all probability she will end up as first lady-in-waiting to the Queen of Night! K., H.

## COSÌ FAN TUTTE

*Opera buffa* in two acts by Wolfgang Amadeus Mozart. Text by Lorenzo da Ponte. First performed at the Burgtheater, Vienna, January 26, 1790, with Ferrarese del Bene, Villeneuve (they were also sisters in real life), Signora Bussani, Calvesi, Benucci, Signor Bussani. First performed London, Haymarket Theatre, 1811. Revived by Sir Thomas Beecham at His Majesty's Theatre, London, 1911, with Ruth Vincent, Lena Maitland, Beatrice La Palme, Walter Hyde, Frederick Austin, and Lewys James; Metropolitan, New York, 1922, with Florence Easton, Frances Peralta, Lucrezia Bori, George Meader, Giuseppe de Luca, Adamo Didur, conductor Artur Bodanzky; Glyndebourne, 1934, with Ina Souez, Luise Helletsgruber, Irene Eisinger, Heddle Nash, Willi Domgraf-Fassbänder. Vincenzo Bettoni, conductor Fritz Busch. Recent revivals include, Sadler's Wells, 1944, with Joan Cross, Margaret Ritchie, Rose Hill, Peter Pears, John Hargreaves, and Owen Brannigan, conductor Lawrance Collingwood; Glyndebourne Opera at the Edinburgh Festival, 1948, with Suzanne Danco, Eugenia Zareska, Hilde Güden, Petre Munteanu, Erich Kunz, Mariano Stabile, conductor Vittorio Gui; at Glyndebourne, 1950, with Sena Jurinac, Blanche Thebom, Alda Noni, Richard Lewis, Erich Kunz, Mario Borriello, conductor Fritz Busch.

## CHARACTERS

Fiordiligi ..................................... Soprano
Dorabella, *her sister* .......................... Soprano
Ferrando, *her fiancé* ........................... Tenor
Guglielmo, *engaged to Fiordiligi* ................... Bass
Don Alfonso ................................. Baritone
Despina, *maid to Fiordiligi and Dorabella* ......... Soprano

*Così fan Tutte, ossia La Scuola degli Amanti* was written by
Mozart to a commission from the Emperor Joseph II; the story
is said to have been based on a real-life incident which was the
talk of Vienna at the time of its occurrence. Two young officers,
confident of the constancy of the sisters to whom they are engaged,
enter into a bet with an old bachelor friend of theirs, who maintains that a woman's memory is shorter than they think. At his
direction, they put on disguises, and start to make love to each
other's fiancée, having already taken the precaution of securing
the aid of Despina, maid to the two sisters. After a short resistance, the sisters succumb to their wooing, but at the wedding
party the two young men disappear to emerge a moment later in
their uniforms and confront the inconstant sisters with their
original lovers.

The story is slight, but one of da Ponte's neatest, and its
symmetrical cast—two pairs of lovers, a third of worldly-wise
cynics—and equally symmetrical construction provide Mozart
with opportunities for some incomparable music. He was at the
very summit of his creative powers, and anyone who knows the
opera cannot help being surprised at the nineteenth-century
suggestion that he in any way disliked the plot he was to use.
The truth is inescapable: in *Così fan Tutte* Mozart surpassed even
himself in the richness and variety of his invention, in the im-
peccable skill with which the slenderest drama is adorned with
music, in the creation of beauty. The idea is as light as a feather,
and yet the music which clothes it suggests not only the comedy
which is on the surface and which remains the most important
part of the opera, but also the heartbreak which is behind the
joke that goes too far and occasionally takes a serious turn.
All the odder then that various attempts were made in the nineteenth century and later to provide the music with a new libretto,
all of them short-lived—and small wonder in view of the quality

of the original, which, as Professor Dent has emphasised, cannot
be judged from a summary but must be seen in all its details.
The opera 'plays' slower than either *Figaro* or *Don Giovanni*,
and it is by no means short, but the stage action is as full of life
as the music, and the opera is the ideal piece for a musically
sophisticated audience.

The short overture has eight bars of slow introduction before
the theme of the title is enunciated. Most of the rest of it is quick
until just before the end when the motto theme re-occurs.

Act I. The curtain rises on a café where are seated the three
men, in the middle apparently of a heated argument, or so one
assumes from the vigorous defence of Dorabella, his fiancée,
that Ferrando is making as the music begins. There are three
trios, the first with the two lovers answering the sceptical Alfonso,
the second in the form of an accompanied solo for Alfonso:

the third consisting of jubilation on the part of the lovers at the
prospect of winning the bet which they enter upon with Alfonso.
It is a scene of the purest comedy and the music matches the
artificiality of the mood, culminating in a tune of bubbling,
infectious gaiety such as even Mozart himself could not duplicate:

The scene changes, the clarinets play in thirds over the strings,[1]

and we can be sure we are with Fiordiligi and Dorabella, the paragons of faithfulness on whose constancy so much has just been wagered. They are discussing the respective merits of their young men as evinced in their portraits, and their sentimental rapture at what they see is conveyed in music of exquisitely exaggerated cast, which dissolves in the middle into a cadenza in thirds on the word 'Amore'. This day-dreaming is interrupted by the precipitate arrival of Don Alfonso, who makes obvious his distress at the news he is only too anxious to break to the two young ladies: their lovers are ordered to the wars and are to leave immediately. It is Alfonso's nearest approach to an aria in the whole opera—is in fact described as one in the score; its *allegro agitato* perfectly reflects the breathless agitation he counterfeits so well. The situation is admirably summed up in two quintets, which are separated by a short duet for the two officers and a military chorus. In 'Sento, oh Dio' (Courage fails me) [2] the ladies are inconsolable, Don Alfonso builds up the situation, while Guglielmo is inclined to leave specific consolation to Ferrando and himself joins with Alfonso in a more general comment. Twice the two men cannot help nudging the sceptic ('There, you see now'), but he remains quite unconvinced. Ferrando and Guglielmo say good-bye, soldiers march across the stage singing of the joys of a military existence, but the farewells are not complete until all four have sung a protracted and beautiful farewell, to pungent comment from Alfonso ('Di scrivermi ogni giorno': You'll write long letters often).

Their lovers departed, Fiordiligi and Dorabella show real feeling so that even Alfonso joins them in a wonderfully evocative

[1] The richness of the wind writing is unusual, even for Mozart, and there is more than a hint here and elsewhere of the great B flat major Serenade (K.361) for thirteen wind instruments.

[2] Translations throughout by the Rev. Marmaduke Browne.

trio, 'Soave sia il vento', as they pray for calm sea and gentle breezes for the travellers. The idyllic mood does not for one bar survive their joint exit. Alfonso muses in *secco* recitative on his plans, but as he grows animated at the thought of woman's changeability he launches into an accompanied tirade against the whole sex, the one inescapably bitter moment of the score.

The scene changes, and we meet the chattering Despina, maid to the two sisters, who soon show that their loss has left them in no mood for chocolate or any other such consolation. Dorabella is the first to give vent to her feelings, in an aria of exaggeratedly tragic order, 'Smanie implacabili', a parody one may think of the self-consciously tragic Donna Elvira or even of the wholly serious Electra in *Idomeneo*. Despina advises a more moderate line; she is the female counterpart of Don Alfonso, and in her philosophy lover's absence affords an opportunity for sport, not for lamentation: 'In uomini, in soldati.' The ladies go out in disgust, and Alfonso seizes the opportunity to enlist Despina as an ally in his attempt to win the wager. Enter the two supposedly departed officers, disguised as Albanians; they are introduced to Despina, who laughs at them but does not recognise them, and is quite prepared to help them in their attempt to win the affections of her mistresses. In a moment, the two are back on the stage, indignant at finding two strange men in their house and demanding their withdrawal. Alfonso stays in hiding but comments on the situation, and emerges to embrace the Albanians as old friends of his; will the ladies not be kind to them—for his sake? Fiordiligi makes it quite clear that their protestations of love are entirely unavailing: she and her sister are each of them 'firm as a rock' ('Come scoglio'). The aria is parodistic in tone, and, with its wide intervals and absurd jumps from the top to the bottom of the soprano range, seems likely to have been at any rate partly intended to poke fun at the phenomenal range and technique of Ferrarese del Bene, the original singer of Fiordiligi, who was da Ponte's mistress at the time of the première but seems to have been no favourite of Mozart's either artistically or personally.

con·tra venti e la tem·pe·sta, e la tem·pe· sta

Guglielmo answers for Ferrando as well as himself and is given music of such delicacy and charm—'Non siate ritrosi' [1] (O vision so charming)—that one cannot but be surprised that the objects of the two young men's affections turn on their respective heels and leave the room before he has had time to finish the aria, which dissolves in laughter. The rapid laughing trio is charming, but Don Alfonso has his work cut out to persuade his young friends that he has by no means lost his bet at this early juncture. Let them be ready to meet him in the garden in a few minutes' time. Ferrando is left alone to sing of his love in a beautiful aria, in type romantic or even sentimental but hardly comic ('Un' aura amorosa': Her eyes so alluring). Alfonso and Despina reassure themselves that this is only a pair of women, and that there is as yet no danger of losing the bet.

For the finale we are back in the garden, under the blue Neapolitan sky and with the bay of Naples as background. Small wonder that Fiordiligi and Dorabella reflect jointly on the mutability of pleasure in music of exquisite tenderness, whose end is hardly reached before Ferrando and Guglielmo rush on to the stage brandishing bottles of poison which Alfonso is unable to prevent them drinking. The situation is sufficiently complicated to provide Mozart with exactly what he wanted for an extended finale. As the Albanians sink into a coma, pandemonium breaks loose, and when Alfonso and Despina rush for the doctor, there is even an opportunity for Ferrando and Guglielmo to join in the ensemble. Alfonso returns with a doctor (Despina in disguise) who proceeds to give the corpses the benefit of the most recent scientific discovery, Mesmerism—as much the latest thing in 1790 one may imagine as Psychiatry was in the 1940's and as likely to raise a laugh, particularly when compressed, as here, into the outward form of an oversize, all-healing magnet. The corpses revive, think at first they are in the Elysian Fields, and demand a kiss from the Goddesses to set the seal on their cure. In spite of the promptings of Alfonso and Despina this is denied them, and the curtain falls with the sisters defending what they appear to regard as nothing less than honour itself, to a background of derisive exclamations from Despina and Alfonso, and

---

[1] A magnificent *buffo* aria, 'Rivolgete a lui lo sguardo' (K.584), was originally planned here, but the slighter piece was substituted, one may imagine, as being more in keeping with this situation.

approving comments of 'Great would be my indignation were
they not to answer No' from the Albanians themselves. The
music of the finale ranges from the purest beauty—the opening,
for instance—to sheer farce—Despina in disguise and her trilling,
omnipotent magnet. If there is in this finale less incident than
in, for instance, that of Act II of *Le Nozze di Figaro*, there is
nonetheless a musical variety and invention which places it in the
very highest rank.

Act II. Despina loses her patience with her virtuous employers. Make hay while the sun shines, she says, and behave like
normal women when men are around; she rounds off her point in
an aria, 'Una donna a quindici anni'. The process of persuasion
so well begun is completed by the ladies themselves, who agree
that there can be no harm in something so innocent as talk with
the strangers. Their minds made up, each selects the appropriate
partner—'Prenderò quel brunettino' (Give me then the gentle
dark one)—in typically melodious fashion, to find at the end of
the duet that they are invited to the garden where an entertainment is planned for their delectation. In truth, Alfonso has not
exaggerated: nature has never so well imitated art—not even in
the case of Cosima Wagner and the 'Siegfried Idyll'—as to
serenade a loved one with music as entrancing as the duet and
chorus, 'Secondate aurette amiche' (Gentle zephyr, softly sighing,) which Ferrando and Guglielmo now combine to sing to them.
I have seen it made the subject of a producer's whims—the
singers exchanging copies of the music, dropping them, fumbling;
doing in fact everything except sing—but nothing was hindrance
enough to stand in the way of the entrancing, seductive melody.
If this is Mozart's most hedonistically inclined opera, no other
number so perfectly illustrates its prevailing characteristic.

But, the serenade over, neither Albanian seems able to pursue
the advantage gained, and, in disgust, Alfonso and Despina enact
the scene for them. Neither seems a very apt pupil, but the teachers
steal away at the end of their duet (the few phrases from Ferrando

and Guglielmo make it technically into a quartet), leaving two
rather embarrassed couples behind them talking animatedly about
the weather. Ferrando is led off by Fiordiligi, and, after some
tentative compliments, Guglielmo succeeds in giving Dorabella
a heart-shaped locket, in return for which he removes the medallion (with its portrait of Ferrando) from her neck. Their duet,
'Il core vi dono' (This heart that I give you), is charmingly light
in texture and sentiment, and particularly delightful are the
references to the pit-a-pat of their hearts.

The outer defences of Dorabella's constancy have been rather
easily breached; Fiordiligi's are to prove much harder to carry.
She turns a deaf ear to Ferrando's advances, and he is given a
magnificent aria, 'Ah, lo veggio, quell' anima bella' (Well I knew
that a maid so enchanting), in which he alternately expresses
doubts and confidence as to the eventual outcome of his suit.
Although it is one of the highest pieces Mozart wrote for tenor
voice, perhaps it owes its frequent omission from contemporary
performances not only to this high *tessitura* and its extended
form, but also to the fact that it is immediately followed by an
even longer aria for Fiordiligi which is much too well known to
be omitted under any circumstances. Still, Ferrando's aria is far
too good to be neglected as is present practice. Fiordiligi's great
rondo, 'Per pietà, ben mio, perdona' (Ah, my love, forgive my
madness), is the principal show-piece of the opera; the extensive
range, sudden and precipitous leaps from high soprano to contralto and back again, the passages of exacting coloratura, the
taxing length—all combine to show off the singer's technique,
which is mocked at the same time as it is used to express the
turmoil of conflicting emotions in Fiordiligi's mind. A horn
obbligato adds to the effect.

Ferrando and Guglielmo meet to compare notes on their
progress to date. Guglielmo is suitably smug about the apparent
constancy of Fiordiligi, but Ferrando is furiously indignant when
he hears of Dorabella's conduct and sees the proof in the shape
of the locket he himself had given her. He will have revenge; but,
he asks Guglielmo, in what form? Don't take it so much to heart,
replies his friend: 'Ladies have such variations, permutations,
combinations' ('Donne mie la fate a tanti'). It is a wonderful
example of an *opera buffa* aria, and one of the most delightful
moments in the score, as light of touch and delicate in style as

the best of Mozart's own chamber music. Symmetry being the thing it is, there follows an aria for Ferrando, less formidable and shorter than 'Ah, lo veggio', although by no means easy to sing; it is sometimes omitted, as is almost invariably the aria for Dorabella, 'E' amore un ladroncello' (Young love is unrelenting), in the next scene.

Fiordiligi resolves to make a last effort to extract herself and maybe Dorabella as well from the intolerable situation in which they find themselves. She sends for a couple of old suits of uniform belonging to Ferrando and Guglielmo which happen to be conveniently in the house, and announces her intention of going off to the wars taking her equally disguised sister. She launches into the opening measures of a big aria, but she has hardly started to express her determination to reach her lover's side when she is interrupted by Ferrando, still in his Albanian disguise, and protesting that before she leave him she should run her sword through his heart and end his agony for ever. Once more he protests his love, and, in response to a meltingly beautiful tune, resistance crumbles and she falls into his arms; they sing of their future happiness. Is it Mozart or the romantic Ferrando who has overreached himself in this love duet? There is a school of thought which denies to genius the subtleties which are incidental to the main issue—there is no indication that he ever actually thought of *that*, they say, ignoring presumably the part played by the instinctive and the subconscious in the creative process. If Ferrando is in love with love as well as with Dorabella, he will be no less shattered by his new and involuntary success with her sister than he was by news of her own infidelity. The joke in fact has gone too far, and has involved too many emotional ties, old and new, for detachment to be any more a possibility—which is exactly what is conveyed by the uneasiness of the music. Granted that the lovers who began as puppets have suddenly become warm and real; perhaps it is one of music's (and therefore opera's) fascinations that such a transformation is possible, and, when achieved, so moving.

The whole scene is watched by Guglielmo from the side, and Alfonso has his work cut out to keep him quiet until it is over. 'What about your fond Fiordiligi now?' asks Ferrando; 'Fior di Diavolo!' answers the discomfited Guglielmo. They are no worse than all the other women, affirms Alfonso: 'Tutti accusan le donne' (Everyone berates the ladies), and at the end of his short solo, he makes the crestfallen lovers repeat the motto with him: 'Così fan tutte'. Despina brings the news that her mistresses have made up their minds to make their Albanian suitors happy and marry them on the spot.

The finale carries the plot one stage further and provides the expected dénouement. Servants make ready for the wedding under the direction of Despina, and hail the bridal couples when they appear. The lovers' toast is introduced by one of those unforgettable tunes such as Mozart has a habit of producing at just the moment when abundance has seemed to be sated, and the toast itself is an enchanting canon, led by Fiordiligi, which goes

harmoniously on its way until it is the turn of Guglielmo to take up the tune. He contents himself with an angry aside to the effect that nothing would please him more than that the wine should turn to poison on their lips. It has been suggested that the device, which helps to lend variety to the quartet, was dictated to Mozart for the obvious reason that the tune which goes up to A flat was too high for the bass Guglielmo to sing. Alfonso brings in a notary (Despina in yet another costume) who is to take care of the legal side of the weddings, and, with much vocal disguise and a spate of pseudo-legal patter (including a punning refer-ence to these 'dame Ferraresi'), the contract is prepared and signed.

This is the signal for a burst of military music from outside, which is immediately recognised by the female signatories as the march to which Ferrando and Guglielmo went off to the wars.

Their suspicion turns to consternation when Alfonso confirms that Ferrando and Guglielmo are on their way up to the house at that very moment. The Albanians are bundled out, the sisters try to compose themselves, and their military lovers make an entrance to music which refers back unmistakably to the early part of Act I. Despina is discovered in an ante-room, Alfonso conveniently lets the marriage contracts fall where the young men cannot fail to see them, and they are told that proof of the inconstancy can be found in the next-door room. In a moment they re-appear, bringing with them bits of the Albanian costumes, and moreover singing snatches of the music that helped to bring the wooing to its successful conclusion. Here is a curious anomaly, which I have never yet seen explained. Guglielmo quotes from 'Il core vi dono' and he and Ferrando sing the music associated with Despina's mesmerism in the finale to Act I; but before either of these, Ferrando has quoted something which he in fact never sings at any moment during the opera. Was one of Ferrando's arias changed at rehearsal, and did the second thoughts never get as far as this finale, or is there some deeper explanation?

Everything is forgiven, the four lovers are reunited—whether in the original or Albanian combination we are not told—and the six characters sing a valedictory in praise of him who is able to take the rough with the smooth and who can fall back on reason however the world treats him.

*Così fan Tutte* demands sensitive and beautiful performing, from singers, orchestra, and conductor of course, but no less from producer and designer. It is not the work for the producer who knows nothing in between solemnity and horseplay, nor for the designer who cannot by means of imagination re-create the Mediterranean atmosphere at the same time as he is solving the all-important problem of maintaining continuity, which, here as in Mozart's other operas, is as vital a consideration as it has become in modern Shakespearean production. *Così fan Tutte* is a comedy pure and simple, and, like every comedy of genius, it comments profoundly and movingly and above all naturally on human life and manners during the course of its action.' If the comedy becomes farce at the wrong moment, the result will be as appallingly unstylish as it will if the performance is planned to prove once and for all that the work embodies Mozart's considered reflections on the subject of Sex.                    H.

# LA CLEMENZA DI TITO
## The Clemency of Titus

Opera in two acts by Wolfgang Amadeus Mozart. Text by Mazzolà, adapted from Metastasio. First performed at the National Theatre, Prague, September 6, 1791. First performed in London, King's Theatre, March 27, 1806; revived by the City Opera Club at the Guildhall School of Music, London, 1949; at the Salzburg Festival, 1949, under Josef Krips, with Hilde Zadek, Wilma Lipp, Marta Rohs, Julius Patzak, Richard Holm, and Otto Edelmann (in an arrangement by Bernhard Paumgartner, which included much music from other sources, notably *Idomeneo*). First performances in English (translated by M. and E. Radford), Falmouth, 1930, London, 1931.

### CHARACTERS

Titus, *Roman Emperor* (A.D. 79–81) ................Tenor
Vitellia, *daughter of the deposed Emperor, Vitellius* .Soprano
Sextus ⎫ *young Roman patricians* ⎧..............Contralto
Annius ⎭ ⎩........ Mezzo-Soprano
Servilia, *sister of Sextus* .......................Soprano
Publius, *Captain of the Praetorian Guard* ............Bass

All his life, Mozart had a longing to write *opera seria*; his attempts began with *Mitridate*, written during his years in Italy (1770), reached their height in *Idomeneo* (1781), and culminated in *La Clemenza di Tito* (1791). Even though *opera seria* was already in 1781 an out of date form, it was Mozart not Gluck who was in *Idomeneo* to say the final word on the subject. *La Clemenza di Tito* is a rather different matter. Mazzolà's revised version of Metastasio's libretto (which had been set by Caldara and Gluck in its original state), though dramatically a great improvement on its model, may not, with its conventional glorification of benevolent despotism, have been particularly congenial material for Mozart. The opera was commissioned to celebrate the coronation in Prague in 1791 of the Emperor Leopold II as King of Bohemia. Mozart had not even finished *The Magic Flute* and was engaged on the *Requiem*, yet *Tito* was written and performed within eighteen days of receipt of the commission, during part of which period the composer was travelling from Vienna to Prague. Small wonder that Mozart had to entrust the composition of the *secco* recitatives to his pupil Süssmayr! Three weeks after the première, *The Magic Flute* was brought out in Vienna; nine weeks later still, Mozart was dead. It only remains to add that the work seems to have failed at its first performance, but within a month had turned into a considerable success. It was performed in most German-speaking theatres (in translation of course) before the end of the first decade of the nineteenth century, and was actually the first of Mozart's operas to be heard in London, in 1806, when it was given in Italian for Mrs. Billington's benefit.

The story is dominated by two considerations: the determination of Vitellia, who is in love with Titus, to have revenge on him when he seems disposed to marry another; and the inclination of Titus to show clemency no matter what provocation may be offered him.

Vitellia knows of Titus's plan to marry Berenice, daughter of Agrippa I of Judaea, and she urges Sextus, who is madly in love with her, to fall in with her plans and lead a conspiracy against Titus. No sooner has he agreed than she hears that Berenice has been sent home and that Titus now plans to marry a Roman. Annius asks his friend Sextus to intercede with the Emperor in the matter of his (Annius's) marriage to Servilia, Sextus's sister, but Sextus is forestalled in his plan when Titus tells him that he has chosen none other than Servilia to be Empress. Servilia herself tells the Emperor that she is in love with Annius, and he renounces her, deciding instead to take Vitellia to wife. Vitellia has no knowledge of this change of plans, and sends Sextus off to set fire to the Capitol and murder Titus, only to hear, the moment he is gone, that she is now the destined bride of Titus. Sextus succeeds in the first part of his plan, but the conspiracy against Titus's life fails when someone else, wearing his mantle, is killed in his stead. The act ends in general confusion.

It is known at the beginning of Act II that Titus has escaped death, and moreover that the details of the plot have been revealed to him. Annius advises Sextus to throw himself on the mercy of the Emperor and to show renewed zeal in his cause. Vitellia in contrast is anxious to avoid any risk that her connection with the plot may be discovered, and she urges Sextus to fly the country. Publius, however, settles the matter by arriving to arrest Sextus, who is tried by the Senate and condemned to death. Titus confronts him with proof of his guilt, but when Sextus has left him, tears up the death sentence he has just signed. As Sextus and the other conspirators are about to be thrown to the wild beasts in the arena, Vitellia can bear the load of guilt no longer and confesses her share in the plot, only in her turn to be forgiven by the clement Emperor.

For years, critical opinion has been agreed that the music of *La Clemenza di Tito* was written in a hurry at a time when Mozart was exhausted by illness and overwork, and is therefore of little value. Anyone hearing it again (or maybe for the first time) will find it hard to agree that it is uninspired, although certainly written against time and in an outmoded form. There is almost no dramatic impetus behind the plot of the opera, and few of the arias have powerful situations behind them. But situations and plots were never the strong points of *opera seria*, which aimed rather at providing a dignified and graceful frame for the noble music and virtuoso singing which the aristocracy wanted to hear. Mozart and Mazzolà have between them upset some of the static nature of Metastasio's original libretto but even so they have not succeeded in altering the essentially conventional nature of the entertainment; on the other hand, Mozart has succeeded in providing a very superior example of the sort of music which went with these eighteenth-century occasions—it is pointless to complain that he did not write another *Don Giovanni* when he was in fact being asked to write something entirely and absolutely different.

Of the twenty-six numbers in the score, only eleven are in fact arias—which shows how much alteration was made in Metastasio's original, which made provision for no ensembles of any sort or kind. They range from a simple arietta such as that for Servilia ('S'altro che lagrime') to the great show pieces for Sextus ('Parto, parto') and Vitellia ('Non piu di fiori'). These latter have elaborate instrumental obbligati, for respectively clarinet and basset horn, and Stader went specially to Prague to play them. The vocal writing is no less elaborate, and, in this combination of virtuoso styles for voice and instrument, the arias look back to 'Martern aller Arten' (or even 'Possente spirto' from Monteverdi's *Orfeo*), and forward to such different pieces as Schubert's song 'Der Hirt auf dem Felsen' and the Mad scene in *Lucia*. The duets for Sextus and Annius, and for Servilia and Annius are particularly attractive, and there is a fine trio for Vitellia, Sextus, and Publius in the second act just before the arrest of Sextus. But the most notable section of the score is the finale to Act I, after the Capitol has been set on fire by Sextus. An agitated crowd offstage adds to the terror of the characters onstage, and Mozart builds up the whole finale antiphonally to imposing dimensions. It is genuine dramatic music, and is the only time the composer makes simultaneous use of soloists and chorus together in an extended finale. H.

## DIE ZAUBERFLÖTE
### The Magic Flute

Opera in two acts by Mozart, text by Emanuel Schikaneder. First performed at the Theater an der Wien, Vienna, September 30, 1791, with Nanetta Gottlieb (Pamina), Josefa Hofer (Queen of Night), Schack (Tamino), Gerl (Sarastro), Schikaneder (Papageno). Its first performances in England were at the Haymarket Theatre, London, 1811, and at Covent Garden, 1833 (in German). The opera was revived in 1911 by the Cambridge University Music Society in Professor Dent's translation, with Victoria Hopper, Mrs. Fletcher, Steuart Wilson, Clive Carey, H. G. Hiller; in 1914 at Drury Lane under Sir Thomas Beecham, with Claire Dux, Margarete Siems, Kirchner, Knüpfer, Hans Bechstein; in 1938 at Covent Garden under Beecham, with Lemnitz, Berger, Tauber, Strienz, and Hüsch. It has been in the regular Old Vic and Sadler's Wells repertory since 1921. First performed at Glyndebourne in 1935, with Rautawaara, Kocova, Ludwig, Andresen, Domgraf-Fassbänder and conducted by Fritz Busch. Revived at Salzburg under Toscanini, 1937, with Novotna, Osvath, Roswaenge, Kipnis, Domgraf-Fassbänder; and under Furtwängler in 1949, with Seefried, Lipp, Ludwig, Greindl, and Schmitt-Walter.

### CHARACTERS

Tamino, *an Egyptian Prince* ..................... Tenor
Three Ladies, *in attendance on the Queen of Night* ........
.................. Two Sopranos and Mezzo-Soprano
Papageno, *a bird-catcher* ...................... Baritone
The Queen of Night .......................... Soprano
Monostatos, *a Moor in the service of Sarastro* ....... Tenor
Pamina, *daughter of the Queen of Night* .......... Soprano
Three Genii .......... Two Sopranos and Mezzo-Soprano
The Orator ..................................... Bass
Sarastro, *High Priest of Isis and Osiris* .............. Bass
Two Priests .......................... Tenor and Bass
Papagena ..................................... Soprano
Two men in armour .................... Tenor and Bass
Slaves, Priests, People, etc.
The scene is laid in Egypt in the neighbourhood of a Temple of Isis and Osiris

Emanuel Johann Schikaneder, who wrote the libretto with the aid of a chorister named Gieseke, was a friend of Mozart and a member of the same Masonic Lodge. He was also the manager of a theatrical company and a successful actor,[1] and had persuaded Mozart to compose the music to a puppet show for him. He had selected for this show the story of 'Lulu' by Liebeskind, which had appeared in a volume of Oriental tales brought out by Wieland under the title of *Dschinnistan*. In the original tale a wicked sorcerer has stolen the daughter of the Queen of Night, who is restored by a Prince by means of magic. While Schikaneder was busy on his libretto, a fairy story by Perinet, music by Wenzel Müller, and treating of the same subject, was given at another Viennese theatre. Its great success interfered with Schikaneder's original plan.

At that time, however, freemasonry was a much discussed subject. It had been interdicted by Maria Theresa and armed forces were employed to break up the lodges. As a practical man Schikaneder saw his chance to exploit the forbidden rites on the stage. Out of the wicked sorcerer he made Sarastro, the sage priest of Isis. The ordeals of Tamino and Pamina became copies of the ceremonials of freemasonry. He also laid the scene of the opera in Egypt, where freemasonry believes its rites to have originated. In addition to all this Mozart's beautiful music ennobled the libretto and lent to the whole the force of the mysterious and sacred.

Because of the opera's relationship to freemasonry, commentators[2] have identified Tamino with the Emperor Joseph II, Pamina with the Austrian people, Sarastro with Ignaz von Born, a freemason and a scientist of great eminence; the vengeful Queen of Night was the Empress Maria Theresa, and Monostatos the clergy, especially the Jesuits and the religious orders.

Mozart was engaged on *The Magic Flute* from March until July 1791, and again in September of that year. On September 30, two months before his death, the first performance was given.

In the overture, the heavy reiterated chords represent, it has been suggested, the knocking at the door of the lodge room, especially as they are heard again in the temple scene, when the novitiate of Tamino is about to begin. The brilliance of the fugal *allegro* has been commented upon as well as the resemblance of its theme to that of Clementi's sonata in B flat.

1 According to Einstein, in his youth, one of the first German Hamlets.
2 Beginning with Moritz Zille, 1866.

Act I.   The story opens with Tamino endeavouring to escape from a huge snake. He falls unconscious. Hearing his cries, three black-garbed Ladies-in-Waiting of the Queen of Night appear and kill the serpent with their spears. The opening *allegro* leads to an extended trio for the Ladies, in which they rejoice that they have been able to foil the serpent and comment on the good looks of the youth they have rescued. Quite unwillingly they leave the handsome youth, who, on recovering consciousness, sees dancing towards him an odd-looking man entirely covered with feathers. It is Papageno, the Queen's bird-catcher. His song, 'Der Vogel-fänger bin ich ja' (I am the jolly bird-catcher [1]), is punctuated

with runs on his pipe and shows us at once that he is a jovial, not to say a popular, type of comedian. He tells the astonished Tamino that this is the realm of the Queen of Night. Nor, seeing that the snake is dead, does he hesitate to boast that it was he who killed the monster. For this lie he is immediately punished by the three Ladies, who reappear and place a padlock on his mouth. Then they show Tamino the miniature of a maiden, whose beauty at once fills his heart with an ardent love, which he expresses in one of the most beautiful of Mozart's tenor arias, 'Dies Bildnis ist bezaubernd schön' (O loveliness beyond compare). The Ladies tell him that she is a prisoner in Sarastro's hands, and he has no sooner sworn to deliver her than the Queen herself materialises from the clouds to reinforce his determination with a description of her desolation now that she has lost her daughter, and a promise that Pamina shall be his once she is free. 'O zittre nicht, mein lieber Sohn' (Be not afraid, O noble youth), she sings, and her scena develops into a display of coloratura fireworks designed primarily, we may be sure, to display the agile technique of the original Queen, Josefa Hofer, the composer's sister-in-law, but

[1] Translation by Professor Edward J. Dent (published by O.U.P.).

expressive also of her blind and passionate nature. The Ladies come back, take the padlock from Papageno's mouth and give him a set of chimes and Tamino a golden flute; by means of these magical instruments they will be able to escape the perils of their journey, on which they will be accompanied by three youths or genii. The quintet, 'Hm, hm, hm, der Arme kann von Strafe sagen' ('Tis hard such punishment to suffer), apart from being enchanting in itself, serves also to introduce the music associated later with the Genii, which has a curious quality of its own, which one can only ascribe to the lesser supernatural and call 'magical'.

The scene changes, and a richly furnished apartment in Sarastro's palace is disclosed. A brutal Moor, Monostatos, is pursuing Pamina with unwelcome attentions. Even in this duet, whose basis is surely in comedy, something of the depth which is to be Pamina's can be discerned; compare her feminine warmth with the lack of that quality in the Queen and the three Ladies. The appearance of Papageno puts him to flight. The Bird-catcher recognises Pamina as the daughter of the Queen of the Night and assures her that she will soon be rescued, and, what is more, by someone who has fallen in love with her without even seeing her— not the sort of thing, he laments, that ever seems to happen to him. Pamina consoles him in an exquisitely simple E flat tune and assures him that love will yet be his: 'Bei Männern, welche Liebe fühlen fehlt auch ein gutes Herze nicht' (The kindly voice of mother Nature wakes love in bird and beast and flower).

The finale takes place in a grove on three sides of which stand three Temples, dedicated to Wisdom, Reason, and Nature. Thither the three Genii lead Tamino, and leave him with the advice that he 'be silent, patient, persevering'. In a recitative which admirably expresses the dawning of understanding in his mind, Tamino decides to enter the Temples, but at the first two he is refused admittance, and from the third emerges a priest who informs him that Sarastro is no tyrant, no wicked sorcerer as the Queen had warned him, but a man of wisdom and of noble character. The solemn atmosphere of their dialogue—an extraordinary example of a musical argument which has the force of logic—serves to awaken still further Tamino's desire for knowledge, and his beautiful recitative 'O ew'ge Nacht' (O endless night), takes the form of question and answer, the answer being

supplied by a hidden and encouraging chorus. He takes his flute
and plays and sings to its accompaniment: 'Wie stark ist nicht
dein Zauberton' (O voice of magic melody). The wild animals
come out from their lairs and lie at his feet, but before the end
of the aria he hears Papageno's pan-pipe and at its end he rushes
off to find him. Papageno comes on from the opposite side of
the stage leading Pamina whom he intends to unite with Tamino.
Their duet, 'Schnelle Füsse, rascher Mut' (Let us hasten, quick as
thought) is punctuated with calls on the pipes and answers from
the flute but becomes a trio when they are overtaken by Monostatos, who sends for chains with which to complete their capture.

Disaster seems near, but Papageno remembers that he has a last
remedy and sets the Moor and his slaves dancing by playing on
his magic chimes. He and Pamina rejoice at their escape, but are
interrupted by a flourish of trumpets and the sound of a chorus
of praise to Sarastro. Papageno wonders what they are going to
say to him. 'Die Wahrheit!' (The truth, friend) proudly answers

Pamina, and the phrase serves to end the comedy of the escape and to initiate the solemnity of Sarastro's procession. She kneels at Sarastro's feet and explains that she was trying to escape the unwelcome attentions of the Moor. Sarastro comforts her and assures her that he understands her predicament and that the Gods aim to provide a remedy. Monostatos drags Tamino in, and in phrases whose origin is surely in Mozart's 'Turkish' style (see *Entführung*), denounces him to Sarastro, but, instead of the reward he expects, he is sentenced to a sound flogging. Woven into the structure of this section of the finale is the rapturous moment of the first meeting of Pamina and Tamino. By command of Sarastro, the two of them are brought into the Temple of Ordeals, where they must prove that they are worthy of the higher happiness.

Act II.     A solemn *andante* sets the scene, which is laid in a grove of palms outside the Temple. Sarastro informs the Priests of the plans which he has laid. The gods have decided that Pamina shall become the wife of the noble youth Tamino. Tamino, however, must prove by his own power that he is worthy of admission to the Temple. Therefore, Sarastro has taken under his protection Pamina, daughter of the Queen of Night, to whom is due all darkness and superstition. But the couple must go through severe ordeals in order to be worthy of entering the Temple of Light, and thus of thwarting the sinister machinations of the Queen. In between his pronouncements the Priests blow their trumpets, repeating the chords which were heard in the overture. Sarastro prays to Isis and Osiris that strength may be granted to the two aspirants after the goal of wisdom: 'O Isis und Osiris'. This solemn prayer is of so noble a nature that it has been described as the only music which could without fear of blasphemy be put into the mouth of God. It certainly belongs in quite another category from that in which is often to be found the music associated in opera with High Priests.

The Porch of the Temple. The ordeals of Tamino and Papageno are about to begin. They are warned by the Priests that they may perish in their search for the Truth, and then enjoined to silence as the first step in their probation. Two Priests warn them in a duet of what will happen if they fail to keep their vow of silence ('Bewahret euch vor Weibertücken': Beware of the wiles of woman's weaving), but no sooner are they left alone and in

PLATE VII. Ezio Pinza as Don Giovanni.

PLATE VIII. Julius Patzak as Florestan, Salzburg 1948.

darkness than they are confronted by the three Ladies of the Queen of Night. In the quintet which follows, the Ladies try to persuade them to abandon their quest, but Tamino, and even, with some prompting, Papageno, maintain a rigid silence in the face of the questioning women. The Priests reappear and congratulate them on having passed their first test.

The scene changes to a garden. Pamina is discovered lying asleep. Towards her steals the Moor, and indulges in what Einstein describes as a 'grotesque, phallic dance' and an aria which is not far behind in that quality: 'Alles fühlt der Liebe Freuden' (All with passion's fever tingle). The accompaniment to the aria is 'to be sung and played very softly, as if the music was a very long way off'—so runs Mozart's own direction. Monostatos comes up to Pamina but a cry of 'Zurück' causes him to start back: it is the Queen of Night. She flings her daughter a dagger with the command that she take it and kill Sarastro. In 'Der Hölle Rache kocht in meinem Herzen' (I'll have revenge, no longer can I bear it) one can feel the fires of fury boiling in the music, with its passionate staccato coloratura, its four top F's, and its headlong impetus. Monostatos returns and, threatening that he will reveal the plot (to which Pamina has never agreed to be a party), demands her love as the price of his silence. Sarastro enters just in time to hurl Monostatos from the defenceless Pamina, but the Moor departs promising to try if he will have better luck with the mother than with the daughter. Pamina pleads for her mother, but Sarastro assures her that vengeance is not in his thoughts: 'In diesen heil'gen Hallen kennt man die Rache nicht' (We know no thought of vengeance within these temple

Hal - len kennt man die Ra - che nicht

walls). Again, the nobility of the musical expression equals, perhaps even surpasses, that of 'O Isis und Osiris'. The bass who can sing these two arias evenly throughout their compass, with the flowing *cantilena* they demand and with the necessary expression of their content, will find himself with few rivals.

A Hall. Enjoined once more to keep silent, Tamino and Papageno are once more left by the attendant Priests. Papageno still chatters to himself, and soon enters into a long conversation with an old crone who introduces herself to him as his as yet unknown sweetheart, Papagena. A clap of thunder and she departs, to be replaced by the three Genii who appear bringing with them the flute and magic bells, carrying a table spread with food and drink, and singing in strains similar to those we heard at their first entrance. To the two aspirants comes Pamina, unaware of their vow of silence, but overjoyed to have found Tamino at last. But her delight is short-lived and she suspends belief in human constancy when she can get no answer from her beloved. 'Ach, ich fühl's, es ist verschwunden' (Ah, 'tis gone, 'tis gone for ever) run the words of her G minor aria, in which that mixture of maturity and innocence which she has consistently shown reaches its

*Andante.*

Ach, ich fühl's, es ist ver-

highest level of expression. Nowhere else in the repertory of the lyric soprano is the grief which passes all bounds given musical expression of such poignant simplicity, nor, one may add, a setting which is so exceptionally difficult to realise in terms of practical performance; this aria stands in the same relationship to the soprano as Sarastro's arias do to the bass.

The scene changes to a vault. The Priests sing a solemn *adagio* chorus of praise to Isis and Osiris, after which Sarastro confronts Pamina with Tamino and tells them to take their last farewell of each other: 'Soll ich dich, Teurer, nicht mehr seh'n?' (And shall I never see thee more?). As throughout the opera, the characterisation is preserved in every phrase, and is most marked when the three singers express the same idea by means of imitation:

muss nun wirk - lich fort

fort,     wirk - lich fort.

fort!     Die Stunde schlägt

We return to Papageno, who is told he can have one wish granted but is left vaguely dissatisfied when he has drunk the wine he asks for. What is missing? 'Ein Mädchen oder Weibchen wünscht Papageno sich' ('Tis love they say, love only, that makes the world go round). There are three *andante* verses, each with its *allegro* refrain, the *Glockenspiel ritornelli* growing successively more complicated. At the end of the song, the old woman comes back to him and, threatening him with dire penalties if he does not swear to be true to her, when he does so, reveals herself as a young and attractively feathered mate—but poor Papageno is warned off her by a Priest who pronounces him not yet worthy of her.

The three Genii are discovered in a garden singing of the symbolical joys of the rising sun, whose rays drive away the fears of night and herald the reign of light and love: 'Bald prangt, den Morgen zu verkünden' (The rosy flush that greets us yonder). Nothing more suitable for the beginning of the finale of the opera could be found than these sentiments and the disembodied agents through whom they are expressed. None of the music in the opera stands further away from the conventions of *opera buffa* or *Singspiel* or even *opera seria*—the forms known in Mozart's day—

than the conception of this trio of voices, and the hushed beauty of their music seems to convey that sense of being 'different', dedicated even, that characterises the serious side of the music of *The Magic Flute*, and sets it apart from other operas. Not knowing she is observed, Pamina contemplates suicide ('Du also bist mein Bräutigam? Durch dich vollend' ich meinen Gram': No other way but this remains to make an end of all my pains), but is restrained and comforted by the Genii in music of extraordinary tenderness. Two Men in Armour are seen standing at each side of a doorway, and Tamino is brought in by Priests for the last stage of his initiation. The test of fire and water is heralded by the Men in Armour, whose scene is constructed in the form of a chorale prelude, the orchestra weaving a *fugato* round the chorale 'Ach Gott vom Himmel sieh' darein'. Tamino proclaims his resolution, but is joined by Pamina for these final ordeals. His joy at being not only reunited with her but even allowed to speak to her freely is expressed in an ardent phrase which prepares us for the moving simplicity of their meeting and the duet which follows, and becomes a quartet with the musical entrance of the two guardians of the gates.

Pamina's sufferings appear to have produced an astonishing serenity and even wisdom in her, and she is in a sense Tamino's guide as, to the accompaniment of an *adagio* for the solo flute, they undergo successively the ordeals by fire and by water. At the end they are welcomed into the temple by Sarastro and the Priests.

At this point occurs Papageno's great scene of mock suicide, a parallel trial in comic terms perhaps to the serious trials Tamino and Pamina are expected to surmount. 'Papagena! Papagena!' is a song of a more serious cut than the other two Schikaneder had to himself, but, after an appeal to someone in the audience to volunteer to save him and the subsequent intervention of the Genii, the scena ends happily with a jingle of bells, and is followed by an irresistible patter duet for Papageno and Papagena.

Before the Temple. Monostatos leads on the Queen and her Ladies, who are making a last bid for revenge on Sarastro. But their appearance coincides with the stage being flooded with light, and the forces of night disappear before the short chorus extolling the new initiates and the magic flute which was their faithful companion, brings the opera to an end.

Nothing is so simple as to be absolutely clear-cut, and in life the serious and the comic are intermingled in a way that is frequently disconcerting but is nonetheless inevitable. Mozart, who was far from scorning the operatic conventions of his day, seems to have had no qualms about attempting this mixture in his operas in spite of the lack of precedent. Though both *Figaro* and *Così fan Tutte* partake of this mixture, they are nevertheless comedies pure though by no means simple: the one a comedy of action, the other of conversation; but the remaining two out of his four greatest operas present a more complicated problem. In each of them, the close relationship of the comic and the serious is treated in art as in life as the natural and inevitable thing we know it to be. *Don Giovanni*, comic in theme and predominantly comic in treatment, yet continually takes a turn towards the serious considerations which arise out of the comedy; *The Magic Flute*, serious in its presentation of the urge towards an understanding of truth, nonetheless mingles the digressions of Papageno with the aspirations of Tamino and Pamina. A refusal to take the story of *The Magic Flute* seriously is to turn a blind eye to the immaculate skill of the librettist (or librettists) and also to deny to the genius of Mozart the power of discrimination and choice. To what extent the fortuitous circumstances surrounding the commission of *The Magic Flute*—the fact that Schikaneder was an accomplished and popular comedian and that freemasonry was a controversial topic of the day—may have influenced Mozart in an unexpected direction, is likely to be a matter for speculation as long as opera is played, but it is in the end almost irrelevant. His terms of reference and his plans are interesting, but far more important is the work of art which resulted from them; in the cases of *The Magic Flute* and *Don Giovanni* he succeeded in combining the two elements which go to make up everyday life in a way which may occasionally have been approached since his day, but which had hardly before been attempted and has never been surpassed. K., H.

# PART II

# THE NINETEENTH CENTURY

# CHAPTER 4

## German Opera

# LUDWIG VAN BEETHOVEN
## (1770–1827)

### FIDELIO

OPERA in two acts by Ludwig van Beethoven. Text by Joseph Sonn-leithner and Georg Friedrich Sonnleithner after the drama by Jean Nicolas Bouilly. First produced at the Theater an der Wien, Vienna, November 20, 1805 (in three acts), with Anna Milder, Louise Müller, Demmer, Meier, Rothe, Weinkopf, and Cache, conducted by Beethoven; given in two acts on March 29, 1806. First given in its final form at the Kärnthnerthor Theatre, Vienna, 1814. First performed in London at the Haymarket (in German), 1832, at Covent Garden (in English), 1835, with Malibran; New York (in English) 1839, (in German) 1856; at the Metropolitan, New York, 1884, with Marianne Brandt, Auguste Kraus, Anton Schott, Adolf Robinson, Josef Miller, Josef Staudigl, and Otto Kemlitz, conductor Leopold Damrosch. First performed at Sadler's Wells in Professor Dent's English translation, 1937, with Molly de Gunst, Hamilton-Smith, Tudor Davies, Redvers Llewellyn, Ronald Stear, Arnold Matters, and Ivor Samuel, conductor Braithwaite. Revivals at Covent Garden include those of 1927, with Helene Wildbrunn, Fritz Krauss, and Paul Bender, conductor Bruno Walter; 1934, with Lotte Lehmann, Franz Voelker, and Alexander Kipnis, conductor Beecham; 1938, with Rose Pauly, Helge Roswaenge, Ludwig Weber, conductor Beecham; 1948, with Sylvia Fisher, Thorsteinn Hannesson, David Franklin, conductor Karl Rankl; 1951, with Kirsten Flagstad and Julius Patzak.

### CHARACTERS

Florestan, *a Spanish Nobleman* . . . . . . . . . . . . . . . . . . . . Tenor
Leonora, *his wife, in male attire as Fidelio* . . . . . . . . Soprano
Don Fernando, *the King's Minister* . . . . . . . . . . . . . . . . Bass
Don Pizarro, *Governor of the prison* . . . . . . . . . . . . . . . Bass
Rocco, *chief jailer* . . . . . . . . . . . . . . . . . . . . . . . . . . . . . . Bass
Marcellina, *daughter of Rocco* . . . . . . . . . . . . . . . . . Soprano
Jacquino, *assistant to Rocco* . . . . . . . . . . . . . . . . . . . . . Tenor

Soldiers, Prisoners, People

*Time:* Eighteenth century.     *Place:* A fortress, near Seville, Spain, used as a prison for political offenders

The libretto, which appealed to the composer by reason of its pure and idealistic motive, was not written for Beethoven. It was a French book by Bouilly and had been used by three composers: Pierre Gaveaux (1798); Simon Mayr, Donizetti's teacher and the composer of more than seventy operas (1805); and Paër (1804).
It was Schikaneder, the librettist and producer of Mozart's

*Magic Flute*, who commissioned Beethoven to compose an opera. But it was finally executed for Baron von Braun, who had succeeded to the management of the Theater an der Wien.

Beethoven's heart was bound up in the work. Conscientious to the last detail in everything he did, there are no less than sixteen sketches for the opening of Florestan's first air and 346 pages of sketches for the opera. Nor did his labour in it cease when the opera was completed and performed.

Bouilly's libretto was translated and made over for Beethoven by Schubert's friend Joseph Sonnleithner. The opera was brought out November 20 and repeated November 21 and 22, 1805. It was a failure. The French were in occupation of Vienna, which the Emperor of Austria and the court had abandoned, and conditions generally were upset. But even Beethoven's friends did not blame the non-success of the opera upon these untoward circumstances. It had inherent defects, as was apparent even a century later, when at the *Fidelio* centennial celebration in Berlin, the original version was restored and performed.

To remedy these, Beethoven's friend, Stephen von Breuning, condensed the three acts to two and the composer made changes in the score. This second version was brought forward April 29, 1806, with better success, but a quarrel with von Braun led Beethoven to withdraw it. It seems to have required seven years for the *entente cordiale* between composer and manager to become re-established. Then Baron von Braun had the book taken in hand by a practical librettist, Georg Friedrich Treitschke. Upon receiving the revision, which greatly pleased him, Beethoven in his turn re-revised the score. In this form *Fidelio* was brought out May 23, 1814, in the Theater am Kärnthnerthor. There was no question of failure this time. The opera took its place in the repertoire and when, eight years later, Mme. Schröder-Devrient sang the title role, her success in it was sensational.

There are four overtures to the work, three entitled *Leonore* (Nos. 1, 2, and 3) and one *Fidelio*. The *Leonore* overtures are incorrectly numbered. The No. 2 was given at the original performance and is, therefore, No. 1. The greatest and justly the most famous, the No. 3, is really No. 2. The so-called No. 1 was composed for a projected performance at Prague, which never came off. The score and parts, in a copyist's hand, but with corrections by Beethoven, were discovered after the composer's death. When it was recognised as an overture to the opera, the conclusion that it was the earliest one, which he probably had laid aside, was not unnaturally arrived at. The *Fidelio* overture was intended for the second revision, but was not ready in time. The overture to *The Ruins of Athens* was substituted. The overture to *Fidelio* usually is played before the opera and the *Leonore*, No. 3, is frequently inserted between the two scenes of Act II.[1]

In the story of the opera, Florestan, a noble Spaniard, has aroused the enmity of Pizarro, governor of a gloomy mediaeval fortress, used as a place of confinement for political prisoners. Pizarro has been enabled secretly to seize Florestan and cast him into the darkest dungeon of the fortress, at the same time spreading a report of his death.

One person, however, suspects the truth—Leonora, the wife of Florestan. Her faithfulness, the danger she runs in order to save her husband, and the final triumph of conjugal love over the sinister machinations of Pizarro, form the motive of the story of *Fidelio*, a title derived from the name assumed by Leonora, when, disguised as a man, she obtains employment as assistant to Rocco, the chief jailer of the prison. Fidelio has been at work and has become a great favourite with Rocco, as well as with Marcellina, the jailer's daughter. The latter, in fact, much prefers the gentle, comely youth, Fidelio, to Jacquino, the turnkey, who, before Fidelio's appearance upon the scene, believed himself to be her accepted lover. Leonora cannot make her sex known to the girl. It would ruin her plans to save her husband. Such is the situation when the curtain rises on the first act, which is laid in the courtyard of the prison.

Act I.    The opera opens with a brisk duet between Jacquino and Marcellina, in which he urges her definitely to accept him and she cleverly puts him off. Left alone she expresses her com-

---

[1] But this practice is by no means universally approved (except, maybe, among conductors, since it gives them a solo opportunity). *Leonore* 3 repeats much of the material of the scene it follows; sacrifices the effect of sunshine and of solution which the C major of the final scene can produce when *not* preceded by music in the same key; and entirely destroys the dramatic balance of the whole act. Professor Dent has pointed out in addition that the careful balance of the instrumentation of the opera is upset (compare the dynamic ranges of the *Fidelio* overture and *Leonore* 3) and has suggested that the piece be played at the end of the whole opera for the benefit of those who must have it and of the prima donna conductors who must play it!

H.

passion for Jacquino, but wishes she were united with Fidelio. ('O wär ich schon mit dir vereint'—O, were I but with you united.)

Later she is joined by her father. Then Leonora (as Fidelio) enters the courtyard. Marcellina, seeing how weary Leonora is, hastens to relieve the supposed youth of his burden. Rocco hints not only tolerantly but even encouragingly at what he believes to be the fancy Fidelio and Marcellina have taken to each other. This leads up to the quartet in canon form, one of the notable vocal numbers of the opera, 'Mir ist so wunderbar' (How wondrous the emotion). Being a canon, the theme enunciated by each of the four characters is the same, but if the difference in the sentiments of each character is indicated by subtle nuance of expression on the part of the singers, and the intonation be correct, the beauty of this quartet points the tragic implications of much of the rest of the opera. The participants are Leonora, Marcellina, Rocco, and Jacquino, who appears toward the close. 'After this canon,' say the stage directions, so clearly is the form of the quartet recognised, 'Jacquino goes back to his lodge.'

Rocco sings a song in praise of money and the need of it for young people about to marry. ('Hat man nicht auch Gold beneben': Life is nothing without money.) Its jocular, vulgar character is curiously at variance with the style of the quartet it follows. The situation is awkward for Leonora, but the rescue of her husband demands that she continue to masquerade as a man. Moreover there is an excuse in the palpable fact that before she entered Rocco's service, Jacquino was in high favour with Marcellina and probably will have no difficulty in re-establishing himself therein when the comely youth Fidelio turns out to be Leonora, the faithful wife of Florestan.

Through a description which Rocco gives of the prisoners, Leonora now suspects what she had not been sure of before: her husband is confined in this fortress and in its deepest dungeon. The scene ends with a trio dominated by Leonora's 'Ich habe Muth'.

A short march, with a pronounced and characteristic rhythm covers the change of scenes and announces the approach of Pizarro. He looks over his despatches. One of them warns him that Fernando, the Minister of State, is about to inspect the fortress, representations having been made to him that Pizarro has used his power as governor to wreak vengeance upon his private enemies. A man of quick decision, Pizarro determines to do away with Florestan at once. His aria, 'Ha! welch' ein Augenblick!' (Ah! the great moment!), is one of the heaviest and most difficult solos for bass voice in the dramatic repertory, but its effectiveness is undeniable.

Pizarro posts a trumpeter on the ramparts with a sentry to watch the road from Seville. As soon as a state equipage with outriders is sighted, the trumpeter is to blow a signal. Having thus made sure of being warned of the approach of the Minister, he tosses a well-filled purse to Rocco, and bids him 'for the safety of the State', to make away with the most dangerous of the prisoners—meaning Florestan. Rocco declines to commit murder, but when Pizarro takes it upon himself to do the deed, Rocco consents to dig a grave in an old cistern in the vaults, so that all traces of the crime will be hidden from the expected visitor. The music of this duet, effective enough to begin with, is later subjected to repetition in a way which brings it perilously out of line with the dramatic situation—it provides evidence for those who doubt the existence in Beethoven of a sense of the stage.

Leonora, who has overheard the plot, now gives vent to her feelings in the highly dramatic: 'Abscheulicher! wo eilst du hin!' (Accursed one! Where hasten'st thou!); a deeply moving expression of confidence that her love and faith will enable her, with the aid of Providence, to save her husband's life. The recitative, *andante* air, and quick final section is on the pattern made familiar by Mozart's 'Dove sono', and, later, in the operas of Weber. 'Abscheulicher' is one of the most famous examples of such a scena. Soon afterwards she learns that, as Rocco's assistant, she is to help him in digging the grave. She will be near her husband and either able to aid him or at least die with him.

The prisoners from the upper tiers are now, on Leonora's intercession and because it is the King's birthday, permitted a brief opportunity to breathe the open air. The cells are unlocked and they are allowed to stroll in the garden of the fortress, until Pizarro, hearing of this, angrily puts an end to it. The chorus of the prisoners, subdued like the half-suppressed joy of fearsome beings, is one of the significant passages of the score.

Act II.    The scene is in the dark dungeon where Florestan is in heavy chains. The act opens with Florestan's recitative and air, a fit companion piece to Leonora's 'Komm Hoffnung' in Act I:

The whispered duet between Leonora and Rocco as they dig the grave and the orchestral accompaniment impress one with the gruesome significance of the scene, and with Beethoven's delicate juxtaposition of melodrama and accompanied song.

Leonora thinks she recognises her husband and obtains Rocco's permission to give him some food and drink. His heartfelt thanks for the unexpected kindness, her anguished recognition, and Rocco's premonition that the prisoner is beyond human aid combine in a trio of wonderful beauty.

Pizarro enters the vault, makes himself known to his enemy, and draws his dagger for the fatal thrust. Leonora throws herself in his way. Pushed aside, she again interposes herself between the would-be murderer and his victim, and, pointing at him a loaded pistol, which she has had concealed about her person, cries out: 'First slay his wife!'

At this moment, in itself so tense, a trumpet call rings out from the direction of the fortress wall. Jacquino appears at the head of the stone stairway leading down into the dungeon and announces (in spoken dialogue) that the Minister of State is at the gate. Florestan is saved and the quartet ends with Pizarro's discomfiture. There is a rapturous duet, 'O namenlose Freude' (Joy inexpressible) for him and the devoted wife to whom he owes his life.

In Florestan the Minister of State recognises his friend, whom he believed to have died, according to the reports set afloat by Pizarro, who himself is now apprehended. To Leonora is assigned the joyful task of unlocking and loosening her husband's fetters and freeing him from his chains. A chorus of rejoicing: 'Wer ein solches Weib errungen' (He, whom such a wife has cherished) brings the opera to a close.

It is well said in George P. Upton's book, *The Standard Operas*, that 'as a drama and as an opera, *Fidelio* stands almost alone in its perfect purity, in the moral grandeur of its subject, and in the resplendent ideality of its music.' Even those who do not appreciate the beauty of such a work, and, unfortunately their number is considerable, cannot fail to agree with me that the trumpet call, and, still more, the immaculate timing with which it brings the prison scene to a climax, is one of the most dramatic moments in opera. I was a boy when I first heard *Fidelio* in Wiesbaden, but I still remember the thrill, when that trumpet call split the air with the message that the Minister of State was in sight and that Leonora had saved her husband.

When *Fidelio* had its first American performance (New York, Park Theatre, September 9, 1839) the opera did not fill the entire evening. The entertainment, as a whole, was a curiosity according to present-day standards. First came Beethoven's opera, with Mrs. Martyn as Leonora. Then a *pas seul* was danced by Mme. Araline; the whole concluding with *The Deep, Deep Sea*, in which Mr. Placide appeared as The Great American Sea Serpent. This seems incredible. But I have searched for and found the advertisement in the New York *Evening Post*, and the facts are as stated.

Under Dr. Leopold Damrosch, *Fidelio* was performed at the Metropolitan Opera House in the season of 1884–85; under Anton Seidl, during the season of 1886–87, with Brandt and Niemann, as well as with Lehmann and Niemann as Leonora and Florestan. K.

# CARL MARIA VON WEBER
## (1786–1826)

### DER FREISCHÜTZ

Opera in three acts by Carl Maria von Weber, text by Johann Friedrich Kind. First produced at the Schauspielhaus, Berlin, June 18, 1821, with Mmes. Seidler, Eunicke, Messrs. Stümer and Blume. First performed in London, at the English Opera House, 1824, with Miss Noel, Miss Povey, Mr. Braham, Mr. Baker, Mr. Bartley, and Mr. Bennet; in German at Her Majesty's Theatre, 1832. First performance in New York (in English), 1825; (in German) 1845; at Metropolitan Opera, 1884. For the performance in Italian at Covent Garden in 1825, Costa wrote recitatives to replace the spoken dialogue, as did Berlioz for the production at the Opéra, Paris, 1841. Revived at Metropolitan Opera, 1923, with Rethberg, Taucher, and Bohnen, and conducted by Bodanzky; at Covent Garden, 1935 (in English), with Eva Turner, Walter Widdop, Arthur Fear, and conducted by Beecham; at la Scala 1955, with de los Angeles, Ratti, Albanese, Rossi-Lemeni, conductor Giulini.

### CHARACTERS

Prince Ottokar ................................Baritone
Cuno, *the head ranger* ...........................Bass
Max, *a forester* ...............................Tenor
Caspar, *a forester* .............................Bass
Kilian, *a rich peasant* ..........................Tenor
A Hermit ........................................Bass
Samiel, *the wild huntsman* .................Speaking Part
Agathe, *Cuno's daughter* ......................Soprano
Aennchen, *her cousin* .........................Soprano

*Time:* Middle of seventeenth century     *Place:* Bohemia

The overture to *Der Freischütz* is the first in which an operatic composer unreservedly has made use of melodies from the opera itself. Beethoven, in the *Leonora* overtures, utilises the theme of Florestan's air and the trumpet call. Weber has used not merely thematic material but complete melodies. Following the beautiful passage for horns at the beginning of the overture is the music of Max's outcry when, in the opera, he senses rather than sees the passage of Samiel across the stage, after which comes the sombre music of Max's 'Hatt denn Himmel mich verlassen?' (Am I then by heaven forsaken?). This leads up to the music of Agathe's outburst of joy when she sees her lover approaching.

Act I.    At the target range. Kilian, a peasant, has defeated
Max, the forester, at a prize shooting, a *Schützenfest* maybe.
Max, of course, as a forester accustomed to use of fire-arms,
should have won, and it is disgraceful for him to have been
defeated by a peasant. Kilian rubs it in and the men and girls of
the village join in the mocking of Max—a clever bit of teasing in
music which establishes at the very start the originality of melody,
style, and character of the opera.

The hereditary forester, Cuno, is worried over the poor showing Max has made not only that day, but for some time past.
There is to be a shoot on the morrow before Prince Ottokar. In
order to win the hand in marriage of Agathe, Cuno's daughter,
and the eventual succession as hereditary forester, Max must
carry off the honours in the competition now so near at hand.
There is an expressive trio for Max, Caspar, and Cuno with
chorus ('O diese Sonne!'), which is followed by a short waltz
as the peasants bring the competition to a suitable end. Max is
in despair; life will be worthless to him without Agathe, yet he
seems to have lost all his cunning as a shot, and without it he
cannot win her hand. The first part of his scena, 'Durch die
Wälder, durch die Auen' (Through the forest and o'er the
meadows), is a melody of great beauty, but the music takes on a
more sinister character as Samiel, unseen of course by Max,
hovers, a threatening shadow, in the background. It is now,
when the others have gone, that his comrade Caspar, another
forester of dark visage and of morose and forbidding character,
approaches him. He hands him his gun, points to an eagle circling
far above, and tells him to fire at it. Max shoots, and from its
dizzy height the bird falls dead at his feet. It is a wonderful shot,
but Caspar explains to him that he has shot with a charmed bullet
and that such bullets always hit what the marksman wills them
to. (*Der Freischütz* can only be translated as 'the free-shooter',
i.e. someone who shoots with magic bullets.) If Max will meet him
in the Wolf's Glen at midnight, they will mould bullets with one
of which, on the morrow, he will be able to win Agathe's hand
and the hereditary office of forester. Max, to whom victory means
all that is dear to him, consents. Caspar's effective drinking song,
which precedes his tempting of Max, is forced in its hilarity
and ends in grotesque laughter, Caspar being the familiar of
Samiel, the wild huntsman. The act ends with an aria for Caspar,

whose wide range and rapid passages are taxing for the singer, but which is wholly in keeping with Caspar's sinister character.

Act II.    Agathe's room in the head ranger's house. The music opens with a delightful duet for Agathe and Aennchen and a charmingly coquettish little air for the latter ('Kommt ein schlanker Bursch gegangen'; Comes a comely youth a-wooing). But Agathe has gloomy forebodings, and even her sprightly relative is unable to cheer her up. Left alone, she opens the window and, as the moonlight floods the room, intones the prayer so simple, so exquisite, so expressive: 'Leise, leise, fromme Weise' (Softly sighing, day is dying). This is followed after a

recitative by a rapturous passage leading into an ecstatic melody as she sees her lover approaching. It is one of the best known tunes in all opera, but gains immeasurably from being heard in its context as part of one of the greatest scenes for solo soprano.

Max comes in and is quickly followed by Aennchen. Very soon, however, he says he must leave, because he has shot a deer in the Wolf's Glen and must go after it. The scene ends with a trio in which the girls try vainly to warn him against the locality, which is said to be haunted.

The scene changes to the Wolf's Glen, the haunt of Samiel the wild huntsman (otherwise the devil) to whom Caspar has sold himself, and to whom he now plans to turn over Max as a victim, in order to gain for himself a brief respite on earth, his time to Samiel being up. The younger forester joins him in the Wolf's Glen and together they mould seven magic bullets, six of which go true to the mark, the seventh wherever Samiel wills it. The music has long been considered the most expressive rendering of the gruesome that is to be found in a musical score—its power is undiminished to-day whatever may be thought of the naïveté of the stage apparatus which goes with it. The ghost of Max's mother appears to him and strives to warn him away. Cadaverous, spooky-looking animals crawl out from caves in the rocks and spit flames and sparks. But the music is a fascinating essay in the grotesque—nothing comparable had been tried before—and the way in which it avoids the excessive but yet cunningly mixes the speaking voice and singing, the purely musical effect of Max's entrance with the atmospheric climax of the moulding of the bullets, is entirely admirable. The music remarkably anticipates Wagner, who got more than one hint from this scene—but its merits are particular and far beyond any prophetic qualities it may incidentally possess.

Act III. After a brief introduction, with suggestions of the hunting chorus later in the action, the act opens with Agathe's lovely cavatina 'Und ob die Wolke' (And though a cloud the sun obscure), a melody of such pure and expressive beauty that even Weber was never able to surpass it. Agathe is attired for the shooting test, which will make her Max's bride if he is successful. Aennchen sings a solo (composed after the rest of the opera), and then comes the enchanting chorus of bridesmaids who enter and wind the bridal garland. This is the piece which Richard Wagner, then seven years old, was playing in a room adjoining that in which his stepfather, Ludwig Geyer, lay in his last illness. As he listened to him playing the bridesmaids' chorus, Geyer turned to his wife, Wagner's mother, and said: 'What if he should have a talent for music!'

The concluding scene—the shooting test—begins with the spirited hunting chorus. Only the seventh bullet, the one which Samiel controls, remains to Max, the others having been used up during the hunt. Caspar, who expects Max to be Samiel's victim, climbs a tree to watch the proceedings from a safe place of concealment. Before the whole village and Prince Ottokar himself the test shot is to be fired. The Prince points to a flying dove and Max raises his gun. At that moment Agathe appears, accompanied by a Hermit, and calls out to Max not to shoot, that she is the dove. But Max has already pulled the trigger; Agathe falls —but only in a swoon—and it is Caspar who tumbles from the tree and rolls, fatally wounded, on the turf. Samiel has had no power over Max, for the young forester had not come to the Wolf's Glen of his own free will, but only after being tempted by Caspar; therefore Caspar had himself to be the victim of the seventh bullet. There is general uproar, Agathe is seen to be alive and Caspar dying, but Max's confession results in a sentence of banishment from the Prince. Only through the intercession (in a chorale-like aria) of the Hermit, a holy man revered by the whole district, is disaster for Max averted and the Prince's forgiveness obtained. The opera ends with the jubilant melody from Agathe's second act scene.

No less notable as portent than as music, *Der Freischütz* holds an important position in the logical development of music and particularly of opera. If anyone can be said to qualify for such a title, Weber was the founder of the German romantic school—a school which reached its climax with Wagner, its culmination perhaps with Strauss. Weber is as truly the forerunner of Wagner as Haydn is of Mozart, and Mozart of Beethoven. From *Der Freischütz*, Wagner derived his early predilection for legendary subjects, as witness *The Flying Dutchman*, *Tannhäuser*, and *Lohengrin*, from which it was but a step to the mythological subject of the *Ring* dramas.

The structure of the overture to this opera is much like that to Wagner's *Tannhäuser*. There is also a resemblance in contour between the music of Agathe's jubilation and that of Tannhäuser's hymn of Venus—Wagner worshipped Weber. Without a suggestion of plagiarism, the contour of Wagner's melodic idiom is that of Weber's. The resemblance to Weber in the general structure of the finales to the first acts of both *Tannhäuser* and *Lohengrin* is obvious, and even in some of the leading motives of the Wagner music dramas, the student will find hints of Weber still persisting.

But Weber is much more than just Wagner's forerunner—just as Bellini has importance of his own beyond being the predecessor of Verdi. He is one of the great melodists of musical history, and perhaps no other composer of the romantic movement so completely preserved musical freshness at the same time as he introduced the literary element into music.     K., H.

# EURYANTHE

Opera in three acts by Weber. Book, by Helmine von Chezy, adapted from
*L'Histoire de Gérard de Nevers et de la belle et vertueuse Euryanthe, sa mie.*
This is Weber's only 'Grand opera', i.e. without spoken dialogue. Produced,
Vienna, Kärnthnerthor Theatre (Theatre at the Carinthian Gate), October 25,
1823; London, Covent Garden (in German), 1833; Drury Lane (in German),
1882, with Mmes. Sucher, Peschka-Leutner, Messrs. Nachbaur, Gura, conductor Hans Richter. Probable American première, Metropolitan, New York,
1887, with Lilli Lehmann, Marianne Brandt, Max Alvary, Emil Fischer, conductor Anton Seidl. Revived Salzburg Festival, 1937, with Maria Reining,
Kerstin Thorborg, Karl Friedrich, Alexander Sved, conductor Bruno Walter.

## CHARACTERS

Euryanthe of Savoy............................Soprano
Eglantine of Puiset ......................Mezzo-Soprano
Count Lysiart of Forêt.........................Baritone
Count Adolar of Nevers..........................Tenor
Louis VI ........................................Bass
Rudolph, *a knight* ..............................Tenor
Bertha .......................................Soprano

*Time:* Beginning of the twelfth century          *Place:* France

Act I.   The Palace of the King. Count Adolar chants the
beauty and virtue of his betrothed, Euryanthe. Count Lysiart
sneers and boasts that he can lead her astray. The two noblemen
stake their possessions upon the result.

Garden of the Palace of Nevers. Euryanthe sings of her longing
for Adolar. Eglantine, the daughter of a rebellious subject who,
made a prisoner, has, on Euryanthe's plea, been allowed the
freedom of the domain, is in love with Adolar. She has sensed that
Euryanthe and her lover guard a secret. Hoping to estrange
Adolar from her, she seeks to gain Euryanthe's confidence and
only too successfully. For Euryanthe confides to her that Adolar's
dead sister, who lives in the lonely tomb in the garden, has appeared to Adolar and herself and confessed that, her lover having
been slain in battle, she has killed herself by drinking poison from
her ring; nor can her soul find rest until someone, innocently
accused, shall wet the ring with tears. To hold this secret inviolate
has been imposed upon Euryanthe by Adolar as a sacred duty.
Too late she repents of having communicated it to Eglantine who,
on her part, is filled with malicious glee. Lysiart arrives to conduct
Adolar's betrothed to the royal palace.

Act II.   Lysiart despairs of accomplishing his fell purpose when Eglantine emerges from the tomb with the ring and reveals to him its secret. In the royal palace, before a brilliant assembly, Lysiart claims to have won his wager, and, in proof, produces the ring, the secret of which he claims Euryanthe has communicated to him. She protests her innocence, but in vain. Adolar renounces his rank and estates with which Lysiart is forthwith invested and endowed, and, dragging Euryanthe after him, rushes into the forest where he intends to kill her and then himself.

Act III. In a rocky mountain gorge Adolar draws his sword and is about to slay Euryanthe, who in vain protests her innocence. At that moment a huge serpent appears. Euryanthe throws herself between it and Adolar in order to save him. He fights the serpent and kills it; then, although Euryanthe vows she would rather he slew her than not love her, he goes his way leaving her to heaven's protection. She is discovered by the King, who credits her story and promises to vindicate her when she tells him that it was through Eglantine, to whom she disclosed the secret of the tomb, that Lysiart obtained possession of the ring.

Gardens of Nevers, where preparations are being made for the wedding of Lysiart and Eglantine. Adolar enters in black armour with visor down. Eglantine, still madly in love with him and dreading her union with Lysiart, is so affected by the significance of the complete silence with which the assembled villagers and others watch her pass, that, half out of her mind, she raves about the unjust degradation she has brought upon Euryanthe.

Adolar, disclosing his identity, challenges Lysiart to combat. But before they can draw, the King appears. In order to punish Adolar for his lack of faith in Euryanthe, he tells him that she is dead. Savagely triumphant over her rival's end, Eglantine now makes known the entire plot and is slain by Lysiart. At that moment Euryanthe rushes into Adolar's arms. Lysiart is led off a captive. Adolar's sister finds eternal rest in her tomb because the ring has been bedewed by the tears of the innocent Euryanthe.

The libretto of *Euryanthe* is accounted extremely stupid, and the work is rarely given. The opera, however, is important historically and contains some magnificent music.

Apart from its overture *Euryanthe* has never been popular. The overture consists of two vigorous, stirringly dramatic sections separated by the weird tomb motive. The opening chorus in the King's palace is sonorous and effective. There is a very beautiful romanza for Adolar (''Neath almond trees in blossom'). In the challenge of the knights to the test of Euryanthe's virtue occurs the vigorous phrase with which the overture opens. Euryanthe has an exquisite cavatina ('Chimes in the valley'); there is an effective duet for Euryanthe and Eglantine ('Threatful gather clouds about me'). A scene for Eglantine is followed by the finale—a chorus with solo for Euryanthe.

Lysiart's recitative and aria ('Where seek to hide?'), expressive of hatred and defiance—a powerfully dramatic number—opens the second act. There is a darkly premonitory duet for Lysiart and Eglantine. Adolar has a tranquil aria ('When zephyrs waft me peace') with a beautiful woodwind introduction; its *allegro* melody is prominent in the overture. There is a duet full of abandon with Euryanthe ('To you my soul I give'). The finale is a quartet with chorus. The hunting chorus in the last act, previous to the King's discovery of Euryanthe, has been called Weber's finest inspiration.

Many efforts have been made by means of a new libretto or by re-editing to give *Euryanthe* the position it deserves in the modern operatic repertory. An attempt at a new libretto was made in Paris in 1857, at the Théâtre Lyrique. It failed. Having read a synopsis of that libretto, I can readily understand why. It is, if possible, more absurd than the original. Shakespeare's *Cymbeline* is derived from the same source as *Euryanthe*, which shows that, after all, something could be made of the story.        K.

# OBERON

Opera in three acts, by Carl Maria von Weber. Text, in English, by James Robertson Planché. The original story appeared in *La Bibliothèque Bleue* under the title of *Huon de Bordeaux*. Wieland adapted this story to form his poem *Oberon*, and Planché took his libretto from Sotheby's translation of Wieland. First performed at Covent Garden, April 12, 1826, with Miss Paton as Reiza (Rezia only in German versions), Mme. Vestris as Fatima, Braham as Huon, and Bland as Oberon, the composer conducting. First performance in New York, 1828. Revived, Metropolitan Opera, 1918, with Ponselle, Alice Gentle, Martinelli, Althouse, conducted by Bodanzky (with recitatives composed by Bodanzky, instead of spoken dialogue); Salzburg, in German under Walter, with, in 1932, Maria Müller, Lotte Schoene, Helge Roswaenge, and, in 1934, Anny Konetzni, Anday, Kullman; Holland Festival, 1950, with Gré Brouwenstijn, Anna Pollak, Frans Vroons, conducted by Monteux (in German); Florence Festival, 1952, in the Boboli Gardens in a production by Herbert Graf, with Doris Doree, Gianna Pederzini, Tyge Tygesen, Gino Penno, conducted by Fritz Stiedry (in Italian); Opéra, Paris, 1953, with Araujo, Gedda, conducted by Cluytens, producer Maurice Lehmann.

## CHARACTERS

Sir Huon of Bordeaux ..........................Tenor
Sherasmin, *his squire* .......................Baritone
Oberon, *King of the Fairies* ......................Tenor
Puck ........................................Soprano
Reiza, *daughter of Haroun el Rashid* .............Soprano
Fatima, *her attendant* ...................Mezzo-Soprano
A Sea Nymph ..............................Soprano
Charlemagne, *Emperor of the Franks* ⎤
Haroun el Rashid, *Calif*
Babekan, *a Saracen Prince*
Almanzor, *Emir of Tunis*
Abdullah, *a Corsair*                        } Speaking Parts
Titania, *Oberon's wife*
Roshana, *wife of Almanzor*
Namouna, *Fatima's grandmother*
Nadina, *a female of Almanzor's Harem* ⎦

The overture, which is one of the best known and most popular of concert pieces, is made up entirely of music which is employed elsewhere in the opera. The horn call (ex. 1) with which it opens, plays a prominent part throughout and is used in rather the same way as the magic instruments in *The Magic Flute*. It is followed

by a figure of soft, quickly descending woodwind chords (ex. 2), which at once suggests the atmosphere of fairyland; its light, airy quality sets the scene for the opening fairy chorus. Two themes follow, still played softly and mysteriously; they are heard again at the end of the opera, as a triumphant march. Atmosphere and tempo change and we hear a stormy figure in the strings (ex. 3);

this returns as an accompanying figure to the quartet in Act II, when the four lovers escape to the ship. The fairy chords have the effect of calming down the violent *allegro* section, and a theme of great beauty (ex. 4), which Huon later sings in the big scena, is

Ex. 4

heard on the clarinet and is then taken over by the strings. This leads straight into an exultant tune (ex. 5), which is typically and unmistakably Weber—most people will recognise it as from the closing section of Reiza's great aria 'Ocean, thou mighty monster'.

Ex. 5

As is so often his way with his triumphant themes, Weber first introduces it quietly and unpretentiously, and it is not till after a recapitulation of the existing material and the introduction of a new, strong theme (later associated with Puck; ex. 6), that he

Ex. 6

allows us to feel the full force of this exhilarating tune. It brings the overture to an exciting close.

Act I. The curtain rises to reveal Oberon's bower, where a group of fairies sing over their sleeping King a chorus which breathes the very atmosphere of enchantment. Example 2 punctuates the various sentences, and the composer's marking is *Andante quasi allegretto* (sempre tutto pianissimo possibile). Puck appears and explains that Oberon, having quarrelled with his fairy partner Titania, has vowed never to be reconciled to her until he shall have found two lovers constant through every peril and temptation. To seek such a pair, Puck, his 'tricksy spirit', has ranged through the world in vain. Oberon wakes and, in an aria which fulfils the implications of its *agitato* introduction, laments the 'fatal oath' he has sworn. He hears that Puck has heard sentence passed on Sir Huon of Bordeaux, a young knight, who, having been insulted by the son of Charlemagne, has killed him in single combat and for this has been condemned by the Emperor to proceed to Bagdad, slay him who sits on the Caliph's right hand, and claim the Caliph's daughter as his bride.

Oberon instantly resolves to make this pair the instrument of his reunion with his Queen, and for this purpose he conjures up Huon and Sherasmin asleep before him, and enamours the knight by showing him Reiza, daughter of the Caliph, in a vision. Introduced by the horn call of the overture (ex. 1) she begs for help. (Reiza is the original form, as found in the libretto and in the first English edition of the score. It appears as Rezia in the earliest German score, where Huon becomes Hüon.)

Oberon wakes Huon to the sound of fairy music, Huon promises to be faithful to his mission, and Oberon with a wave of his wand transports him and his squire to Bagdad. The contrast between the utterances of the mortal Huon and the immortal Oberon is most marked, and the transformation (an enharmonic change from F minor to D major) makes as lovely an effect musically as it should when staged. Huon rejoices at the prospect before him in music of florid cast accompanied by the chorus, and prepares, with the help of the magic horn Oberon has given him, to fulfil his mission.

Two non-musical episodes follow. In the first, Huon and Sherasmin rescue Prince Babekan from a lion. He turns out to be the betrothed of Reiza, but his evil disposition is soon apparent when he and his followers set on their rescuers; they are, however, put to flight. The knight next learns from an old woman, Namouna, that Reiza is to be married next day, but the Princess has been influenced, like her lover, by a vision and is resolved to be his alone. She believes that fate will protect her from her nuptials with Babekan.

Huon exults in his chivalrous role in a great scena, whose

music exactly fits his youthful heroic character. The magnificent flourish of the opening section is succeeded by a lovely *andante* for the cello which later expresses Huon's sentiments as opposed to his heroic resolves. This scena returns to the *allegro energico* of the beginning and the close is strenuous and forthright. It has been said with more than a little truth that to do justice to this music the singer requires the voice of a Wagnerian tenor and the technique of a coloratura soprano. The combination, if it ever existed, is by no means easy to find in the twentieth century.

The scene changes to the palace of Haroun el Rashid, where Reiza tells Fatima that nothing will induce her to marry anyone other than her destined knight; better death than union with the hated Babekan. The finale begins with a big solo for Reiza, in which she swears to be true to the knight she has as yet seen only in a vision. Fatima tells Reiza that her deliverer is at hand, and mistress and maid contemplate their coming bliss in a simple duettino. The sound of a march is heard and Reiza sings jubilantly above a soft chorus of palace guards and eunuchs.

Act II.    We are at the court of Haroun el Rashid. A chorus of attendants and slaves sings the praises of the mighty Caliph, who sits serenely in their midst with Prince Babekan at his right. The Prince asks that there shall be no more delay before he is married to his promised Reiza, and Haroun orders that she be led into his presence. Preceded by dancing girls (to a short orchestral *allegretto grazioso*) she comes in. No sooner is the music ended than the clash of swords is heard outside and in a moment Reiza is in the arms of her rescuer. Huon fights Babekan and vanquishes him, and having spellbound the rest by a blast of the magic horn, he and Sherasmin carry off Reiza and Fatima.

A scene without music serves to establish the flight of the four fugitives (they are set on by palace guards, but frighten them off with the help of the horn); it also gives them an opportunity to lose the horn in the course of the fight. Later, we find Fatima and Sherasmin together, and, in the course of a love scene, Fatima finds occasion to sing a song of nostalgic import, 'A lonely Arab maid', marked by the composer *moderato amoroso*. The four lovers take ship to the sound of a quartet, the two women answering the two men, all four later joining in a rapturous ensemble to the accompaniment of the string figure of the overture (No. 3).

The scene changes to a rocky seashore. Puck calls together his spirits and instructs them to bring about the wreck of the ship in which Reiza and Huon are crossing the sea; the music ends with the rousing of the storm. No sooner are they gone about their work than Huon appears supporting the fainting figure of Reiza. His short *adagio* prayer for her recovery is one of the most beautiful passages in the score and reveals a tender, poetic side to Huon's character which is hitherto unsuspected. His prayer is answered, Reiza revives, and Huon goes off to see if there are other survivors of the wreck.

Reiza is alone. She apostrophises the sea, whose very repose carries menace but whose fury is terrible indeed. 'Ocean thou mighty monster' is a justly famous aria for dramatic soprano, and, with the overture, it is the one number of *Oberon* which will be familiar to everybody. It is an extended scena, modelled on the lines of Agathe's big solo in *Freischütz*, but more dramatic in content. It opens with a grand recitativic introduction, continues with a swelling *allegro con moto* section describing the storm which is still in progress, sinks to the comparative calm of the *maestoso assai*, but rises again steeply as Reiza catches sight of something moving, reaching a climax of excitement as she realises it is a ship; the concluding *Presto con fuoco* is one of the most thrilling passages in opera and is familiar to everyone as the final section of the overture.

But the ship Reiza has seen turns out to be manned by pirates, who pause only to make her prisoner, and leave Huon, who attempts to rescue her, senseless on the shore.

For the finale, we are back in an atmosphere which is Weber at his most idyllic. The sensuously graceful song of the Sea Nymphs in 6/8 has a magic of its own, but the whole scene, with its short duet for Oberon and Puck and its extended and mostly *pianissimo* chorus of fairies, is wonderfully beautiful. This is pure fairy music, such as even such a specialist as Mendelssohn never excelled (*Midsummer Night's Dream*, like *Oberon*, was written in 1826), and its delicacy and soft charm can never fail to astonish an unsuspecting listener and ravish his musical susceptibilities.

Act III.    Fatima, saved with Sherasmin from the wreck but now like him a slave in Tunis, laments her changed fortune in a song with pronounced character-flavour, 'O Araby, dear Araby, my own, my native land'. But she cannot prevent her natural cheerfulness breaking into the refrain with its repeated 'Al, al, al, al, al, al'. Sherasmin, who works in the same establishment for one Ibrahim, joins her and together they reflect sadly on the distance each of them has come since childhood; again, they finish by looking on the bright side—at least they are together in their slavery, and have a kind master. But a surprise is round the corner and Puck brings in Huon. There is a great recognition, and Fatima says she has even heard that Reiza is in Tunis, but where she does not know. They plan to dress Huon up and get him employment with Ibrahim.

The scene changes to the palace of the Emir of Tunis, where Reiza lies a captive, and has become, like Mozart's Constanze before her, the principal object of her noble master's affections. She grieves for her lost love in an F minor aria of pure and mournful beauty, the counterpart of Huon's prayer in the previous act, 'Mourn thou poor heart'. Like the Pasha Selim, Almanzor respects the grief of his prisoner and tells her he will not use force to compel her to yield to his love.

Huon receives a message, conveyed in the symbolic language of the East by means of flowers. Fatima interprets it for him and tells him it is from Reiza; he is to go at once to her. Huon's rondo, 'I revel in hope and joy again', is likely to test the agility of the tenor but it is of comparatively conventional musical value. He is led to the Emir's palace where, in fact, Reiza is incarcerated, but is confronted instead with the Emir's wife, Roshana, thirsting for revenge on the husband who has discarded her in favour of the beautiful captive. She assures Huon that he will have earned her love and the throne of Tunis if he will help her dispose of her erring husband. Neither the prospect of power nor of her love can turn the hero from his purpose, which is to free Reiza, and he has little difficulty in resisting the efforts which Roshana employs to seduce him; his musical answers to the vocal and balletic blandishments of Roshana's attendants are nothing if not firm.

As Huon is rushing from her presence he is surprised and seized by Almanzor and his guard; Roshana tries to stab her husband, and is arrested in her turn and led off by negro attendants. Almanzor commands that a pyre be erected and Huon burnt within the hour, and the efforts of Reiza to obtain his pardon only succeed in gaining for her a similar sentence. At this juncture, Sherasmin, who has contrived entrance to the palace, has the magic horn miraculously restored to him, and with its help he is able to change the situation completely.

The sound of music has an exactly similar effect on Almanzor's court as it had on Monostatos's slaves; they no longer have a desire to do anything but dance, and the four lovers, now re-united, resolve to summon the aid of Oberon in an effort not only to suspend but to dissolve completely the nightmare situation in which they find themselves. The god appears in answer to the horn's blast, and in a short but beautiful aria hails the faithful, loving pair and tells them that their prayers are answered and he will restore them to safety and happiness. They are transported to the court of Charlemagne, who takes his place with his entour-age to the sound of a march. Huon tells him his commands have been fulfilled, and he is here with Reiza to claim the promised pardon. This is granted and the opera ends with a chorus of praise and thanksgiving.

*Oberon* has always resisted the efforts which have from time to time been made to fit it neatly into the category of German romantic opera. Its pattern is undeniably unconventional, and the signs are that Weber himself was disturbed by several aspects of the dramatic plan. Various attempts have been made to adapt the opera for performance, and it is safe to say that it has been heard far less often in the form in which Weber left it than in the various arrangements to which it has been subjected.

Bodanzky composed recitatives in place of the spoken dialogue for the production at the Metropolitan in 1918, but otherwise left the score intact. More important is the version prepared by Mahler in conjunction with the scenic designer Alfred Roller, with a new German translation by Gustav Brecher. Mahler arranged a number of musical sections, usually (but not always) in conjunction with spoken dialogue as opposed to singing, which he designated 'Melodram'; these are not given separate numbers in his edition but are clearly indicated as 13a and 13b in the score. There are eight of these additions, and they have the effect of connecting certain sections of the music very closely with the dramatic action, most particularly of course the horn call, which is heard at the beginning of the overture, and which in Mahler's arrangement assumes a musical status comparable to that of Papageno's pipes. A section of music is introduced to lead up to the vision of Reiza in Act I, and another to reinforce the giving of the magic horn by Oberon to Sherasmin before the ensemble during which takes place the transformation from France to Bagdad. In Act II, the bewitching of Haroun's court is made more plausible by means of musical accompaniment, and the flight of the two pairs of lovers has orchestral accompaniment from the moment the horn invokes Oberon's aid, Oberon and Reiza later between them singing the short aria of Oberon which occurs in the finale of the third act (in Mahler's version it is thus heard twice). After Reiza has been carried away by the pirates (which occurs immediately after she has sung 'Ocean, thou mighty monster'), Oberon laments the hard nature of their trials in a shortened version of his first aria, and Puck anticipates the fairy music of the finale by singing a reminiscence (shortened, and in C instead of F) of the fairy chorus at the opening of Act I. In Act III, Huon's return just before the trio with Fatima and Sherasmin is heralded by a melodrama for Puck, and Mahler omits entirely the rondo for Huon which should follow Reiza's F minor aria. The preparations for the public burning of Huon are made to the sound of the march which, later in the finale, reintroduces Huon to the court of Charlemagne.

The fact that arrangements of the score have been made should not influence one to think that *Oberon* is impracticable; it is unconventional in much the same way as *The Magic Flute* is unconventional, with of course the important difference that Mozart was increasing the stature of a form—*Singspiel*—which he understood exceedingly well, whereas Weber, with whom drama and continuity were never the strongest points, was attempting a form—English pantomime in its original state (Planché founded pantomime)—which he found completely strange. There is no need to elevate Weber to Mozart's level: *Oberon* is musically strong enough to stand on its own merits. No one would deny that it would be extremely difficult to achieve a perfect performance nowadays; and it is not easy to find a singer for Reiza, almost impossible to think of one to do justice to Huon. The production would have to give the impression of being lavish as well as imaginative. On the other hand the intrinsic merits of the opera are so great that attempts to stage it are likely to increase in frequency rather than the reverse; one wonders how long the country for which Weber originally wrote the work will continue to ignore it.                                   H.

# ALBERT LORTZING

## ZAR UND ZIMMERMANN
### Tsar and Carpenter

COMIC opera in three acts by Albert Lortzing. Text by the composer, founded on a French play by J. T. Merle. First produced, Leipzig, December 22, 1837; New York, 1857; London, Gaiety Theatre, 1871 (in English, as *Peter the Shipwright*), with Santley and Blanche Cole. Still popular in German-speaking theatres.

### CHARACTERS

Peter I, *Tsar of Russia* .........................Baritone

Peter Ivanov, *a runaway Soldier* ...................Tenor

van Bett, *Burgomaster of Sardam* ...................Bass

Marie, *his niece* ..............................Soprano

Admiral Lefort, *Russian Ambassador* ...............Bass

Lord Syndham, *English Ambassador* .................Bass

Marquis de Chateauneuf, *French Ambassador* .......Tenor

Witwe Browe ...............................Contralto

**Act I.** Peter the Great of Russia, under the name of Peter Michaelov, is working in the ship-building yards at Sardam, in Holland, with a view to gaining experience and knowledge such as he could never find in Russia itself. He has become friends with Peter Ivanov, another Russian and a deserter from the armed forces. Peter Ivanov has fallen in love with Marie, the Burgomaster's niece, a coquette who cannot resist showing him that he is not the only attractive man about the place. Van Bett, the comically self-opinionated Burgomaster, has been approached by the Ambassadors of England and France to find out if the Tsar is secretly working in Sardam. He calls together the ship-workers, and finding many are called Peter, determines on a subtle and, he thinks, foolproof strategem: which of them, he asks, is a foreigner? To his consternation, two step forward—Peter Ivanov and Peter Michaelov. He needs time to fathom it all out; let everyone go back to work—he has all the information he requires. He decides that Peter Ivanov is the man he is looking for, and accordingly offers him whatever he chooses, even the hand of his niece in marriage, if he will admit his identity to the foreign gentleman he will presently introduce him to. At the end of the act, the French Ambassador has recognised the Tsar and even made contact with him, while Syndham and van Bett, thinking Ivanov is the man they are looking for, start to pay court to him.

Act II.    A local festivity is in progress. All the principals of the opera watch the dancing and listen to the singing, and the French Ambassador even sings a song in praise of Flemish beauty, much to the chagrin of Peter Ivanov, who takes it to be aimed at Marie. The principal characters divide into two groups: Peter Michaelov, the French and Russian Ambassadors on one side, Peter Ivanov, van Bett, and Lord Syndham on the other, and negotiations proceed. Van Bett has had a good deal to drink, and he thinks the time has come for him to solve his problem in his own way. He demands, with more forthrightness than manners, the names and identification of the three Ambassadors present in the inn. Somewhat taken aback by their answers, he announces he will arrest the two Peters, and is only prevented from carrying out his design—in spite of the remonstrance of all present—when the Tsar draws his sword and announces he will not be taken alive.

Act III.    Van Bett prepares to send 'the Tsar' on his way with full musical honours. He rehearses his choir and tells them that he himself will sing the solo part; nothing is too much trouble if it will honour their noble visitor. The Tsar himself has in the meanwhile found the means to provide himself with a ship in which to sail home, promising before he leaves a safe conduct for Peter Ivanov. Van Bett starts off his anthem (which he directs at Ivanov, still thinking him the Tsar), but is interrupted by the sound of a cannon shot; the real Tsar is about to leave the harbour. He pauses for a moment to take leave of his friends, and is gone to the acclamation of the crowd.

The music of *Zar und Zimmermann* is anything but complicated, and its square-cut choruses and straightforward solos reveal little unusual in the imagination of their composer. The best role is for van Bett, whose entrance aria in Act I, with its catch phrase, 'Oh, ich bin klug und weise', is a favourite with German comic basses. Perhaps the most enjoyable moment in the opera is his rehearsal in the last act; this is capital fun, with van Bett's 'diddle-dum, diddle-dum, diddle-dum' to show when the orchestra plays alone, and his relish of the excellence of his own words. In Act II, the French Ambassador has a charming solo, 'Lebewohl mein flandrisch' Mädchen', and in the last act occur the Tsar's song, 'Sonst spielt ich mit Szepter und Kron' and the Clog dance, the latter a direct forerunner of Wagner's apprentices.     H.

## DER WILDSCHÜTZ
### The Poacher

Opera in three acts by Albert Lortzing. Text by the composer based on a play by A. von Kotzebue. First produced at Leipzig, December 31, 1842. First performance in England, Drury Lane, 1895 (in German); New York, 1831. Still current in Germany.

### CHARACTERS

Count of Eberbach ............................ Baritone
The Countess, *his wife* ........................ Contralto
Baron Kronthal, *her brother* ..................... Tenor
Baroness Freimann, *a young widow,*
　　　　　　　　　　　*sister of the Count* ....... Soprano
Nanette, *her maid* ............................. Soprano
Baculus, *a schoolmaster on the Count's estate* ... Buffo-Bass
Gretchen, *his fiancée* ......................... Soprano
Pancratius, *majordomo to the Count* ......... Speaking Part
Servants, Huntsmen, Peasants, Schoolboys

*Der Wildschütz* is perhaps, after *Zar und Zimmermann*, Lortzing's most popular opera; the story is amusing, and the excellent comic role of Baculus has the additional merit of being unique—there can be no other poaching schoolmaster in operatic annals. His 'Fünftausend Thaler' aria is one of the most celebrated solos in the repertory of the German bass.

Act I.     Baculus has accidentally shot a buck in a wood belonging to Count Eberbach, on whose estate he is employed as schoolmaster. He is filled with consternation when he receives a summons to the castle to account for his poaching. Gretchen, his bride-to-be, says she will intercede for him, but Baculus mistrusts this offer and will not allow her to go. A young student offers to help them in their dilemma and go dressed as Gretchen to ask for the Count's pardon (the student is in reality the Baroness Freimann in disguise; accompanied by her maid Nanette—also dressed as a boy—she wishes, unknown to him, to observe her betrothed, Baron Kronthal). Count Eberbach and the Baron arrive at the school and the Count, taking an instant liking to the supposed Gretchen, invites her and her friends to his birthday celebrations next day.

Act II. Baculus accompanies the disguised Baroness to the castle. Here everybody is enchanted by her country airs, the Count tries to make love to her on the sly, Baron Kronthal even goes so far as to contemplate matrimony. To save the situation, the Countess takes the 'village girl' into her own room for the night. Meanwhile the Baron offers Baculus no less than 5,000 thalers if he will give up his bride. It is more than the schoolmaster can resist.

Act III. Baculus sets about persuading Gretchen to fall in with the new situation, only to find to his consternation that the Baron is interested in the Gretchen he first met, not in the real bearer of that name. Baculus's admission that this was a student in disguise has unforeseen consequences: Baron Kronthal is furious that a man should have passed the night in his sister's room—for the Countess, it appears, is his sister. The discovery that the supposed Gretchen is really a student who is really Baroness Freimann solves all problems: the Count, who has been caught kissing her, is able to pass it off as only natural that he should kiss his sister, and the Countess is cleared of all blame.

As for the unhappy Baculus, he receives a full pardon from the Count, and he is even reconciled to Gretchen. H.

school and the Count fitting an locked lling to the surprised
Charming Ipytice for and her Count to his birthday celebration
next da

# OTTO NICOLAI

## DIE LUSTIGEN WEIBER VON WINDSOR
### The Merry Wives of Windsor

OPERA in three acts by Otto Nicolai. Text by Hermann von Mosenthal, after Shakespeare's play. First produced at the Berlin Hofoper, March 9, 1849 (the composer died in May), with Zschiesche as Falstaff and the composer conducting. First produced, Philadelphia, 1863; London, Her Majesty's, 1864 (in Italian), with Tietjens, Vitali, Jura, Santley; Adelphi Theatre, London, 1878 (in English); Metropolitan, New York, 1900 (in German), with Sembrich, Fritz Friedrichs, Dippel, conducted by Emil Paur; Covent Garden, 1907 (in German), with Jenny Fischer, Minnie Nast, Max Lohfing, Franz Naval. Revived by the Carl Rosa Company, 1943, with Ruth Packer, Gladys Parr, Norman Allin, Robert Sydney, conductor Charles Webber; hundredth anniversary production in Berlin, Staatsoper, 1949, with Irma Beilke, Margarete Klose, Otto Hopf, Helmut Krebs, conductor Johannes Schüler.

### CHARACTERS

| | |
|---|---|
| Sir John Falstaff | Bass |
| Herr Fluth (*Mr. Ford*) | Baritone |
| Herr Reich (*Mr. Page*) | Bass |
| Fenton | Tenor |
| Junker Spärlich (*Slender*) | Tenor |
| Dr. Caius | Bass |
| Frau Fluth (*Mistress Ford*) | Soprano |
| Frau Reich (*Mistress Page*) | Mezzo-Soprano |
| Jungfer Anna Reich (*Anne Page*) | Soprano |
| Erster Bürger | Tenor |

Nicolai, who died before he was thirty-nine, had a busy life of professional music-making, and his career embraced such diverse activities as organist at the Prussian Embassy in Rome, Kapellmeister in Vienna, composer in Italy, founder and conductor of the Berlin Philharmonic, and head of the opera in that city. He composed a number of operas, of which *Die lustigen Weiber von Windsor* is by far the most successful, as is hardly surprising in view of the wit, neatness of construction, and light-hearted gaiety for which it is distinguished.

Act I.    After an overture which is one of the most popular in the concert repertory, we find ourselves in the garden between the houses of Messrs. Ford and Page (to give them their Shake-spearean names), where their respective spouses are comparing notes on the love-letters they have each received that day from no less a person than Sir John Falstaff. They leave the stage to the men. Page has promised the hand of his daughter in marriage to Slender, whom he prefers to her other suitors, Caius and Fenton, in spite of the impassioned pleading of the last-named; Fenton is told Anne is not for a have-not like himself.

Inside Ford's house, his wife waits for the promised visit from Falstaff. She is furious with all men, and rehearses what she shall say to this particular specimen. She will make as if to give in to him—woman's heart is weak, she observes; he will be taken in and believe her. This is a big-scale coloratura aria, 'Nun eilt herbei', with an elaborate recitative and much exacting passage work for the singer.

Falstaff duly arrives, his love scene is interrupted by loud knocking, he hides in the linen basket, and Ford storms in, announcing he has caught his wife at last and bringing a crowd of witnesses to watch the proceedings. The search begins and the women laugh at the way their well-planned joke is taking shape—Falstaff is to be dumped into the river. The light touch of the duet contrasts well with Mistress Ford's scolding of Ford for his base, unworthy suspicion of her. The act ends with a general ensemble.

Act II.    We meet Falstaff on home ground for a change, and he leads a drinking song at the 'Gasthaus zum Hosenbande'—'The Garter' in fact. 'Als Büblein klein' has always been popular and it is still a war-horse in the repertory of the German operatic bass; it is in fact an admirably simple and highly effective piece. Ford, calling himself Brook (or 'Bach' in the German), comes to pump Falstaff on the subject of his relations with Mistress Ford. Their comic duet is capital fun, Falstaff's patter being interspersed with horrified interjections from Ford. 'Wie freu' ich mich' each sings in turn, the one rejoicing at the prospect of his rendezvous, the other at the possibility of catching Falstaff in the act.

The scene changes to Page's garden, where no less than three suitors are preparing to serenade Anne. Two of them, Slender and Caius, make a decidedly comic effect, the other, Fenton, is dis-tinctly romantic; in fact his 'Horch, die Lerche singt im Hain' is a deliciously pretty tune. There follows a pleasant little love duet for Anne and Fenton and a most ingenious 'quartettino' (as

Nicolai calls it) for Anne and the three lovers, the comic pair overhearing what the other two are saying to each other, and handing the tune, which was first sung by Anne, backwards and forwards from one to another until all four are engaged on it. The whole of this garden scene is controlled by the lightest of hands and its delicacy is quite unusual amongst German comic operas of the period—by comparison it makes Lortzing sound the clodhopper he unfortunately so often turns out to be.

We are back in Ford's house, as in Act I. Ford tells his wife she will be found out this time; nothing will prevent him catching her lover. He is furious—he even examines the laundry basket which the servants happen to bring through the room at this moment—and his wife laughs at him. Caius, Slender, Page knock at the door saying they are there, as Ford has instructed them. Falstaff is smuggled through dressed as an old woman and guided by Mistress Page. He pretends not to be able to hear Ford's questions and is got rid of to general acclamation. There is another unsuccessful search, and the act ends with an ensemble.

Act III.    The first scene is laid in Mistress Page's house, and there she sings her ballad of Herne the Hunter, an agreeable 6/8 tune. Later Anne delivers herself of the aria which alone makes the role worth a prima donna's while.

The last scene is laid in Windsor Forest, near what the score describes as 'die Eiche des Jägers Herne', or Herne the Hunter's Oak—an English description of *Freischütz* probably sounds just as odd to a German. Here the music we know so well from the overture comes into its own, and is deployed in a succession of choruses and dance movements associated with the preparation and tormenting of Falstaff by the disguised company. Falstaff himself has a trio with the wives of Ford and Page—he makes love to them both—Anne and Fenton, disguised as Titania and Oberon, have a short duet between ballet movements, and finally the big tune of the overture makes its presence felt. All is resolved and the opera ends with a short trio with chorus.        H.

# CHAPTER 5

## *Wagner*

# WEBER TO WAGNER

IN the evolution of opera from Weber to Wagner what might otherwise be a gap is filled by composers whose reputations endure, but whose music is seldom heard to-day. Heinrich Marschner (1795–1861) composed in *Hans Heiling*, Berlin, 1833, an opera based on legendary material. Its success may have confirmed Wagner's bent toward dramatic sources of this kind already aroused by his admiration for Weber. *Hans Heiling*, *Der Vampyr* (The Vampire), and *Der Templer und Die Judin* (Templar and Jewess, a version of *Ivanhoe*) long held an important place in the operatic repertory of their composer's native land. On the other hand *Faust* (1818) and *Jessonda* (1823), by Ludwig Spohr (1784–1859), have completely disappeared. Spohr, however, deserves mention as being one of the first professional musicians of prominence to encourage Wagner. Incapable of appreciating either Beethoven or Weber, strange to say, he at once recognised the merits of *The Flying Dutchman* and *Tannhäuser*, and even of *Lohengrin*—at the time sealed volumes to most musicians and music lovers. As court conductor at Kassel, he brought out the first two Wagner operas mentioned respectively in 1842 and 1853; and was eager to produce *Lohengrin*, but was prevented by opposition from the court.

Meyerbeer and his principal operas will be considered at length in the chapters in this book devoted to French opera. There is no doubt, however, that what may be called the 'largeness' of Meyerbeer's style and the effectiveness of his instrumentation had their influence on Wagner.

Gasparo Spontini (1774–1851) was an Italian by birth, but I believe can be said to have made absolutely no impression on the development of Italian opera. His principal works, *La Vestale* (The Vestal Virgin), *Olimpia*, and *Fernando Cortez*, were brought out in Paris and later in Berlin, where he was general music director, 1820–1841. His operas were heavily scored, especially for brass, but the three works mentioned have all been successfully revived, *La Vestale* for Rosa Ponselle at the Florence Festival and at the Metropolitan, *Olimpia* in Florence in 1950, and *Fernando Cortez* in Naples in 1951 (the last two productions with Renata Tebaldi).

# RICHARD WAGNER

## (1813–1883)

### RIENZI

OPERA in five acts by Richard Wagner. Text by the composer after Bulwer Lytton's novel of the same name. First performed at the Hofoper, Dresden, October 20, 1842, with Mmes. Schröder-Devrient, Wüst, Thiele, Messrs. Tichatscheck, Dettmer, Wächter, Vestri, Reinhold, Risse; New York, 1878; London, Her Majesty's (in English), 1879, with Helene Crosmond, Mme. Vanzini, and Joseph Maas, conductor Carl Rosa; Metropolitan, New York, 1886, with Lilli Lehmann, Marianne Brandt, Eloi Sylva, Emil Fischer, conductor Anton Seidl; revived Berlin, 1933, with de Stroggi, Klose, Lorenz, Helgers, List, conductor Blech; Berlin 1941 with Scheppan, Klose, Lorenz, Prohaska.

### CHARACTERS

| | |
|---|---|
| Cola Rienzi, *Roman Tribune and Papal Notary* | Tenor |
| Irene, *his sister* | Soprano |
| Steffano Colonna | Bass |
| Adriano, *his son* | Mezzo-Soprano |
| Paolo Orsini | Bass |
| Raimondo, *Papal Legate* | Bass |
| Baroncelli<br>Cecco del Vecchio } *Roman citizens* | { Tenor<br>Bass |
| Messenger of Peace | Soprano |

Ambassadors, Nobles, Priests, Monks, Soldiers, Messengers, and Populace in General

*Time:* Middle of the fourteenth century          *Place:* Rome

The overture of *Rienzi* gives a vivid idea of the action of the opera. Soon after the beginning there is heard the broad and stately melody of Rienzi's prayer, and then the Rienzi motive, a typical phrase, which is used with great effect later in the opera. It is followed in the overture by the lively melody heard in the concluding portion of the finale of the second act. These are the three most conspicuous portions of the overture, in which there are, however, numerous tumultuous passages reflecting the dramatic excitement which pervades many scenes.

Orsini, a Roman patrician, attempts to abduct Irene, the sister of Rienzi, a papal notary, but is opposed at the critical moment by Colonna, another patrician. A fight ensues between the two factions, in the midst of which Adriano, Colonna's son, who is in love with Irene, appears to defend her. A crowd is attracted by the tumult, and among others Rienzi comes upon the scene. Enraged at the insult offered his sister, and stirred on by Cardinal Raimondo, he urges the people to resist the outrages of the nobles. Adriano is impelled by his love for Irene to cast in his lot with her brother. The nobles are overpowered, and appear at the capitol to swear allegiance to Rienzi, but during the festal proceedings Adriano warns him that the nobles have plotted to kill him. An attempt which Orsini makes to murder him is foiled by the steel breastplate which Rienzi wears under his robe.

The nobles are seized and condemned to death, but on Adriano's pleading they are spared. However, when they violate their oath of submission, the people under Rienzi's leadership rise and exterminate them, in spite of Adriano's pleas. In the end the people prove fickle. The popular tide turns against Rienzi, especially in consequence of the report that he is in league with the German emperor, and intends to restore the Roman pontiff to power. As a festive procession is escorting him to church, Adriano, infuriated at the slaughter of his family, rushes upon him with a drawn dagger, but again the blow is averted. Instead of the 'Te Deum', with which Rienzi expected to be greeted on his entrance to the church, he hears the malediction and sees the ecclesiastical dignitaries placing the ban of excommunication against him upon the doors. Adriano hurries to Irene to warn her of her brother's danger, and urges her to seek safety with him in flight. She, however, repels him, and seeks her brother, determined if need be to die with him. She finds him at prayer in the capitol, but rejects his counsel to save herself with Adriano. Rienzi appeals to the infuriated populace which has gathered around the capitol, but they do not heed him. They fire the capitol with their torches, and hurl stones at Rienzi and Irene. As Adriano sees his beloved one and her brother doomed to death in the flames, he throws away his sword, rushes into the capitol, and perishes with them.

The opening of the first act is full of animation, the orchestra depicting the tumult which prevails during the struggle between the nobles. Rienzi's brief recitative is a masterpiece of declamatory music, and his call to arms is spirited. It is followed by a trio between Irene, Rienzi, and Adriano, and this in turn by a duet for the two last-named which is full of fire. The finale opens with a double chorus for the populace and the monks in the Lateran, accompanied by the organ. Then there is a broad and energetic appeal to the people from Rienzi, and amid the shouts of the populace and the ringing tones of the trumpets the act closes.

The insurrection of the people against the nobles is successful, and Rienzi, in the second act, awaits at the capitol the patricians who are to pledge him their submission. The act opens with a broad and stately march, to which the messengers of peace enter. They sing a graceful chorus. This is followed by a chorus for the senators, and the nobles then tender their submission. There is a terzetto, between Adriano, Colonna, and Orsini, in which the nobles express their contempt for the young patrician. The finale which then begins is highly spectacular. There is a march for the ambassadors, and a grand ballet, historical in character, and supposed to be symbolical of the triumphs of ancient Rome. In the midst of this occurs the assault upon Rienzi. Rienzi's pardon of the nobles is conveyed in a broadly beautiful melody, and this is succeeded by the animated passage heard in the overture. With it are mingled the chants of the monks, the shouts of the people who are opposed to the cardinal and nobles, and the tolling of bells.

The third act opens tumultuously. The people have been aroused by fresh outrages on the part of the nobles. Rienzi's emissaries disperse, after a furious chorus, to rouse the populace to vengeance. After they have left, Adriano has his great air, a number which can never fail of effect when sung with all the expression of which it is capable. The rest of the act is a grand accumulation of martial music, and includes the stupendous battle hymn, which is accompanied by the clashing of sword and shields, the ringing of bells, and all the tumult incidental to a riot. After Adriano has pleaded in vain with Rienzi for the nobles, and the various bands of armed citizens have dispersed, there is a duet between Adriano and Irene, in which Adriano takes farewell of her. The victorious populace appears and the act closes with their triumphant shouts. The fourth act is brief, and beyond the description given in the synopsis of the plot, requires no further comment.

The fifth act opens with the beautiful prayer of Rienzi,

already familiar from the overture. There is a tender duet between Rienzi and Irene, an impassioned aria for Rienzi, a duet for Irene and Adriano, and then the finale, which is chiefly choral.                                                                                K.

## DER FLIEGENDE HOLLÄNDER
### The Flying Dutchman

Opera in three acts by Richard Wagner. Text by the composer, founded on an episode in Heine's Memoirs of Herr von Schnabelewopski. Performed at the Hofoper, Dresden, January 2, 1843, with Mmes. Schröder-Devrient, M. Wachter, Messrs. Wächter, Reinhold, Risse, Bielezizky, conductor Wagner; Drury Lane, 1870 (in Italian; first Wagner opera to be performed in London), with Ilma di Murska, Mme. Corsi, Messrs. Santley, Perotti, Foli, Rinaldini, conductor Arditi; Lyceum, 1876 (in English), by Carl Rosa Company; Philadelphia, 1876 (in Italian); Metropolitan, 1889, with Sophie Weisner, Charlotte Huhn, Reichmann, Kalisch, Fischer, Mittelhauser, conductor Seidl. Interpreters of the title role have included Theodor Bertram, Anton van Rooy, Friedrich Schorr, Rudolf Bockelmann, Herbert Janssen, Joel Berglund, and Hans Hotter; famous Sentas have included Emmy Destinn, Maria Müller, Frieda Leider, and Kirsten Flagstad.

#### CHARACTERS

Daland, *a Norwegian sea captain* ................... Bass
Senta, *his daughter* .......................... Soprano
Eric, *a huntsman* ............................. Tenor
Mary, *Senta's nurse* ......................... Contralto
Daland's Steersman ........................... Tenor
The Dutchman ............................. Baritone
Sailors, Maidens, Hunters, etc.

*Time:* Eighteenth century     *Place:* A Norwegian Fishing Village

From *Rienzi* Wagner took a great stride forwards to *The Flying Dutchman*. This is the first milestone on his road from opera to music-drama. Of his *Rienzi* the composer was in after years ashamed, writing to Liszt: 'I, as an artist and man, have not the heart for the reconstruction of that, to my taste, superannuated work, which in consequence of its immoderate dimensions, I have had to remodel more than once. I have no longer the heart for it, and desire from all my soul to do something new instead.' He spoke of it as a youthful error, but in *The Flying Dutchman* there is little, if anything, which could have troubled his artistic conscience.

One can hardly imagine the legend more effective dramatically and musically than it is in Wagner's libretto and score. It is a work of wild and sombre beauty, relieved only occasionally by touches of light and grace, and has all the interest attaching to a work in which for the first time a genius feels himself conscious of his greatness. If it is not as impressive as *Tannhäuser* or *Lohengrin*, nor as tremendous as the music-dramas, that is because the subject of the work is lighter. As his genius developed, his choice of subjects and his treatment of them passed through as complete an evolution as his musical theory, so that when he finally abandoned the operatic form and adopted his system of leading motives, he conceived, for the dramatic bases of his scores, dramas which it would be difficult to fancy set to music of any other type than that which is so characteristic of his music-dramas.

Wagner's present libretto is based upon the picturesque legend of the Flying Dutchman—the Wandering Jew of the ocean. A Dutch sea-captain, who, we are told, tried to double the Cape of Good Hope in the teeth of a furious gale, swore that he would accomplish his purpose even if he kept on sailing forever. The devil, hearing the oath, condemned the captain to sail the sea until Judgment Day, without hope of release, unless he should find a woman who would love him faithfully unto death. Once in every seven years he is allowed to go ashore in search of a woman who will redeem him through her faithful love.

The opera opens just as a term of seven years has elapsed. The Dutchman's ship comes to anchor in a bay of the coast of Norway, in which the ship of Daland, a Norwegian sea-captain, has sought shelter from the storm. Daland's home is not far from the bay, and the Dutchman, learning he has a daughter, asks permission to woo her, offering him in return all his treasures. Daland readily consents. His daughter, Senta, is a romantic maiden upon whom the legend of the Flying Dutchman has made a deep impression. As Daland ushers the Dutchman into his home Senta is gazing dreamily upon a picture representing the unhappy hero of the legend. The resemblance of the stranger to the face in this picture is so striking that the emotional girl is at once attracted to him, and pledges him her faith, deeming it her mission to save him. Later on, Eric, a young huntsman, who is in love with her, pleads his cause with her, and the Dutchman, overhearing them, and thinking himself again forsaken, rushes off to his vessel. Senta cries out that she is faithful to him, but is held back by Eric, Daland, and her friends. The Dutchman, who really loves Senta, then proclaims who he is, thinking to terrify her, and at once puts to sea. But she, undismayed by his words, and truly faithful unto death, breaks away from those who are holding her, and rushing to the edge of a cliff casts herself into the ocean, with her arms outstretched toward him. The phantom ship sinks, the sea rises high and falls back into a seething whirlpool. In the sunset glow the forms of Senta and the Dutchman are seen rising in each other's embrace from the sea and floating upward.

In *The Flying Dutchman* Wagner employs several leading motives, not, indeed, with the resource which he displays in his music-dramas, but with considerably greater freedom of treatment than in *Rienzi*. There we had but one leading motive, which never varied in form. The overture, which may be said to be an eloquent and beautiful musical narrative of the whole opera, contains all these leading motives. It opens with a stormy passage, out of which there bursts the strong but sombre Motive of the Flying Dutchman himself, the dark hero of the legend. The orchestra fairly seethes and rages like the sea roaring under the lash of a terrific storm. And through all this furious orchestration there is heard again and again the motive of the Dutchman, as if his figure could be seen amid all the gloom and fury of the elements. There he stands, hoping for death, yet indestructible. As the excited music gradually dies away, there is heard a calm, somewhat undulating phrase which occurs in the opera when the Dutchman's vessel puts into the quiet Norwegian harbour. Then, also, there occurs again the motive of the Dutchman, but this time played softly, as if the storm-driven wretch had at last found a moment's peace.

We at once recognise to whom it is due that he has found this moment of repose, for we hear like prophetic measures the strains of the beautiful ballad which is sung by Senta in the second act of the opera, in which she relates the legend of The Flying Dutchman and tells of his unhappy fate. She is the one whom he is to meet when he goes ashore. The entire ballad is not heard at this point, only the opening of the second part, which may be taken as indicating in this overture the simplicity and beauty of Senta's character. In fact, it would not be too much to call this opening phrase the Senta Motive. It is followed by the phrase which indicates the coming to anchor of the Dutchman's vessel; then we hear the Motive of the Dutchman himself, dying away with the faintest possible effect. With sudden energy the orchestra dashes into the surging ocean music, introducing this time the wild, pathetic plaint sung by the Dutchman in the first act of the opera. Again we hear his motive, and again the music seems to represent the surging, swirling ocean when aroused by a furious tempest. Even when we hear the measures of the sailors' chorus the orchestra continues its furious pace, making it appear as if the sailors were shouting above the storm.

Characteristic in this overture, and also throughout the opera, especially in Senta's ballad, is what may be called the Ocean Motive, which most graphically depicts the wild and terrible aspect of the ocean during a storm. It is varied from time to time, but never loses its characteristic force and weirdness. The overture ends with an impassioned burst of melody based upon a portion of the concluding phrases of Senta's ballad; phrases which we hear once more at the end of the opera when she sacrifices herself in order to save her lover.

A wild and stormy scene is disclosed when the curtain rises upon the first act. The sea occupies the greater part of the scene, and stretches itself out far toward the horizon. A storm is raging. Daland's ship has sought shelter in a little cove formed by the cliffs. The orchestra, chiefly with the wild ocean music heard in the overture, depicts the raging of the storm, and above it are heard the shouts of the sailors at work: 'Ho-jo-he! Hal-lo-jo!'

As the storm seems to be abating the sailors descend into the hold and Daland goes down into the cabin to rest, leaving his Steersman in charge of the deck. The Steersman, as if to force himself to remain awake, intones a sailor song, but sleep overcomes him and the phrases become more and more detached, until at last he falls asleep.

The storm begins to rage again and it grows darker. Suddenly the ship of the Flying Dutchman, with blood-red sails and black mast, enters the harbour over against the ship of the Norwegian; then silently and without the least noise the spectral crew furl the sails. The Dutchman goes on shore.

Here now occur the weird, dramatic recitative and aria: 'Die Frist ist um' (The term is passed, and once again are ended seven long years). Daland perceives the Dutchman and going ashore questions him. It is then that the Dutchman, after relating a mariner's story of ill luck and disaster, asks Daland to take him to his home and allow him to woo his daughter, offering him his treasures. At this point we have a graceful and pretty duet, Daland readily consenting that the Dutchman accompany him. The storm having subsided and the wind being fair, the crews of the vessels hoist sail to leave port, Daland's vessel disappearing just as the Dutchman goes on board his ship.

Act II.    After an introduction in which we hear a portion of the Steersman's song, and also that phrase which denotes the appearance of the Dutchman's vessel in the harbour, the curtain rises upon a room in Daland's house. On the walls are pictures of vessels, charts, and on the farther wall the portrait of a pale man with a dark beard. Senta, leaning back in an armchair, is absorbed in dreamy contemplation of the portrait. Her old nurse, Mary, and her young friends are sitting in various parts of the room, spinning. Here we have that charming musical number famous all the musical world over, partly through Liszt's admirable piano arrangement of it, the 'Spinning Chorus'. It may be cited as a striking instance of Wagner's gift of melody, should anybody at this late day be foolish enough to require proof of his genius in that respect. The girls tease Senta for gazing so dreamily at the portrait of the Flying Dutchman, and finally ask her if she will not sing his ballad.

This ballad is a masterpiece of composition, vocally and instrumentally. It begins with the storm music familiar from the overture, and with the weird measures of the Flying Dutchman's motive  which sound like a voice calling in distress across the sea.

Senta repeats the measures of this motive, and then we have the simple phrases beginning: 'A ship the restless ocean sweeps'. Throughout this portion of the ballad the orchestra depicts the surging and heaving of the ocean, Senta's voice ringing out dramatically above the accompaniment. She then tells how he can be delivered from his curse, this portion being set to the measures which were heard in the overture, Senta finally proclaiming, in the broadly delivered, yet rapturous phrases with which the overture ends, that she is the woman who will save him by

being faithful to him unto death. The girls about her spring up
in terror and Eric, who has just entered the door and heard her
outcry, hastens to her side. He brings news of the arrival of
Daland's vessel, and Mary and the girls hasten forth to meet the
sailors. Senta wishes to follow, but Eric restrains her and pleads
his love for her in melodious measures. Senta, however, will not
give him an answer at this time. He then tells her of a dream he
has had, in which he saw a weird vessel from which two men,
one her father, the other a ghastly-looking stranger, made their
way. Her he saw going to the stranger and entreating him for his
regard.

Senta, worked up to the highest pitch of excitement by Eric's
words, exclaims: 'He seeks for me and I for him.' and Eric, full
of despair and horror, rushes away. The door opens and the
Dutchman and Daland appear. Senta turns from the picture to
him, and, uttering a loud cry of wonder, remains standing as if
transfixed without removing her eyes from the Dutchman. Daland
in an aria tells her of the stranger's request, and leaves them
alone. There follows a duet for Senta and the Dutchman, with its
broad, smoothly flowing melody and its many phrases of dramatic
power, in which Senta gives herself up unreservedly to the hero
of her romantic attachment, Daland finally entering and adding
his congratulations to their betrothal. This scene closes the act.

Act III.    The music of it re-echoes through the introduction
of the next act and goes over into a vigorous sailors' chorus and
dance. The scene shows a bay with a rocky shore, with Daland's
house in the foreground on one side, and the background occupied
by his and the Dutchman's ships. The sailors and the girls in their
merry-making call loudly toward the Dutch ship to join them,
but no reply is heard from the weird vessel. Finally the sailors
call louder and louder and taunt the crew of the other ship.
Suddenly the sea, which has been quite calm, begins to rise. The
storm wind whistles through the cordage of the strange vessel,
and as dark bluish flames flare up in the rigging, the weird crew
show themselves, and sing a wild chorus, which strikes terror into

all the merrymakers. The girls have fled, and the Norwegian sailors quit their deck, making the sign of the cross. The crew of the Flying Dutchman observing this, disappear with shrill laughter.

Senta now comes with trembling steps out of the house. She is followed by Eric. He pleads with her and entreats her to remember his love for her, and speaks also of the encouragement which she once gave him. The Dutchman has entered unperceived and has been listening. Eric seeing him, at once recognises the man of ghastly mien whom he saw in his vision. When the Flying Dutchman bids her farewell, because he deems himself abandoned, and Senta endeavours to follow him, Eric holds her and summons others to his aid. But, in spite of all resistance, Senta seeks to tear herself loose. Then it is that the Flying Dutchman proclaims who he is and puts to sea. Senta, however, freeing herself, rushes to a cliff overhanging the sea, and calling out,

> 'Praise thou thine angel for what he saith;
> Here stand I faithful, yea, to death,'

casts herself into the sea. The work ends with the portion of the ballad which brought the overture and spinning scene to a close.

Wagner intended *The Flying Dutchman* to be played in a single act—another example of his efforts to break with tradition—and at Bayreuth in 1901 his original design was adhered to. For this purpose, Ernest Newman tells us in his invaluable *Wagner Nights*, cuts were made from bar 26 before the end of the orchestral postlude to Act I to bar 19 of the prelude to Act II, and a dozen bars were omitted at the end of Act II.                    K.

# TANNHÄUSER
## Und der Sängerkrieg auf dem Wartburg
### (and the Song Contest at the Wartburg)

Opera in three acts by Richard Wagner, text by the composer. Première Dresden, October 19, 1845. with Johanna Wagner, Schröder-Devrient, Tichatschek, Mitterwurzer, Dettmer, conductor Wagner. Revised and performed (in what is now known as the 'Paris version') Opéra, Paris, 1861. with Marie Saxe, Fortunata Tedesco, Niemann, Morelli, Cazaux, conductor Dietsch. First performed New York 1859; Covent Garden 1876 (in Italian) with Albani, d'Angeri, Carpi, Maurel, Capponi, conductor Vianesi; Her Majesty's, London, 1882 (in English) with Valleria, Burns, Schott, Ludwig, Pope, conductor Randegger; Metropolitan, New York, 1884, with Seidl-Kraus, Slach, Schott, Adolf Robinson; Covent Garden in French.

in 'Paris version') 1896, with Eames, Adini, Alvarez, Ancona, Plançon, conductor, Mancineli. Famous Tannhäusers include Max Alvary, Winkelmann, Slezak, Schmedes, Melchior.

## CHARACTERS

| | |
|---|---|
| Hermann, *Landgrave of Thuringia* ................. | Bass |
| Tannhäuser | Tenor |
| Wolfram von Eschenbach | Baritone |
| Walter von der Vogelweide    *Knights and* | Tenor |
| Biterolf    *Minnesinger* .... | Bass |
| Heinrich der Schreiber | Tenor |
| Reinmar von Zweter | Bass |
| Elisabeth, *niece of the Landgrave* ............... | Soprano |
| Venus ........................................ | Soprano |
| A Young Shepherd .......................... | Soprano |
| Four Noble Pages ................... | Soprano and Alto |

Nobles, Knights, Ladies, elder and younger Pilgrims,
Sirens, Naiads, Nymphs, Bacchantes

*Time:* Early thirteenth century      *Place:* Near Eisenach

The story of *Tannhäuser* is laid in and near the Wartburg, where, during the thirteenth century, the Landgraves of the Thuringian Valley held sway. They were lovers of art, especially of poetry and music, and at the Wartburg many peaceful contests between the famous minnesingers took place. Near this castle rises the Venusberg. According to tradition the interior of this mountain was inhabited by Holda, the Goddess of Spring, who, however, in time became identified with the Goddess of Love. Her court was filled with nymphs and sirens, and it was her greatest joy to entice into the mountain the knights of the Wartburg and hold them captive to her beauty.

Among those whom she had thus lured into the rosy recesses of the Venusberg is Tannhäuser. In spite of her beauty, however, he is weary of her charms and longs for a glimpse of the world. With the cry that his hope rests in the Virgin, he tears himself away from her. The court of Venus disappears and in a moment we see Tannhäuser prostrate before a cross in a valley upon which the Wartburg peacefully looks down. Pilgrims on their way to Rome pass him by and Tannhäuser thinks of joining them in order that at Rome he may obtain forgiveness for his crime in allowing himself to be enticed into the Venusberg. But at that moment the Landgrave and a number of minnesingers on their return from the chase come upon him and, recognising him, endeavour to persuade him to return to the Wartburg with them. Their pleas, however, are vain, until one of them, Wolfram von Eschenbach, tells him that since he has left the Wartburg a great sadness has come over the niece of the Landgrave, Elisabeth. It is evident that Tannhäuser has been in love with her, and that it is because of her beauty and virtue that he regrets so deeply having been lured into the Venusberg. For Wolfram's words stir him profoundly. To the great joy of all, he agrees to return to the Wartburg, the scene of his many triumphs as a minnesinger in the contests of song.

The Landgrave, feeling sure that Tannhäuser will win the prize at the contest of song soon to be held, offers the hand of his niece to the winner. The minnesingers sing tamely of the beauty of virtuous love, but Tannhäuser, suddenly remembering the seductive and magical beauties of the Venusberg, cannot control himself, and bursts out into a reckless hymn in praise of Venus. Horrified at his words, the knights draw their swords and would slay him, but Elisabeth throws herself between him and them. Crushed and penitent, Tannhäuser stands behind her, and the Landgrave, moved by her willingness to sacrifice herself for her sinful lover, announces that he will be allowed to join a second band of pilgrims who are going to Rome and to plead with the Pope for forgiveness.

Elisabeth prayerfully awaits his return; but, as she is kneeling by the crucifix in front of the Wartburg, the pilgrims pass her by and in the band she does not see her lover. Slowly and sadly she returns to the castle to die. When the pilgrims' voices have died away, and Elisabeth has returned to the castle, leaving only Wolfram, who is also deeply enamoured of her, upon the scene, Tannhäuser appears, weary and dejected. He has sought to obtain forgiveness in vain. The Pope has cast him out forever, proclaiming that no more than that his staff can put forth leaves can he expect forgiveness. He has come back to re-enter the Venusberg. Wolfram seeks to restrain him, but it is not until he invokes the name of Elisabeth that Tannhäuser is saved. A cortège approaches, and, as Tannhäuser recognises the form of Elisabeth on the bier, he sinks down on her coffin and dies. Just then the second band of pilgrims arrive, bearing Tannhäuser's staff, which has put forth blossoms, thus showing that his sins have been forgiven.

The overture of the opera has long been a favourite piece on concert programmes. Like that of *The Flying Dutchman* it is the story of the whole opera told in music. It certainly is one of the most brilliant and effective pieces of orchestral music and its popularity is easily understood. It opens with the melody of the pilgrims' chorus, beginning softly as if coming from a distance and gradually increasing in power until it is heard in all its grandeur.

Having reached a climax, this chorus gradually dies away, and suddenly, and with intense dramatic contrast, we have all the seductive spells of the Venusberg displayed before us—that is, musically displayed; but then the music is so wonderfully vivid, it depicts with such marvellous clearness the many-coloured alluring scene at the court of the unholy goddess, it gives vent so freely to the sinful excitement which pervades the Venusberg, that we actually seem to see what we hear. This passes over in turn to the impassioned burst of song in which Tannhäuser hymns Venus's praise, and immediately after we have the boisterous and vigorous music which accompanies the threatening action of the Landgrave and minnesingers when they draw their swords upon Tannhäuser in order to take vengeance upon him for his crimes. Upon these three episodes of the drama, which so characteristically give insight into its plot and action, the overture is based, and it very naturally concludes with the pilgrims' chorus which seems to voice the final forgiveness of Tannhäuser.

The curtain rises, disclosing all the seductive spells of the Venusburg. Tannhäuser lies in the arms of Venus, who reclines upon a flowery couch. Nymphs, sirens, and satyrs are dancing about them and in the distance are grottoes alive with amorous figures. Various mythological amours, such as that of Leda and the swan, are supposed to be in progress.

Much of the music familiar from the overture is heard during this scene, but it gains in effect from the distant voices of the sirens and, of course, from the dances of the denizens of Venus's court.

Very dramatic is the scene between Venus and Tannhäuser, when the latter sings his hymn in her praise, but at the same time proclaims that he desires to return to the world. In alluring strains she endeavours to tempt him to remain with her, but when she discovers that he is bound upon going, she vehemently warns him of the misfortunes which await him upon earth and prophesies that he will some day return to her and penitently ask to be taken back into her realm.

Dramatic and effective as this scene is in the original score, it has gained immensely in power by the additions which Wagner made for the production of the work in Paris, in 1861. The overture does not, in this version, come to a formal close, but after the manner of Wagner's later works, the transition is made directly from it to the scene of the Venusberg. The dances have been elaborated and laid out upon a more careful allegorical basis and the music of Venus has been greatly strengthened from a dramatic point of view, so that now the scene in which she pleads with him to remain and afterwards warns him against the sorrows to which he will be exposed, are among the finest of Wagner's compositions, rivalling in dramatic power his ripest work.

Wagner's knowledge of the stage is shown in the wonderfully dramatic effect in the change of scene from the Venusberg to the landscape in the valley of the Wartburg. One moment we have the variegated allures of the court of the Goddess of Love, with its dancing nymphs, sirens, and satyrs, its beautiful grottoes and groups; the next all this has disappeared and we are transported to a peaceful scene whose influence upon us is deepened by the crucifix in the foreground, before which Tannhäuser kneels in penitence. The peacefulness of the scene is further enhanced by the appearance upon a rocky eminence to the left of a young

Shepherd who pipes a pastoral strain. Before he has finished piping his lay the voices of the pilgrims are heard in the distance, their solemn measures being interrupted by little phrases piped by the Shepherd. As the pilgrims approach, the chorus becomes louder, and as they pass over the stage and bow before the crucifix, their praise swells into an eloquent psalm of devotion.

Tannhäuser is deeply affected and gives way to his feelings in a lament, against which are heard the voices of the pilgrims as they recede in the distance. This whole scene is one of marvellous beauty, the contrast between it and the preceding episode being enhanced by the religiously tranquil nature of what transpires and of the accompanying music. Upon this peaceful scene the notes of hunting-horns now break in, and gradually the Landgrave and his hunters gather about Tannhäuser. Wolfram recognises him and tells the others who he is. They greet him in an expressive septet, and Wolfram, finding he is bent upon following the pilgrims to Rome, asks permission of the Landgrave to inform him of the impression which he seems to have made upon Elisabeth. This he does in a melodious solo, and Tannhäuser, overcome by his love for Elisabeth, consents to return to the halls which have missed him so long. Exclamations of joy greet his decision, and the act closes with an enthusiastic *ensemble*, which is a glorious piece of concerted music, and never fails of brilliant effect when it is well executed, especially if the representative of Tannhäuser has a voice that can soar above the others.

The scene of the second act is laid in the singers' hall of the Wartburg. The introduction depicts Elisabeth's joy at Tannhäuser's return, and when the curtain rises she at once enters and joyfully greets the scenes of Tannhäuser's former triumphs in broad phrases. Wolfram then appears, conducting Tannhäuser to her. Elisabeth seems overjoyed to see him, but then checks herself, and her maidenly modesty, which veils her transport at meeting him, again finds expression in a number of hesitating but exceedingly beautiful phrases. She asks Tannhäuser where he has been, but he, of course, gives misleading answers. Finally, however, he tells her she is the one who has attracted him back to the castle. Their love finds expression in a swift and rapidly flowing dramatic duet, which unfortunately is rarely given in its entirety, although as a glorious outburst of emotional music it certainly deserves to be heard in the exact form and length in which the composer wrote it.

There is then a scene of much tender feeling between the Landgrave and Elisabeth, in which the former tells her that he will offer her hand as prize to the singer whom she shall crown as winner. The first strains of the brilliantly effective grand march are then heard. After an address by the Landgrave, which can hardly be called remarkably interesting, the singers draw lots to decide who among them shall begin. This prize singing is, unfortunately, not so great in musical value as the rest of the score, and, unless a person understands the words, it is decidedly long drawn out. What, however, redeems it is a gradually growing dramatic excitement as Tannhäuser voices his contempt for what seem to him the tame tributes paid to love by the minnesingers, an excitement which reaches its climax when, no longer able to restrain himself, he bursts forth into his hymn in praise of the unholy charms of Venus.

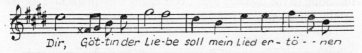

Dir,  Göt-tin der Lie-be soll mein Lied er-tö--nen

The women cry out in horror and rush from the hall and the men, drawing their swords, attack him. This brings us to the great dramatic moment, when, with a shriek, Elisabeth, in spite of his betrayal of her love, throws herself protectingly before him, and thus appears a second time as his saving angel. In short and excited phrases the men pour forth their wrath at Tannhäuser's crime in having sojourned with Venus, and he, realising its enormity, seems crushed with a consciousness of his guilt. Of great beauty is the septet, 'An angel has from heaven descended', which rises to a magnificent climax and is one of the finest pieces of dramatic writing in Wagner's scores, though all too often execrably sung. The voices of young pilgrims are heard in the valley. The Landgrave then announces the conditions upon which Tannhäuser can again obtain forgiveness, and Tannhäuser joins the pilgrims on their way to Rome.

The third act displays once more the valley of the Wartburg, the same scene as that to which the Venusberg changed in the first act. Elisabeth, arrayed in white, is kneeling, in deep prayer, before the crucifix. At one side, and watching her tenderly, stands

Wolfram. After a sad recitative from Wolfram, the chorus of returning pilgrims is heard in the distance. They sing the melody heard in the overture and in the first act; and the same effect of gradual approach is produced by a superb *crescendo* as they reach and cross the scene. With anxiety and grief Elisabeth scans them as they go by, to see if Tannhäuser is among them, and when the last one has passed and she realises that he has not returned, she sinks again upon her knees before the crucifix and sings the prayer, 'Almighty Virgin, hear my sorrow', music in which there is most beautifully combined the expression of poignant grief with trust in the will of the Almighty. As she rises and turns toward the castle, Wolfram, by his gesture, seems to ask her if he cannot accompany her, but she declines his offer and slowly goes her way up the mountain.

Meanwhile night has fallen upon the scene and the evening star glows softly above the castle. It is then that Wolfram, accompanying himself on his lyre, intones the tender and beautiful 'Song to the Evening Star', confessing therein his love for the saintly Elisabeth.

Then Tannhäuser, dejected, footsore, and weary, appears and in broken accents asks Wolfram to show him the way back to the Venusberg. Wolfram bids him stay his steps and persuades him to tell him the story of his pilgrimage. In fierce, dramatic accents, Tannhäuser relates all that he has suffered on his way to Rome and the terrible judgment pronounced upon him by the Pope. This is a highly impressive episode, clearly foreshadowing Wagner's dramatic use of musical recitative in his later music-dramas. Only a singer of the highest rank can do justice to it.

Tannhäuser proclaims that, having lost all chance of salvation, he will once more give himself up to the delights of the Venusberg. A roseate light illumines the recesses of the mountain and the unholy company of the Venusberg again is seen, Venus stretching out her arms for Tannhäuser, to welcome him. But at last, when Tannhäuser seems unable to resist Venus's enticing voice any longer, Wolfram conjures him by the memory of the sainted Elisabeth. The light dies away and the magic charms of the

Venusberg disappear. Amid tolling of bells and mournful voices a funeral procession comes down the mountain. Recognising the features of Elisabeth, the dying Tannhäuser falls upon her corpse. The younger pilgrims arrive with the staff, which has again put forth leaves, and amid the hallelujahs of the pilgrims the opera closes.

K.

## LOHENGRIN

Opera in three acts, by Richard Wagner, text by the composer. Première, Weimar, August 28, 1850, with Agthe, Fasztlinger, Beck, von Milde, Hoder, conductor Liszt. First performed Covent Garden, 1875 (in Italian), with Albani, d'Angeri, Nicolini, Maurel, Seiderman, conductor Vianesi; Her Majesty's, London, 1880 (in English); Drury Lane, 1882 (in German), with Sucher, Dily, Winkelmann, Kraus, Koegel, conductor Richter; New York, 1871; Academy of Music, New York, 1874 (in Italian), with Nilsson, Cary, Campanini, Del Puente; Metropolitan (in German), 1885, with Seidl-Kraus, Brandt, Stritt, Robinson, Fischer, conducted by Seidl. Famous interpreters of the title role have included Jean de Reszke, van Dyck, Dalmores, Urlus, Slezak, Völker.

### CHARACTERS

Henry the Fowler, *King of Germany* ................Bass
Lohengrin .......................................Tenor
Elsa of Brabant .............................Soprano
Duke Godfrey, *her brother*
Frederick of Telramund, *Count of Brabant* .......Baritone
Ortrud, *his wife* .......................Mezzo-Soprano
The King's Herald ...............................Bass
Saxon, Thuringian, and Brabantian Counts and Nobles,
Ladies of Honour, Pages, Attendants

*Time:* First half of the tenth century        *Scene:* Antwerp

*Lohengrin,* at the time of its composition so novel and so strange, yet filled with beauties of orchestration and harmony that are now quoted as leading examples in books on these subjects, was composed in less than a year. The acts were finished almost, if not quite, in reversed order. For Wagner wrote the third act first, beginning it in September 1846, and completing it March 5, 1847. The first act occupied him from May 12 to June 8, less than a month; the second act from June 18 to August 2.

Wagner's music, however, was so little understood at the time, that even before *Lohengrin* was produced and not a note of it had been heard, people made fun of it. A lithographer named Meser had issued Wagner's previous three scores, but the enterprise had not been a success. People said that before publishing

*Rienzi* Meser had lived on the first floor. *Rienzi* had driven him to the second; *The Flying Dutchman* and *Tannhäuser* to the third; and now *Lohengrin* would drive him to the garret—a prophecy that didn't come true, because he refused to publish it.

In 1849, *Lohengrin* still not having been accepted by the Dresden Opera, Wagner took part in the May revolution, which, apparently successful for a very short time, was quickly suppressed by the military. The composer is said to have made his escape from Dresden in the disguise of a coachman. Occasionally there turns up in sales as a great rarity a copy of the warrant for Wagner's arrest issued by the Dresden police. As it gives a description of him at the time when he had but recently composed *Lohengrin*, I will quote it:

'Wagner is thirty-seven to thirty-eight years of age, of medium stature, has brown hair, an open forehead; eyebrows, brown; eyes, greyish blue; nose and mouth, proportioned; chin, round, and wears spectacles. Special characteristics: rapid in movements and speech. Dress: coat of dark green buckskin, trousers of black cloth, velvet vest, silk neckerchief, ordinary felt hat and boots.'

Much fun has been made of the expression 'chin, round, and wears spectacles'. Wagner got out of Dresden on the pass of a Dr. Widmann, whom he resembled. It has been suggested that he made the resemblance still closer by discontinuing the habit of wearing spectacles on his chin.

I saw Wagner several times in Bayreuth in the summer of 1882, when I attended the first performance of *Parsifal*, as correspondent by cable and letter for one of the large New York dailies. Except that his hair was grey (and that he no longer wore his spectacles on his chin) the description in the warrant still held good, especially as regards his rapidity of movement and speech, to which I may add a marked vivacity of gesture. There, too, I saw the friend, who had helped him over so many rough places in his early career, Franz Liszt, his hair white with age, but framing a face as strong and keen as an eagle's. I saw them seated at a banquet, and with them Cosima, Liszt's daughter, who was Wagner's second wife, and their son, Siegfried Wagner; Cosima the image of her father, and Siegfried a miniature replica of the composer to whom we owe *Lohengrin* and the music-dramas that followed it. The following summer one of the four was missing. I have the *Parsifal* programme with mourning border signifying that the performances of the work were in memory of its creator.

In April 1850, Wagner, then an exile in Zurich, wrote to Liszt: 'Bring out my *Lohengrin*! You are the only one to whom I would put this request; to no one but you would I entrust the production of this opera; but to you I surrender it with the fullest, most joyous confidence.'

Wagner himself describes the appeal and the result, by saying that at a time when he was ill, unhappy, and in despair, his eye fell on the score of *Lohengrin* which he had almost forgotten. 'A pitiful feeling overcame me that these tones would never resound from the deathly-pale paper; two words I wrote to Liszt, the answer to which was nothing else than the information that, as far as the resources of the Weimar Opera permitted, the most elaborate preparations were being made for the production of *Lohengrin*.'

Liszt's reply to which Wagner refers, and which gives some details regarding 'the elaborate preparations', while testifying to his full comprehension of Wagner's genius and the importance of his new score as a work of art, may well cause us to smile to-day at the small scale on which things were done in 1850.

'Your *Lohengrin*,' he wrote, 'will be given under conditions that are most unusual and most favourable for its success. The direction will spend on this occasion almost 2,000 thalers [about $1,500]—a sum unprecedented at Weimar within memory of man . . . the bass clarinet has been bought,' etc. Ten times fifteen hundred dollars might well be required to-day for a properly elaborate production of *Lohengrin*, and the opera orchestra that had to send out and buy a bass clarinet would be a curiosity. But Weimar had what no other opera house could boast of—Franz Liszt as conductor.

Under his brilliant direction *Lohengrin* had at Weimar its first performance on any stage, August 28, 1850. This was the anniversary of Goethe's birth, the date of the dedication of the Weimar monument to the poet, Herder, and, by a coincidence that does not appear to have struck either Wagner or Liszt, the third anniversary of the completion of *Lohengrin*. The work was performed without cuts and before an audience which included some of the leading musical and literary men of Germany. The performance made a deep impression. The circumstance that Liszt added the charm of his personality to it and that the weight of his influence had been thrown in its favour alone gave vast importance to the event.

On May 15, 1861, when, through the intervention of Princess Metternich, he had been permitted to return to Germany, fourteen years after he had finished *Lohengrin* and eleven years after its production at Weimar, Wagner himself heard it for the first time at Vienna. A tragedy of fourteen years—to create a masterpiece of the lyric stage, and be forced to wait that long to hear it!

Before proceeding to a complete descriptive account of the *Lohengrin* story and music I will give a brief summary of the plot and a similar characterisation of the score.

The story of *Lohengrin* is briefly as follows: The Hungarians have invaded Germany, and King Henry I visits Antwerp for the purpose of raising a force to combat them. He finds the country in a condition of anarchy. The dukedom is claimed by Frederick, who has married Ortrud, a daughter of the Prince of Friesland. The legitimate heir, Godfrey, has mysteriously disappeared, and his sister, Elsa, is charged by Frederick and Ortrud with having done away with him in order that she might obtain the sovereignty. The King summons her before him so that the cause may be tried by the ordeal of single combat between Frederick and a champion who may be willing to appear for Elsa. None of the knights will defend her cause. She then describes a champion whose form has appeared to her in a vision, and she proclaims that he shall be her champion. Her pretence is derided by Frederick and his followers, who think that she is out of her mind; but after a triple summons by the Herald, there is seen in the distance on the river, a boat drawn by a swan, and in it a knight clad in silver armour. He comes to champion Elsa's cause, and before the combat betroths himself to her, but makes a strict condition that she shall never question him as to his name or birthplace, for should she do so, he would be obliged to depart. She assents to the conditions, and the combat which ensues results in Frederick's ignominious defeat. Judgment of exile is pronounced on him.

Instead, however, of leaving the country he lingers in the neighbourhood of Brabant, plotting with Ortrud how they may compass the ruin of Lohengrin and Elsa. Ortrud by her entreaties moves Elsa to pity, and persuades her to seek a reprieve for Frederick, at the same time, however, using every opportunity to instil doubts in Elsa's mind regarding her champion, and rousing her to such a pitch of nervous curiosity that she is on the point of asking him the forbidden question. After the bridal ceremonies, and in the bridal chamber, the distrust which Ortrud and Frederick have engendered in Elsa's mind so overcomes her faith that she vehemently puts the forbidden question to her champion. Almost at the same moment Frederick and four of his followers force their way into the apartment, intending to take the knight's life. A single blow of his sword, however, stretches Frederick lifeless, and his followers bear his corpse away. Placing Elsa in the charge of her ladies-in-waiting, and ordering them to take her to the presence of the King, he repairs thither himself.

The Brabantian hosts are gathering, and he is expected to lead them to battle, but owing to Elsa's question he is now obliged to disclose who he is and to take his departure. He proclaims that he is Lohengrin, son of Parsifal, Knight of the Holy Grail, and that he can stay no longer in Brabant, but must return to the place of his coming. The swan has once more appeared, drawing the boat down the river; bidding Elsa farewell he steps into the little shell-like craft. Then Ortrud, with malicious glee, declares that the swan is none other than Elsa's brother, whom she, Ortrud, bewitched into this form, and that he would have been changed back again to his human shape had it not been for Elsa's rashness. But Lohengrin, through his supernatural powers, is able to undo Ortrud's work, and at a word from him the swan disappears and Godfrey stands in its place. A dove now descends, and, hovering in front of the boat, draws it away with Lohengrin, while Elsa expires in her brother's arms.

Owing to the lyric character of the story upon which *Lohengrin* is based, the opera, while not at all lacking in strong dramatic situations, is characterised by a subtler and more subdued melodiousness than *Tannhäuser*, is more exquisitely lyrical in fact than any Wagnerian work except *Parsifal*.

There are typical themes in the score, but they are hardly handled with the varied effect that entitles them to be called leading motives. On the other hand there are fascinating details of orchestration. He uses the brass chiefly to accompany the

King, and, of course, the martial choruses; the plaintive, yet
spiritual high woodwind for Elsa; the English horn and sombre
bass clarinet—the instrument that had to be bought—for Ortrud;
the violins, especially in high harmonic positions, to indicate the
Grail and its representative, for Lohengrin is a Knight of the
Holy Grail. Even the keys employed are distinctive. The Herald's
trumpets blow in C and greet the King's arrival in that bright key.
F sharp minor is the dark, threatful key that indicates Ortrud's
appearance. The key of A, which is the purest for strings and the
most ethereal in effect, on account of the greater ease of using
'harmonics', announces the approach of Lohengrin and the subtle
influence of the Grail.

The Prelude is based entirely upon one theme, a beautiful one
and expressive of the sanctity of the Grail, of which Lohengrin is
one of the knights. Violins and flutes with long-drawn-out,
ethereal chords open the Prelude. Then is heard on the violins,
so divided as to heighten the delicacy of the effect, the Motive of
the Grail, the cup in which the Saviour's blood is supposed to
have been caught as it flowed from the wound in His side, while
He was on the Cross. No modern book on orchestration is considered complete unless it quotes this passage from the score,
which is at once the earliest and, after seventy years, still the most
perfect example of the effect of celestial harmony produced on
the high notes of the divided violin choir. This interesting passage
in the score is as follows:

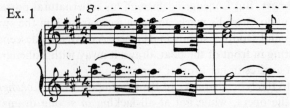

Ex. 1

Although this is the only motive that occurs in the Prelude, the
ear never wearies of it. Its effectiveness is due to the wonderful
skill with which Wagner handles the theme, working it up through
a crescendo to a magnificent climax, with all the splendours of
Wagnerian orchestration, after which it dies away again to the
ethereal harmonies with which it first greeted the listener.

Act I.    The curtain, on rising, discloses a scene of unwonted life on the plain near the River Scheldt, where the stream winds toward Antwerp. On an elevated seat under a huge oak sits King Henry I. On either side are his Saxon and Thuringian nobles. Facing him with the knights of Brabant are Count Frederick of Telramund and his wife, Ortrud, of dark, almost forbidding beauty, and with a treacherous mingling of haughtiness and humility in her carriage.

It is a strange tale the King has just heard fall from Frederick of Telramund's lips. Henry has assembled the Brabantians on the plain by the Scheldt in order to summon them to join his army and aid in checking the threatened invasion of Germany by the Hungarians. But he has found the Brabantians themselves torn by factional strife, some supporting, others opposing Frederick in his claim to the ducal succession of Brabant.

'Sire,' says Frederick, when called upon by the King to explain the cause of the discord that has come upon the land, 'the late Duke of Brabant upon his death-bed confided to me, his kinsman, the care of his two children, Elsa and her young brother Godfrey, with the right to claim the maid as my wife. But one day Elsa led the boy into the forest and returned alone. From her pale face and faltering lips I judged only too well of what had happened, and I now publicly accuse Elsa of having made away with her brother that she might be sole heir to Brabant and reject my right to her hand. Her hand! Horrified, I shrank from her and took a wife whom I could truly love. Now as nearest kinsman of the duke I claim this land as my own, my wife, too, being of the race that once gave a line of princes to Brabant.'

So saying, he leads Ortrud forward, and she, lowering her dark visage, makes a deep obeisance to the King. To the latter but one course is open. A terrible accusation has been uttered, and an appeal must be made to the immediate judgment of God in trial by combat between Frederick and whoever may appear as champion for Elsa. Solemnly the King hangs his shield on the oak, the Saxons and Thuringians thrust the points of their swords into the ground, while the Brabantians lay theirs before them. The royal Herald steps forward. 'Elsa, without delay appear!' he calls in a loud voice.

A sudden hush falls upon the scene, as a slender figure robed in white slowly advances toward the King. It is Elsa. With her fair brow, gentle mien, and timid footsteps it seems impossible that she can be the object of Frederick's dire charge. But there are dark forces conspiring against her, of which none knows save her accuser and the wife he has chosen from the remoter North. In Friesland the weird rites of Odin and the ancient gods still had many secret adherents, Ortrud among them, and it is the hope of this heathenish woman, through the undoing of Elsa and the accession of Frederick whom she has completely under her influence, to check the spread of the Christian faith toward the North and restore the rites of Odin in Brabant. To this end she is ready to bring into play all the black magic of which she secretly is mistress. What wonder that Elsa, as she encounters her malevolent gaze, lowers her eyes with a shudder!

Up to the moment of Elsa's entrance, the music is harsh and vigorous, reflecting Frederick's excitement as, incited by Ortrud, he brings forward his charge against Elsa. With her appearance a change immediately comes over the music. It is soft, gentle, and plaintive; not, however, entirely hopeless, as if the maiden, being conscious of her innocence, does not despair of her fate.

'Elsa,' gently asks the King, 'whom name you as your champion?' She answers as if in a trance; and it is at this point that the music of 'Elsa's Dream' is heard. In the course of this, violins whisper the Grail Motive and in dreamy rapture Elsa sings, 'I see, in splendour shining, a knight of glorious mien. His eyes rest upon me with tranquil gaze. He stands amid clouds beside a house of gold, and resting on his sword. Heaven has sent him to save me. He shall my champion be!'

Ex. 2

The men regard each other in wonder. But a sneer curls around Ortrud's lips, and Frederick again proclaims his readiness to prove his accusation in trial by combat for life and death. 'Elsa,' the King asks once more, 'whom have you chosen as your champion?' 'Him whom Heaven shall send me; and to him, whatever he shall ask of me, I freely will give, e'en though it be myself as bride!' Again there is heard the lovely, broad, and flowing melody of which I have already spoken and which may be designated as the Elsa Motive (Ex. 2).

The Herald now stations his trumpeters at the corners of the plain and bids them blow a blast toward the four points of the compass. When the last echo has died away he calls aloud:

'He who in right of Heaven comes here to fight for Elsa of Brabant, let him step forth!'

The deep silence that follows is broken by Frederick's voice. 'No one appears to repel my charge. 'Tis proven.'

Again the trumpeters blow toward the four points of the compass, again the Herald cries his call, again there is the fateful silence. Suddenly there is a commotion among the men nearest the river bank.

'A wonder!' they cry. 'A swan—drawing a boat by a golden chain! In the boat stands a knight!'

There is a rush toward the bank and a great shout of acclaim, as the swan brings the shell-like boat, in which stands a knight in dazzling armour and of noble mien, up to the shore. Not daring to trust her senses and turn to behold the wondrous spectacle, Elsa gazes in rapture heavenward, while Ortrud and Telramund, their fell intrigue suddenly halted by a marvel that surpasses their comprehension, regard each other with mingled amazement and alarm.

Lohengrin bids farewell to the swan, which gently inclines its head and then glides away with the boat, vanishing as it had come. The men fall back and the Knight of the Swan, for a silver swan surmounts his helmet and is blazoned upon his shield, having made due obeisance to the King, advances to where Elsa stands and, resting his eyes upon her pure and radiant beauty, questions her.

'Elsa,' he says slowly, as if wishing her to weigh every word, 'if I champion your cause and take you to wife, there is one promise I must exact: Never must you ask me whence I come or what my name.' 'I promise,' she answers, serenely meeting his warning look.

'Elsa, I love you!' he exclaims, as he clasps her in his arms. Then addressing the King he proclaims his readiness to defend her innocence in trial by combat.

In this scene occurs one of the significant themes of the opera, the Motive of Warning—for it is Elsa's disregard of it and the breaking of her promise that brings her happiness to an end.

Ex. 3.

Three Saxons for the Knight and three Brabantians for Frederick solemnly pace off the circle within which the combatants are to fight. The King, drawing his sword, strikes three resounding blows with it upon his shield. At the first stroke the Knight and Frederick take their positions. At the second they draw their swords. At the third they advance to the encounter. Frederick is no coward. His willingness to meet the Knight whose coming had been so strange proves that. But his blows are skilfully warded off until the Swan Knight, finding an opening, fells him with a powerful stroke. Frederick's life is forfeited, but his conquerer, perchance knowing that he has been naught but a tool in the hands of a woman leagued with the powers of evil, spares it and bids his fallen foe rise. The King leads Elsa to the victor, while all hail him as her deliverer and betrothed.

The scenes here described are most stirring. Before the combat begins, the King intones a prayer, in which first the principals and then the chorus join with noble effect, while the music of rejoicing over the Knight's victory has an irresistible onsweep.

Act II.     That night in the fortress of Antwerp, the palace where live the knights is brilliantly illuminated and sounds of revelry issue from it. But in the shadow of the walls sit two figures, a man and a woman; the man, his head bowed in despair, the woman looking vindictively toward the palace. They are Frederick and Ortrud, who have been condemned to banishment, he utterly dejected, she still trusting in the power of her heathenish gods. Not knowing that Ortrud still darkly schemes to ruin Elsa and restore him to power, Frederick denounces her in an outburst of rage and despair.

As another burst of revelry, another flash of light, causes Frederick to bow his head in deeper gloom, Ortrud begins to unfold her plot to him. Let Frederick conceal himself within the minster, and when the bridal procession reaches the steps, come forth and, accusing the Knight of treachery and deceit, demand that he be compelled to disclose his name and origin. He will refuse, and thus, even before Elsa enters the minster, she will begin to be beset by doubts. She herself meanwhile will seek to enter the kemenate and play upon her credulousness. 'She is for me; her champion is for you. Soon the daughter of Odin will teach you all the joys of vengeance!' is Ortrud's sinister exclamation as she finishes.

Indeed it seems as if Fate were playing into her hand. For at that very moment Elsa comes out upon the balcony and breathes out upon the night air her rapture at the thought of what bliss the coming day has in store for her. As she lets her gaze rest on the calm night she hears a piteous voice calling her name, and looking down sees Ortrud, her hands raised in supplication to her. Moved by the spectacle of one but a short time before so proud and now apparently in such utter dejection, the guileless maid descends and gently leads her in, while Ortrud pours doubts regarding her champion into Elsa's mind. The whole closes with a beautiful duet, which is repeated by the orchestra, as Ortrud is conducted by Elsa into the apartment.

It is early morn. People begin to gather in the open place before the minster and, by the time the sun is high, the space is crowded with folk eager to view the bridal procession. They sing a fine and spirited chorus.

A great shout, 'Hail! Elsa of Brabant!' goes up, as the bride herself appears followed by her ladies-in-waiting. For the moment Ortrud's presence in the train is unnoticed, but as Elsa approaches the minster, Frederick's wife suddenly throws herself in her path.

'Back, Elsa!' she cries. 'I am not a menial, born to follow you! Although your Knight has overthrown my husband, you cannot boast of who he is—his very name, the place whence he came, are unknown. Strong must be his motives to forbid you to question him. To what foul disgrace would he be brought were he compelled to answer!'

Fortunately the King, the bridegroom, and the nobles approaching from the palace, Elsa shrinks from Ortrud to her champion's side and hides her face against his breast. At that moment Frederick of Telramund, taking his cue from Ortrud, comes out upon the minster steps and repeats his wife's accusation. Then, profiting by the confusion, he slips away in the crowd. The insidious poison, however, has already begun to take effect. For even as the King taking the Knight on his right and Elsa on his left conducts them up the minster steps, the trembling bride catches sight of Ortrud whose hand is raised in threat and warning; and it is clinging to her champion, in love indeed, but love mingled with doubt and fear, that she passes through the portal and into the edifice.

Act III.     The wedding festivities are described in the brilliant Introduction. This is followed in the opera by the 'Bridal Chorus', which, whenever heard—on stage or in church—falls with renewed freshness and significance upon the ear. The King ceremoniously embraces the couple and then the procession makes its way out, until, as the last strains of the chorus die away, Elsa and her champion are for the first time alone.

The love duet is exquisite—one of the sweetest and tenderest passages of which the lyric stage can boast.

It should be a moment of supreme happiness for both, and indeed, Elsa exclaims as her bridegroom takes her to his arms that words cannot give expression to all its hidden sweetness. Yet, when he tenderly breathes her name, it serves only to remind her that she cannot respond by uttering his. 'How sweetly sounds my name when spoken by you, while I, alas, cannot reply with yours. Surely, some day, you will tell me, all in secret, and I shall be able to whisper it when none but you is near!'

In her words the Knight perceives but too clearly the seeds of the fatal mistrust sown by Ortrud and Frederick. Gently he leaves her side and throwing open the casement, points to the flowery close below, softly illumined by the moon, and sings to an accompaniment of what might be called musical moonbeams, 'Say, dost thou breathe the incense sweet of flowers?' The same subtle magic that can conjure up this scene from the night has brought him to her, made him love her and give unshakable credence to her vow never to question his name or origin. Will she now wantonly destroy the wondrous spell of moonlight and love?

In spite of the tender warning which he conveys to her, she begins to question him, but he turns toward her and in a passionate musical phrase begs her to trust him and abide with him in loving faith. Her dread that the memory of the delightful place from which he has come will wean him from her; the wild vision in which she imagines she sees the swan approaching to bear him away from her, and when she puts to him the forbidden questions, are details expressed with wonderful vividness in the music.

After the attack by Frederick and his death, there is a dramatic silence during which Elsa sinks on her husband's breast and faints. When I say silence I do not mean that there is a total cessation of sound, for silence can be more impressively expressed in music than by actual silence itself. It is done by Wagner in this case by long drawn-out chords followed by faint taps on the tympani. When the Knight bends down to Elsa, raises her, and gently places her on a couch, echoes of the love duet add to the mournfulness of the music. The scene closes with the Motive of Warning, which resounds with dread meaning.

The second scene takes place on the banks of the Scheldt; on the very spot where he had disembarked, the Knight elects to make reply to Elsa's questions. There the King, the nobles, and the Brabantians, whom he was to lead, are awaiting him, and as their leader they hail him when he appears. This scene, 'Promise of Victory', is in the form of a brilliant march and chorus, during which the Counts of Brabant, followed by their vassals, enter on horseback from various directions. In the average performance of the opera, however, much of it is sacrificed in order to shorten the representation.

The Knight answers their hail by telling them that he has come to bid them farewell, that Elsa has been lured to break her vow and ask the forbidden questions which he now is there to answer. From distant lands he came, from Montsalvat, where stands the temple of the Holy Grail, his father, Parsifal, its King, and he, Lohengrin, its Knight. And now, his name and lineage known, he must return, for the Grail gives strength to its knights to right wrong and protect the innocent only so long as the secret of their power remains unrevealed.

Even while he speaks the swan is seen floating down the river. Sadly Lohengrin bids Elsa farewell. Sadly all, save one, look on. For Ortrud, who now pushes her way through the spectators, it is a moment of triumph.

'Depart in all your glory,' she calls out. 'The swan that draws you away is none other than Elsa's brother Godfrey, changed by my magic into his present form. Had she kept her vow, had you been allowed to tarry, you would have freed him from my spell. The ancient gods, whom faithfully I serve, thus punish human faithlessness!'

By the river bank Lohengrin falls upon his knees and prays in silence. Suddenly a white dove descends over the boat; the swan vanishes; in its place Godfrey stands upon the bank, and Lohengrin, entering the boat, is drawn away by the dove. At sight of the young Duke, Ortrud falls with a shriek, while the Brabantian nobles kneel before him as he advances and make obeisance to the King. Elsa gazes on him in rapture until, mindful of her own sorrow, as the boat in which Lohengrin stands vanishes around the upper bend of the river, she cries out, 'My husband! My husband!' and falls back in death in her brother's arms.

Lohengrin's narrative of his origin is beautifully set to music familiar from the Prelude; but when he proclaims his name we hear the same measures which Elsa sang in the second part of her dream in the first act. Very beautiful and tender is the music which he sings when he hands Elsa his horn, his sword, and his ring to give to her brother, should he return, and also his greeting to the swan when it comes to bear him back. The work is brought to a close with a repetition of the music of the second portion of Elsa's dream, followed by a superb climax with the Motive of the Grail.                                                    K.

# TRISTAN UND ISOLDE
## Tristan and Isolde

Opera in three acts, by Richard Wagner, text by the composer. Première, Munich, June 10, 1865, with Malvini Schnorr von Carolsfeld, Anne Deinet, Ludwig Schnorr von Carolsfeld (the Tristan was thus in real life the husband of the Isolde), Zottmayer, Mitterwurzer, Heinrich, conductor Hans von Bülow. Bülow it will be remembered was still married to Cosima at the time of the première of *Tristan* and did not in fact divorce her until a year later. First performed Drury Lane, London, 1882, with Rose Sucher, Brandt, Winkelman, Gura, Landau, conductor Richter; Bayreuth 1886, with Malton, Gisela, Staudigl, Gudehus, Gura, Plank, conductor Mottl; Metropolitan, New York, 1886, with Lilli Lehmann, Brandt Nieman, Robinson, Fischer, conductor Seidl; Covent Garden, 1892, with Rosa Sucher, Schumann-Heink, Alvary, Knapp, conductor Mahler. Jean de Reszke is generally accounted the greatest Tristan heard at the Metropolitan. Others particularly famous in this role were Schmedes, Vogel, Urlus, Melchior. Famous Isoldes have included Nordica, Ternina, Fremstad, Mildenburg, Wittich, Gadski, Litvinne, Kappel, Leider, Larsen-Todsen, Marta Fuchs, Flagstad, Lubin,

Traubel, Bispham, van Rooy, and Hotter were famous Kurwenals in their time; and Eduard de Reszke, Mayr, Bohnen, Kipnis, and Weber as King Marke. Amongst Italian singers, Giuseppe Borgatti and Giuseppina Cobelli were particularly well-known exponents of the title roles.

## CHARACTERS

Tristan, *a Cornish knight, nephew to King Marke* ....Tenor
King Marke, *of Cornwall* ..........................Bass
Isolde, *an Irish princess* ........................Soprano
Kurwenal, *one of Tristan's retainers* .............Baritone
Melot, *a courtier* ...............................Baritone
Brangäne, *Isolde's attendant* ..............Mezzo-Soprano
A Shepherd ......................................Tenor
A Sailor ........................................Tenor
A Helmsman ................................Baritone
Sailors, Knights, Esquires, and Men-at-Arms

*Time:* Legendary   *Place:* A ship at sea; outside King Marke's palace, Cornwall; the platform at Kareol, Tristan's castle

Wagner remodelled the *Tristan* legend thoroughly before turning it into a music-drama.[1] He has shorn it of all unnecessary incidents and worked the main episodes into a concise, vigorous, swiftly moving drama, admirably adapted for the stage. He shows keen dramatic insight in the manner in which he adapts the love-potion of the legends to his purpose. In the legends the love of Tristan and Isolde is merely 'chemical'—entirely the result of the love-philtre. Wagner, however, presents them from the outset as enamoured of one another, so that the potion simply quickens a passion already active.

To the courtesy of G. Schirmer, Inc., publishers of my *Wagner's Music-Dramas Analysed*, I am indebted, as I have already stated elsewhere, for permission to use material from that book. I have there placed a brief summary of the story of *Tristan and Isolde* before the descriptive account of the 'book' and music, and, accordingly do so here.

In the Wagnerian version the plot is briefly as follows: Tristan, having lost his parents in infancy, has been reared at the court of his uncle, Marke, King of Cornwall. He has slain in combat Morold, an Irish knight, who had come to Cornwall to collect

[1] Cf. Frank Martin's *Le Vin Herbé* based on Bédier's version of the legend.

the tribute that country had been paying to Ireland. Morold was affianced to his cousin Isolde, daughter of the Irish King. Tristan, having been dangerously wounded in the combat, places himself, without disclosing his identity, under the care of Morold's affianced, Isolde, who comes of a race skilled in magic arts. She discerns who he is; but, although she is aware that she is harbouring the slayer of her affianced, she spares him and carefully tends him, for she has conceived a deep passion for him. Tristan in his turn becomes enamoured of her, but both deem their love unrequited. Soon after Tristan's return to Cornwall, he is dispatched to Ireland by Marke, that he may win Isolde as Queen for the Cornish King.

The music-drama opens on board the vessel in which Tristan bears Isolde to Cornwall. Thinking that Tristan does not love her, she determines to end her sorrow by quaffing a death-potion; and Tristan, feeling that the woman he loves is about to be wedded to another, readily consents to share it with her. But Brangäne, Isolde's companion, substitutes a love-potion for the death-draught, and this rouses their love to irresistible passion. Not long after they reach Cornwall, they are surprised in the castle garden by the King and his suite, and Tristan is severely wounded by Melot, one of Marke's knights. Kurwenal, Tristan's faithful retainer, bears him to his native place, Kareol. Hither Isolde follows him, arriving in time to fold him in her arms as he expires. She breathes her last over his corpse.

All who have made a study of opera, and do not regard it merely as a form of amusement, are agreed that the score of *Tristan and Isolde* is the greatest setting of a love-story for the lyric stage. It is a tale of tragic passion, culminating in death, unfolded in the surge and palpitation of immortal music.

This passion smouldered in the heart of the man and woman of this epic of love. It could not burst into clear flame because over it lay the pall of duty—a knight's to his king, a wife's to her husband. They elected to die; drank, as they thought, a death potion. Instead it was a magic love-philtre, craftily substituted by the woman's confidante. Then love, no longer vague and hesitating, but roused by sorcerous means to the highest rapture, found expression in the complete abandonment of the lovers to their ecstasy—and their fate.

What precedes the draught of the potion in the drama, is narrative, explanatory, and prefatorial. Once Tristan and Isolde have shared the goblet, passion is unleashed. The goal is death.

The magic love-philtre is the excitant in this story of rapture and gloom. The Vorspiel therefore opens most fittingly with a motive which expresses the incipient effect of the potion upon Tristan and Isolde. It clearly can be divided into two parts, one descending, the other ascending chromatically. The potion overcomes the restraining influence of duty in two beings and leaves them at the mercy of their passions. The first part, with its descending chromatics, is pervaded by a certain sadness of mood, as if Tristan were still vaguely forewarned by his conscience of the impending tragedy. The second soars ecstatically upward. It is the woman yielding unquestioningly to the rapture of requited love. Therefore, while the phrase may be called the Motive of the Love-Potion, or, as Wolzogen calls it, of Yearning, it seems best to divide it into the Tristan and Isolde Motives (A and B).

The two motives having been twice repeated, there is a *fermata*. Then the Isolde Motive alone is heard, so that the attention of the hearer is fixed upon it. For in this tragedy, as in that of Eden, it is the woman who takes the first decisive step. After another *fermata*, the last two notes of the Isolde Motive are twice repeated, dying away to *pp*. Then a variation of the Isolde Motive leads

with an impassioned upward sweep into another version, full of sensuous yearning, and distinct enough to form a new motive, the Motive of the Love Glance.

This occurs again and again in the course of the Vorspiel. Though readily recognised, it is sufficiently varied with each repetition never to allow the emotional excitement to subside. In fact, the Vorspiel gathers impetus as it proceeds, until, with an inversion of the Love Glance Motive, borne to a higher and higher level of exaltation by upward rushing runs, it reaches its

climax in a paroxysm of love, to die away with repetitions of the Tristan, the Isolde, and the Love Glance Motives.

In the themes it employs this prelude tells, in music, the story of the love of Tristan and Isolde. We have the motives of the hero and heroine of the drama, and the Motive of the Love Glance. When, as is the case in concerts, the finale of the work, 'Liebestod,' [1] is linked to the Vorspiel, we hear the beginning and the end of the music-drama, forming an eloquent epitome of the tragic story.

Act I.    Wagner refrains from actually placing before us on the stage the events that transpired in Ireland before Tristan was despatched thither to bring Isolde as a bride to King Marke. The events, which led to the two meetings between Tristan and Isolde, are told in Isolde's narrative, which forms an important part of the first act. This act opens aboard the vessel in which Tristan is conveying Isolde to Cornwall.

The scene shows Isolde reclining on a couch, her face hid in soft pillows, in a tent-like apartment on the forward deck of a vessel. It is hung with rich tapestries, which hide the rest of the

[1] But the word, now customarily applied to the music of Isolde's death, was intended by Wagner to characterise the Prelude, which contains the seeds of Death through Love.

ship from view. Brangäne has partially drawn aside one of the
hangings and is gazing out upon the sea. From above, as though
from the rigging, is heard the voice of a young Sailor singing a
farewell song to his 'Irish maid'. It has a wild charm and is a
capital example of Wagner's skill in giving local colouring to his
music. The words, 'Frisch weht der Wind der Heimath zu' (The
wind blows freshly toward our home), are sung to a phrase which
occurs frequently in the course of this scene. It represents most
graphically the heaving of the sea and may be appropriately
termed the Ocean Motive. It undulates gracefully through
Brangäne's reply to Isolde's question as to the vessel's course,
surges wildly around Isolde's outburst of impotent anger when she
learns that Cornwall's shore is not far distant, and breaks itself
in savage fury against her despairing wrath as she invokes the
elements to destroy the ship and all upon it. Ocean Motive:

It is her hopeless passion for Tristan which has prostrated
Isolde, for the Motive of the Love Glance accompanies her first
exclamation as she starts up excitedly.

Isolde calls upon Brangäne to throw aside the hangings, that
she may have air. Brangäne obeys. The deck of the ship, and,
beyond it, the ocean, are disclosed. Around the mainmast
sailors are busy splicing ropes. Beyond them, on the after deck,
are knights and esquires. A little aside from them stands Tristan,
gazing out upon the sea. At his feet reclines Kurwenal, his esquire.
The young Sailor's voice is again heard.

Isolde beholds Tristan. Her wrath at the thought that he whom
she loves is bearing her as bride to another vents itself in an angry
phrase. She invokes death upon him. This phrase is the Motive of
Death. The Motive of the Love Glance is heard—and gives away
Isolde's secret—as she asks Brangäne in what estimation she
holds Tristan. It develops into a triumphant strain as Brangäne
sings his praises. Isolde then bids her command Tristan to come

into her presence. This command is given with the Motive of
Death, for it is their mutual death Isolde wishes to encompass.

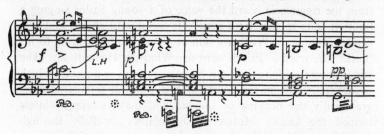

As Brangäne goes to do her mistress's bidding, a graceful variation of the Ocean Motive is heard, the bass marking the rhythmic
motions of the sailors at the ropes. Tristan refuses to leave the
helm and when Brangäne repeats Isolde's command, Kurwenal
answers with a song in praise of Tristan. Knights, esquires, and
sailors repeat the refrain. The boisterous measures—'Hail to
our brave Tristan!'—form the Tristan Call.

Heil un-ser Held Tris - tan,

Isolde's wrath at Kurwenal's taunts finds vent in a narrative in
which she tells Brangäne that once a wounded knight calling
himself Tantris landed on Ireland's shore to seek her healing art.
Into a niche in his sword she fitted a sword splinter she had found
imbedded in the head of Morold, which had been sent to her in
mockery after he had been slain in a combat with the Cornish
foe. She brandished the sword over the knight, whom thus by
his weapon she knew to be Tristan, her betrothed's slayer. But
Tristan's glance fell upon her. Under its spell she was powerless.
She nursed him back to health, and he vowed eternal gratitude
as he left her. The chief theme of this narrative is derived from the
Tristan Motive.

'What of the boat, so bare, so frail,
    That drifted to our shore?
What of the sorely stricken man feebly extended there?
Isolde's art he humbly sought;

With balsam, herbs, and healing salves,
From wounds that laid him low,
She nursed him back to strength.'

Exquisite is the transition of the phrase 'His eyes in mine were gazing', to the Isolde and Love Glance Motives. The passage beginning: 'Who silently his life had spared', is followed by the Tristan Call, Isolde seeming to compare sarcastically what she considers his betrayal of her with his fame as a hero. Her outburst of wrath as she inveighs against his treachery in now bearing her as bride to King Marke, carries the narrative to a superb climax. Brangäne seeks to comfort Isolde, but the latter, looking fixedly before her, confides, almost involuntarily, her love for Tristan.

It is clear, even from this brief description, with what constantly varying expression the narrative of Isolde is treated. Wrath, desire for vengeance, rapturous memories that cannot be dissembled, finally a confession of love to Brangäne—such are the emotions that surge to the surface.

They lead Brangäne to exclaim: 'Where lives the man who would not love you?' Then she weirdly whispers of the love-potion and takes a phial from a golden salver. The motives of the Love Glance and of the Love-Potion accompany her words and action. But Isolde seizes another phial, which she holds up triumphantly. It is the death-potion. Here is heard an ominous phrase of three notes—the Motive of Fate.

A forceful orchestral climax, in which the demons of despairing wrath seem unleashed, is followed by the cries of the sailors greeting the sight of the land, where she is to be married to King Marke. Isolde hears them with growing terror. Kurwenal brusquely calls to her and Brangäne to prepare soon to go ashore. Isolde

orders Kurwenal that he command Tristan to come into her
presence; then bids Brangäne prepare the death-potion. The
Death Motive accompanies her final commands to Kurwenal
and Brangäne, and the Fate Motive also drones threateningly
through the weird measures. But Brangäne artfully substitutes
the love-potion for the death-draught.

Kurwenal announces Tristan's approach. Isolde, seeking to
control her agitation, strides to the couch, and, supporting herself by it, gazes fixedly at the entrance where Tristan remains
standing. The motive which announces his appearance is full of
tragic defiance, as if Tristan felt that he stood upon the threshold
of death, yet was ready to meet his fate unflinchingly. It alternates
effectively with the Fate Motive, and is used most dramatically
throughout the succeeding scene between Tristan and Isolde.
Isolde claims that she wants to drink to their reconciliation.
Sombrely impressive is the passage when he bids Isolde slay him
with the sword she once held over him.

Shouts of the sailors announce the proximity of land. In a
variant of her narrative theme Isolde mockingly anticipates
Tristan's praise of her as he leads her into King Marke's presence.
At the same time she hands him the goblet which contains, as she
thinks, the death-potion and invites him to quaff it. Again the
shouts of the sailors are heard, and Tristan, seizing the goblet,
raises it to his lips with the ecstasy of one from whose soul a great
sorrow is about to be lifted. When he has half emptied it, Isolde
wrests it from him and drains it.

The tremor that passes over Isolde loosens her grasp upon the
goblet. It falls from her hand. She faces Tristan.

Is the light in their eyes the last upflare of passion before the
final darkness? What does the music answer as it enfolds them in
its wondrous harmonies? The Isolde Motive;—then what? Not
the glassy stare of death; the Love Glance, like a swift shaft of
light penetrating the gloom. The spell is broken. Isolde sinks into
Tristan's embrace.

Voices! They hear them not. Sailors are shouting with joy
that the voyage is over. Upon the lovers all sounds are lost, save
their own short, quick interchange of phrases, in which the rapture
of their passion, at last uncovered, finds speech. Music surges
about them. But for Brangäne they would be lost. It is she who
parts them, as the hangings are thrust aside.

Knights, esquires, sailors crowd the deck. From a rocky height King Marke's castle looks down upon the ship, now riding at anchor in the harbour. Peace and joy everywhere save in the lovers' breasts! Isolde faints in Tristan's arms. Yet it is a triumphant climax of the Isolde Motive that is heard above the jubilation of the ship-folk, as the act comes to a close.

Act II.   This act also has an introduction which, together with the first scene between Isolde and Brangäne, constitutes a wonderful mood picture in music. Even Wagner's bitterest critic, Eduard Hanslick, of Vienna, was disposed to compare it with the loveliest creations of Schubert, in which that composer steeps the senses in dreams of night and love.

And so, this introduction of the second act opens with a motive of peculiar significance. During the love scene in the previous act, Tristan and Isolde have inveighed against the day which jealously keeps them apart. They may meet only under the veil of darkness. Even then their joy is embittered by the thought that the blissful night will soon be succeeded by day. With them, therefore, the day stands for all that is inimical, night for all that is friendly. This simile is elaborated with considerable metaphysical subtlety, the lovers even reproaching the day with Tristan's willingness to lead Isolde to King Marke, Tristan charging that in the broad light of the jealous day his duty to win Isolde for his King stood forth so clearly as to overpower the passion for her which he had nurtured during the silent watches of the night. The phrase, therefore, which begins the act as with an agonised cry is the Day Motive.

The Day Motive is followed by a phrase whose eager, restless

measures graphically reflect the impatience with which Isolde awaits the coming of Tristan—the Motive of Impatience.

Over this there hovers a dulcet, seductive strain, the Motive of the Love Call, which is developed into the rapturous measures of the Motive of Ecstasy.

When the curtain rises, the scene it discloses is the palace garden, into which Isolde's apartments open. It is a summer night, balmy and with a moon. The King and his suite have departed on a hunt. With them is Melot, a knight who professes devotion to Tristan, but whom Brangäne suspects.

Brangäne stands upon the steps leading to Isolde's apartment. She is looking down a wooded clearing in the direction taken by the hunt. She fears the hunt is but a trap; and that its quarry is not the wild deer, but her mistress, and the knight who conveyed her for bride to King Marke. Meanwhile against the open door of Isolde's apartment is a burning torch. Its flare through the night is to be the signal to Tristan that all is well, and that Isolde waits.

The first episode of the act is one of those exquisite tone paintings in the creation of which Wagner is supreme. The notes of the hunting-horns become more distant. Isolde comes from her apartment into the garden. She asks Brangäne if she cannot now signal for Tristan. Brangäne answers that the hunt is still within hearing. Isolde chides her—is it not some lovely, prattling rill she hears? The music is deliciously idyllic—conjuring up a dream-picture of a sylvan spring night bathed in liquescent moonlight. Brangäne warns Isolde against Melot; but Isolde laughs at her fears. In vain Brangäne entreats her mistress not to signal for Tristan. The seductive measures of the Love Call and of the Motive of Ecstasy tell throughout this scene of the yearning in Isolde's breast. When Brangäne informs Isolde that she substituted the love-potion for the death-draught, Isolde scorns the suggestion that her guilty love for Tristan is the result of her quaffing the potion. This simply intensified the passion already in her breast. She proclaims this in the rapturous phrases of the Isolde Motive; and then, when she declares her fate to be in the hands of the goddess of love, there are heard the tender accents of the Love Motive.

In vain Brangäne warns once more against possible treachery rom Melot. The Love Motive rises with ever increasing passion until Isolde's emotional exaltation finds expression in the Motive of Ecstasy as she bids Brangäne hie to the lookout, and proclaims that she will give Tristan the signal by extinguishing the torch, though in doing so she were to extinguish the light of her life. The Motive of the Love Call ringing out triumphantly accompanies her action, and dies away into the Motive of Impatience as she gazes in the direction from which she seems to expect Tristan to come to her. Then the Motive of Ecstasy and Isolde's rapturous gesture tell that she has discerned her lover; and, as this motive reaches a fiercely impassioned climax, Tristan and Isolde rush into each other's arms.

The music seethes with passion as the lovers greet one another, the Love Motive and the Motive of Ecstasy vying in the excitement of this rapturous meeting. Then begins the exchange of phrases in which the lovers pour forth their love for one another. This is the scene dominated by the Motive of the Day, which, however, as the day sinks into the soft night, is softened into the Night Motive, which soothes the senses with its ravishing caress. This motive throbs through the rapturous harmonies of the duet: 'Oh, sink upon us, Night of Love', and there is nothing in the realms of music or poetry to compare in suggestiveness with these caressing, pulsating phrases.

The duet is broken in upon by Brangäne's voice warning the lovers that night will soon be over. The arpeggios accompanying her warning are like the first grey streaks of dawn. But the lovers heed her not. In a smooth, soft melody—the Motive of Love's Peace—whose sensuous grace is simply entrancing, they whisper their love.

It is at such a moment, enveloped by night and love, that death should have come to them; and, indeed, it is for such a love-death they yearn. Hence we have here, over a quivering accompaniment, the Motive of the Love-Death,

Once more Brangäne calls. Once more Tristan and Isolde heed her not.

'Night will shield us for aye!'

Thus exclaims Isolde in defiance of the approach of dawn while the Motive of Ecstasy, introduced by a rapturous mordant, soars ever higher.

A cry from Brangäne, Kurwenal rushing upon the scene calling to Tristan to save himself—and the lovers' ravishing dream is ended. Surrounded by the King and his suite, with the treacherous Melot, they gradually awaken to the terror of the situation.

Almost automatically Isolde hides her head among the flowers, and Tristan spreads out his cloak to conceal her from view while phrases reminiscent of the love scene rise like mournful memories.

Now follows a soliloquy for the King, whose sword instead should have leapt from its scabbard and buried itself in Tristan's breast. For it seems inexplicable that the monarch, instead of slaying the betrayer of his honour, should indulge in a philosophical discourse, ending:

> 'The unexplained,
> Unpenetrated
> Cause of all these woes,
> Who will to us disclose?'

Tristan turns to Isolde. Will she follow him to the bleak land of his birth? Her reply is that his home shall be hers. Then Melot draws his sword. Tristan rushes upon him, but as Melot thrusts, allows his guard to fall and receives the blade. Isolde throws herself on her wounded lover's breast.

Act III.    The introduction to this act opens with a variation of the Isolde Motive, sadly prophetic of the desolation which broods over the scene to be disclosed when the curtain rises. On its third repetition it is continued in a long-drawn-out ascending phrase, which seems to represent musically the broad waste of ocean upon which Tristan's castle looks down from its craggy height.

The whole passage appears to represent Tristan hopelessly yearning for Isolde, letting his fancy travel back over the watery waste to the last night of love, and then giving himself up wholly to his grief.

The curtain rises upon the desolate grounds of Kareol, between the outer walls of Tristan's castle and the main structure, which stands upon a rocky eminence overlooking the sea. Tristan is stretched, apparently lifeless, under a huge linden-tree. Over him, in deep sorrow, bends the faithful Kurwenal. A Shepherd is heard piping a strain, whose plaintive notes harmonise most beautifully with the despairing desolation and sadness of the scene. It is the Lay of Sorrow, and by it the Shepherd, who scans the sea, conveys to Kurwenal information that the ship he has dispatched to Cornwall to bear Isolde to Kareol has not yet hove in sight.

The Lay of Sorrow is a strain of mournful beauty, with the simplicity and indescribable charm of a folk-song. Its plaintive notes cling like ivy to the grey and crumbling ruins of love and joy.

The Shepherd peers over the wall and asks if Tristan has shown any signs of life. Kurwenal gloomily replies in the negative. The Shepherd departs to continue his lookout, piping the sad refrain. Tristan slowly opens his eyes. 'The old refrain; why wakes it me? Where am I?' he murmurs. Kurwenal is beside himself with joy at these signs of returning life. His replies to Tristan's feeble and wandering questions are mostly couched in a motive which beautifully expresses the sterling nature of this faithful retainer, one of the noblest characters Wagner has drawn.

When Tristan loses himself in sad memories of Isolde, Kurwenal seeks to comfort him with the news that he has sent a trusty man to Cornwall to bear Isolde to him that she may heal the wound inflicted by Melot as she once healed that dealt Tristan by Morold. In Tristan's jubilant reply, during which he draws Kurwenal to his breast, the Isolde Motive assumes a form in which it becomes a theme of joy.

But it is soon succeeded by the Motive of Anguish, when

Tristan raves of his yearning for Isolde. 'The ship! the ship!' he exclaims. 'Kurwenal, can you not see it?' The Lay of Sorrow, piped by the Shepherd, gives the sad answer. It pervades his sad reverie until, when his mind wanders back to Isolde's tender nursing of his wound in Ireland, the theme of Isolde's Narrative is heard again. Finally his excitement grows upon him, and in a paroxysm of anguish bordering on insanity he even curses love.

Tristan sinks back apparently lifeless. But no—as Kurwenal bends over him and the Isolde Motive is breathed by the orchestra, he again whispers of Isolde. In ravishing beauty the Motive of Love's Peace caressingly follows his vision as he seems to see Isolde gliding toward him o'er the waves. With ever-growing excitement he orders Kurwenal to the lookout to watch the ship's coming. What he sees so clearly cannot Kurwenal also see? Suddenly the music changes in character. The ship is in sight, for the Shepherd is heard piping a joyous lay. It pervades the music of

Tristan's excited questions and Kurwenal's answers as to the vessel's movements. The faithful retainer rushes down toward the shore to meet Isolde and lead her to Tristan. The latter, his strength sapped by his wound, his mind inflamed to insanity by his passionate yearning, struggles to rise. He raises himself a little. The Motive of Love's Peace, no longer tranquil, but with frenzied rapidity, accompanies his actions as, in his delirium, he tears the bandage from his wounds and rises from his couch.

Isolde's voice! Into her arms, outstretched to receive him, staggers Tristan. Gently she lets him down upon his couch, where he has lain in the anguish of expectancy.

'Tristan!'

'Isolde!' he answers in broken accents. This last look resting rapturously upon her, while in mournful beauty the Love Glance Motive rises from the orchestra, he expires.

In all music there is no scene more deeply shaken with sorrow.

Tumultuous sounds are heard. A second ship has arrived. Marke and his suite have landed. Kurwenal and his men, thinking the King has come in pursuit of Isolde, attack the newcomers, but are overpowered, and Kurwenal, having avenged Tristan by slaying Melot, sinks, himself mortally wounded, and dies by Tristan's side. He reaches out for his dead master's hand, and his last words are: 'Tristan, chide me not that faithfully I follow you.'

When Brangäne rushes in and hurriedly announces that she has informed the King of the love-potion, and that he comes bringing forgiveness, Isolde heeds her not. As the Love-Death Motive rises softly over the orchestra and slowly swells into the impassioned Motive of Ecstasy, to reach its climax with a stupendous crash of instrumental forces, she gazes with growing transport upon her dead lover, until, with rapture in her last glance, she sinks upon his corpse and expires.

In the Wagnerian version of the legend this love-death for which Tristan and Isolde prayed and in which they are united, is more than a mere farewell together to life. It is tinged with Oriental philosophy, and symbolises the taking up into and the absorption of by nature of all that is spiritual, and hence immortal, in lives rendered beautiful by love.                                    K.

## DIE MEISTERSINGER VON NÜRNBERG
### The Mastersingers of Nuremberg

Opera in three acts by Richard Wagner. Text by the composer. Première at the Royal Court Theatre, Munich, June 21, 1868, with Mathilde Mallinger, Sophie Dietz, Franz Betz, Bausewein, Gustav Hölzel, Fischer, Nachbauer, Schloser, conductor Hans von Bülow. First performed Theatre Royal, Drury Lane, 1882, with Rose Sucher, Schefsky, Gura, Koegel, Ehrke, Landau, Winkelmann, Kraus, conductor Richter; Metropolitan, New York, 1886, with Seidl-Kraus, Marianne Brandt, Emil Fischer, Josef Staudigl, Kemlitz, Stritt, Krämer, conductor Anton Seidl; Covent Garden, 1889 (in Italian), with Albani, Miranda, Lassalle, Isnardon, Abramoff, Winagradow, Jean de Reszke, Montariol, conductor Mancinelli. Famous interpreters of the part of Hans Sachs have included Reichmann, van Rooy, Whitehill, Weil, Soomer, Schorr, Bockelmann, Nissen, Rode, Prohaska, Schöffler, Berglund, Hotter and Edelmann.

### CHARACTERS

| | | |
|---|---|---|
| Hans Sachs, *Cobbler* | | Bass |
| Veit Pogner, *Goldsmith* | | Bass |
| Kunz Vogelgesang, *Furrier* | | Tenor |
| Conrad Nachtigall, *Buckle-Maker* | | Bass |
| Sixtus Beckmesser, *Town Clerk* | *Mastersingers* | Bass |
| Fritz Kothner, *Baker* | | Bass |
| Balthasar Zorn, *Pewterer* | | Tenor |
| Ulrich Eisslinger, *Grocer* | | Tenor |
| Augustin Moser, *Tailor* | | Tenor |

Hermann Ortel, *Soap-Boiler* ..... ⎫                        ⎧ Bass
Hans Schwarz, *Stocking-Weaver*. ⎬ *Mastersingers* ⎨ Bass
Hans Foltz, *Coppersmith* ........ ⎭                        ⎩ Bass
Walther von Stolzing, *a young Franconian knight* ....Tenor
David, *apprentice to Hans Sachs* ..................Tenor
A Night Watchman ..............................Bass
Eva, *daughter of Pogner* .......................Soprano
Magdalena, *Eva's nurse* .................Mezzo-Soprano
Burghers of the Guilds, Journeymen, Apprentices, Girls

*Time:* Middle of the Sixteenth Century          *Place:* Nuremberg

Walther von Stolzing is in love with Eva. Her father having
promised her to the singer to whom at the coming midsummer
festival the Mastersingers shall award the prize, it becomes
necessary for Walther to seek admission to their art union. He
is, however, rejected, his song violating the rules to which the
Mastersingers slavishly adhere. Beckmesser, the town clerk who
is the 'marker' of the union, is instrumental in securing Walther's
rejection. His duty is to mark all violations of the rules against a
candidate, and since he is a suitor for Eva's hand, he naturally
makes the most of every chance to put down a mark against
Walther, whom he recognises as a rival.

Sachs alone among the Mastersingers has recognised the
beauty of Walther's song. Its very freedom from rule and rote
charms him, and he discovers in the young knight's untrammelled
genius the power which, if properly directed, will lead art from
the beaten path of tradition toward a new and loftier ideal.

After Walther's failure before the Mastersingers the impetuous
young knight persuades Eva to elope with him. But at night as
they are preparing to escape, Beckmesser comes upon the scene
to serenade Eva. Sachs, whose house is opposite Pogner's, has
meanwhile brought his work-bench out into the street and insists
on 'marking' what he considers Beckmesser's mistakes by bringing his hammer down upon his last with a resounding whack.
The louder Beckmesser sings, the louder Sachs bangs. Finally the
neighbours are aroused. David, who is in love with Magdalena
and thinks Beckmesser is serenading her, falls upon him with a
cudgel. The whole neighbourhood turns out and a general *mêlée*
ensues, during which Sachs separates Eva and Walther and draws
the latter into his home.

The following morning Walther sings to Sachs a song which has come to him in a dream; Sachs transcribes the words and passes friendly criticism upon them and the music. The midsummer festival is to take place that afternoon, and through a ruse Sachs manages to get Walther's poem into Beckmesser's possession, who, thinking the words are by the popular cobbler-poet, feels sure he will be the chosen master. Eva, coming into the workshop to have her shoes fitted, finds Walther, and the lovers depart with Sachs, David, and Magdalena for the festival. Here Beckmesser, as Sachs had anticipated, makes a wretched failure, as he has utterly missed the spirit of the poem, and Walther, being called upon by Sachs to reveal its beauty in music, sings his prize song, winning at once the approbation of Mastersingers and populace. After a momentary hesitation on his part he is received into their art union and at the same time wins Eva as his bride.

The Mastersingers were of burgher extraction. They flourished in Germany, chiefly in the imperial cities, during the fourteenth, fifteenth, and sixteenth centuries. They did much to generate and preserve a love of art among the middle classes. Their musical competitions were judged according to a code of rules which distinguished by particular names thirty-two faults to be avoided. Scriptural or devotional subjects were usually selected and the judges or Markers were, in Nuremberg, four in number, the first comparing the words with the Biblical text, the second criticising the prosody, the third the rhymes, and the fourth the tune. He who had the fewest marks against him received the prize.

Hans Sachs, the most famous of the Mastersingers, born November 5, 1494, died January 1576, in Nuremberg, is said to have been the author of some six thousand poems. He was a cobbler by trade—

> 'Hans Sachs war ein Schuh-
> Macher und Poet dazu.'

A monument was erected to him in the city of his birth in 1874.

*The Mastersingers* is a parable of art told in terms of a simple, human love story, with many touches of humour to enliven it, and its interest enhanced by highly picturesque, historical surroundings. As a drama it conveys also a perfect picture of the life and customs of Nuremberg of the time in which the story plays. Wagner must have made careful historical researches, but his book lore is not thrust upon us. The work is so spontaneous that the method and manner of its art are lost sight of in admiration of the result. Hans Sachs himself could not have left a more faithful portrait of life in Nuremberg in the middle of the sixteenth century.

*The Mastersingers* has a peculiarly Wagnerian interest. It is Wagner's protest against the narrow-minded critics and the prejudiced public who so long refused him recognition. Eduard Hanslick,[1] the bitterest of Wagner's critics, regarded the libretto as a personal insult to himself. Being present by invitation at a private reading of the libretto—at this stage, Beckmesser was called Hans Lick—Hanslick rose abruptly and left after the first act. Walther von Stolzing is the incarnation of new aspirations in art; the champion of a new art ideal, and continually chafing under the restraints imposed by traditional rules and methods. Hans Sachs is a conservative. But, while preserving what is best in art traditions, he is able to recognise the beautiful in what is new. He represents enlightened public opinion. Beckmesser and the other Mastersingers are the embodiment of rank prejudice—the critics. Walther's triumph is also Wagner's. Few of Wagner's dramatic creations equal in life-like interest the character of Sachs. It is drawn with a loving, firm hand, and filled in with many delicate touches.

The Vorspiel gives a complete musical epitome of the story. It is full of life and action—pompous, impassioned, and jocose in turn, and without a suggestion of the overwrought or morbid. Its sentiment and its fun are purely human. In its technical construction it has long been recognised as a masterpiece.

In the sense that it precedes the rise of the curtain, this orchestral composition is a Vorspiel, or prelude. As a work, however, it is a fully-fledged overture, rich in thematic material. These themes are Leading Motives heard many times, and in wonderful variety in the three acts of *The Mastersingers*. To a great extent an analysis of this overture forecasts the work itself. Accordingly, again through the courtesy of G. Schirmer Inc., I avail myself of my *Wagner's Music-Dramas Analysed*, in the account of the Vorspiel and of the action and music that follow it.

The pompous Motive of the Mastersingers opens the Vorspiel.

[1] But not so bitter that he could not recognise beauty when he heard it, nor give reasons for his likes and dislikes.

This theme gives capital musical expression to the characteristics of these dignitaries; eminently worthy but self-sufficient citizens who are slow to receive new impressions and do not take kindly to innovations. Our term of 'old fogy' describes them imperfectly, as it does not allow for their many excellent qualities. They are slow to act, but if they are once aroused their ponderous influence bears down all opposition. At first an obstacle to genuine reform, they are in the end the force which pushes it to success. Thus there is in the Motive of the Mastersingers a certain ponderous dignity which well emphasises the idea of conservative power.

In great contrast to this is the Lyric Motive, which seems to express the striving after a poetic ideal untrammelled by old-fashioned restrictions, such as the rules of the Mastersingers impose.

But, the sturdy conservative forces are still unwilling to be persuaded of the worth of this new ideal. Hence the Lyric Motive is suddenly checked by the sonorous measures of the Master-singers' March.

In this the majesty of law and order finds expression. It is followed by a phrase of noble breadth and beauty, obviously developed from portions of the Motive of the Mastersingers, and so typical of the goodwill which should exist among the members of a fraternity that it may be called the Motive of the Art Brotherhood.

PLATE IX. *Die Walküre*, Act III; Covent Garden 1947. Kirsten Flagstad as Brünnhilde and Hans Hotter as Wotan.

PLATE X. Bayreuth 1952. Wieland Wagner's new settings for Act II of *Siegfried*, and Act III of *Tristan*; Ramon Vinay as Tristan, Hans Hotter as Kurwenal.

It reaches an eloquent climax in the Motive of the Ideal.

Opposed, however, to this guild of conservative masters is the restless spirit of progress. Hence, though stately, the strains of the Mastersingers' March and of the Guild Motive soon yield to a theme full of emotional energy and much like the Lyric Motive. Walther is the champion of this new ideal—not, however, from a purely artistic impulse, but rather through his love for Eva. Being ignorant of the rules and rote of the Mastersingers, when he presents himself for admission to the fraternity, he sings measures which soar untrammelled into realms of beauty beyond the imagination of the masters. But it was his love for Eva which impelled him to seek admission to the brotherhood, and love inspired his song. He is therefore a reformer only by accident; it is not his love of art, but his passion for Eva, which really brings about through his prize song a great musical reform. This is one of Wagner's finest dramatic touches—the love story is the main-spring of the action, the moral is pointed only incidentally. Hence all the motives in which the restless striving after a new ideal, or the struggles of a new art form to break through the barriers of conservative prejudice, find expression, are so many love motives, Eva being the incarnation of Walther's ideal. Therefore the motive which breaks in upon the Mastersingers' March and Guild Motive with such emotional energy expresses Walther's desire to possess Eva more than his yearning for a new ideal in art. So I call it the Motive of Longing.

A portion of 'Walther's Prize Song', like a swiftly whispered

declaration of love, leads to a variation of one of the most beautiful themes of the work—the Motive of Spring.

And now Wagner has a fling at the old fogyism which was so long an obstacle to his success. He holds the masters up to ridicule in a delightfully humorous passage which parodies the Mastersingers' and Art Brotherhood Motives, while the Spring Motive vainly strives to assert itself. In the bass, the following quotation is the Motive of Ridicule, the treble being a variant of the Art Brotherhood Motive (associated with the Apprentices):

The passage is followed by the Motive of the Mastersingers, which in turn leads to an imposing combination of phrases. We hear the portion of the Prize Song already quoted—the Motive of the Mastersingers as bass—and in the middle voices portions of the Mastersingers' March; a little later the Motive of the Art Brotherhood and the Motive of Ridicule are added, this grand massing of orchestral forces reaching a powerful climax, with the Motive of the Ideal, while the Motive of the Mastersingers brings the Vorspiel to a fitting close. In this noble passage, in which the 'Prize Song' soars above the various themes typical of the masters, the new ideal seems to be borne to its triumph upon the shoulders of the conservative forces which, won over at last, have espoused its cause with all their sturdy energy.

This concluding passage in the Vorspiel thus brings out with great eloquence the inner significance of *Die Meistersinger*. In whatever the great author and composer of this work wrote for the stage, there always was an ethical meaning at the back of the

words and music. Thus we draw our conclusion of the meaning of *Die Meistersinger* story from the wonderful combination
of leading motives in the peroration of its Vorspiel.

In his fine book, *The Orchestra and Orchestral Music*, W. J.
Henderson relates this anecdote: 'A professional musician was
engaged in a discussion of Wagner in the corridor of the Metropolitan Opera House, while inside the orchestra was playing the
*Meistersinger* overture. "It is a pity," said this wise man, in a
condescending manner, "but Wagner knows absolutely nothing
about counterpoint."

'At that instant the orchestra was singing five different melodies
at once; and, as Anton Seidl was the conductor, they were all
audible.'

In a rare book by J. C. Wagenseil, printed in Nuremberg in
1697, are given four 'Prize Master Tones'. Two of these Wagner
has reproduced in modern garb, the former in the Mastersingers'
March, the latter in the Motive of the Art Brotherhood.

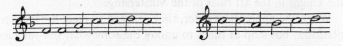

Act I.    The scene of this act is laid in the Church of St.
Catherine, Nuremberg. The congregation is singing the final
chorale of the service. Among the worshippers are Eva and
Magdalena. Walther stands at the side, and, by means of nods
and gestures, communicates with Eva. This mimic conversation
is expressively accompanied by interludes between the verses of
the chorale, interludes based on the Lyric, Spring, and Prize Song
Motives, and contrasting with the strains of the chorale.

The service over, the Motive of Spring, with an impetuous
upward rush, seems to express the lovers' joy that the restraint is
removed, and the Lyric Motive resounds exultingly as the congregation departs, leaving Eva, Magdalena, and Walther behind.

Eva, in order to gain a few words with Walther, sends Magdalena
back to the pew to look for a kerchief and hymn-book she has
purposely left there. Magdalena urges Eva to return home, but
just then David appears in the background and begins putting
things to rights for the meeting of the Mastersingers. Magdalena
is therefore only too glad to linger. The Mastersinger and Guild
Motives, which naturally accompany David's activity, contrast

soberly with the ardent phrases of the lovers. Magdalena explains to Walther that Eva is already affianced, though she herself does not know to whom. Her father wishes her to marry the singer to whom at the coming contest the Mastersingers shall award the prize; and, while she shall be at liberty to decline him, she may marry none but a master. Eva exclaims: 'I will choose no one but my knight!' Very pretty and gay is the theme heard when David joins the group—the Apprentice Motive.

How capitally this motive expresses the light-heartedness of gay young people, in this case the youthful apprentices, among whom David is as gay and buoyant as any.

The scene closes with a beautiful little terzet, after Magdalena has ordered David, under penalty of her displeasure, to instruct the knight in the art rules of the Mastersingers.

When the apprentices enter, they proceed to erect the marker's platform, but stop at times to annoy the somewhat self-sufficient David, while he is endeavouring to instruct Walther in the rules of the Mastersingers. The merry Apprentice Motive runs through the scene and brings it to a close as the apprentices sing and dance around the marker's box, suddenly, however, breaking off, when the Mastersingers appear.

Pogner and Beckmesser lead the way, and the latter is established straight away as a suitor for the hand of Eva, and, musically, as a cantankerous and prickly figure. Pogner renews his acquaintance with Walther, and is surprised to hear that the knight means to present himself as a candidate for the Masters' Guild.

The other Masters enter, there is a roll-call and Beckmesser is chosen as marker. Pogner rises and, in a fine passage for bass voice, offers Eva's hand in marriage to the winner of the coming song contest—with the proviso that Eva adds her consent. The passage is known on concert programmes as 'Pogner's Address'.

Hans Sachs proposes an amendment: let the voice of the people be heard as well as Eva's before a decision is given. This will not only widen the basis of the competition but will also serve as a corrective to the very rules by which the singer is judged and will prevent them becoming stereotyped. But all are against the suggestion, and Pogner proposes that the extra innovation be postponed at any rate for a year.

Walther is introduced by Pogner. The Knight Motive:

The prospective candidate is questioned as to his qualifications and answers in the three verses of 'Am stillen Herd'. Finally Beckmesser, jealous of a prospective rival for Eva's hand and determined that Walther shall fail, enters the marker's box.

Kothner now begins reading off the rules of singing established by the masters; his music is a capital take-off on old-fashioned forms of composition, but if it is not to fail in its humour, requires to be delivered with precision as well as considerable pomposity and unction. Unwillingly enough Walther takes his seat in the candidate's chair. Beckmesser shouts from the marker's box: 'Fanget an!' (Now begin!). After a brilliant chord, followed by an ascending run on the violins, Walther, in ringing tones, enforced by a broad and noble chord, repeats Beckmesser's words. But such a change has come over the music that it seems as if that upward rushing run had swept away all restraint of ancient rule and rote, just as the spring wind whirling through the forest tears up the spread of dry, dead leaves, thus giving air and sun to the yearning mosses and flowers. In Walther's song the Spring Motive forms an ever-surging, swelling accompaniment, finally joining in the vocal melody and bearing it higher and higher to an impassioned climax. He is, however, interrupted by the scratching made by Beckmesser as he chalks the singer's violations of the rules on the slate, and Walther, who is singing of love and spring, changes his theme to winter, which, lingering behind a thorny hedge, is plotting how it can mar the joy of the vernal season. The knight then rises from the chair—another breach of the rules—and sings a second stanza with defiant enthusiasm. As he concludes it Beckmesser tears open the curtains which concealed him in the marker's box, and exhibits his board completely covered with chalk marks. Walther protests, but the masters, with the exception of Sachs and Pogner, refuse to listen further, and deride his singing. We have here the Motive of Derision.

Sachs protests that, while he found the knight's artistic method new, he did not find it formless. The Sachs Motive is here introduced.

The Sachs Motive betokens the genial nature of this sturdy, yet gentle man—the master spirit of the drama. He combines the tolerance of a conservative character with the force of a progressive one, and is thus the incarnation of the idea which Wagner is working out in this drama, in which the union of a proper degree of conservative caution with progressive energy produces a new ideal in art. To Sachs's innuendo that Beckmesser's marking hardly could be considered just, as he is a candidate for Eva's hand, Beckmesser, by way of reply, chides Sachs for having delayed so long in finishing a pair of shoes for him, and as Sachs makes a humorously apologetic answer, the Cobbler Motive is heard.

The sturdy burgher calls to Walther to finish his song in spite of the masters. And now a finale of masterful construction begins. In short, excited phrases the masters chaff and deride Walther. His song, however, soars above all the hubbub. The apprentices see their opportunity in the confusion, and joining hands they dance around the marker's box, singing as they do so. We now have combined with astounding skill Walther's song, the apprentices' chorus, and the exclamations of the masters. The latter finally shout their verdict: 'Rejected and outsung!' The knight, with a proud gesture of contempt, leaves the church. The apprentices put the seats and benches back in their proper places, and in doing so greatly obstruct the masters as they crowd toward the doors. Sachs, who has lingered behind, gazes thoughtfully at the singer's empty chair, then, with a humorous gesture of discouragement, turns away.

Act II.    The scene of this act represents a street in Nuremberg. There are two corner houses—on the right corner of the alley Pogner's, on the left Sachs's. Before the former is a linden-tree, before the latter a lilac. It is a lovely summer evening.

The opening scene is a merry one. David and the apprentices are closing shop. After a brisk introduction based on the Midsummer Festival Motive the apprentices quiz David on his love affair with Magdalena. The latter appears with a basket of dainties for her lover, but on learning that the knight has been rejected, she snatches the basket away from David and hurries back to the house. David is now mockingly congratulated on his successful wooing. He loses his temper and shows fight, but Sachs, coming upon the scene, sends the apprentices on their way and then enters his workshop with David. The music of this episode, especially the chorus, is bright and graceful.

Pogner and Eva, returning from an evening stroll, come down the alley. Before retiring into the house the father, obviously disturbed by the events of the day, questions the daughter as to her feelings concerning the duty she is to perform at the Mastersinging on the morrow. Her replies are discreetly evasive. The music beautifully reflects the affectionate relations between Pogner and Eva. When Pogner, his daughter seated beside him under the linden-tree, speaks of the morrow's festival and Eva's part in it in awarding the prize to the master of her choice before the assembled burghers of Nuremberg, the stately Nuremberg Motive is ushered in.

Magdalena appears at the door and signals to Eva. The latter persuades her father that it is too cool to remain outdoors and, as they enter the house, Eva learns from Magdalena of Walther's failure before the masters. Magdalena suggests she seek the advice of Sachs.

The Cobbler Motive shows us Sachs and David in the former's workshop. When the master has dismissed his apprentice till morning, he yields to his poetic love of the balmy midsummer night and, laying down his work, leans over the half-door of his shop lost in reverie. The Cobbler Motive dies away to *pp*, and then there is wafted from the orchestra, like the sweet scent of the lilac, the Spring Motive, while tender notes on the horn blossom beneath a nebulous veil of tremolo violins into memories of Walther's song. Its measures run through Sachs's head until, angered at the stupid conservatism of his associates, he resumes his work to the brusque measures of the Cobbler's Motive. As his ill humour yields again to the beauties of the night, this motive yields once more to that of spring, which, with reminiscences of Walther's first song before the masters, imbues this masterful monologue, 'Wie duftet doch der Flieder', with poetic beauty of the highest order. The last words in praise of Walther ('The bird who sang to-day', etc.) are sung to a broad and expressive melody.

Eva now comes out into the street and, shyly approaching the shop, stands at the door unnoticed by Sachs until she speaks to him. The theme which pervades this scene seems to breathe forth the very spirit of lovely maidenhood which springs from the union of romantic aspirations, feminine reserve, and rare physical graces. It is the Eva Motive, which, with the delicate touch of a master, Wagner so varies that it follows the many subtle dramatic suggestions of the scene. The Eva Motive, in its original form, is as follows:

When at Eva's first words Sachs looks up, there is this elegant variation of the Eva Motive:

Then, the scene being now fully ushered in, we have the Eva Motive itself. Eva leads the talk up to the morrow's festival, and when Sachs mentions Beckmesser as her chief wooer, roguishly hints, with evident reference to Sachs himself, that she might prefer a widower to a bachelor of such disagreeable characteristics as the marker. There are sufficient indications that the sturdy master is not indifferent to Eva's charms, but, whole-souled, genuine friend that he is, his one idea is to further the love affair between his fair neighbour and Walther. The music of this passage is very expressive. The melodic leading of the upper voice in the accompaniment, when Eva asks: 'Could not a widower hope to win me?' is identical with a variation of the Isolde Motive in *Tristan and Isolde,* while the Eva Motive, shyly *pp,* seems to indicate the artfulness of Eva's question. The reminiscence from *Tristan* can hardly be regarded as accidental, for Sachs afterwards boasts that he does not care to share the fate of poor King Marke. Eva now endeavours to glean particulars of Walther's experience in the morning, and we have the Motive of Envy, the Knight Motive, and the Motive of Ridicule. Eva does not appreciate the fine satire in Sachs's severe strictures on Walther's singing—he re-echoes not his own views, but those of the other masters, for whom, not for the knight, his strictures are really intended—and she leaves him in anger. This shows Sachs which way the wind blows, and he forthwith resolves to do all in his power to bring Eva's and Walther's love affair to a successful conclusion. While Eva is engaged with Magdalena, who has come out to call her, he busies himself in closing the upper half of his shop door so far that only a gleam of light is visible, he himself being completely hidden. Eva learns from Magdalena of Beckmesser's intended serenade, and it is agreed that the maid shall personate Eva at the window

Steps are heard coming down the alley. Eva recognises Walther and flies to his arms, Magdalena discreetly hurrying into the house. The ensuing ardent scene between Eva and Walther brings

familiar motives. The knight's excitement is comically broken in
upon by the Night Watchman's cow-horn, and, as Eva lays her
hand soothingly upon his arm and counsels that they retreat
within the shadow of the linden-tree, there steals over the orchestra,
like the fragrance of the summer night, a delicate variant of the
Eva Motive—The Summer Night Motive.

Eva vanishes into the house to prepare to elope with Walther.
The Night Watchman crosses the stage intoning a mediaeval
chant, which makes a quaint effect in the middle of music of
such different character.

As Eva reappears and she and the knight are about to make
their escape, Sachs, to prevent this precipitate and foolish step,
throws open his shutters and allows his lamp to shed a streak of
brilliant light across the street.

The lovers hesitate; and now Beckmesser sneaks in after the
Night Watchman and, leaning against Sachs's house, begins to
tune his lute, the peculiar twang of which, contrasted with the
rich orchestration, sounds irresistibly ridiculous.

Meanwhile, Eva and Walther have once more retreated into
the shade of the linden-tree, and Sachs, who has placed his work
bench in front of his door, begins hammering at the last and
intones a song which is one of the rough diamonds of musical
invention, for it is purposely brusque and rough, just such a song
as a hearty, happy artisan might sing over his work. It is aptly
introduced by the Cobbler Motive. Beckmesser, greatly disturbed
lest his serenade be ruined, entreats Sachs to cease singing. Sachs
argues that he must finish Beckmesser's shoes, or else he will
again publicly blame him for neglecting his work in favour of
his poetry. In the end, he agrees, but with the proviso that he shall
'mark' each of Beckmesser's mistakes with a hammer stroke.
As if to bring out as sharply as possible the ridiculous character
of the serenade, the orchestra breathes forth once more the
summer night's music before Beckmesser begins his song, and this
is set to a parody of the Lyric Motive. Wagner, with keen satire,
seems to want to show how a beautiful melody may become

absurd through old-fogy methods. Beckmesser has hardly begun before Sachs's hammer comes down on the last with a resounding whack, which makes the town clerk fairly jump with anger. He resumes, but soon is rudely interrupted again by a blow of Sachs's hammer. The whacks come faster and faster. Beckmesser, in order to make himself heard above them, sings louder and louder. Some of the neighbours are awakened by the noise and coming to their windows bid Beckmesser hold his peace. David, stung by jealousy as he sees Magdalena listening to the serenade, leaps from his room and falls upon the town clerk with a cudgel. The neighbours, male and female, run out into the street and a general *mêlée* ensues, the masters, who hurry upon the scene, seeking to restore quiet, while the apprentices vent their high spirits by doing all in their power to add to the hubbub. All is now noise and disorder, pandemonium let loose upon the dignified old town.

Musically this tumult finds expression in a fugue whose chief theme is the Cudgel Motive.

From beneath the hubbub of voices—those of the apprentices and journeymen, delighted to take part in the shindy, of the women who are terrified at it, and of the masters who strive to stop it—is heard the theme of Beckmesser's song, the real cause of the row.

Sachs finally succeeds in shoving the apprentices and journeymen out of the way. The street is cleared, but not before the cobbler-poet has pushed Eva, who was about to elope with Walther, into her father's arms and drawn Walther after him into his shop.

The street is quiet. And now, the rumpus subsided and all concerned in it gone, the Night Watchman appears, rubs his eyes and chants his mediaeval call. The street is flooded with moonlight. The Watchman with his clumsy halberd lunges at his own shadow, then goes up the alley.

We have had hubbub, we have had humour, and now we have

a musical ending elfish, roguish, and yet exquisite in sentiment. The effect is produced by the Cudgel Motive played with the utmost delicacy on the flute, while the theme of Beckmesser's serenade merrily runs after itself on clarinet and bassoon, and the muted violins softly breathe the Midsummer Festival Motive.

Act III.     During this act the tender strain in Sachs's sturdy character is brought out in bold relief. Hence the prelude develops what may be called three Sachs themes, two of them expressive of his twofold nature as poet and cobbler, the third standing for the love which his fellowburghers bear him.

The prelude opens with the 'Wahn' Motive or Motive of Poetic Illusion. This reflects the deep thought and poetic aspirations of Sachs the poet. It is followed by the theme of the beautiful chorus, sung later in the act, in praise of Sachs: 'Awake! draws nigh the break of day'. This theme, among the three heard in the prelude, points to Sachs's popularity. The third consists of portions of the cobbler's song in the second act. This prelude has long been considered one of Wagner's masterpieces. The themes are treated with the utmost delicacy, so that we recognise through them both the tender, poetic side of Sachs's nature and his good-humoured brusqueness. The Motive of Poetic Illusion is deeply reflective, and it might be preferable to name it the Motive of Poetic Thought, were it not that it is better to preserve the significance of the term Wahn Motive, which, there is ample reason to believe, originated with Wagner himself. The prelude is, in fact, a subtle analysis of character expressed in music.

How peaceful the scene on which the curtain rises. Sachs is sitting in an arm-chair in his sunny workshop, reading a large folio. The Illusion Motive has not yet died away in the prelude, so that it seems to reflect the thoughts awakened in Sachs by what he is reading. David, dressed for the festival, enters just as the prelude ends. He is at first afraid of Sachs's anger, but sings his song (by a slip of the tongue, he starts off with the tune of Beckmesser's serenade, but corrects himself). At the end he realises that it is Sachs's name-day. When David has withdrawn, Sachs is lost in thought: 'Wahn! Wahn! Ueberall Wahn!' (Fools, fools, all of them fools).

While the Illusion Motive seems to weave a poetic atmosphere about him, Sachs, buried in thought, rests his head upon his arm over the folio. The Illusion Motive is followed by the Spring Motive, which in turn yields to the Nuremberg Motive as Sachs sings the praises of the stately old town. At his reference to the tumult of the night before there are in the score corresponding allusions to the music of that episode. 'A glowworm could not find its mate,' he sings, referring to Walther and Eva. The Midsummer Festival, Lyric, and Nuremberg Motives in union foreshadow the triumph of true art through love on Nuremberg soil, and thus bring the monologue to a stately conclusion.

Walther now enters from the chamber, which opens upon a gallery, and, descending into the workshop, is heartily greeted by Sachs with the Sachs Motive, which dominates the immediately ensuing scene. Very beautiful is the theme in which Sachs protests against Walther's derision of the masters; for they are, in spite of their many old-fogyish notions, the conservators of much that is true and beautiful in art.

Walther tells Sachs of a song which came to him in a dream during the night, and sings two stanzas of this *Prize Song*, Sachs making friendly critical comments as he writes down the words. The Nuremberg Motive in sonorous and festive instrumentation closes this melodious episode.

When Sachs and Walther have retired Beckmesser is seen peeping into the shop. Observing that it is empty he enters hastily. He is ridiculously overdressed for the approaching festival, limps, and occasionally rubs his muscles as if he were still stiff and sore from his drubbing. By chance his glance falls on the manuscript of the *Prize Song* in Sachs's handwriting on the table, when he breaks forth in wrathful exclamations, thinking now that he has in the popular master a rival for Eva's hand. Hearing the chamber door opening he hastily grabs the manuscript and thrusts it into his pocket. Sachs enters. Beckmesser accuses him of being a secret candidate for Eva's hand; his behaviour of the night before is now plain. Observing that the manuscript is no longer on the table, Sachs realises that Beckmesser has stolen it, and conceives the idea of allowing him to keep it, knowing that the marker will fail most wretchedly in attempting to give musical expression to Walther's inspiration.

The scene places Sachs in a new light. A fascinating trait of his character is the dash of scapegrace with which it is seasoned. Hence, when he thinks of allowing Beckmesser to use the poem the Sachs Motive takes on a somewhat facetious, roguish grace. There now ensues a charming dialogue between Sachs and Eva, who enters when Beckmesser has departed. This is accompanied by a transformation of the Eva Motive, which now reflects her shyness and hesitancy in taking Sachs into her confidence.

With it is joined the Cobbler Motive when Eva places her foot upon the stool while Sachs tries on the shoes she is to wear at the festival. When, with a cry of joy, she recognises her lover as he appears upon the gallery, and remains motionless, gazing upon him as if spellbound, the lovely Summer Night Motive enhances the beauty of the tableau. While Sachs cobbles and chats away, pretending not to observe the lovers, the Motive of Maidenly Reserve passes through many modulations until there is heard a phrase from *Tristan and Isolde* (the Isolde Motive), an allusion which is explained below. The Lyric Motive introduces the third stanza of Walther's *Prize Song*, with which he now greets Eva, while she, overcome with joy at seeing her lover, sinks upon Sachs's breast. The Illusion Motive rhapsodises the praises of the generous cobbler-poet, who seeks relief from his emotions in bantering remarks, until Eva glorifies him in a noble burst of love and gratitude ('O Sachs, mein Freund') in a melody derived from the Isolde Motive.

It is after this that Sachs, alluding to his own love of Eva, exclaims that he will have none of King Marke's sad experience; and the use of the King Marke Motive at this point shows that the previous echoes of the Isolde Motive were premeditated rather than accidental.

Magdalena and David now enter, and Sachs gives to Walther's *Prize Song* its musical baptism, utilising chiefly the first and second lines of the chorale which opens the first act. David then kneels down and, according to the custom of the day, receives from Sachs a box on the ear in token that he is advanced from apprentice to journeyman. Then follows the beautiful quintet, in which the *Prize Song*, as a thematic germ, puts forth its loveliest blossoms. This is but one of many instances in which Wagner proved that when the dramatic situation called for it he could conceive and develop a melody of most exquisite fibre.

After the quintet the orchestra resumes the Nuremberg Motive and all depart for the festival. The stage is now shut off by a curtain behind which the scene is changed from Sachs's workshop to the meadow on the banks of the Pegnitz, near Nuremberg. After a tumultuous orchestral interlude, which portrays by means of motives already familiar, with the addition of the fanfare of the town musicians, the noise and bustle incidental to preparations for a great festival, the curtain rises upon a lively scene. Boats decked out in flags and bunting and full of festively clad members of the various guilds and their wives and children are constantly arriving. To the right is a platform decorated with the flags of the guilds which have already gathered. People are making merry under tents and awnings where refreshments are served. The apprentices are having a jolly time of it heralding and marshalling the guilds who disperse and mingle with the merrymakers after the standard-bearers have planted their banners near the platform.

Soon after the curtain rises the cobblers arrive, and as they march down the meadow, conducted by the apprentices, they sing in honour of St. Crispin, their patron saint, a chorus, based on the Cobbler Motive, to which a melody in popular style is added. The town watchmen, with trumpets and drums, the town pipers, lute makers, etc., and then the journeymen, with comical sounding toy instruments, march past, and are succeeded by the tailors, who sing a humorous chorus, telling how Nuremberg was saved from its ancient enemies by a tailor, who sewed a goatskin around him and pranced around on the town walls, to the terror of the hostile army, which took him for the devil. The bleating of a goat is capitally imitated in this chorus.

With the last chord of the tailors' chorus the bakers strike up their song and are greeted in turn by cobblers and tailors with their respective refrains. A boatful of young peasant girls in gay costumes now arrives, and the apprentices make a rush for the bank. A charming dance in waltz time is struck up. The apprentices with the girls dance down toward the journeymen, but as soon as these try to get hold of the girls, the apprentices veer off with them in another direction. David joins in. This veering should be timed to fall at the beginning of those periods of the dance to which Wagner has given, instead of eight measures, seven and nine, in order by this irregularity to emphasise the ruse of the apprentices.

The dance is interrupted by the arrival of the masters, the apprentices falling in to receive, the others making room for the procession. The Mastersingers and Eva advance to the stately strains of the Mastersinger Motive, which, when Kothner appears bearing their standard with the figure of King David playing on his harp, goes over into the sturdy measures of the Mastersingers' March. Sachs rises and advances. At sight of him the populace intone the noblest of the choruses: 'Awake! draws nigh the break of day', the words of which are a poem by the real Hans Sachs.

At its conclusion the populace break into shouts in praise of Sachs, who modestly yet most feelingly gives them thanks. When Beckmesser is led to the little mound of turf upon which the singer is obliged to stand, we have the humorous variation of the Mastersinger Motive from the Prelude. Beckmesser's attempt to sing Walther's poem ends, as Sachs had anticipated, in utter failure. His attempt at the words is as muddled as his efforts at a tune. The town clerk's effort is received with jeers. Before he rushes away, infuriated but utterly discomfited, he proclaims that Sachs is the author of the song they have derided. The cobbler-poet declares to the people that it is not by him; that it is a beautiful poem if sung to the proper melody and that he will show them the author of the poem, who will in song disclose its beauties. He then introduces Walther. The knight easily succeeds in winning over people and masters, who repeat the closing melody of his

*Prize Song* in token of their joyous appreciation of his new and wondrous art. Eva crowns him to the accompaniment of a beautiful vocal phrase—and Sachs's rejected suggestion of letting the people help in the judging is thus brought about.

In more ways than one the *Prize Song* is a mainstay of *Die Meistersinger*. It has been heard in the previous scene of the third act, not only when Walther rehearses it for Sachs, but also in the quintet. Moreover, versions of it occur in the overture and indeed throughout the work, adding greatly to the romantic sentiment of the score. For *Die Meistersinger* is a comedy of romance.

Pogner advances to decorate Walther with the insignia of the Masters' Guild, but, with an impulsive gesture, the knight rejects the honour. It is a moment of embarrassment but Sachs saves the situation. In measures easily recognised from the Prelude, to which the Nuremberg Motive is added, he praises the masters and explains their noble purpose as conservators of art. Eva takes the wreath with which Walther has been crowned, and with it crowns Sachs, who has meanwhile decorated the knight with the insignia. Pogner kneels, as if in homage, before Sachs, the masters point to the cobbler as to their chief, and Walther and Eva remain on either side of him, leaning gratefully upon his shoulders. The chorus repeats Sachs's final admonition to the closing measures of the Prelude.          K.

# DER RING DES NIBELUNGEN
## The Ring of the Nibelung

A stage-festival play for three days and a preliminary evening (Ein Bühnen-festspeil für drei Tage und einen Vorabend), words and music by Richard Wagner.

The first performance of the entire cycle took place in August 1876 at Bayreuth (for details, see below). The first complete cycle in London was given at Her Majesty's Theatre, May 5, 6, 8, 9, 1882, conducted by Anton Seidl and sung in German. The first complete New York cycle was given at the Metropolitan, March 4, 5, 8, 11, 1889, under Seidl; previously, there had been performances of the cycle apart from *Das Rheingold* in 1887–8 also under Seidl. The first cycle at Covent Garden took place in June 1892, but the four operas were given in the wrong order so that Alvary could make his debut as the young Siegfried! The first complete cycle in English was at Covent Garden in 1908, under Richter.

Famous Brünhildes have also included Ellen Gulbranson, Saltzmann-Stevens, Litvinne, Mildenburg, Kappel, Leider, Larsen-Todsen, Ohms, Flagstad, Marta Fuchs, Traubel; Sieglindes: Marie Wittich, Fremstad, Lotte Lehmann, Rethberg, Marie Müller, Lemnitz; Siegmunds: Jacques Urlus, Melchior, Schmedes, Völker, Lorenz; Wotans: van Rooy, Reichmann, Schorr, Bockelmann, Rode, Hotter, Berglund.

In 1863, while working upon *Die Meistersinger*, at Penzing, near Vienna, Wagner published his *Nibelung* dramas, expressing his hope that through the bounty of one of the German rulers the completion and performance of his *The Ring of the Nibelung* would be made possible. But in the spring of 1864, worn out by his struggle with poverty and almost broken in spirit by his contest with public and critics, he actually determined to give up his public career, and eagerly grasped the opportunity to visit a private country seat in Switzerland. Just at this very moment, when despair had settled upon him, the long wished-for help came. King Ludwig II, of Bavaria, bade him come to Munich, where he settled in 1864. *Tristan* was produced there June 10, 1865. June 21, 1868, a model performance of *Die Meistersinger*, which he had finished in 1867, was given at Munich under the direction of von Bülow, Richter acting as chorus master and Wagner supervising all the details. Wagner also worked steadily at the unfinished portion of the *Ring*, completing the instrumentation of the third act of *Siegfried* in 1869 and the introduction and first act of *The Twilight of the Gods* in June 1870.

In August 25, 1870, his first wife having died January 25, 1866, after five years' separation from him, he married the divorced wife of von Bülow, Cosima Liszt. In 1869 and 1870, respectively, *The Rhinegold* and *The Valkyr* were performed at the Court Theatre in Munich.

Bayreuth having been determined upon as the place where a theatre for the special production of his *Ring* should be built, Wagner settled there in April 1872. By November 1874, *The Twilight of the Gods* received its finishing touches, and rehearsals had already been held at Bayreuth. During the summer of 1875, under Wagner's supervision, Hans Richter held full rehearsals there, and at last, twenty-eight years after its first conception, on

August 13, 14, 16, and 17, again from August 20 to 23, and from August 27 to 30, 1876, *The Ring of the Nibelung* was performed at Bayreuth with the following cast: Wotan, Betz; Loge, Vogel; Alberich, Hill; Mime, Schlosser; Fricka, Frau Grün; Donner and Gunther, Gura; Erda and Waltraute, Frau Jaide; Siegmund, Niemann; Sieglinde, Frl. Schefsky; Brünnhilde, Frau Materna; Siegfried, Unger; Hagen, Siehr; Gutrune, Frl. Weckerin; Rhine-daughters, Lilli and Marie Lehmann, and Frl. Lammert. First violin, Wilhelmj; conductor, Hans Richter. The first Rhine-daughter was the same Lilli Lehmann who, in later years, at the Metropolitan Opera House, New York, became one of the greatest of prima donnas and, as regards the Wagnerian repertory, set a standard for all time. Materna appeared at that house in the *Walküre* production under Dr. Damrosch, in January 1885, and Niemann was heard there later.

*The Ring of the Nibelung* consists of four music-dramas— *Das Rheingold* (The Rhinegold), *Die Walküre* (The Valkyr), *Siegfried*, and *Götterdämmerung* (Twilight of the Gods). The books of these were written in inverse order. Wagner made a dramatic sketch of the Nibelung myth as early as the autumn of 1848, and between then and the autumn of 1850 he wrote the *Death of Siegfried*. This subsequently became *The Twilight of the Gods*. Meanwhile Wagner's ideas as to the proper treatment of the myth seem to have undergone a change. *Siegfried's Death* ended with Brünnhilde leading Siegfried to Walhalla—dramatic, but without the deeper ethical significance of the later version, when Wagner evidently conceived the purpose of connecting the final catastrophe of his trilogy with *The Twilight of the Gods*, or end of all things, in Northern mythology, and of embodying a profound truth in the action of the music-dramas. This meta-physical significance of the work is believed to be sufficiently explained in the brief synopsis of the plot of the trilogy and in the descriptive musical and dramatic analyses below.

In the autumn of 1850 when Wagner was on the point of sketching out the music of *Siegfried's Death*, he recognised that he must lead up to it with another drama, and *Young Siegfried*, afterwards *Siegfried*, was the result. This in turn he found incomplete, and finally decided to supplement it with *The Valkyr* and *The Rhinegold*.

Of the principal characters in *The Ring of the Nibelung*, Alberich, the Nibelung, and Wotan, the chief of the gods, are symbolic of greed for wealth and power. This lust leads Alberich to renounce love—the most sacred of emotions—in order that he may rob the Rhinedaughters of the Rhine gold, which they guard, and forge from it the ring which is to make him all-powerful. Wotan by strategy obtains the ring, but instead of returning it to the Rhinedaughters, he gives it to the giants, Fafner and Fasolt, as ransom for Freia, the goddess of youth and beauty, whom he had promised to the giants as a reward for building Valhalla. Alberich has cursed the ring and all into whose possession it may come. The giants no sooner obtain it than they fall to quarrelling over it. Fafner slays Fasolt and then retires to a cave in the heart of a forest where, in the form of a dragon, he guards the ring and the rest of the treasure which Wotan wrested from Alberich and also gave to the giants as ransom for Freia. This treasure includes the Tarnhelmet, whose wearer can assume any guise.

Wotan, having witnessed the slaying of Fasolt, is filled with dread lest the curse of Alberich be visited upon the gods. To defend Walhalla against the assaults of Alberich and the host of Nibelungs, he begets in union with Erda, the goddess of wisdom, the Valkyrs (chief among them Brünnhilde), wild maidens who course through the air on superb chargers and bear the bodies of departed heroes to Walhalla, where they revive and aid the gods in warding off the attacks of the Nibelungs. But it is also necessary that the curse-laden ring should be wrested from Fafner and restored through purely unselfish motives to the Rhinedaughters, and the curse thus lifted from the race of the gods. None of the gods can do this because their motive in doing so would not be unselfish. Hence Wotan, for a time, casts off his divinity, and, disguised as Wälse, begets in union with a human woman the Wälsung twins, Siegmund and Sieglinde. Siegmund he hopes will be the hero who will slay Fafner and restore the ring to the Rhinedaughters. To nerve him for this task, Wotan surrounds the Wälsungs with numerous hardships. Sieglinde is seized and forced to become the wife of Hunding. Siegmund, storm-driven, seeks shelter in Hunding's hut, but he and his sister recognise one another and flee into the night together. Hunding overtakes them and Wotan, as Siegmund has been guilty of a crime against the marriage vow, is obliged, in response to the urging of his spouse Fricka, the Juno of Northern mythology, to give victory to Hunding. Brünnhilde, contrary to Wotan's command, takes pity on Siegmund, and seeks to shield him against Hunding. As punishment for this, Wotan causes her to fall into a profound slumber. The hero who will penetrate the barrier of fire with which Wotan has surrounded the rock upon which she slumbers can claim her as his bride.

After Siegmund's death Sieglinde gives birth to Siegfried, the son of their illicit union, who is reared by one of the Nibelungs, Mime, in the forest where Fafner guards the Nibelung treasure. Mime is seeking to weld the pieces of Siegmund's sword (*Nothung*, or Needful) in order that Siegfried may slay Fafner, Mime hoping then to kill the youth and to possess himself of the treasure. But he cannot weld the sword. At last Siegfried, learning that it was his father's weapon, welds the pieces and slays Fafner. His lips having come in contact with the dragon's blood which is on his fingers, he is enabled, through its magic power, to understand the language of the birds, one of which warns him of Mime's treachery. Siegfried slays the dwarf and is then guided to the fiery barrier around the Valkyr rock. Penetrating this, he comes upon Brünnhilde, and enraptured with her beauty, awakens her and claims her as his bride. She, the virgin pride of the goddess yielding to the love of the woman, gives herself up to him. He plights his troth with the curse-laden ring which he has wrested from Fafner.

Siegfried goes forth in quest of adventure. On the Rhine lives the Gibichung Gunther, his sister Gutrune, and their half-brother Hagen, none other than the son of the Nibelung Alberich. Hagen, knowing of Siegfried's coming, plans his destruction in order to regain the ring for the Nibelungs. Therefore, craftily concealing the relationship of Brünnhilde and Siegfried from Gunther, he incites a longing in the latter to possess Brünnhilde as his bride. Carrying out a plot evolved by Hagen, Gutrune on Siegfried's arrival presents to him a drinking-horn filled with a love-potion. Siegfried drinks, is led through the effect of the potion to forget that Brünnhilde is his bride, and, becoming enamoured of Gutrune, asks her in marriage of Gunther. The latter consents, provided Siegfried will disguise himself in the Tarnhelmet as Gunther and lead Brünnhilde to him as bride. Siegfried readily agrees, and in the guise of Gunther overcomes Brünnhilde and delivers her to the Gibichung. But Brünnhilde, recognising on

Siegfried's finger the ring, which her conquerer had taken from her, accuses him of treachery in delivering her, his own bride, to Gunther. The latter, unmasked and also suspicious of Siegfried, conspires with Hagen and Brünnhilde, who, knowing naught of the love-potion, is roused to a frenzy of hate and jealousy by Siegfried's seeming treachery, to compass the young hero's death. Hagen slays Siegfried during a hunt, and then, in a quarrel with Gunther over the ring, also kills the Gibichung.

Meanwhile Brünnhilde has learned through the Rhinedaughters of the treachery of which she and Siegfried have been the victims. All her jealous hatred of Siegfried yields to her old love for him and a passionate yearning to join him in death. She draws the ring from his finger and places it on her own, then hurls a torch upon the pyre. Mounting her steed, she plunges into the flames. One of the Rhinedaughters, swimming in on the rising waters, seizes the curse-laden ring. Hagen rushes into the flooding Rhine hoping to regain it, but the other Rhinedaughters grasp him and draw him down into the flood. Not only the flames of the pyre, but a glow which pervades the whole horizon illumine the scene. It is Walhalla being consumed by fire. Through love—the very emotion Alberich renounced in order to gain wealth and power—Brünnhilde has caused the old order of things to pass away and a human era to dawn in place of the old mythological one of the gods.

The sum of all that has been written concerning the book of *The Ring of the Nibelung* is probably larger than the sum of all that has been written concerning the librettos used by all other composers. What can be said of the ordinary opera libretto beyond Voltaire's remark that 'what is too stupid to be spoken is sung'? But *The Ring of the Nibelung* produced vehement discussion. It was attacked and defended, praised and ridiculed, extolled and condemned. And it survived all the discussion it called forth. It is the outstanding fact in Wagner's career that he always triumphed. He threw his lance into the midst of his enemies and fought his way up to it. No matter how much opposition his music-dramas excited, they gradually found their way into the repertory.

It was contended on many sides that a book like *The Ring of the Nibelung* could not be set to music. Certainly it could not be after the fashion of an ordinary opera. Perhaps people were so accustomed to the books of nonsense which figured as opera librettos that they thought *The Ring of the Nibelung* was so great a work that its action and climaxes were beyond the scope of musical expression. For such, Wagner has placed music on a higher level. He has shown that music makes a great drama greater.

One of the most remarkable features of Wagner's works is the author's complete absorption of the times of which he wrote. He seems to have gone back to the very period in which the scenes of his music-dramas are laid and to have himself lived through the events in his plots. One cannot imagine Hans Sachs leaving a more faithful portrayal of life in the Nuremberg of his day than Wagner has given us in *Die Meistersinger*. In *The Ring of the Nibelung* he has done more—he has absorbed an imaginary epoch; lived over the days of gods and demigods; infused life into mythological figures. *The Rhinegold*, which is full of varied interest from its first note to its last, deals entirely with beings of mythology. They are presented true to life—if that expression may be used in connection with beings that never lived—that is to say, they are so vividly drawn that we forget such beings never lived, and take as much interest in their doings and sayings as if they were lifelike reproductions of historical characters. Was there ever a love scene more thrilling than that between Siegmund and Sieglinde? It represents the gradations of the love of two souls from its first awakening to its rapturous greeting in full self-consciousness. No one stops to think during that impassioned scene that the close relationship between Siegmund and Sieglinde is in fact incestuous. For all we know, in those moments when the impassioned music of that scene whirls us away in its resistless current, not a drop of related blood courses through their veins. It has been said that we could not be interested in mythological beings—that *The Ring of the Nibelung* lacked human interest. In reply, I say that, wonderful as is the first act of *The Valkyr*, there is nothing in it to compare in wild and lofty beauty with the last act of that music-drama—especially the scene between Brünnhilde and Wotan.

Brünnhilde is Wagner's noblest creation. She takes upon herself the sins of the gods and by her expiation frees the world from the curse of lust for wealth and power. She is a perfect dramatic incarnation of the profound and beautiful metaphysical motive upon which the plot of *The Ring of the Nibelung* is based.

That there are faults of dramatic construction in *The Ring of the Nibelung* I admit. In what follows I have not hesitated to point them out. But there are faults of construction in Shakespeare. With all its faults of dramatic construction *The Ring of the Nibelung* is a remarkable drama, full of life and action and logically developed, the events leading up to superb climaxes. Wagner was doubly inspired. He was both a great dramatist and a great musician.

The chief faults of dramatic construction of which Wagner was guilty in *The Ring of the Nibelung* are certain unduly prolonged scenes which are merely episodic—that is, unnecessary to the development of the plot, so that they delay the action and weary the audience to a point which endangers the success of the really sublime portions of the score. In several of these scenes there is a great amount of narrative, the story of events with which we have become familiar being retold in detail with the addition of some incidents which connect the plot of the particular music-drama with that of the preceding one. But, as narrative on the stage makes little impression, and when it is sung perhaps none at all, because it cannot be well understood, it would seem as if prefaces to the dramas could have taken the place of these narratives. Certain it is that these long drawn-out scenes did more to retard the popular recognition of Wagner's genius than the activity of hostile critics and musicians. Still, it should be remembered that these music-dramas were composed for performance under the circumstances which prevail at Bayreuth, where the performances begin in the afternoon and there are long waits between the acts, during which you can refresh yourself by a stroll or by the more mundane pleasures of the table. Then, after an hour's relaxation of the mind and of the sense of hearing, you are ready to hear another act. Under these agreeable conditions one remains sufficiently fresh to enjoy the music even of the dramatically faulty scenes.

There now follow descriptive accounts of the stories and music of the four component parts of this work by Wagner—perhaps his greatest.                                        K.

# DAS RHEINGOLD
## The Rhinegold

Prologue (in four scenes) to the trilogy *Der Ring des Nibelungen* by Richard Wagner  text by the composer. First performed at Munich, September 22,

1869, with August Kindermann, Nachbar, Vogel, Fischer, Schlosser, Polzer, Bausewein, Sophie Stehle, Frau Müller, Frau Seehofer, Frau Kaufman, Therese Vogel, Frau Ritte, conductor Franz Wüllner. First performed Her Majesty's Theatre, London, 1882, with Emil Scaria, Vogel, Schelper, Schlosser, Reicher-Kindermann, Schreiber, Riegler, Krauss, Klafsky, Schulze, Eilers, Wiegand, Bürgen, conductor Seidl; Metropolitan, New York, 1889, with Fischer, Grienauer, Mittelhauser, Alvary, Beck, Sedlmayer, Mödlinger, Weiss, Moran-Oldern, Bettaque, Reill, Traubmann, Koschoska, conductor Seidl; Covent Garden, 1892, with Grengg, Alvary, Lissman, Lieban, Ende-Andriessen, Bettaque, Fröhlich, Traubman, Ralph, Schumann-Heink, Dome, Simon, Wiegand, Litter, conductor Mahler; in English, 1908, with Whitehill, Hedmont, Meux, Bechstein, Borghyld Bryhn, Walter Hyde, Radford, Thornton, conductor Richter.

## CHARACTERS

| | | |
|---|---|---|
| Wotan | ⎫ | Bass-Baritone |
| Donner | ⎪ *Gods* | Bass-Baritone |
| Froh | ⎬ | Tenor |
| Loge | ⎭ | Tenor |
| Fasolt | ⎫ *Giants* | Bass-Baritone |
| Fafner | ⎭ | Bass |
| Alberich | ⎫ *Nibelungs* | Bass-Baritone |
| Mime | ⎭ | Tenor |
| Fricka | ⎫ | Mezzo-Soprano |
| Freia | ⎬ *Goddesses* | Soprano |
| Erda | ⎭ | Mezzo-Soprano |
| Woglinde | ⎫ | Soprano |
| Wellgunde | ⎬ *Rhinedaughters* | Soprano |
| Flosshilde | ⎭ | Mezzo-Soprano |

*Time:* Legendary     *Place:* The bed of the Rhine; a mountainous district near the Rhine; the subterranean caverns of Nibelheim

In *The Rhinegold* we meet with supernatural beings of German mythology—the Rhinedaughters Woglinde, Wellgunde, and Flosshilde, whose duty it is to guard the precious Rhine gold; Wotan, the chief of the gods; his spouse Fricka; Loge, the God of Fire (the diplomat of Walhalla); Freia, the Goddess of Youth and Beauty; her brothers Donner and Froh; Erda, the all-wise woman; the giants Fafner and Fasolt; Alberich and Mime of the race of Nibelungs, cunning, treacherous gnomes who dwell in the bowels of the earth.

The first scene of *The Rhinegold* is laid in the Rhine, at the bottom of the river, where the Rhinedaughters guard the Rhine gold.

The work opens with a wonderfully descriptive Prelude, which depicts with marvellous art (marvellous because so simple) the transition from the quietude of the water-depths to the wavy life of the Rhinedaughters. The double basses intone E flat. Only this note is heard during four bars. Then three contra bassoons add a B flat. The chord, thus formed, sounds until the 136th bar. With the sixteenth bar there flows over this seemingly immovable triad, as the current of a river flows over its immovable bed, the Motive of the Rhine.

A horn intones this motive. Then one horn after another takes it up until its wave-like tones are heard on the eight horns. On the flowing accompaniment of the 'cellos the motive is carried to the woodwind. It rises higher and higher, the other strings successively joining in the accompaniment, which now flows on in gentle undulations until the motive is heard on the high notes of the woodwind, while the violins have joined in the accompaniment. When the theme thus seems to have stirred the waters from their depth to their surface the curtain rises.

The scene shows the bed and flowing waters of the Rhine, the light of day reaching the depths only as a greenish twilight. The current flows on over rugged rocks and through dark chasms.

Woglinde is circling gracefully around the central ridge of rock. To an accompaniment as wavy as the waters through which she swims, she sings to the Motive of the Rhinedaughters.

Meanwhile Alberich has clambered from the depths up to one of the cliffs, and watches the gambols of the Rhinedaughters. As he speaks to them there is a momentary harshness in the music, whose flowing rhythm is broken. In futile endeavours to clamber up to them, he inveighs against the 'slippery slime' which causes him to lose his foothold.

Woglinde, Wellgunde, and Flosshilde in turn gambol almost within his reach, only to dart away again. He curses his own weakness in the Motive of the Nibelungs' Servitude.

Swimming high above him the Rhinedaughters incite him to chase them. Alberich tries to ascend, but always slips and falls. Then his gaze is attracted and held by a glow which suddenly pervades the waves above him and increases until from the highest point of the central cliff a bright, golden ray shoots through the water. Amid the shimmering accompaniment of the violins is heard on the horn the Rhinegold Motive:

With shouts of triumph the Rhinedaughters swim around the rock:

As the river glitters with golden light the Rhinegold Motive rings out brilliantly on the trumpet. The Rhinedaughters gossip with one another, and Alberich thus learns that the light is that of the Rhinegold, and that whoever shall shape a ring from this gold will become invested with great power. We hear the Ring Motive.

Flosshilde bids her sisters cease their prattle, lest some sinister foe should overhear them. Wellgunde and Woglinde ridicule their sister's anxiety, saying that no one would care to filch the gold, because it would give power only to him who abjures or renounces love. At this point is heard the darkly prophetic Motive of the Renunciation of Love.

Alberich reflects on the words of the Rhinedaughters. The Ring Motive occurs both in voice and orchestra in mysterious pianissimo (like an echo of Alberich's sinister thoughts), and is followed by the Motive of Renunciation. Then is heard the sharp, decisive rhythm of the Nibelung Motive. Alberich fiercely springs over to the central rock. The Rhinedaughters scream and dart away in different directions. Alberich has reached the summit of the highest cliff.

'Hark, ye floods! Love I renounce forever!' he cries, and amid the crash of the Rhinegold Motive he seizes the gold and disappears in the depths. With screams of terror the Rhinedaughters dive after the robber through the darkened water, guided by Alberich's mocking laugh.

There is a transformation. Waters and rocks sink. As they disappear, the billowy accompaniment sinks lower and lower in the orchestra. Above it rises once more the Motive of Renunciation. The Ring Motive is heard, and then, as the waves change into nebulous clouds, the billowy accompaniment rises pianissimo until, with a repetition of the Ring Motive, the action passes to the second scene. One crime has already been committed—the theft of the Rhine gold by Alberich. How that crime and the ring which he shapes from the gold inspire other crimes is told in the course of the following scenes of *The Rhinegold*. Hence the significance of the Ring Motive as a connecting link between the first and second scenes.

Scene II.     Dawn illumines a castle with glittering turrets on a rocky height at the back. Through a deep valley between this and the foreground flows the Rhine.

The Walhalla Motive now heard is a motive of superb beauty. It greets us again and again in *The Rhinegold* and frequently in the later music-dramas of the cycle. Walhalla is the abode of gods and heroes. Its motive is divinely, heroically beautiful. Though essentially broad and stately, it often assumes a tender mood, like the chivalric gentleness which every hero feels toward woman.

Fricka lies asleep at Wotan's side. As she awakens, her eyes fall on the castle. In her surprise she calls to her spouse. Wotan dreams on, the Ring Motive and later the Walhalla Motive being heard in the orchestra, for with the ring Wotan is planning to compensate the giants for building Walhalla, instead of rewarding them by presenting Freia to them as he has promised. As he opens his eyes and sees the castle you hear the Spear Motive, which is a characteristic variation of the Motive of Compact. For Wotan should enforce, if needful, the compacts of the gods with his spear.

Wotan sings of the glory of Walhalla. Fricka reminds him of his compact with the giants to deliver over to them for their work in building Walhalla, Freia, the Goddess of Youth and Beauty. This introduces on the 'cellos and double basses the Motive of Compact, a theme expressive of the binding force of law and with the inherent dignity and power of the sense of justice.

Wotan charges Fricka that she was as anxious as he to have Walhalla built. Fricka answers that she desired to have it erected in order to persuade him to lead a more domestic life. At Fricka's words,

'Halls, bright and gleaming,'

the Fricka Motive is heard, a caressing motive of much grace and beauty.

It is also prominent in Wotan's reply immediately following.

Wotan tells Fricka that he never really intended to give up Freia to the giants. Chromatics, like little tongues of flame, appear in the accompaniment. They are suggestive of the Loge Motive, for with the aid of Loge the God of Fire, Wotan hopes to trick the giants and save Freia.

'Then save her at once!' calls Fricka, as Freia enters in hasty flight. The following is the Freia Motive:

With Freia's exclamations that the giants are pursuing her, the first suggestion of the Giant Motive appears and as these 'great, hulking fellows' enter, the heavy, clumsy Giant Motive is heard in its entirety:

For the giants, Fasolt and Fafner, have come to demand that Wotan deliver up to them Freia, according to his promise when they agreed to build Walhalla for him. In the ensuing scene, in which Wotan parleys with the giants, the Giant Motive, the Walhalla Motive, the Motive of the Compact, and the first bar of the Freia Motive figure until Fasolt's threatening words,

'Peace wane when you break your compact,'

when there is heard a version of the Motive of Compact characteristic enough to be distinguished as the Motive of Compact with the Giants:

The Walhalla, Giant, and Freia Motives again are heard until Fafner speaks of the golden apples which grow in Freia's garden. These golden apples are the fruit of which the gods partake in order to enjoy eternal youth. The Motive of Eternal Youth, which now appears, is one of the loveliest in the cycle. It seems as though age could not wither it, nor custom stale its infinite variety.

Its first bar is reminiscent of the Ring Motive, for there is subtle relationship between the Golden Apples of Freia and the Rhine gold. Here is the Motive of Eternal Youth:

It is finely combined with the Giant Motive at Fafner's words:

'Let her forthwith be torn from them all.'

Froh and Donner, Freia's brothers, enter hastily to save their sister. Froh clasps her in his arms, while Donner confronts the giants, the Motive of Eternal Youth rings out triumphantly on the horns and woodwind. But Freia's hope is short-lived. For though Wotan desires to keep Freia in Walhalla, he dare not offend the giants. At this critical moment, however, he sees his cunning adviser, Loge, approaching. These are Loge's characteristic Motives:

Wotan upbraids Loge for not having discovered something which the giants would be willing to accept as a substitute for Freia. Loge says he has travelled the world over without finding aught that would compensate man for the renunciation of a lovely woman. This leads to Loge's narrative of his wanderings. With great cunning he tells Wotan of the theft of the Rhine gold and of the wondrous worth of a ring shaped from the gold. Thus he incites the listening giants to ask for it as a compensation for giving up Freia. Hence Wagner, as Loge begins his narrative, has blended, with a marvellous sense of musical beauty and dramatic fitness, two phrases: the Freia Motive and the accompaniment to the Rhinedaughters' Shout of Triumph in the first scene. This music continues until Loge says that he discovered but one person (Alberich) who was willing to renounce love. Then the Rhinegold Motive is sounded in a minor key and immediately afterward is heard the Motive of Renunciation.

Loge next tells how Alberich stole the gold. He has already excited the curiosity of the giants, and when Fafner asks him what power Alberich will gain through the possession of the gold, he dwells upon the magical attributes of the ring shaped from Rhine gold.

Loge's diplomacy is beginning to bear results. Fafner tells Fasolt that he deems the possession of the gold more important than Freia. Notice here how the Freia Motive, so prominent when the giants insisted on her as their compensation, is relegated to the bass and how the Rhinegold Motive breaks in upon the Motive of Eternal Youth, as Fafner and Fasolt again advance toward Wotan, and bid him wrest the gold from Alberich and give it to them as ransom for Freia. Wotan refuses, for he himself now lusts for the ring made of Rhine gold. The giants, having proclaimed that they will give Wotan until evening to determine upon his course, seize Freia and drag her away. Pallor now settles upon the faces of the gods; they seem to have grown older. They are affected by the absence of Freia, the Goddess of Youth, whose motives are but palely reflected by the orchestra. At last Wotan proclaims that he will go with Loge to Nibelung and wrest the entire treasure of Rhine gold from Alberich as ransom for Freia.

Loge disappears down a crevice in the side of the rock. From it a sulphurous vapour at once issues. When Wotan has followed Loge into the cleft the vapour fills the stage and conceals the remaining characters. The vapours thicken to a black cloud, continually rising upward until rocky chasms are seen. These have an upward motion, so that the stage appears to be sinking

PLATE XI. Bayreuth 1952; *Götterdämmerung*. Wieland Wagner's production and sets for the gathering of the Gibichung vassals, and Siegfried's funeral procession.

PLATE XII. Bayeuth 1951; *Parsifal*. George London is Amfortas, and sets and production are by Wieland Wagner.

deeper and deeper. With a *molto vivace* the orchestra dashes into the Motive of Flight. From various distant points ruddy gleams of light illumine the chasms, and when the Flight Motive has died away, only the increasing clangour of the smithies is heard from all directions. This is the typical Nibelung Motive, characteristic of

Alberich's Nibelungs toiling at the anvil for him. Gradually the sounds grow fainter. Then as the Ring Motive resounds like a shout of malicious triumph (expressive of Alberich's malignant joy at his possession of power), there is seen a subterranean cavern, apparently of illimitable depth, from which narrow shafts lead in all directions.

Scene III. Alberich enters from a side cleft dragging after him the shrieking Mime. The latter lets fall a helmet which Alberich at once seizes. It is the Tarnhelmet, made of Rhine gold, the wearing of which enables the wearer to become invisible or assume any shape. As Alberich closely examines the helmet the Motive of the Tarnhelmet is heard.

It is mysterious, uncanny. To test its power Alberich puts it on and changes into a column of vapour. He asks Mime if he is visible, and when Mime answers in the negative Alberich cries out shrilly, 'Then feel me instead,' at the same time making poor Mime writhe under the blows of a visible scourge. Alberich then departs—still in the form of a vaporous column—to announce to the Nibelungs that they are henceforth his slavish subjects. Mime cowers down with fear and pain.

Wotan and Loge enter from one of the upper shafts. Mime tells them how Alberich has become all-powerful through the ring and the Tarnhelmet made of the Rhine gold. Then Alberich, who has taken off the Tarnhelmet and hung it from his girdle, is seen in the distance, driving a crowd of Nibelungs before him from the caves below. They are laden with gold and silver, which he forces them to pile up in one place and so form a hoard. He suddenly perceives Wotan and Loge. After abusing Mime for permitting strangers to enter Nibelheim, he commands the Nibelungs to descend again into the cavern in search of new treasure for him. They hesitate. You hear the Ring Motive. Alberich draws the ring from his finger, stretches it threateningly towards the Nibelungs, and commands them to obey their master.

They disperse in headlong flight, with Mime, into the cavernous recesses. Alberich looks with mistrust upon Wotan and Loge. Wotan tells him they have heard report of his wealth and power and have come to ascertain if it is true. The Nibelung points to the hoard. He boasts that the whole world will come under his sway (Ring Motive), that the gods who now laugh and love in the enjoyment of youth and beauty will become subject to him (Freia Motive); for he has abjured love (Motive of Renunciation). Hence, even the gods in Walhalla shall dread him (Walhalla Motive) and he bids them beware of the time when the night-begotten host of the Nibelungs shall rise from Nibelheim into the realm of daylight. (Rhinegold Motive followed by Walhalla Motive, for it is through the power gained by the Rhine gold that Alberich hopes to possess himself of Walhalla.) Loge cunningly flatters Alberich, and when the latter tells him of the Tarnhelmet, feigns disbelief of Alberich's statements. Alberich, to prove their truth, puts on the helmet and transforms himself into a huge serpent. The Serpent Motive expresses the windings and writhings of the monster. The serpent vanishes and Alberich reappears. When Loge doubts if Alberich can transform himself into something very small, the Nibelung changes into a toad. Now is Loge's chance. He calls Wotan to set his foot on the toad. As Wotan does so, Loge puts his hand to its head and seizes the Tarnhelmet. Alberich is seen writhing under Wotan's foot. Loge binds Alberich; both seize him, drag him to the shaft from which they descended and disappear.

Accompanied by the orchestra, the scene changes in the reverse direction to that in which it changed when Wotan and Loge were descending to Nibelheim. The Ring Motive dies away from crashing fortissimo to piano, to be succeeded by the dark Motive of Renunciation. Then is heard the clangour of the Nibelung smithies. The Giant, Walhalla, Loge, and Servitude Motives follow the last with crushing force as Wotan and Loge emerge from the cleft, dragging the pinioned Alberich with them. His lease of power was brief. He is again in a condition of servitude.

Scene IV.    A pale mist still veils the prospect as at the end
of the second scene. Loge and Wotan place Alberich on the ground
and Loge dances around the pinioned Nibelung, mockingly
snapping his fingers at the prisoner. Wotan joins Loge in his
mockery of Alberich. The Nibelung asks what he must give for
his freedom. 'Your hoard and your glittering gold,' is Wotan's
answer. Alberich assents to the ransom and Loge frees the gnome's
right hand. Alberich raises the ring to his lips and murmurs a
secret behest. The Nibelungs emerge from the cleft and heap up
the hoard. Then, as Alberich stretches out the ring toward them,
they rush in terror toward the cleft, into which they disappear.
Alberich now asks for his freedom, but Loge throws the Tarnhelmet on to the heap. Wotan demands that Alberich also give
up the ring. At these words dismay and terror are depicted on the
Nibelung's face. He had hoped to save the ring, but in vain.
Wotan tears it from the gnome's finger. Then Alberich, impelled
by hate and rage, curses the ring. The Motive of the Curse:

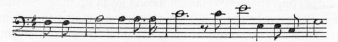

To it should be added the syncopated measures expressive of
the ever-threatening and ever-active Nibelung's Hate:

Amid heavy thuds of the Motive of Servitude Alberich vanishes
in the cleft.

The mist begins to rise. It grows lighter. The Giant Motive and
the Motive of Eternal Youth are heard, for the giants are approaching with Freia. Donner, Froh, and Fricka hasten to greet Wotan.
Fasolt and Fafner enter with Freia. It has grown clear except
that the mist still hides the distant castle. Freia's presence seems
to have restored youth to the gods. Fasolt asks for the ransom for
Freia. Wotan points to the hoard. With staves the giants measure
off a space of the height and width of Freia. That space must be
filled out with treasure. Loge and Froh pile up the hoard, but the
giants are not satisfied even when the Tarnhelmet has been added.
They wish also the ring to fill out a crevice. Wotan turns in anger
away from them.

A bluish light glimmers in the rocky cleft to the right, and through it Erda rises. She warns Wotan against retaining possession of the ring. The Erda Motive bears a strong resemblance to the Rhine Motive. The syncopated notes of the Nibelung's Malevolence, so threateningly indicative of the harm which Alberich is plotting, are also heard in Erda's warning.

Wotan, heeding her words, throws the ring upon the hoard. The giants release Freia, who rushes joyfully towards the gods. Here the Freia Motive combined with the Flight Motive, now no longer agitated but joyful, rings out gleefully. Soon, however, these motives are interrupted by the Giant and Nibelung Motives, and later the Nibelung's Hate and Ring Motive. For Alberich's curse already is beginning its dread work. The giants dispute over the spoils, their dispute waxes to strife, and at last Fafner slays Fasolt and snatches the ring from the dying giant, while, as the gods gaze horror-stricken upon the scene, the Curse Motive resounds with crushing force.

Loge congratulates Wotan on having given up the curse-laden ring. But even Fricka's caresses, as she asks Wotan to lead her into Walhalla, cannot divert the god's mind from dark thoughts, and the Curse Motive accompanies his gloomy reflections—for the ring has passed through his hands. It was he who wrested it from Alberich—and its curse rests on all who have touched it.

Donner ascends to the top of a lofty rock. He gathers the mists around him until he is enveloped by a black cloud. He swings his hammer. There is a flash of lightning, a crash of thunder, and lo! the cloud vanishes. A rainbow bridge spans the valley to Walhalla, which is illumined by the setting sun. Wotan eloquently greets Walhalla, and then, taking Fricka by the hand, leads the procession of the gods into the castle.

The music of this scene is of wondrous eloquence and beauty. Six harps are added to the ordinary orchestral instruments, and as the variegated bridge is seen their arpeggios shimmer like the colours of the rainbow around the broad, majestic Rainbow Motive:

Then the stately Walhalla Motive resounds as the gods gaze,

lost in admiration, at the Walhalla. It gives way to the Ring
Motive as Wotan speaks of the day's ills; and then as he is
inspired by the idea of begetting a race of demigods to conquer
the Nibelungs, there is heard for the first time the Sword Motive:

The cries of the Rhinedaughters greet Wotan. They beg him
to restore the ring to them. But Wotan must remain deaf to their
entreaties. He gave the ring, which he should have restored to
the Rhinedaughters, to the giants, as ransom for Freia.

The Walhalla Motive swells to a majestic climax and the gods
enter the castle. Amid shimmering arpeggios the Rainbow Motive
resounds. The gods have attained the height of their glory—but
the Nibelung's curse is still potent, and it will bring woe upon all
who have possessed or will possess the ring until it is restored to
the Rhinedaughters. Fasolt was only the first victim of Alberich's
curse.                                                            K.

## DIE WALKÜRE
### The Valkyr

Music-drama in three acts, words and music by Richard Wagner. Première,
Munich, June 26, 1870, with Sophie Stehle, Therese Thoma, Frau Kauf-
mann, Heinrich Vogel, August Kinderman, Bausewein, conductor Franz
Wüllner. First performed Beyreuth, 1876, with Materna, Schafsky, Niemann,
Betz, conductor Richter; Academy of Music, New York, in an incomplete
and inadequate performance with Pappenheim, Canissa, Bischoff, Preusser,
conductor Neuendorff; Her Majesty's, London, 1882, with Frau Vogel,
Sachse-Hofmeir, Reicher-Kindermann, Niemann, Scaria, Wiegand, conductor Seidl; Metropolitan, New York, 1885, with Materna, Seidl-Kraus,
Brandt, Schott, Staudigl, Koegel, conductor Damrosch; Covent Garden,
1892, with Ende-Andriessen, Bettaque, Schumann-Heink, Alvary, Reichmann, Weigand, conductor Mahler; 1895 (in English), with Lillian Tree,
Susan Strong, Rose Olitzka, Charles Hedmont, Bispham, Alexander Bevan,
conductor George Henschel.

### CHARACTERS

| | |
|---|---|
| Siegmund | Tenor |
| Hunding | Bass |
| Wotan | Bass-Baritone |
| Sieglinde | Soprano |
| Brünnhilde | Soprano |
| Fricka | Mezzo-Soprano |

Valkyrs (Sopranos and Mezzo-Sopranos): Gerhilde,
Ortlinde, Waltraute, Schwertleite, Helmwige, Siegrune,
Grimgerde, Rossweisse

*Time:* Legendary    *Place:* Interior of Hunding's hut; a rocky
height; the peak of a rocky mountain
(the Brünnhilde rock)

The dramatis personæ in *Die Walküre* are Brünnhilde, the
Valkyr, and her eight sister Valkyrs; Fricka, Sieglinde, Siegmund,
Hunding (the husband of Sieglinde), and Wotan. The action
begins after the forced marriage of Sieglinde to Hunding. The
Wälsungs are in ignorance of the divinity of their father, they
know him only as Wälse.

Act I.    In the introduction to *Das Rheingold*, we saw the
Rhine flowing peacefully toward the sea and the innocent gambols
of the Rhinedaughters. But *Die Walküre* opens in storm and stress.
The peace and happiness of the first scene of the cycle seem to
have vanished from the earth with Alberich's abjuration of love,
his theft of the gold, and Wotan's equally treacherous acts.

This *Walküre* Vorspiel is a masterly representation in tone of
a storm gathering for its last infuriated onslaught. The elements
are unleashed. The wind sweeps through the forest. Lightning
flashes in jagged streaks across the black heavens. There is a
crash of thunder and the storm has spent its force.

The two leading motives are employed in this introduction.
They are the Storm Motive and the Donner Motive. The Storm
Motive is as follows:

These themes are elemental. From them Wagner has composed
storm music of convincing power.

The storm gradually dies away. Before it has quite passed over,
the curtain rises, revealing the large hall of Hunding's dwelling.
This hall is built around a huge ash-tree, whose trunk and branches
pierce the roof. In the right foreground is a large open hearth; in
the background a large door. A few steps in the left foreground
lead up to the door of an inner room. The furniture of the hall
is primitive and rude. It consists chiefly of a table, bench, and
stools in front of the ash-tree.

The door in the background is opened from without. Siegmund stands in the entrance. He seems exhausted, like a fugitive who has reached the limit of his powers of endurance. Seeing no one in the hall, he staggers toward the hearth and sinks upon a bearskin rug before it.

Wagner's treatment of this scene is masterly. As Siegmund stands in the entrance we hear the Siegmund Motive. This is a sad, weary strain on 'cellos and basses. It seems the wearier for the burden of an accompanying figure on the horns, beneath which it seems to stagger as Siegmund staggers toward the hearth. Thus the music not only reflects Siegmund's weary mien, but accompanies most graphically his weary gait. Perhaps Wagner's intention was more metaphysical. Maybe the burden beneath which the Siegmund Motive staggers is the curse of Alberich. It is through that curse that Siegmund's life has been one of storm and stress.

When the storm-beaten Wälsung has sunk upon the rug the Siegmund Motive is followed by the Storm Motive, *pp*—and the storm has died away. The door of the room to the left opens and a young woman—Sieglinde—appears. She has heard someone enter, and, thinking her husband returned, has come forth to meet him—not impelled to this by love, but by fear. For Hunding had, while her father and kinsmen were away on the hunt, laid waste their dwelling and abducted her and forcibly married her. Ill-fated herself, she is moved to compassion at sight of the storm-driven fugitive before the hearth, and bends over him.

Her compassionate action is accompanied by a new motive, which by Wagner's commentators has been entitled the Motive of Compassion. But it seems to me to have a further meaning as expressing the sympathy between two souls, a tie so subtle that it is at first invisible even to those whom it unites. Siegmund and Sieglinde, it will be remembered, belong to the same race; and though they are at this point of the action unknown to one another, yet, as Sieglinde bends over the hunted, storm-beaten Siegmund, that subtle sympathy causes her to regard him with more solicitude than would be awakened by any other

unfortunate stranger. Hence I have called this motive the
Motive of Sympathy—taking sympathy in its double meaning of
compassion and affinity of feeling:

The beauty of this brief phrase is enhanced by its unpretentiousness. It wells up from the orchestra as spontaneously as pity
mingled with sympathetic sorrow wells up from the heart of a
gentle woman. As it is Siegmund who has awakened these feelings
in Sieglinde, the Motive of Sympathy is heard simultaneously
with the Siegmund Motive.

Siegmund, suddenly raising his head, ejaculates, 'Water, water!'
Sieglinde hastily snatches up a drinking-horn and hands it to
Siegmund. As though new hope were engendered in Siegmund's
breast by Sieglinde's gentle ministration, the Siegmund Motive
rises higher and higher, gathering passion in its upward sweep
and then, combined again with the Motive of Sympathy, sinks
to an expression of heartfelt gratitude. This passage is scored
entirely for strings.

Having quaffed from the proffered cup the stranger lifts a
searching gaze to her features, as if they awakened within him
memories whose significance he himself cannot fathom. She, too,
is strangely affected by his gaze.

Here occurs the Love Motive played throughout as a violoncello solo, with accompaniment of eight violoncellos and two
double basses; exquisite in tone colour and one of the most
tenderly expressive phrases ever penned.

The Love Motive is the mainspring of this act.

Siegmund asks with whom he has found shelter. Sieglinde
replies that the house is Hunding's, and she his wife, and requests
Siegmund to await her husband's return.

> 'Weaponless am I:
> The wounded guest,
> He will surely give shelter,'

is Siegmund's reply. With anxious celerity, Sieglinde asks him to show her his wounds. But, refreshed by the draught of cool spring water and with hope revived by her sympathetic presence, he gathers force and, raising himself to a sitting posture, exclaims that his wounds are but slight; his frame is still firm, and had sword and shield held half so well, he would not have fled from his foes. His strength was spent in flight through the storm, but the night that sank on his vision has yielded again to the sunshine of Sieglinde's presence. At these words the Motive of Sympathy rises like a sweet hope. Sieglinde fills the drinking-horn with mead and offers it to Siegmund. He asks her to take the first sip. She does so and then hands it to him. His eyes rest upon her while he drinks. As he returns the drinking-horn to her there are traces of deep emotion in his mien. He sighs and gloomily bows his head. The action at this point is most expressively accompanied by the orchestra. Specially noteworthy is an impassioned upward sweep of the Motive of Sympathy as Siegmund regards Sieglinde.

In a voice that trembles with emotion, he says: 'You have harboured one whom misfortune follows wherever he wends his footsteps. Lest through me misfortune enter this house, I will depart.' With firm, determined strides he already has reached the door, when she, forgetting all in the vague memories that his presence has stirred within her, calls after him:

'Tarry! You cannot bring sorrow to the house where sorrow already reigns!'

Her words are followed by a phrase weighted with sorrow, the Wälsung Motive:

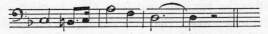

Siegmund returns to the hearth, while she, as if shamed by her outburst of feeling, allows her eyes to sink toward the ground. Leaning against the hearth, he rests his calm, steady gaze upon her, until she again raises her eyes to his, and they regard each other in long silence and with deep emotion. The woman is the first to start. She hears Hunding, and soon afterward he stands upon the threshold looking darkly upon his wife and the stranger.

With the approach of Hunding there is a sudden change in the character of the music. We hear the Hunding Motive, *pp*. Then

as he stands upon the threshold, this motive resounds with dread
power on the tubas:

The woman, anticipating her husband's inquiry, explains that
she had discovered the stranger lying exhausted at the hearth
and given him shelter. With an assumed graciousness that makes
him, if anything, more forbidding, Hunding orders her prepare
the meal.

'Your name and story?' he asks, after they have seated themselves at the table in front of the ash-tree. Slowly, as if oppressed
by heavy memories, he begins his story, carefully, however, continuing to conceal his name, since, for all he knows, Hunding may
be one of the enemies of his race. Amid incredible hardships,
surrounded by enemies against whom he and his kin constantly
were obliged to defend themselves, he grew up in the forest. He
and his father returned from one of their hunts to find the hut
in ashes, his mother a corpse, and no trace of his twin sister. In
one of the combats with their foes he became separated from his
father.

At this point you hear the Walhalla Motive, for Siegmund's
father was none other than Wotan, known to his human descendants, however, only as Wälse. In Wotan's narrative in the next
act it will be discovered that Wotan purposely created these
misfortunes for Siegmund, in order to strengthen him for his task.

Continuing his narrative Siegmund says that, since losing track
of his father, he has wandered from place to place, ever with
misfortune in his wake. That very day he has defended a maid
whom her brothers wished to force into marriage. But when, in
the combat that ensued, he had slain her brothers, she turned
upon him and denounced him as a murderer, while the kinsmen
of the slain, summoned to vengeance, attacked him from all
quarters.

Those whom Siegmund slew were Hunding's kinsmen. Thus
Siegmund's dark fate has driven him to seek shelter in the house
of the very man who is the arch-enemy of his race and is bound
by the laws of kinship to avenge on Siegmund the death of
kinsmen.

As Siegmund concludes his narrative the Wälsung Motive is heard. Gazing with ardent longing toward Sieglinde, he says:

> 'Now know'st thou, questioning wife,
> Why "Peaceful" is not my name.'

These words are sung to a lovely phrase. Then, as Siegmund rises and strides over to the hearth, while Sieglinde, pale and deeply affected by his tale, bows her head, there is heard on the horns, bassoons, violas, and 'cellos a motive expressive of the heroic fortitude of the Wälsungs in struggling against their fate. It is the Motive of the Wälsung's Heroism, a motive steeped in the tragedy of futile struggle against destiny.

The sombre visage at the head of the table has grown even darker and more threatening. Hunding rises. 'I know a ruthless race to whom nothing is sacred, and hated of all,' he says. 'Mine were the kinsmen you slew. I, too, was summoned from my home to take blood vengeance upon the slayer. Returning, I find him here. You have been offered shelter for the night, and for the night you are safe. But to-morrow be prepared to defend yourself.

Left alone, Siegmund's gloomy thoughts are accompanied by the threatening rhythm of the Hunding Motive and the Sword Motive in a minor key, for Siegmund is still weaponless.

> 'A sword my father did promise
> .      .      .      .      .      .      .
> Wälse! Wälse! Where is thy sword!'

The Sword Motive rings out like a shout of triumph. As the embers of the fire collapse, there is seen in the glare, that for a moment falls upon the ash-tree, the hilt of a sword whose blade is buried in the trunk of the tree at the point upon which Sieglinde's look last rested. While the Motive of the Sword gently rises and falls, like the coming and going of a lovely memory, Siegmund apostrophises the sheen as the reflection of Sieglinde's glance. And although the embers die out, and night falls upon the scene,

in Siegmund's thoughts the memory of that pitying, loving look
glimmers on.

A moment later, Sieglinde is by his side. She has given Hunding
a sleeping-potion. She will point out a weapon to Siegmund—a
sword. If he can wield it she will call him the greatest hero, for
only the mightiest can wield it. The music quickens with the
subdued excitement in the breasts of the two Wälsungs. You hear
the Sword Motive and above it, on horns, clarinet, and oboe, a
new motive—that of the Wälsung's Call to Victory:

for Sieglinde hopes that with the sword the stranger, who has
so quickly awakened love in her breast, will overcome Hunding.
This motive has a resistless, onward sweep. Sieglinde, amid the
strains of the stately Walhalla Motive, followed by the Sword
Motive, narrates the story of the sword. While Hunding and his
kinsmen were feasting in honour of her forced marriage with
him, an aged stranger entered the hall. The men knew him not
and shrank from his fiery glance. But upon her his look rested
with tender compassion. With a mighty thrust he buried a sword
up to its hilt in the trunk of the ash-tree. Whoever drew it from
its sheath to him it should belong. The stranger went his way.
One after another the strong men tugged at the hilt—but in vain.
Then she knew who the aged stranger was and for whom the sword
was destined.

The Sword Motive rings out like a joyous shout, and Sieglinde's
voice mingles with the triumphant notes of the Wälsung's Call
to Victory as she turns to Siegmund:

'O, found I in thee
The friend in need!'

Then is heard the Motive of the Wälsung's Heroism, now no
longer full of tragic import, but forceful and defiant—and Siegmund holds Sieglinde in his embrace.

There is a rush of wind. The woven hangings flap and fall. As
the lovers turn, a glorious sight greets their eyes. The landscape
is illumined by the moon. All nature seems to be throbbing in

unison with the hearts of the lovers, and, turning to the woman, Siegmund greets her with the Love Song:

The Love Motive, impassioned, irresistible, sweeps through the harmonies—and Love and Spring are united. The Love Motive also pulsates through Sieglinde's ecstatic reply after she has given herself fully up to Siegmund in the Flight Motive—for before his coming her woes have fled as winter flies before the coming of spring. With Siegmund's exclamation:

> 'Oh, wondrous vision!
> Rapturous woman!'

there rises from the orchestra like a vision of loveliness the Motive of Freia, the Venus of German mythology. In its embrace it folds this pulsating theme:

It throbs on like a love-kiss until it seemingly yields to the blandishments of this caressing phrase:

This throbbing, pulsating, caressing music is succeeded by a moment of repose. The woman again gazes searchingly into the man's features. She has seen his face before. It was when she saw her own reflection in a brook! And his voice? It seems to her like an echo of her own. And his glance; has it never before rested on her? She is sure it has; it was when the stranger thrust the sword into the ash-tree.

He who thrust the sword into the tree was of her own race, the Wälsungs. Who is he?

'I, too, have seen that light, but in your eyes!' exclaimed the fugitive. 'I, too, am of your race. I, too, am a Wälsung, my father none other than Wälse himself."

'Was Wälse your father?' she cries ecstatically. 'For you, then, this sword was thrust in the tree! Let me name you, as I recall you from far back in my childhood, Siegmund—Siegmund—Siegmund!'

'Yes, I am Siegmund; and you, too, I now know well. You are Sieglinde. Fate has willed that we two of our unhappy race, shall meet again and save each other or perish together.'

Then, leaping upon the table, he draws the sword from the tree as a blade from its scabbard. Brandishing it in triumph, he leaps to the floor and, clasping Sieglinde, rushes forth with her into the night.

And the music? It fairly seethes with excitement. As Siegmund leaps upon the table, the Motive of the Wälsung's Heroism rings out as if in defiance of the enemies of the race. The Sword Motive —and he has grasped the hilt; the Motive of Compact, ominous of the fatality which hangs over the Wälsungs; the Motive of Renunciation, with its threatening import; then the Sword Motive —brilliant like the glitter of refulgent steel—and Siegmund has unsheathed the sword. The Wälsung's Call to Victory, like a song of triumph; a superb upward sweep of the Sword Motive; the Love Motive, now rushing onward in the very ecstasy of passion, and Siegmund holds in his embrace Sieglinde, his bride—of the same doomed race as himself!

Act II.    In the Vorspiel the orchestra dashes into the Motive of Flight. The Sword Motive in 9–8 rhythm closely resembles the Motive of the Valkyr's Ride, and the Flight Motive in the version in which it appears is much like the Valkyr's Shout. The Ride and the Shout are heard in the course of the Vorspiel, the former with tremendous force on trumpets and trombones as the curtain rises on a wild, rocky mountain pass, at the back of which, through a natural rock-formed arch, a gorge slopes downward.

In the foreground stands Wotan, armed with spear, shield, and helmet. Before him is Brünnhilde in the costume of the Valkyr. The stormy spirit of the Vorspiel pervades the music of Wotan's command to Brünnhilde that she bridle her steed for battle and spur it to the fray to do combat for Siegmund against Hunding. Brünnhilde greets Wotan's command with the joyous Shout of the Valkyrs:

Ho -jo -to ho . . . . . !

The accompanying figure is based on the Motive of the Ride of the Valkyrs:

Brünnhilde faces Wotan, and with delightful banter calls to him that Fricka is approaching in her ram-drawn chariot. Fricka advances toward Wotan, Brünnhilde having meanwhile disappeared behind the mountain height. Fricka is the protector of the marriage vow, and as such she has come in anger to demand from Wotan vengeance on behalf of Hunding. Her angry, passionate demeanour is reflected by the orchestra, and this effective musical expression of Fricka's ire is often heard in the course of the scene. Wotan, though knowing well what has brought Fricka upon the scene, feigns ignorance of the cause of her agitation and asks what it is that harasses her. Her reply is preceded by the stern Hunding Motive. She tells Wotan that she, as the protectress of the sanctity of the marriage vow, has heard Hunding's voice calling for vengeance upon the Wälsung twins. Her words, 'His voice for vengeance is raised,' are set to a phrase strongly suggestive of Alberich's curse. It seems as though the avenging Nibelung were pursuing Wotan's children and thus striking a blow at Wotan himself through Fricka. The Love Motive breathes through Wotan's protest that Siegmund and Sieglinde only yielded to the music of the spring night. Wotan argues that Siegmund and Sieglinde are true lovers, and Fricka should smile instead of venting her wrath on them. The Motive of the Love Song, the Love Motive, and the caressing phrase heard in the love scene are beautifully blended with Wotan's words. In strong contrast to these motives is the music in Fricka's outburst of wrath, introduced by the phrase reflecting her ire, which is repeated several times in the course of this episode. Wotan explains to her why he begat the Wälsung race and the hopes he has founded upon it. But Fricka mistrusts him. What can mortals accomplish that the gods, who are far mightier than mortals, cannot accomplish? Hunding must be avenged on Siegmund and Sieglinde. Wotan must withdraw his protection from Siegmund. Now appears a phrase which expresses Wotan's impotent wrath —impotent because Fricka brings forward the unanswerable argument that if the Wälsungs go unpunished by her, as guardian

of the marriage vow, she, the Queen of the gods, will be held up
to the scorn of mankind.

Wotan would fain save the Wälsungs. But Fricka's argument is
conclusive. He cannot protect Siegmund and Sieglinde, because
their escape from punishment would bring degradation upon the
Queen-goddess and the whole race of the gods, and result in their
immediate fall. Wotan's wrath rises at the thought of sacrificing
his beloved children to the vengeance of Hunding, but he is
impotent. His far-reaching plans are brought to nought. He sees
the hope of having the ring restored to the Rhinedaughters by
the voluntary act of a hero of the Wälsung race vanish. The curse
of Alberich hangs over him like a dark, threatening cloud. The
Motive of Wotan's Wrath is as follows:

Brünnhilde's joyous shouts are heard from the height. Wotan
exclaims that he had summoned the Valkyr to do battle for
Siegmund. In broad, stately measures, Fricka proclaims that her
honour shall be guarded by Brünnhilde's shield and demands of
Wotan an oath that in the coming combat the Wälsung shall fall.
Wotan takes the oath and throws himself dejectedly down upon
a rocky seat. Fricka strides toward the back.

In this scene we have witnessed the spectacle of a mighty god
vainly struggling to avert ruin from his race. That it is due to
irresistible fate and not merely to Fricka that Wotan's plans
succumb, is made clear by the darkly ominous notes of Alberich's
Curse, which resound as Wotan, wrapt in gloomy brooding,
leans back against the rocky seat, and also when, in a paroxysm
of despair, he gives vent to his feelings, a passage which, for over-
powering intensity of expression, stands out even from among
Wagner's writings. The final words of this outburst of grief:

<blockquote>'The saddest I among all men,'</blockquote>

are set to this variant of the Motive of Renunciation; the meaning
of this phrase having been expanded from the renunciation of
love by Alberich to cover the renunciation of happiness which is
forced upon Wotan by avenging fate:

Brünnhilde casts away shield, spear, and helmet, and sinking down at Wotan's feet looks up to him with affectionate anxiety. Here we see in the Valkyr the touch of tenderness, without which a truly heroic character is never complete.

Musically it is beautifully expressed by the Love Motive, which, when Wotan, as if awakening from a reverie, fondly strokes her hair, goes over into the Siegmund Motive. It is over the fate of his beloved Wälsungs that Wotan has been brooding. There is a wonderfully soft yet rich melody on four horns. It is one of those beautiful details in which Wagner's works abound.

In Wotan's narrative, which now follows, the chief of the gods tells Brünnhilde of the events which have brought this sorrow upon him. The motives heard in Wotan's narrative will be recognised, except one, which is new. This is expressive of the stress to which the gods are subjected through Wotan's crime. It is first heard when Wotan tells of the hero who alone can regain the ring. It is the Motive of the Gods' Stress.

Excited by remorse and despair Wotan bids farewell to the glory of the gods. Then he in terrible mockery blesses the Nibelung's heir—for Alberich has wedded and to him has been born a son, upon whom the Nibelung depends to continue his death struggle with the gods. Terrified by this outburst of wrath, Brünnhilde asks what her duty shall be in the approaching combat. Wotan commands her to do Fricka's bidding and withdraw protection from Siegmund. In vain Brünnhilde pleads for the Wälsung whom she knows Wotan loves, and wished a victor until Fricka exacted a promise from him to avenge Hunding. But her pleading is in vain. Wotan is no longer the all-powerful chief of the gods—through his breach of faith he has become the slave of fate.

Slowly and sadly Brünnhilde bends down for her weapons, her actions being accompanied by the Valkyr Motive. Bereft of its stormy impetuosity it is as sad as her thoughts. Lost in these reflections, which find beautiful expression in the orchestra, she turns toward the background.

Suddenly the sadly expressive phrases are interrupted by the

Motive of Flight. Looking down into the valley the Valkyr
perceives Siegmund and Sieglinde approaching in hasty flight.
For hours they have toiled forward, yet never have the fugitives
been able to shake off the dread sound of Hunding's horn as he
called upon his kinsmen to redouble their efforts to overtake the
two Wälsungs. Terror has begun to unsettle Sieglinde's reason.
When Siegmund bids her rest she stares wildly before her, then
gazes with growing rapture into his eyes and throws her arms
around his neck, only to shriek suddenly: 'Away, away!' as she
hears the distant horn-calls, then to grow rigid and stare vacantly
before her as Siegmund announces to her that here he proposes
to end their flight, here await Hunding, and test the temper of
Wälse's sword. At last, utterly overcome by the strain of flight
with the avenger on the trail, she faints. Slowly Siegmund lets
himself down on a rocky seat, drawing her with him, so that
when he is seated her head rests on his lap. Tenderly he looks
down upon the companion of his flight, and, while, like a mournful memory, the orchestra intones the Love Motive, he presses a
kiss upon her brow. As he looks up from Sieglinde he sees standing on the rock above them a shining apparition in flowing robes,
breastplate, and helmet, and leaning upon a spear. It is Brünnhilde.

The Motive of Fate—so full of solemn import—is heard.

While her earnest look rests upon him, there is heard the
Motive of the Death-Song, a prophetic strain.

Brünnhilde gazes upon Siegmund. Then there rises from the
orchestra, in strains of rich, soft, alluring beauty, an inversion of
the Walhalla Motive. The Fate, Death-Song, and Walhalla
Motives recur, and Siegmund, raising his eyes and meeting
Brünnhilde's look, questions her and receives her answers. The
episode is so fraught with solemnity that the shadow of death
seems to have fallen upon the scene. The solemn beauty of the
music impresses itself the more upon the listener, because of the
agitated, agonised scene which preceded it.

To the Wälsung, who meets her gaze so calmly, Brünnhilde speaks in solemn tones: 'Siegmund, look on me. I am she whom soon you must prepare to follow.' Then she paints for him in glowing colours the joys of Walhalla, where Wälse, his father, is awaiting him and where he will have heroes for his companions, himself the hero of many valiant deeds. Siegmund listens unmoved. In reply he frames but one question: 'When I enter Walhalla, will Sieglinde be there to greet me?'

When Brünnhilde answers that in Walhalla he will be attended by valkyrs and wishmaidens, but that Sieglinde will not be there to meet him, he scorns the delights she has held out. Let her greet Wotan from him, and Wälse, his father, too, as well as the wishmaidens. He will remain with Sieglinde.

Then the radiant Valkyr, moved by Siegmund's calm determination to sacrifice even a place among the heroes of Walhalla for the woman he loves, makes known to him the fate to which he has been doomed by Wotan. Let Siegmund therefore prepare for Walhalla, but let him leave Sieglinde in her care. She will protect her.

'No other living being but I shall touch her,' exclaims the Wälsung, as he draws his sword. 'If the Wälsung sword is to be shattered on Hunding's spear, to which I am to fall a victim, it first shall bury itself in her breast and save her from a worse fate!' He poises the sword ready for the thrust above the unconscious Sieglinde.

'Hold!' cries Brünnhilde, thrilled by his heroic love. 'Whatever the consequences which Wotan, in his wrath, shall visit upon me, to-day, for the first time I disobey him. Sieglinde shall live, and with her Siegmund!'

Hunding's horn-calls sound nearer and nearer. With a last look and a last kiss for Sieglinde, Siegmund gently lays her down and begins to ascend toward the peak. Slowly Sieglinde regains her senses. She looks for Siegmund. Instead of seeing him bending over her she hears Hunding's voice as if from among the clouds, calling him to combat; then Siegmund's accepting the challenge. Suddenly a bright light pierces the clouds. Above her she sees the men fighting, Brünnhilde protecting Siegmund who is aiming a deadly stroke at Hunding.

At that moment, however, the light is diffused with a reddish glow. In it Wotan appears. As Siegmund's sword cuts the air on its errand of death, the god interposes his spear, the sword breaks in two and Hunding thrusts his spear into the defenceless Wälsung's breast. The second victim of Alberich's curse has met his fate.

With a wild shriek, Sieglinde falls to the ground, to be caught up by Brünnhilde and swung upon the Valkyr's charger, which, urged on by its mistress, now herself a fugitive from Wotan's anger, dashes down the defile in headlong flight for the Valkyr rock.

Act III.    The third act opens with the famous 'Ride of the Valkyrs'. The wild maidens of Walhalla coursing upon winged steeds through storm-clouds, their weapons flashing in the gleam of lightning, their weird laughter mingling with the crash of thunder, have come to hold tryst upon the Valkyr rock.

When eight of the Valkyrs have gathered upon the rocky summit of the mountain, they espy Brünnhilde approaching. Instead of a slain hero across her pommel, Brünnhilde bears a woman, and instead of urging her horse to the highest crag, she alights below.

In frantic haste the Valkyr tells her sisters what has transpired, and how Wotan is pursuing her to punish her for her disobedience. One of the Valkyrs ascends the rock and, looking in the direction from which Brünnhilde has come, calls out that even now she can descry the red glow behind the storm-clouds that denotes Wotan's approach. Quickly Brünnhilde bids Sieglinde seek refuge in the forest beyond the Valkyr rock. The latter, who has been lost in gloomy brooding, starts at her rescuer's supplication and in strains replete with mournful beauty begs that she may be left to her fate and follow Siegmund in death. The glorious prophecy in which Brünnhilde now foretells to Sieglinde that she is to become the mother of Siegfried, is based upon the Siegfried Motive:

Sieglinde, in joyous frenzy, blesses Brünnhilde and hastens to find safety in a dense forest to the eastward, the same forest in which Fafner, in the form of a serpent, guards the Rhinegold treasures.

Wotan, in hot pursuit of Brünnhilde, reaches the mountain summit. In vain her sisters entreat him to spare her. He harshly threatens them unless they cease their entreaties, and with wild cries of fear they hastily depart.

In the ensuing scene between Wotan and Brünnhilde, in which the latter seeks to justify her action, is heard one of the most beautiful themes of the cycle.

It is the Motive of Brünnhilde's Pleading, which finds its loveliest expression when she addresses Wotan in the passage beginning:

'Thou, who this love within my breast inspired.'

Brünnhilde is Wotan's favourite daughter, but instead of the loving pride with which he always has been wont to regard her, his features are dark with anger at her disobedience of his command. Throwing herself at her father's feet, she pleads that he himself had intended to save Siegmund and had been turned from his purpose only by Fricka's interference. But Wotan is obdurate: She must be punished. He will cause her to fall into a deep sleep upon the Valkyr rock, which shall become the Brünnhilde rock, and to the first man who finds her and awakens her, she, no longer a Valkyr, but a mere woman, shall fall prey.

This great scene between Wotan and Brünnhilde is introduced by an orchestral passage. The Valkyr lies in penitence at her father's feet. In the expressive orchestral measures the Motive of Wotan's Wrath mingles with that of Brünnhilde's Pleading. The motives thus form a prelude to the scene in which the Valkyr seeks to appease her father's anger, not through a specious plea, but by laying bare the promptings of a noble heart, which forced her, against the chief god's command, to intervene for Siegmund. The Motive of Brünnhilde's Pleading is heard in its simplest form at Brünnhilde's words: 'Was it so shameful what I have done,' and it may be noticed that as she proceeds the Motive of Wotan's Wrath, heard in the accompaniment, grows less stern, until with her plea, 'Soften thy wrath', it assumes a tone of regretful sorrow.

Wotan's feelings toward Brünnhilde have softened for the time from anger to grief that he must mete out punishment for her disobedience. In his reply excitement subsides to gloom. It would be difficult to point to other music more touchingly expressive of deep contrition than the phrase in which Brünnhilde pleads that Wotan himself taught her to love Siegmund. It is here that the Motive of Brünnhilde's Pleading assumes the form in the notation given above. Then we hear from Wotan that he had abandoned Siegmund to his fate, because he had lost hope in the cause of the gods and wished to end his woe in the wreck of the world. The weird terror of the Curse Motive hangs over this outburst of despair. In broad and beautiful strains Wotan then depicts Brünnhilde yielding to her emotions when she intervened for Siegmund.

Brünnhilde makes her last appeal. She tells her father that Sieglinde has found refuge in the forest, and that there she will give birth to a son, Siegfried—the hero for whom the gods have been waiting to overthrow their enemies. If she must suffer for her disobedience, let Wotan surround her sleeping form with a fiery circle which only such a hero will dare penetrate. The Motive of Brünnhilde's Pleading and the Siegfried Motive vie with each other in giving expression to the beauty, tenderness, and majesty of this scene.

Gently the god raises her and tenderly kisses her brow; and thus bids farewell to the best beloved of his daughters. Slowly she sinks upon the rock. He closes her helmet and covers her with her shield. Then, with his spear, he invokes the god of fire. Tongues of flame leap from the crevices of the rock. Wildly fluttering fire breaks out on all sides. The forest beyond glows like a furnace, as Wotan, with a last look at the sleeping form of Brünnhilde, vanishes beyond the fiery circle.

A majestic orchestral passage opens Wotan's farewell to Brünnhilde. In all Wagner's music this scene has no peer. Such tender, mournful beauty has never found expression in music— and this, whether we include the vocal part or the orchestral accompaniment in which figures the lovely Slumber Motive:

Wotan leads Brünnhilde to the rock, upon which she sinks, closes her helmet, and covers her with her shield, then invokes Loge, and, after gazing fondly upon the slumbering Valkyr, vanishes amid the magic flames. The Slumber Motive, the Magic Fire Motive, and the Siegfried Motive combine to place the music of the scene with the most brilliant and beautiful portion of our heritage from the great master-musician. But here, too, lurks Destiny. Towards the close of this glorious finale we hear again the ominous muttering of the Motive of Fate. Brünnhilde may be saved from ignominy, Siegfried may be born to Sieglinde—but the crushing weight of Alberich's curse still rests upon the race of the gods. K.

## SIEGFRIED

Music-drama in three acts, words and music by Richard Wagner. Première, Bayreuth, August 16, 1876, with Unger, Schlosser, Betz, Hill, von Reichenberg, Materna, conductor Richter. First performed Her Majesty's Theatre, London, 1882, with Scaria, Vogel, Schlosser, Schelper, Frau Vogel, Reigler, Schreiber, conductor Seidl; Metropolitan, New York, 1887, with Fischer, Alvary, von Milde, Fererczy, Elmbald, Lilli Lehmann, Brandt, Seidl-Krauss, conductor Seidl; Covent Garden, 1892, with Grengg, Alvary, Lieban, Lorent, Wiegand, Rosa Sucher, Schumann-Heink, Traubmann, conductor Mahler; Manchester (in English), 1901; Covent Garden (in English), 1908, with Clarence Whitehall, Cornelieus, Meux, Bechstein, Agnes Nicholls, Thornton, Hatchard, conductor Richter.

### CHARACTERS

Siegfried ........................................Tenor
Mime .........................................Tenor
Wotan (*disguised as the Wanderer*) ..........Bass-Baritone
Alberich .............................Bass-Baritone
Fafner .........................................Bass
Erda .......................................Contralto
Forest Bird ................................Soprano
Brünnhilde ................................Soprano

*Time:* Legendary      *Place:* A rocky cave in the forest; deep in
                                the forest; wild region at foot of a rocky
                                mount; the Brünnhilde Rock.

The Nibelungs were not present in the dramatic action of *The Valkyr,* though the sinister influence of Alberich shaped the tragedy of Siegmund's death. In *Siegfried* several characters of *Das Rheingold,* who do not take part in *Die Walküre,* reappear. These are the Nibelungs, Alberich and Mime; the giant Fafner, who in the guise of a serpent guards the Nibelung hoard in a cavern, and Erda.

Siegfried has been born of Sieglinde, who died in giving birth to him. This scion of the Wälsung race has been reared by Mime, who found him in the forest by his dead mother's side. Mime is plotting to obtain possession of the ring and of Fafner's other treasures, and hopes to be aided in his designs by the lusty youth. Wotan, disguised as a wanderer, is watching the course of events, again hopeful that a hero of the Wälsung race will free the gods from Alberich's curse. Surrounded by magic fire, Brünnhilde still lies in deep slumber on the Brünnhilde Rock.

The Vorspiel of *Siegfried* is expressive of Mime's planning and plotting. It begins with music of a mysterious brooding character. Mingling with this is the Motive of the Hoard, familiar from *The Rhinegold*. Then is heard the Nibelung Motive. After reaching a forceful climax it passes over to the Motive of the Ring, which rises from pianissimo to a crashing climax. The ring is to be the prize of all Mime's plotting. He hopes to weld the pieces of Siegmund's sword together, and that with this sword Siegfried will slay Fafner. Then Mime will slay Siegfried and possess himself of the ring. Thus it is to serve his own ends only that Mime is craftily rearing Siegfried.

The opening scene shows Mime forging a sword at a natural forge formed in a rocky cave. In a soliloquy he discloses the purpose of his labours and laments that Siegfried shivers every sword which has been forged for him. Could he (Mime) but unite the pieces of Siegmund's sword! At this thought the Sword Motive rings out brilliantly, and is jubilantly repeated, accompanied by a variant of the Walhalla Motive. For if the pieces of the sword were welded together, and Siegfried were with it to slay Fafner, Mime could surreptitiously obtain possession of the ring, slay Siegfried, rule over the gods in Walhalla, and circumvent Alberich's plans for regaining the hoard.

Mime is still at work when Siegfried enters, clad in a wild forest garb. The sturdy youth has captured a bear. He leads it by a rope, with which he gives it full play so that it can make a dash at Mime. As the latter flees terrified behind the forge, Siegfried gives vent to his high spirits in shouts of laughter. Musically his buoyant nature is expressed by a theme inspired by the fresh, joyful spirit of a wild, woodland life. It may be called, to distinguish it from the Siegfried Motive, the Motive of Siegfried the Fearless.

It pervades with its joyous impetuosity the ensuing scene, in which Siegfried has his sport with Mime until, tiring of it, he loosens the rope from the bear's neck and drives the animal back into the forest. In a pretty, graceful phrase Siegfried tells how he blew his horn, hoping it would be answered by a pleasanter companion than Mime. Then he examines the sword which Mime has been forging. The Siegfried Motive resounds as he inveighs against the weapon's weakness, then shivers it on the anvil. The orchestra, with a rush, takes up the Motive of Siegfried the Impetuous.

This is a theme full of youthful snap and dash. Mime tells Siegfried how he tenderly reared him from infancy. The music here is as simple and pretty as a folk-song, for Mime's reminiscences of Siegfried's infancy are set to a charming melody, as though Mime were recalling to Siegfried's memory a cradle song of those days. But Siegfried grows impatient. If Mime really tended him so kindly out of pure affection, why should Mime be so repulsive to him; and yet why should he, in spite of Mime's repulsiveness, always return to the cave? The dwarf explains that he is to Siegfried what the father is to the fledgling. This leads to a beautiful lyric episode. Siegfried says that he saw the birds mating, the deer pairing, the she-wolf nursing her cubs. Whom shall he call Mother? Who is Mime's wife? This episode is pervaded by the lovely Motive of Love-Life.

Mime endeavours to persuade Siegfried that he is his father and mother in one. But Siegfried has noticed that the young of birds and deer and wolves look like the parents. He has seen his features reflected in the brook, and knows he does not resemble the hideous Mime. The notes of the Love-Life Motive pervade this episode. When Siegfried speaks of seeing his own likeness, we also hear the Siegfried Motive. Mime, forced by Siegfried to speak the truth, tells of Sieglinde's death while giving birth to Siegfried. Throughout this scene we find reminiscences of the first act of *The Valkyr*, the Wälsung Motive, the Motive of Sympathy, and the Love Motive. Finally, when Mime produces as evidence of the truth of his words the two pieces of Siegmund's sword, the Sword Motive rings out brilliantly. Siegfried exclaims that Mime must weld the pieces into a trusty weapon. Then follows

Siegfried's 'Wander Song', so full of joyous abandon. Once the sword is welded, he will leave the hated Mime for ever. As the fish darts through the water, as the bird flies so free, he will flee from the repulsive dwarf. With joyous exclamations he runs from the cave into the forest.

The frank, boisterous nature of Siegfried is charmingly portrayed. His buoyant vivacity finds capital expression in the Motives of Siegfried the Fearless, Siegfried the Impetuous, and his 'Wander Song', while the vein of tenderness in his character seems to run through the Love-Life Motive.

Mime has a gloomy soliloquy. It is interrupted by the entrance of Wotan, disguised as a wanderer. At the moment Mime is in despair because he cannot weld the pieces of Siegmund's sword. When the Wanderer departs, he has prophesied that only he who does not know what fear is—only a fearless hero—can weld the fragments, and that through this fearless hero Mime shall lose his life. This prophecy is reached through a somewhat curious process which must be unintelligible to anyone who has not made a study of the libretto. The Wanderer, seating himself, wagers his head that he can correctly answer any three questions which Mime may put to him. Mime then asks: 'What is the race born in the earth's deep bowels?' The Wanderer answers: 'The Nibelungs.' Mime's second question is: 'What race dwells on the earth's back?' The Wanderer replies: 'The race of giants.' Mime finally asks: 'What race dwells on cloudy heights?' The Wanderer answers: 'The race of the gods.' The Wanderer, having thus answered correctly Mime's three questions, now puts three questions to Mime: 'What is that noble race which Wotan ruthlessly dealt with, and yet which he deemeth most dear?' Mime answers correctly: 'The Wälsungs.' Then the Wanderer asks: 'What sword must Siegfried then strike with, dealing to Fafner death?' Mime answers correctly: 'With Siegmund's sword.' 'Who,' asks the Wanderer, 'can weld its fragments?' Mime is terrified, for he cannot answer. Then Wotan utters the prophecy of the fearless hero.

Several motives familiar from *The Rhinegold* and *The Valkyr* are heard here. The Motive of Compact so powerfully expressive of the binding force of law, the Nibelung and Walhalla motives from *The Rhinegold*, and the Wälsung's Heroism Motives from the first act of *The Valkyr*, are among these.

When the Wanderer has vanished in the forest Mime sinks back on his stool in despair. Staring after Wotan into the sunlit forest, the shimmering rays flitting over the soft green mosses with every movement of the branches and each tremor of the leaves seem to him like flickering flames and treacherous will-o'-the-wisps. We hear the Loge Motive familiar from *The Rhinegold* and the finale of *The Valkyr*. At last Mime rises to his feet in terror. He seems to see Fafner in his serpent's guise approaching to devour him, and in a paroxysm of fear he falls with a shriek behind the anvil. Just then Siegfried bursts out of the thicket, and with the fresh, buoyant 'Wander Song' and the Motive of Siegfried the Fearless, the weird mystery which hung over the former scene is dispelled. Siegfried looks about him for Mime until he sees the dwarf lying behind the anvil.

Laughingly the young Wälsung asks the dwarf if he has thus been welding the sword. 'The sword? The sword?' repeats Mime confusedly, as he advances, and his mind wanders back to Wotan's prophecy of the fearless hero. Regaining his senses he tells Siegfried there is one thing he has yet to learn, namely, to be afraid; that his mother charged him (Mime) to teach fear to him (Siegfried). Mime asks Siegfried if he has never felt his heart beating when in the gloaming he heard strange sounds and saw weirdly glimmering lights in the forest. Siegfried replies that he never has. If it is necessary before he goes forth in quest of adventure to learn what fear is, he would like to be taught. But how can Mime teach him?

The Magic Fire Motive and Brünnhilde's Slumber Motive, familiar from Wotan's Farewell and the Magic Fire scene in the third act of *The Valkyr*, are heard here, the former depicting the weirdly glimmering lights with which Mime has sought to infuse dread into Siegfried's breast, the latter prophesying that, penetrating fearlessly the fiery circle, Siegfried will reach Brünnhilde. Then Mime tells Siegfried of Fafner, thinking thus to strike terror into the young Wälsung's breast. But far from it! Siegfried is incited by Mime's words to meet Fafner in combat. Has Mime welded the fragments of Siegmund's sword, asks Siegfried. The dwarf confesses his impotency. Siegfried seizes the fragments. He will forge his own sword. Here begins the great scene of the forging of the sword. Like a shout of victory the Motive of Siegfried the Fearless rings out and the orchestra fairly glows as Siegfried heaps a great mass of coal on the forge-hearth, and, fanning the heat, begins to file away at the fragments of the sword.

The roar of the fire, the sudden intensity of the fierce white heat to which the young Wälsung fans the glow—these we would respectively hear and see were the music given without scenery or action, so graphic is Wagner's score. The Sword Motive leaps like a brilliant tongue of flame over the heavy thuds of a forceful variant of the Motive of Compact, till brightly gleaming runs add to the brilliancy of the score, which reflects all the quickening, quivering effulgence of the scene. How the music flows like a fiery flood and how it hisses as Siegfried pours the molten contents of the crucible into a mould and then plunges the latter into water! The glowing steel lies on the anvil and Siegfried swings the hammer. With every stroke his joyous excitement is intensified.

No - thung! No - thung! Neid - li - ches Schwert!

At last the work is done. He brandishes the sword and with one stroke splits the anvil from top to bottom. With the crash of the Sword Motive, united with the Motive of Siegfried the Fearless, the orchestra dashes into a furious *prestissimo*, and Siegfried, shouting with glee, holds aloft the sword!

Act II.   The second act opens with a darkly portentous
Vorspiel. On the very threshold of it we meet Fafner in his motive,
which is so clearly based on the Giant Motive that there is no
necessity for quoting it. Through themes which are familiar from
earlier portions of the work, the Vorspiel rises to a crashing
*fortissimo*.

The curtain lifts on a thick forest. At the back is the entrance
to Fafner's cave, the lower part of which is hidden by rising
ground in the middle of the stage, which slopes down toward the
back. In the darkness the outlines of a figure are dimly discerned.
It is the Nibelung, Alberich, haunting the domain which hides
the treasures of which he was despoiled. From the forest comes a
gust of wind. A bluish light gleams from the same direction.
Wotan, still in the guise of a Wanderer, enters.

The ensuing scene between Alberich and the Wanderer is, from
a dramatic point of view, episodical. Suffice it to say that the fine
self-poise of Wotan and the maliciously restless character of
Alberich are superbly contrasted. When Wotan has departed the
Nibelung slips into a rocky crevice, where he remains hidden when
Siegfried and Mime enter. Mime endeavours to awaken dread in
Siegfried's heart by describing Fafner's terrible form and powers.
But Siegfried's courage is not weakened. On the contrary, with
heroic impetuosity, he asks to be at once confronted with Fafner.
Mime, well knowing that Fafner will soon awaken and issue from
his cave to meet Siegfried in mortal combat, lingers on in the
hope that both may fall, until the young Wälsung drives him
away.

Now begins a beautiful lyric episode. Siegfried reclines under
a linden-tree, and looks up through the branches. The rustling
of the trees is heard. Over the tremulous whispers of the orchestra
—known from concert programmes as the 'Waldweben' (forest-
weaving)—rises a lovely variant of the Wälsung Motive. Siegfried
is asking himself how his mother may have looked, and this variant
of the theme which was first heard in *The Valkyr*, when Sieglinde
told Siegmund that her home was the home of woe, rises like a
memory of her image. Serenely the sweet strains of the Love-
Life Motive soothe his sad thoughts. Siegfried, once more
entranced by forest sounds, listens intently. Birds' voices greet
him.

The forest voices—the humming of insects, the piping of the

birds, the amorous quiver of the branches—quicken his half-defined aspirations. He listens, but cannot catch the meaning of the song. Perhaps, if he can imitate it, he may understand it. He cuts a reed with his sword and quickly fashions a pipe from it. He blows on it, but it sounds shrill. He may not be able to imitate the song on the reed, but on his silver horn he can wind a wood-land tune. Putting the horn to his lips he makes the forest ring with its notes.

The notes of the horn have awakened Fafner who now, in the guise of a huge dragon, crawls toward Siegfried. Perhaps the less said about the combat between Siegfried and Fafner the better. This scene, which seems very spirited in the libretto, is ridiculous on the stage. The music is highly dramatic. The exultant force of the Motive of Siegfried the Fearless, which rings out as Siegfried rushes upon Fafner, the crashing chord as the serpent roars when Siegfried buries the sword in its heart, the rearing, plunging music as the monster rears and plunges with agony—these are some of the most graphic features of the score.

Siegfried raises his fingers to his lips and licks the blood from them. Immediately after the blood has touched his lips he seems to understand the bird, which has again begun its song, while the forest voices once more weave their tremulous melody. The bird tells Siegfried of the ring and helmet and of the other treasures in Fafner's cave, and Siegfried enters it in quest of them. With his disappearance the forest-weaving suddenly changes to the harsh, scolding notes heard in the beginning of the Nibelheim scene in *The Rhinegold*. Mime slinks in and timidly looks about him to make sure of Fafner's death. At the same time Alberich issues forth from the crevice in which he was concealed. This scene, in which the two Nibelungs berate each other, is capitally treated, and its humour affords a striking contrast to the preceding scenes.

As Siegfried comes out of the cave and brings the ring and helmet from darkness to the light of day, there are heard the Ring Motive, the Motive of the Rhinedaughters' Shout of Triumph, and the Rhinegold Motive. The forest-weaving again begins, and the birds bid the young Wälsung beware of Mime. The dwarf now approaches Siegfried with repulsive sycophancy. But under a smiling face lurks a plotting heart. Siegfried is enabled through the supernatural gifts with which he has become endowed to fathom the purpose of the dwarf, who unconsciously discloses his scheme to poison Siegfried. The young Wälsung slays Mime, who, as he dies, hears Alberich's mocking laugh. Though the Motive of Siegfried the Fearless predominates at this point, we also hear the Nibelung Motive and the Motive of the Curse—indicating Alberich's evil intent towards Siegfried.

Siegfried again reclines under the linden. His soul is tremulous with an undefined longing. As he gazes in almost painful emotion up to the branches and asks if the bird can tell him where he can find a friend, his being seems stirred by awakening passion.

The music quickens with an impetuous phrase, which seems to define the first joyous thrill of passion in the youthful hero. It is the Motive of Love's Joy:

It is interrupted by a beautiful variant of the Motive of Love-Life, which continues until, above the forest-weaving, the bird again thrills him with its tale of a glorious maid who has so long slumbered upon the fire-guarded rock. With the Motive of Love's Joy coursing through the orchestra, the bird flutters from the linden branch, hovers over Siegfried, and hesitatingly flies before him until it takes a definite course towards the background. Siegfried follows the little singer, the Motive of Love's Joy, succeeded by that of Siegfried the Fearless, bringing the act to a close.

Act III.    The third act opens with a stormy introduction in which the Motive of the Ride of the Valkyrs accompanies the Motive of the Gods' Stress, the Compact, and the Erda motives.

Then to the sombre, questioning phrase of the Motive of Fate, the action begins to disclose the significance of this Vorspiel. A wild region at the foot of a rocky mountain is seen. It is night. A fierce storm rages. In dire distress and fearful that through Siegfried and Brünnhilde the rulership of the world may pass from the gods to the human race, Wotan summons Erda from her subterranean dwelling.

But Erda has no counsel for the storm-driven, conscience-stricken god.

The scene reaches its climax in Wotan's noble renunciation of the empire of the world. Weary of strife, weary of struggling against the decree of fate, he renounces his sway. Let the era of human love supplant this dynasty, sweeping away the gods and the Nibelungs in its mighty current; perhaps the twilight of the gods will be the dawn of a more glorious epoch. A phrase of great dignity gives force to Wotan's utterances. It is the Motive of the World's Heritage:

Siegfried enters, guided to the spot by the bird; Wotan checks his progress with the same spear which shivered Siegmund's sword. Siegfried must fight his way to Brünnhilde. With a mighty blow the young Wälsung shatters the spear and Wotan disappears amid the crash of the Motive of Compact—for the spear with which it was the chief god's duty to enforce compacts is shattered. Siegfried stands at the rim of the magic circle. Winding his horn he plunges into the seething flames. Around the Motive of Siegfried the Fearless and the Siegfried Motive flash the Magic Fire and Loge Motives.

The flames, having flashed forth with dazzling brilliancy, gradually pale before the red glow of dawn till a rosy mist envelops the scene. When it rises, the rock and Brünnhilde in deep slumber under the fir-tree, as in the finale of *The Valkyr*, are seen. Siegfried appears on the height in the background. As he gazes upon the scene there are heard the Fate and Slumber Motives and then the orchestra weaves a lovely variant of the Freia Motive. This is followed by the softly caressing strains of the Fricka Motive. Fricka sought to make Wotan faithful to her by bonds of love, and hence the Fricka Motive in this scene does not reflect her personality, but rather the awakening of the love which is to thrill Siegfried when he has beheld Brünnhilde's features. As we see Brünnhilde's charger slumbering in the grove, we hear the Motive of the Valkyr's Ride, and when his gaze is attracted by the sheen of Brünnhilde's armour, the theme of Wotan's Farewell. Approaching the armed slumberer under the fir-tree, Siegfried raises the shield and discloses the figure of the sleeper, the face being almost hidden by the helmet.

Carefully he loosens the helmet. As he takes it off Brünnhilde's face is disclosed and her long curls flow down over her bosom. Siegfried gazes upon her enraptured. Drawing his sword he cuts the rings of mail on both sides, gently lifts off the corselet and greaves, and Brünnhilde, in soft female drapery, lies before him. He starts back in wonder. Notes of impassioned import—the Motive of Love's Joy—express the feelings that well up from his heart as for the first time he beholds a woman. The fearless hero is infused with fear by a slumbering woman. The Wälsung Motive, afterwards beautifully varied with the Motive of Love's Joy, accompanies his utterances, the climax of his emotional excitement being expressed in a majestic *crescendo* of the Freia Motive. A sudden feeling of awe gives him at least the outward appearance of calmness. With the Motive of Fate he faces his destiny; and then, while the Freia Motive rises like a vision of loveliness, he sinks over Brünnhilde, and with closed eyes presses his lips to hers.

Brünnhilde awakens, and with a noble gesture greets in majestic accents her return to the sight of earth. Strains of loftier eloquence than those of her greeting have never been composed. Brünnhilde rises from her magic slumbers in the majesty of womanhood:

With the Motive of Fate she asks who is the hero who has awakened her. The superb Siegfried Motive gives back the proud answer. In rapturous phrases they greet one another. It is the Motive of Love's Greeting,

which unites their voices in impassioned accents until, as if this motive no longer sufficed to express their ecstasy, it is followed by the Motive of Love's Passion,

which, with the Siegfried Motive, rises and falls with the heaving of Brünnhilde's bosom.

These motives course impetuously through this scene. Here and there we have others recalling former portions of the cycle—the Wälsung Motive, when Brünnhilde refers to Siegfried's mother, Sieglinde; the Motive of Brünnhilde's Pleading, when she tells him of her defiance of Wotan's behest; a variant of the Walhalla Motive when she speaks of herself in Walhalla; and the Motive of the World's Heritage, with which Siegfried claims her, this last leading over to a forceful climax of the Motive of Brünnhilde's Pleading, which is followed by a lovely, tranquil episode introduced by the Motive of Love's Peace,

succeeded by a motive, ardent yet tender—the Motive of Siegfried the Protector:

These motives accompany the action most expressively. Brünnhilde still hesitates to cast off for ever the supernatural characteristics of the Valkyr and give herself up entirely to Siegfried. The young hero's growing ecstasy finds expression in the Motive of Love's Joy. At last it awakens a responsive note of purely human passion in Brünnhilde and, answering the proud Siegfried Motive with the jubilant Shout of the Valkyrs and the ecstatic measures of Love's Passion, she proclaims herself his.

With a love duet the music-drama comes to a close. Siegfried, a scion of the Wälsung race, has won Brünnhilde for his bride, and upon her finger has placed the ring fashioned of Rhine gold.

K.

# GÖTTERDÄMMERUNG
## Dusk of the Gods

Music-drama in a prologue and three acts, words and music by Richard Wagner. First performed Bayreuth, August 17, 1876, with Unger, Gura, Seihr, Hill, Materna, conductor Richter. First performed Her Majesty's, London, 1882, with Vogel, Wiegand, Schelper, Biberti, Frau Vogel, Schreiber, Reicher-Kindermann, conductor Seidl; Metropolitan, New York, 1888, with Niemann, Robinson, Fischer, von Milde, Seidl-Krauss, Brandt, Lilli Lehmann, conductor Seidl; Covent Garden, 1892, with Alvery, Knapp, Wiegand, Lissmann, Klafsky, Bettaque, Schumann-Heink, conductor Mahler; 1908 (in English), with Cornelius, Frederick Austin, Meux, Knowles, Perceval Allen, Edith Evans, conductor Richter.

### CHARACTERS
Siegfried ........................................Tenor
Gunther .....................................Baritone
Alberich .............................. Bass-Baritone
Hagen .........................................Bass
Brünnhilde ..................................Soprano

Gutrune ........................................Soprano
Waltraute .............................Mezzo-Soprano
First, Second, and Third Norn ................Contralto,
　　　　　　　　　　　　Mezzo-Soprano, and Soprano
Woglinde, Wellgunde, and Flosshilde ...........Sopranos
　　　　　　　　　　　　　　　and Mezzo-Soprano

Vassals and Women

*Time:* Legendary　　　*Place:* On the Brünnhilde Rock; Gunther's
　　　　　　　　　　castle on the Rhine; wooded district by
　　　　　　　　　　the Rhine.

### THE PROLOGUE

The first scene of the prologue is a weird conference of the
three grey sisters of fate—the Norns who wind the skein of life.
They have met on the Valkyrs' rock and their words forebode the
end of the gods. At last the skein they have been winding breaks
—the final catastrophe is impending.

An orchestral interlude depicts the transition from the unearthly
gloom of the Norn scene to break of day, the climax being reached
in a majestic burst of music as Siegfried and Brünnhilde, he in
full armour, she leading her steed by the bridle, issue forth from
the rocky cavern in the background. This climax owes its eloquence
to three motives—that of the Ride of the Valkyrs and two new
motives, the one as lovely as the other is heroic, the Brünnhilde
Motive,

and the Motive of Siegfried the Hero:

The Brünnhilde Motive expresses the strain of pure, tender
womanhood in the nature of the former Valkyr, and proclaims
her womanly ecstasy over wholly requited love. The Motive of
Siegfried the Hero is clearly developed from the Motive of Siegfried the Fearless. Fearless youth has developed into heroic man.
In this scene Brünnhilde and Siegfried plight their troth, and

Siegfried having given to Brünnhilde the fatal ring and having received from her the steed Grane, which once bore her in her wild course through the storm-clouds, bids her farewell and sets forth in quest of further adventure. Here occur the two new motives already quoted, and a third—the Motive of Heroic Love.

Siegfried disappears with the steed behind the rocks and Brünnhilde stands upon the cliff looking down the valley after him; his horn is heard from below and Brünnhilde with rapturous gesture waves him farewell. The orchestra accompanies the action with the Brünnhilde Motive, the Motive of Siegfried the Fearless, and finally with the theme of the love-duet with which *Siegfried* closed.

The curtain then falls, and between the prologue and the first act an orchestral interlude describes Siegfried's voyage down the Rhine to the castle of the Gibichungs where dwell Gunther, his sister Gutrune, and their half-brother Hagen, the son of Alberich. Through Hagen the curse hurled by Alberich in *The Rhinegold* at all into whose possession the ring shall come, is to be worked out to the end of its fell purpose—Siegfried betrayed and destroyed and the rule of the gods brought to an end by Brünnhilde's expiation.

In the interlude between the prologue and the first act we first hear the brilliant Motive of Siegfried the Fearless and then the gracefully flowing Motives of the Rhine, and of the Rhine-daughters' Shout of Triumph with the Motives of the Rhinegold and Ring. Hagen's malevolent plotting, of which we are soon to learn in the first act, is foreshadowed by the sombre harmonies which suddenly pervade the music.

Act I.    On the river lies the hall of the Gibichungs, where live Gunther, his sister Gutrune, and Hagen, their half-brother. Gutrune is a maiden of fair mien, Gunther a man of average strength and courage, Hagen a sinister plotter, large of stature and sombre of visage. Long he has planned to possess himself of the ring fashioned of Rhine gold. He is aware that it was guarded by the dragon, has been taken from the hoard by Siegfried, and by him given to Brünnhilde.

A descendant, through his father, Alberich, the Nibelung, of a race which practised the black art, Hagen plots to make Siegfried forget Brünnhilde through a love-portion to be administered to him by Gutrune. Then, when under the fiery influence of the potion and all forgetful of Brünnhilde, Siegfried demands Gutrune to wife, the price demanded will be that he win Brünnhilde as bride for Gunther. Before Siegfried comes in sight, before Gunther and Gutrune so much as even know that he is nearing the hall of the Gibichungs, Hagen begins to lay the foundation for this seemingly impossible plot. For it is at this opportune moment Gunther chances to address him:

'Hark, Hagen, and let your answer be true. Do I head the race of the Gibichungs with honour?'

'Aye,' replies Hagen, 'and yet, Gunther, you remain unwived while Gutrune still lacks a husband.' Then he tells Gunther of Brünnhilde—'a circle of flame surrounds the rock on which she dwells, but he who can brave that fire may win her for wife. If Siegfried does this in your stead, and brings her to you as bride, will she not be yours?' Hagen craftily conceals from his half-brother and from Gutrune the fact that Siegfried already has won Brünnhilde for himself; but having aroused in Gunther the desire to possess her, he forthwith unfolds his plan and reminds Gutrune of the magic love-potion which it is in her power to administer to Siegfried.

At the very beginning of this act the Hagen Motive is heard. Particularly noticeable in it are the first two sharp, decisive chords. They recur with dramatic force in the third act when Hagen slays Siegfried. The Hagen Motive is as follows:

This is followed by the Gibichung Motive, the two motives being frequently heard in the opening scene.

Added to these is the Motive of the Love-Potion which is to cause Siegfried to forget Brünnhilde, and conceive a violent passion for Gutrune.

Whatever hesitation may have been in Gutrune's mind, because of the trick which is involved in the plot, vanishes when soon afterwards Siegfried's horn-call announces his approach from the river, and, as he brings his boat up to the bank, she sees this hero among men in all his youthful strength and beauty. She hastily withdraws, to carry out her part in the plot that is to bind him to her.

The three men remain to parley. Hagen skilfully questions Siegfried regarding his combat with the dragon. Has he taken nothing from the hoard?

'Only a ring, which I have left in a woman's keep,' answers Siegfried; 'and this.' He points to a steel network that hangs from his girdle.

'Ha,' exclaims Hagen, 'the Tarnhelmet! I recognise it as the artful work of the Nibelungs. Place it on your head and it enables you to assume any guise.' He then flings open a door and on the platform of a short flight of steps that leads up to it, stands Gutrune, in her hand a drinking-horn which she extends toward Siegfried.

'Welcome, guest, to the house of the Gibichungs. A daughter of the race extends to you this greeting.' And so, while Hagen looks grimly on, the fair Gutrune offers Siegfried the draught that is to transform his whole nature. Courteously, but without regarding her with more than friendly interest, Siegfried takes the horn from her hands and drains it. As if a new element coursed through his veins, there is a sudden change in his manner. Handing the horn back to her he regards her with fiery glances, she blushingly lowering her eyes and withdrawing to the inner apartment. New in this scene is the Gutrune Motive:

'Gunther, your sister's name? Have you a wife?' Siegfried asks excitedly.

'I have set my heart on a woman,' replies Gunther, 'but may not win her. A far-off rock, fire-encircled, is her home.'

'A far-off rock, fire encircled,' repeats Siegfried, as if striving to remember something long forgotten; and when Gunther utters Brünnhilde's name, Siegfried shows by his mien and gesture that it no longer signifies aught to him. The love-potion has caused him to forget her.

'I will press through the circle of flame,' he exclaims. 'I will seize her and bring her to you—if you will give me Gutrune for wife.'

And so the unhallowed bargain is struck and sealed with the oath of blood-brotherhood, and Siegfried departs with Gunther to capture Brünnhilde as bride for the Gibichung. The compact of blood-brotherhood is a most sacred one. Siegfried and Gunther each with his sword draws blood from his arm, which he allows to mingle with wine in a drinking-horn held by Hagen; each lays two fingers upon the horn, and then, having pledged blood-brotherhood, drinks the blood and wine. This ceremony is significantly introduced by the Motive of the Curse followed by the Motive of Compact. Phrases of Siegfried's and Gunther's pledge are set to a new motive whose forceful simplicity effectively expresses the idea of truth. It is the Motive of the Vow:

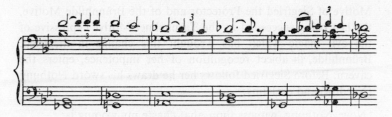

Abruptly following Siegfried's pledge:

'Thus I drink thee troth,'

are those two chords of the Hagen Motive which are heard again
in the third act when the Nibelung has slain Siegfried. It should
perhaps be repeated here that Gunther is not aware of the union
which existed between Brünnhilde and Siegfried, Hagen having
concealed this from his half-brother, who believes that he will
receive the Valkyr in all her goddess-like virginity.

When Siegfried and Gunther have departed and Gutrune,
having sighed her farewell after her lover, has retired, Hagen
broods with wicked glee over the successful inauguration of his
plot. During a brief orchestral interlude a drop-curtain conceals
the scene which, when the curtain again rises, has changed to the
Valkyr's rock, where sits Brünnhilde, lost in contemplation of
the ring, while the Motive of Siegfried the Protector is heard on
the orchestra like a blissful memory of the love scene in *Siegfried*.

Her rapturous reminiscences are interrupted by the sounds of
an approaching storm and from the dark cloud there issues one
of the Valkyrs, Waltraute, who comes to ask of Brünnhilde that
she cast back the ring Siegfried has given her—the ring cursed by
Alberich—into the Rhine, and thus lift the curse from the race of
gods. But Brünnhilde refuses.

It is dusk. The magic fire rising from the valley throws a glow
over the landscape. The notes of Siegfried's horn are heard.
Brünnhilde joyously prepares to meet him. Suddenly she sees a
stranger leap through the flames. It is Siegfried, but through the
Tarnhelmet (the motive of which, followed by the Gunther
Motive, dominates the first part of the scene) he has assumed the
guise of the Gibichung. In vain Brünnhilde seeks to defend herself
with the might which the ring imparts. She is powerless against
the intruder. As he tears the ring from her finger, the Motive of
the Curse resounds with tragic import, followed by echoes of the

Motive of Siegfried the Protector and of the Brünnhilde Motive,
the last being succeeded by the Tarnhelmet Motive expressive of
the evil magic which has wrought this change in Siegfried.
Brünnhilde, in abject recognition of her impotence, enters the
cavern. Before Siegfried follows her he draws his sword Nothung
(Needful) and exclaims:

'Now, Nothung, witness thou, that chaste my wooing is;
 To keep my faith with my brother, separate me from his bride.'

Phrases of the pledge of Brotherhood followed by the Brünnhilde, Gutrune, and Sword Motives accompany his words. The
thuds of the typical Nibelung rhythm resound, and lead to the
last crashing chord of this eventful act.

Act II.    The ominous Motive of the Nibelung's Malevolence
introduces the second act. The curtain rises upon the exterior of
the hall of the Gibichungs. It is night. Hagen, spear in hand and
shield at side, leans in sleep against a pillar of the hall. Alberich
appears to urge Hagen to murder Siegfried and to seize the ring
from his finger. After hearing Hagen's oath that he will be faithful
to the hate he has inherited, Alberich disappears. The weirdness of
the surroundings, the monotony of Hagen's answers, uttered
seemingly in sleep, as if, even when the Nibelung slumbered, his
mind remained active, imbue this scene with mystery.

A charming orchestral interlude depicts the break of day. Its
serene beauty is, however, broken in upon by the Motive of
Hagen's Wicked Glee, which I quote, as it frequently occurs in
the course of succeeding events.

All night Hagen has watched by the bank of the river for the
return of the men from the quest. It is daylight when Siegfried
returns, tells him of his success, and bids him prepare to receive
Gunther and Brünnhilde. On his finger he wears the ring—the
ring made of Rhine gold, and cursed by Alberich—the same with
which he pledged his troth to Brünnhilde, but which in the struggle
of the night, and disguised by the Tarnhelmet as Gunther, he has
torn from her finger—the very ring the possession of which

Hagen craves, and for which he is plotting. Gutrune has joined them. Siegfried leads her into the hall.

Hagen, placing an ox-horn to his lips, blows a loud call toward the four points of the compass, summoning the Gibichung vassals to the festivities attending the double wedding—Siegfried and Gutrune, Gunther and Brünnhilde; and when the Gibichung brings his boat up to the bank, the shore is crowded with men who greet him boisterously, while Brünnhilde stands there pale and with downcast eyes. But as Siegfried leads Gutrune forward to meet Gunther and his bride, and Gunther calls Siegfried by name, Brünnhilde starts, raises her eyes, stares at Siegfried in amazement, drops Gunther's hand, advances, as if by sudden impulse, a step toward the man who awakened her from her magic slumber on the rock, then recoils in horror, her eyes fixed upon him, while all look on in wonder. The Motive of Siegfried the Hero, the Sword Motive, and the Chords of the Hagen Motive emphasise with a tumultuous crash the dramatic significance of the situation. There is a sudden hush—Brünnhilde astounded and dumb, Siegfried unconscious of guilt quietly self-possessed, Gunther, Gutrune, and the vassals silent with amazement—it is during this moment of tension that we hear the motive which expresses the thought uppermost in Brünnhilde, the thought which would find expression in a burst of frenzy were not her wrath held in check by her inability to grasp the meaning of the situation or to fathom the depth of the treachery of which she has been the victim. This is the Motive of Vengeance:

'What troubles Brünnhilde?' composedly asks Siegfried, from whom all memory of his first meeting with the rock maiden and his love for her have been effaced by the potion. Then, observing that she sways and is about to fall, he supports her with his arm.

'Siegfried knows me not!' she whispers faintly, as she looks up into his face.

'There stands your husband,' is Siegfried's reply, as he points to Gunther. The gesture discloses to Brünnhilde's sight the ring upon his finger, the ring he gave her, and which to her horror Gunther, as she supposed, had wrested from her. In the flash of its precious metal she sees the whole significance of the wretched situation in which she finds herself, and discovers the intrigue, the trick, of which she has been the victim. She knows nothing, however, of the treachery Hagen is plotting, or of the love-potion that has aroused in Siegfried an uncontrollable passion to possess Gutrune, has caused him to forget her, and led him to win her for Gunther. There at Gutrune's side, and about to wed her, stands the man she loves. To Brünnhilde, infuriated with jealousy, her pride wounded to the quick, Siegfried appears simply to have betrayed her to Gunther through infatuation for another woman.

'The ring,' she cries out, 'was taken from me by that man,' pointing to Gunther. 'How came it on your finger? Or, if it is not the ring'—again she addresses Gunther—'where is the one you tore from my hand?'

Gunther, knowing nothing about the ring, plainly is perplexed. 'Ha,' cries out Brünnhilde in uncontrollable rage, 'then it was Siegfried disguised as you and not you yourself who won it from me! Know then, Gunther, that you, too, have been betrayed by him. For this man who would wed your sister, and as part of the price bring me to you as bride, was wedded to me!'

In all but Hagen and Siegfried, Brünnhilde's words arouse consternation. Hagen, noting their effect on Gunther, sees in the episode an added opportunity to mould the Gibichung to his plan to do away with Siegfried. The latter, through the effect of the potion, is rendered wholly unconscious of the truth of what Brünnhilde has said. He even has forgotten that he ever has parted with the ring, and, when the men, jealous of Gunther's honour, crowd about him, and Gunther and Gutrune in intense excitement wait on his reply, he calmly proclaims that he found it among the dragon's treasure and never has parted with it. To the truth of this assertion, to a denial of all Brünnhilde has accused him of, he announces himself ready to swear at the point of any spear which is offered for the oath, the strongest manner in which the asseveration can be made and, in the belief of the time, rendering his death certain at the point of that very spear should he swear falsely.

How eloquent the music of these exciting scenes!—Crashing chords of the Ring Motive followed by that of the Curse, as Brünnhilde recognises the ring on Siegfried's finger, the Motive of Vengeance, the Walhalla Motive, as she invokes the gods to witness her humiliation, the touchingly pathetic Motive of Brünnhilde's Pleading, as she vainly strives to awaken fond memories in Siegfried; then again the Motive of Vengeance, as the oath is about to be taken, the Murder Motive and the Hagen Motive at the taking of the oath, for the spear is Hagen's; and in Brünnhilde's asseveration, the Valkyr music coursing through the orchestra.

It is Hagen who offers his weapon for the oath. 'Guardian of honour, hallowed weapon,' swears Siegfried, 'where steel can pierce me, here pierce me; where death can be dealt me, there deal it me, if ever I was wed to Brünnhilde, if ever I have wronged Gutrune's brother.'

At his words, Brünnhilde, livid with rage, strides into the circle of men, and thrusting Siegfried's fingers away from the spearhead, lays her own upon it.

'Guardian of honour, hallowed weapon,' she cries, 'I dedicate your steel to his destruction. I bless your point that it may blight him. For broken are all his oaths, and perjured now he proves himself.'

Siegfried shrugs his shoulders. To him Brünnhilde's imprecations are but the ravings of an overwrought brain. 'Gunther, look to your lady. Give the tameless mountain maid time to rest and recover,' he calls out to Gutrune's brother. 'And now, men, follow us to table, and make merry at our wedding feast!' Then with a laugh and in highest spirits, he throws his arm about Gutrune and draws her after him into the hall, the vassals and women following them.

But Brünnhilde, Hagen, and Gunther remain behind; Brünnhilde half stunned at sight of the man with whom she has exchanged troth, gaily leading another to marriage, as though his vows had been mere chaff; Gunther, suspicious that his honour wittingly has been betrayed by Siegfried, and that Brünnhilde's words are true; Hagen, in whose hands Gunther is like clay, waiting the opportunity to prompt both Brünnhilde and his half-brother to vengeance.

'Coward,' cries Brünnhilde to Gunther, 'to hide behind another in order to undo me! Has the race of the Gibichungs fallen so low in prowess?'

'Deceiver, and yet deceived! Betrayer, and yet myself betrayed,' wails Gunther. 'Hagen, wise one, have you no counsel?'

'No counsel,' grimly answers Hagen, 'save Siegfried's death.'

'His death!'

'Aye, all these things demand his death.'

'But, Gutrune, to whom I gave him, how would we stand with her if we so avenged ourselves?' For even in his injured pride Gunther feels that he has had a share in what Siegfried has done.

But Hagen is prepared with a plan that will free Gunther and himself of all accusation. 'To-morrow,' he suggests, 'we will go on a great hunt. As Siegfried boldly rushes ahead we will fell him from the rear, and give out that he was killed by a wild boar.'

'So be it,' exclaims Brünnhilde; 'let his death atone for the shame he has wrought me. He has violated his oath; he shall die!'

At that moment as they turn toward the hall, he whose death they have decreed, a wreath of oak on his brow and leading Gutrune, whose hair is bedecked with flowers, steps out on the threshold as though wondering at their delay and urges them to enter. Gunther, taking Brünnhilde by the hand, follows him in. Hagen alone remains behind, and with a look of grim triumph watches them as they disappear within. And so, although the valley of the Rhine re-echoes with glad sounds, it is the Murder Motive that brings the act to a close.

Act III.    How picturesque the *mise-en-scène* of this act—a clearing in the primeval forest near a spot where the bank of the Rhine slopes towards the river. On the shore, above the stream, stands Siegfried. Baffled in the pursuit of game, he is looking for Gunther, Hagen, and his other comrades of the hunt, in order to join them.

One of the loveliest scenes of the cycle now ensues. The Rhinedaughters swim up to the bank and, circling gracefully in the current of the river, endeavour to coax from him the ring of Rhinegold. It is an episode full of whimsical badinage and more charming even than the opening of *Rheingold*.

Siegfried refuses to give up the ring. The Rhinedaughters swim off leaving him to his fate.

Here is the principal theme of their song in this scene:

Distant hunting-horns are heard. Gunther, Hagen, and their attendants gradually assemble and encamp themselves. Hagen fills a drinking-horn and hands it to Siegfried whom he persuades to relate the story of his life. This Siegfried does in a wonderfully picturesque, musical, and dramatic story in which motives, often heard before, charm us anew.

In the course of his narrative he refreshes himself by a draught from the drinking-horn into which Hagen meanwhile has pressed the juice of an herb. Through this the effect of the love-potion is so far counteracted that tender memories of Brünnhilde well up within him and he tells with artless enthusiasm how he penetrated the circle of flame about the Valkyr, found Brünnhilde slumbering there, awoke her with his kiss, and won her. Gunther springs up aghast at this revelation. Now he knows that Brünnhilde's accusation is true.

Two ravens fly overhead. As Siegfried turns to look after them the Motive of the Curse resounds and Hagen plunges his spear into the young hero's back. Gunther and the vassals throw themselves upon Hagen. The Siegfried Motive, cut short with a crashing chord, the two murderous chords of the Hagen Motive forming the bass—and Siegfried, who with a last effort has heaved his shield aloft to hurl it at Hagen, lets it fall, and, collapsing, drops upon it. So overpowered are the witnesses—even Gunther —by the suddenness and enormity of the crime that, after a few disjointed exclamations, they gather, bowed with grief, around Siegfried. Hagen, with stony indifference, turns away and disappears over the height.

With the fall of the last scion of the Wälsung race we hear a new motive, simple yet indescribably fraught with sorrow, the Death Motive:

Siegfried, supported by two men, rises to a sitting posture, and with a strange rapture gleaming in his glance, intones his death-song. It is an ecstatic greeting to Brünnhilde. 'Brünnhilde!' he exclaims, 'thy wakener comes to wake thee with his kiss.' The ethereal harmonies of the Motive of Brünnhilde's Awakening, the Motive of Fate, the Siegfried Motive swelling into the Motive of Love's Greeting and dying away through the Motive of Love's Passion to Siegfried's last whispered accents—'Brünnhilde beckons to me'—in the Motive of Fate—and Siegfried sinks back in death.

Full of pathos though this episode be, it but brings us to the threshold of a scene of such overwhelming power that it may without exaggeration be singled out as the supreme musico-dramatic climax of all that Wagner wrought. Siegfried's last ecstatic greeting to his Valkyr bride has made us realise the blackness of the treachery which tore the young hero and Brünnhilde asunder and led to his death; and now as we are bowed down with a grief too deep for utterance—like the grief with which a nation gathers at the grave of its noblest hero—Wagner voices for us, in music of overwhelmingly tragic power, feelings which are beyond expression in human speech.

Motionless with grief the men gather around Siegfried's corpse. Night falls. The moon casts a pale, sad light over the scene. At the silent bidding of Gunther the vassals raise the body and bear it in solemn procession over the rocky height. Meanwhile with majestic solemnity the orchestra voices the funeral oration of the 'world's greatest hero'. One by one, but tragically interrupted by the Motive of Death, we hear the motives which tell the story of the Wälsung's futile struggle with destiny—the Wälsung Motive, the Motive of the Wälsung's Heroism, the Motive of Sympathy, and the Love Motive, the Sword Motive, the Siegfried Motive, and the Motive of Siegfried the Hero, around which the Death Motive swirls and crashes like a black, death-dealing, all-wrecking flood, forming an overwhelmingly powerful climax that dies away into the Brünnhilde Motive with which, as with a heart-broken sigh, the heroic dirge is brought to a close.

Meanwhile the scene has changed to the Hall of the Gibichungs as in the first act. Gutrune is listening through the night for some sound which may announce the return of the hunt.

Men and women bearing torches precede in great agitation the funeral train. Hagen grimly announces to Gutrune that Siegfried is dead. Wild with grief she overwhelms Gunther with violent accusations. He points to Hagen whose sole reply is to demand the ring as spoil. Gunther refuses. Hagen draws his sword and after a brief combat slays Gunther. He is about to snatch the ring from Siegfried's finger, when the corpse's hand suddenly raises itself threateningly, and all—even Hagen—fall back in consternation.

Brünnhilde advances solemnly from the back. While watching on the bank of the Rhine she has learned from the Rhinedaughters the treachery of which she and Siegfried have been the victims. Her mien is ennobled by a look of tragic exaltation. To her the grief of Gutrune is but the whining of a child. When the latter realises that it was Brünnhilde whom she caused Siegfried to forget through the love-potion, she falls fainting over Gunther's body. Hagen leaning on his spear is lost in gloomy brooding.

Brünnhilde turns solemnly to the men and women and bids them erect a funeral pyre. The orchestral harmonies shimmer with the Magic Fire Motive through which courses the Motive of the Ride of the Valkyrs. Then, her countenance transfigured by love, she gazes upon her dead hero and apostrophises his memory in the Motive of Love's Greeting. From him she looks upward and in the Walhalla Motive and the Motive of Brünnhilde's Pleading passionately inveighs against the injustice of the gods. The Curse Motive is followed by a wonderfully beautiful combination of the Walhalla Motive and the Motive of the Gods' Stress at Brünnhilde's words:

'Rest thee! Rest thee! O, God!'

For with the fading away of Walhalla, and the inauguration of the reign of human love in place of that of lust and greed—a change to be wrought by the approaching expiation of Brünnhilde for the crimes which began with the wresting of the Rhine gold from the Rhinedaughters—Wotan's stress will be at an end. Brünnhilde, having told in the graceful, rippling Rhine music how she learned of Hagen's treachery through the Rhinedaughters, places upon her finger the ring. Then turning toward the pyre upon which Siegfried's body rests, she snatches a firebrand from one of the men, and flings it upon the pyre, which kindles brightly. As the moment of her immolation approaches the Motive of Expiation begins to dominate the scene.

Brünnhilde mounts her Valkyr charger, Grane, who oft bore her through the clouds, while lightning flashed and thunder reverberated. With one leap the steed bears her into the blazing pyre.

The Rhine overflows. Born on the flood, the Rhinedaughters swim to the pyre and draw, from Brünnhilde's finger, the ring. Hagen, seeing the object of all his plotting in their possession, plunges after them. Two of them encircle him with their arms and draw him down with them into the flood. The third holds up the ring in triumph.

In the heavens is perceived a deep glow. It is Götterdämmerung —the dusk of the gods. An epoch has come to a close. Walhalla is in flames. Once more its stately motive resounds, only to crumble, like a ruin, before the onsweeping power of the Motive of Expiation. The Siegfried Motive with a crash in the orchestra; once more then the Motive of Expiation. The sordid empire of the gods has passed away. A new era, that of human love, has dawned through the expiation of Brünnhilde. As in *The Flying Dutchman* and *Tannhäuser*, it is through woman that comes redemption.

K.

## PARSIFAL

Stage Dedication Festival Play (Bühnenweihfestspiel) in three acts, words and music by Richard Wagner. Produced Bayreuth, July 26, 1882. Save in concert form, the work was not given elsewhere until December 24, 1903, when it was produced at the Metropolitan Opera House at that time under the direction of Heinrich Conried.

At the Bayreuth performances there were alternating casts. Winkelmann was the Parsifal of the première, Gudehus of the second performance, Jäger of the third. The alternating Kundrys were Materna, Marianne Brandt, and Malten; Gurnemanz: Scaria and Siehr; Amfortas: Reichmann; Klingsor: Hill and Fuchs. Hermann Levi conducted.

In the New York cast Ternina was Kundry, and others in the cast were Burgstaller (Parsifal), van Rooy (Amfortas), Blass (Gurnemanz), Goritz (Klingsor), Journet (Titurel); Hertz conducted. First performed in England, Covent Garden, February 2, 1914, with von der Osten, Heinrich Hansel, Bender, Knüpfer, August Kiess, Murray Davey, conductor Bodansky; Covent Garden, 1919 (in English), with Gladys Ancrum, Mullings, Heming

Allin, Hubert Langley, Foster Richardson, conductor Albert Coates. Famous Kundrys have included Sucher, Brema, Mildenburg, Wittich, Gulbranson, Edyth Walker, Saltzmann-Stevens, Fremstad, Kurt, Matzenauer, Kemp, Leider, Marta Fuchs, Thorborg, Lubin. In the title role, in addition to the above: van Dyck, Schemedes, Burrian, Sembach, Urlus, Hutt, Laubenthal, Melchior, Fritz Wolff; as Gurnemanz; Karl Grengg, Felix von Krauss, Karl Braun, Mayr, Andresen, Bohnen, Kipnis, von Manowarda, Weber; as Amfortas: Eugen Gura, Scheidemantel, Karl Perron, Whitehill, Hermann Weil, Plaschke, Scheidl, Janssen, Schlusnus, Schorr, George London.

## CHARACTERS

Amfortas, *son of Titurel, and ruler of the Kingdom of the Grail* ................................. Bass-Baritone
Titurel, *former ruler* ............................. Bass
Gurnemanz, *a veteran Knight of the Grail* ............ Bass
Klingsor, *a Magician* ............................. Bass
Parsifal ........................................ Tenor
Kundry ....................................... Soprano
First and Second Knights ................ Tenor and Bass
Four Esquires ................... Sopranos and Tenors
Six of Klingsor's Flower Maidens .............. Sopranos
Brotherhood of the Knights of the Grail; Youths and Boys; Flower Maidens (two choruses of sopranos and altos)

*Time:* The Middle Ages   *Place:* Spain, near and in the Castle of the Holy Grail; in Klingsor's enchanted castle and in the garden of his castle

Parsifal is a familiar name to those who have heard *Lohengrin*. Lohengrin, it will be remembered, tells Elsa that he is Parsifal's son and one of the knights of the Holy Grail. The name is written Percival in Tennyson's *Idylls of the King*. Wagner, however, returns to the quainter and more Teutonic form of spelling. *Parsifal* deals with an earlier period in the history of the Grail knighthood than *Lohengrin*. But there is a resemblance between the Grail music in *Parsifal* and the *Lohengrin* music—a resemblance not in melody, nor even in outline, but merely in the purity and spirituality that breathe through both.

Three legends supplied Wagner with the principal characters in this music-drama. They were *Percival le Galois; or Contes de Grail*, by Chrétien de Troyes (1190); *Parsifal*, by Wolfram von Eschenbach, and a manuscript of the fourteenth century called by scholars the *Mabinogion*. As usual, Wagner has not held himself strictly to any one of these, but has combined them all, and revived them through the alchemy of his own genius.

Into the keeping of Titurel and his band of Christian knights has been given the Holy Grail, the vessel from which the Saviour drank when He instituted the Last Supper. Into their hands, too, has been placed, as a weapon of defence against the ungodly, the Sacred Spear, the arm with which the Roman soldier wounded the Saviour's side. The better to guard these sanctified relics Titurel, as King of the Grail knighthood, has reared a castle, Montsalvat, which, from its forest-clad height, facing Arabian Spain, forms a bulwark of Christendom against the pagan world and especially against Klingsor, a sorcerer and an enemy of good. Yet time and again this Klingsor, whose stronghold is near-by, has succeeded in enticing champions of the Grail into his magic garden, with its lure of flower-maidens and its arch-enchantress Kundry, a rarely beautiful woman, and in making them his servitors against their one-time brothers-in-arms.

Even Amfortas, Titurel's son, to whom Titurel, grown old in service and honour, has confided his reign and wardship, has not escaped the thrall of Klingsor's sorcery. Eager to begin his reign by destroying Klingsor's power at one stroke, he penetrated into the garden to attack and slay him. But he failed to reckon with human frailty. Yielding to the snare so skilfully laid by the sorcerer and forgetting, at the feet of the enchantress Kundry, the mission upon which he had sallied forth, he allowed the Sacred Spear to drop from his hand. It was seized by the evil-doer he had come to destroy, and he himself was grievously wounded with it before the knights who rushed to his rescue could bear him off.

This wound no skill has sufficed to heal. It is sapping Amfortas's strength. Indecision, gloom, have come over the once valiant brotherhood. Only the touch of the Sacred Spear that made the wound will avail to close it, but there is only one who can regain it from Klingsor. For to Amfortas, prostrate in supplication for a sign, a mystic voice from the sanctuary of the Grail replied that only through a youth 'guileless' and wholly ignorant of sin could the King's salvation be wrought. Instead of succumbing to the temptations of Klingsor's magic garden, he would become, through resisting them, cognisant of Amfortas's guilt, and, stirred by pity for him, make his redemption the mission of his life, regain the Spear and heal him with it. And so the Grail warders are waiting for the coming of the 'guileless fool'.

The working out of this prophecy forms the absorbing subject of the story of *Parsifal*. The plot is allegorical. Parsifal is the personification of Christianity, Klingsor of Paganism, and the triumph of Parsifal over Klingsor is the triumph of Christianity over Paganism.

The character of Kundry is one of Wagner's most striking creations. She is a sort of female Ahasuerus—a wandering Jewess. In the *Mabinogion* manuscript she is no other than Herodias, condemned to wander for ever because she laughed at the head of John the Baptist. Here Wagner makes another change. According to him she is condemned for laughing in the face of the Saviour as He was bearing the cross. She seeks forgiveness by serving the Grail knights as messenger on her swift horse, but ever and anon she is driven by the curse hanging over her back to Klingsor, who changes her to a beautiful woman and places her in his garden to lure the Knights of the Grail to destruction. She can be freed only by one who resists her temptations. Finally, she is freed by Parsifal and is baptised. In her character of Grail messenger she has much in common with the wild messengers of Valhalla, the Valkyrs. Indeed, in the Edda Saga, her name appears in the first part of the compound Gundryggja, which denotes the office of the Valkyrs.

### THE VORSPIEL

The Vorspiel to *Parsifal* is based on three of the most deeply religious motives in the entire work. It opens with the Motive of the Sacrament, over which, when it is repeated, arpeggios hover, as in the religious paintings of old masters angel forms float above the figure of virgin or saint.

Through this motive we gain insight into the office of the Knights of the Grail, who from time to time strengthen themselves for their spiritual duties by partaking of the communion, on which occasions the Grail itself is uncovered. This motive leads to the Grail Motive (the so-called 'Dresden Amen'), effectively swelling to *forte* and then dying away in ethereal harmonies, like the soft light with which the Grail illumines the hall in which the knights gather to worship.

The trumpets then announce the Motive of Faith, severe but sturdy:

The Grail Motive is heard again and then the Motive of Faith is repeated, its severity exquisitely softened, so that it conveys a sense of peace which 'passeth all understanding'.

The rest of the Vorspiel is agitated. That portion of the Motive of the Sacrament which appears later as the Spear Motive here assumes through a slight change a deeply sad character, and becomes typical throughout the work of the sorrow wrought by Amfortas's crime. I call it the Elegiac Motive.

Thus the Vorspiel depicts both the religious duties which play so prominent a part in the drama, and the unhappiness which Amfortas's sinful forgetfulness of these duties has brought upon himself and his knights.

Act I.   One of the sturdiest of the knights, the aged Gurnemanz, grey of head and beard, watches near the outskirts of the
forest. One dawn finds him seated under a majestic tree. Two
young Esquires lie in slumber at his feet. Far off, from the direction of the castle, sounds a solemn reveille.

'Hey! Ho!' Gurnemanz calls with brusque humour to the
Esquires. 'Not forest, but sleep warders I deem you!' The youths
leap to their feet; then, hearing the solemn reveille, kneel in prayer.
The Motive of Peace echoes their devotional thoughts. A wondrous
peace seems to rest upon the scene. But the transgression of the
King ever breaks the tranquil spell. For soon two knights come
in the van of the train that thus early bears the King from a
bed of suffering to the forest lake near-by, in whose waters he
would bathe his wound. They pause to parley with Gurnemanz,
but are interrupted by outcries from the youths and sounds of
rushing through air.

'Mark the wild horsewoman!'—'The mane of the devil's mare
flies madly!'—'Aye, 'tis Kundry!'—'She has swung herself off,'
cry the Esquires as they watch the approach of the strange creature
that now rushes in. Precipitately she thrusts a small crystal flask
into Gurnemanz's hand.

'Balsam—for the King!' There is a savagery in her manner
that seems designed to ward off thanks, when Gurnemanz asks her
whence she has brought the flask, and she replies: 'From farther
away than your thought can travel. If it fail, Arabia bears
naught else that can ease his pain. Ask no further. I am weary.'

Throwing herself upon the ground and resting her face on her
hands, she watches the King borne in, replies to his thanks for
the balsam with a wild, mocking laugh, and follows him with her
eyes as they bear him on his litter toward the lake, while
Gurnemanz and four Esquires remain behind.

Kundry's rapid approach on her wild horse is accompanied
by a furious gallop in the orchestra. Then, as she rushes upon

the stage, the Kundry Motive—a headlong descent of the string instruments through four octaves—is heard.

Kundry's action in seeking balsam for the King's wound gives us insight into the two contradictory natures represented by her character. For here is the woman who has brought all his suffering upon Amfortas striving to ease it when she is free from the evil sway of Klingsor. She is at times the faithful messenger of the Grail; at times the evil genius of its defenders.

When Amfortas is borne in upon a litter there is heard the Motive of Amfortas's Suffering, expressive of his physical and mental agony. It has a peculiar heavy, dragging rhythm, as if his wound slowly were sapping his life.

A beautiful idyll is played by the orchestra when the knights bear Amfortas to the forest lake.

One of the youths, who has remained with Gurnemanz, noting that Kundry still lies where she had flung herself upon the ground, calls out scornfully, 'Why do you lie there like a savage beast?'

'Are not even the beasts here sacred?' she retorts, but harshly, and not as if pleading for sufferance. The other Esquires would have joined in harassing her had not Gurnemanz stayed them.

'Never has she done you harm. She serves the Grail, and only when she remains long away, none knows in what distant lands, does harm come to us.' Then, turning to where she lies, he asks: 'Where were you wandering when our leader lost the Sacred Spear? Why were you not here to help us then?'

'I never help!' is her sullen retort, although a tremor, as if caused by a pang of bitter reproach, passes over her frame.

'If she wants to serve the Grail, why not send her to recover the Sacred Spear!' exclaims one of the Esquires sarcastically; and the youths doubtless would have resumed their nagging of Kundry, had not mention of the holy weapon caused Gurnemanz to give voice to memories of the events that have led to its capture by Klingsor. Then, yielding to the pressing of the youths who gather at his feet beneath the tree, he tells them of Klingsor— how the sorcerer has sued for admission to the Grail brotherhood, which was denied him by Titurel, how in revenge he has sought its destruction and now, through possession of the Sacred Spear, hopes to compass it.

Prominent with other motives already heard is a new one, the Klingsor Motive:

During this recital Kundry still lies upon the ground, a sullen, forbidding-looking creature. At the point when Gurnemanz tells of the sorcerer's magic garden and of the enchantress who has lured Amfortas to his downfall, she turns in quick, angry unrest, as if she would away, but is held to the spot by some dark and compelling power.

Gurnemanz concludes by telling the Esquires that while Amfortas was praying for a sign as to who could heal him, phantom lips pronounced these words:

> 'By pity lightened
>     The guileless fool;
> Wait for him,
>     My chosen tool.'

This introduces an important motive, that of the Prophecy, a phrase of simple beauty, as befits the significance of the words to which it is sung. Gurnemanz sings the entire motive and then the Esquires take it up. They have sung only the first two lines

when suddenly their prayerful voices are interrupted by shouts of dismay from the direction of the lake. A moment later a wounded swan, one of the sacred birds of the Grail brotherhood, flutters over the stage and falls dead near Gurnemanz. The knights follow in consternation. Two of them bring Parsifal, whom they have seized and accuse of murdering the sacred bird. As he appears the magnificent Parsifal Motive rings out on the horns:

It is a buoyant and joyous motive, full of the wild spirit and freedom of this child of nature, who knows nothing of the Grail and its brotherhood or the sacredness of the swan, and freely boasts of his skilful marksmanship. During this episode the Swan Motive from *Lohengrin* is effectively introduced. Then follows Gurnemanz's noble reproof, sung to a broad and expressive melody. Even the animals are sacred in the region of the Grail and are protected from harm. Parsifal's gradual awakening to a sense of wrong is one of the most touching scenes of the music-drama. His childlike grief when he becomes conscious of the pain he has caused is so simple and pathetic that one cannot but be deeply affected.

After Gurnemanz has ascertained that Parsifal knows nothing of the wrong he committed in killing the swan he plies him with questions concerning his parentage. Parsifal is now gentle and tranquil. He tells of growing up in the woods, of running away from his mother to follow a cavalcade of knights who passed along the edge of the forest and of never having seen her since.

In vain he endeavours to recall the many pet names she gave him. These memories of his early days introduce the sad motive of his mother, Herzeleid (Heart's Sorrow), who has died in grief.

'I do not know,' is the youth's invariable answer to all questions. His ignorance, coupled, however, with his naïve nobility of bearing and the fact that he has made his way to the Grail domain, engender in Gurnemanz the hope that here at last is the 'guileless fool' for whom prayerfully they have been waiting, and, the King having been borne from the lake toward the castle where the holy rite of unveiling the Grail is to be celebrated that day, thither Gurnemanz in kindly accents bids the youth follow him.

Then occurs a dramatically effective change of scene. The scenery becomes a panorama drawn off toward the right, and as Parsifal and Gurnemanz face toward the left they appear to be walking in that direction. The forest disappears; a cave opens in rocky cliffs and conceals the two; they are then seen again in sloping passages which they appear to ascend. Long sustained trombone notes softly swell; approaching peals of bells are heard. At last they arrive at a mighty hall which loses itself overhead in a high vaulted dome, down from which alone the light streams in.

The change of scene is ushered in by the solemn Bell Motive, which is the basis of the powerful orchestral interlude accompanying the panorama, and also of the scene in the hall of the Grail Castle.

As the communion, which is soon to be celebrated, is broken in upon by the violent grief and contrition of Amfortas, so the majestic sweep of this symphony is interrupted by the agonised Motive of Contrition, which graphically portrays the spiritual suffering of the King.

This subtly suggests the Elegiac Motive and the Motive of Amfortas's Suffering, but in greatly intensified degrees. For it is like an outcry of torture that affects both body and soul.

With the Motive of the Sacrament resounding upon the trombones, followed by the sonorous Bell Motive, Gurnemanz and Parsifal enter the hall, the old knight giving the youth a position from which he can observe the proceedings. From the deep colonnades on either side the knights march with stately tread, and arrange themselves at the horseshoe-shaped table, which encloses a raised couch. Then, while the orchestra plays a solemn processional based on the Bell Motive, they intone the chorus: 'To the last love feast'. After the first verse a line of pages crosses the stage and ascends into the dome. The graceful interlude here is based on the Bell Motive.

The chorus of knights closes with a glorious outburst of the Grail Motive as Amfortas is borne in, preceded by pages who bear the covered Grail. The King is lifted upon the couch and the holy vessel is placed upon the stone table in front of it. When the Grail Movement has died away amid the pealing of the bells, the youths in the gallery below the dome sing a chorus of penitence based upon the Motive of Contrition. Then the Motive of Faith floats down from the dome as an unaccompanied chorus for boys' voices—a passage of ethereal beauty—the orchestra whispering a brief postludium like a faint echo. This is, when sung as it was at Bayreuth, where I heard the first performance of *Parsifal* in 1882, the most exquisite effect of the whole score. For spirituality it is unsurpassed. It is an absolutely perfect example of religious music—a beautiful melody without the slightest worldly taint.

Titurel now summons Amfortas to perform his sacred office—to uncover the Grail. At first, tortured by contrition for his sin, of which the agony from his wound is a constant reminder, he refuses to obey his aged father's summons. In anguish he cries out that he is unworthy of the sacred office. But again ethereal voices float down from the dome. They now chant the prophecy of the 'guileless fool' and, as if comforted by the hope of ultimate redemption, Amfortas uncovers the Grail. Dusk seems to spread over the hall. Then a ray of brilliant light darts down upon the sacred vessel, which shines with a soft purple radiance that diffuses itself through the hall. All are on their knees save the youth, who has stood motionless and obtuse to the significance of all he has heard and seen save that during Amfortas's anguish he has clutched his heart as if he too felt the pang. But when the rite is over—when the knights have partaken of communion—and the glow has faded, and the King, followed by his knights, has been borne out, the youth remains behind, vigorous, handsome, but to all appearances a dolt.

'Do you know what you have witnessed?' Gurnemanz asks harshly, for he is grievously disappointed.

For answer the youth shakes his head.

'Just a fool, after all,' exclaims the old knight, as he opens a side door to the hall. 'Begone, but take my advice. In future leave our swans alone, and seek yourself, gander, a goose!' And with these harsh words he pushes the youth out and angrily slams the door behind him.

This jarring break upon the religious feeling awakened by the scene would be a rude ending for the act, but Wagner, with exquisite tact, allows the voices in the dome to be heard once more, and so the curtains close, amid the spiritual harmonies of the Prophecy of the Guileless Fool and of the Grail Motive.

Act II. This act plays in Klingsor's magic castle and garden. The Vorspiel opens with the threatful Klingsor motive, which is followed by the Magic and Contrition Motives, the wild Kundry Motive leading over to the first scene.

In the inner keep of his tower, stone steps leading up to the battlemented parapet and down into a deep pit at the back, stands Klingsor, looking into a metal mirror, whose surface, through his necromancy, reflects all that transpires within the environs of the fastness from which he ever threatens the warders of the Grail. Of all that has just happened in the Grail's domain it has made him aware; and he knows that of which Gurnemanz is ignorant—that the youth, whose approach the mirror divulges, once in his power, vain will be the prophecy of the 'guileless fool' and his own triumph assured. For it is that same 'guileless fool' the old knight impatiently has thrust out.

Klingsor turns toward the pit and imperiously waves his hand. A bluish vapour rises from the abyss and in it floats the form of a beauteous woman—Kundry, not the Kundry of a few hours before, dishevelled and in coarse garb girdled with snake-skin; but a houri, her dark hair smooth and lustrous, her robe soft, rich Oriental draperies. Yet even as she floats she strives as though she would descend to where she has come from, while the sorcerer's harsh laugh greets her vain efforts. This then is the secret of her strange actions and her long disappearances from the Grail domain, during which so many of its warders have fallen into Klingsor's power! She is the snare he sets, she the arch-enchantress of his magic garden. Striving, as he hints while he mocks her impotence, to expiate some sin committed by her during a previous existence in the dim past, by serving the brotherhood of the Grail knights, the sorcerer's power over her is such that at any moment he can summon her to aid him in their destruction.

Well she knows what the present summons means. Approaching the tower at this very moment is the youth whom she has seen in the Grail forest, and in whom she, like Klingsor, has recognised the only possible redeemer of Amfortas and of—herself. And now she must lure him to his doom and with it lose her last hope of salvation, now, aye, now—for even as he mocks her, Klingsor once more waves his hand, castle and keep vanish as if swallowed up by the earth, and in its place a garden heavy with the scent of gorgeous flowers fills the landscape.

The orchestra, with the Parsifal Motive, gives a spirited description of the brief combat between Parsifal and Klingsor's knights. It is amid the dark harmonies of the Klingsor Motive that the keep sinks out of sight and the magic garden, spreading out in all directions, with Parsifal standing on the wall and gazing with astonishment upon the brilliant scene, is disclosed.

The Flower Maidens in great trepidation for the fate of their lover knights rush in from all sides with cries of sorrow, their confused exclamations and the orchestral accompaniment admirably enforcing their tumultuous actions.

The Parsifal Motive again introduces the next episode, as Parsifal, attracted by the grace and beauty of the girls, leaps down into the garden and seeks to mingle with them. It is repeated several times in the course of the scene. The girls, seeing that he does not seek to harm them, bedeck themselves with flowers and crowd about him with alluring gestures, finally circling around him as they sing this caressing melody:

The effect is enchanting, the music of this episode being a marvel of sensuous grace. Parsifal regards them with childlike, innocent joy. Then they seek to impress him more deeply with their charms, at the same time quarrelling among themselves over him. When their rivalry has reached its height, Kundry's voice—'Parsifal, tarry!'—is wafted from a flowery nook near-by.

'Parsifal!' In all the years of his wandering none has called him by his name; and now it floats toward him as if borne on the scent of roses. A beautiful woman, her arms stretched out to him, welcomes him from her couch of brilliant flowers. Irresistibly drawn toward her, he approaches and kneels by her side; and she, whispering to him in tender accents, leans over him and presses a long kiss upon his lips. It is the lure that has sealed the fate of many a knight of the Grail. But in the youth it inspires a sudden change. The perilous subtlety of it, that is intended to destroy, transforms the 'guileless fool' into a conscious man, and that man conscious of a mission. The scenes he has witnessed in the Grail castle, the stricken King whose wound ever bled afresh, the part he is to play, the peril of the temptation that has been placed in his path—all these things become revealed to him in the rapture of that unhallowed kiss. In vain the enchantress seeks to draw him towards her. He thrusts her from him. Maddened by the repulse, compelled through Klingsor's arts to see in the handsome youth her lawful prey, she calls upon the sorcerer to aid her. At her outcry Klingsor appears on the castle wall, in his hand the Spear taken from Amfortas, and, as Parsifal faces him, hurls it full at him. But lo, it rises in its flight and remains suspended in the air over the head of him it was aimed to slay.

Reaching out and seizing it, Parsifal makes with it the sign of the Cross. Castle and garden wall crumble into ruins, the garden shrivels away, leaving in its place a sere wilderness, through which Parsifal, leaving Kundry as one dead upon the ground, sets forth in search of the castle of the Grail, there to fulfil the mission with which now he knows himself charged.

Act III.    Not until after long wanderings through the wilderness, however, is it that Parsifal once more finds himself on the outskirts of the Grail forest. Clad from head to foot in black armour, his visor closed, the Holy Spear in his hand, he approaches the spot where Gurnemanz, now grown very old, still holds watch, while Kundry again in coarse garb, but grown strangely pale and gentle, humbly serves the brotherhood. It is Good Friday morn, and peace rests upon the forest.

Kundry is the first to discern the approach of the black knight. From the tender exaltation of her mien, as she draws Gurnemanz's look toward the silent figure, it is apparent that she divines who it is and why he comes. To Gurnemanz, however, he is but an armed intruder on sanctified ground and upon a holy day, and, as the black knight seats himself on a little knoll near a spring and remains silent, the old warder chides him for his offence. Tranquilly the knight rises, thrusts the Spear he bears into the ground before him, lays down his sword and shield before it, opens his helmet, and removing it from his head, places it with the other arms, and then himself kneels in silent prayer before the Spear. Surprise, recognition of man and weapon, and deep emotion succeed each other on Gurnemanz's face. Gently he raises Parsifal from his kneeling posture, once more seats him on the knoll by the spring, loosens his greaves and corselet, and then places upon him the coat of mail and mantle of the knights of the Grail, while Kundry, drawing a golden flask from her bosom anoints his feet and dries them with her loosened hair. Then Gurnemanz takes from her the flask, and, pouring its contents upon Parsifal's head, anoints him king of the knights of the Grail. The new king performs his first office by taking up water from the spring in the hollow of his hand and baptising Kundry, whose eyes, suffused with tears, are raised to him in gentle rapture.

Here is heard the stately Motive of Baptism:

The 'Good Friday Spell', one of Wagner's most beautiful mood paintings in tone colour, is the most prominent episode in these scenes.

Once more Gurnemanz, Kundry now following, leads the way toward the castle of the Grail. Amfortas's aged father, Titurel, uncomforted by the vision of the Grail, which Amfortas, in his passionate contrition, deems himself too sullied to unveil, has died, and the knights having gathered in the great hall, Titurel's bier is borne in solemn procession and placed upon a catafalque before Amfortas's couch.

'Uncover the shrine!' shout the knights, pressing upon Amfortas. For answer, and in a paroxysm of despair, he springs up, tears his garments asunder and shows his open wound. 'Slay me!' he cried. 'Take up your weapons! Bury your sword-blades deep—deep in me, to the hilts! Kill me, and so kill the pain that tortures me!'

As Amfortas stands there in an ecstasy of pain, Parsifal enters, and, quietly advancing, touches the wound with the point of the Spear.

'One weapon only serves to staunch your wounded side—the one that struck it.'

Amfortas's torture changes to highest rapture. The shrine is opened and Parsifal, taking the Grail, which again radiates with light, waves it gently to and fro, as Amfortas and all the knights kneel in homage to him, while Kundry, gazing up to him in gratitude, sinks gently into the sleep of death and forgiveness for which she has longed.

The music of this entire scene floats upon ethereal arpeggios. The Motive of Faith especially is exquisitely accompanied, its spiritual harmonies finally appearing in this form.

There are also heard the Motives of Prophecy and of the Sacrament, as the knights on the stage and the youths and boys in the dome chant. The Grail Motive, which is prominent throughout the scene, rises as if in a spirit of gentle religious triumph and brings, with the Sacrament Motive, the work to a close.

K.

# CHAPTER 6

# German Opera Continued

# PETER CORNELIUS

## DER BARBIER VON BAGDAD
### The Barber of Bagdad

OPERA in two acts by Peter Cornelius (1824–1874); text, based on a story from the *Arabian Nights*, by the composer. First performed at Weimar, conducted by Liszt on December 15, 1858. As a result of the feud between Liszt, Weimar's head of music, and Dingelstedt, the manager of the theatre, the first night was made the occasion of a showdown on the part of their rival adherents, and the opera was a fiasco; Liszt resigned his position, and the opera was not given again during the composer's lifetime. Revived Hanover, 1877, and again a failure. Revised and re-orchestrated by Felix Mottl, produced at Karlsruhe, 1885, and in many other German theatres. Metropolitan, New York, 1890, with Sophie Traubmann, Kalisch and Fischer, conducted by Damrosch; Savoy Theatre, London, 1891, by students of the Royal College of Music; Covent Garden, 1906, with Burchardt, Jörn, Knüpfer, and conducted by Richter. Revived Metropolitan, 1925, with Rethberg, Laubenthal, and Bender; London Opera Club, 1949, with Victoria Sladen, Owen Brannigan; Vienna Volksoper, 1949, with Jurinac, Dermota and Edelmann; Edinburgh Festival, 1956, by Hamburg Opera, with Muszely, Konya, van Mill.

### CHARACTERS

| | |
|---|---|
| The Caliph | Baritone |
| Baba Mustapha, *a Cadi* | Tenor |
| Margiana, *his daughter* | Soprano |
| Bostana, *a servant of the Cadi's* | Mezzo-Soprano |
| Nureddin | Tenor |
| Abul Hassan Ali Ebn Bekar, *a Barber* | Bass |

Nureddin's Servants, Friends of the Cadi, People of Bagdad, Wailing Women, the Caliph's entourage

*Place:* Bagdad

When he was twenty-five, Cornelius wrote that he was clear in his mind that his natural bent was towards operatic comedy. Considering the success which he achieved in his one attempt at this genre (a posthumous success unfortunately, as the opera had only a single performance in his lifetime), it seems a pity that his two other operas should have been on serious subjects; neither has had anything like the number of performances *Der Barbier* has collected since the composer's death.

Originally Cornelius planned *Der Barbier* in one act, with an extended final scene occupying something like a third of the whole work (see Ernest Newman's *Opera Nights*). Later, he decided on two acts of equal length, and it was in this form that the opera was given in Weimar. After the unsuccessful première, Liszt (who liked the opera but would, apparently, have preferred it to have been a serious rather than a comic work!) persuaded the composer to re-write his overture, and instead of the comedy prelude to substitute something based on the themes of the opera itself. Cornelius died before he could orchestrate the new overture, and this was done after his death by Liszt. For the revivals they conducted, both Mottl and Levi made a number of changes in the orchestration, and it was not until 1904 that the opera was given in the form (and orchestral dress) Cornelius had intended.

The D major overture—that is to say the one written at Liszt's suggestion—is based on references to the Barber's theme, his patter song, Nureddin's appeal to the absent Margiana, the assignation duet between Nureddin and Bostana, and the chorus of Nureddin's servants.

Act I.　　Nureddin is lying on a couch at his house, nursing his apparently hopeless love for Margiana. He and his servants, scorning the more scientific forms of diagnosis, fear that his life is in danger. The servants' chorus and Nureddin's love song are delightfully sentimental, and he repeats the name Margiana in the apparent hope that it will ameliorate his sufferings. Left alone, Nureddin again conjures up a vision of his beloved, 'Vor deinem Fenster die Blumen versengte der Sonne Strahl', a song of charmingly romantic character.

To assuage his sufferings comes Bostana, an aged relation of Margiana's father, the Cadi. She tells him that Margiana will receive him that very day when her father goes to the mosque at noon. Bostana gives him his instructions and he repeats them in a quick, canonic duet. Before she goes, she prescribes a bath and a shave for him; he agrees, and again they go over the plan they have formulated. With a last 'Don't forget the Barber' (she has recommended her own favourite to him), she leaves the lover to contemplate his prospective bliss, which he does in an ecstatic *allegro*, 'Ach, das Leid hab' ich getragen, wie ertrag' ich nun mein Glück?'

He is far too much occupied with his daydreams to notice the entrance of the Barber, Abul Hassan Ali Ebn Bekar, carrying with him his towel, his basin, a looking-glass, and other apparatus of his calling, and, in addition, an astrolabe, with which he is accustomed to foretell his clients' futures. Nureddin is anxious to be shaved straight away, but he has to do with the most garrulous man in Bagdad, and the Barber tells him at length and in a series of ingenious multiple rhymes exactly how fortunate it is that Nureddin should have chosen him to perform the necessary offices.

Nureddin tries to stop him and make him get on with the shaving, but Abul must first cast his horoscope. This he does to the accompaniment of Nureddin's rapidly rising impatience, and having finished, once again puts forward his own qualifications in a brilliant patter song. Nureddin, not without justification by now, tells him he is nothing but a chatterbox. This fills the Barber with righteous indignation; his brothers it is true were talkative, but he, the youngest of the family, has always been known for his virtue and his taciturnity. Things seem to be out of hand, and Nureddin yells for his servants to come and deliver him from this plague of a Barber. Their attempts are successful up to a point, but, just as they get him to the door, the Barber flourishes his razor and succeeds in turning them out.

Nureddin resorts to tact, and the Barber is soon ready to begin operations, ready that is to say until his client lets fall the word 'Margiana' from his lips. This starts a flood of reminiscence; the Barber himself was once in love with a Margiana—and this is the song he used to sing to her. As a lover, he is more philosophical than Osmin would be, and one cannot imagine that worthy favouring the object of his affections with the elaborate and apparently endless cadenza with which Abul rounds off his song. He is delighted that Nureddin is in love, but horrified to hear that his Margiana is the daughter of Cadi Baba Mustapha, a villain, he says, who shaves himself. There is no hope unless he accompanies his new-made friend to the assignation.

Nureddin advises him to go back to his doubtless innumerable other customers, but the Barber soliloquises in his absence on the disastrous effect women can have on a man's life: 'So schwärmet Jugend'. What was the ruin of all his six brothers? Love—and the catalogue of their respective misfortunes is punctuated by references to the word 'Lieben'. Cornelius's ingenuity in varying this repetition is no less to be admired than the old man's ability to find a topic to suit every occasion and, having found it, to dilate upon it endlessly.

Nureddin returns, and is horrified to find the Barber still there and fully purposing to accompany him to Margiana's house. He calls his servants again, and instructs them to minister to the Barber, who, he tells them, is very ill; let them put him to bed and keep him there, sparing no remedy whatsoever. The servants are delighted at the prospect of getting their own back, and they succeed in catching the elusive Abul, whom they deposit on the couch, covering him with cushions and preparing razors and lancets as they sing. The last we hear of them is their recital of the Barber's names in five part harmony.

Act II.     The Intermezzo is based on the figure associated with the Muezzin's call to prayer. The melody is varied throughout and the effect is a delightful anticipation in music of the moment when Nureddin can meet his Margiana for the first time. When the curtain rises, we are for the first time in the Cadi's house, in that part of it reserved for the women. Margiana expresses her delight at the prospect of Nureddin's arrival: 'Er kommt, er kommt, o Wonne meiner Brust!' No sooner has she finished the long phrase than Bostana rushes in and expresses the same sentiment in an identical melody, only to be joined some moments later by the Cadi, whose sentiments are made known in exactly similar terms, but of course for very different reasons. The women rejoice that Nureddin is coming, the Cadi is excited at the thought of his rich friend Selim's arrival from Damascus, bringing with him splendid presents and a request for the hand of Margiana in marriage. The trio is one of the most beautiful numbers in the score. A chest arrives from Damascus full of the expected treasures, and Margiana is dutifully pleased that her father is happy. Into the general rejoicings comes the sound of the Muezzin, sung offstage by a bass and two tenors; the chant is taken up by the three characters onstage, and the Cadi goes off to the mosque.

In a moment Nureddin is in the room, and he launches into a declaration of his love, which is taken up by Margiana: 'O holdes Bild in Engelschöne'. The alternating triple and quadruple time gives way to a decided 3/4 for the second half of the duet sung in octaves throughout. The duet has a cool, almost innocent feel about it, as is suitable for a first, almost formal declaration of love. The idyllic scene is interrupted by the sound of the Barber's voice from down below. He assures Nureddin that he is safe with so faithful a watchdog, and starts to sing his own love song. The lovers make little progress with so much distraction outside, and to Abul's song are added a moment later the howls of a slave who has broken the Cadi's favourite vase and is being punished out of hand by his master immediately on his return from the mosque.

The situation is a tricky one for Nureddin, and it takes a turn for the worse when Abul, hearing the screams of the slave, construes them as meaning that the Cadi is murdering Nureddin, and yells for help. The sound of a crowd shouting hostile remarks about the Cadi can be heard down below, as Nureddin is bundled into the treasure chest, which is quickly emptied. When Abul bursts into the room, bringing with him some of Nureddin's servants, Bostana tries to tell him that the unlucky lover has been hidden in the chest, but he takes it into his head that the box contains nothing but his friend's corpse. The servants are on the point of carrying out the chest when the Cadi returns and thinks they are stealing his treasure. The ensuing alliterative abuse is thought by Ernest Newman to have been intended as a parody of Wagner's alliterative methods in *The Ring*: Cornelius was Liszt's secretary and must certainly have seen the printed copy of the libretto which Liszt had as early as 1853. A misunderstanding occurs over the word 'Schatz', which the Cadi uses in its literal sense of 'treasure', and which the Barber understands as meaning more colloquially 'darling'.

The Cadi, the Barber, the Cadi's friends and retainers, Nureddin's servants, women already in mourning for him, and a mixed crowd of inhabitants of Bagdad join in an ensemble of accusation and counter-accusation, during which the chest is turned upside down. It is only brought to an end by the arrival of the Caliph, suitably attended by magnificently uniformed soldiers. The Cadi explains that Abul is a thief who is stealing his daughter's treasure. Abul, after contrasting his silent habits with his brothers' loquacity and after running through a list of his own accomplishments, denies that he is a thief but accuses the Cadi of having murdered his friend and hidden the body in the chest. Margiana and Bostana return, and the Caliph tells Margiana to open the chest and show him what her father persists in describing as her treasure.

Nobody's consternation could be more genuine than the Cadi's when the senseless body of Nureddin is disclosed in the chest.

'He! Mustapha!' he exclaims, and the cry is taken up by the Caliph and Abul in an ensemble, which is later joined by Margiana and Bostana, who lament the untimely death of the young man. Abul has been bending over the 'dead' body and he brings the lamentation to an end by announcing that Nureddin is not dead after all, but only unconscious. The Caliph suggests that this is the moment when the Barber's miraculous healing powers can suitably be brought into use. Abul starts off with a line from his love song to Margiana but with no result; he tweaks Nureddin's nose and ears and tries smelling salts on him. But the simultaneous application to his nose of the rose Margiana has given him, and to his ears of the second line of the love song works the trick: Nureddin opens his eyes and gets up.

The Cadi joins the lovers' hands and tells his soldiers to arrest the Barber—merely, he assures him, in order that he may benefit from his advice and his story-telling which have been denied him so long. Abul leads the assembly in a song of praise to the Caliph: 'Heil diesem Hause' and everyone repeats the refrain, 'Salamaleikum'.                                                              H.

# KARL GOLDMARK

## DIE KÖNIGIN VON SABA
### The Queen of Sheba

OPERA in four acts by Karl Goldmark, text by Hermann von Mosenthal. Première at the Hofburgtheater, Vienna, March 10, 1875, with Materna, Wild, and Beck. First performed Metropolitan, New York, 1885, with Lilli Lehmann (Sulamith; in 1889 at the same house, she sang the Queen of Sheba), Krämer-Wiedl, Marianne Brandt, Albert Stritt, Adolf Robinson, Emil Fischer, conducted by Anton Seidl; Metropolitan, 1905, with Rappold (Sulamith), Walker, Alten, Knote, van Rooy, Blass, and conducted by Hertz; Manchester, 1910; London, Kennington Theatre, 1910. The opera was in the repertory of the Vienna Staatsoper continuously from 1875 to 1938.

### CHARACTERS

King Solomon ................................ Baritone
Baal Hanan, *the Palace overseer* ................ Baritone
Assad ........................................ Tenor
The High Priest ............................... Bass
Sulamith, *his daughter* ....................... Soprano
The Queen of Sheba .................... Mezzo-Soprano
Astaroth, *her slave* .......................... Soprano
Voice of the Temple-Watchman ................... Bass

*Time:* Tenth Century B.C.             *Place:* Jerusalem

Act I.    In Solomon's magnificent palace everybody is preparing for the reception of the Queen of Sheba. But nobody is more delighted than Sulamith, the daughter of the High Priest, for Assad, whom she is to marry and who had gone to meet the foreign queen, will return with her. Here he comes already into the hall. But Assad, growing pale, draws back before his betrothed. He confesses to King Solomon that he has not yet seen the Queen of Sheba but at a cedar grove in Lebanon a wonderful woman favoured him with her love and since then his mind has been confused. The King tells the young man that God will restore his peace of mind through marriage to Sulamith. Now the Queen's train approaches; she greets Solomon and unveils herself. Assad rushes toward her; this was the woman of the cedar grove! What does the young man want of her? She does not know him.

Act II.    The Queen did not want to recognise Assad but the woman in her is consumed with longing for him. He comes and happy love unites them. The scene changes and shows the interior of the Temple, where the wedding of Assad and Sulamith is about to be solemnised. At a decisive moment the Queen appears, and Assad throws the ring on the floor and hurries to the Queen, who, for her part, declares a second time that she has never seen him; she came only to bring a wedding gift for Sulamith. Assad, who has offended the Almighty, has incurred the penalty of death.

Act III.    Solomon is alone with the Queen. She has one request to make of him, that he shall release Assad. Why? He is nothing to her but she wants to see whether the King has regard for his guest. However, Solomon understands his guest's scheme and refuses her request; the Queen, breathing vengeance, strides out of the palace. Sulamith is in the depths of despair but Solomon consoles her; Assad will shake off the unworthy chains. Far away on the borders of the desert, she will find peace with him.

Act IV.    Again the scene changes. On the border of the desert stands the asylum of the young women consecrated to God in which Sulamith has found rest from the deceitful world. Assad staggers thither, a weary, banished man. Again the Queen of Sheba appears before him offering him her love, but he flees from the false woman for whom he had sacrificed the noble Sulamith. A desert storm arises, burying Assad in the sand. When the sky becomes clear again Sulamith, taking a walk with her maidens, finds her lover. She pardons the dying man and sings of the eternal joys which they will taste together.

*Die Königin von Saba* belongs in the category of operas whose music is basically conventional and which require a lavish scenic display if they are to be seen at their best. Much of the music in its day must have sounded agreeably exotic; on the other hand, such a section as Assad's narration to Solomon (Act I) reaches an almost Wagnerian length without displaying anything like a Wagnerian expressiveness. The beginning of the second act, however, with the big scena for the Queen followed by Astaroth's luring song (marvellously effective in the hands of a great artist), Assad's well-known 'Magische Töne' and the big love duet for him and the Queen is, musically speaking, by no means negligible. Sulamith's two big scenes with the chorus ('Der Freund ist dein' in the opening scene, and the wailing lament in Act III) have a passionate, exotic colouring and demand considerable powers of execution on the part of the singer. The Queen has a striking duet with Solomon at the beginning of Act III, when she attempts to seduce him from the path of duty and to obtain Assad for herself. K.W., H.

## DAS HEIMCHEN AM HERD
### The Cricket on the Hearth

Opera in three acts, by Carl Goldmark, text by M. Willner, after the story by Charles Dickens. Produced, Berlin, 1896; in America, 1910.

### CHARACTERS

John ........................................Baritone
Dot, *his wife* ...............................Soprano
May .......................................Soprano
Edward Plummer ...........................Tenor
Tackleton ....................................Basso
The Cricket .................................Soprano

*Time:* Early Nineteenth Century *Place:* An English Village

Act I. Room in John's house. Invisible chorus of elves. To the Cricket, the guiding spirit of the house, Dot confides her secret: she hopes soon to have a child. May, a pretty young girl, a toymaker, is to be married the next day to Tackleton, her employer. She bemoans her fate. She still loves Edward Plummer, who disappeared several years before. After May's departure John appears with Edward, disguised as a sailor; he is not recognised either by John or the villagers.

Act II. A garden. May and Tackleton are supping together. John makes Tackleton jealous of the stranger, Edward, who, seeing that May is only marrying Tackleton because his wealth will save her old foster-father from want, reveals his identity to Dot. Tackleton now succeeds in making John in his turn jealous of Edward, but John is lulled to sleep by the Cricket, and dreams of himself as a happy father.

Act III. May resolves to be true to Edward. Recognising him (after his song, 'Hulla, list to the Seas'), they drive off in Tackleton's carriage. John is told of Dot's secret. Reconciliation, with the Cricket chirping merrily. There is much pretty music (for instance, the quintet on the hearth in the second act, and Edward's song), which, however, has not sufficed to keep the piece in the international repertory. K.W.

# JOHANN STRAUSS

## DIE FLEDERMAUS
### The Bat

OPERA in three acts by Johann Strauss. Text by Haffner and Genée, from a French vaudeville 'Le Reveillon' by Meilhac and Halévy. First performed at the Theater an der Wien, Vienna, April 5, 1874, with Marie Geistinger, Mme. Charles Hirsch, Mme. Nittingwe, Herr Szika, Herr Rudinger, Herr Lebrecht, Herr Rott and conducted by the composer. First performed in London, Alhambra Theatre, 1876, with Mlle. Cabella, Miss Chambers, Loredan, Rosenthal, Jarvis, Shaw, conducted by M. G. Jacobi; New York, 1879; Vienna Opera, 1894, conducted by Mahler; Metropolitan Opera, New York, 1905, with Sembrich, Alten, Edyth Walker, Dippel, Reiss, Greder, Goritz, conducted by Nathan Franko. Revived in London at His Majesty's Theatre, 1910, with Carrie Tubb, Beatrice de la Palme, Muriel Terry, Joseph O'Mara, John Bardsley, Frederick Ranalow, Arthur Royd, conducted by Hamish McCunn; Covent Garden, 1930, with Lotte Lehmann, Schumann, Olszewska, Willi Wörle, Karl Jöken, Hüsch, Habich, conducted by Bruno Walter; Sadler's Wells, 1934, with Joan Cross, Ruth Naylor, Gladys Parr, Tudor Davies, Arthur Cox, Redvers Llewelyn, Percy Heming, conducted by Warwick Braithwaite. Revived at Metropolitan, New York, 1950, with Welitsch, Munsel, Stevens, Svanholm, Tucker, Brownlee, Hugh Thompson, conducted by Eugene Ormandy.

### CHARACTERS

Gabriel von Eisenstein ........................... Tenor
Rosalinda, *his wife* ........................... Soprano
Frank, *the governor of the prison* ............... Baritone
Prince Orlofsky, *a rich Russian* .......... Mezzo-Soprano
Alfred, *a singer* ................................ Tenor
Dr. Falke, *a friend of Eisenstein's* ............. Baritone
Dr. Blind, *Eisenstein's attorney* ................ Tenor
Adele, *Eisenstein's maid* ....................... Soprano
Frosch, *the gaoler* ...................... Speaking Part

Johann Strauss the younger was already famous as a composer of Viennese dance music before he turned his hand to operetta, his first being *Indigo* (1871), his second *Der Karneval in Rom* (1873), his third *Die Fledermaus*. Whether the spirited action and the predominance of dialogue make it preferable to cast the main roles in *Fledermaus* with actors who can sing, or whether the difficult nature of the vocal music suggests rather singers who can act, has never been settled once and for all. There are disadvantages in either solution: few actresses have the singing technique to encompass the music of Rosalinda and Adele adequately, few singers have the lightness of touch, vocal and dramatic, which is so essential if the spirited nature of the whole entertainment is not to suffer. What is quite certain is that the moment *Fledermaus* becomes a vehicle for a star conductor (and the danger is less remote than one might think), then disaster is round the corner, and we are treated to the unwelcome spectacle of portentous gaiety—as unreal as a gifted elephant dancing a waltz.

The overture, a potpourri, is one of the most popular ever written. The first three tunes are from the prison scene in the last act, the third being associated with the dénouement. Then comes the famous waltz with its lilting refrain, followed after a short interlude by a mournful tune on the oboe (also in 3/4), with a contrasting section (the tunes associated with Eisenstein's mock-serious farewell before going to prison). The material is repeated, the overture as a whole being dominated by its waltz.

Act I.    We are in Eisenstein's house. The stage is empty, but outside can be heard the sound of Alfred's voice, as he serenades Rosalinda. He is, it appears, an old flame of hers, and he addresses her fittingly as his dove. Adele, the Eisensteins' maid, makes her entrance on a cadenza and proceeds to read a letter from her sister, Ida. The Ballet, of which Ida is a member, has been invited *en bloc* that night to a party which is being given by Prince Orlofsky, the rich and eccentric young Russian; if Adele can get hold of a dress, Ida can take her along—the orchestra fairly bubbles with Adele's excitement. But Rosalinda, who has heard Alfred's serenade and suspects who it is, is far too preoccupied to pay much attention to Adele's plea that she be allowed to go and look after her sick aunt. With Eisenstein going off that night for the beginning of his five-day prison sentence, she cannot possibly think of sparing anybody; he must have a good supper before he leaves. Alfred waits until Adele has gone and then tells Rosalinda he has heard that Eisenstein will be away for a few days; he will call again that evening. Rosalinda is beside herself: as long as he doesn't sing she is all right—but he is a tenor and who could resist the sound of his top A?

Eisenstein storms in with his advocate, Dr. Blind, who, says Eisenstein, is to blame for the whole affair of the prison sentence, most of all that he is now being sent down for eight days, not five. There is a lively trio for Rosalinda, Eisenstein, and Blind, in which Rosalinda protests her grief—perhaps a shade too much—Eisenstein rages at Blind, and the lawyer runs through a list of legal expedients he will call into play once he has a chance of appealing against the sentence.

The lawyer leaves, Adele, still in tears about her mythical aunt, is sent off to order a delicious supper for the master, and Rosalinda goes to look out some old clothes for him to go to prison in. Enter Dr. Falke, a friend of Eisenstein's, who has, we should know, been nursing a grievance against him ever since the last Carnival. It seems that Falke, who was dressed as a bat (hence the title), was left by Eisenstein to find his way home in broad daylight and in his unconventional costume. He has a plan, though Eisenstein has not the least suspicion of it, for revenge. Why, he says, should Eisenstein not accept the invitation from Prince Orlofsky, which Falke brings him, and go in disguise to the ball, giving himself up to the prison authorities next morning? Rosalinda need never know—nor need Eisenstein guess that Rosalinda is also being asked to the party, at which she will wear a mask. The Bat's revenge is taking shape, and Eisenstein receives the invitation to the strains of the same polka which accompanied Adele's reading of the letter from her sister earlier on. He accepts it with a minimum of shilly-shallying.

Rosalinda is astonished to hear that her husband is going off to prison in style, in evening dress in fact, but she is so preoccupied with the prospect of Alfred's disturbing promise to come back at supper-time that she accepts a flimsy excuse. All is prepared; Rosalinda, Adele (who has been given the night off after all, in preparation for Alfred's expected visit), and Eisenstein sing a farewell trio, which is one of the most delicious moments of the score. Rosalinda still grieves in exaggerated fashion in the *moderato espressivo*, but none of the three can keep these long faces for ever, and the refrain to each of Rosalinda's utterances glitters and sparkles as gaily as the parties they each of them enjoy in anticipation. Rosalinda ends with a ringing top C, and Eisenstein bustles off.

Alfred keeps his promise, and Eisenstein is hardly out of the house before his wife's admirer is eating the supper that was originally prepared for him. 'Trinke, Liebchen, trinke schnell',

sings the tenor, and Rosalinda joins in the refrain, although she
cannot help noticing that her companion is beginning to show the
effects of the wine he so melodiously urges her to drink. The
drinking song is interrupted by the sound of voices below and
Frank, the new prison governor, appears, with the information
that he has come to escort Herr von Eisenstein, who is to be his
guest for the next eight days, to prison. Alfred ropes him in to
sing the chorus of his song, but denies hotly that he is Eisenstein
when Frank addresses him by name. The situation looks compromising, but Rosalinda carries it off with impressive bravado:
does the governor think she would be at supper as late as this
with someone who is not her husband? 'Mein Herr, was dächten
sie von mir?' (What inferences would you draw?) she sings, and
reconciles Frank to the delay and Alfred to his probable fate in
the enchanting slow waltz refrain to her song. Rosalinda fears the
worst—Alfred and her husband will almost certainly meet in
prison—but what can she do? A farewell kiss, and Frank, who is
also going to Orlofsky's party, hurries Alfred off, a brisk trio
bringing the act to its end.

Act II.    The party at Prince Orlofsky's is in full swing, and
the opening chorus leaves us in no doubt as to its successful
nature. Although he is too blasé to enjoy them himself, Prince
Orlofsky likes his parties to go well—but woe betide anyone who
refuses to drink with him; he will get a bottle thrown at his head.
His song, 'Ich lade gern mir Gäste ein', a mixture of languid
nonchalance and adolescent gaucherie, is perfect characterisation.
With its repeated A flats, it is not exactly the easiest music for
a mezzo-soprano to sing, but it requires a rich lower register if
the refrain (ending with a reiterated 'Chacun à son gout') is to
make its full effect.

Eisenstein, who is introduced as Marquis Renard, feels sure
that he can recognise in one of the guests his wife's maid, Adele,
but Orlofsky and the rest laugh at him for his curious mistake and
Adele herself sings a delightful soubrette song, 'Mein Herr
Marquis', in whose laughing refrain she is able to make fun of
her employer to her heart's content. Apart from the famous waltz,
this is possibly the best-known number of the score—but then,
Fledermaus is so unfailingly tuneful that there seems no necessity
to emphasise the popularity of one piece at the expense of the
rest.

Eisenstein recognises his maid, although he is persuaded to the contrary, but he does not know his wife when she comes in masked and is announced as a Hungarian Countess. She excites his curiosity straight away, and it is not long before he is showing her his chiming watch, a bait which has worked the trick on many an unsuspecting Miss. This time, though all seems to be beginning well, and Eisenstein is soon timing his Countess's heart-beats, something goes wrong, and the lady ends up with the watch, which is not at all according to plan. It is a delicious moment, this seduction duet, as anyone who has heard Julius Patzak and Hilde Güden sing it in the recording of the opera will know; we hear the watch chime before the singers launch into a gallop, and Rosalinda ends with peals of triumphant coloratura.

Rosalinda will not unmask and it is suggested by Adele that the reason for this is that she is not a Hungarian at all. 'I will prove it,' says Rosalinda; 'the music of my native country shall speak for me.' It is a flimsy enough pretext for the Czardas and Frischka which follows, but once it starts the music is exhilarating enough to make us forget why it began in the first place. If there were no other reason—and there are, in fact, plenty of reasons— this Czardas would make it certain that nobody but a really capable soprano could do justice to the role of Rosalinda. It is not only a display piece of a high order, but it demands something unusual in the way of a dramatic technique. In fact, Ernest Newman has said that the Czardas 'shows what depths of expression there were in Strauss had he chosen to explore them more consistently. No genuine Hungarian could sing more movingly of the pain of separation from the beloved homeland, or of the fire in the Hungarian breast that drives them to the dance . . .'

The finale begins. It opens with a short section in praise of champagne, *allegro con brio*. First Orlofsky, then Adele and finally Eisenstein leads the company, which joins in the chorus after the three verses. Eisenstein and Frank (who has been introduced as the Chevalier Chagrin) toast each other, and Falke, looking round at the assembled couples, proposes in a slow waltz tune that they shall pledge each other in eternal brother- and sisterhood. Coherent expression seems out of place, and, in their efforts to do justice to the toast, they resort to 'Duidu' and 'la, la, la', relapsing before long into silence for the ballet which, with its dancers, has been mentioned all along as one of the attractions of the party. It is customary to introduce the 'Blue Danube' waltz or some other of Strauss's most famous dances and subject them to balletic treatment at this point. At the end of the dance, Orlofsky suggests that the professional dancers should have a rest, and that the guests should show that they are no less adept at the waltz themselves. It is the famous *Fledermaus* waltz, heard first in the overture but now come into its own in the biggest way. It takes the foreground for most of the time, but also serves as background for the continued flirtation of Eisenstein and Rosalinda and for much comic byplay between Eisenstein and Governor Frank. Finally, the clock strikes six, Eisenstein remembers it is high time for him to go to prison, and the curtain comes down as he and Frank help each other from the ballroom.

Act III.   An entr'acte, part march, part waltz, introduces us to the prison, where Frosch, the gaoler (a speaking part), has been doing his best to emulate in his own quiet way the grander drinking exploits of Governor Frank; in a word, he is drunk, a situation of which full advantage is taken by the professional comic who is engaged to play the role. His inebriated gambollings are interrupted from time to time by snatches of song from cell No. 12, where Alfred is relieving the tedium of prison life with reminiscences of his serenade to Rosalinda, and with snatches of tunes from other operas as well, if the truth be known. Frosch staggers off to make another attempt to curb this nuisance, and no sooner has he gone than Frank comes in, no less the worse for wear than his underling. He makes his entrance to musical accompaniment, whistles the tune of the ball-room waltz, sings a bit of the champagne song, and eventually falls asleep to reminiscences of the waltz.

But his is not to be the sleep of the just, for Frosch has pulled himself together sufficiently to be able to make his morning report in the usual way. Nothing untoward has happened, he says, except that Herr von Eisenstein has been restless and, having asked for a lawyer, is to see Dr. Blind almost immediately. The door-bell rings, and Frosch announces the two young ladies who have so taken Frank's fancy at the ball, to wit Adele and her sister. Adele, it is explained, is not yet an artist in fact, only one by nature. Cannot Frank help her to start a stage career? She sings to him of her versatility ('Spiel ich die Unschuld vom Lande') and says there is nothing she cannot do on the stage, from country wench to Queen—to say nothing of a flirtatious French Marquise. There is another ring at the door, and the Marquis Renard is admitted. When he hears that the Chevalier Chagrin (whom he at first assumes to have been arrested for insobriety) is none other than the prison governor, he laughs aloud at what he thinks is a particularly good jest. Frank for his part cannot take seriously the announcement that his friend from the ball is Herr von Eisenstein; did he not himself escort that gentleman from his home to the prison, and is he not at this moment incarcerated within twenty feet of where they sit?

Frosch announces that another lady is without (the first two have been shown into cell No. 13, the only empty room), and Frank goes to greet her, leaving Eisenstein to waylay Blind and borrow his wig, glasses, and legal paraphernalia in the hope that he may discover who it was who was arrested in his place the previous night.

Rosalinda (it was she who rang just now) has come to see what can be done about getting Alfred out of prison, with the help maybe of the lawyer who is waiting for them. Eisenstein comes in in place of Blind and proceeds to cross-question the two with a vigour more becoming to a prosecuting counsel than to someone engaged for the defence, and they begin to wonder why he is so very strict. He demands the unvarnished truth, which he gets from Alfred in an agreeable tune, punctuated by his own frequent bursts of indignation as the story unfolds. After one of them, Rosalinda defends herself as the victim of a husband who is himself a monster of deceitfulness. Eventually, unable to bear the insults any longer—Alfred asks how they can between them throw dust in the husband's eyes—Eisenstein rises in fury and denounces (in the tune which opens the overture) what he describes as their treachery to him.

The explanation is not long in forthcoming. No sooner is the lively trio between Rosalinda, Eisenstein, and Alfred over, than the rest of the company at last night's ball appears as if summoned by magic, all that is to say apart from Adele and her sister—and news of them is quickly forthcoming when Frosch complains to Frank that the two ladies in No. 13 are proving obstructive and have refused to let him give them their regulation bath! Falke explains that Eisenstein's predicament is of his engineering, is in fact his vengeance for the shabby trick played on him a year ago. Alfred and Rosalinda are quick to take advantage of the situation and add that their supper was also an invention designed as part of the joke. Eisenstein is delighted at the way things have turned out, and Rosalinda sings the only possible moral: let all join with her in praising the sovereign reconciling power of King Champagne! H.

## DER ZIGEUNERBARON

### The Gipsy Baron

Operetta in three acts by Johann Strauss, text by J. Schnitzer, adapted from a libretto by M. Jokai, based on her story *Saffi*. First performed at the Theater des Westerns, Vienna, October 24, 1885; at the Staatsoper, Vienna, 1910; New York, 1886; London, Rudolf Steiner Theatre, 1935 (amateur production). Revived, New York City Center, 1944; Volksoper, Vienna, 1948, with Esther Réthy, Laszlo Szemere, Walter Höfermayer, Alfred Jerger, conducted by Anton Paulik.

### CHARACTERS

Graf Peter Homonay ......................... Baritone
Conte Carnero ............................... Baritone
Sandor Barinkay .............................. Tenor
Kalman Zsupan, *a pig-farmer* ................. Baritone
Arsena, *his daughter* ......................... Soprano
Mirabella, *her governess* ..................... Contralto
Ottokar ..................................... Tenor
Czipra, *a gipsy leader* .................. Mezzo-Soprano
Saffi, *her foster-daughter* ...................... Soprano
Pali, *a gipsy* ................................... Bass

Act I.    The overture, as is Strauss's custom, is based on tunes from the opera. We are in Hungary in the middle of the eighteenth century. The scene is the edge of a village, where stands a deserted and partly ruined castle, and a small peasant house. Nearby is a gipsy's hut. Rustic noises in the orchestra introduce a lazy, typically Straussian tune in 6/8 rhythm which is sung by the chorus. Ottokar, a young peasant, comes in vigorously cursing his continued lack of success in finding the treasure which is supposed to be hidden in the castle. Czipra, an old gipsy woman, taunts him for his love of Arsena, daughter of the rich pig-farmer, Zsupan, who lives nearby.

On to the scene comes a little group, headed by Sandor Barinkay, to whom by rightful inheritance belongs the castle; he is about to get it back with the help of Conte Carnero, Commissioner of Morals, who accompanies him. Barinkay gives a vivid account of his experiences in a song ('Als flotter Geist') which has a swinging waltz refrain in which the chorus joins and which is familiar to anyone who has ever seen a Strauss film. Carnero wants witnesses for the official reinstatement, but Czipra, pressed into service, says she cannot write and proceeds to read the hands of Barinkay and Carnero. Barinkay will find both happiness and fortune through a faithful wife, who will tell him through a dream how he can discover hidden treasure. Carnero too will find a treasure, now much increased in size, which he had thought lost years before. This mystifies the Commissioner, who cannot remember any such loss.

Zsupan is to be the other witness, and he appears, explaining in the thickest of country accents and the most comical of tunes ('Ja, das Schreiben und das Lesen') that reading and writing have never come his way; he is content with his pigs, and their products. When he hears that Barinkay is to be his neighbour, he warns him to expect some litigation in the matter of property; Barinkay suggests that a match with Zsupan's daughter would prevent any such unpleasantness, and Zsupan calls his daughter from the house. It is not Arsena who answers his summons but Mirabella, her governess, who turns out to be no other than Carnero's long-lost wife (Schatz=darling, as well as treasure). She explains in a song that she had thought him lost these twenty-four years. Czipra's first prophecy is fulfilled.

Arsena eventually makes her appearance, veiled and by no means overjoyed at the prospect of another suitor, as she makes quite clear in a charming song with interjections from the chorus. In spite of Barinkay's graceful proposal of marriage, in spite of the charm of her song, Arsena has fully made up her mind not to marry Barinkay, for the very good reason that she already has a lover; she says she requires a noble suitor and warns Barinkay not, moth-like, to singe his wings at the candle flame.

Barinkay is left alone, disconsolate at his failure. He overhears Saffi, Czipra's daughter, sing a gipsy song in praise of the loyalty the gipsy prides himself on showing to his friend ('So elend und so treu'); it ends with an impassioned *allegretto*. Barinkay is not slow to accept the invitation of the beautiful gipsy girl and her mother and joins them for supper.

It turns out to be Ottokar with whom Arsena is in love, and their after-dark flirtation is observed and overheard by Barinkay, Saffi, and Czipra, the former swearing to be revenged on Arsena for her cavalier treatment of him. The gipsies can be heard in the distance singing the song Saffi has already made known to us, and when they appear Czipra tells them that Barinkay is the true owner of the castle. They make him their chief, and he loses no time in knocking on Zsupan's door and telling him that he now has the title on which Arsena insisted: he is a Gipsy Baron. 'Er ist Baron' sings the ensemble, and Saffi welcomes him to the land of his childhood in a tune already familiar from the overture. Zsupan starts to tell Barinkay he is not the right sort of Baron, but Barinkay makes it quite clear that his ideas have changed; he does not want to marry Arsena, but Saffi! Zsupan is furious, but all join in the big tune of the overture which comes as it were as the coda of the finale.

Act II.    The entr'acte, made up of the tune of the opening chorus of Act I, introduces the dawn. Barinkay has spent the night in the ruins of the castle, with Czipra and Saffi, and the three greet the day in a trio ('Mein Aug' bewacht') which ends in something more like a love duet for the two young people. Czipra tells of a dream she has had in which she found the treasure which legend has always associated with the castle; Barinkay laughs at the idea, but agrees to look where she directs—what's the harm? Czipra and Saffi have a little tune in which they mock his scepticism, and all three join in the rapturous treasure waltz ('Ha, seht es winkt') when they uncover the treasure itself. This is one of Strauss's most charming inspirations, and a comparison between it and the ensemble at the end of the previous act shows how much more at home he is writing a simple tune, simply harmonised, than trying to devise something more complicated.

The gipsies arrive to start work at their forge. They sing as they come, and the skit on the anvil chorus from *Trovatore* is unmistakable; the chorus finishes in a gallop. Zsupan appears with the object of getting help for a wagon which has stuck in the mud, but he insults the gipsies who get their own back by stealing his money and his watch. His cries of fury bring Carnero, Mirabella, Ottokar, and Arsena on to the scene, and they are followed by Barinkay and Saffi. Barinkay is by now dressed as a Gipsy Baron, and he greets them with the information that he and Saffi are man and wife. Carnero starts to ask certain questions about the legal side of the affair, and Saffi and Barinkay answer him in a duet which has become the most famous number of the opera: 'Wer uns getraut?' (Who married us?) The birds have performed the ceremony and acted as witness, says Barinkay, and he joins Saffi in the slow refrain.

This is too much for Carnero, who leads Mirabella and Zsupan in a comic ode to morality, the so-called 'Sittencommissions Couplets'.

There is a diversion when Ottokar finds a few pieces of gold and thinks he is on the track of the treasure at last, but Barinkay disillusions him, and next moment the stage is full of a recruiting party, headed by Barinkay's old friend, Graf Peter Homonay. Led by Homonay, they sing a recruiting song and follow it up with a stirring Csardas. Homonay refuses to be shocked at Barinkay and Saffi and in spite of the protestations of Carnero congratulates them on the match.

During the course of the finale, Czipra makes it known that Saffi is not really her daughter but a Princess whom she has brought up, and who is descended from the last Pasha of Hungary —she even has documentary proof. 'Ein Fürstenkind', sings the whole company to the music of a gallop, and Saffi joins in with a couple of top C's. Barinkay alone cannot play his part in the rejoicing: Saffi is now unapproachably above him, and he will join Ottokar and Zsupan, who have been impressed, and go off to the wars. His regret is touchingly shown, but the Act ends with the 'Werberlied' repeated by the whole company, topped by repeated B's and C's from Saffi.

Act III. The entr'acte makes use of the treasure waltz, and the scene is laid in Vienna, where all are assembled to welcome the victorious army, among which are Barinkay, Ottokar, and Zsupan. Arsena sings a little song about the incompatibility of courtship and propriety, but the little group is soon joined by the returning heroes. Zsupan sings to them of his exploits, which are hardly of the most military nature but which seem to have been entirely successful. Again, this is an opportunity for the comedian. The rest of the army comes marching on, and we are soon told of the distinguished service of both Barinkay and Ottokar, each of whom is to be rewarded with a title of nobility. In the finale, all difficulties are resolved, Arsena flies into Ottokar's arms, and Saffi appears from nowhere to greet Barinkay, who leads the full company in a final statement of the waltz refrain of his opening song. H.

# KARL MILLÖCKER
## (1842–1899)

### DER BETTELSTUDENT
#### The Beggar Student

COMIC opera in three acts by Karl Millöcker. Text by Zell and Genée. First performed at the Theater an der Wien, Vienna, December 6, 1882; New York, 1883; London, Alhambra Theatre, 1884 (in English), Royalty Theatre, 1895 (in German). Revived at Vienna, Staatsoper, 1936, with Margit Bokor, Dora Komarek, Richard Sallaba, Alfred Jerger, Frederick Gynrod, conductor Josef Krips; Volksoper, 1949, with Maria Cebotari, Lorna Sidney, Fred Liewehr, Kurt Preger, Walter Höfermayer, conductor Anton Paulik.

### CHARACTERS

Palmatica, *Countess Nowalska* ............ Mezzo-Soprano
Countess Laura, *her daughter* .................. Soprano
Countess Bronislawa, *Laura's sister* ............. Soprano
Simon, *the Beggar Student* ....................... Tenor
Jan Janitzky, *Simon's friend* ..................... Tenor
Colonel Ollendorf ............................... Bass
Enterich, *Prison Governor* ..................... Baritone
Richthofen ⎤
Wangenheim ⎬ *Saxon officers*
Henrici ⎦

Colonel Ollendorf, Cracow's irascible governor, has been badly hurt: he was just starting to make advances to Countess Laura, a proud Polish beauty, when she struck him in the face with her fan—in public, and at an official ball! Honour must be satisfied and he will have his revenge.

Act I.   We are in the prison; the prisoners' wives try to persuade Enterich, the prison governor, to let them see their husbands. He is disposed to grant their request, but he confiscates the various delicacies which are intended to cheer the prisoners' lot. To the prison comes Ollendorf, complaining loudly at the treatment meted out to him the night before. His entrance song, with its waltz refrain 'Ach, ich hab' sie ja nur auf die Schulter geküsst', gives an excellent opportunity to a comic bass. The object of Ollendorf's visit is to find two young prisoners and persuade them in return for their freedom to aid him in his scheme of revenge: they are to make love to Countess Laura and her sister, and he will then be able to expose the joke and so revenge the insult to his honour. The two Poles he chooses— political prisoners, both of them—seem light-hearted enough to judge by their duet; they agree to fall in with the scheme, and promise to say nothing about its origin. Ollendorf will fit them out as Prince Wibicky and his secretary—and they will be free.

The scene changes to a fair in the Rathausplatz in Cracow, which is ushered in with a brisk 6/8 chorus and a march. Palmatica and her daughters are there, too poor to buy anything, but doing their best in their 3/8 trio to disguise this painful fact by sneering at what is exposed for sale. Ollendorf introduces the Prince Wibicky and his companion to the Countess and her daughters, and Simon proceeds to tell them of his wanderings over the earth; the flirtations he has indulged in wherever he has been have only proved to him how far superior Polish girls are to those in the rest of the world. His romance, 'Ich knüpfte manche zarte Bande' (Full many a tender knot I've tied), is an excellent example of the unpretentiousness and graceful charm which is to be found in Millöcker at his best. Simon proposes to Laura, and all sit down to table to celebrate the betrothal with—since Ollendorf has to pay—the best mine host can bring them. Laura sings a Polish song—joy and grief, she says, are closely allied; its solemn *andante* opening soon gives way to a sparkling *allegretto*. The town band puts in an appearance with a march which takes its cue from Schubert rather than Sousa, and the act comes to an end with general rejoicing.

Act II.     Laura is at home trying on her wedding dress, assisted by her mother and her sister. She repeats the advice her mother has given her, that husbands can and should be dominated by their wives—not by direct precept but by persuasion, by tears not threats. The Prince's secretary is announced, and Jan makes love to Bronislawa in a charming duet.

Jan reminds Simon that plans are afoot to restore Cracow to the Poles, that the King's nephew, Duke Adam, is preparing a coup, and that only money is wanting. It looks as though their schemes are coming to fruition. Simon is alone with Laura; would she still love him, he asks, if he were poor, untitled, even an impostor? She tells him her love were proof against any such change in his status, and asks him whether he would love her if someone prettier came along, rich and well-born? Simon reassures her in his turn. The music of the second part of this duet ('Ich setz den Fall') is the same as that of the first, the only difference being that Laura in the second half sings what Simon had sung in the first, and he takes over what she had originally sung. Taking courage from what Laura has told him, Simon writes her a note telling her the truth about his deception; he is astonished when he sees later that its reception seems to have made no difference in her attitude towards him, but he does not know that Ollendorf has had it intercepted. The marriage is performed, and Ollendorf waits to savour his triumph, which will not be long delayed. The happy couple are congratulated, their healths drunk in the bride's shoe, the mazurka is danced, when suddenly the sound of rowdy singing is heard outside: Simon's fellow-prisoners have come to join in the fun. All must come out. Ollendorf explains that the joke was his revenge: after all, he only kissed her on the shoulder, but she slapped his face in public. She may repent now at her leisure.

Act III.   The aftermath of Ollendorf's disclosure is still to be reckoned with. People comment on Simon's dastardly behaviour, and on the punishment which they cannot help thinking Laura has earned by her behaviour. Bronislawa confesses that she is still secure in her love, and that the day's tragedy has not had the effect of removing her appetite, which she had hoped would be assuaged at the wedding feast.

Simon is disconsolate, but Jan explains to him that all will yet be well. He seems disgraced but he has yet a part to play in the freeing of Cracow. Ollendorf has approached Jan and bribed him—with the 200,000 of money they need to finance Duke Adam's insurrection—if he will give the patriot away. He for his part has promised to do so after the wedding feast, and Simon must pretend, for the sake of Poland, to be the Duke; only by this means can enough time be gained to enable the Duke himself to get inside the gates with his troops. Simon confesses that the game is up for him in his best known aria, 'Ich hab' kein Geld, bin Vogelfrei' (I'm quite cleaned out, my money's gone), with its refrain challenging Dame Fortune to another game of chance.

Palmatica takes to abusing poor Simon, in spite of the comment of Ollendorf and Jan, and much to the Beggar Student's rage.

Eventually, Ollendorf reveals what he describes as the fact of the matter: he has discovered that Simon is none other than Duke Adam, and he must take him off to prison and there chop off his head. Consternation is general, not least as far as Simon is concerned; Palmatica says she suspected he was noble all along and is delighted to have him as son-in-law, Laura frantically announces she will die with him, and Jan trembles in case Simon should not play his part adequately. All is well, however; a cannon shot is heard, and the news arrives that Duke Adam has won control of the city. Ollendorf admits there is nothing more for him to do but give himself up—whereupon Bronislawa says *she* has already surrendered herself, to the Secretary. Laura says she has done no less, to the Beggar Student, but Jan hastens to correct her: in future he will be known as Count Simon Rymanowitsch. The opera ends in rejoicing. H.

# ENGELBERT HUMPERDINCK

## 1854–1921

### HAENSEL UND GRETEL

OPERA in three acts by Engelbert Humperdinck; text by Adelheid Wette (the composer's sister). First performed at the Hoftheater, Weimar, December 23, 1893; Daly's Theatre, London, 1894 (in English), with Marie Elba, Jeanne Douste, Edith Miller, Julia Lennox, Charles Copland, conductor Arditi; Drury Lane, 1895 (in German), by the Ducal Court Company of Saxe-Coburg and Gotha; Covent Garden, 1896, with Marie Elba, Jessie Huddleston, Lilian Tree, Luise Meisslinger, David Bispham, conductor Mancinelli; New York, Daly's Theatre, 1895 (in English); Metropolitan, 1905 (in German), with Lina Abarbanell, Bella Alten, Louise Homer, Marion Weed, Otto Goritz, conductor Alfred Hertz; Covent Garden, by B.N.O.C., January 1923 (first broadcast of a complete opera from an opera house in Europe), with Doris Lemon, Lillian Stanford, Sydney Russell, Richard Collins.

### CHARACTERS

Haensel .............................. Mezzo-Soprano
Gretel, his sister............................. Soprano
The Witch ............................ Mezzo-Soprano
Gertrude, mother of Haensel and Gretel.......... Soprano
Peter, their father ............................ Baritone
Sandman ................................... Soprano
Dew Fairy .................................. Soprano

The opera has established itself in the repertory and is played in almost every town at Christmas.

The first act represents the hut of a broom-maker. Haensel is binding brooms and Gretel is knitting. The children romp, quarrel, and make up. When their mother, Gertrude, enters she is angry to see them idle, and trying to smack them she upsets a pitcher of milk instead. With all hope of supper vanished she sends the children out into the woods with little baskets to look for strawberries, while she herself, bemoaning their poverty, sinks exhausted upon a chair and falls asleep. A riotous song announces the approach of her husband, drunk as usual. She is about to reproach him when she notices that he has brought sausages, bread and butter, coffee—enough for a feast. He tells her that he has had good luck at the Kirmes and bids her prepare supper. When he asks for the children he is horrified to hear that

PLATE XIII. (above) 'Fredda ed immobile'; *Il Barbiere di Siviglia* in an imaginative production (Günther Rennert) and set (Alfred Siercke) on the very shallow stage at Hamburg 1948.

(below) Giulietta Simionato and Mario Petri in *L'Italiana in Algeri*, la Scala, Milan 1953.

PLATE XIV. Maria Meneghini Callas in *Norma*, Covent Garden 195

they have been sent into the woods, for a wicked fairy lives near the Ilsenstein who entices children to bake them in her oven and devour them. Both parents rush off in search of Haensel and Gretel.

The second act takes place near the Ilsenstein. Haensel has filled his basket with berries and Gretel has made a wreath with which her brother crowns her. Before they realise what they are doing the children eat all the berries. Then they see that it is too dark to look for any more or to find their way home. Gretel weeps with fear and Haensel comforts her. They grow sleepy. The sandman sprinkles sand into their eyes, but before going to sleep the children are careful not to forget their evening prayer. Fourteen guardian angels are seen descending the heavenly ladder to protect them.

Morning comes with the third act. The dew fairy sprinkles dew on the children. Suddenly they notice a little house made of cake and sugar. They start to break off little bits when a voice cries out from within and the witch opens the door. She throws a rope around Haensel's throat, and tells them both to come in. Frightened, they try to escape, but after binding them with a magic spell she imprisons Haensel in a kennel, and forces Gretel to go into the house.

When she believes Haensel to be asleep she turns her attention to the oven, then rides around the house on her broom-stick. When she alights she orders Haensel to show her his finger. But he pokes a stick through the bars and, thinking it is still thin, the witch orders more food for him. While she turns her back, Gretel seizes the juniper bough with which the old woman makes her spells, speaks the magic words and breaks her brother's enchantment. Then the witch tells Gretel to get into the oven and see if the honey cakes are done. But Gretel pretends to be stupid and asks her to show her how to get in. Together the children push the old witch into the oven and slam the door. The oven soon falls to pieces. The children then see a row of boys and girls standing stiffly against the house. Gretel breaks the spell for them as she had done for Haensel. There is general rejoicing, Gertrude and Peter appear, the old witch is pulled out of the ruined oven as a gigantic honey cake and everyone on the stage joins in a hymn of thanksgiving.

The overture, based on motives from the opera, is very well

known. In Act I, there is a long duet for the two children, culminating in their dance, and the rollicking 'Tra-la-la-la' entrance song of the father. Act II begins with the Witches' Ride, and contains the Sandman's song, the children's evening prayer, and the Wagnerian Angels' pantomime. Act III has the Dew Fairy's song, the Witch's big solo, and the Witch waltz in which Haensel and Gretel celebrate their triumph.  K.W.

# HUGO WOLF
## (1860–1903)

## DER CORREGIDOR
### The Magistrate

OPERA in four acts by Hugo Wolf; text by Rosa Mayreder-Obermeyer founded on P. de Alarcon's story *El sombrero de tres picos*. Première in Mannheim, June 7, 1896. First performed in Vienna, under Mahler, 1904, with Förster-Lauterer (Frasquita), Breuer (Corregidor), Demuth (Tio Lucas), and Hesch (Repela); London, Royal Academy of Music, 1934; Salzburg Festival, 1936, with Novotna (Frasquita), Thorborg (Mercedes), Bella Paalen, Gunnar Graarud, Jerger, Zec, Ludwig Hoffmann, conductor Bruno Walter.

### CHARACTERS

Don Eugenio de Zuniga, *the Corregidor*
(*magistrate*) .............................Buffo Tenor
Doña Mercedes, *his wife* ......................Soprano
Repela, *his valet* ...........................Buffo Bass
Tio Lucas, *a miller* ..........................Baritone
Frasquita, *his wife* .....................Mezzo-Soprano
Juan Lopez, *the alcalde* (*mayor*) ...................Bass
Pedro, *his secretary* ...........................Tenor
Manuela, *a maid* ......................Mezzo-Soprano
Tonuelo, *a court messenger* .......................Bass
A Neighbour ...................................Tenor
A Duenna, *employed by the Corregidora* ...Mezzo-Soprano

Act I.   The miller, Tio Lucas, is living a happy life with his beautiful wife, Frasquita. Her love is so true that jealousy, to which he is inclined, cannot thrive. Jealous? Yes, he has a bump of jealousy. True, the Corregidor, who is keenly interested in the miller's pretty wife, has one too. But no matter, he is a high, very influential functionary. Meanwhile Frasquita loves her Tio Lucas so truly that she can even allow herself a dance with the Corregidor. Perhaps she will cure him so, perhaps she will obtain in addition the wished-for official place for her nephew. The Corregidor too does not keep her waiting long and Frasquita makes him so much in love with her that he becomes very impetuous.

Thereupon he loses his balance and the worthy official falls in the dust, out of which the miller, without suspecting anything, raises him up. But the Corregidor swears revenge.

Act II.    The opportunity for this comes very quickly. As the miller one evening is sitting with his wife in their cosy room, there comes a knock at the door. It is the drunken court messenger, Tonuelo, who produces a warrant of arrest. Tio Lucas must follow him without delay to the alcalde who has lent himself as a willing instrument to the Corregidor's scheme. Frasquita is trying to calm her anxiety with a song when outside there is a cry for help. She opens the door and before it stands the Corregidor dripping with water. He has fallen in the brook. Now he begs admission from Frasquita who is raging with anger. He has even brought with him the appointment of the nephew. But the angry woman will pay no attention and sends the Corregidor away from her threshold. Then he falls in a swoon. His own servant now comes along. Frasquita admits both of them to the house and herself goes into town to look for her Tio Lucas. When the Corregidor, awakened out of his swoon, hears this, full of anxiety, he sends his valet after her; he himself, however, hangs his wet clothes before the fire and goes to bed in the miller's bedroom.

(Change of scene.) In the meantime Tio Lucas drinks the alcalde and his fine comrades under the table and seizes the occasion to flee.

Act III.    In the darkness of the night, Tio Lucas and Frasquita pass by without seeing each other. The miller comes to his mill. (Change of scene.) Everything is open. In the dust lies the deed of appointment for the nephew; before the fire hang the Corregidor's clothes. A frightful suspicion arises in Tio Lucas's mind which becomes certainty when through the keyhole he sees the Corregidor in his own bed. He is already groping for his rifle to shoot the seducer and the faithless woman when another thought strikes him. The Corregidor also has a wife, a beautiful wife. Here the Corregidor's clothes are hanging close at hand. He quickly slips into them and goes back to town. In the meantime the Corregidor has awakened. He wants to go back home now. But he does not find his clothes and so he crawls into those of the miller, and in them is almost arrested by the alcalde who now enters with his companions and Frasquita. When the

misunderstanding is cleared up, they all go with different feelings
into the town after the miller.

Act IV.    Now comes the explanation and the punishment of
the Corregidor, at least in so far as he receives a sound thrashing
and becomes really humbled. In reality the miller also has not
yet had his 'revenge', but he is recognised and is likewise beaten
blue—*that* he must suffer in reparation for his churlish doubt of
the faithful Frasquita.

The comedy of *Der Corregidor* is *durchkomponiert*. The overture opens with the Corregidor theme (later played on the trombones), and makes play also with the E major love music, which
is later heard in the first scene of the second act. Two of Wolf's
songs are worked into the libretto of the work, the first, 'In dem
Schatten meiner Locken', sung by Frasquita to the Corregidor,
the second to words by Heine, 'Herz, verzage nicht geschwind',
sung by the Corregidor at the end of the first scene of Act II.

K.W.

# CHAPTER 7

## *Italian Opera*

# DOMENICO CIMAROSA
## 1749–1801

### IL MATRIMONIO SEGRETO

OPERA buffa in two acts by Domenico Cimarosa. Text by Giovanni Bertati after Colman's *The Clandestine Marriage.* First performed at the Burgtheater, Vienna, February 7, 1792; la Scala, Milan, 1793; London, 1794; Her Majesty's, 1842; Covent Garden, 1849. Recent revivals include Metropolitan, 1937, with Natalie Bodanya, Muriel Dickson, Ira Petina, George Rasely, Julius Huehn and Louis D'Angelo; Rome, 1948, with Alda Noni, Angela Tuccari, Palmira Vitali-Marini, Cesare Valletti, Antonio Cassinelli and Vito de Taranto; la Scala, Milan, 1949, with Alda Noni, Hilde Güden, Fedora Barbieri, Tito Schipa, Boris Christoff, and Sesto Bruscantini; Fortune Theatre, London, by the London Opera Club, 1949, with Maureen Springer, Pamela Woolmore, Bruna Maclean, Richard Lewis, Bruce Boyce, and Owen Brannigan; Edinburgh, by Piccola Scala, 1957, with Sciutti, Ratti, Alva, cond. Sanzogno.

### CHARACTERS

| | |
|---|---|
| Geronimo | Buffo |
| Elisetta, *his daughter* | Soprano |
| Carolina, *another daughter* | Soprano |
| Fidalma, *Geronimo's sister* | Mezzo-Soprano |
| Count Robinson, *an English milord* | Bass |
| Paolino | Tenor |

*Time:* Eighteenth Century          *Place:* Bologna

Cimarosa's most famous opera has the distinction of being reputedly the only work ever encored *in toto* on the occasion of its first performance. History has it that the Emperor Leopold II, for whom Mozart wrote *La Clemenza di Tito* a few months earlier, so enjoyed the work that he invited all the participants to supper, after which the performance was repeated!

The story is concerned with events at the house of one Geronimo, a wealthy citizen of Bologna, whose sister Fidalma is installed as mistress of his house, and who has two daughters, Elisetta and Carolina. At the opening of the first act we meet Carolina and Paolino, the latter a junior business associate of Geronimo's and secretly married to Carolina. In their first duet she urges him to hide the secret of their marriage no longer but to reveal it to everyone. There is another duet in lighter vein as

Carolina says 'Goodbye' to her husband. Geronimo appears, inclined to deafness and definitely afflicted by the golden malady of the *nouveau riche*. He learns from Paolino that the latter's friend, the English Count Robinson, is on his way to Bologna with the firm intention of arranging a match with no other than Elisetta, Geronimo's daughter. Nothing will please him but to recount the news with all its imports to his family, which he does in a *buffo* aria. The sisters immediately find cause to quarrel, much to Fidalma's annoyance; a trio brings the quarrel to a musical climax.

Fidalma admits to Elisetta that she herself is in love—she underlines it in a song—but she will not admit with whom, though she whispers in an aside to the audience that it is Paolino.

Geronimo cannot wait for the Count's arrival. The English nobleman duly appears and proceeds to address everyone with a maximum of words and a minimum of content—he hates a man who cannot be brief, he says. The situation develops until it becomes, musically speaking, a sextet, and the Count mistakes both the other ladies in turn for the Elisetta who is his bride-to-be. In conversation with Paolino shortly afterwards he reveals that the prospect of marriage with Elisetta fills him with consternation, while he looks with nothing but favour on union with Carolina—a fact which causes Paolino not a little consternation. He proposes to Carolina, but is told as politely as possible that she is not disposed to welcome his proposal; she even lists in her aria the faults which she says she possesses.

Preparations are being made for the banquet which is to be given in the Count's honour, when that worthy himself enters, protesting his love to Carolina. Elisetta interrupts and upbraids them for their conduct, but Fidalma manages to silence the quarrel which ensues by warning them that Geronimo approaches. He does his best to discover what is the cause of all the fuss, but his deafness, Paolino's unwillingness to let him find out that the Count wishes to marry Carolina (not unnaturally, since she is already Paolino's wedded wife), Fidalma's preoccupation with avoiding a family quarrel, and the fact that everyone talks at once, prevents him from carrying out his intention.

At the beginning of the second act Geronimo is still trying to find out what it is all about, and he is found alone with the Count. After some misunderstanding, he gathers that his prospective son-in-law has not taken kindly to his bride-to-be. After voicing their mutual dissatisfaction, the two parties come to an agreement when the Count suggests that he resign half the dowry he has been promised if Geronimo will allow him to marry the younger of his two daughters. This arrangement suits Geronimo admirably, and their duet ends in complete accord.

Paolino is told of the new arrangement, and in his desperation is just going to throw himself on Fidalma's mercy, when she, encouraged by what she takes to be glances and sighs directed at her, says that she will accept his proposal and marry him! Paolino can stand the strain no longer and faints away. It is while Fidalma is trying to revive him that Carolina comes on the scene. Fidalma goes to fetch some smelling-salts, and the wretched Paolino tries to explain the situation to Carolina, but it is not until the trio is over and he is able to embark on an aria that he manages to convince her that his protestations of love are not mere deceit.

The Count now tries, by depicting himself as an ogre and a monster of iniquity, to persuade Elisetta to break off the marriage. He fails in this object, and Elisetta and Fidalma (who has revealed that Carolina, though the object of the Count's affections, is herself in love with Paolino) plot to rid themselves of their rival and send her to a convent. Geronimo agrees, and tells her himself of his decision. Poor Carolina is broken-hearted, and her music takes on a moving character as she thinks of the future without her husband. The Count offers his help in her distress, and she is just about to tell him the whole truth when her sister, her aunt, and her father jump out on them, declaring that there can be no further doubt since they have caught them in the act. Geronimo sends Paolino off at once with a letter to the lady superior of the convent.

The finale begins. The Count is out of his room, although it is night, and muses on the possibility of helping Carolina when he is surprised by the watchful Elisetta; they say good-night to each other and depart, to be succeeded by Paolino and Carolina planning an elopement. Disturbed by a noise, they quickly hide in Carolina's room, and in a moment the suspicious Elisetta is on the scene. She listens at the door, hears whispers, and rouses the house to come and catch the Count in her sister's room. Everyone rushes to the spot and together they demand that the Count shall come forth and reveal his perfidy. He does—but from his own room, where he has been asleep until woken up by the din. A moment later, Carolina and Paolino come out of the room and admit that they were married two months ago. Eventually, all is forgiven, the Count agrees to marry Elisetta, and happiness reigns supreme.

Cimarosa's main disadvantage *vis-à-vis* a modern audience is that his music reminds them, now of Mozart, now of Rossini, and that in each case they are inclined to compare him unfavourably with the more familiar master. But there is a great deal of excellent music in this opera, and the two finales are models of their kind, as are the arias for Carolina and Paolino, and the comedy duet between Geronimo and the Count.          H.

# GIOACCHINO ANTONIO ROSSINI

## (1792–1868)

### L'ITALIANA IN ALGERI

OPERA in two acts by Gioacchino Rossini; text by A. Anelli (originally written for L. Mosca and performed at the Scala in 1808). Première on May 22, 1813, at Teatro San Benedetto, Venice. First performed in London, Haymarket Theatre, 1819 (in Italian); Princess's Theatre, 1844 (in English); New York, 1832 (in Italian). Revived Metropolitan, New York, 1919, with Besanzoni, Hackett, Didur, de Luca, conductor Papi; Turin, 1925, with Supervia, conductor Gui; Rome, 1927, with Supervia, Folgar, Bettoni, Scattola; Paris, 1933; la Scala, Milan, 1933, with Castagna; Covent Garden, 1935, with Supervia, Ederle, Bettoni, Scattola, conductor Bellezza; Colon, Buenos Aires, 1938, with Pederzini, conductor Serafin; Basle, 1938, with Else Böttcher; Florence Festival, 1941, with Pederzini; Fenice, Venice, 1946, with Danco; Rome Opera, 1948, with Pederzini, Sinimberghi, Bettoni, Ghirardini, conductor Gui; la Scala, 1953, with Simionato, Dobbs, Valletti, Bruscantini, Petri; Glyndebourne 1957, with Dominguez, Oncina, Montarsolo, Cortis, cond. Gui.

### CHARACTERS

Mustafa, *Bey of Algiers* ............................Bass
Elvira, *his wife* .................................Soprano
Zulma, *her confidante* ..........................Contralto
Haly, *in the service of the Bey* ......................Bass
Lindoro, *an Italian in love with Isabella* ............Tenor
Isabella ........................................Contralto
Taddeo, *an old Italian*..........................Baritone

Rossini's *L'Italiana in Algeri* is *commedia dell'arte* set to music. The plot and the words are less those of a well-constructed play, rather the situations used by the actors of the *commedia dell'arte* for their free invention. The nearest parallel to it is the modern music hall, where the comedian is accustomed to 'gag' at will, and in fact relies very largely on this method to hold his audience's attention. Improvisation was out of the question the moment music entered into partnership, but the plot provides plenty of evidence as to its origin.

On its first performance, the opera was immediately successful. 'When Rossini wrote *L'Italiana*', notes Stendhal, 'his youthful genius was bursting into flower.' And the brilliant character of the work shows clearly the spirit, optimism, and geniality of youth (Rossini was only twenty-one at the time). The whole work was written in twenty-seven days.

Act I.    The overture, one of the composer's most famous, begins with a strong feeling of latent drama, but this soon gives way to an enchanting *allegro*. The interplay of the woodwind, and in fact the writing for this section of the orchestra throughout the opera, is particularly attractive.

We are in the palace of the Bey of Algiers. A chorus of the eunuchs of the harem (tenors and basses, surprisingly enough) laments the sad lot of women, while Elvira, the Bey's wife, assisted by her confidante, Zulma, bemoans her own tragedy—her husband no longer loves her. Enter the Bey in person. With a multitude of roulades he inveighs against the arrogance of women, and, the moment Elvira speaks directly to him, protests that his eardrums are broken. A lively ensemble ensues (it is a quartet, Haly, the captain of the Bey's corsairs, having joined the family quarrel), and at its end Haly is told by the Bey that he must go off and find him an Italian wife—nothing else will satisfy him. (Haly's name will impress the Englishman as more apt to the context if he imagines it without the initial 'H'.)

The Bey has in his service an Italian, now one of the slaves, by name Lindoro. In a slow cavatina, 'Languir per una bella', he laments the absence of his beloved. It is a particularly attractive example of Rossini's highly decorated lyric style, and is followed by a vigorous *cabaletta*, no less full of *coloratura* and, with its high C's, B naturals, and B flats, calculated to try the technique of any but the most agile of tenors. The Bey asks Lindoro whether he would like to get married. Not unless he was in love, is Lindoro's reply. A charming duet ensues between the two. The subject is marriage, with particular reference to the qualifications necessary in the prospective partner, and in style it is not unlike that between Almaviva and Figaro in the first act of *Il Barbiere*.

The scene changes. Isabella, who has been roaming the seas in search of her lost lover Lindoro, is involved in a shipwreck, conveniently on the shore of Algeria. Haly's men exclaim on the beauty of the slaves, and on Mustafa's good fortune in securing so many additions to his harem. 'Cruda sorte!' (Cruel fate) sings Isabella; she is in this danger only because of her faithfulness to Lindoro—but the cabaletta leaves us in no doubt whatsoever as to her confidence in her own ability to look after herself. All are made prisoner, and Haly is overjoyed to find that Isabella and Taddeo, an ageing and comic admirer she has brought with her for company on the voyage, are indeed Italians; they shall go to the Bey. Left alone with Taddeo, Isabella seems less dismayed than he at the indication that she is destined for the Bey's Seraglio. They quarrel and argue about the situation in their duet, 'Ai capricci della sorte', but all is made up in a charming *allegro vivace*, in which they agree that the status of uncle and niece (which they have decided shall be their official relationship) has its advantages. The tune is enchantingly silly, and an excellent example of Rossini's ability to write music that is genuinely comic as well as being, in the hands of the right singers, extremely pretty.

We return to the palace. Elvira and Zulma remonstrate with Lindoro because he seems disinclined to marry the former, even though the Bey has offered him freedom (and money) if he will take her off his hands. Haly brings the news of Isabella's capture, and the Bey rejoices at his good fortune in an aria whose coloratura difficulties rival those of a Handel bass aria: 'Gia d'insolito ardore'. After he has gone, Elvira admits she still loves her inconstant husband, but Lindoro comforts her: if she comes to Italy with him, she will find husbands and lovers as she pleases.

The finale begins with the eunuchs singing the praises of 'Mustafa the scourge of women, who changes them from tigresses to lambs'. Isabella is led in and cannot contain her amusement at the sight of Mustafa; her tune is irresistibly comic, and the duet as she makes up to the bemused Mustafa is very funny. Taddeo pushes himself forward: is he not her uncle? A quartet follows between Isabella, Taddeo, Haly, and Mustafa, and at its end, Elvira, Zulma, and Lindoro enter the hall. Isabella and Lindoro recognise each other, and the quartet becomes a septet, dominated by a florid figure for Lindoro and Mustafa. Isabella makes a fuss when she discovers that Elvira is the Bey's wife whom he is discarding, and the complications mount until the end of the act.

Act II. The eunuchs comment on Mustafa's love-lorn condition. Haly advises Elvira and Zulma to keep on the right side of Mustafa; he may change his mind again. At the moment, there appears no prospect of this, for, no sooner has he come in, than he sends his wife and her slave to tell the Italian girl he wishes to drink coffee with her later. Isabella, alone with Lindoro, reproaches him because of his forthcoming marriage to Elvira, but eventually accepts his protestations of unchanging affection for herself, and together they plan an escape, the prospect of which spurs Lindoro to an even more exuberant expression of devotion than heretofore. Mustafa tells Taddeo that he will make him, in honour of his niece, Grand Kaimakan of Algeria. The chorus sing his praises, and Taddeo follows with an amusing aria, 'Ho un gran peso sulla testa'.

Isabella is in front of her looking-glass, finishing dressing. Elvira and Zulma come to deliver the Bey's message, and Isabella orders coffee for three from her slave, Lindoro, saying she would not dream of excluding the Bey's wife from the party. She will in fact, as woman to woman, give her a much needed lesson in man-management. Sitting in front of her looking-glass and watched from behind by Lindoro, Haly and Mustafa, she sings 'Per lui, che adoro', which is in effect an aria with comments and later accompaniment from the three men. Mustafa cannot wait to be alone with Isabella and tells Taddeo that it is his duty as Kaimakan to conduct her to his presence and leave them alone together. At the beginning of the quintet, Mustafa makes formal and florid presentation to Isabella of Taddeo, Grand Kaimakan; this over he sets about getting rid of the men, but with little success. Coffee comes in, and, after a moment, so does Elvira, and what has begun as a quartet becomes a quintet. Mustafa becomes enraged, and the ensemble ends in a *crescendo* of pandemonium.

Haly is found alone; in a pleasantly straightforward aria 'Le femine d'Italia', he praises the wiles of Italian women and the way in which they insinuate themselves into men's affections. No sooner has he left the stage than Taddeo and Lindoro appear, the former telling the latter in confidence that he loves Isabella, whom he once thought loved a certain Lindoro, but whom he finds loves him (Taddeo) truly after all. Lindoro is suitably impressed by the announcement, but privately finds time to express pleasure that his rival should be so obviously insignificant. As Mustafa comes in, Lindoro whispers to his compatriot to back him up in the plan he is about to put forward. Mustafa seems disposed to complain of the treatment he has received at Isabella's hands, but he is reassured, and told she waits only until he joins that ancient and noble Italian order of the 'Pappatacci' (literally 'eat and be silent', but having the significance of a complacent husband). Mustafa, who is quite unaware of what it implies, consents to be enrolled, and the trio which ensues, known as the trio of the 'Pappatacci', once sent the public raving with delight—indeed, it might well do so again. Lindoro has a flowing, high tune and he is supported by the two lower voices to make a very comic effect. It is a charming piece and one of the gems of the score. Haly meanwhile is suspicious: why, he asks Zulma, does Isabella give too much to drink to the eunuchs and the Moors? For fun, she tells him, and to make it into a true holiday.

In preparation for the ceremony to enrol Mustafa in the inglorious ranks, Isabella gathers together all the Italians in the Bey's service and appeals to their patriotism to help her carry out her plans, which include escape for them all during the course of the initiation ceremony. They greet her in a chorus, and she sings her recitative ('Amici, in ogni evento') and rondo ('Pensa alla patria'), taking the chance of having a dig at Taddeo and a kind word for Lindoro. This is a big-scale bravura aria, and contains in its first words one of Rossini's few overt references to patriotism.

Announced by Lindoro, the 'Pappatacci' chorus comes on with horns blowing. Mustafa, prompted by Isabella, swears to obey all the rules of the order, which he then repeats after Taddeo; what it amounts to is that the duty of the model husband is to eat and sleep soundly—nothing else. Isabella and Lindoro indulge in public love-making as a 'test' for Mustafa—he fails, but is prompted by Taddeo, and swears he will not offend against the rules again. A chorus of European slaves can be heard from outside, where the boat Isabella has chartered to take them all home is waiting in full sight of the Bey's palace. Isabella and Lindoro prepare to go on board, and Mustafa treats it all as part of his initiation, although Taddeo is worried at the turn events are taking. In an *allegro*, Mustafa discovers his mistake through the intervention of Elvira, Zulma, and Haly, who convince him he has been hoodwinked. He turns to Elvira as his true love—Italians were only a passing fancy. Isabella and her party are still within sight of the palace, and the opera ends with mutual congratulations from both parties, escapers, and erstwhile captors as well.                                                                      H.

# IL BARBIERE DI SIVIGLIA

## The Barber of Seville

Opera in two acts by Rossini; text by Sterbini founded on Beaumarchais Première on February 20, 1816, at the Teatro Argentina, Rome, with Giorgi-Righetti, M. Garcia, L. Lamboni, Vitanelli, Botticelli, conductor Rossini (as *Almaviva or L'Inutile precauzione*; title of *Il Barbiere* first used at Bologna, 1816). Haymarket, London, 1818, with Fodor, Garcia, Naldi, Angrisani, Ambrogetti; Covent Garden, 1818, with Mrs. Dickons, Mr. Jones, Mr. Liston, Mr. Fawcett, Mr. Isaacs; New York, 1819 (in English) with Thomas Phillips and Miss Leesugg; 1825 (in Italian), with Garcia the Elder as Almaviva, Garcia the Younger as Figaro, Malibran as Rosina; Metropolitan, 1883, with Sembrich, Stagno, del Puente, Mirabella, Corsini, conductor Vianesi; Covent Garden, 1919, with Borghi-Zerni, Tom Burke, Sammarco, Cotreuil, Malatesta, conductor Mugnone; 1925, with dal Monte, Borgioli, Franci, Cotreuil, Malatesta, conductor Votto; 1926, with Capsir, Hackett, Badini, Chaliapin, Malatesta; 1935, with Pons, Dino Borgioli, de Luca, Pinza, Scattola, conductor Bellezza; 1946, with Carosio, Infantino, Franci, Luise, Colella; La Scala, Milan, 1952, with Simionato, Tagliavini, Bechi, Rossi-Lemeni, Luise, conductor de Sabata.

## CHARACTERS

Count Almaviva ............................... Tenor

Doctor Bartolo ......................... Basso-Comico

Basilio, *a singing teacher* ......................... Bass

Figaro, *a barber* ........................... Baritone

Fiorello, *servant to the count* ....................... Bass

Ambrogio, *servant to the doctor* ................... Bass

Rosina, *the doctor's ward* ............... Mezzo-Soprano

Berta (or Marcellina), *Rosina's governess* ........ Soprano

Notary, Constable, Musicians, and Soldiers

*Time:* Seventeenth Century          *Place:* Seville, Spain

Upon episodes in Beaumarchais's trilogy of *Figaro* comedies, two composers, Mozart and Rossini, based operas that have long maintained their hold upon the repertory. The three Beaumarchais comedies are *Le Barbier de Seville*, *Le Mariage de Figaro*, and *La Mère Coupable*. Mozart selected the second of these, Rossini the first; so that although in point of composition Mozart's *Figaro* (May 1786) antedates Rossini's *Barbiere* (February 1816) by nearly thirty years, *Il Barbiere di Siviglia* precedes *Le Nozze di Figaro* in point of action. In both operas Figaro is a prominent character, and, while the composers were of wholly different nationality and race, their music is genuinely and equally sparkling and witty.

There is much to say about the first performance of *Il Barbiere
di Siviglia*; also about the overture, the origin of Almaviva's
graceful solo, 'Ecco ridente in cielo', and the music selected by
prima donnas to sing in the 'lesson scene' in the second act. But
these details are better preceded by some information regarding
the story and the music.

Act I, Scene i.    A street by Dr. Bartolo's house. Count
Almaviva, a Grandee of Spain, is desperately in love with Rosina,
the ward of Doctor Bartolo. Accompanied by his servant Fiorello
and a band of musicians, he serenades her with the smooth,
flowing measures of 'Ecco ridente in cielo' (Lo, smiling in the
eastern sky).

He pays off the musicians and tells them to go away quietly,
but his generosity provokes a hubbub as they crowd round him
to say 'thank you'.

Just then *Figaro*, the barber, the general factotum and busy-
body of the town, dances in, singing the famous patter air, 'Largo
al factotum della città' (Room for the city's factotum).

As a bravura aria for high baritone it is perhaps unequalled,
and certainly it has no rival in point of popularity for voices of
this type.

Figaro is Dr. Bartolo's barber, and, learning from the Count
of his heart's desire, immediately plots with him to bring about
an introduction to Rosina.

Rosina is strictly watched by her guardian, Doctor Bartolo,
who himself plans to marry his ward, since she has both beauty
and money. In this he is assisted by Basilio, a music-master.
Rosina, however, returns the affection of the Count although she
has never met him, and, in spite of the watchfulness of her
guardian, she contrives to drop a letter from the balcony to

Almaviva, declaring her passion, and at the same time requesting to know her lover's name. He tells her in an aria that it is Lindoro.

Two clever duets between Figaro and the Count bring the scene to a close—one in which Almaviva promises money to the Barber; the other in praise of love and pleasure, and Figaro's skill in providing them.

Scene ii.     A room in Dr. Bartolo's house. Rosina enters. She sings the brilliant 'Una voce poco fa' (A little voice I heard just

U - na vo - ce po - co fà    qui nel cor mi ri -suo - no

now), followed by 'Io sono docile' (With mild and docile air).

Io  so  -  no    do - ci - le,  son ris - pet - to - - sa,

Meanwhile Bartolo has made known to Basilio his suspicions that Count Almaviva is in town and moreover in love with Rosina. Basilio advises to start a scandal about the Count and, in an aria ('La calunnia') remarkable for its descriptive *crescendo*, depicts how calumny may spread from the first breath to a tempest of scandal.

La  ca - lun-nia      è un ven - ti  - cel - lo

Figaro, who has left Almaviva, tells Rosina that Signor Lindoro is his cousin, and adds that the young man is deeply in love with her. Rosina is delighted. She gives him a note to convey to the supposed Signor Lindoro. (Duet, Rosina and Figaro: 'Dunque io son, tu non m'inganni?'—Am I his love, or dost thou mock me?)

Bartolo taxes Rosina with having dropped a note from the balcony, and, even though she has a ready answer to all his questions, he continues to disbelieve her excuses and reads her a lecture on the futility of trying to deceive him. His aria, 'A un dottor della mia sorte' is a fine *buffo* piece, and far superior to 'Manca un foglio', which is often sung in its place and is anyhow not by Rossini at all.

To obtain an interview with Rosina, the Count disguises himself as a drunken soldier, and forces his way into Bartolo's house. The disguise of Almaviva is penetrated by the guardian, and the pretended soldier is placed under arrest, but is at once released upon secretly showing the officer his order as a Grandee of Spain. There is an irresistibly comic sextet for Rosina, Almaviva, Bartolo, Berta, Figaro, and Basilio—'Fredda ed immobile' (Awestruck and immovable), and the act ends in a general finale.

Act II.     The Count again enters Bartolo's house. He is now disguised as a music-teacher, and pretends that he has been sent by Basilio to give a lesson in music, on account of the illness of the latter. He obtains the confidence of Bartolo by producing Rosina's letter to himself, and offering to persuade Rosina that the letter has been given him by a mistress of the Count. In this manner he obtains the desired opportunity, under the guise of a music lesson—the 'music lesson' scene, which is discussed below —to hold a whispered conversation with Rosina. Figaro also manages to obtain the keys of the balcony, an escape is determined on at midnight, and a private marriage arranged. Now, however, Basilio makes his appearance. The lovers are disconcerted, but manage, by persuading the music-master that he really is ill—an illness accelerated by a full purse slipped into his hand by Almaviva—to get rid of him. He departs after the quintet, 'Buona sera, mio Signore' (Fare you well then, good Signore).

Buo-na  se - ra, mio Si- gno-re  Buo-na se-ra, buo-na, se-ra.

Figaro starts to shave the Doctor, while Almaviva and Rosina plan an elopement. But Bartolo becomes suspicious, gets out of his chair when no one is looking, and catches the lovers in compromising conversation.

When the Count and Figaro have gone, Bartolo, who possesses the letter Rosina wrote to Almaviva, succeeds, by producing it, and telling her he secured it from another lady-love of the Count, in exciting the jealousy of his ward. In her anger she discloses the plan of escape and agrees to marry her guardian. At the appointed time, however, Figaro and the Count make their appearance— the lovers are reconciled, and a notary, procured by Bartolo for his own marriage to Rosina, celebrates the marriage of the loving pair. When the guardian enters, with officers of justice, into whose hands he is about to consign Figaro and the Count, he is too late, but is reconciled by a promise that he shall receive the equivalent of his ward's dowry.

Just before Almaviva and Figaro enter for the elopement there is a storm. The delicate trio for Almaviva, Rosina, and Figaro, 'Zitti, zitti, piano' (Softly, softly and in silence), bears, probably without intention, a resemblance to a passage in Haydn's *Seasons*.

The first performance of *Il Barbiere di Siviglia*, an opera tha has held its own for over a century, was a scandalous failure, which, however, was not without its amusing incidents. Castil-Blaze, Giuseppe Carpani in his *Rossiniane* and Stendhal in *Vie de Rossini* (a lot of it 'cribbed' from Carpani) have told the story. Moreover the Rosina of the evening, Mme. Giorgi-Righetti, who was both pretty and popular, has communicated her reminiscences.

On December 26, 1815, Duke Cesarini, manager of the Argentine Theatre, Rome, for whom Rossini had contracted to write two operas, brought out the first of these, *Torvaldo e Dorliska*, which was poorly received. Thereupon Cesarini handed to the composer the libretto of *Il Barbiere di Siviglia*, which Paisiello, who was still living, had set to music more than a quarter of a century before. A pleasant memory of the old master's work still lingered with the Roman public. The honorarium was 400 Roman crowns (about $400) and Rossini also was called upon to preside over the orchestra at the pianoforte at the first three performances. It is said that Rossini composed his score in a fortnight. Even if not strictly true, from December 26 to the February 5 following is but little more than a month. The young composer had too much sense not to honour Paisiello, or, at least, to appear to. He hastened to write to the old composer. The latter, although reported to have been intensely jealous of the young maestro (Rossini was only twenty-five) since the sensational success of the latter's *Elisabetta, Regina d'Inghilterra* (Elizabeth, Queen of

England), Naples, 1815, replied that he had no objection to another musician dealing with the subject of his opera. In reality, it is said, he counted on Rossini's making a glaring failure of the attempt. The libretto was rearranged by Sterbini, and Rossini wrote a preface, modest in tone, yet not without a hint that he considered the older score out of date. But he took the precaution to show Paisiello's letter to all the music lovers of Rome, and insisted on changing the title of the opera to *Almaviva, ossia l'Inutile Precauzione* (Almaviva, or the Useless Precaution).

Mme. Giorgi-Righetti reports that 'hot-headed enemies' assembled at their posts as soon as the theatre opened, while Rossini's friends, disappointed by the recent ill luck of *Torvaldo e Dorliska*, weret imid in their support of the new work. Furthermore, according to Mme. Giorgi-Righetti, Rossini weakly yielded to a suggestion from Garcia, and permitted that artist, the Almaviva of the première, to substitute for the air which is sung under Rosina's balcony, a Spanish melody with guitar accompaniment. The scene being laid in Spain, this would aid in giving local colour to the work—such was the idea. But it went wrong. By an unfortunate oversight no one had tuned the guitar with which Almaviva was to accompany himself, and Garcia was obliged to do this on the stage. A string broke. The singer had to replace it, to an accompaniment of laughter and whistling. This was followed by Figaro's entrance air. The audience had settled down for this. But when they saw Zamboni, as Figaro, come on the stage with another guitar, another fit of laughing and whistling seized them, and the racket rendered the solo completely inaudible. Rosina appeared on the balcony. The public greatly admired Mme. Giorgi-Righetti and was disposed to applaud her. But, as if to cap the climax of absurdity, she sang: 'Segui, o caro, deh, segui cosi' (Continue, my dear, do always so). Naturally the audience immediately thought of the two guitars, and went on laughing, whistling, and hissing during the entire duet between Almaviva and Figaro. The work seemed doomed. Finally Rosina came on the stage and sang the 'Una voce poco fa' (A little voice I heard just now) which had been awaited with impatience (and which to-day is still considered an operatic *tour de force* for soprano). The youthful charm of Mme. Giorgi-Righetti, the beauty of her voice, and the favour with which the public regarded her, 'won her a sort of ovation' in this number. A triple round of prolonged applause raised hopes for the fate of the work. Rossini rose from his seat at the pianoforte, and bowed. But realising that the applause was chiefly meant for the singer, he called to her in a whisper, 'Oh, natura!' (Oh, human nature!).

'Give her thanks,' replied the artist, 'since without her you would not have had occasion to rise from your seat.'

What seemed a favourable turn of affairs did not, however, last long. The whistling was resumed louder than ever at the duet between Figaro and Rosina. 'All the whistlers of Italy,' says Castil-Blaze, 'seemed to have given themselves a rendezvous for this performance.' Finally, a stentorian voice shouted: 'This is the funeral of Don Pollione,' words which doubtless had much spice for Roman ears, since the cries, the hisses, the stamping, continued with increased vehemence. When the curtain fell on the first act Rossini turned toward the audience, slightly shrugged his shoulders, and clapped his hands. The audience, though greatly offended by this show of contemptuous disregard for its opinion, reserved its revenge for the second act, not a note of which it allowed to be heard.

For the second performance of *Il Barbiere* Rossini replaced the unlucky air introduced by Garcia with the 'Ecco ridente in cielo', as it now stands. This cavatina he borrowed from an earlier opera of his own, *Aureliano in Palmira* (Aurelian in Palmyra). It also had figured in a cantata (not an opera) by Rossini, *Ciro in Babilonia* (Cyrus in Babylon)—so that measures first sung by a Persian king in the ancient capital of Nebuchadnezzar, and then by a Roman emperor and his followers in the city which flourished in an oasis in the Syrian desert, were found suitable to be intoned by a love-sick Spanish count of the seventeenth century as a serenade to his lady of Seville. It is amusing to note in tracing this air to its original source, that 'Ecco ridente in cielo' figured in *Aureliano in Palmira* as an address to Isis—'Sposa del grande Osiride' (Spouse of the great Osiris).

Equally curious is the relation of the overture to the opera. The original is said to have been lost. The present one has nothing to do with the ever-ready Figaro, the coquettish Rosina, or the sentimental Almaviva, although there have been writers who have dilated upon it as reflecting the spirit of the opera and its characters. It came from the same source as 'Lo, smiles the morning in the sky'—from *Aureliano*, and in between had figured as the overture to *Elisabetta, Regina d'Inghilterra*.

It is a singular fact that the reception of *Il Barbiere* in Paris was much the same as in Rome. The first performance in the Salle Louvois was coldly received. Newspapers compared Rossini's *Barber* unfavourably with that of Paisiello. Fortunately the opposition demanded a revival of Paisiello's work. Paer, musical director at the Théâtre Italien, not unwilling to spike Rossini's guns, pretended to yield to a public demand, and brought out the earlier opera. But the opposite of what had been expected happened. The work was found to be superannuated. It was voted a bore, and Rossini triumphed. The elder Garcia, the Almaviva of the production in Rome, played the role in Paris, as he also did in London, and at the first Italian performance of the work in New York.

Rossini had the reputation of being indolent in the extreme—when he had nothing to do. We have seen that when the overture to *Il Barbiere di Siviglia* was lost (if he really ever composed one), he did not take the trouble to compose another, but replaced it with an earlier one. A similar legend exists in connection with the lesson Almaviva is supposed to give Rosina in Dr. Bartolo's house. This is said to have been lost with the overture—quite erroneously; it exists and is now usually sung in performance. As with the overture, according to the stories, Rossini did not attempt to recompose this number either. He simply let his prima donna sing anything she wanted to. 'Rosina sings an air, ad libitum, for the occasion,' reads the direction in the libretto. Perhaps it was Giorgi-Righetti who first selected 'La Biondina in gondoletta', which was frequently sung in the lesson scene by Italian prima donnas. Later there was substituted the air 'Di tanti palpiti' from the opera *Tancredi*, which is known as the 'aria dei rizzi', or 'rice aria', because Rossini, who was a great gourmet, composed it while cooking his rice. Pauline Viardot-Garcia (Garcia's daughter), like her father in the unhappy première of the opera, sang a Spanish song. This may have been La Calesera', which Adelina Patti also sang in Paris about 1867. Patti's other selections at this time included the laughing song, the so-called 'L'Eclat de Rire' (Burst of Laughter) from Auber's *Manon Lescaut*, as highly esteemed in Paris in years gone by as Massenet's *Manon* now is. In New York I have heard Patti sing,

in this scene, the Arditi waltz, 'Il Bacio' (The Kiss); the bolero
of Hélène, from *Les Vêpres Siciliennes* (The Sicilian Vespers), by
Verdi; the 'Shadow Dance' from Meyerbeer's *Dinorah*, and, in
concluding the scene, 'Home, Sweet Home', which never failed
to bring down the house, although the naïveté with which she
sang it was more affected than affecting.

Among prima donnas much earlier than Patti there were at
least two, Grisi and Alboni (after whom boxes were named at
the Academy of Music), who adapted a brilliant violin piece,
Rode's 'Air and Variations', to their powers of vocalisation and
sang it in the lesson scene. I mention this because the habit of
singing an air with variations persisted until Mme. Sembrich's time.
She sang those by Proch, a teacher of many prima donnas, among
them Tietjens and Peschka-Leutner, who sang at the Peace
Jubilee in Boston (1872) and was the first to make famous her
teacher's coloratura variations, with 'flauto concertante'. Besides
these variations, Mme. Sembrich sang Strauss's 'Voce di Prima-
vera' waltz, 'Ah! non giunge' from *La Sonnambula*, the bolero
from *The Sicilian Vespers*, and 'O luce di quest 'anima' from *Linda
di Chamounix*. The scene was charmingly brought to an end by
her seating herself at the pianoforte and singing, to her own
accompaniment, Chopin's 'Maiden's Wish'. Mme. Melba sang
Arditi's waltz, 'Se Saran Rose', Massenet's 'Sevillana', and the
mad scene from *Lucia*, ending, like Mme. Sembrich, with a song
to which she played her own accompaniment, her choice being
Tosti's 'Mattinata'. Mme. Galli-Curci was apt to begin with the
brilliant vengeance air from *The Magic Flute*, her encores being
'L'Eclat de Rire' by Auber and 'Charmant Oiseau' (Pretty
Bird) from David's *La Perle du Brésil*' (The Pearl of Brazil).
'Home, Sweet Home' and 'The Last Rose of Summer', both sung
by her to her own accompaniment, conclude this interesting
'lesson', in which every Rosina, although supposedly a pupil
receiving a lesson, must be a most brilliant and accomplished
prima donna.

Readers familiar with the history of opera, therefore aware
that Alboni was a contralto, will wonder at her having appeared
as Rosina, when that rôle is associated with prima donnas whose
voices are extremely high and flexible. But the rôle was written
for low voice. Giorgi-Righetti, the first Rosina, was a contralto.
As it is now sung by high sopranos, the music of the rôle is

transposed from the original to higher keys in order to give full scope for brilliant vocalisation on high notes.

Many liberties have been taken by prima donnas in the way of vocal flourishes and a general decking out of the score of *Il Barbiere* with embellishments. The story goes that Patti once sang 'Una voce poco fa', with her own frills added, to Rossini in Paris.

'A very pretty song! Whose is it?' is said to have been the composer's cutting comment.

There is another anecdote about *Il Barbiere* which brings in Donizetti, who was asked if he believed that Rossini really had composed the opera in thirteen days.

'Why not? He's so lazy,' is the reported reply.

If the story is true, Donizetti was a very forward young man. He was only nineteen when *Il Barbiere* was produced, and had not yet brought out his first opera.

The first performance in America of *The Barber of Seville* was in English at the Park Theatre, New York, May 3, 1819. (May 17, cited by some authorities, was the date of the third performance, and is so announced in the advertisements.) Thomas Phillips was Almaviva and Miss Leesugg Rosina. 'Report speaks in loud terms of the new opera called *The Barber of Seville* which is announced for this evening. The music is said to be very splendid and is expected to be most effective.' This primitive bit of 'publicity', remarkable for its day, appeared in *The Evening Post*, New York, Monday, May 3, 1819. The second performance took place May 7. Much music was interpolated. Phillips, as Almaviva, introduced 'The Soldier's Bride', 'Robin Adair', 'Pomposo, or a Receipt for an Italian Song', and 'the favourite duet with Miss Leesugg, of "I love thee"'. (One wonders what was left of Rossini's score.) In 1821 he appeared again with Miss Holman as Rosina.

That Phillips should have sung Figaro, a baritone rôle in *Le Nozze di Figaro*, and Almaviva, a tenor part, in *Il Barbiere*, may seem odd. But in the Mozart opera he appeared in Bishop's adaptation, in which the Figaro rôle is neither too high for a baritone, nor too low for a tenor. In fact the liberties Bishop took with Mozart's score were so great (and so outrageous) that Phillips need have hesitated at nothing.

On Tuesday, November 22, 1825, Manuel Garcia, the elder

issued the preliminary announcement of his season of Italian opera at the Park Theatre, New York. The printers appear to have had a struggle with the Italian titles of operas and names of Italian composers. For *The Evening Post* announces that 'The Opera of *H. Barbiora di Seviglia*, by Rosina, is now in rehearsal and will be given as soon as possible.' That 'soon as possible' was the evening of November 29, and is regarded as the date of the first performance in America of opera in Italian.     K.

# LA CENERENTOLA
## Cinderella

Opera in two acts by Gioacchino Rossini, text by Jacopo Ferretti (founded on Etienne's French libretto for Isouard's *Cendrillon*, 1810). Première at the Teatro Valle, Rome, January 25, 1817, with Giorgi-Righetti in the title rôle. First performed in London, Haymarket Theatre, 1820 (in Italian); New York, 1826 (in Italian); Covent Garden, 1830 (in English). Revived Pesaro, 1920, with Fanny Anitua; Rome, 1920; Paris, 1929, with Supervia, Ederle, Bettoni; Vienna, 1930, with Kern, von Pataky; Berlin, 1931, with Schoene, Hüsch, Kandl; Florence Festival, 1933, with Supervia, conductor Serafin; Covent Garden, 1934, with Supervia, Dino Borgioli, Ghirardini, Pinza, conductor Marinuzzi; la Scala, 1937, with Pederzini, conductor Marinuzzi; Buenos Aires, 1939, with Pederzini; Florence Festival, 1942, with Barbieri; la Scala, 1946, with Barbieri, conductor Serafin; Trieste, 1951, with Simionato; Glyndebourne, 1952, with de Gabarain, Oncina, Bruscantini, Ian Wallace, conductor Gui.

### CHARACTERS

Don Ramiro, *Prince of Salerno* .................... Tenor
Dandini, *his valet* ................................. Bass
Don Magnifico, *Baron of Mountflagon* ......... Buffo-Bass
Clorinda⎫ *his daughters* ............... ⎧ Soprano
Thisbe ⎭ ⎩ Mezzo-Soprano
Angelina, *known as Cinderella, his step-daughter* .. Contralto
Alidoro, *a philosopher* ........ ..................... Bass

The action takes place partly in the house of Don Magnifico, partly in the palace of the Prince.

With the exception of *The Barber of Seville* perhaps no other opera of Rossini has been performed more often than this.

Act I.    Cenerentola is, of course, Cinderella, and as the curtain rises she is seen making coffee for her half-sisters, singing a pathetic little song the while. The friend and counsellor of the Prince, Alidoro, enters disguised as a beggar. The two sisters

curtly dismiss him; Cinderella pities him and offers him refreshment, to the intense annoyance of her sisters. The quarrel is interrupted by the entrance of the Prince's followers. Clorinda and
Thisbe feel convinced that he must fall an easy victim to their
charms. They listen rather reluctantly while their father tells them
at length of a dream he has had, and then go to make ready for
the Prince, who arrives disguised as his valet, Dandini, to find
Cinderella alone.

Cinderella and the Prince fall in love at first sight and express
their feelings in a love duet which has all the wit and melodiousness characteristic of its composer.

Cinderella must go to the sisters, who clamour for her services.
The Prince, left alone, does not know what to think of his
charmer. His musings are interrupted by the arrival of Dandini
(masquerading as the Prince).

While Dandini misquotes Latin to give himself an air, the voice
of Cinderella is heard begging the Baron to allow her to go to
the ball. Neither the Baron nor her sisters will listen to her; the
third daughter is dead, they tell the Prince, and Cinderella is only
a servant. They tell her to sweep the house, and leave, but Alidoro
promises to help her.

The next scene takes place in the Prince's palace. The Baron
has been appointed chief butler to the Prince and is busy tasting
the wines. The disguised Prince has seen enough of Clorinda and
Thisbe by this time to know that neither could make him happy.
The girls, for their part, set about capturing Dandini, and when
the arrival of a distinguished but unknown lady is announced,
their jealousy is up in arms. The unknown, however, looks too
much like Cinderella to arouse their alarm.

Act II.    Clorinda and Thisbe are no longer on friendly terms,
as both believe they have made a conquest of the Prince, but
Dandini is himself in love with Cinderella and asks her to marry
him. Cinderella refuses and confesses her love for his 'valet'. The

Prince overhears her, comes forward, and himself proposes to her. Cinderella admits that she loves him, but before consenting to be his bride the Prince must find out who she is. She gives him a bracelet which matches another she is wearing and departs.

The Baron enters and asks Dandini whether it would be possible to speed up the wedding. Dandini has a secret to impart; if he were to marry one of the Baron's daughters, he asks, how should she be treated? The Baron tells him: thirty lackeys always at hand; sixteen horses; a dozen dukes, a coach with six footmen and 'dinners with ices' always ready. Dandini thereupon confesses that he is but a valet and that marriage with a daughter of the Baron is unthinkable.

The next scene is at the Baron's house, where Clorinda and Thisbe scowl at Cinderella, who resembles the hateful stranger of the ball. A storm rages outside—brought about by the incantations of the philosopher, Alidoro. The Prince and Dandini seek refuge while another coach is got ready; the Baron orders Cinderella to bring the best chair forward for the Prince. Cinderella, trying to hide herself, puts her hands up to cover her face, and the Prince notices the bracelet, the companion of which he holds. All the knots are gradually unravelled. The Baron, Clorinda, and Thisbe, unable to understand, rudely order Cinderella away. The Prince grows angry and threatens them with his displeasure. The scene changes to the palace, where the intercession of Cinderella results in the pardon of the Baron and his daughters, and all ends merrily.                                                    F. B.

Not the least reason for the comparative lack of popularity of Rossini's operas in the twentieth century—only *The Barber* survives in the regular repertory—is the florid nature of the vocal writing; *Cenerentola* is no exception to this rule, in fact it emphasises it, since the title rôle, like that of *L'Italiana*, is written for that *rara avis* a coloratura contralto. Though attempts have been made to arrange the music for a soprano (as has been done with Rosina), the opera generally has to wait for revival until a low voice with phenomenal agility comes along. When it does, we have an opportunity of hearing the brilliant rondo, 'Nacqui all'affanno, al pianto', with which the opera ends, in its proper context and not on gramophone record or (more rarely) concert platform; and the unmatched ensembles for which Rossini is renowned show a modern audience the stuff a comic opera was made of in the days when every singer was a master of the bravura coloratura style, and most of them brilliant actors and actresses as well. Nobody has surpassed Rossini in the surface brilliance of his comic invention, and only Mozart and (in one opera) Verdi have added to it a depth of feeling of which Rossini was seemingly incapable but which turns comedy from the most artificial of media into the truest. In *Cenerentola*, it is not the motives of the characters which matter—apart from the charming duet early in Act I, the love of Prince Ramiro for Cinderella's plays little part in the music—nor even primarily their reactions to their own and other people's motives, but the situations these motives get them into. And situations with Rossini lead not so much to arias as to ensembles. Rossini's ability to catch hold of the verbal rhythm of a chance phrase and turn it into music (e.g. the ensemble after Alidoro's announcement of Cinderella's arrival at the ball), his dexterity with patter, his astonishing manipulation of the simplest material until it becomes a towering invention of quicksilver sound—these qualities are heard at their best in the quintet which begins 'Signore, una parola', in the finale of Act I, which ends with the *crescendo* first heard in the overture, in the brilliantly comic duet of Dandini and Magnifico in Act II. The climax of the opera comes, not with the rondo at the end, good though it is, but with the great E flat ensemble of stupefaction after the Prince and Dandini have taken refuge from the storm in the astonished Don Magnifico's house. This sextet is built up on a slow, *staccato* tune (marked *maestoso*: majestically) from which each singer in turn breaks away with a florid phrase, the others meanwhile keeping up the steady rhythm with a constant repetition of the tune and a maximum use of the words and particularly of the opportunities given by the rolled Italian 'r'.                                                          H.

## SEMIRAMIDE

Opera in two acts by Gioacchino Rossini; text by Gaetana Rossi, founded on Voltaire's tragedy. First performed on February 3, 1823, at the Fenice Theatre, Venice; London, Haymarket, 1824; Covent Garden, 1842 (in English), with Adelaide Kemble, Mrs. Shaw, Mr. Giubilei, Mr. Leffler; opened the Royal Italian Opera, Covent Garden, 1847, with Grisi, Alboni, Tamburini, Lavia, Tagliafico, conductor Costa; New York, 1845; Metropolitan, New York, 1893, with Melba, Scalchi, Guetary, Castelmary, E. de Reszke; Florence Festival, 1940, with Gatti, Stignani, Tagliavini, Pasero, Colella, conductor Serafin.

Semiramide, *Queen of Babylon* .................. Soprano
Arsace, *Commander of the Assyrian Army* ....... Contralto

Ghost of Nino ......................................Bass
Oroe, *High Priest of the Magi* ......................Bass
Assur, *a Prince* ...............................Baritone
Azema, *a Princess* ............................Soprano
Idreno, *an Indian Prince* ........................Tenor
Mitrane, *Captain of the Guard* ....................Tenor
Magi, Guards, Satraps, Slaves

*Time:* Antiquity                          *Place:* Babylon

*Semiramide* seems to have had its day. Yet, were a soprano and a contralto, capable of doing justice to the rôles of Semiramide and Arsace, to appear in conjunction in the operatic firmament, the opera might be successfully revived, as it was for Patti and Scalchi. The latter, in her prime when she first appeared in America, was one of the greatest of contraltos. I think that all who, like myself, had the good fortune to hear that revival of *Semiramide*, still consider the singing by Patti and Scalchi of the duet , 'Giorno d'orrore' (Day of horror), the finest example of *bel canto* it has been their privilege to listen to. For beauty and purity of tone, smoothness of phrasing, elegance, and synchronisation of embellishment it has not been equalled here since.

In the first act of the opera is a brilliant aria for Semiramide, 'Bel raggio lusinghier' (Bright ray of hope),—the one piece that has kept the opera in the gramophone repertory.

Bel rag - gio lusin - - - - - ghier.

A priests' march and chorus, which leads up to the finale of the first act, is accompanied not only by orchestra, but also by full military band on the stage, the first instance of the employment of the latter in Italian opera. The duet, 'Giorno d'orrore,' is in the second act.

PLATE XV. Margherita Carosio as Violetta in Act II of *La Traviata*, Covent Garden 1946.

PLATE XVI. The Council Chamber scene of *Simon Boccanegra*, Sadler's Wells 1948. John Moody was the producer, and the sets were by John Piper.

For many years the overture to *Semiramide* was a favourite
at popular concerts. It was admired for the broad, hymnlike air
in the introduction, which in the opera becomes an effective
chorus,

and for the graceful, lively melody, which is first announced on
the clarinet. I call it 'graceful' and 'lively,' and so it would be
considered to-day. But in the opera it accompanies the cautious

entrance of priests into a darkened temple where a deep mystery
is impending, and, at the time the opera was produced, this music,
which now we would describe as above, was supposed to be
'shivery' and gruesome. In fact the scene was objected to by
audiences of that now seemingly remote period, on the ground
that the orchestra was too prominent and that, in the treatment
of the instrumental score to his operas, Rossini was leaning too
heavily toward German models! But this, remember, was in 1823.

The story of *Semiramide* can be briefly told. Semiramide,
Queen of Babylon, has murdered her husband, Nino, the King.
In this deed she was assisted by Prince Assur, who expects to win
her hand and the succession to the throne.

Semiramide, however, is enamoured of a comely youth, Arsace,
victorious commander of her army, and supposedly a Scythian,
but in reality her own son, of which relationship only Oroe, the
chief priest of the temple, is aware. Arsace himself is in love
with the royal Princess Azema.

At a gathering in the temple, the gates of the tomb of Nino
are opened as if by invisible hands. The shade of Nino announces
that Arsace shall be his successor; and summons him to come to
the tomb at midnight there to learn the secret of his assassination.

Enraged at the prophecy of the succession of Arsace and

knowing of his coming visit to the tomb of Nino, Assur contrives to enter it; while Semiramide, who now knows that the young warrior is her son, comes to the tomb to warn him against Assur. The three principal personages in the drama are thus brought together at its climax. Arsace makes what would be a fatal thrust at Assur. Semiramide interposes herself between the two men and receives the death wound. Arsace is proclaimed king and the avenger of his father's murder.

According to legend, Semiramis, when a babe, was fed by doves; and, after reigning for forty-two years, disappeared or was changed into a dove and flew away. For the first New York performance Garcia announced the work as *La Figlia dell Aria, or Semiramide.*                                                K.

# GUILLAUME TELL
## William Tell

Opera in four acts by Gioacchino Rossini; text by V. J. Etienne de Jouy and H. L. F. Bis after Schiller. Première on August 3, 1829, at the Opéra, Paris, with Nourrit as Arnold; the four acts were reduced to three in June 1831. First performed in London, Drury Lane, 1830 (in English); Her Majesty's, 1839 (in Italian); Covent Garden, 1845 (in French); New York, 1831 (in English), 1845 (in French), 1855 (in Italian). Last London performance, London Opera House, 1911, with Victoria Fer, Orville Harrold, conductor Ernaldy. Revived Metropolitan, New York, 1923, with Ponselle, Martinelli, and 1931 with Lauri-Volpi; Colon, Buenos Aires, 1923, with Spani; la Scala, Milan, 1930, with Bruna Rasa, Lauri-Volpi, Franci; Rome Opera, 1930, with Arangi-Lombardi; Paris Opéra, 1932, with Norena, O'Sullivan, Huberty, Journet; Berlin, 1934, with Heidersbach, Roswaenge, Bockelmann, Bohnen, Kipnis, conductor Heger; Florence Festival, 1939, with Gatti, Mazaroff, Sved, Pasero, conductor Marinuzzi; Rome, 1950, with Gatti, Filippeschi, Silveri; Florence Festival, 1952, with Rossi-Lemeni (Tell), Tebaldi, Baum, and Serafin conducting.

### CHARACTERS

Guillaume Tell ............................... Baritone
Hedwige, *Tell's wife* .......................... Soprano
Jemmy, *Tell's son* .......................... Soprano
Arnold, *suitor of Mathilde* ...................... Tenor
Melcthal, *Arnold's father* ......................... Bass
Gessler, *governor of Schwitz and Uri* ................ Bass
Mathilde, *Gessler's sister* ...................... Soprano
Rudolph, *captain in Gessler's guard* ................ Tenor
Walter Furst ..............     .................... Bass

Leuthold, *a shepherd* ............................Bass
Ruedi, *a fisherman* ............................Tenor
Peasants, Knights, Pages, Ladies, Hunters, Soldiers, Guards,
and three Bridal Couples

*Time:* Thirteenth Century                    *Place:* Switzerland

Arnold, a Swiss patriot and son of the venerable Swiss leader,
Melcthal, has saved from drowning Mathilde, sister of the
Austrian tyrant Gessler, whom the Swiss abhor. Arnold and
Mathilde have fallen in love with each other.

Act I.    A beautiful May morning has dawned over the Lake
of Lucerne, on which Tell's house is situated. It is the day of the
Shepherd Festival. According to ancient custom the grey-haired
Melcthal blesses the loving couples among them. But his own
son, Arnold, does not ask a blessing of the old man; although he
loves Mathilde, his heart belongs to his native land. The festival
is interrupted by the sound of horns. It is the train of Gessler,
the hated tyrant. Leuthold rushes in, breathless. In order to protect his daughter from dishonour, he has been obliged to kill one
of Gessler's soldiers. He is pursued. To cross the lake is his only
means of escape. But who will take him in the face of the storm
that is coming up? Tell wastes no time in thinking. He acts. It is
the last possible moment. Gessler's guards are already in sight,
Rudolph at their head. With Tell's aid the fugitive escapes them,
but they turn to the country folk, and seize and carry off old
Melcthal.

Act II.    In a valley by a lake Arnold and Mathilde meet and
again pledge their love. Arnold learns from Tell and Walter that
his father has been slain by Gessler's order. His thoughts turn to
vengeance. The three men bind themselves by oath to free
Switzerland. The cantons gather and swear to throw off the
Austrian yoke.

Act III.    The market-place in Altdorf. It is the hundredth
anniversary of Austrian rule in Switzerland. Fittingly to celebrate
the day Gessler has ordered his hat to be placed on top of a pole,
and the Swiss are commanded to make obeisance to it. Tell comes
along holding his son Jemmy by the hand. He refuses to pay
homage to the hat. As in him is also recognised the man who
saved Leuthold, he must be punished. Gessler cynically orders
him to shoot an apple from Jemmy's head. The shot succeeds.

Fearless, as before, Tell informs Gessler that the second arrow was intended for him, had the first missed its mark. Tell's arrest is ordered, but the armed Swiss, who have risen against Austria, approach. Gessler falls by Tell's shot; the fight ends with complete victory for the Swiss. Mathilde who still loves Arnold finds refuge in his arms.

*Guillaume Tell* is the only opera by an Italian of which it can be said that the overture has gained world-wide fame, and justly so, while the opera itself is so rarely heard that it may almost be said to have passed out of the repertory. Occasionally it is revived for the benefit of a high tenor like Tamagno. In point of fact, however, it is too good a work to be made the vehicle of a single operatic star. It is quite likely that, with a fine ensemble, *Guillaume Tell* could be restored to the list of operas regularly given.

The care which Rossini bestowed on this work is seen in the layout and composition of the overture, which as an instrumental number is as fine a *tour de force* as his 'Una voce poco fa', 'Bel raggio', or 'Giorno d'orrore' are for voice. The slow introduction denotes Alpine calm. There is a beautiful passage for violoncellos, which has been quoted in books on instrumentation. In it Rossini may well have harked back to his student years, when he was a pupil in violoncello playing at the conservatory in Bologna. The calm is followed by a storm and this, in turn, by a 'Ranz des Vaches.' The final section consists of a trumpet call, followed by a fast movement, which can be played so as to leave the hearer quite breathless. It is supposed to represent the call to arms and the uprising of the Swiss against their Austrian oppressors, whose yoke they threw off.

The most striking musical number in the first act of the opera, is Arnold's 'Ah, Mathilde'.

A tenor with powerful high tones in his voice can always render this with great effect. In fact it is so effective that its coming so early in the work is a fault of construction which in my opinion has been a factor in the non-success of the opera as a whole. Even a tenor like Mierzwinski, 'a natural singer of short-lived celebrity', with remarkable high notes, could in this number rouse to a high pitch of enthusiasm an audience that remained comparatively calm the rest of the evening.

The climax of the second act is the trio between Arnold, Tell, and Walter, followed by the assembly of the cantons and the taking of the oath to conquer or die (May glory our hearts with courage exalt).

Its most effective passage begins as follows:

Another striking musical number is Arnold's solo in the last act, at sight of his ruined home, 'Asile héréditaire' (O, silent abode).

At the initial performance of *Guillaume Tell* in Paris, there was no indication that the opera was not destined to remain for many years in the repertory. It was given fifty-six times. Then, because of the great length of the opera, only the second act was performed in connection with some other work, until the sensational success of Duprez, in 1837, led to a revival.

*Guillaume Tell*, given in full, would last nearly five hours. The poor quality of the original libretto by 'Jouy' led to the revision by Bis, but even after that there had to be cuts.

'Ah, Maestro,' exclaimed an enthusiastic admirer of Rossini to that master, 'I heard your *William Tell* at the Opera last night!'

'What?' asked Rossini. 'The whole of it?'

Clever; but by his question Rossini unconsciously put his finger on the weak spot of the opera he intended to be his masterpiece. Be it never so well given, it is long-winded.          K.

# VINCENZO BELLINI

## (1802–1835)

## LA SONNAMBULA

### The Sleepwalker

OPERA in two acts by Vincenzo Bellini; text by Felice Romani. Première at the Teatro Carcano, Milan, on March 6, 1831, with Pasta, Rubini, Mariani. First performed in London, Haymarket, 1831, with Pasta, Rubini, Santini; Drury Lane, 1833 (in English), with Malibran (her début), Templeton, Seguin; Covent Garden, 1835, with same cast; New York, 1835 (in English); 1844 (in Italian). Last performed at Covent Garden 1910 with Tetrazzini, McCormack, E. Burke; revived Metropolitan, New York, 1932, with Pons, Bourskaya, Gigli, Pinza, conductor Serafin; Scala, Milan, 1935, with dal Monte, Schipa, Pasero, conductor Guarnieri; 1939, with Carosio, Malipiero, Pasero, conductor Marinuzzi; Florence, 1942, with Carosio, Tagliavini, Pasero; Rome Opera, 1951, with Carosio, Valletti, Christoff, conductor Gavazzeni; la Scala, 1955, with Callas in Visconti's production (also Edinburgh 1957).

### CHARACTERS

Count Rodolpho, *lord of the castle* .................. Bass
Teresa, *proprietress of the mill* .................. Soprano
Amina, *her foster-daughter* .................... Soprano
Lisa, *proprietress of the village inn* .............. Soprano
Elvino, *a young farmer* .......................... Tenor
Alessio, *a villager* ................................ Bass
Notary, Villagers, etc.

*Time:* Early Nineteenth Century   *Place:* A Village in Switzerland

Act I.   The village green. On one side an inn, in the background a water mill, in the distance mountains. As the curtain rises the villagers are making merry, for they are about to celebrate a nuptial contract between Amina, an orphan brought up as the foster child of Teresa, the mistress of the village mill, and Elvino, a young landowner of the neighbourhood. These preparations, however, fill with jealousy the heart of Lisa, the proprietress of the inn, for she is in love with Elvino. Nor do Alessio's ill-timed attentions please her. Amina enters under the care of Teresa, and returns her thanks to her neighbours for their good wishes. She has two attractive solos; these are 'Come per me sereno' (How, for me brightly shining) and 'Sovra il sen la man mi posa' (With this heart its joy revealing). Both are replete with grace and charm.

When the village notary and Elvino appear, the contract is signed and attested, and Elvino places a ring on Amina's finger. Duet: 'Prendi, l'anel ti dono' (Take now the ring I give you), a composition in long-flowing expressive measures.

The village is startled by the crack of whips and the rumble of wheels. A handsome stranger in officer's fatigue uniform appears, and desires to have his horses watered and fed, before he proceeds to the castle. The road is bad, night is approaching. Counselled by the villagers, and urged by Lisa, the officer consents to remain the night at the inn.

The villagers know it not at this time, but the officer is Rodolpho, the lord of the castle. He looks about him and recalls the scenes of his youth: 'Vi ravviso' (As I view).

Vi rav - vi - so      o luoghu a - me - - - ni,

He then gallantly addresses himself to Amina in a charming cabaletta, 'Tu non sai in quei begli occhi' (You know not, maid, the light your eyes within).

Elvino is piqued at the stranger's attentions to his bride, but Teresa warns all present to retire, for the village is said to be haunted by a phantom. The stranger treats the superstition lightly, and, ushered in by Lisa, retires to the village inn. All then wend their several ways homeward. Elvino, however, finds time to upbraid Amina for seemingly having found much pleasure in the stranger's gallant speeches, but before they part there are mutual concessions and forgiveness.

Rodolpho's sleeping apartment at the inn. He enters, conducted by Lisa. She is coquettish, he quite willing to meet her halfway in taking liberties with her. He learns from her that his identity as the lord of the castle has now been discovered by the villagers, and that they will shortly come to the inn to offer their congratulations.

He is annoyed, but quite willing that Lisa's attractions shall atone for the discovery. At that moment, however, there is a noise without, and Lisa escapes into an adjoining room, in her haste dropping her handkerchief, which Rodolpho picks up and hangs over the bedpost. A few moments later he is amazed to see Amina, all in white, raise his window and enter his room. He realises almost immediately that she is walking in her sleep, and that it is her somnambulism which has given rise to the superstition of the village phantom. In her sleep Amina speaks of her approaching marriage, of Elvino's jealousy, of their quarrel and reconciliation. Rodolpho, not wishing to embarrass her by his presence should she suddenly awaken, extinguishes the candles, steps out of the window and closes it lightly after him. Still asleep Amina sinks down upon the bed.

The villagers enter to greet Rodolpho. As the room is darkened, and, to their amusement, they see the figure of a woman on the bed, they are about to withdraw discreetly, when Lisa, who knows what has happened, enters with a light, brings in Elvino, and points out Amina to him. The light, the sounds, awaken her. Her natural confusion at the situation in which she finds herself is mistaken by Elvino for evidence of guilt. He casts her off. The others, save Teresa, share his suspicions. Teresa, in a simple, natural way, takes the handkerchief hanging over the bedpost and places it around Amina's neck, and when the poor, grief-stricken girl swoons, as Elvino turns away from her, her foster-mother catches her in her arms.

In this scene, indeed in this act, the most striking musical number is the duet near the end. It is feelingly composed, and is almost wholly devoid of vocal embellishment. It begins with Amina's protestations of innocence: 'D'un pensiero, e d'un accento' (Not in thought's remotest region).

When Elvino's voice joins hers there is no comfort for her in his words. He is still haunted by dark suspicions.

An unusual and beautiful effect is the closing of the duet with an expressive phrase for tenor alone: 'Questo pianto del mio cor' (With what grief my heart is torn).

Act II.    A shady valley between the village and the castle.
The villagers are proceeding to the castle to beg Rodolpho to
intercede with Elvino for Amina. Elvino meets Amina. Still enraged at what he considers her perfidy, he snatches from her
finger the ring he gave her. Amina still loves him. She expresses
her feelings in the air: 'Ah! perche non posso odiarti' (Ah! Why
is it I cannot hate him).

Scene ii.    The village, near Teresa's mill. Water runs through
the race and the wheel turns rapidly. A slender wooden bridge,
spanning the wheel, gives access from some dormer lights in the
millroof to an old stone flight of steps leading down to the foreground.

Lisa has been making hay while the sun shines. She has induced
Elvino to promise to marry her. Preparations for the wedding are
on foot. The villagers have assembled. Rodolpho endeavours to
dissuade Elvino from the step he is about to take. He explains
that Amina is a somnambulist. But Elvino has never heard of
somnambulism. He remains utterly incredulous.

Teresa begs the villagers to make less disturbance, as poor
Amina is asleep in the mill. The girl's foster-mother learns of
Elvino's intention of marrying Lisa. Straightway she takes from
her bosom Lisa's handkerchief, which she found hanging over
Rodolpho's bedpost. Lisa is confused. Elvino feels that she, too,
has betrayed him. Rodolpho again urges upon Elvino that
Amina never was false to him—that she is the innocent victim
of sleepwalking.

'Who can prove it?' Elvino asks in agonised tones.

'Who? She herself!—See there!' exclaims Rodolpho.

For at that very moment Amina, in her nightdress, lamp in
hand, emerges from a window in the mill roof. She passes along,
still asleep, to the lightly built bridge spanning the mill wheel,
which is still turning round quickly. Now she sets foot on the
narrow, insecure bridge. The villagers fall on their knees in prayer
that she may cross safely. Rodolpho stands among them, head
uncovered. As Amina crosses the bridge a rotting plank breaks
under her footsteps. The lamp falls from her hand into the torrent
beneath. She, however, reaches the other side, and gains the stone
steps, which she descends. Still walking in her sleep, she advances
to where stand the villagers and Rodolpho. She kneels and prays
for Elvino. Then rising, she speaks of the ring he has taken from

her, and draws from her bosom the flowers given to her by him on the previous day. 'Ah! non credea mirarti, si presto estinto o flore' (Scarcely could I believe it that so soon thou would'st wither, O blossoms).

Ah! non credea mi-rar----ti si presto es-tin-to, o fio---re

Gently Elvino replaces the ring upon her finger, and kneels before her. 'Viva Amina!' cry the villagers. She awakens. Instead of sorrow, she sees joy all around her, and Elvino, with arms outstretched, waiting to beg her forgiveness and lead her to the altar:

Ah! non giun-ge u-man pen-sie-ro.. Al con-ten-to ond'io son pie-na

It ends with this brilliant passage:

The 'Ah! non giunge' is one of the show pieces of Italian opera. Nor is its brilliance hard and glittering. It is the brightness of a tender soul rejoicing at being enabled to cast off sorrow. Indeed, there is about the entire opera a sweetness and a gentle charm, that go far to account for its having endured so long in the repertory, out of which so many works far more ambitious have been dropped.

Opera-goers of the old Academy of Music days recalled the bell-like tones of Etelka Gerster's voice in 'Ah! non giunge'; nor were they ever able to forget the bird-like, spontaneous singing in this rôle of Adelina Patti, gifted with a voice and an art such as those who had the privilege of hearing her in her prime did not hear since, nor are likely to hear again. Admirers of Mme. Sembrich's art also were justly numerous, and it was fortunate for habitués o the Metropolitan that she was so long in the company singing at that house. She was a charming Amina. Tetrazzini was brilliant in *La Sonnambula*.

The story of *La Sonnambula* is simple and thoroughly intelligible. The mainspring of the action is the interesting psycho-physical manifestation of somnambulism. This is effectively worked out, and the crossing of the bridge in the last scene is a tense moment in the simple story. It calls for an interesting stage 'property'— the plank that breaks without precipitating Amina, who sometimes may have more embonpoint than voice, into the mill-race. All these elements contribute to the success of *La Sonnambula*, which, produced in 1831, still is a good evening's entertainment.

Amina was one of Jenny Lind's favourite rôles. There is a beautiful portrait of her in the character by Eichens. It shows her, in the last act, kneeling and singing 'Ah! non credea', and is somewhat of a rarity. It is far more interesting than her better known portraits.                                              K.

# NORMA

Opera in two acts by Vincenzo Bellini; text by Felice Romani, founded on L. A. Soumet's tragedy. Première on December 26, 1831, at la Scala, Milan, with Pasta, Grisi, Donzelli, Negrini; London, Haymarket, 1833, with Pasta, de Meric, Donzelli, Galli; Drury Lane, 1837; Covent Garden, 1841, with Adelaide Kemble, Rainforth, Harrison, Leffler; New York, 1841 (in English); 1843 (in Italian); Metropolitan, New York, 1891, with Lilli Lehmann, 1927, with Ponselle, Telva, Lauri-Volpi, Pinza, conductor Serafin; Covent Garden, 1929, with Ponselle, Cattaneo, Fusati, Manfrini, conductor Bellezza; Metropolitan, New York, 1936, with Cigna, Castagna, Martinelli, Pinza, conductor Panizza; 1943, with Milanov, Castagna, Jagel, Cordon, conductor Sodero; Scala, 1952, with Callas, Stignani, Penno, Rossi-Lemeni, conductor Ghione; Covent Garden, 1952, with Callas, Stignani, conductor Gui.

### CHARACTERS

Pollione, *Roman Pro-consul in Gaul* ................ Tenor

Oroveso, *Archdruid, father of Norma* ................ Bass

Norma, *High priestess of the druidical temple* ..... Soprano

Adalgisa, *a virgin of the temple* ................. Soprano

Clotilda, *Norma's confidante* .................... Soprano

Flavio, *a centurion* ............................. Tenor

Priests, Officers of the Temple, Gallic Warriors, Priestesses and Virgins of the Temple, and Two Children of Norma and Pollione.

*Time:* Roman Occupation, about 50 B.C.          *Place:* Gaul

Act I.    Sacred grove of the Druids. The high priest Oroveso comes with the Druids to the sacred grove to beg of the gods to rouse the people to war and aid them to accomplish the destruction of the Romans. Scarcely have they gone than the Roman Pro-consul Pollione appears and confides to his Centurion, Flavio, that he no longer loves Norma, although she has broken her vows of chastity for him and has borne him two sons. He has seen Adalgisa and his heart is now hers.

At the sound of the sacred instrument of bronze that calls the Druids to the temple, the Romans disappear. The priests and priestesses approach the altar, and Norma, the high priestess, daughter of Oroveso, ascends the steps. No one suspects her intimacy with the Roman enemy. But she loves Pollione and seeks to avert the danger that would threaten him, should Gaul rise against the Romans, by prophesying that Rome will fall through its own weakness, and declaring that it is not yet the will of the gods that Gaul shall go to war. She also prays to the goddess for the return of the Roman leader, who has left her.

In the next scene, which also takes place in the sacred grove, Adalgisa is shown waiting for Pollione, who joins her and begs her to fly with him to Rome, where their happiness would be secure. After some hesitation, she agrees to go with him.

The scene changes and shows Norma's dwelling. The priestess is steeped in deep sadness, for she knows that Pollione plans to desert her and their offspring, although she is not yet aware of her rival's identity. Adalgisa comes to unburden her heart to her superior. She confesses that she has become untrue to her faith through love—and, moreover, love for a Roman. Norma, thinking of her own unfaithfulness to her vows, is about to free Adalgisa from hers, when Pollione appears. For the first time Norma learns the identity of the Roman Adalgisa loves. When she learns the truth the latter turns from Pollione; she loves Norma too well to go away with the betrayer of the high priestess.

Act II.    Norma, filled with despair, is beside the cradle of her little ones. An impulse to kill them comes over her, but motherhood triumphs over unrequited love. She will renounce her lover, and Adalgisa shall become the happy spouse of Pollione, but shall promise to take the place of mother to her children. Adalgisa, however, will not hear of treachery to Norma. She will go to Pollione, but only to remind him of his duty.

The scene changes again to a wooded region of the temple in which the warriors of Gaul have gathered. Norma awaits the result of Adalgisa's plea to Pollione; then learns that she has failed and has come back to the grove to pass her life as a priestess. Norma's wrath is now beyond control. She strikes the brazen shield, and, when the warriors have gathered, joyfully proclaims her message: War against the Romans! But with the deep war song now mingles the sound of tumult from the temple. A Roman has broken into the sacred edifice, and has been captured. It is Pollione, who Norma knows has attempted to carry off Adalgisa. The penalty for his intrusion is death. But Norma, moved by love to pity and still hoping to save her recreant lover, submits a new victim to the enraged Gauls—a perjured virgin of the priesthood.

'Speak, then, and name her!' they cry.

To their amazement she utters her own name, then confesses all to her father, and to his care confides her children.

A pyre has been erected. She mounts it, but not alone. Pollione, his love rekindled at the spectacle of her greatness of soul, joins her. In the flames he, too, will atone for their offences before God.

K.

*Norma* is a work of great lyrical beauty and considerable dramatic tension—the combination which Bellini only this once succeeded in achieving. The music unfolds in long scenes, but the listener never loses the feeling that the threads are drawing gradually and inevitably together towards the final tragic dénouement.

The overture is in the nature of a dramatic prelude. The Druids are shown first in a solemn introduction (in which occurs a haunting wood-wind phrase), followed by an inflammatory pronouncement by Oroveso, which leads to a typical early nineteenth-

century Italian march. Next we are introduced to the Romans, in the persons of Pollione and his friend Flavio; Pollione has a cavatina, 'Meco all' altar di Venere', whose ending is interrupted by the sounds of the Druids gathering for their ceremony, but he has time for a cabaletta before he disappears from view.

The introduction to the great scene of Druidical rites is in the form of a march which is later used for the quick section of Norma's great and justly famous 'Casta diva', which forms the centre-piece of this scene and indeed of the whole opera. This prayer to the 'chaste goddess' is one of the most cele-

brated of soprano arias, and its form and melodic contour are said (with other pieces of the same kind in Bellini's works) to have had the strongest influence on the character and mood of Chopin's nocturnes, a view which is easy to understand when one hears the aria well sung. Even transposed, the fioriture ornaments are taxing to the average soprano—but the truth is that the average soprano cannot (and never could) tackle the title rôle.

Adalgisa is the fourth character to be presented musically; her impressive recitative, 'Sgombra e la sacra selva', is her only solo opportunity, but it leads to a big-scale duet with Pollione, 'Va crudele, al dio spietato', and is followed by an extensive scene with Norma herself as she confesses her guilt, and a trio

which ends the Act. Better known and even more beautiful is the great scene for the two sopranos in Act II, 'Mira, o Norma' after Norma has begged Adalgisa to marry Pollione and to

look after the two children Norma has had by him. Adalgisa's devotion is touchingly and beautifully shown in this duet, which contains one of Bellini's finest melodies. Norma and Adalgisa sing in thirds together in the slow section and again in the decorated quick section, with which it ends.

The last part of the opera begins with Oroveso's solo, 'Ah, del Tebro' (marked 'con ferocia' in the score), gathers momentum

when Norma summons the Druids and with them sings a determined chorus, 'Guerra!' but reaches its climax when Pollione is
left alone with Norma. Their two great duets, of which 'In mia
man alfin tu sei' takes place in private, 'Qual cor tradisti' in
public and with choral support, form the climax of the opera.
Bellini's vocal writing is at its most expressive, and the drama is
hardly less intense than in, for instance, the duet between Radames
and Amneris in the last act of *Aida*. The opera ends fittingly with
a beautiful trio, 'Deh non volerli vittime', for Norma, Pollione,
Oroveso and the chorus.                                    H.

# I PURITANI
## The Puritans

Opera in three acts, by Vincenzo Bellini; words by Count Pepoli. Produced,
Paris, Théâtre des Italiens, January 25, 1835, with Grisi as Elvira, Rubini as
Arturo, Tamburini as Riccardo, and Lablache as Giorgio. London, King's
Theatre, May 21, 1835 (in Italian); la Scala, Milan, 1835; New York, Feb-
ruary 3, 1844; Academy of Music, 1883, with Gerster. Revived, Manhattan
Opera House, December 3, 1906, with Bonci as Arturo, and Pinkert as Elvira;
and in 1909 with Tetrazzini as Elvira; Metropolitan, 1918, with Barrientos,
Lazaro, de Luca, Mardones; Florence, 1933, with Capsir, Lauri-Volpi,
Basiola, Pinza, conductor Serafin; la Scala, Milan, 1942, with Carosio, Salva-
rezza, Pasero; Rome Opera, 1948, with Pagliughi, Filippeschi, Tagliabue,
Neroni; la Scala, 1949, with Carosio, Conley, Tagliabue, Siepi, conductor
Capuana; Fenice, Venice, 1949, with Callas, Perino, Savarese, Christoff,
conductor Serafin.

### CHARACTERS

Lord Gaultiers Walton, *of the Puritans* .............. Bass
Sir George Walton, *his brother, of the Puritans* ........ Bass
Lord Arthur Talbot, *of the Cavaliers* .............. Tenor
Sir Richard Forth, *of the Puritans* .............. Baritone
Sir Benno Robertson, *of the Puritans* .............. Tenor
Henrietta, *of France, widow of Charles I* ......... Soprano
Elvira, *daughter of Lord Walton* ................ Soprano

Puritans, Soldiers of the Commonwealth, Men-at-Arms,
Women, Pages, etc.

*Time:* During the Wars between Cromwell and the Stuarts
*Place:* Near Plymouth, England
(The leading characters are customarily called Enrichetta,
Arturo, Riccardo, and Giorgio in Italian.)

Act I is laid in a fortress, near Plymouth, held by Lord Walton
for Cromwell. Lord Walton's daughter, Elvira, is in love with

Lord Arthur Talbot, a cavalier and adherent of the Stuarts, but her father has promised her hand to Sir Richard Forth, like himself a follower of Cromwell. He relents, however, and Elvira is bidden by her uncle, Sir George Walton, to prepare for her nuptials with Arthur, for whom a safe conduct to the fortress has been provided.

Queen Henrietta, widow of Charles I, is a prisoner in the fortress. On discovering that she is under sentence of death, Arthur, loyal to the Stuarts, enables her to escape by draping her in Elvira's bridal veil and conducting her past the guards, as if she were the bride. There is one critical moment. They are met by Sir Richard, who had hoped to marry Elvira. The men draw their swords, but a disarrangement of the veil shows Sir Richard that the woman he supposes to be Lord Arthur's bride is not Elvira. He permits them to pass. When the escape is discovered, Elvira, believing herself deserted, loses her reason. Those who had gathered for the nuptials, now, in a stirring chorus, invoke maledictions upon Arthur's head.

Act II plays in another part of the fortress. It concerns itself chiefly with the exhibition of Elvira's madness. But it has also the famous martial duet, 'Suoni la tromba' (Sound the trumpet), in which Sir George and Sir Richard announce their readiness to meet Arthur in battle and strive to avenge Elvira's sad plight.

Act III is laid in a grove near the fortress. Arthur, although proscribed, seeks out Elvira. Her joy at seeing him again temporarily lifts the clouds from her mind, but renewed evidence of her disturbed mental state alarms her lover. He hears men, whom he knows to be in pursuit of him, approaching, and is aware that capture means death, but he will not leave Elvira. He is apprehended and is about to be executed when a messenger arrives with news of the defeat of the Stuarts and a pardon for all prisoners. Arthur is freed. The sudden shock of joy restores Elvira's reason. The lovers are united.

As an opera *I Puritani* lacks the naïveté of *La Sonnambula*, nor has it any one number of the celebrity of 'Casta diva' in *Norma*. Occasionally, however, it is revived for a tenor like Bonci, whose elegance of phrasing finds exceptional opportunity in the rôle of Arthur; or for some renowned prima donna of the brilliant coloratura type, for whom Elvira is a grateful part.

The principal musical numbers are, in Act I, Sir Richard
Forth's cavatina, 'Ah! per sempre io ti perdei' (Ah! forever have
I lost thee); Arthur's romance, 'A te o cara' (To thee, beloved);

A te o ca-ra,... a-mor ta-lo-ra,

and Elvira's sparkling polacca, 'Son vergin vezzosa' (I am a
blithesome maiden).

Son ver - - gin vez - zo - - sa      in

ve - - sto    di      spo - - - sa,

In Act II we have Sir George's romance, 'Cinta di fiori', and
Elvira's mad scene, 'Qui la voce sua soave' (It was here in
sweetest accents).

Qui la vo-ce sua so- a- ve

This is a *legato* melody of infinite pathos and beauty—one of
Bellini's finest inspirations and perhaps the loveliest and most
purely musical of all nineteenth-century mad scenes. It is followed
by a beautiful, quicker air, 'Vien, diletto' (Come, dearest love).

The act closes with the duet for baritone and bass, between Sir
Richard and Sir George, 'Suoni la tromba', a fine sonorous proclamation of martial ardour.

Maestoso

Suo-ni la tromba in-tre-pi-do! Io pug-ne-rò da    for-te,

It was in this duet, on the occasion of the opera's revival for
Gerster, that I heard break and go to pieces the voice of Antonio
Galassi, the great baritone of the heyday of Italian opera at the
Academy of Music. 'Suoni la tromba!'—he could sound it no
more. The career of a great artist was at an end.

'A una fonte aflitto e solo' (Sad and lonely by a fountain), a beautiful number for Elvira, occurs at the beginning of the third act. There is also in this act the impassioned 'Vieni fra queste braccia' (Come to these arms) for Arthur and Elvira, with its two top D's for the tenor. It is followed by a big ensemble, 'Credeasi misera', dominated by the tenor's part, in which occurs what must be the only example of a top F written for the tenor.

Bellini's simplicity of style amounts at its best to genius, but it is too often companioned by his fatal dramatic naïveté. There are a few dramatic strokes in *Puritani*—the sound of Elvira's voice offstage as she interrupts the stage action with the beginning of 'Son vergin vezzosa' is one of them—but even such scenes as this, or the exquisite 'Qui la voce', require to be integrated to the drama if they are to achieve a genuine dramatic as well as a musical effect. One is too often in *Puritani* excited by the lyrical beauty of the music, but at the same time exasperated by its lack of direction and its aimless relationship with the drama, a situation which does not arise when *Norma* is the opera in question.                              K., H.

# GAETANO DONIZETTI
## (1797–1848)

### L'ELISIR D'AMORE
### The Elixir of Love

OPERA in two acts by Gaetano Donizetti; text by Felice Romani. Première at the Teatro della Canobbiana, Milan, May 12, 1832, with Sabina Heinefetter, Genero, Dabadie, Frezzolini. First performed in London, Lyceum Theatre, 1836; New York, 1838; Metropolitan, New York, 1904, with Sembrich, Caruso, Scotti, Rossi, conductor Vigna; 1916, with Hempel, Caruso, Scotti, Didur, conductor Papi; revived 1941, with Sayao, Landi, Valentino, Baccaloni, conductor Panizza; Covent Garden, 1950, with Carosio, Tagliavini, Gobbi, Tajo, conductor Capuana. Always in repertory of Italian Opera Houses; famous Nemorinos of this generation also include Schipa and Gigli.

### CHARACTERS

Nemorino, *a young peasant* ....................... Tenor
Adina, *wealthy, and owner of a farm* ............. Soprano
Belcore, *a sergeant* ........................... Baritone
Dulcamara, *a quack doctor* ....................... Bass
Gianetta, *a peasant girl* ........................ Soprano

*Time:* Nineteenth Century          *Place:* A small Italian village

Act I.    Beauty and riches have made the youthful Adina exacting. She laughs at the embarrassed courting of the true-hearted peasant lad, Nemorino, mocks at the story of *Tristan and Isolde*, and rejoices that there are now no more elixirs to bring the merry heart of woman into slavish dependence on love. Yet she does not seem so much indifferent to Nemorino as piqued over his lack of courage to come to the point.

Sergeant Belcore arrives in the village at the head of a troop of soldiers. He seeks to win Adina's heart by storm. The villagers tease Nemorino about his soldier rival, and he is driven almost to despair by their raillery. Enter the peripatetic quack, Dr. Dulcamara. For a ducat Nemorino eagerly buys of him a flask of cheap Bordeaux, which the quack assures him is an elixir of love that within twenty-four hours will enable him to win Adina. Nemorino empties the flask at a draught. A certain effect shows itself at once. Under the influence of the Bordeaux he falls into extravagant mirth, sings, dances—and grieves no more about Adina, who becomes piqued and, to vex Nemorino, engages herself to marry Sergeant Belcore. An order comes to the troops to move. The Sergeant presses for an immediate marriage. To this Adina, still under the influence of pique, consents. Nemorino seeks to console himself by louder singing and livelier dancing.

Act II.    The village is assembled on Adina's farm to celebrate her marriage with the Sergeant. But it is noticeable that she keeps putting off signing the marriage contract. Nemorino awaits the effect of the elixir. To make sure of it, he buys from Dulcamara a second bottle. Not having the money to pay for it, and Belcore being on the look-out for recruits, Nemorino enlists and, with the money he receives, pays Dulcamara. The fresh dose of the supposed elixir makes Nemorino livelier than ever. He pictures to himself the glory of a soldier's career. He also finds himself greatly admired by the village girls for enlisting. Adina also realises that he has joined the army out of devotion to her, and indicates that she favours him rather than Belcore. But he now has the exalted pleasure of treating her with indifference, so that she goes away very sad. He attributes his luck to the elixir.

The villagers have learned that his rich uncle is dead and has left a will making him his heir. But because this news has not yet been communicated to him, he thinks their attentions due to the love philtre, and believes the more firmly in its efficacy. In any event, Adina has perceived, upon the Sergeant's pressing her to sign the marriage contract, that she really prefers Nemorino. Like a shrewd little woman, she takes matters into her own hands, and buys back from Sergeant Belcore her lover's enlistment paper. Having thus set him free, she behaves so coyly that Nemorino threatens to seek death in battle, whereupon she faints right into his arms. The Sergeant bears this unlucky turn of affairs with the bravery of a soldier, while Dulcamara's fame becomes such that he can sell the villagers his entire stock of Bordeaux at a price that makes him rich.

The elixir of life of this *Elixir of Love* is the romance for tenor in the second act, 'Una furtiva lagrima' (A furtive tear), which Nemorino sings as Adina sadly leaves him, when she thinks that he has become indifferent to her. It was because of Caruso's admirable rendition of this beautiful romance that the opera was revived at the Metropolitan Opera House, New York, in 1904.

Even the instrumental introduction to it, in which the bassoons carry the air, is captivating.

Act I is laid on Adina's farm. Nemorino sings a charming song, 'Quanto e bella', and Adina has a florid air, 'Chiedi all' aura lusinghiera' (Go, demand of yon light zephyr), with which she turns aside from Nemorino's attentions.

The scene then changes to a square in the village. Here Dr. Dulcamara makes his entry, singing his *buffo* air, 'Udite, udite, o rustici' (Give ear, now, ye rustic ones). There are two attractive duets in this scene. One is for Nemorino and Dr. Dulcamara, 'Obbligato! obbligato!' (Thank you kindly! thank you kindly!).

The other, for Adina and Nemorino, is 'Esulti pur la barbara per poco alle mie pene' (Tho' now th' exalting cruel one can thus deride my bitter pain).

Act II, which shows a room in Adina's farm house, opens with a bright chorus of rejoicing at her approaching wedding. Dulcamara brings out a piece of music, which he says is the latest thing from Venice, a barcarole for two voices. He and Adina sing it; a dainty duet, 'Io son ricco, e tu sei bella' (I have riches, thou hast beauty) which figures in all the old potpourris of the opera.

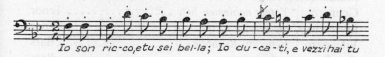

There is a scene for Nemorino, Gianetta, and the peasants, in which Nemorino praises the elixir, 'Dell' elisir mirabile' (Of this most potent elixir). Later comes another duet for Adina and

Dulcamara, 'Quanto amore!' (What affection!) in which Adina expresses her realisation of the death of Nemorino's affection for her.

'The score of *Elisir d'Amore*,' says the *Dictionnaire des Opéras* 'is one of the most pleasing that the Bergamo composer has written in the comic vein. It abounds in charming motifs and graceful melodies. In the first act the duet for tenor and bass between the young villager and Dr. Dulcamara is a little master-piece of animation, the accompaniment of which is as interesting as the vocal parts. The most striking passages of the second act are the chorus, "Cantiamo, facciam brindisi"; the barcarole for two voices, "Io son ricco, e tu sei bella"; the quartet, "Dell' elisir mirabile"; the duet between Adina and Dulcamara, "Quanto amore"; and finally the lovely and smoothly flowing romance of Nemorino, "Una furtiva lagrima", which is one of the most remarkable inspirations of Donizetti.'

To these one may add the melodious passage in which Adina makes her peace with Nemorino.                    K.

## LUCREZIA BORGIA

Opera in a prologue and two acts by Gaetano Donizetti; text by Felice Romani (after Victor Hugo). Première at la Scala, Milan, on December 26, 1833, with Lalande, M. Brambilla, Pedrazzi, Mariani, Spiaggi; Her Majesty's Theatre, London, 1839, with Grisi, Ernesta Grisi, Mario, Tamburini; New York, 1844; Covent Garden, 1847, with Grisi, Alboni, Mario, Tamburini; Metropolitan, 1904, with de Macchi, Edyth Walker, Caruso, Scotti, conductor Vigna. Revived Colon, Buenos Aires, 1919, with Mazzoleni, Gigli; Florence, 1933, with Arangi-Lombardi, Pederzini, Gigli, Pasero, conductor Marinuzzi; la Scala, 1951, with Mancini, Pirazzini, Picchi, Rossi-Lemeni, conductor Capuana. Teresa Tietjens was one of the most famous exponents of the title rôle.

### CHARACTERS

Alfonso d'Este, *Duke of Ferrara* . . . . . . . . . . . . . . . . . Baritone

Lucrezia Borgia . . . . . . . . . . . . . . . . . . . . . . . . . . . . . . Soprano

Maffio Orsini . . . . . . . . . . . . . . . . . . . . . . . . . . . . . . . . Contralto

Gennaro ⎰ *Young noblemen in* ⎱ . . . . . . . . . . . . . . . . Tenor

Liverotto ⎰ *the service of the* ⎱ . . . . . . . . . . . . . . . Tenor

Vitellozzo ⎱ *Venetian Republic* ⎰ . . . . . . . . . . . . . . . . Bass

Gazello . . . . . . . . . . . . . . . . . . . . . . . . . . . . . . . . . . . . Bass

Rustighello, *in the service of Don Alfonso* . . . . . . . . . . Tenor

Gubetta ⎱ *in the service of Lucrezia* . . . . . . . . . . . . . . ⎰ Bass

Astolfo ⎰ . . . . . . . . . . . . . . . . ⎱ Bass

Gentlemen-at-Arms, Officers, and Nobles of the Venetian
Republic; same, attached to court of Alfonso; Ladies-in-
Waiting, Capuchin Monks, etc.

*Time:* Early Sixteenth Century      *Place:* Venice and Ferrara

When an opera, without actually maintaining itself in the
repertory, nevertheless is an object of occasional revival, it is sure
to contain striking passages that seem to justify the experiment
of bringing it forward again. *Lucrezia Borgia* has a male character,
Maffio Orsini, sung by a contralto. Orsini's ballata, 'Il segreto
per esser felice' (O the secret of bliss in perfection), is a famous
contralto air which Ernestine Schuman-Heink, with her voice of
extraordinary range, made well known all over the United States.

The music has all the dash and abandon that the words suggest.
Orsini sings it at a banquet in Ferrara. Suddenly from a neighbouring room comes the sound of monks' voices chanting a dirge.
A door opens. The penitents, still chanting, enter. The lights grow
dim and one by one go out. The central doors swing back.
Lucrezia Borgia appears in the entrance. The banqueters are her
enemies. She has poisoned the wine they have just quaffed to
Orsini's song. They are doomed. The dirge is for them. But—and
this she did not know—among them is Gennaro, her illegitimate
son, whom she dearly loves. She offers him an antidote, but in
vain. He will not save himself, while his friends die. She then
discloses the fact that she is his mother. But, even then, instead of
accepting her proffered aid to save his life, he repulses her.
Lucrezia herself then drains the poisoned cup from which he has
quaffed, and sinks, dying, upon his prostrate form. Such is the
sombre setting for the Brindisi when heard in the opera.

*Il se-gre-to per es-ser fe-li · · · ce s o per prova el'in seg-noaghami-ce*

The tenor rôle of Gennaro has also been responsible for occasional revivals of the work. Mario introduced for this character
as a substitute for a scene in the second act, a recitative and air
by Lillo, 'Com' è soave quest' ora di silenzio' (Oh! how delightful
this pleasing hour of silence), a change which is sometimes
followed.

Prologue. Terrace of the Grimani palace, Venice. Festival by night. Gennaro, weary, separates from his friends and falls asleep on a stone bench of the terrace. Here he is discovered by Lucrezia, who is masked. She regards him with deep affection. 'Com' e bello quale incanto' (Holy beauty, child of nature) she sings.

Com' è bel-lo quale in-can-to

Gennaro awakens. In answer to her questions he tells her that he has been brought up by a poor fisherman 'Di pescatore ignobile' (Deem'd of a fisher's lowly race).

Larghetto

Di pes-ca-to-re i-gno-bi-le.

The youth's friends come upon the scene. Maffio Orsini tears the mask from Lucrezia's face, and in a dramatic concerted number he and his friends remind Lucrezia, for the benefit of Gennaro, who had been struck by her beauty and was unaware that she was the hated Borgia, how each has lost a brother or other relative through her. 'Maffio Orsini, signora, son' io cui svenasto il dormente fratello' (Madam, I am Orsini. My brother you did poison, the while he was sleeping). And so each one in order.

Gennaro turns from her in loathing. She faints.

Act I.    A public place in Ferrara. On one side a palace. Alfonso, who, incidentally, is Lucrezia's fourth husband, she having done away with his predecessors by poison, or other murderous means, is jealous of Gennaro. Like the youth himself, he is ignorant that Lucrezia is Gennaro's mother, and is persuaded that he is her paramour. He has two solos. The first is 'Vieni, la mia vendetta' (Haste then to glut a vengeance); the second, 'Qualunque sia l'evento' (On this I stake my fortune).

Qua lun-gue sia l'e-van-to, che può re-car for-tu-na.

Gennaro and his friends come into the Plaza. They see the letters BORGIA under the escutcheon of the palace. Gennaro, to show his detestation of Lucrezia's crimes, rushes up the steps and with his sword hacks away the first letter of the name, leaving only ORGIA. At the command of the Duke he is arrested.

Lucrezia, not knowing who has committed the outrage, demands of her husband that its perpetrator be put to death. Alfonso, with cynical readiness, consents. Gennaro is led in. Lucrezia now pleads for his life. The Duke is firm, even though Lucrezia quite casually reminds him that he is her fourth husband and may share the fate of the other three. His comment is the command that Gennaro shall meet death by quaffing a goblet of poisoned wine handed to him by Lucrezia herself. There is here a strong trio for Lucrezia, Gennaro, and Alfonso, as Alfonso pours wine for himself and Lucrezia from a silver flagon, while he empties the poisoned contents of a gold vessel, 'the Borgia wine', into Gennaro's cup. But Lucrezia has the antidote; and, the Duke having left her with Gennaro in order that she shall have the pleasure of watching the death of the man of whom he suspects her to be enamoured, she gives it to Gennaro, and bids him flee from Ferrara.

Act II is laid in the Negroni palace, and is the scene of the banquet, which has already been described.                K.

## LUCIA DI LAMMERMOOR

Opera in three acts by Gaetano Donizetti; text by Salvatore Cammarano after Sir Walter Scott's novel. Première at Teatro San Carlo, Naples, September 26, 1835, with Persiani, Duprez, Cosselli, Porto; Her Majesty's, 1838; New York, 1843; Metropolitan, New York, 1883, with Sembrich, Campanini, Kaschmann, Augier, conductor Vianesi; last performed at Covent Garden, 1925, with Toti dal Monte, Dino Borgioli, Badini, Cotreuil, conductor Votto; la Scala, Milan, 1923, with dal Monte, Pertile, Stracciari, Pinza, conductor Toscanini; 1936, with dal Monte, Schipa; 1938, with Pagliughi, Gigli, conductor Marinuzzi; 1947, with Pagliughi, Gigli, Savarese, Siepi, conductor Panizza. Among celebrated Lucias have been Lucca, Patti, Gerster, Melba, Sembrich, Tetrazzini, Galli-Curci, Barrientos, Pacini, Pareto, Callas; among Edgardos, Italo Campanini and Caruso.

### CHARACTERS

Lord Henry Ashton, *of Lammermoor* ............Baritone
Lucy, *his sister* ..............................Soprano
Edgar, *Master of Ravenswood* ....................Tenor
Lord Arthur Bucklaw .........................Tenor
Raymond, *chaplain at Lammermoor* .................Bass
Alice, *companion to Lucy*.................Mezzo-Soprano

Norman, *follower of Lord Ashton* ..................Tenor
Relatives, Retainers, and Friends of the House of Lammer
                              moor

*Time:* About 1700                    *Place:* Scotland
(Note. The characters in Italian are Enrico, Lucia, Edgardo,
Arturo, Raimondo, Alisa, and Normando.)

*Lucia di Lammermoor* is generally held to be Donizetti's finest
work, apart perhaps from *Don Pasquale.* 'In it the vein of melody
—now sparkling, now sentimental, now tragic—which embodies
Donizetti's best claim on originality and immortality, finds, perhaps, freest and broadest development.' These words are quoted
from Baker's *Biographical Dictionary of Musicians,* a volume that
rarely pauses to comment on an individual work. The melodies
of *Lucia* are many and beautiful, and even when ornate in passages, are basically expressive of the part of the tragic story to
which they relate. Moreover, the sextet at the end of the second
act when Edgar of Ravenswood appears upon the scene just as
Lucy with trembling hand has affixed her signature to the contract of marriage between Lord Bucklaw and herself, ranks as
one of the finest pieces of dramatic music in all opera, and for
popularity is rivalled, in Italian opera, by only one other composition, the quartet in *Rigoletto.*

Another number, the mad scene in the third act, gives coloratura sopranos an opportunity for technical display equal to that
afforded by the lesson scene in *Il Barbiere di Siviglia*; and, unlike
the latter, the music does not consist of interpolated selections,
but of a complete *scena* with effective recitatives and brilliant
solos, that belong to the score.

In the story of *Lucia* the heroine's brother, Lord Henry Ashton
of Lammermoor, in order to retrieve his fallen fortunes, and
extricate himself from a perilous situation in which his participation in political movements directed against the King has placed
him, arranges a marriage between his sister and Lord Arthur
Bucklaw. Lucy herself knows nothing of this arrangement. Henry,
on the other hand, is equally ignorant of an attachment which
exists between Lucy and Edgar of Ravenswood, between whose
family and his own there has long been a deadly feud. When he
discovers it, he uses the most underhand methods to break it off.

Edgar of Ravenswood is the last of his race. While he is absent
on a mission to France in the interests of Scotland, he despatches

many letters to Lucy. These letters are intercepted by Henry, who also arranges that a forged paper, tending to prove the infidelity of Edgar, is shown to Lucy. Urged by the importunity of her brother, and believing herself deserted by her lover, Lucy unwillingly consents to become the bride of Lord Arthur Bucklaw. But, just as she has signed the marriage contract, Edgar of Ravenswood suddenly appears. He has returned from France, and now comes to claim the hand of Lucy—but too late. Convinced that Lucy has betrayed his love, he casts the ring she gave him at her feet and invokes imprecations upon her and his ancient enemies, the House of Lammermoor.

At night he is sought out in his gloomy castle by Henry. They agree upon a duel to be fought near the tombs of the Ravenswoods, on the ensuing morning, when Edgar, weary of life, and the last of a doomed race, intends to throw himself on his adversary's weapon. But the burden of woe has proved too much for Lucy to bear. At night, after retiring, she goes out of her mind, slays her husband, and dies of her sorrows.

Edgar awaits his enemy in the churchyard of Ravenswood. But Ashton has fled. Instead, Edgar's solitude is interrupted by a train of mourners coming from the Castle of Lammermoor. Upon hearing of Lucy's death he plunges his dagger into his breast, and sinks down lifeless in the churchyard where repose the remains of his ancestors.

On the stage this story is developed so that shortly after the curtain rises on Act I, showing a grove near the Castle of Lammermoor, Henry learns from Norman the latter's suspicions that Lucy and Edgar have been meeting secretly in the park of Lammermoor. Norman has despatched his huntsmen to discover, if they can, whether or not his suspicions are correct. 'Cruda funesta smania' (Each nerve with fury trembleth) sings Henry.

Returning, the hunters relate, in a brisk chorus, that

> Long they wander'd o'er the mountain,
> Search'd each cleft around the fountain,

finally to learn by questioning a falconer that the intruder upon the domain of Lammermoor was none other than Edgar of Ravenswood. Rage and the spirit of revenge are expressed in Henry's vigorous aria, 'La pietade in suo favore' (From my breast I mercy banish).

The scene changes to the park near a fountain. What now occurs is usually as follows. The curtain rises, and shows the scene—evening and moonlight. There is played a beautiful harp solo, an unusual and charming effect in opera. Having prepared the mood for the scene which is to follow, it is promptly encored and played all over again. Then Lucy appears with her companion, Alice. To her she relates the legend of the fountain, 'Regnava nel silenzio' (Silence o'er all was reigning).

Reg-na-va  nel  si - len - zio

*(This is generally sung in D, but was written in E)*

This number gives an idea of the characteristics of Lucy's principal solos. It is brilliant in passages, yet its melody is dreamy and reflective. Lucy's solo following the legend of the fountain, dispels the dark forebodings it had inspired. This second solo for Lucy, one of the best known operatic numbers for soprano, is the 'Quando rapita' (Then swift as thought).

Quando rapita in  es - ta - si  del più co-cen-te ardo-re.

Another beautiful and familiar number is the duet between Lucy and Edgar, who has come to tell her of his impending departure for France and to bid her farewell: 'Verranno a te sull' aure' (My sighs shall on the balmy breeze).

*Moderato legato*

Ver-ran-no ate sull au - re i  miei sos-pi-ri ar-den-ti

Act II.    Apartment in the Castle of Lammermoor. In a sad tune Lucy protests to her brother against the marriage which he has arranged for her with Bucklaw. Henry then shows her the forged letter, which leads her to believe that she has been betrayed by her lover. 'Soffriva nel pianto languia nel dolore' (My sufferings and sorrow I've borne without repining) begins the duet between Lucy and Henry with an especially effective cadenza—a dramatic number.

Though believing herself deserted by Edgar, Lucy still holds back from the thought of marriage with another, and yields only to save her brother from a traitor's death, and even then not until she has sought counsel from Raymond, the chaplain of Lammermoor, who adds his persuasions to Henry's.

The scene of the signing of the dower opens with a quick, bright chorus of guests who have assembled for the ceremony. There is an interchange of courtesies between Henry and Arthur; and then Lucy enters. The sadness of her mien is explained by her brother to Arthur on the ground that she is still mourning the death of her mother. Desperate, yet reluctant, Lucy signs the contracts of dower; and at that moment, Edgar, a sombre figure, but labouring under evident tension, appears at the head of the broad flight of steps in the background, and slowly comes forward.

The orchestra preludes briefly, and the great sextet has begun. Edgar and Henry: 'Chi mi frena in tal momento? Chi troncò dell' ire il corso?' (What restrains me at this moment? Why my sword do I not straightway draw?):

Because he sees Lucy 'as a rose 'mid tempest bending'

Even Henry is moved to exclaim, 'To my own blood I am a traitor':

The chorus swells the volume of sound, but Lucy's voice soars despairingly above all:

Lucy and Edgar—they are the victims of Henry's treachery, as will soon transpire.

Act III.     The first scene is laid in Edgar's gloomy castle, whither at night comes Henry to challenge him to a duel at morn.

The scene then changes back to Lammermoor, where the wedding guests are still feasting. Their revels are halted by Raymond, who, horror-stricken, announces to them that Lucy has gone mad and slain her husband; and soon the unhappy bride herself appears. Then follows the mad scene, one of the greatest show numbers for soprano, with the further merit that it fits perfectly into the scheme of the work.

This is an elaborate *scena*. In an earlier part of the opera Donizetti made effective use of a harp. In the mad scene he introduces a flute obbligato, which plays around the voice, joins with it, touches it with sharp, brilliant accentuations, and glides with it up and down the scale in mellifluous companionship.

In a brief article in *The Musician*, Thomas Tapper writes that 'to perform the mad scene has been an inspiration and incentive to attainment for many singers. Its demands are severe. There must be the "mood", that is, the characterisation of the mental state of Lucy must be evidenced both in vocal tone and physical movement. The aria requires an unusual degree of facility. Its transparency demands adherence to pitch that must not vary a shade from the truth (note the passage where voice and flute are in unison). The coloratura soprano is here afforded unusual opportunity to display fluency and flexibility of voice, to portray the character that is "as Ophelia was"; the dramatic intensity is paramount and must be sustained at a lofty eminence. In brief, the aria is truly a *tour de force*.'

One of the best things in the above is its insistence on the 'mood', the emotional situation that underlies the music. However brilliant the singing of the prima donna, something in her performance must yet convey to her hearers a sense of the sad fortunes of Lucy of Lammermoor.

To the accomplishment of this Donizetti lends a helping hand by introducing, as a mournful reminiscence, the theme of the first act love duet for Lucy and Edgar ('My sighs shall on the balmy breeze'); also by the dreaminess of the two melodies, 'Alfin son tua' (Thine am I ever):

and 'Spargi d'amaro pianto' (Shed thou a tear of sorrow):

The *scena* ends with a *stretto*, a concluding passage taken in more rapid tempo in order to enhance the effect.

There is a point in the mad scene where it is easy to modulate into the key of G major. Donizetti has written in that key the aria 'Perchè non ho del vento' (Oh, for an eagle's pinions) which sopranos sometimes introduce during the scene, since it was composed for that purpose.

Probably the air is unfamiliar to opera-goers in this country.

Lionel Mapleson, once the librarian of the Metropolitan Opera House, never heard it sung there, and was interested to know where I had found it. As it is a florid, brilliant piece of music, and well suited to the scene, I quote a line of it, as a possible hint to some prima donna.

Per - chè non ho del ven - - - - to
l'in - fa - ti - ca - - bil vo - o - le

During the finale of the opera, laid near the churchyard where lie the bones of Edgar's ancestors, Lucy's lover holds the stage. His final aria, 'Tu che a Dio spiegasti l'ali' (Tho' from earth thou'st flown before me), is a passage of mournful beauty, which has few equals in Italian opera.

Tu che a Dio spie-gas-ti l'a-li o bell' alma in-na-mo-ra-ta

Of the singers of former days who have been heard as Lucia, Adelina Patti interpreted the rôle with the least effort and the greatest brilliancy. Hers was a pure flexible soprano, which seemed to flow forth spontaneously from an inexhaustible reservoir of song. Unfortunately she was heard by many long after her day had passed. She had too many 'farewells'. But those who heard her at her best will always remember her as the possessor of a naturally beautiful voice, exquisitely trained.

Italo Campanini, a tenor who was in his prime when Mapleson was impresario at the Academy of Music, was one of the great Edgars. He was an elder brother of Cleofonte Campanini, orchestral conductor and director of the Chicago Opera Company.

As for Caruso, rarely have I witnessed such excitement as followed the singing of the sextet the evening of his first appearance as Edgar at the Metropolitan Opera House. It is a fact that the policeman in the lobby, thinking a riot of some sort had broken loose in the auditorium, grabbed his night stick and pushed through the swinging doors—only to find an audience

vociferously demanding an encore. Even granted that some of
the excitement was 'worked up', it was, nevertheless, a remarkable demonstration.

The rôle of Henry, though, of course, of less importance than
Edgar, can be made very effective by a baritone of the first
rank. Such, for example, was Antonio Galassi, who, like Campanini, was one of Mapleson's singers. He was a tall, well-put-up
man; and when, in the sextet, at the words 'E mio rosa inaridita'
(Of thine own blood thou'rt the betrayer), he came forward in
one stride, and projected his voice into the proceedings, it seemed
as if, no matter what happened to the others, he could take the
entire affair on his broad shoulders and carry it through to success

K.

## LA FIGLIA DEL REGGIMENTO
### La Fille du Régiment—The Daughter of the Regiment

Opera in two acts by Gaetano Donizetti; text by J. H. Vernoy de Saint-
Georges and F. Bayard. Première at the Opéra-Comique, Paris, February 11,
1840. First performed in Milan, 1840; New York, 1843 (in French); London,
Her Majesty's, 1847; Metropolitan, New York, 1902, with Sembrich, Salignac,
Gilibert, conductor Flon; revived 1917, with Hempel, Carpi, Scotti, conductor
Papi, and 1940, with Pons, Jobin, Baccaloni, conductor Papi; la Scala, Milan,
1928, with dal Monte, Lomanto, di Lelio, conductor Santini. Famous Maries
have also included Lind, Sontag, Lucca, Patti, Tetrazzini.

#### CHARACTERS

Marie, *the 'Daughter of the Regiment'* . . . . . . . . . . . . Soprano
Sulpice, *sergeant of French Grenadiers* . . . . . . . . . . . . . . . Bass
Tonio, *a Tyrolese peasant in love with Marie* . . . . . . . . Tenor
Marquise de Birkenfeld . . . . . . . . . . . . . . . . . . . . . . . Soprano
Hortensio, *steward to the Marquise* . . . . . . . . . . . . . . . . Bass
Corporal . . . . . . . . . . . . . . . . . . . . . . . . . . . . . . . . . . . . . . Bass
A Peasant . . . . . . . . . . . . . . . . . . . . . . . . . . . . . . . . . . . . Tenor
Duchesse de Krakenthorp . . . . . . . . . . . . . . . . . . . . Soprano
Soldiers, Peasants, Friends of the Marquise, etc.

*Time:* 1815           *Place:* Mountains of the Swiss Tyro

Act. I.   A valley in the Tyrolese mountains. On the right is
a cottage, on the left the first houses of a village. Heights in the
background. Tyrolese peasants are grouped on rising ground, as
if on the lookout. Their wives and daughters kneel before a shrine
to the Virgin. The Marquise de Birkenfeld is seated on a rustic

bench. Beside her stands Hortensio, her steward. They have been
caught in the eddy of the war. An engagement is in progress not
far away. The Tyrolese chorus sings valiantly, the women pray;
the French are victorious. And why not? Is not the unbeaten
Twenty-first Regiment of Grenadiers among them?

One of them is coming now, Sergeant Sulpice, an old grumbler.
After him comes a pretty girl in uniform, a vivandière—Marie,
the daughter of the regiment, found on the field of battle when
she was a mere child, and brought up by a whole regiment of
fathers, the spoiled darling of the grenadiers. She sings 'Apparvi

alla luce, sul campo guerrier' (I first saw the light in the camp of
my brave grenadiers), which ends in a brilliant cadenza.

The Sergeant puts her through a drill. Then they have a 'Rataplan' duet, which may be called a repetition of Marie's solo with
an accompaniment of rataplans. The drum is the music that is
sweetest to her; and, indeed, Marie's manipulation of the drum-
sticks is a feature of the rôle.

But for a few days Marie has not been as cheerful as formerly.
She has been seen with a young man. Sulpice asks her about him.
She tells the Sergeant that this young man saved her life by pre-
venting her from falling over a precipice. That, however, establishes no claim upon her. The regiment has decreed that only a
grenadier shall have her for wife.

There is a commotion. Some soldiers drag in Tonio, whom
they charge as a spy. They have discovered him sneaking about
the camp. His would have been short shrift had not Marie
pleaded for him, for he is none other than her rescuer. As he
wants to remain near Marie, he decides to become a soldier. The
grenadiers celebrate his decision by drinking to his health and
calling upon Marie to sing the 'Song of the Regiment', a dapper
tune, which is about the best known number of the score: 'Ciascun
lo dice, ciascun lo sà! E il Reggimento, ch'egual non ha'.

> (All men confess it,
> Go where we will!
> Our gallant Regiment
> Is welcome still.

Maestoso

Ciascun lo di-ce, Ciascun lo sa! E il Reg-gi-men-to Ch'e-gual non ha

There is then a love scene for Marie and Tonio, followed by a duet for them, 'A voti cosi ardente' (No longer can I doubt it).

Afterwards the grenadiers sing a 'Rataplan' chorus. But, alas, the Sergeant has been informed that the Marquise de Birkenfeld desires safe conduct. Birkenfeld! That is the very name to which were addressed certain papers found on Marie when she was discovered as a baby on the battlefield. The Marquise examines the papers, declares that Marie is her niece and henceforth must live with her in the castle. Poor Tonio has become a grenadier in vain. The regiment cannot help him. It can only lament with him that their daughter is lost to them. She herself is none too happy. She sings a sad farewell, 'Convien partir! o miei compagni d'arme' (Farewell, a long farewell, my dear companions).

Act II.    In the castle of the Marquise. Marie is learning to dance the minuet and to sing classical airs. But in the midst of her singing she and Sulpice, whom the Marquise also has brought to the castle, break out into the 'Song of the Regiment' and stirring 'rataplans'. Their liveliness, however, is only temporary, for poor Marie is to wed, at her aunt's command, a scion of the ducal house of Krakenthorp. The march of the grenadiers is heard. They come in, led by Tonio, who has been made a captain for valour. Sulpice can now see no reason why Marie should not marry him instead of the nobleman selected by her aunt. And, indeed, Marie and Tonio decide to elope. But the Marquise confesses to the Sergeant, in order to win his aid in influencing Marie, that the girl is really her daughter, born out of wedlock. Sulpice informs Marie, who now feels that she cannot go against her mother's wishes.

In the end, however, it is Marie herself who saves the situation. The guests have assembled for the signing of the wedding contract, when Marie, before them all, sings fondly of her childhood with the regiment, and of her life as a vivandière. 'Quando il destino in mezzo a stragiera' (When I was left, by all abandoned).

The society people are scandalised. But the Marquise is so touched that she leads Tonio to Marie and places the girl's hand in that of her lover. The opera ends with an ensemble, 'Salute to France!'                                                               K.

## LA FAVORITA
### The Favourite

Opera in four acts by Gaetano Donizetti; text by Alphonse Royer and Gustav Waez after a drama *Le Comte de Commingues,* by Baculard d'Arnaud. Première at the Paris Opéra, December 2, 1840. First performed in London, Drury Lane, 1843 (in English); New York, 1843 (in French); Covent Garden, 1845 (in French); Her Majesty's, 1847 (in Italian); Metropolitan, New York, 1895, with Mantelli, Cremonini, Ancona, Plançon; 1905, with Edyth Walker, Caruso, Scotti, Plançon; last London performance, 1912, at London Opera House, with Augusta Doria, Orville Harrold. Recent revivals: la Scala, Milan, 1934, with Stignani, Pertile; Rome Opera, 1935, with Cobelli, Gigli; la Scala, 1939, with Stignani, Malipiero, Tagliabue, Pasero; Rome, 1946, with Stignani, Lauri-Volpi, Bechi; la Scala, 1949, with Stignani, Poggi, Silveri, Siepi, conductor Capuana; Rome, 1951, with Barbieri, Lauri-Volpi.

### CHARACTERS

Alfonso XI, *King of Castile* .....................Baritone
Ferdinand, *a young novice of the Monastery of St.*
    *James of Compostella* (Fernando) ................Tenor
Don Gaspar, *the King's Minister* ..................Tenor
Balthazar, *Superior of the Monastery of St. James*
    (Baldassare) ...................................Bass
Leonora di Gusmann .........................Soprano
Inez, *her confidante* ..........................Soprano
Courtiers, Guards, Monks, Ladies of the Court, Attendants

*Time:* About 1340          *Place:* Castile, Spain

With Campanini as her Fernando, Leonora was, for a number of seasons, one of the principal rôles of Annie Louise Cary at the Academy of Music. Mantelli as Leonora, Cremonini as Fernando, Ancona as King Alfonso, and Plançon as Balthazar, appeared, 1895–96, at the Metropolitan, where *La Favorita* was heard again in 1905; but the work never became a fixture, as it had been at the Academy of Music.

There is in *La Favorita* a strong, dramatic scene at the end of the third Act. As if to work up to this as gradually as possible, the opera opens quietly.

Ferdinand, a novice in the Monastery of St. James of Compostella, has chanced to see and has fallen in love with Leonora, the mistress of Alfonso, King of Castile. He neither knows her name, nor is he aware of her equivocal position. So deeply conceived is his passion, it causes him to renounce his novitiate and seek out its object.

Act I.   The interior of the monastery. Ferdinand makes known to Balthazar, the Superior, that he desires to renounce his novitiate, because he has fallen in love, and cannot banish the woman of his affections from his thoughts. He describes her to the priest as 'Una vergine, un angiol di Dio' (A virgin, an angel of God).

Although this air bears no resemblance to 'Celeste Aida' its flowing measures and melodious beauty, combined with its position so early in the opera, recall the Verdi aria—and prepare for it the same fate—which is to be marred by the disturbance caused by late-comers and to remain unheard by those who come still later.

Balthazar's questions elicit from Ferdinand that his only knowledge of the woman, whose praises he has sung, is of her youth and beauty. Name and station are unknown to him, although he believes her to be of high rank. Balthazar, who had hoped that in time Ferdinand would become his successor as superior of the monastery, releases him reluctantly from his obligations, and prophesies, as the novice turns away from the peaceful shades of the cloister, that he will retrace his steps, disappointed and heartbroken, to seek refuge once more within the monastery's walls.

The scene changes to an idyllic prospect on the island of St. Leon, where Leonora lives in splendour. She, for her part, is deeply enamoured of Ferdinand, yet is convinced that, because of her relations with King Alfonso, he will despise her once he discovers who she is. But so great is her love for him, that, without letting him learn her name or station, she has arranged that he shall be brought, blindfolded, to the island.

'Bei raggi lucenti' (Bright sunbeams, lightly dancing), a graceful solo and chorus for Inez, Leonora's confidante, and her woman companions, opens the scene. It is followed by 'Dolce zeffiro il seconda' (Gentle zephyr, lightly wafted), which is sung by the chorus of women, as the boat conveying Ferdinand touches the island and he, after disembarking, has the bandage withdrawn from over his eyes, and looks in amazement upon the charming surroundings amid which he stands. He questions Inez regarding the name and station of her who holds gentle sway over the island, but in vain. Inez and her companions retire, as Leonora enters. She interrupts Ferdinand's delight at seeing her by telling him—but without giving her reasons—that their love can lead only to sorrow; that they must part. He protests vehemently. She, however, cannot be moved from her determination that he shall not be sacrificed to their love, and hands him a parchment, which she tells him will lead him to a career of honour.

He still protests. But at that moment Inez, entering hurriedly, announces the approach of the King. Leonora bids Ferdinand farewell and goes hastily to meet Alfonso. Ferdinand now believes that the woman with whom he has fallen in love is of rank so high that she cannot stoop to wed him, yet expresses her love for him by seeking to advance him. This is confirmed when, on reading the scroll she has given him, he discovers that it gratifies his highest ambition and confers upon him a commission in the army. The act closes with his martial air, 'Si, che un tuo solo accento' (Oh, fame, thy voice inspiring).

He sees the path to glory open up before him, and with it the hope that some great deed may yet make him worthy to claim the hand of the woman he loves.

Act II.    Gardens of the Palace of the Alcazar. Ferdinand's dream of glory has come true. We learn, through a brief colloquy between Alfonso and Don Gaspar, his minister, that the young officer has led the Spanish army to victory against the Moors. Indeed, this very palace of the Alcazar has been wrested from the enemy by the young hero.

Gaspar having retired, the King, who has no knowledge of the love between Ferdinand and Leonora, sings of his own passion for her in the expressive air, 'Vien, Leonora, a' piedi tuoi' (Come, Leonora, before thee kneeling).

The object of his love enters, accompanied by her confidante. The King has prepared a fête in celebration of Ferdinand's victory, but Leonora, while rejoicing in the honours destined to be his, is filled with foreboding because of the illicit relations between herself and the King, when she truly loves another. Moreover, these fears find justification in the return of Gaspar with a letter in Ferdinand's handwriting, and intended for Leonora, but which the minister has intercepted in the hand of Inez. The King's angry questions regarding the identity of the

writer are interrupted by confused sounds from without. There
enters Balthazar, preceded by a priest bearing a scroll with the
Papal seal. He faces the King and Leonora while the lords and
ladies, who have gathered for the fête, look on in apprehension,
though not wholly without knowledge of what is impending.

For there is at the Court of Alfonso a strong party that condemns the King's illicit passion for Leonora, so openly shown.
This party has appealed to the Papal throne against the King.
The Pope has sent a Bull to Balthazar, in which the Superior of
the Monastery of St. James is authorised to pronounce the inter-
dict on the King if the latter refuses to dismiss his favourite from
the Court and restore his legitimate wife to her rights. It is with
this commission Balthazar has now appeared before the King,
who at first is inclined to refuse obedience to the Papal summons.
He wavers. Balthazar gives him time till the morrow, and until
then withholds his anathema.

Balthazar's vigorous yet dignified denunciation of the King,
'Ah paventa il furor d'un Dio vendicatore' (Do not call down
the wrath of God, the avenger, upon thee), forms a broadly
sonorous foundation for the finale of the act.

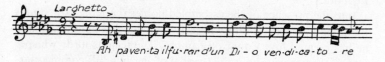

Ah paven-ta ilfu·rar d'un Di - o ven·di·ca·to - re

Act III.   A salon in the Palace of the Alcazar. In a brief
scene the King informs his minister that he has decided to heed
the behest of the church and refrain from braving the Papal malediction. He bids Gaspar send Leonora to him, but, at the first
opportunity, to arrest Inez, her accomplice.

It is at this juncture, as Gaspar departs, that Ferdinand appears
at court, returning from the war, in which he has not only distinguished himself by his valour, but actually has saved the
kingdom. Alfonso asks him to name the prize which he desires
as recompense for his services. Leonora enters. Ferdinand, seeing
her, at once asks for the bestowal of her hand upon him in
marriage. The King, who loves her deeply, and has nearly risked
the wrath of the Pope for her sake, nevertheless, because immediately aware of the passion between the two, gives his assent,
but with reluctance, as indeed appears from the irony that

pervades his impressive solo, 'A tanto amor' (Thou flow'r belov'd).

He then retires with Ferdinand.

Leonora, touched by the King's magnanimity, inspired by her love for Ferdinand, yet shaken by doubts and fears, because aware that he knows nothing of her past, now expresses these conflicting feelings in her principal air, 'O, mio Fernando,' one of the great Italian airs for mezzo-soprano.

She considers that their future happiness depends upon Ferdinand's being truthfully informed of what her relations have been with the King, thus giving him full opportunity to decide whether, with this knowledge of her guilt, he will marry her, or not. Accordingly she despatches Inez with a letter to him. Inez, as she is on her way to deliver this letter, is intercepted by Gaspar, who carries out the King's command and orders her arrest. She is therefore unable to place in Ferdinand's hands the letter from Leonora.

Into the presence of the assembled nobles the King now brings Ferdinand, decorates him with a rich chain, and announces that he has created him Count of Zamora. The jealous lords whisper among themselves about the scandal of Ferdinand's coming marriage with the mistress of the King; but Leonora, who enters in bridal attire, finds Ferdinand eagerly awaiting her, and ready to wed her, notwithstanding, as she believes, his receipt of her communication and complete knowledge of her past.

While the ceremony is being performed in another apartment, the nobles discuss further the disgrace to Ferdinand in this marriage. That Leonora was the mistress of the King is, of course, a familiar fact at court, and the nobles regard Ferdinand's elevation to the rank of nobility as a reward, not only for his defeat of the Moors, but also for accommodatingly taking Leonora off the hands of the King, when the latter is threatened with the malediction of Rome. They cannot imagine that the young officer is ignorant of the relations that existed between his bride and the King.

Ferdinand re-enters. In high spirits he approaches the courtiers,

offers them his hand, which they refuse. Balthazar now comes to
learn the decision of the King. Ferdinand, confused by the taunting words and actions of the courtiers, hastens to greet Balthazar,
who, not having seen him since he has returned victorious and
loaded with honours, embraces him, until he hears Gaspar's
ironical exclamation, 'Leonora's bridegroom!' Balthazar starts
back, and it is then Ferdinand learns that he has just been wedded
'alla bella del Re'—to the mistress of the King.

At this moment, when Ferdinand has but just been informed
of what he can only interpret as his betrayal by the King and the
royal favourite, Alfonso enters, leading Leonora, followed by
her attendants. In a stirring scene, the dramatic climax of the
opera, Ferdinand tears from his neck the chain Alfonso has
bestowed upon him, and throws it contemptuously upon the
floor, breaks his sword and casts it at the King's feet, then
departs with Balthazar, the nobles now making a passage for them.

Act IV.    The cloisters of the Monastery of St. James. Ceremony of Ferdinand's entry into the order. 'Splendon piu belle in
ciel le stelle' (Behold the stars in splendour celestial), a distinguished solo and chorus for Balthazar and the monks.

Left alone, Ferdinand gives vent to his sorrow, which still
persists, in the romance, 'Spirto gentil' (Spirit of Light), one of
the most exquisite tenor solos in the Italian repertory.

Spir-to gen-til  ne'so-gni mie - i   bril-las-ti un di ma ti per-de-i

Balthazar and the monks return. With them Ferdinand enters
the chapel. Leonora, disguised as a novice, comes upon the scene.
She hears the chanting of the monks, Ferdinand's voice enunci-
ating his vows. He comes out from the chapel, recognises Leonora,
bids her be gone. 'Ah! va, t'invola! e questa terra' (These cloisters
fly).

She, however, tells him of her unsuccessful effort to let him
know of her past, and craves his forgiveness for the seeming
wrong she has wrought upon him. 'Pietoso al par del Nume'
(Forgiveness through God I crave of thee).

All of Ferdinand's former love returns for her. 'Vieni, ah!
vieni' (Joy once more fills my breast).

He would bear her away to other climes and there happily pass his days with her. But it is too late. Leonora dies in his arms. 'By to-morrow my soul, too, will want your prayers', are Ferdinand's words to Balthazar, who, approaching, has drawn Leonora's cowl over her dishevelled hair. He calls upon the monks to pray for a departed soul.          K.

# LINDA DI CHAMOUNIX
## Linda of Chamounix

Opera in three acts by Gaetano Donizetti; text by Gaetano Rossi. Première at the Kärnthnerthor Theater, Vienna, May 19, 1842. First performed London, Her Majesty's Theatre, 1843; New York, 1847, with Clothilda Barili; last London performance, 1888, with Fursch-Madi, Trebelli, Navarini; revived Metropolitan, New York, 1934, with Pons, Swarthout, Crooks, de Luca, Pinza, conductor Serafin; San Carlo, Naples, 1934, with dal Monte, Kovaceva, Manuritta, Montesanto, Badini, conductor Baroni; la Scala, Milan, 1939, with dal Monte, Elmo, Malipiero, Basiola, Pasero, conductor Marinuzzi; Trieste, 1949, with Carosio, Palombini, Valletti, Taddei, Mongelli.

### CHARACTERS

Marquis de Boisfleury ........................Baritone
Charles, *Vicomte de Sirval* .......................Tenor
Prefect .........................................Bass
Pierotto ....................................Contralto
Linda .......................................Soprano
Antonio......................................Baritone
Maddalena ..................................Soprano
Intendant....................................Tenor

Peasant men and women, Savoyards, etc.

*Time:* 1760, during the reign of Louis XV

*Place:* Chamounix and Paris

*Linda di Chamounix* contains an air for soprano without which no collection of opera arias is complete. This is Linda's aria in the first act, 'O luce di quest' anima' (Oh! star that guid'st my fervent love). When Donizetti was composing *Linda di Chamounix* for Vienna, with this air and its fluent embellishments, he also was writing for the Imperial chapel a 'Miserere' and an 'Ave Maria' which were highly praised for a style as severe and restrained as 'O luce di quest' anima' is light and graceful.

*Linda di Chamounix* is in three acts, entitled 'The Departure',

'Paris', 'The Return'. The story is somewhat naïve, as its exposition will show.

Act I.    The village of Chamounix. On one side a farmhouse; on an eminence a church. Antonio and Maddalena are poor villagers. Linda is their daughter. She has fallen in love with an artist, Charles, who is really the Vicomte de Sirval, but has not yet disclosed his identity to her. When the opera opens Linda's parents are in fear of being dispossessed by the Marquis de Boisfleury, who is Charles's uncle, but knows nothing of his nephew's presence in Chamounix, or of his love for Linda. She, it may be remarked, is one of those pure, sweet, unsophisticated creatures who exist only on the stage, and possibly only in opera.

When the opera opens, Antonio returns from a visit to the Marquis's agent, the Intendant. Hopes have been held out to him that the Marquis will relent. Antonio communicates these hopes to his wife in the beautiful solo, 'Ambo nati in questa valle' (We were both in this valley nurtured).

Ambo nati in questa valle,

There are shouts of 'Viva!' without. The Marquis has arrived. He seems kindness itself to the old couple. He asks for Linda, but she has gone to prayers in the chapel. We learn from an aside between the Marquis and his Intendant, that the Marquis's apparent benevolence is merely part of a libidinous scheme which involves Linda, whose beauty has attracted the titled roué.

After this scene, Linda comes on alone and sings 'O luce di quest' anima'.

O luce di quest'a ni ma, Delizia amore e vi ta;

I also quote the concluding phrase:

u ni ta nostra sor te,... In ciel, in ciel sarà

Savoyards are preparing to depart for Paris to go to work there. Among them is Pierrot, with his hurdy-gurdy. He sings a charming ballad, 'Per sua madre ando una figlia' (Once a better fortune seeking).

There is then a love scene between Linda and Charles, with the effective duet, 'A consolarmi affretisi' (Oh! that the blessed day were come, when standing by my side), a phrase which is heard again with significant effect in the third act.

A con-so-la - mi af -fret -ti - si, . . Tal gior-no so-spi-ra -to

Antonio then learns from the good Prefect of the village that the latter suspects the Marquis of sinister intentions toward Linda. Indeed at that moment Linda comes in with a paper from the Marquis, which assures to her parents their home; but, she adds, naïvely, that she has been invited by the Marquis to the castle. Parents and Prefect are alarmed for her safety. The Prefect has a brother in Paris. To his protection it is decided that Linda shall go with her Savoyard friends, who even now are preparing to depart.

Act II.    Room in a handsome, well-furnished apartment in Paris. This apartment is Linda's. In it she has been installed by Charles. The natural supposition, that it has been paid for by her virtue, is in this instance a mistake, but one, I am sure, made by nine people out of ten of those who see the opera, since the explanation of how she got there consists merely of a few incidental lines in recitative.

Linda herself, but for her incredible naïveté, would realise the impossibility of the situation.

A voice singing in the street she recognises as Pierrot's, calls him up to her, and assists him with money, of which she appears to have plenty. She tells him that the Prefect's brother, in whose house she was to have found protection, had died. She was obliged to support herself by singing in the street. Fortunately she had by chance met Charles, who disclosed to her his identity as the Vicomte de Sirval. He is not ready to marry her yet on account of certain family complications, but meanwhile has placed her in this apartment, where he provides for her. There is a duet, in which Linda and Pierrot sing of her happiness.

Pierrot having left, the Marquis, who has discovered her retreat, but does not know that it is provided by his nephew

Charles, calls to force his unwelcome attentions upon her. He
laughs, as is not unnatural, at her protestations that she is supported here in innocence; but when she threatens him with
possible violence from her intended, he has a neat little solo of
precaution, ending 'Guardati, pensaci, marchese mio' (Be
cautious—ponder well, Marquis most valiant).

The Marquis, having prudently taken his departure, Linda
having gone to another room, and Charles having come in, we
learn from his recitative and air that his mother, the Marquise
de Sirval, has selected a wife for him, whom she insists he shall
marry. He hopes to escape from this marriage, but, as his mother
has heard of Linda and also insists that he shall give her up, he
has come to explain matters to her and temporarily to part from
her. But when he sees her, her beauty so moves him that his
courage fails him, although, as he goes, there is a sadness in his
manner that fills her with sad forebodings.

For three months Linda has heard nothing from her parents.
Letters, with money, which she has sent them, have remained
unanswered—another of the situations in which this most artless
heroine of opera discovers herself, without seeking the simple
and obvious way of relieving the suspense.

In any event, her parents have become impoverished through
the Marquis de Boisfleury's disfavour, for at this moment her
father, in the condition of a mendicant, comes in to beg the
intercession in his behalf of the Vicomte de Sirval (Charles). Not
recognising Linda, he mistakes her for Charles's wife. She bestows
bounteous alms upon him, but hesitates to make herself known,
until, when he bends over to kiss her hand, she cannot refrain
from disclosing herself. Her surroundings arouse his suspicions,
which are confirmed by Pierrot, who comes running in with the
news that he has learned of preparations for the marriage of
Charles to a lady of his mother's choice. In a scene (which a
fine singer like Galassi was able to invest with real power) Antonio
hurls the alms Linda has given him at her feet, denounces her,
and departs. Pierrot seeks to comfort her. But alas! her father's
denunciation of her, and, above all, what she believes to be
Charles's desertion, have unseated her reason.

Act III.    The village of Chamounix. The Savoyards are returning and are joyfully greeted. Charles, who has been able to
persuade his mother to permit him to wed Linda, has come in

search of her. Incidentally he has brought solace for Antonio and Maddalena. The de Sirvals are the real owners of the farm, the Marquis, Charles's uncle, being only their representative. Linda's parents are to remain in undisturbed possession of the farm— but where is she?

Pierrot is heard singing. Whenever he sings he is able to persuade Linda to follow him. Thus her faithful friend gradually has led her back to Chamounix. And when Charles chants for her a phrase of their first act duet, 'O consolarmi affretisi', her reason returns, and it is 'Ah! di tue pene sparve il sogno' (Ah! the vision of my sorrow fades).

In this drama of naïveté, an artlessness which I mention again because I think it is not so much the music as the libretto that has become old-fashioned, even the Marquis comes in for a good word. For when he too offers his congratulations, what does Linda do but refer to the old libertine, who has sought her ruin, as 'him who will be my uncle dear'. K.

# DON PASQUALE

Opera in three acts by Gaetano Donizetti; text by Cammarano from Anelli's *Ser Marc Antonio*. Première at the Théâtre-Italien, Paris, January 3, 1843, with Grisi, Mario, Tamburini, Lablache. First performed, la Scala, Milan, 1843; Her Majesty's, London, 1843; New York, 1846. Revived Metropolitan, 1899, with Sembrich, Salignac, Scotti, Pini-Corsi, conductor Mancinelli; 1935, with Bori, Schipa, de Luca, Pinza, conductor Panizza; 1940, with Sayao, Martini, Valentino, Baccaloni, conductor Papi (1945, conductor Busch); Covent Garden, 1920, with Pareto, Govoni, Paterna, Badini, conductor Bavagnoli; 1937, with Favero, Dino Borgioli, Biasini, di Lelio, conductor Salfi; Glyndebourne, 1938, with Mildmay, Dino Borgioli, Stabile, Baccaloni, conductor Busch; Cambridge Theatre, London, 1946, with Noni, MacPherson, Stabile, Lawrence, conductor Erede. Revived la Scala, Milan, 1930, with dal Monte, Lomanto, Stabile, Autori, conductor Calusio; 1936, with Carosio, Schipa, de Luca, Badini, conductor Marinuzzi; 1950, with Noni, Prandelli, Taddei, Pasero, conductor Capuana. Revived Vienna, 1944, with Noni, Dermota, Kunz, Vogel, conductor Paulik.

## CHARACTERS

Don Pasquale, *an old bachelor* .....................Bass
Dr. Malatesta, *his friend* ......................Baritone
Ernesto, *nephew of Don Pasquale* ..................Tenor
Norina, *a young widow* .......................Soprano
A Notary ....................................Baritone
*Time:* Early Nineteenth Century          *Place:* Rome

The overture is mainly concerned with Ernesto's serenade from the last act, and Norina's aria from the first. It admirably suggests the lively tone of the opera.

Act I. The first scene is set in Don Pasquale's room. The wealthy Don Pasquale is about to marry. Though determined himself to have a wife, he is very angry with his nephew Ernesto for wishing to do likewise, and threatens to disinherit him on that account. Ernesto is greatly disturbed by these threats, and so is his lady-love, the sprightly young widow Norina, when he reports them to her.

When the curtain rises, Don Pasquale is impatiently waiting for Malatesta, who, not being able to dissuade his friend from marriage and still less able to influence him to allow his nephew to follow the dictates of his heart, pretends to acquiesce in the mad-cap scheme. He proposes that his 'sister' shall be the bride (Don Pasquale has no one in particular in mind), and describes her in a graceful aria, 'Bella siccome un' angelo', as a timid, naïve, ingenuous girl, brought up, he says, in a convent. She is, however, none other than Norina, who is in no way related to Malatesta. At this description, Don Pasquale is quite unable to contain his delight, in spite of Malatesta's attempts to restrain him, and, when he is alone, he breaks into a gay cavatina, 'Ah, un foco insolito'.

Don Pasquale prepares to give his nephew a lecture on the subject of his future conduct, and tells him in the course of it that he is proposing to take a wife himself. This arouses Ernesto's irreverence, and his uncle is obliged to repeat it several times before he can take it in. When he does, it is to realise that it finally cuts him off from the marriage he himself proposed to enter into. 'Sogno soave e casto' (Fond dream of love thou hast perished) he sings, in one of Donizetti's soaring inspirations, while the old uncle grumbles away in the bass. When Don Pasquale says he has already consulted Malatesta, Ernesto's last remaining hope vanishes; there is no one now to dissuade the old fool.

The scene changes to Norina's room, where she is reading. 'Quel guardo il cavaliere' (Glances so soft and bright) begins her recitative—but she is only reading a novel aloud; her aria, 'So anch' io la virtu magica' (I know what spells a glance can dart), shows her sprightly nature in an enchanting tune. A letter is

So anch'io la vir-tu ma-gi-ca, D'un guar-do a tem-po e lo-co

brought to her, and when Malatesta comes to tell her that
Ernesto's old uncle has fallen for the scheme which shall finally
make him agree to his nephew's marriage, she is anything but
pleased with the way things have gone; they have not had time
to tell Ernesto about their scheme and he has written that he is
furious. However, Malatesta is convinced all is going well, and
he and Norina rehearse how they shall behave with Don Pasquale
when finally he meets his convent-bred bride. The music is pure
effervescence, with its sparkling coloratura and its gaily changing
tunes, and no one who heard Mariano Stabile sing it with Alda
Noni in London during the revival in 1946–8 will ever forget the
effect it made.

Act II.   We are in Ernesto's lodgings. The owner is in
despair at the prospect of losing his bride and his home (Don
Pasquale has told him to clear out of the house). A long horn
prelude ushers in the recitative and aria, 'Cerchero lontana terra',
one of the most famous of the opera.

At home, Don Pasquale receives his prospective bride and her
sponsor, his friend, Malatesta. She is shy, he urges her on, and
the husband-to-be watches every manœuvre enraptured. Norina
is eventually persuaded to speak to Pasquale, and assures him
that she is only interested in the things of the household—sewing,
making clothes, and looking after the kitchen. A notary has been
sent for, and Malatesta dictates the terms of the marriage, the
others, including the notary, repeating his words after him. A
witness is needed, but none seems forthcoming until Ernesto
rushes in, proclaiming his betrayal to anyone who chooses to
listen. Malatesta has his work cut out to explain the situation to
him, without letting Don Pasquale know the way the wind is
blowing.

The moment the contract is signed, Norina's temper seems to
change, and she spits fire at every one of Don Pasquale's attempts
at either conciliation or authority. He is confounded at the contrast, and dumb with horror when she says that Ernesto is just
the person to take her out walking, something that is plainly
beyond the capacity of a man of his years—or girth, for that

matter. The quartet redoubles in vigour, and Norina and Ernesto have a charming lyrical aside which leaves no one in any doubt as to their mutual feelings. When Norina calls together the servants, and, finding there are only three in all, laughingly directs that more be engaged and that the wages of those at present in service be doubled, Don Pasquale can bear it no more. 'Son tradito, son tradito' (I'm a victim of collusion) he shouts in his rage, and the *stretta* of the quartet brings the act to a spirited conclusion.

Act III. The room is the same as that of the previous scene. Servants are rushing hither and thither executing Norina's commands, and disposing of what she has ordered for the house. Don Pasquale sees her dressed up to the nines and about to go out of the house; may he ask where? To the theatre she says—without him. Their duet works the quarrel up until Norina finds occasion to box her 'husband's' ears. As far as Don Pasquale is concerned, it is the end of his hopes and pretensions as well as his hateful marriage, and even Norina is sorry that she has had to go so far to bring the foolish old man to what is, from hers and Ernesto's point of view, a reasonable frame of mind. She rushes from the room, but takes care to drop a note as she goes. It purports to be from Ernesto, and makes an assignation for that very evening in the garden. Don Pasquale reads it, and sees in it his chance of getting quit of the whole affair; he will send for Malatesta.

When he has left the room, the servants flock back into it, and comment on the happenings in the house in a charming chorus. Malatesta arrives and proceeds to give Don Pasquale the benefit of his advice. The two men confer in a famous comic duet, whose every performance has reduced an audience somewhere to helpless laughter. Its *buffo* 6/8 finish is one of the funniest pieces of music in the post-Rossinian repertory.

The scene changes to the garden, where Ernesto sings to Norina the beautiful serenade, 'Com' è gentil'. The story is that

Com'è gen-til, la notte a mezzo April,...

after one of the rehearsals Donizetti asked the music publisher, Dormoy, to go with him to his lodgings. There he rummaged among a lot of manuscripts until, finding what he was looking for, he handed it to Dormoy. 'There,' he said, 'give this to Mario and tell him to sing it in the last scene in the garden as a serenade to Norina.' When the opera was performed, Mario sang it, while Lablache, behind the scenes, played an accompaniment on the lute. It was the serenade. It is in truth the very essence of a light-handed nocturnal piece, and most of the great lyric tenors of history, from Mario to Schipa, have tried at one time or another to prove that never before has it been so stylishly sung.

It is immediately followed by a duet that is no less charming and hardly less well known, 'Tornami a dir'. This is all thirds and sixths for the two voices, but the effect is entrancing. Don Pasquale and Malatesta surprise the lovers, Ernesto escapes, but Norina stays as if to brave it out. Malatesta twists everything round to everyone's satisfaction, and soon Ernesto and Norina are waiting to be married, and moreover with the full approval of Don Pasquale. Suitably, Malatesta leads off the *Rondo finale* with which the work ends.                                K., H.

CHAPTER 8

*Verdi*

# GIUSEPPE VERDI
## (1813–1901)

### NABUCCO

OPERA in four acts by Giuseppe Verdi; text by Temistocle Solera (refused by Nicolai). Première at la Scala, Milan, March 9, 1842, with Giuseppina Strepponi (who, years later, became Verdi's wife). Bellinzaghi, Miraglia, Ronconi, Derivis. First performed in London, Her Majesty's Theatre, 1846, as *Nino* (in Italian); Covent Garden, 1850, as *Anato*, with Castellan, Costi, Tamberlik, Ronconi, Tagliafico, conductor Costa; New York, 1848. Revived Florence Festival and la Scala, 1933, with Cigna, Stignani, Dolci (in Milan, Voyer), Galeffi, Pasero, conducted by Gui and produced by Ebert; Verona Arena, 1938, with Jacobo, Stignani, Voyer, Tagliabue, Pasero, conductor Capuana; la Scalà, 1946, for the reopening of the rebuilt theatre, with Pedrini, Barbieri, Binci, Bechi, Siepi, conductor Serafin; Rome, 1951, with Caniglia, Pirazzini, Franceso Albanese, Bechi, Rossi-Lemeni, conductor Gui; South Wales (Clydach and District), 1952, with di Leo, Tom Williams; Glasgow, 1952.

### CHARACTERS

Abigaille, *a slave, believed to be the elder daughter of Nabucco* .................................... Soprano

Fenena, *daughter of Nabucco* ................... Soprano

Ismaele, *nephew of the King of Jerusalem* .......... Tenor

Nabucco, *King of Babylon* .................... Baritone

Zaccaria, *high priest of Jerusalem* ................. Bass

High Priest of Babylon .......................... Bass

Abdallo, *an old officer in Nabucco's Service* ........ Tenor

Anna, *sister of Zaccaria* ...................... Soprano

*Nabucco* was Verdi's first great success, the opera that established him as one of the leading composers of Italy, the theme which identified him for the first time publicly with his country's political aspirations. Its success was huge, mainly because of its musical quality but also to some extent because of the vivid way in which the composer gave expression to his countrymen's aspirations towards the liberty and self-government which had never yet been theirs. No Italian who heard 'Va, pensiero' could fail to identify himself with the chorus of exiles who were singing it, and it soon became one of the most popular tunes of the day. Franz Werfel, in his collection of Verdi's letters, has described the scene of Verdi's second funeral in Milan a few months after his death (the first, as directed in his will, was very simple): '. . . then came one of the great and rare moments when people and music become one. Without any preconcerted plan, by some inexplicable inspiration, there suddenly rose out of the monstrous soul of the multitude the chorus from *Nabucco* with which Giuseppe Verdi had become the voice of consolation and hope for his people, sixty years before. "Va, pensiero sull' ali dorate!" The song of the enslaved by the waters of Babylon, after the words of the Psalm . . .'

The rather conventional overture makes use of various tunes from the opera, notably the big choral themes.

Act I.    In passionate choruses, the priests and people of Jerusalem lament their defeat at the hands of Nabucodonosor, King of Babylon (hereinafter, as in the opera, called 'Nabucco'), and beg Jehovah to prevent the capture of the Temple. In an impressive solo, 'Sperate, o figli', Zaccaria exhorts them to have faith in God, but the news that Nabucco is advancing on the Temple itself throws them once more into consternation.

Ismaele, who brought the news of the enemy's further advance, is left alone with Fenena, a hostage in the hands of the Jews, whom he has loved ever since she rescued him when, as Jewish envoy in Babylon, he had been thrown into prison. Their colloquy is interrupted by the appearance of Abigaille, Fenena's supposed sister, at the head of a band of Babylonian soldiers. She threatens the two lovers with instant death, but admits to Ismaele that she loves him and says she has it in her power to save him if he were disposed to return her love. The trio which follows has that mixture of intensity and suave vocal writing which distinguishes similar moments in *Norma* (though the dramatic situation is by no means similar). Zaccaria rushes in saying he has seen the King riding towards the Temple itself; in a moment Babylonian troops fill the Temple, and Nabucco himself rides to the door. Zaccaria threatens to kill Fenena, Nabucco's daughter, if he desecrates the holy place, but Nabucco taunts the defeated Jews ('Tremin

gl'insani'), and Zaccaria's attempt on Fenena's life is frustrated
by Ismaele. Nebucco's anger now flows unrestrained, and he
orders the sacking of the Temple.

Act II.   The Jews have been carried captive into Babylon,
and Nabucco, away at the wars, has left Fenena as Regent in his
stead. Abigaille, jealous of her sister's position and burning to
know whether or not she is Nabucco's daughter or, as rumour
has it, only a slave, finds a document which proves that the latter
estimation of her birth is the true one. Her fury is unbridled, but
she remembers her love for Ismaele, and the first part of her
great aria is smooth and expressive. The High Priest of Bel informs her that Fenena is setting free the Jewish prisoners; he
urges her to seize power, and says he has already spread the
report that Nabucco has been killed in battle. Abigaille's cabaletta
is suitably vigorous and determined.

The Hebrews are gathered together in a room of the palace,
and, in a noble example of Verdian prayer ('Tu sul labbro'),
Zaccaria invokes the guidance of God. The people curse Ismaele,
but Zaccaria reminds them that Fenena, for whose sake he committed the act of treachery, has become a convert to their faith.

Abdallo rushes in to tell them that the popular cry goes up
the King is dead, and that Abigaille plans Fenena's death. In a
moment Abigaille, surrounded by court officials, comes to
demand the crown from Fenena. It is, however, Nabucco who
steps between them, seizes it, and places it on his own head,
defying Abigaille to take it from him. Nabucco, predicting that
the incident will have dire consequences, leads off the ensemble,
which is extraordinarily effective and notable for its excellent
contrasting of soloists and chorus. Nabucco proclaims himself
God, and commands the protesting Zaccaria and Fenena to bow
down before him. There is a clap of thunder, and the crown is
torn from his head by a supernatural force. When the crowd has
recovered from its consternation, the King is seen to be mad,
babbling of persecution and complaining that not even his
daughter will help him. Zaccaria proclaims the punishment of
heaven on the blasphemer, but Abigaille takes the crown from
where it has fallen, crying that the glory of Babylon is not yet
departed.

Act III.   Abigaille has been installed as Regent, with the
support of the priests, who demand the death of the captive Jews,

amongst them Fenena. Nabucco is led into Abigaille's presence by his faithful Abdallo, and the rest of the first scene consists of an extended duet between the King and his supposed daughter. At first, he is enraged at finding someone else on his throne, but Abigaille taunts him into sealing the death sentence of the Jews, and, when she tells him he is a prisoner in her hands, his mood changes to one of supplication and desperation. Throughout his career, Verdi was to entrust crucial scenes of his operas to these lengthy, highly developed duets. Already in *Oberto*, there is a long scene of reconciliation between Oberto (bass) and his estranged daughter (soprano), and these two examples from his first and third operas are the forerunners, in manner if not in shape, of that great line which was to include the scene for Macbeth and his wife after the murder, the second act duet for Rigoletto and Gilda, the meeting between Violetta and Germont, the two great duets for Simon Boccanegra and Fiesco, the love duet from *Ballo*, Leonora's scene with Padre Guardiano in *Forza*, Philip's interviews with Posa and the Grand Inquisitor in *Don Carlos*, the two examples in the third act of *Aida*, the love duet in *Otello* and the second act scene between Otello and Iago, and Falstaff's conversation with Ford. The two earliest examples may not have the quality of their descendants, but they are by no means unworthy of the remarkable series they inaugurate.

The second scene of the act takes place on the banks of the Euphrates, where the enslaved Jews sing the psalms of their lost fatherland. 'Va, pensiero' is the first of Verdi's patriotic choruses, and its poignant melody is typical of the composer's writing in this vein. Zaccaria upbraids the Jews for their defeatist attitude and tries to galvanise them into life and resistance by prophesying the imminent fall of Babylon.

Act IV.    Nabucco in prison wakens from a nightmare (suggested in the prelude) to hear the crowd down below crying 'Death to Fenena'. He sees her being led to execution, and prays movingly to Jehovah to pardon him his sin of pride and spare her life: 'Dio di Giuda'. Abdallo appears at the head of the guard and frees his master, who rushes out to rescue his daughter.

The scene changes to the place of execution. A funeral march is heard and Fenena has a beautiful prayer as she and the Jews prepare for death. The arrival of Nabucco and his followers arrests the sacrifice, the false idol is thrown down as if by magic, and all join in a prayer of thanksgiving to Jehovah. The general rejoicing is interrupted by the arrival of Abigaille, who in her remorse has taken poison and presently dies, calling on God, as she does so, for forgiveness. Zaccaria promises glory to his convert, Nabucco.

There is no doubt that *Nabucco* represents a tremendous advance on Verdi's two earlier operas, *Oberto*, a story of the struggle for power in Northern Italy in the thirteenth century, and *Un Giorno di Regno* (King for a day), his ill-fated comedy, but it is difficult to agree with those commentators who find in it the most satisfactory of the operas written before *Rigoletto*. The frequent and highly successful revivals which it has enjoyed in recent years prove that it is still a living force, but few people who have heard *Macbeth* would be inclined to estimate it above that near-masterpiece, and there would be many (the present writer amongst them) to prefer *Ernani* to the earlier work. *Nabucco*, however, represents something important in Verdi's output: it was his first success. In it he can be seen making a serious attempt at the musical portrayal of character, and, in spite of obvious dependence on the operatic formulas of his day and age, there is usually more interest attached to the immature efforts of genius than to the finished products of mere talent.          H.

## ERNANI

Opera in four acts by Giuseppe Verdi; text by Francesco Maria Piave, after the drama by Victor Hugo. Première at the Fenice Theatre, Venice, March 9, 1844, with Löwe, Guasco, Superchi, Selva. First performed Her Majesty's Theatre, London, 1845; New York, 1847; Metropolitan, 1903, with Sembrich, de Marchi, Scotti, Edouard de Reszke, conductor Mancinelli; 1921, with Ponselle, Martinelli, Danise, Mardones, conductor Papi; 1928, with Ponselle, Martinelli, Ruffo, Pinza, conductor Bellezza; 1956 with Milanov, del Monaco, Warren, Siepi; revived la Scala, 1935, with Cigna, Merli, Armando Borgioli, Pasero, conductor Marinuzzi; Berlin, 1935, with Lemnitz, Wittrisch, Janssen, Bohnen, conductor Blech; la Scala 1941, with Castellani, Merli, Bechi, Pasero, conductor Marinuzzi; Rome, 1951, with Mancini, Penno, Silveri, Christoff, conductor Santini.

### CHARACTERS

Don Carlos, *King of Castile* ....................Baritone
Don Ruy Gomez di Silva, *Grandee of Spain* ..........Bass
Ernani, or John of Aragon, *a bandit chief*...........Tenor
Don Riccardo, *esquire to the King* .................Tenor

Jago, *esquire to Silva* .............................Bass
Elvira, *kinswoman to Silva* ....................Soprano
Giovanna, *in Elvira's service* ...................Soprano
Mountaineers and Bandits, Followers of Silva, Ladies of
Elvira, Followers of Don Carlos, Electors and Pages

*Time:* Early Sixteenth Century                    *Place:* Spain

His father, the Duke of Segovia, having been slain by order of
Don Carlos's father, John of Aragon has become a bandit. Proscribed and pursued by the emissaries of the King, he has taken
refuge in the fastnesses of the mountains of Aragon, where, under
the name of Ernani, he is leader of a large band of rebel mountaineers. Ernani is in love with Donna Elvira, who, although she
is about to be united to her relative, the aged Ruy Gomez di
Silva, a grandee of Spain, is deeply enamoured of the handsome,
chivalrous bandit chief.

Don Carlos, afterwards the Emperor Charles V, also has fallen
violently in love with Elvira. By watching her windows he has
discovered that at dead of night a young cavalier (Ernani) gains
admission to her apartments. He imitates her lover's signal, gains
admission to her chamber, and declares his passion. Being
repulsed, he is about to drag her off by force, when a secret panel
opens, and he finds himself confronted by Ernani. In the midst
of a violent scene Silva enters. To allay his jealousy and anger at
finding two men, apparently rival suitors, in the apartment of
his affianced, the King, whom Silva does not recognise, reveals
himself, and pretends to have come in disguise to consult him
about his approaching election to the empire, and a conspiracy
that is on foot against his life. Then the King, pointing to Ernani,
says to Silva, 'It doth please us that this, our follower, depart,'
thus insuring Ernani's temporary safety—for a Spaniard does
not hand an enemy over to the vengeance of another.

Believing a rumour that Ernani has been run down and killed
by the King's soldiers, Elvira at last consents to give her hand in
marrlage to Silva. On the eve of the wedding, however, Ernani,
pursued by the King with a detachment of troops, seeks refuge
in Silva's castle, in the disguise of a pilgrim. Although not known
to Silva, he is, under Spanish tradition, his guest, and from that
moment entitled to his protection.

Elvira enters in her bridal attire. Ernani is thus made aware that her nuptials with Don Silva are to be celebrated on the morrow. Tearing off his disguise, he reveals himself to Silva, and demands to be delivered up to the King, preferring death to life without Elvira. But true to his honour as a Spanish host, Silva refuses. Even his enemy, Ernani, is safe in his castle. Indeed he goes so far as to order his guards to man the towers and prepare to defend the castle, should the King seek forcible entry. He leaves the apartment to make sure his orders are being carried out. The lovers find themselves alone. When Silva returns they are in each other's arms. But as the King is at the castle gates, he has no time to give vent to his wrath. He gives orders to admit the King and his men, bids Elvira retire, and hides Ernani in a secret cabinet. The King demands that Silva give up the bandit. The grandee proudly refuses. Ernani is his guest. The King's wrath then turns against Silva. He demands the surrender of his sword and threatens him with death, when Elvira interposes. The King pardons Silva, but bears away Elvira as hostage for the loyalty of her kinsman.

The King has gone. From the wall Silva takes down two swords, releases his guest from his hiding-place, and bids him cross swords with him to the death. Ernani refuses. His host has just protected his life at the danger of his own. But, if Silva insists upon vengeance, let grandee and bandit first unite against the King, with whom the honour of Elvira is unsafe. Elvira rescued, Ernani will give himself up to Silva, to whom, handing him his hunting-horn, he avows himself ready to die, whenever a blast upon it shall be sounded from the lips of the implacable grandee. Silva, who has been in entire ignorance of the King's passion for Elvira, grants the reprieve, and summons his men to horse.

He sets on foot a conspiracy against the King. A meeting of the conspirators is held in the Cathedral of Aix-la-Chapelle, in the vault, within which stands the tomb of Charlemagne. Here it is resolved to murder the King. A ballot decides who shall do the deed. Ernani's name is drawn.

The King, however, has received information of the time and place of this meeting. From the tomb he has been an unobserved witness of the meeting and purpose of the conspirators. Booming of cannon outside tells him of his choice as head of the Holy Roman Empire. Emerging from the tomb, he shows himself to the awed conspirators, who imagine they see Charlemagne issuing forth to combat them. At the same moment the doors open. The electors of the Empire enter to pay homage to Charles V.

'The common herd to the dungeon, the nobles to the headsman,' he commands.

Ernani advances, discovers himself as John of Aragon, and claims the right to die with the nobles—'to fall, covered, before the King'. But upon Elvira's fervent plea, the King, now also Emperor, commences his reign with an act of grace. He pardons the conspirators, restores to Ernani his titles and estates, and unites him with Elvira.

Silva, thwarted in his desire to marry Elvira, waits until Ernani and Elvira, after their nuptials, are upon the terrace of Ernani's castle in Aragon. At their most blissful moment he sounds the fatal horn. Ernani, too chivalrous to evade his promise, stabs himself in the presence of the grim avenger and of Elvira who falls prostrate upon his lifeless body.

In the opera, this plot develops as follows: Act I opens in the camp of the bandits in the mountains of Aragon. In the distance is seen the Moorish castle of Silva. The time is near sunset. Of Ernani's followers, some are eating and drinking, or are at play, while others are arranging their weapons. They sing, 'Allegri, beviamo' (Haste! Clink we our glasses).

Ernani sings Elvira's praises in the air 'Come rugiada al cespite' (Balmier than dew to drooping bud).

Co - me ru - gia - da al ce - spi - te

This expressive number is followed by one in faster time, 'O tu, che l'alma adora' (O thou toward whom, adoring soul).

O tu, che l'al-maa-do-ra Vien, vien, la mia vi-ta in - fio - - ra,

Enthusiastically volunteering to share any danger Ernani may incur in seeking to carry off Elvira, the bandits, with their chief at their head, go off in the direction of Silva's castle.

The scene changes to Elvira's apartment in the castle. It is night. She is meditating upon Ernani. When she thinks of Silva, 'the frozen, withered spectre', and contrasts with him Ernani, who 'in her heart ever reigneth', she voices her thoughts in that famous air for sopranos, one of Verdi's loveliest inspirations, 'Ernani! involami' (Ernani! fly with me).

It ends with a brilliant cadenza, 'Un Eden quegli antri a me' (An Eden that opens to me).

Young maidens bearing wedding gifts enter. They sing a chorus of congratulation. To this Elvira responds with a graceful cabaletta, the sentiment of which, however, is expressed as an aside, since it refers to her longing for her young, handsome, and chivalrous lover. 'Tutto sprezzo che d'Ernani' (Words that breathe thy name Ernani).

The young women go. Enter Don Carlos, the King. There is a colloquy, in which Elvira protests against his presence; and then a duet, which the King begins, 'Da quel di che t'ho veduta' (From the day, when first thy beauty).

A secret panel opens. The King is confronted by Ernani, and by Elvira, who has snatched a dagger from his belt. She interposes between the two men. Silva enters. What he beholds draws from him the melancholy reflections—'Infelice! e tu credevi' (Unhappy me! and I believed thee), an exceptionally fine bass

solo. He follows it with the vindictive 'Infin, che un brando vindice' (In fine a swift, unerring blade).

Men and women of the castle and the King's suite have come on. The monarch makes himself known to Silva, who does him obeisance, and, at the King's command, is obliged to let Ernani depart. An ensemble brings the act to a close.

Act II.    Grand hall in Silva's castle. Doors lead to various apartments. Portraits of the Silva family, surmounted by ducal coronets and coats-of-arms, are hung on the walls. Near each portrait is a complete suit of equestrian armour, corresponding in period to that in which lived the ancestor represented in the portrait.

The persistent chorus of ladies, though doubtless aware that Elvira is not thrilled at the prospect of marriage with her 'frosty' kinsman, and has consented to marry him only because she believes Ernani dead, enters and sings 'Esultiamo!' (Exultation!), then pays tribute to the many virtues and graces of the bride.

To Silva, in the full costume of a Grandee of Spain, and seated in the ducal chair, is brought in Ernani, disguised as a monk. He is welcomed as a guest; but, upon the appearance of Elvira in bridal array, throws off his disguise and offers his life, a sacrifice to Silva's vengeance, as the first gift for the wedding. Silva, however, learning that he is pursued by the King, offers him the protection due to a guest under the roof of a Spaniard.

'Ah, morir potessi adesso' (Ah, to die would be a blessing) is the impassioned duet sung by Elvira and Ernani, when Silva leaves them together.

Ah, mo-rir  po-tes-sia-des-so O mio Er-na-ni sul tuo net-to

Silva, even when he returns and discovers Elvira in Ernani's arms, will not break the law of Spanish hospitality, preferring to wreak vengeance in his own way. He therefore hides Ernani so securely that the King's followers, after searching the castle, are obliged to report their complete failure to discover a trace of him. Chorus: 'Fu esplorato del castello' (We have now explored the castle).

Then come the important episodes described—the King's demand for the surrender of Silva's sword and threat to execute him; Elvira's interposition; and the King's sinister action in carrying her off as a hostage, after he has sung the significant

Vie - ni me-co, sol di  ro - se

air, 'Vieni meco, sol di rose' (Come with me, a brighter dawning waits for thee).

Ernani's handing of his hunting horn to Silva, and his arousal of the grandee to an understanding of the danger that threatens Elvira from the King, is followed by the finale, a spirited call to arms by Silva, Ernani, and chorus, 'In arcione, in arcione, cavalieri!' (To horse, to horse, cavaliers!).

Act III.    The scene is a sepulchral vault, enclosing the tomb of Charlemagne in the Cathedral of Aix-la-Chapelle. The tomb is entered by a heavy door of bronze, upon which is carved in large characters the word 'Charlemagne'. Steps lead to the great door of the vault.

It is to this sombre but grandiose place that the King has come in order to overhear, from within the tomb of his greatest ancestor, the plotting of the conspirators. His soliloquy, 'Oh, de' verd' anni miei' (Oh, for my youthful years once more), derives impressiveness both from the solemnity of the situation and the music's flowing measure.

Oh de' verd'an - ni mie - - i

The principal episode in the meeting of the conspirators is their chorus, 'Si ridesti il Leon di Castiglia' (Let the lion awake in Castilia). Dramatically effective, too, in the midst of the plotting, is the sudden booming of distant cannon. It startles the conspirators. Cannon boom again. The bronze door of the tomb swings open, and the King presents himself at the entrance of the tomb. Three times he strikes the door of bronze with the hilt of his dagger. The principal entrance to the vault opens. To the sound of trumpets electors enter, dressed in cloth of gold. They are followed by pages carrying, upon velvet cushions, the sceptre, crown, and other imperial insignia. Courtiers surround the Emperor. Elvira approaches. The banners of the Empire are displayed. Many torches borne by soldiers illuminate the scene. The act closes with the pardon granted by the King, and the stirring finale, 'Oh, sommo Carlo!' (Charlemagne!).

Act IV, on the terrace of Ernani's castle, is brief, and there is nothing to add to what has been said of its action. Ernani asks

Silva to spare him till his lips have tasted the chalice filled by love. He recounts his sad life: 'Solingo, errante misero' (To linger in exiled misery).

Silva's grim reply is to offer him his choice between a cup of poison and a dagger. He takes the latter. 'Ferma, crudele, estinguere' (Stay thee, my lord, for me at least) cries Elvira, wishing to share his fate. In the end there is left only the implacable avenger, to gloat over Ernani, dead, and Elvira prostrate upon his form.

*Ernani*, brought out in 1844, is, with *Nabucco*, the earliest work by Verdi that maintains a foothold in the modern repertory, though by no means a firm one. Hanslick, the Viennese critic, pointed out that whereas in Victor Hugo's drama the mournful blast upon the hunting horn, when heard in the last act, thrills the listener with tragic forebodings, in the opera, after listening to solos, choruses, and a full orchestra all the evening, the audience is but little impressed by the sounding of a note upon a single instrument. That comment, however, presupposes considerable subtlety, so far undiscovered, on the part of operatic audiences.

Early in its career the opera experienced various vicissitudes. The conspiracy scene had to be toned down for political reasons before the production of the work was permitted. Even then the chorus, 'Let the lion awake in Castilia', caused a political demonstration. In Paris, Victor Hugo, as author of the drama on which the libretto is based, raised objections to its representation, and it was produced in the French capital as *Il Proscritto* (The Proscribed) with the characters changed to Italians. Victor Hugo's *Hernani* was a famous play in Sarah Bernhardt's repertory during her early engagements in America, and her Doña Sol (Elvira in the opera) was one of her finest achievements.

*Ernani* is in many respects a fine opera. Since 1844, the whirligig of time has made one, two, three, perhaps even four revolutions, and now, over a hundred years since the first performance and after a period when it was looked upon as crude and empty, the opera is once again, in adequate performances and with singers who can do justice to the music, accepted by audiences as a thrilling and rewarding experience. Its whipcrack melodies have the energy of youth, and, for all its frequent lack of subtlety, the genius of the composer is very much in evidence.        K.

# MACBETH

Opera in four acts by Giuseppe Verdi; text by Francesco Maria Piave. Première in Florence, March 14, 1847, with Barbieri-Nini, Varesi. First performed in New York, 1850; Dublin, 1859, with Pauline Viardot-Garcia as Lady Macbeth and Arditi conducting. Revised for Paris and first performed there in the new version, April 21, 1865. Revived Dresden, 1928; Berlin, 1931, with Bindernagel and Onegin (Lady Macbeth), Reinmar, Andresen; Rome, 1932, with Scacciati, Franci, conductor Guarnieri; Vienna, 1933, with Rose Pauly; Glyndebourne, 1938 (for the first time in England, though productions had been scheduled for seasons of 1861 and 1870 but abandoned), with Vera Schwarz (in 1939, Grandi), Valentino, Franklin, David Lloyd, conductor Busch, producer Ebert; la Scala, Milan, 1938, with Cigna and Jacobo, Sved, Pasero, Parmeggiani, conductor Marinuzzi; Buenos Aires, 1939, with Spani, Sved, Vaghi, conductor Panizza; Edinburgh Festival, 1947, with Grandi, Valentino, Tajo, Midgley, conductor Goldschmidt (Glyndebourne production); Zürich, 1949, with Malaniuk and Dow; Berlin, 1950, with Mödl, Metternich, Herrmann, conductor Keilberth; Florence Festival, 1951, with Varnay, Petroff, Tajo, Penno, conductor Gui; la Scala, 1952, with Callas Mascherini, conductor de Sabata.

## CHARACTERS

Lady Macbeth .............................. Soprano
Macbeth, *a general* ........................... Baritone
Banquo, *a general* ............................. Bass
Macduff, *a Scottish nobleman* .................... Tenor
Duncan, *King of Scotland* ........................ Mute
Lady-in-Waiting to Lady Macbeth .............. Soprano
Malcolm, *son of Duncan* ........................ Tenor
Fleance, *son of Banquo* .......................... Mute
Doctor ........................................ Bass

After the première in Paris of the revised version of *Macbeth* (1865), Verdi was accused amongst other things of not knowing Shakespeare. The accusation moved him to fury, and he, the most modest of composers, wrote: 'I may not have rendered *Macbeth* well, but that I do not know, do not understand and feel Shakespeare, no, by heavens, no! He is one of my very special poets, and I have had him in my hands from my earliest youth, and I read and re-read him continually.'

*Macbeth* remained a favourite of Verdi's amongst his own works. He spent a considerable time revising it, and its comparative lack of success in his lifetime was a continual source of irritation to him. Piave the librettist was provided with a detailed scenario by the composer before he was allowed to put pen to paper, so that the dramatic construction is Verdi's. Faced with the difficulty of putting a fairly long play on to the operatic stage, Verdi concentrated on three principals: Lady Macbeth, Macbeth, and the Witches—he was emphatic on this last point. Lady Macbeth is explicitly (as in Shakespeare implicitly) the dominating figure, although her husband remains at the centre of the tragedy; Macduff is reduced to little more than a member of the ensemble (even his solitary aria forms part of the moment of stillness before the turning point in the action); and Banquo, a considerable figure until his murder, disappears well before the half-way mark. Malcolm is almost entirely eliminated, and the Doctor and the Gentlewoman are retained mainly for the sleep-walking scene, although the Gentlewoman is used as well in the finale of Act I, and to bring Macbeth the news of his wife's death.

Act I, which takes the action up to the end of Shakespeare's Act II, scene iii, begins with Macbeth's first encounter with the Witches, then moves to Lady Macbeth's reading of the letter, the message from her husband, and

> '. . . come you spirits
> That tend on mortal thoughts, unsex me here'.

There follow the arrival of Macbeth and Duncan, the murder, Macbeth's horror, and finally the discovery of the crime and general consternation.

Act II begins with the decision that Banquo now threatens Macbeth's position, and proceeds to his murder, finishing with the Banquet scene and the appearance of the ghost.

In Act III, Macbeth again goes to the Witches for reassurance, is found by his wife in a state of collapse after the various apparitions, and, with her, vows Macduff's death.

The last act opens with a group of Scottish refugees, among them Macduff, singing of Macbeth's reign of terror in Scotland; their gloom is dispelled by the arrival of Malcolm with the relieving army. The scene changes to Dunsinane for the sleep-walking episode, Macbeth's reception of the news that Birnam Wood is on the march, and the final triumph of Malcolm and death of Macbeth. Only essentials are preserved, but they form the core of Shakespeare's drama, and might have been the framework from which he produced the play, as they were to be the framework of Verdi's opera.

The prelude concentrates on material later used in the sleep-walking scene. The first scene takes place on the heath, where the Witches sing a fantastic chorus while waiting for Macbeth, and then prophesy his future in awesome tones. A messenger arrives to announce that Macbeth has been granted the title and estates of the rebel Cawdor, and Macbeth and Banquo meditate in a duet on the implications of the prophecy, half of which has already come true. The scene concludes with a chorus and dance for the Witches.

Lady Macbeth reads the letter from her husband in which he tells her of the meeting with the weird band, and launches into a determined recitative. 'Vieni, t'affretta' has been described by some as an inadequate setting of the great soliloquy of Act I, but it is strikingly effective in its context, and anyone who heard Margherita Grandi sing it at Glyndebourne or Edinburgh knows that it can, with its *cabaletta*, 'Or tutti, sorgete, ministri in-fernali', produce an effect of tigerish ferocity, and it is not un-reasonable to assume that this is what Verdi had in mind and could obtain in his own day.

Macbeth arrives and in a few pregnant sentences and with hardly a direct word spoken, the murder is decided upon, as the march which announces the King's arrival is heard offstage. The march itself is commonplace enough, but by no means unsuitable to accompany the pantomime which goes with the King's pro-cession—no word is spoken throughout his passage across the stage.

Macbeth, alone, sees a dagger in front of him, and with his soliloquy, in itself highly expressive, begins the great duet between the two principal characters. The murder done, Macbeth staggers down the stairs with the dagger still in his hands: 'Fatal mia donna! un murmure, com' io, non intendesti?' He describes the

scene and the murmuring of the grooms in the ante-chamber, and the way 'Amen' stuck in his throat, and in the end it is Lady Macbeth who has to take the dagger back into the King's chamber.

Characteristically, this duet is marked to be sung 'sotto voce, e cupa', that is to say in a half voice and with dark, stifled tone. Only a few phrases, such as Macbeth's outburst of agonised horror when he catches sight of his blood-stained hands, 'Oh, vista orribile', are to be sung out, and they are specifically marked 'a voce aperta'. The original Lady Macbeth records that there were 151 rehearsals of this duet before the composer was satisfied, and that the sleep-walking scene—Verdi always maintained that these were the opera's two crucial moments—cost her three months of ceaseless worry before her movements and singing were judged to be satisfactory.

Banquo and Macduff arrive to accompany the King on his way, and Banquo broods impressively in C minor on the horrid portents of the night, while his companion goes to rouse the King. The murder is discovered, and all gather together for the magnificently sonorous and excitingly written finale, one of the most splendid (and, for the principal female singer, one of the most exacting) in any of Verdi's earlier operas.

Act II. Macbeth is discovered on stage (the orchestral prelude is a reminiscence of 'Fatal mia donna'), where he is quickly joined by Lady Macbeth, who accuses him of avoiding her. They decide that the death of Banquo is necessary to their schemes, and Lady Macbeth is left alone to sing an expressive aria, 'La luce langue', whose ferocious determination (it dates from 1865) puts it into quite another class from the much tamer piece it replaces, and whose layout reminds us that 'O don fatale' (Don Carlos) was written less than two years after the revision of Macbeth.

The scene changes to a park, where a band of assassins is waiting for Banquo. Their chorus is a particularly fortunate example of the conventional music given to bands of murderers in Italian opera of the period (or indeed to any felonious nocturnal gathering for that matter; cf. the chorus at the end of Act I of Rigoletto). Banquo's aria which follows is a beautiful example of Verdi's writing for bass voice; at its end, the murderers fall upon him, but his son escapes.

The opening music of the banquet scene has a feverish, spurious gaiety, which it may be going too far to ascribe solely to the composer's sense of dramatic character (as if it were the inn scene in Wozzeck) but which is uncannily apt in its context. The same quality is evident in the graceless, nerve-ridden *Brindisi*,

which Lady Macbeth sings to the assembled guests; the close relationship of its tune to the flowing 6/8 *Brindisi* in *Traviata* and the strong contrast of mood between the two has been pointed out by Desmond Shawe-Taylor, writing in the *New Statesman*. In between verses, Macbeth has a conference with a representative of the band charged to murder Banquo and learns that Fleance, his son, has escaped. Returning to his guests, he complains that Banquo's absence detracts from the pleasure of the occasion and says he himself will sit for a moment in his place. As he goes to the chair, he sees the ghost of the murdered man, and bursts into an agonised denial of his guilt, to the astonishment of the company, which naturally sees nothing. Lady Macbeth's remonstrances finally nerve him to face his guests again, which he does with an attempt at making light of the lapse. Lady Macbeth sings another verse of the *Brindisi*, but Macbeth's frenzy breaks out again as the ghost makes another appearance. His nerve has gone, and the assembly draws away from him, sensing the guilt he makes little attempt any longer to conceal. His sombre tune, 'Sangue a me', begins the finale, which is musically and dramatically no less effective than that to Act I.

Act III.    The Witches sit round their cauldron in a dark cave. Their chorus is in the same vein as that of the first act, and is succeeded by a ballet, written, of course, for Paris (1865) and interrupted in the middle by the appearance of Hecate to instruct her followers as to their conduct when they are visited, as they will shortly be, by Macbeth. The dance continues and at its end Macbeth appears and demands to know his future destiny. The music is extraordinarily suggestive and Verdi has perhaps nowhere else so successfully invoked the supernatural as in the scene of the apparitions, which is punctuated by the distraught comments of Macbeth himself. The King loses consciousness, and the Witches dance and sing round him before disappearing.

The mood changes, Lady Macbeth appears searching for her

husband, and asks what he has learnt from the Witches. He tells her and finishes by revealing that he has seen foretold the line of kings which Banquo will sire. The energy of Lady Macbeth's denial that this shall come to pass communicates itself to her husband and arouses something of his old military spirit, so that their short but vigorous duet makes a very striking end to the act.

Act IV.    We are at the turning-point in the drama, the zenith of the ambitious career of the Macbeths, and the nadir of the fortunes of the people of Scotland. As we might expect from the Verdi of 1847, the force opposed to Macbeth's tyranny is not only retribution but the less tragic and more immediately topical one of patriotism, which is implied throughout and personified in Macduff, Banquo, the Chorus, and, of course, in the minor figure of Malcolm. 'Patria oppressa', the chorus of the Scottish exiles in Act IV, is in direct line from 'Va, pensiero' in *Nabucco*, with its wailing minor second in the accompaniment, sometimes ascending, sometimes descending (it appears again in the sleep-walking scene) and its wonderfully evocative contours.

Macduff's beautiful aria completes the still moment at the centre of the dramatic action, and is succeeded by a quick movement as Malcolm's army crosses the stage; Malcolm and Macduff sing a duet with the chorus.

Nothing in the score of *Macbeth* is more worthy of admiration than the sleep-walking scene, which is cast in the form of the old soprano 'mad scene', but has a freedom of movement and an expressiveness that Verdi was not to excel in a similar set piece, one is tempted to say, until Aida's arias nearly twenty-five years later. Much of the preliminary orchestral music has been heard

macchia          è   qui   tut - to - - ra!

in the prelude, but the expressive quality of the vocal writing is quite extraordinary, and the scene itself very exacting for the singer, comprising as it does every shade of expression, and a very wide compass, from C flat at the bottom to top D flat in the last phrase of all (marked 'un fil di voce').

Macbeth is at bay, furious that Malcolm is marching on him with an army reinforced by English troops but confident in his knowledge that the Witches have prophesied for him immunity from death at the hands of anyone 'born of woman'. He curses the low, friendless state to which his way of life has brought him, but leads his men defiantly to war when he hears that his wife is dead. The battle is accompanied by a fugue, which persists through the short encounter of Macbeth and Macduff and eventually gives way to a general chorus of rejoicing at the defeat of the tyrant.

Apart from the ballet, which was written specially for Paris, four pieces were inserted in 1865 in place of material which now finds no place in the revised opera: in Act II, Lady Macbeth's aria, 'La luce langue'; in Act III the final duet; in Act IV the chorus of exiles (replacing one similar in feeling and with the same words), and the whole of the battle scene (i.e. after Macbeth's aria). Originally, the opera ended with a short *scena* for Macbeth and this has in fact always been used in Glyndebourne's production of the opera, Busch and Ebert inserting it after the fugue and before the entrance of Macduff and Malcolm. Even with the inclusion of this material, which the composer himself had discarded, there is no doubt that the last section of the opera, with its brilliantly descriptive fugue and firm, 'national' final chorus, is a vast improvement on the rather ordinary ending of the original version.

There are quite a number of changes in the rest of the opera, notably in the *presto* section of the big duet of Act I, Macbeth's reaction to the first appearance of the ghost in the banquet scene, the E major section of the first chorus of Act III, and the apparitions scene. These are usually designed to give more prominence to climaxes and moments of extreme intensity, and the composer has been so successful in his tidying up of his score that one must be grateful that he did not decide to re-write the whole opera, as some commentators, notably Francis Toye, have suggested would have been his best course.

All his life, Verdi strove towards an expression of character, and nowhere previously had he been so successful in its portrayal as in *Macbeth*. Macbeth himself is shown as dominated, even more than in the play, by the other two main characters, his wife and the Witches; that is to say, his own personality plays proportionately a lesser part in determining events, and he is shown often at his worst and most susceptible, hardly ever at his best as poet or soldier. All the same, the working of remorse on his conscience—Verdi, like Shakespeare, obviously thinks of him as a better man than his actions—is excellently shown, and the long duet after the murder subtly and admirably expresses his terror at his deed and its inevitable consequences, and constitutes, with the sleep-walking scene, the most complete musical expression of the element of tragedy and destiny in the composition of the two leading figures.

Macbeth's loss—if loss it can be called—is, of course, Lady Macbeth's gain, and she dominates music and action alike. Judged purely as a rôle for a singing actress, it is one of the finest Verdi ever wrote, but its significance goes further than that and it is perhaps the earliest Verdian rôle in which a complete musical development can be traced along with the dramatic and psychological growth in a character. The progress from the aria in the first act, 'Vieni, t'affretta', which is in form a conventional aria with *cabaletta* (although a most exciting and successful one), through the increasingly unnerving events of the intermediate scenes, to the final, long, wailing curve of the sleep-walking scene is a remarkable musical study of gradual disintegration under the influence of conscience.

*Macbeth* may be said to sum up, better perhaps than any other opera, this period of Verdi's career; for the first time he had achieved a really successful combination of the three characteristics which dominate his music: the theatre, patriotism, and character. In *Macbeth*, uneven though it may be, the artist, the man of the theatre, and the patriot combine to produce a near-masterpiece.

H.

# LUISA MILLER

Opera in three acts by Giuseppe Verdi; text by S. Cammarano from Schiller's play *Kabale und Liebe*. Première at the Teatro San Carlo, Naples, December 8, 1849, with Gavazzaniga, della Salandri, Malvezzi, Selva, de Bassini. First performed in New York, 1852; London, Her Majesty's Theatre, 1858, with Piccolomini, Giuglini, Vialetti, Beneventaro. Revived Berlin, 1927; Metropolitan, 1929, with Ponselle, Lauri-Volpi, de Luca, Pasero, Ludikar, conductor Serafin; Florence Festival, 1937, with Caniglia, Lauri-Volpi, Armando Borgioli, Pasero, conductor Gui; Rome, 1949, with Caniglia, Pirazzini, Lauri-Volpi, Silveri, Baronti, conductor Santini.

## CHARACTERS

Count Walter ................................... Bass
Rodolfo, *his son* .............................. Tenor
Miller, *an old soldier* ......................... Baritone
Luisa, *his daughter* ........................... Soprano
Federica, Duchess of Ostheim, *Walter's niece* .... Contralto
Laura, *a peasant girl* ......................... Contralto
Wurm ......................................... Bass
Ladies attending the Duchess, Pages, Servants, Archers, and Villagers

*Place:* The Tyrol.    *Time:* First half of the Eighteenth Century.

Act I.    A village in the Tyrol. Luisa is the daughter of Miller, an old soldier. There is ardent love between her and Rodolfo, the son of Count Walter, who has concealed his real name and rank from her and her father and is known to them as a peasant named Carlo. Old Miller, however, has a presentiment that evil will result from their attachment. This is confirmed in his mind on his being informed by Wurm that Carlo is Rodolfo, his master's son. Wurm is himself in love with Luisa.

The Duchess Federica, Count Walter's niece, arrives at the castle. She had been brought up there with Rodolfo, and has from childhood cherished a deep affection for him; but, compelled by her father to marry the Duke d'Ostheim, has not seen Rodolfo for some years. The Duke, however, having died, she is now a

widow, and, on the invitation of Count Walter, who has, unknown to Rodolfo, made proposals of marriage to her on his
son's behalf, she arrives at the castle, expecting to marry at once
the love of her childhood. The Count, having been informed by
Wurm of his son's love for Luisa, resolves to break off their
intimacy. Rodolfo reveals to the Duchess that he loves another.
He also discloses his real name and position to Luisa and her
father. The Count interrupts this interview between the lovers.
Enraged at his son's persistence in preferring a union with Luisa,
he calls in the guard and is about to consign her and her father
to prison, when he is, for the moment, deterred and appalled by
Rodolfo's threat to reveal that the Count, aided by Wurm,
assassinated his predecessor in order to obtain possession of the
title and estates.

Act II.    Luisa's father has been seized and imprisoned by the
Count's order. She, to save his life, consents, at the instigation of
Wurm, to write a letter in which she states that she had never
really loved Rodolfo, but only encouraged him on account of his
rank and fortune, of which she was always aware; and finally
offers to fly with Wurm. She even manages to convince the
Duchess that her love for Rodolfo was never more than pretence.
The letter, as the Count and his steward have arranged, falls into
the hands of Rodolfo, who, enraged by the supposed treachery
of the woman he loves, consents to marry the Duchess, but
ultimately resolves to kill Luisa and himself.

Act III.    Luisa also has determined to put an end to her
existence. Rodolfo enters her home in the absence of Miller, and,
after extracting from Luisa's own lips the avowal that she did
write the letter, he pours poison into a cup, from which they both
drink. She had sworn to Wurm that she would never reveal the
fact of the compulsion under which she had written the letter,
but feeling herself released from her oath by fast approaching
death, she confesses the truth to Rodolfo. The lovers die in the
presence of their horror-stricken parents, but not before Rodolfo
has summoned the strength to draw his sword and run Wurm
through the body with it.

The overture has been much praised, the finale to Act I is
excellent, and earlier in the act there are three effective arias for
Luisa, Miller, and Walter. The duet between Wurm and Walter
and Rodolfo's aria are the best passages in Act II; the latter,

'Quando le sere al placido', is one of the most beautiful arias

Verdi ever wrote, and its wistful loveliness is unsurpassed in his music. Francis Toye describes Act III as the best of the opera, because of its uncommon dramatic fitness. Luisa's 'Piangi, piangi' in the scene with Rodolfo, and the final trio are singled out for particular praise.                                                    K.

## RIGOLETTO

Opera in three acts by Giuseppe Verdi; text by Francesco Maria Piave after Victor Hugo's *Le Roi s'amuse*. Première at the Teatro la Fenice, Venice, March 11, 1851, with Brambilla, Casaloni, Mirate, Varesi, Pons, Damini. First performed Covent Garden, 1853, with Bosio, Mario, Ronconi; New York, 1857, with Bignardi, Frezzolini; Covent Garden (in English), 1909, with Beatrice Miranda, Wheatley, L. Turner; Sadler's Wells (Dent's translation), 1937, with Ruth Naylor, Edith Coates, Francis Russell, Redvers Llewellyn. Famous Gildas of this century include Melba, Tetrazzini, Galli-Curci, dal Monte, Norena, Pagliughi, Pons, Sayao; in the rôle of the Duke, Caruso, Bonci, Hislop, Piccaver, D. Borgioli, Gigli, Schipa, Björling; of Rigoletto, Scotti, Ruffo, de Luca, Sammarco, Formichi, Joseph Schwarz, Franci, Stabile, Basiola, Warren.

### CHARACTERS

| | |
|---|---|
| The Duke of Mantua | Tenor |
| Rigoletto, *his jester, a hunchback* | Baritone |
| Count Ceprano ⎱ *Nobles* | Bass |
| Count Monterone ⎰ | Baritone |
| Sparafucile, *a bravo* | Bass |
| Matteo Borsa, *a courtier* | Tenor |
| Cavaliere Marullo, *a courtier* | Baritone |
| Countess Ceprano | Mezzo-Soprano |
| Gilda, *daughter of Rigoletto* | Soprano |
| Giovanna, *her duenna* | Mezzo-Soprano |
| Maddalena, *sister to Sparafucile* | Contralto |

Courtiers, Nobles, Pages, Servants

*Time:* Sixteenth Century                      *Place:* Mantua

*Rigoletto* is a distinguished opera. Composed in forty days in 1851, it still retains its vitality. Twenty years, with all they imply in experience and artistic growth, lie between *Rigoletto* and *Aida*. Yet the earlier opera, composed so rapidly as to constitute a *tour de force* of musical creation, seems destined to remain a close second in popularity to the more mature work of its great composer.

There are several reasons for the public's abiding interest in *Rigoletto*. It is based upon a most effective play by Victor Hugo, *Le Roi s'amuse*, known to English play-goers in Tom Taylor's adaptation as *The Fool's Revenge* (the jester was one of Edwin Booth's great rôles). Rigoletto, the hunchback, has been vividly characterised by Verdi in his music, and it is a rôle which has appealed to many famous artists. Ronconi (who taught singing in New York for a few years, beginning in 1867) was a notable Rigoletto; so was Galassi, whose intensely dramatic performance was once vividly recalled by the older opera-goers; Renaud at the Manhattan Opera House, Titta Ruffo at the Metropolitan Opera House, Philadelphia, both made their American débuts as Rigoletto.

But the opera offers other rôles of distinction. Mario was a famous Duke in other days. Caruso made his sensational début at the Metropolitan in the character of the volatile Duke of Mantua, November 23, 1903. We have had as Gilda, Adelina Patti, Melba, and Tetrazzini, to mention but a few; and the heroine of the opera was one of the rôles of Galli-Curci, who appeared in it in Chicago, November 18, 1916. No coloratura soprano can, so to speak, afford to be without it.*

Thus the opera has plot, a central character of vital dramatic importance, and at least two other characters of strong interest. But there is even more to be said in its behalf. For, with the sextet in *Lucia*, the quartet in the last act of *Rigoletto* is the finest piece of concerted music in Italian opera.

The argument of *Rigoletto* deals with the amatory escapades of the Duke of Mantua, in which he is aided by Rigoletto, his jester, a hunchback. Rigoletto, both by his caustic wit and unscrupulous conduct, has made many enemies at court. Count

---

* Although Verdi never looked upon it as anything but a lyrical rôle, and Toscanini even cast it (in a concert performance) with a heavy dramatic soprano.

Monterone, who comes to the court to demand the restoration of his daughter, who has been dishonoured by the Duke, is met by the jester with laughter and derision. The Count curses Rigoletto, who is stricken with superstitious terror.

Rigoletto has a daughter, Gilda, whom he keeps in strict seclusion. But the Duke, without being aware who she is, has seen her, unknown to her father, and fallen in love with her. Count Ceprano, who many times has suffered under Rigoletto's biting tongue, knowing that she is in some way connected with the jester (in fact believing her to be his mistress, and glad of any opportunity of doing him an injury), forms a plan to carry off the young girl, and so arranges it that Rigoletto unwittingly assists in her abduction. When he finds that it is his own daughter whom he has aided to place in the power of the Duke, he determines to murder his master, and engages Sparafucile, a bravo, to do so. This man has a sister, Maddalena, who entices the Duke to a lonely inn. She becomes fascinated with him, however, and begs her brother to spare his life. This he consents to do if before midnight anyone shall arrive at the inn whom he can kill and pass off as the murdered Duke. Rigoletto, who has recovered his daughter, brings her to the inn so that, by being a witness of the Duke's inconstancy, she may be cured of her unhappy love. She overhears the plot to murder her lover, and Sparafucile's promise to his sister. Determined to save the Duke, she knocks for admittance, and is stabbed on entering. Rigoletto comes at the appointed time for the body. Sparafucile brings it out in a sack. The jester is about to throw it into the water, sack and all, when he hears the Duke singing. He tears open the sack, only to find his own daughter, at the point of death.

The prelude sets forth the music associated with the curse.

Act I opens in a salon in the Duke's palace. A suite of other

apartments is seen extending into the background. All are brilliantly lighted for the fête that is in progress. Courtiers and ladies are moving about in all directions. Pages are passing to and fro. From an adjoining salon music is heard and bursts of merriment.

There is effervescent gaiety in the orchestral accompaniment to the scene. The Duke and Borsa enter from the back. They are conversing about an 'unknown charmer'—none other than Gilda —whom the Duke has seen at church. He says that he will pursue the adventure to the end, although a mysterious man visits her nightly.

Among a group of guests the Duke sees the Countess Ceprano, whom he has been wooing quite openly, in spite of the Count's visible annoyance. The dashing gallant cares nothing about what anyone may think of his escapades, least of all the husbands or other relatives of the ladies. 'Questa o quella per me pari sono' (This one, or that one, to me 'tis the same).

The music floats on air. It gives at once the cue to the Duke's character. Like Don Giovanni he is indifferent to fate, flits from one affair to another, and is found as fascinating as he is dangerous by all women, of whatever degree, upon whom he confers his doubtful favours. The Duke dances with Countess Ceprano to the strains of a minuet that is curiously reminiscent of the one in *Don Giovanni*.

Rigoletto, hunchbacked but agile, sidles in. He is in cap and bells, and carries the jester's bauble. The immediate object of his satire is Count Ceprano, who is watching his wife, as she is being led off on the Duke's arm. Rigoletto then goes out looking for other victims. Marullo joins the nobles. He tells them that Rigoletto, despite his hump, has an *inamorata*. The statement makes a visible impression upon Count Ceprano, and when the nobles, after another sally from the jester, who has returned with the Duke, inveigh against his bitter tongue, the Count bids them meet him at night on the morrow and he will guarantee them revenge upon the hunchback for the gibes they have been obliged to endure from him.

The gay music, which forms a restless background to the scene of which I have given the gist, trips buoyantly along, to be sud-

denly broken in upon by the voice of one struggling without, and who, having freed himself from those evidently striving to hold him back, bursts in upon the scene. It is the aged Count Monterone. His daughter has been dishonoured by the Duke, and he denounces the ruler of Mantua before the whole assembly. His arrest is ordered. Rigoletto mocks him until, drawing himself up to his full height, the old noble not only denounces him, but calls down upon him a father's curse.

Rigoletto is strangely affrighted. He cowers before Monterone's malediction. It is the first time since he has appeared at the gathering that he is not gibing at some one. Not only is he subdued; he is terror-stricken.

Monterone is led off between halberdiers. The gay music again breaks in. The crowd follows the Duke. But Rigoletto?

The scene changes to the street outside his house. It is secluded in a courtyard, from which a door leads into the street. In the courtyard are a tall tree and a marble seat. There is also seen at the end of the street, which has no thoroughfare, the gable end of Count Ceprano's palace. It is night.

As Rigoletto enters, he remembers Monterone's curse. His entrance to the house is interrupted by the appearance of Sparafucile, an assassin for hire. In a colloquy, to which the orchestra

supplies a subtly contrived 'nocturne' accompaniment, he offers to Rigoletto his services, should they be needed, in putting enemies out of the way—and his charges are reasonable.

(The scoring is for muted solo cello and double bass, accompanied by *pizzicato* strings.)

Rigoletto has no immediate need of him, but ascertains where he can be found.

Sparafucile goes. Rigoletto has a soliloquy, 'Pari siamo'; 'How like are we!—the tongue, my weapon, the dagger his! to make others laugh is my vocation—his to make them weep! . . . Tears, the common solace of humanity, are to me denied. . . . ''Amuse me, buffoon''—and I must obey.' His mind still dwells on the curse—a father's curse, pronounced upon him, a father to whom his daughter is a jewel. He refers to it, even as he unlocks the door that leads to his house, and also to his daughter, who, as he enters, throws herself into his arms.

He cautions her about going out. She says she never ventures beyond the courtyard save to go to church. He grieves over the death of his wife—Gilda's mother—that left her to his care while she was still an infant. 'Deh non parlare al misero' (Speak not of one whose loss to me).

He charges her attendant, Giovanna, carefully to guard her. Gilda endeavours to dispel his fears. The result is the tender duet for Rigoletto and Gilda, beginning with his words to Giovanna, 'Veglia, o donna, questo fiore' (Ah, watch I pray this tender flower), a duet considerably improved when given in its entirety and not with the cut which has become almost invariable.

Rigoletto hears footsteps in the street and rushes out through the door of the courtyard to see who may be there. As the door swings out, the Duke, for it is he, in the guise of a student, whose stealthy footsteps have been heard by the jester, conceals himself behind it, then slips into the courtyard, tosses a purse to Giovanna, and hides in the shadow of the tree. Rigoletto reappears for a brief moment to say good-bye to Gilda and once more to warn Giovanna to guard her carefully.

When he has gone Gilda worries because fear drove her to

refrain from revealing to her father that a handsome youth has several times followed her from church. This youth's image is installed in her heart. 'I long to say to him "I lo'—"'

The Duke steps out of the tree's shadow, motions to Giovanna to retire and, throwing himself at Gilda's feet, takes the words out of her mouth, exclaiming, 'I love thee!'

No doubt taken by surprise, yet also thrilled with joy, she hearkens to him rapturously as he declares, 'E il sol dell' anima, la vita e amore' (Love is the sun by which passion is kindled).

*E il sol dell'a- ni-ma, la vi-ta è a- mo-re,*

The meeting is brief, for again there are footsteps outside. But their farewell is an impassioned duet, 'Addio speranza ed anima' (Farewell, my hope, my soul, farewell).

He has told her that he is a student, by name Walter Maldè. When he has gone, she muses upon the name, and, when she has lighted a candle and is ascending the steps to her room, she sings the enchanting air, 'Caro nome che il mio cor' (Dear name, my heart enshrines).

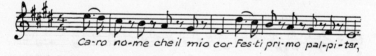

*Ca-ro no-me che il mio cor Fes-ti pri-mo pal-pi-tar,*

If the Gilda be reasonably slender and pretty, the scene, with the courtyard, the steps leading up to the room, and the young maiden gracefully and tenderly expressing her heart's first romance, is charming, and in itself sufficient to account for the attraction which the rôle holds for prima donnas.

Tiptoeing through the darkness outside come Marullo, Ceprano, Borsa, and other nobles and courtiers, intent upon seeking revenge for the gibes Rigoletto at various times has aimed at them, by carrying off the damsel, whom they assume to be his *inamorata*. At that moment, however, the jester himself appears. They tell him they have come to abduct the Countess Ceprano and bear her to the ducal palace. To substantiate this statement Marullo quickly has the keys to Ceprano's house passed to him by the Count, and in the darkness holds them out to Rigoletto, who, his suspicions allayed because he can feel the Ceprano crest in bas-relief on the keys, volunteers to aid in the escapade. Marullo gives him a mask and, as if to fasten it securely, ties it with a handkerchief, which he passes over the piercings for his eyes. Rigoletto, confused, holds a ladder against what he believes to be the wall of Ceprano's house. By it, the abductors climb his own wall, enter his house, gag, seize, and carry away Gilda, making their exit from the courtyard, but in their hurry failing to observe a scarf that has fluttered from their precious burden.

Rigoletto is left alone in the darkness and silence. He tears off his mask. The door to his courtyard is open. Before him lies Gilda's scarf. He rushes into the house, into her room; reappears, staggering under the weight of the disaster, which, through his own unwitting connivance, has befallen him.

'Ah! La maledizione!' he cries out. It is Monterone's curse.

Act II has its scene laid in a salon of the ducal palace.

The Duke is disconsolate. He has returned to Rigoletto's house, found it empty, the bird flown. The scamp mourns his loss—in affecting language and music, 'Parmi veder le lagrime' (Fair maid, each tear of mine that flows).

In a capital chorus he is told by Marullo and the others that they have abducted Rigoletto's *inamorata*.

Scor-ren-do u-ni - ti  re-mo-ta  vi - - a

The Duke well knows that she is the very one whose charms are the latest that have enraptured him. 'Possente amor mi chiama' (To her I love with rapture)—the aria is usually omitted in performance.

He learns from the courtiers that they have brought her to the palace. He hastens to her, 'to console her', in his own way. It is at this moment Rigoletto enters. He knows his daughter is in the palace, and has come to search for her. Aware that he is in the presence of those who took advantage of him and thus secured his aid in the abduction of the night before, he yet, in order to accomplish his purpose, must appear light-hearted, question craftily, and be diplomatic, although at times he cannot prevent his real feelings breaking through. It is the ability of Verdi to give expression to such varied emotions which makes this scene one of the most remarkable in his early operas. It is dominated by an orchestral motive, that of the clown who jests while his heart is breaking.

Finally he turns upon the crowd that taunts him and hurls invective upon them—'Cortigiani, vil razza dannata' (Ah, ye courtiers, vile race accursed). When a door opens and Gilda, whose story can be read in her aspect of despair, rushes into his arms, he orders the courtiers out of sight with a sense of outrage so justified that, in spite of the flippant words with which they comment upon his command, they obey it.

Father and daughter are alone. She tells him her story—of the handsome youth, who followed her from church—'Tutte le feste al tempio' (On every festal morning).

Then follows her account of their meeting, his pretence that he was a poor student, when, in reality, he was the Duke—to whose chamber she was borne after her abduction. It is from there she has just come. Her father strives to comfort her—'Piangi, fanciulla' (Weep, my child)—in one of Verdi's loveliest duets.

At this moment he is again reminded of the curse pronounced upon him by the father he had mocked. Count Monterone, between guards, is conducted through the apartment to the prison where he is to be executed for denouncing the Duke. Rigoletto vows vengeance upon the betrayer of Gilda. 'Si, vendetta, tremenda vendetta.'

It was a corrupt, care-free age. Victor Hugo created a debonair character—a libertine who took life lightly and flitted from pleasure to pleasure. And so Verdi lets him flit from tune to tune —gay, melodious, sentimental. There still are plenty of men like the Duke, and plenty of women like Gilda to love them; and other women, be it recalled, as discreet as the Duchess, who does not appear in this opera save as a portrait on the wall, from which she calmly looks down upon a jester invoking vengeance upon her husband, because of the wrong he has done the girl, who weeps on the breast of her hunchback father.

To Act III might be given as a sub-title, 'The Fool's Revenge', the title of Tom Taylor's adaptation into English of Victor Hugo's play. The scene shows a desolate spot on the banks of the Mincio. On the right, with its front to the audience, is a house two stories high, in a very dilapidated state, but still used as an inn. The doors and walls are so full of crevices that whatever is going on within can be seen from without. In front are the road and the river; in the distance is the city of Mantua. It is night.

The house is that of Sparafucile. With him lives his sister, Maddalena, a handsome young gipsy woman, who lures men to the inn, there to be robbed—or killed, if there is more money to be had for murder than for robbery. Sparafucile is seen within, cleaning his belt and sharpening his sword.

Outside are Rigoletto and Gilda. She cannot banish the image of her despoiler from her heart. Hither the hunchback has brought her to prove to her the faithlessness of the Duke. She sees him in the garb of a soldier coming along the city wall. He descends, enters the inn, and calls for wine and a room for the night. Shuffling a pack of cards, which he finds on the table, and pouring out the wine, he sings of woman. This is the famous 'La donna è mobile' (Fickle is woman fair).

La don-na è mo-bi-le  Qual piu-ma al ven-to

It has been highly praised and violently criticised; and usually gets as many encores as the singer cares to give. As for the criticisms, the cadenzas so ostentatiously introduced by singers for the sake of catching applause, are no more Verdi's than is the high C in *Il Trovatore*. The song is perfectly in keeping with the Duke's character. It has grace, verve, and buoyancy; and, what is an essential point in the development of the action from this point on, it is easily remembered. In any event I am glad that among my operatic experiences I can count having heard 'La donna è mobile' sung by such great artists as Campanini, Caruso, and Bonci, the last two upon their first appearances in the rôle in America.

At a signal from Sparafucile, Maddalena joins the Duke. He presses his love upon her. With professional coyness she pretends to repulse him. This leads to the quartet, with its dramatic interpretation of the different emotions of the four participants. The Duke is gallantly urgent and pleading: 'Bella figlia dell' amore' (Fairest daughter of the graces).

Maddalena laughingly resists his advances: 'I am proof, my gentle wooer, 'gainst your vain and empty nothings'.

Gilda is moved to despair: 'Ah, thus to me of love he spoke.'

Rigoletto mutters of vengeance.

They continue so to the end. Gilda's voice, in brief cries of grief, rising twice to effective climaxes, then becoming even more poignant through the syncopation of the rhythm.

This quartet is usually sung as the *pièce de résistance* of the opera, and is supposed to be the great event of the performance. I cannot recall a representation of the work with Nilsson and Campanini in which this was not the case, and it was so at the

Manhattan when *Rigoletto* was sung there by Melba and Bonci.
But at the Metropolitan, after Caruso's advent, *Rigoletto* became
a 'Caruso opera', and the stress was laid on 'La donna è mobile',
for which numerous encores were demanded, while with the
quartet the encore was deliberately side-stepped—a most
interesting process for the initiated to watch.

After the quartet, Sparafucile comes out and receives from
Rigoletto half of his fee to murder the Duke, the balance to be
paid when the body, in a sack, is delivered to the hunchback.
Sparafucile offers to throw the sack into the river, but that does
not suit the jester's desire for revenge. He wants the grim satisfaction of doing so himself. Satisfied that Gilda has seen enough
of the Duke's perfidy, he sends her home, where, for safety, she
is to don male attire and start on the way to Verona, where he
will join her. He himself also goes out.

A storm now gathers. There are flashes of lightning; distant
rumblings of thunder. The wind moans (indicated by the chorus,
*à bouche fermée*, behind the scenes). The Duke has gone to his
room, after whispering a few words to Maddalena. He lays down
his hat and sword, throws himself on the bed, sings a few snatches
of his song, and in a short time falls asleep. Maddalena, below,
stands by the table. Sparafucile finishes the contents of the bottle
left by the Duke. Both remain silent for a while.

Maddalena, fascinated by the Duke, begins to plead for his
life. The storm is now at its height. Lightning plays vividly across
the sky, thunder crashes, wind howls, rain falls in torrents.
Through this uproar of the elements, to which night adds its
terrors, comes Gilda, drawn as by a magnet to the spot where
she knows her false lover to be. Through the crevices in the wall
of the house she can hear Maddalena pleading with Sparafucile
to spare the Duke's life. 'Kill the hunchback', she counsels,
'when he comes with the balance of the money.' But there is
honour even among assassins as among thieves. The bravo will
not betray a customer.

Maddalena pleads yet more urgently. Well—Sparafucile will
give the handsome youth one desperate chance for life: should
any other man arrive at the inn before midnight, that man will
he kill and put in the sack to be thrown into the river, in place
of Maddalena's temporary favourite. A clock strikes the half-
hour. Gilda is in male attire. She determines to save the Duke's

life—to sacrifice hers for his. She knocks. There is a moment of surprised suspense within. Then everything is made ready. Maddalena opens the door, and runs forward to close the outer one. Gilda enters. For a moment one senses her form in the darkness. A half-stifled cry; then all is buried in silence and gloom.

The storm is abating. The rain has ceased; the lightning becomes fitful, the thunder distant and intermittent. Rigoletto returns. 'At last the hour of my vengeance is nigh.' A bell tolls midnight. He knocks at the door. Sparafucile brings out the sack, receives the balance of his money, and retires into the house. 'This sack his winding sheet!' exclaims the hunchback, as he gloats over it. The night has cleared. He must hurry and throw it into the river.

Out of the second storey of the house and on to the wall steps the figure of a man and proceeds toward the city. Rigoletto starts to drag the sack with the body towards the stream. Lightly upon the night fall the notes of a familiar voice singing:

> La donn' è mobile
> Qual piuma al vento;
> Muta d'accento,
> E di pensiero.
>
> (Fickle is woman fair,
> Like feather wafted;
> Changeable ever,
> Constant, ah, never.)

It is the Duke. Furiously the hunchback tears open the sack. In it he beholds his daughter. Not yet quite dead, she is able to whisper, 'Too much I loved him—now I die for him.' There is a duet: 'Lassu—in cielo' (From yonder sky).

'Maledizione!' The music of Monterone's curse upon the ribald jester, now bending over the corpse of his own despoiled daughter, resounds from the orchestra. The fool has had his revenge.

For political reasons the performance of Victor Hugo's *Le Roi s'amuse* was forbidden in France after the first representation. In Hugo's play the principal character is Triboulet, the jester of François I. The King, of course, also is a leading character; and there is a pen-portrait of Saint-Vallier. It was considered unsafe, after the revolutionary uprisings in Europe in 1848, to present on

454 THE COMPLETE OPERA BOOK

the stage so licentious a story involving a monarch. Therefore, to avoid political complications, and copyright ones possibly later, the Italian librettist laid the scene in Mantua. Triboulet became Rigoletto, François I the Duke, and Saint-Vallier the Count Monterone. Early in its career the opera was also given under the title of *Viscardello*. K.

# IL TROVATORE
## The Troubadour

Opera in four acts by Giuseppe Verdi; text by S. Cammarano, from the Spanish drama of the same title by Antonio Garcia Gutierrez. Première at the Teatro Apollo, Rome, January 19, 1853, with Penco, Goggi, Baucarde, Guicciardi, Balderi. First performed New York, 1855, with Steffanone, Vestvali, Brignoli, Amodio; Covent Garden, 1855, with Ney, Viardot, Tamberlik, Tagliafico; Drury Lane, 1856 (in English), with Louisa Pyne, Susan Pyne, Harrison, Good; Metropolitan, 1883, with Valleria, Trebelli, Stagno, Kaschmann. Revived Covent Garden, 1927, with Leider, Olszewska, Pertile, A. Borgioli; Sadler's Wells, 1939 (Dent's translation), with Jeanne Dusseau, Edith Coates, Henry Wendon, Redvers Llewellyn; Covent Garden, 1939, with Cigna, Wettergren, Björling, Basiola, conductor Gui; Florence Festival, 1939, with Caniglia, Stignani, Lauri-Volpi, A. Borgioli, conductor Gui. Famous Manricos also include Caruso, Zenatello, Slezak, Martinelli.

### CHARACTERS

Count di Luna, *a young noble of Aragon*..........Baritone
Ferrando, *di Luna's captain of the guard* .............Bass
Manrico, *a chieftain under the Prince of Biscay, and
reputed son of Azucena* ........................Tenor
Ruiz, *a soldier in Manrico's service* ...............Tenor
An Old Gypsy ...............................Baritone
Duchess Leonora, *lady-in-waiting to the Princess of
Aragon* ...................................Soprano
Inez, *confidante of Leonora* ....................Soprano
Azucena, *a Biscayan gypsy woman*........Mezzo-Soprano
Followers of Count di Luna and of Manrico; Messenger,
Gaoler, Soldiers, Nuns, Gypsies
*Time:* Fifteenth Century   *Place:* Biscay and Aragon

For many years *Il Trovatore* has been an opera of world-wide popularity, and for a long time could be accounted the most popular work in the operatic repertory of practically every land.

The libretto of *Il Trovatore* is considered the acme of absurdity; and the popularity of the opera is believed to be entirely due to the almost unbroken melodiousness of Verdi's score.

While it is true, however, that the story of this opera seems to be a good deal of a mix-up, it is also a fact that, under the spur of Verdi's music, even a person who has not a clear grasp of the plot can sense the dramatic power of many of the scenes. It is an opera of immense verve, of temperament almost unbridled, of genius for the melodramatic so unerring that its composer has taken dance rhythms, like those of mazurka and waltz, and on them developed melodies most passionate in expression and dramatic in effect. The music of *Il Trovatore* is swift, spontaneous, and stirring. Absurdities, complexities, unintelligibilities of story are swept away in its unrelenting progress. *Il Trovatore* is the Verdi of forty working at white heat.

One reason why the plot of *Il Trovatore* seems such a jumbled-up affair is that a considerable part of the story is supposed to have transpired before the curtain goes up. These events are narrated by Ferrando, the Count di Luna's captain of the guard, soon after the opera begins. Could the audience be sure of knowing what Ferrando is singing about, the subsequent proceedings would not appear so hopelessly involved, or appeal so strongly to humorous rhymesters, who usually begin their parodies on the opera with,

This is the story
of *Il Trovatore*

What happened before the curtain goes up on the opera is as follows: The old Count di Luna, some time deceased, had two sons nearly of the same age. One night, when they still were infants, and asleep in a nurse's charge in an apartment in the old Count's castle, a gypsy hag, having gained stealthy entrance into the chamber, was discovered leaning over the cradle of the younger child, Garzia. Though she was instantly driven away, the child's health began to fail and she was believed to have bewitched it. She was pursued, apprehended, and burned alive at the stake.

Her daughter, Azucena, at that time a young gypsy woman with a child of her own in her arms, was a witness to the death of her mother, which she swore to avenge. During the following night she stole into the castle, snatched the younger child of the Count di Luna from its cradle, and hurried back to the scene of execution, intending to throw the baby boy into the flames that still raged over the spot where they had consumed her mother. Almost bereft of her senses, however, by her memory of the horrible scene she had witnessed, she seized and hurled into the flames her own child, instead of the young Count (thus preserving, with an almost supernatural instinct for opera, the baby that was destined to grow up into a tenor with a voice high enough to sing 'Di quella pira').

Thwarted for the moment in her vengeance, Azucena was not to be completely baffled. With the infant Count in her arms she fled and rejoined her tribe, entrusting her secret to no one, but bringing him up—Manrico, the Troubadour—as her own son; and always with the thought that through him she might wreak vengeance upon his own kindred.

When the opera opens, Manrico has grown up; Azucena has become old and wrinkled, but is still unrelenting in her quest for vengeance. The old Count has died, leaving the elder son, Count di Luna of the opera, sole heir to his title and possessions, but always doubting the death of the younger, despite the heap of infant's bones found among the ashes about the stake.

Each of the four acts of this opera has a title: Act I, 'Il Duello' (The Duel); Act II, 'La Gitana' (The Gypsy); Act III, 'Il Figlio della Zingara' (The Gypsy's Son); Act IV, 'Il Supplizio' (The Penalty).

Act I.    Atrium of the palace of Aliaferia, with a door leading to the apartments of the Count di Luna. Ferrando, the captain of the guard, and retainers, are reclining near the door. Armed men are standing guard in the background. It is night. The men are on guard because Count di Luna desires to apprehend a minstrel knight, a troubadour, who has been heard on several occasions serenading the Duchess Leonora, for whom a deep but unrequited passion sways the Count.

Weary of the watch, the retainers beg Ferrando to tell them the story of the Count's brother, the stolen child. This Ferrando proceeds to do in the ballad, 'Abbietta zingara' (Sat there a gypsy hag).

Ferrando's gruesome ballad and the comments of the horror-stricken chorus dominate the opening of the opera. The scene is an unusually effective one for a subordinate character like Ferrando, but in *Il Trovatore* Verdi is lavish with his melodies—more so, perhaps, than in any of his other operas.

The scene changes to the gardens of the palace. On one side a flight of marble steps leads to Leonora's apartment. Heavy clouds obscure the moon. Leonora and Inez are in the garden. From the confidante's questions and Leonora's answers it is gathered that Leonora is enamoured of an unknown but valiant knight who, lately entering a tourney, won all contests and was crowned victor by her hand. She knows her love is requited, for at night she has heard her Troubadour singing below her window. In the course of this narrative Leonora has two solos. The first of these is the romantic 'Tacea la notte placida' (The night calmly and peacefully in beauty seemed reposing).

It is followed by the graceful and engaging 'Di tale amor che dirsi' (Of such a love how vainly),

with its brilliant cadenza.

Leonora and Inez then ascend the steps and retire into the palace. The Count di Luna now comes into the garden. He has hardly entered before the voice of the Troubadour, accompanied on a lute, is heard from a nearby thicket singing the familiar romanza, 'Deserto sulla terra' (Lonely on earth abiding).

From the palace comes Leonora. Mistaking the Count in the shadow of the trees for her Troubadour, she hastens toward him. The moon emerges from a cloud, she sees the figure of a masked cavalier, and recognising it as that of her lover, turns from the Count toward the Troubadour. The Troubadour discloses his identity as Manrico, one who as a follower of the Prince of Biscay is proscribed in Aragon. The men draw their swords. There is a trio that fairly seethes with passion—'Di geloso amor sprezzato' (Fires of jealous, despised affection).

The men rush off to fight their duel. Leonora faints.

Act II.     An encampment of gypsies. There is a ruined house at the foot of a mountain in Biscay, the interior partly exposed to view; within, a great fire is lighted. Day begins to dawn.

Azucena is seated near the fire. Manrico, enveloped in his mantle, is lying upon a mattress; his helmet is at his feet; in his hand he holds a sword, which he regards fixedly. A band of gypsies are sitting in scattered groups around them.

Since an almost unbroken sequence of melodies is a characteristic of *Il Trovatore*, it is not surprising to find at the opening of this act two famous numbers in quick succession—the famous Anvil Chorus,

in which the gypsies, working at the forges, swing their hammers and bring them down on clanking metal in rhythm with the music; and Azucena's equally well-known 'Stride la vampa' (Upward the flames roll).

In this air, which the old gypsy woman sings as a weird but impassioned outpouring of memories and hatreds, she relates the story of her mother's death. 'Avenge thou me!' she murmurs to Manrico, when she has concluded.

Swept along by the emotional stress under which she labours, Azucena concludes her narrative of the tragic events at the pyre, voice and orchestral accompaniment uniting in a vivid musical setting of her memories. Naturally, her words arouse doubts in

Manrico's mind as to whether he really is her son. She hastens to dispel these; they were but wandering thoughts she uttered. Moreover, after the recent battle of Petilla, between the forces of Biscay and Aragon, when he was reported slain, did she not search for and find him, and has she not been tenderly nursing him back to strength?

The forces of Aragon were led by Count di Luna, who but a short time before had been overcome by Manrico in a duel in the palace garden; why, on that occasion, asks the gypsy, did he spare the Count's life?

Manrico's reply is couched in a bold, martial air, 'Mal reggendo all' aspro assalto' (Ill sustaining the furious encounter). But at the end it dies away to *pp*, when he tells how, with the Count's life his for a thrust, a voice, as if from heaven, bade him spare it—a suggestion, of course, that although neither Manrico nor the Count know that they are brothers, Manrico unconsciously was swayed by the relationship, a touch of psychology rare in Italian opera librettos.

Enter now Ruiz, a messenger from the Prince of Biscay, who orders Manrico to take command of the forces defending the stronghold of Castellor, and at the same time informs him that Leonora, believing reports of his death at Petilla, is about to take the veil in a convent near the castle.

The scene changes to the cloister of this convent. It is night. The Count and his followers, led by Ferrando, and heavily cloaked, advance cautiously. It is the Count's plan to carry off Leonora before she becomes a nun. He sings of his love for her in the air, 'Il balen del suo sorriso' (Bright her smiles, as when bright morning), which is justly regarded as one of the most chaste and beautiful baritone solos in Italian opera.

It is followed by an air *alla marcia*, also for the Count, 'Per me ora fatale' (Oh, fatal hour impending).

A chorus of nuns is heard from within the convent, and Leonora, with Inez, and her ladies, comes upon the scene. They are about to proceed from the cloister into the convent when the Count interposes, but before he can seize Leonora, another figure stands between them. It is Manrico, with him Ruiz and his followers. The Count is foiled.

'E deggio!—e posso crederlo?' (And can I still my eyes believe?) exclaims Leonora, as she beholds before her Manrico, whom she had thought dead. It is here that begins the impassioned finale, an ensemble consisting of a quartet for Leonora, Manrico, the Count di Luna, and Ferrando, with chorus.

Act III.  The camp of Count di Luna, who is laying siege to Castellor, whither Manrico has safely borne Leonora. There is a stirring chorus for Ferrando and the soldiers.

The Count comes from his tent. He casts a lowering gaze at the stronghold from where his rival defies him. There is a commotion. Soldiers have captured a gypsy woman found prowling about the camp. They drag her in; it is Azucena. Questioned, she sings that she is a poor wanderer who means no harm. 'Giorni poveri vivea' (I was poor, yet uncomplaining).

But Ferrando, though she thought herself masked by the grey hairs and wrinkles of age, recognises her as the gypsy who, to avenge her mother, threw the infant brother of the Count to the flames. In the vehemence of her denials, she cries out to Manrico, whom she names as her son, to come to her rescue. This still further enrages the Count, who orders that she be cast into prison and then burned at the stake. She is dragged away.

The scene changes to a hall adjoining the chapel in the stronghold of Castellor. Leonora is about to become the bride of Manrico, who sings the beautiful lyric, 'Ah si, ben mio coll' essere' (Ah yes, thou art my spouse by right).

Its serenity makes all the more effective the tumultuous scene that follows, and it assists in giving to that episode, one of the most famous in Italian opera, its true significance as a dramatic climax.

Just as Manrico takes Leonora's hand to lead her to the altar of the chapel, Ruiz rushes in with word that Azucena has been captured by the besiegers and is about to be burned to death. Already through the windows of Castellor the glow of flames can be seen. Her peril would render delay fatal. Dropping the hand of his bride, Manrico draws his sword, and, as his men gather, sings 'Di quella pira' (See the pyre blazing), and rushes forth at the head of his soldiers to attempt to save Azucena. The line 'O teco almeno, corro a morir' (Or, all else failing, to die with thee), contains the famous high C.

This is a *tour de force*, which has been condemned as vulgar and ostentatious, but which undoubtedly adds to the effectiveness of the number. There is, it should be remarked, no high C in the score of 'Di quella pira'. It was introduced by a tenor, who saw a chance to make an effect with it, and succeeded so well that it became a fixture.

Dr. Frank E. Miller, author of *The Voice* and *Vocal Art Science*, the latter the most complete exposition of the psycho-physical functions involved in voice-production, informed me that a series of photographs were made (by an apparatus too complicated to describe) of the vibrations of Caruso's voice as he takes and holds the high C in 'Di quella pira'. The record measured fifty-eight feet. While it might not be correct to say that Caruso's high C is fifty-eight feet long, the record is evidence of its being superbly taken and held.

Not infrequently the high C in 'Di quella pira' is faked for tenors who cannot reach it, yet have to sing the rôle of Manrico, or who, having been able to reach it in their younger days and at the height of their prime, still wish to maintain their fame as robust tenors. For such the number is transposed. The tenor, instead of singing high C, sings B flat, a tone lower, and much easier to take. By flourishing his sword and looking very fierce he usually manages to get away with it. Transpositions of operatic airs requiring unusually high voices are not infrequently made for singers, both male and female, no longer in their prime, but still good for two or three more 'farewell' tours. All they have to do is to step up to the footlights with an air of perfect confidence, which indicates that the great moment in the performance has arrived, deliver, with a certain assumption of effort—the semblance of a real *tour de force*—the note which has conveniently been transposed, and receive the enthusiastic plaudits of their devoted admirers. But the assumption of effort must not be omitted. The tenor who sings the high C in 'Di quella pira' without getting red in the face will hardly be credited with having sung it at all.

Act IV.    Manrico's sortie to rescue his supposed mother has failed. His men have been repulsed, and he himself captured and thrown into the dungeon tower of Aliaferia, where Azucena is already enchained. The scene shows a wing of the palace of Aliaferia. In the angle is a tower with window secured by iron bars. It is night, dark and clouded.

Leonora enters with Ruiz, who points out to her the place of Manrico's confinement, and retires. That she has conceived a desperate plan to save her lover appears from the fact that she wears a poison ring, a ring with a swift poison concealed under the jewel, so that she can take her own life, if driven thereto.

Unknown to Manrico, she is near him. Her thoughts wander to him 'D'amor sull' ali rosee' (On rosy wings of love depart).

It is followed by the 'Miserere', which was for many years and perhaps still is the world over the most popular of all melodies from opera.

The 'Miserere' is chanted by a chorus within. Against this as a sombre background are projected the heart-broken ejaculations of Leonora. Then Manrico's voice in the tower intones 'Ah! che la morte ognora' (Ah! how death still delayeth).

One of the most characteristic phrases, suggestions of which occur also in *La Traviata* and even in *Aida*, is the following:

A chi de - si - a, a chi de - si - a mo - rir!

Familiarity may breed contempt, and nothing could well be more familiar than the 'Miserere' from *Il Trovatore*. Yet, well sung, it never fails of effect; and the gaoler always has to let Manrico come out of the tower and acknowledge the applause of an excited house, while Leonora stands by and pretends not to see him, one of those little fictions and absurdities of old-fashioned opera that really add to its charm.

The Count enters, to be confronted by Leonora. She promises to become his wife if he will free Manrico. Di Luna's passion for her is so intense that he agrees. There is a solo for Leonora, 'Mira, d'acerbe lagrime' (Witness the tears of agony), followed by a duet between her and the Count, who little suspects that, Manrico once freed, she will escape a hated union with himself by taking the poison in her ring.

The scene changes to the interior of the tower. Manrico and Azucena sing a duet of mournful beauty, 'Ai nostri monti' (Back to our mountains).

Ai no-stri mon-ti          Ri-po-sao ma-dre; so pro-noe mu-to

Leonora enters and bids him escape. But he suspects the price she has paid; and his suspicions are confirmed by herself, when the poison she has drained from beneath the jewel in her ring begins to take effect and she feels herself sinking in death, while Azucena, in her sleep, sings dreamily, 'Back to our mountains'.

The Count di Luna, coming upon the scene, finds Leonora dead in her lover's arms. He orders Manrico to be led to the block at once and drags Azucena to the window to witness the death of her supposed son.

'It is over!' exclaims di Luna, when the executioner has done his work.

'The victim was thy brother!' shrieks the gypsy hag. 'Thou art avenged, O mother!' She falls near the window.

'And I still live!' exclaims the Count.

With that exclamation the cumulative horrors, set to one of the most tuneful scores in Italian opera, are over.    K.

# LA TRAVIATA
## The Frail One

Opera in three acts by Giuseppe Verdi; text by Francesco Maria Piave, after Alexandre Dumas's play *La Dame aux Camélias*. Première at Teatro la Fenice, Venice, March 6, 1853, with Salvini Donazelli, Graziani, Vanesi. First performed at Her Majesty's Theatre, London, 1856, with Piccolomini, Calzolari, Beneventato; New York, 1856, with La Grange, Brignoli, Amodio; Covent Garden, 1858, with Bosio, Mario; Metropolitan, 1883, with Sembrich, Capoul, del Puente, conductor Vianesi. Revivals at Covent Garden include 1930, with Ponselle, Gigli, Noble; 1939, with Caniglia, Gigli, Basiola, conductor Gui; 1946, with Carosio, Gallo, Tagliabue, conductor Capuana; 1948, with Schwarzkopf, Neate, Silveri; la Scala 1955, with Callas, di Stefano, Bastianini, in Visconti's production, cond. Giulini. Famous Violettas have also included Patti, Nilsson, Bellincioni, Melba, Tetrazzini, Galli-Curci, Selma Kurz, Muzio.

### CHARACTERS

Alfredo Germont, *lover of Violetta* ............ Tenor
Giorgio Germont, *his father* ................... Baritone
Gastone de Letorières .......................... Tenor
Baron Douphol, *a rival of Alfredo* ............. Baritone
Marchese d'Obigny .............................. Bass
Doctor Grenvil ................................. Bass
Giuseppe, *servant to Violetta* ................. Tenor
Violetta Valery, *a courtesan* .................. Soprano
Flora Bervoix, *her friend* ............... Mezzo-Soprano
Annina, *confidante of Violetta* ................ Soprano

Ladies and gentlemen who are friends and guests in the houses of Violetta and Flora; servants and masks; dancers and guests as matadors, picadors, and gypsies.

*Time:* Louis XIV            *Place:* Paris and vicinity

At its production in Venice in 1853 *La Traviata* was a failure, for which various reasons can be advanced. The younger Dumas's play, *La Dame aux Camélias*, familiar to English playgoers under the incorrect title of *Camille*, was a study of modern life and played in modern costume. When Piave reduced his *Traviata* libretto from the play, he retained the contemporary period. This is said to have nonplussed an audience accustomed to operas laid in the past and given in 'costume'. But the chief blame for the fiasco appears to have rested with the singers. Graziani, the Alfredo, was hoarse. Salvini-Donatelli, the Violetta, was inordinately stout. The result was that the scene of her death as a consumptive was received with derision. Varesi, the baritone, who sang Giorgio Germont, considered the rôle beneath his reputation—notwithstanding Germont's beautiful solo, 'Di Provenza'—and was none too cheerful over it. There is evidence in Verdi's correspondence that the composer had complete confidence in the merits of his score, and attributed its failure to its interpreters and its audience.

When the opera was brought forward again a year later, the same city which had decried it as a failure acclaimed it a success. On this occasion, however, the period of the action was set back to the time of Louis XIV, and costumed accordingly. There is, however, no other opera to-day in which this matter of costume is so much a go-as-you-please affair for the principals, as it is in *La Traviata*. I do not recall whether Christine Nilsson dressed Violetta according to the Louis XIV period, or not; but certainly Adelina Patti and Marcella Sembrich, both of whom I heard many times in the rôle (and each of them the first time they sang it in America), wore the conventional evening gown of modern times. To do this has become entirely permissible for prima donnas in this character. Meanwhile the Alfredo may dress according to the Louis XIV period, or wear the swallow-tail costume of Victorian times, or compromise, as some do, and wear the swallow-tail coat and modern waistcoat with knee-breeches and black silk stockings. As if even this diversity were not yet quite enough, one of the most notable Germonts of the twentieth century, Renaud, who, at the Manhattan Opera House, sang the rôle with the most exquisite refinement, giving a portrayal as finished as a genre painting by Meissonnier, wore the costume of a gentleman of Provence of, perhaps, the middle of the last century. But, as I have hinted before, in old-fashioned opera, these incongruities, which would be severely condemned in a modern work, don't amount to a row of pins. Given plenty of melody, beautifully sung, everything else can go hang.

Act I. A salon in the house of Violetta. In the back scene is a door, which opens into another salon. In the centre of the apartment is a dining-table, elegantly laid. Violetta is conversing with Dr. Grenvil and some friends. Others are receiving the guests who arrive, among whom are Baron Douphol and Flora on the arm of the Marquis.

The opera opens with a brisk ensemble. Violetta is a courtesan (*traviata*=the frail one). Her house is the scene of a revel. Early in the festivities Gaston, who has come in with Alfred, informs Violetta that his friend is seriously in love with her. She treats the matter with outward levity, but it is apparent that she is touched by Alfred's devotion. Already, too, in this scene, there are slight indications, more emphasised as the opera progresses, that consumption has undermined Violetta's health.

First in the order of solos in this act is a spirited drinking song for Alfred, which is repeated by Violetta. After each measure the chorus joins in. This is the 'Libiamo ne'lieti calici' (Let us quaff from the wine-cup o'erflowing).

Li - bia . . . mo li - bia - mo ne' lie - - ti ca - - li - ci

Music is heard from an adjoining salon, toward which the guests proceed. Violetta is about to follow, but is seized with a coughing spell and sinks upon a sofa to recover. Alfred has remained behind. She asks him why he has not joined the others. He protests his love for her. At first answering his words with banter, she becomes more serious, as she begins to realise the depth of his affection for her. How long has he loved her? A year, he answers—'Un di felice eterea' (One day a rapture ethereal), he sings.

In this the words 'Di quell' amor ch'e palpito' (Ah, 'tis with love that palpitates) are set to a phrase which Violetta repeats in the famous 'Ah, fors è lui', just as she has previously repeated the drinking song.

*Con espansione*

Di quell' a - mor, quell'a - mor ch'è pal - pi - to

Verdi thus seems to intend to indicate in his score the effect upon her of Alfred's genuine affection. She repeated his drinking song; now she repeats, like an echo of heart-beats, his tribute to a love of which she is the object.

It is when Alfred and the other guests have retired that Violetta, lost in contemplation, her heart touched for the first time, sings 'Ah fors' è lui che l'anima' (For him, perchance, my longing soul).

Then she repeats, in the nature of a refrain, the measures already sung by Alfred. Suddenly she changes, as if there were no hope of lasting love for a woman of her character, and dashes into the brilliant 'Sempre libera' (Ever free shall I still hasten madly on from pleasure to pleasure).

With this solo the act closes.

Act II.    Salon on the ground floor of a country house near Paris, occupied by Alfred and Violetta, who for him has deserted the allurements of her former life. Alfred enters in sporting costume. He sings of his joy in possessing Violetta: 'De' miei bollenti spiriti' (Wild my dream of ecstasy).

From Annina, the maid of Violetta, he learns that the expenses of keeping up the country house are much greater than Violetta has told him, and that, in order to meet the cost, which is beyond her own means, she has been selling her jewels. He immediately leaves for Paris, his intention being to try to raise money there so that he may be able to reimburse her.

After he has gone, Violetta comes in. She has a note from Flora inviting her to some festivities at her house that night. She smiles at the absurdity of the idea that she should return, even for an evening, to the scenes of her former life. Just then a visitor is announced. She supposes he is her business agent, whom she is expecting. But, instead, the man who enters announces that he is Alfred's father. His dignity, his courteous yet restrained manner, at once fill her with apprehension. She has foreseen separation from the man she loves, and now senses that the dread moment is impending.

The elder Germont's plea that she leave Alfred is based both upon the blight which threatens his career by his liaison with her, and upon another misfortune that will result to the family. There is not only the son; there is a daughter—'Pura siccome un angelo' (Pure as an angel) sings Germont, in the familiar air.

Should the scandal of Alfred's liaison with Violetta continue, the family of a youth, whom the daughter is to marry, threaten to break off the match. Therefore it is not only on behalf of his son, it is also for the future of his daughter, that the elder Germont pleads. As in the play, so in the opera, the reason why the rôle of the heroine so strongly appeals to us is that she makes the sacrifice demanded of her—though she is aware that, among other unhappy consequences to her, it may aggravate the disease of which she is a victim and hasten her death, wherein, indeed, she even sees a solace. She cannot yield at once. She prays, as it were, for mercy: 'Non sapete' (Ah, you know not).

Finally she yields in a tune of infinite beauty: 'Dite alla giovine' (Say to thy daughter);

then 'Imponete' (Now command me); and, after that, 'Morrò—la mia memoria' (I shall die—but may my memory).

Germont retires. Violetta writes a note, rings for Annina, and hands it to her. From the maid's surprise as she reads the address, it can be judged to be for Flora, and, presumably, an acceptance of her invitation. When Annina has gone, she writes to Alfred informing him that she is returning to her old life, and that she will look to Baron Douphol to maintain her. Alfred enters. She conceals the letter about her person. He tells her that he has received word from his father that the latter is coming to see him in an attempt to separate him from her. Pretending that she leaves so as not to be present during the interview, she takes an emotional farewell of him: 'Amami, Alfredo'.

Alfred is left alone. He picks up a book and reads listlessly. A messenger enters and hands him a note. The address is in Violetta's handwriting. He breaks the seal, begins to read, staggers as he realises the import, and would collapse, but that his father, who has quietly entered from the garden, holds out his arms, in which the youth, believing himself betrayed by the woman he loves, finds refuge.

'Di Provenza il mar, il suol chi dal cor ti cancellò' (From fair Provence's sea and soil, who hath won thy heart away), sings the elder Germont, in an effort to soften the blow that has fallen upon his son.

Alfred rouses himself. Looking about vaguely, he sees Flora's letter, glances at the contents, and at once concludes that Violetta's first plunge into the vortex of gaiety, to return to which she has, as he supposes, abandoned him, will be at Flora's fête.

'Thither will I hasten, and avenge myself!' he exclaims, and departs precipitately, followed by his father.

The scene changes to a richly furnished and brilliantly lighted salon in Flora's house. The fête is in full swing. There is a ballet of women gypsies, who sing as they dance 'Noi siamo zingarelle' (We're gypsies gay and youthful).

Gaston and his friends appear as matadors and others as picadors. Gaston sings, while the others dance, 'E Piquillo, un bel gagliardo' ('Twas Piquillo, so young and so daring).

It is a lively scene, upon which there enters Alfred, to be followed soon by Baron Douphol with Violetta on his arm. Alfred is seated at a card table. He is steadily winning. 'Unlucky in love, lucky in gambling!' he exclaims. Violetta winces. The Baron shows evidence of anger at Alfred's words and is with difficulty restrained by Violetta. The Baron, with assumed nonchalance, goes to the gaming table and stakes against Alfred. Again the latter's winnings are large. A servant's announcement that the banquet is ready is an evident relief to the Baron. All retire to an adjoining salon. For a brief moment the stage is empty.

Violetta enters. She has asked Alfred to come and speak to her. He joins her. She begs him to leave. She fears the Baron's anger will lead him to challenge Alfred to a duel. The latter sneers at her apprehensions and intimates that it is the Baron she fears for. Violetta's emotions almost betray her, but she remembers her promise to the elder Germont, and exclaims that she does indeed love the Baron.

Alfred tears open the doors to the salon where the banquet is in progress. 'Come hither, all!' he shouts.

They crowd upon the scene. Violetta, almost fainting, leans against the table for support. Facing her, Alfred hurls at her invective after invective. Finally, in payment of what she has spent to help him maintain the house near Paris in which they have lived together, he furiously casts at her feet all his winnings at the gaming table. She faints in the arms of Flora and Dr. Grenvil.

The elder Germont enters in search of his son. He alone knows the real significance of the scene, but for the sake of his son and daughter cannot disclose it. A dramatic ensemble, in which Violetta sings, 'Alfredo, Alfredo, di questo core non puoi comprendere tutto l'amore' (Alfred, Alfred, little canst thou fathom the love within my heart for thee) brings the act to a close.

Act III.     Violetta's bedroom. At the back is a bed with the curtains partly drawn. The prelude to this act, like that to Act I, is a notably beautiful piece.

Violetta awakens. In a weak voice she calls Annina, who, waking up confusedly, opens the shutters and looks down into the street, which is gay with carnival preparations. Dr. Grenvil is at the door. Violetta endeavours to rise, but falls back again. Then, supported by Annina, she walks slowly toward the settee. The doctor enters in time to assist her. Annina places cushions about her. To Violetta the physician cheerfully holds out hope of recovery, but to Annina he whispers, as he is leaving, that her mistress has but a few hours more to live.

Violetta has received a letter from the elder Germont telling her that Alfred has been told by him of her sacrifice and has been sent for to come to her bedside as quickly as possible. But she has little hope that he will arrive in time. She senses the near approach of death. 'Addio del passato' (Farewell to bright visions)

Ad - di - o.. del pas - sa - to.. bei - sog - ni .. ri - - den - ti

is more like a sigh from the depths of a once frail but now purified soul, than an aria.

A bacchanalian chorus of carnival revellers floats up from the street. Annina, who had gone out with some money which Violetta had given her to distribute as alms, returns. Her manner is excited. Violetta is quick to perceive it and divine its significance. Annina has seen Alfred. The dying woman bids Annina hasten to admit him. A moment later he holds Violetta in his arms. Approaching death is forgotten; nothing again shall part them. They will leave Paris for some quiet retreat. 'Parigi, o cara, noi lasceremo' (We shall fly from Paris, beloved), they sing.

Andante mosso

Pa - ri - gi, o ca - ra, noi la - sce - re - mo

But it is too late. The hand of death is upon the woman's brow. 'Gran Dio! morir si giovane' (O, God! to die so young).

The elder Germont and Dr. Grenvil have come in. There is nothing to be done. The cough that racked the poor frail body has ceased. La Traviata is dead.

Not only were *Il Trovatore* and *La Traviata* produced in the same year, but *La Traviata* was written between the date of *Trovatore*'s première at Rome (January 19) and March 6. Only four weeks in all are said to have been devoted to it, and part of the time Verdi was working on *Trovatore* as well. Nothing could better illustrate the fecundity of his genius, the facility with which he composed. But it was not the fatal facility that sacrifices real merit for temporary success. There are a few echoes of *Trovatore* in *Traviata*; but the remarkable achievement of Verdi is not only in having written so beautiful an opera as *La Traviata* in so short a time, but in having produced in it a work in a style wholly different from *Il Trovatore*. The latter palpitates with the passions of love, hatred, and vengeance. The setting of the action encourages these, consisting as it does of palace gardens, castles, dungeons. *La Traviata* in contrast plays in drawing-rooms. The music corresponds with these surroundings, and is vivacious, graceful, gentle. When it palpitates, it is with sorrow.

Oddly enough, although *Il Trovatore* is by far the more robust and at one time was, as I have stated, the most popular opera in the world, I believe that to-day the advantage lies with *La Traviata*, and that, as between the two, there belongs to that opera the ultimate chance of survival. I explain this on the ground that, in *Il Trovatore*, the hero and heroine are purely musical creations, the real character drawing, dramatically and musically, being in the rôle of Azucena, which, while a principal rôle, has not the prominence of Leonora or Manrico. In *La Traviata*, on the other hand, we have in the original of Violetta—the Marguerite Gauthier of Alexandre Dumas, *fils*—one of the great creations of modern drama, the frail woman redeemed by the touch of an artist. Piave, in his libretto, preserves the character. In the opera, as in the play, one comprehends the injunction, 'Let him who is not guilty throw the first stone'. For Verdi has clothed Violetta in music that brings out the character so vividly and so beautifully that whenever I see *Traviata* I recall the first performance in America of the Dumas play by Bernhardt, then in her slender and supple prime, and the first American appearance in it of Duse, with her exquisite intonation and restraint of gesture.

In fact, operas survive because the librettist has known how to create a character and the composer how to match it with his musical genius. Recall the dashing Don Giovanni; the resourceful Figaro, both in the Mozart and the Rossini opera; the real interpretive quality of a mild and gracious order in the heroine of *La Sonnambula*—innocence personified; the gloomy figure of Edgar stalking through *Lucia di Lammermoor*; the hunchback and the titled gallant in *Rigoletto*, and you can understand why these very old operas have lived so long. They are not make-believe; they are real.　　　　　　　　　　　　　　　K.

# I VESPRI SICILIANI
## The Sicilian Vespers

Opera in five acts by Giuseppe Verdi; text by Scribe and Charles Duveyier. Première at the Opéra Paris, with Cruvelli as Hélène, January 13, 1855.

First performed in Italy, Parma, 1855; at la Scala, Milan, 1856 (as *Giovanna di Guzman*); at San Carlo, Naples, 1857 (as *Batilde di Turenna*); Drury Lane, London, 1859; New York, 1859. Revived Stuttgart, 1929 (in a new German version by G. Bundi); Berlin, 1932, with Anni Konetzni, Roswaenge, Schlusnus, List, conductor Kleiber; Palermo, 1937, with Arangi-Lombardi, Franco lo Giudice, Guicciardi, Vaghi, conductor Capuana; Genoa, 1939, with Scacciati, Olivato, Armando Borgioli, Pasero, conductor Gui; Florence Festival, 1951, with Callas, Kokolios, Mascherini, Christoff, conductor Kleiber; la Scala, Milan, 1951, with substantially the same cast, conductor de Sabata.

## CHARACTERS

Duchess Elena, *sister of Frederick of Austria* ...... Soprano

Arrigo, *a young Sicilian* .......................... Tenor

Guido di Monforte, *Governor of Sicily* ........... Baritone

Giovanni da Procida, *a Sicilian doctor* ............. Bass

di Béthune, *a French officer* ........................ Bass

Count Vaudemont, *a French officer* ................. Bass

Ninetta, *in attendance on Elena* ................. Soprano

Danieli, *a young Sicilian* ..................•...... Tenor

Tebaldo, *a French soldier* ........................ Tenor

Roberto, *a French soldier* ......................... Bass

Manfredo, *a Sicilian* ............................ Tenor

*Place:* Palermo                                    *Time:* 1282

*I Vespri Siciliani* (as we now know it, or *Les Vêpres Siciliennes* as it was originally called) was commissioned especially for the Great Exhibition of 1855. Much as Verdi disliked the conditions of work in Paris, he could not but find it an honour to be asked to write music for so great an occasion in the artistic capital of the world, as Paris unquestionably was in those days. In the event, he disliked the libretto, which he said offended the French because of the massacre at the end, and offended the Italians because of the treacherous behaviour of the Sicilian patriots, and his relations with Scribe were even the subject of comment in the newspapers. As if the unsatisfactory conditions of his task were not enough for the composer to bear, Cruvelli, the admirable soprano entrusted with the rôle of Elena, elected to disappear without a word to anyone during rehearsals. The scandal spread over the whole continent, but, a month after her disappearance, the lady reappeared just as suddenly as she had vanished. 'She seems to have gone', says Francis Toye, 'on a kind of anticipatory honeymoon with one Baron Vigier, whom she married shortly afterwards'.

The opera is concerned with the occupation of Sicily by French troops during the thirteenth century, and the efforts of the Sicilians to dislodge them. The overture is one of Verdi's best, and is dominated by the long cello tune, taken from the duet in Act III between Arrigo and Monforte.

Act I.    A detachment of French troops is in the great square at Palermo, some of them drinking, others watching the crowd of Sicilians which eyes them sullenly from the other side of the square. The French sing of their enforced absence from their native land, the Sicilians of their hatred of their oppressors. An exchange between di Béthune, Roberto, and Tebaldo (I have used the Italian names throughout, as the opera is almost always nowadays given in that language) indicates that there is nothing new about the proprietary attitude of occupying troops towards the women of the country.

At this moment the French notice Elena crossing the square. She has been praying for her brother, who was executed by order of Monforte for his patriotic activities. A drunken soldier is struck by her beauty and orders her to sing to entertain the French conquerors. Somewhat to his surprise she consents, but her song is not at all what it was expected to be. The loosely knit opening phrases and the long *cantabile* line lead to a sudden and inflammatory *allegro giusto*, which whips up the courage of the downcast Sicilians. It is a scene of considerable theatrical power and makes a great effect when sung by a soprano of the calibre of Maria Callas, who was in the revival at the Florence Festival in 1951. No one who heard her will forget her repeated 'il vostro fato è in vostra man' (votre salut est dans vos mains), nor the brilliant effect of her coloratura and top notes in the *cabaletta* itself.

The Sicilians rush at the French, but the abortive rising is quelled by the appearance of Monforte, alone and unarmed, at the door of his palace. The square clears as if by magic, and Elena, supported by her attendants Ninetta and Danieli, is left alone with Monforte. Their quartet is mostly unaccompanied, and at its end Arrigo, who has been imprisoned, rushes up to Elena with the news of his release. He does not notice Monforte, but, in spite of his openly expressed patriotic sentiments, is

ordered by him to remain behind. The act ends with a duet
between the two, in which Monforte offers Arrigo fame in the
service of the French. His offer is indignantly spurned, as is his
command that Arrigo associate no more with the rebel Elena,
into whose palace without more ado Arrigo betakes himself.

Act II takes place outside the city, in a valley, to which comes
Procida, until his banishment leader of the Sicilian patriots and
now returned secretly to stir up resistance. He salutes his beloved
native land in a recitative and aria which has become perhaps
the most famous number of the opera, 'O tu Palermo' (O toi,

Palerme). In a *cabaletta*, he exhorts the small band of chosen
patriots to prepare with him the deliverance of Sicily.

Elena and Arrigo have been bidden to meet the exiled patriot,
and he leaves them together while he goes off to set plans afoot,
but not before he has enrolled Arrigo as one of the leaders of the
projected revolt. Arrigo declares his love to Elena and swears to
avenge the death of her beloved brother. A messenger arrives
from Monforte bringing an invitation to Arrigo to attend a ball.
He indignantly refuses it, and is immediately surrounded by
soldiers and led away.

Procida returns to learn of this new mishap, but he sees an
opportunity of stirring up feeling against the French in the
betrothal festivity which is about to take place, and for which a
crowd can be seen approaching. He will suggest to the French
that they carry off the young women, an outrage which may
perhaps rouse the Sicilians from their apathy. Couples in festive
attire dance a *tarantella*, but Procida's plan works all too well,
and in a moment the French soldiers have fallen on the women,
carried off some and put the rest to flight.

Only a few patriots are left behind with Procida and Elena,
and together in half-strangled sentences they give vent to their
feelings, which are further exacerbated by the sound of a complacent *barcarolle* being sung at sea by a boat-load of French
pleasure-seekers. The two choruses combine most effectively as
the act comes to an end.

Act III.    Monforte is found alone in his palace. He reflects
on the injustice he did years ago to the woman who became the
mother of his son, but escaped from him and brought up that
son to hate his father as the oppressor of the Sicilians. Now, on
her death-bed, she has written to him that the son he has not seen
for eighteen years is no other than Arrigo, his sworn enemy.
Monforte's soliloquy 'In braccio alle dovizie' (Au sein de la

puissance) gives effective expression to his indecision and agony
of mind, and is in many ways more satisfactory than the big duet
between Monforte and his newly found son which immediately
follows it. Here occurs the tune first heard on the celli in the
overture, which, memorable though it no doubt is, has more than
a little complacency about it when heard in its proper context—
and complacency is the last thing felt by either father or son in
their peculiar predicament.

The scene ends with Arrigo calling on his mother's memory,
but at the beginning of the ballroom scene he is apparently
sufficiently reconciled, at any rate temporarily, to accompany his
father to the great hall, where together they watch the lengthy
ballet of the seasons, which Monforte has planned for the entertainment of his guests. This is a French ballet on a grand scale
and, whatever its importance to the devotees of Grand Opera in
its heyday, it is in the habit nowadays of impressing listeners
mostly with its length—it lasts for half an hour—and the way it
holds up the dramatic action at a crucial point. On the other
hand, to leave it out is no solution, as the ball is then left as it
were without its core. In any case, much of the music is most
attractive, and it is delightfully scored; perhaps its salvation
would be to incorporate it in a separate ballet, as was once done
by Constant Lambert with the ballet music from Le Prophète,
and to give only one of the four sections when the opera is
revived.

Amongst the invited guests are to be seen a number of masked
figures with silk ribbons fastened to their cloaks. These are the
Sicilian conspirators, led by Procida and Elena. The tension of

Arrigo's predicament—whether to allow his father to be murdered, or to betray his friends—is skilfully suggested by the snatched conversations he has with Elena and Procida in the midst of the general festivity. Finally, he makes an attempt to warn Monforte that his life is in danger, but the governor refuses to leave the ball. When Procida advances upon him, Arrigo steps in between, the conspirators are arrested, and the act ends with an impressive concerted piece, in which the Sicilians unite in cursing the treachery of Arrigo.

Act IV takes place in the great courtyard of the fortress, whither Arrigo has come, armed with a pass from Monforte, to see the prisoners. In a sombre E minor aria, 'Giorno di pianto' (O jour de peine), he reflects on the situation he is in, when his dearest friends are likely to look upon him as their worst enemy. The thought of Elena's hate is too much for him, he thinks he hears her coming up from her cell, and in an ecstasy he prays for her forgiveness. When Elena appears, she does in fact greet him as a traitor, and repeats his words, 'Non son reo' (Malheureux et non coupable), after him ironically, until he admits to her that their enemy is his own father. Her tone changes to one of pity, and later she admits in a ravishing Bellini-like *cantilena* that her greatest sorrow in prison was the necessity to think of the man she loves as a traitor. Their music takes on the character of a love duet, before Procida is led out of the prison by the guards. He sees Arrigo, but ascribes his apparent repentance to yet another treacherous trick.

Monforte enters and orders that the preparations for the double execution shall go forward straight away, in spite of the pleading of Arrigo, who demands to die with them—such an honour, says Procida, is too great for so notorious a traitor. Monforte bids Arrigo pay no attention to the insults of his erstwhile comrades; let him but remember that he is his son. Procida is stupefied at this totally unexpected revelation, and in a few moving phrases bids farewell to the country for whose ideals he has fought. His phrases lead to a quartet (with Elena, Arrigo, Monforte) of considerable beauty, which in its turn gives way to the execution music, heard already in the overture but now assuming an unbearable poignancy, with Monforte urging that pardon will only be given if Arrigo will address him as Father; Arrigo is hesitant, Elena and Procida emphatic that death is preferable to dishonour, and all the time the sound of the funeral hymn accompanies the victims as they draw nearer to the block and the headsman's axe.

At last Arrigo gives in to Monforte's dearest wish, pardon is forthwith granted and with it a general amnesty. The troth of Elena and Arrigo is announced, and the curtain falls on a general ensemble.

Act V is set in the gardens of Monforte's palace, where the wedding of Elena and Arrigo is about to be celebrated. After a chorus, Elena sings her well-known *Bolero*, 'Merce, dilette amiche' (Merci, jeunes amies), a lively and appropriate display piece. Arrigo joins her and sings a charming air, 'La brezza aleggia intorno a carrezzarmi il viso' (La brise souffle au loin plus légère et plus pure), an entirely lyrical interlude in what is by no means otherwise a predominantly lyrical score.

Arrigo disappears and Elena is joined by Procida, now more than ever the plotter with a dagger ever conveniently to hand, for whose over-simplified drawing Verdi so much reproached Scribe. He congratulates Elena on having provided with her wedding the opportunity for the Sicilian patriots to fall on the unarmed French, and tells her that the ringing of the bells will be the signal for the massacre. Nothing she can say will deflect the fanatic from his purpose and he defies her to denounce him to the French and so prevent the carrying out of his plan. Elena's only reply is to refuse to go through with the wedding, much to Arrigo's consternation. There is an impressive and extended trio for Elena, Arrigo, and Procida, which is one of the best numbers in the opera and which dominates the finale. Monforte enters, sweeps aside Elena's objections, the cause of which has not been revealed to him, and himself pronounces the betrothal, at the same time ordering the bells to ring out. The Sicilians rush from their hiding-places, and Procida's revenge is complete.

*I Vespri Siciliani* has been much criticised as being one of Verdi's weakest pieces, and it is true that it does not reach the heights of *Don Carlos* or *Simon Boccanegra*. On the other hand, recent revivals have been attended by a good deal of success, and the unfamiliar music is in the habit of striking its listeners as vastly better than the commentators have made out. In fact, the least satisfactory thing about *Vespri* is its unwieldy shape: Verdi himself complained about the enormous length of the five acts required for a French Grand Opera, and the spectacular nature of the work makes it difficult (though I think not impossible) to combine two acts in one, just as the careful positioning of the ballet rules out its omission *in toto*. There is, of course, a further difficulty, not peculiar to this score but none the less potent: the rôle of Elena requires a coloratura dramatic soprano of a very high order if the possibilities of the rôle are to be realised. Whenever one can be found, and a tenor of similar attainments to go with her, the opera seems likely to be revived for many years to come.

It would be a pity if it were not, as there is much music of fine quality in this score. In the first act, Elena's aria and the unaccompanied quartet are brilliantly successful numbers, and in the second, 'O tu Palermo' is one of Verdi's most famous bass arias. Monforte's monologue at the beginning of Act III is of an expressive quality worthy of Philip himself, and the choral finale after the attempted murder is most effective. The whole of the fourth act seems to me on Verdi's highest level, the solo for Arrigo and that for Elena in the middle of the duet being outstandingly successful, and the moment of suspense before the execution most movingly done. The fifth act can seem rather long in performance, but Arrigo's lyrical tune and the large-scale trio are first-rate.                                                    H.

## SIMON BOCCANEGRA

Opera in three acts and a prologue by Giuseppe Verdi; text by Francesco Maria Piave, from a play by Gutierrez. Première at the Teatro la Fenice, Venice, March 12, 1857, with Bendazzi, Negrini, Giraldoni, Echeveria Viallini. First performed in revised version (alterations by Boito), la Scala, Milan, 1881, with d'Angeri, Tamagno, Maurel, Edouard de Reszke, conductor Faccio. Revived Vienna (in Werfel's version), 1930, with Nemeth, von Pataky, Rode, Manowarda, conductor Krauss; Berlin, 1930; Metropolitan, New York, 1932, with Müller, Martinelli, Tibbett, Pinza, conductor Serafin; la Scala, 1932; Florence Festival, 1938, with Caniglia, Civil, Sved, Pasero, conductor Gui; Sadler's Wells, 1948, with Gartside, Johnston, Matters, Glynne, Sharp, conductor Mudie; Rome, 1949, with Fineschi, Picchi, Gobbi, Siepi, conductor Serafin; Venice, 1950, with Mancini, Penno, Tagliabue, Christoff, Panerai. The revival at Sadler's Wells was outstandingly successful and the work has been frequently performed there in subsequent seasons.

### CHARACTERS

Amelia Boccanegra (*sometimes called Maria, and under the name of Amelia Grimaldi during Act I*) . Soprano
Gabriele Adorno, *a patrician* ..................... Tenor

Simon Boccanegra, *a plebeian, later Doge*........Baritone
Jacopo Fiesco, *a patrician* .........................Bass
Paolo Albiani, *a plebeian* .....................Baritone
Pietro, *a plebeian* ...............................Bass
A Captain .....................................Tenor

*Place:* In and near Genoa          *Time:* Fifteenth century

*Simon Boccanegra* was unsuccessful when first performed in
Venice, and indeed Verdi himself referred to this first version as
'monotonous and cold', so that it is not surprising that he chose
to revise the opera over twenty years after the first performance.
At this time he had written *Aida* and the *Requiem* and plans for
*Otello* already existed in his mind, and it was to Boito, as his
prospective collaborator in the greater enterprise of *Otello*, that
he entrusted the revision. In this version the opera has gradually
won its way into the international repertory, but one is bound
to admit that Boito's contribution, while it included the insertion
of a scene of nothing short of genius, stopped short of clarifying
the complications of the plot. This small but important task has
been attempted with a very fair measure of success by Franz
Werfel, working in Germany in the 1920's, and by Norman
Tucker in his English translation of 1948.

Genoa in the fourteenth century was ruled by an elected Doge,
who had hitherto always been chosen from the ranks of the
patricians. Fiesco, who is in office when the story begins, has a
daughter, Maria, who has fallen in love with a plebeian, Simon
Boccanegra, and borne him a daughter. His seafaring exploits, in
the course of which he cleared the seas of the African pirates who
so impeded the smooth course of Genoa's trade, have won him
considerable fame but not the right to treat the Doge's daughter
as his equal. Their child was looked after at Pisa by an old
woman while he was at sea, until one day on his return home he
found her dead, and his daughter vanished. Since then, he has
sought her in vain, and he does not know that she was found
wandering on the sea shore by Count Grimaldi, a patrician, and
brought up by him as his own child.

Prologue.    Paolo, political leader of the plebeians, and Pietro,
an influential member of the movement, are in conversation, the
latter proposing that Lorenzino shall be the plebeian choice for

Doge, the former suggesting that Boccanegra would be a better candidate. Pietro agrees to organise the people's vote for Boccanegra in return for honour and riches for himself. (Tucker simplifies the plot, omitting all mention of Lorenzino, a nebulous figure who plays an important part in the drama but never appears on the stage, and making Paolo renounce the honour for himself, before suggesting Boccanegra's name.) Boccanegra has been specially called to Genoa by Paolo, and agrees to accept the position, which should win him permission to marry his beloved Maria. The people are called together, and Paolo announces to them that Boccanegra is to be their candidate; they unite in cursing Fiesco, in whose adjoining palace they see mysterious lights moving.

The whole of this movement is set to music that is extraordinarily suggestive of underground movement and conspiracy under the cover of darkness, from the mysterious prelude to Paolo's cursing of the haughty patricians and his *sotto voce* working up of the crowd in fear of the nameless doings in Fiesco's palace.

The square empties, and Fiesco leaves his home, lamenting the loss of his daughter, from whose death-bed he has just come. His noble, restrained cry of grief, 'Il lacerato spirito' (Weary and worn with suffering*), with its moving orchestral postlude, establishes him straight away as a flesh-and-blood personality whose emotions may be subdued to his sense of rank, but who is none the less anything but an insensitive, cardboard figure:

He sees Boccanegra enter the square and confronts him again with an accusation of the wrong he has done Maria. It is the first of the two great duets between the adversaries, Fiesco's fury contrasting well with Boccanegra's pleading as he tells the story of the loss of the little daughter, which has robbed one of them

---

* English translation by Norman Tucker

of his only child, the other of the grand-daughter he has never seen.

Fiesco leaves Boccanegra, telling him that only the sight of his grand-daughter can bring peace between them. He watches from a distance as the distracted man knocks on the palace door, then, finding it open, goes up, only to find that his Maria is dead. Boccanegra reappears to hear the plaudits of the mob, as they crowd into the square (to a most democratic-sounding march) and salute their new Doge.

Act I.    Twenty-five years have passed. Amelia, Boccanegra's daughter, is standing in the garden of the Grimaldi palace, near the sea. It is dawn, and she salutes the beauty of the scene and memories of her childhood in a lovely aria, 'Come in quest' ora bruna' (See how sky and ocean), whose shimmering accompaniment might have been written by a French Impressionist. She hears the voice of Gabriele, her lover, serenading her from a distance, and when he appears, tells him of her fears for his safety and that of Andrea (in reality, Fiesco in disguise), who she knows is plotting against the Doge. Her warning, and Gabriele's answer, turn to thoughts of their mutual love, which take on greater urgency when Pietro comes to announce that the Doge asks to be received by Amelia on his way back from hunting, for no other purpose, as she well knows, than that of asking her hand in marriage for his henchman, Paolo. Gabriele resolves immediately to ask the blessing of Andrea, Amelia's guardian now that Count Grimaldi has been banished from Genoa for political intrigue, on their marriage. When he does so, Fiesco tells him the story of Amelia's adoption (he has, of course, no idea of her actual identity), Gabriele swears eternal love to her, and Fiesco blesses Gabriele in his affection for Amelia and his patriotic love of Genoa.

The Doge greets Amelia, shows her the pardon he is granting to Count Grimaldi, and asks her if she is content with her life of seclusion. She answers that she has a lover, and is pursued by one she hates—Paolo. In any case she confides to the Doge that she is not Grimaldi's daughter, but an orphan, whose only clue to her identity is a locket containing the portrait of her mother. With great emotion, Boccanegra recognises it as that of Maria and knows he has found his daughter at last. Their duet mounts in intensity, through Simon's lyrical reaction to the possibility of having found his daughter, until uncertainty gives way to proof, and

he gratefully acknowledges her. The direct expression of the later part of the duet gives way to unique tenderness as it comes to an end, and the orchestral postlude, with Boccanegra's final, ecstatic 'Figlia!' (Daughter) on a top F, makes a fitting end to a remarkable scene. It remains only for Boccanegra to deny any hope of Amelia to the waiting Paolo and for Paolo to plot her abduction with his crony Pietro, before the scene changes and we return to the political struggle.

The finale of Act I. which plays in the Council Chamber of the Doge, dates entirely from Boito's revision, and amounts to fifty pages of vocal score, or almost one half of the entire act. It is one of the finest scenes in all Verdi, and an extraordinary and entirely worthy anticipation of the work of the composer and librettist in *Otello*; it has been not inaccurately said that if Otello had ever been shown in council, this is how it might have sounded.

We find the Doge, surrounded by the plebeian and patrician members of his Council (the former in the majority), receiving emissaries from the King of Tartary, who pledges himself to keep his waters open to the ships of Genoa. He goes on to read and support a message from Petrarch, which urges that peace should immediately be made with Venice, which, like Genoa, acknowledges a common fatherland, Italy. (In Tucker's version, the message is from the Pope, and concerns the internal strife of patrician and plebeian, rather than that of the rival sea powers of Genoa and Venice.) A noise of rioting is heard in the distance, and Paolo sees through the window that the crowd is dragging Adorno to the palace; the words 'Morte ai patrizi' (Death to the nobles) can now be distinguished. In a moment, the Council has divided itself into patricians and plebeians, each group with swords drawn. Simon hears the cry 'Morte al Doge', and sends his herald to open the doors of the palace and say to the crowd that he awaits them in his Council Chamber, if they wish to find him. The sound of the trumpet can be heard calling them to silence, but the herald's words cannot be distinguished, only the sound of the yell of 'Evviva il Doge' at the end of his announcement.

It is a scene of breathless drama achieved by the simplest means, and the domination of Boccanegra is nowhere better shown than in his efforts to keep peace, not only in the city but within his own Council as well.

The mob rushes in, crying for vengeance on Gabriele Adorno and Andrea (or Fiesco), whom they drag into the Doge's presence. It seems from Adorno's own account that he has slain Lorenzino, who had abducted Amelia, and that before he died, the villain admitted he was the agent of a mightier man than he, 'a man of high position'. He is about to stab Boccanegra for the crime which he supposes to be his when Amelia, who has entered through the crowd, throws herself between the two men. Her story corroborates Gabriele's, but before she can name the offender, patrician and plebeian accuse and counter-accuse each other of

the crime; only Boccanegra's intervention prevents further bloodshed.

His great plea for peace and unity, 'Piango su voi, sul placido
raggio del vostro clivo' (Sadly I see the sweet bloom of spring
on our native hillsides), leads to an extended ensemble, led
by Amelia, who echoes the prayer that peace may return to
all their hearts. (In Tucker's version, it is not Lorenzino who
abducts Amelia at Paolo's behest, but Pietro, who is thu
absent from the Council Chamber scene, where his part is
slight (see page 486).)

Adorno surrenders his sword to Boccanegra, who accepts it,
before turning 'con forza terribile' to Paolo. He speaks with
ever-increasing intensity of his determination to find the traitor
who raised his hand against Amelia, and in a terrible voice calls
on Paolo to join with him in cursing the villain. This Paolo cannot avoid doing, and his curse is taken up by the bystanders, in
whom the scene seems to induce something approaching hysteria,

to judge from their first *forte* cry of 'Sia maledetto!!' (He is accursed), and the subsequent and ever softer repetitions. The crowd disperses, Paolo rushes out and only Boccanegra and his daughter are left alone at the end of a scene whose atmosphere has been at any rate partly induced by the uncanny nature of the principal motive, played by cello and double-bassoon.

Act II.    Paolo is alone, the prey to acute fear of the consequences of his action and of the curse he was obliged by the implacable Boccanegra to deliver against himself. He sees himself as rejected by all, patricians and plebeians alike, but rears himself like a snake to threaten the absent Doge with the most terrible and the most secret vengeance at his command poison. Fiesco and Adorno are brought in, and he offers the former his liberty if he will perform one vital action: kill the Doge. If he refuses, the details of the patrician plot, as well as the names of the men who lead them, both of which are known to him, shall go forthwith to the Doge himself. Fiesco indignantly refuses the offer, but Paolo has one weapon left; as Adorno prepares to leave with Fiesco, he asks him if he knows that Amelia is here in the palace, as Boccanegra's mistress? (Tucker has changed the order of events: the interview with Fiesco, who enters alone, begins the act, is followed by Paolo's soliloquy, at the end of which Adorno is brought in alone.)

Adorno accepts Paolo's slander all too easily, and launches into a magnificent tirade in A minor against the Doge, who once ordered his father's execution and has now ravished his mistress. He prays, in the dominant major, that his fears may be groundless and that Amelia's love may still be his. Amelia comes in and he confronts her with the accusation, which she indignantly denies. She attempts to persuade him to leave, but the Doge can be heard approaching, and Adorno hides, still breathing threats of revenge.

Boccanegra notices that his daughter has tears in her eyes, and tells her that he knows the reason, which she has already revealed to him: she is in love. When he hears the name of Adorno, his worst fears are realised; Adorno is a traitor and a plotter against the state. She entreats him to pardon Gabriele, with whom she would rather die than live on alone. The Doge tells her to leave him, and wonders whether it is strength or weakness which prompts him to pardon an enemy. He pours water from the jug which Paolo has poisoned, drinks from it, and, in a sad phrase, reflects on the melancholy destiny of those who wear a crown. He feels himself falling asleep, and murmurs Amelia's name while the orchestra softly adumbrates the theme of their duet in Act I.

Adorno steps from concealment; the man who murdered his father and who is now his rival is at his mercy. But Amelia steps between the two men, Boccanegra awakes, takes in the situation, and defies Adorno to kill a defenceless man. Gabriele says Boccanegra's life is forfeit in return for his father's. Boccanegra replies that his revenge is already complete since he has taken from him the thing in life that he valued most, his daughter. Adorno is overcome at the news, and begs for forgiveness from Amelia, whom he says he has pursued with too jealous a love. He begs for death at the Doge's hands, in music whose virility and youthful, heroic quality is as good as anything of the kind Verdi ever wrote. Boccanegra's humanity does not desert him and he pardons his would-be murderer in a phrase whose nobility dominates the latter part of the splendid trio:

Warlike sounds are heard outside, and Boccanegra, remembering the conspiracy, orders Adorno to join his friends, whose rebellion has evidently started. But Adorno swears loyalty to the Doge and the act ends as he promises to do what he can to put an end to the fighting.

Act III.   The scene changes from Simon's private apartments to a great hall, whose window reveals a view of Genoa harbour. The city is lit up with torches in honour of the crushing of the revolt. Fiesco's sword is returned to him and he is released. As he turns to go, he sees Paolo with an escort of guards, and learns that he took part in the rebellion and, when captured, was immediately condemned to death by Boccanegra—but Paolo can exult in the knowledge that the Doge will follow him quickly to the grave, slain by the slow poison he has prepared for him. The sound of the wedding hymn of Gabriele and Amelia can be heard, and Paolo is conducted to the scaffold with its sound ringing in his ears, leaving Fiesco full of regret that Boccanegra's end should be brought about in so treacherous and dishonourable a manner, but still determined to see him again.

· A proclamation is read from the balcony, ordering that the lights be extinguished in honour of the valiant dead. The Doge himself enters the hall, already affected by the poison he has taken. The sight of the sea and the feel of the salt wind on his brow restores his confidence, and brings back to him memories of the life he once led as a free man on the sea he loved and understood so well. It is a moving, expansive moment, one of those pieces of unforced self-revelation in which this opera abounds, and whose beauty is so intense that one finds oneself waiting for them at every performance one hears. Why, asks Boccanegra, did he not find death at this early, happy stage of his career? As if in answer to his question comes an echo from the concealed Fiesco. The Doge makes an effort to summon his guards, but Fiesco reveals himself as the ancient enemy long thought dead. It is the moment, not of Fiesco's revenge, but of Boccanegra's atonement, and he proudly announces that there can be peace between them now that in Amelia he has found the daughter he had lost. Fiesco's hate turns to pity for the man he knows has only a short time to live. As is appropriate the second of the two great duets is on an even more generous scale than that of the prologue, when Fiesco first imposed his conditions for reconciliation on the unfortunate Boccanegra. The passionate declamation of the bass is matched here by the mature, conciliatory tone of Boccanegra's music.

Boccanegra summons up strength to tell Amelia of her descent, and to appoint Adorno as his successor before he dies in the arms of his children and surrounded by his friends and counsellors. Fiesco goes to the balcony and announces to the assembled crowd that Gabriele Adorno is their new Doge; when they shout for Boccanegra, he reveals to them that he is dead.

Much has been made of the complication of the original libretto, and of the difficulty Boito apparently had in tidying it up, but the truth is that very little more is needed to make the story entirely comprehensible, even easy to follow, provided it is heard by an audience in its own language; at any rate, that was the common experience at Sadler's Wells. Apart from a general tidying up of the dialogue, Boito was responsible for the finale of Act I, generally conceded to be the finest section of the opera. Verdi's revision was even more thorough. Details of the orchestration, of the vocal line, and of the harmony are altered all over the place, in much the same way as they had been in *Macbeth* but on a far more extensive scale. Entirely new is the opening scene of the prologue up to Fiesco's aria (apart from Paolo's 'L'altra magion'); the introduction to Act I, the duet for Gabriele and Fiesco, the climax of the recognition duet, and of course the Council Chamber scene; Boccanegra's short solo in Act II and Paolo's *Credo*-like soliloquy which precedes it; the opening of Act III up to the entrance of Boccanegra and to a large extent the final quartet with chorus.

That Verdi entertained such high regard for the opera is perhaps to some extent due to his love for Genoa itself. Certainly his music communicates this love as well as the city's dependence for life on the sea. But the most remarkable thing about the opera is its central figure, a puissant character and amongst Verdi's greatest creations; all the way through, one cannot help but be impressed by the amazing consistency of the characterisation. Never before had a composer succeeded in putting the rather unspectacular quality of statesmanship on to the stage, although quite a number had tried, e.g. Mozart in *La Clemenza di Tito*. Boccanegra is a mature creation, whose insight and integrity are expressed in music as well as in the drama. It is not only that Verdi has been provided with striking situations for his main character—the sudden recognition of a long-lost daughter, the cursing of the abductor, the falling asleep and waking to find his daughter's prospective bridegroom standing over him with a dagger, the confronting by his ancient enemy apparently risen from the dead—but that the music shows exactly the same consistent understanding that we are asked to believe was Boccanegra's. Not a bar of recitative, not a note in the great solos and ensembles in which he takes part but contributes to this picture of the central figure, which is in addition perhaps the most exacting baritone part Verdi ever wrote, certainly one of the most rewarding.                                                                    H.

## UN BALLO IN MASCHERA
### A Masked Ball

Opera in three acts by Giuseppe Verdi; text by Somma, based on Scribe's libretto for Auber's opera *Gustave III, ou Le Bal Masqué*. Première at Apollo Theatre, Rome, February 17, 1859, with Scotti, Sbriscia, Fraschini, Giraldoni. First performed New York, 1861; London, Lyceum Theatre, 1861, with Tietjens, Lemaire, Gussier, Giuglini, Sedie; Metropolitan, 1889 (in German), with Lilli Lehmann, Perotti, Reichmann, conductor Seidl. Revived Metropolitan, 1903, with Jean de Reszke; 1905, with Caruso, Eames, Homer, Scotti, Plançon, Journet; Covent Garden, 1919, with Destinn, Martinelli, Dinh Gilly; 1935, with Eva Turner, Dino Borgioli, Fear, conductor Raybould; Florence Festival, 1935, with Cigna, Grani, Buades, Lauri-Volpi,

Armando Borgioli, conductor Serafin; 1941, with Caniglia, Grani, Stignani, Gigli, Bechi; Metropolitan, 1940, with Milanov, Thorborg, Björling, Sved, conductor Panizza; 1949, Edinburgh Festival, with Welitsch and Grandi, Noni, Picchi, Silveri, conductor Gui. Bonci was one of the most famous exponents of the rôle of Riccardo, and Selma Kurz's trill was apparently never heard to better advantage than as Oscar.

## CHARACTERS

Riccardo, *Count of Warwick* (Gustavus III) ......... Tenor
Amelia ..................................... Soprano
Renato, *Secretary to the Governor* (Anckarstroem) Baritone
Samuele (Count Ribbing) ⎱ *enemies of the Governor* . ⎰ Bass
Tomaso (Count Horn) ⎰ ⎱ Bass
Silvano, *a sailor* (Cristian) .................... Baritone
Oscar, *a page* ............................... Soprano
Ulrica, *a fortune-teller* (Arvidson) .............. Contralto
A Judge, a Servant of Amelia, Populace, Guards, Courtiers, etc. (The names used when the opera is set in Boston appear first, those when it is restored to its Swedish setting are added in brackets.)

The English libretto of *Un Ballo in Maschera*, literally *A Masked Ball* but always called *The Masked Ball*, has the following note:

'The scene of Verdi's *Ballo in Maschera* was, by the author of the libretto, originally laid in one of the European cities. But the government censors objected to this, probably because the plot contained the record of a successful conspiracy against an established prince or governor. By a change of scene to the distant and, to the author, little-known city of Boston, in America, this difficulty seems to have been obviated. The fact should be borne in mind by Bostonians and others, who may be somewhat astonished at the events which are supposed to have taken place in the old Puritan city.'

Certainly the events in *The Masked Ball* are amazing for the Boston of Puritan or any other time, and the reason is not far to seek.

Auber produced, in 1833, an opera on a libretto by Scribe, entitled *Gustave III, ou Le Bal Masqué*, and it is upon this Scribe libretto that the book of *Un Ballo in Maschera* is based. Verdi's opera was originally called *Gustavo III*, and, like the Scribe-Auber work, was written around the assassination of Gustavus III, of Sweden, who, March 16, 1792, was shot in the back during a masked ball at Stockholm.

Verdi composed the work for the San Carlo Theatre, Naples, where it was to have been produced for the carnival of 1858. But on January 14 of that year, while the rehearsals were in progress, Felice Orsini, an Italian revolutionist, made his attempt on the life of Napoleon III. In consequence the authorities forbade the performance of a work dealing with the assassination of a king. The suggestion that Verdi adapt his music to an entirely different libretto was put aside by the composer, and the work was withdrawn, with the result that a revolution nearly broke out in Naples. People paraded the street, and by shouting 'Viva Verdi!' proclaimed, under guise of the initials of the popular composer's name, that they favoured the cause of a united Italy, with Victor Emanuel as King; viz. Vittorio Emmanuele Re D'Italia (Victor Emanuel, King of Italy). Finally the censor in Rome suggested, as a way out of the difficulty, that the title of the opera be changed to *Un Ballo in Maschera* and the scene transferred to Boston— for, however nervous the authorities were about having a king murdered on the stage, they regarded the assassination of an English governor in far-off America as a quite harmless diversion. So, indeed, it proved to be, the only excitement evinced by the audience of the Apollo Theatre, Rome, on the evening of February 18, 1859, being the result of its enthusiasm over the various musical numbers of the work, this enthusiasm not being at all reduced by the fact that, with the transfer to Boston, two of the conspirators, Samuel and Tommaso, became negroes, and the astrologer who figures in the opera, a negress!

The change of scene from Boston to Naples (where the scene has often been laid) is said to have been initiated in Paris upon the instance of Mario, who 'would never have consented to sing his ballad in the second act in short pantaloons, silk stockings, red dress, and big epaulettes of gold lace. He would never have been satisfied with the title of Earl of Warwick and the office of governor. He preferred to be a grandee of Spain, to call himself the Duke of Olivares, and to disguise himself as a Neapolitan fisherman, besides paying little attention to the strict accuracy of the rôle, but rather adapting it to his own gifts as an artist.' The ballad referred to in this quotation undoubtedly is Riccardo's barcarolle, 'Di' tu se fedele il flutto m'aspetta' (Declare if the waves will faithfully bear me).

Far more sensible is it to put the setting back to the original Sweden, and so restore the correct historical background to a set of happenings that is substantially based on historical fact. Gustavus III was a monarch distinguished for his liberal views, Richard, Count of Warwick, is a librettist's makeshift. Similarly, Anckarstroem, Horn, and Ribbing were sincere fighters for a reactionary, aristocratic cause—which we can understand even if we cannot sympathise with it—and they bear little resemblance to the ludicrous Tom and Sam, or the implausible half-breed Renato. If the change from the negress Ulrica to the society go-between Mam'zelle Arvidson is rather more difficult to reconcile with the music, the enormous gain to the other characters surely affords ample compensation. It is not that the change affects the music, only that the motivation of the action becomes imme-diately much stronger.

Act I.   Reception hall in the Governor's house. Riccardo is giving an audience. Oscar, his page, brings him the list of guests invited to a masked ball. Riccardo is especially delighted at seeing on it the name of Amelia, the wife of his secretary, Renato, although his conscience bitterly reproaches him for loving Amelia, for Renato is his most faithful friend, ever ready to defend him. The secretary has recently discovered a conspiracy against his master, but as yet has been unable to learn the names of the conspirators.

At the audience a judge is announced, who brings for signature the sentence of banishment against an old fortune-teller, by name Ulrica. Oscar, however, intercedes for the old woman. Riccardo decides to visit her in disguise and test her powers of divination.

The scene changes to Ulrica's hut, which Riccardo enters dis-guised as a fisherman. Without his knowledge, Amelia also comes to consult the sorceress. Concealed by a curtain he hears her ask for a magic herb to cure her of the love which she, a married woman, bears to Riccardo. The old woman tells her of such an herb, but Amelia must gather it herself at midnight in the place where stands the gibbet. Riccardo thus learns for the first time that she loves him, and of her purpose to be at the place of the gibbet at midnight. When she has gone he comes out of his concealment and has his fortune told. Ulrica predicts that he will die by the hand of a friend. The conspirators, who are in his retinue, whisper among themselves that they are discovered. 'Who will be the slayer?' asks Riccardo. The answer is, 'Whoever first shall shake your hand.' At this moment Renato enters, greets his friend with a vigorous shake of the hand, and Riccardo laughs at the evil prophecy. His retinue and the populace rejoice with him.

Act II.    Midnight, beside the gallows. Amelia, deeply veiled, comes to pluck the magic herb. Riccardo arrives to protect her. Amelia is unable to conceal her love for him. But who comes there? It is Renato. Concern for his master has called him to the spot. The conspirators are lying in wait for him nearby. Riccardo exacts from Renato a promise to escort back to the city the deeply veiled woman, without making an attempt to learn who she is, while he himself returns by an unfrequented path. Renato and his companion fall into the hands of the conspirators. The latter do not harm the secretary, but want at least to learn who the Governor's sweetheart is. They lift the veil. Renato sees his own wife. Rage grips his soul. He bids the leaders of the conspiracy meet with him at his house in the morning.

Act III.    A room in Renato's dwelling. For the disgrace he has suffered he intends to kill Amelia. Upon her plea she is allowed to embrace her son once more. He reflects that, after all, Riccardo is much the more guilty of the two. He refrains from killing her, but when he and the conspirators draw lots to determine who shall kill Riccardo, he calls her in, and, at his command, she draws a piece of paper from an urn. It bears her husband's name, drawn unwittingly by her to indicate the person who is to slay the man she loves. Partly to remove Amelia's suspicions, Renato accepts the invitation to the masked ball which Oscar brings him, Riccardo, of course, knowing nothing of what has transpired.

In the brilliant crowd of maskers, the scene having changed to that of the masked ball, Renato learns from Oscar what disguise is worn by Riccardo. Amelia, who, with the eyes of apprehensive love, has also recognised Riccardo, implores him to flee the danger that threatens him. But Riccardo knows no fear. In order that the honour of his friend shall remain secure, he has determined to send him as an envoy to England, accompanied by his

PLATE XVII. The finale of Act III, *Un Ballo in Maschera*, Covent Garden 1952. The producer was Günther Rennert, designs by Alan Barlow.

PLATE XVIII. *La Forza del Destino*: 'Rataplan' Chorus at Metropolitan, New York, Mildred Miller as Preziosilla.

wife. Her, he tells Amelia, he will never see again. 'Once more I bid thee farewell, for the last time, farewell.'

'And thus receive thou my farewell!' exclaims Renato stabbing him in the side.

With his last words Riccardo assures Renato of the guiltlessness of Amelia, and admonishes all to seek to avenge his death on no one.

Even outside Italy, the opera is the subject of frequent revival; it contains a considerable amount of excellent music and a quintet of exceptional quality.

Early in the first act comes Riccardo's solo, 'La rivedrà nell' estasi' (I shall again her face behold), which also forms the main theme of the prelude.

La ri-ve-drà nel-le-sta-si

This is followed by the faithful Renato's 'Alla vita che t'arride' (To thy life with joy abounding), with horn solo.

Strikingly effective is Oscar's song, in which the page vouches for the fortune-teller, 'Volta la terrea fronte alle stelle' (Lift up thine earthly gaze to where the stars are shining).

Allegretto

Vol - ta la ter-re-a... frontealle stel-le

In the scene in the fortune-teller's hut, after her invocation come a trio for Amelia, Ulrica, and Riccardo (during which the latter overhears Amelia's welcome confession of love for himself),

Con espressione

Con - sen - ti - mi, o Si - gno - - re.

and Riccardo's charming barcarolle addressed to the sorceress, a Neapolitan melody, 'Di tu se fedele il flutto m'aspetta' (Declare if the waves will faithfully bear me).

The quintet begins with Riccardo's laughing disbelief in Ulrica's prophecy regarding himself, 'E scherzo ed e follia' ('Tis an idle folly):

Andante mosso

È scher-zo o dè fol - li - - a si f-fat-ta pro-fe-zi - a

Concluding the scene is the chorus, in which, after the people have recognised Riccardo, they sing what has been called 'a kind of "God Save the King" tribute to his worth'—'O figlio d' Inghilterra' (O son of mighty England).

The second act opens with a beautiful air for Amelia, 'Ma dall' arido stelo divulsa' (From the stem, dry and withered, dissevered).

An impassioned duet occurs during the meeting at the place of the gibbet between Riccardo and Amelia: 'O qual soave brivido' (Oh, what delightful ecstasies).

Allegro
dolciss

Oh qual so-a-ve bri-vi-do l'ac-ce-so pet-to ir - ro - ra

The act ends with a quartet for Amelia, Renato, Samuel, and Tom.

In the last act is Amelia's touching supplication to her husband, in which 'the weeping of the violoncello and the veiled key of E flat minor stretch to the last limits of grief this prayer of the wife and mother' ('Morrò, ma prima in grazia': I die, but first in mercy).

'Eri tu' (It was you) sings her husband, in a musical inspiration prefaced by harp and flute.

In the scene at Renato's house there is a quintet for Amelia, Oscar, Renato, Samuel, and Tom, from which the sprightly butterfly *allegro* of Oscar, 'Di che fulgor, che musiche' (What brilliant lights, what music gay) detaches itself. Later on at the Ball the Page has a buoyant 'tra-la-la' solo, beginning, in reply to Renato's question concerning Riccardo's disguise, 'Saper vorreste, di che si veste' (You'd fain be hearing what mask he's wearing).

There is a colloquy between Riccardo and Amelia carried on to the accompaniment of dance music, then the catastrophe.

K.

# LA FORZA DEL DESTINO
## The Force of Destiny

Opera in four acts by Francesco Maria Piave, founded on a Spanish drama by the Duke of Rivas, *Don Alvaro o Le Fuorza de Sino*. Première at St. Petersburg on November 10, 1862, with Barbot, Didiée, Tamberlik, Graziani, Angelini. First performed, New York, 1865; London, Her Majesty's Theatre, 1867, with Tietjens, Trebelli, Mongini, Santley, Gassie, conductor Arditi. Revived Metropolitan, 1918, with Ponselle, Caruso, de Luca, Mardones, conductor Papi; 1942, with Milanov, Baum, Tibbett, Pinza, conductor Walter; Dresden, 1926, with Seinemeyer, Pattiera, Burg, Plaschke, conductor Busch; Vienna, 1926, with Angerer, Piccaver, Schipper, Mayr; la Scala, 1928, with Scacciati, Merli, Franci, Pasero, conductor Toscanini; Covent Garden, 1931, with Ponselle, Pertile, Franci, Pasero, conductor Serafin; Buenos Aires, 1933, with Muzio, Gigli, conductor Marinuzzi; la Scala, 1940, with Cigna, Gigli, A. Borgioli, Pasero, conductor Marinuzzi; 1949, with Barbato, Filippeschi, Silveri, Christoff, conductor de Sabata; Edinburgh Festival, 1951, with Wegner, Poleri, Rothmüller, Dargavel, conductor Busch.

### CHARACTERS

Donna Leonora di Vargas .....................Soprano

Preziosilla, *a gypsy* ....................Mezzo-Soprano

Don Alvaro, *lover of Donna Leonora* ..............Tenor

Don Carlo di Vargas, *Leonora's brother* ..........Baritone

Padre Guardiano, *a Franciscan monk* ...............Bass

Marchese di Calatrava, *Leonora's father* .............Bass

Fra Melitone, *a Franciscan monk* ...............Baritone

Curra, *Leonora's maid* ..................Mezzo-Soprano

The Mayor of Hornachuelos ......................Bass

Trabucco, *a muleteer*...........................Tenor

A Surgeon .....................................Tenor

*Time:* Middle of Eighteenth Century    *Place:* Spain and Italy

*Forza* is customarily criticised for its rambling libretto, and because the destiny which is proclaimed in the title tends to be replaced in the story by the less compelling factor of coincidence. Francis Toye is at some pains to point out that Rivas's play, *Don Alvaro*, is dominated by the principle of the blood-feud, in which facts were more important than intentions, and that to understand the original significance of the play entails an imaginative reconstruction of this outmoded attitude. He also suggests that Rivas, a liberal, may have intended to show that life should be influenced by other considerations than that of the honour of noble Spanish families—in any case, his scenes of popular life were particularly successful.

The overture is a vividly exciting affair, dominated by Leonora's aria from Act II, and the music concerned with 'fate':

Reference is also made to Alvaro's *cantabile con espressione* tune (in A minor) from the fourth act duet, and to themes from the duet between Leonora and Padre Guardiano.

Act I takes place in Leonora's room. She says good night to her father and is then overcome with remorse at the idea of leaving him so suddenly—for she has arranged that very night to elope with her lover, Don Alvaro. In an aria, 'Me pellegrina ed orfana' (As wanderer and orphan), she pictures her friendless lot in a foreign country, for which even the prospect of marriage with her lover cannot console her. It is late; he surely cannot come now—but no sooner are the words spoken than the sound of his horses is heard and he has bounded in through the window, protesting his eternal love for her. His passionate description of the preparations for their elopement evokes, after some hesitation, an equally demonstrative response from Leonora, but the delay proves disastrous, and, before they can escape, the Marchese is in the room, denouncing his daughter's seducer. Alvaro protests his and her innocence, and throws down his pistol in token of his surrender to the mercy of the Marchese. It goes off as it falls and fatally wounds the old man, who curses Leonora as he dies.

Act II. Leonora has been separated from Alvaro in their flight; each believes the other dead, but Don Carlo, Leonora's brother, knows that they are alive and scours the land to revenge himself on the murderer of his father and the sister who has brought dishonour to his family.

The first scene is laid in the inn at the village of Hornachuelos, where are gathered various village worthies, muleteers, servants and a mysterious student, who is no other than Don Carlo in disguise. The company sings and dances until the meal is

announced; Leonora appears for a moment at the door seeking
shelter, just as the student says grace, but she recognises in him
her brother and withdraws. Presently Preziosilla, a gypsy, enters,
telling the guests that war has broken out and that all should
lose no time in going to Italy to fight the Germans. She sings a
song in praise of war and its delights, and proceeds to tell the
fortunes of the assembled company, incidentally informing the
student that his being in disguise cannot be hidden from a fortune-
teller.

Pilgrims can be heard outside, and all join in their prayer, not
least Leonora, who observes from the door and prays to be
delivered from her brother's vengeance. It is a splendid example
of choral writing. Don Carlo plies the muleteer with questions
about the traveller he brought to the inn, and is asked in his turn
and since he is so curious about others, to tell the company his
own story. This he does in a ballad; he is Pereda, a young student,
who has followed his friend Vargas in his quest for the murderer
of his father. The murderer it appears has escaped to South
America, and the sister of Vargas, whom the murderer seduced,
is dead. The mayor says it is late, all bid each other good night,
and, after a final dance, the scene comes to an end.

Leonora continues on her way and at the opening of the next
scene we find her outside the monastery of the 'Madonna degli
Angeli', near Hornachuelos, whither she has been sent for
sanctuary. In the most extended aria of the opera, she prays for
forgiveness for her sin, and takes courage from the sound of the
hymn which can be heard coming from the church. At the beginning of the scene can be heard the 'fate' motive familiar from
the overture, then, after a dramatic recitative, the aria, 'Madre,
pietosa Vergine' (Holy Mother, hear my prayer), whose climax
comes with the great phrase (in the major) of which such use has
already been made in the overture: 'Deh, non m'abbandonar':

Leonora rings the bell, and a window in the door opens to
reveal the head of Fra Melitone, who is impressed to hear that
Father Cleto sent her and agrees to inform the Father Superior
of her presence. He receives her kindly, and knows immediately

who she is when she tells him who sent her. He warns her of the extreme loneliness of the solitary life she proposes to lead in the cave where once before a female penitent lived out her life, but she is determined to go through with her plan, and he, convinced of her steadfastness of purpose, agrees to allow her request. He himself will bring her food daily and in case of urgent danger or the approach of death she can ring a bell to summon help; otherwise, she will never again set eyes on a human being. He gathers the monks together and tells them that once again the cave will be occupied; no one is to approach it or make any attempt to discover the identity of the penitent.

Leonora's scene with the Padre Guardiano is one of the finest in all Verdi, and belongs to the line of great duets to which reference has been made earlier in these pages. The expressive vocal line is enhanced by the contrasting nature of the various sections, whether it be the loose-limbed tune in which Leonora first tells of the gradual awakening of peace in her soul, or the closely knit E major duet in which Padre Guardiano immediately afterwards warns her of the danger she runs in living alone, the long sentences in which Padre Guardiano urges her to draw closer to God, or the passionate phrases she employs to voice her thanks to the salvation she feels she has found. The finale (the short service in which the Father Superior blesses Leonora and warns the monks in future not to approach her solitary cell) is the perfect pendant to a great scene. Padre Guardiano leads them in pronouncing a curse on anyone who violates the sanctity of the cell, and then the sound of Leonora's voice floats out over the male voices of the monks in the prayer to the Virgin, 'La Vergine degli angeli'. It would be difficult to imagine music that more perfectly combined simplicity of means and beauty of effect (see opposite).

Act III.    The scene changes to Italy, near Velletri, where the fighting referred to at the beginning of the previous act is taking place. Don Alvaro and Don Carlo di Vargas, each under assumed names and unknown to the other, have enlisted in the Spanish contingent which is taking part in the fighting. The sound of gambling is heard as Alvaro comes forward to sing his long recitative and aria, 'O tu che in seno agli angeli' (O sainted soul, in rest above), a fitting expression of the torture his lonely soul has suffered since the death of the Marchese di Calatrava, and

before that when his father, related to the last of the Incas, tried to free his country from foreign rule only to meet death on the scaffold.

In response to a cry for help, he rushes offstage, to reappear with none other than his old enemy Don Carlo, whom he has saved from death at the hands of a gang of ruffians. Having exchanged false names, they swear friendship and go off together in answer to an urgent call to arms.

The scene changes, and we see a military surgeon surrounded by soldiers watching the battle from a distance. Victory is to the Italians and the Spaniards, but Don Carlo brings in Alvaro grievously wounded. When Carlo seeks to give his friend the military decoration of the order of Calatrava, he shudders at the name, but a moment later he entrusts Carlo with his last instructions. He has a small casket which contains a letter which must be burnt unopened after his death; will his friend do this for him? Carlo swears to carry out the commission faithfully. The duet, 'Solenne in quest' ora' (In this solemn hour), has become world-famous, partly, perhaps, because of the celebrity of the gramophone record made of it by Caruso and Scotti, but also because of its graceful tune and remarkably apt relationship to the situation (an appropriateness which would be the more frequently noticed if the tenor singing Alvaro paid more attention to the portrayal of a dying man and less to the display of his own voice):

Alvaro is carried away by the surgeon, and Carlo reflects on the secret which lies hidden in the fateful box. His friend trembled at the name of Calatrava; could it be his enemy in disguise? He soliloquises on the temptation the casket presents even to a man of honour, 'Urna fatale del mio destin' (Fatal urn of my destiny), but finds a portrait inside which no oath prevents him from inspecting. It is Leonora's! The secret is out, and his newly found friend is recognised as his old enemy! At this moment a messenger tells him that Alvaro's life is saved; in an *allegro* he rejoices at the prospect of revenge.

The scene changes to a military camp near Velletri. A military patrol passes, and as dawn approaches Don Alvaro can be seen crossing the camp. Carlo calls him, and asks him if he is strong enough to fight a duel. With whom? Has he had no message lately from Don Alvaro, the Indian? Alvaro's protests and offers of friendship are in vain; Carlo insults him until he has provoked the duel he is seeking, only to be interrupted by the patrol on its way home. Alvaro, left alone, resolves to seek sanctuary in a monastery. The scene is in the splendid tradition of the duets for tenor and baritone which Verdi did so incomparably, and it is the greatest pity that recent custom in Italy is to omit it altogether, either with a view to shortening the long opera, or else to save the tenor in what is anyhow a rôle of considerable weight. In any case, the duet is in a false position, as Toye points out, and was originally designed to end the act.

It is dawn. Soldiers polish their equipment, pedlars offer their wares, food and drink is for sale, and Preziosilla offers to tell fortunes until the appearance of a band of recruits gives her an opportunity of leading a tarantella in an effort to dispel their gloom. Mixed up in the dance is Fra Melitone, who extricates himself and treats the company to a discourse on its several vices, the whole thing dressed up in a series of outrageous puns. The soldiers make an attempt to give him a drubbing, but Preziosilla interrupts them and sings a spirited though hardly imaginative 'Rataplan', which ends the act.

Act IV.     The scene shows the cloister of the Convent of the 'Madonna degli Angeli', where a crowd of beggars is assembling to collect the free soup which the monks dole out regularly. Fra Melitone is in charge, and his marked lack of patience and his intense annoyance at being compared unfavourably by the crowd with Padre Raffaello (in reality Alvaro in disguise) make him more than usually short with his customers. Finally, he can bear their torments and their importunities no longer, and he kicks over the cauldron with what remains of the soup inside. The Father Superior, who has been watching, reproaches him gently for his lack of patience, and bids him not complain if Raffaello be preferred to him. Melitone says he likes Raffaello but cannot understand his odd, haunted look—caused, says the Father Superior, by his frequent fasts and his concentration on his duty.

The music of Melitone is always cited as amongst the most interesting in *Forza*, as giving a foretaste of the methods Verdi was to employ years later when writing *Falstaff*. There is a good deal of truth in this view; the rhythms and orchestral accompaniment as well as the shape of the vocal line certainly suggest an entirely new type of character for Verdi.

The monastery door-bell rings violently, and Melitone admits Don Carlo himself, asking for Padre Raffaello. Melitone says there are two of that name in the monastery, but from the description he easily knows which is meant. He goes off to fetch him, while Don Carlo muses on how his hatred for Alvaro was sufficient to penetrate the most unlikely of hiding-places. Alvaro comes in, Carlo discloses himself and immediately challenges him to a duel, producing two swords as he does so from under his cloak. Alvaro pleads with him to renounce his thoughts of vengeance, and believe what he now hears from the mouth of a priest, that his sister Leonora was never dishonoured, that he has nought to avenge but the misfortune which has dogged them both. Alvaro will even do what he says he has never before done, kneel at Don Carlo's feet. Carlo says this act proclaims the baseness of his birth and for a moment Alvaro's feelings threaten to get the better of his self-control, but he chokes down his anger until Carlo strikes him across the face, branding him a coward with the blow. Alvaro's vows are forgotten and he proclaims that he is ready to fight him. They rush off to expiate the blood-feud which has followed them for so long.

The duet is a magnificent passage, perhaps the finest and most expressive for tenor and baritone which Verdi achieved before the days of *Otello*. It is immediately followed by a quick change of scene; the 'fate' motive sounds, and Leonora is seen outside her grotto. In great long phrases of supplication she prays

for the peace which she has never known since the day she first
secluded herself from the world: 'Pace, pace, mio Dio' (Peace,
grant me peace, O Lord). She sees the bread which has been left
for her and which serves only to prolong, as she says, a wretched
life. Suddenly, the sound of fighting can be heard, and, calling
down a curse on whoever dares to profane her solitude, she
returns to her cell.

In a moment, the voice of Carlo can be heard begging for
absolution; he is dying, and Alvaro, distracted that he has once
again the blood of a Vargas on his hands, bangs on the door of
Leonora's cell and begs for help for the dying man. Leonora rings
the bell in her alarm but a moment later appears and is recognised
by Alvaro, who tells her what has happened. She goes to the spot
where her brother lies dying and a few seconds later her cry is
heard as Carlo stabs her, revenge uppermost in his mind even at
his last moment. Alvaro can restrain his anger no longer when
he sees Leonora supported by Padre Guardiano, and he curses
the fate which has brought so much misery on them all. The old
Father Superior in music of great nobility bids him not to curse
but to prostrate himself before the might of Heaven, whither the
angel, who now lies dying, is going. In the presence of her lover
and of the old priest who brought her such salvation as earth can
offer, Leonora dies, and so expiates the curse which fell on them
all with the death of her father.

The final trio is extraordinarily beautiful, and the opera, which
has been attended with so much strife and bloodshed, ends with
music of true serenity. In this last scene we have a typical example
of the prodigality with which Verdi lavished melody on this
opera—and it is primarily for its almost unique melodic richness
that *Forza* is loved by so many; it is one of the most popular of
all Verdi's works in Italy, though its length and the disconnected
nature of the scenes together make it one of the more difficult to
perform satisfactorily.                                    H.

# DON CARLOS

Opera in five acts by Giuseppe Verdi; text by G. Méry and C. du Locle (in French), after Schiller. Première at Opéra, Paris, March 11, 1867, with Marie Sass, Gueymard, Morera, Jean Baptiste Faure, Obin, David, conductor Emil Perrin. First performed at Covent Garden, 1867, with Pauline Lucca, Fricci, Naudin, Grazziani; New York, 1877. Produced in revised version at la Scala, Milan, 1884, with Bianchi-Chiatti, Pasqua, Tamagno, Lhérie, Silvestri, Navarini. Revived Metropolitan, 1920, with Ponselle, Matzenauer, Martinelli, de Luca, Didur, conductor Papi; la Scala, 1926, with Scacciati, Cobelli, Trantoul, conductor Toscanini; Vienna, 1932 (in revised version by Werfel), with Ursuleac, Rünger, Völker, Schipper, Manowarda, conductor Krauss; Covent Garden, 1933, with Cigna, Giani, Lappas, Rimini, Autori, Tomei, conductor Beecham; Venice, 1938, with Grandi, Merli, Valentino, conductor Gui; Sadler's Wells, 1938, with Dusseau, Coates, Tudor Davies. 5-Act version: Florence Festival, 1950, with Caniglia, Stignani, Picchi, Silveri, Christoff, Neri, conductor Serafin; Metropolitan, 1950, with Delia Rigal, Barbieri, Björling, Merrill, Siepi, Hines, conductor Stiedry; Covent Garden, 1958, with Brouwenstijn, Barbieri, Vickers, Gobbi, Christoff, cond. Giulini, producer Visconti.

## CHARACTERS

Elisabetta di Valois, *Queen of Spain* . . . . . . . . . . . . . . Soprano
Principessa Eboli, *her lady-in-waiting* . . . . . . Mezzo-Soprano
Don Carlos, *heir to the Spanish throne* . . . . . . . . . . . . . . Tenor
Rodrigo, *Marquis of Posa* . . . . . . . . . . . . . . . . . . . . . Baritone
Filippo II, *King of Spain* . . . . . . . . . . . . . . . . . . . . . . . . Bass
The Grand Inquisitor . . . . . . . . . . . . . . . . . . . . . . . . . . . Bass
A Monk . . . . . . . . . . . . . . . . . . . . . . . . . . . . . . . . . . . . . Bass
Tebaldo, *Elisabetta's page* . . . . . . . . . . . . . . . . . . . . Soprano
Count Lerma . . . . . . . . . . . . . . . . . . . . . . . . . . . . . . . . Tenor
The Royal Herald . . . . . . . . . . . . . . . . . . . . . . . . . . . . Tenor
A heavenly voice . . . . . . . . . . . . . . . . . . . . . . . . . . . Soprano

*Time:* Mid 16th Century.          *Place:* France and Spain

*Don Carlos* has always suffered from an inherent defect; it was written for Paris, in the five-act, display-conscious tradition which Meyerbeer did so much to establish at that house, and it is therefore too long for modern tastes. In 1884 Verdi undertook, with Ghislanzoni, his librettist for *Aida*, to produce a shorter version, but this entailed, as well as the omission of the ballet music, the jettisoning of most of the important first act, which it is hard to justify artistically. Since then, the most satisfactory revivals of the opera have usually made an attempt at including the first act, whatever they may have cut later on.

Spain is nearing the end of a war with France, and one of the conditions of peace is that the heir to the throne of Spain, Don Carlos (in reality an epileptic and a monster, but represented in Verdi as well as in Schiller as a brilliant young man), should marry Elizabeth the daughter of the King of France.

Act I.    Don Carlos has come secretly to France to see the bride who has been chosen for him. A hunt is in progress near Fontainebleau (there is no prelude to the opera) and Elizabeth and her page Tebaldo are separated from the main body of riders. They disappear in search of their companions and Carlos, alone, sings of the love which the sight of his bride has awakened in his heart. His romance was salvaged in an altered version when Verdi discarded Act I in his attempt at revision. Elizabeth re-appears and Don Carlos offers to escort her home, saying he is a member of the staff of the Spanish envoy. He lights a fire and is questioned by the Princess about the young Spanish Prince to whom she is betrothed but whom she has never met. She fears for her marriage if love does not enter into it. Carlos tells her she need have no fear; the Prince will love her—and he shows her a portrait, which she naturally recognises as his. He declares his love, which she admits she returns. Their duet, which was omitted in the 1884 version, is a particularly lovely inspiration, and the delicate beauty of Elizabeth's phrase, 'Di qual amor, di quant' ardor' (Ah yes, 'tis love), as she recognises the love in her heart, is something that can ill be spared, not only for its own sake but because it is used later in the opera in something approaching the manner of a motive.

Tebaldo returns and warns Elizabeth that the Spanish envoy is approaching to make a formal request for her hand in marriage for his master, the King of Spain himself, not for Don Carlos as had originally been arranged. The two lovers are filled with consternation, but Elizabeth accedes to the prayers of the crowd of courtiers who beg her to acquiesce and so put an end to the war. The acclamations of the crowd mingle with the agonised regrets of Elizabeth and Carlos as the curtain falls.

Act II.   In an effort to forget the misery of the world, Carlos
has taken refuge in the Convent of San Giusto, where his grandfather, Charles V, before him had gone to end his days. Monks
are praying before the tomb of the great Emperor, and one of
them proclaims the uselessness of expecting peace in this life.
Don Carlos remembers the curious stories to the effect that
Charles V is not really dead at all but still living peacefully as a
forgotten monk, and fancies he sees and hears a resemblance to
his grandfather. The bass solo with the chorus is highly impressive, the more particularly since this is the first contact we have
with the influence of the Church, which is to be one of the
dominating features of the opera.

Carlos is overjoyed to see Rodrigo, Marquis of Posa, his
greatest friend, lately returned from Flanders. Carlos confides to
him that he loves none other than his own stepmother—will his
friend turn from him at the news? Rodrigo expresses his determination to help him, and bids him devote himself to the cause
of the oppressed people of Flanders, and forget his own troubles
in his efforts to right their wrongs. They swear eternal friendship,
'Dio, che nell' alma infondere amor' (God, who has filled our
hearts), to a theme which is heard frequently throughout the
opera. It has always seemed to me a noble expression of feeling,
but it has sometimes been criticised for its supposed banality, a
quality which I have never been able to detect in it.

A procession passes in front of the tomb, and the King himself
is seen leading his Queen by the hand. The sight is almost too
much for Carlos, but he is sustained by Rodrigo, and by the
voice of the mysterious monk, who leads the chanting. The scene
ends with a reiteration of the friendship theme.

The scene changes to a garden outside the monastery. The
Queen's entourage wait for their mistress, and Princess Eboli,

supported by the irrepressible Tebaldo, wiles away the time by singing the song of the veil, a Moorish love-romance. With its ambitious cadenzas and rapid coloratura, it is a fine display piece for the mezzo-soprano who sings Eboli.

The Queen leaves the church and makes her way to where her adies are waiting for her. Rodrigo is announced, and gives her a letter he has brought from her mother in Paris, at the same time slipping a note from Carlos into her hand. She reads the message, while Rodrigo takes Eboli apart to tell her the latest news from Paris. The conversation between the two and the asides from Elizabeth are carried on to the accompaniment of a graceful dance rhythm, which most successfully suggests the elegant court atmosphere. Elizabeth thanks Rodrigo and bids him ask some favour. He will, but not for himself. In a short aria he asks for her help and influence with the King in acquiring for Carlos what he most desires, an interview with his father. Eboli, who is in love with Carlos, is struck with the thought that the agitation she has noticed in him when she has been in attendance on the Queen may be due to undeclared love for herself. Elizabeth signifies to Rodrigo that she will see her son, and he contrives to manoeuvre the ladies out of hearing so that the interview takes place in private.

Carlos enters and greets his mother formally, asking for her influence in persuading the King to send him to Flanders. But his outward calm is not proof against contact with the person he loves, and he bitterly reproaches her for her seeming indifference, which, she tells him, is no more than the duty she owes his father. In music of melting tenderness, Carlos shows that he understands her meaning, but it is clear that love for her still dominates his thoughts (example opposite).

Suddenly, he passes into a mood of exaltation and falls senseless at Elizabeth's feet (the only reference in the opera to the fits which appear to have been so common with the real Don Carlos). Elizabeth for a moment fears he is dying, but in his delirium he once again proclaims his love for her. Coming to himself, he takes her in his arms, but she tears herself away, demanding whether he means to murder his father and then lead his mother to the altar? With a cry of grief, Carlos rushes from her presence, and she is left asking for Heaven's assistance in her predicament.

The King leaves the Church to find that his orders have been

disobeyed and that the Queen is unattended. He orders the offending lady-in-waiting, whose turn of duty it was, to return forthwith to her native France. Elizabeth ignores the affront to herself, and does her best to console the unhappy woman in a tender aria.

Philip watches until the Queen withdraws, followed by her ladies, but bids the Marquis of Posa remain behind. Why, he asks, has so tried and trusted a servant of Spain never asked him for a favour—preferment, or even an audience? Rodrigo answers that service is his reward; but there is a favour he would like to ask, not for himself, but for others. He pleads for a relaxation of the measures being taken against the people of Flanders, who are even now dying by the sword and of starvation. Only severity, answers the King, can cure such infidels and rebels of their heresies; and he cites the contentment and peace of the people of Spain as an example of what he hopes to bring to the Flemish. It is a peace of desolation that he brings, replies Rodrigo. Let the King beware lest history say of him: 'This man was Nero!' Let him instead build an empire founded on freedom. The King tells him his dreams are those of youth; but let him have no fear of the throne, rather beware of the Grand Inquisitor, not only for his own sake but because the King wants him as counsellor. He confides his fear over Elizabeth and Carlos to Rodrigo, who takes this confidence in him as a sign that happier times may be at hand for all whom he loves. With a last warning to beware the Inquisition, the King dismisses Rodrigo from his presence.

The second act is dominated by the two duets. That for Elizabeth and Don Carlos is a most moving affair, with its wonderful characterisation of Carlos's hopeless love for Elizabeth and the suggestive description of his delirium. The interview between Philip and Rodrigo shows Verdi's mastery in setting to music not only the clash involved between differing personalities but also the logical type of argument which takes place when the personalities involved are what we would call reasonable, intelligent beings.

Act III.     A masked ball is in progress at the palace in Madrid (it was here that the ballet music originally occurred), and Carlos waits in the Queen's gardens in response to an anonymous note which he has received making the assignation. He sees what he thinks is Elizabeth, and pours out his love to her, until she unmasks and reveals that it is Eboli. He cannot conceal his dismay, and she accuses him of loving the Queen just as the watchful Rodrigo comes upon them. Carlos, he says, is not well and can be held responsible for neither his words nor his actions; but Eboli is not deceived, and in spite of Rodrigo's threat against her life, she promises to exert her power in bringing about their downfall. Rodrigo persuades Carlos to give him any incriminating papers he may have in his possession in case Eboli carries out her threats, and the curtain falls on a *fortissimo* statement in the orchestra of the theme of the oath of friendship.

The second scene is placed in the great square in Madrid, where preparations are afoot for an *auto-da-fé*, the ceremonial punishment of heretics at the stake. The people rejoice in the might of Spain as a procession of monks precedes the mournful band of victims of the Inquisition. The members of the court, headed by the Queen, enter in procession, and, to the acclamation of the crowd and announced by a herald, Philip himself comes ceremoniously through the door of the Cathedral, the Crown of Spain on his head. He repeats the oath which he swore before his coronation, to wage war against the enemies of the Faith. Led by Carlos, six deputies from Flanders fling themselves at his feet protesting their own loyalty and that of his Flemish subjects but begging for relief from their suffering. The King is adamant in his attitude toward them, and an ensemble develops in which some of the court and part of the crowd join in begging for mercy, others, led by the priests, demand death for the traitors and heretics.

Don Carlos stands before his father and asks that he may begin his training for the Crown which will one day adorn his brow by being put as the King's deputy at the head of his Flemish subjects. The King refuses a demand which would create a weapon which might one day be used against Spain itself. Carlos in desperation draws his sword and announces that he will save Flanders; consternation fills the bystanders that he should have dared to draw his sword in the presence of the King. Philip orders that he be disarmed, but no one dare obey, until Rodrigo, who sees that he is otherwise lost, quietly asks for his sword and gives it to the King. The procession advances, the sound of the monks singing the death-knell of the heretics can be heard, and over all a voice from heaven promises peace in the next world to those who are suffering so much in this.

Act IV. The first scene takes place in Philip's own room, where, for the first time in the opera, we see him alone, as a man and not only as a king. In his monologue he betrays his anxiety, more, his acute misery over the failure of his marriage, his loneliness not only as a king, because his state demands it, but as a man, because his wife has no love for him in her heart. The Grand Inquisitor is announced, an old man, ninety years of age, blind but walking erect with the aid of a stick.

He has been sent for; may he know why? The King explains that his son has offended grievously and has publicly taken the part of the heretic Flemish; he intends to exact no penalty from him at all, or else to punish him with nothing less than death. If he decides on the latter alternative, has he the support of Holy Church in so extreme a measure? The Inquisitor says that God was not afraid to give His only Son that the world might be saved. Has the King nothing more to ask of him? No. Then it is his duty, as Inquisitor, to speak to him as the King. The fault of the impetuous Carlos is as nothing to that committed by the man he wishes to denounce; the Marquis of Posa. The King will not agree to this sacrifice, and is castigated by the Inquisitor as a man whose heart is not wholly given to God. Refusing to make any concession whatsoever, the Inquisitor goes his way, leaving behind him a sadder man.

No sooner has the Inquisitor left than Elizabeth rushes into Philip's presence, demanding the King's help in regaining her casket of jewels, which has disappeared from her room. He asks her coldly if what she seeks is the casket on his table; she opens it to reveal a portrait of Carlos. Philip denounces what he describes as her adultery in phrases of ever mounting tension, and Elizabeth faints. Eboli and Rodrigo answer the King's call for help, and Philip himself expresses his bitter regret at his rash and cruel suspicion. Eboli is stricken with conscience at what her jealousy of Carlos and Elizabeth have brought about—it was she who suggested the King look in the jewel case—and Rodrigo sees in the crisis a situation from which he can only rescue Carlos by taking his place as an offering on the altar of liberty. The Queen revives and voices her loneliness and desolation. The two men leave the room and Eboli throws herself at the feet of the Queen to confess a double fault: that she has excited the King's suspicions because of her own jealousy, and that she herself has been guilty of the adultery of which she suspected Elizabeth—she has in fact been the King's mistress. Elizabeth's dignity remains unshaken, but she orders Eboli to leave her presence for ever and choose exile or life in a nunnery if she is to expiate her crime. Left alone, Eboli pours forth her grief and misery at what her fatal beauty has brought about; one thing only remains for her to do before she leaves the court for the last time—she must do whatever is in her power to save Carlos from the threat of death which hangs over him.

The first scene of Act IV of *Don Carlos* is one of the finest in all Verdi's operas. A mere catalogue of what it contains is perhaps enough to give some idea of its varied, many-sided nature,

*Andante mosso cantabile.*

Dor - mi - rò sol      nel manto mio re - gal

and yet to suggest the strong dramatic line which runs through it all. It begins with the greatest of all Verdi's bass arias, the *scena* 'Ella giammai m'amo' (She has no love for me), a remarkable portrayal of the King's anguish and loneliness.

There follows the duet between the two basses, a uniquely varied piece of writing, whose strength is unsurpassed, one makes bold to say, in any operatic music. The clash of personalities is extraordinary, the King, bigot though he is, still relying on logic and reason for his argument, the Inquisitor, impregnable in his privileged stronghold, carrying logic and argument before him in his religious conviction.

At the end, after the King has twice made unsuccessful attempts at reconciliation or at any rate at a kind of working peace, his reserve breaks down, and in a mighty two-octave phrase spanning the bass's top and bottom F's he demands rhetorically whether the throne must always bow the knee to the altar. The short scene between Philip and Elizabeth, particularly the King's measured cursing of his wife's infidelity, is excellent, as is the equally brief but no less expressive scene between Eboli and Elizabeth, but the quartet which divides the two is equally remarkable. It is dominated by Philip's rising phrase, but the Queen's

revival from her swoon is marvellously done, and the whole
quartet is a splendid example of Verdi's ensemble writing. To
crown an act of almost unmatched richness, we have 'O don
fatale' (O fatal beauty), a superb, economical piece of construction, which brings the act to an appropriate close and ends
Eboli's appearances in a blaze of musical glory.

Scene ii is set in Carlos's prison. To him comes Rodrigo,
knowing that the letters from Flanders which were originally
addressed to Carlos have been found in his possession and that
his days are therefore numbered. He bids farewell to his friend
in an expressive aria, 'Per me giunto e il di supremo' (The last
day for me has dawned). A shot rings out and he falls mortally
wounded by an assassin who has crept into the prison after him,
and discharged his arquebus into his back. He tells Carlos ('O
Carlo ascolta') that the Queen will wait for him on the following
day outside the Convent of San Giusto and will see him for the
last time. He dies happy, he says, at the thought that a champion
of liberty survives him in the person of his friend.

Philip makes an attempt to give back his sword to his son, but
Carlos spurns him as the murderer of his friend. A noise can be
heard; it is a mob which has gained entrance to the prison building, crying for liberty and the release of Don Carlos. Eboli herself
is with them, making a last effort to save Carlos from the fate of
his folly. The people demand that Carlos be given up to them,
but at this moment the Inquisitor appears as if from nowhere
and castigates the crowd which has dared to raise its hand against
the Lord's anointed; let them get down on their knees before him.
Once more, the Church has come to the rescue of the throne.

Act V.   The scene is the cloister of San Giusto, as in the first
scene of Act II. Elizabeth sings sadly of the joys she once knew,
of her native France and her love for the youthful Don Carlos,
and of the sorrow she now has in parting from him for ever: 'Tu
che le vanità conoscesti del mondo' (God, who knowest the
hearts and the frailty of mortals). The wide-ranging melody
shows Elizabeth at her full stature as a mature person, and does

S'an-cor si pian-ge in cie - - lo,

something to give the lie to those who look upon this as one of Verdi's less interesting heroines.

The exquisite phrase, originally heard in the duet in Act I and since then associated with her youth in France, recurs as she remembers her past happiness (example on p. 506). The aria finishes with a renewal of her prayer for peace, ending exquisitely *ppp*.

Elizabeth and Carlos meet for a last farewell, and recall the happiness that might have been theirs, turning their attention however from the past and present toward the future, which holds for Carlos a career devoted to the liberal causes that Rodrigo loved so well. It is the last of their three extensive duets, and worthy of the richness of the two that went before. As they take their leave of one another, Philip comes from his hiding-place, seizes Elizabeth, and demands that the Grand Inquisitor, who is with him, shall do his duty towards Carlos. The old priest orders his guards to seize the prince, but Carlos defends himself and backs toward the tomb of Charles V at the rear of the cloister. Suddenly, a voice can be heard coming from it, and the Emperor himself (or a monk in his guise) appears and takes his grandson into the safety of the cloister. The ending has been much criticised as a weakened version of Schiller, where Philip hands his son over to the mercy of the Inquisition, and in some productions an attempt has been made to return to Schiller's original.

*Don Carlos* is in most respects a magnificent opera, weakened only by one less than first-class scene (the spectacular *auto-da-fè*, which obstinately refuses to touch the heights, unlike the triumph scene in *Aida*), and by its excessive length—the five-act production in Florence in 1950, even with some cuts, played with intervals for over five hours! It contains Verdi's greatest bass rôle and one of the greatest of his mezzo-soprano rôles; two superb singing rôles in Elizabeth and Carlos; and an opportunity for a notable baritone to re-create out of the slightly reduced figure of Posa the great liberal of Schiller's play. It also contains one of the most perfect climactic scenes in all Verdi, the first of the fourth act, in which the diverse threads of the drama, which have been developed in the five preceding scenes, are drawn together. The two scenes which follow resolve the conflicts which it has brought to a head—in Act IV, scene ii, Catholic Spain *v.* Protestant Flanders, liberal Rodrigo *v.* established authority (Crown and Church),

Church *v*. State; in Act V, Elizabeth *v*. Eboli (over Carlos), and Philip *v*. Carlos (over Elizabeth and Flanders). With these five major issues at stake, it is hardly surprising that the opera is a long one, any more than it is surprising that the subject elicited some of Verdi's most memorable music.                          H.

## AIDA

Opera in four acts by Giuseppe Verdi; text by Antonio Ghislanzoni from the French prose of Camille du Locle, plot by Mariette Bey. Première at Cairo on December 24, 1871, with Pozzini, Grossi, Mongini, Stella, Medini, Costa, Bottardi, conductor Bottesini. First performed at la Scala, Milan, February 8, 1872, with Stolz, Waldmann, Fancelli, Pandolfini, Maini, conductor Verdi; New York, 1873; Covent Garden, 1876, with Patti, Gindele, Nicolini, Graziani, Capponi, Feitlinger, conductor Bevignani; Her Majesty's Theatre, 1880 (in English), with Minnie Hauk, J. Yorke, Maas, Ludwig, Conly, conductor Randegger. Continuously in the repertories of all leading opera houses. Famous as Aida have been Lilli Lehmann, Nordica, Eames, Gadski, Destinn, Russ, Boninsegna, Raisa, Muzio, Rethberg, Giannini, Ponselle, Arangi-Lombardi, Turner, Cigna, Caniglia, Milanov, Welitsch; as Radames: Jean de Reszke, Tamagno, Caruso, Zenatello, Slezak, Martinelli, Pertile, Lauri-Volpi, Merli, Vinay, del Monaco; as Amneris: Mantelli, Homer, Kirkby Lunn, Mildenburg, Edyth Walker, Matzenauer, Onegin, Minghini-Cattaneo, Stignani, Castagna, Wettergren.

### CHARACTERS

Aida, *an Ethiopian, slave of Amneris* . . . . . . . . . . . . . Soprano
Amneris, *daughter of the King of Egypt* . . . . Mezzo-Soprano
Amonasro, *King of Ethiopia, father of Aida* . . . . . . . Baritone
Radames, *captain of the Egyptian Guard* . . . . . . . . . . . Tenor
Ramphis, *High Priest of Egypt* . . . . . . . . . . . . . . . . . . . Bass
King of Egypt . . . . . . . . . . . . . . . . . . . . . . . . . . . . . . . . . Bass
Messenger . . . . . . . . . . . . . . . . . . . . . . . . . . . . . . . . . . . Tenor
Priests, Soldiers, Ethiopian Slaves, Prisoners, Egyptians, etc.
*Time:* Epoch of the Pharaohs      *Place:* Memphis and Thebes

*Aida* was commissioned by Ismail Pasha, Khedive of Egypt, for the Italian Theatre in Cairo, which opened in November, 1869. The opera was produced there December 24, 1871; not at the opening of the house, as sometimes is erroneously stated. Its success was sensational.

Equally enthusiastic was its reception when brought out at la Scala, Milan, February 8, 1872, under the direction of Verdi himself, who was recalled thirty-two times and presented with an ivory baton and diamond star with the name of Aida in rubies and his own in other precious stones.

It is an interesting fact that *Aida* reached New York before it did any of the great European opera houses save la Scala. It was produced at the Academy of Music under the direction of Max Strakosch, November 26, 1873. I am glad to have heard that performance and several other performances of it that season. For the artists who appeared in it gave a representation that for brilliancy has not been surpassed if, indeed, it has been equalled. In support of this statement it is only necessary to say that Italo Campanini was Radames, Victor Maurel Amonasro, and Annie Louise Cary Amneris. No greater artists have appeared in these rôles in America. Mlle. Torriani, the Aida, while not so distinguished, was entirely adequate. Nanneti as Ramphis, the high priest, Scolara as the King, and Boy as the Messenger, completed the cast.

I recall some of the early comment on the opera. It was said to be Wagnerian. In point of fact *Aida* is Wagnerian only as compared with Verdi's earlier operas. Compared with Wagner himself, it is Verdian—purely Italian. It was said that the fine melody for the trumpets on the stage in the pageant scene was plagiarised from a theme in the Coronation March of Meyerbeer's *Prophète*. Slightly reminiscent the passage is, and, of course, stylistically the entire scene is on Meyerbeerian lines; but these resemblances are no longer of importance.

Paris failed to hear *Aida* until April 1876, and then at the Théâtre Italien, instead of at the Grand Opéra, where it was not heard until March 1880, when Maurel was the Amonasro and Edouard de Reszke, later a favourite basso at the Metropolitan Opera House, the King. In 1855 Verdi's opera, *Les Vêpres Siciliennes* (The Sicilian Vespers) had been produced at the Grand Opéra and occurrences at the rehearsals had greatly angered the composer. The orchestra clearly showed a disinclination to follow the composer's minute directions regarding the manner in which he wished his work interpreted. When, after a conversation with the chef d'orchestre, the only result was plainly an attempt to annoy him, he put on his hat, left the theatre, and did not return. In 1867 his *Don Carlos* met only with a *succès d'estime* at the Opéra. He had not forgotten these circumstances, when the Opéra wanted to give *Aida*. He withheld permission until

1880. But when at last this was given, he assisted at the production, and the public authorities vied in atoning for the slights put upon him so many years before. The President of France gave a banquet in his honour and he was created a Grand Officer of the National Order of the Legion of Honour.

When the Khedive asked Verdi to compose a new opera especially for the new opera house at Cairo, and inquired what the composer's terms would be, Verdi demanded $20,000. This was agreed upon and he was then given the subject he was to treat, *Aida*, which had been suggested to the Khedive by Mariette Bey, the great French Egyptologist. The composer received the rough draft of the story. From this Camille du Locle, a former director of the Opéra Comique, who happened to be visiting Verdi at Busseto, wrote a libretto in French prose, 'scene by scene, sentence by sentence', as he has said, adding that the composer showed the liveliest interest in the work and himself suggested the double scene in the finale of the opera. The French prose libretto was translated into Italian verse by Antonio Ghislanzoni, who wrote more than sixty opera librettos, *Aida* being the most famous. Mariette Bey brought his archaeological knowledge to bear upon the production. 'He revived Egyptian life of the time of the Pharaohs; he rebuilt ancient Thebes, Memphis, the Temple of Phtah; he designed the costumes and arranged the scenery. And under these exceptional circumstances, Verdi's new opera was produced.'

Verdi's score was ready a year before the work had its première, the production being delayed by force of circumstances. Scenery and costumes were made by French artists, but before these accessories could be shipped to Cairo, the Franco-Prussian war broke out. They could not be got out of Paris, and their delivery was delayed accordingly.

Does the score of *Aida* owe any of its charm, passion, and dramatic stress to the opportunity thus afforded Verdi of going over it and carefully revising it, after he had considered it finished? Quite possibly. For we know that he made changes, eliminating, for instance, a chorus in the style of Palestrina, which he did not consider suitable to the priesthood of Isis. Even this one change resulted in condensation, a valuable quality, and in leaving the exotic music of the temple scene entirely free to exert to the full its fascination of local colour and atmosphere.

The story is unfolded in four acts and seven scenes.

Act I. Scene i.    After a very brief but beautiful prelude, based on the theme associated with Aida (heard at the outset) and a descending figure later connected with the priests, the curtain rises on a hall in the King's palace at Memphis. Through a high gateway at the back are seen the temples and palaces of Memphis and the pyramids.

It had been supposed that, after the invasion of Ethiopia by the Egyptians, the Ethiopians would be a long time in recovering from their defeat. But Amonasro, their king, has swiftly rallied the remnants of his defeated army, gathered new levies to his standard, and crossed the frontier—all this with such extraordinary rapidity that the first news of it has reached the Egyptian court in Memphis through a messenger hot-foot from Thebes with the startling word that the sacred city itself is threatened.

While the priests are sacrificing to Isis in order to learn from the goddess whom she chooses as leader of the Egyptian forces, Radames, a young warrior, indulges in the hope that he may be the choice. To this hope he joins the further one that, returning victorious, he may ask the hand in marriage of Aida, an Ethiopian slave of the Egyptian King's daughter, Amneris. To these aspirations he gives expression in the romance, 'Celeste Aida' (Radiant Aida).

Ce - leste A - i - da

It ends effectively with the following phrase:

un tro-no vicino al sol, un tro-no vicino al sol

He little knows that Aida is of royal birth or that Amneris herself, the King's daughter, is in love with him and, having noted the glances he has cast upon Aida, is fiercely jealous of her—a jealousy that forms the mainspring of the story and leads to its tragic dénouement.

A premonition of the emotional forces at work in the plot is given in the 'Vieni, o diletta' (Come dearest friend), beginning as

a duet between Amneris and Aida and later becoming a trio for
them and Radames. In this the Princess feigns friendship for
Aida, but, in asides, discloses her jealous hatred of her.

Meanwhile the Egyptian hosts have gathered before the temple.
There the King announces that the priests of Isis have learned
from the lips of that goddess the name of the warrior who is to
lead the army—Radames! It is the Princess herself who, at this
great moment in his career, places the royal standard in his hands.
But amid the acclaims that follow, as Radames, to the strains of
march and chorus, is conducted by the priests to the temple of
Phtah to be invested with the consecrated armour, Amneris notes
the fiery look he casts upon Aida. Is this the reason Radames,
young, handsome, brave, has failed to respond to her own
guarded advances? Is she, a princess, to find a successful rival in
her own slave?

Meanwhile Aida herself is torn by conflicting emotions. She
loves Radames. When the multitude shouts 'Ritorna vincitor!'
(Victorious return!) she joins in the acclamation. Yet it is against
her own people he is going to give battle, and the Ethiopians are
led by their king, Amonasro, her father. For she, too, is a princess,
as proud a princess in her own land as Amneris herself, and it is
because she is a captive and a slave that her father has so swiftly
rallied his army and invaded Egypt in a desperate effort to rescue
her, facts which for obvious reasons she has carefully concealed
from her captors.

It is easy to imagine Aida's agonised feelings since Radames
has been chosen head of the Egyptian army. If she prays to her
gods for the triumph of the Ethiopian arms, she is betraying her
lover. If she asks the gods of victory to smile upon Radames, she
is a traitress to her father, who has taken up arms to free her,
and to her own people. Small wonder if she exclaims, as she
contemplates her own wretched state:

'Never on earth was heart torn by more cruel agonies. The
sacred names of father, lover, I can neither utter nor remember.
For the one—for the other—I would weep, I would pray!'

The lines to which Aida's aria is set have been highly praised.
They furnished the composer with opportunity, of which he made
full use, to express conflicting emotions in music of dramatic
force and the concluding passage, 'Numi pieta' (Pity, kind
heaven), is of extraordinary beauty:

Nu-mi pie-tà Del mio sof-frir! Spe-me non v'ha del mio do lor

Scene ii.  Ramphis, the high priest, at the foot of the altar; priests and priestesses; and afterwards Radames are shown in the Temple of Vulcan at Memphis. A mysterious light descends from above. A long row of columns, one behind the other, is lost in the darkness; statues of various deities are visible; in the middle of the scene, above a platform rises the altar, surmounted by sacred emblems. From golden tripods comes the smoke of incense.

A chant of the priestesses, accompanied by harps, is heard from the interior. Radames enters unarmed. While he approaches the altar, the priestesses execute a sacred dance. On the head of Radames is placed a silver veil. He is invested with consecrated armour, while the priests and priestesses resume the religious chant and dance.

The entire scene is saturated with local colour—piquant, exotic, it is as Egyptian to the ear as to the eye. You see the temple, you hear the music of its devotees, and that music sounds as distinctively Egyptian as if Mariette Bey had unearthed two examples of ancient Egyptian temple music and placed them at the composer's disposal. It is more likely, however, that the themes are original with Verdi and that the Oriental tone colour, which makes the music of the scene so fascinating, is due to his employment of certain intervals peculiar to the music of Eastern people. The interval, which, falling upon Western ears, gives an Oriental sound to the scale, consists of three semi-tones. In the very Eastern sounding themes in the temple scenes in *Aida*, these intervals are G to F flat, and D to C flat.

The sacred chant,

twice employs the interval between D and C flat, the first time descending, the second time ascending, in which latter it sounds more characteristic to us, because we regard the scale as having an upward tendency, whereas in Oriental systems the scale seems to have been regarded as tending downward.

In the sacred dance,

the interval is from G to F flat. The intervals, where employed in the two music examples just cited, are bracketed. The interval of three semi-tones—the characteristic of the Oriental scale—could not be more clearly shown than it is under the second bracket of the sacred dance.

Act II. Scene i.    In this scene, which takes place in a hall in the apartments of Amneris, the Princess adopts strategy to discover if Aida returns the passion which she suspects in Radames. Messengers have arrived from the front with news that Radames has put the Ethiopians to utter rout and is returning with many trophies and captives. Naturally Aida is distraught. Is her lover safe? Was her father slain? It is while Aida's mind and heart are agitated by these questions that Amneris chooses the moment to test her feelings and wrest from her the secret she longs yet dreads to fathom.

The Princess is reclining on a couch in her apartment in the palace at Thebes, whither the court has repaired to welcome the triumphant Egyptian army. Slaves are adorning her for the festival or agitating the air with large feather fans. Moorish slave boys dance for her delectation and her attendants sing:

> While on thy tresses rain
> Laurels and flowers interwoven,
> Let songs of glory mingle
> With strains of tender love.

In the midst of these festive preparations Aida enters, and Amneris, craftily feigning sympathy for her lest she be grieving over the defeat of her people and the possible loss in battle of someone dear to her, affects to console her by telling her that Radames, the leader of the Egyptians, has been slain.

It is not necessary for the Princess to watch the girl intently in order to note the effect upon her of the sudden and cruelly contrived announcement. Almost as suddenly, having feasted her eyes on the slave girl's grief, the Princess exclaims: 'I have deceived you; Radames lives!'

'He lives!' Tears of gratitude instead of despair now moisten Aida's eyes as she raises them to Heaven.

'You love him; you cannot deny it!' cries Amneris, forgetting in her furious jealousy her dignity as a Princess. 'But know, you have a rival. Yes—in me. You, my slave, have a rival in your mistress, a daughter of the Pharaohs!'

Having fathomed her slave's secret, she vents the refined cruelty of her jealous nature upon the unfortunate girl by commanding her to be present at the approaching triumphant entry of Radames and the Egyptian army:

' Come, follow me, and you shall learn if you can contend with me—you, prostrate in the dust, I on the throne beside the king!'

What has just been described is formulated by Verdi in a duet for Amneris and Aida, 'Fu la sorte dell' armi a' tuoi funesta ('Neath the chances of battle succumb thy people), which expresses the craftiness and subtlety of the Egyptian Princess, the conflicting emotions of Aida, and the dramatic stress of the whole episode.

This phrase especially expresses the combined haughtiness and jealousy in the attitude of Amneris toward Aida:

Scene ii.    Brilliant indeed is the spectacle to which Aida is compelled to proceed with the Princess. It is near a group of palms at the entrance to the city of Thebes that the King has elected to give Radames his triumph. Here stands the temple of Ammon. Beyond it a triumphal gate has been erected. When the King enters to the cheers of the multitude and followed by his gaudily clad court, he takes his seat on the throne surmounted by a purple canopy. To his left sits Amneris, singling out for her disdainful glances the most unhappy of her slaves.

A blast of trumpets, and the victorious army begins its defile past the throne. After the foot-soldiers come the chariots of war; then the bearers of the sacred vases and statues of the gods, and a troupe of dancing girls carrying the loot of victory. A great flourish of trumpets, an outburst of acclaim, and Radames, proudly standing under a canopy borne high on the shoulders of twelve of his officers, is carried through the triumphal gate and into the presence of his King. As the young hero descends from the canopy, the monarch, too, comes down from the throne and embracing him exclaims:

'Saviour of your country, I salute you. My daughter with her own hand shall place the crown of laurels upon your brow.' And when Amneris, suiting her action to her father's words, crowns Radames, the King continues: 'Now ask of me whatever you most desire. I swear by my crown and by the sacred gods that nothing shall be denied to you this day!'

But although no wish is nearer the heart of Radames than to obtain freedom for Aida, he does not consider the moment as yet opportune. Therefore he requests that first the prisoners of war be brought before the King. When they enter, one of them, by his proud mien and spirited carriage, easily stands forth from the rest. Hardly has Aida set eyes upon him than she utters the startled exclamation, 'My father!'

It is indeed none other than Amonasro, the Ethiopian king, who, his identity unknown to the Egyptians, has been made captive by them. Swiftly gliding over to where Aida stands, he whispers to her not to betray his rank to his captors. Then, turning to the Egyptian monarch, he craftily describes how he has seen the king of Ethiopia dead at his feet from many wounds, and concludes by entreating clemency for the conquered. Not only do the other captives and Aida join in his prayer, but the people, moved by his words and by his noble aspect, beg their king to spare the prisoners. The priests, however, protest. The gods have delivered these enemies into the hands of Egypt; let them be put to death lest, emboldened by a pardon so easily obtained, they should rush to arms again.

Meanwhile Radames has had eyes only for Aida, while Amneris notes with rising jealousy the glances he turns upon her hated slave. At last Radames, carried away by his feelings, himself joins in the appeal for clemency. 'Oh, King,' he exclaims, 'by the sacred gods and by the splendour of your crown, you swore to grant my wish this day! Let it be life and liberty for the Ethiopian prisoners.' But the high priest urges that even if freedom is granted to the others, Aida and her father be detained as hostages and this is agreed upon. Then the King, as a crowning act of glory for Radames, leads Amneris forth, and addressing the young warrior, says:

'Radames, the country owes everything to you. Your reward shall be the hand of Amneris. With her one day you shall reign over Egypt.'

A great shout goes up from the multitude. Unexpectedly Amneris sees herself triumphant over her rival, the dream of her heart fulfilled, and Aida bereft of hope, since for Radames to refuse the hand of his king's daughter would mean treason and death. And so while all seemingly are rejoicing, two hearts are sad and bewildered. For Aida, the man she adores appears lost to her for ever and all that is left to her, the tears of hopeless love; while to Radames the heart of Aida is worth more than the throne of Egypt, and its gift, with the hand of Amneris, is like the unjust vengeance of the gods descending upon his head.

This is the finale of the second act. It has been well said that not only is it the greatest effort in this style of the composer, but also one of the grandest conceptions of modern musical and specifically operatic art. The importance of the staging, the magnificence of the spectacle, the diversity of characterisation, and the strength of action of the drama all conspire to keep at an unusually high level the inspiration of the composer.

The triumphal chorus, 'Gloria all' Egitto' (Glory to Egypt), is sonorous and can be rendered with splendid effect. It is preceded by a march.

Then comes the chorus of triumph.

Voices of women join in the acclaim.

The priests sound a warning note.

Del - la vit - to - ria a - gliarbi-tri su - pre-mi

The trumpets of the Egyptian troops execute a most brilliant modulation from A flat to B natural. The reference here is to the long, straight trumpets with three valves (only one of which, however, is used). These trumpets, in groups of three, precede the divisions of the Egyptian troops. The trumpets of the first group are tuned in A flat.

When a second group enters and intones the same stirring march theme in B natural, the enharmonic modulation to a tone higher gives a immediate and vastly effective 'lift' to the music and the scene

The entrance of Radames, borne on high under a canopy by

PLATE XIX. *Don Carlos*: Gobbi and Brouwenstijn in Act II of Visconti's production at Covent Garden, 1958.

PLATE XX. Renata Tebaldi and Ramon Vinay in Act III of *Otello*, during the visit of la Scala, Milan, to Covent Garden 1950.

twelve officers, is a dramatic climax to the spectacle. But a more emotional one is to follow.

The recognition of King Amonasro by his daughter; the supplication of the captives; the plea of Radames and the people in their favour; the vehement protests of the priests who, in the name of the gods of Egypt, demand their death; the diverse passions which agitate Radames, Aida, and Amneris; the hope of vengeance that Amonasro cherishes—all these conflicting feelings are musically expressed with complete success. The structure is reared upon Amonasro's plea to the King for mercy for the Ethiopian captives, 'Ma tu, re, tu signore possente' (But thou, O king, thou puissant lord).

When the singer, who takes the rôle of Amonasro, is also a good actor, he will know how to convey, between the lines of this supplication, his secret thoughts and unavowed hope for the reconquest of his freedom and his country. After the Egyptian King has bestowed upon Radames the hand of Amneris, the chorus, 'Gloria all' Egitto', is heard again, and, above its sonorous measures, Aida's cry:

> What hope now remains for me?
> To him, glory and the throne;
> To me, oblivion—the tears
> Of hopeless love.

It is to some extent due to Verdi's management of the score to this elaborate scene that *Aida* not only has superseded all spectacular operas that came before it, but has held its own against and survived all those that have come since. The others were merely spectacular; in *Aida* the surface radiates and glows because beneath it seethe the fires of conflicting human passion. In other operas spectacle is merely spectacle; in *Aida* it clothes in brilliant habiliments the forces of impending and on-rushing tragedy.

Act III.     That tragedy further advances toward its consummation in the present act.

It is a beautiful moonlight night on the banks of the Nile— moonlight whose silvery rays are no more exquisite than the

music that seems steeped in them. Half concealed in the foliage
is the temple of Isis, from which issues the sound of women's
voices, softly chanting. A boat approaches the shore and out of
it steps Amneris and the high priest, with a train of closely veiled
women and several guards. The Princess is about to enter upon
a vigil in the temple to implore the favour of the goddess before
her nuptials with Radames.

For a while after they have entered the temple, the shore seems
deserted. But from the shadow of a grove of palms Aida cautiously
emerges into the moonlight. In song she breathes forth memories
of her native land: 'Oh, patria mia, mai più ti rivedrò' (Oh,
native land, I ne'er shall see thee more).

O cieli az-zur-ri a dol-ci au-re na-ti - - ve.

It is an aria whose freedom of form and richly expressive
melodies have won it admirers ever since the first performance,
and there is no better known aria in the repertory of the Italian
dramatic soprano. Here Radames has asked Aida to meet him.
Is it for a last farewell? If so, the Nile shall be her grave. She
hears a swift footfall, and turning, in expectation of seeing
Radames, beholds her father. He has fathomed her secret and
divined that she is here to meet Radames—the betrothed of
Amneris! Cunningly Amonasro works upon her feelings. Would
she triumph over her rival? The Ethiopians again are in arms.
Again Radames is to lead the Egyptians against them. Let her
discover from him the path which he intends to take with his
army and that path shall be converted into a fatal ambush.

At first the thought is abhorrent to Aida, but her father by
craftily inciting her love of country and no less her jealousy and
despair, at last is able to wrest consent from her; then draws
back into the shadow as he hears Radames approaching.

It is difficult to bring Aida to make the designs of her father
agree with her love for the young Egyptian chief. But the subtlety
of the score, its warmth, its varied and ably managed expression,
make plausible the submission of the young girl to the adjurations
of Amonasro, and excusable a decision of which she does not
foresee the consequences. To restore the crown to her father, to

view again her own country, to escape an ignominious servitude, to prevent her lover becoming the husband of Amneris, her rival, —such are the thoughts which assail her during this duet, and they are quite capable of disturbing for a moment her better reason.

As she is still reluctant to lure from her lover the secret of the route by which, in the newly planned invasion of her country, the Egyptians expect to enter Ethiopia, Amonasro changes his tactics and conjures up for her in music a vision of the carnage among her people, and finally invokes her mother's ghost, until, in pianissimo, dramatically contrasting with the force of her father's savage imprecation, she whispers, 'O patrio! quanto mi costi!' (Oh, native land! how much thou demandest of me!).

This duet of Aida and Amonasro is in the line of Verdi's most famous duets. Its dramatic effectiveness is enormous and no-where is there a better example of his skill in advancing the drama in purely musical terms. Amonasro clinches his ascendancy over Aida in a great phrase which is a close descendant of Leonora's in *Forza*.

Pen - sa che un po    po - lo vin - to, straz - zia - to

Amonasro leaves. Aida awaits her lover. When she somewhat coldly meets Radames's renewed declaration of love with the bitter protest that the rites of another love are awaiting him, he unfolds his plan to her. He will lead the Egyptians to victory, and on returning with these fresh laurels, he will prostrate him-self before the King, lay bare his heart to him, and ask for the hand of Aida as a reward for his services to his country. But Aida is well aware of the power of Amneris and that her vengeance would swiftly fall upon them both. She can see but one course to safety—that Radames join her in flight to her native land, where, amid forest groves and the scent of flowers, and all for-getful of the world, they will dream away their lives in love. This is the beginning of the dreamy yet impassioned love duet— 'Fuggiam gli ardori inospiti' (Ah, fly from where these burning skies). She implores him in passionate accents to escape with her.

Enthralled by the rapture in her voice, thrilled by the vision of
happiness she conjures up before him, he forgets for the moment
country, duty, all else save love; and exclaiming, 'Love shall be
our guide!' turns to fly with her.

This duet, charged with exotic rapture, opens with recitativo
phrases for Aida. I have selected two passages for quotation: 'Là
tra foreste vergini' (There 'mid the virgin forest groves) and 'In

estasi la terra scorderem' (In ecstasy the world forgotten).

But Aida, feigning alarm, asks:

'By what road shall we avoid the Egyptian host?'

'The path by which our troops plan to fall upon the enemy
will be deserted until to-morrow.'

'And that path?'

'The pass of Napata.'

A voice echoes his words, 'The pass of Napata.'

'Who hears us?' exclaims Radames.

'The father of Aida and king of the Ethiopians,' and Amonasro
issues forth from his hiding-place. He has uncovered the plan of
the Egyptian invasion, but the delay has been fatal. For at the
same moment there is a cry of 'Traitor!' from the temple.

It is the voice of Amneris, who with the high priest has overheard all. Amonasro, baring a dagger, would throw himself upon
his daughter's rival, but Radames places himself between them
and bids the Ethiopian king fly with Aida. Amonasro, drawing
his daughter away with him, disappears in the darkness; while
Radames, with the words, 'Priest of Isis, I remain with you,'
delivers himself a prisoner into his hands.

Act IV. Scene i.   In a hall of the Royal Palace Amneris
awaits the passage, under guard, of Radames to the dungeon
where the priests are to sit in judgment upon him. She now bitterly repents the doom her jealousy is about to bring upon the

man she loves and calls to the guard to bring Radames to her.
Their duet is a magnificently dramatic passage as Amneris alter-

nately implores Radames to exculpate himself, and rages at his
refusal to do so. Radames's world has fallen around him: not
being able to possess Aida he will die.

He is conducted to the dungeon, from where, as from the
bowels of the earth, she hears the sombre voices of the priests.

Three times Ramphis accuses Radames of treason, and three
times Radames is silent in face of the accusation.

The dramatically condemnatory 'Traditor!' is a death-knell
for her lover in the ears of Amneris. And after each accusation,
silence from Radames, and a cry from the priests of 'Traitor!'
Amneris realises only too well that his approaching doom is to
be entombed alive. Her revulsions of feeling from hatred to love
and despair find vent in highly dramatic musical phrases. In fact
Amneris dominates this scene, which, with its frenzied curse of
the cold-hearted priests, is one of the most powerful passages for
mezzo-soprano in all opera.

Scene ii.    This is the famous double scene. The stage setting
is divided into two floors. The upper floor represents the interior
of the Temple of Vulcan, resplendent with light and gold; the
lower floor a subterranean hall and long rows of arcades which
are lost in the darkness. A colossal statue of Osiris, with the
hands crossed, sustains the pilasters of the vault.

In the temple Amneris and the priestesses kneel in prayer. And
Radames? Immured in the dungeon and, as he thinks, doomed
to perish alone, he sees a form slowly take shape in the darkness,
and his own name, uttered by the tender accents of a familiar
voice, falls upon his ear. It is Aida. Anticipating the death to
which he will be sentenced, she has secretly made her way into
the dungeon before his trial and there hidden herself to find reunion with him in death. And so, while in the temple above them
the unhappy Amneris kneels and implores the gods to vouchsafe
Heaven to him whose death she has compassed, Radames and
Aida, blissful in their mutual sacrifice, await the end.

From 'Celeste Aida', Radames's apostrophe to his beloved, with which the opera opens, to the muted passion and unearthly stillness of 'O, terra, addio' (Oh, earth, farewell!), which is the

swan song of Radames and Aida, united in death in the stone-sealed vault—such is the tragic fate of love, as set forth in this beautiful and eloquent score by Giuseppe Verdi.     K.

# OTELLO

Opera in four acts by Giuseppe Verdi; text by Arrigo Boito, after Shakespeare's play. Première at la Scala, Milan, February 5, 1887, with Pantaleone, Tamagno, Maurel, conductor Faccio. First performed in New York, 1888, with Eva Tetrazzini, Marconi (later Campanini), Galassi; Lyceum Theatre, London, 1889, with Cataneo, Tamagno, Maurel, conductor Faccio; Covent Garden, 1891, with Albani, Jean de Reszke, Maurel; Metropolitan, New York, 1894, with Albani, Tamagno, Maurel. Revived Covent Garden, 1926, with Lehmann, Zenatello, Stabile; 1928, with Sheridan, Zanelli, Inghilleri; 1933, with Pampanini, Melchior, Rimini; 1937, with Ciani (later Norena), Martinelli, Formichi (later Tibbett), conductor Beecham; 1950, by Company of la Scala, Milan, with Tebaldi, Vinay, Bechi, conductor de Sabata. Revived at Metropolitan, 1902, with Eames, Alvarez, Scotti; 1937, with Rethberg, Martinelli, Tibbett, conductor Panizza. Revived at la Scala, 1927, with Scacciati, Trantoul, Stabile, conductor Toscanini; 1935, with Caniglia, Merli, Stabile, conductor Marinuzzi; 1938, with Caniglia, Merli, Biasini, conductor de Sabata; 1942, with Caniglia, Lauri-Volpi, Stabile, conductor Marinuzzi; 1947, with Caniglia, Vinay, Bechi, conductor de Sabata. After Tamagno's death, Zenatello and Slezak became the leading international exponents of the title rôle, to be followed by Zanelli and later Martinelli, and (after 1945) by Vinay. Other famous singers of the title rôle have included Pertile and (in England) Frank Mullings.

## CHARACTERS

Otello, *a Moor, general in the Venetian army* . . . . . . . . Tenor

Iago, *his ensign* . . . . . . . . . . . . . . . . . . . . . . . . . . . . . . Baritone

Cassio, *his lieutenant* . . . . . . . . . . . . . . . . . . . . . . . . Tenor

Roderigo, *a Venetian gentleman* . . . . . . . . . . . . . . . . . . Tenor

Lodovico, *ambassador of the Venetian republic* . . . . . . . . Bass

Montano, *predecessor of Otello in Cyprus* . . . . . . . . . . . Bass

A Herald . . . . . . . . . . . . . . . . . . . . . . . . . . . . . . . . . . . . . . . Bass

Desdemona, *wife to Otello* . . . . . . . . . . . . . . . . . . . . Soprano

Emilia, *Iago's wife and Desdemona's lady* ...Mezzo-Soprano
Soldiers and Sailors of the Republic, Venetian ladies and
gentlemen, Cypriot men and women
*Time:* End of the Fifteenth Century *Place:* A seaport in Cyprus

*Otello* has been described as the 'perfect' opera. It first appeared nearly sixteen years after Aida, since when only the composition of the *Manzoni Requiem* (1884), itself a work on the very
highest level, showed the public that the ageing composer had
not actually given up composition. In *Otello* Verdi was working
with one of Italy's foremost poets, Boito, who was in his own
right a composer of rank, to produce an opera at the very height
of his powers. The enthusiasm engendered by its first performances gave way to something closer to respect as the years went
by, and for some time it was regarded as an opera which would
never be popular, an impression which lasted until quite recently.
Now, however, a performance of *Otello* which is not sold out is
a rarity, and the opera is as much a part of the repertory—in
spite of the difficulty of casting the title rôle—as *Don Giovanni*
or *Tristan*.

In *Otello* as in *Macbeth*, his previous Shakespearean opera,
Verdi had a hand in the construction of the libretto, although
Boito must have the credit for the remarkable feat of compression
which has gone toward it. In Shakespeare's play there are
nearly 3,500 lines; in the opera under 800. The Venetian scenes
have been cut out, and the four acts are each continuous with
(in the modern, not the Shakespearean sense) no more than a
single change of scene (in Act III).

In Act I, the chorus waits for the arrival of the victorious
Otello's ship out of the storm. Iago meanwhile plots with
Roderigo and succeeds later in making Cassio drunk; there is a
fight which is interrupted by Otello, who deprives Cassio of his
office. Desdemona enters and the act ends with a duet.

In Act II, Iago advises Cassio to look for reinstatement as
Otello's lieutenant through Desdemona's influence, and, left
alone, soliloquises on the futility of life and the glory of evil (the
'Credo'). There follows the first phase of the planting of the seed
of jealousy in Otello's heart, an interruption from women of the
island who come to serenade Desdemona, her pleading of
Cassio's cause, the offer of the handkerchief to bind Otello's head

and Iago's theft of it as it falls. Iago presses his advantage and Otello's peace is gone. The account of Cassio's dream leads to the joint oath of vengeance which ends the act.

The Venetian ambassadors are announced as in harbour at the beginning of Act III, when Otello asks Desdemona for the handkerchief, is put off, and finishes by insulting her. Iago stations him behind a column to see Cassio play unwittingly with the handkerchief, and the two plot Desdemona's death in half a dozen sentences as the ambassadors enter. Their reception, the striking of Desdemona, and a general ensemble lead to Otello's frantic dismissal of the assembly; he lies prostrate as the curtain falls.

Act IV, in Desdemona's bedroom, consists of the Willow Song and prayer, murder, and the death of Otello.

Act I.    In the background, a quay and the sea; a tavern with an arbour; it is evening. After the crashing opening chord, Otello's ship can be seen making for port through a heavy storm. Among the crowd of watchers who exclaim upon the danger to the vessel, are Iago and Roderigo. The storm prepares vividly for our first encounter with Otello, who is, as it is obvious he must be, the dominating figure of the opera. His opening shout of triumph, 'Esultate! l'orgoglio musulmano sepolto e in mar' (Hear glad tidings. Our wars are done. The ocean has whelmed the Turk), makes a splendid entrance, and shows the warrior in all his glory, unhurried and unrivalled, in a way that perhaps Shakespeare without the help of music never quite achieves.

Otello ascends the steps to the quay, is acclaimed by the crowd, and proceeds to the castle followed by Cassio, Montano, and soldiers. The people start a wood fire and gather about it dancing and singing: 'Fuoco di gioia' (Flame brightly burning). It transpires in talk between Iago and Roderigo that Iago hates Otello,

to whom he is outwardly so devoted, because he has advanced
Cassio over him, and that Roderigo is in love with Desdemona.

The fire dies out, the storm has ceased. Now comes the scene
in which Iago purposely makes Cassio drunk, in order to cause
his undoing. He sings a drinking song, 'Inaffia l'ugola' (Then let

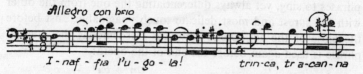

me the canakin clink), which Cassio tries unsuccessfully to repeat
after him; under the influence of the liquor Cassio resents the
taunts of Roderigo, which Iago has instigated. Montano tries to
quiet them, Cassio draws, and, in the fight that follows, Montano
is wounded. The tumult brings Otello to the scene, and, with an
imperious call, he brings the brawl to an end (Boito's use of
'Keep up your bright swords'—'Abasso le spade'—at this point
is evidence of his care for detail). Cassio is dismissed from the
Moor's service, and Iago has scored his first triumph.

The people disperse, quiet settles upon the scene, and Otello
and Desdemona are alone. At her first musical entrance, Desdemona is to some extent characterised by her very isolation, far
more so than if she had been shown on the quayside to welcome
her husband. Her presence brings forth an entirely new aspect of
Otello's character. So far, we have seen only the man of authority,
but in the love duet Otello the poet is put forward with a per-
suasiveness that is to keep this side of him fresh in the minds of
the audience, however low he may fall for the rest of the drama.

For the duet Boito has used lines from the Senate scene of Shakespeare's Act I, and also from Othello's welcome to Desdemona
in Cyprus.

This is Verdi's only full-scale love duet in which there is no sense of urgency or restriction; all the previous examples, however beautiful, have been either illicit or liable to interruption at every moment. In his music, the composer encompasses the sensitivity of both lovers, the mature yet impetuous Otello, the serene but passionate Desdemona, frequently giving them the same phrases to sing, yet always differentiating the one from the other with the surest and most delicate touch imaginable. Just before the close of the act, Otello embraces Desdemona; the musical phrase is used again before the end of the opera:

The music is in the form of one of those long, quasi-conversational duets which the composer made so peculiarly his own, and which, from his very earliest operas to this one, are to be the vehicles of some of his most subtle expression. There would be many to support the claim that this is the most beautiful love music ever written.

Act II.    A hall on the ground floor of the castle. Iago, planning to make Otello jealous of Desdemona, counsels Cassio to induce the Moor's wife to plead for his reinstatement. When he is alone, Iago sings his famous Credo: 'Credo in un Dio crudel che m'ha creato simile a se' (I believe in a cruel God, who has fashioned me in his own image). Though this is generally looked on as a masterpiece of invective, it can be regarded as a simplification of Shakespeare's Iago, the lines and the sentiments being original to Boito. Trumpets, employed in what may be termed a declamatory manner, are conspicuous in the accompaniment.

Iago, seeing Otello approach, leans against a column and looks fixedly in the direction of Desdemona and Cassio, exclaiming, as Otello enters, 'Ha! I like not that.' As in the corresponding scene in the play, this leads up to the questioning of him by Otello and to Iago's crafty answers, which not only apply the match to, but also fan the flame of Otello's jealousy. The temptation of Otello by Iago is set to music that is suggestive and fluid to a marked degree. Every word has due weight, and the rising temperature of the music throughout the act is exactly calculated to fit the growing and unremitting intensity of the play at this point.

Now comes the interruption of the madrigal; by its end, Otello is once more under the spell of Desdemona's beauty and transparent innocence, and is prepared to put suspicion behind him. But in a moment she has asked him to pardon Cassio, has asked again when he refuses gently to consider the subject at such a juncture, and then accused him of ill-temper in his answer. In the quartet which follows, between Desdemona, Emilia, Otello, and Iago, the poison works, and at its end Otello dismisses Desdemona, but not before Iago has had the opportunity to steal the handkerchief round which so much of the rest of the plot is to turn.

Otello and Iago are left alone again, and Otello voices his grief at the loss of his peace of mind in his present wretched and suspicious state: 'Ora e per sempre addio' (Now and for ever, farewell). It is the equivalent of the farewell to arms in the play, and the type of musical expression used here is far more straightforward than in the earlier part of the act, as befits Otello decided as compared with Otello perplexed.

Iago makes pretence of calming him, but to such a fury is the Moor aroused that he seizes Iago, hurls him to the ground, and threatens to kill him should his accusations against Desdemona prove false. Iago ventures on yet another and bolder step, and describes a dream he says Cassio has had while sharing a room with him. He talked openly in his sleep of his love for Desdemona, and Iago describes what ensued in wonderfully suggestive music:

He caps it all by telling Otello that he has even seen the handkerchief, which Otello gave his wife when they were married, in the hands of Cassio.

Otello's rage knows no limits, and in music of relentless fury, he pledges himself to prove Desdemona's guilt and to avenge it; Iago joins with him in his oath: 'Si, pel ciel marmoreo giuro' (Witness yon marble heaven).

*Si, pel ciel mar-mo-reo giu - ro! per  leat-tor-te fol-ger-i*

Act III.    The great hall of the castle; at the back a terrace. After a brief scene in which the approach of the ambassadors is announced, Desdemona enters. Wholly unaware of the cause of Otello's strange actions towards her, she again begins to plead for Cassio's restoration to favour:

Allegro moderato

*Dio ti gio-con-dyospo-so    del-l'alma mi-a so-vra - - no*

Boito has used Otello's insistence on the handkerchief while Desdemona urges Cassio's reinstatement, and combined it with part of the so-called 'brothel' scene. Upon her knees, Desdemona vows her constancy: 'Esterrefata fisso' (Upon my knees before thee), but Otello's mixture of wrath, irony, and hysteria proves too much for her, and she rushes from his presence.

Left alone, Otello soliloquises in the introspective mood of the temptation scenes ('Had it pleased Heaven to try me with affliction'), and there is nothing of the character of the outburst at the end of Act II about his monologue until its end, when Iago re-enters and tells him that Cassio is at hand, and the music rises suddenly to a strident climax.

Otello hides and Iago brings in Cassio, who is led into banter about Bianca, which Otello half hears and takes to refer to Desdemona. During the course of the trio, Iago contrives that Cassio shall reveal the handkerchief so that Otello may see it (Iago has conveyed it to Cassio's chambers, after stealing it from Emilia). Cassio disappears when the trumpets are heard announcing the arrival of the Venetian ambassadors, and, in a few bars of music and with the acclamation of the crowd as background, Otello plots with Iago that Desdemona shall die that very night in the bed she has fouled.

The Venetian ambassadors arrive. There follows the scene in which the recall of Otello to Venice and the appointment of Cassio as Governor of Cyprus in his stead are announced. In the presence of the ambassadors, the Moor strikes down Desdemona, and all join her in a plea for mercy, at the end of which ensemble Otello orders them to leave the hall. Overcome by his rage and emotion, Otello falls in a swoon, while the people, believing that their deliverer is to return to Venice to receive new honours at the hands of the Republic, shout his praises from outside. Iago reaches the heights of his power with his triumphant 'Ecco il Leon!' over the prostrate body of the general who trusts him and has just granted him promotion, but whom he hates so much.

Act IV. The scene is Desdemona's bedchamber. There is an orchestral introduction of great beauty; then, as in the play, comes the brief dialogue between Desdemona and Emilia. Desdemona sings the pathetic Willow song: 'Piangea cantando'. Her

singing is interrupted as she talks to Emilia, and at its end she says good-night, the song dying away into silence as Emilia goes out, only to be called back by Desdemona's heartrending cry of 'Ah! Emilia, Emilia, addio!' It is the most moving moment of a moving scene.

Emilia leaves, and Desdemona kneels down before the image of the Virgin and intones an exquisite 'Ave Maria', beginning and ending in pathetic monotone. The violins end Desdemona's prayer on a high A flat, and the double basses herald Otello's entrance with a *pianissimo* bottom E, five octaves and a half below. He moves toward Desdemona's bed, hesitates, and then kisses her three times. He vainly tries to force her to admit the crime he thinks she has committed, and then strangles her in spite of her pleas for mercy. The sound of knocking is heard and Emilia runs into the room crying that Cassio has killed Roderigo. She hears a dying gasp from Desdemona, and rushes from the room screaming at the top of her voice that her mistress has been murdered.

Cassio, Iago, and Lodovico answer her summons, and Emilia reveals Iago's villainy, which is confirmed by Montano, who has heard the confession of the dying Roderigo. Iago escapes, and Otello seizes his sword from the table, defying anyone present to require it of him. 'Niun mi tema' (Let no one fear me) he sings, before addressing himself to the dead Desdemona in music whose pathos is doubled by its contrast with what has gone before. He stabs himself, and the music associated in the Love Duet with his kiss is heard: 'Un bacio, un bacio ancora, un altro bacio', before he lies dead beside his wife. In this last utterance he has resumed the nobility of the earlier part of the opera, and his death scene musically has some of the quality of the great closing speech of the last act of Shakespeare's play.      K., H.

## FALSTAFF

Opera in three acts by Giuseppe Verdi; text by Arrigo Boito. Première at la Scala, Milan, February 9, 1893, with Stehle, Zilla, Pasqua, Garbin, Maurel, Pini-Corsi, Paroli, Arimondi, conductor Mascheroni. First performed Opéra-Comique, Paris, 1894; Covent Garden, 1894, with Ravogli, de Lussan, Olgina, Pessina, Arimondi; Metropolitan, New York, 1895, with Eames, de Lussan, Schalchi, Russitano, Maurel, Campanari, conductor Mancinelli. Revived at la Scala, 1921, with Canetti, Marmora, Casazza, de Paolis, Stabile, Badini, conductor Toscanini; 1926, with Raisa, Rimini, conductor Panizza; 1931, with dalla Rizza, Stabile, conductor Panizza; 1936, with Caniglia, Favero, Casazza, Landi, Stabile, Badini, conductor de Sabata; 1950, with Tebaldi, Noni, Barbieri, Francesco Albanese, Stabile, Silveri, Siepi, conductor de Sabata. Covent Garden, 1926, with Stabile; 1937, with Caniglia, Albanese, Cravcenco, Fort, Formichi, Biasini, conductor Beecham; Sadler's Wells, 1938, with Parry, Cross, Matters; Cambridge Theatre, 1948, with Stabile, conductor Erede; Covent Garden, 1950, by la Scala company. Metropolitan, 1925, with Bori, Alda, Telva, Gigli, Scotti, Tibbett, conductor Serafin; 1938, with Tibbett, conductor Panizza. Salzburg, 1935, with Caniglia, Mason, Cravcenco, Dino Borgioli, Stabile, Biasini, conductor Toscanini.

### CHARACTERS

Sir John Falstaff ..............................Baritone
Fenton, *a young gentleman* ......................Tenor
Ford, *a wealthy burgher* ........................Baritone
Dr. Cajus .......................................Tenor
Bardolph ⎫ *followers of Falstaff* ......⎧ Tenor
Pistol ⎭ ......⎩ Bass
Alice Ford, *Ford's wife* ....................... Soprano
Nanetta, *her daughter* ..........................Soprano
Mistress Page ....................... Mezzo-Soprano

Dame Quickly ...............................Contralto
Burghers and Street-folk, Ford's servants, etc.
*Time:* Reign of Henry IV                    *Place:* Windsor

If Verdi surrounded the writing of *Otello* with mystery, this was as nothing compared with the secrecy which shrouded its successor, which Verdi insisted, almost until it was finished, was being written purely for his own pleasure and with no thought or intention of public performance. The aged composer seems to have laid down the score with a feeling of real regret and a conviction that his life's work was ended with its completion. As far as opera was concerned, this turned out to be true, but the anything but negligible 'Quattro Pezzi Sacri' testify to his continued energy as a musical creator.

Shakespeare's comedy, *The Merry Wives of Windsor*, did not by any means have its first lyric adaptation when Verdi penned the score of his last work for the stage. *Falstaff* by Salieri was produced in Vienna in 1798; another *Falstaff* by Balfe came out in London in 1838, and Otto Nicolai's *The Merry Wives of Windsor* is mentioned on pages 152–154 of this book. The character of Falstaff also appears in *Le Songe d'une Nuit d'Eté* (Midsummer Night's Dream) by Ambroise Thomas (who also wrote a *Hamlet*), which came out at Paris in 1850; 'the type is treated with an adept's hand, especially in the first act, which is a masterpiece of pure comedy in music'—so says a contemporary. A one-act piece, *Falstaff*, by Adolphe Adam, was produced at the Théâtre Lyrique in 1856. Since Verdi, only Vaughan Williams seems to have attempted to set *Falstaff* to music, his *Sir John in Love* having appeared for the first time in 1935. Holst's short opera, *At the Boar's Head*, sets the tavern scenes of *Henry IV*.

In both *Otello* and *Macbeth*, Verdi and his librettists had kept as close to Shakespeare as operatic form would allow them; and that, in essentials, as I have tried to indicate, was very close. But in *Falstaff*, they contrived to inject a considerable measure of the great Falstaff of *Henry IV* into the veins of the Falstaff of *The Merry Wives of Windsor*, and so the operatic adaptation is in many ways an improvement over the original.

Act I.    A room at the Garter Inn—the 'Giarrettiera', as the Italian has it. Dr. Caius comes to complain that Falstaff has beaten his servants, and that Bardolph (Bardolfo) and Pistol (Pistola) made him drunk and then robbed him. Falstaff laughs and talks him out of countenance, and he swears that he will never get drunk again, save in the society of honest, sober people, noted for their piety. As he leaves after this grandiloquent statement, Pistol and Bardolph, beating time as they do so, sing an antiphonal 'Amen', until Falstaff stops them with his complaint that they sing out of time.

He looks at his bill, compares the total with what is left in his purse, and starts to complain that the prodigal living of his two cronies is reducing him to a state of beggary, and, what is worse, is bringing him perilously close to reducing his weight—and Falstaff, as he rightly says, without his corporation would be a shadow of his real self. The others applaud such self-revelation— 'Falstaff immenso! enorme Falstaff!'—and Falstaff proceeds to tell them that he is currently enamoured of no less than two ladies, the wives of Ford and Page. He has written two love letters, and Bardolph and Pistol are to bear them to their destinations. But this the two worthies refuse to do; their honour will not allow them to take part in such a transaction. Cursing them, Falstaff sends the notes off by a page, and rounds on the pair of them. What right have they to talk of honour, ruffians that they are? Boito has transplanted the Honour monologue, and here Verdi sets it with incomparable aptness and relish: 'L'onore! Ladri!'

At its end, Falstaff picks up a broom and chases Bardolph and Pistol out of the room.

The scene changes to the garden of Ford's house, and the orchestra tells us clearly we are in presence of the merry wives, Alice Ford, Meg Page, and Mistress Quickly. With them is Anne

Ford (Nanetta). In company with Quickly, Meg has come to pay a visit to Alice Ford to show her a letter which she has just received from Falstaff. Alice matches Meg's with one she also has received from him, and the four read the two letters which, save for the change of address, are exactly alike. The women are half amused, half annoyed at the presumption of the fat knight, and plan to avenge themselves upon him.

Meanwhile Ford goes walking before his house in company with Caius, young Fenton (who is in love with Nanetta, but frowned on as a suitor by Ford), Bardolph and Pistol. The last two have betrayed their master, and from them Ford has learned that Falstaff is after his wife. He too meditates revenge, and the female quartet and the male quintet sometimes mingle, sometimes are heard on their own. Fenton and Nanetta remain behind for a fleeting kiss, and sing a miniature love duet together, ending with a phrase of melting beauty: 'Bocca baciata non perde

ventura'. The women return, but quickly disappear when they think they are being overheard, and once again the two young lovers are alone and can indulge in their battle of kisses. The men reappear, so do the women, and separately they put the finishing touches to their schemes of revenge. This is the famous ensemble in which Verdi combines what was previously sung separately by the men and the women; the fact that the men are singing *alla breve* and the women in 6/8 makes this notoriously difficult to perform:

Act II reverts to the Garter Inn, where Falstaff is still at table. Beating their breasts in mock penitence, Bardolph and Pistol ask to be forgiven for their previous infidelity, and tell Falstaff that an old woman is outside asking to be admitted to his presence. Dame Quickly comes in, and, with the orchestra, makes deep obeisance to the knight: 'Reverenza' is set characteristically to a musical representation of a curtsey. Falstaff is all condescension

and affability—'Buon giorno, buona donna'—and Quickly delivers her messages, one from each of the ladies, to the effect that Alice will receive the knight, but that Meg's husband guards her too jealously ever to leave her alone. Alice can see him from two till three ('Dalle due alle tre') when her husband is always out. Falstaff repeats the words with evident delight, and assures Quickly that he will not default on the assignation. Quickly starts to leave, and is tipped by Falstaff as he dismisses her, again with a magnificent sense of the appropriate gesture. He is left alone with thoughts of his impending success: 'Alice è mia' (Alice is mine) he sings (orchestrally this is the epitome of Falstaff's delight and anticipation):

and has time for a little strutting march of self-satisfied triumph ('Va, vecchio John') before his next visitor is announced.

It is Ford. He introduces himself to Falstaff under the name of Master Brook (Signor Fontana), presents the knight with a purse of silver as a bait, then tells him that he is in love with Mistress Ford, whose chastity he cannot conquer, and begs Falstaff to lay siege to her and so make the way easier for him. Falstaff catches up the suggestion of music from him, and breaks mockingly into a little song of delicious triumph:

L'a-mor, l'a-mor che non ci dà mai tre-que Fin-chè la vi-ta strug-ge.

Falstaff gleefully tells him that he has a rendezvous with her that very afternoon, and that he (Master Brook) may be quite sure that he will be able eventually to attain what he so much desires. When Ford asks if Falstaff knows the husband of Alice, he hears himself described with contumelious abuse. The comedy is rich and yet highly subtle, and this duet stands as the last of the long line of similarly conceived scenes which occur all through Verdi's work.

Falstaff goes out for a moment to change his clothes, and Ford s left alone, a prey to jealousy in its most tormenting form. His soliloquy in praise of jealousy might be expected to put Verdi in a dangerous position after his completely successful creation of a tragic jealous passion in *Otello*, but not a note is out of place, and this is one of the great moments of the opera, and moreover a complete re-creation of the Elizabethan delight in the comedy of the enraged cuckold. Falstaff returns, and, after some argument as to who shall go through the door first, they go off arm in arm.

The scene changes to Ford's house, where the four women get ready to give Falstaff the reception he deserves. We learn, quite casually from talk between Mistress Ford and Nanetta, that Ford wants to marry off the girl to the aged pedant, Dr. Caius, while she of course will marry none but Fenton, with whom she is in love. Her mother promises to aid her plans. Alice leads an ensemble with a *staccato* melody, and Quickly gives warning of Falstaff's approach.

Alice sits herself down and starts to play on the lute, to whose accompaniment Falstaff begins to sing her praises in extravagant terms. He sings a little song of irresistible melody: 'Quand' ero paggio del Duca di Norfolk' (When I was page to the Duke of Norfolk's grace), in which he describes his own slender and comely build when he was a boy. They are interrupted by Quickly, who announces that Ford can be seen approaching. The fat lover must be concealed. This is accomplished by getting him behind a screen, just before Ford enters with his followers, hoping to surprise the man who has thus invaded his home. With them he begins a search of the rooms.

While they are off exploring another part of the house, the women hurry Falstaff into a big washbasket, pile the soiled clothes over him, and fasten it down. Scarcely has this been done when Ford comes back and hears the sound of kissing behind the screen. No longer any doubt! Falstaff is hidden there with his wife. He gathers everyone together and knocks down the screen—to find behind it Nanetta and Fenton, who have used to their own purpose the diversion of attention from them by the hunt for Falstaff. Ford, more furious than ever, rushes out, while his wife and her friends call in the servants, who lift the basket and empty it out of the window into the Thames below. When Ford comes back, his wife leads him to the window and shows him Falstaff striking out for the shore.

Act III.    Falstaff is sitting in an armchair at the Garter. His thoughts are gloomy and he calls for more wine, but even that prospect does not seem to make him more cheerful. The world is in a sorry state, he reflects, when such a pearl of knighthood as himself can be bundled unceremoniously into a basket full of dirty linen and dropped into the water. Everything is going to the dogs—even a subdued memory of the little march only reminds him that he is the last of the old brigade. Suddenly, the host appears with a bottle of wine, and Falstaff's mood alters perceptibly at the prospect of swamping some of the Thames water inside him with some good wine. The scene has begun as invective against an ungrateful world, but it finishes as a panegyric in praise of wine, with the full orchestra trilling in sympathy as the wine mounts to colour his view of humanity.

Once more Quickly curtseys to him (considerably, it must be admitted, to his dismay), and offers him a rendezvous with Alice.

But Falstaff wants to hear no more of such things, and it takes all Quickly's powers of persuasion to get him even to listen, much less to agree to a meeting-place. However, in the end, he cannot resist the temptation which is being dangled in front of him, and settles for midnight at Herne the Hunter's Oak in Windsor forest, where he is to appear (as we learn a moment later from the concealed Alice and her friends) disguised as the black huntsman himself, who, according to legend, hanged himself from the oak, with the result that the spot is haunted by witches and sprites.

The scene ends with an ensemble as the women and Fenton arrange the details of the evening's fun, and Ford and Caius plot that Caius's betrothal to Nanetta shall be announced that very night. The women call to each other offstage and the strings offer fifteen bars of idyllic commentary as darkness falls.

The last scene takes place by moonlight under Herne's Oak. Horn-calls and references to the love music form the basis for the prelude to Fenton's aria, which begins the act. It is filled with

the same sweetness as can be found in the love music and it ends with their love motive. Disguises are hastily donned, and in a moment Falstaff is heard arriving. He is wearing a brace of antlers on his head and is wrapped in a heavy cloak. Midnight strikes, echoed at each stroke by Falstaff, who consoles himself for the incongruity of his disguise by remembering that Jove disguised himself as a bull for love of Europa. For a moment he is alone with Alice, but they are immediately interrupted by noises, and Alice disappears into the darkness leaving Falstaff to fend for himself.

Nanetta, who is disguised as Queen of the Fairies, calls her followers around her, and they pirouette until she begins to sing. Verdi has given them music of exquisite delicacy and the choral writing is as delicious as that for the soloist: 'Sul fil d'un soffio etesio' (From secret caves and bowers).

Bardolph in disguise stumbles on the recumbent figure of Falstaff (who has hidden his face so as not to see the fairies), and calls everyone to him. The merry women, Ford's entourage, and about a hundred others, all disguised and masked, unite in mystifying, taunting, and belabouring Falstaff, until the knight at last recognises Bardolph amongst his tormentors. Everyone unmasks in turn, and Falstaff's enormity and folly is brought to light for his delectation. He makes a valiant attempt to recapture the initiative by complaining that without his participation a joke seems to have no wit in it, and all—even Ford—agree that his wit alone is sufficient to redeem him, in spite of his egregious faults.

Ford takes Nanetta by the hand and announces her betrothal to Caius, and does the same to another disguised young couple whom Alice leads up to him. He bids them all unmask—to find that Bardolph has been dressed up in Nanetta's clothes and is now therefore betrothed to Caius, and that the other couple were Nanetta and Fenton in disguise. Falstaff cannot resist the temptation to turn Ford's question back on him: who is the dupe now? But Alice will not let him get away with it; he is to be placed beside Ford and Caius; if they are dupes, so is he. Ford is induced to bless his daughter and her sweetheart, and Falstaff leads the company in a final fugue: 'Tutto nel mondo è burla. L'uom è nato burlone' (Jesting is man's vocation. Wise is he who is jolly):

*Tutt·o nel mondo è bur-la. L'uom .. è na-to bur-lo-ne, bur-lo-ne, bur-lo-ne*

For the second time in his career, Verdi, who despised academic-ism with unabating scorn, finished a Shakespearean opera with what is traditionally the most academic of forms, a fugue.

It would take most of a book to describe *Falstaff* in sufficient detail to do anything like justice to the kaleidoscopic variety of the score. There is a sparkle, a rapidity of utterance, a speed of movement, an economy of means in the ensemble writing that has no equal in music written since Mozart, and every bar is endowed with a refinement of expression and a restraint that it would be difficult to imagine in the composer of the operas written before *Macbeth*. The music is even more fluid than in *Otello*, and rhythmic ideas are caught up, dropped, and used again with a dexterity that Shakespeare himself never excelled in his own medium. It is all as light as air, and yet out of it has been fashioned Shakespeare's Falstaff drawn (without intending any pun) completely in the round, speaking Italian but more English at heart than in any English musical re-creation of him.

H.

CHAPTER 9

*Italian Opera Continued*

# ARRIGO BOITO
## (1842–1918)

### MEFISTOFELE

OPERA in four acts by Arrigo Boito, words by the composer. Première at la Scala, Milan, March 5, 1868, with Reboux, Flory, Spallazzi, Junca (not a success). In a revised version, produced at Bologna, 1875, with Borgi-Manno, Campanini, Nannetti, with great success. First performed Her Majesty's Theatre, London, 1880, with Nilsson, Trebelli, Campanini, Nannetti, Grazzi, conductor Arditi; New York, Academy of Music, 1880, with Valleria, Cary, Campanini, Novara; Metropolitan, 1883, with Nilsson, Trebelli, Campanini, Mirabella. Revived Metropolitan, 1889 (Lehmann), 1896 (Calvé), 1907 (Farrar, Martin, Chaliapin); Covent Garden, 1914, with Muzio, Raisa, McCormack, Didur; 1926, with Scacciati, Merli, Chaliapin; la Scala, 1918, with Canetti, Gigli, de Angelis, conductor Toscanini; 1924, with Spani, Arangi-Lombardi, Pertile, de Angelis; 1934, with Caniglia, Bruna Rasa, Masini, Pinza; 1936, with Tassinari, Bruna Rasa, Pertile, Pasero; 1952, with Tebaldi, Martinis, Tagliavini, Rossi-Lemeni, conductor de Sabata; Metropolitan, 1920, with Alda, Easton, Gigli, Didur.

### CHARACTERS

Mefistofele ....................................... Bass
Faust .......................................... Tenor
Margherita .................................... Soprano
Martha ...................................... Contralto
Wagner ....................................... Tenor
Elena ........................................ Soprano
Pantalis ..................................... Contralto
Nereo ........................................ Tenor

Mystic choir, celestial phalanxes, cherubs, penitents, wayfarers, men-at-arms, huntsmen, students, citizens, populace, townsmen, witches, wizards, Greek chorus, sirens, naiads, dancers, warriors

*Time:* Middle Ages  *Place:* Heaven; Frankfurt, Germany; Vale of Tempe, Ancient Greece

*Mefistofele* is in a prologue, four acts, and epilogue. In Gounod's *Faust*, the librettists were circumspect, and limited the book of the opera to the first part of Goethe's *Faust*, the story of Faust and Marguerite—succinct, dramatic, and absorbing. Only for the ballet did they reach into the second part of Goethe's play and appropriate the scene on the Brocken, which, however, is frequently omitted.

Boito, himself a poet, based his libretto on both parts of Goethe's work, and endeavoured to give it the substratum of philosophy upon which the German master reared his dramatic structure. This, however, resulted in making *Mefistofele* two operas in one. Wherever the work touches on the familiar story of Faust and Marguerite, it is absorbingly interesting, and this in spite of the similarity between some of its scenes and those of Gounod's *Faust*. When it strays into Part II of Goethe's drama, the main thread of the action suddenly seems broken. That is why one of the most profound works for the lyric stage, one of the most beautiful scores that has come out of Italy, figures comparatively rarely in programmes outside its native country.

The Prologue opens in the nebulous regions of space, in which float the invisible legions of angels, cherubs, and seraphs. These lift their voices in a hymn of praise to the Supreme Ruler of the universe. Mefistofele comes on the scene at the close of the anthem, and, standing erect amid the clouds, with his feet upon the border of his cloak, mockingly addresses the Deity: 'Ave Signor'. In answer to the question from the mystic choir, 'Knowest thou Faust?', he replies contemptuously, and offers to wager that he will be able to entice Faust to evil, and thus gain a victory over the powers of good. The wager is accepted, and the spirits resume their chorus of praise.

Musically the Prologue is full of interest. There are five distinct periods of music, varied in character, so that a scene in which there is but little stage action has the necessary movement. There is the prelude with mystic choir; the sardonic scherzo foreshadowing the entry of Mefistofele; his scornful address, in which he engages to bring about the destruction of Faust's soul; a vivacious chorus of cherubs (impersonated by twenty-four boys); a psalmody of penitents and spirits.

Act I. The drama opens on Easter Sunday, at Frankfort-on-Main. Crowds of people of all conditions move in and out of the city gates. Among them appears a grey friar, an object of both reverence and dread to those near him. The aged Dr. Faust and his pupil Wagner descend from a height and enter upon the scene, shadowed by the friar, whose actions they discuss. Faust returns to his laboratory, still at his heels the friar, who, unheeded, enters with him, and conceals himself in an alcove. Faust gives himself to meditation, and upon opening the sacred volume, is startled by a shriek from the friar as he rushes from his place of concealment. Faust makes the all-potent 'sign of Solomon', which compels Mefistofele to throw off his friar's disguise and to appear in his own person in the garb of a cavalier, with a black cloak upon his arm. In reply to Faust's questionings, he declares himself the spirit that denieth all things, desiring only the complete ruin of the world, and a return to chaos and night. He offers to make Faust the companion of his wanderings, upon certain conditions, to which the latter agrees, saying: 'If thou wilt bring me one hour of peace, in which my soul may rest—if thou wilt unveil the world and myself before me—if I may find cause to say to some flying moment, "Stay, for thou art blissful"', then let me die, and let hell's depths engulf me'. The contract completed. Mefistofele spreads his cloak, and both disappear through the air.

The first scene of this act gains its interest from the reflection in the music of the bustle and animation of the Easter festival. The score plastically follows the many changing incidents of the scene upon the stage. Conspicuous in the episodes in Faust's laboratory are Faust's beautiful air, 'Dai campi, dai prati' (From the fields and from the meadows); Mefistofele's proclamation of his identity, 'Son lo spirito che nega sempre tutto' (I am the spirit that denieth), and the duet beginning 'Se tu mi doni un'ora'.

Act II opens with the garden scene. Faust, rejuvenated, and under the name of Henry, Margaret, Mefistofele, and Martha stroll here and there in couples, chatting and love-making. Thence Mefistofele takes Faust to the heights of the Brocken, where he witnesses the orgies of the Witches' Sabbath. The fiend is welcomed and saluted as their king. Faust, benumbed and stupefied, gazes into the murky sky, and experiences there a vision of Margaret, pale, sad, and fettered with chains.

In this act the garden scene is of entrancing grace. It contains Faust's 'Colma il tuo cor d'un palpito' (Flood thou thy heart with all the bliss), and the quartet of farewell, with which the scene ends, Margaret, with a gay and reckless laugh of ineffable bliss, exclaiming to Faust that she loves him. The scene on the Brocken, besides the whirl of the witches' orgy, has a solo for Mefistofele, when the weird sisters present to him a glass globe, reflected in which he sees the earth: 'Ecco il mondo' (Behold the earth).

Act III.    The scene is a prison. Margaret lies extended upon a heap of straw, mentally wandering, and singing to herself. Mefistofele and Faust appear outside the grating. They converse hurriedly, and Faust begs for the life of Margaret. Mefistofele promises to do what he can, and bids him haste, for the infernal steeds are ready for flight. He opens the cell, and Faust enters it. Margaret thinks the jailors have come to release her, but at length recognises her lover. She describes what followed his desertion of her, and begs him to lay her in death beside her loved ones— her babe, whom she drowned, her mother whom she is accused of having poisoned. Faust entreats her to fly with him, and she finally consents, saying that in some far distant isle they may yet be happy. But the voice of Mefistofele in the background recalls her to the reality of the situation. She shrinks away from Faust, prays to Heaven for mercy, and dies. Voices of the celestial choir are singing softly 'She's saved!' Faust and Mefistofele escape as the executioner and his escort appear in the background.

The act opens with Margaret's lament, 'L'altra notte in fondo al more' (To the sea, one night in sadness), in which she tells of the drowning of her babe.

There is an exquisite duet, for Margaret and Faust, 'Lontano, sui flutti d'un ampio oceano' (Far away, o'er the waves of a far-spreading ocean), and a fine passage for Margaret, 'Spunta l'aurora pallida', before her death.

Act IV.    Mefistofele takes Faust to the shores of the Vale of Tempe. Faust is ravished with the beauty of the scene while Mefistofele finds that the orgies of the Brocken were more to his taste.

It is the night of the classic Sabbath. A band of young maidens appear, singing and dancing. Mefistofele, annoyed and confused, retires. Helen enters with chorus, and, absorbed by a terrible vision, rehearses the story of Troy's destruction. Faust enters, richly clad in the costume of a knight of the fifteenth century, followed by Mefistofele, Nereo, Pantalis, and others. Kneeling before Helen, he addresses her as his ideal of beauty and purity. Thus pledging to each other their love and devotion, they wander through the bowers and are lost to sight.

Helen's ode, 'La luna immobile inonda l'etere' (Motionless floating, the moon floods the dome of night); her dream of the destruction of Troy; the love duet for Helen and Faust, 'Forma ideal purissima' and 'Ah! Amore! misterio celeste' ('Tis love, a mystery celestial); and the dexterous weaving of a musical background by orchestra and chorus, are the chief features in the score to this act.

In the Epilogue, we find Faust in his laboratory once more—an old man, with death fast approaching, mourning over his past life, with the holy volume open before him. Fearing that Faust may yet escape him, Mefistofele spreads his cloak, and urges Faust to fly with him through the air. Appealing to Heaven, Faust is strengthened by the sound of angelic songs, and resists. Foiled in his efforts, Mefistofele conjures up a vision of beautiful sirens. Faust hesitates a moment, flies to the sacred volume, and cries, 'Here at last I find salvation'; then falling on his knees in prayer, effectually overcomes the temptations of the evil one. He dies amid a shower of rosy petals, and to the triumphant song of a celestial choir. Mefistofele has lost his wager, and holy influences have prevailed.

We have here Faust's lament, 'Giunto sul passo extremo' (Nearing the utmost limit); his prayer, and the choir's message of salvation.                                                         K.

# NERONE
## Nero

Opera in four acts by Arrigo Boito; text by the composer. Première May 1, 1924, at la Scala, Milan, with Raisa, Bertana, Pertile, Galeffi, Journet, Pinza, conductor Toscanini. First performed Rome, 1928, with Scacciati, Bertana, Lauri-Volpi, Franci, Maugeri, conductor Marinuzzi; Buenos Aires, 1926, with Arangi-Lombardi, Bertana, Pertile, Franci, Formichi, Pinza, conductor Marinuzzi. Revived la Scala, 1939, with Cigna, Stignani, Voyer, Sved, Baronti, conductor Marinuzzi; Rome, 1950, with Laszlo, Minarchi, Annaloro, Tagliabue, Mongelli, conductor Santini.

## CHARACTERS

Nerone, *Emperor of Rome* ..........................Tenor
Simon Mago, *a sorcerer* ........................Baritone
Fanuèl, *a Christian leader* ......................Baritone
Asteria .........................................Soprano
Rubria, *a Vestal Virgin, but secretly a*
   *Christian* .............................Mezzo-Soprano
Tigellino, *follower of Nerone*.......................Bass
Gobrias, *follower of Simon Mago* ..................Tenor
Dositeo, *a Roman* ..............................Baritone
Perside, *a Christian* .............................Soprano
Cerinto ........................................Contralto

In *Mefistofele* Boito sought to express, in words and music, the conflict between good and evil; in *Nerone* the contrast is between the dying pagan world and Christianity. On the one hand decay and luxury and power; on the other faith, simplicity and a new idea.

Act I. The Appian Way. Simon Mago and Tigellino are waiting for Nero, who comes to bury the ashes of his mother, Agrippina, whom he has murdered. He arrives fearful and trembling and almost penitent but for the fact that in the Oresteia he finds a precedent for matricide. He has heard an unearthly voice saying 'I am Orestes', and he finds comfort in the thought that he is the reincarnation of Orestes. Tigellino has dug a deep trench where the ashes of Agrippina, which Nero carries, must be buried, He apostrophises the grave: 'Queste ad un lido fatal'. When this is accomplished Simon Mago gives him absolution. Just as the rite is ending the figure of a woman, whose neck is encircled by snakes, seems to rise from the ground. Nero flies, followed by Tigellino. Simon stays and boldly challenges her.

The newcomer is Asteria, who loves Nero and follows him everywhere. Simon believes she may be of use to him and promises to bring her to Nero if she will do his bidding. Simon descends to the crypt where the Christians are wont to gather, while two Christians, Rubria and Fanuèl, meet above. Rubria loves Fanuèl, but Fanuèl has no other thought than his mission. Rubria recites the Lord's Prayer, watched by Asteria. When the two Christians see their arch-enemy, Simon, issuing from the crypt, Rubria is sent to warn the Christians, while Fanuèl remains to face whatever danger there is. But Simon has no hostile intentions. He sees the old world going to ruin and now offers power and wealth to Fanuèl if Fanuèl will but teach him to work miracles. The music at this point works in the traditional 'intonation' of the 'Credo'. Fanuèl, dreaming of a world in which neither power nor wealth has a share, indignantly refuses. The two must henceforth be enemies.

The news of Nero's return has reached Rome and a great procession comes to meet him. A scene of triumph closes the act.

Act II. The temple of Simon Mago. The stage is divided in two by the altar where Simon pretends to work a miracle. Before the altar are the faithful; behind, Simon's adepts. The faithful worship and pray; the adepts laugh and count their gains. When the mock ceremony is over, Simon prepares the temple for the expected visit of Nero. The Emperor must be made to believe that Simon can work miracles Asteria will therefore pretend to be a goddess; echoes must be arranged to give the voice of god or goddess an awful timbre; mirrors must be placed so as to make it appear that phantoms visit the temple. Nero appears and addresses the supposed goddess: 'Oh, come vieni a errar'; everything follows the appointed course until Nero touches Asteria and the goddess reveals herself as a woman. In vain the metallic voice of the oracle is heard warning Nero. The emperor no longer fears these gods. He snatches a torch and throws it in the mouth of the bronze shell in which an adept of Simon played the part of the oracle. He calls to his guards, who arrest Simon and his followers, and sets about destroying the temple. Simon has boasted that he could fly; on the next festival he will be thrown from a tower of the circus and fly—if he can. Then, standing over the ruins, Nero takes a cithara and sings.

Act III. In an orchard away from the noise of Rome the Christians meet. Solemnly their leader, Fanuèl, expounds to them the beatitudes; Rubria tells the parable of the foolish virgins in music of utmost suavity. The lesson is interrupted by the arrival of Asteria who has escaped from her prison house to warn them that Simon has tried to purchase freedom by betraying the Christians to Nero. Rubria urges Fanuèl to fly but he refuses. Two beggars come to them in the darkness; they are Simon and Gobrias, one of his assistants disguised, who come to spy. Discovering Fanuèl, Simon sends to warn the guards; there is a short scene of considerable power between Fanuèl and Simon Mago. When the guards arrive, the Christians would attack Simon, but Fanuèl orders them to submit. He turns to his followers and tells them his journey is ended. As he goes the women make a path of flowers before him. Rubria is left alone while the Christians' hymn dies away in the distance. The whole passage, with its mixture of Christian serenity and dramatic power, is most impressive.

Act IV. The first scene takes place in the 'Oppidum', where the mob attending the games in the circus has gathered to applaud the victors and abuse the vanquished. Here are Simon, closely followed by two guards, and Gobrias. They are plotting to burn Rome and escape the punishment which awaits Simon. The conspiracy is made known by Tigellino to Nero, who refuses to interfere. He has planned the games; he is determined to succeed and to please the mob; if the mob demands victims it shall have them. Fanuèl is brought in together with other Christians, who go to their martyrdom in the circus. A vestal appears, preceded by a lictor, and demands their pardon. Nero angrily orders the veil to be torn from her. It is Rubria, who has come to help Fanuèl. Her efforts are in vain. She, too, is condemned. The Christians go to their death; Simon follows, and then the light of the flames which are consuming the city are seen in the distance.

The second scene takes us to the 'spoliarium', where those who died in the circus are thrown. Asteria and Fanuèl, who, thanks to the fire, have escaped, have come to seek Rubria. They find her wounded to death. Before dying she confesses her sin. She was a vestal; she worshipped with the Christians and then returned every day to Vesta. Now she would kneel and beg forgiveness; she cannot move. There is time for another confession; she loves Fanuèl. He too loves and now calls her his bride, his beloved. As Rubria feels life ebbing, she asks Fanuèl to tell her once more of Galilee and of the sea on whose strand Christ prayed. Fanuèl obeys, and with that image in her eyes and in her mind, Rubria dies.

The scene of Rubria's death is one of the most successful of the opera, and Boito achieves a moving effect without even momentary recourse to the tear-jerking methods which were so much in evidence in Italy in the early twentieth century.

*Nerone* was planned originally in five acts. It is known that Boito worked at the opera all his life, adding and cancelling and improving till old age made him desist. When he had finally revised the fourth act he wrote on the last page: 'The End: Arrigo Boito and Kronos'.

*Nerone* was never produced in the author's lifetime. It aims, perhaps, too high. Boito obviously meant to give the three arts of the music drama equal importance. The first and the fourth act exploit in superb fashion the resources of theatrical presentation; the libretto is a masterpiece of learning leavened by a true poets' emotion; but the music has lost some of the easy charm that was the great merit of Boito's first opera, *Mefistofele*.

If it lacks lyrical force, *Nerone* has nevertheless pages of great beauty, and it is still the subject of occasional revival.

F. B.

# AMILCARE PONCHIELLI
### (1834–1886)

## LA GIOCONDA
### The Ballad Singer

OPERA in four acts by Amilcare Ponchielli; text by Arrigo Boito. Première at la Scala, Milan, April 8, 1876, with Mariani, Biancolini-Rodriguez, Barlani-Dini, Gayarre, Aldighieri, Maini. First performed Covent Garden, 1883, with Maria Durand, Stahl, Tremelli, Marconi, Cotogni, Edouard de Reszke; Metropolitan, 1883, with Nilsson, Fursch-Madi, Stagno, del Puente, Novarre. Revived Metropolitan, 1904, with Nordica, Homer, Walker, Caruso, Giraldoni, Plançon; Covent Garden, 1907, with Destinn, Kirkby Lunn, Thornton, Bassi, Sammarco, Journet, conductor Campanini; Metropolitan, 1925, with Ponselle, Telva, Gigli, Danise, Mardones, conductor Serafin; la Scala, Milan, 1927, with Arangi-Lombardi, Stignani, Merli, Franci, Pasero, conductor Toscanini; Covent Garden, 1929, with Ponselle, Minghini-Cattaneo, Merli, Inghilleri, conductor Bellezza; la Scala, Milan, 1934, with Cigna, Stignani, Ziliani, Galeffi; Metropolitan, 1937, with Cigna, Castagna, Martinelli, Morelli; 1939, with Milanov; 1943, with Roman, Castagna, Tucker, Bonelli.

### CHARACTERS

La Gioconda, *a ballad singer* .................Soprano
La Cieca, *her blind mother* ...................Contralto
Alvise Badoero, *one of the heads of the State Inquisi-*
   *tion* ..........................................Bass
Laura, *his wife*........................Mezzo-Soprano
Enzo Grimaldo, *a Genoese noble*..................Tenor
Barnaba, *a spy of the Inquisition* ..............Baritone
Zuane, *a boatman* ...............................Bass
Isèpo, *a public letter-writer*.....................Tenor
A Pilot .........................................Bass

Monks, senators, sailors, shipwrights, ladies, gentlemen,
populace, masquers, guards, etc.

*Time:* Seventeenth Century                    *Place:* Venice

Twenty-one years elapsed between the production of *La Gioconda* at the Metropolitan Opera House and its revival. After its reawakening, it took good hold on the repertory, which made it difficult to explain why it should have been allowed to sleep so

long. It may be that possibilities of casting it did not suggest
themselves; not always does 'Cielo e mar' flow as suavely as it
did from the throat of Caruso. Then, too, managers are superstitious, and may have hesitated to make re-trial of anything that
had been attempted at that first season of opera at the Metropolitan, one of the most disastrous on record. Even Praxede
Marcelline Kochanska (in other words Marcella Sembrich), who
was a member of Henry E. Abbey's troupe, was not re-engaged,
and did not reappear at the Metropolitan until fourteen years
later.

There was in the course of the first Metropolitan performance
of the opera in 1883 an unusual occurrence and one that is
interesting to hark back to. Nilsson had a voice of great beauty
—pure, limpid, flexible—but not one conditioned to a severe
dramatic strain. Fursch-Madi, on the other hand, had a large,
powerful voice and a singularly dramatic temperament. When La
Gioconda and Laura appeared in the great duet in the second act,
'L'amo come il fulgor del creato' (I love him as the light of
creation), Fursch-Madi, without great effort, 'took away' this
number from Mme. Nilsson, and completely eclipsed her. When
the two singers came out in answer to the recalls, Mme. Nilsson
as etiquette demanded, was slightly in advance of the mezzo-
soprano, for whom, however, most of the applause was intended.

Each act of *La Gioconda* has its separate title: Act I, 'The
Lion's Mouth'; Act II, 'The Rosary'; Act III, 'The House of
Gold'; Act IV, 'The Orfano Canal'. The title of the opera can
be translated as 'The Ballad Singer', but the Italian title appears
invariably to be used.

Act I.    Grand courtyard of the Ducal palace, decorated for
festivities. At back, the Giant's Stairway, and the Portico della
Carta, with doorway leading to the interior of the Church of St.
Mark. On the left, the writing-table of a public letter-writer. On
one side of the courtyard one of the historic Lion's Mouths, with
the following inscription cut in black letters into the wall:

> FOR SECRET DENUNCIATIONS
> TO THE INQUISITION
> AGAINST ANY PERSON,
> WITH IMPUNITY, SECRECY, AND
> BENEFIT TO THE STATE.

It is a splendid afternoon in spring. The stage is filled with holiday-makers, monks, sailors, shipwrights, masquers, etc., and amidst the busy crowd are seen some Dalmatians and Moors.

Barnaba, leaning his back against a column, is watching the people. He has a small guitar, slung around his neck.

The populace gaily sings, 'Feste e pane' (Sports and feasting). They dash away to watch the regatta, when Barnaba announces that it is about to begin. He watches them disdainfully. 'Above their graves they are dancing!' he exclaims. Gioconda leads in La Cieca, her blind mother. There is a scene of much tenderness between them: 'Figlia, che reggi il tremulo piè' (Daughter, in thee my faltering steps).

Barnaba is in love with the ballad singer, who has several times repulsed him. She is in love with Enzo, a nobleman, who has been proscribed by the Venetian authorities, but is in the city in the disguise of a sea captain. His ship lies in the Fusina Lagoon.

Barnaba again presses his love upon the girl. She escapes from his grasp and runs away, leaving her mother seated by the church door. Barnaba is eager to get La Cieca into his power in order to compel Gioconda to yield to his sinister desires. Opportunity soon offers. For, now the regatta is over, the crowd returns bearing in triumph the victor in the contest. With them enter Zuane, the defeated contestant, Gioconda, and Enzo. Barnaba subtly insinuates to Zuane that La Cieca is a witch, who has caused his defeat by sorcery. The report quickly spreads among the defeated boatman's friends. The populace becomes excited, La Cieca is seized and dragged from the church steps. Enzo calls upon his sailors, who are in the crowd, to aid him in saving her.

At the moment of greatest commotion the palace doors swing open. From the head of the stairway where stand Alvise and his wife, Laura, who is masked, Alvise sternly commands an end to the rioting, then descends with Laura.

Barnaba, with the keenness that is his as chief spy of the Inquisition, is quick to observe that, through her mask, Laura is gazing intently at Enzo, and that Enzo, in spite of Laura's mask, appears to have recognised her and to be deeply affected by her presence. Gioconda kneels before Alvise and prays for mercy for her mother. When Laura also intercedes for La Cieca, Alvise immediately orders her freed. In one of the most expressive airs of the opera, 'Voce di donna, o d' angelo' (Voice thine of woman, or angel fair), La Cieca thanks Laura and gives to her a rosary, at the same time extending her hands over her in blessing.

She also asks her name. Alvise's wife, still masked, and looking significantly in the direction of Enzo, answers, 'Laura!' ''Tis she!' exclaims Enzo.

The episode has been observed by Barnaba, who, when all the others save Enzo have entered the church, goes up to him and, despite his disguise as a sea captain, addresses him by his name and title, 'Enzo Grimaldo, Prince of Santa Fior'. The spy knows the whole story. Enzo and Laura were betrothed. Although they were separated and she obliged to wed Alvise, and neither had seen the other since then until the meeting a few moments before, their passion is still as strong as ever. Barnaba, cynically explaining that, in order to obtain Gioconda for himself, he wishes to show her how false Enzo is, promises him that he will arrange for Laura, that very night, to be aboard Enzo's vessel, ready to escape with him to sea. The duet is justly famous.

Enzo departs. Barnaba summons one of his tools, Isèpo, the public letter-writer, whose stand is near the Lion's Mouth. At that moment Gioconda and La Cieca emerge from the church, and Gioconda, seeing Barnaba, swiftly draws her mother behind a column, where they are hidden from view. The girl hears the spy dictate to Isèpo a letter, for whom intended she does not know, informing someone that his wife plans to elope that evening with Enzo. Having thus learned that Enzo no longer loves her, she vanishes with her mother into the church. Barnaba drops the letter into the Lion's Mouth. Isèpo goes. The spy addresses in soliloquy the Doge's palace. 'O monumento! Regia e bolgia dogale!' (O mighty monument, palace and den of the Doges).

The masquers and populace return, singing. They dance *La Furlana*. In the church a monk and then the chorus chant. Gioconda and her mother come out. Gioconda laments that Enzo should have forsaken her. La Cieca seeks to comfort her. In the church the chanting continues.

Act II.   Night. A brigantine, showing its starboard side. In front, the deserted bank of an uninhabited island in the Fusina Lagoon. In front, a smaller altar of the Virgin, lighted by a red lamp.

At the rise of the curtain sailors are discovered; some seated on the deck, others standing in groups, each with a speaking trumpet. They sing a Marinaresca, in part a sailors' shanty, in part a regular melody.

In a boat Barnaba appears with Isèpo. They are disguised as fishermen. Barnaba sings a fisherman's ballad, 'Ah! Pescator affonda l'esca' (Fisher-boy, thy net now lower).

He has set his net for Enzo and Laura, as well as for Gioconda, as his words, 'Some sweet siren, while you're drifting, in your net will coyly hide', imply. The scene is full of 'atmosphere'.

Enzo comes up on deck, gives a few orders; the crew go below. He then sings the famous 'Cielo! e mar!' (O sky, and sea)—an impassioned voicing of his love for her whom he awaits. The scene, the moon having emerged from behind a bank of clouds, is of great beauty.

A boat approaches. In it Barnaba brings Laura to Enzo. There is a rapturous greeting and a passionate love duet: 'Laggiu, nelle nebbie remote'. They are to sail away as soon as the setting of the moon will enable the ship to depart undetected. There is distant singing. Enzo goes below. Laura kneels before the shrine and prays, 'Stella del marinar! Vergine Santa!' (Star of the mariner! Virgin most holy).

Gioconda steals on board and confronts her rival. The duet between the two women, who love Enzo, and in which each defies the other, 'L'amo come il fulgor del creato' (I adore him as the light of creation), is the most dramatic number in the score.

Gioconda is about to stab Laura, but stops suddenly and, seizing her with one hand, points with the other out over the lagoon, where a boat bearing Alvise and his armed followers is seen approaching. Laura implores the Virgin for aid. In doing so she lifts up the rosary given to her by La Cieca. Through it Gioconda recognises in Laura the masked lady who saved her mother from the vengeance of the mob. Swiftly the girl summons the boat of two friendly boatmen who have brought her thither, and bids Laura make good her escape. When Barnaba enters, his prey has evaded him; Gioconda has saved her. Barnaba hurries back to Alvise's galley, and, pointing to the fugitive boat in the distance, bids the galley start in pursuit.

Enzo comes on deck. Instead of Laura he finds Gioconda. There is a dramatic scene between them. Venetian galleys are seen approaching. Rather than that his vessel shall be captured by them, Enzo sets fire to it.

Act III.   A room in Alvise's house. Alvise sings of the vengeance he will wreak upon Laura for her betrayal of his honour. 'Si! morir ella de'' (Yes, to die is her doom).

He summons Laura and accuses her of faithlessness. Nocturnal serenaders are heard singing without, as they wend their way in gondolas along the canal. Alvise draws the curtains from before a doorway and points to a funeral bier erected in the chamber beyond. To Laura he hands a phial of swift poison. She must drain it before the last note of the serenade they now hear has died away. He will leave her; the chorus ended, he will return to find her dead.

When he has gone, Gioconda, who, anticipating the fate that might befall the woman who has saved her mother, has been in hiding in the palace, hastens to Laura, and hands her a flask containing a narcotic that will create the semblance of death. Laura drinks it, and disappears through the curtains into the funeral chamber. Gioconda pours the poison from the phial into her own flask, and leaves the empty phial on the table.

The serenade ceases. Alvise re-entering, sees the empty phial on the table. He enters the funeral apartment for a brief moment. Laura is lying as one dead upon the bier. He believes that he has been obeyed and that Laura has drained the phial of poison.

The scene changes to a great hall in Alvise's house, where he is receiving his guests. Here occurs the immensely popular 'Dance of the Hours', a ballet suite which, in costume changes, light effects and choreography represents the hours of dawn, day, evening, and night. It is also intended to symbolise, in its mimic action, the eternal struggle between the powers of darkness and light. A more satirical, and extremely funny, interpretation was put on it by Walt Disney in his film *Fantasia*.

Barnaba enters, dragging in with him La Cieca, whom he has found concealed in the house. Enzo also has managed to gain admittance. La Cieca, questioned as to her purpose in the House of Gold, answers, 'For her, just dead, I prayed'. A hush falls upon the fête. The passing bell for the dead is heard slowly tolling. 'For whom?' asks Enzo of Barnaba. 'For Laura', is the reply. The guests shudder. 'D'un vampiro fatal l'ala fredda passo' (As if over our brows a vampire's wing had passed), chants the chorus. 'Già ti veggo immota e smorta' (I behold thee motionless and pallid), sings Enzo. Barnaba, Gioconda, La Cieca, and Alvise add their voices to an ensemble of great power. Alvise draws back the curtains of the funeral chamber, which also gives upon the festival hall. He points to Laura extended upon the bier. Enzo, brandishing a dagger, rushes upon Alvise, but is seized by guards.

Act IV.     The vestibule of a ruined palace on the island of Giudeca. In the right-hand corner an opened screen, behind which is a bed. On a couch are various articles of mock jewellery belonging to Gioconda.

On the right of the scene a long, dimly lighted street. From the end two men advance, carrying in their arms Laura, who is enveloped in a black cloak. The two *cantori* (street singers) knock at the door. It is opened by Gioconda, who motions them to place their burden upon the couch behind the screen. As they go, she pleads with them to search for her mother, whom she had not been able to find since the scene in the House of Gold.

She is alone. Her love for Enzo, greater than her jealousy of Laura, has prompted her to promise Barnaba that she will give herself to him, if he will aid Enzo to escape from prison and guide him to the Orfano Canal. Now, however, despair seizes her. In a dramatic soliloquy—a 'terrible song', it has been called—she invokes suicide. 'Suicidio! . . . in questi fieri momenti tu sol mi resti' (Aye, suicide, the sole resource now left me). For a moment she even thinks of carrying out Alvise's vengeance by stabbing

Laura and throwing her body into the water—'for deep is yon lagoon'.

Through the night a gondolier's voice calls in the distance over the water: 'Ho! gondolier! hast thou any fresh tidings?' Another voice, also distant: 'In the Orfano Canal there are corpses.'

In despair Gioconda throws herself down weeping near the table. Enzo enters. In a tense scene Gioconda excites his rage by telling him that she has had Laura's body removed from the burial vault and that he will not find it there. He seizes her. His dagger is already poised for the thrust. Hers—so she hopes—is to be the ecstacy of dying by his hand!

At that moment, however, the voice of Laura, who is coming out of the narcotic, calls, 'Enzo!' He rushes to her, and embraces her. In the distance is heard a chorus singing a serenade. It is the same song, before the end of which Alvise had bidden Laura drain the poison. Both Laura and Enzo now pour out words of gratitude to Gioconda, who has provided everything for flight. A boat, propelled by two of her friends, is ready to convey them to a barque, which awaits them. What a blessing, after all, has proved to be the rosary, bestowed upon the queenly Laura by an old blind woman. Enzo and Laura voice their thanks: 'Sulle tue mani l'anima tutta stempriamo in pianto' (Upon thy hands thy generous tears of sympathy are falling), and the scene works up to a powerful climax.

Once more Gioconda is alone. The thought of her compact with Barnaba comes over her. She starts to flee the spot, when the spy himself appears in the doorway. Pretending that she wishes to adorn herself for him, she begins putting on the mock jewellery, and, utilising the opportunity that brings her near the table, seizes the dagger that is lying on it. 'Gioconda is thine!' she cries, facing Barnaba, then stabs herself to the heart.

Bending over the prostrate form, the spy furiously shouts into her ear, 'Last night thy mother did offend me. I have strangled her!' But no one hears him. La Gioconda is dead. With a cry of rage, he rushes down the street.                                    K.

# ALFREDO CATALANI
## (1854–1893)

### LA WALLY

OPERA in four acts by Alfredo Catalani, text by Luigi Illica. Première at la Scala, Milan, on January 20, 1892, with Darclée, Stehle, Guerrini, Suagnes, Pessina, Cesari, Brancaleoni, conductor Mascheroni. First performed Metropolitan, 1909, with Emmy Destinn, Riccardo Martin, Amato, Campanari, conductor Toscanini; Manchester, 1919. Revived la Scala, 1922, with Sheridan, de Voltri, Bertana, Piccaluga, Noto, di Lelio, conductor Panizza; 1936, with Cigna, Carosio, Palombini, Merli, Armando Borgioli; Rome, 1944, with Caniglia, Renato Gigli; 1946, with Caniglia, Ziliani, Silveri; Venice, 1951, with Guerrini, Voyer, Panerai, Baronti, conductor Votto; la Scala 1953, with Tebaldi, Scotto, del Monaco, Guelfi, cond. Giulini.

### CHARACTERS

| | |
|---|---|
| Wally | Soprano |
| Stromminger, *her father* | Bass |
| Afra, *a landlady* | Contralto |
| Walter, *a strolling minstrel* | Soprano |
| Giuseppe Hagenbach, *of Sölden* | Tenor |
| Vincenzo Gellner, *of Hochstoff* | Baritone |
| The Messenger of Schnals | Tenor |

*Time:* 1800                                          *Place:* Tyrol

Act I. Stromminger is celebrating his seventieth birthday. There is shooting, and Gellner hits the target. Hagenbach of Sölden would not have thought much of that, says Stromminger, adding that he cares little for the boasts of this individual, who is anyhow the son of his greatest enemy. While Stromminger and Gellner drink, Walter sings a song, which, he says, has been written by Wally. Hagenbach enters, flushed with triumph and holding the skin of a bear he has shot. Stromminger mocks his skill, and then insults his father, so that Hagenbach throws Stromminger to the ground.

Wally rushes to protect her father, and recognises Hagenbach, who does not know her, as the youth she has been secretly in love with for some time. Gellner, who himself is in love with Wally, warns Stromminger that his daughter has fallen for his enemy, and Stromminger tells Wally she must marry Gellner within the month. Wally tries to persuade Gellner to give her up, but becomes indignant when he seems determined to carry out her father's scheme. Stromminger threatens to throw her out of his house if she does not agree to his suggestion, and Wally retorts that if he does she will go off alone into the snow.

Act II. The Eagle Tavern at Sölden. The landlady Afra is engaged to Hagenbach. Stromminger is now dead, and Wally has inherited a fortune. Gellner is no longer gay and care-free, but taciturn and even sinister. A festival is in progress, to which Wally is sure to come, they say, particularly since she will there meet her adored Hagenbach. He comes in, and seems to have little regard for Wally, whom he thinks of as better able to hate than to love. He is bet that he will not succeed in snatching a kiss from Wally, and, in spite of the warnings of Afra that you cannot play with love, he accepts the challenge.

When Wally comes in, someone suggests the kissing game, but Wally says that this is not the sort of thing that amuses her, as it does the other village girls, who use it as an excuse for what they cannot otherwise have. The people go in to Mass, and Wally, who has not seen Gellner since she left home on his account, offers him money if he will go away. He protests that he still loves her madly, and that in any case there is no use her setting her cap at Hagenbach as he is engaged to Afra. Wally is furious, and insults Afra; Hagenbach tells her that he will avenge her.

The dance starts. Hagenbach has turned the eagle's wing in his hat upside down, which means that any promise made has no value. Only Gellner notices, but Wally dances all the same with Hagenbach. In the end, he finds her passionate fascination is too much for him, and what has started as a game has gone rather further. He kisses her, but is then dragged away amid shouts of 'Hagenbach has won his bet and Afra is revenged'. Wally turns to Gellner, asks if he still wants her, and then says that Hagenbach, for what he has done to her, must die.

Act III. Hochstoff. Wally's bedroom can be seen on one side, on the other is the bridge over the Ache. Wally returns from the dance, dismisses Walter who had accompanied her, and retires to her room, not however before hearing that Hagenbach has started for Hochstoff on some unidentified mission. Wally laments her broken dream of love, but finds enough forgiveness in her heart to wonder whether she should tell Gellner that he must not do her bidding and rid the world of Hagenbach. Suddenly there is a knock at the door; Gellner tells her he has taken advantage of the dark and has just pushed Hagenbach into the abyss below.

Wally is horror-stricken, and drags Gellner out. A crowd collects in answer to her cries for help. Wally promises Afra that Giuseppe shall be hers if he survives, and herself goes down with a rope to rescue him. He is brought up unconscious. Wally tells Afra that he has been restored to her by the grace of God. She kisses him, and says that Afra should tell him she has returned the kiss he gave her at the dance.

Act IV.    Tired and hopeless, Wally contemplates the glacier near her house. Walter comes by and tells her that she is in danger from the avalanches which are prevalent at that time of the year —it is Christmas; why does she not come down to celebrate with them? She says good-bye to Walter, asking him only that he will pause on his way down and sing for her the song of the Edelweiss which was heard earlier in the opera.

He leaves her sadly, and she prepares to die like the girl in the song. Suddenly, she hears another voice, not Walter's. She thinks at first that it is the elves of the glacier who are coming to fetch her, but soon understands that it is Hagenbach, recovered from his injuries and come to confess his love for her. Wally does not like to believe him, even when he tells her that his accident occurred when he was on his way to tell her he loved her. She admits her share in his 'accident', and he embraces her and tells her that it makes no difference to his love. The sky is overcast, and a fog comes up. Hagenbach goes to look for the path down. He shouts up to Wally, but the sound of an avalanche is heard. Wally calls anxiously to him, but all is silent. Opening her arms wide, she throws herself after the avalanche.                    H.

# RUGGIERO LEONCAVALLO
## (1858–1919)

### I PAGLIACCI
### The Strolling Players

OPERA in two acts, words and music by Ruggiero Leoncavallo. Première, Teatro dal Verme, Milan, May 21, 1892, with Stehle, Giraud, Maurel, Ancona, Daddi. First performed Grand Opera House, New York, June 15, 1893, under the direction of Gustav Hinrichs, with Selma Kronold, Montegriffo, and Campanari; Covent Garden and Metropolitan later the same year, with Melba, De Lucia, and Ancona. Constantly performed at all opera houses. Famous Canios have included Caruso, Martinelli, Gigli, Zenatello.

### CHARACTERS

Canio (*in the play 'Pagliaccio'*), *head of a troupe of strolling players* .................................Tenor
Nedda (*in the play 'Columbine*), *wife of Canio* .....Soprano
Tonio (*in the play 'Taddeo'*), *a clown* .........Baritone
Beppe (*in the play 'Harlequin'*) ....................Tenor
Silvio, *a villager* .............................Baritone
Villagers

*Time:* The Feast of the Assumption, about 1865–70
*Place:* Montalto, in Calabria.

*Pagliacci* opens with a prologue. There is an instrumental introduction. Then Tonio pokes his head through the curtains,— 'Si puo? Signore, Signori' (By your leave, Ladies and Gentlemen) —comes out, and sings. The prologue rehearses, or at least hints at, the story of the opera, and does so in musical phrases, which we shall hear again as the work progresses—the bustle of the players as they make ready for the performance; Canio's lament that he must be merry before his audiences, though his heart be breaking; part of the lovemaking music between Nedda and Silvio; and the theme of the intermezzo, to the broad measures of which Tonio sings, 'E voi piuttosto che le nostre povere gabbane' (Ah, think then, sweet people, when you behold us clad in our motley):

E vo-i, piut-to-sto che le no-stre po-ve-re gabbane di-strio-ni

The prologue, in spite of ancient prototypes, was a bold stroke on the part of Leoncavallo, and, as the result proved, a successful one. Besides its effectiveness in the opera, it has made a favourite concert number.

Act I.    The edge of the village of Montalto, Calabria. People are celebrating the Feast of the Assumption. In the background is the tent of the strolling players. These players, Canio, Nedda, Tonio, and Beppe, in the costume of the characters in the play they are to enact, are parading through the village.

The opening chorus, 'Son qua' (They're here), proclaims the innocent joy with which the village hails the arrival of the players. The beating of a drum, the blare of a trumpet are heard. The players, having finished their parade through the village, are returning to their tent. Beppe, in his Harlequin costume, enters leading a donkey drawing a gaudily painted cart, in which Nedda is reclining. Behind her, in his Pagliaccio costume, is Canio, beating the big drum and blowing the trumpet. Tonio, dressed as Taddeo, the clown, brings up the rear. The scene is full of life and gaiety.

Men, women, and boys, singing sometimes in separate groups, sometimes together, form the chorus. The rising inflection in their oft-repeated greeting to Canio as 'il principe se dei pagliacci' (the prince of players), adds materially to the lilt of joy in their greeting to the players whose coming performance they evidently regard as the climax to the festival.

Canio addresses the crowd. At seven o'clock the play will begin. They will witness the troubles of poor Pagliaccio, and the vengeance he wreaked on the Clown, a treacherous fellow. 'Twill be a strange combination of love and of hate. Again the crowd acclaims its joy at the prospect of seeing the players on the stage behind the flaps of the tent.

Tonio comes forward to help Nedda out of the cart. Canio boxes his ears, and lifts Nedda down himself. Tonio, jeered at by the women and boys, angrily shakes his fists at the youngsters, and goes off muttering that Canio will have to pay high for what he has done. Beppe leads off the donkey with the cart, comes back, and throws down his whip in front of the tent. A villager asks Canio to drink at the tavern. Beppe joins them. Canio calls to Tonio. Is he coming with them? Tonio replies that he must stay behind to groom the donkey. A villager suggests that Tonio is remaining in order to make love to Nedda. Canio takes the intended humour of this sally rather grimly: 'Un tal gioco, credetemi' (Such a game, believe me, friends). He says that in the play, when he interferes with Tonio's lovemaking, he lays himself open to a beating. But in real life—let anyone, who would try to rob him of Nedda's love, beware. The emphasis with which he speaks causes comment.

'What can he mean?' asks Nedda in an aside.

'Surely you don't suspect her?' question the villagers of Canio. 'Of course not,' protests Canio, kissing Nedda on the forehead.

Just then the bagpipers from a neighbouring village are heard approaching. The musicians, followed by the people of their village, arrive to join in the festival. All are made welcome, and the villagers, save a few who are waiting for Canio and Beppe, go off down the road toward the village. The church bells ring. The villagers sing the pretty chorus, 'Din, don—suona vespero' (Ding, dong—the vespers bell). Canio nods good-bye to Nedda. He and Beppe go toward the village.

Nedda is alone. Canio's words and manner worry her. 'How fierce he looked and watched me!—Heavens, if he should suspect me!' But the birds are singing, the birds, whose voices her mother understood. Her thoughts go back to her childhood. She sings, 'Oh! che volo d'augelli' (Ah, ye beautiful song-birds), which leads up to her vivacious *ballatella*, 'Stridono lassu' (Forever flying through the boundless sky).

Tonio comes out from behind the theatre. He makes violent love to Nedda. The more passionately the clown pleads, the more she mocks him, and the more angry he grows. He seeks forcibly to grasp and kiss her. She backs away from him. Spying the whip where Beppe threw it down, she seizes it, and with it strikes Tonio across the face. Infuriated, he threatens, as he leaves her, that he will yet be avenged on her.

A man leans over the wall. He calls in a low voice, 'Nedda!' 'Silvio!' she cries. 'At this hour . . . what madness!'

He assures her that it is safe for them to meet. He has just left Canio drinking at the tavern. She cautions him that, if he had been a few moments earlier, his presence would have been discovered by Tonio. He laughs at the suggestion of danger from a clown.

Silvio has come to secure the promise of the woman he loves, and who has pledged her love to him, that she will run away with him after the performance that night. She does not consent at

once, not because of any moral scruples, but because she is afraid.
After a little persuasion, however, she yields. The scene reaches its
climax in an impassioned love duet, 'E allor perchè, di', tu m'ai
stregato' (Why hast thou taught me Love's magic story). The
lovers prepare to separate, and agree not to see each other again
until after the play, when they are to meet and elope.

But the jealous and vengeful Tonio has overheard them, and
has run to the tavern to bring back Canio. He comes just in time
to hear Nedda call after Silvio, who has climbed the wall, 'To-
night, love, and forever I am thine.'

Canio, with drawn dagger, makes a rush to overtake and stay
the man, who was with his wife. Nedda places herself between
him and the wall, but he thrusts her violently aside, leaps the
wall, and starts in pursuit. 'May Heaven protect him now,' prays
Nedda for her lover, while Tonio chuckles.

The fugitive has been too swift for Canio. The latter returns.
'His name!' he demands of Nedda, for he does not know who
her lover is. Nedda refuses to give it. Silvio is safe! What matter
what happens to her. Canio rushes at her to kill her. Tonio and
Beppe restrain him, and Tonio whispers to him to wait: Nedda's
lover surely will be at the play—a look, or gesture from her will
betray him. Then Canio can wreak vengeance. Canio thinks well
of Tonio's ruse. Nedda escapes into the theatre.

It is time to prepare for the performance. Beppe and Tonio
retire to do so.

Canio's grief over his betrayal by Nedda finds expression in
one of the most famous numbers in Italian opera, 'Vesti la
giubba' (On with the motley), with its tragic 'Ridi Pagliaccio'
(Laugh then, Pagliaccio), as Canio goes toward the tent, and
enters it. It is the old and ever effective story of the buffoon
who must laugh, and make others laugh, while his heart is breaking.

Act II.    The scene is the same as that of the preceding act.
Tonio with the big drum takes his position at the left angle of
the theatre. Beppe places benches for the spectators, who begin
to assemble, while Tonio beats the drum. Silvio arrives and nods
to friends. Nedda, dressed as Columbine, goes about with a plate
and collects money. As she approaches Silvio, she pauses to
speak a few words of warning to him, then goes on, and re-enters
the theatre with Beppe. The brisk chorus becomes more insistent
that the play begin. Most of the women are seated. Others stand
with the men on slightly rising ground.

A bell rings loudly. The curtain of the tent theatre on the stage
rises. The mimic scene represents a small room with two side
doors and a practicable window at the back. Nedda, as Columbine, is walking about expectantly and anxiously. Her husband,
Pagliaccio, has gone away till morning; Taddeo is at the market;
she awaits her lover, Harlequin. A dainty minuet forms  the
musical background.

A guitar is heard outside. Columbine runs to the window with
signs of love and impatience. Harlequin, outside, sings his pretty
serenade to his Columbine, 'O Colombina, il tenero fido Arlec-
chin' (O Columbine, unbar to me thy lattice high).

The ditty over, she returns to the front of the mimic stage, seats
herself, back to the door, through which Tonio, as Taddeo, a
basket on his arm, now enters. He makes exaggerated love to
Columbine, who, disgusted with his advances, goes to the window,
opens it, and signals. Beppe, as Harlequin, enters by the window.
He makes light of Taddeo, whom he takes by the ear and turns
out of the room, to the accompaniment of a few kicks. All the
while the minuet has tripped its pretty measure and the village
audience has found plenty to amuse it.

Harlequin has brought a bottle of wine, also a phial with a
sleeping potion, which she is to give her husband, when opportunity offers, so that, while he sleeps, she and Harlequin may fly
together. Love appears to prosper, till, suddenly, Taddeo bursts
in. Columbine's husband, Paggliaccio, is approaching. He suspects her, and is stamping with anger. 'Pour the philtre in his
wine, love!' admonishes Harlequin, and hurriedly gets out
through the window.

Columbine calls after him, just as Canio, in the character of
Pagliaccio, appears in the door. 'To-night, love, and forever, I

am thine!'—the same words Canio had heard his wife call after
her lover a few hours before.

Columbine parries Pagliaccio's questions. He has returned too
early. He has been drinking. No one was with her, save the harmless Taddeo, who has become alarmed and has sought safety in
the closet. From within, Taddeo expostulates with Pagliaccio.
His wife is true, her pious lips would ne'er deceive her husband.
The audience laughs.

But now it is no longer Pagliaccio but Canio who calls out
threateningly, not to Columbine, but to Nedda, 'His name!'

'Pagliaccio! Pagliaccio!' protests Nedda, still trying to keep
up the play, 'No!' cries out her husband—in a passage dramatically almost as effective as 'Ridi Pagliaccio!'—'I am Pagliaccio
no more! I am a man again, with anguish deep and human!' The
audience thinks his intensity is wonderful acting—all save Silvio,
who shows some signs of anxiety.

'Thou had'st my love,' concludes Canio, 'but now thou hast
my hate and scorn.'

'If you doubt me,' argues Nedda, 'why not let me leave
you?'

'And go to your lover!—His name! Declare it!'

Still desperately striving to keep up appearances, and avert the
inevitable, Nedda, as if she were Columbine, sings a chic gavotte,
'Suvvia, cosi terribile' (I never knew, my dear, that you were such
a tragic fellow).

She ends with a laugh, but stops short, at the fury in Canio's
look, as he takes a knife from the table.

'His name!' 'No!'—Save her lover she will, at whatever cost
to herself.

The audience is beginning to suspect that this is no longer
acting. The women draw back frightened, overturning the
benches. Silvio is trying to push his way through to the
stage.

Nedda makes a dash to escape into the audience. Canio pursues
and catches up with her.

'Take that—and—that!' (He stabs her in the back.) 'Soccorso
... Silvio!' (Help! Help!—Silvio!)

A voice from the audience cries, 'Nedda!' A man has nearly
reached the spot where she lies dead. Canio turns savagely,
leaps at him. A steel blade flashes. Silvio falls dead beside
Nedda.

'Gesumaria!' shriek the women; 'Ridi Pagliaccio!' sob the
instruments of the orchestra. Canio stands stupefied. The knife
falls from his hand:

'La commedia è finita' (The comedy is ended).

There are plays and stories in which, as in *Pagliacci*, the drama
on a mimic stage suddenly becomes real life, so that the tragedy
of the play changes to the life-tragedy of one or more of the
characters. *Yorick's Love*, in which I saw Lawrence Barrett act,
and of which I wrote a review for *Harper's Weekly*, was adapted
by William D. Howells from *Drama Nuevo* by Estebanez, which
is at least fifty years older than *Pagliacci*. In it the actor Yorick
really murders the actor whom, in character, he is supposed to
kill in the play. In the plot, as in real life, this actor had won away
the love of Yorick's wife, before whose eyes he is slain by the
wronged husband. About 1883, I should say, I wrote a story, *A
Performance of Othello*, for a periodical published by students of
Columbia University, in which the player of Othello, impelled by
jealousy, actually kills his wife, who is the Desdemona, and then,
as in the play, slays himself. Yet, although the *motif* is an old
one, this did not prevent Catulle Mendès (who himself had been
charged with plagiarising, in *La Femme de Tabarin*, Paul Ferrier's
earlier play, *Tabarin*) from accusing Leoncavallo of plagiarising
*Pagliacci* from *La Femme de Tabarin*, and from instituting legal
proceedings to enjoin the performance of the opera in Brussels.
Thereupon Leoncavallo, in a letter to his publisher, stated that
during his childhood at Montalto a jealous player killed his wife
after a performance, that his father was the judge at the criminal's
trial—circumstances which so impressed the occurrence on his
mind that he was led to adapt the episode for his opera. Catulle
Mendès accepted the explanation and withdrew his suit.

K.

# ZAZÀ

Opera in four acts by Ruggiero Leoncavallo, text by the composer. Première at the Teatro Lirico, Milan, on November 10, 1900, with Storchio, Clorinda Pini-Corsi, Garbin, Sammarco, conductor Toscanini. First performed in London at Coronet Theatre, 1909; Metropolitan, New York, 1920, with Farrar, Crimi, Amato. Revived la Scala, 1940, with Favero, Gigli, Bechi; Naples, 1950, with Favero, Prandelli, Tagliabue.

## CHARACTERS

Zazà, *a music-hall singer* ........................ Soprano
Anaide, *her mother* ........................... Contralto
Floriana, *a music-hall singer* .................... Soprano
Natalia, *Zazà's maid* .................... Mezzo-Soprano
Mme. Dufresne ........................ Mezzo-Soprano
Milio Dufresne, *a young man-about-town* ............ Tenor
Cascart, *a music-hall performer* ................. Baritone
Bussy, *a journalist* ............................. Baritone
Marlardot, *proprietor of a music-hall* ............... Tenor
Lartigon, *monologist* ............................. Bass
Duclou, *stage manager* ........................ Baritone
Michelin, *journalist* ........................... Baritone
Courtois ....................................... Bass
Marco, *Dufresne's butler* .......................... Tenor
Toto, *Dufresne's child* .......................... Soprano
Auguste ........................................ Tenor
Claretta ....................................... Soprano
Simona ........................................ Soprano

*Time:* The present                      *Place:* Paris

Leoncavallo is supposed to have preferred *Zazà* to *Pagliacci*, but the public has been reluctant to accept the later opera at the composer's own valuation. All the same, it has enjoyed a certain success whenever a singing actress of sufficient personal attraction has been available for the title rôle.

Act I.    The scene is back-stage at the music-hall where Zazà is the star attraction. On one side of the stage can be seen her dressing-room, on the other the back of a stage set. Zazà and her stage partner Cascart are lovers, but Zazà has taken a fancy to Milio Dufresne, and she boasts to the journalist Bussy that it will not be long before Dufresne in his turn succumbs to her charms. Zazà and Cascart behind the scenes have a charming 'kiss' duet, a parody on the sentimental music-hall song of the period. Dufresne waits for Zazà to come off the stage, and gossips with Bussy, revealing as he does so that he is considerably attracted to Zazà. He describes her smile with more rapture than caution: 'E un riso gentil'. It is obvious to Bussy that Zazà's conquest is already made.

Act II.    The love affair between Dufresne and Zazà is quickly under way, and the two of them go off to Zazà's house in the suburbs of Paris. Dufresne says that he must go away on business, and Zazà accepts this philosophically enough, until Cascart comes to see her. He hints that the trip may have other reasons than business behind it, and says that Dufresne has been seen with another woman in Paris. The scene includes a well-known aria for Cascart, 'Buona Zazà'. Zazà resolves to see for herself whether these suspicions are justified or not; she will follow Dufresne to Paris.

Act III.    Dufresne's Paris residence. Zazà, accompanied by Natalia, goes to the address she has been given. She sees a letter addressed to Madame Dufresne and realises with a shock that the 'other woman' in Dufresne's life is his wife. Dufresne's little child tells Zazà that her mother is out, and, when she is alone, Zazà gives way to her grief: 'Mamma usciva di casa.' She makes an excuse that she has come to the wrong address and leaves.

Act IV.    Zazà's house. Cascart tries to persuade Zazà to give up Dufresne, who is likely to bring nothing but sorrow and suffering into her life. The stage is her career, and his old affection for her is just as strong as ever: 'Zazà, piccola zingara.' But she cannot go against the dictates of her heart, for all her affection for Cascart, and she sends him away. When Dufresne returns to the house, Zazà taxes him with what she has discovered. She says that his being married makes no difference to her love for him, but, in an effort to punish him for his deception, pretends that she revealed their liaison to Madame Dufresne. Dufresne furiously curses her for what she has done to him, and throws her to the floor in his anger. Zazà's love is cured, and she sends Dufresne away, after telling him that she revealed nothing to his wife, who does not even know of her existence.                H.

# UMBERTO GIORDANO
## (1867–1948)

### ANDREA CHÉNIER

OPERA in four acts by Umberto Giordano; text by Luigi Illica. Première at la Scala, Milan, on March 28, 1896, with Carrera, Borgatti, Sammarco. First performed New York, 1896; Manchester, 1903 (in English); Camden Town Theatre, London, 1903 (in English); Covent Garden, 1905, with Strakosch, Zenatello, Sammarco, conductor Mugnone; Metropolitan, New York, 1921, with Muzio, Gigli, Danise, conductor Moranzoni. Revived Covent Garden, 1925, with Sheridan, Lauri-Volpi, Franci; 1930, with Sheridan, Gigli, Inghilleri; la Scala, fiftieth anniversary performance in 1946, with Caniglia, Beval, Guelfi, conductor Giordano; 1949, Giordano Commemoration performance, with Tebaldi, del Monaco, Silveri, conductor de Sabata.

### CHARACTERS

| | |
|---|---|
| A Major-domo | Baritone |
| Charles Gérard | Baritone |
| Madeleine de Coigny | Soprano |
| Countess de Coigny, *her mother* | Mezzo-Soprano |
| Bersi, *Madeleine's mulatto maid* | Mezzo-Soprano |
| Fléville, *a cavalier ('Romanziere')* | Baritone |
| The Abbé | Tenor |
| Andrea Chénier, *a poet* | Tenor |
| Mathieu, *a waiter* | Baritone |
| Incredibile, *a spy* | Tenor |
| Roucher, *a friend of Chénier's* | Bass |
| Madelon, *an old woman* | Mezzo-Soprano |
| Dumas, *president of the tribunal* | Baritone |
| Fouquier-Tinville, *attorney-general* | Baritone |
| Schmidt, *gaoler at St. Lazare prison* | Baritone |

Ladies and gentlemen of the court, citizens of France, soldiers, servants, peasants, prisoners, members of revolutionary tribunal

*Time:* Before and after French Revolution          *Place:* Paris

Historical as a character though André Chénier was, Giordano's librettist, Luigi Illica, has turned his life into fiction. Chénier was a poet, dreamer, and patriot; he was born in Constantinople, but

returned to Paris for his education, and there became a partici-
pant in the Revolution, and later a victim of it.

Act I.    Ballroom in a chateau. Preparations are in train for
a big party, and Gérard is amongst the servants setting the room
to rights. He mocks at the falsities and conventionalities of aristocratic life, but his words take on a more menacing character
when, provoked by the sight of his old father carrying in some
furniture, he launches forth into a denunciation of the masters he
works for and the system which keeps them in their unearned
luxury: 'Son sessant' anni.' The Countess, her daughter Madeleine, and Bersi come to see that the last-minute preparations for
the party are going well. The Countess checks up on endless
details, Madeleine discusses with her maid what she shall wear,
and Gérard comments on the beauty of the daughter of the
house, with whom he is secretly in love.

The guests arrive, notable amongst them the Abbé, and Fléville,
the latter of whom introduces an Italian musician, and the poet
Chénier. The Abbé talks of politics, but with some graceful
phrases Fléville bids the guests turn their minds to the serious
business of the Pastoral they are about to see and hear. There is
a pastoral chorus, and then Chénier, who has declined the Countess's request that he read a poem, agrees to recite at Madeleine's
invitation.

He sings the well-known *Improvviso di Chénier*, 'Un di, all'
azzurro spazio', in which he contrasts the beauty of nature with
the misery man makes around him; he denounces the selfishness
of those in authority—priests, politicians, aristocrats—and his
extremist sentiments find little favour with the guests (though the
aria itself has become enormously popular in the fifty years and
more since it was first sung).

Madeleine apologises to him for the situation her request has
put him in, but the Countess quickly gets the band to strike up
a gavotte. Even that is interrupted when Gérard bursts in at the
head of a band of beggars, announcing, butler-like, 'His Lord-
ship, Misery'. The major-domo gets them to leave, but not before
Gérard has torn his coat from his back, and denounced it as a
sign of slavery. The gaiety recommences, and amusement goes
on as if nothing has happened.

Act II.    The Café Hottot in Paris. The first phase of the
Revolution is over, and at one side of the stage is an altar-like

affair, on which stands a bust of Marat. Chénier sits alone at a table, and at another are Bersi and Incredibile, the spy. Bersi asks whether it is true that there are spies about, and says she herself has nothing to fear; is she not a true daughter of the Revolution, who thoroughly enjoys the new freedom, the drinking, and even watching a tumbril go by? Incredibile reads aloud from the note he is making about Bersi and about Chénier, both of whom he thinks suspicious characters.

Roucher appears and goes up to Chénier with a passport which he has been influential in getting for him. It is important he should fly at once, as he has powerful enemies. Chénier rejects such counsel of despair, and sings of his confidence in his own destiny: 'Credo a una possanza arcana.' Chénier moreover has received several anonymous letters from a woman, whose image has been built up in his mind until she is the most beautiful creature he has ever imagined. Chénier is about to leave, when Robespierre and several other leading Revolutionaries appear, followed by a cheering crowd. Gérard is one of the leaders, and Incredibile stops him to enquire more details about the woman he is trying to find. Gérard gives him a lyrical description of the beauty of Madeleine. Roucher is approached by Bersi, who tells him that someone wishes to see Chénier, who is in danger.

Madeleine arrives at the meeting-place and is soon joined by Chénier. It is some minutes before he recognises her and discovers that it was she who wrote the letters he has been receiving; at the same time, Incredibile looks from his hiding-place, makes up his mind that this is the woman Gérard is looking for, and goes off to inform him of her whereabouts. Madeleine asks Chénier for help in her loneliness, and he avows his love in a passionate duet. They are about to rush away together, when Gérard appears in their path, closely followed by the spy and by Roucher. Chénier shouts to his friend Roucher to take Madeleine into his charge, and he and Gérard draw their swords, neither having recognised the other. They fight, Gérard falls wounded, and recognises his opponent; he murmurs to him to be on his guard—he is on Fouquier-Tinville's list as a counter-revolutionary.

Incredibile returns with police, a crowd collects and demands vengeance on the assailant of a leader of the people; but Gérard says he did not recognise his attacker.

Act III.   The Revolutionary Tribunal. Mathieu speaks to the crowd which has assembled to watch the proceedings and tries to get them to contribute money and valuables to the common fund. The response is listless, until Gérard comes in and makes an impassioned speech. Immediately, all are ready to give, not least amongst them an old woman (Madelon), who says that she has already lost two sons fighting for France, but now offers the youngest, a boy of about fifteen. The crowd disperses singing the revolutionary song, *La Carmagnole*.

Gérard asks Incredibile, who has appeared, whether there is news of either Chénier or Madeleine—as to the former, a newsboy can be heard crying that he is arrested, and the latter, says the spy, will not be long in coming to look for her lover. Gérard is shocked by the spy's cynicism, still more so when Incredibile urges him to write out the indictment against Chénier; it will be needed for the forthcoming session of the Tribunal.

Gérard is haunted by conscience, and memory of his former patriotic enthusiasm. Can he denounce Chénier as 'an enemy of his country' ('Nemico della patria')? His revolutionary zeal, which formerly fed on such ideals as brotherly love, is now kept alive by jealousy and lust. It is an effective outburst, and one of the most popular arias in the opera. Swayed by his desire for Madeleine, he quickly signs the indictment and gives it to Incredibile.

Madeleine is brought in by Mathieu, and Gérard explains that Chénier has been arrested by his orders, and because of his own passion for her. She repulses him, but then offers her love in exchange for Chénier's freedom. She tells Gérard the story of her mother's dreadful death, in the flames of her house as it was burned by the mob: 'La mamma morta.' The tribunal is ready to sit and people crowd into the court. Gérard tells Madeleine he will do what he can for Chénier, and writes a note to the President.

The Tribunal is in session. Several prisoners are summarily condemned, to the applause of the crowd, and when Chénier's turn comes, he is refused permission by the court to answer the charge. On Gérard's insistence, he is finally allowed to defend himself: 'Si, fui soldato.' He has fought for his country and his ideals with sword and with pen; let them now take his life, but leave his honour unstained. Gérard raises his voice in Chénier's defence; the indictment was false, he says. But all is in vain, and the death sentence is duly passed and acclaimed.

Act IV.    In the courtyard of the Prison of St. Lazare, Chénier waits for the tumbril. Roucher is with him, and when he finishes writing, his friend asks him to read the poem he has written. 'Come un bel di di Maggio' he sings in a beautiful aria which describes his feelings as a poet in the face of death.

Roucher bids him farewell and leaves him to return to his cell.

Gérard appears at the outer gate, with Madeleine, and the gaoler lets them in. He agrees to allow Madeleine to take the place of a female prisoner condemned to death, and so to die with Chénier. Gérard leaves, determined to make a last effort in their defence, and Chénier is brought in. Their love duet is on a big scale; they exult in their love and rejoice that death will unite them for ever: 'Vicino a te.' In an opera in which Giordano has

indulged to the full his gift for passionate, lyrical melody, it is fitting that the most lyrical and the most passionate moments should come in the short last act, in the shape of Chénier's aria and the big duet.

*Andrea Chénier* is easily Giordano's most popular opera, and also his best; it is in the regular Italian repertory.  H.

## FEDORA

Opera in three acts by Umberto Giordano; text by A. Colautti from the play by Sardou. Première on November 17, 1898, at the Teatro Lirico, Milan, with Bellincioni, Caruso, Delfino Menotti, conductor Giordano. First performed Covent Garden, 1906, with Giachetti, Zenatello, Sammarco, conductor Mugnone; New York, Metropolitan, 1906, with Cavalieri, Caruso, Scotti, conductor Vigna. Revived Metropolitan, 1923, with Jeritza, Martinelli, Scotti, conductor Papi; Covent Garden, 1925, with Jeritza, Lappas, Badini, conductor Failoni; la Scala, Milan, 1932, with Cobelli, Pertile, Stabile, conductor de Sabata; 1939, with Pacetti, Gigli, Manacchini, conductor Marinuzzi; 1941, with Pederzini, Pigni, Gobbi, conductor Ghione; 1948, with Caniglia, Prandelli, Mascherini, conductor de Sabata.

### CHARACTERS

| | |
|---|---|
| Princess Fedora Romanov | Soprano |
| Count Loris Ipanov | Tenor |
| De Siriex, *a French diplomat* | Baritone |
| Countess Olga Sukarev | Soprano |
| Grech, *a police officer* | Bass |
| Cirillo, *a coachman* | Baritone |
| Dmitri, *a groom* | Contralto |
| A little Savoyard | Mezzo-Soprano |
| Désiré, *a valet* | Tenor |
| Baron Rouvel | Tenor |
| Lorek, *a surgeon* | Baritone |
| Borov, *a doctor* | Baritone |
| Nicola ⎫ *footmen* | ⎰ Tenor |
| Sergio ⎭ | ⎱ Baritone |
| Boleslao Lazinski, *a pianist* | Mime |

*Fedora* is, after *Andrea Chenier*, Giordano's most successful opera, and it is still popular all over Italy. It is written in the composer's familiar style—a mixture of the mellifluous and the stressful—and Sardou's effective story (and the fact that it offers excellent rôles to good singing actors) keeps it well in the forefront of the Italian repertory.

Act I plays in St. Petersburg, at the house of Count Vladimir Andrejevich; the time is 'the present'. The Count's servants are waiting for his return home, playing dominoes and gossiping about his way of life—gambling, drinking, and women are his diversions, which, they say, will have to stop now that he is marrying the rich widow, Princess Fedora. A bell rings; it is the Princess herself, asking where her fiancé is.

The sound of a sleigh is heard, and Grech enters quickly, asking where the Count's room is. He is carried to it, gravely wounded; doctors arrive, and we catch a glimpse of the end of the bed before the doctors close the door. No one knows who has wounded him, and Grech, the police officer in charge of the case, proceeds to question everyone present, beginning with Dmitri, Désiré, and Cirillo. The coachman gives his evidence dramatically and with emotion as he thinks about his master. He drove him to the shooting gallery, he said, and, a quarter of an hour after arriving, he heard two shots. Someone rushed out, leaving bloody footprints on the snow, and disappeared into the darkness. He (Cirillo) hailed a passing cab (in which was de Siriex) and together they went into the house, to find the Count upstairs covered in blood. It comes to light that the Count received a letter that very morning, brought by an old woman—and the building in which he was found wounded was let to an old woman. Was anyone else seen in the house during the morning? Yes, a young man, who sat down without giving his name, and eventually rushed out.

Suddenly, one of the servants remembers that it was Count Loris Ipanov who was there that morning—and Fedora jumps at the idea that it must have been he who committed the murder. Grech goes to his rooms—he lives just opposite—but returns to say that their quarry has escaped them. In the meanwhile the doctor summons Fedora, whose shriek of consternation tells us conclusively that Vladimir is dead.

Act II.    Fedora has determined to devote herself to the pursuit and capture of the man she presumes is her fiancé's murderer, Count Loris Ipanov, and to extract a confession of his guilt from him. A reception is in progress at her house in Paris, and Countess Olga introduces her friend the pianist, Boleslao Lazinski, to the guests. Fedora comes up to de Siriex, now French Foreign Secretary, and says to him with peculiar emphasis: 'I may need your help. You are an old friend, this is a newer one—Count Loris

Ipanov.' De Siriex is astonished at the speed with which Fedora has caught up with Loris.

Fedora is alone with Loris, and he declares his love in the passionate *arioso*, 'Amor ti vieta' (Love doth forbid you not to love). This flowing *cantilena* is one of the best-known songs in the repertory of the Italian tenor, and its performance customarily sends an Italian audience into a delirium of delight.

Fedora tells Borov, who asks her if she would like to give him a message for any Russian friend, that she too is going back to Russia almost immediately. She has been pardoned and her possessions restored to her. Loris is disconsolate, and admits that he cannot go. Fedora says she will intercede for him, but he tells her that in itself is unlikely to prove sufficient to have his sentence revoked. While Lazinski, with much comic pantomime, starts to play for the guests, Loris confesses to Fedora that he was in fact responsible for the death of Count Vladimir, but that he is innocent of his murder. Fedora can hardly contain her triumph. Loris says he can bring proof of his innocence, and she bids him return that very night with his documents.

Fedora, alone, sits down at her writing table. She calls to Grech and confirms that he and his men are to kidnap Loris once he has given her proof of his guilt and convey him on board a Russian ship. She has written to General Jarischkin in St. Petersburg to inform him of the way events have been moving, and has added the names of Loris's brother and of his friend Sokolev, who have been, she says, accomplices in his crime.

Loris arrives, and Fedora immediately accuses him of being a Nihilist and implicated in the plot against the Tsar's life, as well as guilty of the murder of Count Vladimir. He denies that his act was murder, and tells her the story of the Count's duplicity in carrying on a clandestine affair with Loris's wife, Wanda. He discovered the liaison by chance, and found proof in the shape of a letter from Wanda to Vladimir, which he took from a drawer in Vladimir's house the day of the murder. He shows Fedora letters from Vladimir to Wanda, and she knows that he is speaking the truth. Loris's confession, 'Mia madre, la mia vecchia madre', is one of the best-known passages in the score. He continues his story: he went to the place of assignation and caught the guilty pair together, was shot at by Vladimir and wounded, and, when he fired in his turn, inflicted a mortal wound on his enemy. Wanda escaped, only to die later.

Fedora is overcome at the story, but Loris tells her he is still pursued by an unknown adversary, who sets spies on him and will not let him live out his exile in peace. 'Vedi, io piango' (See, I am weeping) he sings, thinking of the mother and the native land he cannot see again. The signal is heard, and Fedora with difficulty prevents Loris from rushing out to meet his accusers. Only when she admits she loves him and will keep him with her, does he succumb to her persuasion.

Act III.    Fedora's villa in Switzerland. Mountaineers sing a Swiss song as a prelude to a short but passionate interchange between Fedora and Loris, who are now married and living happily together. Olga interrupts the idyllic scene, and is prepared to be enthusiastic about everything—even the bicycle she sees propped up against the wall. Loris recommends a tandem as better suited to her amatory purposes. Loris goes to collect his mail as de Siriex enters. He cannot resist telling Olga that her Polish pianist was in reality a spy, set on her trail to pump information from her.

When they are alone, de Siriex tells Fedora that Jarischkin had pursued his vengeful career until his dismissal by the new Tsar. Two young men, accomplices so it was said in the murder of Count Vladimir, were arrested; one disappeared, the other was shut up in a prison on the banks of the Neva, where, the tide rising suddenly, he was slowly drowned in his dungeon. It was Valerian, Loris's brother. The news of his death proved such a shock to his aged mother that she fell ill and died.

Fedora is left alone, and prays that Loris may be saved from the net she has unwittingly drawn around him: 'Dio di giustizia' (O God of justice). Loris enters and finds a telegram telling him he has been pardoned and is free to return to Russia. His joy knows no bounds. But he has had a letter from his friend Borov, who also sent the telegram, in which he indicates that a woman's accusation has been the means of prolonging his exile, and has even caused the deaths of his supposed 'accomplices', Valerian and Sokolev, which in their turn have broken the heart of his mother, who has died of shock.

Loris will not listen to Fedora's attempt to suggest that the woman in question may have done what she did believing him

PLATE XXI. Leonard Warren as Iago.

PLATE XXII. Mariano Stabile as Falstaff.

to have been guilty of a monstrous crime, but a renewal of her pleading shows him that his enemy has been none other than Fedora herself. He rushes at her in fury, but she drinks the poison she has carried concealed in the Byzantine crucifix she wore, and Borov arrives to find her dying. Loris's grief knows no bounds, and to the tune of 'Amor ti vieta', he forgives the woman who has brought such hate and such love into his life.          H.

# FRANCESCO CILEA
## (1866–1950)

### L'ARLESIANA
### The Maid of Arles

OPERA in three acts by Francesco Cilea; text by Leopoldo Marenco, based on Daudet's play. Première on November 27, 1897, at Teatro Lirico, Milan, with Fraces, de Paz, Caruso, Pasini, conductor Ferrari. Reduced to three acts (from the original four) in October 1898. Revived San Carlo, Naples, 1912; la Scala, Milan, 1936, with Pederzini, Carosio, Schipa, Basiola, conductor Antonicelli; 1943, with Stignani, Ferris, Schipa, Gobbi, conductor Questa. Still played all over Italy.

### CHARACTERS

Rosa Mamai .......................... Mezzo-Soprano
Federico, *her son* ............................... Tenor
Vivetta, *Rosa's god-daughter* .................... Soprano
Baldassare, *an old shepherd* .................... Baritone
Metifio, *a horse tender* ........................ Baritone
Marco, *Rosa's brother* ........................... Bass
L'Innocente, *Rosa's second son* ........... Mezzo-Soprano

Act I.    The action takes place in Provence, and the first scene is laid at the farm-house of Rosa Mamai, who has two children, one—Federico—grown up, the other—known as the Innocent—still a child, and feeble-minded. Baldassare is sitting with the Innocent, whom he alone cares for and loves. For the hundredth time, he tells him the story of the wolf and the kid, in a melodious lyrical passage: 'Come due tizzi accesi.' Rosa appears and asks what he thinks about Federico's determination to marry a girl from Arles—a girl moreover she has never met. She is even now waiting for her brother Marco, who lives in Arles and is adept at finding out about other people.

Vivetta comes on the scene, ostensibly to help with the work at the farm but really in order to be near Federico, with whom she is secretly in love. Rosa tells her that Federico is planning to get married, and she can hardly conceal her distress, the more so when Federico himself arrives, full of delight that his uncle has so good a report to make to his mother. Only Baldassare pays any attention to Vivetta's misery.

On the arrival of Marco, all go inside to celebrate. Metifio comes into the farm and asks Baldassare where he can find Rosa. She comes out to him, and, to the accompaniment of the rejoicing inside, he tells Rosa that the woman her son proposes to marry is nothing less than a strumpet. She was living with him, with the consent of her parents, until Federico offered her marriage; from that moment, she threw him out like a dog, and put all her energies into making sure that the marriage came off. He shows Rosa two letters he once received from the girl, and Baldassare persuades him to leave them behind, on condition they are returned the next day.

Federico calls them inside, and he continues to sing the drinking song until Rosa forbids him ever again to mention the name of the Arlesiana. She shows him the letters, and the curtain comes down as he despairingly understands their import.

Act II. By the pond of Vacares in the Camargue, Rosa and Vivetta are distractedly searching for Federico, who has left home. They cannot find him, but Rosa suggests to Vivetta that another woman, even more attractive than the Arlesiana, could make him forget; why should not Vivetta be that woman? Vivetta admits that she loves Federico, but says she cannot bring herself to say as much to Federico.

The Innocent comes up to them with Baldassare. The shepherd tells him he will find food in the bag he has left in the hut, but the Innocent cries out when he goes to fetch it; Federico himself is inside. Baldassare tries to persuade him to join his mother, but he refuses, although he admits eventually that he is mad with jealousy and even asks Baldassare for a potion against his hopeless love.

The Innocent repeats a line from Baldassare's story, and Federico takes up the idea, covering the Innocent, who has gone to sleep, with his coat: 'E la solita storia del pastore.' He envies his brother the sleep that allows him to forget, but says it is in vain; he sees always in front of his eyes the image of his beloved. Why, oh why, must he suffer so? The 'Lamento di Federico' is the best-known passage in the opera, and, with its graceful melody and easy, unforced lyricism, it is in strict contrast to most arias of the *verismo* period (see example page 594).

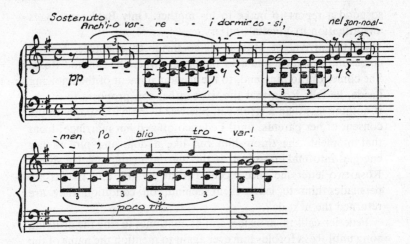

The sleeping child reminds Federico of the last time he saw the Arlesiana; the Innocent was lying asleep just as he is, and she called to Federico by name. The illusion is prolonged when Vivetta calls his name now, and admits that she loves him. Federico will however have none of her, and he escapes just as his mother returns to console Vivetta.

When Vivetta has left, Rosa leads back Federico, Baldassare and the Innocent. Federico is struck with his mother's misery, and affirms that he will not marry anyone who is not able to bring a spotless reputation into his family. He sees Vivetta, and asks her if she will still undertake to heal him from the 'illness' from which she told him he was suffering. They fall into one another's arms, and the act ends as Rosa and Baldassare congratulate them both.

Act III is preceded by an *intermezzo*. A large room inside Rosa's farm. Girls sing as they make garlands of flowers. Baldassare tells them that the marriage is fixed for the coming Saturday; he, who gave away the brides to Federico's father and grandfather, is planning after the ceremony to retire to the mountains where he was born.

To Baldassare comes Metifio. He admits that he has taken up again with the Arlesiana, who has forgiven him for his behaviour over the letters. He is going to carry her off that very night on horse back; he cannot bear the uncertainty in which he lives. Federico catches Metifio's last words, and at the sight of his rival, all his old jealousy, which he had thought dead, rekindles. He runs at Metifio with a hammer, and is only just prevented by the others from attacking him. The singing of the girls goes on, as Rosa emerges to pray to heaven to protect her son: 'Esser madre è un inferno.'

The Innocent comes out to her, with an unusual expression of life and intelligence on his face. He explains to his mother that he seems suddenly to understand, and will watch over Federico and see that no harm comes to him that night. Rosa cannot make out what has happened; is she mad herself, she wonders. She goes to her room. Day dawns slowly, and suddenly Federico appears, distraught; he repeats the story of the battle between the wolf and the kid which the shepherd has so often told his brother, and in some way connects it with the idea of Metifio eloping with the Arlesiana. He curses what he cannot help imagining. In vain his mother and his fiancée try to restrain him. He has taken on the look of an idiot and does not understand them. He rushes up the stairs leading to the roof, bolting the door at the bottom as he goes. His mother shouts to him to open the door, Vivetta calls for help, but a dull thud is heard. Rosa collapses on the ground, and Vivetta throws herself by her side. The Innocent kneels, sobbing, beside them.                                         H.

# ADRIANA LECOUVREUR

Opera in four acts by Francesco Cilea; text by Colautti, from the play by Scribe and Legouve. Première on November 26, 1902, at the Teatro Lirico, Milan, with Pandolfini, Ghibaudo, Caruso, de Luca, conductor Campanini. First performed Covent Garden, 1904, with Giachetti, Anselmi, Sammarco, conductor Campanini; Metropolitan, New York, 1907, with Cavalieri, Caruso, Scotti, conductor Ferrari. Revived la Scala, Milan, 1932, with Cobelli, Pederzini, Pertile, Ghirardini, conductor Ghione; 1939, with Oltra-bella, Elmo, Voyer, Valentino; 1942, with Cobelli; 1945, with Favero; Rome, 1952, with Caniglia, Benedetti, Campora, Gobbi. Magda Olivero has been one of the most famous of recent exponents of the title rôle.

## CHARACTERS

Maurizio, *Count of Saxony* ...................... Tenor
Prince de Bouillon ............................... Bass
L'Abate di Chazeuil ............................ Tenor
Michonnet, *stage director of the Comédie-*
     *Française* .................................. Baritone

Quinault  ⎱
Poisson   ⎰ *members of the company* { . . . . . . . . . . . . . . Bass
                                       { . . . . . . . . . . . . . Tenor
Major-domo . . . . . . . . . . . . . . . . . . . . . . . . . . . . . . . . . . . . . . Tenor
Adriana Lecouvreur . . . . . . . . . . . . . . . . . . . . . . . . Soprano
Princesse de Bouillon  . . . . . . . . . . . . . . . . . . Mezzo-Soprano
Mlle. Jouvenot   ⎱
Mlle. Dangeville ⎰ *members of the company* { . . . . . . Soprano
                                             { Mezzo-Soprano
A Chamber Maid . . . . . . . . . . . . . . . . . . . . . . . .

Ladies, Gentlemen, Servants

*Time:* 1730                                        *Place:* Paris

Act I.    The foyer of the Comédie-Française. Actors and
actresses going on to the stage demand their swords, hats, coats
from Michonnet, who complains that everyone expects him to
do everything at the same time. The Prince de Bouillon comes
in with the Abate and greets the actors and actresses. The visitors
look through at the stage, and comment on the fullness of the
house; hardly surprising, says Michonnet, since both Duclos and
Adriana Lecouvreur are playing to-night. Adriana comes in trying
over her speech. She acknowledges the cries of admiration
modestly, and says that she is only the handmaid of the arts: 'Io
son l'umile ancella.' It is one of Cilea's finest inspirations, and
the tune is heard frequently throughout the opera as a 'motto'
theme for Adriana.

Michonnet is her best friend, she tells them all, and the faithful
Michonnet bursts into tears of emotion; when all have left he
admits the reason—he has been in love with Adriana ever since
she joined the company. Dare he tell her now? He starts to, but
she tells him that she is in love with an unknown cavalier, attached
to the Count of Saxony. Michonnet leaves her alone, and in a
moment her as yet unknown lover is at her side. He addresses
her in a passionate *arioso*: 'La dolcissima effigie.' Adriana says
she will play only for him tonight, and leaves him, giving him
before she does so violets for his buttonhole.

The Prince and the Abate come in, and the latter reads a letter
which they have intercepted; it is from the Prince's wife, but

because it makes an assignation for eleven o'clock in the villa of the Prince's mistress, the actress Duclos, they think it is from her. Their plan to surprise the lovers is overheard by some of the actors and actresses, and a spritely ensemble ensues.

Act II. The Princesse de Bouillon—it is she who has arranged the assignation—is seated, listening to the voices of the night. She reflects agitatedly on the torments of love in a big soliloquy: 'Acerba voluttà.' Maurizio arrives, and excuses his lateness; he was followed. She notices the violets and asks whether they had nothing to do with his lateness; he says it was for her he brought them: 'L'anima ho stanca'.

Their conversation is interrupted by the sound of a carriage outside; it is her husband, exclaims the Princess—she must hide. This she does, and the Prince de Bouillon, accompanied by the Abate, comes in to find Maurizio alone. They taunt him that he is caught, and are astonished when he threatens a duel. Why should he make so much fuss? The Prince is tired of la Duclos; why should not the Count of Saxony take her on as his mistress? Maurizio begins to understand, when, a moment later, Adriana is led in and introduced to him. This time, the astonishment is hers; the man she had thought a retainer, turns out to be the Count of Saxony himself. The Prince and the Abate go out to see that they are not kept waiting longer for supper, and Adriana and Maurizio are alone.

In a short duet they renew their passionate vows. Michonnet comes in, asking that he may speak to Duclos, as an important decision has to be made over a new rôle before morning. She is here, says the Abate; Maurizio tries to silence him, but Michonnet takes the decision into his own hands and goes firmly into the room which Maurizio has tried to bar. Maurizio swears to Adriana that Duclos is not there; his appointment had to do with his political position, not with love. She believes him, and when Michonnet comes out saying it was not the Duclos, and the Abate wishes to discover the lady's identity, it is Adriana who prevents him. She says to Michonnet that she means to keep her word to Maurizio and help whoever it is.

Adriana knocks at the door and says she can save the lady inside with the aid of the key of the garden which she has in her hand. The Princess plies her with questions, and eventually admits that she loves Maurizio. Adriana proudly claims his love as her own, to the tune of her recent duet with him. The act ends as the Princess escapes just before the Prince and his followers return.

Act III.    A party is being prepared in the house of the Prince de Bouillon. The Princess wonders where she has heard the voice of her rival; she cannot place it. The guests arrive, amongst them Adriana, whom the Princess naturally recognises immediately, and who sings the tune originally heard to the words of 'Io son l'umile ancella'. The Princess mutters something about a duel which she says Maurizio has taken part in, and in which he was gravely wounded—and Adriana shows obvious signs of emotion. Maurizio comes in, and is persuaded to talk about his battle experiences. A ballet entertainment has been arranged, and during its course the conversation continues, developing in the end into a battle of wits between the Princess and Adriana.

Act IV.    The scene is the same as that of Act I. Michonnet waits for Adriana who presently appears in a mood bordering on suicide. Various actors and actresses come in to congratulate her on her birthday, and presently a casket is brought in. Adriana opens it as the others leave, and sees in it violets, the very ones she had given Maurizio the previous evening, but by now shrivelled and old. She sings sadly to the violets, in whose shrivelled appearance she sees the dying of Maurizio's love for her: 'Poveri fiori.' Michonnet tries to comfort her, and smiles when he hears Maurizio's voice outside. Adriana cannot resist Maurizio's protestation of innocence, least of all when he proposes marriage to her, and tells her in the same breath that all his claims have been met and he is once more in possession of his rightful titles. For a moment she tries to impress him by saying that the stage is the only throne she can ever mount, but her love is too much for her, and she and Maurizio rest happily in each other's arms.

Suddenly, she turns pale and would fall if Maurizio did not catch her. She thinks it has something to do with the flowers which she gave Maurizio and which he returned to her; but he denies having ever done such a thing. Adriana is convulsed with pain, and for a moment does not recognise her lover. Maurizio sends for help, and Michonnet comes in; he thinks the flowers may have been poisoned and suggests that a rival has done it. After a further convulsion, Adriana dies in their arms. The Princess's revenge is complete.                                    H.

# PIETRO MASCAGNI

## (1863–1945)

### CAVALLERIA RUSTICANA
### Rustic Chivalry

OPERA in one act by Pietro Mascagni; text by G. Menasci and G. Targioni-Tozzetti, based on the play of G. Verga. Première on May 17, 1890, at Teatro Costanzi, Rome, with Bellincioni, Stagno, Salasso, conductor Mugnone. First performed Philadelphia, 1891, with Kronold, Guille, del Puente; Metropolitan, New York, 1891, with Eames, Valero; Shaftesbury Theatre, London, 1891, with Masiani, Brema, Damian, Vignas, Brombara, conductor Arditi; Covent Garden, 1892, with Calvé, de Lucia. Special fiftieth anniversary performances under the direction of the composer took place in Italy in 1940, including Rome, with Bruna Rasa, Masini, Franci.

### CHARACTERS

Turiddu, *a young soldier* ........................Tenor
Alfio, *the village teamster* .....................Baritone
Lola, *his wife* .........................Mezzo-Soprano
Mamma Lucia, *Turiddu's mother* ...............Contralto
Santuzza, *a village girl* .......................Soprano

Villagers, Peasants, Boys

*Time:* The present, on Easter day      *Place:* A village in Sicily

*Cavalleria Rusticana* in its original form is a short story, compact and tense, by Giovanni Verga. From it was made the stage tragedy, in which Eleonora Duse displayed her great powers as an actress. It is a drama of swift action and intense emotion; of passion, betrayal, and retribution. Much has been made of the rôle played by the 'book' in contributing to the success of the opera. It is a first-rate libretto—one of the best ever put forth. It inspired the composer to what so far has remained his only significant achievement. But only in that respect is it responsible for the success of *Cavalleria Rusticana* as an opera. The hot blood of the story courses through the music of Mascagni, who in his score also has quieter passages, that make the cries of passion the more poignant. Like practically every enduring success, that of *Cavalleria Rusticana* rests upon merit. From beginning to end it is an inspiration. In it, in 1890, Mascagni, at the age of twenty-one, 'found himself', and ever afterwards was trying, unsuccessfully, to find himself again.

The prelude contains three passages of significance in the development of the story. The first of these is the phrase of the despairing Santuzza, in which she cries out to Turiddu that, despite his betrayal and desertion of her, she still loves and pardons him. The second is the melody of the duet between Santuzza and Turiddu, in which she implores him to remain with her and not to follow Lola into the church. The third is the air in Sicilian style, the *Siciliana*, which, as part of the prelude, Turiddu sings behind the curtain, in the manner of a serenade to Lola: 'O Lola, ch'ai di latti' (O Lola, fair as a smiling flower).

With the end of the *Siciliana* the curtain rises. It discloses a public square in a Sicilian village. On one side, in the background, is a church, on the other Mamma Lucia's wineshop and dwelling. It is Easter morning. Peasants, men, women, and children cross or move about the stage. The church bells ring, the church doors swing open, people enter. A chorus, in which, mingled with gladness over the mild beauty of the day, there is also the lilt of religious ecstasy, follows. Like a refrain the women voice and repeat 'Gli aranci olezzano sui verdi margini' (Sweet is the air with the blossoms of oranges). The men, meanwhile, pay a tribute to the industry and charm of women. Those who have not entered the church go off singing. Their voices die away in the distance.

Santuzza, sad of mien, approaches Mamma Lucia's house, just as her false lover's mother comes out. There is a brief colloquy between the two women. Santuzza asks for Turiddu. His mother answers that he has gone to Francofonte to fetch some wine. Santuzza tells her that he was seen during the night in the village. The girl's evident distress touches Mamma Lucia. She bids her enter the house.

'I may not step across your threshold,' exclaims Santuzza. 'I cannot pass it, I, most unhappy excommunicated outcast!'

Mamma Lucia may have her suspicions of Santuzza's plight. 'What of my son?' she asks. 'What have you to tell me?'

But at that moment the cracking of a whip and the jingling of bells are heard from off-stage. Alfio, the teamster, comes upon the scene. He is accompanied by the villagers. Cheerfully he sings the praises of a teamster's life, also of Lola's, his wife's, beauty.

The villagers join him in chorus, 'Il cavallo scalpita' (Gaily moves the tramping horse).

Alfio asks Mamma Lucia if she still has on hand some of her fine old wine. She tells him it has given out; Turiddu has gone away to buy a fresh supply of it.

'No,' says Alfio. 'He is here. I saw him this morning standing not far from my cottage.' Mamma Lucia is about to express great surprise. Santuzza is quick to check her.

Alfio goes his way. A choir in the church intones the 'Regina Cœli'. The people in the square join in with 'Allelujas'. Then they kneel and, led by Santuzza's voice, sing the Resurrection hymn, 'Inneggiamo, il Signor non è morto' (Let us sing of the Lord now victorious).

Mamma Lucia asks the girl why she signalled her to remain silent when Alfio spoke of Turiddu's presence in the village. 'Voi lo sapete' (Now you shall know), exclaims Santuzza, and in one of the most impassioned numbers of the score, pours into the ears of her lover's mother the story of her betrayal. Before Turiddu left to serve his time in the army, he and Lola were in love with each other. But, tiring of awaiting his return, the fickle Lola married Alfio. Turridu, after he had come back, made love to Santuzza and betrayed her; now, lured by Lola, he has taken advantage of Alfio's frequent absences, and has gone back to his first love. Mamma Lucia pities the girl, who begs that she go into church and pray for her.

Turiddu comes, a handsome fellow. Santuzza upbraids him for pretending to have gone away, when instead he has surreptitiously been visiting Lola. It is a scene of vehemence. But when Turiddu intimates that his life would be in danger were Alfio to know of his visits to Lola, the girl is terrified: 'Battimi, insultami, t'amo e perdono' (Beat me, insult me, I still love and forgive you).

Such is her mood—despairing, yet relenting. But Lola's voice is heard off-stage. Her song is carefree, a key to her character, which is fickle and selfish, with a touch of the cruel. 'Fior di giaggiolo' (O gentle flower of gold) runs her song. It conveys in its melody, its pauses, and inflections, a quick sketch in music of the heartless coquette, who, to gratify a whim, has stolen Turiddu from Santuzza. She mocks the girl, then enters the church. Only a few minutes has she been on the stage, but Mascagni has let us know all about her.

A highly dramatic scene, one of the most impassioned out-bursts of the score, occurs at this point. Turiddu turns to follow Lola into the church. Santuzza begs him to stay. 'No, no, Turiddu, rimani, rimani, ancora—Abbandonarmi dunque tu vuoi?' (No, no, Turiddu! Remain with me now and forever! Love me again! How can you forsake me?).

A highly dramatic phrase, already heard in the prelude, occurs at 'La tua Santuzza piange et'implora' (Lo! here thy Santuzza, weeping, implores thee).

Turiddu repulses her. She clings to him. He loosens her hold and casts her from him to the ground. When she rises, he has followed Lola into the church.

But the avenger is nigh. Before Santuzza has time to think, Alfio comes upon the scene. He is looking for Lola. To him in the fewest possible words, and in the white voice of suppressed passion, Santuzza tells him that his wife has been unfaithful with Turiddu. His outburst has real strength. In the brevity of its recitatives, the tense summing up in melody of each dramatic situation as it develops in the inexorably swift unfolding of the tragic story, lies the strength of *Cavalleria Rusticana.*

Santuzza and Alfio leave. The square is empty. But the action goes on in the orchestra. For the *intermezzo*—the famous *inter-mezzo*—which follows, recapitulates, in its forty-eight bars, what has gone before, and foreshadows the tragedy that is impending. There is no restating here of leading motives. The effect is accomplished by means of terse, vibrant melodic progression. It is melody and yet it is drama. Therein lies its merit. For no piece of serious music can achieve the world-wide popularity of this intermezzo and not possess merit.

What is to follow in the opera is quickly accomplished. The people come out of church. Turiddu, in high spirits, because he is with Lola and because Santuzza no longer is hanging around to reproach him, invites his friends over to his mother's wineshop. Their glasses are filled. Turiddu dashes off a drinking song, 'Viva il vino spumeggiante' (Hail! the ruby wine now flowing).

Alfio joins them. Turiddu offers him wine. He refuses it. The women leave, taking Lola with them. In a brief exchange of words Alfio gives the challenge. In Sicilian fashion the two men embrace, and Turiddu, in token of acceptance, bites Alfio's ear. Alfio goes off in the direction of the place where they are to test their skill with the stiletto.

Turiddu calls for Mamma Lucia. He is going away, he tells her. At home the wine cup passes too freely. 'Mamma, quel vino è generoso' (Mother the red wine burns me like fire). He must leave. If he should not come back she must be like a kindly mother to Santuzza—'Santa, whom I have promised to lead to the altar'.

He goes. Mamma Lucia wanders aimlessly to the back of the stage. She is weeping. Santuzza comes on, throws her arms around the poor woman's neck. People crowd upon the scene. All is suppressed excitement. There is a murmur of distant voices. A woman is heard calling from afar: 'They have murdered neighbour Turiddu!'

Several women enter hastily. One of them , the one whose voice was heard in the distance, repeats, but now in a shriek, 'Hanno ammazzato compare Turiddu!'—(They have murdered neighbour Turiddu!).

Santuzza falls in a swoon. Mamma Lucia is supported by some of the women.

A tragedy of Sicily, hot in the blood, is over.

K.

To *Cavalleria Rusticana* we owe the succession of short operas, usually founded on debased and sordid material, in which other composers have paid Mascagni the doubtful compliment of imitation in hopes of achieving similar success. Of all these, *Pagliacci*, by Leoncavallo, is the only one that has shared the vogue of the Mascagni opera. The two make a remarkably effective double bill, but their 'heart-on-the-sleeve' manner (and, in all fairness, that of their less successful competitors) has spurred on singers all over the world to exhibitions of lacrymose vocalism that would make the singers of the 'golden age' turn in their graves. How much *Cavalleria* and its companions benefit when sung seriously and 'straight', only those who have been lucky enough to hear it will know; how vulgar (in the wrong sense) the music can sound when sung by exhibitionists, most of us know all too well.

H.

# L'AMICO FRITZ
## Friend Fritz

Opera in three acts by Pietro Mascagni; text by P. Suardon (N. Daspuro), founded on Erckmann-Chatrian's novel. Première on November 1, 1891, at Teatro Costanzi, Rome, with Calvé, Synnemberg, de Lucia, Lhérie, conductor Ferrari. First performed Covent Garden, 1892, with Calvé, Ravogli, de Lucia, Dufriche; Philadelphia, 1892; Metropolitan, New York, 1893, with Calvé, Schalchi, de Lucia, Ancona. Revived Metropolitan, 1923, with Bori, Fleta, Danise; la Scala, Milan, 1930, with Marengo, Dino Borgioli, Ghirardini, conductor Mascagni; 1937, with Favero, Schipa, Danise; Florence Festival, 1941, with Magnoni, Tagliavini, Poli, conductor Mascagni.

### CHARACTERS

Fritz Kobus, *a rich bachelor landowner* . . . . . . . . . . . . . Tenor
Suzel, *a farmer's daughter* . . . . . . . . . . . . . . . . . . . . . Soprano
Beppe, *a gypsy* . . . . . . . . . . . . . . . . . . . . . . . . . Mezzo-Soprano
David, *a Rabbi*. . . . . . . . . . . . . . . . . . . . . . . . . . . . . . . Baritone
Hanezò ⎫ *friends of Fritz* . . . . . . . . . . . . . . . . . . . ⎧ Bass
Federico ⎭ . . . . . . . . . . . . . . . . . . . . . . . . . . . . . . . ⎩ Tenor
Caterina, *Fritz's housekeeper* . . . . . . . . . . . . . . . . . . . Soprano

*Time:* The present                         *Place:* Alsace

Act I.    The dining-room of Fritz's house. He complains to his friend David that he has once again been asked to provide the dowry for two neighbours who want to get married. He himself cannot understand this business of falling in love and sighing for a woman. Two friends, Hanezò and Federico, come in with Caterina his housekeeper to wish him luck on his fortieth birthday. They are all coming to sup with him, but David must leave them to give the good news to the young lovers. Fritz laughs at him, but he prophesies that within a year Fritz himself will be married.

Caterina brings in Suzel, the daughter of one of Fritz's tenants, who gives him flowers as a present: 'Son pocchi fiori' she sings, a pretty little aria. Fritz makes her sit beside him; before long they hear the sound of Beppe's fiddle outside. There is general admiration for his music-making, and, when he comes in, he is asked to sing for the company. This he does, and at the same time contrives to pay Fritz a graceful compliment on the subject of his charitable disposition: 'Laceri, miseri.'

Suzel leaves to rejoin her family, and all exclaim on her attractiveness now that she is nearly grown-up. David comments that he is likely soon to be marrying her off to someone or other, and Fritz protests that she is only a girl. David says he is prepared to bet Fritz that he will soon be married himself, and they agree that Fritz's vineyard shall be the subject of their wager. A party of orphans who have been befriended by Fritz come in to the sound of a march, and the act ends in general rejoicing.

Act II.　　An orchard near a farm. Suzel is picking cherries; she sings a little ditty to express her happiness and the whole scene is full of pastoral charm. Fritz comes in ('Suzel, buon di'), compliments Suzel on her singing, and thanks her for the flowers she has picked him; she tells him the cherries are already ripe.

Han del-la por-po-ra vi-vo co-lo-re, son dol-cie te-ne-re

She mounts a ladder, picks the cherries and throws them down to Fritz, who is charmed and captivated by her youth and freshness. Where else can he find such peace and innocence ('Tutto tace'); when but in spring ('Tu sei bella, o stagion primaverile')?

Tu sei bel-la, o ..... sta-gion pri-ma-ve-ri-le! Rin-no-vel-la fiorie amor il dol-ce a-pri-le!

The feeling is very different from the coarse, full-blooded energy of *Cavalleria Rusticana*, but it is doubtful whether Mascagni ever elsewhere wrote music of such delicacy and genuine inspiration.

The sound of bells and cracking whips heralds the arrival of David, Beppe, Hanezò, and Federico. They suggest a drive round the countryside, but David pleads fatigue and stays behind. When Suzel offers him some water to drink, he tells her the scene reminds him of the story of Isaac and Rebecca, and makes her read the appropriate passage from the Bible. This she does,

David thinks, with evident understanding of its relevance to her situation. When Fritz and the others return, David determines to test Fritz's reaction and tells him that he has found a suitable husband for Suzel and that her father approves. Fritz is horrified at the idea, and when David has left him, he admits to himself that he must be in love, but immediately determines to evade the consequences and return with his friends to town. David does his best to comfort the unhappy Suzel, who watches him go—he has not even said good-bye—with a sad heart.

Act III.　　The intermezzo which begins the act has attained considerable popularity with Italian audiences, and is nearly as often encored as the famous vocal numbers of the score. The scene is the same as that of the first act. Fritz is distracted with the worry that the discovery of love has brought him. Beppe comes in and tries to comfort him, even going so far as to sing him a song he wrote while himself under the influence of unhappy love. Fritz is aghast that Beppe should have joined his persecutors.

Left alone, he laments that even Beppe should have been troubled with love; what hope, he implies, is there for him? He launches into a full-scale aria on the subject of the fatal passion: 'O amore, o bella luce del core.' David comes to him and tells him that all is arranged for Suzel's wedding; only his consent is now needed. Fritz distractedly refuses it, and rushes from the room. David calls in Suzel, who has brought fruit for Fritz. Why does she look so sad, he asks? She sings plaintively of her love for Fritz: 'Non mi resta che il pianto.'

Fritz himself comes in and asks her if it is true that she is going to be married. She begs him to save her from a match she does not want. He finally admits that he loves her himself, and they sing happily of their future bliss. David wins his bet, and all congratulate Fritz on his new-found happiness.

L'Amico Fritz is still frequently played in Italy. If there is nothing else in it to equal the Cherry duet, perhaps Mascagni's most purely musical composition, it has a consistent gentleness and charm. It also contains one of the few rôles in which a tenor has the chance to impersonate a middle-aged lover; perhaps on that account, and for the Cherry duet, it will not fail of revival for many years to come.　　　　　　　　　　　　　　　H.

# IRIS

Opera in three acts by Pietro Mascagni, text by Luigi Illica. Première on November 27, 1898, at the Teatro Costanzi, Rome, with Darclée, de Lucia, conductor Mascagni; revised version performed at la Scala, Milan, 1899, with the same singers. First performed Philadelphia, 1902; New York, 1902, with Farneti; Metropolitan, 1907, with Eames, Caruso, Scotti, Journet; Covent Garden, 1919, with Sheridan, Capuzzo, Couzinou, Huberdeau, conductor Mugnone. Revived Metropolitan, 1915, with Bori; Chicago, 1929, with Mason, Cortis; Metropolitan, 1931, with Rethberg, Gigli, de Luca, Pinza; la Scala, 1924, with Vigano, Pertile, Badini, conductor Toscanini; 1936, with Pampanini, Bertelli; 1944, with Carbone, conductor Guarnieri.

## CHARACTERS

Il Cieco, *the blind man* ........................... Bass
Iris, *his daughter* ............................. Soprano
Osaka, *a rich young man*......................... Tenor
Kyoto, *a takiomati* ........................... Baritone
Ragpickers, Shopkeepers, Geishas, *Mousmés* (laundry girls), *Sumarai*, Citizens, Strolling Players, Three Women representing Beauty, Death, and the Vampire; a Young Girl

*Time:* Nineteenth Century                    *Place:* Japan

Act I.    The home of Iris near the city. The hour is before dawn. The music depicts the passage from night into day. It rises to a crashing climax—the instrumentation including tamtams, cymbals, drums, and bells—while voices reiterate, 'Calore! Luce! Amor!' (Warmth! Light! Love!). In warmth and light there are love and life. A naturalistic philosophy, to which this opening 'Hymn to the Sun' gives the key, runs through *Iris.*

Fujiyama glows in the early morning light, as Iris, who loves only her blind father, comes to the door of her cottage. She has dreamed that monsters sought to injure her doll, asleep under a rosebush. With the coming of the sun the monsters have fled.

Iris is young and beautiful. She is desired by Osaka, a wealthy rake, and Kyoto, keeper of a questionable resort, plots to obtain her for him. While her father prays and *mousmés* sing on the bank of the stream, Iris tends her flowers: 'In pure stille.' Osaka and Kyoto come to her cottage with a marionette show. The play starts, and after a while Osaka, in the person of Jor, son of the sun god, sings a serenade: 'April la tua finestra.' While Iris is intent upon the performance, three geisha girls, representing Beauty, Death, and the Vampire, dance about her. They conceal her from view by spreading their skirts. She is seized and carried off. Osaka, by leaving money for the blind old father, makes the abduction legal. When Il Cieco returns, he is led to believe that his daughter has gone voluntarily to the Yoshiwara. In a rage he starts out to find her.

Act II.　　Interior of the 'Green House' in the Yoshiwara. Kyoto and Osaka regard the sleeping Iris, who awakens. At first she thinks it is an awakening after death. But death brings paradise, while she is unhappy. Osaka, who has placed jewels beside her, comes to woo, but vainly seeks to arouse her passions. In her purity she remains unconscious of the significance of his words and caresses. His brilliant attire leads her to mistake him for Jor, the sun god, but he tells her he is Pleasure. That frightens her. For, as she narrates to him, one day, in the temple, a priest told her that pleasure and death were one: 'Un di (ero piccina) al tempio.'

Osaka embraces her in a last effort to win her love ('Or dammi il braccio tuo'), then wearies of her innocence and leaves her. But Kyoto, wishing to lure him back, attires her in transparent garments and places her upon a balcony. The crowd in the street cries out in amazement over her beauty. Again Osaka wishes to buy her. She hears her father's voice, and joyously makes her presence known to him. He, ignorant of her abduction and believing her a voluntary inmate of the 'Green House', takes a handful of mud from the street, flings it at her, and curses her. In terror, she leaps from a window into the sewer below.

Act III.　　Ragpickers and scavengers are dragging the sewer before daylight. In song they mock the moon. A flash of light from the mystic mountain awakens what is like an answering gleam in the muck. They discover and drag out the body of Iris. They begin to strip her of her jewels. She shows signs of life. The sordid men and women flee. The rosy light from Fujiyama spreads over the sky. Warmth and light come once more. Iris regains consciousness. Spirit voices whisper of earthly existence and its selfish aspirations typified symbolically by the knavery of Kyoto, the lust of Osaka, the desire of Iris's father, Il Cieco, for the comforts of life through her ministrations.

Enough strength comes back to her for her to acclaim the

sanctity of the sun. In its warmth and light—the expression of Nature's love—she sinks, as if to be absorbed by Nature, into the blossoming field that spreads about her. Again, as in the beginning, there is the choired tribute to warmth, light, love—the sun!

K.

# GIACOMO PUCCINI

## (1858–1924)

### MANON LESCAUT

OPERA in four acts by Giacomo Puccini; text by Praga, Oliva, and Illica. Première on February 1, 1893, at the Teatro Reggio, Turin, with Cesira-Ferrani, Cremonini, Moro, Polinini, conductor Pome. First performed at Covent Garden, 1894, with Olgina, Beduschi, Pini-Corsi; Philadelphia, 1894; New York, 1898; Metropolitan, 1907, with Cavalieri, Caruso, Scotti. Revived Covent Garden, 1920, with Quaiatti (later dalla Rizza), Burke, Badini; 1929, with Sheridan (later Pampanini), Pertile, Badini; 1937, with Oltrabella, Menescaldi, Noble; Metropolitan, 1927, with Alda, Gigli, Scotti, Didur, conductor Serafin; 1949, with Kirsten, Björling, Valdengo; la Scala, Milan, 1922, with Carraciolo, Pertile, Badini, conductor Toscanini; 1934, with Pacetti, Ziliani, Biasini; 1941, with Caniglia, Gigli, Poli, conductor Marinuzzi; 1944, with Favero, Beval, Stabile, conductor Marinuzzi; 1949, with Barbato, del Monaco, Colombo.

### CHARACTERS

Manon Lescaut ............................Soprano

Lescaut, *sergeant of the King's Guards* ...........Baritone

Chevalier des Grieux ...........................Tenor

Geronte di Ravoir, *Treasurer-General*...............Bass

Edmondo, *a student*...........................Tenor

The Innkeeper ................................Bass

A Music Master .............................Tenor

A Musician ...........................Mezzo-Soprano

A Lamp-lighter ...............................Tenor

A Naval Captain ...............................Bass

A Wig-maker ................................Mime

A Sergeant of Archers .........................Bass

*Time:* Second half of Eighteenth Century

*Place:* Amiens, Paris, Havre, Louisiana

Act I plays in front of an inn at Amiens. Edmondo has a solo with chorus of students and girls. Des Grieux is teased for looking unhappy; perhaps he has had an unsuccessful love affair? He replies by mockingly serenading them all: 'Tra voi, belle, brune e bionde.' Lescaut, Geronte, and Manon arrive in a diligence. Lescaut is taking his sister to a convent to complete her education, but finding her to be greatly admired by the wealthy Geronte, is quite willing to play a negative part and let the old satyr plot with the landlord to abduct Manon. Des Grieux, however, sees her and asks her what her name is. 'Donna non vidi mai simile a questa' (Never did I behold so fair a maiden), he sings in praise of her beauty:

*Don-na non vi - di ma-i si - mi -le a questa*

It is the turn of the students to laugh at him.

With Manon, as with des Grieux, it is love at first sight. When she rejoins him, as she had promised to, they have a love duet. 'Vedete. Io son fedele alla parola mia' (Behold me! I have been faithful to my promise), she sings. Edmondo, who has overheard Geronte's plot to abduct Manon, informs des Grieux, who has little trouble in inducing the girl to elope with him. They drive off in the carriage Geronte had ordered. Lescaut, who has been carousing with the students, hints that, as des Grieux is not wealthy and Manon loves luxury, he will soon be able to persuade her to desert her lover for the rich Treasurer-General.

Such, indeed, is the case, and in Act II she is found ensconced in luxurious apartments in Geronte's house in Paris. But to Lescaut, who prides himself on having brought the business with her wealthy admirer to a successful conclusion, she complains that in these silken curtains ('In quelle trine morbide') there is a chill that freezes her. She wishes she might be back in the humble dwelling where she knew love. The aria is one of the most beautiful Puccini ever wrote.

*Moderato In quel-le tri-ne morbide*

A dancing master enters. Manon, Lescaut, Geronte, and old beaux and abbés, who have come in with Geronte, form for the dance, and a lesson in the minuet begins.

Manon is carried away, and expresses her delight in a brilliant aria with chorus: 'L'ora o Tirsi, è vaga e bella.' The soprano who can float a *pianissimo* top C can make a ravishing effect at the end.

Lescaut hurries off to inform des Grieux, who has made money in gambling, where he can find Manon. When the lesson is over and all have gone, her lover appears at the door: 'Tu, tu, amore! Tu?' At first he reproaches her, but soon is won by her beauty. There is an impassioned love duet, 'Vieni! Colle tue braccia stringi Manon che t'ama' (Oh, come love! In your arms enfold Manon, who loves you).

Geronte surprises them, and goes out to get the police. Lescaut urges them to make a precipitate escape. Manon, however, now loath to leave the luxuries Geronte has lavished on her, insists on gathering up her jewels in order to take them with her. Des Grieux reproaches her for her love of luxury, and all the unhappiness she has caused them in the past and will cause them in the future: 'Ah, Manon, mi tradisce il tuo folle pensier.' The delay is fatal. The police arrive. She is arrested on the charge made by Geronte that she is an abandoned woman.

Her sentence is banishment, with other women of loose character, to the then French possession of Louisiana. The journey to Havre for embarkation is represented by an *intermezzo* in the score, and an extract from Abbé Prévost's story in the libretto. The theme of the *intermezzo*, a striking composition, is as follows:

Act III.    The scene is laid in a square near the harbour at Havre. Des Grieux and Lescaut have a plan to free Manon from imprisonment, but are foiled. A lamp-lighter goes across the stage. There is much hubbub when the roll is called of the women who are to be transported. As they step forward, the crowd comments upon their looks. When it is Manon's turn, des Grieux stays at her side. The guard threatens him, but he is distracted with grief at the prospect of losing her and will stand no opposition: 'Ah, non v'avvicinate.' He appeals to the ship's captain, whose attention has been drawn by the noise, to be taken along with Manon, no matter how lowly the capacity in which he may be required to serve on board: 'Guardate, pazzo son.' It is a scene of powerful drama, and can make a splendid effect—must make such an effect, in fact, since the captain is sufficiently impressed to grant his request.

Act IV.    A vast plain on the borders of the territory of New Orleans. The country is bare and undulating, the horizon is far distant, the sky is overcast. Night falls. Thus the stage directions. Manon and des Grieux have left New Orleans—the victims of jealousy and intrigue—and Manon is exhausted with the journey. They sing sadly of the fate which has overtaken them, and Manon begs des Grieux to leave her to die alone. He goes off to look for help and, left alone, she gives expression to her terror and misery in a despairing aria: 'Sola, perduta abbandonata.' When he returns, she is dying. Des Grieux collapses by her side.

K.

## LA BOHÈME
### The Bohemians

Opera in four acts by Giacomo Puccini; text by Giacosa and Illica. Première on February 1, 1896, at the Teatro Reggio, Turin, with Cesari-Ferrani, Pasini, Gorga, Wilmant, Mazzara, Pini-Corsi, conductor Toscanini. First performed in England in Manchester, 1897, with Alice Esty, Robert Cunningham; Covent Garden (in English), 1897, with Alice Esty, Bessie McDonald, Umberto Salvi, Maggi; 1899 (in Italian), with Melba, de Lussan, de Lucia, Ancona, Journet, Gilibert, conductor Mancinelli; New York, 1898; Metropolitan, 1900, with Melba, Occhiolini, Saleza, Campanari, conductor Mancinelli. Revived at la Scala, Milan, 1924, with Zamboni, Ferraris, Pertile, Franci, conductor Toscanini; 1947, with Favero, Menotti, Lauri-Volpi, Tagliabue. Covent Garden revivals include 1935, with Grace Moore, Naylor, Dino Borgioli, Brownlee, Pinza; 1938, with Perli, Andreva, Gigli, Rossi-Morelli, conductor Gui.

#### CHARACTERS

Rodolfo, *a poet* .................................Tenor
Marcello, *a painter* ...........................Baritone
Colline, *a philosopher* ...........................Bass
Schaunard, *a musician* ........................Baritone
Benoit, *a landlord* ................................Bass

Alcindoro, *a state councillor and follower of Musetta* ..Bass
Parpignol, *an itinerant toy vendor* ..................Tenor
Custom-house Sergeant  ..........................Bass
Musetta,  *a grisette* ..........................Soprano
Mimi, *a maker of embroidery* ..................Soprano
Students, Work Girls, Citizens, Shopkeepers, Street Vendors,
Soldiers, Waiters, Boys, Girls, etc.

*Time:* About 1830                    *Place:* Latin Quarter, Paris

*La Bohème* is considered by many Puccini's finest score. It
chances that, as the opera is laid in the Quartier Latin, the
students' quarter of Paris, where gaiety and pathos touch elbows,
it laughs as well as weeps. Authors and composers who can tear
passion to tatters are more numerous than those who have the
light touch of high comedy. The latter, a rare gift, confers distinction upon many passages in the score of *La Bohème*, which
now sparkles with merriment, now is eloquent of love, now is
filled with despair.

Act I.    The garret in the Latin Quarter, where live the in-
separable quartet—Rodolfo, poet; Marcello, painter; Colline,
philosopher; Schaunard, musician—who defy hunger with cheerfulness and play pranks upon the landlord of their meagre lodging,
when he importunes them for his rent.

When the act opens, Rodolfo is at a table writing, and Marcello
is at work on a painting, 'The Passage of the Red Sea'. He remarks that, owing to lack of fuel for the garret stove, the Red
Sea is rather cold.

'Questo mar rosso' (This Red Sea) runs the duet, in the course
of which Rodolfo says that he will sacrifice the manuscript of
his tragedy to the needs of the stove. They tear up the first act,
throw it into the stove, and light it. Colline comes in with a
bundle of books he has vainly been attempting to pawn. Another
act of the tragedy goes into the fire, by which, still hungry, they
warm themselves.

But relief is nigh. Two boys enter, bringing provisions and fuel.
After them comes Schaunard. He tosses money on the table. The
boys leave. In vain Schaunard tries to tell his friends the ludicrous
details of his three-days' musical engagement to an eccentric
Englishman. It is enough for them that it has yielded fuel and
food, and that some money is left over for the immediate future.

Between their noise in stoking the stove and unpacking the provisions, Schaunard cannot make himself heard.

Rodolfo locks the door. Then all go to the table and pour out wine. It is Christmas Eve. Schaunard suggests that, when they have emptied their glasses, they repair to their favourite resort, the Café Momus, and dine. Agreed. Just then there is a knock. It is Benoit, their landlord, come for the rent. They let him in and invite him to drink with them. The sight of the money on the table reassures him. He joins them. The wine loosens his tongue. He boasts of his conquests of women at shady resorts. The four friends feign indignation. What! He, a married man, engaged in such disreputable proceedings! They seize him, lift him to his feet, and eject him, locking the door after him.

The money on the table was earned by Schaunard, but, according to their custom, they divide it. Now, off for the Café Momus —that is, all but Rodolfo, who will join them soon, when he has finished an article he has to write for a new journal, the *Beaver*. He stands on the landing with a lighted candle to aid the others in making their way down the rickety stairs.

With nothing that could be designated as a set piece, there nevertheless has not been a dull moment in the music of these scenes. It has been brisk, merry and sparkling, in keeping with the careless gaiety of the four dwellers in the garret.

Re-entering the room, and closing the door after him, Rodolfo clears a space on the table for pens and paper, then sits down to write. Ideas are slow in coming. Moreover, at that moment, there is a timid knock at the door.

'Who's there?' he calls.

It is a woman's voice that says, hesitatingly, 'Excuse me, my candle has gone out.'

Rodolfo runs to the door, and opens it. On the threshold stands a frail, appealingly attractive young woman. She has in one hand an extinguished candle, in the other a key. Rodolfo bids her come in. She crosses the threshold

She lights her candle by his, but, as she is about to leave, collapses with a fit of coughing in a chair. When she has recovered, the draught again extinguishes the candle. Rodolfo's candle also is blown out, as he hastens to relight hers. The room is dark, save for the moonlight that, over the snow-clad roofs of Paris, steals in through the garret window. Mimi exclaims that she has dropped the key to the door of her room. They search for it. He finds it but slips it into his pocket. Guided by Mimi's voice and movements, he approaches. As she stoops, his hand meets hers. He clasps it.

'Che gelida manina' (Your tiny hand is frozen), he exclaims with tender solicitude. 'Let me warm it into life.' He then tells her who he is, in what has become known as the *Racconto di Rodolfo* (Rodolfo's Narrative); the gentle and solicitous phrase, 'Che gelida manina', followed by the proud exclamation, 'Sono un poeta' (I am a poet), leads up to an eloquent avowal of his dreams and fancies. Then comes the girl's charming 'Mi chiamano Mimi' (They call me Mimi), in which she tells of her work and how the flowers she embroiders for a living transport her from her narrow room out into the broad fields and meadows.

Her frailty, which one can see is caused by consumption in its early stages, makes her beauty the more appealing to Rodolfo.

His friends call him from the street below. Their voices draw Mimi to the window. In the moonlight she appears even lovelier to Rodolfo. 'O soave fanciulla' (Lovely maid in the moonlight), he exclaims, as he takes her to his arms. This is the beginning of the love duet, which, though it be sung in a garret, is as impassioned as any that has echoed through the corridors of operatic palaces, or the moonlit colonnades of forests by historic rivers. The theme is quoted here in the key in which it occurs, like a premonition, a little earlier in the act.

The theme of the love duet is used by the composer several times in the course of the opera, and always in association with Mimi. Especially in the last act does it recur with poignant effect.

Act II. A meeting of streets, where they form a square, with shops of all sorts, and the Café Momus. The square is filled with a happy Christmas Eve crowd. Somewhat aloof from this are Rodolfo and Mimi. Colline stands near the shop of a clothes dealer. Schaunard is haggling with a tinsmith over the price of a horn. Marcello is chaffing the girls who jostle against him in the crowd.

There are street vendors crying their wares; citizens, students, and work-girls, passing to and fro and calling to each other; people at the café giving orders—a merry whirl, depicted in the music by snatches of chorus, bits of recitative, and an instrumental accompaniment that runs through the scene like a many-coloured thread, and holds the pattern together.

Rodolfo and Mimi enter a bonnet shop. The animation outside continues. When the two lovers come out of the shop, Mimi is wearing a new bonnet trimmed with roses. She looks about.

'What is it?' Rodolfo asks suspiciously.

'Are you jealous?' asks Mimi.

'The man in love is always jealous.'

Rodolfo's friends are at a table outside the café. Rodolfo joins them with Mimi. He introduces her to them as one who will make their party complete, for he 'will play the poet, while she's the muse incarnate'.

Parpignol, the toy vendor, crosses the square and goes off, followed by children, whose mothers try to restrain them. The toy vendor is heard crying his wares in the distance. The quartet of Bohemians, now a quintet through the accession of Mimi, order food and wine.

Shopwomen, who are going away, look down one of the streets, and exclaim over someone whom they see approaching.

''Tis Musetta! My, she's gorgeous!—Some stammering old dotard is with her.'

Musetta and Marcello have loved, quarrelled, and parted. She has recently put up with the aged but wealthy Alcindoro de Mittoneaux, who, when she comes upon the square, is out of breath trying to keep up with her.

Despite Musetta's and Marcello's attempt to appear indifferent to each other's presence, it is plain that they are not so. Musetta has a chic waltz song, 'Quando me'n vo' soletta per la via' (As through the streets I wander onward merrily), one of the

best-known numbers of the score, which she deliberately sings at
Marcello, to make him aware, without arousing her aged gallant's
suspicions, that she still loves him. Marcello joins *fortissimo* in
the reprise.

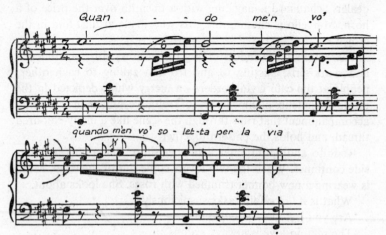

Feigning that a shoe hurts her, she makes the ridiculous
Alcindoro undo and remove it, and trot off with it to the cobbler's. She and Marcello then embrace, and she joins the five
friends at their table, and the expensive supper ordered by
Alcindoro is served to them with their own.

The military tattoo is heard approaching from the distance.
There is great confusion in the square. A waiter brings the bill
for the Bohemians' order. Schaunard looks in vain for his purse.
Musetta comes to the rescue. 'Make one bill of the two orders.
The gentleman who was with me will pay it.'

The patrol enters, headed by a drum major. Musetta, being
without her shoe, cannot walk, so Marcello and Colline lift her
between them to their shoulders, and carry her through the
crowd, which, sensing the humour of the situation, gives her an
ovation, then swirls around Alcindoro, whose foolish figure,
appearing from the direction of the cobbler's shop with a pair of
shoes for Musetta, it greets with jeers. For his gay ladybird has
fled with her friends from the *Quartier*, and left him to pay all
the bills.

Act III.    A gate to the city of Paris on the Orleans road. A
toll house at the gate. To the left a tavern, from which, as a sign-

board, hangs Marcello's picture of the Red Sea. Several plane trees. It is February. Snow is on the ground. The hour is that of dawn and it is cold (as the open fifths of the orchestra aptly illustrate). Scavengers, milk women, truckmen, peasants with produce, are waiting to be admitted to the city. Custom-house officers are seated, asleep, around a brazier. Sounds of revelry are heard from the tavern. These, together with characteristic phrases, when the gate is opened and people enter, enliven the first scene.

Into the square comes Mimi from the Rue d'Enfer, which leads from the Latin Quarter. She looks pale, distressed, and frailer than ever. A cough racks her. Now and then she leans against one of the bare, gaunt plane trees for support.

A message from her brings Marcello out of the tavern. He tells her he finds it more lucrative to paint signboards than pictures. Musetta gives music lessons. Rodolfo is with them. Will not Mimi join them? She weeps, and tells him that Rodolfo is so jealous of her she fears they must part. The duet has real feeling. When Rodolfo, having missed Marcello, comes out to look for him, Mimi hides behind a plane tree, from where she hears her lover tell his friends that he wishes to give her up because of their frequent quarrels. 'Mimi è una civetta' (Mimi is a heartless creature) is the burden of his song. Her violent coughing reveals her presence. They decide to part—not angrily, but regretfully. Tenderness runs through Mimi's farewell: 'Donde lieta usci,' with its closing line: 'Addio, senza rancore' (Farewell, then, I wish you well).

Meanwhile Marcello, who has re-entered the tavern, has caught Musetta flirting with a stranger. This starts a quarrel, which brings them out into the street. The lovers' joint farewell thus becomes a quartet: 'Addio, dolce svegliare' (Farewell, sweet love),

sing Rodolfo and Mimi, while Marcello and Musetta upbraid each other. The temperamental difference between the two women, Mimi gentle and melancholy, Musetta aggressive and disputatious, and the difference in the effect upon the two men, are admirably brought out by the composer. 'Viper!' 'Toad!'

Marcello and Musetta call out to each other, as they separate; while the frail Mimi sighs, 'Ah! that our winter night might last forever', and she and Rodolfo sing, 'Our time for parting's when the roses blow'.

Act IV.    The scene is again the attic of the four Bohemians. Rodolfo is longing for Mimi, of whom he has heard nothing, Marcello for Musetta, who, having left him, is indulging in one of her gay intermezzos with one of her wealthy patrons. 'Ah, Mimi, tu piu non torni' (Ah, Mimi, fickle-hearted), sings Rodolfo, as he gazes at the little pink bonnet he bought her at the milliner's shop Christmas Eve. Schaunard comes in and thrusts the water bottle into Colline's hat as if the latter were a champagne cooler. The four friends seek to forget sorrow and poverty in assuming mock dignities and then indulging in a frolic about the attic. When the fun is at its height, the door opens and Musetta enters. She announces that Mimi is dying and, as a last request, has asked to be brought back to the attic, where she had been so happy with Rodolfo. He rushes out to get her, and supports her feeble and faltering footsteps to the cot, on which he gently lowers her.

She coughs; her hands are very cold. Rodolfo takes them in his to warm them. Musetta hands her earrings to Marcello, and bids him go out and sell them quickly, then buy a tonic for the dying girl. There is no coffee, no wine. Colline takes off his overcoat, and, having apostrophised it in the 'Song of the Coat', goes out to sell it, so as to be able to replenish the larder. Musetta runs off to get a muff for Mimi, her hands are still so cold.

Rodolfo and the dying girl are now alone. This tragic moment, when their love revives too late, finds expression, at once passionate and exquisite, in the music. The phrases 'Che gelida manina' and 'Mi chiamano Mimi', from the love scene in the first act, recur like mournful memories.

Mimi whispers of incidents from early in their love. 'Te lo rammenti' (Ah! do you remember).

Musetta and the others return. There are tender touches in the good offices they would render the dying girl. They are aware before Rodolfo that she is beyond aid. In their faces he reads what has happened. With a cry, 'Mimi! Mimi!' he falls sobbing upon her lifeless form. Musetta kneels weeping at the foot of the bed. Schaunard, overcome, sinks back into a chair. Colline stands dazed at the suddenness of the catastrophe. Marcello turns away to hide his emotion.

'Mi chiamano Mimi'!

K.

## TOSCA

Opera in three acts by Giacomo Puccini, text by Giacosa and Illica, after the play by Sardou. Première on January 14, 1900, at the Teatro Constanzi, Rome, with Darclée, de Marchi, Giraldoni, conductor Mugnone. First performed at la Scala, Milan, 1900, with Darclée, Borgatti, Giraldoni, conductor Toscanini; Covent Garden, 1900, with Ternina, de Lucia, Scotti, conductor Mancinelli; Metropolitan, 1901, with Ternina, Cremonini, Scotti, conductor Mancinelli. Revived la Scala, 1927, with Scacciati, Pertile, Galeffi, conductor Toscanini. Famous Toscas have included Cavalieri, Destinn, Edvina, Eames, Muzio, Jeritza, Pacetti, Lotte Lehmann, Cobelli, Cigna, Caniglia, Grandi, Welitsch. Amongst the best-known singers of Scarpia have been Scotti, Baklanoff, Formichi, Franci, Stabile, Tibbett, Rothmüller, Gobbi, Guelfi.

### CHARACTERS

Floria Tosca, *a celebrated singer* ...............Soprano
Mario Cavaradossi, *a painter*......................Tenor
Baron Scarpia, *Chief of Police* .................Baritone
Cesare Angelotti, *a political prisoner* ...............Bass
A Sacristan ...................................Baritone
Spoletta, *police agent*...........................Tenor
Sciarrone, *a gendarme* ...........................Bass

A Gaoler ........................................Bass
A Shepherd Boy ............................Contralto
Roberti, Executioner; a Cardinal, Judge, Scribe, Officer, and
    Sergeant, Soldiers, Police Agents, Ladies, Nobles, Citizens,
    Artisans, etc.

*Time:* June 1800                              *Place:* Rome

Three chords played *fff, tutta forza*, and denoting the imperious
yet sinister and vindictive character of Scarpia—such is the
introduction to 'Tosca'.

Act I.     The church of Sant' Andrea della Valle.[1] To the right
the Attavanti chapel; left a scaffolding, dais.

Enter Angelotti. He has escaped from prison and is seeking a
hiding-place. Looking about, he recognises a pillar shrine containing an image of the Virgin, and surmounting a receptacle for
holy water. Beneath the feet of the image he searches for and
discovers a key, unlocks the Attavanti chapel and disappears
within it. The Sacristan comes in. He has a bunch of brushes that
he has been cleaning, and evidently is surprised not to find
Cavaradossi at his easel. He looks into the basket, finds the
luncheon in it untouched, and now is sure he was mistaken in
thinking he had seen the painter enter.

The Angelus is rung. The Sacristan kneels. Cavaradossi enters.
He uncovers the painting—a Mary Magdalen with large blue
eyes and masses of golden hair. The Sacristan recognises in it
the portrait of a lady who lately has come frequently to the
church to worship. The good man is scandalised at what he considers a sacrilege. Cavaradossi, however, has other things to
think of. He compares the face in the portrait with the features
of the woman he loves, the dark-eyed Floria Tosca, famous as a
singer. 'Recondita armonia di bellezza diverse' (Strange harmony
of contrasts deliciously blending), he sings in a celebrated lyrical
passage.

Meanwhile the Sacristan, engaged in cleaning the brushes in a
jug of water, continues to growl over the sacrilege of putting
frivolous women into religious paintings. Finally, his task with

---

1 Sardou describes the church as 'L'Eglise Saint Andréa des Jésuites à
Rome. Architecture du Bernin'. He meant Sant' Andrea al Quirinale, but
this being an oval church may account for the librettists having made the
transfer.

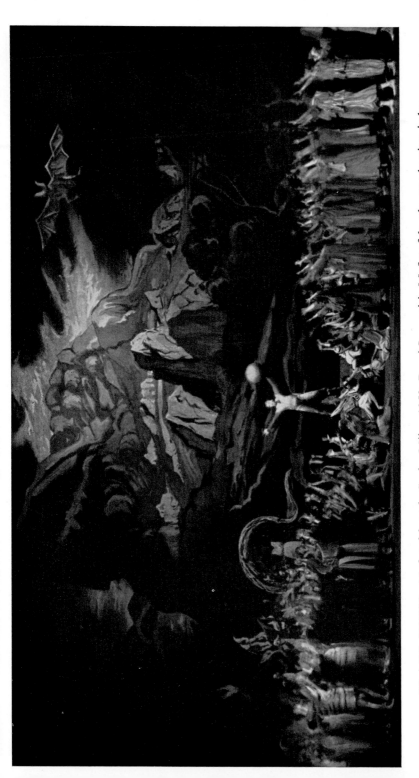

PLATE XXIII. *Mefistofele* at la Scala, Milan 1952. Rossi-Lemeni is Mefistofele, the production is by Frigerio and the sets by Chirico.

PLATE XXIV. Tito Gobbi as Scarpia.

the brushes over, he points to the basket and asks, 'Are you fasting?' 'Nothing for me,' says the painter. The Sacristan casts a greedy look at the basket, as he thinks of the benefit he will derive from the artist's abstemiousness. The painter goes on with his work. The Sacristan leaves.

Angelotti, believing no one to be in the church, comes out of his hiding-place. He recognises Cavaradossi as a political sympathiser and explains that he has just escaped from the prison in the castle of Sant' Angelo. The painter at once offers to help him. Just then, however, Tosca's voice is heard outside. The painter presses the basket with wine and viands upon the exhausted fugitive, and urges him back into the chapel, while from without Tosca calls more insistently, 'Mario!'

Feigning calm, for the meeting with Angelotti, who had been concerned in the abortive uprising to make Rome a republic, has excited him, Cavaradossi admits Tosca. Jealously she insists that he was whispering with someone, and that she heard footsteps and the swish of skirts. Her lover reassures her, tries to embrace her. Gently she reproves him. She cannot let him kiss her before the Madonna until she has prayed to her image and made an offering. She adorns the Virgin's figure with flowers she has brought with her, kneels in prayer, crosses herself and rises. She tells Cavaradossi to await her at the stage door that night, and they will steal away together to his villa. He is still distrait. When he replies, absent-mindedly, he surely will be there, her comment is, 'Thou say'st it badly'. Then, beginning the love duet, 'Non la sospiri la nostra casetta' (Dost thou not long for our dovecote secluded), she conjures up for him a vision of that 'sweet, sweet nest in which we love-birds hide'.

For the moment Cavaradossi forgets Angelotti; then, however, urges Tosca to leave him, so that he may continue with his work. She is vexed and, when she recognises in the picture of Mary Magdalen the fair features of the Marchesa Attavanti, she becomes jealous to the point of rage. But her lover soon soothes her; what eyes could be more beautiful than hers ('Qual' occhio al mondo')? The various episodes of the duet make this one of the most effective passages of its kind Puccini ever wrote.

Tosca having departed, Cavaradossi lets Angelotti out of the chapel. He is a brother of the Marchesa Attavanti, of whom Tosca is so needlessly jealous, and who has concealed a suit of woman's clothing for him under the altar. They talk with hatred of the man responsible for keeping Angelotti in prison—Scarpia, 'a bigoted satyr and hypocrite, secretly steeped in vice, yet most demonstratively pious'—the first hint we have in the opera of the relentless character, whose desire to possess Tosca is the mainspring of the drama.

A cannon shot startles them. It is from the direction of the castle and announces the escape of a prisoner—Angelotti. Cavaradossi suggests the grounds of his villa as a place of concealment from Scarpia and his police agents, especially the old dried-up well, from which a secret passage leads to a dark vault. It can be reached by a rough path just outside the Attavanti chapel. The painter even offers to guide the fugitive. They leave hastily.

The Sacristan enters excitedly; he has great news—word has been received that Bonaparte has been defeated. The old man now notices, greatly to his surprise, that the painter has disappeared. Acolytes, penitents, choristers, and pupils of the chapel crowd in from all directions There is to be a *Te Deum* in honour of the victory, and that very evening, in the Farnese palace, a cantata with Floria Tosca as soloist. It means extra pay for the choristers. They are jubilant.

Scarpia's sudden entrance immediately quietens the hubbub. A hush falls upon all. For a while they are motionless, as if spellbound, while he gives his orders. While preparations are being made for the *Te Deum*, Scarpia orders a search in the Attavanti chapel. He finds a fan which, from the coat-of-arms on it, he recognises as having been left there by Angelotti's sister. A police agent also finds a basket. As he comes out with it, the Sacristan unwittingly exclaims that it is Cavaradossi's, and empty, although the painter had said that he would eat nothing. It is plain to Scarpia, who has also discovered in the Mary Magdalen of the picture the likeness to the Marchesa, that Cavaradossi has given the basket of provisions to Angelotti, and been an accomplice in his escape.

Tosca comes in and quickly approaches the dais. She is greatly surprised not to find Cavaradossi at work on the picture. Scarpia dips his fingers in holy water and deferentially extends them to Tosca. Reluctantly she touches them, then crosses herself. Scarpia insinuatingly compliments her on her religious zeal. She comes to church to pray, not, like certain frivolous wantons—he points to the picture—to meet their lovers. He now produces the fan. 'Is this a painter's brush?' he asks, and adds that he found it on the easel. Quickly, jealously, Tosca examines it, sees the arms of the Attavanti. She had come to tell her lover that, because she is obliged to sing in the cantata, she will be unable to meet him that night. Her reward is this evidence, offered by Scarpia, that he has been carrying on a love affair with another woman, with whom he probably has gone to the villa. She gives way to an outburst of jealous rage; then, weeping, leaves the church, to the doors of which Scarpia gallantly escorts her. He beckons to his agent Spoletta, and orders him to trail her and report to him at evening at the Farnese palace.

Church bells are tolling. Intermittently, from the castle of Sant' Angelo comes the boom of the cannon. A Cardinal has entered and is advancing to the high altar. The *Te Deum* begins. Scarpia soliloquises vindictively: 'Va, Tosca! Nel tuo cuor s'annida Scarpia' (Go, Tosca! There is room in your heart for Scarpia).

He pauses to bow reverently as the Cardinal passes by. Still soliloquising, he exults in his power to send Cavaradossi to execution, while Tosca he will bring to his own arms; for her, he exclaims, he would renounce his hopes of heaven. He kneels and fervently joins in the *Te Deum*.

This finale, with its elaborate apparatus, its complex emotions and the sinister and dominating figure of Scarpia set against a brilliant and constantly shifting background, is a stirring and effective climax to the act.

Act II. The Farnese palace. Scarpia's apartments on an upper floor. A large window overlooks the palace courtyard. Scarpia is seated at table supping. At intervals he breaks off to reflect. His manner is anxious. An orchestra is heard from a lower story of the palace, where Queen Caroline is giving an entertainment in honour of the reported victory over Bonaparte. They are dancing, while waiting for Tosca, who is to sing in the cantata. Scarpia summons Sciarrone and gives him a letter, which is to be handed to the singer upon her arrival. Alone, he exults on the probable outcome of the affair: Tosca will yield to his desires. It is in violent conquests like this that he finds his greatest pleasure: 'Ella verrà' (She will come).

Spoletta returns from his mission. Tosca was followed to a

villa almost hidden by foliage. She remained but a short time. When she left it, Spoletta and his men searched the house, but could not find Angelotti. Scarpia is furious, but is appeased when Spoletta tells him that they discovered Cavaradossi, put him in irons, and have brought him with them.

Through the open window there is now heard the beginning of the cantata, showing that Tosca has arrived and is on the floor below, where are the Queen's reception rooms. Upon Scarpia's order there are brought in Cavaradossi, Roberti, the executioner, and a judge with his clerk. Cavaradossi's manner is indignant, defiant, Scarpia's at first suave. Now and then Tosca's voice is heard singing below. Finally Scarpia closes the window, thus shutting out the music. His questions addressed to Cavaradossi are now put in a voice more severe. He has just asked, 'Once more and for the last time, where is Angelotti?' when Tosca, evidently alarmed by the contents of the note received from Scarpia, hurries in and, seeing Cavaradossi, fervently embraces him. Under his breath he manages to warn her against disclosing anything she saw at the villa.

Scarpia orders that Cavaradossi be removed to an adjoining room and his deposition there taken. Tosca is not aware that it is the torture chamber whose door has closed upon her lover. With Tosca Scarpia begins his interview quietly, deferentially. He has deduced from Spoletta's report of her having remained but a short time at the villa that, instead of discovering the Attavanti with her lover, as she jealously had suspected, she had found him making plans to conceal Angelotti. In this conjecture he has just been confirmed by her frankly affectionate manner toward Cavaradossi.

At first she answers Scarpia's questions as to the presence of someone else at the villa lightly; then, when he becomes more insistent, her replies show irritation, until, turning on her with 'ferocious sternness', he tells her that his agents are attempting to wring a confession from Cavaradossi by torture. Even at that moment a groan is heard. Tosca implores mercy for her lover. Yes, if she will disclose the hiding-place of Angelotti. It looks as though she will give in, and Scarpia orders that the pressure be slackened; but the sound of Cavaradossi's voice reassures Tosca and she denies that she knows anything. Scarpia orders that the treatment be started again. Groan after groan escapes from the torture chamber. Tosca, overcome, bursts into convulsive sobs and sinks back upon a sofa. Spoletta kneels and mutters a Latin prayer. Scarpia remains cruelly impassive, silent, until, seeing his opportunity in Tosca's collapse, he steps to the door and signals to the executioner, Roberti, to apply still greater pressure. The air is rent with a prolonged cry of pain. Unable longer to bear her lover's anguish and, in spite of warnings to say nothing which he has called out to her between his spasms, she says hurriedly and in a stifled voice to Scarpia, 'The well . . . in the garden'.

Cavaradossi is borne in from the torture chamber and deposited on the sofa. Kneeling beside him Tosca lavishes tears and kisses upon him. Sciarrone, the judge, Roberti, and the clerk go. In obedience to a sign from Scarpia, Spoletta and the agents remain behind. Still loyal to his friend, Cavaradossi, although racked with pain, asks Tosca if unwittingly in his anguish he has disclosed aught. She reassures him.

In a loud and commanding voice Scarpia says to Spoletta: 'In the well in the garden—go, Spoletta!'

From Scarpia's words Cavaradossi knows that Tosca has betrayed Angelotti's hiding-place. He tries to repulse her.

Sciarrone rushes in much perturbed. He brings bad news. The victory they have been celebrating has turned into defeat. Bonaparte has triumphed at Marengo. Cavaradossi is roused to enthusiasm by the tidings. 'Victory! Tremble, Scarpia, thou butcherly hypocrite,' he cries.

It is his death warrant. At Scarpia's command Sciarrone and the agents seize him and drag him away to be executed.

Quietly seating himself at table, Scarpia invites Tosca to a chair. Perhaps they can discover a plan by which Cavaradossi may be saved. He carefully polishes a wineglass with a napkin, fills it with wine, and pushes it toward her.

'Your price?' she asks, contemptuously.

Imperturbably he fills his glass. 'Gia mi dicon venal' (Venal my enemies call me) he sings in a passage of great power (the

Già mi strug - gea l'a-mor del- la di - va!

*Cantabile di Scarpia* it used to be called at the time the opera first appeared). *She* is the price that must be paid for Cavaradossi's life. The horror with which she shrinks from the proposal, her unfeigned detestation of the man putting it forward, make her seem the more fascinating to him. There is a sound of distant drums. It is the escort that will conduct Cavaradossi to the scaffold. Scarpia has almost finished supper. Imperturbably he peels an apple and cuts it in quarters, occasionally looking up and scanning his chosen victim's features.

Distracted, not knowing whither or to whom to turn, Tosca now utters the famous 'Vissi d'arte, vissi d'amore, non feci mai male ad anima viva'. It is to passages of surpassing eloquence like this that Puccini owes his fame, and his operas are indebted for their strong power of appeal.

Beginning quietly, 'Vissi d'arte' works up to the impassioned,

heart-rending outburst of grief with which it comes to an end:

A knock at the door. Spoletta comes to announce that Angelotti, on finding himself discovered, swallowed poison. 'The other,' he adds, meaning Cavaradossi, 'awaits your decision.' The life of Tosca's lover is in the hands of the man who has told her how she may save him. Softly Scarpia asks her, 'What say you?' She nods consent; then, weeping for the shame of it, buries her head in the sofa cushions.

Scarpia says it is necessary for a mock execution to be gone through with, before Tosca and Cavaradossi can flee Rome. He directs Spoletta that the execution is to be simulated—'as we did in the case of Palmieri. You understand'.

'*Just* like Palmieri,' Spoletta repeats with emphasis and goes. Scarpia turns to Tosca. 'I have kept my promise.' She, however, demands safe conduct for Cavaradossi and herself. Scarpia goes to his desk to write the paper. With trembling hand Tosca, standing at the table, raises to her lips the wineglass filled for her by Scarpia. As she does so she sees the sharp, pointed knife with which he peeled and quartered the apple. A rapid glance at the desk assures her that he still is writing. With infinite caution she reaches out, secures possession of the knife, conceals it on her person. Scarpia has finished writing. He folds up the paper, advances toward Tosca with open arms to embrace her.

'Tosca, at last thou art mine!'

With a swift stroke of the knife, she stabs him full in the breast.

'It is thus that Tosca kisses!'

He staggers, falls. Ineffectually he strives to rise; makes a final effort; falls backward; dies.

Glancing back from time to time at Scarpia's corpse, Tosca goes to the table, where she dips a napkin in water and washes her fingers. She arranges her hair before a looking-glass, then looks on the desk for the safe-conduct. Not finding it there, she searches elsewhere for it, finally discovers it clutched in Scarpia's dead fingers, lifts his arm, draws out the paper from between the fingers, and lets the arm fall back stiff and stark, as she hides the paper in her bosom. For a brief moment she surveys the body, then extinguishes the lights on the supper table.

About to leave, she sees one of the candles on the desk still burning. With a grace of solemnity, she lights with it the other candle, places one candle to the right, the other to the left of Scarpia's head, takes down a crucifix from the wall, and, kneeling, places it on the dead man's breast. There is a roll of distant drums. She rises; steals out of the room.

In the opera, as in the play, which was one of Sarah Bernhardt's triumphs, it is a wonderful scene—one of the greatest in all melodrama. Anyone who has seen it adequately acted, knows what it has signified in the success of the opera, even after giving Puccini credit for 'Vissi d'arte' and an expressive accompaniment to all that transpires on the stage.

Act III.     A platform of the Castle Sant' Angelo. Left, a casement with a table, a bench, and a stool. On the table are a lantern, a huge register book, and writing materials. Suspended on one of the walls are a crucifix and a votive lamp. Right, a trap door opening on a flight of steps that lead to the platform from below. The Vatican and St. Paul's are seen in the distance. The clear sky is studded with stars. It is just before dawn. The jangle of sheep bells is heard, at first distant, then nearer. Without, a shepherd sings his lay. A dim, grey light heralds the approach of dawn.

The firing party conducting Cavaradossi ascends the steps through the trap door and is received by a jailer. From a paper handed him by the sergeant in charge of the picket, the jailer makes entries in the register, to which the sergeant signs his name, then descends the steps followed by the picket. A bell strikes. 'You have an hour,' the jailer tells Cavaradossi. The latter craves the favour of being permitted to write a letter. It being granted, he begins to write, but soon loses himself in memories of Tosca. 'E lucevan le stelle ed olezzava la terra' (When the stars were brightly shining, and faint perfumes the air pervaded)— a tenor air of great beauty, which reaches its climax with

O dolce baci, o languide ca-rezze

He buries his face in his hands. Spoletta and the sergeant conduct Tosca up the steps to the platform, and point out to her where she will find Cavaradossi. A dim light still envelops the scene as with mystery. Tosca, seeing her lover, rushes up to him and, unable to speak for sheer emotion, lifts his hands and shows him—herself and the safe-conduct.

'At what price?' he asks.

Swiftly she tells him what Scarpia demanded of her and how, having consented, she thwarted him by slaying him with her own hand. Lovingly he takes her hands in his: 'O dolci mani mansuete e pure' (Oh! gentle hands, so pitiful and tender).

Their voices join in a love duet that is half wistful, half resolute with determination to forget the past. 'Amaro sol per te m'era il morire' (The sting of death, I only felt for thee, love).

She informs him of the necessity of going through a mock execution. He must fall naturally and lie perfectly still, as if dead, until she calls to him. They laugh over the ruse. It will be amusing. The firing party arrives. The sergeant offers to bandage Cavaradossi's eyes. The latter declines. He stands with his back to the wall. The soldiers take aim. Tosca stops her ears with her hands so that she may not hear the explosion. The officer lowers his sword. The soldiers fire. Cavaradossi falls.

'How well he acts it!' exclaims Tosca.

A cloth is thrown over Cavaradossi. The firing party marches off. Tosca cautions her lover not to move yet. The footsteps of the firing party die away—'Now get up.' He does not move. Can he not hear? She goes nearer to him. 'Mario! Up quickly! Away!—Up! up! Mario!'

She raises the cloth. To the last Scarpia has tricked her. He had ordered a real, not a mock execution just like Palmieri. Her lover lies at her feet—a corpse.

There are cries from below the platform. Scarpia's murder has been discovered, and his myrmidons are hastening to apprehend her. She springs upon the parapet and throws herself into space.

K.

# MADAMA BUTTERFLY
## Madam Butterfly

Opera in two acts by Giacomo Puccini, text by Giacosa and Illica. Première at la Scala, Milan, on February 17, 1904, with Storchio, Giaconia, Zenatello, de Luca, conductor Campanini. The work was a fiasco, and there was only one performance, but a revision was hugely successful in May 1904 at Brescia, with Krusceniski and Zenatello, conducted by Toscanini. First performed Covent Garden, 1905, with Destinn, Lejeune, Caruso, Scotti, conductor Campanini; New York, 1906 (in English); Metropolitan, 1907, with Farrar, Homer, Caruso, Scotti. Revived la Scala, 1925, with Pampanini, Pertile, Paci, conductor Toscanini; 1938, with Adami-Corradetti, Lugo, de Franceschi, conductor de Sabata; 1940, with Favero, Pigni, Poli, conductor Guarnieri. Famous Butterflies have included Tamaki Miura, Rethberg, Giannini Sheridan, dal Monte, Maggie Teyte, Joan Cross, Cebotari, de los Angeles.

## CHARACTERS

Madam Butterfly (Cio-Cio-San) ................Soprano
Suzuki, *her servant* .....................Mezzo-Soprano
Kate Pinkerton, *Pinkerton's American wife*  Mezzo-Soprano
B. F. Pinkerton, *Lieutenant, U.S. Navy* ............Tenor
Sharpless, *U.S. Consul at Nagasaki* ..............Baritone
Goro, *a marriage broker* ........................Tenor
Prince Yamadori, *a rich Japanese* ...............Baritone
The Bonze, *Cio-Cio-San's uncle* ....................Bass
The Imperial Commissioner .......................Bass
The Official Registrar .......................Baritone
Trouble, *Cio-Cio-San's Child* ...................
Cio-Cio-San's relations and friends; servants

*Time:* Present day                        *Place:* Nagasaki

Although *Madama Butterfly* is in two acts, the division of the second act into two parts by the fall of the curtain, there also being an instrumental introduction to part two, in effect gives the opera three acts.

Act I.   There is a prelude, based on a Japanese theme. This theme runs through the greater part of the act. It is employed as a background and as a connecting link, with the result that it imparts much exotic tone colour to the scenes. The prelude passes over into the first act without a break.

Lieutenant B. F. Pinkerton, U.S.N., is on the point of contracting a 'Japanese marriage' with Cio-Cio-San, whom her friends call Butterfly. At the rise of the curtain Pinkerton is looking over a little house on a hill facing the harbour. This house he has leased and is about to occupy with his Japanese wife. Goro, the nakodo or marriage broker who has arranged the match, has also found the house for him and is showing him over it, enjoying the American's surprise at the clever contrivances found in Japanese house construction. Three Japanese servants are in the house, one of whom is Suzuki, Butterfly's faithful maid.

Sharpless, the American Consul at Nagasaki, arrives. In the chat which follows between the two men it becomes apparent that Sharpless looks upon the step Pinkerton is about to take with disfavour. He argues that what may be a mere matter of pastime to the American Naval lieutenant, may have been taken seriously by the Japanese girl and, if so, may prove a matter of life or death to her. Pinkerton laughs off his friend's fears and, having poured out drinks for both, recklessly pledges his real American wife of the future. Further discussion is interrupted by the arrival of the bride with her relatives and friends.

After greetings have been exchanged, the Consul on conversing with Butterfly becomes thoroughly convinced that he was correct in cautioning Pinkerton. For he discovers that she is not contemplating the usual Japanese marriage of arrangement, but, actually being in love with Pinkerton, is taking it with complete seriousness. She has even gone to the extent, as she confides to Pinkerton, of secretly renouncing her religious faith, the faith of her forefathers, and embracing his, before entering on her new life with him. This step, if discovered by her relatives, will mean that she has cut herself loose from all her old associations and belongings, and entrusted herself and her future entirely to her husband.

Minor officials whose duty it is to see that the marriage contract, even though it be a 'Japanese marriage', is signed with proper ceremony, arrive. In the midst of drinking and merry-making on the part of all who have come to the wedding, they are startled by fierce imprecations from a distance, gradually drawing nearer. A weird figure, shouting and cursing wildly, appears upon the scene. It is Butterfly's uncle, the Bonze (a Japanese priest). He has discovered her renunciation of faith, now calls down curses upon her head for it, and insists that all her relatives, even her immediate family, renounce her. Pinkerton enraged at the disturbance turns them out of the house. The air shakes with their imprecations as they depart. Butterfly is weeping bitterly, but Pinkerton soon is enabled to comfort her. The act closes with a passionate love scene.

The Japanese theme, which I have spoken of as forming the introduction to the act, and acting as background to the greater part of it, never becomes monotonous because it is interrupted by several other musical episodes. Such are the short theme to which Pinkerton sings 'Tutto è pronto' (All is ready), and the skippy little theme when Goro tells Pinkerton about those who will be present at the ceremony. When Pinkerton sings 'Dovunque al mondo' (The whole world over, on business or pleasure the Yankee travels), a motif based on the *Star Spangled Banner* is heard for the first time.

In the duet between Pinkerton and Sharpless, which Pinkerton begins with the words, 'Amore o grillo' (Is it love or fancy), Sharpless's serious argument and its suggestion of the possibility of Butterfly's genuine love for Pinkerton are well brought out in the music. When Butterfly and her party arrive, her voice soars above those of the others to the strains of the same theme which occurs as a climax to the love duet at the end of the act and which, in the course of the opera, is heard on other occasions so intimately associated with herself and her emotions that it may be regarded as a motif expressing the love she has conceived for Pinkerton.

Full of feeling is the music of her confession to Pinkerton that he has renounced the faith of her forefathers, in order to be a fit wife for the man she loves: 'Ieri son salita' (Yesterday I crept softly to the Mission). An episode, brief but of great charm, is the chorus 'Kami! O Kami!' (Let's drink to the newly married couple). Then comes the interruption of the cheerful scene by the appearance of the Bonze, which forms a dramatic contrast.

The love scene between Pinkerton and Butterfly is extended. From its beginning, 'Viene la sera' (Evening is falling), to the end, its interest never flags. It is full of beautiful melody charged with sentiment and passion, yet varied with lighter passages, like Butterfly's 'I am like the moon's little goddess'; 'I used to think if anyone should want me'; and the exquisite, 'Vogliatemi bene' (Ah, love me a little). There is a beautiful melody for Pinkerton, 'Love, what fear holds you trembling'. The climax of the love duet is reached in two impassioned phrases: 'Dolce notte! Quante stelle' (Night of rapture, stars unnumbered),

'Oh! Quanti occhi fisi, attenti' (Oh, kindly heavens).

Act II: part I.   Three years have elapsed. It is a long time since Pinkerton has left Butterfly with the promise to return to her

'when the robins nest'. When the curtain rises, after an introduction, in which another Japanese theme is employed, Suzuki,
although convinced that Pinkerton has deserted her mistress, is
praying for his return. Butterfly is full of faith and trust. In chiding
her devoted maid for doubting that Pinkerton will return, she
draws in language and song a vivid picture of his home-coming
and of their mutual joy therein: 'Un bel di vedremo' (Some
day he'll come).

In point of fact, Pinkerton really is returning to Nagasaki, but
with no idea of resuming relations with his Japanese wife. Indeed,
before leaving America he has written to Sharpless asking him to
let Butterfly know that he is married to an American wife, who
will join him in Nagasaki. Sharpless calls upon Butterfly, and
attempts to deliver his message, but is unable to do so because
of the emotions aroused in Butterfly by the very sight of a letter
from Pinkerton. It throws her into a transport of joy because,
unable immediately to grasp its contents, she believes that in
writing he has remembered her, and must be returning to her.
Sharpless endeavours to make the true situation clear to her, but
is interrupted by a visit from Yamadori, a wealthy Japanese
suitor, whom Goro urges Butterfly to marry. For the money left
by Pinkerton with his little Japanese wife has dwindled almost
to nothing, and poverty stares her in the face. But she will not
hear of an alliance with Yamadori. She protests that she is already
married to Pinkerton, and will await his return.

When Yamadori has gone, Sharpless makes one more effort
to open her eyes to the truth. They have a duet, 'Ora a noi' (Now
at last), in which he again produces the letter, and attempts to
persuade her that Pinkerton has been faithless to her and has
forgotten her. Her only reply is to fetch in her baby boy, born
since Pinkerton's departure. Her argument is, that when the boy's
father hears what a fine son is waiting for him in Japan, he will
hasten back. She sings to Trouble, as the little boy is called: 'Sai
cos' ebbe cuore' (Do you hear, my sweet one, what that bad man
is saying), and the aria rises to a dramatic climax. Sharpless makes

a final effort to disillusion her, but in vain. If Pinkerton does not come back? There are two things, she says, she can do—return to her old life and sing for people; or die. She sings a touching little lullaby to her baby boy, Suzuki twice interrupting her with the pathetically voiced exclamation, 'Poor Madam Butterfly!'

A salute of cannon from the harbour announces the arrival of a man-of-war. Looking through the telescope, Butterfly and Suzuki discover that it is Pinkerton's ship, the *Abraham Lincoln*. Now Butterfly is convinced that Sharpless is wrong. Her faith is about to be rewarded, and the man she loves is returning to her. The home must be decorated and made cheerful and attractive to greet him. She and Suzuki distribute cherry blossoms wherever their effect will be most charming. The music accompanying this is the enchanting duet of the flowers, 'Scuoti quella fronda di ciliegio' (Shake that cherry tree till every flower). Most effective is the joint phrase, 'Gettiamo a mani piene mammole e tuberose' (In handfuls let us scatter violets and white roses).

Butterfly adorns herself and the baby boy. Then with her fingers she pierces three holes in the paper wall of the dwelling. She, Suzuki, and the baby peer through these, watching for Pinkerton's arrival. Night falls. Suzuki and the boy drop off to sleep. Butterfly rigid, motionless, waits and watches, her faith still unshaken, for the return of the man who has forsaken her. The pathos of the scene is profound; the music, with the hum of voices, borne upon the night from the distant harbour, exquisite.

Act II: part II.   When the curtain rises, night has passed, dawn is breaking. Suzuki and the baby are fast asleep, but Butterfly still is watching. Again Puccini employs a Japanese melody (the 'vigil' theme).

When Suzuki awakes, she persuades the poor little 'wife' to go to rest, which Butterfly does only upon Suzuki's promise to awaken her as soon as Pinkerton arrives. Pinkerton and Sharpless appear. Suzuki at first is full of joyful surprise, which, however, soon gives way to consternation, when she learns the truth. Pinkerton himself, seeing about him the proofs of Butterfly's complete loyalty to him, realises the heartlessness of his own conduct. There is an excellent trio for Pinkerton, Sharpless, and Suzuki: 'Io so che alle sue pene.' Pinkerton, who cannot bear to face the situation, sings a tearful farewell to the house he once knew so well ('Addio fiorito asil'), and rushes away, leaving it to Sharpless to settle matters as best he can.

Butterfly has become aware that people are below. Suzuki tries to prevent her coming in, but she appears radiantly happy, for she expects to find her husband. The pathos of the scene in which she learns the truth is difficult to describe. She does not burst into lamentations. With a gentleness which has been characteristic of her throughout, she bears the blow. She even expresses the wish to Kate, Pinkerton's real wife, that she may experience all happiness, and sends word to Pinkerton that, if he will come for his son in half an hour, he can have him.

Sharpless and Mrs. Pinkerton withdraw. In a scene of tragic power, Butterfly mortally wounds herself with her father's sword (the blade of which bears the inscription, 'To die with honour when one can no longer live with honour'), drags herself across the floor to where the boy is playing with his toys and waving a little American flag, and expires just as Pinkerton enters to take away the son whom thus she gives up to him.

Much was once made of Puccini's use of Japanese tunes as a 'background' to the opera, and he was contrasted favourably with the older composers who cared nothing for 'atmosphere' and relied solely on melody. The 'atmosphere' of *Butterfly* now seems of only secondary importance, and it is in the delineation of character that the opera seems strongest. In this respect, Butterfly dominates.

The use of the *Star Spangled Banner* motif as a personal theme for Pinkerton always has had a disagreeable effect upon me, and from now on should be objected to by all Americans.[1]

I 'did' the first night of David Belasco's play *Madam Butterfly* for the New York *Herald*. The production occurred at the Herald Square Theatre, Broadway, and Thirty-fifth Street, New York,

[1] It never has been, apparently, and seems now to cause no comment after fifty years of repeated hearings.    H.

March 5, 1900, with Blanche Bates as Butterfly. It was given with *Naughty Anthony*, a farce-comedy also by Belasco, which had been a failure. The tragedy had been constructed with great rapidity from John Luther Long's story, but its success was even swifter. At the Duke of York's Theatre, London, it was seen by Francis Nielsen, stage-manager of Covent Garden, who immediately sent word to Puccini urging him to come from Milan to London to see a play which, in his hands, might well become a successful opera. Puccini came at once, with the result that he created a work which has kept its popularity until to-day.

The Milan production was a complete failure—one of the great fiascos of operatic history. The revision which followed was important, but it is hard even now to see why the work was a flop in February and a huge success the following May.     K.

## LA FANCIULLA DEL WEST
### The Girl of the Golden West

Opera in three acts by Giacomo Puccini; text by G. Civinini and C. Zangarini, from the play by David Belasco. Première at Metropolitan, New York, December 10, 1910, with Destinn, Caruso, Amato, conductor Toscanini. First performed Covent Garden, 1911, with Destinn, Bassi, Dinh Gilly, conductor Campanini; la Scala, Milan, 1912, with Poli-Randaccio, Martinelli, Galeffi. Revived Metropolitan, 1929, with Jeritza, Martinelli, Tibbett; la Scala, 1930, with dalla Rizza, Thill, Viglione-Borghese, conductor de Sabata; 1937, with Cobelli, Merli, Armando Borgioli; 1943, with Carbone, Lauri-Volpi, Reali, conductor Erede; San Francisco, 1943, with Kirk, Jagel, Weede; Rome, 1947, with di Giulio, Ferrauto, Franci; Buenos Aires, 1951, with Barbato, Annaloro, Galeffi, conductor Panizza; Rome, 1952, with Caniglia, Lauri-Volpi, de Falchi.

### CHARACTERS

| | | |
|---|---|---|
| Minnie, *owner of ' The Polka'* | | Soprano |
| Jack Rance, *the Sheriff* | | Baritone |
| Dick Johnson, Ramerrez, *a bandit* | | Tenor |
| Nick, *bar-tender at ' The Polka'* | | Tenor |
| Ashby, *agent of the Wells Fargo Transport Co.* | | Bass |
| Sonora | | Baritone |
| Trim | | Tenor |
| Sid | | Baritone |
| Handsome | *miners* | Baritone |
| Harry | | Tenor |
| Joe | | Tenor |
| Happy | | Baritone |
| Larkens | | Bass |

Billy Jackrabbit, *a Red Indian* ....................... Bass

Wowkle, *Billy's squaw* ................... Mezzo-Soprano

Jake Wallace, *a travelling minstrel* ............... Baritone

José Castro, *a 'greaser' from Ramerrez's band* ....... Bass

A Courier ..................................... Tenor

*Time:* 1849–1850       *Place:* A mining camp at the foot of
the Cloudy Mountains in California

The score is prefaced with a note which quotes from an early history of California: 'In those strange days, people coming from God knows where, joined forces in that far Western land, and, according to the rude custom of the camp, their very names were soon lost and unrecorded, and here they struggled, laughed, gambled, cursed, killed, loved, and worked out their strange destinies in a manner incredible to us of to-day. Of one thing only we are sure—they lived.' In such an atmosphere, Puccini designed that his opera should be played.

Act I.     A large room, roughly built in the shape of a triangle, forming the inside of 'The Polka', the inn where the miners came to drink and gamble. It is presided over by Minnie, whom they respect, love and protect, and who in return has even ventured to set up a sort of elementary school for the roughest of the inhabitants. She is looked after by two Red Indian servants, Billy and Wowkle. There is a bar, various trophies of the chase, a notice offering a reward for the arrest of Ramerrez, and a sheet-iron screen to protect a person from pistol shots.

Miners greet each other, and a game of faro starts up. Larkens is observed to be melancholy—he has got gold fever, says Nick. Jake comes through singing a melancholy song, in whose refrain all join. Larkens breaks down, and Sonora takes up a collection for him. Sid is caught cheating, and the miners are for meting out justice to him themselves, but Rance, the Sheriff, who has been in and out of the bar since the beginning, dominates the scene, and tells them rather to pin a card on Sid's chest as a token that he must not play. Pass the word round the camp, and string him up if he takes off the mark of shame. Ashby comes in, asks after Minnie, and tells Rance that he is close on the heels of the notorious Ramerrez. Minnie sends in hot whisky and lemon, and they all drink to her, Rance taking the opportunity of mentioning that she is likely soon to be Mrs. Rance. Sonora mocks him, and they fight, but are separated after a moment by a woman's strong arm. It is Minnie. She tells them all off, and they bring one or two small gifts they have got for her. Rance and Ashby talk apart, as Minnie takes down the Bible and starts to teach from it.

The post arrives, and Ashby has a letter from Nina Michel-torena, a cast-off girl-friend of Ramerrez's, indicating where he is to be found that night. He rejoices at the prospect of catching him at last. Everyone reads letters and newspapers and comments on what he finds inside.

A stranger is outside, Nick says, asking for whisky with water. They all laugh at the notion. Rance comes up to Minnie and starts to tell her how much he loves her, but she interrupts and will have none of it. He goes sulkily away, and, when she asks whether he is angry with her, bursts out into an avowal of his passion: 'Minnie della mia casa son partito.' He left everything without regret when his gambler's heart impelled him to come out West, but now he would give a fortune for a kiss from her. Minnie says that love is not like that; she has happy memories of her parents and her home-life, and would not take a husband unless she loved him as they loved each other: 'Laggiù nel Soledad.'

Nick brings in the stranger, Dick Johnson. Rance is rude to him, but Minnie recognises him and talks about the time they first met. Rance comes over and knocks his glass off the counter, saying that he is Sheriff and demanding to know what is the stranger's business. The miners are about to take Rance's part when Minnie says she will vouch for him. Johnson takes Minnie off to dance. While they are away, Castro is brought in; he is a member of Ramerrez's band and has been captured. He says he will lead them to the bandit's camp if they will spare him, then, seeing Johnson's saddle lying on the ground, thinks to himself that they have already captured him. A moment later he notices his chief come from the other room. Asking for something to drink, he tells Johnson that he has given nothing away, and that the gang is all round, only waiting until the Sheriff and his men are out of the way before they fall on the defenceless camp and pillage it.

Johnson remains behind with Minnie when the others ride off. He comments on her defenceless state and on the strange fact that she is guarding the miners' gold. She tells him that she loves the life she lives and would have no other. They are interrupted by Nick who says that a bandit has been seen skulking round the camp quite near at hand. Johnson comforts her, and yields to her suggestion that he should come up later that evening to her cabin to continue the conversation and have a meal. As he goes out, she bursts into tears, but he tells her: 'You've the face of an angel.'

Act II. Minnie's hut—a single room, above which is a loft. When the curtain goes up, Wowkle is singing a lullaby to her papoose. She and Billy talk for a moment—shall they get married?—before Minnie comes in, sends Billy about his business and tells Wowkle that there will be two for supper. She starts to dress up in what little finery she has, obviously hoping to make a real impression on Johnson when he comes. He knocks at the door and comes in. They sit down to supper, and Johnson comments that the life up here must be lonely. 'Oh, you've no notion how exciting my life is,' says Minnie. The mountains and the wild flowers, and her school for the miners—these keep her very busy: 'Oh, se sapeste.'

They sing of their happiness, and Minnie makes up a bed for herself in front of the fire. She has persuaded Johnson to spend the night there, as he would inevitably get lost in the heavy snow. There is a noise from outside, and voices demand admittance. Minnie hides Johnson behind the curtains of the bed, and lets in Rance, Nick, Ashby, and Sonora. They were worried for her safety—Dick Johnson, they have discovered, is none other than the notorious Ramerrez. They were led by Castro to his hiding-place, where they found his girl, Nina Micheltorena, who showed them a photograph of him—Rance hands it to Minnie, who laughs loudly.

She says good-night to them, then rounds furiously on Johnson. He admits that he came to rob, but at sight of her, changed his purpose. In an aria he explains his upbringing: his father was a bandit, and when he died six months ago ('Or son sei mesi') left nothing for him, his mother and his brothers, but the gang of thieves he led. He was fated to take the road, but from the moment he met Minnie he longed to lead an honest life. He does not expect forgiveness, only understanding.

Johnson rushes out, and a moment later there is the sound of a shot. A body falls against the door; Minnie opens it, and he staggers in, telling her not to shut the door as he will leave again. She cries that she loves him and will help him, and, putting the ladder in place, drags him to concealment in the loft. No sooner is he in hiding than Rance is again at the door. He searches everywhere for his quarry, then, asking Minnie to swear that he is not hidden there, tries to embrace her. She backs away from him; he accuses her of loving the bandit. With a gesture of defiance, Rance swears to Minnie that she shall never be Johnson's. A drop of blood falls on his outstretched hand, then another. Rance calls to Johnson to come out of hiding; he descends the ladder, helped by Minnie, and collapses at the bottom. Minnie tries a last desperate expedient. She suggests to Rance that they should play a game of poker: if she wins, Johnson's life is hers, if she loses, Rance wins her love. He cannot resist the gamble. They play two hands, each winning one, but before the last Minnie shows signs of distress and asks Rance to get her a drink from the bottle in the corner. She has previously secreted some cards in her stocking, and now, unable to bear the thought of losing at one stroke love and honour, she substitutes the cards for the hand she has been dealt. Rance returns, and against his three kings, Minnie is able to show three aces and a pair. He leaves the house, and Minnie is left alone with the lover whose life she has saved.

Act III. A clearing in the forest. Nick, Rance, and Ashby are resting there round a fire. They are members of a party which is hunting for Ramerrez. They reflect bitterly on the change that Johnson's arrival has brought into their lives. A noise is heard and Ashby shouts that his men seem to have caught up with their quarry. But it is a false alarm, although they are hard on his tracks. Ashby goes off with them, while Rance raises his arms towards Minnie's cabin, and shouts triumphantly that she will not see her lover again, except at the end of a rope. There is another false alarm, and then Sonora gallops in shouting that they have caught him at last. They prepare the rope from which he will shortly swing. Ashby hands over Johnson to the Sheriff, who suggests that they string him up forthwith. All unite in calling down curses on his head, each ascribing a different crime to him and his gang. He protests that he stopped short of murder, and asks for one thing only, that he be allowed to speak before he dies. He makes an impassioned plea that Minnie shall think he has gone free, that she shall wait for him, but never know the ignominious fate which overtook him: 'Ch'ella mi creda libero e lontano' (Let her believe that I have gained my freedom). It is one of Puccini's most famous arias, and one that is familiar to every Italian that has ever been to the opera, and to most that have not. In the 1914–18 war it was even a favourite song for troops on the march.

Almost before Johnson has finished speaking, Rance rushes up to him and hits him in the face, to sounds of disapproval from the bystanders. They are about to hang their prisoner, when Minnie's voice is heard. In a moment she is among them, threatening the first man that takes a step towards Johnson, and defying them all to do their worst. Which one was ever ready to cry 'enough' when she was working for them, sharing their troubles and their want—will they deny her the first thing she has ever asked of them? She and Johnson were planning to start a new life together, the bandit having died in her cabin a week before, when the honest man was born. Sonora goes to her side and takes her part; they agree that they owe her too much to deny her this. She and Johnson go off arm-in-arm, to seek out a new existence together. H.

## LA RONDINE
### The Swallow

Lyric comedy in three acts by Giacomo Puccini; text by G. Adami, from the German libretto by A. M. Willner and H. Reichert. Première at Monte Carlo on March 27, 1917, with dalla Rizza, Ferraris, Schipa, Francesco Dominici, Huberdeau, conductor Marinuzzi. First performed Bologna, 1917; Rome, 1918; Metropolitan, New York, 1928, with Bori, Fleischer, Gigli, Tokatyan, Ludikar, conductor Bellezza. Revived Metropolitan, 1936, with Bori, Martini, conductor Panizza; la Scala, Milan, 1940, with Favero, Malipiero, conductor Marinuzzi; Rome, 1940, with Favero, Gigli, Gobbi, Taddei.

### CHARACTERS

Magda, *Rambaldo's mistress* .................... Soprano
Lisette, *her maid* .............................. Soprano
Ruggero, *a young man* ........................... Tenor
Prunier, *a poet* ................................ Tenor
Rambaldo, *a wealthy Parisian* ... ............. Baritone
Périchaud........................ ......... Bass-Baritone
Gobin ⎫ *his friends* ⎧ ................ .............. Tenor
Crébillon ⎭            ⎩ ......... ......... Bass-Baritone

Yvette ⎫                              ⎧ ................Soprano
Bianca ⎬ *ladies of pleasure, and*   ⎨ ...............Soprano
Suzy ⎭     *friends of Magda*         ⎩ ........Mezzo-Soprano
A steward ........................................Bass

Ladies and Gentlemen of the world, Citizens, Students,
Artists, Demi-Mondaines, Dancers, etc.

*Time:* The Second Empire                    *Place:* Paris

It was while he was in Vienna in 1912 that Puccini was asked
by an Austrian publisher to write a light opera in something
approaching the Viennese manner. The war prevented fulfilment
of the suggested contract, but Puccini decided to set the libretto
which had been prepared for him, albeit in a somewhat different
form from that originally envisaged. The music is light in
character and frequently employs waltz rhythms, but the composer has abandoned any attempt to write an operetta.

Act I.    A luxuriously furnished room in Magda's house in
Paris. Magda and Rambaldo are entertaining their friends,
amongst whom is Prunier, a poet. He sings his latest song, sitting
at the piano. It tells the story of one Doretta, who dreams that
the King looked upon her one day. When Prunier says that the
end evades him, Magda takes up the tale ('Chi il bel sogno di
Doretta'). Rambaldo produces a necklace he has been meaning all
evening to give Magda, and she is immediately the centre of an
admiring and envious circle. Lisette the maid, about whose cheeky
habits Prunier is not slow to complain but whom Magda praises
as a ray of sunshine in her life, asks Rambaldo whether he will
at last see the young man who has been waiting for nearly
two hours to see him. He is the son of an old friend of Rambaldo's.

Magda talks to her friends of the old days when she was still
an innocent girl and went to Bullier's café in search of adventure
and, maybe, love. The dancing was something that she can never
forget, nor the memory of the man she met there, into whose
eyes she gazed, but whose name she never knew. 'Ore dolce e
divine' (Happy hours, golden hours) she sings, and the music
traces every stage of that never-to-be-forgotten experience of her
carefree youth.

Ruggero is brought in just as Prunier starts to tell everyone's
future from their hands; Magda's is that, like a swallow, she will
migrate far away from Paris, perhaps to find love. The conversa-

tion turns to where Ruggero shall spend his first evening in Paris; Bullier's is chosen, and Lisette (whom Prunier continues to object to, as impertinent) proclaims that the choice is a good one.

All leave, except Prunier who stays on the verandah. It is Lisette's day off, she reminds Magda, who dismisses her and goes off to her room. The stage is empty for a moment, before Lisette reappears, dressed in an assortment of her mistress's finery. She runs into Prunier, who takes her in his arms and makes love to her—objecting, though, a moment later, that her clothes have been badly chosen and do not match. She rushes out and re-appears more suitably dressed and they go off together for the evening. Magda herself comes in, hardly recognisable in that her hair has been re-done and she is dressed simply and as a grisette. She takes a look in the glass, is satisfied, and leaves the room.

Act II.    Chez Bullier; the ballroom. The room is crowded with artists, grisettes, demi-mondaines, men about town, etc. Flower-girls offer their wares for sale. Ruggero is sitting alone at one of the tables, apparently oblivious of the confusion and noise and gaiety around him, and quite unresponsive to the various girls who try to entice him away with them. Magda comes in and has some difficulty in fending off any number of would-be escorts, which she succeeds in doing by saying she is meeting the young man sitting by himself in the corner.

Ruggero is delighted when she sits by him and will not let her go, as she suggests she should the moment her molesters are out of the way. They dance, and Magda is irresistibly reminded of her adventure long ago; they even write their names in pencil on the marble-topped table at which they are sitting. Prunier and Lisette come in, and Lisette thinks she recognises her mistress, but is persuaded by her escort that she is mistaken. They are introduced to each other, and sing a quartet expressing their different views and requirements of love.

Some of the other dancers shower flowers on them, but Magda suddenly sees Rambaldo come in, and Prunier hastens to get Ruggero and Lisette out of the way. Rambaldo comes over to Magda, brushes Prunier aside, and asks her if she is coming home with him. She tells him she has found love and is not leaving with him, now or at any time. In spite of the blow he preserves his dignity, and leaves her sitting where he has found her. Ruggero returns and together they leave the restaurant.

Act III.    A little cottage, near Nice, in which live Magda and Ruggero, secure in their love. The two lovers are having tea, and the sea can be heard in the distance. They are blissfully happy, and Ruggero, who says he has written to ask his father's consent to their marriage, tells her of his confidence that his family will receive her as one of themselves. Magda wonders how best to let him know the details of her past.

Lisette and Prunier can be heard in the distance, and they appear just after Ruggero and Magda have left the stage. It appears that Prunier tried to make Lisette a successful actress, only to have to listen to the hisses of the audience at her one and only appearance. Lisette now wants to see if she can get back her old job with Magda. Magda agrees, and Lisette immediately seems more natural in her accustomed surroundings—so too would Magda, hints Prunier, if she were to return to Paris and gaiety, as she surely will, some time, some day. Magda understands that Rambaldo has sent her a message through Prunier, and that she can return to him whenever she wishes.

Prunier prepares to go, saying he has finished with Lisette for ever—but he does not omit to find out when she is going out that night, so as to be ready to meet her. Ruggero comes in with a letter he has had from his mother, and makes Magda read it, which she does with aching heart. She tells him she cannot deceive him any longer; he must know that she has been ready to sell her favours for money, that she has lived in guilty splendour. She can love him, but she cannot marry him and come to meet his mother as if she were a virgin bride. They must part, she insists, and, supported by Lisette and with breaking heart, she goes out, back to her own existence, leaving behind her the one love of her life.

H.

# IL TABARRO
## The Cloak

Opera in one act by Giacomo Puccini; text by G. Adami, after the play by Didier Gold, *La Houppelande*. Première at Metropolitan, New York, on December 14, 1918, with Muzio, Crimi, Montesanto, Didur, conductor Moranzoni. First performed at Rome, 1919, with Maria Labia, di Giovanni (Edward Johnson), Galeffi, conductor Marinuzzi; Buenos Aires, 1919, with Labia, Grassi, Viglioni-Borghese, conductor Serafin; Covent Garden, 1920, with Quaiatti, Burke, Gilly; la Scala, Milan, 1922, with Concato, Piccaluga, Noto, conductor Panizza; Sadler's Wells, 1935 (in English), with Winifred Kennard, Wendon, Matters. Revived la Scala, 1936, with Carbone, Merli, Franci, conductor Marinuzzi; Metropolitan, 1946, with Albanese, Jagel, Tibbett.

## CHARACTERS

Michele, *owner of a barge, aged fifty* .............Baritone
Luigi, *a stevedore, aged twenty* ....................Tenor
'Tinca', *a stevedore, aged thirty-five* ...............Tenor
'Talpa', *a stevedore, aged fifty-five* .................Bass
Giorgetta, *Michele's wife, aged twenty-five* ........Soprano
Frugola, *Talpa's wife, aged fifty* ..........Mezzo-Soprano

Puccini's *Trittico* consists of an example of Grand Guignol, a piece of sentimentality, and a comedy. *Suor Angelica*, which came second in the original performances, has never caught on with either public or managements, but *Gianni Schicchi*, the comedy, was an immediate success and has remained one ever since, being frequently played apart from its companions. *Tabarro*, the melo-dramatic opening, was slower to find favour, but recently seems to have come into its own, and indeed this is hardly surprising. In it the *verismo* side of Puccini's make-up, which found its best-known expression in *Tosca*, had a subject to which it was entirely suited. The rather commonplace ambitions and desires of the characters are uncomplicated by such ideas as Freedom and there is no need, as in *Tosca*, to bring in Napoleon and the Battle of Marengo as what amount to no more than stage props. From the point of view of directness of expression, and indeed from that of melodic interest as well, *Tabarro* is something of a master-piece, and certainly amongst Puccini's most successful works.

The action takes place on board a barge, whose master is Michele. It is moored in the Seine and the imposing shape of Notre-Dame can be seen in the distance. The barge takes up most of the stage, but beyond it can be seen the shore, to which it is connected by a companion-way.

The curtain rises before the music begins. A swaying orchestral figure denotes the gentle movement of a boat tied up to the shore:

It is the end of the day, and workmen are finishing their job of loading the barge. Michele and Giorgetta take little notice of them as they work, but Giorgetta suggests that they should be offered a drink before they go. Michele goes up to embrace her, but she only offers him her cheek, and he goes discontentedly on shore. The workmen crowd round Giorgetta, and drink to her in a well-defined triple time. An organ-grinder goes by on the shore and Luigi calls to him to play for them. Giorgetta says she only understands one kind of music, that which sets her feet dancing.

The phrase is later considerably developed in her love scene with Luigi.

Tinca is immediately at her side offering himself as a partner. His clumsiness becomes too much for her, and Luigi pushes him aside and takes his place, holding Giorgetta closer than is perhaps necessary. Talpa sees Michele coming and the dancing stops hurriedly, as the workmen disappear. Giorgetta asks Michele about arrangements for the morrow, when they are due to leave for Rouen; he will take the three—Tinca, Talpa, and Luigi—who have been helping him in Paris.

Frugola, Talpa's wife, appears and talks of her curious occupation as a rag-picker. Her one love, it appears, is her cat, for whom she buys the best meat available. Talpa, Tinca and Luigi with other stevedores come up from the hold, and Tinca explains that he drinks to forget his sorrows. Luigi takes up the cue: he is right, their fate is a poor one ('Hai ben ragione'). The solution, says Tinca, is to follow his example: drink!

Talpa and Frugola prepare to go wearily home, dreaming of the cottage in the country that they have always wanted but are never going to be able to afford. Giorgetta admits that her dream is for something quite different; she was born in the suburbs of Paris, and wishes that Michele might one day give up their nomadic existence and settle down: 'E ben altro il mio sogno.' This is one of the opera's purple passages, and Luigi joins his voice to hers as they agree that this former life was the happiest they have known: 'Ma chi lascia il sobborgo.'

Giorgetta and Luigi are alone. They listen to voices singing off-stage (to example 1); then Luigi moves quickly towards Giorgetta, who stops him with a gesture. They are lovers and Luigi complains of the barrier which prevents them being happy together; their duet is founded on example 2. There is a short interruption as Michele comes up from down below. Luigi asks him to put him ashore next day at Rouen; he means to try his luck there as a labourer. Michele advises strongly against such a course of action, and Luigi agrees to go on working for him. Michele says good-night. Luigi's enthusiasm carries Giorgetta away, and the duet rises to a climax as Luigi agrees to come for Giorgetta in an hour's time; they will use the same signal as last night, a lighted match will mean that all is safe.

Luigi leaves Giorgetta, who reflects sadly on the difficulties in the way of being happy in this life, as Michele comes back and asks her why she has not yet gone to bed. They talk for a moment of their crew, and then Michele comes close to her with an affectionate gesture. Why can they not renew their old love, which seems to have cooled since the death of their child: 'Perchè, perchè non m'ami più?' (Ah, why do you love me no more?). Why does she no longer come for warmth beneath his cloak? 'Resta vicino a me' (Stay close by my side) he begs; but Giorgetta prosaically explains the cooling of affection between them—they are both getting older.

She goes off to bed, and Michele stays on deck apparently reconciled to what she has told him. But the moment she has gone, he exclaims in fury: 'You whore.' He listens for a moment while two lovers on shore say good-night, and a bugle sounds from the near-by barracks, then peers in at the window to see Giorgetta still dressed and apparently waiting: for what? What has changed her? Who is her lover? He goes through the men with whom he knows her to be in fairly frequent contact, but dismisses each one in turn. Who can it be? Would he could catch him and crush the life out of him between his hands. His monologue is a powerful passage, and as his anger rises, so the orchestra boils with his emotions.

He raises his pipe and lights it with a match, giving as he does so, all unwittingly, the signal agreed upon by Luigi and Giorgetta. Michele sees a movement, and quickly hides himself, then throws himself on the figure which creeps towards the boat. It is Luigi.

Michele's hands are round his throat as he demands an admission of guilt. He chokes Luigi, then, as Giorgetta, roused by the noise, appears, hides the body under his cloak and stands as if nothing had happened. Giorgetta comes up to him, and asks him to warm her under his cloak. With a terrible cry, he opens his cloak and reveals what is concealed beneath it.                                    H.

# SUOR ANGELICA
## Sister Angelica

Opera in one act by Giacomo Puccini; text by G. Forzano. Première at Metropolitan, New York, on December 14, 1918, with Farrar, Perini, conductor Moranzoni (in conjunction with premières of *Gianni Schicchi* and *Il Tabarro*). First performed Rome, 1919, with dalla Rizza, conductor Marinuzzi; Buenos Aires, 1919, with Mazzoleni, conductor Serafin; Covent Garden, 1920, with dalla Rizza; la Scala, Milan, 1922, with Carena, Casazza, conductor Panizza. Revived la Scala, 1936, with Oltrabella, Casazza, conductor Marinuzzi; 1944, with Oltrabella, Palombini, conductor Marinuzzi; 1947, with same principals, conductor Capuana.

### CHARACTERS

Suor Angelica....................................Soprano
The Princess, *her aunt*.........................Contralto
The Abbess ...........................Mezzo-Soprano
The Alms Collector............................Soprano
Mistress of the Novices ..................Mezzo-Soprano
Suor Genoveva ..............................Soprano
Suor Osmina ................................Soprano
Suor Dolcina .........................Mezzo-Soprano
Aspirant Sisters ......................Mezzo-Sopranos
Nursing Sister ..............................Soprano

Novices, Sisters

*Time:* Seventeenth Century    *Place:* The cloister of a nunnery

Suor Angelica, the daughter of a noble Florentine family, has taken the veil to expiate the scandal which has overshadowed her life; she is the unmarried mother of a little baby. Seven years she has spent in the peace and seclusion of a convent, in a state of mind that has alternated between repentance and longing for the child she has never really known. The Abbess tells her that she has a visitor, her aunt, the Princess, towards whom her attitude must be one of reverence and humility.

The Princess has come to obtain from Angelica her signature to a legal document in connection with her sister's forthcoming marriage. She impresses upon her that her life must be given up now and for ever to atoning for the sin she once committed. When Angelica asks for news of the little child which has had to live its life in the great outside world without its mother, she is told coldly that it died two years ago.

In a frenzy of despair, Angelica resolves on suicide. She gathers herbs and flowers and makes from them a poisonous draught, which she drinks. She prays to the Virgin that she may not die in mortal sin, and, as if in answer to her prayer, sees a vision of the Blessed Virgin leading a little child towards her. An invisible chorus sings of salvation as she dies.

The opera has never been popular, and more often than not the *Trittico* is given without it. Only Angelica's lament, 'Senza mamma', has attained the fame which has attended some of Puccini's other arias, and this is fairly frequently heard in concerts and recitals in Italy.                              H.

# GIANNI SCHICCHI

Opera in one act by Giacomo Puccini, text by G. Forzano. Première at Metropolitan, New York, on December 14, 1918, with Easton, Crimi, de Luca, conductor Moranzoni. First performed at Rome, 1919, with dalla Rizza, di Giovanni (Edward Johnson), Galeffi, conductor Marinuzzi; Buenos Aires, with Vanni Marcoux, conductor Serafin; Covent Garden, 1920, with dalla Rizza, Tom Burke, Badini, conductor Bavagnoli; la Scala, Milan, 1922, with de Voltri, Marion, Badini, conductor Panizza. Revived Covent Garden, 1926, with Torri, Minghetti, Badini; 1931, with Rettore, Nash, Badini, conductor Barbirolli; 1937 with Ziffado, Nash, Crabbé; la Scala, 1928, with Galeffi; 1944, with Menotti, Malipiero, Stabile, conductor Marinuzzi; 1947, with Forti, Sinimberghi, Stabile, conductor Capuana; Metropolitan, 1936, with Tibbett; 1944, with Albanese, Martini, Baccaloni; Sadler's Wells, 1935 (in English), with Naylor, Tudor Davies, Sumner Austin, conductor Menges.

## CHARACTERS

Gianni Schicchi, *aged fifty* ....................Baritone
Lauretta, *his daughter, aged twenty-one* ..........Soprano
Relations of Buoso Donati:
  Zita, *called La Vecchia, cousin of Buoso, aged*
    *sixty* ..................................Contralto
  Rinuccio, *nephew of Zita, aged twenty-four* .......Tenor

Gherardo, *nephew of Buoso, aged forty* ...........Tenor

Nella, *his wife, aged thirty-four* ...............Soprano

Gherardino, *their son, aged seven* ............Contralto

Betto di Signa, *brother-in-law of Buoso, poor and*
    *badly dressed, of indefinite age* .................Bass

Simone, *Buoso's cousin, aged seventy* .............Bass

Marco, *his son, aged forty-five*................Baritone

La Ciesca, *Marco's wife, aged thirty-eight* Mezzo-Soprano

Maestro Spinelloccio, *doctor* ......................Bass

Ser Amantio di Nicolao, *lawyer* ................Baritone

Pinellino, *cobbler* ...............................Bass

Guccio, *painter* .................................Bass

*Time:* 1299                          *Place:* Florence

Gianni Schicchi, an historical character, has the honour of
being mentioned by Dante in the 30th Canto of *The Inferno,*
where he appears in company with the incestuous Myrrha of
Cyprus as a 'pallid, naked shape' (the connection between the
two is that both counterfeited the shape of another for their own
ends).

Before the curtain rises, there are a few bars of rapid music,
whose impetus is however tempered to become a lament (in the
minor) by the time the action begins. A chuckling figure, Ernest
Newman suggests, is used to indicate that the shadow of Gianni
Schicchi is already over them:

The opera takes place in a bedroom in the house of Buoso
Donati, who has recently died. The dead man is lying in bed, and
his relations are kneeling round him, behaving with proper
solemnity, that is all except Gherardino, who is heartily bored by
the whole proceeding. A whisper goes round; 'it is rumoured in
Signa' that Buoso's wealth has been left to the monks, and the
agitation of the mourners resolves itself in a request for the
advice of Simone, he having once been mayor of Fucecchio and
therefore of them all the wisest as well as the oldest. Simone tells
them that if the will is already in the hands of lawyers, there is

no hope for them, but if it is still in the room, something may yet be done about it.

A search for the will begins, and gets ever more feverish as first one, then another thinks he or she has discovered it, only to find that it is a false alarm. At last Rinuccio holds it triumphantly aloft, but before giving it up asks for a reward for having found it in the shape of permission to marry Lauretta, Gianni Schicchi's daughter. Zita is far too much concerned with the will to worry about a little thing like that, and eventually it is opened (in the meanwhile, Rinuccio sends Gherardino off to fetch Gianni Schicchi and his daughter). The will is addressed to Zita and Simone; expectation runs high, and speculation as to what is the portion of each even higher. They read the will in silence and, as they begin to understand its import, mounting horror; the rumour in Signa was by no means an exaggeration. Simone speaks for them all, and gradually they collect their wits sufficiently to be able to utter a rapid curse on the monks who will grow fat on *their* portions. Who would ever have thought, reflects Zita broken-heartedly, that they would ever shed so many genuine tears when Buoso was taken from them?

A thought seems to strike them all at the same time; if only it were possible. . . . They appeal to Simone but he can offer them no comfort. Rinuccio suggests that only one man can help them: Gianni Schicchi. Zita furiously says they have heard enough of him and his brood for one day, but Rinuccio is not to be put off, least of all when Gherardino bursts into the room and says the man they are discussing is on his way. He praises Schicchi's resourcefulness and cunning, and urges them to stop their spiteful gossip about his origins and lack of family tree. Has not majestic Florence herself got her roots in the countryside? Rinuccio's song, 'Firenze è come un albero fiorito,' has an antique flavour about it, as if it were a traditional song. It contains in the middle a broad phrase which is later to blossom out into Lauretta's well-known song:

Gianni Schicchi arrives with his daughter, and wonders if the long faces he can see are to be taken as meaning that Donati is better. He is told the sad facts of the will, and comments that this means they are disinherited. Zita repeats the word, and snaps out that he can take himself and his daughter back to where they came from; her nephew shall never marry a nobody. Schicchi bursts out into a vivid denunciation of the snobbish, money-grabbing old hag, who would sacrifice young people's happiness to her own greed. An ensemble develops, through which runs the lovers' sad plaint that they had hoped (vainly it seems) to be married before midsummer. Rinuccio prevents Schicchi leaving unceremoniously, and begs him at least to look at the will. Schicchi is reluctant, but Lauretta adds her plea to Rinuccio's and he gives way. 'O mio babbino caro' (O my beloved daddy), built up on the phrase from Rinuccio's aria (now in A flat, rather than B flat), has become enormously popular over the years, and is now nearly as well known as 'Un bel di' or 'Mi chiamano Mimi'. Its lyrical charm must be taken in this context as a masterly piece of tongue-in-cheek writing.

Schicchi walks up and down considering the will; 'it can't be done', he concludes, and immediately there is an outburst of sorrow from the lovers. More consideration, same conclusion, another lament, before finally a ray of hope presents itself to Schicchi's agile mind (the lovers react appropriately). Lauretta is sent out on to the balcony to feed the bird, and he asks if anyone apart from themselves yet knows of Buoso's death. No one, comes the answer: then there is hope, he concludes, and immediately gives orders that the funeral ornaments, etc., be removed from the room (to the sound of a muffled funeral march rhythm). Just then, a knock is heard, and in comes the doctor, not however before Schicchi has had time to jump behind the curtains of the bed. Schicchi answers the doctor's queries in what he hopes is Donati's voice, and tells him he is feeling better; they all bid the doctor good-night and breathe a sigh of relief at his departure. Schicchi outlines his plan: let them send for a lawyer, giving out that Buoso has had a relapse and wishes to make his will. Schicchi's monologue is slyness and good humour personified, and at its end the relatives shriek with delight and the ensemble takes on break-neck speed as all congratulate Schicchi (and themselves) on the possibilities of the scheme.

Collectively they tell him to divide the possessions equally amongst them, but each one then asks for the plums for himself.

Schicchi laughs at them all, just at the moment the passing bell
is heard—but it is for the servant of the mayor, they are told, and
heave a sigh of relief. Simone suggests that the division should
be left to the sense of justice of their friend, but again, as Schicchi
is helped into Buoso's nightclothes, each one in turn offers him
some reward if he will leave the particularly coveted things to
him. He agrees to each. When he is dressed, Zita, Ciesca, and
Nella gather round and admire his get-up, which they say is
perfect; they lead a chorus of praise for him.

When all is ready, he says that before going to bed he must
warn them of the danger they are collectively running. The law
provides penalties for falsifying a will—exile, and the loss of the
right hand for the malefactor and his accomplices—and they are
each one of them liable to these penalties. With mock solemnity
he bids a sad farewell to the Florence they all love, and the relations, seeing the force of his argument, sadly repeat the phrases
after him: 'Farewell, dear Florence. . . . I wave good-bye with
this poor handless arm.'

Ad-dio, Fi - ren - ze, ad - dio, cie -lo di - vi - no

Then, a knock is heard at the door, all is ready, and the lawyer
and the two witnesses who are to assist him are admitted. Schicchi
answers their questions in a thin, assumed voice, and, with many
comic touches, they go through the terms of the new will. The
inexpensive funeral which Schicchi orders pleases the relations,
and something is left in turn to each of them, until the moment
arrives when there remain only the prizes—the villa in Florence,
the saw-mills at Signa, and the mule. Amidst protests from the
relations he leaves each in turn to 'his devoted friend, Gianni
Schicchi', commenting, when they interrupt, that he knows best
what is good for Schicchi. When the interruptions look like becoming too violent, he sings a line or two of the farewell to
Florence, and they understand only too well that they are caught
in their own trap, and that there is nothing they can do. As if to
add insult to injury, he directs Zita to give twenty florins to each
of the witnesses and a hundred to the lawyer.

As soon as the lawyer has gone, they all rush at Schicchi and tear the night-shirt off his back. He picks up Donati's stick and deals some shrewd blows with it, as he chases them out of the house, which is now his, and which they attempt to pillage before leaving. Lauretta and Rinuccio sing of the happiness they will know together, and Schicchi returns, bringing with him some of the things the relations have carried off. He turns to the audience: 'Could you imagine a better use for Buoso's money? . . . if you have enjoyed yourselves this evening, I trust you will applaud a verdict of "Extenuating Circumstances".'

Puccini owes an obvious debt to Verdi for his example in *Falstaff*, but it would be churlish to deny him his achievement in writing music of such dexterity and brilliance, however short it may fall of the magnitude and humanity of its greater predecessor. *Gianni Schicchi* makes use of a side of the composer's make-up hitherto only revealed in such passages as the interplay of the Bohemians in *Bohème*, the entrance of the Sacristan in *Tosca*; in *Schicchi*, however, the wit is sharper and the tempo of movement faster than anywhere else in his output.

H.

# TURANDOT

Opera in three acts by Giacomo Puccini; text by Adami and Simoni based on Gozzi's fable. Première at la Scala, Milan, on April 25, 1926, with Raisa, Zamboni, Fleta, Rimini, Nessi, Palai, Carlo Walter, conductor Toscanini. First performed in Rome, 1926, with Scacciati, Torri, Merli, conductor Vitale; Buenos Aires, 1926, with Muzio, Pampanini, Lauri-Volpi, conductor Marinuzzi; Metropolitan, 1926, with Jeritza, Attwood, Lauri-Volpi, conductor Serafin; Covent Garden, 1927, with Scacciati (later Easton), Schoene, Merli, conductor Bellezza. Revived Covent Garden, 1929, with Eva Turner; 1931, with Nemeth, Norena, Cortis, conductor Barbirolli; 1937, with Turner, Favero, Martinelli; 1946, with Turner, Terry, Midgley, conductor Lambert. Other famous exponents of the title rôle have included Mafalda Salvatini, Cigna, Grob-Prandl.

## CHARACTERS

| | |
|---|---|
| Princess Turandot | Soprano |
| The Emperor Altoum | Tenor |
| Timur, *exiled King of Tartary* | Bass |
| Calaf, *his son* | Tenor |
| Liù, *a slave girl* | Soprano |
| Ping, *Grand Chancellor of China* | Baritone |
| Pang, *supreme lord of provisions* | Tenor |
| Pong, *supreme lord of the Imperial Kitchen* | Tenor |
| A Mandarin | Baritone |

*Turandot* is a version of the ancient fairy tale of the cruel Eastern Princess who slays those who love her. The fame of Turandot's beauty has spread far and wide; her wooers come to Pekin from distant lands. But before they can approach her they must submit to a trial. If they can answer three riddles they win the bride and, with her, the throne of China. But if they fail they must accept the penalty—and the penalty is death.

As the curtain rises on the first act the mob is waiting to learn the result of a trial which has just taken place in the Imperial Palace. When they hear from a Mandarin that the Prince of Persia has failed and must lose his life their joy is unbounded. They exchange rude jests with the headsman and look eagerly for the moon whose rising is the signal for the execution.

In the crowd is also the blind banished King of Tartary, Timur, accompanied by a faithful slave girl, Liù; the joy of their meeting with his son Calaf, whom he had thought dead, has, however, a dark shadow; the plotters who have usurped the crown of Tartary would not hesitate to slay Calaf if they knew that he was alone and defenceless. Timur has determined therefore to keep his name and birth a secret. He tells Calaf the story of his flight, aided only by Liù. Why has she risked so much, asks the Prince; because he once smiled at her in the Palace, she tells him.

The crowd urges on the executioner and his assistants to sharpen the ceremonial sword ('Gira la cote'). This done, they wait for the rising of the moon, to music subtly suggestive of half-dark, half-light. The moon rises, but as the funeral procession, led by the pathetic figure of the victim, wends its way slowly up the hill leading to the place of execution there is a change of heart in the mob. Voices are heard calling for a pardon, and Calaf curses the beauty which sends to the scaffold noble and innocent lovers. Turandot herself appears for a moment on the balcony of the Palace. The clamour for a reprieve rises from all sides. It is answered by Turandot with a gesture which means death to the unhappy Prince of Persia, and the halted procession moves on again.

But the beauty of Turandot has claimed another victim. The sight of her has been enough to stifle in Calaf all feeling other than the desire to win her. He, too, will submit to the test and either win her or end like the Prince of Persia.

In vain his father and Liù (who loves him) implore him to

desist. In vain the three ministers of the Imperial Household, Ping, Pang, and Pong, attempt to dissuade him with material arguments. They make their entrance to music of characteristic cast:

Liù pathetically begs him in an exquisite passage to relinquish his attempt: 'Signore ascolta' (My Lord, hear me).

In an aria he comforts her: 'Non piangere Liù' (Do not weep, Liù), but his determination is not to be shaken, and as the curtain descends he gives the signal which announces the arrival of a new claimant to the hand of Turandot.

Act II.    The first scene (a pavilion) shows the three ministers, Ping, Pang, and Pong (a re-incarnation of stock characters of the *Commedia dell' Arte*) lamenting the state of China.

Surely, they say, this is the end of its kingly race of rulers. Heads fall like rotten apples and no one can bring peace to the distracted country. They think longingly of their distant homes. The music is remarkable for the consistent way in which Puccini suggests the kaleidoscopic nature of the three dignitaries. If the scene of the enigmas is the opera's slow movement, this is un-doubtedly its *scherzo*.

Drums are heard in the distance; the hour of the trial draws near and they retire meekly 'to enjoy the latest torture'. The sounds of a majestic march are heard; the curtains are drawn apart and disclose the throne room where the trial is to take place.

High above all others sits the old Emperor, surrounded by his sages and guards. Calaf is led to the Imperial presence with noble-men and soldiers who carry strange banners. Last to come is

Turandot. When the loyal acclamations have died down the Emperor addresses Calaf and asks him to retire from the contest; the victims of Turandot are too many already. When Calaf answers with a refusal, Turandot tells, in her turn, the story of her ancestress who 'thousands and thousands of years ago' was betrayed by a foreign conqueror who sacked the city and carried her into exile where she died of grief: 'In questa reggia' (Within this Palace). It is to avenge her that Turandot has devised the trial. She, too, tells Calaf to desist and warns him that while the riddles are three, there is but one chance of escaping death. Calaf answers her somewhat rhetorically but with immense confidence, and their joint voices in their excitement soar thrillingly to a top C.

The first riddle is no sooner asked than it is answered. The 'phantom that is born every night and dies every day', says Calaf, 'is what now inspires me: it is Hope.' Turandot, alarmed by the prompt solution, hastens to ask the second riddle. 'Tell me,' she asks, 'what is it that at times is like a fever, yet grows cold when you die; that blazes up if you think of great deeds?' Calaf hesitates a moment, then gives the right answer: it is The Blood. His reply arouses the joy of the courtiers, who encourage him: 'Keep up your heart, reader of riddles.' It only annoys Turandot. She orders silence, and then puts the third question: 'What is the ice that sets you on fire?' and as Calaf seems at a loss she taunts him: 'You are afraid, death is near.' But after awhile Calaf guesses: 'You are the ice that sets me on fire'; the answer to the last riddle is 'Turandot'. He has won the contest and he receives the praise of the courtiers. But Turandot is not yet won.

Angry and fearful she begs the Emperor not to treat her like a slave given to the foreign prince, for she would die of shame. The Emperor objects that his oath is sacred and that the contest has been fairly won. Magnanimously Calaf himself comes to her rescue. 'I have answered three riddles,' he says; 'if before morning you can discover but one secret—the name I bear, and which you do not know, I will die as I would have died if I had never answered your riddles.'

Act III takes us back to the scene of the first. It is night and the voice of the herald is heard: Turandot's orders are that no one shall sleep in Pekin until the name of the strange prince is discovered; the penalty for disregarding her injunction is death. Calaf hears the proclamation, but is unmoved. In a delightful aria ('Nessun dorma': None shall sleep) typical of Puccini's happiest work, he expresses the conviction that he alone will reveal the secret. When the sun is high in the heavens Turandot will be his bride.

Ping, Pang, and Pong come to him offering any prize he chooses to ask, slaves, riches, power and a safe way out of China, if he will but tell them his name. Neither bribes nor threats can move Calaf. Turandot's guards now come on the scene; they have arrested Timur and Liù, who had been seen speaking to Calaf; they must know his name. Turandot, apprised of the capture, comes to order that torture be applied to Timur to make him reveal the secret. Fearing for the old man's life, Liù boldly steps forward: 'I know the name,' she says, 'and I alone.' She is taken; she is tortured, but refuses to tell. 'What gives you this power of resistance?' asks Turandot; 'Princess, it is love' ('Tanto amore segreto'). The executioner is called for, but Liù says she can bear the pain no longer. She addresses Turandot directly: 'Tu, che di gel sei cinta' (Thou, who with ice art girdled). This aria is the emotional climax of the opera; Liù embodies the female virtues which are so conspicuously lacking in Turandot, and Puccini has perfectly captured the qualities of this last of the 'frail women' he always dealt with so lovingly in his music. At the end of the aria, she snatches the dagger of a soldier and stabs herself to death. There is an outburst of rage from Timur, then the body is carried away followed by the crowd. Calaf and Turandot are alone.[1]

Calaf upbraids the Princess with her cruelty; then he takes hold of her and boldly kisses her on the mouth. Turandot's strength is gone and with it all thought of revenge, all her fierceness and courage. The dawn comes to herald a new day; she weeps in the arms of Calaf: 'Del primo pianto.' The reign of Turandot is over. She humbly begs Calaf to go and carry away his secret. But Calaf knows that he has won her. 'I have no longer a secret,' he replies. 'I am Calaf, the son of Timur. I give you my name and with it my life.'

Trumpets are heard announcing the meeting of the court. The scene is switched back to the throne room. There Turandot addresses the assembled courtiers and the Emperor: 'I have discovered the stranger's secret and his name is—Love.'

The music of *Turandot* retains much of Puccini's directness with a richer and bolder harmonic structure. The composer's faith in the power of melody was unshaken; his last opera is extremely melodious. Yet he dreamt of something lovelier than anything he had ever written for the last love duet, which was to be the crowning incident of *Turandot*, as the love duet of *Tristan* is the central pivot of that opera. This he did not live to write.

F. B.

[1] Of the concluding duet only some sketches were found at the composer's death. Out of these Signor Alfano has found the material for the last scenes which were added by him.

## CHAPTER 10

*French Opera*

# FRANÇOIS ADRIEN BOIELDIEU

## (1775–1834)

### LA DAME BLANCHE
### The White Lady

OPERA in three acts by Boieldieu, text by Scribe, founded on Scott's *Guy Mannering* and *The Monastery*. Première at the Opéra-Comique, Paris, December 10, 1825, with Mmes. Rigaut, Boulanger, MM. Ponchard, Henri. First performed Drury Lane, London, 1826 (in English); Haymarket, 1834 (in German); New York, 1827 (in French). Revived Metropolitan, 1904, with Gadski, Naval, Blass, conductor Mottl; Paris, 1926, with Féraldy, Faroche, Villabella, Marrio; Brussels, 1936.

### CHARACTERS

Gaveston, *steward to the late Comte d'Avenel* ........ Bass
Anna, *his ward* .............................. Soprano
Georges Brown, *a young English officer* ........... Tenor
Dickson, *tenant on the estate* .................... Tenor
Jenny, *his wife* .............................. Soprano
Marguerite, *old servant of the Comte d'Avenel* ..... Soprano
Gabriel, *employed by Dickson* .................... Bass
MacIrton, *Justice of the Peace* .................... Bass

*Time:* 1759                          *Place:* Scotland

*La Dame Blanche* had one of the most successful premières in all operatic history, and still stands as one of the most notable hits in the history of opéra-comique. The 1,000th performance at the Opéra-Comique in Paris was in 1862, the 1,675th in 1914. The score is full of delightful and skilfully written music, and the work still appears to have a sparkle and lightness of touch which distinguish it from its many less praiseworthy successors.

Act I takes place in front of Dickson's house. Dancing and singing are in progress in honour of the christening of Dickson's small child. Georges Brown arrives, makes himself known as an officer in the King's service, and accepts to take the place of the child's missing godfather. He enquires about the history of the castle of Avenel, which dominates the countryside, and is told that, amongst other things, it boasts a ghost, not a malicious one as is so often the case, but a female, known as 'The White Lady', whose special office is to protect her sex from their false-hearted suitors. Everyone believes in her, and most are firmly convinced that at one time or another they have seen her. Dickson is summoned to meet her that very night, and, in spite of his very definite fears, he dare not disobey. Georges offers to go in his stead, and the offer is gratefully accepted. They wish him god-speed.

Act II.     A Gothic room in the Castle. It is only half-lit, and Marguerite is sitting there spinning. Anna comes in and Marguerite hears from her something of the story of the old Count's missing heir, whom Gaveston is thought to have spirited away so as to obtain the castle and the Count's lands for himself. Gaveston enters and tries unsuccessfully to discover from Anna where the Countess hid the treasure before she died. Someone rings the door-bell and Gaveston says he will not allow anyone to enter; but Anna pleads with him—has he not enemies enough without making any more? She knows that it is Dickson, come at the order of the 'white lady' (for it is Anna who appears as the ghost, and who has summoned Dickson, hoping to be able through him to prevent the castle falling into Gaveston's hands). Anna tells Gaveston that she will the next day reveal the Countess's secret if he will allow the traveller in. Anna disappears and Marguerite goes to open the doors.

Georges Brown, who has come in Dickson's place, says that he has heard that the castle has a ghost, and he would like to have the opportunity of seeing it. He is left alone in the great room, when the other two go to bed. He stokes up the fire, and sings a serenade, hoping to entice the ghost to appear. She does, believing at first that it is Dickson come to meet her as she had ordered. She discovers that it is Georges Brown and recognises him as a wounded officer she had once tended and nursed and grown fond of. He is astonished that the ghost should know such details of his past as that he was wounded—he has been trying ever since to find his benefactress, whom he loves—and promises, as she asks, that he will perform whatever she orders on the morrow.

She disappears and Gaveston comes in, and, after some talk, invites Georges to stay for the auction which is just about to begin. Jenny and Dickson ply him with questions, but he reveals nothing of what he has seen.

Dickson has been charged by his fellow farmers to bid as high as he dare in order to prevent the castle falling into Gaveston's hands. The bidding advances, Dickson is obliged to drop out, but then Georges Brown comes into the reckoning. He is about to give in when the sight of Anna spurs him on to greater efforts, and eventually the castle is knocked down to Georges. He must pay, says the justice, by midday. Gaveston is beside himself with fury.

Act III. The same room. Anna and Marguerite discuss the whereabouts of a certain statue of the 'white lady' in which, says Anna, all the family money was once hidden. Marguerite remembers a secret passage, and they go off to explore it. The crowd meanwhile assembles to do honour to the new owner, and sings to him a version of the old Scottish tune 'Robin Adair', which he recognises and is able to finish.

Gaveston asks Georges for some explanation of his extraordinary behaviour of that morning; has he the money to pay for the castle? No, says Georges, but the 'white lady' will provide it. Georges leaves and his place is taken by MacIrton, a friend of Gaveston's, who warns him that the once lost son of the house has turned up in England and now goes under the name of Georges Brown. Anna, in hiding, overhears.

Just before midday, MacIrton comes with representatives of the law to collect the money; Georges asks for time to communicate with the white lady, who is financing the whole transaction, he says. Anna appears in the guise of the white lady, bringing the treasure chest with her—she has found it after all. Moreover she declares that Georges Brown is the missing heir to the estates of Avenel.

The freshness of the tunes, the gaiety of the personalities at work in it—these qualities seem to survive the passing of years as far as *La Dame Blanche* is concerned. Such passages as Georges' invigorating 'Ah, quel plaisir d'être soldat', the agreeable ballad of 'la dame blanche' sung by Jenny and Dickson, and the charming *allegretto* section of the duet in Act II for Anna and Georges —these have the lightness of touch and distinction that even now is implied by the expression 'opéra-comique'. Anna's aria at the beginning of Act III has an almost Weber-like feeling about it, and several of the tunes are cut in his style. The figure of Georges Brown himself (the combination of the French spelling of the Christian name with this surname is irresistible) is particularly attractive. His part in the action is romantic, debonair and devil-may-care and yet it never for a moment goes against the logic of the drama; he does not behave like a hero without good reason. Highly successful are his two romantic solos, the one when he is waiting for the ghost to appear ('Viens gentille dame'), the other equally charming when he tries to catch the tune of 'Robin Adair' as the chorus start to sing it in Act III.

H.

# DANIEL FRANÇOIS AUBER
## (1782–1871)

### LA MUETTE DE PORTICI
#### The Dumb Girl of Portici

OPERA in five acts by Auber, text by Scribe, and Delavigne. Première at the Opéra, Paris, February 29, 1828, with Mlles. Noblet, Cinti-Damoreau, MM. Nourrit, Dabadie. First performed at Drury Lane, London (in English), 1829; New York, 1831 (in French); Covent Garden, 1845 (in French); 1849 (in Italian), with Grisi and Mario; Metropolitan, 1884, with Bely, Schott, Kögel, conductor Damrosch. Braham was a noted Masaniello. Revived Berlin, Staatsoper, 1953, with Stolze.

### CHARACTERS

Alfonso d'Arcos, *son of the Spanish Viceroy of Naples* .......................................... Tenor
Lorenzo, *his confidant* ............................ Tenor
Selva, *an officer of the Viceroy's guard* ............... Bass
Masaniello, *a fisherman of Naples* ................. Tenor
Pietro, *his friend* ............................. Baritone
Fenella, *Masaniello's sister* ...................... Dancer
Borella ⎫
Moreno ⎬ *fishermen* ........................... ⎰ Bass
         ⎭                                         ⎱ Bass
Elvira, *a Spanish Princess* ...................... Soprano
A Maid of Honour of the Princess ........ Mezzo-Soprano

*Time:* 1647                                 *Place:* Naples

The story of *La Muette de Portici* is based on the historical happenings of the year 1647, when the people of Naples rose against their Spanish oppressors. The opera is perhaps the most successful Auber ever wrote; within twelve years of the first performance, there had been 100 representations at the Paris Opéra, and the 500th occurred in 1880. 'It is well known', says Loewenberg, 'that a performance (not the first performance though as sometimes stated) at Brussels, August 25, 1830, gave the signal to the outbreak of the Belgian revolution, which led to the independence of the country.'

The overture has an almost Rossinian animation, and its popularity is still considerable. Act I takes place in the gardens next to the palace of the Duke of Arcos, Spanish Viceroy of

Naples. A chapel can be seen. Against a chorus of rejoicing, the Viceroy's son, Alfonso, laments his conduct in seducing an innocent and poor Neapolitan maid, Fenella, who loved him but whom he has had to cast off in view of his approaching marriage with Elvira, the Spanish Princess whom he loves. Fenella, who is dumb, has disappeared, and for a month there has been no sign of her. In a big aria, Elvira proclaims her happiness to the young girls who are attending her to the altar. Dances are performed for her entertainment, but Elvira is informed that a fishermaid, pursued by soldiers, is asking for her protection. Elvira questions Fenella, who tells her story in dumb show.

The Princess with her attendants goes into the chapel. When she emerges with her bridegroom, Alfonso recognises Fenella, whom Elvira beckons towards them. Fenella indicates that it is Alfonso who has betrayed her. Elvira is horrified, and the act ends in general consternation at the turn events have taken.

Act II. Portici, on the seashore between Naples and Mount Vesuvius. Fishermen are assembling, and greet their leader, Masaniello. He sings a barcarolle ('Amis la matinée est belle'), which is fuller of foreboding than of the joy of living. As yet only Pietro, Masaniello's friend, knows of the sad fate of Fenella, but he now reports that he has been unable to find her anywhere, or indeed to gather any news of her whereabouts. The two friends swear vengeance on the tyrants, who have oppressed their people for so long and who have now done so grievous an injury to the most defenceless of their subjects; 'Amour sacré de la patrie' runs the refrain of the famous patriotic duet, which history says was the signal for the start of the Belgian revolution.

Fenella comes to seek Masaniello, and tells him her story. She will not admit her lover's name, but signifies that he is married and so cannot redeem her shame. Masaniello swears to be revenged, and calls the fishermen to arms. They swear perdition to the enemies of the country.

Act III. A public square in Naples. Alfonso tries to persuade Elvira that he loves her, and that his penitence for the wrong he did the fishermen is sincere. She yields to his entreaty, and he commands the guards to find Fenella and bring her before Elvira. The market is in full swing, and people buy and sell; a *tarantella* is danced. The guards think they see Fenella and attempt to arrest her. Masaniello intervenes and, when the guards would arrest him too, calls on the people to rise. The soldiers are driven off, but before leading his improvised army off to further conquests, Masaniello calls on them to pray for God's guidance in their just enterprise. The act comes to an end as they prepare to subdue the city.

Act IV.    Portici; the hut of Masaniello. Masaniello laments that the battle for liberty should have bred licence and destructiveness amongst the conquering rabble he led to victory. Fenella appears, pale and with faltering steps, and her brother gently sings her to sleep. Pietro and his companions come to incite Masaniello once more to place himself at their head and lead them to victory and revenge. He pleads for moderation, and for a cessation of bloodshed.

They go to the back of the house, and shortly afterwards a knock is heard. Alfonso and Elvira come to seek shelter from the bloodthirsty mob, little knowing from whom they are asking it. At first Fenella does not want to save Elvira, whom she thinks of as her rival, but Elvira's pleading wins her pity, and she vows to save them or die with them in the attempt. Much to Fenella's joy, Masaniello agrees to shelter the two fugitives.

Pietro appears with representatives of the people to ask Masaniello to take the keys of government and rule over them. Pietro recognises Alfonso, and an ensemble ensues between the two Spanish fugitives, Masaniello, Pietro, and the chorus. Pietro wishes to put them straightway to death, Masaniello urges that his oath of hospitality is binding. In the end Masaniello gives the Spaniards safe-conduct and threatens to slay anyone who makes a move against them. Pietro and his followers swear that Masaniello shall be the next to fall—their words are spoken against a background of praise for Masaniello as victor of the day.

Act V.    In front of the Viceroy's palace at Naples. Pietro sings a barcarolle with the chorus; in between the two verses he confides to a friend that he has already administered poison to Masaniello, who bad fair to become a greater tyrant than those they deposed in his favour. Even as he sings, the 'king of the day' is lying dying, and no human power can save him.

News comes that Alfonso is marching against them at the head of troops, and, almost as bad, that Vesuvius is in irruption; the credulous peasants think that the wrath of heaven is being visited on the rebels. Only Masaniello can save them, cry the people, but Pietro and his friends reveal that the poison has made the hero the victim of hallucinations. Masaniello himself comes out of the palace, and is obviously not in his right mind. All appeal to him as their only hope; but he takes no notice and sings the barcarolle we heard in the first act. Not until Fenella appears can he grasp the import of the situation, but then he places himself at the head of the rebels and marches off with them.

Fenella prays for his safe return. A moment later Elvira appears, explaining that Masaniello has saved her life from the murderous stroke of one of his followers; Alfonso, who follows her, continues the story—Masaniello himself was struck down in revenge for his saving of Elvira. Fenella is overcome by the news and commits suicide.                                    H.

# FRA DIAVOLO

Opera in three acts by Auber, text by Scribe. Première at Opéra-Comique, Paris, January 28, 1830, with Mmes. Prévost, Boulanger, M. Chollet. First performed Drury Lane, 1831; New York, 1831; Lyceum, 1857 (in Italian), with Borsio, Gardoni, Ronconi, Tagliafico. Last performance at Covent Garden, 1896, with Engle, de Lucia, Pini-Corsi, Arimondi, Bispham. Revived Metropolitan, 1910, with Alten and Clément, conductor Hertz; Berlin, 1934, with Eisinger, Pattiera, Schützendorf, Hüsch, conductor Blech; la Scala, Milan, 1934, with Carosio, Pertile, Autori, Bettoni, Nessi, conductor Santini; Sadler's Wells, 1935 (in English), with Naylor, Arthur Cox (Carron), Matters, Stear, Lloyd; Berlin, 1936, with Berger, Völker, Eugen Fuchs, Helgers; Stockholm, 1948. Fra Diavolo was a favourite rôle of many famous tenors, the most recent having been Bonci and Schipa.

## CHARACTERS

Fra Diavolo, *a bandit chief* ...................... Tenor
Lord Cockburn, *an English tourist* ................. Tenor
Lady Pamela, *his wife* .................. Mezzo-Soprano
Lorenzo, *an officer of caribiniers* ................... Tenor
Matteo, *an innkeeper* ........................... Bass
Zerlina, *his daughter* ........................... Soprano
Giacomo, *a bandit* .............................. Bass
Beppo, *a bandit* ................................ Tenor

*Fra Diavolo*, one of the most popular of all opéras-comique, is now remembered chiefly through its overture. All the same, its admirable music and excellent story seem to entitle it to more frequent revival than in fact, outside Germany, it seems to receive.

The story is concerned with Fra Diavolo, a famous bandit leader in the district round Naples. His reputation is to some extent that of a Robin Hood, his chivalry being above question and his tendency to give extensively to the poor out of what he has taken from the rich. At the time of the story, he is travelling under the name of the Marquis of San Marco.

Act I. Matteo's tavern. A reward of 10,000 *piastres* has been offered for the apprehension of the bandit Fra Diavolo. Lorenzo and his troop of caribiniers are drinking at the inn, but the brigadier seems unusually preoccupied. It soon turns out that he is full of sadness at the prospect of losing his sweetheart, Zerlina, the innkeeper's daughter, whom her father has destined for a wealthier suitor, the farmer Francesco. The party is interrupted by the precipitate arrival of Lord Cockburn, wealthy English traveller, and his wife, Lady Pamela, complaining loudly that they have been set upon and robbed, only escaping with their lives because they had the presence of mind to abandon their coach. Lorenzo starts off to look for the brigand, after hearing that Lord Cockburn means to offer a reward of 6,000 *scudi* for the return of his wife's jewels.

The English couple have only just finished an altercation on the subject of the attentions of a certain Marquis of San Marco to her ladyship—in one case welcome, in the other not so welcome —when a carriage draws up at the door, and the Marquis himself is announced. He seems delighted to see Pamela, and says that he is going to stay the night. Matteo hastens to see that he is suitably provided with food, and then bids his daughter look after the Marquis well while he himself is away for the night making the final arrangements for her wedding to Francesco.

The Marquis asks why the English lord seems in such a bad temper and is told that he has just been robbed by the notorious Fra Diavolo. The Marquis expresses incredulity at the idea that there should be bandits in such civilised parts of the country, but Zerlina is told to sing him the local ballad of Fra Diavolo. He joins in the last verse. A couple of beggars come in, and the Marquis says he will pay for their board and lodging. When the innkeeper and his daughter have gone out, these turn out to be

Giacomo and Beppo, two members of Fra Diavolo's band, and they discuss the affair of the English nobleman with him, admitting that they were unable to find the gold he was reputed to have with him. Fra Diavolo says he will try to find out its whereabouts from Lady Pamela, whom at that moment he spies coming towards them. He dismisses his retainers, and starts to pay compliments to the lady, turning their emotional duet into a barcarolle when he catches sight of her husband. The Marquis flatters Milord into giving away the secret hiding-place of his money; he boasts that it is in bills, sown into his cloak and his wife's gown.

There is a noise outside; it is the troop of caribiniers returning after a most successful sortie against the bandits. They report that they have killed at least twenty and recaptured the stolen property. Lady Pamela insists that Lorenzo be given his reward straight away, so that he can convince Matteo that he is wealthy enough to marry Zerlina. The act ends with Lorenzo and the soldiers announcing their intention to capture the bandit chief himself, Fra Diavolo swearing to be revenged for the loss of his followers.

Act II.    The curtain rises to show Zerlina's bedroom. Lord Cockburn and his wife are sleeping next door, and the only way to their room is through hers. Zerlina prepares the rooms, singing a brilliant aria the while. Their occupants come up to bed, quarrelling as they do so sufficiently for Zerlina to remark that she and her husband will not be like that a year after their wedding day. Zerlina goes with them to their room to help Lady Pamela undress and to see if there is anything they need.

Enter Fra Diavolo, who has discovered that Zerlina's room is next to that of the English travellers, and who means to hide there himself, with his two followers, so as to relieve them for the second time of their valuables. He sings a barcarolle to attract the attention of Giacomo and Beppo, and lets them in through the window. They hear Zerlina's voice and all go to hide, Beppo and Giacomo going through some glass doors from which the bedroom is in full view. Zerlina undresses and pauses for a moment to admire her face and figure in the looking-glass; this is too much for the watchers who cannot restrain their laughter. Zerlina says her prayers and goes to bed, soon to fall asleep. It is the moment for Diavolo and his two followers to make their way towards Milord's rooms. Giacomo is about to stab Zerlina —might she not give them away if there were to be any noise?— but she murmurs a prayer in her sleep and he cannot bring himself to do the deed.

Suddenly, there is a noise downstairs; Zerlina wakes up to hear Lorenzo calling for her. He and his men have not found Fra Diavolo and would like food and shelter for the rest of the night. She admits them; Lord Cockburn makes an appearance to complain about the noise but that is forgotten when Beppo knocks something over in the cupboard in which he is hidden. All is not lost however, Fra Diavolo taking it upon himself to step out and confront the brigadier and the Englishman. He had, he confesses to each of them separately, a rendezvous; he whispers the names of Zerlina and Lady Pamela into the appropriate ear. He is challenged by Lorenzo, and accepts. When Zerlina and Lady Pamela appear, they are met with nothing but coldness by respectively the lover and the husband on whom they were counting for comfort.

Act III.    The mountains, not far from Matteo's inn. Fra Diavolo has laid his plans carefully. He means to be revenged on Lorenzo for what he and his soldiers have done to the rest of his band. Meanwhile, he sings of the charms of a bandit's life. The Easter procession is about to start out from the inn, watched by Beppo and Giacomo, who have orders to wait until Lorenzo and his soldiers have moved off, then ring the church bell to indicate to Fra Diavolo that the way is clear. Lorenzo, in a romance, sings sadly of the love he had thought faithful but has found to be false. Suddenly, he remembers that he has a debt of honour to pay at exactly this hour. He reproaches Zerlina for her unfaithfulness, which she indignantly denies. Just then Beppo and Giacomo catch sight of her and recognise her as the girl they watched going to bed the previous night. They laugh at the memory and repeat some of her phrases, just a little too loudly it appears, for she hears them and demands that someone find out the truth about how they overheard her when she was alone in her own bedroom. A paper giving Fra Diavolo's plan is found on one of them and the plot is revealed.

Lorenzo orders that Giacomo be taken to ring the bell, and that when Fra Diavolo appears Beppo tell him the way is clear. He will then fall into their hands. All goes as he has hoped. Diavolo appears and descends to the square, where he is surrounded by caribiniers and made prisoner. All is explained and forgiven. (In an alternative ending to the opera, Fra Diavolo is shot by the soldiery in the ambush.)                                     H.

# ADOLPHE ADAM
## (1803–1856)

### LE POSTILLON DE LONGJUMEAU
#### The Coachman of Longjumeau

OPERA in three acts by Adolphe Adam, text by A. de Leuven and L. L. Brunswick. Première at Opéra-Comique, Paris, October 13, 1836, with Mme. Roy, MM. Chollet, Henri. First performed St. James's Theatre, London, 1837 (in English); Drury Lane, 1845 (in French); New York, 1840 (in English). Revived Berlin, 1930, with de Garmo, Roswaenge, Helgers, conducted by Blech. The most famous of all Chappelous was Theodor Wachtel, who himself began life as a stableman.

### CHARACTERS

Madeleine, *Chappelou's wife* ....................Soprano
Rose..........................................Soprano
Chappelou, *a postillion* ..........................Tenor
Le Marquis de Corcy, *head of the Paris Opéra* ......Tenor
Bijou, *Chappelou's friend* ......................Baritone
Bourdon .......................................Bass

Act I.    Chappelou, the coach-driver of Longjumeau, is about to be married to the young mistress of the post-house, Madeleine. The wedding over, his friends make him stay behind—as is the custom—to sing. He says he has no heart for it, but in response to their urging chooses a favourite song, on the subject of the Postillion of Longjumeau, who wins the love of a beautiful princess, mainly, one gathers from the music, because of his exquisitely beautiful post-horn playing. This is the song which has made the opera famous, and the tenor who can imitate the post-horn when it comes to the top D's is sure of a success.

The effect of the song is further-reaching than either singer or those who asked for it could have guessed. Chappelou is heard by the Marquis de Corcy, who is head of the Opéra in Paris, and who urges Chappelou to come with him to augment the sadly depleted ranks of the tenors of his company. Chappelou tries to postpone his departure, but the Marquis is adamant; if he wants to come to Paris, he must leave straight away. Chappelou charges his friend Bijou, who also has a voice, to tell Madeleine he will be back to-morrow, or next week, but that he has had to leave hurriedly, to meet the King in Paris and to make his fortune. Madeleine is broken-hearted and furious with her inconstant lover, but Bijou makes up his mind to follow Chappelou the next day, so that his voice may be given to the world as well.

Act II.    Madeleine is now in Paris under the assumed name of Madame de Latour. Having inherited a fortune from an old aunt who had died, she passes as a rich and noble lady, but the whole object of her expedition is to find her errant husband and punish him for what he has done to her. These sentiments she puts forward in an aria at the beginning of the act; but it is clear that in spite of ten years of absence she still loves her husband.

A rehearsal is in progress at the Opéra, where Chappelou, under the name of St. Phar, has become principal tenor, and where his friend Bijou (called Alcindor) is leader of the chorus. St. Phar protests that they are all asked to sing too much, and he at any rate has a sore throat. The Marquis is in despair; the performance they are rehearsing is to be given in honour of Madame Latour, and the Marquis is in love with her. Immediately, St. Phar seems better—he too is violently in love with the lady—and he is able to sing his song, top C, top D, and all.

There is an interview between St. Phar and Madame Latour in which the tenor lays bare his heart and Madame eventually agrees to marry him. He is congratulated by his comrades and invites them all to the wedding. St. Phar, it should be mentioned, unwilling to commit bigamy, has persuaded his friend Bijou to dress up as a priest and take the wedding ceremony, but Madame has somehow got to know about this and has locked Bijou up, together with the second leader of the chorus, so that the ceremony is performed by a real priest.

Act III.    The Marquis remembers that St. Phar has a wife at home and so is fully conscious that bigamy is being committed; however, since he is himself in love with the beautiful Madame Latour, he does nothing to prevent the marriage going through, but he rejoices to himself that to-morrow he will be able to bring the police to arrest his rival. St. Phar is full of happiness in his marriage, but it is short-lived. Bijou escapes, and reveals the horrid truth to him; it was not he but a priest who officiated at the wedding, which is thus not mock, but real.

Madeleine has not yet finished with her husband, but comes

to him in her original country clothes, and with Madeleine's voice. Then, blowing out the candle, she proceeds to hold a conversation with herself, altering her voice from that of Madeleine to that of Madame Latour and back again. Chappelou does not know what to say, and his despair is complete when the police are heard knocking at the door. Headed by the Marquis, they prepare to take him away—to be hanged, says the Marquis. Madeleine demands to be allowed to go with him—and then suddenly puts on her 'grand' voice, saying that there are two witnesses to the crime. She reveals the truth, and all is forgiven.

H.

# JACQUES FRANÇOIS HALÉVY
## (1799–1862)

### LA JUIVE
### The Jewess

OPERA in five acts by Halévy, text by Scribe. Première at the Opéra, Paris, February 23, 1835, with Mmes. Falcon, Dorus-Gras, Nourrit, Levasseur. First performed New York, 1845; Drury Lane, London 1846; Covent Garden, 1850 (in Italian), with Pauline Viardot, Tamberlik, Pololini; Metropolitan, 1885, with Materna, Udvardy, Kögel, conductor Damrosch. Revived Metropolitan, 1887, with Lilli Lehmann, Niemann, Fischer; 1919, with Ponselle, Caruso, Rothier, conductor Bodanzky; 1924, with Easton, Martinelli, Rothier; 1936, with Rethberg, Martinelli, Pinza; Paris, 1933, with Hoerner, Franz, Huberty; Brussels, 1938; New York, 1944, with Doree, Carron; Karlsruhe, 1952. Rosa Raisa was famous in the rôle of Rachel, and Duprez one of Nourrit's most famous successors in the rôle of Eléazar.

### CHARACTERS

| | |
|---|---|
| Princess Eudoxia, *niece of the Emperor* | Soprano |
| Rachel, *daughter of Eléazar* | Soprano |
| Eléazar, *Jewish goldsmith* | Tenor |
| Léopold, *prince of the Empire; employed by Eléazar under the name of Samuel* | Tenor |
| Ruggiero, *provost of the city of Constance* | Baritone |
| Albert, *sergeant in the army of the Emperor* | Bass |
| Cardinal de Brogni, *president of the Council* | Bass |

*Time:* 1414         *Place:* Constance, in Switzerland

Halévy was thirty-five at the time of the first performance of *La Juive*; later he wrote a number of other operas, and many of them were most successful, but *La Juive* remains the work by which his name goes down to posterity. Wagner had more than a little admiration for this work, and it seems likely that he was, apart from Verdi and Berlioz, the most talented of the composers who tackled the specifically French form of 'grand opera'—more so on the evidence of *La Juive* than Meyerbeer, but unfortunately quite without Meyerbeer's drive and energy.

The original plan was to give the rôle of Eléazar, one of the greatest in the nineteenth-century tenor repertory, to a high bass, and to place the scene of the opera in Spain at the time of the Inquisition's greatest power, but in the end the chief rôle was written for the great tenor Nourrit, who himself, if history is to be believed, had a hand in the writing of certain portions of the opera, notably the famous aria, 'Rachel, quand du Seigneur'.

Before the opera opens, various relevant events have taken place. De Brogni was once chief magistrate of Rome. During one of his periodical absences from the city, Rome was captured by the besieging Neapolitans, and considerable portions of the city burnt. Amongst the houses pillaged and destroyed was Brogni's own; he returned to find his wife dead and his child vanished, and therefore presumably dead too. In his agony, Brogni gave up his civic dignities and joined the Church, later rising to become the Cardinal who is one of the principal figures of the story.

Act I.    The overture is concerned with contrasting the themes representing the Jewish and the Christian elements of the story, and the curtain goes up to reveal a square in the city of Constance, in Switzerland (the action takes place throughout in this city). On one side of the square can be seen the great door of a church; on the other, amongst other shops, the house and workroom of Eléazar, the Jewish goldsmith and jeweller. Inside the church, the choir is chanting a *Te Deum*, outside a bystander resents the fact that some Jew seems to be working on a Christian feast-day. Léopold, the young general who has just triumphantly led his armies to victory over the Hussites, is in Constance in disguise— on a previous visit he had met and fallen in love with Eléazar's daughter, Rachel, and he wishes to resume the acquaintance. He is recognised by one of his own soldiers, but enjoins the fellow to silence, at the same time enquiring the cause of the festivity he seems to have stumbled upon. Albert tells him that it is in honour of the state visit of the Emperor, who has called a great council with a view to uniting all the Christians of the world into one solid faith, an undertaking only envisaged since Léopold's own victories over the dissident Hussites.

A great choral 'Hosanna' resounds from the church, and the congregation pours out, to listen to the proclamation in the Emperor's name of a public holiday by Ruggiero, the provost of the town. Nothing could suit the temper of the people better, but no sooner have they voiced their enthusiastic reaction than

Ruggiero hears the sound of work going on in Eléazar's shop and orders the occupants to be brought before him. Eléazar is dragged out with his daughter by his side. He answers Ruggiero's questions with defiance; did he not watch his own sons burned by Christians? Why should he bow to their laws? Ruggiero threatens him with a similar death, but intervention comes from an unexpected source. Cardinal Brogni is passing with his retinue, and asks what is the cause of the noise. He recognises Eléazar, and the jeweller reminds him that it was in Rome that they formerly knew each other, in the days before the Cardinal had entered the service of the Church (there is no mention of it in the opera, but in Scribe's original story it is made clear that Brogni had banished Eléazar from Rome, thus saving his life after he had been condemned to death as an usurer). Brogni sings a calmly flowing *cavatina*, 'Si la rigeur et la vengeance', in which he prays that enlightenment

may come to the Jewish unbelievers; the aria develops into an ensemble, after which the stage clears.

Only Léopold is left behind. He takes up a position outside Eléazar's house (he has been taken on there as a workman, under the name of Samuel, and they believe him to be Jewish), and proceeds to serenade Rachel. It is a charming, high-lying melody, and it is not long before Rachel answers it from inside. She bids him come that very evening, when her father and his fellow-believers will be celebrating the feast of the Passover. Léopold is about to object when a crowd precipitates itself into the square, intent on making the most of the Emperor's largesse. The choruses pile up on one another, there is a brisk dance, and the drinking is general. Eléazar and Rachel, trying to cross the square, are recognised as Jews by Ruggiero and set upon by the mob. Eléazar confronts them with dignity, but they are for throwing him in the lake, when salvation comes in the person of Léopold who, though still disguised, is immediately recognised by Albert, who causes the crowd to leave the Jewish pair alone. Rachel is astonished at the effect Samuel has on the Christians and at first tries to restrain him from intervening.

Rachel is left wondering at Léopold's inexplicable power;
Eléazar continues to pour scorn on the hated Christians.

Act II.    A room in Eléazar's house, where the feast of the
Passover is being celebrated. Eléazar leads the chant ('O dieu,
dieu de nos pères'), which the others, together with Rachel,
repeat after him. Eléazar pronounces a curse against anyone who
dares profane the holy feast ('Si trahison ou perfidie') and then
distributes the unleavened bread, Samuel being the last to receive
it. He thinks he has escaped notice when he drops it without
tasting it, but Rachel has seen his gesture, and is worried by
what it may import. The scene is immensely impressive, and the
measured incantation of the opening is one of the most remarkable moments in the opera:

Eléazar's supplication to God ('Dieu, que ma voix tremblante')
is barely finished when there is a knock at the door. He commands the Jews to put away the ritual vessels and candles, and
the table is removed, the Jews themselves going out through a
back door. Léopold is about to depart, when Eléazar commands
him to stay with him. The door is opened, and in comes the
Princess Eudoxia. She makes herself known, and Eléazar kneels
before her. Her object is to buy from him a fine chain which she
hears he has; it once belonged, Eléazar tells her, to the Emperor
Constantine himself. She wishes to buy it for her husband
Léopold, whom that day she expects back from the wars, where he
has defeated the Hussites. Léopold overhears the conversation,
and is filled with remorse at his deceit. Eudoxia orders that the
chain be brought the next day to her palace.

While Eléazar sees Eudoxia to the door, Rachel returns and
asks Samuel to explain his conduct when saving them from the
mob, and also, that evening, at the Passover service. He protests
that he must see her in greater privacy.

Rachel comes back to keep her rendezvous with Léopold. Her
heart is full of foreboding, even fear: 'Il va venir! et d'effroi je

me sens frémir'. The aria admirably expresses the mixture of feelings of which she is conscious, and is full of the apprehension with which she awaits their meeting. Léopold admits to her that he has deceived her, and is in fact a Christian. Rachel bitterly reproaches him for his deception; he can but defend himself by saying that there was no thought in his mind but love of her. Léopold's pleading is so passionate (the music expresses it most convincingly) that Rachel is on the point of yielding, when her father confronts them.

Eléazar declares that their offence is such that they shall not escape punishment. In a trio they admit their guilt and express terror at the wrath of Eléazar, who tells them that only the fact that Samuel is a Jew prevents him from striking him dead on the spot for his falsity. Léopold bids him strike; he is a Christian. Rachel intercepts the blow, and pleads distractedly for her lover; she also is guilty. Eléazar declares himself willing to agree to the marriage, but his wrath knows no bounds when Léopold says that he is unable to marry Rachel.

Act III in some versions begins with a scene for Eudoxia and Rachel, who asks to be allowed to serve as a slave in her palace for one day only; she has trailed Léopold to the palace, but does not yet know his real identity, although she believes that such a position would make revenge possible. Eudoxia agrees to her request.

When this scene is omitted, the act begins in the gardens of the Emperor's palace, where a festival in honour of Léopold is in progress. The Emperor himself is seated at the high table, together with Brogni, Léopold and Eudoxia. A ballet is performed for their entertainment, and at its end, Eléazar and Rachel come to bring Eudoxia the chain she has bought for Léopold. When she is about to place it round her husband's neck, Rachel snatches it from her and announces that Léopold has committed the heinous crime of consorting with a Jewess, and that she herself is the Jewess in question.

There is a moment of stupefied horror. When Eléazar asks if the Christian laws are directed only against Jews or apply equally to themselves—Léopold has silently admitted the charge— Cardinal Brogni rises to his feet and pronounces a terrible anathema on all three, who have dared to break the laws of heaven: 'Vous, qui du Dieu vivant'.

Act IV.  All have been condemned to death, but Eudoxia resolves to risk humiliation in order to save Léopold, whom she still loves. She begs Rachel to retract her charge against Léopold. Rachel at first proudly refuses, then says she will do as she has been asked, saying to herself that a Jewess can outdo a Christian in magnanimity. The scene is highly dramatic and is succeeded by one hardly less compelling when the Cardinal confronts Rachel and begs her to abjure her faith and so save herself from death. She refuses.

Brogni resolves to send for Eléazar in a last effort to save Rachel's life. He pleads with him to renounce his faith, and in so doing to save her life; but the old man is resolute in the face of temptation, and refuses to deny his fathers' creed. He reminds Brogni of the time when his house and his family perished in the conflagration; his daughter was saved by a Jew who came to fight the flames, and she is alive now. But though her whereabouts are known to him, he will take his revenge by carrying the secret with him to death. Brogni implores him to reveal what he knows, but he will say no more.

Eléazar is torn with doubts; can he bear, by his orthodoxy and his own uncompromising hatred of Christians, to send his daughter to her death? The thought tortures him, and resolves itself into a great expression of emotion: 'Rachel, quand du Seigneur'. This is the climax of the opera, and Eléazar is at one

Ra-chel, quand du Sei-gneur la grâ-ce tu - té - lai-re

and the same time at his noblest and his most human. He hears the savage cries: 'Au bûcher, les Juifs' from outside, and is strengthened in his decision; Rachel shall die a victim of their hate. The end of the act is hardly less moving than the great aria a little earlier.

Act V.  From a tent, a view is to be had of the ground on which the scaffold is erected for the martyrdom of the two Jews —Léopold's sentence has been commuted to one of banishment. The people howl for the death of the Jews, and presently Eléazar and Rachel are seen coming slowly towards the scaffold. Just as she is about to mount the scaffold, Eléazar asks Rachel if she would like at the last moment to abjure her faith and adopt Christianity, but she proudly disdains any such idea. She is thrown into the cauldron by the executioners, at the very moment when Brogni is told by Eléazar, 'Your daughter perished in those flames'.                                                    H.

# GIACOMO MEYERBEER
## (1791–1864)

ALTHOUGH he was born in Berlin (September 5, 1791), studied pianoforte and theory in Germany, and attained in that country a reputation as a brilliant pianist, besides producing several operas there, Meyerbeer is regarded as the founder of what is generally understood as French Grand Opera. It has been said of him that 'he joined to the flowing melody of the Italians the solid harmony of the Germans, the poignant declamation and varied, piquant rhythm of the French'; which is a good description of the opera that flourished on the stage of the Académie or Grand Opéra, Paris. The elaborate spectacular scenes and finales in Meyerbeer's operas were the models for many of his successors, Italian as well as French and German. He understood how to write effectively for the voice, and he was an opera composer who made a point of striving for tone colour in the instrumental accompaniment. Sometimes the effect may be too calculated, too cunningly contrived, too obviously sought for. But what he accomplished had decided influence on the enrichment of the instrumental score in operatic composition.

Much criticism has been directed at Meyerbeer, and much of his music has disappeared from the stage. Meyerbeer had the pick of the great artists of his day. His works were written for and produced with brilliant casts, and had better not be sung at all than indifferently. His greatest work, *Les Huguenots*, is still capable of leaving a deep impression, if adequately performed.

Meyerbeer came of a Jewish family. His real name was Jacob Liebmann Beer. He prefixed 'Meyer' to his patronymic at the request of a wealthy relative who made him his heir. He was a pupil in pianoforte of Clementi; also studied under Abbé Vogler, being a fellow pupil of C. M. von Weber. His first operas were German. In 1815 he went to Italy and composed a series of operas in the style of Rossini. Going to Paris in 1826, he became 'immersed in the study of French opera, from Lully onward'. The first result was *Robert le Diable* (Robert the Devil), Grand

Opéra, Paris, 1831. This was followed by *Les Huguenots*, 1836; *Le Prophète*, 1849; *L'Étoile du Nord*, Opéra-Comique, 1854; *Dinorah, ou le Pardon de Ploërmel* (Dinorah, or the Pardon of Ploërmel), Opéra-Comique, 1859. Much of the music of *L'Étoile du Nord* came from an earlier score, *Das Feldlager in Schlesien* (The Camp in Silesia), Berlin, 1843. Meyerbeer died May 2, 1864, in Paris, where his *L'Africaine* was produced at the Grand Opéra in 1865.

## ROBERT LE DIABLE
### Robert the Devil

Opera in five acts by Meyerbeer; words by Scribe and Delavigne. Première Grand Opéra, Paris, November 22, 1831, with Mmes. Dorus-Gras, Cinti-Damoreau, MM. Nourrit, Levasseur. First performed Drury Lane, London, 1832 (in English), as *The Demon, or the Mystic Branch*; Covent Garden, 1832 (in English), as *The Fiend Father, or Robert of Normandy*; Her Majesty's Theatre, 1847 (in Italian), with Jenny Lind (her London début); New York, 1834 (in English), with Mrs. Wood as Isobel and Wood as Robert, the opera being followed by a *pas seul* by Miss Wheatley, and a farce, *My Uncle John*; Astor Place Opera House, 1851, with Steffanone, Bosio, Bettini, Marini; Academy of Music, 1857, with Formes as Bertram; Metropolitan, 1883, with Fursch-Madi, Valleria, Stagno, Mirabella. Last Covent Garden performance, 1890, with Fanny Moody, Stromfield, Charles Manners, Guetray, conductor Arditi.

### CHARACTERS

Alice, *foster-sister of Robert*...................Soprano
Isabella, *Princess of Sicily* .....................Soprano
The Abbess ...................................Dancer
Robert, *Duke of Normandy* .....................Tenor
Bertram, *the Unknown* ..........................Bass
Raimbaut, *a minstrel* ...........................Tenor

*Time:* Thirteenth Century                  *Place:* Sicily

The production of *Robert le Diable* in Paris was such a sensational success that it made the fortune of the Grand Opéra. Whatever criticism may now be directed against this opera, it was a remarkable creation for its day. Meyerbeer's score not only saved the libretto, in which the grotesque is carried to the point of absurdity, but actually made a brilliant success of the production as a whole.

The story is legendary. Robert is the son of the arch-fiend by a human woman. Robert's father, known as Bertram, but really the devil, ever follows him about, and seeks to lure him to destruction. The strain of purity in the drama is supplied by Robert's foster-sister, Alice, who, if Bertram is the prototype of Mephistopheles in *Faust*, may be regarded as the original of Micaela in *Carmen*.

Robert, because of his evil deeds (inspired by Bertram), has been banished from Normandy, and has come to Sicily. He has fallen in love with Isabella, she with him. He is to attend a tournament at which she is to award the prizes. Tempted by Bertram, he gambles and loses all his possessions, including even his armour. These facts are disclosed in the first act. This contains a song by Raimbaut, the minstrel, in which he tells of Robert's misdeeds; he is saved from the latter's fury by Alice, who is betrothed to Raimbaut, and who, in an expressive air, pleads vainly with Robert to mend his ways and especially to avoid Bertram, from whom she instinctively shrinks. In the second act Robert and Isabella meet in the palace. She bestows upon him a suit of armour to wear in the tournament. But, misled by Bertram, he seeks his rival elsewhere than in the lists, and, by his failure to appear there, loses his honour as a knight. In the next act, laid in the cavern of St. Irene, occurs an orgy of evil spirits, to whose number Bertram promises to add Robert. Next comes a scene that verges upon the grotesque, but which is converted by Meyerbeer's genius into something highly fantastic. This is in the ruined convent of St. Rosalie. In a big solo ('Nonnes, qui reposez') Bertram summons from their graves the nuns who, in life, were unfaithful to their vows. The fiend has promised Robert that if he will but seize a mystic cypress branch from over the grave of St. Rosalie, and bear it away, whatever he wishes for will become his. The ghostly nuns, led by their Abbess (Taglioni at the Paris première), dance about him. They seek to inveigle him with gambling, drink, and love, until, dazed by their enticements, he seizes the branch. Besides the ballet of the nuns, there are two duets for Raimbaut and Bertram—'Du rendezvous' (Our meeting place), and 'Le bonheur est dans l'inconstance' (Our pleasure lies in constant change).

The first use Robert makes of the branch is to effect entrance into Isabella's chamber. He threatens to seize her and bear her away, but yields to her entreaties, breaks the branch, and destroys the spell. In this act—the fourth—occurs the famous air for Isabella, 'Robert, toi que j'aime' (Robert, whom I love).

Once more Bertram seeks to make a compact with Robert, the price for which shall be paid with his soul. But Alice, by repeating to him the last warning words of his mother, delays the signing of the compact until the clock strikes twelve. The spell is broken. Bertram disappears. The cathedral doors swing open disclosing Isabella, who, in her bridal robes, awaits Robert. The finale contains a trio for Alice, Robert, and Bertram, which is considered one of Meyerbeer's finest inspirations.      K.

# LES HUGUENOTS
## The Huguenots

Opera in five acts by Giacomo Meyerbeer; text by A. E. Scribe after Deschamps. Première at the Opéra, Paris, February 29, 1836, with Mmes. Falcon, Dorus-Gras, Nourrit, Levasseur, Serda. First performed Covent Garden, 1842 (in German); 1845 (in French); 1848 (in Italian); New York, 1845 (in French); 1850 (in Italian). Revived Metropolitan, 1883, with Nilsson, Sembrich, Campanini, Mirabella, Kaschmann, conductor Vianesi; performed frequently at Covent Garden in the 1900's with Destinn, Tetrazzini, Caruso, Scotti, Journet; revived Buenos Aires, 1921, with Borina, Barrientos, Martinelli, Crabbé, Melnik, conductor Panizza; Rome, 1923, with Llacer, Pasini, O'Sullivan, Parvis, Donaggio, conductor Gui; Covent Garden, 1927, with Scacciati, Guglielmetti, O'Sullivan, Stabile, Kipnis, conductor Bellezza; Verona Arena, 1933, with Raisa, Saraceni, Lauri-Volpi, Rimini, Pasero, conductor Votto; Paris, 1936, with Hoerner, Delmas, Thill, Huberty, Pernet.

### CHARACTERS

Valentine, *daughter of St. Bris and betrothed to de Nevers* ..................................... Soprano

Marguerite de Valois, *betrothed to Henry IV, of Navarre* ..................................... Soprano

Urbain, *page to Marguerite de Valois* ...... Mezzo-Soprano

Count de St. Bris ⎱ *Catholic noblemen* ⎰ Baritone
Count de Nevers ⎰               ⎱ Baritone

Cossé ......................................... Tenor

Méru ⎱
Thoré ⎰ *Catholic gentlemen* ................ ⎰ Baritone
Tavannes ⎰               ⎰ Baritone
               ⎱ Tenor

de Retz ....................................... Baritone

Raoul de Nangis, *a Huguenot nobleman* ........... Tenor

Marcel, *a Huguenot soldier, servant to Raoul* ........ Bass

Bois-Rosé, *a Huguenot soldier* ................... Tenor

Maurevert, *a Catholic nobleman*.....................Bass
Catholic and Huguenot Ladies, and Gentlemen of the Court;
Soldiers, Pages, Citizens, and Populace; Night Watch,
Monks, and Students.

*Time:* August 1572          *Paris:* Touraine and Paris

It has been said that, because Meyerbeer was a Jew, he chose
for two of his operas, *Les Huguenots* and *Le Prophète*, subjects
dealing with bloody uprisings due to religious differences among
Christians. *Les Huguenots* is written around the massacre of the
Huguenots by the Catholics, on the night of St. Bartholomew's,
Paris, August 24, 1572; *Le Prophète* around the seizure and occupation of Münster, in 1555, by the Anabaptists, led by John of
Leyden. Even the ballet of the spectral nuns, in *Robert le Diable*,
has been suggested as due to Meyerbeer's racial origin and a
tendency covertly to attack the Christian religion. Far-fetched, I
think. Most likely his famous librettist was chiefly responsible
for choice of subjects and Meyerbeer accepted them because of
the effective manner in which they were worked out. Even so, he
was not wholly satisfied with Scribe's libretto of *Les Huguenots*.
He had the scene of the benediction of the swords enlarged, and
it was upon his insistence that Deschamps wrote in the love duet
in Act IV. As it stands, the story has been handled with keen
appreciation of its dramatic possibilities.

Act I.    Touraine. Count de Nevers, one of the leaders of the
Catholic party and a great lady-killer, has invited friends to a
banquet at his château. Among these is Raoul de Nangis, a
Huguenot. He is accompanied by an old retainer, the Huguenot
soldier, Marcel. In the course of the fête it is proposed that everyone shall toast his love in a song. Raoul is the first to be called
upon. The name of the beauty whom he pledges in his toast is
unknown to him. He had come to her assistance while she was
being molested by a party of students. She thanked him most
graciously, and he lives in the hope of meeting her again.

Marcel is a fanatic Huguenot. Having followed his master to
the banquet, he finds him surrounded by leaders of the party belonging to the opposite faith. He fears for the consequences. In
strange contrast to the glamour and gaiety of the festive proceedings, he intones Luther's hymn 'Ein feste Burg' (A Stronghold Sure). The noblemen of the Catholic party instead of

becoming angry are amused. Marcel repays their levity by singing a fierce Huguenot battle song. That also amuses them.

At this point the Count de Nevers is informed that a lady is in the garden and wishes to speak with him. He leaves his guests who, through an open window, watch the meeting. Raoul, to his surprise and consternation, recognises in the lady none other than the fair creature whom he saved from the molestations of the students and with whom he has fallen in love. Naturally, however, from the circumstances of her meeting with de Nevers he cannot but conclude that a liaison exists between them.

De Nevers returns, rejoins his guests. Urbain, the page of Queen Marguerite de Valois, enters. He is in search of Raoul, having come to conduct him to a meeting with a gracious and noble lady whose name, however, is not disclosed. Raoul's eyes having been bandaged, he is conducted to a carriage and departs with Urbain, wondering what his next adventure will be.

Act II. In the Garden of Chenonceaux, Queen Marguerite de Valois receives Valentine, daughter of the Count de St. Bris. The Queen knows of her rescue from the students by Raoul. Desiring to put an end to the differences between Huguenots and Catholics which have already led to bloodshed, she has conceived the idea of uniting Valentine, daughter of one of the great Catholic leaders, to Raoul. Valentine, however, was already pledged to de Nevers. It was at the Queen's suggestion that she visited de Nevers and had him summoned from the banquet in order to ask him to release her from her engagement to him—a request which, however reluctantly, he granted.

Here, in the Gardens of Chenonceaux, Valentine and Raoul are, according to the Queen's plan, to meet again, but she intends first to receive him alone. He is brought in, the bandage is removed from his eyes, he does homage to the Queen, and when, in the presence of the leaders of the Catholic party, Marguerite de Valois explains her purpose and her plan through this union of two great houses to end the religious differences which have disturbed her reign, all consent.

Valentine is led in. Raoul at once recognises her as the woman of his adventure but also, alas, as the woman whom de Nevers met in the garden during the banquet (he has, as yet, no knowledge of the purpose of this meeting). Believing her to be unchaste, he refuses her hand. General consternation. St. Bris, his followers, all draw their swords. Raoul's flashes from its sheath. Only the Queen's intervention prevents bloodshed.

Act III.     The scene is an open place in Paris before a chapel, where de Nevers, who has renewed his engagement with Valentine, is to take her in marriage. The nuptial cortège enters the building. The populace is restless, excited. Religious differences still are the cause of enmity. The presence of Royalist and Huguenot soldiers adds to the restlessness of the people. De Nevers, St. Bris, and another Catholic nobleman, Maurevert, come out from the chapel, where Valentine has desired to linger in prayer. The men are still incensed over what appears to them the shameful conduct of Raoul toward Valentine. Marcel at that moment delivers to St. Bris a challenge from Raoul to fight a duel. When the old Huguenot soldier has retired, the noblemen conspire together to lead Raoul into an ambush. During the duel, followers of St. Bris, who have been placed in hiding, are suddenly to issue forth and murder the young Huguenot nobleman.

From a position in the vestibule of the chapel, Valentine has overheard the plot. She still loves Raoul and him alone. How shall she warn him of the certain death in store for him? She sees Marcel and counsels him that his master must not come here to fight the duel unless he is accompanied by a strong guard. As a result, when Raoul and his antagonist meet, and St. Bris's soldiers are about to attack the Huguenot, Marcel summons the latter's followers from a nearby inn. A street fight between the two bodies of soldiers is imminent, when the Queen and her suite enter. A gaily bedecked barge comes up the river and lays to at the bank. It bears de Nevers and his friends. He has come to convey his bride from the chapel to his home. And now Raoul learns, from the Queen, and to his great grief, that he has refused the hand of the woman who loved him and who had gone to de Nevers in order to ask him to release her from her engagement with him.

Act IV.     Raoul seeks Valentine, who has become the wife of de Nevers, in her home. He wishes to be assured of the truth of what he has heard from the Queen. During their meeting footsteps are heard approaching and Valentine barely has time to hide Raoul in an adjoining room when de Nevers, St. Bris, and other noblemen of the Catholic party enter, and form a plan to be carried out that very night—the night of St. Bartholomew—

to massacre the Huguenots. Only de Nevers refuses to take part in the conspiracy. Rather than do so, he yields his sword to St. Bris and is led away a prisoner. The priests bless the swords, St. Bris and his followers swear loyalty to the bloody cause in which they are enlisted, and depart to await the signal to put it into effect, the tolling of the great bell from St. Germain.

Raoul comes out from his place of concealment. His one thought is to hurry away and notify his brethren of their peril. Valentine seeks to detain him, entreats him not to go, since it will be to certain death. As the greatest and final argument to him to remain, she proclaims that she loves him. But already the deep-voiced bell tolls the signal. Flames, blood-red, flare through the windows. Nothing can restrain Raoul from doing his duty. Valentine stands before the closed door to block his egress. Rushing to a casement, he throws back the window and leaps to the street.

Act V.    Covered with blood, Raoul rushes into the ballroom of the Hotel de Nesle, where the Huguenot leaders, ignorant of the massacre that has begun, are assembled to celebrate the marriage of Marguerite de Valois and Henry IV, and summons them to battle. Already Coligny, their great commander, has fallen. Their followers are being massacred.

The scene changes to a Huguenot churchyard, where Raoul and Marcel have found temporary refuge. Valentine hurries in. She wishes to save Raoul, and adjures him to adopt her faith. De Nevers has met a noble death and she is free—free to marry Raoul. But he refuses to marry her at the sacrifice of his religion. Now she decides that she will die with him and that they will both die as Huguenots and united. Marcel blesses them. The enemy has stormed the churchyard and begins the massacre of those who have sought safety in the edifice itself. Again the scene changes, this time to a square in Paris. Raoul, who has been severely wounded, is supported by Marcel and Valentine. St. Bris and his followers approach. In answer to St. Bris's summons, 'Who goes there?' Raoul, calling to his aid all the strength he has left, cries out, 'Huguenots'. There is a volley. Raoul, Valentine, Marcel lie dead on the ground. Too late St. Bris discovers that he has been the murderer of his own daughter.

Originally in five acts, the version of *Les Huguenots* usually performed contains but three. The first two acts are drawn into one by converting the second act into a scene and adding it to the first. The fifth act (or in the usual version the fourth) is nearly always omitted. This is due to the length of the opera. The audience takes it for granted that, when Raoul leaves Valentine, he goes to his death. I have seen a performance of *Les Huguenots* with the last act. So far as an understanding of the work is concerned, it is unnecessary. It also involves as much noise and smell of gunpowder as Massenet's opera, *La Navarraise*—and that is saying a good deal.

The performances of *Les Huguenots*, during the most brilliant revivals of that work at the Metropolitan Opera House, New York, under Maurice Grau, were known as 'les nuits de sept étoiles' (the nights of the seven stars). The cast to which the performances owed this designation is given in the summary above. A manager, in order to put *Les Huguenots* satisfactorily upon the stage, should be able to give it with seven first-rate principals, trained as nearly as possible in the same school of opera. The work should be sung preferably in French and by singers who know something of the traditions of the Grand Opéra, Paris. Mixed casts of Latin and Teutonic singers mar a performance of this work. That *Les Huguenots* has lost almost all its former popularity since 'the nights of the seven stars', is due to the dearth of singers of the necessary calibre almost as much as to the change in public taste. What would have been Meyerbeer singers now concentrate on Wagner, and Meyerbeer is given no more.

After a brief overture, in which 'Ein feste Burg' is prominent, the first act opens with a sonorous chorus for the diners in the salon of de Nevers's castle. Raoul, called upon to propose in song a toast to a lady, pledges the unknown beauty, whom he rescued from the insolence of a band of students. He does this in the romance, 'Plus blanche que la blanche hermine' (Whiter than the whitest ermine). The accompaniment to the melodious measures, with which the romance opens, is supplied by a viola solo, the effective employment of which in this passage shows Meyerbeer's knowledge of the instrument and its possibilities This romance is a perfect example of a certain phase of Meyerbeer's art—a suave and elegant melody for voice, accompanied in a highly original manner, part of the time, in this instance, by a single instrument in the orchestra, which however, in spite of its effectiveness, leaves an impression of simplicity not wholly uncalculated.

Raoul's romance is followed by the entrance of Marcel, and the scene for that bluff, sturdy old Huguenot campaigner and loyal servant of Raoul, a splendidly drawn character, dramatically and musically. Marcel tries to drown the festive sounds by intoning the stern phrases of Luther's hymn. This he follows with the Huguenot battle song, with its 'Piff, piff, piff', which has been rendered famous by the great bassos who have sung it, not least Edouard de Reszke.

De Nevers is then called away to his interview with the lady, whom Raoul recognises as the unknown beauty rescued by him from the students, and whom, from the circumstances of her visit to de Nevers, he cannot but believe to be engaged in a liaison with the latter. Almost immediately upon de Nevers's rejoining his guests there enters Urbain, the page of Marguerite de Valois. He greets the assembly with the brilliant recitative, 'Nobles Seigneurs salut!' This is followed by a charming cavatina, 'Une dame noble et sage' (A wise and noble lady). Originally this was a soprano number, Urbain having been composed as a soprano rôle, which it remained for twelve years. Then, in 1844, when *Les Huguenots* was produced in London, with Alboni as Urbain, Meyerbeer transposed it, and a contralto, or mezzo-soprano, part it has remained ever since, its interpreters having included Annie Louise Cary, Trebelli, Scalchi, and Homer.

The letter brought by Urbain is recognised by the Catholic noblemen as being in the handwriting of Marguerite de Valois. As it is addressed to Raoul, they show by their obsequious demeanour toward him the importance they attach to the invitation. In accordance with its terms Raoul allows himself to be blindfolded and led away by Urbain.

Following the original score and regarding what is now the second scene of Act I as the second act, this opens with Marguerite de Valois's apostrophe to the fair land of Touraine ('O beau pays de la Touraine'), which, with the air immediately following, 'A ce mot tout s'anime et renait la nature' (At this word everything revives and Nature renews itself), constitutes an animated and brilliant scene for coloratura soprano.

There is a brief colloquy between Marguerite and Valentine, then the graceful female chorus, sung on the bank of the Seine and known as the 'bathers' chorus', this being followed by the entrance of Urbain and his engaging song—the rondeau composed for Alboni—'Non!—non, non, non, non, non! Vous n'avez jamais, je gage' (No!—no, no, no, no, no! You have never heard, I wager).

Raoul enters, the bandage is removed from his eyes, and there follows a duet, 'Beauté divine, enchanteresse' (Beauty brightly divine, enchantress), between him and Marguerite, all graciousness on her side and courtly admiration on his. The nobles and their followers come upon the scene. Marguerite de Valois's plan to end the religious strife that has distracted the realm meets with their approbation. The finale of the act begins with the swelling chorus in which they take oath to abide by it. There is the brief episode in which Valentine is led in by St. Bris, presented to Raoul, and indignantly spurned by him. The act closes with a turbulent ensemble. Strife and bloodshed, then and there, are averted only by the interposition of Marguerite.

Act III opens with the famous chorus of the Huguenot soldiers in which, while they imitate with their hands the beating of drums, they sing their spirited 'Rataplan'. By contrast, the Catholic maidens, who accompany the bridal cortège of Valentine and de Nevers to the chapel, intone a litany, while Catholic citizens, students, and women protest against the song of the Huguenot soldiers. These several choral elements are skilfully worked out in the score. Marcel, coming upon the scene, manages to have St. Bris summoned from the chapel, and presents Raoul's challenge to a duel. The Catholics form their plot to assassinate Raoul, of which Valentine finds opportunity to notify Marcel, in a long duet which is one of the most striking scenes of the opera. The duel scene is preceded by a stirring septet, a really great passage, 'En mon bon droit j'ai confiance' (On my good cause relying). The music, when the ambuscade is uncovered and Marcel summons the Huguenots to Raoul's aid and a street combat is threatened, reaches an effective climax in a double chorus. The excitement subsides with the arrival of Marguerite de Valois, and of the barge containing de Nevers and his retinue. A brilliant chorus, supported by the orchestra and by a military band on the stage, with ballet to add to the spectacle forms the finale, as de Nevers conducts Valentine to the barge, and is followed on board by St. Bris and the nuptial cortège.

The fourth act, in the home of de Nevers, opens with a romance for Valentine, 'Parmi les pleurs' (Amid my tears, by dreams once more o'ertaken), which is followed by a brief scene between her and Raoul, whom the approach of the conspirators quickly obliges her to hide in an adjoining apartment. The scene of the consecration of the swords is one of the greatest in the opera; but that it shall have its full effect St. Bris must be an artist like Plançon, who, besides being endowed with a powerful and beautifully managed voice, was superb in appearance and as St. Bris had the bearing of the dignified, commanding yet fanatic nobleman of old France. Musically and dramatically the scene rests on St. Bris's shoulders, and broad they must be, since his is the most conspicuous part in song and action, from the intonation of his solo, 'Pour cette cause sainte, obéisses sans crainte' (With sacred zeal and ardour let now your soul be burning),

to the end of the savage *stretta*, when the conspirators, having tiptoed almost to the door, in order to disperse for their mission, suddenly turn, once more uplift sword hilts, poignards, and crucifixes, and, after a frenzied adjuration of loyalty to a cause that demands the massacre of an unsuspecting foe, steal forth into the shades of fateful night.

Powerful as this scene is, Meyerbeer has made the love duet which follows even more gripping. For now he interprets the conflicting emotions of love and loyalty in two hearts. It begins with Valentine's exclamation, 'Oh, ciel! Où courez-vous?' and reaches its climax in a *cantilena* of supreme beauty, 'Tu l'as dit, oui tu m'aimes' (Thou hast said it; aye, thou lov'st me),

Andante amoroso

which is broken in upon by the sinister tolling of a distant bell—the signal for the massacre to begin. An air for Valentine, an impassioned *stretta* for the lovers, Raoul's leap from the window, followed by a discharge of musketry, from which, in the curtailed version, he is supposed to meet his death, and this act, still an amazing achievement in opera, is at an end.

In the fifth act, there is the fine scene of the blessing by Marcel of Raoul and Valentine, during which strains of Luther's hymn are heard, intoned by Huguenots, who have crowded into their church for a last refuge.

*Les Huguenots* has been the subject of violent attacks, beginning with Robert Schumann's essay indited as far back as 1837, and starting off with the assertion, 'I feel to-day like the young warrior who draws his sword for the first time in a holy cause'. Schumann's most particular 'holy cause' was, in this instance, to praise Mendelssohn's oratorio, *St. Paul*, at the expense of Meyerbeer's opera *Les Huguenots*, notwithstanding the utter dissimilarity of purpose in the two works. On the other hand, Hanslick remarks that a person who cannot appreciate the dramatic power of this Meyerbeer opera, must be lacking in certain elements of the critical faculty. Even Wagner, one of Meyerbeer's bitterest detractors, found words of the highest praise for the passage from the love duet, which is quoted immediately above. The composer of *The Ring of the Nibelung* had a much broader outlook upon the world than Schumann, in whose genius there was, after all, a good deal of the *bourgeois*.

Pro or con, when *Les Huguenots* is sung with a fully adequate cast, it cannot fail to make a deep impression—as witness 'les nuits de sept étoiles'.

A typical night of the seven stars at the Metropolitan Opera House, New York, was that of December 26, 1894, when the prices for the first time were raised to $7.

The *sept étoiles* were Nordica (Valentine), Scalchi (Urbain), Melba (Marguerite de Valois), Jean de Reszke (Raoul), Plançon (St. Bris), Maurel (de Nevers), and Edouard de Reszke (Marcel). Two Academy of Music casts are worth referring to. April 30, 1872, Parepa Rosa, for her last appearance in America, sang Valentine. Wachtel was Raoul and Santley St. Bris. The other Academy cast was a 'Night of six stars', and is noteworthy as including Maurel twenty years, almost to the night, before he appeared in the Metropolitan cast. The date was December 24, 1874. Nilsson was Valentine; Cary, Urbain; Maresi, Marguerite de Valois; Campanini, Raoul; del Puente, St. Bris; Maurel, de

Nevers; and Nanneti, Marcel. With a more distinguished Marguerite de Valois, this performance would have anticipated the 'nuits de sept étoiles'. K.

# LE PROPHÈTE
## The Prophet

Opera in five acts by Meyerbeer; words by Scribe. Première Grand Opéra, Paris, April 16, 1849, with Pauline Viardot and Roger. First performed London, Covent Garden, July 24, 1849, with Mario, Viardot-Garcia, Miss Hayes, and Tagliafico. New Orleans, April 2, 1850. New York, Niblo's Garden, November 25, 1853, with Salvi (John of Leyden), Steffanone and Mme. Maretzek. Revived in German, Metropolitan Opera House, by Dr. Leopold Damrosch, December 17, 1884, with Anton Schott as John of Leyden, Marianne Brandt as Fides and Schroeder-Hanfstaengl as Bertha. It was given ten times during the season, in which it was equalled only by *Tannhäuser* and *Lohengrin*. Revived Covent Garden, 1890 (in French), with Richard, Jean de Reszke, Edouard de Reszke; last performed there 1895, with Ravogli, Tamagno. Also, Metropolitan Opera House, 1898–99, with Jean de Reszke, Brema (Fides), Lehmann (Bertha); January 22, 1900, Alvarez, Schumann-Heink, Suzanne Adams, Plançon and Edouard de Reszke; by Gatti-Casazza, February 7, 1918, with Caruso, Matzenauer, Muzio, Didur, and Mardones; and 1927, with Corona, Matzenauer, Martinelli. Schumann-Heink was a celebrated Fides.

### CHARACTERS

John of Leyden .................................Tenor
Fides, *his mother* .......................Mezzo-Soprano
Bertha, *his bride*............................Soprano
Jonas ⎤                                ⎱ Tenor
Matthisen ⎬ Anabaptists ......................⎨ Bass
Zacharias ⎦                              ⎰ Bass
Count Oberthal .............................Baritone

Nobles, Citizens, Anabaptists, Peasants, Soldiers, Prisoners, Children

*Time:* 1534–35       *Place:* Dordrecht, Holland, and Münster

Act I. At the foot of Count Oberthal's castle, near Dordrecht, Holland, peasants and mill hands are assembled. Bertha and Fides draw near. The latter is bringing to Bertha a betrothal ring from her son John, who is to marry her on the morrow. But permission must first be obtained from Count Oberthal as lord of the domain. The women are here to seek it.

There arrive three sombre-looking men, who strive to rouse the people to revolt against tyranny. They are the Anabaptists,

Jonas, Matthisen, and Zacharias. The Count, however, who chances to come out of the castle with his followers, recognises in Jonas a steward who was discharged from his employment. He orders his soldiers to beat the three men with the flat of their swords. John's mother and Bertha make their plea to Oberthal. John and Bertha have loved ever since he rescued her from drowning in the Meuse. Admiring Bertha's beauty, Oberthal refuses to give permission for her to marry John, but, instead, orders her seized and borne to the castle for his own diversion. The people are greatly agitated and, when the three Anabaptists reappear, throw themselves at their feet, and on rising make threatening gestures toward the castle.

Act II.    In John's inn at Leyden are the three Anabaptists and a throng of merrymaking peasants. Full of longing for Bertha, John is thinking of the morrow. The Anabaptists discover that he bears a remarkable resemblance to the picture of King David in the Cathedral of Münster. They believe this resemblance can be made of service to their plans. John tells them of a strange dream he has had, in which he found himself standing under the dome of a temple with people prostrate before him. They interpret it for him as evidence that he will mount a throne, and urge him to follow them. But for him there is but one throne—that of the kingdom of love with Bertha.

At that moment, however, she rushes in and begs him quickly to hide her. She has escaped from Oberthal, who is in pursuit. Oberthal and his soldiers enter. The Count threatens that if John does not deliver over Bertha to him, his mother, whom the soldiers have captured on the way to the inn, shall die. She is brought in and forced to her knees. A soldier with a battle-axe stands over her. After a brief struggle John's love for his mother conquers. He hands over Bertha to Oberthal. She is led away. Fides is released.

The three Anabaptists return. Now John is ready to join them, if only to wreak vengeance on Oberthal. They insist that he come at once, without even saying farewell to his mother, who must be kept in ignorance of their plans. John consents and hurries off with them.

Act III.    In the winter camp of the Anabaptists in a forest of Westphalia, before Münster. On a frozen lake people are skating. The people have risen against their oppressors. John has been proclaimed a prophet of God. At the head of the Anabaptists he is besieging Münster.

The act develops in three scenes. The first reveals the psychological medley of fanaticism and sensuality of the Anabaptists and their followers. In the second John enters. Oberthal is delivered into his hands. From him John learns that Bertha again has escaped from the castle and is in Münster. The three Anabaptist leaders wish to put the Count to death. But John, saying that Bertha shall be his judge, puts off the execution, much to the disgust of the three fanatics, who find John assuming more authority than is agreeable to them. This scene, the second of the act, takes place in Zacharias's tent. The third scene shows again the camp of the Anabaptists. The leaders, fearing John's usurpation of power, have themselves headed an attack by their followers on Münster and met with defeat. The rabble they had led is furious and ready to turn even against John. He, however, by sheer force of personality coupled with his assumption of superhuman inspiration, rallies the crowd to his standard, and leads it to victory.

Act IV.    A public place in Münster. The city is in possession of the Anabaptists. John, once a plain innkeeper of Leyden, has been swept along on the high tide of success and decides to have himself proclaimed Emperor. Meanwhile Fides has been reduced to beggary. The Anabaptists, in order to make her believe that John is dead—so as to reduce to a minimum the chance of her suspecting that the new Prophet and her son are one and the same—left in the inn a bundle of John's clothes stained with blood, together with a script stating that he had been murdered by the Prophet and his followers.

The poor woman has come to Münster to beg. There she meets Bertha, who, when Fides tells her that John has been murdered, vows vengeance upon the Prophet.

Fides follows the crowd into the cathedral, to which the scene changes. When, during the coronation scene, John speaks, and announces that he is the elect of God, the poor beggar woman starts at the sound of his voice. She cries out, 'My son!' John's cause is thus threatened and his life at stake. He has claimed divine origin. If the woman is his mother, the people, whom he rules with an iron hand, will denounce and kill him. With quick wit he meets the emergency, and even makes use of it to enhance his authority by improvising an affirmative scene. He bids his followers draw their swords and thrust them into his breast, if the beggar woman again affirms that he is her son. Seeing the swords held ready to pierce him, Fides, in order to save him, now declares that he is not her son—that her eyes, dimmed by age, have deceived her.

Act V. The three Anabaptists, Jonas, Matthisen, and Zacharias, had intended to use John only as an instrument to attain power for themselves. The German Emperor, who is moving on Münster with a large force, has promised them pardon if they will betray the Prophet and usurper into his hands. To this they have agreed, and are ready on his coronation day to betray him.

At John's secret command Fides has been brought to the palace. Here her son meets her. He, whom she has seen in the hour of his triumph and who still is all powerful, implores her pardon, but in vain, until she, in the belief that he has been impelled to his usurpation of power and bloody deeds only by thirst for vengeance for Bertha's wrongs, forgives him, on condition that he return to Leyden. This he promises in full repentance.

They are joined by Bertha. She has sworn to kill the Prophet whom she blames for the supposed murder of her lover. To accomplish her purpose, she has set a slow fire to the palace. It will blaze up near the powder magazine, when the Prophet and his henchmen are at banquet in the great hall of the palace, and blow up the edifice.

She recognises her lover. Her joy, however, is short-lived, for at that moment a captain comes to John with the announcement that he has been betrayed and that the Emperor's forces are at the palace gates. Thus Bertha learns that her lover and the blood-stained Prophet are one. Horrified, she plunges a dagger into her heart.

John determines to die, a victim to the catastrophe which Bertha has planned, and which is impending. He joins the banqueters at their orgy. At the moment when all his open and secret enemies are at the table and pledge him in a riotous bacchanale, smoke rises from the floor. Tongues of fire shoot up. Fides, in the general uproar and confusion, calmly joins her son, to die with him, as the powder magazine blows up, and, with a fearful crash the edifice collapses in smoke and flame.

John of Leyden's name was Jan Beuckelszoon. He was born in 1509. In business he was successively a tailor, a small merchant, and an innkeeper. After he had had himself crowned in Münster, that city became a scene of orgy and cruelty. It was captured by the imperial forces June 24, 1535. The following January the 'prophet' was put to death by torture. The same fate was meted out to Knipperdölling, his henchman, who had conveniently rid him of one of his wives by cutting off her head.

The music of the first act of *Le Prophète* contains a cheerful chorus for peasants, a cavatina for Bertha, 'Mon cœur s'élance' (My heart throbs wildly), in which she voices her joy over her expected union with John; the Latin chant of the three Anabaptists, gloomy yet stirring; the music of the brief revolt of the peasantry against Oberthal; the plea of Fides and Bertha to Oberthal for his sanction of Bertha's marriage to John, 'Un jour, dans les flots de la Meuse' (One day in the waves of the Meuse); Oberthal's refusal, and his abduction of Bertha; the reappearance of the three Anabaptists and the renewal of their efforts to impress the people with a sense of the tyranny by which they are oppressed.

Opening the second act, in John's tavern, in the suburbs of Leyden, are the chorus and dance of John's friends, who are rejoicing over his prospective wedding. When the three Anabaptists have recognised his resemblance to the picture of David in the cathedral at Münster, John, observing their sombre yet impressive bearing, tells them of his dream, and asks them to interpret it: 'Sous les vastes arceaux d'un temple magnifique' (Under the great dome of a splendid temple). They promise him a throne. But he knows a sweeter empire than the one they promise, that which will be created by his coming union with Bertha: 'Pour Berthe moi, je soupire'. Her arrival in flight from Oberthal and John's sacrifice of her in order to save his mother from death, lead to Fides's solo, 'Ah, mon fils' (Ah, my son), one of the great airs for mezzo-soprano.

Most attractive in the next act is the ballet of the skaters on the frozen lake near the camp of the Anabaptists.* The scene is brilliant in conception, the music delightfully rhythmic and

* Now frequently heard as the music for *Les Patineurs*, Frederick Ashton's successful ballet for Sadler's Wells.

graceful. There is a stirring battle song for Zacharias, in which he sings of the enemy 'as numerous as the stars', yet defeated. Another striking number is the fantastic trio for Jonas, Zacharias, and Oberthal, especially in the descriptive passage in which. in rhythm with the music, Jonas strikes flint and steel, ignites a lantern and by its light recognises Oberthal. When John rallies the Anabaptists, who have been driven back from under the walls of Münster, and promises to lead them to victory, the act reaches a superb climax in a 'Hymne Triomphal' for John and chorus: 'Roi du Ciel et des Anges' (Ruler of Heaven and the Angels):

At the most stirring moment of this finale, as John is being acclaimed by his followers, mists that have been hanging over the lake are dispelled. The sun bursts forth in glory.

In the next act there is a scene for Fides in the streets of Münster, in which, reduced to penury, she begs for alms. There also is the scene at the meeting of Fides and Bertha. The latter believing, like Fides, that John has been slain by the Anabaptists, vows vengeance upon the Prophet.

The great procession in the cathedral with its march and chorus has been, since the production of *Le Prophète* in 1849, a model of construction for striking spectacular scenes in opera. The march is famous. Highly dramatic is the scene in which Fides first proclaims and then denies that John is her son. The fifth contains a striking solo for Fides ('O Prêtres de Baal') and a duet for her and John. The climax, however, comes with the drinking song, 'Versez, que tout respire l'ivresse et le délire' (Quaff, quaff, in joyous measure; breathe, breathe delirious pleasure), in the midst of which the building is blown up, and John perishes with those who would betray him.

During the season of opera which Dr. Leopold Damrosch conducted at the Metropolitan Opera House, 1884–85, when this work of Meyerbeer's led the repertory in number of performances, the stage management produced a fine effect in the scene at the end of Act III, when the Prophet rallies his followers. Instead of soldiers tamely marching past, as John chanted his battle hymn, he was acclaimed by a rabble, wrought up to a high pitch of excitement, and brandishing cudgels, scythes, pitchforks, and other implements that would serve as weapons. The following season, another stage-manager, wishing to outdo his predecessor, brought with him an electric sun from Germany, a horrid thing that almost blinded the audience when it was turned on.

K.

# DINORAH

## ou

## LE PARDON DE PLOERMEL

Opera in three acts by Giacomo Meyerbeer, words by Barbier and Carré. Première Opéra-Comique, Paris, April 4, 1859, with Mme. Cabel, MM. St. Foy, Faure. First performed Covent Garden, 1859 (in Italian), with Miolan-Carvalho, Gardoni, Graziani; New York, 1862; Metropolitan, 1892, with van Zandt, Giannini, Lassalle. Revived Paris, 1912, with Vauchelet, Capitaine, Albers; Metropolitan, 1925, with Galli-Curci, Tokatyan, de Luca; Brussels, 1939. Apart from Galli-Curci, famous in the title rôle were Ilma di Murskal, Patti, Tetrazzini.

### CHARACTERS

Dinorah, *a peasant girl* ....................... Soprano
Hoël, *a goat-herd* ............................ Baritone
Corentino, *a bag-piper* ......................... Tenor
Huntsman ...................................... Bass
Harvester...................................... Tenor
Goat-herds ................... Soprano and Contralto

Dinorah is betrothed to Hoël. Her cottage has been destroyed in a storm. Hoël, in order to rebuild it, goes into a region haunted by evil spirits, in search of hidden treasure. Dinorah, believing herself deserted, loses her reason and, with her goat, whose tinkling bell is heard, wanders through the mountains in search of Hoël.

The opera is in three acts. It is preceded by an overture during which there is sung by the villagers behind the curtain the hymn to Our Lady of the Pardon. The scene of the first act is a rough mountain passage near Corentino's hut. Dinorah finds her goat asleep and sings to it a graceful lullaby, 'Dors, petite, dors tranquille' (Little one, sleep; calmly rest). Corentino, in his cottage, sings of the fear that comes over him in this lonely region. To dispel it, he plays on his cornemuse. Dinorah enters the hut, and makes him dance with her, while she sings.

When someone is heard approaching, she jumps out of the

window. It is Hoël. Both he and Corentino think she is a sprite.
Hoël sings of the gold he expects to find, and offers Corentino a
share in the treasure if he will aid him lift it. According to the
legend, however, the first one to touch the treasure must die, and
Hoël's seeming generosity is a ruse to make Corentino the victim
of the discovery. The tinkle of the goat's bell is heard. Hoël
advises that they follow the sound as it may lead to the treasure.
The act closes with a trio, 'Ce tintement que l'on entend' (The
tinkling tones that greet the ear). Dinorah stands among the high
rocks, while Hoël and Corentino, the latter reluctantly, make
ready to follow the tinkle of the bell.

A wood of birches by moonlight is the opening scene of the
second act. It is here Dinorah sings of 'Le vieux sorcier de la
montagne' (The ancient wizard of the mountain), following it
with the 'Shadow Song', 'Ombre legère qui suis mes pas' (Fleet
shadow that pursues my steps)—'Ombra leggiera' is the more
familiar Italian version:

This is a passage so graceful and, when sung and acted by an
Adelina Patti, was so appealing, that I am frank to confess it suggested to me the chapter entitled 'Shadows of the Stage', in my
novel of opera behind the scenes, *All-of-a-Sudden Carmen*.

The scene changes to a wild landscape. A ravine bridged by
an uprooted tree. A pond, with a sluiceway which, when opened,
gives on the ravine. The moon has set. A storm is rising.

Hoël and Corentino enter; later Dinorah. Through the night,
that is growing wilder, she sings the legend of the treasure,
'Sombre destinée, âme condamnée' (O'ershadowing fate, soul
lost for aye).

Her words recall the tragic story of the treasure to Corentino,
who now sees through Hoël's ruse, and seeks to persuade the girl
to go after the treasure. She sings gaily, in strange contrast to the
gathering storm. Lightning flashes show her her goat crossing the
ravine by the fallen tree. She runs after her pet. As she is crossing
the tree, a thunderbolt crashes. The sluice bursts, the tree is
carried away by the flood, which seizes Dinorah in its swirl. Hoël
plunges into the wild waters to save her.

Not enough of the actual story remains to make a third act. But as there has to be one, the opening of the act is filled in with a song for a Hunter (bass), another for a Reaper (tenor), and a duet for Goat-herds (soprano and contralto). Hoël enters bearing Dinorah, who is in a swoon. Hoël here has his principal air, 'Ah! mon remords te venge' (Ah, my remorse avenges you). Dinorah comes to. Her reason is restored when she finds herself in her lover's arms. The villagers chant the 'Hymn of the Pardon'. A procession forms for the wedding, which is to make happy Dinorah and Hoël, everyone, in fact, including the goat.

Except for the scene of the 'Shadow Dance', the libretto is incredibly inane—far more so than the demented heroine. But Meyerbeer evidently wanted to write a pastoral opera. He did so; with the result that now, instead of pastoral, it sounds pasteurised.                                             K.

## L'AFRICAINE
### The African Maid

Opera in five acts by Meyerbeer; words by Scribe. Première Grand Opéra, Paris, April 28, 1865, with Marie Sasse, Battu, Naudin, Faure. First performed in London (in Italian), Covent Garden, July 22, 1865, with Lucca, Fioretti, Wachtel, Graziani; (in English) Covent Garden, October 21, 1865. New York, Academy of Music, December 1, 1865, with Mazzoleni as Vasco, and Zucchi as Selika; September 30, 1872, with Lucca as Selika; Metropolitan Opera House, January 15, 1892, with Nordica, Pettigiani, Jean de Reszke, Edouard de Reszke, Lassalle. Revived Arena, Verona, 1932, with Bruna Rasa, Gigli, Armando Borgioli, Righetti; Metropolitan, 1933, with Ponselle, Martinelli, Armando Borgioli, Lazzari, conductor Serafin; Rome, 1937, with Caniglia, Licia Albanese, Gigli, Basiola, Vaghi, conductor Serafin; Vienna, 1937, with Anny Konetzni, Gerhart, Piccaver, Jerger, Zec, conductor Alwin; Berlin, 1951, with Wasserthal, Beilke, Beirer, Metternich, Greindl, conductor Ludwig.

### CHARACTERS

Selika, *a slave* ................................ Soprano
Inez, *daughter of Don Diego* .................... Soprano
Anna, *her attendant* ..................... Mezzo-Soprano
Vasco da Gama, *an officer in the Portuguese Navy* ... Tenor
Nelusko, *a slave* ............................. Baritone
Don Pedro, *President of the Royal Council* ........... Bass
Don Diego ⎱ *Members of the Council* ............ ⎰ Bass
Don Alvar ⎰                                      ⎱ Tenor

Grand Inquisitor ...............................Bass
High Priest of Brahma .......................Baritone
Priests, Inquisitors, Councillors, Sailors, Indians, Attendants,
Ladies, Soldiers

*Time:* Early Sixteenth Century    *Place:* Lisbon; on a ship at
sea; and India

In 1838 Scribe submitted to Meyerbeer two librettos: that of
*Le Prophète* and that of *L'Africaine.* For the purposes of immediate composition he gave *Le Prophète* the preference, but worked
simultaneously on the scores of both. As a result, in 1849, soon
after the production of *Le Prophète,* a score of *L'Africaine* was
finished.

The libretto, however, had never been entirely satisfactory to
the composer. Scribe was asked to retouch it. In 1852 he delivered
an amended version to Meyerbeer who, so far as his score had
gone, adapted it to the revised book, and finished the entire work
in 1860. 'Thus,' says the *Dictionnaire des Opéras,* 'the process of
creating *L'Africaine* lasted some twenty years and its birth
appears to have cost the life of its composer, for he died, in the
midst of preparations for its production, on Monday, May 2,
1864, the day after a copy of his score was finished in his own
house in the Rue Montaigne and under his eyes.'

Act I.    Lisbon. The Royal Council Chamber of Portugal.
Nothing has been heard of the ship of Bartholomew Diaz, the
explorer. Among his officers was Vasco da Gama, the affianced
of Inez, daughter of the powerful nobleman, Don Diego. Vasco
is supposed to have been lost with the ship and her father now
wishes Inez to pledge her hand to Don Pedro, head of the Royal
Council of Portugal.

During a session of the Council, it is announced that the King
wishes to send an expedition to search for Diaz, but one of the
councillors, Don Alvar, informs the meeting that an officer and
two captives, the only survivors from the wreck of Diaz's vessel,
have arrived. The officer is brought in. He is Vasco da Gama,
whom all have believed to be dead. Nothing daunted by the
perils he has been through, he has formed a new plan to discover
the new land that, he believes, lies beyond Africa. In proof of
his conviction that such a land exists, he brings in the captives,
Selika and Nelusko, natives, apparently, of a country still

unknown to Europe. Vasco then retires to give the Council opportunity to discuss his enterprise.

In his absence Don Pedro, who desires to win Inez for himself (he knows that she loves Vasco), and to head a voyage of discovery, surreptitiously gains possession of an important chart from among Vasco's papers. He then, in spite of Don Alvaro's efforts, persuades the Grand Inquisitor and the Council that the young navigator's plans are futile. Through his persuasion they are rejected. Vasco, who has again come before the meeting, when informed that his proposal has been set aside, insults the Council by charging it with ignorance and bias. Don Pedro, utilising the opportunity to get him out of the way, has him seized and thrown into prison.

Act II.    Vasco has fallen asleep in his cell. Beside him watches Selika. In her native land she is a queen. Now she is a captive and a slave, her rank, of course, unknown to her captor, since she and Nelusko have carefully kept it from the knowledge of all. Selika is deeply in love with Vasco and is broken-hearted over his passion for Inez, of which she has become aware. But the love of this supposedly savage slave is greater than her jealousy. She protects the slumbering Vasco from the thrust of Nelusko's dagger. For her companion in captivity is deeply in love with her and desperately jealous of the Portuguese navigator for whom she has conceived so ardent a desire. Not only does she save Vasco's life, but on a map hanging on the prison wall she points out to him a route known only to herself and Nelusko, by which he can reach the land of which he has been in search.

Inez, Don Pedro, and their suite enter the prison. Vasco is free. Inez has purchased his freedom through her own sacrifice in marrying Don Pedro. Vasco, through the information received from Selika, now hopes to undertake another voyage of discovery and thus seek to make up in glory what he has lost in love. But he learns that Don Pedro has been appointed commander of an expedition and has chosen Nelusko as pilot. Vasco sees his hopes shattered.

Act III.    The scene is on Don Pedro's ship at sea. Don Alvar, the leader of the faction in the Royal Council which supported da Gama's claim to head the expedition, has become suspicious of Nelusko. Two ships of the squadron have already been lost;

Don Alvar fears for the safety of the flagship. At that moment a Portuguese vessel is seen approaching. It is in command of Vasco da Gama, who has fitted it out at his own expense. Although Don Pedro is his enemy, he comes aboard the admiral's ship to warn him that the vessel is on a wrong course and likely to meet with disaster. Don Pedro, however, accuses him of desiring only to see Inez, who is on the vessel, and charges that his attempted warning is nothing more than a ruse, with that purpose in view. At his command, Vasco is seized and bound. A few moments later, however, a violent storm breaks over the ship. It is driven upon a reef. Savages, for whom Nelusko has signalled, clamber up the sides of the vessel and massacre all save a few whom they take captive.

Act IV. On the left, the entrance to a Hindu temple; on the right, a palace. Tropical landscape. Selika is welcomed back as Queen and takes the sacred oath. Among those saved from the massacre is Vasco. He finds himself in the land which he has sought to discover—a tropical paradise. He is threatened with death by the natives, but Selika, in order to save him, protests to her subjects that he is her husband. The marriage is now celebrated according to East Indian rites. Vasco, deeply touched by Selika's fidelity, is almost determined to abide by his nuptial vow and remain here as Selika's spouse, when suddenly he hears the voice of Inez. His passion for her revives.

Act V. The gardens of Selika's palace. Again Selika makes a sacrifice of love. How easily she could compass the death of Vasco and Inez! But she forgives. She persuades Nelusko to provide the lovers with a ship and bids him meet her, after the ship has sailed, on a high promontory overlooking the sea.

To this the scene changes. On the promontory stands a large mancanilla tree. The perfume of its blossoms is deadly to anyone who breathes it in from under the deep shadow of its branches. From here Selika watches the ship set sail. It bears from her the man she loves. Breathing in the poison-laden odour from the tree from under which she has watched the ship depart, she dies. Nelusko seeks her, finds her dead, and himself seeks death beside her under the fatal branches of the mancanilla.

Meyerbeer considered *L'Africaine* his masterpiece, and believed that through it he was bequeathing to posterity an immortal monument to his fame. But although he had worked over the music for many years, and produced a wonderfully well-contrived score, his labour upon it was more careful and self-exacting than inspired; and this despite moments of intense interest in the opera. Not *L'Africaine*, but *Les Huguenots*, is considered his most striking work.

*L'Africaine* calls for one of the most elaborate stage-settings in opera. This is the ship scene, which gives a lengthwise section of a vessel, so that its between-decks and cabin interiors are seen—like the compartments of a huge but neatly partitioned box laid on its oblong side; in fact an amazing piece of stage architecture.

Scribe's libretto has been criticised, and not unjustly, on account of the vacillating character which he gives Vasco da Gama. In the first act this operatic hero is in love with Inez. In the prison scene, in the second act, when Selika points out on the map the true course to India, he is so impressed with her as a teacher of geography, that he clasps the supposed slave-girl to his breast and addresses her in impassioned song. Selika, being enamoured of her pupil, naturally is elated over his progress. Unfortunately Inez enters the prison at this critical moment to announce to Vasco that she has secured his freedom. To prove to Inez that he still loves her Vasco glibly makes her a present of Selika and Nelusko. Selika, so to speak, is no longer on the map so far as Vasco is concerned, until, in the fourth act, she saves his life by pretending he is her husband. Rapturously he pledges his love to her. Then Inez's voice is heard—and Selika again finds herself deserted. There is nothing for her to do but to die under the mancanilla tree.

'Is the shadow of this tree so fatal?' asks a French authority. 'Monsieur Scribe says yes, the naturalists say no.' With this question and answer *L'Africaine* may be left to its future fate upon the stage, save that it seems proper to remark that, although the opera is called *The African Maid*, Selika appears to have been an East Indian.

Early in the first act of the opera occurs Inez's ballad, 'Adieu, mon doux rivage' (Farewell, beloved shores). It is gracefully accompanied by flute and oboe. This is the ballad to the river Tagus, which Vasco hears her sing in the fourth act and which revives his love for her. The finale of the first act—the scene in which Vasco defies the Royal Council—is a powerful ensemble.

The slumber song for Selika in the second act, as she watches over Vasco, 'Sur mes genous, fils du soleil' (On my knees, off-spring of the sun) is charming, and entirely original, with many exotic and fascinating touches. Nelusko's air of homage, 'Fille des rois, à toi l'hommage' (Daughter of Kings, my homage thine), expresses a sombre loyalty characteristic of the savage whose passion for his queen amounts to fanaticism. The finale of the act is an impressive unaccompanied septet for Inez, Selika, Anna, Vasco, Alvar, Nelusko, and Don Pedro.

In the act which plays aboard ship, are the graceful chorus of women, 'Le rapide et léger navire' (The swiftly gliding ship), the prayer of the sailors, 'O grand Saint Dominique,' and Nelusko's song, 'Adamastor, roi des vagues profondes' (Adamastor, monarch of the trackless deep), a savage invocation of sea and storm, chanted to the rising of a hurricane, by the most dramatic figure among the characters in the opera. For like Marcel in *Les Huguenots* and Fides in *Le Prophète*, Nelusko is a genuine dramatic creation.

The Indian march and the ballet, which accompanies the cere-mony of the crowning of Selika, open the fourth act. The music is exotic, piquant, and in every way effective. The scene is a master-piece of its kind. There follow the lovely measures of the prin-cipal tenor solo of the opera, Vasco's 'O Paradis, sorti di l'onde' (Paradise, lulled by the lisping sea). Nelusko sings movingly of his love for Selika: 'L'avoir tant aimée' (To have loved her so much). Then comes the love duet between Vasco and Selika, 'O transport, ô douce extase' (Oh transport, oh sweet ecstacy). One authority says of it that 'rarely have the tender passion, the ecstacy of love been expressed with such force'. Now it would be set down simply as a tiptop love duet of the old-fashioned operatic kind.

The scene of Selika's death under the mancanilla tree is pre-ceded by a famous prelude for strings in unison supported by clarinets and bassoons, a brief instrumental recital of grief that makes a powerful appeal. The opera ends dramatically with a soliloquy for Selika—'D'ici je vois la mer immense' (From here I gaze upon the boundless deep).                      K.

# HECTOR BERLIOZ

## (1803–1869)

### BENVENUTO CELLINI

OPERA in three acts by Berlioz. Words by du Wailly and Barbier. Première Grand Opéra, Paris, September 10, 1838, with Dorus-Gras, Stolz, Duprez, Derivis; there were twenty-nine rehearsals, seven performances. Revived London, Covent Garden, 1853, under Berlioz's own direction, with Julienne, Tamberlik, Tagliafico (in Italian); by Liszt, at Weimar, 1852; by von Bülow, Hanover, 1879. Vienna, 1911; Théâtre des Champs-Elysées, Paris, 1912, conducted by Weingartner; Dresden, 1929; Glasgow, 1939 (in English); Carl Rosa in London, 1957, with Craig, cond. Hammond.

#### CHARACTERS

| | |
|---|---|
| Cardinal Salviati | Bass |
| Balducci, *Papal treasurer* | Bass |
| Teresa, *his daughter* | Soprano |
| Benvenuto Cellini, *a goldsmith* | Tenor |
| Ascanio, *his apprentice* | Mezzo-Soprano |
| Francesco ⎱ *artisans in Cellini's workshop* | Tenor |
| Bernardino ⎰ | Bass |
| Fieramosca, *sculptor to the Pope* | Baritone |
| Pompeo, *a bravo* | Baritone |

*Time:* 1532                                      *Place:* Rome

The overture, which makes use of material from the opera, is one of Berlioz's best known.

Act I.    The carnival of 1532. Shrove Monday. We are in the house of the Papal treasurer, Balducci, who has scolded his daughter Teresa for having looked out of the window. The old man is quite vexed, because the Pope has summoned the Florentine goldsmith Cellini to Rome.

Balducci's daughter Teresa, however, thinks quite otherwise and is happy. For she has found a note from Cellini in a bouquet that was thrown in to her from the street by a mask—Cellini, of course. She sings of her pleasure and delight in a nice cavatina, followed by an *allegro con fuoco*. A few moments later Cellini appears at her side. There is a gloriously broad, *andante* tune for

them both to sing (it is later used for the *Carnaval Romain* over-ture). Cellini proposes a plan of elopement. In the morning, during the carnival mask, he will wear a white monk's hood, his apprentice Ascanio a brown one. They will join her and they will flee together. But a listener has sneaked in—Fieramosca, the Pope's sculptor, and no less Cellini's rival in love than in art. He overhears the plot and also the unusually rude remarks made about him by Teresa and Cellini. Unexpectedly, too, Teresa's father, Balducci, comes back. His daughter still up? In her anxiety to find an excuse, she says she heard a man sneak in. During the search Cellini disappears, and Fieramosca is appre-hended. Before he can explain his presence, women neighbours, who have hurried in, drag him off to the public bath house and treat him to a ducking.

Act II.* In the courtyard of a tavern Cellini is seated, with his assistants. In a romance, he sings that he is happy in his love, for he places it even higher than fame, which alone heretofore he has courted. He must pledge his love in wine. Unfortunately the host will no longer give him credit. Just then Ascanio brings some money from the Papal treasurer, but in return Cellini must promise to complete his *Perseus* by morning. He promises, although the avaricious Balducci has profited by his necessity and has sent too little money. Ascanio is informed by Cellini of the disguises they are to wear at the carnival, and of his plan that Teresa shall flee with him.

Again Fieramosca has been spying, and overhears the plot. Accordingly he hires the bravo Pompeo to assist him in carrying off Teresa.

A change of scene shows the crowd of maskers on the Piazza di Collona. It is carnival time and the music is a brilliant repre-sentation of the gaiety and spirit of the scene. Balducci comes along with Teresa and together they see the play in which, in revenge for his niggardly payment to them, Cellini and his friends have arranged that the snoring Midas shall look like Balducci.

* Here, or between the scenes of this act, must be played the splendid *Carnaval Romain* overture, composed in 1844.

Cellini takes advantage of the confusion, caused by Balducci's protests, to approach Teresa with Ascanio. At the same time, from the other side come two more monks, also in the disguise she and her lover agreed upon. Which is the right couple? Soon the two couples fall upon each other. A scream, and one of the brown-hooded monks (Pompeo) falls mortally wounded to the ground. A white-hooded monk (Cellini) has stabbed him. The crowd hurls itself upon Cellini. But at that moment the boom of a cannon gives notice that the carnival celebration is over. It is Ash Wednesday. In the first shock of surprise Cellini escapes, and in his place the other white-hooded monk, Fieramosca, is seized.

Act III.   Before Cellini's house, in the background of which, through a curtain, is seen the foundry, the anxious Teresa is assured by Ascanio that her lover is safe. Soon he comes along himself, and describes his escape. With his white habit he was able to join a procession of monks similarly garbed and so make his way safely home. While Ascanio prepares for their flight, Cellini and Teresa have a duet; the beautiful line of the tune makes this one of the most magnificent episodes of the score.

Balducci and Fieramosca rush in. Balducci wants to force his daughter to become Fieramosca's bride. The scene is interrupted by the arrival of Cardinal Salviati to see the completed *Perseus*. Poor Cellini! Accused of murder and the attempted kidnapping of a girl, the *Perseus* unfinished, the money received for it spent! Heavy punishment awaits him, and another shall receive the commission to finish the *Perseus*.

The artist flies into a passion. Another finish his masterpiece! Never! The casting shall be done on the spot! He is left alone and sings a beautiful 6/8 *andante* aria. Then the casting begins. Not metal enough? He seizes his completed works and throws them into the molten mass. Eventually, the master shatters the mould. The *Perseus* in all its glory appears before the eyes of the astonished onlookers—a potent plea for the inspired master. Once more have Art and her faithful servant triumphed over all rivals.

The statue of Perseus by Benvenuto Cellini, one of the most famous creations of Renaissance Italy, is one of the art treasures of Florence.                                        K., H.

# LA DAMNATION DE FAUST
## The Damnation of Faust

In its original form a 'dramatic legend' in four parts for the concert stage. Music by Hector Berlioz. Words, after Gerald de Nerval's version of Goethe's play, by Berlioz, Gérard, and Gandonnière. Produced in its original form as a concert piece at the Opéra-Comique, Paris, December 6, 1846; London, two parts of the work, under Berlioz's direction, Drury Lane, February 7, 1848; first complete performance in England, Free Trade Hall, Manchester, February 5, 1880. New York, February 12, 1880, by Dr. Leopold Damrosch. Adapted for the operatic stage by Raoul Gunsbourg, and produced by him at Monte Carlo, February 18, 1893, with Jean de Reszke as Faust; Liverpool, 1894. Revived Monte Carlo, March 1902, with Melba, Jean de Reszke, and Maurice Renaud. Given in Paris with Calvé, Alvarez, and Renaud, to celebrate the centennial of Berlioz's birth, December 11, 1903. New York, Metropolitan, 1906, with Farrar, Rousselière, Plançon; Manhattan Opera House, 1907, with Dalmores and Renaud. Revived la Scala, Milan, 1929, with Cobelli, Merli, Galeffi, conductor de Sabata; Covent Garden, 1933, with Cigna, Voyer, Formichi, conductor Beecham; Buenos Aires, 1941, with Djanel, Maison, Romito; la Scala, 1947, with Gatti, Binci, Gobbi, conductor Serafin.

### CHARACTERS

Marguerite ................................... Soprano
Faust ......................................... Tenor
Méphistophélès ................................ Bass
Brander ....................................... Bass
Students, Soldiers, Citizens, Men and Women, Fairies, etc.

In the first part of Berlioz's dramatic legend Faust is supposed to be on the plains of Hungary. Introspectively he sings of nature and solitude. There are a chorus and dance of peasants and a recitative. Soldiers march past to the stirring measures of the *Rákoczy March*, the national air of Hungary.

This splendid march Berlioz orchestrated in Vienna, during his tour of 1845, and conducted it at a concert in Pesth, when it created the greatest enthusiasm. It was in order to justify the interpolation of this march that he laid the first scene of his dramatic legend on the plains of Hungary. In the operatic version, Gunsbourg, who originally adapted the work for the stage, shows Faust in a mediaeval chamber, with a view, through a window, of the sally-port of a castle, out of which the soldiers march.

The next part of the dramatic legend only required a stage setting to make it operatic. Faust is in his study, lamenting his joyless existence. He is about to quaff poison, when the walls part and disclose a church interior. The congregation, kneeling, sings the Easter canticle, 'Christ is Risen', and Faust is comforted by their singing. Méphistophélès however appears and offers to show Faust all that his soul can desire. The two start off together to sample what joy and pleasure can be had on earth. Change of scene to Auerbach's cellar, Leipzig. Revel of students and soldiers. Brander sings the 'Song of the Rat', whose death is mockingly grieved over by a 'Requiescat in pace' and a fugue on the word 'Amen', sung by the roistering crowd. Méphistophélès follows this up with the 'Song of the Flea', in which the skipping about of the elusive insect is depicted in the accompaniment.

In the next scene in the dramatic legend, Faust is supposed to be asleep on the banks of the Elbe. Méphistophélès sings the beautiful 'Voici des roses', after which comes the most exquisite effect of the score, the 'Dance of the Sylphs', a masterpiece of delicate and airy illustration. Violoncellos, *con sordini*, hold a single note as a pedal point, over which is woven a gossamer fabric of melody and harmony, ending with the faintest possible *pianissimo* from drum and harps. Gunsbourg employed here, with admirable results, the aerial ballet, and gave a rich and beautiful setting to the scene, including a vision of Marguerite. The ballet is followed by a chorus of soldiers and a students' song in Latin.

Part III.    The scenic directions of Gounod's *Faust* call Marguerite's house—so much of it as is projected into the garden scene—a pavilion. Gunsbourg made it more like an arbour, into which the audience could see through the elimination of a supposedly existing wall, the same as in Sparafucile's house, in the last act of *Rigoletto*. Soldiers and students are strolling and singing in the street. Faust sings 'Merci doux crépuscule', and rejoices to be in Marguerite's room. He hides; Marguerite comes in and sings the ballad of the King of Thulé. Berlioz's setting of the song is primitive, and he aptly characterises the number as a *Chanson Gothique*. It is a marvellously effective re-creation of the mediaeval spirit. The Invocation of Méphistophélès is followed by the 'Minuet of Will-o'-the-Wisps'.

PLATE XXV. Victoria de los Angeles as Butterfly.

PLATE XXVI. *Les Troyens*: Act III at Covent Garden, with Jon Vickers (Aeneas) and Blanche Thebom (Dido).

Then comes Méphistophélès' serenade, 'Devant la maison', a brilliant, elusive, piece of mockery.

Faust enters Marguerite's house. There is a love duet, 'Ange adorable', which becomes a trio when Méphistophélès joins the lovers and urges Faust's departure.

Part IV. Marguerite is alone. Berlioz, instead of using Goethe's song, 'Meine Ruh ist hin' (My peace is gone), the setting of which by Schubert is famous, substitutes a poem of his own. Introduced by the sad strains of the cor anglais, the unhappy Marguerite sings, 'D'Amour, l'ardente flamme' (Love, devouring fire), an aria of extraordinary beauty.

The singing of the students and the soldiers grows fainter. The 'retreat'—the call to which the flag is lowered at sunset—is sounded by the drums and trumpets. Marguerite, overcome by remorse, swoons at the window.

A mountain gorge. The scene begins with Faust's soliloquy, 'Nature, immense, impénétrable et fière' (Nature, vast, unfathomable and proud), an invocation to nature that is enormously impressive. The *Ride to Hell*; moving panorama; pandemonium; redemption of Marguerite, whom angels are seen welcoming in the softly illumined heavens far above the town, in which the action is supposed to have transpired.

The production by Dr. Leopold Damrosch of *La Damnation de Faust* in its original concert form in New York, was one of the sensational events in the concert history of America. As an opera, however, the work has failed outside France to make the impression that might have been expected from its effect on concert audiences; ... 'the experiment, though tried in various theatres', said Grove's *Dictionary of Music and Musicians*, 'has happily not been permanently successful'. Why 'happily'? It would be an advantage to operatic art if a work by so distinguished a composer as Berlioz could find a permanent place in the repertory.

Berlioz's *Faust* is in fact an extraordinarily imaginative work. Every opera-lover who knows it will be filled with regret that Berlioz wrote it in cantata form; the result is a mixture which is, like the same composer's *Roméo et Juliette*, too dramatic for the concert hall, insufficiently stage-worthy for the opera house.  K.

# LES TROYENS
## The Trojans

Opera in five acts by Hector Berlioz, text by the composer after Virgil. The work was not produced in its entirety until twenty-one years after the composer's death. Part II (*Les Troyens à Carthage:* see below for details of the division) was first performed at the Théâtre Lyriqûe, Paris, November 4, 1863, with Charton-Demeur as Dido and Monjauze as Aeneas. Between that date and December 20, 1863, there were twenty-one performances of the opera, which was then dropped. The entire work was given at Carlsruhe on December 5 and 6, 1890, in a German version by O. Neitzel, conducted by Mottl (Part I, known separately as *La Prise de Troie*, thus had its world première on December 5, 1890). Part I was first performed in French at Nice, 1891; in Paris, Opéra, 1899, with Mme. Delna, MM. Lucas, Renaud, conducted by Taffanel; it was revived in Geneva, 1932. Part II was revived Opéra, Paris, 1892; first performed Liverpool (in concert form), 1897; first performed in Italy, Naples, 1951, with Cavelti, Tygesen, Tajo, conductor Cluytens. Both parts (i.e. *Les Troyens* as Berlioz conceived it) were performed in Cologne, 1898 (in German); Stuttgart, 1913 (arr. Schillings); Opéra, Paris, 1921 (in a reduced version), and revived there 1939; Berlin, 1930 (in four acts), with Leider, Roswaenge, conductor Blech; Glasgow, 1935 (English translation, E. J. Dent), conductor Erik Chisholm; Oxford (reduced version), 1950, with Arda Mandikian and John Kentish, conductor Westrup; Covent Garden (complete in English) 1957, with Thebom, Shuard, Vickers, cond. Kubelik.

## CHARACTERS

Part I: *La Prise de Troie*

Cassandre, a Trojan prophetess ................Soprano
Ascagne, son of Aeneas......................Soprano
Hécube, wife of Priam..................Mezzo-Soprano
Polyxène, daughter of Priam...................Soprano

Enée (Aeneas), a Trojan hero ..................... Tenor
Chorèbe, fiancé of Cassandre ................. Baritone
Panthée, a Trojan priest .......................... Bass
Ghost of Hector................................ Bass
Priam, King of Troy............................. Bass
A Trojan soldier .............................. Baritone
A Greek Captain ................................. Bass
Helenus, son of Priam ......................... Tenor
Andromaque, widow of Hector .................. Mime
Astyanax, her son ............................. Mime

Soldiers of Greece and Troy, Citizens, Women, Children,
Shepherds

Part II: *Les Troyens à Carthage*

Didon (Dido), Queen of Carthage ......... Mezzo-Soprano
Anna, her sister.............................. Contralto
Ascagne....................................... Soprano
Enée.......................................... Tenor
Iopas, a Carthaginian poet ...................... Tenor
Hylas, a young Trojan sailor..................... Tenor
Narbal, Dido's minister ......................... Bass
Panthée ....................................... Bass
First soldier ................................. Baritone
Second soldier................................. Bass
Two Trojan Captains ................... Baritone, Bass
The Ghost of Cassandre............... Mezzo-Soprano
The Ghost of Chorèbe ...................... Baritone
The Ghost of Hector .......................... Bass
The Ghost of Priam ............................ Bass
The God Mercury.............................. Bass

Trojan Captains, Courtiers, Hunters, Carthaginians, Invisible Ghosts, Workmen, Sailors, Labourers, Naiads, Fauns,
Satyrs, Wood Nymphs

*Les Troyens* is Berlioz's greatest opera, and in many respects
his greatest achievement. In it he unites his yearning for the
classicism of Gluck, for design and form, with his own passion
for what is expressive and vivid. The work is on the grandest
scale, and Berlioz himself noted the timings which the five acts
would require: Act I, 52 minutes; Act II, 22 minutes; Act III,
40 minutes; Act IV, 47 minutes; Act V, 45 minutes—a total of

206 minutes. With four intervals, each lasting a quarter of an hour (*if* the elaborate sets did not require more), the performance would thus take four hours and twenty-six minutes, he calculated. But he was fated never to hear his opera in the form in which he conceived it; when it was performed at the Théâtre-Lyrique, the first two acts were removed, and only the second part—known in vocal scores, and in most performances for that matter, as *Les Troyens à Carthage*—was given. The scale was too exacting for most managements to tackle, and so it has proved to the present day.

*Les Troyens* is in fact one of the few neglected masterpieces of opera from the past which remains to be rediscovered. On this subject, Donald Grout, in his *A Short History of Opera* (O.U.P.), has written: '. . . *Les Troyens* is the most important French opera of the nineteenth century, the masterpiece of one of France's greatest composers, the Latin counterpart of Wagner's Teutonic *Ring*; its strange fate is paralleled by nothing in the history of music unless it be the century-long neglect of Bach's *Passion according to St. Matthew* . . . in a country properly appreciative of its cultural monuments it would seem that *Les Troyens* ought to be produced regularly at state expense until singers, conductors and public are brought to realise its greatness. Of all the works of the French grand-opera school in the nineteenth century, this is the one most worthy of being so preserved.'

The difficulties in the way of performance are many, and Berlioz had neither a Ludwig of Bavaria to start him off with ideal, or nearly ideal productions, nor subsequently a Bayreuth Festival at which to produce works requiring more than the normal time, both for rehearsal and performance. The staging is prodigiously exacting, with its frequent changes of scene, its huge chorus, its several ballets—including the inordinately difficult-to-stage *Chasse royale*—and its unusually large scale. The principal singing rôles are formidable, those of Dido and Aeneas particularly so, and moreover two of them disappear after two acts—Cassandra and Chorèbe (though the latter can, if need be, double Narbal). There is no doubt that Berlioz has put many obstacles in between his score and the public, some of them probably unavoidable. There is equally little doubt that the work ranks amongst the masterpieces of opera.

Berlioz's life-long enthusiasm for Virgil was second only to his love for Shakespeare; in point of fact, both contribute to the libretto of *Les Troyens*, the former for the narrative of the love of Dido for Aeneas as told in the first, second and fourth books of the *Aeneid*, the latter for the interpolation of the scene for Jessica and Lorenzo from *The Merchant of Venice*, which is used for the great love duet between Dido and Aeneas in Act IV.

*Les Troyens* begins at the point in the Trojan war when the Trojans have lost Hector, the Greeks Achilles and Patroclus, and the Trojans have reason to believe that their enemies have had enough. The war has gone on for over nine years already, and the Greeks have retired, leaving behind them the wooden horse.

## PART I

Act I. The scene is the abandoned camp of the Greeks on the wooded plain in front of Troy. On one side stands a throne, on the other an altar, at the back the tomb of Achilles, on which sit three shepherds playing the double-flute. The people rejoice that their ten years of confinement are over: 'Quel bonheur de respirer l'air pur des champs'. There is talk of the wooden horse, and everyone rushes off to see this curiosity, everyone except Cassandra, who remains behind prophesying the doom of Troy: 'Malheureux roi!' Even Chorèbe, her lover, believes that her mind is deranged. He tries to console her, but she continues to predict the fall of the city, and his death. She is unable to persuade him to leave Troy, but resigns herself to death on the morrow.

The character of Cassandra is splendidly depicted in the opening scene, Cassandra of whom Berlioz exclaimed when he finally gave up hope of hearing the first part of his opera: 'Ah, my noble Cassandra, my heroic virgin, I must needs resign myself to never hearing thee'. The classical feeling of the opening aria shows Berlioz's affinity to his beloved Gluck, and the duet between her and Chorèbe is full of feeling.

The second scene is set in front of the Citadel, again with an altar on one side, a throne on the other. The Trojans celebrate their deliverance from the Greeks with a procession and public games. The music is a great hymn of thanksgiving. Hector's widow and her son Astyanax, dressed in white clothes of mourning, place flowers at the foot of the altar, while Cassandra foretells for them an even greater sorrow than they have yet known.

The peaceful scene is broken in upon by the arrival of Aeneas, who distractedly describes the terrible scene he has just witnessed on the seashore. The priest, Laocoon, suspecting some hidden design of the Greeks, threw a javelin into the side of the wooden horse, whereupon two serpents came up out of the sea and devoured him before the eyes of the Trojans. All assembled express their horror and fear at this phenomenon in a magnificent octet with chorus: 'Châtiment effroyable'. Aeneas suggests that the disaster may have been brought upon them by Pallas, outraged at the insult to the horse, which has been dedicated to her. They should placate her by bringing the image within the walls and taking it to her temple. Cassandra alone remains behind as they leave to give effect to Aeneas's suggestion. She laments the step they are taking, which, she predicts, will lead to sure disaster.

To the sound of a march, the horse is dragged inside the city walls (this is the 'Trojan March' often heard in concerts). In

spite of the rumour that the sound of arms has been heard coming from inside the horse, the people persist in greeting its arrival with joy, and the sound of their song grows gradually in volume until it fills the whole city. Only Cassandra dissents from the rejoicing but her suggestion that the horse should be destroyed forthwith meets with no favourable response from the crowd.

Act II.   The first scene plays in Aeneas's palace. Aeneas's son, Ascagne, comes in, but seeing his father asleep, dare not wake him, and leaves the room. The ghost of Hector appears and marches slowly across the room. Aeneas wakes, greets the hero, and hears from him that Troy has fallen. He is instructed to take his son and the images of the gods and to take ship across the seas there—in Italy— to found a new empire. Hector's speech is set to a descending chromatic octave, each sentence delivered on one note, a semitone below the previous one. It is an impressive scene. At its end, Panthée comes to Aeneas bringing the images of the Trojan gods. He tells Aeneas of the happenings in the centre of the town; in the middle of the night, the horse opened to disgorge a troop of well-armed Greek soldiers. Priam is dead, and the town sacked and on fire. Aeneas rushes off to lead his men into battle.

The second scene takes place in the Temple of Vesta, where the Trojan women are gathered together, lamenting the fall of Troy. To them comes Cassandra, announcing the escape of Aeneas. For herself nothing remains, she says, since Chorèbe is dead. She urges the women to take their own lives rather than fall as slaves into the hands of the Greeks, and drives out the few who are not willing to die rather than go to certain dishonour, herself staying as leader of those who are resolved on death. The tension mounts, some Greeks come in and demand to know where the treasure is hidden. Cassandra answers by stabbing herself. Some of the women throw themselves from the gallery of the temple, others follow her example, and as they die, all cry 'Italie!'

When this first section of *Les Troyens* is played as a separate opera (under the title of *La Prise de Troie*), it is divided into three acts; the first comprises the opening chorus, Cassandra's aria and her duet with Chorèbe, the second opens with the rejoicings and continues until the end of Act I proper, the third consists of Berlioz's Act II.

## PART II

The rest of the opera takes place in Carthage. Originally, there was no prelude to the opera (which of course was designed to begin with the episodes in Troy itself), but when it was decided to give the second part alone, Berlioz composed a prelude to it, which is now printed in the vocal scores (although not in the one Berlioz prepared). At the first performance he made up his mind that it was essential for the audience to know the events that should have taken place in the first half, and of which they were necessarily ignorant; he therefore had the story recited by a speaker in Greek costume, and followed this with a performance of the Trojan march together with the chorus which accompanies the entrance of the wooden horse within the walls of Troy. This he felt was essential, since the march plays so important a rôle in

the second part of the opera, and much of its significance would
be lost upon an audience which had never heard it before in
their lives.

Act III.    An amphitheatre in the garden of Dido's palace at
Carthage. A festival is taking place to celebrate the progress
which has been made in building the city. Dido herself is greeted
with a rapturous chorus, 'Gloire à Didon', when she takes her
place on the throne. In a majestic aria ('Chers Tyriens'), she
speaks of the work required to raise the city from nothing, and
of what still remains to be done. The people for their part swear
to protect her and her kingdom against Iarbas, who has demanded
her hand in marriage and is now daring to invade their territory.

A sort of harvest festival now takes place. Each section of
national life files past the queen, and is rewarded for its industry.
Singing 'Gloire à Didon', the people march out, leaving Dido
alone with her sister, Anna. A conversation ensues, in which it
is made clear that Anna thinks Dido is badly in need of a husband
(she is a widow), and that Carthage needs a king just as much.
Dido thinks sadly of her dead husband, and Anna does not press
the point, which she feels is already gained.

Iopas comes in to tell the Queen that a foreign fleet has
anchored in their harbour, driven apparently by the recent storm;
the leaders are asking to see the Queen. She gives orders that they
be informed she will receive them, then recalls her own experiences
on the sea as a fugitive from Tyre. The Trojan march is heard
(this time in the minor), and the survivors are led in by Ascagne,
Aeneas having assumed a disguise and allowing his son to speak
for the whole company. Dido welcomes them, and says that
Aeneas, the noble warrior and friend of the great Hector, cannot
be anything but an honoured guest at her court. At that moment,
Narbal enters in great perturbation; Iarbas at the head of a horde
of Numidian troops has advanced into their territory, laying
waste the country, and even now threatening Carthage itself. Instantly Aeneas proclaims himself leader of the Trojans and offers
his services and theirs to help repel the Queen's enemies. His
offer is accepted, and at the head of the army he marches out to
repel the invader, leaving his son in Dido's hands.

In Berlioz's original plan, the third act ended with the great
symphonic intermezzo, the 'Chasse royale et orage'. In modern
scores this appears at the end of the following act, where it is

perhaps no less happily placed, being a self-contained episode, and supplying its own context.

The scene is a virgin forest near Carthage. Naiads cross the glade and swim in the stream. The sound of the hunt can be heard in the distance; the naiads listen anxiously, then disappear. Huntsmen cross the stage; there are signs that a storm is approaching, and one of them takes shelter under a tree. Ascagne is seen, and after him come Dido and Aeneas, the former dressed as Diana, the latter as a warrior, and both take shelter. Naiads dash off, fauns and satyrs dance, and cries of 'Italie!' are heard. A tree falls struck by lightning and bursts into flames; the fauns pick up its burning branches and dance off. The scene is covered with thick clouds, the storm dies down, and gradually peace returns. Ernest Newman* has described this scene as 'the finest and most sustained piece of nature painting in all music; it is like some noble landscape of Claude come to life in sound'. Later on he adds: 'The reader who knows his Vergil will not make the mistake, however, of seeing in *the Royal Hunt and Storm* only a piece of nature painting in music, dragged in for its own pictorial sake. He will listen imaginatively to it, as Berlioz certainly intended him to do, as the passionate climax to the realisation by Dido and Aeneas of their love for each other.'

Act IV.    Dido's gardens, by the sea. Everything is decorated to celebrate Aeneas's victorious return. Narbal confides to Anna his fear that Aeneas's coming will not be for Carthage's and for Dido's good. Already she neglects affairs of state. Anna asks him if he cannot see that Dido is in love with her guest; where else could Carthage find a better king? But Narbal's forebodings are by no means quieted by this thought.

To an orchestral reminiscence of the crowd's greeting early in the previous act, Dido comes in with her royal guest. A ballet is danced for their entertainment. At its end, Dido asks Iopas to sing; he does so, charmingly, to the accompaniment of a harp and various instruments: 'O blonde Cérès'. But Dido can find no pleasure in anything that keeps her attention from Aeneas. She asks him to continue his recital of the fate of Troy. What happened to Andromaque, she asks. Though at first determined to die, in the end she submitted to love's urgings and married her captor Pyrrhus. 'O Pudeur', sings Dido, 'Tout conspire à vaincre

* In *Opera Nights*: Putnam.

*Allegro moderato*

O pu-deur tout con-spi - re, tout con-spire à vain -cre mes re-mords.

mes remords'. Ascagne removes her ring, and Anna comments on his likeness to Cupid. Aeneas's voice has already been heard, but now Iopas and Narbal add theirs to make up the quintet. It is one of the loveliest moments in the score, and the ensemble is built up like one of Verdi's, on the individual reactions to the now apparent love of Dido for Aeneas. It is followed by a septet (Dido, Aeneas, Anna, Ascagne, Iopas, Narbal, Panthée, and the chorus) which is no less beautiful: 'Tout n'est que paix et charme'.

Everyone leaves the stage except Dido and Aeneas, who are alone in the garden: 'Nuit d'ivresse et d'extase infinie'. It is the beginning of the incomparable Shakespearean love duet, one of

*Andante*

Nuit d'i - vresse et d'ex - ta - se in -fi - ni - e

the finest in all opera: 'Par une telle nuit' (In such a night as this). Idea succeeds idea, and a reference to their own names brings the duet to an idyllic close. They go off with Dido leaning on Aeneas's shoulder, just as a shaft of moonlight reveals a statue of the god Mercury which comes to life and reiterates the knell of their hopes: 'L'Italie!'

Act V. The harbour at night. The Trojan ships are lying at anchor, and the tents of the Trojans cover the beach. A young sailor, Hylas, sings sadly of his homeland: 'Vallon sonore'. Panthée and the Trojan chiefs direct that preparations be made for the fleet's departure, which is only delayed because of Aeneas's love for Dido; every moment wasted is likely to bring down the anger of the gods—even now the disembodied cry of 'L'Italie' can be heard again. Two soldiers on sentry duty have little use for what they undoubtedly think of as the high-falutin' talk about 'L'Italie'. They are perfectly content in Carthage, where the food and the women are entirely to their liking. This new voyage is likely to lead to nothing but inconvenience for them—but they break off as they see Aeneas coming towards them.

Aeneas is torn between his overwhelming love for Dido, to whom he has broken the news that he must leave, and his sense of duty and of destiny: 'Inutiles regrets. Je dois quitter Carthage'. But he thinks longingly of Dido, and cannot bear the thought of their farewell: 'Ah, quand viendra l'instant des suprèmes adieux'. His initial agitation returns: 'En un dernier naufrage'. Once again he hears the voices, and now sees the spectre of his father Priam, followed by those of Chorèbe, Cassandra, and Hector; each in turn orders him to follow his destiny. His mind is made up and he orders the Trojans to their boats: 'Debout, Troyens', ending with a sad, slow farewell to the absent Dido. The scena is one of the most magnificent in the tenor repertory.

Dido has followed Aeneas, and a short scene takes place between them, Dido reproaching, weeping, begging him to stay, Aeneas almost prepared to give way until the sound of the Trojan march is heard in the distance. Then, with a cry of 'Italie', Aeneas rushes on to one of his vessels.

The second scene takes place in Dido's palace. Dido tries to persuade her sister Anna to go to the harbour to intercede for her. Anna says Aeneas's departure had become inevitable, if the gods were to be obeyed; but she maintains that, in spite of the gods, he still loves her. Dido says this is impossible; if *she* loved, she would disobey Jove himself. When Iopas describes the ships putting out to sea, Dido bursts out in fury, ordering the Carthaginians to pursue and destroy the traitorous Trojans. She herself has done wrong by not from the start treating the Trojans as they have finished by treating her. Why did she not serve up the body of Ascagne to Aeneas at a feast? One thing only is left her: to raise an awful pyre to the god of the underworld, and on it burn everything that was ever connected with the traitorous Aeneas.

Anna and Narbal leave her, and Dido's grief overflows; she tears her hair and beats her breast in her anguish: 'Ah, je vais mourir'. She will burn on the pyre, and perhaps from his ship Aeneas will catch sight of the flames which will signal her terrible end. She bids farewell to the great city: 'Adieu, fière cité'.

The last scene takes place on a terrace overlooking the sea. A funeral pyre is presided over by priests of Pluto. Dido, preceded by Anna and Narbal, comes slowly in. Anna and Narbal solemnly curse the Trojans, after which Dido prepares to mount the steps of the pyre. She looks sadly at Aeneas's accoutrements on it; then, taking his sword, stands with it while she prophesies that her people will one day produce a warrior to avenge on his descendants the shame now brought by Aeneas. Then she plunges the sword into her breast. Anna tries to help her, but Dido revives only long enough to communicate her further vision, in which she sees Rome triumphant. She dies as the Carthaginians hurl further curses at the Trojans. But the Trojan March contradicts them, and a vision of eternal Rome rises behind Dido's pyre.

H.

# BÉATRICE ET BÉNÉDICT

Opera in two acts by Berlioz. Words by the composer, after Shakespeare's comedy, *Much Ado about Nothing*. Produced at Baden-Baden, August 9, 1862, with Charton-Demeur, Monrose, Montaubry. First performed Weimar, 1863; Carlsruhe, 1888, conducted by Mottl; Vienna, 1890; Opéra-Comique, Paris, 1890; Glasgow (in English), 1936.

## CHARACTERS

Don Pedro, *a general* ............................Bass
Leonato, *governor of Messina*......................Bass
Hero, *his daughter* ...........................Soprano
Béatrice, *his niece* ......................Mezzo-Soprano
Claudio, *an officer* ..........................Baritone
Bénédict, *an officer* ............................Tenor
Ursula, *Hero's companion* ....................Contralto
Somarona, *orchestral conductor* ....................Bass

The story is an adaptation of the short version of Shakespeare's play, which preserves the spirit of the comedy, but omits the saturnine intrigue of Don John against Claudio and Hero. The gist of the comedy is the gradual reaction of the brilliant but captious Béatrice from pique and partially feigned indifference toward the witty and gallant Bénédict, to love. Both have tempers. In fact they reach an agreement to marry as a result of a spirited quarrel.

The overture, like that for *Benvenuto Cellini*, is made up from tunes used elsewhere in the opera. Thus the opening *allegretto scherzando* later accompanies the duet at the end of the opera, and

the *andante* tune is Béatrice's 'Il m'en souvient'. The overture
is a brilliant and gay piece of music, and it has become very
popular in the concert hall, where, doubtless, many of its admirers
are entirely ignorant of the fact that it belongs to an opera.

Act I.    The action takes place in the garden of Leonato, the
governor of Messina. There is general rejoicing that the town
is no longer in danger from the besieging army of Moors, which
has finally been driven off. After some dialogue—this is an
opéra-comique, with much of the action carried on in ordinary
speech —the chorus starts to repeat its praises of the victorious
general and his troops, much to Béatrice's dissatisfaction. There
is a dance, a Sicilienne in 6/8 time, of charming individuality,
and the stage empties.

Hero has a splendid aria in which she looks forward to seeing
Claudio again. The lovely, calm tune of the opening *larghetto*
section, 'Je vais le voir', is a good example of that stylistic refinement and purity which is a feature of Berlioz's music, and the
quick section, ' Il me revient fidèle', makes an exhilarating
finish. Bénédict and Claudio arrive, and the skirmishing of the
protagonists begins. 'Comment le dédain pourrait-il mourir?' (Is
it possible disdain should die?), begins their duet, a really lovely
number. It is followed by a trio for the three men, Bénédict,
Claudio, and Don Pedro: 'Me marier! Dieu me pardonne', a
3/8 *allegretto*, in which Bénédict makes furious answer when he
is twitted on the subject of marriage. It is dominated by long
musical sentences for Bénédict, upon which the others comment.

Berlioz introduces a non-Shakespearean character, Somarona.
a *maître de chapelle*, who rehearses his chorus and orchestra in an
*Epithalame grotesque*, a choral fugue on the subject of love.
Gradually Bénédict is brought to realise that all is not well with
his plans for perpetual bachelordom. He sings a spirited *rondo*
'Ah, je vais l'aimer', a charming and original piece of the greatest
vitality.

It is evening, and Hero and Ursula close the act with a slow
duet—a Nocturne, 'a marvel of indescribable lyrical beauty in

which Berlioz's feeling for nature is wonderfully expressed' (so says W. J. Turner). One has to turn to *Così fan Tutte* to find idyllic writing for combined female voices of comparable beauty.

Act II opens with a version of the *Sicilienne* already heard. There is a dialogue between the servants and Somarona starts up a drinking song, whose accompaniment is provided by guitars, trumpets, and tambourines (the guitar was the instrument on which Berlioz most enjoyed performing). The stage empties, and Béatrice comes in. Bénédict loves her; how to overcome her own increasing feeling for him? She has an aria on the grand scale, 'Il m'en souvient', whose tune has already been heard in the overture. The impressive *scena* finishes with an *allegro agitato*, 'Je l'aime donc'.

There is a flowing, 6/8 trio of great beauty for Hero, Béatrice, and Ursula, in which Béatrice reveals that her feelings have undergone a considerable change since we first met her. She positively welcomes the tenderness which she earlier despised: 'Et ton époux restera ton amant'. This and the succeeding number, an offstage chorus with guitar accompaniment, Berlioz added to the score after returning from Baden, where the opera was first produced.

Béatrice and Bénédict both try to conceal their mutual love, but it is in vain. After a general *Marche nuptiale*, the two marriage contracts are signed between Béatrice and Bénédict, and Hero and Claudio—and the opera finishes with a brilliant duet for Béatrice and Bénédict: 'L'amour est un flambeau'. This, called a *scherzo-duettino* by the composer, is accompanied by the opening figure of the overture, and its sparkle and gaiety make the perfect comedy ending. That it is a love duet is never concealed, but it is informed with a spirit of liveliness and wit which give it a quality hardly realised otherwise in opera outside Verdi's *Falstaff*.

*Béatrice et Bénédict*, for all Berlioz's love of Shakespeare, remains more Berlioz than Shakespeare. One cannot but regret that the composer decided to do away with the sub-plot of Don John and the near-defection of Claudio—the 'serious' side of the story—but that should not blind one to the quality of what has all the same resulted from the collaboration of England's greatest poet and France's greatest composer.

H.

# FRIEDRICH von FLOTOW
## (1812–1883)

### MARTHA

OPERA in five acts by Friedrich von Flotow; text by W. Friedrich after a ballet-pantomime, *Lady Henriette ou La Servante de Greenwich*, by St. Georges, for which Flotow wrote part of the music. Première at the Kärnthnerthor Theater, Vienna, on November 25, 1847, with Anna Zerr, Alois Ander, Formes. First performed New York, 1852, with Anna Bishop; London, Drury Lane, 1849 (in German), 1858 (in English), Covent Garden, 1858, with Bosio, Didiée, Mario, Graziani; Paris, Théâtre-Lyrique, December 16, 1865, when was interpolated the famous air 'M'Appari', from Flotow's two-act opera, *L'Ame en Peine*, produced at the Opéra, Paris, June, 1846; Metropolitan, New York, 1884, with Sembrich, Trebelli, Stagno, Novina; 1905, with Sembrich, Walker, Caruso, Plançon; 1923, with Alda, Howard, Gigli, de Luca; revived Covent Garden, 1930, with Edith Mason, Gigli; la Scala, 1931, with Favero, Pederzini, Pertile, Stabile; 1938, with Favero, Elmo, Gigli, Maugeri.

### CHARACTERS

Lady Harriet Durham, *Maid of Honour to Queen Anne* ...................................... Soprano
Lord Tristan de Mikleford, *her cousin* .............. Bass
Plunkett, *a young farmer* ......................... Bass
Lionel, *his foster-brother; afterwards Earl of Derby* .. Tenor
Nancy, *waiting-maid to Lady Harriet* .......... Contralto
Sheriff ........................................ Bass
Three Man Servants ...... ⎰ ⎱      Tenor and two Basses
Three Maid Servants ..... ⎰ ⎱ Soprano and Mezzo-Soprano
Courtiers, Pages, Ladies, Hunters and Huntresses, Farmers, Servants, etc.

*Time:* About 1710        *Place:* In and near Richmond

The first act opens in Lady Harriet's boudoir. The second scene of this act is the fair at Richmond. The scene of the second act is laid in Plunkett's farm-house; that of the third in a forest near Richmond. The fourth act opens in the farm-house and changes to Lady Harriet's park.

Act I. Scene i.    The Lady Harriet yawned. It was dull even at the court of Queen Anne. The simple fact is that Lady Harriet, like many others whose pleasures come so easily that they lack zest, was bored. Even the resourceful Nancy was at last driven to exclaim: 'If your ladyship only would fall in love!'

But herein, too, Lady Harriet had the surfeit that creates indifference. She had bewitched every man at court only to remain unmoved by their protestations of passion. Even as Nancy spoke, a footman announced the most persistent of her ladyship's suitors, Sir Tristan of Mikleford, an elderly cousin who presumed upon his relationship to ignore the rebuffs with which she met his suit.

'Most respected cousin, Lady in Waiting to Her Most Gracious Majesty,' he began sententiously, and would have added all her titles had she not cut him short with an impatient gesture, 'will your ladyship seek diversion by viewing the donkey races with me to-day?'

'I wonder,' Nancy whispered, 'if he is going to run in the races himself?' which evoked from the Lady Harriet the first smile that had played around her lips that day.

Likely enough Sir Tristan's fair cousin would soon have sent him on some errand that would have taken him out of her presence. But when he opened the window, in came the strains of a merry chorus sung by fresh, happy voices of young women who, evidently, were walking along the highway. The Lady Harriet's curiosity was piqued. Who were these women over whose lives ennui never seemed to have hung like a pall? Nancy knew all about them. They were servants on the way to Richmond fair to hire themselves out to the farmers, according to time-honoured custom.

The Richmond fair! To her ladyship's jaded sense it conveyed a suggestion of something new and frolicsome. 'Nancy,' she cried, carried away with the novelty of the idea, 'let us go to the fair dressed as peasant girls and mingle with the crowd! Who knows, someone might want to hire us! I will call myself Martha, you can be Julia, and you, cousin, can drop your title for the nonce and go along with us as plain Bob!'

Scene ii.   Meanwhile Richmond fair was at its height. From a large parchment the pompous Sheriff had read the law by which all contracts for service made at the fair were binding for at least one year as soon as money had passed. Among those who had come to bid were a sturdy young farmer, Plunkett, and his foster-brother Lionel. The latter evidently was of a gentler birth, but his parentage was shrouded in mystery. As a child he had been left with Plunkett's mother by a fugitive, an aged man who, dying from exposure and exhaustion, had confided the boy to her care, first, however, handing her a ring with the injunction, if misfortune ever threatened the boy, to show the ring to the Queen.

One after another the girls proclaimed their deftness at cooking, sewing, gardening, poultry tending, and other domestic and rural accomplishments, the Sheriff crying out, 'Four guineas! Who'll have her?—Five guineas! Who'll try her?'

Just then they heard a young woman's voice behind them call out, 'No, I won't go with you!' and, turning, they saw two sprightly young women arguing with a testy-looking old man. Lionel and Plunkett nudged each other. Never had they seen such attractive-looking girls. And when they heard one of them call out again to the old man, 'No, we won't go with you!'—for Sir Tristan was urging the Lady Harriet and Nancy to leave the fair—the young men hurried over to the group.

'Can't you hear her say she won't go with you?' asked Lionel, while Plunkett called out to the girls near the Sheriff's stand, 'Here, girls, is a bidder with lots of money!' A moment later the absurd old man was the centre of a rioting, shouting crowd of girls, who followed him when he tried to retreat, so that finally 'Martha' and 'Julia' were left quite alone with the two men. The young women were in high spirits. They had sallied forth in quest of adventure and here it was. After a few slyly reassuring glances from them, Plunkett overcame his hesitancy and spoke up:

'You're our choice, girls!'

'Done!' cried the girls, who thought it all a great lark, and a moment later the Lady Harriet had placed her hand in Lionel's and Nancy hers in Plunkett's and money had passed to bind the bargain.

The escapade seemed to have gone far enough and the two girls looked about for Sir Tristan to take them away. 'None of that,' said the two farmers, and, when the crowd again gathered about Sir Tristan, they hurried off the girls and drove away, while the crowd blocked the blustering knight and jeered as he vainly tried to break away in pursuit.

Act II.    The adventure of the Lady Harriet and her maid Nancy, so lightly entered upon, was carrying them further than they had expected. To find themselves set down in a humble farm-house, and to be told to go into the kitchen and prepare supper, was more than they had bargained for.

Lionel suggested as a substitute for the kitchen that they be allowed to try their hands at the spinning wheels. But they were so awkward at these that the men sat down to show them how to spin, until Nancy brought the lesson to an abrupt close by saucily overturning Plunkett's wheel and dashing away with the young farmer in pursuit, leaving Lionel and 'Martha' alone.

It was an awkward moment for her ladyship; to relieve the situation she began to hum and, finally, to sing, choosing her favourite air, 'The Last Rose of Summer'. But it had the very opposite effect of what she had planned. Lionel, completely carried away, exclaimed: 'Ah, Martha, if you were to marry me, you no longer would be a servant, for I would raise you to my own station!'

Just then, fortunately, Plunkett dragged in Nancy, whom he had pursued into the kitchen, where she had upset things generally before he had been able to seize her; and a distant tower clock striking midnight, the young farmers allowed their servants, whose accomplishments as such, if they had any, so far remained undiscovered, to retire to their room, while they sought theirs, but not before Lionel had whispered:

'Perchance by the morrow, Martha, you will think differently of what I have said and not treat it so lightly.'

Act III. But when morning came the birds had flown the cage. There was neither a Martha nor a Julia in the little farm-house, while at the court of Queen Anne a certain Lady Harriet and her maid Nancy were congratulating themselves that, after all, an old fop named Sir Tristan of Mikleford had had sense enough to be in waiting with a carriage near the farm-house at midnight and helped them escape through the window. The Lady Harriet was no longer bored; and even Nancy had lost her sprightliness. The simple fact is that the Lady Harriet and Nancy, without being certain of it themselves, were in love.

It chanced that Lionel, in much the same state of mind and heart as her ladyship, was wandering, when, suddenly looking up, he saw a young huntress in whom, in spite of her different costume, he recognised the 'Martha' over whose disappearance he had been grieving. But she was torn by conflicting feelings. However her heart might go out toward Lionel, her pride of birth still rebelled against permitting a peasant to address words of love to her. 'You are mistaken. I do not know you!' she exclaimed. And when he in anger began to upbraid her for denying her identity to him who was by law her master, she cried out for help, bringing not only Sir Tristan but the entire hunting train to her side. Noting the deference with which she was treated and hearing her called 'My Lady' Lionel now perceived the trick that had been played upon himself and Plunkett at the fair.

Act IV. Before very long, however, there was a material change in the situation. In his extremity, Lionel remembered about his ring and he asked Plunkett to show it to the Queen and plead his cause. The ring proved to have been the property of the Earl of Derby. It was that nobleman who, after the failure of a plot to recall James II from France and restore him to the throne, had died a fugitive and confided his son to the care of Plunkett's mother, and that son was none other than Lionel, now discovered to be the rightful heir to the title and estates.

Despite his new honours, however, Lionel was miserably unhappy. He was deeply in love with the Lady Harriet. Yet he hardly could bring himself to speak to her, let alone appear so much as even to notice the advances which she, in her contrition, so plainly made toward him.

This sad state of affairs might have continued indefinitely had not Nancy's nimble wit come to the rescue. She and Plunkett, after meeting again, had been quick in coming to an understanding, and now the first thing they did was to plan how to bring together Lionel and the Lady Harriet. One afternoon Plunkett joined Lionel in his lonely walk and, unknown to him, gradually guided him into her ladyship's garden. A sudden turn in the path brought them in view of a bustling scene. Then above it Lionel heard a sweet, familiar voice singing "'Tis the last rose of summer'. A moment later, he held his 'Martha' in his arms.

*Martha* teems with melody. The best known airs are 'The Last Rose of Summer' and Lionel's 'M'appari' (Like a dream). The best ensemble piece, a quintet with chorus, occurs near the close of Act III—'Ah! che a voi perdoni Iddio' (Heaven alone may grant you pardon). The spinning-wheel quartet in Act II is most sprightly. But, as indicated, there is a steady flow of light and graceful melody in this opera. Almost at the very opening of

Act I, Lady Harriet and Nancy have a duet, 'Questo duol che si v'affano' (Sure, some noble lord attending). Bright, clever music abounds in the Richmond fair scene, and Lionel and Plunkett express their devotion to each other in 'Solo, profugo, reietto' (Lost, proscribed, a friendless wanderer), and 'Ne giammai saper potemmo' (Never have we learned his station). Then there is the gay quartet when the two girls leave the fair with their masters, while the crowd surrounds Sir Tristan and prevents him from breaking through and interfering. It was in this scene that the bass singer Castelmary, the Sir Tristan of a performance of *Martha* at the Metropolitan Opera House, February 10, 1897, was stricken with heart failure and dropped dead upon the stage.

A capital quartet opens Act II, in the farm-house, and leads to the spinning-wheel quartet, 'Di vederlo' (What a charming occupation). There is a duet between Lady Harriet and Lionel, in which their growing attraction for each other finds expression, 'Il suo sguardo e dolce tanto' (To his eye, mine gently meeting). Then follows 'Qui sola, vergin rosa' ('Tis the last rose of summer), the words a poem by Tom Moore, the music an old Irish air, 'The Groves of Blarney', to which Moore adapted 'The Last Rose of Summer'. A new and effective touch is given to the old song by Flotow in having the tenor join with the soprano at the close. Moreover, the words and music fit so perfectly into the situation on the stage that for Flotow to have 'lifted' and interpolated them into his opera was a master-stroke. To it *Martha* owed much of its one-time popularity.

'Tis the last rose of sum-mer, Left blooming a - lone

There is a duet for Lady Harriet and Lionel, 'Ah! ride del mio pianto' (She is laughing at my sorrow). The scene ends with another quartet, one of the most beautiful numbers of the score, and known as the 'Good Night Quartet', 'Dormi pur, ma il mio riposo' (Cruel one, may dreams transport thee).

Act III, played in a hunting park in Richmond forest, on the left a small inn, opens with a song in praise of beer, the 'Canzone del Porter' by Plunkett, 'Chi mi dira' (Will you tell me). The pièces-de-résistance of this act are the 'M'appari':

a solo for Nancy, 'Il tuo stral nel lanciar' (Huntress fair, hastens where); Martha's song, 'Qui tranquilla almen posso' (Here in deepest forest shadows); and the stirring quintet with chorus.

In Act IV there are a solo for Plunkett, 'Il mio Lionel perira' (Soon my Lionel will perish), and a repetition of some of the sprightly music of the fair scene.

It is not without considerable hesitation that I have classed *Martha* as a French opera. For Flotow was born in Teutendorf, April 27, 1812, and died in Darmstadt, January 24, 1883. Moreover, *Martha* was produced in Vienna, and his next best known work, *Alessandro Stradella*, in Hamburg (1844).

The music of *Martha*, however, has an elegance that not only is quite unlike any music that has come out of Germany, but is typically French. Flotow, in fact, was French in his musical training, and both the plot and score of *Martha* were French in origin. The composer studied composition in Paris under Reicha, 1827–30, leaving Paris solely on account of the July revolution, and returning in 1835, to remain until the revolution in March 1848 once more drove him away. After living in Paris again, 1863–8, he settled near Vienna, making, however, frequent visits to that city, the French capital, and Italy.

During his second stay in Paris he composed for the Grand Opera the first act of a ballet, *Harriette, ou la Servante de Greenwiche*. This ballet, the text by Vernoy de St. Georges, was for Adèle Dumilâtre. The reason Flotow was entrusted with only one of the three acts was the short time in which it was necessary to complete the score. The other acts were assigned, one each, to Robert Bergmuller and Edouard Deldevez. Of this ballet, written and composed for a French dancer and a French audience, *Martha* is an adaptation. This accounts for its being so typically French and not in the slightest degree German.

K.

# CHARLES
# FRANÇOIS GOUNOD
## (1818–1893)

### FAUST

OPERA in five acts by Gounod; words by Barbier and Carré. Produced Théâtre Lyrique, Paris, March 19, 1859, with Miolan-Carvalho, Faivre, Duclos, Barbot, Reynald, Balanque. Opéra, Paris, March 3, 1869, with Christine Nilsson, Colin, and Faure. London, Her Majesty's Theatre, June 11, 1863, with Tietjens, Trebelli, Giuglini, Santley, Gassier; Covent Garden, July 2, 1863 (in Italian), with Miolan-Carvalho, Tamberlik, Faure; Her Majesty's Theatre, January 23, 1864, in an English version by Chorley, for which, Santley being the Valentine, Gounod composed what was destined to become one of the most popular numbers of the opera, 'Even bravest heart may swell'. New York, Academy of Music, November 26, 1863 (in Italian), with Clara Louise Kellogg, Henrietta Sulzer, Francesco Mazzoleni, Hannibal Biachi. Metropolitan Opera House, opening night, October 22, 1883, with Nilsson, Scalchi, Lablache, Campanini, Novara, Del Puente. *Faust* is in the repertory of virtually every opera house in the world. Famous interpreters have included:—Marguérite: Patti, Melba, Eames, Nordica, Suzanne Adams, Calvé, Farrar, Sayao, de los Angeles; Faust: Jean de Reszke, Capoul, Campanini, Caruso, Muratore, Dalmorès, Ansseau; Méphistophélès: Edouard de Reszke, Plançon, Delmas, Journet, Vanni-Marcoux, Chaliapin, Pinza.

### CHARACTERS

Faust, *a learned doctor* ......................Tenor
Méphistophélès ...............................Bass
Marguérite ...................................Soprano
Valentine, *a soldier, brother to Marguérite* .......Baritone
Siebel, *a village youth, in love with*
    Marguérite .........................Mezzo-Soprano
Wagner, *a student* ...........................Baritone
Martha Schwerlein, *neighbour to*
    Marguérite .........................Mezzo-Soprano
Students, Soldiers, Villagers, Angels, Demons, Cleopatra,
Lais, Helen of Troy, and others

*Time:* Sixteenth Century        *Place:* Germany

Gounod's librettists, Michel Carré and Jules Barbier, with a true Gallic gift for practicable stage effect, did not seek to utilise the whole of Goethe's *Faust* for their book, but contented themselves with the love story of Faust and Marguérite, which also happens to have been entirely original with the author of the play, since it does not occur in the legends. But because the opera does not deal with the whole of *Faust*, Germany, where Gounod's work enjoys great popularity, refuses to accept it under the same title as the play, and calls it *Margarethe* after the heroine.

As reconstructed for the Opéra, where it was brought out ten years after its production at the Théâtre-Lyrique, *Faust* develops as follows:

There is a brief prelude. A *ff* on a single note, then mysterious, chromatic chords, and then the melody which Gounod composed for Santley.

Act I. Faust's study. The philosopher is discovered alone, seated at a table on which an open tome lies before him. His candle flickers in its socket. Night is about to turn to dawn.

Faust despairs of solving the riddle of the universe. Aged, his pursuit of science vain, he seizes a flask of poison, pours it into a crystal goblet, and is about to drain it, when, day having dawned, the cheerful song of young women on their way to work arrests him. The song dies away. Again he raises the goblet, only to pause once more, as he hears a chorus of labourers, with whose voices those of the women unite. Faust, beside himself at these sounds of joy and youth, curses life and advancing age, and calls upon Satan to aid him.

There is a flash of red light and out of it, up through the floor, rises Méphistophélès, garbed as a cavalier, in vivid red. Alternately suave, satirical, and demoniacal in bearing, he offers to Faust wealth and power. The philosopher, however, wants neither, unless with the gift also is granted youth: 'Je veux la jeunesse' (What I long for is youth). That is easy for his tempter, if the aged philosopher, with pen dipped in his blood, will but sign away his soul. Faust hesitates. At a gesture from Méphistophélès the scene at the back opens and discloses Marguérite seated at her spinning wheel, her long blond braid falling down her back. 'O Merveille!' (A miracle!) exclaims Faust, at once signs the parchment, and drains to the vision of Marguérite a goblet proffered him by Méphistophélès. The scene fades away, the philosopher's garb drops off Faust. The grey beard and all other marks of old age vanish. He stands revealed a youthful gallant, eager for adventure, instead of the disappointed scholar weary of life. There is an impetuous duet for Faust and Méphistophélès: 'A moi les plaisirs' ('Tis pleasure I covet). They dash out of the cell-like study in which Faust has vainly devoted himself to science.

Act II.    Outside one of the city gates. To the left is an inn, bearing as a sign a carved image of Bacchus astride a keg. It is kermesse time. There are students, among them Wagner, burghers old and young, soldiers, maidens, and matrons.

The act opens with a chorus. *Faust* has been given so often that this chorus probably is accepted by most people as a commonplace. In point of fact it is an admirable piece of characterisation. The groups of people are effectively differentiated in the score. The toothless chatter of the old men (in high falsetto) is an expecially amusing detail. In the end the choral groups are deftly united.

Valentine and Siebel join the throng. The former is examining a medallion which his sister, Marguérite, has given him as a charm against harm in battle. He sings the number which Gounod composed for Santley, 'Even bravest heart may swell' (Avant de quitter ces lieux).

Wagner mounts a table and starts the 'Song of the Rat'. After a few lines he is interrupted by the sudden appearance of Méphistophélès, who, after a brief parley, sings 'Le veau d'or' (The golden calf), a cynical dissertation on man's worship of mammon. He reads the hands of those about him. To Siebel he prophesies that every flower he touches shall wither. Rejecting the wine proffered him by Wagner, he strikes with his sword the sign of the inn, the keg, astride of which sits Bacchus. Like a stream of wine fire flows from the keg into the goblet held under the spout by Méphistophélès, who raising the vessel, pledges the health of Marguérite.

This angers Valentine and leads to the 'Scène des épées'. Valentine unsheathes his blade. Méphistophélès, with his sword, describes a circle about himself. Valentine makes a pass at his foe. As the thrust carries his sword into the magic circle, the blade breaks. He stands in impotent rage, while Méphistophélès mocks him. At last, realising who his opponent is, Valentine grasps his sword by its broken end, and extends the cruciform hilt toward the red cavalier. The other soldiers follow their leader's example. Méphistophélès, no longer mocking, cowers before the cross-shaped sword hilts held toward him, and slinks away. A sonorous chorus, 'Puisque tu brises le fer' (Since you have broken the blade) for Valentine and his followers distinguishes this scene.

The crowd gathers for the kermesse dance—'the waltz from *Faust*', familiar the world round, and undulating through the score to the end of the gay scene, which also concludes the act. While the crowd is dancing and singing, Méphistophélès enters with Faust. Marguérite approaches, on her way from church, prayerbook in hand. Siebel seeks to join her. But every time the youth steps toward her he confronts the grinning yet sinister visage of Méphistophélès, who dexterously manages to get in his way. Meanwhile Faust has joined her. There is a brief colloquy, he offers his arm to conduct her through the crowd, but she modestly declines. The episode, though short, is charmingly melodious. The phrases for Marguérite can be made to express coyness, yet also show that she is not wholly displeased with the attention paid her by the handsome stranger. She goes her way. The dance continues: 'Valsons toujours' (Waltz alway!).

Act III.     Marguérite's garden. At the back a wall with a wicket door. To the left a bower. On the right Marguérite's house, with a bow window facing the audience. Trees, shrubs, flower beds, etc.

Siebel enters by the wicket. Stopping at one of the flower beds and about to pluck a nosegay, he sings the graceful 'Faites-lui mes aveux' (Bear my avowal to her). But when he picks a flower, it shrivels in his hand, as Méphistophélès had predicted. The boy is much perturbed. Seeing, however, a little font with holy water suspended by the wall of the house, he dips his fingers in it. Now the flowers no longer shrivel as he touches them. He arranges them in a bouquet, which he lays on the house step, where he hopes Marguérite will see it, and leaves.

Faust enters with Méphistophélès, but bids the latter withdraw, as if he sensed the incongruity of his presence near the home of a maiden so pure as Marguérite. The tempter having gone, Faust proceeds to apostrophise Marguérite's dwelling in the exquisite romance, 'Salut! demeure chaste et pure'.

*Larghetto*

Sa - lut! de -meu-re chaste et    pu - re.

Méphistophélès returns. With him he brings a casket of jewels and a handsome bouquet. With these he replaces Siebel's flowers. The two men then withdraw into a shadowy recess of the garden to await Marguérite's return.

She enters by the wicket. Her thoughts are with the handsome stranger—above her in station, therefore the more flattering and fascinating in her eyes—who addressed her at the fair. Pensively she seats herself at her spinning wheel and, while turning it, without much concentration of mind on her work, sings 'Il était un roi de Thulé', the ballad of the King of Thule, her thoughts, however, returning to Faust before she finishes the number, which is set in the simple fashion of a folk-song.

Approaching the house, and about to enter, she sees the flowers, stops to admire them, and to bestow a thought of compassion upon Siebel for his unrequited devotion, then sees and hesitatingly opens the casket of jewels. Their appeal to her feminine vanity is too great to permit her to return them at once to the casket. Decking herself out in them, she regards herself and the sparkling gems in the handglass that came with them, then bursts into the brilliant 'Air des Bijoux' (Jewel Song):

one of the most brilliant airs for coloratura soprano, affording the greatest contrast to the folklike ballad which preceded it, and making with it one of the most effective scenes in opera for a soprano who can rise to its demands, the chaste simplicity required for the ballad, the joyous abandon and faultless execution of elaborate embellishments involved in the 'Air des Bijoux'. When well done, the scene is brilliantly successful; for, added to its own conspicuous merit, is the fact that, save for the very brief episode in Act II, this is the first time in two and a half acts that the limpid and grateful tones of a solo high soprano have fallen upon the ear.

Martha, the neighbour and companion of Marguérite, joins

her. In the manner of the average duenna, whose chief duty in opera is to encourage love affairs however fraught with peril to her charge, she is not at all disturbed by the gift of the jewels or by the entrance upon the scene of Faust and Méphistophélès. Nor, when the latter tells her that her husband has been killed in the wars, does she hesitate, after a few exclamations of rather forced grief, to seek consolation on the arm of the flatterer in red, who leads her off into the garden, leaving Faust with Marguérite. During the scene immediately ensuing the two couples are sometimes in view, sometimes lost to sight in the garden. The music is a quartet, beginning with Faust's 'Prenez mon bras un moment' (Pray lean upon mine arm). It is artistically individualised. The couples and each member thereof are deftly characterised in Gounod's score.

For a moment Méphistophélès holds the stage alone. Standing by a bed of flowers in an attitude of benediction, he invokes their subtle perfume to lull Marguérite into a false sense of security. 'Il était temps!' (It was the hour), begins the soliloquy. For a moment, as it ends, the flowers glow. Méphistophélès withdraws into the shadows. Faust and Marguérite appear. Marguérite plucks the petals of a flower: 'He loves me—he loves me not—he loves!' There are two ravishing duets for the lovers, 'Laisse-moi contempler ton visage' (Let me gaze upon thy beauty), and 'O nuit d'amour . . . ciel radieux!' (Oh, night of love! oh, starlit

sky!). The music fairly enmeshes the listener in its enchanting measures.

Faust and Marguérite part, agreeing to meet on the morrow. She enters the house. Faust turns to leave the garden. He is confronted by Méphistophélès, who points to the window. The casement is opened by Marguérite, who believes she is alone. Kneeling in the window, she gazes out upon the night flooded with moonlight. 'Il m'aime; . . . Ah! presse ton retour, cher bien-aimé! Viens!' (He loves me; ah! haste your return, dearly beloved! Come!).

With a cry, Faust rushes to the open casement, sinks upon his knees. Marguérite, with an ecstatic exclamation, leans out of the embrasure and allows him to take her into his arms. Her head rests upon his shoulder.

At the wicket gate is Méphistophélès, shaking with laughter.

Act IV.    The first scene in this act takes place in Marguérite's room. No wonder Méphistophélès laughed when he saw her in Faust's arms. She has been betrayed and deserted. The faithful Siebel, however, still offers her his love—'Si la bonheur à sourire t'invite' (When all was young and pleasant, May was blooming) —but Marguérite still loves the man who betrayed her, and hopes against hope that he will return.

This episode is followed by the cathedral scene. Marguérite has entered the edifice and knelt to pray. But, invisible to her, Méphistophélès stands beside her and reminds her of her guilt. A chorus of invisible demons calls to her accusingly. Méphistophélès foretells her doom. The 'Dies iræ', accompanied on the organ, is heard. Marguérite's voice joins with those of the worshippers. But Méphistophélès, when the chant is ended, calls out that for her, a lost one, there yawns the abyss. She flees in terror. This is one of the most significant episodes of the work.

Now comes a scene in the street, in front of Marguérite's house. The soldiers return from war and sing their familiar chorus, 'Gloire immortelle' (Glory immortal). Valentine, forewarned by Siebel's troubled mien that all is not well with Marguérite, goes into the house. Faust and Méphistophélès come upon the scene. Facing the house, and accompanying himself on his guitar, the red gallant sings an offensive serenade: 'Vous qui faites l'endormie'. Valentine, aroused by the insult, which he correctly interprets as aimed at his sister, rushes out. There is a spirited trio, 'Allons, messieurs'. Valentine smashes the guitar with his sword, then attacks Faust, whose sword-thrust, guided by Méphistophélès, mortally wounds Marguérite's brother. Marguérite comes into the street, throws herself over Valentine's body. With his dying breath her brother curses her.

Sometimes the order of the scenes in this act is changed. It may open with the street scene, where the girls at the fountain hold themselves aloof from Marguérite. Here the brief meeting between the girl and Siebel takes place. Marguérite then goes into the house; the soldiers return, etc. The act then ends with the cathedral scene.

Act V.   When Gounod revised *Faust* for the Grand Opéra, Paris, the traditions of that house demanded a more elaborate ballet than the dance in the Fair scene afforded. Consequently the authors reached beyond the love story of Faust and Marguérite into the second part of Goethe's drama and utilised the legendary revels of Walpurgis Night (eve of May 1st) on the Brocken, the highest point of the Hartz mountains. Here Faust meets the courtesans of antiquity—Laïs, Cleopatra, Helen of Troy, Phryne. *Les Nubiennes, Cléopatra et la Coupe d'Or* (Cleopatra and the Goblet of Gold), *Les Troyennes* (The Trojan Women), *Variation*, and *Dance de Phryne* are the dances in this ballet. Elsewhere more frequently than not the scene is omitted. To connect it with the main story, there comes to Faust, in the midst of the revels, a vision of Marguérite. Around her neck he beholds a red line, 'like the cut of an axe'. He commands Méphistophélès to take him to her.

They find her in prison, condemned to death for killing her child. There is an impassioned duet for Faust and Marguérite. He begs her to make her escape with him. But her mind is wandering. In snatches of melody from preceding scenes, she recalls the episode at the fair, the night in the garden. She sees Méphistophélès, senses his identity with the arch-fiend. There is a superb trio, in which Marguérite ecstatically calls upon angels to intervene and save her—'Anges purs! Anges radieux!' (Angels pure, radiant, bright). The voices mount higher and higher, Marguérite's

*Moderato Maestoso*

An-ges purs anges ra-di- eux · Portez mon âmes au seindes cieux

soaring to a splendid climax. She dies.

'Condemned!' cries Méphistophélès.

'Saved,' chant ethereal voices.

The rear wall of the prison opens. Angels are seen bearing

Marguérite heavenward. Faust falls on his knees in prayer. Méphistophélès turns away, 'barred by the shining sword of an archangel'.                                        K.

## MIREILLE

Opera in three acts (originally five) by Charles Gounod, text by Carré after Frédéric Mistral's poem *Mireio*. Première at the Théâtre-Lyrique, Paris, March 19, 1864, with Miolan-Carvalho and Michot. The revised version, which involved substantial changes in the music as well as a pastoral ending substituted for the original tragedy, was made later in 1864. First performed at Her Majesty's, London, 1864, with Tietjens, Giuglini, Santley; Philadelphia, 1864; Covent Garden, 1891, with Eames, Lubert, Ceste. Revived at Metropolitan, 1919, with Barrientos, Hackett, Whitehill, conductor Monteux. In open air at the Val d'Enfer, les Baux, with Vivaldi, Gedda, Dens, cond. Cluytens. Currently in the repertory of most French theatres.

### CHARACTERS

Mireille ...................................... Soprano
Vincent, *her lover* ............................. Tenor
Ourrias, *a bull-tender*......................... Baritone
Maître Ramon, *father of Mireille* ................... Bass
Taven, *an old woman, thought to be a witch* Mezzo-Soprano
Andreloux, *a shepherd* ................... Mezzo-Soprano
Maître Ambroise, *father of Vincent* ................. Bass
Clémence.................................... Soprano

*Place:* In and near Arles.

Act I. The overture sets the Provençal atmosphere, with its *cornemuse* tunes. The scene is a mulberry plantation. After a pastoral chorus, Mireille confesses that she is in love with Vincent, who returns her affection. Her song, 'O légère hirondelle', in the waltz rhythm in which Gounod liked to introduce his heroines, is attractively ingenuous. In spite of the warning of Taven that a girl should not give her heart away so openly, least of all when there is little possibility of parental approval for the proposed match, Mireille makes no pretence of hiding her feelings when Vincent comes towards her. In an agreeable duet they repeat their vows, and pledge each other to meet in a particular sanctuary if ever trouble should threaten their lives.

Act II. A festival is in progress at Arles. A *farandole* chorus makes a vigorous introduction to the act. Mireille and Vincent are there together and, when asked by the company to sing, they perform the graceful *Chanson de Magali*: 'La brise est douce'.

Taven warns Mireille that Vincent has a rival, Ourrias, who has admitted his love for her. Mireille is indignant at the idea that she might prove unfaithful to Vincent: 'Trahir Vincent!' She will be true to him all her days: 'Non, jamais, jamais! A toi mon âme'.

Mireille's graceful avowal of her love is followed by the entrance of Ourrias, 'Si les filles d'Arles', a typically bucolic song. Before the act ends, Ourrias has asked for Mireille's hand and been refused, Vincent's father, Ambroise, has likewise pleaded for his son and been told that his reasons were nothing short of mercenary, and Mireille has emphasised the firmness of her attachment for Vincent, in spite of her father's preference for Ourrias.

Act III.  The scene is a desert in the region of Crau, where little has a chance to grow before being burnt up by the heat of the sun. A *Musette* is succeeded by a charming shepherd's song: 'Le jour se lève', sung by Andreloux. Mireille, on her way to the sanctuary she and Vincent agreed upon in Act I, pauses to envy the carefree shepherd: 'Heureux petit berger'. Taven succeeds in catching her up and informing her of an unsuccessful attack made upon Vincent's life by Ourrias; Mireille hurries on towards the sanctuary.

The scene changes to the sanctuary itself, the church of the Saintes Maries. There is a march and chorus for the pilgrims, after which Vincent appears, vainly searching for Mireille. In an effective, high-lying tenor aria, 'Anges du Paradis', he prays that she may win her way to their meeting-place, in spite of the torrid heat of the Provençal sun. Mireille arrives in a state of collapse, but, at sight of her lover waiting for her, she revives, and together they rejoice in their happiness in a charming duet, 'La foi de son flambeau divin'. There is another moment of anxiety when Mireille again appears to lose control of her senses, but the presence of her father blessing her union with Vincent restores her strength.

The alternative ending develops the plot by Ourrias to kill Vincent. There is a short fight between the two rivals which ends in Ourrias stabbing Vincent with his murderous trident, and Ourrias tries to escape across the Val d'enfer, only to be confronted by the reproaching voices of conscience in the shape of the spirits of deceived lovers which haunt the place. Even the

PLATE XXVII. *Faust* at the Metropolitan, New York, in Peter Brook's 1850-style production. *Top:* 'Le veau d'or', with Rossi-Lemeni as Mephistopheles. *Bottom:* the garden scene, with de los Angeles, Björling, Votipka and Rossi-Lemeni.

PLATE XXVIII. Act I of *Carmen* at Covent Garden 1953; production by Anthony Asquith, sets by Georges Wakhevitch. Nell Rankin is Carmen, and James Johnston José.

boatman who comes to his aid seems to know of his crime, and he drowns making his escape.

Mireille herself dies of exhaustion on her way across the desert of Crau to the appointed meeting-place with Vincent. Her big scene, beginning 'Voici la vaste plaine et le désert de feu', is one of the best bits of the score, and it impressively combines the lyrical qualities of Gounod's music with something considerably more dramatic.

*Mireille* has real charm, in spite of the slight nature of much of the music, but it is hard to escape the feeling that if this purports to be a representation of Provençal life, it is one which (at any rate in the revised version) substitutes garlands for garlic—which may please some people, but is hardly true to nature.                                                          H.

# ROMÉO ET JULIETTE
## Romeo and Juliet

Opera in five acts by Gounod; words by Barbier and Carré, after the tragedy by Shakespeare. Produced Paris, Théâtre-Lyrique, April 27, 1867, with Miolan-Carvalho, Michot, Barré, Cazaux; January 1873, taken over by the Opéra-Comique; Opéra, November 28, 1888, with Patti, Jean and Edouard de Reszke, Delmas. London, Covent Garden (in Italian), July 11, 1867, with Patti, Mario, Cotogni, Tagliafico. New York, Academy of Music, November 15, 1867, with Minnie Hauck; Metropolitan Opera House, December 14, 1891, with Eames, Jean and Edouard de Reszke. Chicago, December 15, 1916, with Muratore and Galli-Curci. Revived Covent Garden, 1919, with Melba, Ansseau; Metropolitan, 1922, with Bori, Gigli; Covent Garden, 1930, with Edith Mason, Burdino, Brownlee, Pinza, conductor Barbirolli; Covent Garden Company's Tour, 1937, with Lisa Perli, Nash, Brownlee, Allin, conductor Beecham; Metropolitan, 1937, with Sayao, Crooks, Brownlee, Pinza, conductor d'Abravanel; 1945, with Munsel, Jobin Singher, Pinza. Currently in the repertory of the Paris Opéra.

### CHARACTERS

The Duke of Verona ..................................... Bass
Count Paris ...................................... Baritone
Count Capulet ....................................... Bass
Juliet, *his daughter* ........................... Soprano
Gertrude, *her nurse*...................... Mezzo-Soprano
Tybalt, *Capulet's nephew* ........................ Tenor
Romeo, *a Montague* ............................. Tenor
Mercutio ...................................... Baritone
Stephano, *Romeo's page* ...................... Soprano

Gregory, *a Capulet retainer* .....................Baritone
Friar Lawrence ................................Bass
Benvolio, *retainer to the Montagues* ...............Tenor
Friar Jean .......................................Bass

Nobles and Ladies of Verona, Citizens, Soldiers, Monks,
and Pages

*Time:* Fourteenth Century                *Place:* Verona

Having gone to Goethe for *Faust*, Gounod's librettists, Barbier
and Carré, went to Shakespeare for *Roméo et Juliette*, which, like
*Faust*, reached the Paris Grand Opéra by way of the Théâtre-
Lyrique.

*Roméo et Juliette* has been esteemed more highly in France
than elsewhere. In England it has never enjoyed much popularity,
apart from the period when Patti and after her Melba used to
star in the rôle of Juliet. In America, save for performances in
New Orleans, it was only during the Grau régime at the Metropolitan Opera House, when it was given in French with casts
familiar with the traditions of the Opéra, that it can be said
regularly to have held a place in the repertory. Eames is remembered as a singularly beautiful Juliet, vocally and personally;
Capoul, Jean de Reszke, and Saléza, as Romeos; Edouard de
Reszke as Frère Laurent.

Nicolini, who became Adelina Patti's second husband, sang
Romeo at the Opéra to her Juliet. She was then the Marquise de
Caux, her marriage to the Marquis having been brought about
by the Empress Eugénie. But that this marriage was not to last
long, and that the Romeo and Juliet were as much in love with
each other in actual life as on the stage, was revealed one night
to an Opéra audience, when, during the balcony scene, prima
donna and tenor—so the record says—imprinted twenty-nine
real kisses on each other's lips.

The libretto is in five acts and follows closely, often even to
the text, Shakespeare's tragedy. There is a prologue in which the
characters and chorus briefly rehearse the story that is to unfold
itself.

Act I.     The grand hall in the palace of the Capulets. A masked
ball is in progress. The chorus sings gay measures. Tybalt speaks
to Paris of Juliet, to whom he is engaged and who at that moment
appears with her father. Capulet bids the guests welcome and to

be of good cheer—'Soyez les bienvenus, amis' (Be ye welcome, friends), and 'Allons! jeunes gens! Allons! belles dames!' (Bestir ye, young nobles! And ye, too, fair ladies!).

Romeo, Mercutio, Benvolio, and half-a-dozen followers come masked. Despite the deadly feud between the two houses, they, Montagues, have ventured to come as maskers to the fête of the Capulets. Mercutio sings of Queen Mab, a number as gossamer-like in the opera as the monologue is in the play; hardly ever sung as it should be, because the rôle of Mercutio is rarely assigned to a baritone capable of doing justice to the airy measures of 'Mab, la reine des mensonges' (Mab, Queen Mab, the fairies' midwife).

The Montagues withdraw to another part of the palace. Juliet returns with Gertrude, her nurse. Full of high spirits, she sings the graceful and animated waltz, 'Je veux vivre dans ce rêve, qui m'enivre' (Fair is the tender dream of youth). The nurse is called

away. Romeo, wandering in, meets Juliet. Their love, as in the play, is instantaneous. Romeo addresses her in passionate accents, 'Ange adorable' (Angel! adored one). His addresses, Juliet's replies, make a charming duo.

Upon the re-entry of Tybalt, Romeo, who had removed his mask, again adjusts it. But Tybalt suspects who he is, and from the utterance of his suspicions, Juliet learns that the handsome youth, to whom her heart has gone out, is none other than Romeo, scion of the Montagues, the sworn enemies of her house. The fiery Tybalt is for attacking Romeo and his followers then and there. But old Capulet, respecting the laws of hospitality, orders that the fête proceed.

Act II. The garden of the Capulets. The window of Juliet's apartment, and the balcony, upon which it gives. Romeo's page, Stephano, a character introduced by the librettists, holds a ladder by which Romeo ascends to the balcony. Stephano leaves, bearing the ladder with him.

Romeo sings, in one of Gounod's loveliest tenor arias, 'Ah! levè-toi soleil' (Ah! fairest dawn arise). The window opens, Juliet comes out upon the balcony. Romeo conceals himself. From her soliloquy he learns that, although he is a Montague, she loves him. He discloses his presence. The interchange of pledges is exquisite. Lest the sweetness of so much love music become too cloying, the librettists interrupt it with an episode. The Capulet retainer, Gregory, and servants of the house, suspecting that an intruder is in the garden (they have seen Stephano speeding away), search unsuccessfully and depart.

The nurse calls. Juliet re-enters her apartment. Romeo sings, 'O nuit divine' (Oh, night divine). Juliet again steals out upon the balcony. 'Ah! je te l'ai dit, je t'adore!' (Ah, I have told you that I adore you), sings Romeo. There is a beautiful duet, 'Ah! ne fuis pas encore!' (Ah, do not flee again), a brief farewell, and the curtain falls upon the balcony scene.

Act III, Part I.    Friar Lawrence's cell. Here takes place the wedding of Romeo and Juliet, the good friar hoping that their union may lead to peace between the two great Veronese houses of Montague and Capulet. There are in this part of the act Friar Lawrence's prayer, 'Dieu, qui fis l'homme à ton image' (God, who made man in Thine image); a trio, in which the friar chants the rubric, and the pair respond; and an effective final quartet for Juliet, Gertrude, Romeo, and Friar Lawrence ('O pur bonheur').

Part II.    A street near Capulet's house. Stephano, having vainly sought Romeo, and thinking he still may be in conceal- ment in Capulet's garden, sings a ditty likely to rouse the temper of the Capulet household, and bring its retainers into the street, thus affording Romeo a chance to get away. The ditty is 'Que fais-tu, blanche tourterelle' (Gentle dove, why art thou clinging?). Gregory and Stephano draw and fight. The scene develops, as in the play. Friends of the two rival houses appear. Mercutio fights Tybalt and is slain, and is avenged by Romeo, who kills Tybalt, Juliet's kinsman, and, in consequence, is banished from Verona by the Duke, who appears as the fighting reaches its climax.

Act IV.    It is the room of Juliet, to which Romeo has found access, in order to bid her farewell, before he goes into exile. The lingering *adieux*, the impassioned accents in which the despair of parting is expressed—these find eloquent utterance in the music. There is the duet, 'Nuit d'hyménée, O douce nuit d'amour' (Night hymeneal, sweetest night of love). Romeo hears the lark, sure sign of approaching day, but Juliet protests (Non, non, ce n'est pas le jour' (No, no! 'Tis not yet the day). Yet the parting time cannot be put off longer. Romeo: 'Ah! reste! reste encore dans mes bras enlacés' (Ah! rest! rest once more within mine entwining arms); then both, 'Il faut partir, hélas' (Now we must part, alas).

Hardly has Romeo gone when Gertrude runs in to warn Juliet that her father is approaching with Friar Lawrence. Tybalt's dying wish, whispered into old Capulet's ear, was that the marriage between Juliet and the noble whom Capulet has chosen for her husband, Count Paris, be speeded. Juliet's father comes to bid her prepare for the marriage. Neither she, the friar, nor the nurse dare tell Capulet of her secret nuptials with Romeo. This gives significance to the quartet, 'Ne crains rien' (Fear no more). Capulet withdraws, leaving, as he supposes, Friar Lawrence to explain to Juliet the details of the ceremony. It is then that the friar, in the dramatic 'Buvez donc ce breuvage' (Drink then of this philtre), gives her the potion, upon drinking which she shall appear as dead.

The scene changes to the grand hall of the palace. Guests arrive for the nuptials. There is occasion for the ballet, so essential for a production at the Opéra. Juliet drains the vial, falls as if dead. (This scene, written in 1888, is often omitted.)

Act V. The tomb of the Capulets. Romeo, having heard in his exile that his beloved is no more, breaks into the tomb. She, recovering from the effects of the philtre, finds him dying, plunges a dagger into her breast, and expires with him.

In the music there is an effective prelude. Romeo salutes the tomb, 'Salut, tombeau sombre et silencieux', and sings, to his beloved, apparently lying dead, 'O ma femme! o ma bien aimée' (O wife, dearly beloved). Juliet, not yet aware that Romeo has taken poison, and Romeo forgetting for the moment that death's cold hand already is reaching out for him, they sing, 'Viens, fuyons au bout du monde' (Come, let us fly to the ends of the earth). Then Romeo begins to feel the effect of the poison, and tells Juliet what he has done. 'Console toi, pauvre âme' (Console thyself, sad heart). But Juliet will not live without him, and while he in his wandering mind hears the lark, as at their last parting, she stabs herself.    K.

# AMBROISE THOMAS

## (1811–1896)

### MIGNON

OPERA in three acts by Ambroise Thomas, words, based on Goethe's *Wilhelm Meister*, by Barbier and Carré. Produced, Opéra-Comique, Paris, November 17, 1866, with Galli-Marié. London, Drury Lane, July 5, 1870, with Nilsson, Volpini, Bettini, Faure. New York, Academy of Music, November 22, 1871, with Nilsson, Duval (Philine), Mlle. Ronconi (Frédéric), and Capoul; Metropolitan Opera House, October 21, 1883, with Nilsson, Capoul, and Scalchi (Frédéric). Revived Metropolitan, 1926, with Bori, Gigli; Sadler's Wells, 1932, with Rose Morris, Tudor Davies; la Scala, Milan, 1933, with Besanzoni, Schipa; Metropolitan, 1938, with Risë Stevens; la Scala, 1945, with Pederzini, Schipa; 1947, with Simionato, di Stefano. Frédéric, since Trebelli appeared in the rôle in London, has become a contralto instead of a buffo tenor part. The 'Rondo Gavotte' in Act II, composed for her by Thomas, has since then been a fixture in the score.

### CHARACTERS

Mignon, *stolen in childhood from an Italian castle* .............................. Mezzo-Soprano
Philine, *an actress* ............................ Soprano
Frédéric, *a young nobleman* ..... Buffo Tenor or Contralto
Wilhelm Meister, *a student on his travels* ........... Tenor
Laertes, *an actor* ............................... Tenor
Lothario ...................................... Bass
Giarno, *a gypsy* ................................ Bass
Antonio, *a servant* .............................. Bass

Townspeople, Gypsies, Actors and Actresses, Servants, etc.

*Time:* Late Eighteenth Century   *Place:* Acts I and II, Germany; Act III, Italy

Notwithstanding the popularity of two airs in *Mignon*—'Connais-tu le pays?' and the 'Polonaise'—the opera is beginning to lose its hold on the repertory. It is a work of delicate texture, of charm rather than passion, with a story that is, perhaps, too ingenuous to appeal to the sophisticated audience of the modern opera house. Moreover, the 'Connais-tu le pays?' was at one time done to death, both by concert singers and amateurs. Italian composers are fortunate in having written music so difficult technically that none but the most accomplished singers can risk it.

Act I.    Courtyard of a German inn. Chorus of townspeople and travellers. Lotario, a wandering minstrel, sings, accompanying himself on his harp, 'Fugitif et tremblant' (A lonely wanderer). Philine and Laertes, on the way with their troupe to give a theatrical performance in a neighbouring castle, appear on a balcony. Mignon is sleeping on straw in the back of a gypsy cart. Giarno, chief of the gypsy band, rouses her. She refuses to dance. He threatens her with a stick. Lotario and Wilhelm protect her. Mignon divides a bouquet of wild flowers between them.

Laertes, who has come down from the balcony, engages Wilhelm in conversation. Philine joins them. Wilhelm is greatly impressed with her blonde beauty. He does not protest when Laertes takes from him the wild flowers he has received from Mignon and hands them to Philine.

When Philine and Laertes have gone, there is a scene between Wilhelm and Mignon. The girl tells him of dim memories of her childhood—the land from which she was abducted. It is at this point she sings 'Connais-tu le pays?' (Knowest thou the land?). Wilhelm decides to purchase her freedom, and enters the inn with Giarno to conclude the negotiations. Lotario, who is about to wander on, has been attracted to her, and, before leaving, bids her farewell. They have the charming duet, 'Legères hirondelles' (O swallows, lightly gliding). There is a scene for Philine and Frédéric, a young boy, who is in love with her. Philine is after better game. She is setting her cap at Wilhelm. Lotario wishes to take Mignon with him, but Wilhelm fears for her safety with the old man, whose mind sometimes appears to wander. Moreover Mignon ardently desires to remain in the service of Wilhelm who has freed her from bondage to the gypsies, and, when Wilhelm declines to let her go with Lotario, is enraptured, until she sees her wild flowers in Philine's hand. Already she is passionately in love with Wilhelm, and jealous when Philine invites him to attend the theatricals at the castle. Wilhelm waves adieu to Philine, as she drives away. Lotario, pensive, remains seated. Mignon's gaze is directed toward Wilhelm.

Act II.    The entr'acte is the tune of the famous gavotte. Philine's boudoir at the castle. The actress sings of her pleasure in these elegant surroundings, and of Wilhelm. Laertes is heard without, singing a madrigal to Philine, 'Belle, ayez pitié de nous' (Fair one, pity take on us).

He ushers in Wilhelm and Mignon, then withdraws. Mignon, pretending to fall asleep, watches Wilhelm and Philine. While Wilhelm hands to the actress various toilet accessories, they sing a graceful duet, 'Je crois entendre les doux compliments' (Pray, let me hear now the sweetest of phrases). Meanwhile Mignon's heart is tormented with jealousy. When Wilhelm and Philine leave the boudoir the girl dons one of Philine's costumes, seats herself at the mirror and puts on rouge and other cosmetics, as she has seen Philine do. In a spirit of abandon she sings a brilliant *Styrienne*, 'Je connais un pauvre enfant' (A gypsy lad I well do know). She then withdraws into an adjoining room. Frédéric enters the boudoir in search of Philine. He sings the gavotte, 'Me voici dans son boudoir' (Here am I in her boudoir). Wilhelm comes in, in search of Mignon. The men meet. There is an exchange of jealous accusations. They are about to fight, when Mignon rushes between them. Frédéric recognises Philine's costume on her, and goes off laughing. Wilhelm, realising the awkward situation that may arise from the girl's following him about, tells her they must part. 'Adieu, Mignon, courage' (Farewell, Mignon, have courage). She bids him a sad farewell. Philine re-enters. Her sarcastic references to Mignon's attire wound the girl to the quick. When Wilhelm leads out the actress on his arm, Mignon exclaims: 'That woman! I loathe her!'

The second scene of this act is laid in the castle park. Mignon, driven to distraction, sings a *scena* of real dramatic power: 'Elle est là, près de lui?' She is about to throw herself into the lake, when she hears the strains of a harp. Lothario, who has wandered into the park, is playing. There is an exchange of affection, almost paternal on his part, almost filial on hers, in their duet, 'As-tu souffert? As-tu pleuré?' (Hast thou known sorrow? Hast thou wept?). Mignon hears applause and acclaim from the conservatory for Philine's acting. In jealous rage she cries out that she wishes the building might be struck by lightning and destroyed by fire; then runs off and disappears among the trees. Lothario vaguely repeats her words. 'Fire,' she said! 'Ah, fire! fire!' Through the trees he wanders off in the direction of the conservatory, just as its doors are thrown open and the guests and actors issue forth.

They have been playing *A Midsummer Night's Dream*, and Philine, flushed with success, sings the brilliant *Polonaise*, 'Je suis Titania' (Behold Titania, fair and gay). Mignon appears. Wilhelm, who has sadly missed her, greets her with so much joy that Philine sends her into the conservatory in search of the wild flowers given to Wilhelm the day before. Soon after Mignon has entered the conservatory it is seen to be in flames. Lothario, obedient to her jealous wish, has set it on fire. At the risk of his life Wilhelm rushes into the burning building and reappears with Mignon's fainting form in his arms. He places her on a grassy bank. Her hand still holds a bunch of withered flowers.

Act III.    Gallery in an Italian castle, to which Wilhelm has brought Mignon and Lothario. Mignon has been dangerously ill. A boating chorus is heard from the direction of a lake below. Lothario, standing by the door of Mignon's sick-room, sings a lullaby, 'De son cœur j'ai calmé la fièvre' (I've soothed the throbbing of her aching heart). Wilhelm tells Lothario that they are in the Cipriani castle, which he intends to buy for Mignon. At the name of the castle Lothario is strangely agitated.

Wilhelm has heard Mignon utter his own name in her delirium during her illness. He sings, 'Elle ne croyait pas' (She does not know). When she enters the gallery from her sick-room and looks out on the landscape, she is haunted by memories. There is a duet for Mignon and Wilhelm, 'Je suis heureuse, l'air m'enivre' (Now I rejoice, life reawakens). Philine's voice is heard outside. The girl is violently agitated. But Wilhelm reassures her.

In the scenes that follow, Lothario, his reason restored by being again in familiar surroundings, recognises in the place his own castle and in Mignon his daughter, whose loss had unsettled his mind and sent him, in minstrel's disguise, wandering in search of her. The opera closes with a trio for Mignon, Wilhelm, and Lothario. In it is heard the refrain of 'Connais-tu le pays?'.

K.

# GEORGES BIZET

## (1838–1875)

### LES PÊCHEURS DE PERLES
### (The Pearl Fishers)

OPERA in three acts by Georges Bizet, text by Carré and Cormon. Première at the Théâtre-Lyrique, Paris, on September 30, 1863, with Mlle. de Maesen, Morini, Ismaël, Guyot. First performed Covent Garden, 1887, as *Leïla*, with Fohström, Garulli, Lhérie, Miranda; Philadelphia, 1893; Opéra-Comique, Paris, April 21, 1893, with Calvé, Delmas, Soulacroix, Challet, conductor Danbé; Metropolitan, 1896 (two acts only, in combination with *La Navarraise*), with Calvé, Cremonini, Ancona, Arimondi. Revived Metropolitan, 1916, with Hempel, Caruso, de Luca, Rothier, conductor Polacco; Covent Garden, 1920, with Pareto, Tom Burke, Badini, Edmund Burke, conductor Beecham; Berlin, 1934, with Berger, Wittrisch, Schlusnus, conductor Blech; la Scala, Milan, 1938, with Carosio, Lugo, Biasini, Baronti, conductor Capuana; 1948 with Fineschi, Infantino, Guarrera, Modesti, conductor Capuana. Currently in the repertory of the Opéra-Comique.

### CHARACTERS

Leïla, *priestess of Brahma*......................Soprano
Nadir, *a fisherman* .............................Tenor
Zurga, *king of the fishermen* ...................Baritone
Nourabad, *high priest of Brahma* .................Bass

*Time:* Antiquity                    *Place:* Ceylon

Act I.    The scene is the seashore, where the fishermen are holding fête preparatory to choosing a chief. They sing and dance, and eventually select Zurga as king; he accepts their confidence. Nadir appears, is greeted after his long absence, and describes his adventures in the jungle. There is a fond reunion between Zurga and Nadir. They were formerly friends, but recall their rivalry for the hand of the beautiful priestess, Leïla, whom they had seen together in the Brahmin temple of Candy. Their love for her had brought enmity between them, but they recall that the oath of friendship which they swore has never since been broken. Their duet, 'Au fond du temple saint' (In the depths of the temple), is an example of Bizet's melodic inspiration at its finest, and is one of the most beautiful tenor-baritone duets in all French opera. Its theme is used throughout the opera as a friendship motto:

News is brought that a boat has arrived, bringing with it the unknown virgin whose duty is to pray during the time the fishermen are at sea, so as to ward off evil spirits. Zurga tells Nadir that she is veiled and must not be approached or seen by anyone during the time of her vigil. She is brought in by the old priest Nourabad, and welcomed by the fisherfolk. Zurga swears her in as the inviolate virgin protectress of the fishermen, and threatens her with death if she prove false to her oath.

Leïla and Nadir recognise each other, and he stands watching as if in a dream as she ascends the cliff. In an aria of great beauty he reflects on his love, which has never been dimmed by the passing of time: 'Je crois entendre encore' (I hear as in a dream):

This is the best-known section of the score, not least in its Italian translation, 'Mi par d'udir ancora'. Leïla reappears, and sings an invocation to Brahma, echoed by the chorus, before she is left alone on her rock for her vigil. Before the end of the act, Nadir, gazing up at Leïla, sings ardently of his love for her and swears to protect her from danger.

Act II.   In a ruined temple, the high priest, Nourabad, warns Leïla on pain of death to be faithful to her religious vows. She will be alone but well guarded. Leïla tells him he need have no fear; she never breaks her promise. The necklace she wears was given her by a fugitive, whose hiding-place she refused to reveal although the daggers of his pursuers were pointed at her heart; she had promised not to betray him.

Nourabad leaves her, and she sings of the love which fills her heart: 'Comme autrefois dans la nuit sombre'. Suddenly, not far away, she hears the voice of Nadir singing a serenade: 'De mon amie fleur endormie'. A moment later he is with her, and a passionate duet of almost Verdian character develops: 'Ton cœur n'as pas compris le mien'. Leïla begs Nadir to leave her, and they agree to meet again the next day; but Nourabad has seen Nadir's escape, and he calls down anathema on both their heads, while the chorus mutter that they can see a storm arising. Nadir is captured by the guards, Nourabad accuses the lovers of sacrilege, and the crowd takes up his cry for vengeance. Zurga claims the right, as chief and therefore judge, to settle the case himself, and he inclines to be merciful for the sake of his friend. But Nourabad tears the veil from Leïla's head, and Zurga, recognising Leïla, swears to be revenged on Nadir for his treachery. Leïla and Nadir pray to Brahma for help, while the crowd call on him to avenge the sacrilege.

Act III.   Zurga's tent. The chief contrasts his own restless state of mind with the abated storm, which for a time threatened destruction to the fishing fleet: 'L'orage s'est calmé'. He laments the breaking of his friendship with Nadir: 'O Nadir, tendre ami de mon cœur'. It is a fine lyrical *scena* of considerable power. Leïla appears before him, and expresses her willingness to die, but pleads for Nadir. Zurga eventually gives in to jealousy at the idea of losing Leïla to Nadir, and is cursed by Leïla for his jealous cruelty. Just before leaving him, she asks that a last favour may be granted her; she has a necklace which she would like to have sent to her mother far away. This she puts into Zurga's hands as she leaves him.

The second scene of Act III is set at the place of execution, where has been erected a funeral pyre. There are savage dances and choruses, the sopranos reiterating 'Brahma!' on a high G, before Nourabad leads Leïla out into the middle of the populace. Just as the guilty lovers are to meet death, a distant glow is seen. Zurga dashes in crying out that the camp is on fire, and the people rush out to fight the flames. Zurga tells Leïla and Nadir that it was he who set fire to the camp; the necklace she gave him was once his, and he the fugitive she saved from death long ago. He unfastens their chains and bids them flee; there is a solemn trio 'O lumière sainte'. Zurga impedes their pursuers, but is denounced by Nourabad, who had stayed behind in hiding when the others left. Zurga is stabbed from behind by one of his subjects. The music of 'Au fond du temple sainte' is heard in the orchestra, and the top line is sung by Leïla and Nadir in octaves as they appear on the top of the rock, at whose foot far below Zurga lies dying.                                                    K., H.

# DJAMILEH

Opera in one act by Georges Bizet, text by Louis Gallet. Première at the Opéra-Comique, Paris, May 22, 1872, with Mme. Prelly ('the voiceless Venus' as Gauthier-Villars called her), MM. Duchesne, Potel. First performed Covent Garden, 1893, with Bonnard, Coatellier, Gherlsen; Boston, 1913; Covent Garden, 1919, with Gladys Ancrum, Webstar Millar, Walter Hyde, conductor Pitt; Berlin, 1927; Vienna, 1938, with Brehms and Dermota. Revived Paris, 1938.

## CHARACTERS

Djamileh, *a slave* ...................... Mezzo-Soprano
Haroun, *a prince* .............................. Tenor
Splendiano, *his secretary* ....................... Tenor
A slave merchant

Djamileh, a beautiful slave, is in love with her master, Prince Haroun, a Turkish nobleman, who is tired of her and is about to sell her. She persuades his secretary, Splendiano, who is in love with her, to aid her in regaining her master's affections. She will marry Splendiano if she fails.

Accordingly, with the secretary's aid, when the slave dealer arrives, she is, in disguise, among the slaves offered to Haroun. She dances. Haroun is entranced, and immediately buys her. When she discloses her identity, and pleads that her ruse was prompted by her love for him, he receives her back into his affections.

Djamileh is for mezzo-soprano, the men's rôles for tenor. Besides the dance, there are a duet for the men, 'Que l'esclave soit brune ou blonde' (Let the slave be dark or fair); a trio, 'Je voyais au loin la mer s'étendre' (The distant sea have I beheld extending); and the chorus, 'Quelle est cette belle?' (Who is the charmer?).

K.

# CARMEN

Opera in four acts by Georges Bizet; words by Henri Meilhac and Ludovic
Halévy, founded on the novel by Prosper Mérimée. Première, Opéra-Comique,
Paris, March 3, 1875, the title rôle being created by Galli-Marié with Chapuy,
Lhérie, Bouhy. Her Majesty's Theatre, London (in Italian), June 22, 1878,
with Minnie Hauck; same theatre, February 5, 1879 (in English); same theatre
November 8, 1886 (in French), with Galli-Marié. Covent Garden, 1882, with
Pauline Lucca, Valleria, Lestellier, Bouhy. Minnie Hauck, who created
Carmen in London, also created the rôle in America, October 23, 1879, at
the Academy of Music, New York, with Campanini, Del Puente. The first
New Orleans Carmen, January 14, 1881, was Mme. Ambré. Calvé made her
New York début as Carmen at the Metropolitan Opera House, December 20
1893, with Jean de Reszke and Eames. Campanini, Jean de Reszke, Caruso,
Clément, Saléza, Dalmores, Muratore, Martinelli, Ansseau, Thill, and
Maison have been celebrated as José; Eames and Melba have been un-
approached as Micaela; del Puente, Galassi, Campanari, Plançon, Amato,
and Journet were famous as Escamillo.

Covent Garden Carmens have included de Lussan, Calvé, Bourguignon,
Olszewska, Supervia, Renée Gilly, Coates, Shacklock, Brehms, Mödl. Other
famous interpreters of the title rôle have been Bressler-Gianoli, Maria Gay,
Gutheil-Schoder, Farrar, Mary Garden, Besanzoni, Jeritza, Ponselle, Giannini, Bruna Castagna, Risë Stevens, Swarthout, Djanel, Pederzini.

## CHARACTERS

Don José, *a corporal of dragoons* ................. Tenor
Escamillo, *a toreador* ......................... Baritone
El Dancairo ⎫ *smugglers* ................... ⎰ Baritone
El Remendado ⎭                                   ⎱ Tenor
Zuniga, *a captain* .............................. Bass
Morales, *an officer* ............................ Bass
Micaela, *a peasant girl* ....................... Soprano
Frasquita ⎫ *gypsies, friends of Carmen* ........ ⎰ Soprano
Mercédès ⎭                                        ⎱ Soprano
Carmen, *a cigarette girl and gypsy* ............. Soprano
Innkeeper, Guide, Officers, Dragoons, Boys, Cigarette Girls,
Gypsies, Smugglers, etc.

*Time:* About 1820                    *Place:* Seville, Spain

Act I.    A square in Seville. On the right the gate of a cigarette
factory. At the back, facing the audience, is a practicable bridge.
In front, on the left, is a guard-house. Above it three steps lead
to a covered passage. In a rack, close to the door, are the lances
of the dragoons of Almanza, with their little red and yellow flags.

The prelude, one of the most famous orchestral pieces in all opera, begins with an exhilarating *presto*, but contains a brooding, apprehensive section in the middle. At the end of the work, this music turns out to be connected with the idea of fate.

Morales and soldiers are near the guard-house. People are coming and going. There is a brisk chorus, 'Sur la place' (O'er this square). Micaela comes forward, as if looking for someone.

'And for whom are you looking?' Morales asks of the pretty girl, who has shyly approached the soldiers lounging outside the guard-house.

'I am looking for a corporal,' she answers.

'I am one,' Morales says, gallantly.

'But not *the* one. His name is José.'

The soldiers, scenting amusement in trying to flirt with a pretty creature, whose innocence is as apparent as her charm, urge her to remain until Don José comes at change of guard. But, saying she will return later, she runs away like a frightened deer, past the cigarette factory, across the square, and down one of the side streets.

A fascinating little march of fifes and trumpets is heard, at first in the distance, then gradually nearer.

The change of guard arrives, preceded by a band of street lads, imitating the step of the dragoons. After the lads come Captain Zuniga and Corporal José; then dragoons, armed with lances. The ceremony of changing guard takes place to the accompaniment of a chorus of gamins and grown-up spectators. It is a lively scene.

'It must have been Micaela,' says Don José, when they tell him of the girl with tresses of fair hair and dress of blue, who was looking for him. 'Nor do I mind saying,' he adds, 'that I love her.' And indeed, although there are some sprightly girls in the crowd that has gathered in the square to see the guard changed, he has no eyes for them, but, straddling a chair out in the open, busies himself trying to join the links of a small chain that has come apart.

The bell of the cigarette factory strikes the work hour, and the cigarette girls push their way through the crowd, stopping to make eyes at the soldiers and young men, or lingering to laugh and chat, before passing through the factory gates.

A shout goes up:

'Carmen!'

A girl, dark as a gypsy and lithe as a panther, darts across the bridge and down the steps into the square, the crowd parting and making way for her.

'Love you?' she cries insolently to the men who press around her and ply her with their attentions. 'Perhaps to-morrow. Anyhow not to-day.' Then, a dangerous fire kindling in her eyes, she sways slowly to and fro to the rhythm of a *Habanera*, singing the while, 'L'amour est un oiseau rebelle',

> 'Love is a gypsy boy, 'tis true,
>      He ever was and ever will be free;
> Love you not me, then I love you,
>      Yet, if I love you, beware of me!'

Often she glances toward José, often dances so close to him that she almost touches him, and by subtle inflections in her voice seeks to attract his attention. But he seems unaware of her presence. Whether he is thinking of Micaela, or has steeled himself against the gypsy, in whose every glance, step, and song lurks peril, the handsome dragoon could not be busying himself more obstinately with the broken chain in his hand.

'Yet, if I love you, beware of me!'

Tearing from her bodice a blood-red cassia flower, she flings it at him point-blank. He springs to his feet, as if he would rush at her. But he meets her look, and stops where he stands. Then, with a toss of the head and a mocking laugh, she runs into the factory, followed by the other girls, while the crowd, having had its sport, disperses.

The librettists have constructed an admirable scene. The composer has taken full advantage of it. The *Habanera* establishes Carmen in the minds of the audience—the gypsy girl, passionate yet fickle, quick to love and quick to tire. Hers the dash of fatalism that flirts with death.

At José's feet lies the cassia flower thrown by Carmen, the glance of whose dark eyes had checked him. Hesitatingly, yet as if in spite of himself, he stoops and picks it up, presses it to his nostrils and draws in its subtle perfume in a long breath. Then, still as if involuntarily, or as if a magic spell lies in its odour, he thrusts the flower under his blouse and over his heart.

He has no more than concealed it there, when Micaela again enters the square and hurries to him with joyful exclamations. She brings him tidings from home, and some money from his mother's savings, with which to eke out his small pay. They have a charming duet, 'Parle-moi de ma mère' (Speak to me of my mother).

It is evident that Micaela's coming gives him a welcome change of thought, and that, although she cannot remain long, her sweet, pure presence has for the time being lifted the spell the gypsy has cast over him. For, when Micaela has gone, José grasps the flower under his blouse, evidently intending to draw it out and cast it away.

Just then, however, there are cries of terror from the cigarette factory and, in a moment, the square is filled with screaming girls, soldiers, and others. From the excited utterances of the cigarette girls it is evident that there has been a quarrel between Carmen and another girl, and that Carmen has wounded the latter with a knife. Zuniga promptly orders José to take two dragoons with him into the factory and arrest her. Not the least abashed, and smirking, she comes out with them. When the captain begins questioning her, she answers with a gay 'Tra la la, tra la la', pitching her voice on a higher note after each question with an indescribable effect of mockery, that makes her dark beauty the more fascinating.

Losing patience, the officer orders her hands tied behind her back, while he makes out the warrant for her imprisonment. The soldiers having driven away the crowd, Don José is left to guard Carmen.

Pacing up and down the square, he appears to be avoiding her. But she, as if speaking to herself, or thinking aloud, and casting furtive glances at him, tells of a handsome young dragoon with whom she has fallen in love.

'He is not a captain, nor even a lieutenant—only a corporal. But he will do what I ask—because he is in love with me!'

'I?—I love you?' José pauses beside her.

With a coquettish toss of the head and a significant glance she asks, 'Where is the flower I threw at you? What have you done with it?' Then, softly, she sings another alluring melody in typical Spanish dance measure, a *Seguidilla*, 'Près des remparts de Séville'.

Près des rem-parts de Sé - ville

'Carmen!' cries José, 'you have bewitched me'. . .

'Near by the ramparts of Seville' . . . 'And the dance with my lover I'll share!' she murmurs insinuatingly, and at the same time she holds back her bound wrists toward him. Quickly he undoes the knot, but leaves the rope about her wrists so that she still appears to be a captive, when the captain comes from the guard-house with the warrant. He is followed by the soldiers, and the crowd, drawn by curiosity to see Carmen led off to prison, again fills the square.

José places her between two dragoons, and the party starts for the bridge. When they reach the steps, Carmen quickly draws her hands free of the rope, shoves the soldiers aside, and, before they know what has happened, dashes up to the bridge and across it, tossing the rope down into the square as she disappears from sight, while the crowd, hindering pursuit by blocking the steps, jeers at the discomfited soldiers.

Act II.     The tavern of Lillas Pastia.

Frasquita, Mercédès, and Morales are with Carmen; also other officers, gypsies, etc. The officers are smoking. Two gypsies in a corner play the guitar and two others dance. Carmen looks at them. Zuniga speaks to her; she does not listen to him, but suddenly rises and sings, 'Les tringles des sistres tintaient' (Ah, when of gay guitars the sound).

Frasquita and Mercédès join in the 'Tra la la la' of the refrain. While Carmen clicks the castanets, the dance, in which she and others have joined the two gypsies, becomes more rapid and violent.

There are shouts outside, 'Long live the torero! Long live Escamillo!' The famous bull-fighter, the victor of the bull ring at Granada, is approaching. He sings the famous 'Couplets du Toréador', a rousing song with refrain and chorus. 'Votre toast

je peux vous le rendre' (To your toast I drink with pleasure)
begins the number. The refrain, with chorus, is 'Toréador, en
garde' (Toreador, e'er watchful be).

Tor - e - a - dor    en    gar - - de

Escamillo's debonair manner, his glittering uniform, his reputation for prowess, make him a brilliant and striking figure. In
his turn he is much struck with Carmen. She is impressed by him,
but her fancy is still for the handsome dragoon, who has been
under arrest since he allowed her to escape, and has been freed
only that day. The Toreador, followed by the crowd, which
includes Zuniga, departs.

It is late. The tavern keeper closes the shutters and leaves the
room. Carmen, Frasquita, and Mercédès are quickly joined by
the smugglers, El Dancairo and El Remendado. The men need
the aid of the three girls in wheedling the coastguard, and
possibly others, into neglect of duty. Their sentiments, 'En
matière de tromperie' (When it comes to a matter of cheating . . . let women in on the deal), are expressed in a quintet that
is full of spontaneous merriment—in fact, nowhere in *Carmen*,
not even in the most dramatic passages, is the music forced.

The men want the girls to depart with them at once. Carmen
insists on waiting for José. The men suggest that she win him
over to become one of their band. Not a bad idea, she thinks.
They leave it to her to carry out the plan.

Even now José is heard singing, as he approaches the tavern,
'Halte là! Qui va là? Dragon d'Alcala!' (Halt there! Who goes
there? Dragoon of Alcala!). He comes in. Soon she has made him
jealous by telling him that she was obliged to dance for Zuniga
and the officers. But now she will dance for him.

She begins to dance. His eyes are fastened on her. From the
distant barracks a bugle call is heard. It is the 'retreat', the
summons to quarters. The dance, the bugle call, which comes
nearer, passes by the lithe, swaying figure, the wholly obsessed
look of José. José starts to obey the summons to quarters.
Carmen taunts him with placing duty above his love for her. He
draws from his breast the flower she gave him, and, showing it

to her in proof of his passion, sings the famous 'La fleur que tu m'avais jetée' (The flower that once to me you gave).

La fleur que tu m'a-vais je - té - e

Carmen tries to persuade him to stay with her and later join the band, 'Là-bas, là-bas, dans la montagne', but he hesitates to become a deserter and follow her to the mountains. At that moment Zuniga, thinking to find Carmen alone, bursts open the tavern door. There is an angry scene between Zuniga and José. They draw their sabres. The whole band of smugglers comes in at Carmen's call. El Dancairo and El Remendado cover Zuniga with their pistols, and lead him off.

'And you? Will you now come with us?' asks Carmen of Don José.

He, a corporal who has drawn his sabre against an officer, an act of insubordination for which severe punishment awaits him, has no choice left but to follow his temptress to the mountains.

Act III.    A rocky and picturesque spot among rocks on a mountain. At the rising of the curtain there is complete solitude. After a few moments a smuggler appears on the summit of a rock, then two, then the whole band, descending and scrambling down the mass of rocks. Among them are Carmen, Don José, El Dancairo, El Remendado, Frasquita, and Mercédès.

The opening chorus has a peculiarly attractive lilt.

Don José is unhappy. Carmen's absorbing passion for him has been of brief duration. A creature of impulse, she is fickle and wayward. Don José, a soldier bred, but now a deserter, is ill at ease among the smugglers, and finds cause to reproach himself for sacrificing everything to a fierce and capricious beauty, in whose veins courses the blood of a lawless race. Yet he still loves her to distraction, and is insanely jealous of her—for which she gives him ample cause. It is quite apparent that the impression made upon her by Escamillo is deepening. Escamillo has been caught in the lure of her dangerous beauty, but he does not risk annoying her by sulking in her presence, like Don José, but goes on adding to his laurels by winning fresh victories in the bull ring.

Now that Don José is more than usually morose, she says, with a sarcastic inflection in her voice: 'If you don't like our mode of life here, why don't you leave?' 'And go far from you! Carmen! If you say that again, it will be your death!' He half draws his knife from his belt.

With a shrug of her shoulders Carmen replies: 'What matter —I shall die as fate wills'. And, indeed, she plays with fate as with men's hearts. For whatever else this gypsy may be, she is fearless.

While Don José wanders moodily about the camp, she joins Frasquita and Mercédès, who are telling their fortunes by cards. The superstitious creatures are merry because the cards favour them. Carmen takes the pack and draws.

'Spades!—A grave!' she mutters darkly, and for a moment it seems as if she is drawing back from a shadow that has crossed her path. But the bravado of the fatalist does not long desert her.

'What matters it?' she calls to the two girls. 'If you are to die, try the cards a hundred times, they will fall the same—spades, a grave!' Then, glancing in the direction where Don José stands, she adds, in a low voice, 'First I, then he!'

The Card Trio, 'Mélons! Coupons!' (Shuffle! Throw!) is a brilliant passage of the score, broken in upon by Carmen's fatalistic soliloquy: 'En vain pour éviter'.

A moment later, when the leader of the smugglers announces that it is an opportune time to attempt to convey their contraband through the mountain pass, she is all on the alert and aids in making ready for the departure. Don José is posted behind a screen of rocks above the camp, to guard against a surprise from the rear, while the smugglers make their way through the pass.

Unseen by him, a guide comes out on the rocks, and, making a gesture in the direction of the camp, hastily withdraws. Into this wild passage of nature, where desperate characters but a few moments before were encamped, and where Carmen had darkly hinted at fate, there descends Micaela, the emblem of sweetness and purity in this tragedy of the passions. She is seeking Don José, in hopes of reclaiming him. Her romance, 'Je dis que rien ne m'épouvante' (I try not to own that I tremble), is characterised by Mr. Upton as 'the most effective and beautiful number in the whole work'—a verdict that is a trifle unkind to Carmen and Don José, and might not have pleased Bizet. The introduction

for horns is an exquisite passage, and the expectations it awakens
are fully met by the melodious measures of the romance.

Je dis    que rien ne m'é-pou-vante

Having looked about her, and failing to find Don José, she
withdraws. Meanwhile Don José, from the place where he stands
guard, has caught sight of a man approaching the camp. A shot
rings out; it is Don José who has fired at the man coming up
the defile. He is about to fire again, but the nonchalant manner
in which the stranger comes on, and, waving his hat, calls out,
'An inch lower and it would have been all over with me!' causes
him to lower his gun and advance to meet him.

'I am Escamillo and I am here to see Carmen,' he says gaily.
'She had a lover here, a dragoon, who deserted from his troop
for her. She adored him, but that, I understand, is all over with
now. The loves of Carmen never last long.'

'Slowly, my friend,' replies Don José. 'Before anyone can
take our gypsy girls away, he must pay the price.'

'So, so. And what is it?'

'It is paid with the knife,' grimly answers José, as he draws
his blade.

'Ah,' laughs the Toreador, 'then you are the dragoon of whom
Carmen has wearied. I am in luck to have met you so soon.'

He, too, draws. The knives clash, as the men, the one a soldier,
the other a bullfighter, skilfully thrust and parry. But Don José's
is the better weapon, for, as he catches one of Escamillo's thrusts
on his blade, the Toreador's knife snaps short. It would be a
fatal mishap for Escamillo, did not at that moment the gypsies
and smugglers, recalled by the shot, hurry in and separate the
combatants. Unruffled by his misadventure, especially as his
ardent glances meet an answering gleam in Carmen's eyes, the
Toreador invites the entire band to the coming bullfight in
Seville, in which he is to figure. With a glad shout they accept.

'Don't be angry, dragoon', he adds tauntingly. 'We may meet
again.'

For answer Don José seeks to rush at him, but some of the
smugglers hold him back, while the Toreador leisurely goes his
way.

The smugglers make ready to depart again. One of them, however, spies Micaela. She is led down. Don José is reluctant to comply with her pleas to go away with her. The fact that Carmen urges him to do what the girl says only arouses his jealousy. He bursts out tragically that he will not leave her, should his refusal cost him his life. This is one of the most dramatic moments of the whole score.

*Dût il m'en coûter la vi-e, Non, Carmen, je ne parti-rai pas!*

But when at last Micaela tells him that his mother is dying of a broken heart for him, he makes ready to go.

In the distance Escamillo is heard singing the refrain of his song. Carmen listens, as if enraptured, and starts to run after him. Don José with bared knife bars the way; then leaves with Micaela.

Act IV.    A square in Seville. At the back the entrance to the arena. It is the day of the bullfight. The square is animated. Watersellers, others with oranges, fans, and other articles. Chorus. Ballet.

Gay the crowd that fills the square outside the arena where the bullfights are held. It cheers the first strains of music heard as the festival procession approaches, and it shouts and applauds as the various divisions go by and pass into the arena: 'The Aguacil on horseback!'—'The chulos with their pretty little flags!' —'Look! The bandilleros, all clad in green and spangles, and waving the crimson cloths!'—'The picadors with the pointed lances!'—'The cuadrilla of toreros!'—'Now! Vivo, vivo! Escamillo!' And a great shout goes up, as the Toreador enters, with Carmen on his arm.

There is a brief but beautiful duet for Escamillo and Carmen, 'Si tu m'aimes, Carmen' (If you love me, Carmen), before he goes into the building to make ready for the bullfight, while she waits to be joined by some of the smugglers and gypsies, whom Escamillo has invited to be witnesses, with her, of his prowess.

As the Alcade crosses the square and enters the arena, and the crowd pours in after him, one of the gypsy girls from the smugglers' band whispers to Carmen:

'If you value your life, Carmen, don't stay here. He is lurking in the crowd and watching you.'

'He?—José?—I am no coward.—I fear no one.—If he is here, we will have it over with now,' she answers, defiantly, motioning to the girl to pass on into the arena into which the square is rapidly emptying itself. Carmen lingers until she is the only one left, then, with a shrug of contempt, turns to enter—but finds herself facing Don José, who has slunk out from one of the side streets to intercept her.

'I was told you were here. I was even warned to leave here, because my life was in danger. If the hour has come, well, so be it. But, live or die, yours I shall never be again.'

Her speech is abrupt, rapid, but there is no tremor of fear in her voice.

Don José is pale and haggard. His eyes are hollow, but they glow with a dangerous light. His plight has passed from the pitiable to the desperate stage.

'Carmen,' he says hoarsely, 'leave with me. Begin life over again with me under another sky. I will adore you so, it will make you love me.'

'You never can make me love you again. No one can *make* me do anything. Free I was born, free I die.'

The band in the arena strikes up a fanfare. There are loud vivos for Escamillo. Carmen starts to rush for the entrance. Driven to the fury of despair, his knife drawn, as it had been when he barred her way in the smugglers' camp, Don José confronts her. He laughs grimly.

'The man for whom they are shouting—he is the one for whom you have deserted me!'

'Let me pass!' is her defiant answer.

'That you may tell him how you have spurned me, and laugh with him over my misery!'

Again the crowd in the arena shouts: 'Victory! Victory! Vivo, vivo, Escamillo, the toreador of Granada!'

A cry of triumph escapes Carmen.

'You love him!' hisses Don José.

'Yes, I love him! If I must die for it, I love him! Victory for Escamillo, victory! I go to the victor of the arena!'

She makes a dash for the entrance. Somehow she manages to get past the desperate man who has stood between her and the gates. She reaches the steps, her foot already touches the landing above them, when he overtakes her, and madly plunges his knife into her back. With a shriek heard above the shouts of the crowd within, she staggers, falls, and rolls lifeless down the steps into the square.

The doors of the arena swing open. Acclaiming the prowess of Escamillo, out pours the crowd, suddenly to halt, hushed and horror-stricken, at the body of a woman dead at the foot of the steps.

'I am your prisoner,' says Don José to an officer. 'I killed her.' Then, throwing himself over the body, he cries: 'O Carmen, my beloved Carmen!'

At its production at the Opéra-Comique, *Carmen* was a failure. In view of the world-wide popularity the work was to achieve, that failure has become historic. It had, however, one lamentable result, in that it was a contributory cause of Bizet's death exactly three months after the production, and before he could have had so much as an inkling of the success *Carmen* was to obtain. It was not until four months after his death that the opera, produced in Vienna, celebrated its first triumph. Then came Brussels, London, New York. At last, in 1883, *Carmen* was brought back to Paris for what Pierre Berton calls 'the brilliant reparation'. But Bizet, seriously ill with *angina pectoris*, and mortally wounded in his pride as an artist, had died disconsolate. The 'reparation' was to the public, not to him.

Whoever will take the trouble to read extracts from the reviews in the Paris press of the first performance of *Carmen* will find that the score of this opera, so full of well rounded, individual, and distinctive melodies—ensemble, concerted, and solo—was considered too Wagnerian. More than one trace of this curious attitude toward an opera, in which the melodies crowd upon each other almost as closely as in *Il Trovatore*, and certainly are as numerous as in *Aida*, were still to be found in the article on *Carmen* in the *Dictionnaire des Opéras*, one of the most unsatisfactory essays in that work. Nor, speaking with the authority of Berton, who saw the second performance, was the failure due to defects in the cast. He speaks of Galli-Marié (Carmen), Chapuis (Micaela), Lhérie (Don José), and Bouhy (Escamillo), as 'equal to their tasks . . . an admirable quartet'.

America has had its Carmen periods. Minnie Hauck established an individuality in the rôle, which remained potent until the appearance of Calvé. When Grau wanted to fill the house, all he had to do was to announce Calvé as Carmen. She so dominated the character with her beauty, charm, *diablerie*, and vocal art that, after she left the Metropolitan Opera House, it became impossible to revive the opera there with success, until Farrar made her appearance in it, November 19, 1914, with Alda as Micaela, Caruso as Don José, and Amato as Escamillo.

A season or two before Oscar Hammerstein gave *Carmen* at the Manhattan Opera House, a French company, which was on its last legs when it struck New York, appeared in a performance of *Carmen* at the Casino, and the next day went into bankruptcy. The Carmen was Bressler-Gianoli. Her interpretation brought out the coarse fibre in the character, and was so much the opposite of Calvé's that it was interesting by contrast. It seemed that had the company been able to survive, *Carmen* could have been featured in its repertory, by reason of Bressler-Gianoli's grasp of the character as Mérimée had drawn it in his novel, where Carmen is a much coarser personality than in the opera. The day after the performance I went to see Heinrich Conried, then director of the Metropolitan Opera House, and told him of the impression she had made, but he did not engage her. The Carmen of Bressler-Gianoli (with Dalmores, Trentini, Ancona, and Gilibert) was one of the principal successes of the Manhattan Opera House. It was first given December 14, 1906, and scored the record for the season with nineteen performances, *Aida* coming next with twelve, and *Rigoletto* with eleven.

Mary Garden's Carmen was distinctive and highly individualised on the acting side. It lacked however the lusciousness of voice, the vocal allure, that a singer must lavish upon the rôle to make it a complete success.

One of the curiosities of opera in America was the appearance at the Metropolitan Opera House, November 25, 1885, of Lilli Lehmann as Carmen.

A word is due to Bizet's authors for the admirable libretto they have made from Mérimée's novel. The character of Carmen is, of course, the creation of the novelist. But in his book the Toreador is not introduced until almost the very end, and is but one of a succession of lovers whom Carmen has had since she ensnared Don José. In the opera the Toreador is made a principal character, and figures prominently from the second act on. Micaela, so essential for contrast in the opera, both as regards plot and music, is a creation of the librettists. But their masterstroke is the placing of the scene of the murder just outside the arena where the bullfight is in progress, and in having Carmen killed by Don José at the moment Escamillo is acclaimed victor by the crowd within. In the book he slays her on a lonely road outside the city of Cordova the day after the bullfight.   K.

# JACQUES OFFENBACH

## (1819–1880)

### ORPHÉE AUX ENFERS
#### Orpheus in the Underworld

OPERA in two acts by Jacques Offenbach, text by Hector Cremieux and Halévy. Première at the Bouffes Parisiens, October 21, 1858, with Mme. Tautin, MM. Leonce, Tayau, Désiré. First performed New York, 1861 (in German); London, Haymarket Theatre, 1865; St. James's Theatre, London, 1869, with Hortense Schneider.

### CHARACTERS

Pluton, *god of the underworld; appearing on earth
under name of* Aristée .......................... Tenor
Jupiter, *king of the gods* ...................... Baritone
Orphée, *a violinist* ............................ Tenor
John Styx, *a fool* .............................. Baritone
Mercure ......................................... Tenor
Bacchus ......................................... Speaking rôle
Mars ............................................ Bass
Morphée ......................................... Tenor
Eurydice, *Orphée's wife* ........................ Soprano
Diane ........................................... Soprano
L'Opinion Publique ...................... Mezzo-Soprano
Vénus ........................................... Contralto
Cupidon ......................................... Soprano
Junon ........................................... Mezzo-Soprano
Minerve ......................................... Soprano

Offenbach's parody of the story of Orpheus originally obtained something of a *succés de scandale*; he was accused of blaspheming antiquity, and of satirising the government and prevailing social conditions. Since he was at the time in rather trying financial straits as manager of the Bouffes Parisiens, success in whatever form it came was by no means unwelcome. History suggests that the rôle of John Styx was an afterthought and designed especially for the actor Bache, an excellent musician who had just left the Comédie Française. At a revival of *Orphée* (1867), the notorious

courtesan Cora Pearl sang Cupid, relinquishing the rôle however after only twelve days. On this occasion, Madame Ugalde,
later the first Nicklausse, was Eurydice.

The overture as we know it from concert performances is not
by a long chalk what Offenbach designed to precede his opera,
but was compiled by a certain Carl Binder for the first performance in Vienna; he made use of the overture which Offenbach
wrote (an introduction, minuet, and embryonic canon) and added
to it the famous violin solo and the Can-Can.

Act I. First tableau. Public Opinion introduces the characters.
Eurydice sings lightly and prettily of the extra-marital love she
feels in her heart, while the flutes bill and coo around the vocal
line: 'La femme dont le cœur rêve, N'a pas de sommeil'. Orpheus
sees her with flowers in her hand; who are they for? It appears
that each has lost his or her heart to someone else, and neither
intends to renounce the new-found love in favour of connubial
bliss. They quarrel and it transpires that Eurydice has a morbid
dislike of Orpheus as an artist, hating his fiddle-playing above
everything. This is the crowning insult. Orpheus announces he
will play for her his latest violin concerto (it lasts one and a quarter
hours, he says), and the famous violin tune starts. The duet which
it initiates is charming, and it is not long before the fiddle tune
influences the vocal parts.

Eurydice's lover is Pluto, who appears on earth in the guise of
a shepherd and bee-keeper under the name of Aristée. He charms
Eurydice with a Chanson Pastorale, but admits to her that love
for him involves transporting her to the underworld. She says
good-bye to life most attractively, and leaves a note behind for
Orpheus, telling him that she is dead. This he finds, but his discreet rejoicings are broken in upon by Public Opinion, who
threatens him with scandal if he does not follow his wife to
Hades; the fact that he does not want to get her back means that
his reclamatory action will be even more virtuous than if he did.
They start off on their journey, Orpheus complaining at the way
he is treated, Public Opinion urging him on in a delightful
*marziale* duettino.

The scene changes to Mount Olympus, where the gods are
sleeping peacefully. They introduce themselves one by one, Cupid
being followed by Venus, a wordless chorus dividing their verses.
Jupiter is woken up by Diana's horn. Diana is unhappy, and

admits it is because she could not that morning any longer find Actaeon on earth in his accustomed place. Jupiter reveals that he took it upon himself to change Actaeon into a stag, as he was worried that Diana seemed to be compromising herself rather badly with him. All the gods complain about Jupiter's high-handed, tyrannical ways, but they are interrupted when news comes that Eurydice has arrived amongst them. Pluto makes his entrance and is rebuked by Jupiter for having carried off the delightful Eurydice. He defends himself, and soon the gods join in chorus and announce that they are rebelling against the intolerable domination of Jupiter—to say nothing of the eternal monotony of their diet of nectar and ambrosia. In turn, Minerva, Cupid, Venus, and Diana remind Jupiter of the disguises he has in the past assumed for his earthly amours, and, in charming and witty 'Couplets', they mock him for his obvious interest in the case of Eurydice: 'Ne prends plus l'air patelin, on te connait Jupin'. Pluto adds insult to injury by saying that in his view the disguises were only necessary because Jupiter was so villainously ugly that he would have got nowhere with the girls without them.

At this juncture, Orpheus and Public Opinion are announced, and Jupiter exhorts the gods to be on their best behaviour when he gives audience to the strangers. Pluto leads off the finale to the first act and continues to deny that he has had anything to do with hiding Eurydice. Orpheus starts to ask for Eurydice back, but he has only sung the first phrase of 'J'ai perdu mon Eurydice' when the gods and goddesses take up the tune and sing it for him; his demands are obviously granted in advance, since the appeal of his song has penetrated even to Mount Olympus. Much to Orpheus's dismay, Jupiter orders Pluto to return Eurydice to her husband, and says that he will himself come down to Hades to look for her. Won't he take them too, please, ask the other gods and goddesses, and, when he grants their request, they all join in a hymn of praise which soon becomes a gay gallop tune.

Act II. Tableau iii. An excellent *allegretto* entr'acte introduces the scene in the underworld. Eurydice is being looked after by John Styx, a complete fool on earth and now charged with prison duties in Hades. In a song, with an enchantingly silly melody, he explains that he was once king of Boeotia: 'Quand j'étais roi de Béotie'. Once he is out of the way, Jupiter comes looking for Eurydice, in whom he is considerably interested. He disguises himself as a fly, and imitates its buzzing. Eurydice quickly takes a liking to the fly ('Belle insecte à l'aile dorée'), and they sing and buzz a duet together. At the end, Jupiter in his own voice rejoices at the capture that he seems to have made, and he eventually admits his identity. The scene ends as John Styx repeats his song and is mocked and imitated by Pluto.

Tableau iv.    A splendid *Chœur infernal* opens the scene. Eurydice has by now been turned by Jupiter into a Bacchante, and she is persuaded by Cupid to sing a Bacchic Hymn for their delight. Jupiter proposes a minuet, and all comment on his admirable dancing of it. Then begins the famous Can-Can tune, probably the best-known piece in the opera. Jupiter is about to go off with Eurydice when Pluto stops him, just at the moment when they can hear the sound of Orpheus's fiddle playing 'J'ai perdu mon Eurydice' for all it is worth. He is warned that he must walk in front of his wife, and that even to glance back at her will lead to a revoking of his permission to take her back with him to earth. Public Opinion urges him to obey the god's injunction, but Jupiter has an unexpected card up his sleeve; he hurls a thunderbolt and the noise gives Orpheus such a shock that he involuntarily looks round to see what made it, and so forfeits his right to his bride. Everyone is delighted, Eurydice stays on as a Bacchante, and all join in a final version of the Can-Can to express their pleasure at the turn events have taken.

It is a little hard to explain why in England Johann Strauss is so very much more popular than Offenbach. Is it that the touch of sentimentality which is to be found in almost all Strauss's tunes, even the best, is almost completely absent from Offenbach's, at any rate until the time of the *Barcarolle*? Or is Offenbach's satire too pointedly local for revival almost a hundred years after its time? It is difficult to give a conclusive answer; Offenbach wrote startlingly good comic music, full of excellent tunes and humorous invention, and it seems likely to please almost anyone who is at all interested in the best sort of 'light' music (what else can one call it?). *Orphée* itself is a most accomplished and stylish bit of fooling, at its broadest in the spoofing of Gluck's 'J'ai perdu mon Eurydice', at its most hilarious and catching in the famous Can-Can.

H.

# LES CONTES D'HOFFMANN
## The Tales of Hoffmann

Opera in three acts by Jacques Offenbach, text by Barbier. Première Opéra-Comique, Paris, February 10, 1881, with Adèle Isaac (Stella, Olympia, Giulietta, Antonia), Talazac, Taskin. First performed New York, 1882; London, Adelphi Theatre, 1907; His Majesty's, 1910; Covent Garden, 1910, with Teyte, Nevada, de Lussan, Hyde, conductor Beecham; Metropolitan, New York, 1913, with Hempel, Fremstad, Bori, Macnez, Gilly, conductor Polacco. Revived Metropolitan, 1924, with Morgana, Bori, Fleta, de Luca; Covent Garden, 1936, with Andreva, Delprat, Dino Borgioli, Pinza, conductor Beecham; Florence Festival, 1938, with Menotti, Favero, Novotna, Lomanto, Ghirardini, conductor Gui; Metropolitan 1943, with Munsel, Djanel, Novotna, Jobin, Pinza, Singher, conductor Beecham; Vienna State Opera, 1947, with Lipp, Welitsch, Jurinac, Patzak, Schöffler.

## CHARACTERS

Lindorf, *a councillor of Nuremberg* .................Bass[1]

Andrès, *servant of Stella* ........................Tenor

Hermann, *a student* ...........................Baritone

Nathanael, *a student* ...........................Tenor

Luther, *an innkeeper* ...........................Bass

Hoffmann, *a poet* .............................Tenor

Nicklausse, *his companion* ...............Mezzo-Soprano

Spalanzani, *an inventor* ........................Tenor

Cochenille, *his servant* ........................Tenor

Coppelius, *a scientist and rival of Spalanzani* ......Baritone[1]

Olympia, *a mechanical doll* ....................Soprano

Giulietta, *a courtesan* ........................Soprano

Schlemil, *her lover* .............................Bass

Dapertutto, *a sorcerer* ........................Baritone[1]

Pittichinaccio, *an admirer of Giulietta* ..............Tenor

Antonia, *a singer* ...........................Soprano

Crespel, *her father, a councillor of Munich* ........Baritone

Frantz, *his servant* .............................Tenor

Dr. Miracle, *a doctor* ........................Baritone[1]

The voice of Antonia's mother............Mezzo-Soprano

Stella, *an opera singer* .........................Soprano

The Muse of Poetry ...........................Soprano

*Time:* Nineteenth Century     *Place:* Nuremberg, Venice, Munich

Offenbach died before he had finished *Les Contes d'Hoffmann,*

[1] In performance, it is customary for the incarnations of Hoffmann's evil genius (Lindorf, Coppelius, Dapertutto and Dr. Miracle) to be undertaken by the same singer.

and it was orchestrated by Ernest Guiraud. It was Offenbach's most ambitious work.

Prologue.    Luther's Tavern in Nuremberg, situated next door to the opera house, where a performance of *Don Giovanni* is in progress. A drinking chorus can be heard off-stage. Lindorf comes in with Andrès, the servant of the prima donna Stella, who is singing in *Don Giovanni*. Lindorf obtains from him a letter his mistress has written to Hoffmann, making an assignation for that evening, and enclosing the key of her room. Lindorf, who assumes during the course of the opera and in various forms the rôle of Hoffmann's evil genius, in an aria exults over his prospective victim. A crowd of students enter the tavern and immediately start to celebrate the prospect of the beer which Luther brings them.

Enter Hoffmann, with Nicklausse. They sit down with the students, and Nicklausse, with obvious ironical intent, starts to hum 'Notte e giorno faticar' from the act of *Don Giovanni* they have just been listening to. Hoffmann seems out of humour, and it appears that he is haunted by the sight of Stella, with whom he was once in love. He is prevailed upon to sing a song to the assembled company, and strikes up the Legend of Kleinzack ('Il était une fois à la cour d'Eisenach'). With the chorus echoing his phrases, he goes briskly through the description of the little dwarf whose knees clicked together as he walked, but when he comes to describe his face, suddenly falls into a reverie and instead starts to rhapsodise on the features of his lady-love. He is interrupted, recovers himself, and finishes the song he began.

Hoffmann and the students complain about the quality of Luther's beer, and a punch bowl is brought and duly greeted with song. Hoffmann is by no means pleased to see Lindorf, whom he refers to as haunting his steps and bringing him bad luck. He offers to tell the story of the three great loves of his life, and, in spite of Luther's warning that the curtain is going up on the second act of *Don Giovanni*, all present announce their intention of staying behind to listen. The first, says Hoffmann, was called Olympia.

Act I (Olympia) is introduced by a mocking minuet. When the curtain goes up, we are in Spalanzani's room. He is waiting for the arrival of guests who have been invited to witness the astonishing feats of which his performing doll, Olympia, is capable. Spalanzani mutters about the fortune he hopes to make from his invention, which will recoup him for the loss he suffered when Elias the banker went broke. If only his rival Coppelius does not try to claim a share of the proceeds.

Hoffmann appears, and is immediately impressed by Olympia, whom he takes for Spalanzani's daughter. He sings ardently to her of his love. His aria, 'Ah, vivre deux', is one of the loveliest expressions of his romantic spirit which is to be found in the whole opera. Nicklausse is not at all surprised to find his master in his usual love-lorn condition, but comments ironically on the improbable nature of the new object of his affections—a mechanical doll indeed!

Coppelius comes in and observes Hoffmann gazing fatuously at the doll. He tries to interest him in his own invention: eyes and spectacles to suit every requirement. 'J'ai des yeux' he sings as he shows off his wares. We may guess that the pair he sells to Hoffmann are rose-tinted; at any rate, they seem to increase his delight in beholding Olympia. Spalanzani sees Coppelius, and is forced to acknowledge the latter's share in Olympia; he supplied her eyes, in consideration of which Spalanzani makes him out a bond for five hundred crowns—payable at the bank of Elias.

The guests start to arrive. To the familiar tune of the minuet, they thank Spalanzani for his hospitality. He produces Olympia, whom he describes as his daughter, for their admiration, and accompanies her on the harp while she sings her famous Doll's song to the assembled company: 'Les oiseaux dans la charmille'. The music perfectly imitates the automaton-like delivery that one might expect from a mechanical toy, and in between whiles Spalanzani winds up the spring which brings his 'daughter' to life. She extends her hand to the guests who crowd round to congratulate her, and is left alone with Hoffmann while the others go in to supper. He sings to her, but, when he touches her shoulder, she suddenly rises from the sofa and goes quickly across the room, brushing through the curtains which divide her room from the main part of the house. Hoffmann follows her, in spite of Nicklausse's warning that Olympia is a lifeless doll.

Coppelius returns having found out that he has been cheated by his rival. The dance begins again, and Hoffmann waltzes with Olympia, who, once she is wound up, goes faster and faster so that the other guests wonder if they can save Hoffmann from breaking his neck. When Spalanzani finally manages to catch up

with the doll and stop her, she breaks out into coloratura gyra-
tions over the top of the chorus. Olympia is put away in her
room, and all bend over to see what damage has been done to
the exhausted Hoffmann. Suddenly, the noise of smashing
machinery is heard. Coppelius emerges from Olympia's room,
laughing with triumph, and Hoffmann is left disillusioned at the
discovery that his beloved was only a doll.

Act II (Giulietta).   Venice. The decorated gallery of a palace
overlooking the Grand Canal. The guests of Giulietta are grouped
around, and some of them lie on the sofas. Nicklausse and
Giulietta in a gondola sing the famous Barcarolle, 'Belle nuit, ô
nuit d'amour', one of the world's most popular operatic tunes.

Hoffmann objects to its melancholy strains, and responds with
a lively song, whose refrain is taken up by the chorus. Giulietta
introduces her guests and takes them off for a game of cards,
Nicklausse taking the opportunity of telling Hoffmann that he
means to take him away the moment he shows the least sign of
falling in love with Giulietta. Hoffmann swears that he will not
succumb to her charms—may his soul be forfeit to the devil if
he does!

Dapertutto watches him and, when he has gone out, produces
a great diamond, with which, he says, he will persuade Giulietta
to capture the soul of Hoffmann for him as she has done with that
of Schlemil. They have only to look into his magic mirror, and
their souls stay with their reflections. He is given a powerful aria,
'Scintille diamant', which admirably displays a strong bass voice.

Giulietta agrees to do Dapertutto's command, and upbraids
Hoffmann for wishing to leave just because he has lost his money
gambling. Hoffmann is quite unable to resist her, and he sings
lovingly of the passion which overwhelms him in her presence:
'O dieu de quelle ivresse'. Like his song to Olympia, this is lyrical
expression of a high order.

O Dieu de quelle i - vresse em - brasses-tu mon â - me

There is an ecstatic duet for them, 'Si ta présençe m'est ravie',
during whose course she obtains the reflection which Dapertutto
covets. Then, Schlemil rushes in and furiously denounces
Giulietta's unfaithfulness. Hoffmann discovers that he has no

reflection when he looks into a mirror, but still he will not leave Giulietta, whom he loves madly, he says. A septet begins, in which Hoffmann declares his love, Dapertutto and Pittichinaccio their contempt for the poet; Giulietta admits that she found the diamond irresistible, Schlemil furiously anticipates revenge, and Nicklausse and the chorus look with pity at Hoffmann's predicament.

Giulietta saves the situation by suggesting an excursion on the canal, but Hoffmann and Schlemil fight, the former, using Dapertutto's sword, succeeding in killing his rival and removing from a chain round his neck the key of Giulietta's room. The sound of the Barcarolle can be heard, but, when Hoffmann rushes away to find his Giulietta, it is to see her float away in the gondola, in the arms of Pittichinaccio.

Act III (Antonia). Munich; a room in Crespel's house. Antonia, his daughter, sits singing: 'Elle a fui, la tourterelle'. Crespel comes into the room, and is distressed to find his daughter in a fainting condition. She has broken her promise not to sing, but she says it was the sight of her mother's portrait that prompted her to it. Crespel has already seen signs of the consumption which carried away her mother, and he blames her overwrought condition on Hoffmann, to escape whose attentions he has brought her to Munich. Crespel shouts for his deaf old servant Frantz, to whom he gives orders that no one is to be admitted to the house on any pretext whatsoever. When he is alone, Frantz protests that his crotchety master would make his life a misery were it not for the consolation he gets from his singing and dancing, both of which he does well, he says. After demonstrating the questionable truth of both of these assertions, he falls exhausted into a chair, from which Hoffmann, who comes through the door with Nicklausse, at last manages to rouse him.

Hoffmann looks at the song which is lying open on the harpsichord, and has just begun to sing it when Antonia appears. After an impassioned duet, Antonia hears her father coming, and Hoffmann hides as she leaves the room. Crespel comes in, wishes Hoffmann to the devil, but transfers his spleen to Dr. Miracle, when Frantz tells him the doctor is at the door. He tries to have him kept outside but is too late, and with a burst of laughter, Miracle enters. Hoffmann from hiding sees Miracle's preparations to treat Antonia, and recognises that he is evil; Crespel is in despair at not being able to get rid of the man who, he is certain, killed his wife and means to kill his daughter as well. Although she has not yet appeared, Miracle pretends to feel Antonia's pulse and announces his worry at its irregular movement. In response to his command, she sings a brilliant flourish from her room, but still does not appear. Crespel begs Miracle to leave her alone, but he insists that he can cure Antonia, if he is allowed to try.

Hoffmann is alone, but is soon joined by Antonia, whom he tries to persuade to renounce her singing for the sake of her health and their love. She agrees, but no sooner is Hoffmann safely out of the way than Dr. Miracle is back, pouring temptation into her ear. Can she bear to waste such talent by silencing her voice for ever? Before long, Antonia hears the voice of her mother calling upon her to sing; the portrait glows with life, and Miracle says that he is only there to cause her to give effect to her mother's dearest wish. There is a splendid trio, during whose course Miracle seizes a violin from the walls and plays wildly on it. Antonia's voice rises higher and higher until she falls dying to the ground. Miracle disappears, and Crespel rushes in to hear his daughter's last words. When Hoffmann comes in, Crespel blames him for Antonia's death. Hoffmann wants to call a doctor, but, in answer to his summons, Miracle appears.

There is an intermezzo based on the Barcarolle, and in the epilogue we are back in Luther's tavern. Hoffmann's story is finished; so too is the performance of *Don Giovanni* in which Stella has been taking part. She is doubtless, as Nicklausse observes, the personification of the three types of womanhood that Hoffmann has idealised in his stories. But Hoffmann is too drunk to care—Lindorf is perfectly confident on that score—and, as the students eddy round him singing the drinking song from the prologue, the Muse of Poetry appears by his side claiming him for her own. Hoffmann seems to be in a stupor. As Lindorf leads Stella from the room, she turns and throws a flower from her bouquet to him. He looks blankly in her direction. There is no doubt that he is dead drunk.

*Les Contes d'Hoffmann* was conceived with the Giulietta episode as Act III (i.e. following the Antonia scene), and certain revivals have taken account of this. The foregoing synopsis therefore may vary in different presentations; but in essence Offenbach's glorification of the romantic spirit of love—and his long-established habit of laughing at his own theme—will be as enumerated above.   H.

# SAINT-SAENS

(1835–1921)

## SAMSON ET DALILA

OPERA in three acts by Camille Saint-Saens, text by Ferdinand Lemaire. Première at the Hoftheater, Weimar, December 2, 1877, with Müller, Ferenczy, Milde, conductor Lassen. First performed in France, Rouen, 1890, with Bossy; Paris, Eden Theatre, 1890, with Bloch, Talazac, Bouhy; Opéra, Paris, 1892, with Deschamps-Jéhin, Vergnet, Lassalle, Fournets, conductor Colonne; Covent Garden, 1893 (concert); Metropolitan, 1895, with Mantelli, Tamagno, Campanari, Plançon, conductor Mancinelli. Revived Covent Garden, 1909, with Kirkby Lunn, Fontaine; Metropolitan, 1915, with Matzenauer, Caruso, Amato; Berlin, 1929, with Onegin, Oehmann; Sadler's Wells, 1932, with Willis, Cox; la Scala, Milan, 1936, with Stignani, Merli, Beuf, conductor de Sabata; Metropolitan, 1936, with Wettergren, Maison, Pinza, 1940 with Stevens; la Scala, Milan, 1947, with Stignani, Tasso, 1950 with Barbieri, Vinay, conductor de Sabata.

### CHARACTERS

Dalila .................................. Mezzo-Soprano
Samson ...................................... Tenor
High Priest of Dagon ......................... Baritone
Abimelech, *satrap of Gaza* ....................... Bass
An old Hebrew ................................ Bass
The Philistines' Messenger ...................... Tenor

Hebrews, Philistines

*Time:* B.C.                                        *Place:* Gaza

Act I. Before the curtain rises we hear of the Philistines at Gaza forcing the Israelites to work. When the curtain is raised we see in the background the temple of Dagon, god of the Philistines. The Jews give voice to their despair, but Samson addresses them in an effort to rouse them from their depressed condition ('Arrêtez, ô mes frères', and 'L'as-tu donc oublié?'). At the third attempt, he succeeds to such effect that the new defiance in their voices attracts the attention of Abimelech, who comes in with his guards and pours scorn on the God who so signally fails to come to their aid in their plight. Samson slays Abimelech with the sword he has snatched from him and Israel's champion starts out to complete the work. Dagon's high priest may curse ('Maudite à jamais soit la race'), but the Philistines are not able to offer resistance to the onslaught of the enemy. Already the Hebrews are in a position to rejoice and gratefully praise God, when the Philistines' most seductive maidens, Dalila at their head, appear to do homage to the victorious Samson ('Je viens célébrer la victoire'). Of what use is the warning of an old Hebrew? The memory of the love which she gave him when 'the sun laughed, the spring awoke and kissed the ground', the sight of her ensnaring beauty, the tempting dances ensnare the champion anew. Dalila completes her victory in the seductive aria 'Printemps qui commence'.

Act II. The beautiful seductress waits in her house in the valley of Sorek for her victim. She summons love to her aid in a splendid aria, 'Amour, viens aider ma faiblesse', cast in the same voluptuous mould as the rest of her music. Dalila has never loved the enemy of her country, and she hates him since he left her. Thus, when the high priest comes to her, his exhortation to revenge is not needed, although it has the effect of strengthening her resolve to obtain from Samson the secret on which depends his superhuman strength.

Dalila begins to despair of his coming, but not long after she has gone into the house, he appears, torn by doubt and irresolution, and determined that he is only going to say farewell to Dalila. Her blandishments however gradually break down his resolve, and 'Mon cœur s'ouvre à ta voix' (the most famous number of the score) seems to leave him powerless in her hands. But he summons up reserves of resistance, and refuses to tell her his secret when she demands it of him. She rushes alone into her house, but after a further moment of indecision, Samson follows her in. There destiny is fulfilled. Dalila's cry of triumph summons the Philistines. Deprived of his hair, the betrayed champion is overcome.

Act III. In a dungeon the blinded giant languishes. But more tormenting than the corporal disgrace or the laments of his companions are the reproaches in his own breast. He sings 'Vois ma misère, hélas', and his voice mingles with the reproaches of the Hebrews, who blame him and his weakness for their plight. Now the doors rattle. Soldiers come in to drag him to the Philistines' celebration of their victory. The scene changes. In Dagon's temple the Philistine people are rejoicing. Bitter scorn is poured forth on Samson whom the high priest insultingly invites to sing a love song to Dalila. The false woman herself mocks the powerless man. A Bacchanale is danced. Samson prays to his God. Just once again may he have strength. And while the intoxication of the festival seizes on everybody, he has himself led between the two pillars which support the temple. He clasps them. A terrible crash—the fragments of the temple with a roar bury the Philistine people and their conqueror.                    K.W., H.

# LEO DÉLIBES
## (1836–1891)

### LAKMÉ

OPERA in three acts by Léo Délibes, text by Edmond Gondinet and Philippe Gille, after Pierre Loti's *Le Mariage de Loti*. Première at the Opéra-Comique, Paris, on April 14, 1883, with van Zandt, Frandin, Talazac, Barré, Cobalet, conductor Danbé. First performed London Gaiety Theatre, 1885, with van Zandt, Dupuy, Carroul, conductor Bevignani; New York, 1886, with Pauline L'Allemand; Metropolitan, 1891, with van Zandt, Montariol, Edouard de Reszke; Covent Garden, 1910, with Tetrazzini, McCormack, Edmund Burke. Revived Metropolitan, 1916, with Barrientos, Martinelli, Rothier; 1931, with Pons, Thill; 1938, with Pons, Jagel, Pinza; 1946, with Pons, Jobin, Vaghi, conductor Fourestier. Currently in the repertory of the Opéra-Comique.

### CHARACTERS

| | |
|---|---|
| Lakmé | Soprano |
| Mallika, *her slave* | Mezzo-Soprano |
| Ellen ⎫ *English ladies* | Soprano |
| Rose ⎭ | Soprano |
| Mistress Bentson, *their governess* | Mezzo-Soprano |
| Gérald, *an English officer* | Tenor |
| Nilakantha, *a Brahmin priest* | Bass-Baritone |
| Frédéric, *an English officer* | Baritone |
| Hadji, *servant of Nilakantha* | Tenor |

*Time:* Nineteenth Century          *Place:* India

**Act I.** Lakmé is the daughter of Nilakantha, a fanatical Brahmin priest. While he nurses his hatred of the British invader, who has forbidden him to practise his religion, his daughter and other devotees of his cult sing an invocation to the gods: 'Blanche Dourga, Pâle Silva, Puissant Ganeça'. Lakmé's vocal embroidery over the top of the chorus is full of coloratura work. Nilakantha goes to another gathering of the faithful, and leaves Lakmé alone with her companions in the idyllic garden which surrounds the temple he has built for the practice of his religion. Lakmé and Mallika sing together a most attractive barcarolle as they prepare to bathe in the stream: 'Dôme épais, le jasmin'. The rippling

theme of the music and the oriental beauty of the surroundings perfectly set the tone of the atmosphere in which Lakmé lives and moves.

Lakmé removes her jewellery, placing it on a stone bench, and she and Mallika get into a boat and are quickly lost to sight.

We are next introduced to the English figures of the opera, two army officers, a couple of young girls, and their ineffably comic governess, Mistress Bentson. They are all in varying degrees suspicious of the Orient and its mystery, which they profess to find very queer indeed. They break through the bamboo fence which surrounds the temple, and exclaim with delight at what they can see inside. Frédéric warns them that several of the flowers are poisonous (even some of those which are quite harmless in Europe); he also says that the hut belongs to a dangerous and implacable Brahmin, whose one delight is in his beautiful daughter. In a quintet they speculate on the feelings of such a girl, who is shut off by her priestly vocation from contact with the outside world: 'Quand une femme est si jolie'.

The women want a sketch done of Lakmé's jewels, and Gérald, who is something of an artist, says he will stay behind and do one, if they will go back to the town. Left alone, he is fascinated by the jewels, and he speculates on the beauty and youth of their owner. Gérald's aria, 'Fantaisie aux divins mensonges', is one of the gems of the score; in aptness, melodic freshness and unpretentious charm it is one of the most attractive arias in the French repertory.

Allegretto

Fan-tai-si - e aux di-vins men-son-ges,

Tu re-viens m'é-ga - rer en - cor.

He sees Lakmé and Mallika returning, and hides. Lakmé dismisses Mallika and wonders to herself why she should feel so oddly sad and happy at the same time: 'Pourquoi dans les grands bois'. She sees Gérald, and, filled with alarm, cries for help. But, when Mallika and Hadji come to her aid, she sends them off to look for her father. Alone with Gérald, she tells him that a word from her could have brought about his death; he must leave and forget he ever saw her. But Gérald is obviously infatuated, and he sings passionately of love: 'C'est le dieu de la jeunesse, c'est le dieu du printemps'. Lakmé's voice joins his, until the sound of her father returning brings her back to reality. She begs Gérald to leave, but as he disappears through the gap in the bamboo, Nilakantha appears, and cries for vengeance on whoever has dared profane his temple precincts.

Act II. The scene is a bazaar, with a pagoda in the background. The stage is crowded with soldiers, sailors, and tourists, who mingle with the street-sellers and natives. Mistress Bentson is surrounded by beggars and sellers, who, in the course of conversation, relieve her of her watch and handkerchief, before she is rescued by Frédéric. A bell rings to signal the closing of the market, and the festival begins. Girls perform various exotic dances, and Nilakantha appears, disguised as an old Hindu penitent and accompanied by his daughter. By now Gérald and his fiancée Ellen have appeared on the scene, and Gérald, out of earshot of the girls, has been told by Frédéric that their regiment leaves before dawn to move against a party of rebellious natives. Lakmé hints to her father that Brahma might not be averse to pardoning an offence by a stranger, but her father indignantly denies any such possibility. He sings tenderly of his love for Lakmé: 'Lakmé, ton doux regard se voile'.

Nilakantha demands that his daughter shall sing to attract the

man who has dared to venture on to sacred ground—drawn, Nilakantha is sure, by the beauty of Lakmé herself. A brilliant passage
of roulades is designed to attract the attention of the crowd, to
whom Nilakantha introduces his daughter as a traditional Hindu
singer. She tells the story of the Indian maiden, a pariah, who
one day sees a handsome stranger lost in the forest and defenceless against the wild beasts, who wait to devour him. She plays on
her bells and charms the animals, thus keeping the stranger safe
from them. When he awakens, she discovers that it is Vishnu, the
son of Brahma. He transports her with him to the skies, and ever
since that day, the traveller has heard the sound of bells in that
particular part of the forest. This is the famous Bell Song ('Où
va la jeune Hindoue?'), to which more than to anything else the
opera owes its continued popularity. Its bell effects and seductive

melody have been instrumental in making it a favourite of all
sopranos with any pretensions to vocal agility, but frequent bad
performance should not influence the opera lover against it. In
the hands of a coloratura soprano who is also musically inclined
its effect is still considerable.

To Nilakantha's fury, nobody appears in answer to Lakmé's
singing, and he is still ignorant of the identity of the stranger who
braved his anger by polluting the temple grounds. He bids his
daughter continue her singing, which she reluctantly does, until,
seeing Gérald, she utters a cry of anguish and faints in his arms.
Nilakantha is convinced that he knows his enemy, and plots to
isolate and destroy him during the course of the procession of
the goddess which takes place later that night. The stage has
meanwhile emptied as soldiers cross the square, and are watched
by the gaping crowds.

Lakmé is left alone with the faithful Hadji, who tries to console
her, and promises to do whatever she asks him; whether to help
a friend or dispose of an enemy, she has only to command him.
Hardly has he finished speaking when Gérald returns and rushes
to Lakmé's side. There is a love duet for them ('Dans le vague
d'un rêve'), during whose course Lakmé admits her love for the
young officer whose religion is not her own. Lakmé plans a new

life for them, far away in a part of the forest known only to her and where she has a little hut: 'Dans la forêt près de nous'.

The procession comes into sight, and the English ladies and their escort, Frédéric, watch it as it goes by, the priests chanting their hymn to Dourga. Frédéric comments ironically on Gérald's infatuation for the Hindu 'goddess', and says that he would be really worried were it not that they have to leave that very night, and that Gérald is therefore unlikely to have an opportunity of seeing her again. As the procession passes, Nilakantha's plan is put into operation, and Gérald falls stabbed. Lakmé rushes despairingly to him, but finds that he is only slightly injured. Hadji will help her to remove him to her secret hiding-place, and he will be hers.

Act III. The entr'acte suggests a lullaby, and when the curtain goes up, we are in the hut in the forest, where Gérald is lying on a couch, while Lakmé sings to him: 'Sous le ciel tout étoilé'. When he wakes up, he is at first not sure what has happened to him, but Lakmé reminds him that it was Hadji who carried him to the forest. In one of the happiest pieces of the score, 'Ah, viens dans la forêt profonde', Gérald gives lyrical expression to his happiness far from the world with Lakmé as his only companion.

From afar off can be heard the sound of singing, and Lakmé tells Gérald that it is a band of lovers come to drink of the sacred spring whose waters confer the gift of eternal love on whoever drinks them. She herself will fetch water from the spring in which they may pledge their love. As she goes, Frédéric, who has been watching, appears at Gérald's side. He has followed the traces of blood which were left as Hadji carried the wounded man through the woods to safety. Frédéric reminds Gérald that he is due to go with his regiment that very night, but Gérald is intoxicated with his love for Lakmé. He can forget Ellen, to whom he was engaged, but can he, asks Fréderic, forget his honour as a soldier. As he leaves, Frédéric knows he has triumphed over Gérald's infatuation, and Gérald himself knows it when, a moment after Lakmé's return, he hears in the distance the sound of soldiers marching.

Lakmé notices the change which has come about in her lover during her short absence, and, while his attention is concentrated on the sound of the march, she tears off a leaf of the fatal *datura* tree, and bites it. 'Tu m'as donné le plus doux rêve', she tells

Gérald when he again becomes conscious of her existence. Together they drink water from the cup, and swear to love each other through all eternity. Lakmé admits to Gérald that she thinks he is in no danger of breaking his oath, since she is at that very moment dying. Their voices join again in a duet, but Lakmé dies a moment later, though not before she has had time to tell Nilakantha, who discovers them, that she and her lover have together drunk of the sacred spring. As Gérald cries out in despair, Nilakantha thinks of Lakmé transported to eternal life, and is content.                                              H.

# EDOUARD LALO

## (1823–1892)

### LE ROI D'YS
### The King of Ys

OPERA in three acts by Edouard Lalo, text by Edouard Blau. Première at the Opéra-Comique, Paris, May 7, 1888, with Deschamps, Simonnet, Talazac, conductor Danbé. First performed Covent Garden, 1901, with Paquot, Adams, Jerome, Plançon; Metropolitan, 1922, with Ponselle, Alda, Gigli, Danise, Rothier, conductor Wolff.

### CHARACTERS

| | | |
|---|---|---|
| Le Roi d'Ys | | Bass |
| Margared } *his daughters* | | { Soprano |
| Rozenn } | | { Soprano |
| Mylio | | Tenor |
| Karnac | | Baritone |
| Saint Corentin | | Bass |
| Jahel | | Baritone |

Nobles, Warriors, Soldiers, People

The story is founded upon a Breton legend.

The impressive overture uses themes from the opera, prominent amongst them the duet 'En silence pourquoi souffrir?', which occurs as a cello solo, and Margared's aria in the second act.

Act I. Outside the palace of Ys. The people rejoice that the war in which they have recently been engaged is at an end, and that peace has been brought to them through the betrothal of the King's daughter Margared to the enemy leader, Karnac. As the crowd leaves the stage, the two sisters appear. Rozenn asks Margared why her looks are sad on the day on which her engagement is announced: 'En silence pourquoi souffrir?' At first Margared will not share her grief with anyone else, but eventually she admits that her heart was secretly given to a man, and that man was in the ship on which sailed the soldier Mylio, whom nobody has seen since the cessation of hostilities. She hates Karnac with a double loathing; he takes her away from the man she loves, and he is the enemy of her country. Rozenn tries to comfort her; she must lose no time in admitting her repugnance for Karnac, before it is too late and the marriage contract signed and sealed.

Alone, Rozenn in an aria avows her own love for Mylio himself. He appears suddenly at her side, and they pledge eternal faith to each other. Mylio disappears, and the King leads out Margared to meet Karnac, who appears with his followers. The people rejoice at the marriage which will put an end to their sufferings. During the course of the ceremony, Rozenn whispers to Margared that not only has Mylio returned—she has seen him —but his companions too, and amongst them must be the man for whom Margared languishes. Margared turns impulsively to her father, and repudiates Karnac; she cannot marry, she says, a man she does not love. The general consternation grows when Karnac pledges himself in revenge to carry the war through until Ys is totally destroyed. But at this moment, Mylio pushes his way through the crowd and swears to fight for Ys until the war is brought to a victorious conclusion. The people acclaim their champion.

Act II.    The great hall of the palace. Margared looks from the window at Karnac's troops assembling on the plain below. Mylio will lead the armies of Ys, and Margared is filled with turbulent feelings on his account, which she expresses in a splendid aria: 'Lorsque je t'ai vu soudain'. She suspects that Mylio loves Rozenn; if it is so, her love for her sister and Mylio would turn to implacable hate.

No sooner are the words out of her mouth than Rozenn and the King enter with Mylio. Margared hides, and hears Mylio reassure Rozenn—Saint Corentin has blessed the fight on which he is embarking—and, a moment later, her sister proclaim her love for the valiant general. The King gives his blessing to them, and then leaves with Mylio. Margared confronts Rozenn as her rival for the love of Mylio. May he die rather than be united with Rozenn! Rozenn is horror-stricken at her sister's words and tries to defend herself; were she in Margared's place, her heart might break, but she would not give way to hate: 'Tais-toi, Margared!' But Margared is not to be appeased; she curses her sister and vows vengeance on her for having stolen Mylio.

The scene changes to the great plain in front of the castle of Ys. Mylio is proclaimed victorious, but ascribes the enemy's defeat to the intervention of Saint Corentin, the patron saint of Ys. The stage empties, and Karnac appears, dishevelled and worn after his unsuccessful fight. Margared stands before him, and offers him revenge for his defeat; she will, with his help, open the flood-gates and let in the sea to drown the town. As they go off together past the chapel of Saint Corentin, Margared challenges the saint to avert the disaster she will bring on Ys. The sky darkens, the statue of the Saint animates and calls on her to repent.

Act III. Gallery in the palace. On one side is the door to Rozenn's apartments. In accordance with Breton marriage custom, it is protected by young girls against the efforts of the friends of the bridegroom to force an entrance. Mylio himself joins his retainers and pleads his own cause. He sings the famous *Aubade*, 'Vainement, ma bien-aimée', a tune of delicious fragrance, accompanied by the female chorus. It accomplishes its purpose, and Rozenn to a Breton tune says she will grant his request. The procession forms up, and makes its way into the chapel opposite. As the sound of the *Te Deum* can be heard from the chapel, Margared and Karnac make their way into the castle. Karnac demands that Margared fulfil her promise, and when she seems reluctant to bring disaster on her relations and her countrymen, he taunts her until she is mad with jealousy.

Karnac and Margared leave together, and Mylio and Rozenn emerge from the ceremony, and sing of their love: 'A l'autel j'allais rayonnant'. Margared reappears and overhears Rozenn and her father pray for her return. She is overcome with remorse and, when cries of alarm are heard outside, hastens forward to warn them of their impending fate. She tells them that Karnac has thrown open the gates which keep the sea from drowning the city, but that she herself has killed him for his deed.

The scene changes to the highest point of the city, where the people have taken refuge to escape the fate which threatens them all. The noise of the angry sea can be heard, and the crowd comments on the situation and prays for deliverance from death. The water still mounts, and the King laments that half the city has already disappeared, carrying away most of his subjects. Suddenly, Margared, as if in a trance, reflects that the waters will not recede until they have claimed the required victim. She herself is that victim, she of her own choice has brought this disaster on them, it was her hand that opened the gates. She will die in expiation of her crime. She throws herself into the sea, which immediately grows calmer, and the people thank Saint Corentin for their deliverance. H.

# JULES MASSENET
## (1842–1912)

### MANON

OPERA in five acts by Jules Massenet, text by Meilhac and Gille, based on the story by the Abbé Prévost. Première, Opéra-Comique, Paris, January 19, 1884, with Marie Heilbronn, Talazac, Taskin, Cobalet, conductor Danbé. First performed in England, Liverpool, 1885, with Marie Roze; Drury Lane, London (in English), with Roze, Maas, Ludwig, conductor Eugene Goossens (Snr.); Covent Garden, 1891, with Sybil Sanderson, van Dyck, Isnardon; New York, Academy of Music, 1885, with Minnie Hauck, Giannini, del Puente; 1895 (in Italian), with Sybil Sanderson, Jean de Reszke, Ancona, Plançon. Covent Garden revivals include 1919, with Edvina and Ansseau, conductor Beecham; 1926, with Heldy and Ansseau; since 1947, McWatters, Schwarzkopf and de los Angeles have sung the title rôle in London. Famous interpreters of Manon include also Mary Garden, Farrar, Bori, Grace Moore, Favero, Sayao. Famous des Grieux: Clément, Caruso, Gigli, Schipa, Tagliavini.

### CHARACTERS

Chevalier des Grieux ........................... Tenor
Count des Grieux, *his father* ....................... Bass
Lescaut, *of the Royal Guard, cousin to Manon* ..... Baritone
Guillot de Morfontaine, *Minister of Finance, an
    old roué* ...................................... Tenor
De Brétigny, *a nobleman* ...................... Baritone
Manon Lescaut .............................. Soprano
Pousette, Javotte, Rosette, *actresses* ............. Sopranos
Students, Innkeeper, a Sergeant, a Soldier, Gamblers, Merchants and their Wives, Croupiers, Sharpers, Guards, Travellers, Ladies, Gentlemen, Porters, Postilions, an attendant at the Monastery of St. Sulpice, the People

*Time:* 1721                    *Place:* Amiens, Paris, Havre

Act I.    Courtyard of the inn at Amiens. Guillot and de Brétigny, who have just arrived with the actresses Pousette, Javotte, and Rosette, are shouting for the innkeeper. Townspeople crowd about the entrance to the inn. They descry a coach approaching. Lescaut, who has alighted from it, enters followed by two guardsmen. Other travellers appear amid much commotion, amusement, and shouting on the part of the townspeople.

He is awaiting his cousin Manon, whom he is to conduct to a convent school, and who presently appears and gives a sample of her character, which is a mixture of demureness and vivacity, of serious affection and meretricious preferment, in her opening song, 'Je suis encore tout étourdie' (A simple maiden fresh from home), in which she tells how, having left home for the first time to travel to Amiens, she sometimes wept and sometimes laughed. It is a chic little song.

Lescaut goes out to find her luggage. From the balcony of the inn the old roué Guillot sees her. She is not shocked, but laughs at his hints that he is rich and can give her whatever she wants. De Brétigny, who, accompanied by the actresses, comes out on the balcony in search of Guillot, also is much struck with her beauty. Guillot, before withdrawing with the others from the balcony, softly calls down to her that his carriage is at her disposal, if she will but enter it and await him. Lescaut returns but at the same time his two guardsmen come after hïm. They want him to join with them in gambling and drinking. He pretends to Manon that he is obliged to go to his barracks for a short time. Before leaving her, however, he warns her to be careful of her actions. 'Regardez-moi bien dans les yeux' (Now give good heed to what I say).

Left alone, Manon expresses admiration for the jewels and finery worn by the actresses. She wishes such gems and dresses might belong to her: 'Voyons Manon, plus de chimères'. The Chevalier des Grieux, young, handsome, ardent, comes upon the scene. He falls in love with Manon at first sight. Nor does she long remain unimpressed by the wooing of the Chevalier. Beginning with his words, 'If I knew but your name', and her reply, 'I am called Manon', the music soon becomes an impassioned love-duet. To him she is an enchantress. As for her—'A vous ma vie et mon âme' (To you my life and my soul).

Manon sees Guillot's postilion, who has been told by his master to take his orders from Manon. She communicates to des Grieux that they will run away to Paris in Guillot's conveyance. 'Nous vivrons à Paris tous les deux' (see page 802), they shout in glad triumph, and are off. There is much confusion when the escape is discovered. Ridicule is heaped upon Guillot, for is it not in his carriage, in which the old roué hoped to find Manon awaiting him, that she has driven off with her young lover!

Nous vi-vrons à Pa-ris! Tous les deux. Tous les deux! Et nos

cœurs amoureux. À Pa-ris.

Act II. The apartment of des Grieux and Manon, Rue Vivienne, Paris. Des Grieux is writing at his desk. Discovering Manon looking over his shoulder, he reads her what he has written—a letter to his father extolling her beauty and asking permission to marry her. Musically, it is a scene of great charm.

The scene is interrupted by knocking and voices without. The maid servant announces that two guardsmen demand admission. She whispers to Manon, 'One of them loves you—the nobleman, who lives near here'. The pair are Lescaut and de Brétigny, the latter masquerading as a soldier in Lescaut's regiment. Lescaut scents more profit for himself and for his cousin Manon in a liaison between her and the wealthy nobleman than in her relations with des Grieux. Purposely he is gruff and demands 'yes' or 'no' to his question as to whether or not des Grieux intends to marry the girl. Des Grieux shows the letter he is about to dispatch to his father. Apparently everything is satisfactory. But de Brétigny manages to convey to Manon the information that the Chevalier's father is incensed at his son's mode of life, and has arranged to have him carried off that night. If she will keep quiet about it, he (de Brétigny) will provide for her handsomely and surround her with the wealth and luxury she craves. She protests that she loves des Grieux—but is careful not to warn him of the impending abduction. This lively quartet aptly contrasts the lovesick des Grieux and the practical Lescaut and de Brétigny.

Lescaut and the nobleman depart, after Lescaut, sly fellow, has blessed his 'children', as he calls Manon and des Grieux. Shortly afterwards the latter goes out to despatch the letter to his father. Manon, approaching the table, which is laid for supper, sings the charming air, 'Adieu, notre petite table' (Farewell, dear little table). This is followed by the exquisite air with harp accompaniment, 'Le Rêve de Manon' (A vision of Manon), which is sung by des Grieux, who has re-entered and describes her as he saw her in a dream: 'En fermant les yeux'. Here is an example of Massenet's graceful talent at its best—sensitive, expressive, and full of that indefinable thing we call 'style'.

There is a disturbance outside. Manon knows that the men who will bear away her lover have arrived. She loves des Grieux, but luxury means more to her than love. An effort is made by her to dissuade the Chevalier from going outside to see who is there—but it is a half-hearted attempt. He goes. The noise of a struggle is heard. Manon, 'overcome with grief', exclaims, 'He has gone'.

Act III. Scene i.    The Cours la Reine, Paris, on the day of a popular fête. Stalls of traders are among the trees. There is a pavilion for dancing. After some lively preliminary episodes between the three actresses and Guillot, Lescaut enters singing sentimentally of a certain Rosalinde. After him comes de Brétigny with Manon. She sings frivolously of her gay life, 'Je marche sur tous les chemins', and follows this up with the famous *Gavotte*: 'Obéissons quand leur voix appelle' (List to the voice of youth when it calleth).[1]

The Count des Grieux, father of the Chevalier, comes upon the scene. From a conversation between him and de Brétigny, which Manon overhears, she learns that the Chevalier is about to enter the seminary of St. Sulpice and intends to take holy orders. After a duet between Manon and the Count, one of the most charming of the lesser-known passages of the score and a good example of Massenet's ability to forward the drama in a set-piece, the Count retires, and Guillot returns, bringing with him the ballet from the Opéra. This luxury, we heard a little earlier, Manon had been refused by de Brétigny on the grounds of expense, and has now been brought by Guillot, who hopes to win her away from her current lover. There is dancing by the ballet, at the end of which Manon, who to Guillot's dismay says

[1] At the Opéra-Comique, instead of the Gavotte is sung the *Fabliau*, 'Oui dans les bois'.    H.

she has seen nothing, orders her chair, and bids the amazed
Lescaut have her conveyed to the seminary of St. Sulpice.

Scene ii.    Ante-Chapel of St. Sulpice. Nuns and visitors, who
have just attended religious service, are praising the sermon delivered by des Grieux, who enters a little later attired in the garb
of an abbé. The ladies withdraw, leaving des Grieux with his
father, who has come in unobserved, and now vainly endeavours to
dissuade his son from taking holy orders: 'Epouse quelque brave
fille'. Left alone, des Grieux cannot banish Manon from his thoughts.
'Ah! fuyez douce image' (Ah! depart, image fair), he sings in
an aria which rises almost to a frenzy; then slowly goes out.

Almost as if in answer to his soliloquy, the woman whose
image he cannot put away enters the chapel. From outside chanting is heard. Summoned by the porter of the seminary, des Grieux
comes back. He protests to Manon that she has been faithless
and says that he will not turn from the peace of mind he has
sought in religious retreat.

Gradually, however, he yields to the pleading of the woman
he loves: 'N'est-ce plus ma main que cette main presse? . . .

N'est ce plus ma main que  cet-te main pres-se? N'est ce plus ma voix?

Ah! regarde moi! N'est-ce plus Manon?' (Is it no longer my
hand, your own now presses? . . . Ah! look upon me! Am I no
longer Manon?) The religious chanting continues, but now only
as a background to an impassioned love duet—'Ah! Viens,
Manon, je t'aime!' (Ah, Manon, Manon! I love thee).

Act IV.    Hôtel de Transylvanie, a fashionable gambling house
in Paris. Play is going on. Guillot, Lescaut, Pousette, Javotte,
and Rosette are of the company. Later Manon and des Grieux
come in, and the latter makes impassioned declaration of his
love for Manon, which alone has brought him to such a place:

Manon, who has run through her lover's money, counsels the

Chevalier to stake what he has left on the game. Des Grieux plays with amazing luck against Guillot and gathers in winning after winning. 'Faites vos jeux, Messieurs', cry the croupiers, while Manon joyously sings, 'Ce bruit de l'or, ce rire, et ces éclats joyeux' (Music of gold, of laughter, and clash of joyous sounds). The upshot of it all, however, is that Guillot accuses the Chevalier of cheating, and after an angry scene goes out. Very soon afterwards, the police, whom Guillot has summoned, break in. Upon Guillot's accusation they arrest Manon and the Chevalier. 'O douleur, l'avenir nous sépare' (Oh despair! Our lives are divided for ever), sings Manon, her accents of grief being echoed by those of her lover.

Act V, originally given as a second scene to the fourth act, takes place at a lonely spot on the road to Havre. Des Grieux has been freed through the intercession of his father. Manon, however, has been condemned as a prostitute to deportation to the French colony of Louisiana. Des Grieux and Lescaut are waiting for the prisoners to pass with their escort of soldiers. Des Grieux hopes to release Manon by attacking the convoy, but Lescaut restrains him. The guardsman finds little difficulty in bribing the sergeant to permit Manon, who is already nearly dead from exhaustion, to remain behind with des Grieux, between whom the rest of the opera is a dolorous duet, ending in Manon's death. Even while dying her dual nature asserts itself. Feebly opening her eyes, almost at the last, she imagines she sees jewels and exclaims, 'Oh! what lovely gems!' She turns to des Grieux: 'I love thee! Take thou this kiss. 'Tis my farewell for ever.' It is, of course, this dual nature which makes the character drawn by Abbé Prévost so interesting.

The last act is original with the librettists. In the story the final scene is laid in Louisiana (see Puccini's Manon Lescaut). The effective scene in the convent of St. Sulpice was overlooked by Puccini, as it also was by Scribe, who wrote the libretto for Auber's *Manon*. This latter work survives in the laughing song, 'L'Eclat de Rire', which Patti introduced in the lesson scene in *Il Barbiere di Siviglia*, and which Galli-Curci later revived for the same purpose.

K.

## WERTHER

Opera in four acts by Jules Massenet; text by Edouard Blau, Paul Milliet, and Georges Hartmann, after Goethe's novel. Première in a German version at the Vienna Opera, February 16, 1892, with Marie Renard, Forster, van Dyck, Neidl. First performed Opéra-Comique, Paris, January 16, 1893, with

Marie Delna, Laisné, Ibos, Bouvet; Chicago, 1894; New York, 1894, and Covent Garden the same year, with Eames, Arnoldson, Jean de Reszke. Revived Metropolitan, 1910, with Farrar, Alma Gluck, Clément, Dinh Gilly; His Majesty's Theatre, London (in English), 1910; la Scala, Milan, 1939, with Pederzini, Schipa; 1951, with Simionato, Tagliavini; New York, City Centre, 1948, with Heidt and Conley; Sadler's Wells (in English), 1952, with Marion Lowe and Rowland Jones.

### CHARACTERS

Werther, *a poet, aged twenty-three* ................Tenor
Albert, *a young man, aged twenty-five* ...........Baritone
Le Bailli, *aged fifty* ............................Bass
Schmidt ⎱ *friends of le Bailli* ................⎰ Tenor
Johann  ⎰                            ⎱ Bass
Charlotte, *daughter of le Bailli, aged*
     *twenty* ...............................Mezzo-Soprano
Sophie, *her sister, aged fifteen* ..................Soprano
Children, Neighbours of le Bailli

*Time:* About 1780                    *Place:* Frankfurt

After a prelude consisting of the music associated with the more forceful as well as the idyllic side of Werther's character, the curtain rises on Act I, which takes place in the garden outside the Bailli's house. The owner is rehearsing his children in a Christmas song; they sing it badly, but his comment—that they would not dare sing like that if their sister Charlotte were there—has the effect of reducing their exuberance and improving the performance. Two friends of the Bailli's, Johann and Schmidt, pause to listen to the singing, and remind the Bailli of his promise to meet them later that night at the 'Raisin d'or'. Sophie has come in and mention is made of the dreamer Werther, and the practical Albert; the last-named will make, says Schmidt, a model husband for Charlotte. Schmidt and Johann go off singing 'Vivat Bacchus', and everyone else goes into the house.

Werther appears, asking for the Bailli's house, and expressing his pleasure in the idyllic country atmosphere in a beautiful recitative and aria, 'O nature pleine de grace'. Charlotte, dressed

for the dance which is to take place that night, comes out of the house with the children and takes advantage of the lateness of her escort to cut them their bread and butter. Various guests arrive and are greeted by the Bailli. Charlotte says good-night to the children, who, the Bailli says, have been in her charge since their mother's death. Werther's outburst when confronted with the family scene, 'O spectacle idéal', is sufficiently expressive to banish memories of Thackeray's notorious comment on Goethe's novel:

> 'Charlotte, having seen his body
> Borne before her on a shutter,
> Like a well-conducted person,
> Went on cutting bread-and-butter.'

Most successful is the way Massenet in a few minutes of music suggests the passage of time while Charlotte and Werther are at the ball: a few sentences for the Bailli alone and then with Sophie, an empty stage before the entry of Albert, his recognition by Sophie followed by his aria—and night has fallen completely, the moon risen, and the scene is set for the return of the principals.

The music of the 'Clair de lune' is heard in the orchestra as Charlotte and Werther come into the garden, arm in arm. Their mutual attraction is obvious and Werther declares his passionate love for Charlotte before Massenet interrupts the duet with an effect that is as simple as it is telling: the Bailli calls out from the house that Albert is back—the idyll is shattered, and we have taken the turn towards tragedy which is to be the eventual outcome. The 'Clair de lune' duet shows many of Massenet's qualities at their best—the elegant simplicity of the vocal line, the economical rôle of the orchestra, the shapely, rewarding contours of the tune, the gentle but evocative atmosphere of the whole. It is not undramatic—the vocal line becomes gradually animated as the situation develops, and Charlotte's reticence is influenced by Werther's rising passion—but it is still the world of understatement, of the small gesture as opposed to the large, the world which Massenet knew best.

Lent et soutenu

A few hasty sentences explain that Albert is the fiancé Charlotte's mother wished for her, and the curtain falls on Werther's desperate cry, 'Un autre! son epoux!'

Act II.    In front of the church. The two bon-vivants Johann and Schmidt are drinking at the inn. Inside the church the golden wedding of the village pastor is being celebrated. Charlotte and Albert appear, apparently full of happiness after three months of marriage, and go into the church. Werther catches sight of them as they disappear: 'Un autre est son epoux'. He soliloquises in music of more vigorous character than we have previously heard from him as he laments that marriage with Charlotte is an impossibility for him: 'J'aurais sur ma poitrine'. He sinks down overcome with unhappiness, and, when he comes out of the church, Albert takes the opportunity of talking to his friend, who, he thinks, is, or has been, in love with Charlotte. After a partial admission, Werther affirms his loyalty to both ('Mais, comme après l'orage'). Sophie, in a little song which might have done duty for the immature Manon ('Le gai soleil'), sings of the happiness which is in her heart. Werther resolves to leave, but the sight of Charlotte is too much for him and he renews his protestations of love. She begs him to leave and at all events to stay away until Christmas time. Werther is overcome by the situation; unable to give up his love, he prays at the same time for strength to stay away and for the happiness which his return could bring him: 'Lorsque l'enfant revient d'un voyage'. Seeing Sophie, he tells her he is going away, never to return. She loses no time in informing her sister and brother-in-law of this decision, and Albert comments darkly that this can mean only that Werther is still in love with Charlotte.

Act III.    It is Christmas. Charlotte realises that she returns Werther's love; merely to re-read the letters he has written her

Mais si je ne dois re-pa-raî-tre, Au jour fi-xé de-vant toi, f ne m'ac-cu-se pas, pleure moi!

is enough to bring her to the verge of hysteria. All the efforts of her sister to cheer her up are in vain, and when Sophie refers to

Werther, Charlotte's reserve breaks down and she confesses her
love for him: 'Va! laisse couler mes larmes'. Left alone, she prays
for strength: 'Ah! mon courage m'abandonne'. When she is in
contact with other people, Charlotte's words and behaviour are
as conventional as a Victorian novel (fortunately, this is not by
any means always the case with her music), but this can to a large
extent be forgiven her for the depth and vehemence of feeling
she shows in this scene. Her reading of the letters, the 'Air des
larmes', and her prayer for strength together make up a scene
which is only less powerful and convincing than Tatiana's 'Letter
scene' in *Eugen Onegin*. In a moment Charlotte becomes a real
and believable person, not the prig we have known in the other
two acts.

Suddenly, Werther himself appears, confessing that his reason
had urged him to stay away but instinct had proved too strong;
he is here on the appointed day of Christmas. They look together
at the books they used to read, the harpsichord they used to play,
and Charlotte reminds Werther that he was translating Ossian
before he went away. The sight of the book awakens memories
in Werther's mind, and from it he sings a song of tragic love:
'Pourquoi me réveiller?' This aria has become enormously popular, and in it for the first time in Charlotte's presence Werther
uses the directness of musical expression which has hitherto been
reserved for soliloquies.

When Charlotte's voice betrays her feelings, Werther's restraint
vanishes and he embraces her. The music has a genuine tragic
ring about it as Werther becomes more and more excited, and in

Il  brû - -le sur ma  lèvre  encor i - nas - sou - vi - e

fact, from the beginning of Act III right through to the end of
the opera, there is a directness of expression and a decisiveness
that contrasts with the frustration, the continual second thoughts
of the first two acts. Werther draws back and Charlotte rushes
from the room, locking the door behind her. Albert returns and
connects his wife's agitation with Werther's return, of which he
has already learned. Just then the servant comes in with a message
from Werther: 'I am going on a long journey; will you lend me
your pistols?' Albert tells Charlotte to give them to the servant;

she does so mechanically, but realises the significance of the message a moment after her husband has gone out of the room.

Act IV.    The scene changes to Werther's apartment (Acts III and IV are played without an interval). Charlotte comes in to find Werther dying. He prevents her going for help, and is contented when she tells him she has loved him from the moment they first met. As he dies, the voices of the children celebrating Christmas can be heard outside his room.                                    H.

# THAÏS

Opera in three acts by Jules Massenet; text by L. Gallet after the novel of Anatole France. Première at the Opéra, Paris, February 16, 1894, with Sybil Sanderson, Delmas, and Alvarez. First performed New York, 1907 ; Covent Garden, 1911, with Edvina, Dinh Gilly, conductor Panizza; revived 1919, with Edvina, Couzinou, conductor Beecham; 1926, with Jeritza, Servais, conductor Bellezza. Revived Metropolitan, 1917, with Farrar, Amato; 1922, with Jeritza, Whitehill; 1939, with Jepson, John Charles Thomas; la Scala, Milan, 1942, with Favero, Bechi, conductor Marinuzzi. Currently in the repertory of the Opéra, Paris, with Géori Boué and Bourdin. Amongst the most famous exponents of the title rôle has been Mary Garden.

## CHARACTERS

Athanaël, *a young Cenobite monk* . . . . . . . . . . . . . . Baritone
Nicias, *a young Alexandrian* . . . . . . . . . . . . . . . . . . Tenor
Palémon, *an old Cenobite* . . . . . . . . . . . . . . . . . . . . . Bass
Servant of Nicias . . . . . . . . . . . . . . . . . . . . . . . . . . Baritone
Thaïs, *a courtesan* . . . . . . . . . . . . . . . . . . . . . . . . . Soprano
Crobyle, *a slave* . . . . . . . . . . . . . . . . . . . . . . . . . . . Soprano
Myrtale, *a slave* . . . . . . . . . . . . . . . . . . . . Mezzo-Soprano
Albine, *an abbess* . . . . . . . . . . . . . . . . . . . . . . . . . Contralto

There is no question in *Thaïs* of one of those powerful and passionate dramas, rich in incidents and majestic dramatic strokes, or one of those subjects profoundly pathetic like those of *Les Huguenots*, *La Juive*, or *Le Prophète*. One could extract from the intimate and mystic novel of *Thaïs* only a unity and simplicity of action without circumlocutions or complications, developing between two important persons and leaving all the others in a sort of discreet shadow, the latter serving only to emphasise the scenic movement and to give to the work the necessary life, colour, and variety.

The action of *Thaïs* takes place at the end of the fourth century.

The first act shows us in a corner of the Theban plain on the banks of the Nile a refuge of Cenobites. The good fathers are finishing a modest repast at their common table. One place near them remains empty, that of their comrade Athanaël (Paphnuce in the novel) who has gone to Alexandria. Soon he comes back, greatly scandalised at the sensation caused in the great city by the presence of a shameless courtesan, the famous actress and dancer, Thaïs, who seems to have turned the sceptical and light heads of its inhabitants. Now in his younger days Athanaël had known this Thaïs, and in Alexandria too, which he left to consecrate himself to the Lord and to take the robe of a religious man.

Athanaël is haunted by the memory of Thaïs. He dreams that it would be a pious and meritorious act to snatch her from her unworthy profession and from a life of debauchery which dishonours her and of which she does not even seem to be conscious. He goes to bed and sleeps under the impress of this thought, which does not cease to confront him, so much so that he sees her in a dream on the stage of the theatre of Alexandria, representing the Loves of Venus. He can refrain no longer and on awaking he goes to search her out, firmly resolved to do everything to bring about her conversion.

Arrived at Alexandria, Athanaël meets an old friend, the beau, Nicias, to whom he makes himself known and who is the lover of Thaïs for a day longer because he has purchased her love for a week which is about to end. Athanaël confides his scheme to Nicias who receives him like a brother and makes him put on clothes which will permit him to attend a fête and banquet which he is to give that very night in honour of Thaïs. Soon he finds himself in the presence of the courtesan who laughs at his first words and who engages him to come to see her at her house if he expects to convert her. He does not fail to accept this invitation and once in Thaïs's house tells her to be ashamed of her disorderly life and with eloquent words reveals to her the heavenly joys and the felicities of religion. Thaïs is very much impressed; she is on the point of yielding to his advice when afar off in a song are heard the voices of her companions in pleasure. She repels the monk, who, without being discouraged, goes away, saying to her: 'At thy threshold until daylight I will await thy coming'.

In fact here we find him at night seated on the front steps of Thaïs's house. Time has done its work and a few hours have sufficed for the young woman to be touched by grace. She goes out of her house, having exchanged her rich garments for a rough woollen dress, finds the monk, and begs him to lead her to a convent. The conversion is accomplished.

But Athanaël has deceived himself. It was not love of God but it was jealousy that dictated his course without his being aware of it. When he has returned to the Thebaid after having conducted Thaïs to a convent and thinks he has found peace again, he perceives with horror that he loves her madly. His thoughts without ceasing turn to her and in a new dream, a cruel dream, he seems to see Thaïs, sanctified and purified by remorse and prayer, on the point of dying in the convent where she took refuge. On awaking, under the impression of this sinister vision, he hurries to the convent where Thaïs in fact is near to breathing her last breath. But he does not wish that she die; and while she, in ecstasy, is only thinking of heaven and her purification, he wants to snatch her from death and only talks to her of his love. Thaïs dies and Athanaël falls stricken beside her.

This subject, half mystic, half psychological, was it really a favourable one for theatrical action? Was it even treated in such a way as to mitigate the defects it might present in this connection? We may doubt it. Nevertheless M. Massenet has written on this libretto of *Thaïs* a score which, if it does not present the firm unity of those of *Manon* and of *Werther*, certainly does not lack either inspiration or colour or originality and in which moreover are found in all their force and all their expansion the technical qualities of a master to whom nothing in his art is foreign. All the music of the first act, which shows us the retreat of the Cenobites, is of a sober and severe colour, with which will be contrasted the movement and the gracefulness of the scene at the house of Nicias. There should be noted the peaceful chorus of monks, the entrance of Athanaël ('Hélas, enfant encore'), the fine phrase which follows his dream: 'Toi qui mis la pitié dans nos âmes', and the very curious effect of the scene where he goes away again from his companions to return to Alexandria. In the second act the invocation placed in the mouth of Athanaël, 'Voilà donc la terrible cité', written on a powerful rhythm, is followed by a charming quartet, a passage with an emphasis full of grace and the end of which especially is delightful. I would indicate again in this act the rapid and kindly dialogue of Nicias and of Thaïs, 'Nous nous sommes aimés une longue semaine', which seems to conceal under its apparent indifference a sort of sting of melancholy, and the charming air for Thaïs, 'Qui te fait si sévère'. I pass over the air of Thaïs: 'Dis-moi que je suis belle', an air of bravado solely destined to display the finish of a singer,[1] to which I much prefer the whole scene that follows, which is a long duet in which Athanaël tries to convert Thaïs. The severe and stern accents of the monk put in opposition to the raillery and the voluptuous buoyancy of the courtesan produce a striking contrast which the composer has known how to place in relief with a rare felicity and a real power. The symphonic *intermezzo* which, under the name of Méditation, separates this act from the following, is nothing but an adorable violin solo, supported by the harps and the development of which, on the taking up again of the first motif by the violin, brings about the entrance of an invisible chorus, the effect of which is purely exquisite. The curtain then rises on the scene in which Thaïs, who has put on a rough woollen dress, goes to seek the monk to flee with him. Here there is a duet in complete contrast with the preceding. Athanaël wants Thaïs to destroy and burn whatever may preserve the memory of her past. She obeys, demanding favour only for a little statue of Eros: 'L'amour est une vertu rare'. It is a sort of invocation to the purity of love, written, if one may say so, in a sentiment of chaste melancholy and entirely impressed with gracefulness and poetry. The duet for Athanaël and Thaïs, sung when they arrive at the oasis with her in a state of exhaustion, is moving and simple, and it is the best sustained section of the score. Deserving special praise is the final scene, that of the death of Thaïs. The composer knew wonderfully well how to seize the contrast between the pious thoughts of Thaïs, who at the moment of quitting life begins to perceive eternal happiness, and the powerless rage of Athanaël, who, devoured by an impious love, reveals to her, without her understanding or comprehending it, all the ardour of a passion that death alone can extinguish in him. The touching phrases of Thaïs, the despairing accents of Athanaël, interrupted by the desolate chants of the nuns, companions of

[1] Nevertheless, most people have since found it, with the duet at the oasis, the best movement in the score.   H.

the dying woman, provoke in the hearer a poignant and sincere emotion. That is one of the finest pages we owe to the pen of M. Massenet. We must point out especially the return of the beautiful violin phrase which constitutes the foundation of the intermezzo of the second act.                              K.W.

## LE JONGLEUR DE NOTRE DAME
### Our Lady's Tumbler

Opera in three acts by Jules Massenet; text by M. Lena. Première at Monte Carlo, February 18, 1902, with Charles Maréchal, Renaud. First performed at the Opéra-Comique, Paris, 1904, with Maréchal, Allard, Fugère, Huberdeau (shortly afterwards the part of Jean was taken over by Mary Garden); Covent Garden, 1906, with Laffite, Gilibert, Serveilhac, Crabbé; New York, 1908, with Garden, Renaud, Dufranne; London Opera House, 1912, with Fer, Chadal, Combe. Revived Chicago, 1929, with Garden, Formichi, Cotreuil; la Scala, Milan, 1938, with Malipiero, Maugeri, Bettoni, conductor Marinuzzi; Colon, Buenos Aires, 1944, with Mazella, Romito, Damiani; la Fenice, Venice, 1948, with Malipiero.

### CHARACTERS

| | |
|---|---|
| Jean, *a tumbler* | Tenor (Soprano) |
| Boniface, *cook at the monastery* | Baritone |
| The Prior | Bass |
| A poet-monk | Tenor |
| A painter-monk | Baritone |
| A musician-monk | Baritone |
| A sculptor-monk | Bass |
| Two angels | Soprano, Mezzo-Soprano |

*Time:* Fourteenth Century                    *Place:* Cluny

Act I.    The square of Cluny in the fourteenth century. The façade of the abbey can be seen. It is market-day, and dancing is going on in the square. A hurdy-gurdy is heard in the distance, and Jean, the tumbler, comes into view. He starts his patter, but is mocked by the crowd, and has no sort of success until in desperation and with a bad conscience he sings the so-called 'Alleluiah du vin', in which the chorus joins happily. They are interrupted by the Prior, furious at the near sacrilege which has been committed just outside the monastery.

The Prior vents his wrath on Jean, who alone stays behind. When he finds that the blasphemer is disposed to regret his actions the Prior bids him dedicate himself to the Virgin. Jean is doubtful about renouncing his freedom at so early a stage of his life; he has valued his liberty: 'Liberté! Liberté! c'est elle que mon cœur pour maîtresse a choisie.' Jean's resolve to repent seems to be weakening, but he is particularly anxious not to have to leave behind the cap and bells, which have been the symbols of his trade. The Prior turns on him with some asperity, but decides to make a last attempt to win him over; he shows him the good things being taken by Brother Boniface into the monastery; all are destined for the monks' table. Boniface goes over the splendid array of provisions which he has brought for the greater glory of the Virgin and the greater comfort of her servants: 'Pour la vierge'. The *Benedicite* is heard from inside the monastery, and all cry 'A table'. Jean follows the others inside.

Act II. Interior of the abbey. Monks are at work. A painter is finishing a statue of the Virgin, a musician is rehearsing a hymn with the choir, Boniface prepares vegetables. Only Jean has nothing to do. To the Prior, he confesses that he knows no Latin, and that the songs he used to sing were all profane and in French. His fellow brethren mock him for his idleness, and each advises him that his own profession—be it painting, sculpture, poetry—is the only one for him. The Prior is obliged to intervene and ask for some concord in place of the dispute which seems to be growing. Only Boniface, when the others have gone, tries to comfort Jean; there are other things in life than art—and think of the pride which seems to go with it. He tells him a story to console him—the legend of the humble sage, which opened at the request of the Virgin to hide the Saviour from the sight of the soldiers sent to kill him, and in doing so outshone the rose, which was too proud to perform the service asked of it: 'Fleurissait une rose'. The passage has become the best known in the whole work.

Boniface reflects before dropping the subject that the sage is of course extremely valuable in cooking, and he then leaves to look after his kitchen. Jean is struck with what he has heard, and begins to believe that even the humblest can serve the Virgin in a way acceptable to her. Can he not do so himself?

Act III. The abbey chapel. The painted figure of the Virgin, which we saw early in the previous scene, is now set up, and the monks are singing a hymn. As they leave the chapel, the painter who was responsible for the statue takes a last look at his work. He is about to leave when he catches sight of Jean, coming in with his tumbler's gear. He hides before Jean can see him, and watches while Jean prays at the altar. Jean takes off his monkish garb and arrays himself in his old clothes. He plays a few chords on his hurdy-gurdy, just as he had at his first entrance in the square—but the painter-monk waits for no more; Jean is mad, and he must run and tell the Prior.

In the meanwhile, Jean goes through his repertory, not without some lapses of memory, such as when he starts to hand round his begging bowl. He has not got very far before the Prior arrives, led by the monk who had first seen Jean at his strange occupation. Fortunately Boniface has come too, and he restrains the Prior whose immediate reaction is that Jean is committing sacrilege and must be stopped at once. Eventually Jean dances, just as the monks begin to arrive. They are all horrified by what they can see, but they stay out of sight of Jean, who goes on until he falls exhausted at the foot of the statue.

As they are about to rush forward and seize Jean as a malefactor, Boniface stops them and points to the Virgin, whose arm is miraculously extended to bless the man lying at her feet. Jean awakes from his trance to find the Prior and the others bending over him. He expects punishment, and cannot understand their talk of a miracle. With a last song of praise, he falls back dead.

H.

# DON QUICHOTTE

Opera in five acts by Jules Massenet; text by Henri Cain, after Le Lorrain's play based on Cervantes's novel. Première Monte Carlo, February 19, 1910, with Lucy Arbell, Chaliapin, Gresse. First performed Paris, 1910, with Arbell, Vanni Marcoux, Fugère; London Opera House, 1912, with Kirlord, Lafont, Danse; Philadelphia, 1913; New York, 1914, with Garden, Vanni Marcoux, Dufranne; Metropolitan, 1926, with Easton, Chaliapin, de Luca; Chicago, 1929, with Glade, Vanni Marcoux, Cotreuil. Revived Opéra Comique, 1931; Brussels, 1934; Opéra, Paris, 1947, with Renée Gilly, Vanni Marcoux, Musy, conductor Cluytens.

## CHARACTERS

| | | |
|---|---|---|
| La Belle Dulcinée | | Contralto |
| Don Quichotte | | Bass |
| Sancho | | Baritone |
| Pedro, *burlesquer* | } *admirers of Dulcinée* | { Soprano |
| Garcias, *burlesquer* | | { Soprano |
| Rodriguez | } *admirers of Dulcinée* | { Tenor |
| Juan | | { Tenor |

Two servants .................................Baritone
Tenebrun, Chief, and other Bandits, friends of Dulcinée,
                          and others

*Time:* The Middle Ages.                    *Place:* Spain

Act I.    Square in front of the house of Dulcinée, whose
beauty people praise in song. Into the midst of the throng ride
Don Quichotte and his comical companion, Sancho. They give
money to the beggars who flock round them. Night and moonlight. Don Quichotte serenades Dulcinée ('Quand apparaissent
les étoiles'), arousing the jealousy of Juan, a lover of the professional beauty, who now appears and prevents a duel. She is
amused by the avowals of Don Quichotte, and promises to
become his beloved if he will recover a necklace stolen from her
by brigands.

Act III.    On the way to the camp of the brigands, Don
Quichotte composes a poem in Dulcinée's honour, much to
Sancho's exasperation. Here occurs the fight with the windmill.

Act III.    Camp of the brigands. Don Quichotte attacks them.
Sancho retreats. The Knight is captured. He expects to be put to
death. But his courage, his grave courtesy, and his love for his
Dulcinée, deeply impress the bandits. They free him and give
him the necklace.

Act IV.    Fête at Dulcinée's. To the astonishment of all Don
Quichotte and Sancho put in an appearance. Dulcinée, overjoyed
at the return of the necklace, embraces the Knight. He entreats
her to marry him at once: 'Marchez dans mon chemin'. Touched
by his devotion, Dulcinée disillusions him as to the kind of
woman she is.

Act V.    A forest. Don Quichotte is dying. He tells Sancho
that he has given him the island he promised him in their travels;
the most beautiful island in the world—the 'Island of Dreams'.
In his delirium he sees and hears Dulcinée. The lance falls from
his hand. The gaunt figure in its rusty suit of armour—no longer
grotesque, but tragic—stiffens in death.                    K.W.

# MICHAEL IVANOVITCH GLINKA

## (1804–1857)

### A LIFE FOR THE TSAR

#### (Ivan Susanin)

OPERA in four acts and an epilogue by Michael Ivanovitch Glinka; text by G. F. Rozen. Première December 9, 1836, St. Petersburg. This work opened every new season at St. Petersburg and Moscow until 1917. Since the Russian Revolution it has been known as *Ivan Susanin*. First performed la Scala, Milan, 1874; Covent Garden, 1887, with Albani, Scalchi, Gayerre, Devoyod; Manchester, 1888 (in Russian); Stuttgart, 1937; Berlin, Staatsoper, 1940, with Cebotari, Roswaenge, Prohaska.

### CHARACTERS

Antonida, *Susanin's daughter*....................Soprano
Ivan Susanin, *a peasant* .........................Bass
Sobinjin, *Antonida's bridegroom* ..................Tenor
Vanja, *an orphan boy adopted by Susanin* .......Contralto
A Polish Commander ........................Baritone

*Time:* 1613          *Place:* Domnin, Moscow, and a Polish camp

Act I.    A village street at Domnin. The peasants sing a patriotic song to celebrate the imminent return of Sobinjin from the wars. Antonida, his fiancée, is no less glad, and in a cavatina she pours out her happiness at the prospect of seeing him again. Susanin enters with news that is less to the taste of the company; a Polish army is advancing on Moscow. The chorus is alarmed, but their fears lessen when Sobinjin himself appears and tells them that the Poles have in fact been repulsed. He is anxious that his marriage with Antonida should immediately be celebrated, but Susanin is full of forebodings at the state of the country and will not bless their union until a Tsar has been elected. Sobinjin finds this objection easy to overcome; a Tsar has in fact just been chosen, and it is no other than their own landlord, Romanoff. Susanin withdraws his objections, and, amidst general rejoicing, agrees to the wedding.

Act II.    The Polish headquarters. A magnificent ball is in progress, and the Poles are full of confidence that their forth-coming campaign against the Russians will be crowned with success. A series of dances follows, including a Cracoviak and two Mazurkas. A messenger enters and tells the Polish com-mander of the Polish defeat and of the election of Romanoff as Tsar of Russia. The Poles plan to capture the young Tsar at the monastery where he is at present living.

Act III.    Susanin's house. Vanja sings a song, and Susanin joins in to comment on Russia's present happy state. He goes on to say that he hears rumours that the Poles are planning to cap-ture the young Tsar. Vanja and Susanin look forward to the day when the boy will be old enough to take his place amongst Russia's soldiers. Peasants enter to congratulate Antonida and Sobinjin on their wedding, and a quartet follows for Antonida, Vanja, Sobinjin, and Susanin, in which all comment on their happiness.

In the middle of the rejoicing Polish troops enter and try to force Susanin to tell them the way to the monastery where the Tsar lives. Susanin at first refuses, but then manages to convey to Vanja that he must ride ahead to warn the Tsar while Susanin himself leads the Poles out of their way. He pretends to accept their bribe, and goes off with them, much to the despair of Antonida, who comes in just in time to see her father taken off.

She tells Sobinjin of the disaster which has come upon them; he does his best to console her, and gathers together a band of peasants with whom he goes off in an attempt to rescue Susanin.

Act IV.    A forest, at night. Sobinjin's men are disheartened by the intense cold, but in a vigorous aria he restores their confidence. Glinka composed an alternative version for this scene, and set it in the forest near the monastery. Vanja, who has ridden his horse to death, rushes in, knocks at the monastery doors and convinces the servants of the danger which threatens the Tsar's life.

The scene changes to another part of the forest. Everything is covered in snow, and the Poles accuse Susanin of having lost the way. He denies it, and they light a fire before settling down to rest for the night. Susanin is left alone, and in a famous scene he makes up his mind that it is his duty to give his life for his country. A storm blows up, the Poles awake, and, as day dawns, Susanin tells them that he has deliberately led them astray into the wildest part of the forest; the Tsar is safe and beyond their reach. They kill him.

Epilogue.    A street in Moscow. Everyone is festively dressed and they sing the praises of the Tsar. Antonida, Vanja, and Sobinjin join the crowd. The news of Susanin's death has reached the capital, and the crowd shares the grief of his dependents.

The scene changes to a place in front of the Kremlin. The Tsar's procession can be seen entering the capital.    H.

## RUSSLAN AND LUDMILLA

Opera in five acts by Michael Ivanovitch Glinka, text by V. F. Shirkov and K. B. Bakhturin after Pushkin. Première December 9, 1842, at St. Petersburg. First performed London, Lyceum Theatre, 1931, with Lissitchkina Rebane, Pozemkovsky, Kaidanoff; Berlin, Staatsoper, 1951, with Keplinger Müller, Hülgert, Wolfram, conductor Quennet.

### CHARACTERS

Svietosar, *prince of Kiev* ...........................Bass
Ludmilla, *his daughter* .........................Soprano
Russlan, *a knight* ............................Baritone
Ratmir, *oriental prince* .......................Contralto
Farlaf, *a warrior* ..................................Bass
Gorislava, *Ratmir's slave* ......................Soprano
Finn, *a good fairy* .............................Tenor
Naina, *a bad fairy*.....................Mezzo-Soprano
Bayan, *a bard*...................................Tenor
Tchernomor, *an evil dwarf*

Michael Ivanovitch Glinka's second opera is based upon one of Pushkin's earliest poems. The poet had hardly agreed to prepare a dramatic version of his fairy-tale for the composer when he was killed in a duel incurred owing to the supposed infidelity of his wife. As a result of his untimely end, Glinka employed the services of no less than five different librettists. This, of course, weakened the story.

The opera opens with an entertainment held by the Grand Duke of Kiev in honour of his daughter Ludmilla's suitors. A bard prophesies wonders in the future in connection with Ludmilla and Russlan, and Ludmilla herself welcomes her suitors and sings of her reluctance to leave her own home and the music which has been her joy in it. Of the three suitors, Russlan, a knight, Ratmir, an Oriental poet, and Farlaf, a blustering coward, Russlan is the favoured one. A thunderclap followed by sudden darkness interrupts the festivities. When this is over, Ludmilla has disappeared. After a canon for Ludmilla's father and her three suitors, Svietosar promises her hand in marriage to any one who will rescue her.

The second act takes place in the cave of Finn, the wizard, to whom Russlan has come for advice. The knight hears that the abduction is the work of Tchernomor the dwarf. Finn warns him against the interference of Naina, a wicked fairy. He then starts out on his search. The next scene shows Farlaf in consultation with Naina. Here occurs Farlaf's famous *Rondo*, a brilliant patter song. The fairy advises him to neglect Ludmilla until she is found by Russlan, then to carry her off again. The next scene shows Russlan on a battlefield. He muses on the silent field: perhaps death will come as silently, and he will hear no more of the singing in which he delights. In spite of the mist he finds a lance and shield. When the atmosphere grows clearer he discovers a gigantic head, which by its terrific breathing creates a storm. The head is represented musically by a chorus which sings inside it. Russlan subdues the head with a stroke of his lance. Under it is the magic sword which will make him victorious over Tchernomor. The head then explains that its condition is due to its brother, the dwarf, and reveals to Russlan the use to be made of the sword.

Act III.    The enchanted palace of Naina. Nymphs sing a chorus of enticement. Gorislava, who loves Ratmir, appears. When the object of her passion appears he slights her for a siren of Naina's court. Russlan, too, is imperilled by the sirens, but he is saved from their fascination by Finn.

The fourth act takes place in the dwelling of Tchernomor. Ludmilla, in despair, refuses to be consoled by any distraction. She finally falls asleep, only to be awakened by Tchernomor and his train. The arrival of Russlan interrupts the ensuing ballet. Forcing Ludmilla into a trance, Tchernomor meets Russlan in single combat. The knight is victorious, but unable to awaken Ludmilla from her sleep. He carries her off.

In the fifth act Russlan, with a magic ring, the gift of Finn, breaks Tchernomor's spell and restores Ludmilla to consciousness.                                                    K. W.

# MODEST MOUSSORGSKY
## (1839–1881)

### BORIS GODOUNOV

OPERA in a prologue and four acts by Modest Moussorgsky; text from Pushkin's play of the same name and Karamzin's *History of the Russian State*. There have been no less than four main versions of *Boris*, two by Moussorgsky and two by Rimsky-Korsakov, quite apart from various more recent attempts to prepare performing versions. (A), composed and orchestrated between October 1868 and December 1869, consisted of seven scenes: Courtyard of Novodevichy Monastery; Coronation; Pimen's cell; the inn; the Tsar's apartments; before the Cathedral of St. Basil in Moscow (including the simpleton); death of Boris. This version was submitted to the committee of the Imperial theatres and rejected by them. (B) Moussorgsky immediately started on a second version, accepting the advice of his friends during composition, and finishing by June 1872. In February 1872 the Coronation scene was performed by Napravnik at a concert, and in April Balakirev conducted the Polonaise. This version was also rejected by the committee, but the Inn scene and the two scenes of the Polish act were performed publicly in February 1873 at the Marinsky Theatre with Petrov, the most famous Russian bass of his day, as Varlaam, Komissarzhevsky as Dimitri, Platonova as Marina; the rest of the programme consisted of Act I of *Freischütz* and Act II of *Lohengrin*. As a result of the success of this performance, the entire opera (though with a number of important cuts) was performed on January 27/February 8, 1874, with Melnikov as Boris, and Petrov, Komissarzhevsky, and Platonova in the parts they had played in 1873; Napravnik conducted, and the opera was a great success with the public, although damned by the critics. By 1882 it had dropped from the repertory. In 1896 Rimsky-Korsakov revised and re-scored the work making a large number of cuts and composing some new passages to bridge the gaps caused by the cuts. This (C) was performed in 1896; in 1899 by the Mamontov Company, with Chaliapin in the title rôle; and in 1904 at the Imperial Theatres, again with Chaliapin in the title rôle. In 1906–8, Rimsky, Korsakov worked on another edition of the opera (D) in which he restored the cuts he had previously made, but left in his own additions to the score. It is in version (D) that the opera has usually been performed.

First produced Paris Opéra, 1908; la Scala, Milan, 1909; Metropolitan, New York, 1913, with Didur, conductor Toscanini; London, Drury Lane, 1913, with Chaliapin; Aldwych, London (in English), 1916. Revived, Metropolitan, 1921, with Chaliapin; 1939, with Pinza; 1943, with Kipnis; la Scala, 1922, with Vanni Marcoux, conductor Toscanini; 1930, with Chaliapin; 1941, with Pasero; 1949, with Christoff, conductor Dobrowen; Covent Garden, 1928, with Chaliapin. In 1935 Moussorgsky's (A) was performed at Sadler's Wells, London (in English), with Ronald Stear as Boris; in 1948, Moussorgsky's (B) was produced at Covent Garden (in English), with Silveri in the title rôle; in 1949 Christoff sang the title rôle, in 1950 (by which time a retrograde step to Rimsky-Korsakov's orchestration had been made) Weber was Boris, and in 1952 Rossi-Lemeni sang the title rôle.

## CHARACTERS

Boris Godounov ...............................Baritone
Feodor ...............................Mezzo-Soprano
Xenia .....................................Soprano
The Old Nurse ............................Contralto
Prince Shouisky ...............................Tenor
Andrey Tchelkalov, *clerk of the Douma* ..........Baritone
Pimen, *monk and chronicler* ......................Bass
The Pretender Dimitri, *called Grigory* ..............Tenor
Marina Mnishek, *a Polish princess* ..............Soprano
Rangoni, *a Jesuit in disguise* ......................Bass
Varlaam ⎫ *vagabonds* ⎧ ..................... Bass
Missail ⎭ ⎩ ...............................Tenor
The Hostess of the Inn ..................Mezzo-Soprano
Nikitin (Michael), *constable* ......................Bass
The Idiot .....................................Tenor
Two Jesuits .....................................Bass

*Time:* 1598–1605      *Place:* Russia and Poland

The subject brings to the stage one of the most curious episodes of the history of Russia in the sixteenth and seventeenth centuries. Boris Godounov, the brother-in-law and chief minister of the Tsar Feodor, son of Ivan, has caused to be assassinated the young Dimitri, half-brother of the Tsar and his heir. On the death of Feodor, Boris, who has committed his crime with the sole object of seizing power, has himself acclaimed by the people and ascends the throne. But about the same time, a young monk named Grigory escapes from his convent, discards his habit, and goes to Poland where he passes as the dead tsarevitch Dimitri. The Polish government receives him all the more cordially as it understands the advantage such an event might afford it. Soon the pretended Dimitri, who has married the daughter of the Voyevode of Sandomir, puts himself at the head of the Polish army and marches with it against Russia. Just at this moment they hear of the death of Boris, and the false Dimitri, taking advantage of the circumstances, in turn usurps power.

As a matter of historical fact, Boris's son Feodor was murdered and his daughter Xenia taken by Dimitri as his mistress (Dvorak's opera *Dmitrij* deals with these events). Dimitri's tenure of power was not long, as he was deposed and killed by Shouisky, who reigned in his stead. History has acquitted Boris of the crime of murdering Feodor (although for the purposes of the opera it must of course be accepted as true), but Shouisky goes down as an ambitious and cruel Tsar. Marina seems to have been all that is implied in the opera; after the death of Dimitri, she became the wife of yet another pretender to the throne, whom she claimed to recognise as her lost husband.

Of the poetical drama, a historian of Russian music, himself a musician, César Cui, has written: 'There is no question here of a subject of which the different parts, combined in such a way as to present a necessary sequence of events, one flowing from the other, correspond in their totality to the ideas of a strict dramatic unity. Each scene in it is independent; the rôles, for the greater part, are transitory. The episodes that we see follow each other necessarily have a certain connection; they all relate more or less to a general fact, to a common action; but the opera would not suffer from a rearrangement of the scenes nor even from a substitution of certain secondary episodes by others. This depends on the fact that *Boris Godounov* properly speaking is neither a drama nor an opera, but rather a musical chronicle after the manner of the historical dramas of Shakespeare. Each of the acts, taken separately, awakens a real interest which, however, is not caused by what goes before and which stops brusquely without connection with the scene which is going to follow.' Let us add that some of these scenes are written entirely in prose while others are in verse and we will have a general idea of the make-up of the libretto of *Boris Godounov*, which moreover offered the composer a series of scenes very favourable to music.

K. W.

Prologue.    After a short prelude the curtain goes up to show the courtyard of the Monastery of Novodevichy, near Moscow. It is crowded with people, who are ordered by a police officer to keep up a prayer for guidance. The moment his back is turned they show clearly by their talk among themselves that they are in entire ignorance of why they are there at all. The prayer rises to a frenzy of wailing, but is interrupted by the appearance of Tchelkalov, the secretary of the Douma, who informs them that

Boris has not yet yielded to the petitions of the government and people, who urge him to accept the crown.

The sound of pilgrims nearing the monastery can be heard, and they distribute alms and relics to the people as they pass through their midst.

The second scene of the prologue is laid in the courtyard of the Kremlin in Moscow. Facing the spectators in the background is the Red Staircase leading to the Tsar's apartments; on the right and near the front, the people on their knees occupy the space between the two Cathedrals of the Assumption and the Archangels. The porches of both churches are in view.

Bells are pealing and a procession of boyars and guards crosses the stage. Prince Shouisky cries 'Long life to thee, Tsar Boris Feodorovitch', and the people break into a splendid song in praise of the new Tsar. Boris himself appears, and, in a mood that is introspective rather than triumphant, prays for the guidance of Tsar Feodor in his great task; may he justify the people's confidence during the reign that is just beginning. He bids the boyars come with him to pray before the tombs of Russia's departed rulers; after prayer, the people from beggar to prince shall feast as his guests. The people break out again into acclamation, and the curtain falls.

Act I.    It is five years since Boris's coronation. The background to the story is one of famine and plague, and the people have deserted the ways of law and order and taken to pillage. For Russia's misfortunes, for the death of his sister, Tsar Feodor's widow, for the death of his prospective son-in-law, Boris is blamed—and this in spite of his efforts to rule wisely and well.

The scene is a cell in the monastery of Chudov, where the old monk, Pimen, is engaged on his chronicle of the history of Russia. It is late at night, but Pimen is satisfied that he has reached the end of his labours. He will be able to leave his history to be continued in the future by some monk, as anonymous and little anxious for personal glory as himself. The sound of chanting can be heard from another part of the monastery, and suddenly Grigory, Pimen's young companion in his cell, wakes up. For the third time he has dreamed that he stood on the top of a high tower from which he could see all Moscow lying at his feet. The crowd below mocked him with their laughter, and he, overcome with shame and terror, fell from the tower and awoke from his dream (the reference is to a version of Dimitri's murder; he was thought to have been thrown down from a high tower).

Pimen tries to comfort him, and persuade him to resign himself to a life of contemplation. He himself, before he became a monk and was still young, had fought in the armies of Tsar Ivan the Terrible and had lived a sinful life of fighting and feasting. Grigory continues to lament that his whole life has been spent inside the walls of the monastery, that he has never known action and the world. Pimen reminds him that many of Russia's most famous warriors turned to a solitary existence to end their days in peace, not least of them the war-like Ivan himself, who died in this very cell. The last Tsar, Feodor, was a man of peace, but now God has sent to Russia the fierce Tsar Boris, a regicide. At this, Grigory asks Pimen how old would have been Dimitri, brother of Feodor, had he lived. Pimen tells him that he would have been about his own age, nearly twenty (in version (A) Moussorgsky included a passage in which Pimen described the scene after the murder of the young Tsarevitch at Uglitch, but this was omitted from version (B)). The orchestra gives out a theme which is later to be associated both with Grigory's ambition and the murdered Dimitri, whom he pretends to be:

Pimen expresses his hope that Grigory will carry on his work of chronicler when he is dead and gone, and, the bell for matins being heard, he leans on Grigory's arm as he goes to the door of the cell. Grigory remains behind; Boris shall not escape the judgment of heaven for his crime, he says.

The second scene is set in an inn on the Lithuanian border of Russia. The hostess sings a little song, half ribald in content, half nonsense. She is interrupted by the sound of singing from outside, and sees that her visitors are monks. When they enter, they are seen to be as disreputable a pair of vagabonds as ever took to the road; their names are Varlaam and Missail, and their time is spent, by their own admission, mainly in begging and converting the proceeds into good liquor. With them is Grigory, who has escaped from his monastery, and is even now

on his way to Lithuania and freedom, pursued, owing to an unguarded remark of his own before leaving the monastery, by
the police, who have orders to apprehend him.

The hostess provides her reverend guests with wine, and,
warmed by it, Varlaam launches into a ferocious song about his
achievements as a soldier in Ivan the Terrible's army at the
battle of Kazan. It is a moment of splendid vigour. Varlaam
curses Grigory for not joining him in either drink or song, and
becomes positively maudlin in his reflections. Meanwhile, Grigory
takes the hostess aside and questions her on the best route to
the Lithuanian border. She tells him that patrols are out because
of some fugitive monk from Moscow, but confides that there is
a safe road by which he may reach his goal unobserved.

Varlaam continues to sing and he is obviously on the verge of
falling asleep when the room is suddenly full of the guards of
whom the hostess has just been complaining to Grigory that they
never catch their man and serve only to annoy peaceful citizens
like herself. They question Grigory, who strikes them as harmless enough, then turn their attention to the vagabond monks,
who seem well enough to fit the description of the man they are
after. Varlaam and Missail are perfectly accustomed to such
cross-questioning, and their answers have the whine of long
experience about them. The captain of the police hands the
warrant to Varlaam and orders him to read it, but he pleads
lack of practice. Grigory is instructed to read it aloud; he does
so, substituting a description of Varlaam for what is written on
the paper. When they surround the old monk, he says he will
make an effort to decipher the paper, which plainly does not
say what Grigory has read out, since he is not the renegade they
are after. With much difficulty he spells out the correct sense, and
all realise that Grigory is their man. He jumps out of the window
and escapes.

Act II. The Tsar's apartments in the Kremlin. The Tsarevitch Feodor is sitting reading, while his sister Xenia sings sadly
to herself of the husband who died before they were ever married.
The Nurse tries to comfort her, then sings a nursery song about
a gnat. Feodor complains that it is a very depressing song, and
leads another, a clapping game, in which the Nurse joins. As it
reaches its climax the Tsar himself appears, the Nurse is overcome with terror and vainly tries to explain to Boris that she is

an old woman and easily frightened. Boris comforts his daughter
in her misery, and goes over to where his son is looking at a
map of the Russian empire. He bids him take his lessons seriously;
the time may soon come when he will be called on to rule over
the countries he sees outlined on this map.

In his son's presence Boris pours out his agony of mind, the
doubts and torments which his rule over Russia has brought him,
the enemies who conspire against him, the remorse which fills
his soul when he recalls the murdered Dimitri. This great monologue ('I have attained the highest power') rises to a climax of
intensity, then falls away as Boris himself sinks under the weight
of conscience. Two themes should be quoted; the first is heard
again during the scene of Boris's death:

the second is associated with his guilt in relation to the murdered
Dimitri.

A noise is heard outside, and the Tsar sends Feodor to find
out its cause. The boyar-in-waiting comes to ask for an audience
on behalf of Prince Shouisky. Boris says he will see him. The
boyar goes on to warn his master of the rumours that the dis-
affected nobles have been in touch with the Poles at Cracow,
and that Shouisky himself is in league with them. A messenger
has even arrived from Cracow . . . let him be arrested, says
Boris. As the boyar leaves, Feodor returns, and explains to his
father in a charming song that the fuss was about a parrot
which escaped and flew at the maids in its panic. Boris is pleased
with the way his son tells the story.

Shouisky comes in and is greeted with a storm of abuse from
Boris, who accuses him of double-dealing, hypocrisy and treason.
Shouisky brushes the accusations aside, but tacitly admits his
correspondence with the rebels. He has come he says to bring

Boris grave news; a pretender has arisen in Poland, and has been publicly acknowledged by the King of Poland, and privately by the Pope. After assuring the Tsar that his throne is inviolate and protected by the love his people bear him, he adds that he is in duty bound to warn him that it is possible the Russian people themselves might be attracted to the pretender's cause if he were to cross the border calling himself Dimitri and claiming to be the lost Tsarevitch.

At mention of Dimitri's name the Tsar dismisses his son (illogically, Ernest Newman quite rightly claims, since he has already in his presence mentioned the death of his rival for the throne), and is alone with Shouisky. He orders him to confirm or deny that Dimitri's was the body which was buried at Uglitch; does he not know the story that the dead can walk again? Shouisky makes as if to soothe his fears. The boy was in truth Dimitri, and he himself watched for five days while the bodies of the prince and the men killed by the crowd as his murderers lay on the cathedral steps. The others began to putrefy, but Dimitri's alone was as fresh as when it was killed, in spite of the blood-red circle round his neck. On Dimitri's face, an angelic smile was seen.

Boris can bear the story no more, and signs to Shouisky to leave him. Shouisky looks back as he goes out and sees Boris sink exhausted into a chair. He feels that he is suffocating, as much with terror and remorse as from lack of air. At this very moment a chiming clock (it is known that they were introduced into Russia in Boris's time) begins to strike. The figures begin to move, and Boris takes them for an apparition of the murdered child. His hysteria verges on madness, and he sinks sobbing to the floor as he prays to God for forgiveness. The sinister power of the music is extraordinary, and Ernest Newman has called it 'one of the most tremendous scenes in all opera'.

Act III.    The Polish Act. The first scene is laid in the apartments of Marina Mnishek, daughter of the Voyevode of Sandomir. The girls amuse her with their songs, and she in turn sings of her ambition; she is not interested in love songs but in tales of heroic deeds. She dismisses her attendants and sings an air *alla mazurka*, in which she gives further vent to her ambitious plans, particularly as they concern the pretender Dimitri, through whom she hopes to ascend the throne of Russia.

Her reveries are interrupted by the sudden appearance of Rangoni, a Jesuit, introduced into the story by Moussorgsky. He exhorts her to remember her duty to her faith when she is paramount ruler in Moscow; her aim must be to convert the heretic Russians to the true religion. Marina's angry objections are silenced when he protests that he is heaven's messenger and so the keeper of her soul.

The second scene is laid by a fountain in the garden of Mnishek at Sandomir; it takes place by moonlight. Dimitri has been given a rendezvous by Marina and as he waits for her, he sings ardently of his love. What has been described as an 'oily, snake-like motive' in the shape of a chromatic scale announces that Rangoni has sidled into view. He tells Dimitri (as Grigory is now known by all) that Marina loves him passionately, in spite of the insults she has had to bear on his account. He will lead Dimitri to his beloved, and in return asks for nothing more than that he shall be allowed to follow the Tsarevitch and to watch over his spiritual welfare wherever he goes. Rangoni bids him hide as Mnishek's guests can be seen coming out of the house.

A polonaise is danced, during which the nobles pay court to Marina and plan their march on Moscow. Dimitri watches the scene with jealous eyes, and it stings him to a resolution he has not known before (this to a more heroic version of the Dimitri theme). When Marina comes out into the garden, she finds him full of tender phrases and protestations, and it takes all her haughtiness and pride to sting him once again into a determined frame of mind, so that he reacts to her insults with a declaration of his intention immediately to lead an army on Moscow. Marina has got from him what she wanted, and she can afford in the famous love duet to fawn on him. Poor Dimitri was not hard to catch, and he takes Marina in his arms as he protests his love for her. At the moment of their embrace, Rangoni can be seen looking from his hiding-place, while the orchestra runs down his chromatic scale to show that the triumph is neither Marina's nor Dimitri's, but his and his church's.

Act IV.   Moussorgsky, advised it is said by his friends, in version (B) placed the scene of Boris's death before the so-called revolutionary scene, thus implicitly making the Russian people the real protagonists of his drama. In (C) and (D), Rimsky-Korsakov reversed this order of things, and when his versions have been performed, the death of Boris finishes the opera and is preceded by the revolutionary scene.

In Moussorgsky's definitive version then, the first scene of Act IV takes place in the Granovitaya Palace in the Kremlin, where a session of the Douma is taking place, expressly summoned to discuss the measures necessary for repelling the invasion which is threatened. They seem more interested in deciding on the pretender's fate once he is in their hands than in suggesting means to catch him, but their deliberations are interrupted by the arrival of Prince Shouisky, just as they were beginning to complain that his absence deprives them of invaluable counsel. Straight away he begins to tell them of the curious sight he saw the previous day, when leaving the Tsar's apartments. Boris was muttering to himself, and seemed to be trying to ward off some spectre, crying as he did so 'Away, away'.

No sooner has he uttered the word than Boris's own voice is heard outside, and the same word is on his lips. He staggers into the chamber and seems to see none of the boyars who watch him in frightened silence. Shouisky brings him to his senses, and he takes his seat on the throne, and prepares to listen to the counsel of his boyars. But Shouisky begs to be allowed to speak, and says that a holy man of great age is waiting outside and desires to speak to the Tsar. Boris thinks this may calm his overheated brain and orders that he be admitted.

It is Pimen, and he tells a strange story. A shepherd, blind since birth, was told in a dream to go to the tomb of the Tsarevitch Dimitri at Uglitch and there to pray beside his tomb. He did so, and immediately his sight was restored. Boris is overcome with horror at this mention of Dimitri, and, calling for light, falls unconscious into the arms of the boyars. He understands that he is dying, and sends for his son and for the *skhima* (it was customary for the Tsar to be received into the church as a monk before he died).

When Feodor arrives, Boris orders that they be left alone. He bids farewell to his son, and tells him that he is lawful heir to the throne of Russia. Let him beware of the nobles and their plots, and let him care with his life for the Russian people and for his sister Xenia, who will be under his protection. He feels the hand of death upon him, and prays to God that his children may be blessed. The sound of the passing bell can be heard, and

then, softly from behind the scenes, the chant of monks praying
for the repose of the Tsar's soul. The boyars return to the
chamber, and, with a last cry of 'While I have breath I still am
Tsar', Boris falls dying in their midst.

Perhaps the opera owed its original popularity in the early
years of the twentieth century as much to Chaliapin's performance
of the title rôle as to anything else, and in particular to his singing
and acting of this death scene. But its power is such and its
effect so moving that it would be wrong to think that only a
Chaliapin can do it justice. It is likely to stand for many years to
come as one of the great scenes of opera.

The second scene of Act IV is laid in a clearing in the forest
of Kromy. Dimitri has marched into Russia at the head of his
troops, and the country is in a chaotic state of famine and pillage.
It is hard to imagine the disorder and horror which are the
natural consequences of war, better expressed than in Moussorgsky's music for this scene. During its course, the mob baits a
landlord who has been a supporter of Boris and whom they have
captured. Children mock an idiot, who sings a pathetic song:

and steal the few pence he has managed to collect. Varlaam and
Missail chant the praises of Dimitri, and, when two Jesuits
appear on the scene, denounce them to the crowd, which promptly
prepares to string them up on an improvised gallows.

A procession passes across the scene, heralding the approach
of Dimitri himself, followed by his troops. He releases the boyar
and the Jesuits, and bids the people follow him to Moscow. Then,
at the head of his troops and supporters, he leaves the stage. It
is empty, except for the idiot who has taken no part in welcoming
the new Tsar. Seated on his stone, he bewails the fate of Russia:
'Woe and sorrow always, lament, Russian folk, poor hungry
folk'.

The controversy over whether to use the Rimsky-Korsakov
edition of the score or to return to Moussorgsky's version B—
version A was heard at Sadler's Wells before the war—still seems
to be unresolved. Though most authorities are agreed that the

strength of the original, with its stark scoring, is considerably dissipated by Rimsky-Korsakov's bowdlerisation, managements seem disposed to continue with version D, mostly because singers already know it and are disinclined to re-learn their parts. Audiences which heard the opera when it was produced in English at Covent Garden in 1948 will have some idea of the strength of the work in its original scoring. They will also remember that when a really powerful singing actor was found for the title rôle, considerable portions of Rimsky-Korsakov's scoring had to be introduced as the singer was unfamiliar with the original scoring. The prejudice in fact has still to be broken down.

What has been accepted wherever the work has been performed in virtually whatever version is the extraordinary power of characterisation which Moussorgsky's music possesses. Even as small a rôle as that of the boyar Tchelkalov (whose entire part consists of some thirty bars of music) appears to be a personality and not just a lay figure. The nurse, Feodor and Xenia are more developed, and such characters as Varlaam or Prince Shouisky are superbly portrayed with real economy. Boris himself is a towering creation of demoniac power, and to sing the rôle is the summit of ambition of every bass or bass-baritone with Slav tendencies in his make-up. No less remarkable is the way in which the crowd stands out as one of the main influences in the opera. I have never been convinced that it is projected with even more force than the figure of Boris himself (as some maintain), but the understanding quality of the music Moussorgsky has written for it is extraordinary. *Boris* stands as the finest operatic product of the Russian school.                              H.

# KHOVANTCHINA
## The Khovanskys

Opera in five acts by Modest Moussorgsky; text by the composer and V. V. Stassov. Première February 21, 1886, at St. Petersburg. Completed and orchestrated by Rimsky-Korsakov. Official première St. Petersburg, November 7, 1911, with Zbrueva, Lobinsky, Sharonoff, Chaliapin, conductor Coates; Paris, 1913; London, Drury Lane, 1913, with Petrenko, Damaev, Zaporojetz, Chaliapin, conductor Cooper; Drury Lane, 1917 (in English); Covent Garden, 1919, with Thornton, Millar, Richardson, Allin, conductor Pitt; Paris, 1923, with Charmy, Laval, Journet, Huberty, conductor Koussevitzky; la Scala, Milan, 1926, with Bertana, Dolci, Sdanowsky, Journet; Philadelphia, 1928, with Fedotova, Windheim, Shvetz, Figaniak, conductor Grigaitis; Colon, Buenos Aires, 1933, with Stignani, Ziliani, Morelli, Vaghi;

Florence Festival, 1948, with Pini, Parmeggiani, Inghilleri, Christoff, conductor Gui; la Scala, Milan, 1949, with Barbieri, Francesco Albanese, Inghilleri, Christoff, Rossi-Lemeni, conductor Dobrowen; Metropolitan, New York, 1950, with Stevens, Sullivan, Tibbett, Hines, conductor Cooper; Munich 1956, with Töpper, Hopf, Holm, Metternich, Frick, Engen, cond. Fricsay.

## CHARACTERS

Prince Ivan Khovansky, *leader of the Streltsy* (*Archers*) Bass
Prince Andrew Khovansky, *his son* ................Tenor
Prince Vassily Galitsin ..........................Tenor
The Boyar Shaklovity..........................Baritone
Dositheus, *leader of the Old Believers* ...............Bass
Martha, *young widow, an Old Believer* .....Mezzo-Soprano
A Scrivener ....................................Tenor
Emma, *a young girl from the German quarter of*
    *the city*.....................................Soprano
Varsonofiev, *attendant upon Galitsin* .............Baritone
Kouzka, *an archer* (*Streltsy*) ....................Baritone
1st ⎫                                    ⎧ ...............Bass
2nd ⎬ *archer of the guard* (*Streltsy*) ⎨ ...............Bass
3rd ⎭                                    ⎩ ............. Tenor
Streshniev ......................................Tenor
Susanna, *an Old Believer* ......................Soprano
Archers, Old Believers, Maids-in-Waiting and Persian Slaves
    in the suite of Prince Ivan Khovansky, Bodyguards of Peter
    the Great (Petrovsky-Poteshny), Populace

*Time:* 1682–9

Acts I, II, and III take place in Moscow; Scene 1 of Act IV on the estate of Prince Khovansky; Scene 2 in Moscow; Act V in a wood near Moscow.

. Moussorgsky's aim was to picture the struggle between the old and the new in Russian life at the time of the assumption of power by Peter the Great (1682–9 is the period chosen). On the one hand there are the Princes Khovansky with their Streltsy followers who are engaged in political strife with the Regent (Galitsin's party); on the other, the Old Believers under Dositheus, who had refused to accept the reforms imposed as long before as 1654. The 'new' regime of Peter the Great was victorious in its struggle against both the Streltsy and the Old Believers, and it is with the outcome of this clash rather than of those between the nobles and their followers that *Khovantchina* is concerned.

Moussorgsky, although he began the opera as early as 1872, did not live to finish it himself, the necessary work of scoring and piecing together being done by Rimsky-Korsakov, who also effected a number of changes within the body of the work itself. The score was published in Rimsky-Korsakov's edition in 1883.

Act I.    There is a beautiful prelude beginning *andante tranquillo*. The Red Square in Moscow at sunrise. Kouzka, an archer,[1] lies asleep on guard. A passing patrol sees him but does not wake the sleeping sentry. From their conversation it appears that the Archers were busy during the night 'making short work' of their opponents in the city. The Scrivener (public letter writer) comes to his place in the square where he is soon engaged by the Boyar Shaklovity who dictates a letter to the Tsar and his council warning them of the plots of Prince Khovansky and his son, who, aided by the Old Believers, would become Tsar. The letter must be anonymous and the Scrivener must forget that he wrote it. A chorus splendidly announces the arrival of Prince Khovansky and causes the Scrivener to quit his place in haste. The Prince arrives and addresses the people, telling them that treason is rife in Russia and that he is determined to crush the enemies of the Tsars. The people end with an invocation of the 'White Swan'. With the assent of the people he orders the Archers to patrol the city.

As soon as the procession has departed with the crowd, Emma enters followed by the Prince's son, Andrew Khovansky, who attempts to kiss her in spite of her resistance. Emma's alarm is allayed by the arrival of Martha, whom Andrew Khovansky has loved and deceived. Martha upbraids Andrew and bids him repent. The angry youth answers by attacking her with a dagger. But Martha is also armed and successfully parries the blow. The arrival of Andrew's father and his Archers puts an end to the quarrel. The old Prince likes Emma's looks and orders his guards to take charge of her. His son would rather kill the girl than see her in the hands of the Archers, and would do so but for Dositheus, who arrives in time to arrest Andrew's blow. The chief of the Old Believers restores peace. Martha takes Emma in her care and departs with her. Prince Khovansky and his Archers return

[1] Or streltsy, a band of ill-disciplined troops, who had originally put the Empress Sophia on the throne, but later led by Prince Ivan Khovansky. Many of them were 'Old Believers'.

to the Kremlin, while Dositheus and the Old Believers fall to prayer.

Act II.    An apartment in the house of Prince Galitsin, councillor and one-time lover of the Tsarevna. The Prince is discovered reading a letter from the Tsarevna full of endearing terms. His uneasy conscience tells him, however, not to trust to the favour of his ruler. He has invited Martha to his house to cast his horoscope. Now she is announced by his attendant Varsonofiev. A bowl of water is brought, and gazing intently at it, Martha in her so-called 'Divination', a celebrated and impressive passage, tells of the disgrace and poverty that will be Prince Galitsin's portion in the time that is coming. He dismisses her angrily and gives orders that she must be seized and secretly drowned. Alone he broods on his past services to Russia. His musing is interrupted by the arrival of old Prince Khovansky, who has come to complain of Galitsin's interference in his capacity as adviser to the Tsarevna, and of a slight put upon himself. Angry words pass between them until Dositheus appears and advises that differences be reconciled and a return made to government based on the ancient books and customs. The song of the Old Believers heard in the distance angers Galitsin, while Khovansky sees in them the saviours of Russia. Martha rushes in suddenly to ask Galitsin's protection against his servant who attempted to drown her. He was on the point of doing so but the attempt was foiled by the arrival of the Petrovsky, the bodyguard of Peter the Great. The presence of the Tsar's troops in Moscow, unsuspected hitherto, alarms the Princes. The Boyar Shaklovity comes to tell them that the Tsarevna has proclaimed the Khovanskys traitors.

Act III.    The Streltsy quarter. Martha sits on a mound near the home of Prince Andrew Khovansky and, to a beautiful tune, sings of her past love. She is overheard by Susanna who accuses her of sinful thoughts. Dositheus appears and comforts Martha. As they retire, Shaklovity comes and in an aria, whose mood is almost one of prophetic dedication, expresses the hope that Russia may be freed from a government which oppresses her. The chorus of the Archers approaches and Shaklovity conceals himself. They arrive singing a drinking song and urging one another to repay theft or gossip of neighbours by ravage and destruction. Their women folk now enter and revile them. The uproar is stilled by the arrival of the Scrivener. He has seen foreign mercenaries attack women and children on the outskirts of the Archers' own quarters. The Archers call in alarm to Prince Khovansky asking to be led against the mercenaries. But the Prince advises submission to the will of Tsar Peter.

Act IV, Part 1.    The residence of Prince Ivan Khovansky. As the Prince is listening to the singing of his serving girls, Varsonofiev comes from Prince Galitsin to warn him of the danger which threatens him. Khovansky does not heed the warning and orders his Persian slaves to be brought to him to dance. As the dancing ends the Boyar Shaklovity enters to invite Khovansky to the Tsarevna's council. Khovansky at first refuses to go but later makes ready to accompany him. As he leaves the room, he is stabbed in the back by Shaklovity.

Part 2.    The square in front of the Church of Vassily Blajeny in Moscow. To the sound of impressively solemn music (in concerts, often known as 'Entr'acte, Act IV'), the people watch the departure of Prince Galitsin in a carriage guarded by troopers. He has been condemned to exile. As they follow at the tail of the guards, Dositheus enters lamenting the fall of the two great nobles, Khovansky and Galitsin. After a short dialogue with Martha he leaves her alone to face Prince Andrew Khovansky, who angrily demands news of Emma. Emma, answers Martha, is now safe and perhaps wedded to the man she loved, from whom she had been separated by Andrew. He threatens Martha with the death of a sorceress at the hands of the Archers. Martha defies him and Andrew calls the Archers. They come, but not in answer to his call—a mournful procession, carrying blocks on which their heads soon must fall. Andrew is taken to a secret refuge by Martha. The crowd asks for the death of the Archers, but the herald of the Tsar's guards comes to announce that they have been pardoned. (As a matter of historical fact, the Streltsy were not pardoned but put to death with the cruellest tortures.)

Act V.    A pine wood near Moscow. The Old Believers have come to their hermitage for the last time. Their cause is lost; their sect persecuted throughout Russia. The quarrels of princes have brought about their ruin. Rather than yield to the soldiers who surround their retreat they will perish together. Dositheus sings a beautiful prayer in which he says that the world shall see how men can die for its salvation. The Old Believers, amongst whom are Martha and Andrew, build a funeral pyre which they ascend carrying a lighted taper. As the flames rise and overpower them the troops sent to arrest them arrive and fall back horror-stricken at the sight of the smoking pyre. F. B., H.

## THE FAIR AT SOROTCHINSKI

Opera in three acts by Modest Moussorgsky; text by the composer, founded on an episode from Gogol's *Evenings on a Farm near Dekanka*. Left un-finished at the time of the composer's death, without the greater part of the last act, and unorchestrated. Given at a concert at St. Petersburg, 1911, semi-publicly at the Comedia Theatre, 1911. Another version at the Free Theatre, Moscow, November 3, 1913. In 1917 the opera was produced in a version by Cesar Cui at the Musical Drama Theatre. This version replaced by yet another for which Tcherepnin was responsible. Monte Carlo, 1923, with Luart, John McCormack; Buenos Aires, 1929; Metropolitan, New York, 1930, with Müller, Bourskaya, Jagel, Pinza, conductor Serafin; Fortune Theatre, London, 1934; Covent Garden, 1936, with Danieli, de Villiers, Russell, Kassen, conductor Coates; Trieste, 1940, with Sani, Pauli, Serpo, Bettoni; Savoy Theatre, London, 1942, with Bayan, Slobodskaya, Boleslawski, Parry Jones, Kiriloff, conductor Fistoulari.

### CHARACTERS

Tcherevik, *an old countryman* ..................... Bass
Parassia, *his daughter* .......................... Soprano
Khivria, *his wife* ....................... Mezzo-Soprano
Gritzko, *a young countryman* .................... Tenor
The Priest's Son ............................... Tenor
Tcherevik's Crony .............................. Bass
The Gypsy ...................................... Bass

Young Men and Women, Gypsies, Merchants, Cossacks, Jews, etc.

*Place:* Sorotchinski, in Little Russia.

*Sorotchinski Fair* was written at about the same time as *Khovantchina*. The story is one of Gogol's, the scene Gogol's own birth-place, in the Ukraine. Moussorgsky wrote the libretto himself, though handicapped in doing so by his scanty know-ledge of Ukrainian dialect. Much of the opera was unfinished at his death, but it has had more than a little success outside Russia in Tcherepnin's version.

The introduction is labelled 'A Hot Day in Little Russia', and is an attempt to emulate Gogol's description of the atmosphere in which the story is to take place. The curtain rises on Act I to reveal a market scene: 'Moussorgsky constructs' (says Calvocoressi in his 'Master Musicians' volume on the composer) 'a sort of kaleidoscopic musical mosaic which conveys, as realistically as an opera chorus can hope to convey, the confused impression of a country fair'. Tcherevik has brought his daughter, Parassia, to a fair for the first time, and she is excited at the bustle, and the quantity of things which are for sale. An old gypsy raises his voice above the hubbub to wish everyone well, but also to warn them that the ground on which they stand is cursed by the periodic visitation of a devil—taking the form of a pig and looking, according to legend, for the sleeve (or 'red *svitka*') of a garment he had pawned years ago, but of which he has never been able to recover this one portion.

Parassia has found her young lover, Gritzko, with whom she sits while the gypsy is telling his story. Tcherevik suddenly notices that she is not with him, but Gritzko introduces himself, and asks for Parassia's hand in marriage. The old man can see no harm in such an idea, particularly since Gritzko is the son of an old friend of his, and he gives the couple his blessing. Tcherevik disappears, but presently he and his crony reappear from the inn, happily drunk. They are not left long in peace, Khivria, Tcherevik's wife, putting in an appearance, and showing little disposition to acquiesce in the notion of acquiring a son-in-law whom she has not yet even seen, much less approved of.

They leave the stage, and Gritzko laments the turn his affairs have taken. It is a beautiful aria, but intended by the composer for Act III, not Act I at all, the scene in which Gritzko gives way to his sadness having been indicated in the scenario but not (as far as is known) composed. To Gritzko comes the old gypsy, offering, in return for a reduction in the price of the oxen Gritzko wishes to sell him, to convert Tcherevik (and, through him, Khivria) to the idea of Gritzko's marriage with Parassia. Gritzko gladly accepts the offer and the bargain which goes with it.

The act should end with the *Hopak* (the best known bit of the score), but in Tcherepnin's version this is transferred to the end of the opera, where it makes an excellent finale. In its place is a duet for Parassia and Gritzko, which brings the act to an end.

Act II.    Tcherevik's house. Khivria is busy in the kitchen. Tcherevik is asleep. He wakes up, and there is a short quarrel between husband and wife, during whose course Khivria enquires about the sale of the farm produce. Tcherevik leaves the room, and Khivria waits anxiously for her lover, the priest's son, for whom she has prepared the delicacies he cannot resist. He eventually comes into sight, and makes a splendidly comic figure, his priestly utterances contrasting nicely with his evidently unpriestly intentions. These he is busy making manifest, when suddenly there is a noise outside. Khivria has only just time to hide her lover before Tcherevik and his cronies return home, making a deal of noise, and scared at the idea of being where the 'red sleeve' is liable to be found.

They all drink, and, to keep their spirits up, Tcherevik sings riotously for their entertainment. The unfortunate priest's son knocks over a tin can but this is accepted as the work of the 'red sleeve', and no one takes it for what it is. In the end the crony recites the story for the company. When he reaches the climax, the window blows open, and the head of a pig is seen—it is in this form that the devil is said to roam the world looking for his lost garment. General consternation. In the exclamation of horror which follows the revelation, the priest's son loses his balance, and falls into the midst of the assembly, covered by Khivria's nightdress. Presently he is revealed, and Tcherevik's friends laugh at the resolute, proud Khivria, who has given herself away so badly.

Act III.    The village square: Tcherevik's house visible in the background. Moussorgsky made a special and elaborated version of his *Night on the Bare Mountain* (1867) to act as a ballet-intermezzo between Acts II and III of *Sorotchinski Fair*. The dramatic situation is that Gritzko, the *parobok* (young peasant), is asleep in the open; to him in his dream appears the whole rigmarole of the kingdom of darkness and black magic, and dances round him.

Parassia, alone, sings sadly of her lover, but, looking into a mirror, regains her spirits and sings a charming Hopak (marked *allegretto grazioso*). She dances as she sings. Tcherevik emerges from the house at the same moment as Gritzko appears. Tcherevik loses no time in giving his consent to the marriage—the Gypsy's scheme has worked perfectly—and the two young lovers celebrate their future happiness in a lively duet. The rejoicing becomes more general as the other villagers join in, and even the advent of Khivria, emitting story-book step-mother's disapproval from every pore, cannot put a damper on the jollity; Tcherevik has acquired new authority from the episode of the Priest's son, and will brook no contradiction. The opera ends with the exciting Hopak designed by Moussorgsky to come at the end of Act I but transferred by Tcherepnin.

It must be emphasised that the version referred to is Tcherepnin's, which does not by any means follow Moussorgsky's sketch-plan in every particular. However, as the third act, and even the end of the second, exist in no more than fragmentary form, and as Tcherepnin's is the version usually heard, it seemed more practical to concentrate on that, rather than elaborate on the work in its unfinished state.                                    H.

# PETER ILITSCH TCHAIKOVSKY

## (1840–1893)

TCHAIKOVSKY wrote no fewer than ten operas, which together constitute a bulky argument to set against the idea that he was primarily an instrumental composer with a dramatic work or two to his credit. Their success has been decidedly varied, but at least two of them have established themselves in the world's restricted operatic repertory—*Eugen Onegin* and *The Queen of Spades*. Pointing out the contrast between their continental fame and the typical English attitude towards them, Desmond Shawe-Taylor wrote in 1950: 'It is insular ignorance to regard them as interesting failures, or even as obscure local successes. In Russia their great popularity has not only survived the Revolution but positively increased: Tatiana is now the beloved heroine of the factory, as formerly of the drawing-room; though gambling and superstition are officially frowned upon, Herman and the ghost of the Countess have lost nothing of their glamour'.

## EUGEN ONEGIN

Opera in three acts by Peter Ilitsch Tchaikovsky; text by the composer and K. S. Shilovsky, after Pushkin. Première Imperial College of Music, Little Theatre, Moscow, March 29, 1879; publicly Moscow, 1881; Olympic Theatre, London, 1892 (in English); la Scala, Milan, 1900; Covent Garden, 1906, with Destinn, Battistini, Journet, conductor Campanini; Metropolitan, New York, 1920, with Muzio, Martinelli, de Luca, Didur, conductor Bodanzky; revived 1957, with Amara, Tucker, London, cond. Mitropoulos. Sadler's Wells, 1934, with Cross, Wendon, Austin, conductor Collingwood; revived 1952, with Shuard, Rowland Jones, Sharp; Vienna, 1937, with Lehmann, Maikl, Sved, Hofmann, conductor Walter; Berlin, 1945, with Lemnitz, Witte, Domgraf-Fassbaender; New York City Centre, 1947, with Brenda Miller; Vienna, 1950, with Welitsch, Schock, London, Frick.

### CHARACTERS

Madame Larina, *who owns an estate* ......Mezzo-Soprano
Tatiana ⎫ *her daughters* ⎰ ....................Soprano
Olga ⎭ ⎱ ....................Contralto
Filipievna, *Tatiana's nurse*................Mezzo-Soprano

Lenski, *Olga's fiancé* ............................Tenor
Eugen Onegin, *his friend* ......................Baritone
Prince Gremin, *an old general* ......................Bass
A Captain .......................................Bass
Zaretski .......................................Bass
Monsieur Triquet, *a Frenchman* ...................Tenor
*Time:* Late Eighteenth Century      *Place:* A landed estate;
St. Petersburg

The idea of setting Pushkin's poem, *Eugen Onegin*, as an opera seems to have been suggested to Tchaikovsky in 1877, by which date he had already written four operas. After a short hesitation, he accepted the subject, and with it the risk of being accused of misrepresenting a classic—for Pushkin's poem was already looked upon in Russia as being in that class. He seems to have set the Letter scene straight away, and at the time he wrote that 'he loved Tatiana and was terribly indignant with Onegin, who seemed to him a cold, heartless coxcomb'. It was during the course of work on his opera that he himself received a passionate avowal of love from a girl who had apparently made his acquaintance while he was teaching at the Conservatory in Moscow; his determination not to emulate Onegin was so strong that he took the fatal decision to embark on a loveless marriage. The results were disastrous, and the composer seems to have been lucky to escape with nothing worse than a severe nervous breakdown before the doctors insisted that the marriage come to an end.

Much of Pushkin's social commentary finds no place in the libretto, but in general the latter follows fairly closely the lines of the poem, apart that is to say from the emphasis thrown on Tatiana as opposed to Onegin, and the ending which has been amplified and slightly romanticised so that there is a short duet between Tatiana and Onegin, before Tatiana leaves Onegin to contemplate a future without her.

Act I.    The short prelude is built up on the phrase (Ex. 1):

PLATE XXIX. Carmen (Risë Stevens) and Don José (Richard Tucker) in Act II at Metropolitan, New York.

PLATE XXX. Boris Christoff in Act II of *Boris Godounov*, Covent Garden 1950.

it is wonderfully apt to the purpose, and produces a curious effect of anticipation on the listener.

The curtain rises to reveal Madame Larina's garden. Madame Larina and Filipievna are sitting making jam, and through the open window of the house can be heard the voices of Tatiana and Olga as they practise a duet. The two older women listen to the first stanza in silence but start to talk (like all country house audiences, big or small) during the second, and the duet of necessity becomes a quartet. Outside the garden can be heard the sound of a chorus of reapers coming nearer. They present Madame Larina with a decorated sheaf, singing the while an attractive tune of evident folk-song connections. The chorus is followed by a rapid choral dance.

Tatiana timidly says that these country songs take her in imagination to far-off regions, but Olga takes a matter-of-fact line and says she has no time for such dreams; they do nothing but make her want to dance too. In a little song which is not without tenderness, she gives expression to her light-hearted philosophy. Madame Larina congratulates her daughter, and thanks the reapers for their song; she and Filipievna notice that Tatiana looks pale, but she says (and the clarinet plays a theme associated with her) she is only absorbed in her book, with its tale of lovers' troubles. A carriage is heard on the drive; Lenski must be here—and is it not Onegin with him? Tatiana's imagination flies ahead of her and she tries to get away, but is restrained.

Larina welcomes her two guests, but leaves her daughters to entertain them. A quartet begins, the men and the women conversing separately. Finally, Lenski goes towards Olga, Onegin to Tatiana, and the first pair talk of their mutual pleasure in meeting —they are engaged and have not seen each other since yesterday —and the second of the pleasures, or otherwise, of existence in the country. This conversational music is excellently contrived and sounds, provided the producer can match it as he should, wonderfully natural. Lenski has an *arioso* passage of rapturous import, which is both sincere and immature, conventional and poetic—but then the characters in this opera have a tendency to be life-like persons, rather than romantic giants. The scene often ends at this point, but there is properly a short passage during which Onegin and Tatiana return from their stroll down the garden, the former finishing a story; it gives Filipievna the chance of speculating aloud as to the possibility of Tatiana being interested in the young neighbour.

The scene changes to Tatiana's bedroom, where Filipievna is saying good night to her charge. There is delicate, suggestive orchestral writing in the short prelude. Tatiana and her nurse have been talking, but Tatiana cannot get to sleep and asks Filipievna to tell her a story—about her own early life, and her marriage. Tatiana listens for a bit but her thoughts soon wander and the gradually mounting tension in the orchestra shows the way her feelings are rising. Filipievna asks her if she is ill; no, she is not, but she is in love, Tatiana tells her—and she must keep it a secret.

The moment she is alone, the violence of her emotion is restrained no more, but finds full expression in an orchestral passage which precedes the ecstatic phrase with which she releases her pent-up feelings:

She starts to write and the orchestra with a wealth of detail supplies what she does not say aloud. She makes a fresh start and, as Gerald Abraham[1] has admirably put it, 'the simple oboe line crossed by the dropping fourths and fifths of flute, clarinet and horn and the light splash of the harp magically not only conveys the naive character and romantic mood of the writer but suggests, almost pantomimically, the act of writing in a way comparable with, though not like, the "writing" passages in *Boris Godounov* and *Khovantchina* (the scene in Pimen's cell and the scene of the public scribe)':

[1] In the symposium on Tchaikovsky published by Lindsay Drummond.

Snatches of recitative are interspersed with the letter writing, and the music is now lyrical and reflective, now impassioned and almost declamatory, the contrasting moods being bound together by the commentary of the orchestra. Could she love another, she asks herself? Never!

Everything she has ever done has been done for him, as if in his presence. The horn answers the voice in an expressive phrase:

Gerald Abraham has called it a motto theme for the whole opera, though an unconscious one, which is particularly apt since the Letter scene is known to have been composed before the rest of the opera, Tchaikovsky having even thought at one time of setting it as a song quite apart from its context.

Each stage of the fateful letter which is to change Tatiana's life is expressed in the music until finally it is finished and nothing is left but to send it. Day is dawning, the sound of a shepherd's pipes can be heard, and Filipievna comes to waken Tatiana. She is sent to deliver the note to Onegin, and the curtain falls as the orchestra recapitulates Tatiana's longing.

The third tableau of the first act takes place in a different part of the garden from that we saw in the first scene. Girls sing a graceful, folk-like chorus as they gather the crop of berries, and Tatiana comes on the scene in a state of considerable emotion; she has seen Onegin making his way towards her, and in a minute she will know the answer to her letter; would she had never written it! Onegin, in his aria, expresses himself calmly and collectedly. She has written frankly to him, he will answer her no less frankly, as is her due. He is not cruel, but discouraging within the code of manners. Love and marriage are not for him; he loves her like a brother, no more. The chorus is heard again as Onegin gently leads the humiliated Tatiana from the scene.

Act II.    A ball is in progress at Madame Larina's house in honour of Tatiana's birthday. The guests are engaged in an old-fashioned waltz, and they sing of their enjoyment as they dance (my American score mentions a male semi-chorus of 'Elderly Landed Gentry', which is as nice a designation as is to be found in opera, apart perhaps from the full chorus of Hermits in Verdi's *Attila*). Onegin is there dancing with Tatiana, a combination which gives size to some ill-natured gossip amongst the more senior element of the neighbours, who look upon Onegin with anything but favour. He is bored with the whole business and chooses to direct his spite against Lenski, who insisted he should come, by stealing a dance from Olga that she had promised to her fiancé. Lenski's remonstrances are in vain, and Olga defends her behaviour when he reproaches her with it, giving the cotillon as well to the persistent and—says Lenski—flirtatious Onegin.

There is a diversion as Triquet, the old French tutor, consents to sing a song, which he dedicates to Tatiana. It is a charming piece of pastiche, as good in its way as the equivalent to be found in *Pique Dame*—how well Tchaikovsky did this kind of thing! The Cotillon begins with a Mazurka, and Onegin and Olga dance, watched angrily by Lenski. Onegin provokes him by asking why he does not join in, and a quarrel slowly works up until Lenski challenges his erstwhile friend to give him satisfaction for his behaviour. Madame Larina is in a great state that this sort of thing should happen in her house. In music of melting tenderness, Lenski recalls the happiness he has known in just this house which he has now made the scene of a quarrel and a scandal. In the ensemble which follows, Onegin bitterly regrets his provocative and thoughtless behaviour, and everyone else, including by now Tatiana, is filled with consternation at the prospect of the duel. Onegin makes up his mind that the affair has gone too far for there to be any possibility of a reconciliation, and he and Lenski insult each other, rush together and are separated as the scene comes to an end.

Early next morning the duel is to take place near a mill on the banks of a wooded stream. The melancholy prelude anticipates Lenski's great scene of farewell to life and all he has loved. He and his second, Zaretski, exchange a few words and he is then left alone. He sings of his past, his carefree youth, and contrasts it with his present state, when he cares little whether as a result of the duel he is left alive or dead; the loss of Olga will be his one regret. It is a great lyrical outpouring, supreme amongst tenor scenes in Russian opera, and unbearably pathetic in its context.

Onegin arrives, rather late—Pushkin describes how he over-slept—and Zaretski immediately demands to know where his second is; duels cannot be fought except according to the rules, and he owns that he is a stickler for etiquette. Onegin introduces his servant as his second, and hopes that Zaretski will have no objection; he is a man of the highest character. The two seconds go off to discuss the conditions of the duel, and Lenski and Onegin stand apart without looking at one another and sing a canon. I have read that the duel 'seems rather poor and stagey' (Rosa Newmarch's words) after Lenski's aria, but to me the music at this point seems uncannily right. There is no need to labour the point that the form of a canon exactly expresses the relationship—the thoughts of the two men are similar but divided by form and come together only as they regret that etiquette precludes a reconciliation at this late hour. The bleak tune has just that dead-pan nervousness which the situation might be expected to produce, and the repetition of the word 'No' at the end has a chilling finality. The opponents measure up, and Lenski is killed.

Act III.    Some years have passed and the end of the story takes place in St. Petersburg. A ball is in progress in a fashion-able house—the contrast with the country dance at Madame Larina's cannot be over-emphasised. As the curtain rises, a Polonaise begins (*the* Polonaise often heard in concert perform-ance, just as the Waltz in the previous act was *the* Waltz); it is played through in its entirety with plenty of action but no singing, and a stage production requires presentation in something like ballet form. Onegin is there, just returned at the age of twenty-six to civilisation after the years he has spent in the wilderness

to atone for the death of the friend he has killed in a duel. An
Ecossaise begins but the tempo changes to a slow waltz in D flat

as Prince Gremin and his wife—Tatiana, no less—come into the
ballroom. The guests, Onegin amongst them, comment on her
beauty. The Prince goes to talk to his kinsman, Onegin, who
questions him as to the identity of the lady with whom he has
come to the ball, while Tatiana asks those nearest her who it is
her husband is talking to. The beauty of the waltz theme and the
skill with which Tchaikovsky uses it as a background for conversation are equally notable here.

In an aria Gremin tells Onegin of the love and beauty Tatiana
has brought into his life since their marriage two years ago. The
aria is a favourite of every Russian bass, and it has the important
effect in the opera of turning Gremin from a lay figure into a
thinking, feeling person, part of Tatiana's background it is true,
but real enough to make her loyalty entirely plausible. The single
aria in fact creates the impression of a truly noble figure.

Gremin introduces his wife and his cousin, and Tatiana asks
to be taken home, leaving Onegin to vent his feelings in an impassioned aria, whose final section is the same (a minor third
lower) as the opening section of Tatiana's Letter scene. The
scene ends with a repeat of the Ecossaise.

The last scene plays in a reception room in Prince Gremin's
house. Tatiana has had Onegin's letter and there is no doubt that
he is now passionately in love with her, to such an extent that
words fail him at his entrance and he sinks on his knees at Tatiana's
feet. Tatiana recalls their former meetings—the letter, and his
lecture to her on the subject of maidenly reticence—to a tune
(derived from Gremin's aria) which is heard played by flute and
clarinet in octaves in the orchestral prelude to the scene. She
contrives to make some show of indignation at his return; is he
only looking for the notoriety of having his name coupled with
that of a woman prominent in society? But he is so obviously
sincere and in earnest that she cannot restrain her tears for long.
For a moment they recall the happiness that could have been

theirs long ago, but which, through fate's decree, is now out of
their reach. They must part, says Tatiana, since she is Gremin's
wife. But Onegin urges his love once more, and Tatiana launches
into a big tune in D flat, which is to dominate the rest of the

scene. Characteristically, though it stands for her admission
of her love, it is first heard as she admonishes Onegin to remember
the path of honour and leave her, and only later as an avowal of
love. For a moment they sing this theme together, as Tatiana
prays for courage, but suddenly she finds the strength to go out
of the room, leaving Onegin distraught behind her.

The music of *Onegin* may be said to have grown outwards
from the Letter scene, so much of it is derived from that great
central episode. This is not surprising, since for the most part
the other characters are seen in relation to Tatiana, and therefore
naturally take their cue from her great moment of self-revelation
(the duel scene is the only one in which Tatiana does not appear
at all; otherwise, only the Waltz and the Polonaise may be said
to take place without paying much attention to her or her style
of music). One must assume that it was Tchaikovsky's extraordinary reaction to Tatiana which prompted him to such subtle
development of her music and which enabled him to give the
opera its uncommon unity. One expects a nervous response to
every stimulus from this composer, but the sensitivity he shows
to each contrasting mood, the graded coloration, the concentration on shades and details, all suggest an unusual arousing of his
creative spirit. Its subtlety of detail makes *Onegin* extremely hard
to perform. The opera is not written in sharply defined lengths
(although it is in numbers), and the balance of one section with
another, of one tempo with its near but subtly different neighbour, is no less important than the bringing out of the delicate
colouring of the orchestration. If this is not set about with love
and understanding, quite a lot of what the composer intended
his audience to hear will evaporate before reaching their ears,
and they will thus miss something essential of what is to my
mind one of the great masterpieces yet achieved within the
operatic form.                                        H.

# THE QUEEN OF SPADES
## (Pique Dame)

Opera in three acts by Peter Ilitsch Tchaikovsky; text by Modest Tchaikovsky (the composer's brother), based on Pushkin. Première St. Petersburg, December 19, 1890. First produced at la Scala, Milan, 1906, with Corsi, D'Alberti, de Cisneros, Zenatello, Stracciari, Didur; Metropolitan, New York, 1910, with Destinn, Meitschek, Slezak, Didur, Forsell, conductor Mahler; London Opera House, 1915, with Rosing; Buenos Aires, 1924; Zürich, 1940; Berlin, Staatsoper, 1948, with Scheppan, Rünger, Schuffler, Metternich; Vienna State Opera, 1946, with Hilde Konetzni and Welitsch, Hoengen, Lorenz, Schoeffler, conductor Krips; Covent Garden, 1950 (in English), with Zadek, Coates, Edgar Evans, Rothmüller, Walters, conductor Kleiber.

### CHARACTERS

| | | |
|---|---|---|
| Tchekalinsky | } officers { | .... ................. Tenor |
| Sourin | | .... .................... Bass |

Herman, *a young officer* ......................... Tenor
Count Tomsky ............................. Baritone
Prince Yeletsky ............................. Baritone
The Countess........................... Mezzo-Soprano
Lisa, *her grand-daughter* ....................... Soprano
Pauline, *Lisa's companion* .................. ..... Contralto
Governess ........................... Mezzo-Soprano
Mascha, *Lisa's maid* ......................... Soprano
Master of Ceremonies ......................... Tenor

| | | |
|---|---|---|
| Tchaplitsky | } gamblers { | ...................... Tenor |
| Narumoff | | ........................ Bass |

| | | |
|---|---|---|
| Chloë | | ........... Soprano |
| Daphnis (Pauline) | } in the interlude { | ........... Contralto |
| Plutus (Tomsky) | | ........... Baritone |

Servants, Guests, Gamblers, Children

*Time:* End of Eighteenth Century        *Place:* St. Petersburg

Quite a number of changes of emphasis as well as of detail were made before Pushkin's poem could become an opera libretto—and these have often come in for hostile criticism. Pushkin's story is cynical in character, with a mixture of the grotesque, and his hero is a cold-blooded, unromantic officer, interested only in the secret of the cards and not in any way concerned with Lisa, except in so far as she brings him into contact with the old Countess. Tchaikovsky and his brother have turned Herman into a romantic, almost Byronic character as much in love with Lisa as with gambling, and they have elevated Lisa to become the Countess's grand-daughter, at the same time providing the story with a tragic ending. That they have made something that differs from Pushkin's original story is undeniable; but whether it is any less good, is a moot point.

A short prelude leads to the first scene of Act I, which is laid in an open space in the Summer Garden, St. Petersburg. It is spring, and seated on the benches are nurses and governesses chatting together. Children are playing. After a chorus, in whose course a little group of children play at mounting the guard, Sourin and Tchekalinsky enter, discussing the gambling propensities of Herman; it seems that he was last night at his usual habit of watching the players, but never speaking a word nor even risking a throw.

As they speak, Herman comes in with his friend Tomsky, who is questioning him about the sorrow which seems to hang over his life, and has quite changed him from the spirited boy he once knew. Herman explains the change by saying that he has fallen in love, but does not even know the name of the object of his affections. His *arioso* in praise of the unknown lady has a typical Tchaikovskian freshness. Tomsky suggests that the first thing to do is to learn the lady's name, and then set about wooing her in earnest, but Herman is afraid she is above him in station and will prove beyond his reach. Tomsky is amazed at Herman's mixture of devotion and despair, and they go off together.

The promenade continues, Tomsky and Herman return, and the former greets Prince Yeletsky, who is in the first flush of happiness, having that very morning become engaged. His rejoicings contrast with Herman's bitter despair. A moment later, Yeletsky points out his Lisa to Tomsky, and Herman recognises her as his own beloved. Lisa and her grand-mother, the Countess, exclaim as they catch sight of Herman; they have noticed his ardent looks, but are unaware of his identity. A short quintet ensues, after which Tomsky greets the Countess, who asks Herman's name, and Yeletsky goes towards Lisa.

Presently the Countess takes her grand-daughter away, accompanied by Yeletsky, and the others speculate as to the rumours which surround the Countess's past. She was a great gambler it seems, but has now renounced cards. Is it possible to believe such stories? Tomsky is surprised that her history is not better known, and proceeds to tell it in a ballad. The Countess was a beauty when she was young, and one of her most ardent admirers was the Count Saint Germain; but, alas, she preferred gambling to love. One day at the tables she had lost everything; her depression was noticed by the Count, who followed her from the room, and offered to reveal to her the secret of 'three cards', would she but grant him one rendezvous. Her indignation at such a suggestion was quickly overcome, and next morning she was back at the tables, where nothing could stop her winning run. It was whispered that she subsequently passed the secret on to her husband, and years later to a young gallant who had taken her fancy; but in a dream she had been warned that she would die when next anyone tried to win her secret from her.

The recital is not lost on Herman, and Tchekalinsky and Sourin hasten to repeat the refrain mockingly in his ear. A storm is brewing, and all take shelter except Herman, who stays as if in a trance in the middle of the stage. He broods on the story—what use would the secret be to him with Lisa beyond his reach?—and then gives expression to his determination to win Lisa away from the Prince.

Scene ii.    Lisa's room. A balcony can be seen through the open window, and beyond it the garden. Lisa is sitting at the harpsichord, surrounded by girls of her own age. She and Pauline together sing an old-fashioned duet, which, no less than for instance the opening duet of *Eugen Onegin*, shows how much life Tchaikovsky can breathe into what is no more and no less than pastiche. The listeners duly applaud, and then demand more; Lisa asks Pauline to sing alone, and she follows her romance with a lively peasant song, too lively it appears for the peace of the house, for the governess comes in to ask for a little less noise.

Lisa sees her friends to the door, and tries to fob off Pauline's enquiries about her gloomy look. When she is alone, she gives vent to her feelings in a beautiful aria. Is this marriage to which she is contracted the fulfilment of her dreams? Nobody could have better qualifications than the Prince—he is kind, good-looking, clever, well-born, rich—and yet her heart is full of heavy foreboding.

Suddenly Herman appears at the window. Lisa makes as if to rush through the door, but Herman persuades her to stay and listen to him for a moment. In music of passionate tenderness, he declares his love, and it is immediately evident that Lisa is far from indifferent to what he says. Their conversation is interrupted by a loud knocking at the door; it is the Countess, come to see if Lisa is yet asleep. Herman hides, Lisa calms the Countess's fears, while Herman softly echoes the refrain of Tomsky's ballad; can it be true that she will die when a third man 'impelled by despair' demands to know the secret? When they are left alone, Lisa sinks into Herman's arms, and the curtain falls as they embrace.

Act II.    A large reception room. A masked ball is taking place at the house of a rich dignitary. Theatrical boxes down the sides of the room between the columns. Dances take place, and the movement is general. The Master of Ceremonies invites the guests into the garden to see the firework display, and Tchekalinsky and Sourin plan to play a trick on Herman, who, they say, is obsessed by the idea of the Countess's 'three cards'. The Prince is there with Lisa, to whom he addresses an aria whose sentiments are both noble and touchingly chivalrous: 'I love you, dear, beyond all reck'ning'. They go off together, and Herman appears reading a note which Lisa has sent him; 'After the performance wait for me in the room. I must speak with you'. Did he but know the secret of the 'three cards', he could be wealthy, and then aspire to Lisa's hand. As if in echo of his thoughts, he hears Tchekalinsky and Sourin whisper: 'Are you then that third man? . . . three cards?' Herman wonders whether he is hearing the voice of a ghost.

The Master of Ceremonies announces: 'Our host now prays you all to take your seats, to see a pretty pastoral called *The Faithful Shepherdess*'. The masque begins. It is the story of Daphnis, Chloë, and Plutus. A chorus and saraband are followed by a Mozartian duet for Chloë and Daphnis (the latter is played by Pauline). There is an impressive entry for Plutus (Tomsky), riding in a golden chariot, but Chloë spurns his love, even though it is accompanied by untold wealth, and she and Daphnis plight their troth to the tune of their earlier duet. The chorus rejoices in the happiness of the two lovers.

The interlude over, Herman waits for Lisa. She gives him a key and tells him to gain access to their house through her grandmother's room—the old woman will still be playing cards at midnight—and then with the key open the secret door which is situated behind the portrait of the Countess, and which leads to her own apartments. Herman says he cannot wait until the following day, but will come that very night; Lisa is submissive to his desire. The act ends as the Master of Ceremonies announces the imminent arrival of the Empress herself, and the guests join in welcoming her.

The second scene of Act II is laid in the Countess's bedroom, which is empty. Herman enters, hesitates for a moment, and then hearing the sound of voices conceals himself. The Countess herself, preceded by maids and attendants, comes in. She takes off her evening dress and puts on a night-gown, then stops the sycophantic chorus which has been accompanying her preparations for bed and says she will sit in a chair for a few minutes. Some reflections on the decline of society are followed by reminiscences of 'the old days', when things were done as they should be, when people really could dance, when la Pompadour was queen of Paris, when she herself—the Countess—sang before the King. She sings very softly to herself an air from Grétry's *Richard Cœur de Lion*; then, suddenly aware that the room is still full of servants, their eyes and ears bursting with curiosity, sends them all packing.

She is alone, and again starts to hum the tune which is in her head. But the words die on her lips as she catches sight of Herman in front of her. She does not speak another word, but mouths incoherently as if she had lost the power of speech. Herman begs her not to be frightened; he wants nothing but that she should tell him her secret, the secret of the 'three cards'. In desperation, Herman draws his pistol, and the Countess dies of shock at the sight. With a despairing cry that he can now never know the secret, he turns to find Lisa entering the room, alarmed by the noise. She is horrified by the sight which meets her eyes, and no less horrified to learn why it was that Herman was there. So it was for love of gambling not for her sake that he came here at midnight! She bids him leave.

Act III, Scene i.    Herman's quarters in the barracks. The sound of drums and trumpets, suggestive of a funeral march, can be heard; the wind moans, and Herman sits reading a letter from Lisa, in which she apparently forgives him for the slight she had read into his action, understands that he did not intend to kill her grand-mother, and makes an appointment for midnight by the canal. Herman is overcome by conscience, and obsessed by memories of the Countess's funeral, which he attended. Suddenly, the door opens, the candle is blown out, and the ghost of his victim can be seen in the doorway. She tells Herman that he must marry Lisa, and that the secret of the three cards shall be his: Three! Seven! Ace! He mutters the formula as the curtain falls.

Scene ii.  By the canal. Lisa waits for Herman: 'It is near to midnight'. Can he deceive her, and will she wait in vain? Her nerves are worn with sorrow and waiting. Lisa's aria is particularly fine, and its fame as a concert piece should not blind one to the effect it makes in its original context.

But Lisa's fears are quieted when Herman appears, and sings to her of their future together. All seems well, until Herman tells her they must leave for the gaming-house. Lisa thinks he is mad, but he blurts out his obsession, and, deaf to her pleading, pushes her aside and goes his way. Lisa rushes to the parapet of the canal, and throws herself over the edge.

Scene iii.   The gambling house. Supper is in progress, and a few are playing cards. The praises of wine, youth and merriment are sung. Tomsky greets the Prince with some surprise, since he is no longer a habitual gambler. Yeletsky admits that it is to take his revenge he has come: unlucky in love, lucky at cards. Tomsky is persuaded to sing for their entertainment, which he does to a most lively tune. Herman enters, and asks who will play with him. Tchekalinsky accepts, and Herman stakes hugely and wins twice, on the three and the seven. He rejoices in his fortune: 'What is our life? A game!', then challenges anyone to stake once more. No one accepts, until the Prince steps forward and offers to play with him. Herman reluctantly agrees, and turns up a card, announcing an ace without even looking at it. But the Prince calmly rejoins: 'No, 'tis your Queen of Spades'. With a wild cry, Herman sees the ghost of the Countess. Everyone moves away from him, as he gibbers with fear and rage. He stabs himself, and with his dying breath asks for the Prince's pardon for what he has done to him. A prayer goes up for his soul, and Herman dies.                                                         H.

# ALEXANDER BORODIN

## (1834–1887)

### PRINCE IGOR

OPERA in a prologue and four acts by Borodin; text by the composer after a play by V. V. Stassov; completed by Rimsky-Korsakov and Glazounov. Première November 4, 1890, at St. Petersburg. First performed London, Drury Lane, 1914, with Kousnetzoff, Petrenko, Andreev, Chaliapin; Metropolitan, New York, 1915, with Alda, Amato, Didur; Covent Garden, 1919 (in English), with Licette, Thornton, Millar, Edmund Burke, Allin, conductor Coates. Revivals include Berlin, 1930, with Branzell, Roswaenge, Schorr, Scheidl, conductor Blech; Covent Garden, 1935, with Rethberg, Branzell, Kullman, Janssen, Kipnis, conductor Beecham; 1937, with Karnicka (later Lissitchkina), Renée Gilly, Burdino, Noble, Bernasconi, conductor Goossens; la Scala, 1940, with Scuderi, Alfano, Fratesi, Sved, di Lelio, conductor Capuana; Vienna, 1947, with Hilde Konetzni, Nikolaidi, Rothmüller, Alsen, conductor Krips.

### CHARACTERS

Igor Sviatoslavitch, *Prince of Seversk* . . . . . . . . . . . Baritone
Jaroslavna, *his wife* . . . . . . . . . . . . . . . . . . . . . . . . . . Soprano
Vladimir Igorevitch, *Igor's son* . . . . . . . . . . . . . . . . . Tenor
Vladimir Jaroslavitch, *Prince Galitzky, brother of*
    *Jaroslavna* . . . . . . . . . . . . . . . . . . . . . . . . . . . . . . . . . . Bass
Kontchak ⎱
Gzak    ⎰ *Polovtsian Khans* . . . . . . . . . . . . . . . . . . . . . . Bass
Kontchakovna, *Kontchak's daughter* . . . . . . . Mezzo-Soprano
Ovlour, *a Polovtsian* . . . . . . . . . . . . . . . . . . . . . . . . . . . . Tenor
Skoula   ⎱ *gudok players* ⎰ . . . . . . . . . . . . . . . . . . . . . Bass
Eroshka ⎰               ⎱ . . . . . . . . . . . . . . . . . . . . Tenor
Jaroslavna's Nurse . . . . . . . . . . . . . . . . . . . . . . . . . . . Soprano
A young Polovtsian Maiden . . . . . . . . . . . . . . . . . . . . Soprano

Russian Princes and Princesses, Boyars and their Wives, Old Men, Russian Warriors, Young Women, People. Polovtsian Chiefs, Kontchakovna's Women, Slaves of Khan Kontchak, Russian Prisoners of War, Polovtsian Troops

*Time:* 1185      *Place:* The town of Poutivl, the Polovtsian camp

Borodin, who divided his life between science and music, wrote his opera piece by piece. Rimsky-Korsakov wrote that he often found him working in his laboratory that communicated directly with his house. 'When he was seated before his retorts, which were filled with colourless gases of some kind, forcing them by means of tubes from one vessel to another, I used to tell him that he was spending his time in pouring water into a sieve. As soon as he was free he would take me to his living-rooms and there we occupied ourselves with music and conversation, in the midst of which Borodin would rush off to the laboratory to make sure that nothing was burning or boiling over, making the corridor ring as he went with some extraordinary passage of ninths or seconds. Then back again for more music and talk.'

Borodin, himself, wrote: 'In winter I can only compose when I am too unwell to give my lectures. So my friends, reversing the usual custom, never say to me, "I hope you are well" but "I do hope you are ill." At Christmas I had influenza, so I stayed at home and wrote the Thanksgiving Chorus in the last act of *Igor*.'

He never finished his opera. It was completed by Rimsky-Korsakov and his pupil Glazounov, and three years after his death received its first performance. Borodin never wrote down the overture, but Glazounov heard him play it so frequently that it was an easy matter for him to orchestrate it according to Borodin's wishes. The composer left this note about his opera: 'It is curious to see how all the members of our set agree in praise of my work. While controversy rages amongst us on every other subject, all, so far, are pleased with *Igor*—Moussorgsky, the ultra-realist, the innovating lyrico-dramatist, Cui, our master, Balakirev, so severe as regards form and tradition, Vladimir Stassov himself, our valiant champion of everything that bears the stamp of novelty or greatness.'

The overture, a deservedly popular piece in the concert hall, is composed entirely of music heard later in the opera. It opens with the music which precedes Igor's great aria in the second act, continues with themes later associated with Khan Kontchak and Kontchakovna, before reaching the impassioned No. 1

and No. 2.

p dolce

The Prologue takes place in the market-place of Poutivl, where rules Igor, Prince of Seversk. Although implored to postpone his departure because of an eclipse of the sun, which his people regard as an evil omen, Igor with his son Vladimir departs to pursue the Polovtsi, a Tartar tribe, formerly driven to the plains of the Don by Igor's father, Prince Sviatoslav of Kiev.

Act I takes place in the house of Prince Vladimir Galitzky, brother of Igor's wife, Jaroslavna. Galitzky in Igor's absence has been appointed to govern Poutivl and watch over the Princess Jaroslavna. He is popular with the crowd, on account of his easy-going, profligate ways. In an incisive, vigorous aria, which perfectly sets off his irresponsible character, he makes it clear that he is a man of mettle, and one to be reckoned with.

Some young girls venture into Galitzky's presence to appeal for his help and protection against his hangers-on, who have abducted one of them. He refuses to take any steps in the matter. Skula and Eroshka, a pair of drunken *gudok* players who have deserted from Igor's army, try to stir up the mob against their absent chief. They sing the praises of their patron, Galitzky, and demand rhetorically to know why he should not become their prince and rule over them.

The scene changes to Jaroslavna's room, where the same party of girls as had failed to enlist Galitzky's sympathy comes to ask for aid. This is preceded by a beautiful, warm arioso passage for Jaroslavna alone. That she is a match for her brother she proves a moment later when he enters her room. She compels him to agree to give up the girl who was abducted.

In the finale, an account is given of the disasters which have befallen Igor—he has been defeated, he and the young prince are prisoners, and the enemy is marching on Poutivl. The alarm bell is sounded, but the act ends on a note of defiance, the loyal boyars swearing to defend Jaroslavna, their princess.

Act II takes place in the camp of the Polovtsi. In this and the next act, Borodin has been highly successful in giving his music (to our western ears at any rate) something of an oriental colour. Khan Kontchak sings music that is totally different from Galitzky's (although the two rôles are often sung by one and the same singer), and Kontchakovna obviously inhabits a different world from Jaroslavna. This difference is immediately apparent in the opening scene, when the young Polovtsian maidens sing their languorous song to their mistress. They dance for her, but the day is drawing to an end, and she puts an end to their activities, and herself sings a beautiful nocturne whose languishing, chromatic melody speaks longingly of love: 'Now the daylight dies'.

Kontchakovna sees a group of Russian prisoners coming into the camp, and bids her women give them water to drink. The prisoners sing their thanks, and move on towards captivity, followed by the Polovtsian guards. Prince Vladimir, Igor's son, has already fallen in love with the Khan's daughter, and he expresses his feelings in an aria of exquisite beauty, 'Daylight is fading away'. As Ernest Newman has said, this melody would in itself provide an excuse for the love interest which Borodin has introduced at this point, but the passionate duet which follows is hardly less successful, and one may well think the whole episode entirely justified by the beautiful music it has caused Borodin to write.

Kontchakovna tells Vladimir that she is confident her father will not oppose their marriage, but Vladimir is sure Igor will not even consider giving his approval to a match with the daughter of his enemy. They see a figure approaching, and each goes to his or her tent. It is Igor who, filled with longing for his homeland, is walking through the camp where he is held prisoner. As he appears, we hear the music which began the overture. He sings desperately of his past happiness and present misery (No. 1), and longs for freedom to re-establish his glory and to ensure the safety of his people. There is tenderness in his reference to Jaroslavna (No. 2), but his *scena* dies away in a mood of despair.

To him comes the traitor Ovlour, and, in music of insinuating character, offers to help him escape. He refuses—honour prevents him taking such a course, however much he may be tempted.

Hardly has Ovlour gone than Khan Kontchak himself appears before Igor. In a great bass *scena*, the Khan offers the Prince anything he may desire to make his captivity less irksome. He looks upon him as an honoured guest, not as a prisoner; will he choose hawks, horses, a finer tent, slaves? Igor answers that nothing in his captivity irks him—only his loss of liberty. Even liberty the Khan will restore him, if he will pledge his word not to make war on him again. Why should they not unite? Together, the world would be at their feet. But Igor admits that if he were given his freedom, his first action would be to raise an army and march against the Tartars who threaten the peace of his land. The Khan appears to like his guest's frankness, and gives orders that the dancing slaves should be brought in to perform for their joint entertainment.

Now begin the famous Polovtsian dances, known from frequent performance with or without the chorus (which is in reality an integral part of them), in concert hall, and as a separate ballet. In scope they range from soft enticing melody to real vigour, with more than a touch of the barbaric in it. The name of *Prince Igor* is familiar to probably 1,000 people who know the dances to every one who knows the opera. In their context, they make a thrilling finale to an act whose varied musical splendours constitute perhaps Borodin's most enduring memorial.

Act III.    The prelude is a savage Polovtsian march, well known in the concert hall. In the theatre it continues, augmented by the chorus, to accompany the entrance of Khan Gzak and his warriors, who, like Kontchak, have been victorious over their Russian foes, and who bring in their train a crowd of prisoners. We see the primitive side of Kontchak's character in the vigorous and triumphant aria in which he welcomes his brothers-in-arms and rejoices in the slaughter and devastation they have left behind them. The sound of trumpets announces the division of the spoils, as the two Khans go off to make new plans for their campaigns against the Russians. The Tartars keep up the mood of urgency sounded by Kontchak's aria, but the Russians, when they are left alone by their captors, lament the state into which their country has fallen. Is it not the duty of Igor, they ask, to escape from captivity and lead his countrymen to revenge and freedom? Igor is persuaded that he must sacrifice honour to duty.

In celebration of their victory, the Polovtsi guards make merry, and it is not long before they are in a drunken state, though still capable of rolling out another chorus in praise of their invincible leaders. It is Ovlour's chance. He settles the details of the escape with Igor and Vladimir and arranges to meet them with the horses he has in waiting on the other side of the river. But Kontchakovna has had word that an escape is plotted, and she is full of reproaches, not at the treachery which is planned but that Vladimir should be prepared to leave her without so much as an attempt to take her with him. She pleads that the voice of love should be heard as well as that of duty. Vladimir is undecided, but his father hears what Kontchakovna is suggesting, and a fine trio ensues, in which Igor (to the tune of No. 1) opposes his will to Kontchakovna's. The Khan's daughter finally has recourse to a desperate expedient, and rouses the camp. Igor escapes, but Vladimir is left behind, in the hands of the Polovtsi.

The Polovtsi pursue Igor, and at first cry for the death of Vladimir, in spite of the pleas of Kontchakovna. However, Kontchak appears on the scene, and admits his admiration for Igor; in his position, he would have followed the same course. In a couple of phrases, he shows both sides of his simple yet complex nature; let them hang the guards responsible for Igor's flight, but may Vladimir be spared to live amongst them as Kontchakovna's husband, and their ally. A chorus of praise to Kontchak brings the act to an end.

Act IV.    The city walls and public square of Poutivl. Jaroslavna laments her lost happiness. Her plaintive phrases eventually give way to the passionate theme associated with Igor's love for her (No. 2). After the extensive *scena* for Jaroslavna, who sits absorbed in her gloomy thoughts, some peasants pass by, at least as full of their own woes as she is of hers. There seems no hope in their plight.

But the tide is due to turn for the Russians. Jaroslavna sees in the distance two horsemen riding furiously towards the city; one of them seems arrayed like a prince, the other is evidently from his dress a Polovtsian. Is this a good or evil omen? Dare she hope that this is her husband returned, perhaps with good news? She recognises Igor, and in a moment they are in each other's arms. Their duet is rapturous with delight, and they go off together towards the citadel, pausing however in front of the gate of that building just as Eroshka and Skoula come into sight, slightly drunk as is their habit, and giving vent to disloyal sentiments on the subject of their rightful prince. Igor is the cause of all their woes, they sing—but they are filled with consternation when they recognise the subject of their conversation standing only a few yards from them. What is to be done? their cause is lost! Shall they go into voluntary exile to escape the penalty that must surely be theirs? No! The thought of enforced wandering is hardly less repugnant than the possibility of death; let them stay, and brave it out.

Borodin was much too fond of his drunken rascals to let them finish the opera with anything but a flourish (cf. Moussorgsky with Varlaam and Missail), and Eroshka and Skoula duly emerge on top when they announce the return of Igor to his as yet unsuspecting subjects. They are hailed as at any rate partially responsible for the joy which has come to the city—were they not the first to notice Igor?—and they are allowed to participate in the finale (marked *allegro marziale*), in which the return of Igor and the imminent fall of Galitzky are jointly celebrated.

K. W., H.

# NICHOLAS ANDREIEVICH RIMSKY-KORSAKOV

## (1844–1908)

### PSKOVITYANKA

### (The Maid of Pskov, or Ivan the Terrible)

OPERA in four acts by Rimsky-Korsakov; text by the composer founded on a play by L. A. Mei. Première January 13, 1873, at St. Petersburg. Revived Moscow, 1898, with a new prologue. First performed Paris, 1909 (in Russian); Drury Lane, London, 1913, with Brian, Nicolaewa, Petrenko, Andreev, Zaporojetz, Chaliapin, conductor Emil Cooper; 1917 (in English).

### CHARACTERS

Tsar Ivan Vassilievitch, the Terrible ................. Bass
Prince Youry Ivanovitch Tokmakov, *Tsar's Viceroy* and
   *Mayor of Pskov* ............................... Bass
Boyar Nikita Matouta .......................... Tenor
Prince Afanasy Viazemsky ...................... Tenor
Bomely ........................................ Bass
Michael Andreievitch Toucha, *a Burgher's son* ....... Tenor
Yousko Velebin, *messenger* ........................ Bass
Princess Olga Yourievna Tokmakov ............. Soprano
Boyardin Stephanida Matouta (Stesha), *a com-
   panion of Olga* ............................... Soprano
Vlassievna     } *old nurses* { ...................... Alto
Perfilievna    ............. Mezzo-Soprano
A Sentry ...................................... Tenor
Officers, Judges, Boyars of Pskov, Burghers' Sons, Oprichniki
   (Ivan's Bodyguards), Pages in Waiting, Muscovite Archers
   (Streltsy), Serving Maidens, Boys, the People, the Tsar's
   Huntsmen

*Time:* 1570

The first two acts take place in Pskov. Scene i, Act III, near the Monastery of Pedersk. Scene ii, on the bank of the River Mediedna.

Act I, Scene i. The garden of Prince Tokmakov's mansion. Olga and the two old nurses, Vlassievna and Perfilievna, are watching young girls at play. When the game takes the players to a distant part of the garden the two nurses discuss local gossip and a rumour that Olga is not a Boyar's daughter but comes of 'higher stock'. Vlassievna dismisses the subject as nonsense. Much more important is the news that has been received from Novgorod. Tsar Ivan has led his troops there; and they are now punishing the proud city, slaying the guilty and the innocent alike. The players return and, tired of their game, ask Vlassievna for a story. The nurse consents and begins to tell a legend of a fearsome dragon and the Tsarevna Lada. The story is interrupted by a shrill whistle which frightens the girls and sends them indoors. The whistle was to signal the coming of Olga's lover, Michael Toucha, who climbs over the fence and awaits Olga. She comes to him and learns that Michael is determined to go and seek wealth in distant lands before asking her father, Prince Tokmakov, for her hand. Olga persuades him to stay, afraid lest in his absence she should be affianced to her father's friend, the old Boyar Matouta. The approach of Prince Tokmakov, with the Boyar Matouta, hastens Michael's departure while Olga hides in the bushes. Hidden, she hears the two conversing of Tsar Ivan who is marching on Pskov from Novgorod. Then the conversation becomes more intimate. Tokmakov will give Olga to Matouta, but he must first tell him the secret of her birth. She is not his daughter but his niece. Her mother was his wife's sister. Her father is unknown. Suddenly the bells are heard calling the citizens to the market-place and the distant glow of beacon fires is seen in the sky. The Prince and Matouta hasten to the assembly. A masterly interlude depicts the atmosphere of terror and anxiety.

Scene ii. The market-place of Pskov. The people and Boyars have come to hear the news brought by a messenger from Novgorod. When all are assembled the messenger reports that Novgorod is in ruins, destroyed by order of the cruel Tsar who with his savage guards is now marching to Pskov. The people seem inclined to oppose his coming by force of arms, but Prince Tokmakov persuades the majority that having done no wrong it will be wiser to meet the Tsar with humility and kindness. Michael Toucha alone protests that rather than see Pskov humbled and robbed of her freedom he will go into exile after striking a blow for the cause of the city. The bells ring out again as Michael with a number of followers leaves the market-place singing a martial hymn.

Act II, Scene i.    The market-place is thronged with the crowd awaiting the arrival of the terrible Ivan. At one side of the stage are tables with the ceremonial bread and salt. In the crowd is the nurse Vlassievna vainly attempting to comfort Olga, who grieves over her father's promise to Matouta and her unknown parentage. The advance guard of the Tsar's following, the Tartars, arrive on the stage flourishing their whips; then a procession and finally the ruthless Tsar himself.

Scene ii.    An apartment in Prince Tokmakov's house. The Prince is welcoming the Tsar to his home and trying to avert the tyrant's anger. The Tsar's words give him little confidence. When, however, Olga goes to offer him a salver and a cup the Tsar becomes suddenly agitated. He demands to know who she is, expresses his intention of taking her to Moscow in his train and after dismissing all but Prince Tokmakov, learns from him the mystery of Olga's birth. He is deeply moved by the Prince's recital and after a short prayer promises to end all bloodshed and to forgive Pskov.

Act III, Scene i.    In a dense forest the Tsar and his friends are hunting. The voices of girls are heard singing in the distance. As night falls Olga comes to her tryst with Michael Toucha. He persuades her to leave Pskov and share his fortunes. The lovers are surprised by the servants of Matouta who call their master and capture them. Michael is left senseless on the ground and Olga is carried back to the Tsar.

Scene ii.    The Tsar's tent. In a soliloquy Ivan recalls his past and his love for Olga's mother. Olga is his own daughter. Prince Viazemsky comes to announce the arrival of Matouta who wishes to offer Olga to the Tsar. Ivan orders Matouta to be brought to him with Olga. Matouta he dismisses in anger but he forgives Olga, touched by her faith in him and by her simplicity. As they talk together, Michael Toucha is heard outside urging his companions to attack the Tsar and rescue Olga. Ivan, seizing his sword, stands at the entrance of the tent to cut down any who should dare to enter. But Olga, evading his attention, rushes out to her lover and a shot meant for Michael hits her instead. She is brought in dead by the soldiers. The chorus, which has entered the tent, closes the opera bidding Russians end their quarrels for the sake of one who was sacrificed in the cause of Pskov.

F. B.

# SNEGOUROCHKA
## (The Snow Maiden)

Opera in a prologue and four acts by Rimsky-Korsakov; text by the composer from a play by N. Ostrovsky. Première February 10, 1882, St. Petersburg; first performed Metropolitan, New York, 1922, with Bori, Telva, Harrold, Laurenti, conductor Bodanzky; Buenos Aires, 1929; Sadler's Wells, 1933, with Olive Dyer, Cross, Coates, Tudor Davies, Austin, conductor Collingwood.

### CHARACTERS

Snegourochka..................................Soprano
Shepherd Lehl ...............................Alto
Coupava .....................................Soprano
Fairy Spring .........................Mezzo-Soprano
Bobilicka ............................Mezzo-Soprano
Spirit of the Woods ...........................Tenor
Page ................................Mezzo-Soprano
Tsar Berendey ................................Tenor
Misgir .....................................Baritone
King Frost ....................................Bass
Bobil .......................................Tenor
Bermate ......................................Bass

*Snegourochka* (The Snow Maiden) was written in 1880, and in his autobiography Rimsky-Korsakov tells us how he became enamoured of the subject and how he came to write it in the 'genuine Russian village' of Stlelyovo in the brief period of three months. The orchestration took longer. The full score was begun on September 7, 1880, and completed on May 26 of the following year. When the work was ready, the composer played it through to his friends Balakirev, Borodin, and Stasoff, and all three were pleased, but each in his own way. 'Stasoff and Balakirev were gratified chiefly with the folk-like and fantastic portion of the opera. Borodin, on the other hand, seemed to appreciate it in its entirety.' Balakirev 'could not curb his passion for meddling', and suggested the transposition of the Introduction into B minor. Rimsky-Korsakov declined to do it, because it would have meant, amongst other things, the transposition of the theme representing Spring, which was indissolubly linked in his imagination with the key of A minor. He also tells us without any false modesty that in writing it he felt 'a matured musician and operatic composer who had finally come to stand on his own feet'. This opinion was confirmed by the public, who found the work more ingenious and distinguished than anything Rimsky-Korsakov had previously written.

The action takes place in the fabulous kingdom of Tsar Berendey in prehistoric times. The scene of the Prologue is the Red Mountain near the capital. Act I, in the village of Berendey; Act II, in the Tsar's palace; Act III, in the sacred forest; and Act IV, in the village of Yarilo.

Prologue. It is the early spring, but although the snows are melting the wind is cold. Flocks of birds arrive from the south carrying with them the Fairy Spring. Many years ago, in a whimsical mood she wooed icy Winter, who now treats her like a slave. Hence the cold which endures and makes the very birds shiver. Their love is dead, but Spring and Winter have a bond in the child that was born of their love, the maid, Snegourochka. They fear for her, for she is now sixteen years old and can no longer be kept hidden and protected as she must be; for if the sun-god, Yarilo, should get a glimpse of her she would die. They must go northward now, but before going entrust her to the keeping of the Spirit of the Wood, who promises to guard her from mischance. Snegourochka is free to go into the world.

A carnival rout invades the stage as Spring and Winter depart. Snegourochka goes amongst the people and her beauty makes a deep impression on Bobil and Bobilicka, who adopt her. Particularly to be noted in the prologue is the very beautiful aria given at her entrance to Snegourochka. One of the problems of this opera is to find a soprano with a voice that is equal to the music she has to sing, and physical attributes that do not exceed the limits set by the child-like character she has to play.

Act I. Snegourochka begs Lehl, a young shepherd and singer, to perform for her. He sings two charming folk-like songs for her, but her artless advances are little to his liking, and he goes off eagerly enough at the invitation of the other girls. The little daughter of Spring and Winter knows now the pangs of unrequited love. The situation is complicated by the arrival of the wealthy youth, Misgir, who comes to wed Coupava, but seeing Snegourochka, falls in love with her and bluntly refuses to proceed with the marriage ceremony. Even though Snegourochka refuses to take any notice of Misgir's impassioned love-making, Coupava is desolate, and only saved from suicide by the large-hearted Lehl.

Act II.    In the palace of the Tsar, Coupava comes to claim redress for the affront Misgir has put upon her. The Tsar orders a court of justice to be held and commands the presence of Misgir and Snegourochka. The Tsar, impressed by Snegourochka's beauty, asks her who her lover is. When she replies that she has no lover, the Tsar protests that not to love is a sin against the sun-god, Yarilo, and ends the trial by promising a reward to anyone who succeeds in winning the love of Snegourochka.

The music of this act, with its serene aria for the Tsar, has a unity, and the action an economy and suspense that are not always apparent in the rest of the opera, which often appears rather loosely knit.

Act III.    There is feasting and jollity in the Holy Wood. Even the great Tsar sings a cavatina. It is followed by the celebrated Dance of the Tumblers. Lehl is of the company, and, at the command of the Tsar, sings a delicious song. As a reward he is allowed to claim a kiss from any of the girls present. He passes by Snegourochka, who runs away in tears, and chooses Coupava. Snegourochka, broken-hearted, will not listen to Misgir. When the two are left alone and Misgir would urge his love, Snegourochka vanishes and the Spirit of the Wood, faithful to his trust, bars the way and prevents Misgir from following.

Act IV.    Snegourochka in despair appeals to her mother. She wants to love and be loved. Spring grants her wish, and when Misgir returns she greets him lovingly as her hero. The Tsar greets the couples waiting to be married, amongst them Misgir and Snegourochka. But all is not well. The sun-god has warmed Snegourochka's heart with a ray of sunshine and her destiny must be fulfilled; the little daughter of Spring and Winter must die. As the mist rises she melts away. Misgir throws himself into the lake, but the Tsar interprets his death and that of Snegourochka as a removal of the factor which has influenced Yarilo to withhold his blessing from them. From now on, says the Tsar, Yarilo may be expected to pour his bounty on them. A white-clad youth appears on the mountain top bearing a sheaf of corn in his hand, and the opera ends with an invocation to Yarilo, led by Lehl.                                                F. B., H.

# SADKO

Opera in seven scenes (three or five acts) by Rimsky-Korsakov; text by the composer and V. I. Bielsky. Première Moscow, January 7, 1898; Metropolitan, New York, 1930, with Fleischer, Johnson, Basiola, Ludikar, conductor Serafin; London, Lyceum Theatre, 1931, with Lissitchkina, Sadoven, Pozemkovsky, conductor Goossens; Rome, 1931, with Saraceni, Pederzini, Livi, Damiani, Vaghi, conductor Marinuzzi; la Scala, Milan, 1938, with Carosio, Giani, Parmeggiani, de Franchesci, Sdanowski, conductor Marinuzzi; Staatsoper, Berlin, 1946, with Berger, Klose, Suthaus, Neumann, Prohaska, conductor Schüler.

## CHARACTERS

The King of the Ocean ............................ Bass
Volkhova, *his daughter* ........................ Soprano
Sadko, *a singer of Novgorod* ..................... Tenor
Lubava, *his wife* ....................... Mezzo-Soprano
Nejata, *a gousli player from Kiev* ......... Mezzo-Soprano
A Viking Merchant .............................. Bass
A Hindu Merchant ............................. Tenor
A Venetian Merchant ....................... Baritone
Four Buffoons ....Two Mezzo-Sopranos, Tenor and Bass
Two Elders, *merchants of Novgorod*........ Tenor and Bass
*Place:* Novgorod, and the bottom of the sea

Tableau I.    The merchants of Novgorod sit down to a feast, rejoicing in their prosperity. Nejata, singer and 'gousli' player who comes from Kiev, sings a song about the heroic days of old. The merchants would like one of their own countrymen to perform the same service for Novgorod, and Sadko, who enters at that moment, is asked if he will oblige. But his song worries them; he suggests that Novgorod is on a lake, and that if their ships could only reach the ocean, they could bring back fortunes from all over the world. They laugh at him and bid him good-bye. The feast goes on to the accompaniment of song and dance.

Tableau II.    On the shores of Lake Ilmen, Sadko sings of his distress and disillusionment: 'Oh, yon dark forest'. Fascinated by Sadko's singing, swans swim towards him, and, as they reach him, become young women, Volkhova, the Sea Princess, amongst them. He sings again for them, they dance, and the Princess tells him that he has won her love. When dawn comes, she parts from

Sadko, but tells him that he will catch three golden fish in the lake, that he will make a journey to a foreign land, and that she will wait faithfully for him until he comes to her. She returns to the deep, where her father, the King of the Ocean, holds sway. The sun rises.

Tableau III.    Lubava at home laments the absence of her husband Sadko. Has he gone to seek adventure afar off? Yet only yesterday he assured her of his love. She is overjoyed when he comes in, but broken-hearted when he leaves her again, shouting 'Farewell'.

Tableau IV.    The quayside at Novgorod, on Lake Ilmen. Ships lie at anchor, and the people of the town crowd round the rich foreign merchants, who come from every land known to man. Soothsayers ply their trade, Nejata sings to the accompaniment of his gousli, buffoons sing and dance, the sound of a pilgrim's chant can be heard. Sadko appears and is greeted with laughter, which increases when he tells them he knows a secret; golden fish can be caught in the lake. He bets his head against the wealth of everyone assembled there that he can prove that he speaks the truth. A net is let down, the song of the Sea Princess is heard, and sure enough, when it is drawn up, there are three gold fishes in the net. Sadko invites all the adventurous men of the port to join him in his journey, and they go off to make their preparations.

Nejata sings of the nightingale that became a great merchant. When he returns, Sadko says he will restore the wealth of the merchants, but would take only their ships. He asks three of the merchants, the Viking, the Venetian and the Indian, to sing to him of their native lands, so that he may decide which to visit. The Viking sings first: his country's shores are rugged, the sea rough, and his countrymen fierce fighters. The slow, *pesante* aria is one of the best known in the Russian bass's repertory. Next comes the Indian merchant, with music and story of much more exotic cast. India is a land of gems and mystery, and his song, any hearer would admit, is the stuff of which dreams are made. It is one of the world's famous melodies, known from having been sung by half the sopranos and tenors who have ever appeared on the concert platform, and by its frequent appearance on violin recitalists' programmes. In its original setting it is a tenor melody:

Third representative of the merchants of the world is the Venetian, a baritone, who sings a *barcarolle*. Sadko settles that Venice shall be his destination. He asks the Novgorod people to look after Lubava, and sets sail.

Tableau V.    Sadko is on his way home laden with treasure. The ship is becalmed—due to their not having sacrificed to the King of the Ocean all the twelve years they have been away, says Sadko. They pour treasure over the side, but still the ship remains becalmed. Next at Sadko's command they throw wooden logs over the side: Sadko's sinks, and he descends by a ladder to the water's edge, stepping on to a plank which has been thrown overboard. Immediately a breeze gets up, the ship sails away leaving Sadko abandoned, and a mist comes up.

When it clears away (Tableau VI) we are at the bottom of the sea, at the court of the King of the Ocean. The king and queen sit on thrones, their daughter, Volkhova, sits spinning seaweed. Sadko sings for the king and queen, and is promised the hand of Volkhova in marriage. The wedding guests arrive—every denizen of the deep seems to have been invited—and the marriage is celebrated fittingly. Dances are performed for their entertainment, Sadko sings again and arouses such enthusiasm amongst his hearers that they join in the dance. So fast become the movements of the dancers that the waves are lashed into a fury and ships are sunk. Suddenly an apparition warns them that the reign of the King of the Ocean is at an end. Sadko and Volkhova seated in a shell are drawn away by seagulls.

Tableau VII.    It is morning. Sadko sleeps by the side of Lake Ilmen, watched over by Princess Volkhova, who sings a lullaby as she watches. She bids a last farewell to the still-sleeping minstrel, then vanishes in mist, becoming the great river Volkhova and flowing thenceforth from Lake Ilmen to the sea.

Lubava is still distractedly looking for her husband, and she is filled with delight to see him lying by the lake asleep. He thinks he has been asleep ever since he last saw her, and that he has dreamed his voyage. But the sight of his fleet coming up the new river convinces him that it has all taken place, and that he really has become the richest man of Novgorod. All the citizens of that town welcome him, not least the three merchants who sang to him before he left home. H.

# LE COQ D'OR
## The Golden Cockerel

Opera in three acts by Nicholas Rimsky-Korsakov; text by V. Bielsky after Pushkin. Première Moscow, October 7, 1909. First performed Paris Opéra, 1914; Drury Lane, London, 1914, with Dobrowolska, Petrenko, Petroff, Altechewsky, conductor Emil Cooper; Metropolitan, New York, 1918, with Barrientos, Didur, conductor Monteux. Revived Covent Garden, 1919 (in English), with Nelis, Richardson, conductor Beecham; Buenos Aires, 1937, with Carosio, Melnik; Metropolitan, 1937, with Pons and Pinza, 1942, with Bok and Pinza, 1945 with Munsel and Cordon; Rome, 1940, with Carosio, Pasero, conductor Serafin; Covent Carden, 1954, with Dobbs, Cuénod, Glynne, conductor Markevitch.

### CHARACTERS

King Dodon ....................................Bass
Prince Guidon ...............................Tenor
Prince Afron ...............................Baritone
General Polkan ...............................Bass
Amelfa, the royal housekeeper.................Contralto
The Astrologer ...............................Tenor
The Queen of Shemakha ......................Soprano
The Golden Cockerel .........................Soprano

*Le Coq d'Or* was Rimsky-Korsakov's last opera. The censor refused to sanction its performance—rather surprisingly, unless he found the references to misconduct of war a little too apt to be pleasant—and it was not until after the composer's death that it was performed. When the work was given in Petrograd, it was thought to be over-taxing for the singers who are obliged to dance, or for the dancers who are obliged to sing. Fokine, the choreographer, ingeniously devised the plan of having all the singers seated at each side of the stage, while the dancers interpreted in pantomime what was sung. In spite of the protests made by the composer's family, this was done in Paris, London, and New

York, but the innovation has probably served its purpose in launching the work before the public, and a return can now be made to the directions laid down by Rimsky-Korsakov. In any case, few opera companies have the balletic resources of a Diaghilev, which alone would enable them to mount the work in the opera-ballet style he used for it.

The story of *Le Coq d'Or* is taken from Pushkin, who in his turn got it from his nurse. It is quite possible to fill it with symbolical meaning, although the librettist, Bielsky, preferred to think of it as dealing with human passions and weaknesses in their essence and quite apart from any particular context. Of the work as a whole, Ernest Newman (in *Opera Nights*) has written: 'One of the things that constitute the charm of *The Golden Cockerel* for us to-day is the fact that not only are we not sure what it all means but we are not quite sure that it means anything at all, or that it meant anything in particular for either Bielsky or Rimsky-Korsakov beyond opportunity after opportunity for humour, beauty, burlesque, and, occasionally, sincere feeling. And all the ingredients of the pot are so good in themselves that it does not worry us in the least that we cannot find the right name for the strange dish that is the totality of them'.

A muted trumpet gives out the theme associated with the cockerel, Ex. 1:

and it is immediately followed by a descending chromatic melody on the clarinet, which is characteristic of the Queen of Shemakha, Ex. 2:

Much of the music of this short prelude is derived from the Queen's aria of Act II. The thin, *staccato* sound of the xylophone heralds the appearance of the Astrologer before the curtain. By his art, he says, he will conjure up for the audience a tale from long ago; though it is only a fairy story, its moral is excellent. The Astrologer's music is instrumental rather than vocal in character, and its *tessitura* is abnormally high.

After this short prologue the curtain rises on Act I, which takes place at the court of King Dodon. The council-room is magnificently decorated, and the king is seated in the middle of his ministers and advisers, his two sons, Guidon and Afron, on either side of him. He complains that his neighbours do not treat him fairly; when he was young and vigorous, he used to go out to attack them at the head of his armies; now that he is old, they are inclined to invade him, in spite of the fact that he finds it more and more troublesome to engage in warfare. What advice can his councillors give him to meet the present invasion threat? Guidon, his elder son, is the first to speak. He has naturally given the matter some thought, and his recommendation is that the king withdraw his army inside the capital of his kingdom, and there, supplied with a vast stock of provisions and necessaries, think out the whole problem at leisure. All applaud the suggestion, except old General Polkan, the king's chief minister, who finds the whole notion futile and unpractical. Afron spurns his brother's plan, and advises that the army be disbanded and sent home; once the enemy is past them, they may re-unite and fall upon him from the rear and destroy him. Dodon is delighted, but Polkan demolishes Afron's proposal as quickly as he had Guidon's. There seems no reasonable and practical solution.

Suddenly, preluded by the same music as we had heard in the prologue, the Astrologer appears at the top of the stairs, dressed in a blue robe covered in golden stars, and with a long white astrakan hat on his head. In music of characteristic cast, he offers the king a magic golden cockerel, which has only to be placed so that it has a view of the surrounding country, and it will crow to give warning of any danger. When it is quiet, the king may rest peacefully and take his ease with no fear of danger to cause him worry. Dodon is delighted, and offers the Astrologer any reward he likes to name, but the old man says he will not

PLATE XXXI. George London as Onegin and Lucine Amara as Tatiana in *Eugen Onegin*, Metropolitan, New York, 1957.

PLATE XXXII. Ljuba Welitsch as Salome.

take money or honours, but would like to have the king's promise in writing so as to take advantage of his offer at some future date. This request is refused, the king saying in effect that his word is his bond.

The cock (to the sound of No. 1) bids the king take his ease heedless of danger. Dodon rejoices at the prospect of never again having to be on his guard against the unknown; he will indulge his pleasures and his desire for sleep from now on for ever. He begins to feel sleepy, and the royal nurse, Amelfa, has his bed brought in by servants. He lies down, eats sweetmeats out of a bowl, and plays with his parrot, which sings to him (in the orchestra). As he goes to sleep, watched by the faithful Amelfa, the orchestra begins the slumber scene (as it is known in the orchestral suite), in which the wood-wind quietly repeat the cockerel's assurance that he can rest undisturbed while the cellos play a gentle lullaby. Even Amelfa falls asleep, and the sound of No. 2 shows that the king in his dreams is anticipating his amorous encounter of the next act.

But the king has not slept for long before he is aroused by the warning cry of the cockerel, which is echoed by the instruments of the orchestra. Polkan manages to wake his master, who gives orders for a general mobilisation of the army, which must proceed to the scene of war and return as soon as it has accomplished its duty. It gets under way to the sound of a march. Soon all is quiet, and Dodon is allowed by his watchful bird to return to his slumbers. He cannot recapture his attractive dream—cannot even remember what it was about. Amelfa tries to help him and makes one or two suggestions, finally hitting upon the right one. All go to sleep once more, only to be awakened by an even more urgent summons from the cockerel than previously. The crowd rushes around, and this time Polkan warns the king that he is in danger himself, and that he must gird himself and lead his army to victory. With much grumbling, Dodon prepares to don his armour. It is found to be rusty and dirty, his sword is too heavy, his cuirass is too tight for him and will hardly meet round his middle. But in the end, although it still looks as though nothing fits properly, he is sufficiently arrayed to go off to the wars, which he does to the acclamation of the crowd.

Act II.   But the war goes badly, and the moonlight in a narrow pass reveals the bodies of the soldiers and the king's two sons, lying dead and unattended. The march of the preceding act is now oppressed with gloom, and Dodon bursts into lamentation when he finds the bodies of his slain sons. His lament is typically Russian in character; it may be excessive, but it is certainly not lacking in seriousness.

The mists which have shrouded the pass lift, and reveal a tent. General consternation. Could it belong to the enemy general? Reluctantly the soldiers are persuaded to drag a piece of comic artillery which is trained on the tent, and eventually and with much difficulty fired. But its only effect is that a beautiful young woman emerges from the tent; the soldiers, all but Dodon and Polkan, take to their heels and disappear. The young woman, with nothing but the clarinet phrase of 2 as prelude, sings the praises of the sun, which gives life and beauty to her native land. This is the famous 'Hymn to the Sun', whose sensuously beautiful melody has made it amongst Rimsky-Korsakov's vocal compositions second in popularity only to the Song of the Indian Guest from *Sadko*.

When she is questioned, the girl reveals that she is the Queen of Shemakha, come out to subdue Dodon, not by force of arms, but by her own physical beauty. Dodon is shyer than Polkan, but eventually Polkan's bluntness goes too far and she asks for him to be sent away. Dodon promptly complies, and Polkan watches subsequent proceedings from behind the queen's tent (the bodies of the soldiers have by now been cleared away, and the scene is bathed in sunlight).

Beginning with a little 6/8 tune in which she describes her unclothed beauty, the queen proceeds to vamp Dodon in seductive snatches of song. Even an orchestral reference to the cockerel's warning makes not the slightest difference to the king, who appears to enjoy the process of becoming ensnared. The queen tells him he must sing for her, as he no doubt once did in his youth, and at her orders he starts an incredibly primitive-sounding melody, much to her glee. The queen tries new tactics. At home everyone obeys her slightest whim, and her caprice rules her kingdom; Oh, for contradiction, even domination. Timidly Dodon offers himself as dominator, and she asks him to dance for her—as he must once have danced when he was young. She rigs him up with fan and scarf in place of his cumbersome armour, and has her slaves play a slow melody to accompany him. She joins him and mocks his efforts, which land him, as the music gets quicker, on some cushions in a state of collapse.

By now, the king is completely under the queen's domination. He repeats his offer of his hand, his possessions, his throne, his kingdom. She accepts, with the proviso that Polkan shall forthwith be whipped; Dodon offers to go further and behead him. Preparations are immediately put in hand for a return to Dodon's kingdom, and, while the queen's slaves mock at her newest capture, Dodon's army lines up to escort their monarch and his bride to their capital. The act ends with the grotesque procession.

Act III.  We are back in Dodon's capital. The crowd is wondering if and when he will return. Rumours are noised abroad: he has won a great victory, but lost his two sons, and is escorting home as his bride a young queen whom he rescued from a dragon. All must be well, argue the people, since the cockerel is quiet. Then the cry goes up that the procession is at hand. It files through the crowd, and eventually the king and his bride appear, riding in their gilded chariot, and acclaimed by the crowd.

Suddenly, proceedings are interrupted by the appearance of the Astrologer, preceded naturally by his characteristic music. He has come to claim his reward from the king; it shall be the princess who rides by the king's side! The king angrily refuses, but the Astrologer persists, emphasising his determination to risk marriage even at his age with a sustained top E (Rimsky-Korsakov, in his preface to the score, underlines the fact that the rôle of the Astrologer requires a tenor with a highly developed falsetto voice). The king orders his guards to remove the old man, and when he seems still anxious to continue the dispute, Dodon strikes him on the head with his sceptre, and kills him. The sky darkens, thunder is heard, and Dodon has the grace to appear embarrassed at the turn events have taken; such a bad omen on one's wedding day! The queen laughs at the whole episode, but, when Dodon tries to embrace her, repulses him with disgust. The cockerel suddenly comes to life, utters a piercing cry, flies over the head of the crowd and pecks the king on the head. He falls dead, and the crowd loyally breaks into lamentation for him. The sky becomes completely dark, and when light returns, both queen and cockerel have disappeared.

In the epilogue, the resuscitated Astrologer announces that the story is only a fairy tale and that in Dodon's kingdom only the queen and he himself were mortals.

It seems likely that *Le Coq d'Or* will gradually be accepted as outstandingly the best of Rimsky-Korsakov's operas. It is more compactly shaped than his other stage works, and here the gorgeous orchestration has a new economy and is treated with a more directly pointed sense of style than elsewhere. The spectacular staging which the work requires, and the hardly less spectacular vocal writing for the coloratura-soprano queen are qualities which have contributed towards the opera's popularity; they also constitute a direct link with Rimsky-Korsakov's most famous pupil, Strawinsky, whose first opera, *Le Rossignol*, begun a year after *Le Coq d'Or*, makes use of exactly the same characteristics.

H.

# CHAPTER 12

# English Opera

# MICHAEL WILLIAM BALFE
## (1803–1870)

### THE BOHEMIAN GIRL

OPERA in three acts by Michael William Balfe; text by Alfred Bunn founded on the ballet-pantomime, *The Gipsy*, by St. Georges. Première Drury Lane, London, November 27, 1843. First performed New York, 1844; Her Majesty's Theatre (in Italian), 1858. Revived Sadler's Wells, 1932, with Kemp, Coates, Tudor Davies, Kelsey, Austin; Covent Garden Company at Liverpool, 1951, and subsequently at the Royal Opera House, in a new version by Sir Thomas Beecham and Dennis Arundell with Roberta Peters, Coates, Marlowe and Lanigan, Dickie, Walters, Glynne, conductor Beecham. Like *Maritana*, continuously in the repertories of the British touring companies until the 1930's.

### CHARACTERS

Arline, *daughter of the Count* .................... Soprano
Thaddeus, *a proscribed Pole* ....................... Tenor
Queen of the Gypsies ............................ Alto
Devilshoof, *chief of the gypsies* ..................... Bass
Count Arnheim, *Governor of Presburg* ............... Bass
Florestein, *his nephew* ........................... Tenor
Captain of the Guard ........................... Bass
Officer ......................................... Tenor
Buda, *Arline's attendant* ........................ Soprano

The *Bohemian Girl* owes its popularity to the easy melodies which abound in its score and also, partly, to the fact that it embodies all the elements which commended opera to a certain class of audience fifty years ago. There are no subtleties in the libretto of Alfred Bunn; in fact it has been held up to ridicule ever since it was written. On the other hand, the action is vigorous and as remote from everyday life as one could well imagine. The chief characters are either noblemen or gypsies—noblemen who have the power of life and death over the people, and gypsies who may rob and cheat but also number amongst their companions beings as innocent and pure as the hero and heroine of the story.

The action takes place at Presburg in Poland.

Act I.    Thaddeus, a Polish noble exiled after a rebellion, has sought the company of Devilshoof and his gypsies in order to escape the punishment to which he has been condemned. As a gypsy he saves the life of Arline, the daughter of Count Arnheim, the Austrian governor of the province. The delighted father invites both Thaddeus and Devilshoof to his castle. They go, but refuse to drink the health of the Emperor as loyal subjects should. Devilshoof is cast into prison; Thaddeus, who saved little Arline, is allowed to go free. Devilshoof, however, is the master locksmith for whom locks and bars have no secret. He escapes from prison and, to revenge himself for the slight that has been put on him, steals Arline and hides her amongst the gypsies.

The chief numbers in Act I are Thaddeus's entrance aria, ''Tis sad to leave your fatherland', and, 'In the gypsy's life you lead', the gypsy chorus, which recurs often during the course of the action.

Act II.    Twelve years have gone by and Arline, grown to womanhood, has fallen in love with her rescuer, Thaddeus, who returns her love and wishes to marry her. There is, however, an obstacle. The Queen of the Gypsies is herself in love with Thaddeus, and the Queen is not a woman to be slighted with impunity.

Devilshoof and his friends have robbed Florestein, nephew of Count Arnheim, of all he possessed while he was returning from a feast. The Queen, fearing the Count's power, orders the booty to be returned. The trinkets are returned accordingly, all but a medallion which Devilshoof had taken as his share, but which the Queen retains with a view to its later uses. When she is forced by gypsy custom to unite Thaddeus and Arline, she begins to plot and plan the girl's downfall, and the opportunity is not long in coming.

The gypsies have mingled with the crowds at the fair and there the Queen presents Arline with the medallion stolen from Florestein. This young nobleman, who was at first attracted by Arline and then piqued by her refusals, on seeing the trinket, accuses her of theft and, in spite of the gypsies' resistance, Arline is taken to the castle to be tried. Count Arnheim would be merciful since the accused woman is just the age of his lost daughter, but the evidence is against her and he is forced to find her guilty. Arline does not know the secret of her birth although she has dreamt, as she confided to Thaddeus earlier on, that she 'dwelt in marble halls with vassals and serfs at my side'. Blood, however, will tell; feeling herself disgraced, she is about to stab herself to the heart when the Count himself stops her and in grasping her hand he notices a scar, similar to that his lost daughter bore, on her arm. Recognition follows, to the great joy of all but Thaddeus, who fears that Arline is lost to him.

This act contains the best-known aria in the score, Arline's 'I dreamt that I dwelt in marble halls', a simple tune which, when well sung as it was by, for instance, Roberta Peters in the Covent Garden revival in 1951, is of truly appealing character.

There are also the Count's, 'The heart bowed down', a duet for Arline and Thaddeus, and of course the inevitable repetition of the gypsies' chorus.

Act III.    Arline is faithful to her lover and, in spite of her high station and its advantages, would return to him. The Count, appealed to by the lovers, sternly objects to the marriage of his daughter with a gypsy. Whereupon Thaddeus, stung to the quick, reveals his real identity. The fact that he rebelled against the Austrians is forgotten and forgiven, and a wedding-feast arranged. The Queen alone is angry and disappointed. She aims a shot at Arline, but the bullet richochetting, kills her that fired it. Thaddeus's aria, 'When other lips and other hearts', occurs early in Act III.                                      F. B.

# VINCENT WALLACE
## (1814–1865)

### MARITANA

**O**PERA in three acts by Vincent Wallace; text by Edward Fitzball based on the play, *Don César de Bazan*. Première Drury Lane, London, November 15, 1845. First performed Philadelphia, 1846; New York, 1848; Her Majesty's Theatre, London (in Italian), 1880. Revived Lyceum, London, 1925; Old Vic and Sadler's Wells, 1931, with Kennard (later Cross), Morris, Cox, Austin, Brindle. Continuously in the repertories of the British touring companies until about 1930.

### CHARACTERS

Maritana, *a handsome gitana* . . . . . . . . . . . . . . . . . . Soprano

Don Caesar de Bazan . . . . . . . . . . . . . . . . . . . . . . . . Tenor

Don José de Santarem, *an unscrupulous courtier* . . . Baritone

Lazarillo, *a poor boy* . . . . . . . . . . . . . . . . . . . . Mezzo-Soprano

The Marchioness of Montefiore . . . . . . . . . . Mezzo-Soprano

Captain of the Guard . . . . . . . . . . . . . . . . . . . . . . Baritone

Marquis of Montefiore . . . . . . . . . . . . . . . . . . . . . . . Bass

The King . . . . . . . . . . . . . . . . . . . . . . . . . . . . . . . . . . Bass

The Alcade . . . . . . . . . . . . . . . . . . . . . . . . . . . . . . . . Bass

Soldiers, Gypsies, Populace

*Place:* Madrid

*Maritana* deals, like Balfe's *Bohemian Girl*, on the one hand with the very poor and the very rich and powerful on the other. The essential difference is that while there is no humour of any kind in *The Bohemian Girl*, the librettist of *Maritana*, Edward Fitzball, has contrived to invest the character of Don Caesar de Bazan with a lighthearted, whimsical humour which, if it is not wit, is at least an acceptable substitute for it. As regards the music, the soprano aria 'Scenes that are brightest' and the tenor's 'Yes, let me like a soldier fall' make a perfect match to Balfe's 'I dreamt that I dwelt in marble halls'.

Don José, a young and wealthy courtier of Madrid, is enamoured of the Queen of Spain. Don José believes that the Queen would be his if he could only persuade her that the King does not care for her. The King himself is of a roaming, roving disposition and he has been much attracted lately by the simple charms of Maritana, a street singer, whom we meet at the beginning of Act I engaged in her occupation and surrounded by an admiring crowd. Don José naturally determines to do his utmost to further the King's interests in this quarter, although he well knows that Maritana is above the temptations of wealth and position. Since she does not care for the King, José has to wait until chance comes to aid his desires. The opportunity comes with the return to Madrid of Don Caesar de Bazan, a nobleman as poor as a church mouse and as proud as Satan. Don Caesar, the hero of countless duels, when told by Don José that duelling has been forbidden on pain of death, declares his intention never to fight again. He learns that anyone who forfeits his life to the law on this particular day of the year is not going to be shot in a clean, soldierly fashion, but hanged. But when Lazarillo, a poor apprentice, is pursued by guards, he does not hesitate to challenge their captain so as to give Lazarillo a chance of escaping. Don Caesar wounds the captain, but is himself apprehended and marched to jail.

Act II.    Interior of a fortress. The prospect of dying a felon's death horrifies him and when offered he accepts eagerly a strange proposal from Don José.   Don José, believing that if Maritana could be married to a nobleman he could bring her more easily to comply with the King's wishes, proposes a bargain. Don Caesar will be shot and not hanged if he consents to marry before his execution a veiled lady. Don Caesar is ready to do anything if he can escape the rope, and sings one of the best arias of the opera, exalting the advantages of a soldier's death: 'Yes, let me like a soldier fall'. Don José recalls his first sight of the Queen: 'In happy moments day by day', and resolves to go through with his scheme. The marriage takes place there and then and so, apparently, does the execution—apparently, since Lazarillo, to show his devotion to the man who risked death to serve him, had abstracted the bullets from the executioners' rifles. The soldier of the song fell only to rise again. As soon as the firing squad has gone, Don Caesar walks away and goes in search of the unknown lady he has wedded.

Meanwhile, the King, remembering Don Caesar's former services to the State, had pardoned him. But the pardon fell into the hands of Don José, who did not hesitate to hide it and free himself of Don Caesar's presence.

Scene ii. Maritana has now been taken to the castle of the Marquis of Montefiore. There she is introduced to the King: 'Hear me, gentle Maritana'. Her heart has been given to the gallant Don Caesar and she refuses to listen to the advances of her royal master. Don Caesar comes to the Marquis's house, in search of his wife, whom he is sure he will recognise, although he has only seen her once heavily veiled: 'There is a flower that bloometh'. At Don José's instigation, the Marchioness poses as the wife of Don Caesar, who is completely disillusioned when he sees her age. He is about to sign away all claim on her, when he hears and recognises Maritana's voice and suspects that some intrigue is in progress: 'What mystery?' Don José has Don Caesar re-arrested.

Act III. A magnificent apartment. Maritana laments the loss of her liberty: 'Scenes that are brightest'. The King comes to her pretending to be her husband. Lazarillo, ordered by Don José to guard their privacy and to shoot anyone who attempts to enter, fires on an approaching stranger. His aim is not accurate enough to hit Don Caesar, who climbs in through the window to meet the King, whom Maritana had left to nurse his disappointment alone. 'What are you doing here?' he asks, without recognising the King. 'I am the master here, the Count of Bazan,' replies His Majesty. 'Oh, well', retorts the nobleman, 'I, then, must be the King'. In the course of the wrangle, Don Caesar finds out from the King that he was pardoned and that the execution which nearly cost him his life need never have taken place. The King leaves, and Don Caesar is face to face with Maritana. They recognise each other as husband and wife. The Queen arrives, escorted by Don José, who meant to show her her spouse's infidelity. Explanations ensue (Don Caesar incidentally ran his sword through Don José's body to save the Queen from his importunity) and all ends happily for Don Caesar and his true love, the street singer, Maritana.                F. B.

# BEDRICH SMETANA
## (1824–1884)

### THE BARTERED BRIDE
Prodana Nevesta

OPERA in three acts by Bedrich Smetana; text by Karel Sabina. Première Prague National Theatre, May 30, 1866; some alterations were made to the work in 1869 and the final version produced 1870. First performed Chicago, 1893 (in Czech); Drury Lane, London, 1895 (in German); Covent Garden, 1907 (in German); Metropolitan, New York, 1909 (in German), with Destinn, Jörn, Reiss, Didur, conductor Mahler; Sadler's Wells, 1935 (in English), with Cross, Tudor Davies, Powell Lloyd, Matters, conductor Collingwood; la Scala, Milan, 1935, with Oltrabella, Wesselowski, Nessi, Pasero, conductor Ghione. Revivals include Covent Garden, 1931 (in English), with Phillips, Ben Williams, Dua, Heming, conductor Barbirolli; 1939, with Hilde Konetzni, Tauber, Tessmer, Krenn, conductor Beecham; Metropolitan, 1926, with Müller (later Rethberg), Laubenthal, Meader, Bohnen, conductor Bodanzky; 1941, with Novotna, Kullman, Laufkoetter, Pinza, conductor Walter; Sadler's Wells (at the New Theatre), 1943, with Hill (later Sladen), Servent, Pears, Donlevy, conductor Collingwood; Vienna State Opera, 1951, with Jurinac, Dermota, Christ, Edelmann, conductor Ackermann.

### CHARACTERS

| | |
|---|---|
| Krušina, *a peasant* | Baritone |
| Ludmila, *his wife* | Mezzo-Soprano |
| Marenka, *their daughter* | Soprano |
| Micha, *a landlord* | Bass |
| Hata, *his wife* | Mezzo-Soprano |
| Vasek, *their son* | Tenor |
| Jenik, *Micha's son by a first marriage* | Tenor |
| Kecal, *a marriage broker* | Bass |
| *Ringmaster of a troupe of artists* | Tenor |
| Esmeralda, *a dancer* | Soprano |
| *An Indian* | Bass |

The Bartered Bride is so much of a national institution inside Czechoslovakia, and has more recently been accepted by the outside world as so typical of the very best type of 'folk opera' that it is surprising to remember that Smetana was looked upon during his life-time as insufficiently nationalist in feeling, and his other operas as too strongly under the influence of Wagner. Yet so it was. *The Bartered Bride* won him immediate recognition as a musical patriot, but the public attitude to some of his other works so angered the composer that he claimed to have written this popular comedy without either conviction or much enthusiasm.

The Overture is immensely and justifiably popular as a concert piece, and in fact its infectious tunes and brilliant high spirits fully justify the esteem in which it is held. Very few operas begin with greater *élan*. The themes are all taken from the finale to Act II (the inn scene).

Act I.    Spring in a Bohemian village. The village inn is on one side of the stage. It is holiday time, and the villagers are rejoicing at the prospect of the dancing which will take place to celebrate it. Only Marenka and Jenik seem left out of the general gaiety, and their gloom, we learn, is caused by the fact that Marenka has just learned that her parents plan a rich marriage for her, in spite of her heart having long since been given to the handsome but impecunious Jenik. The villagers go off to dance, and Marenka tells Jenik that her heart would break were he to desert her; her love is his, even though she knows so little of his antecedents and background. Their love duet leaves little doubt of their mutual affection; the lyrical main section is heard fairly frequently during the course of the opera as a love motive.

Marenka and Jenik leave the stage, and are succeeded by Marenka's parents, who are being harangued by that typically Czech institution, the marriage broker. He has the gift of the gab, and it is some time before either of his listeners can get a word in past his apparently endless repetitions of his patter. When they do, it is clear that they are prepared to accept his suggestion that Marenka shall marry the son of Tobias Micha, a rich neighbour. Kruschina thinks the contract should be taken up forthwith; he himself knows Micha, but he cannot so much as remember the names of his two sons. Kecal protests that there is only one; the other, by Micha's first marriage, disappeared from home years ago and is now presumed dead. In spite of Kecal's enthusiastic description of the prospective bridegroom, who was only prevented by his natural modesty from meeting them even now, Ludmila still thinks the final decision should be left in Marenka's hands.

The trio becomes a quartet when Marenka herself appears on the scene. She has one small objection to the scheme, she says; she has become engaged to Jenik. Kecal refuses to take such objections seriously, Kruschina is furious that his permission has not already been asked, and even Ludmila thinks Marenka might have handled the whole affair more tactfully. Marenka knocks the contract out of Kecal's hand, and leaves her parents wishing that Kecal had brought the bridegroom along with him; a sight of him might have caused her to change her mind.

The act ends with a spirited polka, danced and sung by the assembled villagers, and watched by their elders from the tables of the hospitable inn.

Act II.   The scene changes to the inside of the inn, where the men are busy drinking; in a chorus, they sing the praises of beer. Kecal is there looking for Jenik, who seems sunk in reflection. Both, however, join the chorus, Kecal vaunting money as the most desirable of possessions, Jenik objecting that he prefers love. Women join the men, and all dance a brilliant and energetic Furiant, known, like the overture, in the concert hall.

All leave the inn, and the coast is clear for a first sight of Vasek, who comes shyly in, stammering out that he has been sent off by his mother to woo his prospective bride, a frightening business, but one that he does not see how to avoid without making himself a laughing stock. He is an enchantingly silly figure, with his stutter and his transparent simplicity. It does not take long before Marenka, who comes in to find him alone, realises that this is the bridegroom who has been picked out for her. She is horrified, and proceeds to tell him that she, like all the other village girls, is really sorry that so handsome a lad is contracted to Marenka, a flighty girl who will lead him an awful dance once they are married. Vasek is frightened at what his mother may say, but Marenka paints a much brighter prospect for him with another girl, prettier than Marenka and already very much attracted to him from a distance. He eventually agrees to give up Marenka, and tries to kiss the pretty girl in front of him; she evades him, but he follows her out of the room.

Kecal has the prospect of a sizeable commission if he brings off the matter of Marenka's betrothal to the son of Tobias Micha, and he does not intend to lose it. Accordingly, he is prepared to invest a proportion of it in buying off the tiresome suitor whom

Marenka appears to favour. He takes Jenik to the inn for a drink, and talks the matter over. Things do not seem to be getting very far, but Kecal is at pains to point out that there are as good fish in the sea as ever came out of it; why worry so much about this particular girl, when there are others only too anxious to get married? He seems to have made some headway as a result of his monologue, and he attempts to clinch the matter by offering Jenik a match in which there would be some money for him. However, even the brilliant and lively tune of their duet, which Jenik repeats after him, is not enough to persuade the young man to give up his sweetheart, and Kecal is eventually reduced to offering him a substantial sum of money if he will renounce his claim on Marenka. Jenik takes some persuading, but finally agrees to do so—but only to the eldest son of Tobias Micha, the money to be paid to him and to be reclaimable under no circumstances whatsoever.

Kecal goes off well satisfied with the bargain he has made, but he leaves behind him a Jenik who knows quite well that the eldest son of Micha, presumed dead, is none other than himself. He has acquired a marriage contract to his beloved and a dowry from his cheese-paring stepmother at the same time! The plan must succeed! We can have no doubts as to the sincerity of Jenik's love for Marenka after the beautiful love song which he sings the moment Kecal's back is turned. He has not only out-witted the broker, but he deserves his reward!

But he is not left alone for long. Kecal brings in Kruschina and all the villagers to celebrate his successful handling of what turned out to be by no means a simple affair. The finale uses the material already heard in the overture. Kecal calls for silence, as he wants everyone to witness the legality of the document he is now going to have signed in their presence. In legal language, Kecal reads it out; it is to the effect that Jenik has agreed to re-nounce Marenka. Kruschina and Kecal are delighted, so apparently is Jenik, but the villagers cannot quite understand the position until Kecal adds that the whole thing is in consideration of the sum of three hundred gulden. Then popular fury knows no bounds; even Kruschina is shocked that Jenik should abandon Marenka for money, and Jenik signs amidst a general demon-stration of hostility.

Act III has the same set as Act I. Vasek is in stuttering despair that he cannot find the girl who gave him such good advice and whom he found so attractive. His amusing aria is marked *lamentoso*. His thoughts are interrupted by the arrival of a circus troupe, headed by a redoubtable Ringmaster, and heralded by the so-called March of the Comedians. Springer announces that the attractions include the great dancer, Esmeralda, and a real, live, American bear. Let all the bystanders stay and watch a sample of what the company can do! To the accompaniment of the delightfully varied and tuneful Dance of the Comedians, the clowns and dancers go through their paces, watched by an admiring throng.

When all have gone their way, only Vasek is left behind admiring the beautiful Esmeralda. Just then, one of the clowns comes running in to tell the Ringmaster that the man who usually plays the bear is much too drunk to go through with his rôle. He himself has looked for a suitable substitute, but something is wrong with everyone he has asked, and he is at his wits' end. Esmeralda solves the problem by suggesting that the dimwit who has been gawking at her for some minutes would be just the right build. The Ringmaster asks Vasek if he would like to dance with the beautiful girl, Esmeralda assures him that she will teach him how, and the agreement is completed. He will make his début that night.

Vasek is just practising some steps to himself, when he sees his parents. Hata wants him to come with them to meet his future bride, but he is unwilling, and downright determined when he hears that it is Kruschina's Marenka who is his destined spouse. He does not know who it is he wants to marry, or rather he does not know her name, but he *is* sure that it is not Marenka. He escapes, and a moment later in comes Marenka, furious and mortified at the news her father tells her, that Jenik has sold her love for money. The orchestra reminds her of Jenik's protestations of undying affection, and she is inconsolable.

Vasek reappears, and is overjoyed to hear that the girl who stands before him, whom he found so attractive, is Marenka after all. But poor Marenka asks for time in which to make up her mind, and the parents of the prospective bride and bridegroom join with Kecal in exhorting her to give the matter serious thought. This sextet (Marenka joins them just before it finishes) is a lovely, contemplative piece. The mood is continued when

Marenka is left alone, to lament her unhappy position. Everything around her seems dead, she sings, but her misery gives way to melancholy when she reflects that it is she who has changed, and not the spring, which is as lovely as ever.

To her comes Jenik, apparently in the best of spirits. Marenka is furious with him, and even more so when he seems to treat the whole affair as an excellent joke. Nothing he can do will reconcile her to hearing him out. The argument is by no means over when Kecal comes up to them, to tell Jenik he can have his money as soon as Marenka has signed the contract. Jenik urges her to do so, which naturally only increases her fury against him, and gives Kecal an even worse opinion of the type of man with whom he is dealing—these sentiments find expression in a trio.

Everyone in the village comes together for the finale which is to see the betrothal of Marenka and (as Jenik insists the description shall run) 'the son of Tobias Micha'. Everyone congratulates Marenka on the match, nobody louder than Jenik, who has no sooner opened his mouth than he is recognised by Hata and Micha as the long-lost son of the latter. He asks Marenka whether she will have him or Vasek, and her triumphant answer leaves Kecal babbling with fury at having been outwitted. He makes himself so conspicuous in fact that everyone laughs at his discomfiture; he goes out in a real rage.

All is now set for a happy ending, but there is an interruption as a couple of small boys rush in shouting that the bear is loose! He shambles in, but it is not long before the voice of Vasek can be heard from inside the skin saying that nobody need be frightened, as the bear is only him. Hata is overcome with shame at his behaviour, and takes him off, leaving the coast clear for general rejoicing at the betrothal of the bartered bride and her faithful lover.                                                     H.

# DALIBOR

Opera in three acts by Bedrich Smetana, text by J. Wenzig. Première at Prague, May 16, 1868, with Benevic-Mikova (Milada), Lukes (Dalibor). First performed in Vienna, 1892; revived 1938, with Hilde Konetzni, Rethy, Mazaroff, Destal, Kipnis, conductor Walter. First performed Berlin, 1940, with Lemnitz, Scheppan, Völker, Bockelmann, von Manowarda.

## CHARACTERS

Vladislav, *King of Bohemia* ..................... Baritone
Dalibor, *a knight* ................................. Tenor

Budivoj, *captain of the guard* ..................Baritone
Benes, *the gaoler* ...............................Bass
Vitek, *Dalibor's squire* ..........................Tenor
Milada, *sister of the dead Burgrave*..............Soprano
Jitka .......................................Soprano
Zdenek's ghost
          Nobles, soldiers, men and women

*Time:* Fifteenth Century                    *Place:* Prague

The story of *Dalibor* was a legend which symbolised Czech
aspirations long before Smetana took it as a subject for an opera.
It is hard to believe that his librettist's treatment of the story
owed nothing to *Fidelio*, and that dramatic resemblances between
the two are pure coincidence; there are in fact many similarities
of theme and detail. After 1919, when Czech independence ceased
to be a dream and became reality, the opera took on new significance for the Czech people, and it has since then been looked
on, with *The Bartered Bride*, as a national institution, a position
which its theme and the splendid music in which it is clothed
seem amply to justify.

In her *The Music of Czechoslovakia* (O.U.P.), Rosa Newmarch
writes: 'The theme of *Dalibor* seems to have been noted down
by the composer as early as 1863. It appears in the opera soon
after the opening fanfare, and in this form, *largo maestoso*, probably represents the destiny, rather than the personality, of
Dalibor, and is always treated by the orchestra, rather than by
an individual voice or instrument. A modified form of it, in F
major, depicts Dalibor the proud knight and intrepid hero. Out
of this theme grows the melody associated with Dalibor's murdered friend, Zdenek. It is of a softer type and more suited to its
eventual use as a violin solo when the spirit of Zdenek appears
to Dalibor in the dungeon. . . . The motive of deliverance—
another derivative—appears as a brilliant little fanfare in G
major.'

There is no extensive overture, and the curtain rises after fifteen
bars of music on the judgment hall of the king's palace in Prague.
Dalibor has been engaged in strife with the Burgrave of Plosko-
vice; his friend Zdenek was captured and put to death, and, in
revenge, Dalibor has killed the Burgrave. For this he is coming
up for judgment in front of the king. The people, amongst them

Jitka, an orphan whom Dalibor has befriended, are waiting for the assembly of the court; they praise Dalibor as their friend and protector. The king enters with his judges, and rehearses the charges against Dalibor. He calls Milada, the sister of the dead Burgrave, to substantiate her accusations.

Amidst expressions of sympathy for her bereavement, she tells the dramatic story of Dalibor's entry into the castle, and of how he killed her brother. The king assures her Dalibor will pay for his crime with his life, and he orders that the accused may be brought in. As he enters, expressions of admiration are heard on all sides, and even Milada is compelled to comment on his fearless, noble appearance. Dalibor does not deny his action; only, it was not murder but vengeance for murder. In an aria he tells of his love for his friend and of his violin playing (the solo violin is throughout associated with Zdenek). Zdenek was captured in battle, and when Dalibor asked what ransom was required to redeem him, he was sent his head on the end of a lance. Milada begins to feel pity for her former foe. Dalibor defies the king; he has committed no crime, only revenged the murder of his friend.

The verdict of the court is imprisonment for life; Dalibor invokes the free spirit of Zdenek—did he hear the sentence? Dalibor is led away, and Milada pleads for his life. But the judges say he has openly threatened the king; even when Milada protests that she herself, whom he has most wronged, is prepared to forgive him, they are unimpressed. Milada admits to herself that she is in love with Dalibor. Jitka overhears her and begs her to exert herself to free Dalibor.

Act II. Street below the castle in which Dalibor is imprisoned. From an inn comes the sound of gay singing. Jitka and Vitek, Dalibor's page, greet each other eagerly in a charming duet. They discuss Dalibor's plight and Jitka reveals that Milada is already inside the prison disguised as a boy. They are optimistic that their cause has not received so severe a setback in the imprisonment of Dalibor as might have been feared; he will soon be out, and victory and freedom will be theirs. The music has an exuberance that is positively Weberian in character.

The scene changes to the house of Benes, the gaoler, inside the castle. Night is falling and sentries patrol up and down. Budivoj warns Benes that there is danger of a rising in favour of Dalibor; he, as head gaoler, is answerable for the prisoner's safe-keeping with his life. Budivoj looks at Milada who is standing nearby in disguise, and enquires who it is; Benes tells him it is his new assistant. The parallel of the whole situation with that of *Fidelio* is too obvious to need pointing out. In music of sombre character, Benes reflects on the gloomy nature of his calling.

Milada comes to tell Benes that his meal is ready. The gaoler refers most sympathetically to Dalibor, who, he says, has asked for a fiddle to play in his dungeon. He tells Milada to take the instrument down to the prisoner, and says he himself will go to fetch it. Milada left alone rejoices at the prospect of seeing Dalibor for the first time face to face. Benes returns and gives Milada instructions on how to find the appropriate dungeon.

The scene changes again, this time to Dalibor's cell. Dalibor has a vision of Zdenek, who appears to him and plays his violin; when he has gone, Dalibor invokes his reappearance in a beautiful aria. Presently Milada brings him the instrument he has asked for. She admits that she was his accuser at his trial, and that she hated him. She tells him of her useless pleas that he should be allowed to go free, and of the preparations which are in hand for his escape. Will he pardon her for what she has done to him; ever since the trial she has loved him from afar. The whole scene is one of extraordinary power, and the lyrical duet itself of haunting beauty. It seems to me no exaggeration to describe this as one of the greatest love duets in all opera.

Act III.    The throne room of the king, brightly lit. He is surrounded by his councillors. Budivoj and Benes appear in front of him, the former saying that he has news of a rising which is plotted in Dalibor's favour. Benes tells his story; he had an apprentice, who suddenly disappeared, leaving behind him some money and a note of thanks. But at least Benes was in time to prevent Dalibor's escape—the lad had certainly something to do with the preparations he discovered for freeing the prisoner. Benes pleads for leniency for himself. The king, in spite of misgivings as to the justice of his action, takes the step of condemning Dalibor to instant death.

Dalibor in his cell has a brilliant and exciting aria as he thinks of the freedom he can bring to his people when once he has escaped from prison. But Budivoj comes to tell him of the court's decision that he shall die, and he muses on his coming death in music of poignant sadness.

During a march interlude, the scene changes to an open place in front of the castle. Milada, clad for war, with Jitka, Vitek, and their armed supporters, wait for the signal. They hear the tolling of a bell and the sound of a chorus of monks, and Milada is afraid that Dalibor is being done to death inside the prison while they wait for his signal to attack it. They prepare to assault the castle.

Women comment on what they can see, and presently Dalibor comes out of the castle carrying Milada, who is wounded. She dies in his arms, and, when Budivoj appears with troops, Dalibor stabs himself and dies with his beloved. (There is an alternative ending to the opera, in which Dalibor is executed before Milada and the rescue party can reach him: Milada is killed in the attack.)

H.

# THE KISS
## Hubicka

Opera in two acts by Bedrich Smetana, text by E. Krasnohorska. Première, Prague, November 7, 1876. First performed in England, Carl Rosa, 1948, with Packer, Myrrdin, conducted by Tausky (there had been an amateur performance at Liverpool in 1938).

## CHARACTERS

Paloucky, *a peasant* . . . . . . . . . . . . . . . . . . . . . . Bass-Baritone
Vendulka, *his daughter* . . . . . . . . . . . . . . . . . . . . . Soprano
Lukas, *a young widower* . . . . . . . . . . . . . . . . . . . . . . Tenor
Tomes, *brother-in-law of Lukas* . . . . . . . . . . . . . . . Baritone
Martinka, *Vendulka's old aunt* . . . . . . . . . . . . . . . Contralto
Matous, *an old smuggler* . . . . . . . . . . . . . . . . . . . . . . Bass
Barce, *a servant girl* . . . . . . . . . . . . . . . . . . . . . . . Soprano
A frontier guard . . . . . . . . . . . . . . . . . . . . . . . . . . . . Tenor

*Place:* In the mountains on the borders of Bohemia

*The Kiss* is an undemonstrative opera, with the mildest of jokes for subject—the superstitious reluctance of a bride-to-be to give her lover a kiss before their marriage, and their subsequent quarrel (Act I) and reconciliation (Act II, Scene ii). The first scene of Act II is devoted to the frustration of the principal characters, with a band of smugglers (a virtually unexplained interruption) as background. Smetana has provided attractive, melodious and singable music, which may not have quite the point of his *Bartered Bride* score but is full of charm and not without tunes that contain all the elements of popularity.

Act I is set in a room in Paloucky's cottage. Through the open window can be seen the village square. Lukas, a young peasant, was always in love with Vendulka, but, at the wish of his parents, he married another woman. Now she is dead and he is free to marry Vendulka. Martinka is delighted at the way things have worked out, but Vendulka's father has some misgivings; both Vendulka and Lukas are headstrong, determined people—she would do better to refuse him, he tells his daughter. Her unhappiness is so obvious at this piece of advice, that he relents; but he does not appear to alter his view that this marriage is a risky affair.

Barce rushes in to say that the wooing party is about to put in an appearance, and soon Lukas and Tomes appear at the window, followed by a crowd of curious villagers. Tomes explains that Lukas has come a-wooing; Paloucky gives his consent, but in such a way that Lukas takes offence that it was not done more gladly. Paloucky explains that he thinks the prospective couple are too hot-tempered to keep peace for long, but he gives them his blessing and all is forgiven and forgotten in a moment. There is a duet for the two lovers, at the end of which Lukas makes as if to kiss Vendulka; she refuses to allow him to do so. Lukas insists, she continues to refuse, and the fat is in the fire as Paloucky predicted. But all is well again when Tomes starts up a drinking song, in which everyone joins, before leaving the happy couple alone together.

They sing of their love, and presently Lukas's child is brought in a cradle, much to Vendulka's joy. He tries to kiss her again —after all, they are alone now—but she will still not allow him to do so, not until after their wedding. The quarrel breaks out again, and eventually Vendulka threatens to throw Lukas out of the house, to the surprise of everyone except her father, who had anticipated just such a situation arising. Lukas makes a last demand for what he has come to think of as his right, and, when it is refused, leaves in high dudgeon.

Martinka advises Vendulka to make up the quarrel, and bids her good night. Vendulka sits herself by the cradle of the child and sings to it as she rocks it to sleep. She sings two separate songs, which together make a most appealing aria, at the end of which Vendulka herself falls asleep. She is woken up by the sound of a polka outside her window, and she sees Lukas dancing merrily in front of the house, and kissing the girls with whom he dances. She is furious, but even Tomes's endeavours are not sufficient to quieten Lukas, whose blood is up, and who is determined to get his revenge publicly on Vendulka. As the curtain falls, Vendulka exclaims that she must go away from the place where she has been so publicly humiliated.

Act II.    A thick wood near the frontier of Bohemia. Matous appears at the head of a band of smugglers, all carrying heavy bundles. There is a smugglers' chorus, after which the stage is left empty until the arrival of Lukas, who in an aria expresses his despair at the disappearance of Vendulka, whom he dearly loves in spite of his impetuous and odious behaviour. Tomes is looking for him, and presently appears along the same path, to be overjoyed at the sight of his brother-in-law, for whose safety he was becoming really worried. Lukas is anxious to restore himself in Vendulka's favour, and Tomes bids him only have the courage to admit he was in the wrong, and she will have him back at once. It is one of the best of Smetana's tenor-baritone duets, of the type best known from the famous specimen in *The Bartered Bride*.

Matous, who has overheard the conversation between Lukas and Tomes, comes out into the open when they have left and has a good laugh at Lukas's expense. He is waiting for Martinka, who lives nearby and is in league with the smugglers, but when she comes into sight, she has Vendulka with her. Vendulka is frightened by the loneliness of the forest, but Martinka comforts her before giving a signal, which brings Matous out of hiding. Vendulka begins to lament her fate, but Matous knows that the happy ending to her story is being prepared by no one else than Lukas himself, who is only too anxious to make up their quarrel.

When Matous goes his way, he gives some of his contraband to Martinka, who shares the burden with Vendulka. A frontier guard appears but leaves them unmolested. Martinka continues her efforts to persuade Vendulka to return home, where she is sure Lukas will be waiting for her.

Next morning, outside Martinka's cottage. Barce is trying to find Martinka or Vendulka to tell them the news she has heard from Matous. She thinks she can hear them coming—but it is the sound of a lark. She rejoices in the lark's singing in a most attractive aria, but one that is so difficult that it must be beyond the capacity of almost any soprano willing to take secondary rôles.

Up the path to Martinka's cottage come Matous, Paloucky, Lukas and Tomes, with a whole crowd of villagers. Barce rings her hands in frustration that Martinka and Vendulka are not there to welcome them and so make the reconciliation possible. Lukas apologises to Paloucky for his behaviour, and soon afterwards Vendulka appears. She and Lukas are obviously overjoyed to see each other again, but when Vendulka comes towards him with open arms, Lukas refuses to kiss her—until he has openly begged her pardon for his behaviour towards her.          H.

# PART III

# THE TWENTIETH CENTURY

# CHAPTER 14

## *German Opera in the Twentieth Century*

# RICHARD STRAUSS

## (1864–1949)

### SALOME

OPERA in one act by Richard Strauss; words after Oscar Wilde's poem of the same title, translated into German by Hedwig Lachmann. Première in Dresden, December 9, 1905, with Wittich, von Chavanne, Burrian, Perron, conductor von Schuch. Sir Arnold Bax in his autobiographical *Farewell my Youth* wrote that Burrian '. . . created a quite horrifying Herod, slobbering with lust, and apparently almost decomposing before our disgusted but fascinated eyes'. First performed Berlin, 1906, with Destinn, Goetze, Krauss, Baptist Hoffmann, conductor Strauss; la Scala, Milan, 1906, with Krusceniski, Bruno, Borgatti; Metropolitan, 1907, with Fremstad, Weed, Burrian, van Rooy, conductor Hertz (banished after only one public performance); 1909, Manhattan Opera House (in French), with Mary Garden, de Cisneros, Dalmorès, Dufranne; 1910, Covent Garden, with Ackté, Metzger, Ernst Krauss, Whitehill, conductor Beecham. Revivals at Covent Garden: 1924, with Ljüngberg, Olszewska, Kirchoff, Schipper; 1937, with Ranczak (later Schulz), Kalter, Ralf, Schöffler, conductor Knappertsbusch; 1947, with Welitsch (later Cebotari), Höngen, Patzak, Rothmüller, conductor Clemens Krauss; 1949 (in English), with Welitsch, Shacklock, Lechleitner, Schon, conductor Rankl (décor by Salvador Dali); at Metropolitan, 1933, with Ljüngberg, Lorenz, Schorr, conductor Bodanzky; 1937, with Marjorie Lawrence, Branzell, Maison, Huehn, conductor Panizza; 1942, with Djanel, Branzell, Maison, Janssen, conductor Szell; 1949, with Welitsch, Thorborg, Lorenz, Berglund, conductor Reiner; in Berlin, 1942, with Cebotari, Pölzer, Prohaska.

### CHARACTERS

Herod Antipas, *Tetrarch of Judea* . . . . . . . . . . . . . . . . . . Tenor
Herodias, *wife of Herod* . . . . . . . . . . . . . . . . . . Mezzo-Soprano
Salome, *daughter of Herodias* . . . . . . . . . . . . . . . . . . . Soprano
Jokanaan (*John the Baptist*) . . . . . . . . . . . . . . . . . . . . . Baritone
Narraboth, *a young Syrian, Captain of the Guard* . . . . Tenor
The Page of Herodias . . . . . . . . . . . . . . . . . . . . . . . . . . . . Alto
Five Jews . . . . . . . . . . . . . . . . . . . . . . . Four Tenors, One Bass
Two Nazarenes . . . . . . . . . . . . . . . . . . . . . . . . . . . Tenor, Bass
Two Soldiers . . . . . . . . . . . . . . . . . . . . . . . . . . . . . . . . . . Bass
A Cappadocian . . . . . . . . . . . . . . . . . . . . . . . . . . . . . . . . Bass
A Slave

*Time:* About 30 A.D.

*Place:* The great terrace in the palace of Herod at Tiberias Galilee, the capital of his kingdom

On the great terrace of Herod's palace, off the banquet hall, is his body-guard. The ardent looks of the young captain, Narraboth, a Syrian, are directed toward the banquet hall where Salome is seated. In vain the Page, who is aware of the neurotic taint in the woman, warns him. The young captain is consumed with ardent desires.

The night is sultry. The soldiers' talk is interrupted by the sounds from the hall. Suddenly there is heard a loud and deep voice, as from a tomb. Dread seizes even upon the rough soldiers. He who calls is a madman according to some, a prophet according to others, in either case, a man of indomitable courage who with terrifying directness of speech brings the ruling powers face to face with their sins and bids them repent. This is Jokanaan. His voice sounds so reverberant because it issues from the gloomy cistern in which he is held a captive.

Suddenly Salome, in great commotion, steps out on the terrace. The greedy looks with which Herod, her stepfather, has regarded her, as well as the talk and noisy disputes of the gluttons and degenerates within, have driven her out. In her stirs the sinful blood of her mother, who, in order that she might marry Herod, slew her husband. Depraved surroundings, a court at which the satisfying of all desires is the main theme of the day, have poisoned her thoughts. She seeks new pleasures, as yet untasted enjoyments. Now, as she hears the voice of the Prophet, there arises in her the lust to see this man, whom she has heard her mother curse, because he has stigmatised her shame, and whom she knows the Tetrarch fears, although a captive. What she desires is strictly forbidden, but Narraboth cannot resist her blandishments: 'Du wirst das für mich tun, Narraboth.' The strange, gloomy figure of Jokanaan, fantastically noble in the rags of his captivity, emerges from the well to extended orchestral music (including a mature statement of the figure associated with him): No. 1.

The sight of him stirs Salome's morbid desires. There is a lengthy scene between them. When he appears, Jokanaan denounces Herod and Herodias ('Wo ist er dessen Sündenbecher jetzt voll ist?'). Salome is fascinated by him and he turns on her ('Wer ist dies Weib, das mich ansieht?'), and rages at her as the daughter of an iniquitous mother. Salome tells him in music of rising intensity of her desire for his body ('Jokanaan, ich bin verliebt in deinen Leib'), his hair ('In dein Haar bin ich verliebt'), and finally his mouth ('Deinem Mund begehre ich'). A significant phrase emerges: No. 2.

Her arts are brought into full play in her efforts to tempt him, but with the sole result that he bids her do penance. This but adds fuel to the flames. When Narraboth, in despair over her actions, kills himself on his own sword, she does not so much as notice it. Appalled by the wickedness of the young woman, the Prophet warns her to seek for the only one in whom she can find redemption, the Man of Galilee: 'Es lebt nur Einer, der dich retten kann.' But, realising that his words fall on deaf ears, he curses her and retreats into his cistern.

Herod, Herodias and their suite come out on to the terrace: 'Wo ist Salome? Wo ist die Prinzessin?' Herod is suffering under the weight of his crimes—soon after coming in, he has an hallucination that the wind is blowing round his head—but the infamous Herodias is as cold as a serpent. Herod's sinful desire for his step-daughter is the only thing that can stir his blood. He asks Salome to drink from a cup (No. 3) and to eat some fruit so that he may

have the pleasure of putting his teeth and lips in the same place; in spite of Herodias's objections, this he follows up by asking Salome to sit beside him on his throne in her mother's place.

But Salome is weary and indifferent; Herodias full of bitter scorn for him and for her daughter. Against the Prophet, whose voice terrifies whoever hears it, her hatred is fierce. But Herod stands in mysterious awe of the Prophet. He refuses to give him up to the Jews, who clamour to be allowed to judge him, and insists that the Prophet is a holy man who has even beheld God. This starts a theological argument amongst the Jewish guests at the feast, who dispute in a fugal quintet. No sooner is it finished than two Nazarenes proclaim their conviction that the Messiah is in their midst; he has even raised the dead from their graves. Herod is immediately filled with misgivings, which are not quieted by the Prophet's continued prediction of doom.

It is almost as much because of his dread of the future as for longing for her that Herod asks as a diversion for Salome to dance in order that life may flow warm again in his chilled veins. Salome demurs until he swears that he will grant any request she may make of him. She executes the 'Dance of the seven veils', casting one veil after another from her. The dance is long, and is an exacting undertaking for any *prima donna* who has still, be it remembered, the most taxing part of her vocal assignment to come. At the first performance, the dance was performed by a ballerina, and the soprano emerged from the crowd at its end; but at a later performance history relates that Frau Wittich undertook it herself, much to the distress of the composer, who let it be known that he preferred a Salome with two distinct personalities rather than risk a repetition of what he had seen.

When she has finished, Herod asks Salome what her reward shall be. In part prompted by Herodias, but also by her own mad desire to have vengeance for her rejected passion, she demands the head of the Prophet. Herod offers her everything else he can name—precious stones, his unique white peacocks, the mantle of the High Priest, even the Veil of the Temple—but Salome refuses to release him from his promise. At last, almost faint with weariness and fear, he gives in.

The executioner descends into the cistern. Jokanaan is slain (to the eerie sound of a pinched B flat on a solo double-bass) and his severed head presented to Salome upon a silver charger. She is in ecstasy and circles round the head addressing it as though it were still living. Alive he refused her his lips; now, in a frenzy of lust, she presses hers upon them. Even Herod shudders and turns from her revolted. 'Kill that woman!' he commands his guards, who crush her under their shields.

Although *Salome* so far shocked convention at the beginning of the century that it was withdrawn from the Metropolitan after a dress rehearsal and one performance—practically on command, it is said, of the board of directors—it has proved in the long run no exception to the rule of diminishing artistic returns on an investment in the 'shocking'. Certainly it would surprise its early detractors to know that it is now a standard display piece for dramatic soprano, and on the fringe of every repertory.

The passage of time has brought general agreement on the weak points of the score. But, when all is said and done, *Salome* has unusual qualities, not least its unquestioned vitality. What could be more evocative and suggestive of what is to come than the opening music, which so unerringly sets the scene? Strauss's vivid characterisation of persons is equally notable: there are few better musical portrayals of neurasthenia than is to be found in the music of Herod, and his decadence, lust, and fear are implicit in every bar he sings. But the best of the character studies is contained in the title rôle. Each and every change of this emotionally unstable character is reflected in the music, and her final scene with the head of Jokanaan transcends the dramatic implications of the words, and is written, through her eyes as it were, as a sort of psychopathic *Liebestod*.                                    K., H.

## ELEKTRA

Opera in one act by Richard Strauss, text by Hugo von Hofmannsthal, after Sophocles. Première Dresden, January 25, 1909, with Anny Krull, Siems, Schumann-Heink, Sembach, Perron, conductor von Schuch. First performed Berlin, 1909, with Plaichinger, Goetze, Rose, Grüning, Bischof, conductor Blech; Vienna, 1909, with Marie Gutheil-Schoder, Mildenburg, Weidemann; la Scala, Milan, 1909 (in Italian), with Krusceniski, Cannetti, de Cisneros, Gaudenzi, Cirino; New York, Manhattan Opera, 1910 (in French), with Mazarin, Gerville-Réache, Duffault, Huberdeau; Covent Garden, 1910, with Edyth Walker, Rose, Mildenburg, d'Oisly, Weidemann, conductor Beecham; Hull, 1912 (in English), with Florence Easton.

Revived Covent Garden, 1925, with Kappel, Olszewska, Soot, Schorr, conductor Walter; 1938, with Pauly, Hilde Konetzni, Thorborg, Wolff, Janssen, conductor Beecham; 1953 with Schlüter, cond. Kleiber; 1957 with Lammers, cond. Kempe. Metropolitan, 1938, with Pauly, Thorborg, Althouse, Schorr, conductor Bodanzky; la Scala, 1943, with Rünger, Ursuleac, Höngen, conductor von Hoesslin; Vienna State Opera, 1949, with Anny Konetzni, Hilde Konetzni, Höngen, Lorenz, Nissen; Florence Festival, 1950, with Anny Konetzni, Mödl, conductor Mitropoulos; Munich, 1952, with Borkh, Kupper, Fischer, Klarwein, Frantz; Metropolitan, 1952, with Varnay, Wegner, Höngen, Svanholm, Schöffler, conductor Reiner. Gutheil-Schoder was one of the most famous of Elektras.

### CHARACTERS

Klytemnestra, *widow of Agamemnon* . . . . . . . Mezzo-Soprano
Elektra ⎱ *her daughters* ⎰ . . . . . . . . . . . . . . . . Soprano
Chrysothemis ⎰              ⎱ . . . . . . . . . . . . . . . . Soprano

Aegisth, *Klytemnestra's paramour* ..................Tenor

• Orest, *son of Klytemnestra and Agamemnon* .......Baritone

Tutor of Orest....................................Bass

The Confidante of Klytemnestra.................Soprano

The Trainbearer of Klytemnestra...............Soprano

A Young Servant...............................Tenor

An Old Servant ................................Bass

The Overseer ................................Soprano

Five Maidservants ...............
$$\begin{cases} \text{1, Contralto} \\ \text{2, 3, Mezzo-Soprano} \\ \text{4, 5, Soprano} \end{cases}$$

*Time:* Antiquity                    *Scene:* Mycenae

*Elektra* is now accepted as one of Strauss's most successful operas, and one of the strongest candidates amongst them for survival; the 'shocking' element is more part and parcel of the drama than the similar element in *Salome,* and the work as a whole is built on a firmer foundation—so might run a consensus of opinion some fifty years after the first performance. But it was not always so. Mme. Schumann-Heink, the Klytemnestra of the original production in Dresden, said: 'I will never sing the rôle again. It was frightful. We were a set of mad women. . . . There is nothing beyond *Elektra.* We have lived and reached the furthest boundary in dramatic writing for the voice with Wagner. But Richard Strauss goes beyond him. His singing voices are lost. We have come to a full stop. I believe Strauss himself sees it'— and (comments Mr. Kobbé) in his next opera, *Der Rosenkavalier,* the composer shows far more consideration for the voice.

Beyond the fact that Agamemnon was murdered by his wife, Klytemnestra, and her paramour Aegistheus, it is not essential to know the details of the Greek story, but it is nevertheless against this background that even Hoffmannsthal and Strauss, with all their changes of emphasis, have laid their opera. Agamemnon and Menelaus, the sons of King Atreus, married the sisters Klytemnestra and Helen. The latter was carried off by Paris, son of Priam, King of Troy, and it was to procure her return to her husband and to avenge the insult to Greece that the Trojan war began. On their way to Troy, the Greek fleet touched at Aulis and was caught there by the adverse winds, the goddess Artemis being angry with Agamemnon, who had killed one of her sacred hinds.

To appease the goddess and to ensure that the fleet reached Troy in safety, Agamemnon sent for his daughter Iphigenia and sacrificed her. The war over, Menelaus and Helen were driven by storms to Egypt, where they stayed for some years (and formed the subjects of Strauss's *Aegyptische Helene*), and Agamemnon returned to Mycenae. Here he found that Klytemnestra had installed Aegistheus as her lover. With the excuse of the sacrifice of her daughter to salve her conscience Klytemnestra murdered Agamemnon in his bath, and installed Aegistheus as his successor. Three children survived their father: Elektra, who was reduced to menial status, Chrysothemis, and Orestes, who was sent away to safety, according to some legends by a faithful slave, to others by Elektra. Eventually, Orestes returns, gives out that he is dead, gains admittance to the palace, and slays the guilty Klytemnestra and her lover.

The work is in one long act—Strauss was always strongly opposed to having another work given on the same evening—but that act has been divided by analysts into seven sections: (1) Elektra; (2) Chrysothemis; (3) Klytemnestra; (4) Elektra and Chrysothemis; (5) Orestes; (6) the Recognition; (7) the Vengeance.

The curtain rises straight away to show the inner court of the palace of Mycenae. At the back can be seen the palace itself; in the court is a well, from which servants are drawing water as the curtain goes up. They discuss the unpredictable Elektra, who howls like the dogs with whom her mother and stepfather have condemned her to live and eat. Some hate her, others pity her, only the fifth maid reveres and loves her. For her defence of Elektra she is set upon by the others, and when they have gone inside, the fifth maid can be heard crying out that she is being beaten.

The scene is empty before Elektra comes from the house alone. In a great monologue ('Allein! Weh, ganz allein!') she rehearses the story of her father's murder, calls on his name (No. 1), and

A - ga - mem - - non !

looks forward to the time when his death will be avenged by herself and Orestes. When this is accomplished she will dance in triumph round the corpses of her enemies. The motif associated with the children of Agamemnon (No. 2) is important:

The second stage begins when Chrysothemis joins Elektra. Hofmannsthal designs her as a weaker and more human contrast to the implacable Elektra, and she is little inclined to join her sister in the schemes for revenge which are constantly being urged upon her. Instead, she issues a warning that further horrors are in store for Elektra. Poor Chrysothemis feels the fires of love frustrated within her ('Ich hab's wie Feuer in der Brust') and longs to escape from her hateful prison, to which she is doomed by the fear which her sister's weird hatred inspires in Klytemnestra. The ordeal to which both are subjected is leaving its mark on them, she says.

Noises are heard within of running footsteps, torches can be seen, and Chrysothemis says she will not stay to meet Klytemnestra who must surely be coming out. Elektra, however, is determined to speak to her mother.

Stage three begins as Klytemnestra is seen for the first time through the middle window. She is bloated and decayed, and sleepless nights and debauched days have left her looking as though it were an effort to keep her eyes open. She leans on the arm of her Confidante. Her first words are to mourn the evil workings of fate which have given her such a daughter, but presently she comes down to the courtyard, and, dismissing her attendants, is left alone with the daughter she hates and fears so much.

She is tormented by dreams; knows her daughter no remedy for them? Elektra is wise, and alone can help her. She describes her sleepless nights; is there not some sacrifice she can make to the gods to alleviate the torture she suffers? Elektra answers her insinuatingly, and in terms that admit of two meanings. Yes, there is a victim, who is unconsecrated and roams free; it is a woman, married, who can be killed at any time of day or night, with an axe, by a man, a stranger, but of their kin. Klytemnestra becomes impatient, and Elektra asks whether her mother means to call her brother back from exile. Klytemnestra is uneasy at mention of him, and Elektra accuses her of sending money to bribe those who are looking after him to kill him; the trembling of her body at his name proves as much. But Klytemnestra says she fears nobody. She will find means of dragging from Elektra the secret of whose blood must flow to cause her nightmares to abate. Elektra springs at her; it is *her* blood that is required. *She* is the victim the gods have marked down. Elektra describes the chase which will end with Klytemnestra's death. The librettist indicates: 'They stand eye to eye—Elektra in wild intoxication; Klytemnestra breathing in horrible spasms of fear.'

At this moment the Confidante runs out of the palace and whispers in Klytemnestra's ear. A look of triumph comes into the Queen's face, and she goes into the palace, leaving Elektra alone in the courtyard. Stage 4. Not long afterwards, Chrysothemis comes out crying the dread news that Orestes is dead. Elektra at first will not believe it, but Chrysothemis says that two strangers, one old, the other young, brought the news; Orestes was dragged to death by his own horses. A servant comes out of the palace, demanding a horse as quickly as possible so that he may fulfil his mistress's command and carry the news to Aegistheus.

Elektra now demands that Chrysothemis shall help her in her self-appointed task; alone she cannot slay Klytemnestra and Aegistheus but with her sister's help she would be able to accomplish the deed. She flatters Chrysothemis that she is strong, and she promises that she will henceforth look after her as if she were her slave. She holds Chrysothemis fast, but when her sister eventually frees herself and rushes from the courtyard, she hurls a curse after her.

The fifth stage begins as Elektra, left alone, begins to dig like an animal at the side of the courtyard. She looks up twice, and then sees someone standing by the gate. Who is interrupting her thus? He asks her if she works in the palace. She answers bitterly that she does. He tells her that he has business with the Queen; he and another have brought the news of Orestes's death. Elektra's grief at the news is overwhelming; must she look upon him who lives, while someone a thousand times as good as he lies dead? Elektra's utterance takes on the character of a lament for Orestes, whom she will never see again. The stranger asks her if she is of the royal house that she takes Orestes's death as so personal a matter. She reveals her name, and the stranger exclaims in astonishment. He reveals that Orestes is not dead, and, a moment later, servants come in and kiss his hand. Who is he, demands Elektra? Everyone knows him, he answers, except his own sister.

The recognition scene (stage 6) is the emotional climax of the opera. Elektra's ferocity drops from her to be replaced by tenderness, and the unremitting tension of the music gives way to lyricism: 'Orest! Orest! Orest!'

Elektra will not allow her brother to embrace her. She contrasts her former beauty with her present state; everything she has renounced in expiation of the murder of her father. Together they exult in the prospect of the righteous revenge which they will exact on Agamemnon's murderers. They are recalled to the reality of the situation by Orestes's tutor.

The seventh and last stage of the drama begins when the Confidante appears and leads Orestes and the tutor inside. Elektra is alone, in horrible excitement, waiting for the sounds which will tell her that the first part of the revenge is over. A shriek tells her that Orestes has found Klytemnestra. By now the palace is aroused, but Elektra bars the entrance with her body.

Aegistheus saunters into the courtyard, and Elektra offers to light him into the palace. Aegistheus wonders at the change that has come over Elektra, who is circling round him in a strange sort of dance. Aegistheus enters the palace, but re-appears a moment later at a window, yelling for help.

Women rush out of the palace, amongst them Chrysothemis, who has discovered that Orestes is back. Their rejoicings are very different in character, and Elektra breaks away from her sister, throwing back her head like a maenad, and dancing about like a demented creature. Her thirst for vengeance is satisfied, and her dance increases to frenzy. Suddenly she collapses dead upon the ground. With a last cry of 'Orest!' Chrysothemis rushes to the door of the palace, and bangs on it. The orchestra continues to give out the motif associated with Agamemnon.          H.

# DER ROSENKAVALIER
## The Knight of the Rose

Opera in three acts by Richard Strauss; text by Hugo von Hofmannsthal. Première Dresden, January 26, 1911, with Siems, Nast, von der Osten, Perron, conductor Schuch. First performed Berlin, April 1911, with Hempel, Dux, Lola Artôt de Padilla, Knüpfer, conductor Muck; Vienna, 1911, with Weidt, Gutheil-Schoder, Förstel, Mayr; la Scala, Milan, 1911, with Agostinelli, Ferraris, Bori, Ludikar; Covent Garden, 1913, with Siems, Dux, von der Osten, Knüpfer, conductor Beecham; Metropolitan, 1913, with Hempel, Case, Ober, Goritz, conductor Hertz; Sadler's Wells, 1939 (in English), with Cross, Naylor, McArden, Stear, conductor Collingwood. Covent Garden revivals include 1924, with Lehmann (later Leider), Schumann, Reinhardt, Mayr, conductor Walter; 1933, with Lehmann, Kern, Hadrabova, Kipnis, conductor Beecham; 1936, with Rethberg, Andreva, Lemnitz, List, conductor Reiner; 1936 by Dresden company, with Marta Fuchs, Cebotari, Rohs, Ermold, conductor Böhm; 1938, with Lehmann (later Hilde Konetzni), Berger, Lemnitz, Krenn, conductor Kleiber; 1947, with Doree, McWatters, Sladen, Franklin, conductor Rankl; 1950, with Fisher, Graf, Shacklock, Glynne, conductor Kleiber; 1953 cond. Kempe.

## CHARACTERS

Princess von Werdenberg (*The Feldmarschallin*)....Soprano
Baron Ochs von Lerchenau ........................Bass
Octavian, *younger brother of Count Rofrano* Mezzo-Soprano
Herr von Faninal, *a wealthy parvenu* .............Baritone
Sophie, *his daughter* ...........................Soprano
Marianne, *her duenna* ...........................Soprano
Valzacchi, *an Italian intriguer* ....................Tenor
Annina, *his partner in crime* ...................Contralto

A Police Commissar................................Bass
The Major-domo of the Marschallin ..............Tenor
The Major-domo of Faninal .....................Tenor
A Notary .......................................Bass
An Innkeeper ..................................Tenor
A Singer ......................................Tenor
A Flute-player ⎫
A Hairdresser ⎬ *silent*
A Scholar ⎪
A Noble Widow ⎭
Three Noble Orphans .........Soprano, Mezzo, Contralto
A Dressmaker ..................................Soprano
An Animal-tamer...............................Tenor
Four Servants of the Marschallin ..Two Tenors, Two Basses
Four Waiters..................One Tenor, Three Basses
A Little Negro Page

*Time:* The reign of the Empress Maria Theresa    *Place:* Vienna

*Der Rosenkavalier* since its first performance has probably been played more often than any other German opera written in the twentieth century. Perhaps its popularity is partly to be accounted for by its plethora of waltz rhythms—it has even been said: 'It is hardly an exaggeration to call the basic conception . . . that of an immense concert waltz'—that, and the human figure of the Marschallin. What is quite certain is that the work has survived initial attacks made upon it on the grounds that it was immoral; the libretto of *Rosenkavalier* goes no further in suggestiveness than that of *Le Nozze di Figaro* (but then who nowadays bothers their heads with the uncomfortable fact that Beaumarchais's Countess had a baby by Cherubino?).

*Rosenkavalier* requires an enormous orchestra: an examination of the full orchestral score shows that 112 instruments are needed, 19 of them for an orchestra on the stage in the third act. The composer demands for his main orchestra 16 first, 16 second violins, 12 violas, 10 violoncellos, 8 double-basses, 3 flutes (3rd also piccolo), 3 oboes (3rd also cor anglais), 1 bass clarinet (also corno di bassetto), 3 bassoons (3rd also contra bassoon), 4 horns, 3 trumpets, 3 trombones, 1 tuba, timpani, celesta, 2 harps, and 3 players for bass drum, cymbals, triangle, tambourin, Glocken-spiel, tenor drum, side drum, bells, castanets. The conductor is directed to reduce the number of strings in passages 'where the audibility of the words requires it'.

Act I.    Bedroom in the Princess von Werdenberg's palace. Morning. The curtain rises after an impassioned orchestral introduction, which is supposed to represent the incidents immediately preceding the audience's first view of the stage, as suggested by the stage directions which have Octavian kneeling by the side of the bed in which the Marschallin lies; she is hidden but for her arm by the curtain. These directions were not followed in the first production at the Berlin Opera House and their strict observance is now the exception rather than the rule.

The prelude, whose opening bars are quoted below (No. 1)

begins with the excitement of the love-making very much in mind. 1A is the theme of the Rosenkavalier; its continuation perhaps serves to link him with the Marschallin, who is shown in contemplative and passionate moods by Nos. 2

and 3 respectively, the latter bringing the prelude to its end:

When the curtain rises Octavian, a handsome youth just seventeen years old, is taking a passionate leave of the Princess, whose husband, a Field Marshal, is away hunting. Octavian is loath to go, the Princess equally loath to have him depart. For she cannot conceal from herself that in spite of Octavian's present love for her the disparity in their ages will soon cause him to look to women younger than herself for love.

There is a commotion beyond the door of the Marschallin's suite of rooms. Taking alarm—they both think it is her husband returned—Octavian escapes behind the bed, where he disguises himself in the attire of a chambermaid. But the alarm is less serious than the Marschallin had feared. One of her relatives, the country-bred Baron Ochs von Lerchenau, wishes to see her. The servants try to persuade him that the hour is much too early, but he forces his way in.

No sooner is he through the door than his attention is distracted from his noble cousin, whom he so confidently proclaimed would be glad to see him, and focussed on the chambermaid, whom he finds very much to his liking. He ogles her and tries to make an early assignation, and it is only reluctantly that he comes to the point of his visit. Has her highness been able to help in the matter which was set out in his recent letter to her? So occupied has she been with Octavian that she has quite forgotten what it was Ochs wanted her to do, but it transpires that the object of his visit is to have her name for him a Knight of the Rose (Rosenkavalier) to take the customary symbol on his behalf to a certain Sophie, daughter of the wealthy and recently ennobled Herr von Faninal, whom he has decided to take to wife.

Not only does Ochs want help over the matter of the silver rose, he is also anxious that the Marschallin shall recommend an attorney to him, as the details of the marriage contract have yet to be settled. Let him wait, she suggests, not without reluctance, until her morning levée, which is due to begin at any moment. Her own attorney will be there and can help him. Ochs pursues the supposed Mariandel shamelessly, and a chance remark from the Marschallin, to the effect that he seems to know how to take his pleasures where he finds them, sets him off on his favourite subject: love in all its shapes and forms. His monologue consists partly of reminiscence, partly of anticipation, and partly of pure fancy—would he were like Jupiter who could assume a hundred disguises for the purpose of his amours.

The levée begins. In turn we meet the notary, the chef, an Italian singer, three poor orphans, and two Italian scandal-mongers. While the hairdresser attends to the Marschallin's coiffure for the day, the others try to enlist her interest in their various causes. Musically, the most interesting is the Italian singer who demonstrates his art in a *pastiche* aria, 'Di rigori armato il seno', of considerable charm. In the meanwhile, the Marschallin contemptuously rejects the attempts of the Italians to interest her in a scandal-sheet, and Ochs argues with the attorney, his temper spilling over at the suggestion that the dowry is due from him to the bride, not the other way round. In his rage, he bangs the table and shouts—and interrupts the tenor at the climax of the second verse of his song. But calm is restored, and all leave the room, including the down-at-heel servants who have accompanied Ochs to the capital and have handed him the silver rose.

The Marschallin alone is a prey to autumnal thoughts. Was she not herself just such a girl as this poor unsuspecting creature whom Ochs, with all his crudity, is going to marry? 'Kann mich auch an ein Mädel erinnern?' she sings, and even the return of Octavian, booted and spurred and full of chivalrous speeches, cannot change her mood. Whatever his intentions now, it will not be long before he has left her for another, younger woman: 'Die Zeit, sie ist ein sonderbar Ding.' Her sad, reflective, almost bitter mood is something Octavian cannot understand. She tells him he may ride beside her carriage in the afternoon, and he leaves her with an approach to formality. No sooner has he left the room than she remembers she did not even kiss him; she rings for the servants and tells them to run after him and bring him back, but they return to say he has galloped away from the door.

The Marschallin accepts the inevitable and sends for her little black page, Mahomet, and gives him the silver rose in its case, bidding him take it to Count Octavian; he will know what to do with it.

Act II.    Salon in the house of Herr von Faninal. This lately ennobled *nouveau riche* considers it a great distinction that the Baron Ochs von Lerchenau, a member of the old nobility, should apply for the hand of his daughter. That the Baron only does it to mend his broken fortunes does not appear to worry him, although his daughter Sophie is a sweet and modest girl. She and her duenna, Marianne, await her suitor in great agitation, Faninal having been advised by his major-domo that etiquette demands he should be absent at the moment when the bearer of the silver rose arrives in his house.

Marianne comments delightedly on the appearance of Octavian's coach—and on the neighbours who are watching it—and cries of 'Rofrano' are heard from outside. As the music reaches a climax Octavian, escorted by his servants, comes in carrying the silver rose in his right hand (No. 4). He makes a little formal

speech to Sophie, who takes the rose and comments on the scent it gives off, due, Octavian says, to the Persian attar which has been sprinkled on it. In a rapturous, soaring phrase (No. 5), Sophie releases the excitement which has been pent up inside her for so long—excitement caused, we may surmise, as much by the unexpected sight of Octavian as by the rose or anticipation of her bridegroom:

There follows a short duet, after which the two young people sit down and engage in polite conversation, waiting for the arrival of the Baron. Octavian is smitten with the charms of the girl, and she for her part is at once attracted to the handsome young cavalier. So their conversation imperceptibly drifts towards an intimate tone, only to be interrupted when the real suitor enters. His brutal frankness in letting Sophie comprehend that he is condescending in courting her, his looking her over as if she were a new filly for his stable, and his generally rude manners thoroughly repel the girl. Only the humming of his favourite waltz tune

(No. 6) shows a more agreeable side to his character. Octavian meanwhile is boiling with rage and jealousy, as the girl's aversion to the Baron increases.

As if to save the situation, Ochs is called by the notary into an adjoining room where the marriage contract is to be drawn up. Sophie is shocked at what she has just experienced. Never will it be possible for her to marry the detested Baron, especially since she has met the gallant Octavian. The two are quick in agreeing. Sophie sinks into his arms.

At that moment there rush out from behind the two large ornamental stoves which adorn the room the intriguers, Valzacchi and Annina, anxious to be employed by Ochs as spies. Their cries bring the Baron from the next room. The servants rush in. Octavian tells Ochs of Sophie's antipathy, and adds taunt to taunt, until, however reluctant to fight, the Baron is forced to draw his sword. In the encounter, Octavian lightly 'pinks' him. The Baron, a coward at heart, raises a frightful outcry. There ensues the greatest commotion, due to the mix-up of the servants, the doctor, and the rage of Faninal, who orders Sophie to a convent when she positively refuses to give her hand to Lerchenau. The latter meanwhile rapidly recovers when his wound has been dressed and he has drunk some more of Faninal's good wine.

Octavian is determined to win Sophie. For that purpose he decides to make use of the two intriguers, who are so disgusted by the niggardly treatment of the Baron that they readily fall in with the plans of the young cavalier. After the crowd has dispersed and the Baron is left alone lying on the sofa, and humming his favourite waltz tune (No. 6) to himself, Annina approaches and hands him a note. In this the Princess's chambermaid promises him a rendezvous. Ochs is delighted at the new conquest he believes himself to have made.

The finale of the act is dominated by Ochs's famous waltz tune, initially heard soon after he meets Sophie for the first time.

Act III.    After a brilliant orchestral *fugato* the curtain rises on a room in an inn near Vienna. With the help of Valzacchi and Annina, who are now in the service of both the Baron and Octavian, but are more prone to further the latter's plans because he pays them better, Octavian has hired a room in an inn. This room is fitted up with trap-doors, blind windows and the like. Here, at the suggestion of the intriguers, who have the run of the place and know to what uses the trick room can be put, Ochs has made his rendezvous for the evening with the pretty chambermaid. Octavian, in his girl's clothes, is early at the meeting-place.

Between the Baron and the disguised Octavian, as soon as they are alone, develops a rude scene of courtship, mostly to the accompaniment of waltz tunes. Octavian is able to hold him off skilfully, and gradually there is unfolded in all its details the mad practical joke in which the Baron is involved. Strange figures appear at the windows. Lerchenau, ignorant and superstitious, thinks he sees ghosts. Suddenly, what is supposed to be a blind window bursts open and a woman dressed in mourning rushes in. It is the disguised Annina, who claims to be Ochs's deserted wife. Innkeeper and servants hurry in. The clamour and confusion become more and more frantic. Finally the Baron himself calls for the police, without thinking what a 'give away' it may be for himself. When the Commissary of Police arrives, to save his face he gives out that his companion is his affianced, Sophie von Faninal. That, however, only adds to the confusion, for Octavian's accomplices have sought out Faninal and invited him on behalf of the Baron to come to the inn. In his amazement, the Baron can think of no other way out of the dilemma save to act as if he did not know Faninal at all, at which the latter, naturally, is greatly angered.

When the confusion is at its height, the Marschallin suddenly appears. A lackey of the Baron, seeing his master in such difficulties, has run to her to ask for her powerful protection. She quickly takes in the whole situation. The Police Commissary was once her husband's orderly and it is easy for her to persuade him that the whole matter was just a joke and no more. Sophie, who has already informed Ochs that her father never wishes to see him again—nor does she for that matter—is heart-broken at the idea that the 'joke' may even have included Octavian and herself, but her anxiety does not last long. After the Marschallin has got rid of Ochs—he has long since outstayed his welcome, but even his going is attended by more farcical complications— she pushes Octavian towards Sophie. However bitterly Octavian's disaffection grieves her, she is a clever enough woman of the world to recognise that the time for her to give him up has come.

The last section of the opera does something to remove the impression of the musical bustle and purposelessness of the earlier part of Act III. It contains the great trio ('Hab' mir's gelobt, ihn lieb zu haben') for the Marschallin, Sophie, and Octavian, an early example of Strauss's luxuriant writing for combined female voices, always a feature of his scores and here at its finest and most effective:

Octavian and Sophie are forgiven—the stature of the Marschallin can be seen from the great sweep of the first phrase of the trio—and the Marschallin leaves them alone together, saying she will go into the other room to console Faninal for what has happened to him during the day.

There is a little duet for the two lovers ('Ist ein Traum, kann nicht wirklich sein'), set to the simplest tune imaginable and punctuated by No. 4A; their happiness is complete. The Marschallin reappears leaning on Faninal's arm; she says no more than 'Ja, ja', but the orchestra refers gently to music already heard in her monologue at the end of Act I. The lovers are alone again. One more reference to their unexpectedly blissful state, and they go quickly out to the carriage hand in hand. But it is not quite the end of the opera. Sophie has dropped her handkerchief, and Mahomet, the little black page, comes running back to look for it; he finds it, runs out to the carriage, and the curtain falls.

K., H.

# ARIADNE AUF NAXOS
## Ariadne on Naxos

In its original form, opera in one act by Richard Strauss; text by Hugo von Hofmannsthal. The work was designed to follow a condensed version of Molière's *Le Bourgeois Gentilhomme* (translated by Hofmannsthal), for which Strauss provided incidental music. This version was first heard at Stuttgart, October 25, 1912, with Jeritza, Siems, Jadlowker, conductor

Strauss. First performed Berlin, 1913, with Hafgren-Waag, Bosetti, Jadlow-ker, conductor Blech; His Majesty's Theatre, London, 1913, with von der Osten, Bosetti, Marak, conductor Beecham (Tree was Monsieur Jourdain, and the translation was by Somerset Maugham). Revived Edinburgh Festival, 1950 (by Glyndebourne company), with Zadek, Hollweg, Anders, conductor Beecham (Miles Malleson, who translated the play, also played Jourdain). Subsequently, the opera was revised by Strauss, the Molière play dropped altogether (and with it the incidental music), and a scenic prelude involving the characters who later take part in the opera substituted for it. The revised version had its première in Vienna, October 4, 1916, with Jeritza, Selma Kurz, Környey, Duhan, and Lehmann, substituting as the Composer (accord-ing to her autobiography) for the indisposed Gutheil-Schoder; conductor Schalk. First performed Berlin, 1916, with Hafgren-Waag, Hansa, Lola Artôt de Padilla, Kirchner, conductor Blech; Covent Garden, 1924, with Lehmann, Ivogün, Schumann, Fischer-Niemann, conductor Alwin; Turin, 1925, with Arangi-Lombardi, Pasini, Tess, Dolci, conductor Gui; Phila-delphia, 1928; New York, 1934; Rome, 1935, with Anny Konetzni, Kern, Hadrabova, Kalenberg, conductor Krips (ensemble from Vienna Opera); City Centre, New York, most successfully in 1946, with Ella Flesch, MacWat-ters, Stoska, Argyris, conductor Halasz (the first professional performance in New York). Revived Berlin, 1932, with Anny Konetzni, Ivogün, Lorenz; Covent Garden, 1936, with Marta Fuchs, Sack, Wieber, Ralf, conductor Strauss (ensemble of Dresden Opera); Vienna, 1947, with Cebotari, Noni, Jurinac, Friedrich; Munich, 1952, with Cunitz, Lipp, Jurinac, Patzak, conductor Keilberth; Glyndebourne, 1953, with Dow, Dobbs, Jurinac, Lewis, conductor Pritchard.

## CHARACTERS

Characters in the Prologue:

The Major-domo ......................Speaking Rôle

Music Master.................................Baritone

The Composer .................................Soprano

The Tenor (*later Bacchus*) ........................Tenor

An Officer .......................................Tenor

The Dancing Master ............................Tenor

The Wig-maker.................................Bass

A Lackey .......................................Bass

Zerbinetta .....................................Soprano

Prima Donna (*later Ariadne*)....................Soprano

Harlequin .....................................Baritone

Scaramuccio ...................................Tenor

Truffaldino .......................................Bass

Brighella .......................................Tenor

Characters in the Opera:

Ariadne.....................................Soprano

Bacchus.........................................Tenor

| Naiade ⎫ | | ⎧ .................... Soprano |
|---|---|---|
| Dryade ⎬ *three nymphs* | | ⎨ .................... Contralto |
| Echo ⎭ | | ⎩ .................... Soprano |
| Zerbinetta ⎫ | | ⎧ ....... Soprano |
| Harlequin ⎪ | | ⎪ ........ Baritone |
| Scaramuccio ⎬ *characters of Intermezzo* | | ⎨ .......... Tenor |
| Truffaldino ⎪ | | ⎪ ........... Bass |
| Brighella ⎭ | | ⎩ .......... Tenor |

(The characters in the Opera are the same in both versions; those of the Prologue belong only to the second version, the original conception of the opera calling for the cast of Molière's *Le Bourgeois Gentilhomme* for the first part of the evening.)

One of the first things to strike anyone who reads the correspondence of Strauss and Hofmannsthal is the considerable difference there often is between their first thoughts on the subject of one of their operatic collaborations, and their last. Thus *Rosenkavalier* was thought of as a simple comedy with important rôles for a baritone and a soprano in boy's clothes, and in the earlier stages of the correspondence there is no mention of the Marschallin, who was later to become the central figure in the comedy. *Ariadne* went through an even stranger evolution. Originally conceived as a little opera lasting half an hour, and designed as a thank-offering to Max Reinhardt, who produced *Rosenkavalier* in Dresden, it was intended to form the musical divertissement in Molière's *Le Bourgeois Gentilhomme*, taking the place of the Turkish ballet called for by Monsieur Jourdain. In the end the opera became a much more extensive affair than at first envisaged, and lasted about three times as long as projected. Unfortunately, the combination of a theatrical with an operatic company proved beyond the means of most theatres, and the work as it stood was decided to be impracticable. Strauss therefore revised it and substituted a musical prelude (lasting about thirty-five minutes) for the Molière play, making at the same time some alterations in the body of the opera itself (this, however, remains substantially the same as in the first version, although the rôle of Zerbinetta has been slightly shortened and brought a little nearer to the capacity of the ordinarily-gifted coloratura soprano).

*Ariadne* has usually been performed in its second version, but such an authority on Strauss's music as Sir Thomas Beecham wrote (in his autobiographical *A Mingled Chime*): 'In this, the

earlier version of *Ariadne*, I have always considered that the
musical accomplishment of Strauss attained its highest reach,
yielding a greater spontaneity and variety of invention, together
with a subtler and riper style, than anything that his pen had yet
given to the stage . . . the Bacchus section of the opera is one of
the purple patches in the operatic literature of the twentieth
century. . . . The later version has not only failed to hold the
stage, but has dimmed the public recollection of the far superior
and more attractive original.'

The original version of the opera calls for an abbreviated version of *Le Bourgeois Gentilhomme* to form the first part of the
evening's entertainment. The theme of this is that Monsieur
Jourdain, the bourgeois who is determined to become a gentleman
by sheer concentrated hard work and who means to learn to
dance, sing, fence, compose, philosophise, is at the same time
laying siege to the affections of a certain Marquise Dorimène. She
for her part is in love with the shady Count Dorante, who has
undertaken to bring her to the lavish dinner party which is given
in their honour by Jourdain. The play is garnished with some
delightful incidental music by Strauss, and the three principal
characters remain at the side of the stage while the opera is
performed for their benefit.

In the revised version, the Prologue takes place at the house of
a Viennese *nouveau riche* (not in Paris, as in the Molière). We
see musicians, singers, actors, carpenters, and stage hands preparing for the first performance of a serious opera which has been
specially commissioned by the owner of the house to entertain
his guests. There is consternation when the Major-domo announces that after the opera there will be a Harlequinade entertainment; moreover, the two shows must not overrun their allotted
span of time, as the fireworks must begin precisely at nine o'clock!
Worse is to come, as a little later the Major-domo comes in to inform the two troupes that his master has changed his mind, and now
both entertainments will be played simultaneously, the serious
opera being punctuated by intervals of dancing from the comedians.

The dominating figure of the prologue is the composer, a
creation of the second version, and a touching figure which has
found admirable exponents almost every time the opera has been
performed. He extemporises an aria which he intends for the tenor
(this is derived from a little song heard during the course of the

play in the first version), he languishes at the idea of his master-piece being combined with a common dancing show, he tries to explain to Zerbinetta that Ariadne prefers death to the embraces of any man other than her beloved, and, proving unsuccessful in this, he indulges in a duet with Zerbinetta in which he comes perilously close to declaring that he loves her. After some trouble with both tenor and prima donna, the composer brings the prologue to a suitable end by declaring his conviction in the power of music, the most sacred of the arts.

After an interval, the curtain rises on the opera itself, which is watched from boxes by the owner of the house and his guests. The setting, which we have hitherto seen only from its reverse side, is now seen from in front. At one side of the set is a cave, in whose entrance Ariadne can be seen asleep, watched by Naiad, Dryad and Echo. In a trio (of the type made familiar by Wagner's Rhinemaidens), these creatures express a certain sympathy with Ariadne's sorrow, to which however they have become accustomed with the passage of time.

A great *scena* begins for Ariadne. She is speaking as if in a dream, and takes no notice when the Harlequinade quartet and Zerbinetta comment on her distress and try to think of means of comforting her. Ariadne welcomes the idea of death, and not even a determined effort by Harlequin to cure her of her madness—for he thinks it must surely be that which is wrong with her—can stop her for long. 'Es gibt ein Reich, wo alles rein ist; es hat auch einen Namen: Totenreich,' she continues, and at mention of death's messenger, Hermes, her monologue becomes more urgent. The last section of the monologue, where Ariadne rejoices in the idea of the deliverance death will bring to her, is ecstatic in import, and (from the singer's point of view) Wagnerian in weight.

The four comedians make another attempt to cheer up the melancholy Ariadne, but their dancing and singing have not the slightest effect, even when they are joined by the sprightly Zerbinetta. Eventually, Zerbinetta bids them leave her to see what she can do on her own. Her *scena* is one of the most taxing ever written for coloratura soprano—the qualification is hardly neces-

Als ein Gott kam je-der ge-gangen und sein Schritt schon machte mich stumm.

sary; it has really no rival. After a recitative, 'Grossmächtige Prinzessin' (Most gracious sovereign lady), she appeals to Ariadne as woman to woman. Ariadne is not the first to be abandoned by her lover, and will not be the last. Zerbinetta expounds her own fickle philosophy, and is quite unconcerned when Ariadne disappears inside her cave. She goes into details of her amorous career in an *allegretto scherzando* ('So war es mit Pagliazzo') at which point the vocal writing parts company with what is normally considered advisable to write for a singer and becomes a fantastic display of vocal fireworks (even the transposition into D major from the E of the original leaves something which is technically beyond all but the most accomplished of coloratura sopranos).

The section of the opera which begins at her recitative is entirely Zerbinetta's. She is pursued by the four comedians, each of whom seems amorously inclined. Zerbinetta encourages and eludes them all, until only Scaramuccio, Brighella, and Truffaldino are left on the stage. Much to their annoyance, Zerbinetta is immediately heard conversing tenderly with Harlequin, whom they had thought safely out of the way. They rush out to see what they can do about it.

No sooner are they gone than the three attendant nymphs return to the stage, full of the sight they have just seen. A youthful god is coming, Bacchus, fresh from the embraces of Circe, but eager for new adventure. They call to Ariadne, who emerges from the cave in time to hear Bacchus off-stage calling for Circe. The nymphs beg him to continue singing, and Ariadne hails him as the longed-for messenger of death. The opera ends with an extended love duet, Wagnerian in its length and weight if not in its character. In Bacchus's arms, Ariadne finds consolation, and Strauss even allows Zerbinetta to pop in for a moment to comment that all has turned out exactly as she would have expected.

Bacchus and Ariàdne go together into the cave. (In the first version, soon after Bacchus is first heard off-stage, there is a fairly lengthy interruption by Zerbinetta, during which Ariadne is arrayed in fine clothes; it is only after this that the god is first seen on the stage.)

Unlike Strauss's other operas, *Ariadne* is scored for a small orchestra of only thirty-nine players, 2 flutes, 2 oboes, 2 clarinets, 2 bassoons, 2 horns, trumpet, trombone, 6 violins, 4 violas, 4 cellos, 2 double basses, grand piano, 2 harps, harmonium, celesta, drum, tambourin, triangle, a small drum, cymbals, and chimes.                                                                H.

# DIE FRAU OHNE SCHATTEN
## The Woman without a Shadow

Opera in three acts by Richard Strauss; text by Hugo von Hofmannsthal. Première in Vienna, October 10, 1919, with Lehmann, Jeritza, Weidt, Oestvig, Manowarda, Mayr, conductor Schalk. First performed Dresden, 1919; Berlin, 1920, with Kemp, Hafgren-Waag, Branzell; Rome, 1938, with Pauly, Ursuleac, Voyer, Franci, conductor Marinuzzi; la Scala, Milan, 1940, with Pacetti, Roman, Voyer, Franci, conductor Marinuzzi; Buenos Aires 1949, with Hilde Konetzni, Hoerner, Höngen, Suthaus, Weber, conductor, Kleiber. Revivals Salzburg, 1932, with Lehmann, Ursuleac, Rünger, Völker, Manowarda, conductor Krauss; Berlin Staatsoper, 1939, with Rünger, Ursuleac, Klose, Völker, Prohaska; Munich 1954, with Schech, Rysanek, Benningsen, Hopf, Metternich, cond. Kempe.

### CHARACTERS

| | |
|---|---|
| The Emperor | Tenor |
| The Empress, *his wife* | Soprano |
| The Nurse (*Die Amme*) | Mezzo-Soprano |
| A Spirit-messenger | Baritone |
| The Keeper of the Gates of the Temple | Soprano or Tenor (falsetto) |
| Apparition of a Youth | Tenor |
| The Voice of the Falcon | Soprano |
| A Voice from Above | Contralto |
| Barak, *the dyer* | Bass-Baritone |
| His Wife | Soprano |
| The One-eyed ⎱ | Bass |
| The One-armed ⎬ *brothers of Barak* | Bass |
| The Hunchback ⎰ | Tenor |

Six Children's Voices ...Three Sopranos, Three Contraltos
Voices of the Nightwatchmen ..............Three Basses
Servants of the Emperor, Strange Children, Spirits

The Emperor of the South Eastern Islands is married to a supernatural being, the daughter of Keikobad, king of the spirits. She
emerged from a white gazelle which he shot while out hunting.
Their love is mutual and ardent, but their marriage is childless;
in token of her barren state, the Empress throws no shadow. This
is the main theme of the story; to make love complete, the woman
must bear children, and of this the shadow is the outward sign.

Act I.    The opera (which is enormously long, each of the three
acts lasting over an hour) starts when the Emperor and Empress
have been married twelve moons. It is dark, and the Nurse is
crouching on a flat roof above the Imperial gardens. To her
appears a messenger. After reassuring himself that the Empress
still throws no shadow, he tells the Nurse that he is from Keikobad, and he has come to inform her that the Empress may stay
only another three days on earth. She must then go back to
Keikobad, and the Emperor will be turned into stone.

The messenger disappears and the Emperor comes from the
house. He tells the story of how he first saw and won his wife. He
tells the Nurse that he is going hunting for three days, and refers
to his favourite falcon which he has not seen since the day he met
his wife. The Emperor leaves, day dawns, and the Empress comes
from her chamber. She too talks of her love, but then catches
sight of the falcon, whose voice is heard to say: 'The woman
throws no shadow, the Emperor must turn to stone.' The Empress
understands that the only way to save him is to acquire a shadow,
and she begs the Nurse to help her to find one.

The orchestra represents their journey to earth, and the second
scene is set in the hut of the dyer, Barak. It is poorly furnished,
and serves at the same time as workshop and bedroom. When the
curtain rises, the three deformed brothers of the dyer are fighting.

In the scene that ensues, the contrasting characters of Barak
and his wife are made apparent. She nags and complains, he is
patient and full of natural goodness. But he upbraids her for not
having given him a child in the nine months during which they
have been married. He goes off to take his goods to market.

No sooner has he gone than the Empress and her Nurse enter

the hut, dressed simply as servants. The Nurse is immediately aware that in the dyer's wife she has found a good subject for her black arts. She praises her for her beauty, and asks if she does not know that she could sell her shadow and get for it all the luxuries and riches she has always desired. The Nurse tempts her with visions, which she summons to aid her in achieving her object.

The dyer's wife agrees to exchange her own prospect of motherhood for the promise of riches. She will deny her bed to her husband. The Empress and the Nurse go out, saying that they will be back next day. When she is alone, the woman has another vision. This time she hears the voices of her unborn children coming from the flames of the fire. She is terrified.

Barak enters to find his bed separated from his wife's. He is sad, but optimistic that this is only a temporary state of affairs. As they lie down in their beds, the voices of nightwatchmen can be heard coming from outside.

Act II.     In his introduction to the published libretto, Hofmannsthal says: 'The trials continue; all four must be cleansed —the dyer and his wife, the Emperor and the daughter of the spirits. The one pair is too much of the earth earthy, the other too full of pride and remote from the earth.'

The scene is again Barak's hut. The struggle to obtain the shadow continues. The Nurse tempts the woman with the apparition of a handsome youth, who appears each time the dyer is out of the hut. The woman believes she hates her husband and thinks it would be simple to deceive him, and yet does not quite dare to do so. Barak feels the change in her reaction to him, and his simple, good heart grows sad. He invites some beggar children to share in their meal.

The scene changes to the Emperor's falcon house in the forest. The Emperor has found his falcon again, and follows it to the falcon house. There he sees his wife, from whom he has had a letter to the effect that she has been alone and seen no one during his absence hunting. He senses immediately that she has been in contact with the things of the earth.

The scene changes to Barak's hut. It is the third day and the Nurse continues her efforts to gain the shadow of the dyer's wife for the Empress. The Nurse and the dyer's wife go out of the hut together, leaving the Empress and Barak. As the curtain falls, it is obvious that she feels sympathetically towards Barak, and regrets what she is causing to happen to him and his wife.

The Empress's bedroom in the falcon house. She lies on her bed in restless sleep, and the Nurse lies at the foot of the bed. She has a vision of her husband wandering through tomb-like caves, and hears the voice of the falcon: 'The woman throws no shadow, the Emperor must turn to stone.' She is much moved by this, but also touched by Barak's distress, which she is fully aware is caused by her actions.

Back in Barak's hut, the Nurse makes her final attempt to win the woman's shadow from her. Although it is midday, it is growing dark, a storm is brewing, and the three crooked brothers of Barak are howling in terror. The Nurse senses that there are supernatural powers at work, over which she has no control, but assures the Empress of their ultimate attainment of their object. The Empress is appalled by the sufferings of men, but grateful that fate has led her to meet Barak, whose integrity has convinced her of the dignity of humanity. The climax of the scene comes when the woman tells Barak that she has been unfaithful to him and sold her shadow and her unborn children with it. To prove the truth of her words, the brothers light a fire and it is seen that she throws no shadow. Barak threatens to kill her, and as if by magic a sword is there to his hand. The Empress refuses to take the shadow at such a price, but the woman, overcome by remorse when she sees the result of her admission, tells Barak that she has not done what she has confessed, but has only wished to do it.

As the Nurse tears the Empress from the scene, the earth opens and swallows up Barak and his hut.

Act III.    Subterranean vault, divided by a thick wall in the middle. On one side is Barak, on the other his wife, each however unconscious of the presence of the other.

The vault disappears, and when the clouds have dispersed we see the Empress and her Nurse enter in a boat.

Trombone calls summon the Empress to the judgment hall, where her father Keikobad presides. The Nurse wants to prevent her from entering, for she fears Keikobad's anger more than death; her purpose now is to persuade the Empress to return to earth to continue her search for the shadow. But the Empress is determined to enter where she knows her husband is being judged.

She bids the Nurse farewell for ever; the Nurse does not understand men and their struggles and the price they pay for their guilt. She herself has learned to love them and to understand them in their misery. She enters the Temple. The voices of Barak and his wife are heard calling for each other.

The Empress demands to know her place in the scheme of the universe. A voice from above tells her to drink of the Water of Life, and the shadow of the woman will be hers and she will be human. But the voices of Barak and his wife are again heard, and the Empress refuses to drink and be guilty of the crime of their undoing. She feels she belongs to the human race, and yet she refuses to yield to the temptation, which would involve the destruction of innocent beings. She demands to see her father, her judge. The alcove is illuminated, and the Emperor appears, turned to stone except for his eyes, which can be seen pleading with her for life. In her desperation, she wants to rush to her husband's side, and her anguish is increased when she hears a voice call: 'The woman throws no shadow, the Emperor must turn to stone.' She is again urged to drink of the Water of Life, to gain the shadow and save her husband. It is her moment of supreme trial, and she falls to the ground in the agony of her inner struggle. Finally, a cry breaks from her lips: 'I will not.'

As soon as this cry is heard, the water disappears, and the Temple is brightly lit from above. The Empress rises to her feet and it can be seen that she throws a shadow. The Emperor descends from his alcove, the voices of their unborn children are heard singing from above, and in their happiness the Emperor and Empress embrace and fall on their knees to give thanks for deliverance from their trial.

The scene changes to a beautiful landscape, with a waterfall in the middle. The Emperor and Empress stand beside it. Below it can be seen the figures of Barak and his wife, who have found each other. The voices of unborn children complete the happiness of each couple.                                                        H.

## INTERMEZZO

Opera in two acts by Richard Strauss; text by the composer. Premièr Dresden, November 4, 1924, with Lotte Lehmann, Joseph Correck, Theo Strack, Hans Lange, Leisl von Schuch, Ludwig Ermold, conductor Fritz Busch. First performed Berlin, 1925, with Hussa, Scheidl, Guszalewicz, Leo Schützendorf, conductor Szell; Vienna, 1927, with Lehmann, Jerger, conductor Strauss; Berlin, 1930, with Reinhardt, Scheidl, conductor Lert; Zürich, 1951, with Ebers, Wolff, conductor Ackermann.

## CHARACTERS

Christine ..................................... Soprano
Little Franz, *her eight-year-old son* ..............
Hofkapellmeister Robert Storch, *her husband* ..... Baritone
Anna, *the chambermaid* ....................... Soprano
Baron Lummer................................. Tenor
The Notary.................................... Baritone
His Wife ..................................... Soprano
Kapellmeister Stroh ⎱ ⎰ .......... Tenor
Commercial Councillor ⎰ *Storch's skat* ⎱ ........ Baritone
Justizrat ⎰ *partners* ⎱ ........ Baritone
Kammersänger ⎰ ⎱ .......... Bass

*Time:* The Present　　　　　　*Place:* Grundlsee and Vienna

When the opera was first produced, emphasis was laid in newspaper reports on the fact that the basis of the work was taken from incidents in the composer's private life. The emphasis can hardly be thought to have been misplaced, since Strauss himself took care that the sets were made to correspond with his own home at Garmisch, and Josef Correck, the creator of the rôle of Hofkapellmeister Storch, wore a specially constructed mask to make his resemblance to Strauss more marked.

Act I. The dressing-room of the house of Kapellmeister Storch. Seven o'clock in the morning. Open suitcases everywhere indicate that Storch and his wife are busy packing. She is thoroughly bad-tempered, abusing the servants, complaining incessantly at her husband, and, when he seems inclined to answer back, reminding him that she comes of a much better family than he does; who is he, anyway?

After successive exhibitions of her short temper with both maid and cook, Christine admits to the former that not the least of her husband's shortcomings in her view is his incessant kindness and gentleness; if only he would stand up to her like a man and not give way so much, she would have far more respect for him. The telephone rings, and Christine is asked by a neighbour to go skating. She accepts.

An interlude (there are twelve in the course of the opera, and they constitute the chief means of sustained lyrical expression) leads us to a new scene: the toboggan track. Tobogganists cross the stage, but when it is Christine's turn she runs into a young man on skis. She is furious and abuses him, complaining that the fall hurt her very much—there is no word of whether he is injured or not. But when she discovers that he is the well-connected Baron Lummer, she is all over him and only too anxious that he should know she is the wife of the famous composer Storch. She asks him to come and visit her.

An interlude composed of waltzes and other dances takes us to an inn at Grundlsee, where Christine and the Baron are dancing. They converse, and one gathers that he is there for his health. The whole short scene is brilliantly alive; it is the music of the third act of *Rosenkavalier* transferred, shortened, and without any element of farce.

Dining-room in the Storches' house. Christine reads a letter which she is writing to her husband, and in which she talks about the excellent young escort she has acquired for herself. At that very moment, in comes the Baron. They sit opposite each other reading the newspaper, and she asks him when he is going to begin his studies. His family apparently wants him to read law, but he is anxious to take up the study of natural history, for which, without them, he has not the means. She says that he has only to wait until her husband is back, and he will not lack support.

The wistful music from the moment of the Baron's exit is combined with the interlude which follows it to make a concert excerpt, usually known as 'the Interlude from *Intermezzo*'. When the curtain rises, we are in the Baron's room in the house of the notary. He exclaims with impatience at the demands made upon him by Frau Storch. Can she really expect him to sit about with her in the evenings reading the newspapers! And all that talk about his studies . . . and his ill-health. He is interrupted by a girl-friend, obviously come to keep an appointment; he will join her in a minute. He sits down to write a letter to his patroness (as he refers to her); he must have money.

Another interlude brings us again to the Storches' dining-room. Christine has had the letter—a thousand marks, he asks for! He must be mad! At this moment the Baron himself puts in an appearance, and is immediately sent outside to wipe his shoes. She tells him that what he asks for is impossible; but she is sure her husband will help him with his studies when he gets back. Let him not spoil their agreeable relationship by insisting.

At this juncture, the maid brings in a note and hands it to her. It is addressed to Kapellmeister Storch, but Christine opens it, and exclaims in horror. She reads aloud: 'My darling. Do send me two tickets for the opera again to-morrow. Afterwards in the bar as usual! Your Mieze Meier.' The Baron is solicitous, but she sends him away, and when he is gone, she writes out a telegram: 'You know Mieze Meier! Your unfaithfulness proved! We are parted for ever.' She hustles the maid to pack all the suitcases: they are leaving the house—for good.

Another interlude. The child's bedroom. Christine sits by the side of his bed, crying. She abuses her husband, but the child will not hear of this: his father is good and kind, and it is she who is horrid and makes scenes. She replies that she is much too good for the man she married; she kneels melodramatically at the foot of the bed and prays.

Act II. The 'skat' game. The scene is a comfortable sitting-room in the house of the Commercial Councillor. Round the 'skat' table sit the Justizrat, the Commercial Councillor, the Kammersänger, and Kapellmeister Stroh. The conversation which accompanies the game centres round the agreeable character of Storch, which contrasts so markedly with his highly disagreeable wife. When he arrives, Storch apologises for being late and then joins the game. They ask after his wife, and he tells them of the letter he has had in which she talks of her new-found friend the Baron. They cannot keep a hint of criticism from their tone when they refer to Christine, but Storch explains that he finds her extremely stimulating—in any case, her bristling exterior conceals the proverbial heart of gold.

A telegram comes for Storch, whose jocularity falls from him as he reads it. He gives it to Stroh and asks him to read it aloud. Stroh's comment is: 'What, do you know her too?' but Storch hurries out of the room in obvious distress, leaving the others to comment ironically but without malice on the surprising news that such an obviously model husband should turn out to be no better than the rest of them.

The scene changes to the office of the notary. Frau Kapellmeister comes in and demands a divorce. The notary assumes that this is because of the Baron, and is distinctly surprised to hear that Christine is convinced she has evidence against her husband.

A stormy interlude leads to the third scene, in the Prater in Vienna. Storm. Storch is seen wandering about. He has had no answer to his telegrams to Christine, no explanation even of the identity of the mysterious Mieze Meier. He cannot leave Vienna and his work on account of so ridiculous a misunderstanding, but his worry is very real. Stroh finds him and explains that the letter must have been meant for him; the two names are not dissimilar, and probably the volatile Mieze looked up his address in the telephone book, assuming that he—Stroh—was no less a man than the famous Hofkapellmeister. Storch is furious, and demands that Stroh put right the whole ghastly muddle. He must take Christine proof and go at once.

Scene iv.    Christine's dressing-room. Packing and disorder. Christine vents her wrath on everybody and everything in sight. Everyone is against her, she is sure, but she wishes she had not sent the Baron to Vienna to check up on Mieze Meier. Storch's telegrams have caused her to wonder whether there is not some mistake. Another telegram arrives, this time containing the news that Stroh is coming with a full explanation of the whole situation. Stroh is announced and the curtain falls as she goes out to hear what he has to say.

The dining-room, decorated for Storch's return. Christine is wildly excited, she must go and greet him. But she stops herself, and when he rushes in and tries to embrace her, she coldly gives him her hand. She contrives to nag in spite of Storch's obvious delight at seeing her, and seems to think that he must make amends in some way for what has happened. When she tells him she is sick of him and all other men, and he can go and make arrangements for a divorce with the notary, he rounds on her and gives her a long-needed piece of his mind, after which he leaves the stage. She is astonished at his change of attitude, but at this juncture in comes the Baron. It appears from what he says that he has bungled the whole interview with Mieze.

Storch comes back and pretends to be jealous of the Baron. Christine says he was quite agreeable for a bit, but rather a bore, particularly when he asked her for a thousand marks. Storch is delighted at this, and thinks it a great joke. All is set for their reconciliation, and when the curtain falls, they have made up all their differences, and Christine has even gone so far as to comment what a happy marriage theirs is.                    H.

# DIE AEGYPTISCHE HELENA
## The Egyptian Helen

Opera in two acts by Richard Strauss; text by Hofmannsthal. Première at Dresden, June 6, 1928, with Rethberg, Rajdl, Taucher, Burg, conductor Busch. First performed Vienna, 1928; Berlin, 1928, with Müller, Alpar, Laubenthal, Schorr, conductor Blech; Metropolitan, 1928, with Jeritza, Fleischer, Laubenthal, Whitehill, conductor Bodanzky; Salzburg Festival, 1933, with Ursuleac, Völker, conductor Krauss. Revived Berlin, 1935, with Ursuleac, Heidersbach, Völker, Prohaska, conductor Krauss; Munich, 1940, with Ursuleac, Ranczak, Hotter, and 1956 with Rysanek, Aldenhoff, Uhde.

### CHARACTERS

Helena, *wife of Menelaus* ...................... Soprano
Menelaus ....................................... Tenor
Hermione, *their child* ......................... Soprano
Aithra, *the daughter of an Egyptian King; a*
  *sorceress* .................................... Soprano
Altair ......................................... Baritone
Da-Ud, *his son* ................................ Tenor
First and Second Servants of
  Aithra ..................... Soprano, Mezzo-Soprano
Three Elves ................... Two Sopranos, Contralto
The Omniscient Sea-shell (*Die alleswissende*
  *Muschel*) .................................... Contralto

*Time:* 1193–1184 B.C. (after the Trojan war)      *Place:* Egypt

The Trojan war is over, and Menelaus has killed Paris, the ravisher of his wife Helena, and is now returning home with his wife. He has made up his mind that his honour, as well as the blood of the countless Greeks who died fighting for his cause, demands that Helena should pay the supreme price for what has been caused through her beauty, and he is determined to sacrifice her himself, either at sea or when they reach their native soil. But in a storm his ship is wrecked.

Act I. A great room in Aithra's palace. The Sea-shell assures Aithra of Poseidon's love, but conjures up for her a description of Menelaus's ship, bearing the fairest of women, who is about to be murdered by her husband. Aithra causes a storm, which wrecks the ship, and it is not long before Menelaus enters the room, leading a golden-haired woman behind him. He feels that he must fulfil his vow and slay Helena, but she tries to entice him to her arms once again. Aithra intervenes and causes Menelaus to think he sees and hears Paris and the Trojans, whom he has killed, once more rising against him. He rushes from the room after them, and Helena is comforted by Aithra, who gives her a potion to drink, which brings forgetfulness of every ill.

Menelaus returns convinced that he has killed two of the beings he was pursuing—Paris, and Helena. He can see their blood on his dagger—but what he brandishes is spotless and shining. Aithra convinces him that for the past ten years he and the Greeks have been victims of a fantastic delusion; it was not Helena at all who was in Troy—she has been here these ten years, lying in a deep sleep, safe from the touch of man.

Aithra makes a sign, and Helena is visible to Menelaus, waking in all her beauty from her sleep. He is overjoyed, and cannot resist the happiness which the vision affords him. At Helena's insistence, Aithra transports them by her magic arts to a land where the name of Helena means nothing to man or woman. They go together over the threshold of a sleeping chamber, and Aithra watches the triumph of her scheme while she prepares to effect a transformation of their state.

Act II.    A tent opening wide on to a palm grove, behind which the Atlas Mountains are visible. Helena and Menelaus awaken after their magic flight. Helena expresses her ecstasy: 'Zweite Brautnacht! Zaubernacht, überlange!' But Menelaus is only half restored to her; for him, she is still a phantom, conjured up by the magic arts of Aithra, and his conscience is occupied with the murder—he thinks of it as that—of Helena which he accomplished outside the palace of Aithra. It is as the widower of Helena that he thinks of himself.

To visit Helena comes a chieftain of the desert, Altair by name, with his followers. He salutes the queen reverently, and then, as Menelaus takes his place behind her with drawn sword in his hand, commands his followers led by his son, Da-Ud, to do obeisance before her. Menelaus shows signs of being jealous of Da-Ud—is he not like Paris?—but Helena tries to comfort him. Altair invites Menelaus to join the hunt, and offers him Da-Ud as his guide. As he departs, Altair shows his contempt for Menelaus, but makes no secret of his open admiration for Helena.

While Menelaus makes ready for the hunt, Da-Ud throws himself at Helena's feet and declares his devotion and adoration of her, but Helena takes no more notice of his protestations than she has of Altair's. Menelaus departs, but refuses to give up his sword, which Helena wants to take from him but which he insists on having with him for the hunt.

Aithra and attendants come to Helena. Aithra reveals that she has not only given Helena the draught which brings eternal forgetfulness of all that is unpleasant, but has also in error provided her with the antidote. She has come to remove this from Helena, lest she should accidentally taste of it. But Helena proclaims that this alone can save her and Menelaus from the position they are in, this alone can convince Menelaus that she is Helena and not a nymph conjured up by Aithra to take Helena's place in his bed. Helena bids her slaves mix the potion using the remembrance draught.

Altair appears at the entrance of the tent, and declares his passion for Helena. Slaves describe the progress of the hunt, but their voices change from excitement to horror as they perceive that Menelaus and Da-Ud are engaged in deadly combat. Soon it is evident that Menelaus has triumphed, and it is not long before Da-Ud's dead body is borne in by the slaves to the sound of solemn music.

Menelaus appears not to understand that he has slain the son of his host, but, while the slaves gather to bid him and Helena to Altair's feast, Helena and her attendants busy themselves over the mixing of the potion which will restore his memory to him. When it is finally ready, Helena bids him drink, and herself sets the example. Menelaus takes the cup, and, for a moment after he has drunk, it looks as though he will kill her. Then he drops his sword and gazes at his wife, recognising her and stretching out his arms as though to grasp a shadow.

Altair dashes in as though to take Helena by force and with the help of his slaves separate her from her husband. But at the same moment appears Aithra at the head of cohorts of her supernatural followers, and commands Altair not to presume to raise his hand against her or the woman she would protect. In the middle of Aithra's troops stands Hermione, the daughter of Helena and Menelaus. The opera comes to an end after she has asked her father: 'Where is my beautiful mother?' All is forgiven and forgotten, and Helena and Menelaus enter together upon a new life.

H.

# ARABELLA

Opera in three acts by Richard Strauss; text by Hugo von Hofmannsthal. Première Dresden, July 1, 1933, with Ursuleac, Bokor, Kremer, Jerger, Plaschke, conductor Clemens Krauss. First performed Vienna, 1933, with Lehmann, Jerger, conductor Krauss; Berlin, 1933, with Ursuleac, Heidersbach, Wittrisch, Prohaska, Krenn; Covent Garden, 1934, with artists of première; Buenos Aires, 1934, with Teschemacher, Fleischer, Kipnis, Grossmann, conductor Busch; Genoa, 1936, with dalla Rizza, Jerger, conductor Strauss; Salzburg, 1942, with Ursuleac, Eipperle, Taubmann, Reinmar, conductor Krauss; 1947, with Reining, della Casa, Taubmann, Hotter, conductor Böhm; Zürich, 1946, with Cebotari, della Casa, Schöffler; 1950, with della Casa, Harvey, Lechleitner, Wolff, conductor Reinshagen; Vienna, 1952, with della Casa, Felbermayer, Rohs, Edelmann, Poell, Dermota, conductor Moralt; Covent Garden, 1953, with della Casa, Uhde, conductor Kempe.

## CHARACTERS

Graf Waldner .................................... Bass
Adelaide, *his wife* ..................... Mezzo-Soprano
Arabella ⎫ *his daughters* ⎧ .................. Soprano
Zdenka  ⎭            ⎩ .................. Soprano
Mandryka ...,............................... Baritone
Matteo, *officer* ............................... Tenor
Graf Elemer  ⎫           ⎧ ............ Tenor
Graf Dominik ⎬ *suitors of Arabella* ⎨ .......... Baritone
Graf Lamoral ⎭           ⎩ ............ Bass
The 'Fiakermilli'............................ Soprano
A Fortune-teller................................ Soprano
Welko, Servant of Mandryka; Djura, Jankel, Servants of Mandryka; a Servant, Arabella's Duenna, Three Cardplayers, a Doctor, Groom

*Time:* 1860                                     *Place:* Vienna

There is no prelude and the curtain rises to show a salon in an hotel in Vienna; it is richly and newly furnished in the taste of the 1860's. We soon learn that the fortunes of the Waldner family are very low indeed. Graf Waldner is a gambler and has been losing heavily, and the only hope for the future seems to lie in matching the beautiful Arabella with a rich suitor. Zdenka, the younger child, has been brought up as a boy, as her parents always wanted one and Adelaide insists that they cannot possibly afford to have two daughters coming out at the same time.

Adelaide is having her fortune told, and Zdenka, dressed in boy's clothes, is making excuses for her parents to the tradesmen

who call to talk about their unpaid bills. Zdenka is left alone, and
shortly afterwards a young officer, Matteo, who is desperately in
love with Arabella, comes in. He asks for news of his beloved from
Zdenka whom, like everyone else, he believes to be her brother
(and therefore Zdenko). Arabella has not looked at him for days,
and if it were not for the wonderful letter she wrote him a day or
two ago, he would be in complete despair. He threatens to go
away or kill himself if Arabella continues to ignore him. When
he has gone, Zdenka reveals her perturbation; she is in love with
Matteo herself, and it is she who wrote him the letter he believes
to be from Arabella.

There follows a scene between the two sisters. Arabella as usual
has presents from her three noble suitors, and from Matteo as
well, but she has no real interest in any of them, and Zdenka's
pleading for Matteo affects her little. One day the right man will
come along, and she will know him straight away ('Aber der
Richtige wenn's einen gibt für mich'):

The two voices join in a charming and typically Straussian duet,
whose theme is frequently heard in the course of the opera.
Arabella is confident in the future, even though it is the end of
Carnival and she should decide which suitor she will accept before
the night is over.

Elemer, one of the three suitors, comes to take Arabella for a
ride in a sleigh; she says she will be ready in half an hour. When
Elemer has gone, Arabella asks Zdenka if she has noticed the
stranger whom she has seen during the past day or two from
her room, and whom she thinks looks extremely attractive. No
sooner has she spoken than he appears again in the street
below, but he goes away without so much as looking up at the
window.

The parents come back to the hotel and send their daughters
out of the room. The Count has been losing again, and is

depressed that he finds only bills waiting for him, and no word from any of his regimental cronies, to all of whom he had written for help in his financial embarrassment. There was one in particular, rich and eccentric, Mandryka by name, whom he thought would never fail him. Adelaide tells him she has dreamed all will go well, and no sooner has she made this effort to comfort him than a servant announces that there is a gentleman to see Graf Waldner. It turns out to be Mandryka, nephew and heir of the Count's old comrade. He has fallen in love with the photograph of Arabella which Waldner sent with his letter, and he asks for her hand in marriage. To pay for his journey to Vienna he says he sold some woods, and he offers Waldner a couple of thousand-gilder notes. The latter can hardly believe his senses, and when Mandryka has gone, he imitates his tone of voice: 'Teschek, bedien' dich' (Please, help yourself!).

There is a short scene between Zdenka and Matteo, in which the latter shows his desperate anxiety to know whether he can yet have the letter from Arabella which Zdenka promised him she was writing. He is told he may have it that night at the Fiakerball (a ball to which everyone went in costume: a 'Fiaker' was a two-horse cab). He leaves, and Arabella comes in ready for her drive with Elemer. Zdenka refers to him as 'dein Elemer' (your Elemer), and the sound of the words has a romantic ring in Arabella's ears as she repeats them. But the idea of the romantic stranger is much more attractive to her, and even the horrid thought that he may be already married is not enough to damp her enthusiasm.

Act II.    A ballroom. Arabella, very much the queen of the ball, comes downstairs with her mother and several attendant cavaliers, to be introduced by her parents to Mandryka, who is waiting below, and in whom Arabella recognises the stranger she has seen from her window. She is left alone with him, and sits down, refusing a dance to each of her other suitors in turn. His impassioned language astonishes her, but she is completely fascinated and convinced that she has found the right man in him: 'Und du wirst mein Gebieter sein.' Their love duet[1] is quite warm enough to suggest to us that she is right.

[1] During its course, Mandryka conveys the information that in his country a glass of water is given by the girl to her prospective fiancé in token of engagement.

She asks to be allowed an hour at the ball to say good-bye to the things which have made up her girlhood. At that moment, the rest of the guests crowd around her, and the Fiakermilli—a pretty girl dolled up to the nines—curtsies and brings her a bouquet. She sings a brilliant coloratura polka song for Arabella's entertainment, after which Arabella goes off to dance with Dominik.

Waldner's reaction to the news of Arabella's engagement is naturally one of delight. Matteo, however, is heart-broken, not at the news (which he has not heard), but because Arabella has not looked in his direction all evening. Zdenka, however, does her best to reassure him, and says that Arabella relies on his love, though she may not find ways of showing it. Mandryka orders champagne for everyone present at the ball; no one shall be without when he is as happy as he now feels himself. Arabella says good-bye to her three suitors, to whom she is grateful but whom she must relinquish now that she has found the right man. She goes off again to dance.

Zdenka reappears and gives Matteo a letter, which she says is from Arabella. It contains the key of Arabella's room, according to Zdenka, and she insists that if the unbelieving Matteo come to that room in a quarter of an hour, he will receive everything that he most longs for. Mandryka overhears the conversation and cannot believe his ears. He decides there must be another Arabella perhaps in the same hotel, but, when he cannot find his fiancée, is forced to the conclusion that his worst suspicions are justified, and that it must be she who made the assignation. In desperation, Mandryka flirts with the Fiakermilli. A note from Arabella is handed to him: she has gone home but will be his to-morrow. Arabella's parents notice her absence, and they go off to the hotel with Mandryka to find her.

Act III.    A lounge in the hotel, with staircase leading upstairs. Night.

There is a short prelude, and when the curtain goes up Matteo is seen about to come down the stairs. He hides when he hears a bell. Arabella comes in, smiling happily. Music from the ball plays around her as she sings of the happiness which she and Mandryka will enjoy amidst his fields and forests. Matteo reappears and is astonished to see Arabella in the hall. She can make no sense at all of his ardour and his insinuations, and he for his part cannot understand her coldness and apparent heartlessness.

In the middle of their misunderstanding, Arabella's parents arrive with Mandryka, who immediately recognises Matteo as the man he saw receive the key at the ball and is now convinced of the worst. He remains unpersuaded by Arabella's protestations of innocence, tempers rise, and a duel between Mandryka and Matteo is only prevented by the sudden appearance of Zdenka, in a negligée and with her hair down. She rushes down the stairs, and says that she only wants to say good-bye before throwing herself into the Danube. Arabella says she will stand by her whatever her trouble, and Zdenka eventually stammers out that it was she who sent the note to Matteo, and the key inside it was to her room, not Arabella's. The room was dark, and Matteo could not have known that it was not Arabella.

Mandryka tries to put his shame and sorrow into words, but Arabella turns to Zdenka without a glance in his direction and thanks her for teaching her to follow the dictates of her heart. Prompted by Arabella and Mandryka—Arabella bears no malice —Waldner agrees to give Zdenka's hand to Matteo, and the crowd which has been attracted by the noise, begins to disperse. Arabella tells Mandryka that there must be no attempt at explanation between them until morning; she would however be grateful if one of his servants could fetch her a glass of clear, cold water. She would find it refreshing after the tumult of the evening's events. She goes slowly up the stairs without another word.

Mandryka waits dejectedly below, when at the top of the stairs appears Arabella. Holding the glass of water in her hand she makes her way slowly down and offers it to him. The opera ends with their love duet: 'Das war sehr gut, Mandryka.'

H.

## DIE SCHWEIGSAME FRAU
### The Silent Woman

Opera in three acts by Richard Strauss; text by Stefan Zweig, freely adapted from Ben Jonson's comedy *Epicoene, or the Silent Woman*. Première Dresden, June 24, 1935, with Cebotari, Sack, Kremer, Ahlersmeyer, Plaschke, conductor Böhm. The opera was frowned on by the Nazis, and after very few performances was removed from the Dresden repertory. First performed Zürich, 1936, with Moor, Emmerich, Oeggl, conductor Denzler; la Scala, Milan, 1936, with Carosio, Sinnone, Stabile, Bettoni, conductor Marinuzzi; Zürich, 1942, with Moor, Funk, Chabay, Rothmüller, Rehfuss, conductor Reinshagen; Cologne, 1948, with Eipperle; Munich, 1949, with Ebers, Klarwein, Wieter, Dalberg, Kusche; Komische Oper, Berlin 1956, in Felsenstein's production, with Arnold, Reinmar.

## CHARACTERS

| | |
|---|---|
| Sir Morosus........................................ | Bass |
| His Housekeeper ............................. | Contralto |
| The Barber .................................... | Baritone |

| | | |
|---|---|---|
| Henry Morosus | | ......................Tenor |
| Aminta, *his wife* | | .........Coloratura Soprano |
| Isotta | | .........Coloratura Soprano |
| Carlotta | *actors* | .............Mezzo-Soprano |
| Morbio | | ...................Baritone |
| Vanuzzi | | ......................Bass |
| Farfallo | | ......................Bass |

Actors and Neighbours

*Time:* About 1780    *Place:* A room in Sir Morosus's house in a London suburb

Hofmannsthal had died in 1929, leaving behind him the libretto of *Arabella*, but after his death Strauss had to look round for a new collaborator. His choice fell upon Stefan Zweig, and together they turned to Ben Jonson for inspiration, Zweig having already had considerable success with his German version of *Volpone*.

After an overture, described by the composer as a *Potpourri*, the curtain rises on Act I, to show a room in Sir Morosus's house. It is untidy, and the bric-à-brac about the room indicates that it belongs to a former seaman. We are straight away introduced to the mainspring of the action, Schneidebart, the barber, who is approached by Sir Morosus's housekeeper with the suggestion that he should implant the idea in Sir Morosus's head that he wants to get married and that she is just the person. Life is impossible in the house, what with his exaggerated notions about eliminating any kind of noise, and anyhow he needs a wife. The barber is properly scornful of her suggestion, but at this moment Morosus himself comes in, fulminating about the noise his housekeeper is making.

While he is being shaved, he launches forth into a diatribe against the perpetrators of the crime of noise, by which he is surrounded and from which he cannot find any means of escape. He sings sadly of his loneliness; could he only find someone to care for him, his life would acquire the purpose which it lacks. At the end of the opera the melody is developed into a grateful hymn of thanksgiving for peace. The barber suggests he should marry a young and silent wife, and, when told there is no such thing, offers to find one. Morosus, although objecting that he is too old, is obviously not averse to considering the suggestion.

The noise of someone trying to gain admittance to his room causes a further tantrum, but when the intruder turns out to be his nephew Henry, whom he had thought dead, his displeasure turns to extravagant rejoicing. He must be received with all honour. Henry starts to tell him he has his troupe with him. Morosus misunderstands him and thinks he has said 'troops', and the initial joy turns to fury when he discovers Henry is a member of a theatrical company. He refuses even to accept Aminta, Henry's wife, as his niece, insults them all, disinherits Henry, and orders the barber to find him a wife forthwith, and moreover to bring a priest with him when he brings her to the house.

Consternation follows Sir Morosus's withdrawal, but it soon gives place to a discussion of ways and means of taking revenge on the old curmudgeon for his insults. Henry says he is happy in his love and would not barter it for a house made entirely of gold. The barber reminds him that he is throwing away quite a large fortune, but he and Aminta sing a love duet amidst expressions of admiration from the troupe. The barber sees a possible solution in the task which has been set him; it will not be easy to find a silent woman—why should Aminta, Isotta and Carlotta not be dressed up and produced as candidates next morning? Schneidebart says he will take all arrangements into his own hands, and everyone is delighted, except Aminta, who says she would prefer to move the old man to fall in with the situation rather than trick him into it. But she quickly accepts the suggestion, and the curtain falls as they make their plans.

Act II. The same room, the afternoon of the next day. Morosus is warned by his housekeeper that some sort of intrigue is brewing, but he will not listen to her, and continues to array himself in his smartest clothes. The barber comes in to say that he has brought three girls with him, and takes the opportunity of warning the old man that he should not be too ardent with them. Is he likely to eat them? demands Morosus angrily.

When they present themselves for his inspection, the three actresses impersonate three quite different types: Carlotta is a country girl, Isotta a young lady of fashion, and Aminta is dressed simply and unpretentiously. Their conversation matches their clothes: Carlotta is a hopeless bumpkin with a hideous accent, and Morosus soon dismisses her; Isotta's high-flown, pretentious talk culminates in an effort to read his hand, and she also is sent packing; but Aminta behaves naturally and Morosus is obviously impressed by her demeanour. After listening to her for a bit, Morosus tells the barber that Aminta is the one for him (she calls herself Timida). When they are left alone, it becomes apparent that he is genuinely touched by her youth and beauty, and he attempts to apologise for what must look to her a poor bargain; she is so young, and he so old. Aminta also seems to regret the part she has undertaken to play.

But the scheme is well under way, and Schneidebart returns with two members of the company dressed up as a priest and a notary. The mock marriage is concluded, but no sooner is it over than more members of the company come in, proclaiming that they are old shipmates of Sir Morosus and mean to celebrate with him. This they proceed to do, with a maximum of noise, and it is some time before his furious protests are successful in getting rid of them.

Morosus and Aminta are alone, and in an aside she reveals that she has no relish for the part she has to play. It is a question of *Don Pasquale* all over again. Aminta makes scene after scene; she is the mistress of the house, and his wishes have no significance at all. Morosus is dumbfounded, until rescued by Henry, who sends Aminta out and consoles his old uncle. The act ends after a short scene between Henry and Aminta, in which she tells him how she disliked ill-treating the poor old man; but she consoles herself with the thought that it was only done for her husband's sake.

Act III. The scene is the same. Before the curtain rises, the noise of vigorous hammering is heard, and the scene discloses a troop of workmen redecorating the room under Aminta's orders. Henry, in disguise and with another member of his company as accompanist, gives Aminta a singing lesson. This is the last straw, and Morosus is on the verge of despair when the barber comes in to announce that the Chief Justice of England is on his way to the house, and everything is prepared for a divorce. Aminta rejects the idea out of hand, but the legal party makes its appearance and proceeds to rehearse in dog Latin the grounds on which a divorce can be granted. Isotta and Carlotta witness that Sir

Morosus is by no means the first man Timida has known, and Henry, disguised, admits that he has known her intimately. Timida swears she has known but one man—her husband. But the Chief Justice, although agreeing that there is evidence of promiscuity, rules that what took place before marriage is no grounds for divorce. Morosus nears the end of his tether and threatens to commit suicide if he cannot obtain his freedom.

In his misery he throws himself on his bed, and, at a signal from the barber, Henry and Aminta go up to him and explain the truth; it has all been a hoax. He is at first bewildered, then furious, and then bursts out laughing; he may have been close to suicide, but it cannot be denied they put on a wonderful show! He confesses himself willing to hear all their operas if they can make him laugh as much as he has laughed to-day, at himself. The rejoicing is general, and when he, Aminta, and Henry are alone, Morosus sings happily of the peace which he has at last found. He sinks back in his chair, and sighs with contentment.

H.

## FRIEDENSTAG

### Peace Day

Opera in one act by Richard Strauss; text by Josef Gregor. Première, Munich, July 24, 1938, with Ursuleac, Patzak, Ostertag, Hotter, Hann, Weber, Wieter, conductor Clemens Krauss (the opera is dedicated to Ursuleac and Krauss). First performed Berlin, 1939, with Ursuleac, Prohaska, Bockelmann, Sinimberghi, conductor Krauss; Zürich, 1939, with Annie Weber, Stig, Emmerich, conductor Denzler; Venice, 1940, with Grandi, Valentino, Rakowski, Cassinelli, conductor Gui.

### CHARACTERS

Commandant of the Beleaguered Town . . . . . . . . . . Baritone
Maria, *his wife* . . . . . . . . . . . . . . . . . . . . . . . . . . . . . . Soprano
Sergeant . . . . . . . . . . . . . . Bass
Corporal . . . . . . . . . . Baritone
A Private Soldier . . . . . . . . . . . . Tenor
A Musketeer *of the Garrison* . . . . . . . . . . . Bass
A Bugler . . . . . . . . . . . . . . Bass
An Officer . . . . . . . . . . Baritone
A Front-line Officer . . . . . . . . . . Baritone

A Piedmontese ...................................Tenor

The Holsteiner, *commanding the besieging army* ......Bass

Burgomaster ⎱                              ⎰ Tenor
Bishop        ⎰ *of the beleaguered town* ⎱ Baritone
A Woman of the People ⎰            ⎰ Soprano

Soldiers of the garrison and of the besieging army, Elders of the town and women of the deputation to the Commandant, Townspeople

*Time:* October 24, 1648      *Place:* The Citadel of a beleaguered town during the Thirty Years War

The scene shows the great circular room in the citadel. A gallery with loopholes runs round at about a man's height. One staircase leads to the upper storey of the fortress, another descends.

The soldiers sing a ditty, but from afar off can be heard the sound of the townspeople, already afoot and crying that their hunger can no more be borne.

To the sound of a mournful march and with the cries of 'Hunger! Bread!' still sounding from outside, the town elders enter, led by the Burgomaster and the Bishop. Suddenly, the musket-butts strike the ground, and the Commandant appears on the upper stairway. He is a handsome man of about fifty. He warns the deputation that he will hear them but that his answer to anything they may say which involves a cowardly action on his part will be violent—he seizes a musket from a soldier and throws it down at their feet as he speaks. Burgomaster and Bishop plead with him to allow the surrender of the town, but he will not listen to their arguments.

An officer announces to the Commandant that all the ammunition is spent; will he give the order that more be fetched from the secret cellars, where they all know there is a plentiful supply? The Commandant refuses, but bids them trust him. He reads aloud the Emperor's message which reached him only the previous day; it bids them hold out at all costs. But the cries of the deputation redouble in urgency, the crowd shouts for peace, and eventually the Commandant says he is ready to agree to their demands; let them only wait until midday before the surrender takes effect. He himself will give the signal, a rousing, flashing sign which all will recognise.

The deputation departs well content with what it has achieved, but it is clear a moment later that the Commandant, rather than surrender, plans to set fire to his arsenal and so blow himself and his garrison sky-high.

The stage is empty for a moment, but from below comes Maria, the Commandant's wife. She is younger than he is, and she muses on the situation in which all find themselves. Her monologue ends with a pæan of praise to hope, which has returned with the rising sun, which now shines brightly through the loophole.

Maria tries to persuade her husband, who enters at that moment, to confide in her why he looks so different from usual. He urges her to escape since the citadel and all within it are doomed to die. She thanks the sun for the light it has shed on her life; it has melted the heart she had thought frozen, it has removed the look that worried her so much. She will not be parted from the husband she loves so much, be it in life or in death, in peace or in war.

They embrace. The light has grown dimmer during their duet. The soldiers come one by one into the room, last of all the sergeant, with the fuse in his hand. The Commandant motions him towards the arsenal. Suddenly, the sound of a cannon shot is heard. It is the sign the Commandant has hoped for; it means the enemy is attacking. But no enemy can be seen advancing, and instead bells begin to ring out from the town, one after another, bells which have not been heard since the days of peace, almost longer ago than anyone can remember.

A moment later the Burgomaster is up the stairs and into the room, a changed man from the time when he led the deputation to pray for surrender. Peace has now come. The Commandant protests that he will not surrender, but to the sound of a march the Holsteiner's troops enter the citadel, their commander at their head. His voice can be heard from outside demanding to know where his noble, lion-hearted foe is to be found, that he may embrace him. But the Commandant returns harsh words for kind, and refuses to shake the hand which the Holsteiner proffers him. He draws his sword, and the Holsteiner puts his hand on his, but Maria throws herself between the two men. She begs her husband to acknowledge that at long last love and brotherhood have come into the lives of all of them instead of hatred and strife. He looks at her, and then throws away his sword and embraces the Holsteiner leader.

The opera ends with an extended hymn to peace, in which all the soloists join.                                                    H.

# DAPHNE

Opera in one act by Richard Strauss; text by Josef Gregor. Première Dresden, October 15, 1938, with Teschemacher, Jung, Ralf, Kremer, conductor Böhm (given in a double bill with *Friedenstag*). First performed Berlin, 1939, with Cebotari, Focke, Ralf, Anders, conductor Krauss; la Scala, Milan, 1942, with Cigna, Gallo, conductor Marinuzzi; Buenos Aires, 1948, with Bampton, Kindermann, Svanholm, Dermota, Weber, conductor Kleiber. Revived Munich, 1950, with Kupper, Fischer, Fehenberger, Hopf, Hann, conductor Jochum; Vienna, 1950, with Kupper, conductor Moralt.

## CHARACTERS

Peneios, *a fisherman* ............................Bass
Gaea, *his wife*................................Contralto
Daphne, *their daughter* ........................Soprano
Leukippos, *a shepherd*...........................Tenor
Apollo .........................................Tenor
Four Shepherds .............Baritone, Tenor, Two Basses
Two Maids ...................................Soprano

*Time:* Antiquity            *Place:* Near Peneios's hut; Olympus
                                       visible in the distance

There is a short pastoral introduction, after which the curtain rises to show Peneios's hut and the landscape round it. Heralded by the sound of their flocks, the four shepherds appear in pairs and discuss the forthcoming feast-day in honour of Dionysus, which is traditionally the time for lovers' mating. The last rays of the sun light up the stage as Daphne comes in. In a long monologue she reveals her love of nature and identification of herself with the trees and flowers around her; the prospect of the festivity gives her no pleasure.

Leukippos, her childhood's playmate, tells her how much he loves her, and tries to embrace her. She repulses him and refuses to accompany him to the festival, at the same time, however, telling him that her affection for him is by no means gone although she characterises it as sisterly. Gaea has heard the end of their conversation, and she comes to bid her daughter dress herself for the party. The time will come when she will open her heart to love. Daphne listens to her mother, but will not dress up in the clothes the maids bring for her. Gaea follows Daphne from the stage, and the maids are left to comment on the situation. Soon they hear the sound of Leukippos's lamentations. They determine to help him to win Daphne's love, and offer to dress him up in the clothes she has rejected.

As light dies away, the dignified figure of Peneios appears, accompanied by Gaea and the shepherds. He points to the light which still shines on Mount Olympus; the day will yet come when the gods will return amongst men. In spite of murmurs of protest from the shepherds, he affirms his belief that Apollo will come to them, and suggests they prepare a great feast to receive him worthily. Peneios laughs and is answered by a mysterious echo. A stranger appears—Apollo dressed as a herdsman—and greets the company. He tells them his cattle had run wild, and he has only just succeeded in rounding them up. Gaea and the shepherds laugh at Peneios for this mundane realisation of his prophecy that Apollo would visit them. He answers by sending for Daphne and bidding her look after the stranger.

When Daphne appears, Apollo is amazed at her beauty, and calls her 'Sister'. She is taken aback by the compliments he pays her, but starts to do her parents' bidding, and puts a blue cloak round his shoulders. She feels an affinity with him, and asks him his true identity. In enigmatic language, he explains that he saw her from his chariot. She does not understand who he is, but starts to tell him how she hates to be parted from the sun, where-upon he repeats sentences to her from her opening monologue. She sinks on his breast, and rejoices in his promise that she will never again be parted from the sun. For a time she is hidden in the blue of his cloak, but suddenly tears herself free. Apollo declares that he loves her, and tells her to listen to the distant chanting; it is the voice of lovers. But Daphne is full of fear; Apollo told her he was her brother, and now he talks of love.

A procession, led by Peneios and Gaea, approaches, and Daphne joins the women, Apollo the men. They sing the praises of Dionysus, and the feast begins. Leukippos, who is dressed up amongst the women, invites Daphne to join their dancing. No sooner has she done so than Apollo bursts out in complaint that Peneios and his daughter are the victims of deception. With the sound of a thunderclap, he disrupts the feast, whereupon Leukippos reveals himself as a suitor for Daphne's hand. In a fiery passage he begs her to follow him. Daphne complains that she is being doubly deceived, both by the playmate of her youth, and by the stranger, who is not what he seems to be. Apollo reveals himself as the sun, and in the dispute which follows Daphne's refusal to bind herself to either of her suitors, Apollo wounds Leukippos with an arrow.

In a scene with the dying man, Daphne discovers that her lover was a god, and blames herself for Leukippos's death. Apollo watches her, spellbound by her beauty and full of regret for his action in killing Leukippos. He asks Dionysus to forgive him for having caused the death of one of his disciples, and, begging Zeus to pardon him that he strayed outside his sphere in interfering with mortals, he asks that he be given Daphne, not in mortal guise but transformed into imperishable form as one of the trees she loves so well. From her branches, men will in future cut the wreaths reserved for those who are best and bravest amongst them. Gradually Daphne changes into a laurel tree, and her voice is heard celebrating her altered state. H.

## DIE LIEBE DER DANAE
### The Love of Danae

Opera in three acts by Richard Strauss; text by Josef Gregor. The opera was in rehearsal during the late summer of 1944, but a Nazi edict closing the theatres as a result of the plot against Hitler's life prevented a public performance. In the event, *Die Liebe der Danae* was heard at a well-attended dress rehearsal (August 16), conducted by Clemens Krauss and with a cast headed by Ursuleac, Taubmann, and Hotter. The official première was at the Salzburg Festival, August 14, 1952, with Kupper, Gostic, Szemere, Schöffler, conductor Krauss. First performed in Vienna, 1952, with Kupper, Gostic, Patzak, Poell, conductor Krauss; Berlin, 1952, with Richter, Beirer, Poell, conductor Ludwig; la Scala, Milan, with Dow, Gostic, Ego, conductor Krauss; Covent Garden, 1953, with Kupper (later Rysanek), Vandenburg, Frantz, conductor Kempe.

#### CHARACTERS

Jupiter ........................................ Baritone
Mercury........................................ Tenor
Pollux, *King of Eos* ........................... Tenor
Danae, *his daughter* ......................... Soprano

Xanthe, *her servant* . . . . . . . . . . . . . . . . . . . . . . . . . . . . .Soprano

Midas, *King of Lydia* . . . . . . . . . . . . . . . . . . . . . . . . . . .Tenor

Four Kings, *nephews to Pollux* . . . .Two Tenors, Two Basses

Semele ⎤        ⎧ . . . . . . . . . . . . . . . . . . .Soprano

Europa  ⎬ *four queens* ⎨ . . . . . . . . . . . . . . . . . . .Soprano

Alcmene ⎥        ⎩ . . . . . . . . . . . . .Mezzo-Soprano

Leda    ⎦            . . . . . . . . . . . . . . . . . . .Contralto

Four Watchmen . . . . . . . . . . . . . . . . . . . . . . . . . . .Four Basses

Chorus of Creditors, Servants and Followers of Pollux and
Danae, People

As early as the spring of 1920, Hofmannsthal sent Strauss a scenario under the title *Danae, or the prudent marriage*. The suggestion had not been taken up by the composer at the time Hofmannsthal died (in 1929), but Strauss's attention was drawn to it later, and he eventually persuaded Gregor to write a text after Hofmannsthal's theme. The composition was finished in June 1940, so that though *Die Liebe der Danae* was the last of Strauss's operas to reach public performance, its composition in fact antedates that of *Capriccio* by some two years.

Act I. The first scene is laid in the throne-room of King Pollux. It is shabby and there is only part of the golden throne left. One can see the former splendour, but now creditors besiege the hall and demand payment. The King appears and tries to pacify them, telling them that his nieces, the four most beautiful women alive, and their husbands, kings of the islands, have set out to find a husband for Danae, and that Midas, the richest man in the world whose touch turns anything to gold, is on his way to marry her. But the crowd is sceptical and falls on the throne and plunders what is left.

An interlude depicts the Golden Rain. Bedchamber of Danae. She awakes and tells Xanthe, her maid, of her dream, in which she was surrounded and covered with gold. It fell on her lips and on her breasts, and she can hardly believe it was only a dream, so real and wonderful was the sensation of the gold. A march is heard in the distance, and Xanthe announces a new suitor. But Danae says that she will only accept the man who can bring her the gold.

The third scene shows a pillared hall in the palace; in the distance the sea. A large gathering—the King, his councillors, and his creditors—awaits the return of the emissaries. They announce that Midas is the new suitor, whose touch has turned even the portrait of Danae to gold. He sends a golden garland to Danae. A cry is heard—'A ship! A ship of gold!'—and everyone rushes towards the harbour to greet Midas. Only Danae stays behind. It is all like her dream, and she determines that the bringer of gold shall be her bridegroom.

Midas comes in, dressed in simple clothes and saying he is Chrysopher, friend of Midas, come to prepare her to meet the King. She is obviously impressed by him and cannot conceal her disappointment that he is only the forerunner of her suitor. He for his part is reluctant to fulfil his bargain, and hand her over to his master.

The scene changes to the harbour, where the crowd gives a great welcome to the supposed Midas, in reality none other than Jupiter clothed in golden raiment. Danae recognises him as the master of her golden dreams; but is he the master of her love? She faints, and the curtain falls.

Act II. In a magnificent bed-chamber, the four queens are decorating the bridal bed. Jupiter enters, clothed from head to foot in gold. The four queens know him, for in various guises he has been the lover of each of them—as cloud, bull, Amphitryon, and a swan. He warns them not to give his disguise away, but they cannot restrain their jealousy that for Danae he is not content to stay in the form of gold, but has taken the form of a real man—and why the double deception over Midas? He explains that his love for Danae is great, and she is made even more desirable in his eyes because of her coldness and disdain of men. He hopes to find true love at last. As for the impersonation of Midas, that is done to deceive Juno, whose jealousy is stronger than ever, and whose punishments for those he has loved grow ever more severe. As he has taken the outward form of Midas, the real Midas can always take his place should Juno approach in anger. The four queens praise his cunning, and try to entice him back to them.

Midas enters and the women leave the bridal chamber. Jupiter is jealous in case Midas should capture Danae's love, and reminds him that, when he conferred the golden touch upon him, it was with the condition that he should obey his every command. He has been made the richest man on earth, but should he now prove false to his bargain, he will forthwith change back into the donkey-driver Jupiter first knew. Jupiter leaves, a soft march announces the arrival of Danae, and Midas dons the golden clothes which Jupiter has left behind him.

Danae enters accompanied by the four queens, who tell her that the object of her affections has formerly been the lover of each one of them; when they recognise Midas, they take fright, and disappear. Midas explains as much as he dares; he is the master of the gold, and yet not the suitor on the ship. Danae does not understand the mystery, but it is clear that she wants only him, and, when he turns everything in the room to gold, she knows it must be Midas. They fall into each other's arms. A thunderclap . . . darkness . . . and Danae is seen turned to a golden statue.

Midas curses himself and his gift. Jupiter appears and claims Danae as his, but Midas objects that she must come to life only for the sake of him whom she truly loves. They both offer her what it is in their power to give: Jupiter—golden dreams, temples, and god-like honours; Midas—only his human love and poverty. Her voice is heard as though from afar off, choosing Midas. Danae and Midas disappear, and Jupiter alone laments the loss of what might have been. Danae was offered the fate of the gods, and she has chosen the fate of mortals.

Act III.    An open road in the East. Danae and Midas are seen to wake up. Danae slowly begins to understand what has happened. Midas, the favourite of the god, has renounced riches and power and has returned to be the humble donkey-driver on account of his love for her. She is content.

The scene changes to a sunny forest in the mountains. Mercury, half god, half jester, reports to Jupiter that the episode of Danae has caused mirth amongst the gods, but has thrown everyone on Pollux's island into confusion. Jupiter is confronted by the four queens, who have found their way to him with Mercury's help. They flatter him, and affect to regard the episode as an amusing trick played on Danae and designed to draw Juno's attention to her while he diverts himself with them. But soon Jupiter tires of them, and bids a final farewell to them, to his last and dearest love, and to earth.

Unfortunately for his plans, Pollux and his nephews and creditors have found him, and demand satisfaction for the deception which has been practised on them. On Mercury's advice, Jupiter lets money fall from the skies, and they all rush after it. Mercury recommends that Jupiter should not abandon his pursuit of Danae; now that she is poor, how much more easily will she succumb to the lure of gold than when she dwelt in a palace?

Midas's hut, simply but tidily kept. Danae sings of her love. Jupiter enters, dressed in the manner Midas has described to Danae as affected by the man who first gave him the gift of the golden touch. He tries to discover if Danae is discontented with her lot; he reminds her of her golden dreams, but she is proof against his temptations, and finally convinces him that she loves Midas. Jupiter is moved by her obvious faithfulness, and tells her the story of Maia, who was loved by the god and brought forth Spring. The duet is one of Strauss's most inspired passages. At its end, Jupiter recognises Danae's greatness, and she too is full of gratitude for his understanding. He thanks her and leaves. Danae looks after him. Midas's music is heard in the orchestra and she goes out to meet him.                                          H.

# CAPRICCIO

Opera in one act by Richard Strauss; text by Clemens Krauss. Première Munich, October 28, 1942, with Ursuleac, Ranczak, Taubmann, Hotter, Höfermayer, Hann, conductor Krauss. First performed Zürich, 1944, with Cebotari, Rohs, Dermota, Kunz, Schöffler, conductor Böhm; Salzburg, 1950, with della Casa, Höngen, Dermota, Braun, Wolff, Schöffler, conductor Böhm; Vienna, 1951, with Goltz (later della Casa), Höngen, Wenkoff, Braun, Schöffler, conductor Kempe; Covent Garden, 1953, with Cunitz, Holm, Peter, Kusche conductor Heger.

### CHARACTERS

The Countess ................................. Soprano
Clairon, *an actress* ........................... Contralto
Flamand, *a musician* .......................... Tenor
Olivier, *a poet* .............................. Baritone
The Count, *the Countess's brother* .............. Baritone
La Roche, *director of a theatre* ................. Bass
Monsieur Taupe ............................... Tenor
An Italian Singer ............................. Soprano
An Italian Singer ............................. Tenor
A Young Dancer ...............................
The Major-domo ............................... Bass

Eight Servants ...................Four Tenor, Four Bass
Three Musicians ................Violin, 'Cello, Cembalo
*Time:* About 1775, at the time Gluck was beginning his reform
  of operatic theory
*Place:* A castle near Paris

From the earliest times its practitioners have been concerned
with the theory and the re-shaping of opera. Every opera ever
written constitutes an acceptance of an old form or an attempt
to introduce a new, and each example is a particular commentary
on operatic form in general. But the commentary is customarily
implicit in the work and not explicit as in Strauss's last opera
*Capriccio*, in which he and Clemens Krauss took opera itself
as subject (*Capriccio* was finished in 1942, and, though performed before *Danae*, was in fact the last opera on which the
composer worked).

The scene is laid in France, at the time of Gluck's reform. At
the house of the charming Countess, a number of people are discussing the theme 'Prima le parole, dopo la musica', led by
Flamand, a musician, and Olivier, a poet, who are rivals for the
affections of the Countess as well as in their art. Arguing from
a different angle is the Countess's brother, whose interest in
music or poetry is mild, but whose regard for the stage, and most
of all for Clairon, a leading actress, is quite the reverse. More
professional in his practical attitude than the artists, more know-
ledgeable in his cynicism than the Count, is la Roche, a theatrical
manager, who incidentally emerges as the strongest personality
in a cast of types. Each character finds his attitude to opera
reflected symbolically in his relationship to the Countess and the
other guests.

Originally the opera was intended to be a short, one-act affair,
designed to go with *Friedenstag* and *Daphne*, but in its final form
it lasts nearly two hours and a half—and there is of course no
interval. We are confronted in fact with Strauss's old lack of
economy; to take just one example, the string sextet which acts
as overture and which is being played as the curtain rises lasts
nearly twelve minutes. In spite of the composer's skilful craftsmanship, one cannot help being surprised that Strauss did not
perceive that the conversational subject and a large orchestra
were irreconcilable.                                        H.

# EUGEN D'ALBERT

## (1864–1932)

### TIEFLAND

### The Lowlands

OPERA in a prologue and two acts by Eugen d'Albert; text by Rudolph Lothar after a Catalonian play *Tierra Baixa*, by Angel Guimerà. Première at the Neues Deutsches Theater, Prague, November 15, 1903. First performed in Berlin, 1907; Vienna, 1908; Metropolitan, 1908 with Destinn, Schmedes, Feinhals, conductor Hertz; Covent Garden, 1910 with Terry, Teyte, John Coates, Frederick Austin, conductor Beecham. Revived Berlin, 1939, with Rünger, Asserson, Völker, Bockelmann, Hiller; Vienna, 1947, with Helena Braun, Schwaiger, Friedrich, Kamann, conductor Loibner.

### CHARACTERS

Sebastiano, *a rich land owner* .................... Baritone
Tommaso, *the village elder (aged ninety)* ............. Bass
Moruccio, *a miller* ......... Baritone
Marta ......... Soprano
Pepa ......... Soprano
Antonia *in Sebastiano's* ......... Soprano
Rosalia *employment* ........ Contralto
Nuri, *a little girl* ......... Soprano
Pedro, *a shepherd* ........... Tenor
Nandro, *a shepherd* ........... Tenor
The Priest ...................................... Mute

*Scene:* The Pyrenees, and the Lowlands of Catalonia

D'Albert, who was born in Glasgow, was not only a pianist of very high attainments, but also a successful composer, whose operas range from comedy to a German form of *verismo*; *Tiefland* is an example of the latter aspect of his style. D'Albert was married and divorced no less than six times, his second wife being the great pianist Teresa Carreño.

Prologue.  A rocky slope high up in the Pyrenees. A shepherd's hut can be seen. Pedro and Nandro greet each other, Pedro observing that he has not seen anyone for three months, and has not spoken to a soul for six. He protests that he finds the shepherd's life perfect, but that he has sometimes in his prayers asked God to send him a wife ('Zwei Vaterunser bet' ich').

Soon, Sebastiano appears at the top, accompanied by Marta and Tommaso; he sends Tommaso off to look for Pedro, and orders Nandro to bring them milk, bread, and cheese. He himself explains the object of their errand to Marta, who has been his mistress for some time. He has brought her up here to show her Pedro, whom he has picked out as a suitable husband for her!

Pedro tells Nandro of his good fortune, but the latter warns him about conditions down there in the valley. Pedro sings a last greeting to the mountains he knows so well ('ich grüss noch einmal meine Berge') and the curtain falls.

Act I.    The interior of the mill. The millwheel can be seen, various doors leading to other parts of the house, and in the background the huge entrance gate, through which, when it is open, one can see far into the distance. Moruccio is working, but is interrupted by the arrival and importunate questioning of Pepa, Antonia, and Rosalia; is it true that Marta is getting married?

Marta comes in for a moment, but, seeing all the people there, hurries out again. The three women begin to laugh at the curious situation which her marriage will create, not least for the duffer who is going to become her husband. Marta comes back and drives them out of the gate. But she seems pleased to see Nuri, and for a moment it looks as though she will confide in the child.

Nuri goes and Marta reflects on her misery. She is Sebastiano's property, and had not the courage to free herself by drowning herself in the stream. Now she is to marry a mountain lout. . . . She hurries out when she hears what she thinks may be the noise of the escort bringing her bridegroom-to-be. Tommaso comes into the mill, and Moruccio asks him how he came to be a party to the arrangement of such a wicked marriage.

Darkness falls, cries of 'the bridegroom!' can be heard, and Pedro arrives, closely followed by Sebastiano, who orders that Marta be brought from her room.

While Pedro is getting dressed outside, Marta and Sebastiano are alone. There is an extensive duet in which Sebastiano claims that Marta's love will be his even after she is married to Pedro. That very night, if she sees a light in her room, it will be the signal that he is there.

Pedro with other villagers comes for Marta, and they leave for the church. Tommaso, however, asks to speak to Sebastiano. He hints at the accusation which Moruccio has made against Marta, but Sebastiano says it is false; moreover, he who made it shall remain no longer in his service.

The moon rises, the wedding procession can be heard returning, and Marta comes in, followed by Pedro. He attempts to make love to her, but she will have none of him, and even refuses to accept the wedding present he offers her, a silver Taler. It was hard-earned, he says, and proceeds to tell Marta the story of his fight with a wolf which habitually preyed on the sheep, and which he eventually managed to kill with his knife, receiving as a reward the Taler from Sebastiano's own hands ('Wolfserzäh-lung').

Marta seems impressed by his narrative and touched that he wants to give the piece of silver to her. But she bids him good-night, and points to a room which she describes as his in exactly the opposite direction from hers. When he protests, she presumes that he has been told what a shameful bargain he made when he married her. But Pedro knows nothing of her past, and speaks of nothing but his love for her. Suddenly, Pedro sees a light in her room. He feels in his pocket for his knife and is about to approach the curtain which covers the door when the light dis-appears and Marta says that she saw nothing. She resigns herself to spending the night in the main room, and Pedro lies down on the floor, determined to see her vigil through with her.

Act II.    The curtain rises to show Marta and Pedro in the same positions as at the end of Act I. Nuri is heard singing behind the scenes, and Marta gets up and goes out to her room. Nuri wakes up Pedro, who thinks for a moment it is Marta. He says he will not stay any longer; he is sure there was a man in her room last night.

His suspicions are confirmed when Nuri says she is sorry everyone is laughing at him on account of the marriage he has made. He now knows that his dishonour is public property—but at whose hands is he dishonoured?

Marta sees him with Nuri, and has a spasm of jealousy. He goes out with Nuri, and Marta is about to follow them when she meets Tommaso coming to see her. He curses her for what she has let him all unwittingly do to Pedro. In a moving passage ('Ich weiss nicht, wer mein Vater war') she tells him her story, how she was left alone with her mother—she never knew her father—and they earned their living by begging in the streets. One day an old man, a cripple, joined them, and after that he lived with them. Her mother died, and she stayed with the cripple, who would not let her go as she was pretty and her dancing brought them money. Eventually their wanderings led them to this valley, where she was seen by Sebastiano, who spoke the first kind words she had ever heard. The cripple was installed as miller, and she became mistress of Sebastiano, the lord of the manor. She was fourteen years old when she arrived. Now she has been forced into marriage with Pedro; but a wonderful thing happened to her in the chapel when she fancied she heard a voice proclaiming him as her destined mate. Tommaso tells her she must, if she loves Pedro, make up her mind to tell him her secret.

As Tommaso is leaving, the women waylay him and start to question him; what does he know? Nothing, he answers, and goes on his way. Pedro is the next to be cross-questioned. He loses his temper and tries to force them to tell him why they laugh at him, but to no avail. Ask Marta, they tell him. Marta brings him his food, but he tells her that he should kill her, not forgive her, as she asks. He is about to leave her, when she makes a last effort to provoke him. She tells him she was another man's before she was married to him; everyone was laughing at the wedding for that reason, and he was coward enough to sell his honour for money. Beside himself, Pedro stabs her in the arm, and Marta weeps for joy. At last he has punished her for her fault; will he not strike her dead? Pedro is in despair; he admits his love; will she not come with him to the mountains where they can live together in peace, away from these accursed lowlands? Marta joins her voice with his.

They are about to leave arm-in-arm when Sebastiano appears at the gate. Pedro tells him that he must take back his gift of the mill; he and his bride are returning to the mountains—but Sebastiano does not even notice Pedro. He commands Marta to dance for him, as she used to do once ('Hüll in die Mantille'). Peasants support his singing, but Pedro orders Marta to follow him. A quarrel works up, and Pedro is with difficulty restrained from attacking Sebastiano when Marta tells him whose light it was in her room the previous night. But men seize Pedro and drag him away, while Marta falls unconscious.

Tommaso appears and tells Sebastiano that the father of his bride-to-be will not be seeing him that day, as Sebastiano was expecting. He, Tommaso, has made it his business to inform him of the background to the projected marriage, and he will have nothing further to do with Sebastiano. There is a violent duet between Marta and Sebastiano, the latter proclaiming that she is all that is left to him now, Marta objecting that she loves Pedro. At the end Sebastiano defies the absent Pedro to take her from him, only to find that Pedro has gained access to the room and is ready to fight him for Marta.

Sebastiano makes for the gate, but Pedro heads him off, and forces him to stay. Pedro draws his knife, but throws it away, saying that they will fight with bare hands. Sebastiano makes an effort to reach the knife but Pedro forestalls him and seizes him by the throat in a grip of iron, not releasing him until all signs of life are extinct. He drops lifeless to the floor. Pedro goes to the entrance of the mill calling for the villagers. They come in and see the corpse on the floor. Now is the time to laugh, orders Pedro. As for him, he will away into the hills again, taking Marta his wife with him.                                         H.

# HANS PFITZNER

## (1869–1949)

### PALESTRINA

OPERA in three acts by Hans Pfitzner; text by the composer. Première Munich, June 12, 1917, with Karl Erb, Feinhals, Brodersen, Bender, Gustav Schützendorf, Ivogün, conductor Bruno Walter. First performed (by the company from Munich) in Basle, Berne, Zürich, 1917; Vienna 1919, with Emile Schmedes, Fritz Feinhals, Duhan, Mayr, Madin, Maikl, Lotte Lehmann, Kittel; Berlin, 1919, with Josef Mann, Armster, Marherr, conductor Pfitzner. Revived Berlin, 1939, with Wittrisch, Bockelmann, Soot, Spletter; Vienna, 1949, with Patzak, Hotter, Poell, Alsen, Jerger, Pölzer, Jurinac, Rohs, conductor Krips; Munich, 1949, with Fehenberger (later Patzak), Kronnenberg (later Hotter), Nentwig, conductor Heger.

### CHARACTERS

I. Singers:

Pope Pius IV ..................................... Bass
Giovanni Morone } Papal legates { .......... Baritone
Bernardo Novagerio } .............. Tenor
Cardinal Christoph Madruscht ..................... Bass
Carlo Borromeo, *Cardinal from Rome* .......... Baritone
Cardinal of Lorraine ............................. Bass
Abdisu, *Patriarch of Assyria* ..................... Tenor
Anton Brus von Müglitz, *Archbishop of Prague* ...... Bass
Count Luna, *envoy from the King of Spain* ........ Baritone
Bishop of Budoja } Italian Bishops { .......... Tenor
Theophilus of Imola } ........... Tenor
Avosmediano, *Bishop of Cadiz* ............. Bass-Baritone
Giovanni Pierluigi Palestrina ..................... Tenor
Ighino, *his son, aged fifteen* ..................... Soprano
Silla, *his pupil, aged seventeen* ............ Mezzo-Soprano
Bishop Ercole Severolus, *master-of-ceremonies*
  *at Council of Trent* ..................... Bass-Baritone
Five singers from Chapel of Santa Maria
  Maggiore in Rome .......... Two Tenors, Three Basses
Singers from Papal Chapel, Archbishops,
  Bishops, Abbots, Ambassadors, En-
  voys, Theologians, Servants, Soldiers ....... *Chorus*
  People

II. Silent Characters:

Two Papal Nuncios, Jesuits, Massarelli, Bishop of Thelesia, Secretary of Council, Giuseppe, Old Servant of Palestrina

III. Singing Apparitions:

Apparition of Lucretia, Palestrina's dead wife .... Contralto
Apparitions of Nine Dead Composers . . Tenor, Baritone, Bass
Three Angelic Voices ......................... Soprano
Angels ....................................... Chorus

*Time:* November–December 1563, the year of the end of the Council of Trent

*Place:* Rome; Trent

Act I.    A solemn prelude leads straight into the action which is laid in a room in Palestrina's house. Silla, Palestrina's pupil, is sitting there trying over one of his own compositions on the viol (in the last bars of the prelude, this is suggested in the orchestra by two solo violas). Ighino comes in, looking sad. In the course of conversation between the two, it transpires that Ighino is worried by the look of unhappiness he has seen now for so long on his father's face; has Silla not noticed it? Palestrina's pupil admits he can see little wrong with his master, nor can he imagine why he should be unhappy—he, the famous composer. But Ighino pours out his feelings: fame has brought his father little; he has been desperately lonely ever since the loss of his wife, and has written nothing. His life in fact seemed to come to an end with her death.

Palestrina comes into the room with Cardinal Borromeo, and the two boys leave. The Cardinal is astonished at the music he heard when they came in (Silla was practising his song again), and he asks Palestrina whether he likes that kind of music. It is perhaps the new music, the music of the future, replies the master. Borromeo admits that Palestrina's attitude of world-weariness, of submission to the new tendencies, makes him impatient. Without him, what is church music to become? He goes into further detail: his object in coming secretly to Palestrina's house is practical. The Council of Trent, which has been sitting these eighteen years, is now coming to an end. Pope Pius was originally not content with reforming the abuses of church music, but wished to return to Gregorian chant and consign to the flames all other sacred music. Only he—Borromeo—resisted this reactionary view, but he had an ally in the Emperor, who opposed so drastic a change. The case is now won, but has yet to be proved: this can only be done if a Mass is written by a contemporary composer of such calibre as to convince the Pope and his Council. Such a work would be a model for future composers, and would secure the future of church music. It is Palestrina's task to write it!

But Palestrina regretfully says that he is not the right man for the task. Neither the Cardinal's scorn nor his raging nor his pleas are sufficient; Palestrina still insists that even an artist's powers can grow old. Borromeo's anger overflows, and in the end he accuses the composer of blasphemy. He leaves the room in ungovernable fury. Palestrina is moved by what he has seen and heard: there goes my last friend, is his comment. As he muses on the uncertainty of men's conditions and the mysteries of life, looking sadly at the portrait of his dead wife, and reflects that since her death he has been tired and unable to work, he is surrounded by a vision of the composers of the past. He recognises them as his predecessors, and they remind him of his youth, when he first came to know them. They encourage him, and tell him that his ultimate duty is not yet accomplished.

As Palestrina's aversion to composition seems to weaken, the ghosts of the composers watch with an interest that is almost 'knowing'; these are the growing pains once familiar to them all! With Palestrina's resistance overcome, they gradually disappear, but immediately he starts to hear the voices of angels, which dictate his Mass to him. At the height of his inspiration, Palestrina sees the ghost of his wife, Lucretia, who appears to him as she had in life, bringing a message of peace, the peace for which he has longed ever since her death. This scene of the dictation of the Mass is the crux of the opera. It is perhaps sufficient praise to say that it succeeds in giving an impression of the artist's exaltation at the moment of creation.

It is dawn, the angel voices die away, the bells of Rome can be heard in the distance, and Palestrina sinks down exhausted. The floor of the room is covered with music-paper, and, when Silla and Ighino come for their morning lesson, they are overjoyed to see that the master has spent the night working. They gather up the sheets of music, and gradually realise that an entire Mass has been written in a single night. As the curtain falls, Silla

PLATE XXXIII. *Der Rosenkavalier* in Salzburg 1949. (above) Jarmila Novotna (Oktavian) and Jaro Prohaska (Ochs) in the second act.

(below) The presentation of the rose. Josef Gielen was the producer and the sets were by Alfred Roller.

PLATE XXXIV. *Arabella* at Metropolitan, New York, with Eleanor Steber, Ralph Herbert, Blanche Thebom,

wonders whether anything written so quickly can possibly add to the master's fame.

Act II. The agitated prelude is in direct contrast to what preceded the first act. The scene is the great hall in the palace of Cardinal Madruscht at Trent, where preparations are almost complete for renewal of the conference. Cardinal Novagerio makes fun of the farce which always attends the Spanish delegate's efforts to obtain his rightful precedence, and a little later takes the opportunity of warning the servants, who are all of different nationalities, that they will be severely punished if they again start to quarrel in the streets, as has happened recently.

Borromeo arrives, and there is a fairly lengthy political discussion between him and Novagerio. Novagerio congratulates Borromeo on the way he has managed the question of church music, but Borromeo reveals that he has been unsuccessful in getting Palestrina to write the Mass he needs. He has had him thrown into prison, but doubts whether the work can be ready in time, even if gaol were to break Palestrina's self-imposed silence. Novagerio suggests that there are ways to force men to bend to the will of their masters, but Borromeo starts back in horror at the implication of his remarks.

The other delegates begin to arrive, the Italians suspicious of the Germans, the Spaniards commenting on the Italians who, they say, swarm over the place like ants. Some talk in an indignant way of heretics, others are more concerned over whether or not their expenses to and from the conference will be paid by their diocese. The master-of-ceremonies, Bishop Ercole Severolus, announces that the conference is about to begin and invites the delegates to take their places in proper order of precedence. This done, they are addressed by Morone, the papal legate, who prays that wisdom may attend their deliberations and inform their decisions. He calls down a malediction on all heretics, in which the entire conference joins, apart, that is to say, from the liberal-minded but boorish Bishop of Budoja, who makes the mistake of praying that they may be enlightened rather than destroyed, and gets a number of dirty looks from his fellow-delegates.

Discussion begins on the subject of the musical side of the church service. The Pope's approval is dependent on a work being written which satisfies ritual considerations. Borromeo announces that such a Mass is being written, and that Palestrina is the composer. The business of the conference proceeds, but points of order seem to be preferred for discussion to points of doctrine. The Spanish envoy objects to the speed at which business is being transacted, and his quarrelsome attitude brings down upon him the objections of a number of delegates based on precedence and the exalted position he has claimed as his by right. Some sense of responsibility returns when the Bishop of Budoja shouts at the top of his voice that peace is the last thing likely to be obtained by such a conference divided against itself, but the meeting again degenerates into nationalist quarrelling and, after quelling the shouts, Morone decides to end the session. He calls the delegates for the afternoon, but warns them that the co-operation of them all, and not least of the Spanish envoy, will be needed if this last session of the conference is to accomplish the tasks set before it.

As soon as the delegates have gone, not without some more sharp remarks, the Spanish servants gather together and mutter that their delegate has been insulted, and it is not long before a free fight develops between the servants. Madruscht appears with soldiers at his back; seeing the disorder, he commands them to open fire and bids them take any survivors they can catch to the torture chambers. No one shall thus defile the Church's Council with unseemly conduct.

Act III. Palestrina's room as in Act I. The composer is sitting in his chair, barely visible to the audience. Five singers from the chapel stand round him, and Ighino is kneeling by his side. The singers express concern for Palestrina's condition, and when he wakes from his trance, he does not seem to recognise them, though they are from his own choir. He asks Ighino why they are waiting and gazing at him. His son tells him that at that very moment his Mass is being sung at the Pope's Palace. He seems not to grasp the significance of this, but refers to being asked some question about it in prison. The others remind him that they gathered together the pages of the Mass he wrote and that they were subsequently taken away from them.

Suddenly there is a noise from the street, and the people can be heard crying: 'Long life to Palestrina, saviour of music!' People crowd into the room, asking for the master, Palestrina, and saying that the Pope has given it as his opinion that the new Mass is Palestrina's best work. The Pope himself is coming to congratulate him! The Holy Father makes his entrance, followed by his Cardinals, amongst them Borromeo, and tells Palestrina of the enormous impression his Mass has made on them all. He must remain in his service until the end of his life.

The Pope leaves, blessing Palestrina and his singers. The Cardinals follow the Pope, all, that is, except Borromeo, who makes a sign to the singers to leave him alone with Palestrina. They look at each other for a moment, then with a cry Borromeo falls on his knees in front of the composer, who puts his hands gently on the Cardinal's head. Palestrina raises the Cardinal to his feet and they stay for a moment in an embrace, before the Cardinal goes quickly from the room.

Ighino, who has watched the scene from concealment, rushes out to ask his father if he is not the happiest man in the world? Maybe, says his father, but he is old and shows his happiness less demonstratively than Ighino. Where is Silla, he asks. He guesses he has gone to Florence, and Ighino confirms his impression. There is more acclamation for Palestrina from outside, and he bids his son laugh and dance and sing if he wants to. He himself remains alone in his room. He goes quietly towards the portrait of his wife, Lucretia, then walks to his organ and plays softly. The crowd is still below shouting praises to his name, and with these sounds in his ears, the curtain falls.                    H.

# ALBAN BERG
## (1885–1935)

### WOZZECK

OPERA in three acts and fifteen scenes by Alban Berg; text adapted by the composer from Büchner's drama of the same name. Première Berlin Staatsoper, December 14, 1925, with Sigrid Johanson, von Scheele-Müller, Leo Schützendorf, Waldemar Henke, Martin Abendroth, conductor Kleiber. First performed Vienna, 1930, with Pauly, Manowarda, conductor Krauss; Amsterdam, 1930, with Brünn, Bitterauf, conductor Pella; Philadelphia, 1931, with Roselle, Ivantzoff, conductor Stokowski; New York, 1931, same cast; London (Queen's Hall, in concert form), with Blyth, Bitterauf, conductor Boult; Rome, 1942, with Gatti, Gobbi, conductor Serafin. Revived Düsseldorf, 1948, with Mödl, Nillius, conductor Hollreiser; Naples, 1949, with Danco, Gobbi, conductor Böhm; Berne, 1951, with Borkh, Fehr, conductor Aesbacher; Salzburg Festival, 1951, with Goltz, Josef Herrmann, conductor Böhm; Covent Garden, 1952, with Goltz, Rothmüller, Parry Jones, Dalberg, conductor Kleiber; New York, City Centre, 1952, with Neway, Rothmüller, conductor Rosenstock; la Scala, Milan, 1952, with Dow, Gobbi, conductor Mitropoulos; Buenos Aires, 1952, with Goltz, Rothmüller, conductor Böhm.

### CHARACTERS

| | |
|---|---|
| Wozzeck, *a soldier* | Baritone |
| The Drum-major | Tenor |
| Andres | Tenor |
| The Captain | Tenor |
| The Doctor | Bass |
| First and Second Workmen | Baritone and Bass |
| A Fool | Tenor |
| Marie | Soprano |
| Margret | Contralto |
| Marie's Child | Treble |

Soldiers, Maids, Servants, Children

Conceived in 1914, when Berg saw a performance of *Wozzek*, the stylistically prophetic play by Georg Büchner (1813–1837), *Wozzeck*'s composition was interrupted by the first world war, in which Berg served. The music was completed in 1921, and in 1923 Universal Edition undertook to publish the opera. In the meanwhile, Berg tried to persuade some opera house or other to mount the work (he was helped by the noted pianist, Eduard

Steuermann, who played the score to one uninterested General-musikdirektor after another). It was eventually accepted by Kleiber for production at the Staatsoper, Berlin, but, eighteen months before the Berlin première, the public had the opportunity of hearing the so-called Fragments from *Wozzeck* (the first half of Act I, Scene iii; Act III, Scene i; and Act III, Scene v and the interlude which precedes it), sung by Sutter-Kottlar and conducted by Scherchen. From that moment *Wozzeck* became a centre of controversy, and musicians and opera-goers alike divided into those who loved and those who loathed the work—in either case, the reaction was often stronger than the reasons which could be found to support the impression.

*Wozzeck* is in three acts, each of five scenes. The music is continuous and often Berg provides no more than a few seconds of interlude music during which the scene change must be made.

Berg himself has related music and drama in the most succinct way in the following key:

| STAGE | Act I | MUSIC |
|---|---|---|
| *Wozzeck in his relationship to his surroundings* | | *Five Character-Pieces* |
| Wozzeck and the Captain | Scene i | Suite |
| Wozzeck and Andres | Scene ii | Rhapsody |
| Marie and Wozzeck | Scene iii | Military March and Lullaby |
| Wozzeck and the Doctor | Scene iv | Passacaglia |
| Marie and the Drum-major | Scene v | *Andante affettuoso (quasi Rondo)* |
| | Act II | |
| *Dramatic development* | | *Symphony in Five Movements* |
| Marie and the Child, later Wozzeck | Scene i | Sonata Movement |
| Captain and Doctor, later Wozzeck | Scene ii | Fantasy and Fugue |
| Marie and Wozzeck | Scene iii | *Largo* |
| Beer-garden | Scene iv | Scherzo |
| Sleeping quarters in the Barracks | Scene v | *Rondo con introduzione* |
| | Act III | |
| *Catastrophe and Epilogue* | | *Six Inventions* |
| Marie with the Child | Scene i | Invention on a theme |
| Marie and Wozzeck | Scene ii | Invention on one note |
| Inn | Scene iii | Invention on a rhythm |
| Wozzeck's death | Scene iv | Invention on a chord of six notes |
| | Orchestral Interlude: Invention on a key | |
| Children at play | Scene v | Invention on quaver figure |

However, the composer himself (in an article published in the *Neue Musik-Zeitung*, 1928, and reprinted in Willi Reich's book on Berg) has given a warning to those people who may be tempted to perform a mental analysis of *Wozzeck* during performance: 'However thorough one's knowledge of the musical forms which are to be found within the opera . . . from the moment when the curtain rises untill it falls for the last time, nobody in the audience ought to notice anything of these various Fugues and Inventions, Suite and Sonata movements, Variations and Passacaglias—everyone should be filled only by the idea of the opera, an idea which far transcends the individual fate of Wozzeck.'

Berg was a pupil of Schoenberg's, and his musical style is influenced by many of his teacher's theoretical and pratical ideas. *Wozzeck* is not, however, composed according to Schoenberg's so-called Dodecaphonic method, although the theme of the Passacaglia in Act II has twelve notes. Key signatures, except in one important instance, are discarded, and the composer makes considerable and subtle use of the *sprechstimme*, best known from Schoenberg's employment of it in *Pierrot Lunaire*. *Sprechstimme* is best described as 'musically defined speech'. Rhythm and intonation are exactly prescribed, but 'in the execution each note is only defined in the moment when it is articulated, immediately afterwards the voice drops or rises as in natural speech'.[1] All authorities are agreed that an over-vocal and *cantabile* style in *sprechstimme* is disastrous, and that the finished result should sound something like the poetic declamation of a good actor.

Act I. The curtain rises in the third bar of the opera on Scene i, which is laid in the Captain's room. It is morning, and the Captain is being shaved by Wozzeck, his soldier-servant. The Captain is a garrulous, digressive individual, and he moralises to the bewildered Wozzeck: if he hurries so much, what will he do with the ten minutes he saves? He puts aside the subject of Eternity, and asks Wozzeck if the wind is not blowing south-north, laughing at the automatic 'Jawohl, Herr Hauptmann' which he gets as answer. The observation that Wozzeck is a good fellow, but without moral sense—witness the fact that he is unmarried but has a child—finally breaks through Wozzeck's preoccupation. Did not the Lord God say 'Suffer little children to come unto me', asks Wozzeck. The Captain's voice rises to a top C in his astonishment at this answer, and Wozzeck explains

[1] Erwin Stein's article on *Wozzeck*, in *Opera*, January 1952.

that only the rich can afford conventional morality (Example 1).

Wir ar-me Leut!

Wozzeck thinks too much, muses the Captain, and he dismisses him with the admonition that he is not to hurry so dreadfully.

Scene ii.    Wozzeck and Andres are cutting sticks at sundown in a field from which can be seen the town. Andres sings to himself, but Wozzeck cannot rid his mind of an impression that the place they are in is haunted. He imagines every sort of thing, babbles of the intrigues of the Freemasons, thinks the ground is going to open under his feet, and is convinced the whole world is on fire when the setting sun colours the horizon red. This short scene contains some of Berg's most dazzling orchestral invention.

Scene iii.    Marie's room; evening. The sound of a military march played behind the scenes makes it quite plain that what Marie is looking at out of the window is the band going back to barracks. The Drum-major waves to her, and she sings happily to the band's tune, so happily in fact that her neighbour Margret

Sol · da - ten, Sol·da -ten sind schö - ne Bur - - -schen!

cannot resist a malicious comment about her lively interest in soldiers. After an exchange of abuse Marie slams the window and shuts out the sound of the band. She sings a lyrical cradle song

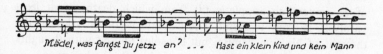

Mädel, was fangst Du jetzt an? - - - Hast ein klein Kind und kein Mann

to her child, before there is a knock at the window, and Wozzeck himself is seen standing there. He cannot come in as it is too late, he has not even time to look at the child which Marie holds up to him. His confused talk worries her and, after he is gone, she rushes out of the door.

Scene iv (the Passacaglia) is laid in the Doctor's study, next day. Wozzeck, in return for a small pittance, is prepared to act as a guinea-pig for the doctor's dietetic experiments. The Doctor complains that Wozzeck does not follow out all his instructions, and his scientific talk further confuses the unhappy man, whose outburst causes the Doctor to suggest that he may well end up in a lunatic asylum. The Doctor is ecstatic about the fame which will result when his new theories are published, and the curtain goes down as he re-examines Wozzeck's tongue.

Scene v.    The street in front of Marie's house, where the Drum-major is posturing to her evident admiration. He assures her that his present finery is as nothing to what he wears on Sundays. Marie repulses him once when he tries to embrace her, but the second time does not resist him, and, with the exclamation 'What does it matter? It's all the same', takes him into her house.

Act II.    In her room, Marie is admiring herself and her new ear-rings in a bit of broken mirror. She tries to get the child to go to sleep, then falls to admiring herself again. Wozzeck comes in, and asks what it is that she is trying to hide. She says she found the ear-rings, and he observes that he has never had the luck to find things like that in pairs. He looks at the sleeping child, then, with a reference to No. 1, reflects that life is nothing but work, and that even in sleep man sweats. He gives Marie the money he has earned from the Captain and the Doctor (to the accompaniment of a string chord of C major) and goes out, leaving her to reflect sadly on her infidelity to him.

Scene ii takes place in the street. The Doctor is hurrying along when he is stopped, in spite of his protests, by his friend the Captain, on whom he revenges himself by giving him details of various fatal cases he has recently seen, ending with a warning that the Captain's own flushed condition may easily be a symptom of an impending apopletic fit, from which death, or at least paralysis, is likely to result. The Captain becomes lyrical at the thought of his own demise, but consoles himself with thoughts of what nice things people will say of him after he has gone.

His reverie is interrupted when Wozzeck comes rapidly down the street—he cuts through the world like one of his own razor blades, says the Captain in a depressed way. The mention of

shaving reminds him of the scandal about Marie and the bearded
Drum-major, and he and the Doctor proceed to torment Wozzeck
with innuendo (has he not lately found a hair of a beard in his
soup?) and even the imitation of a military march. The seriousness with which Wozzeck takes their insinuations quite shocks
his tormentors, and he bursts out with a *fortissimo* imprecation
at the impossibility of finding satisfaction in life. The Doctor feels
his pulse to see if emotion is affecting it, and both he and the Captain
exclaim in surprise as their victim rushes off down the street.

Scene iii takes place in the street in front of Marie's house. It
is the slow movement of the symphony (*largo*) and is scored for
a chamber orchestra of fourteen players, composed according to
the distribution of Schoenberg's *Kammersymfonie*. Marie is standing in front of her house when Wozzeck comes up to her. She is
as beautiful as sin, he says—but how can sin be beautiful? Did *he*
stand there? Marie replies that she cannot control who walks in
the street, and, when Wozzeck looks as though he will strike her:
'Better a knife blade in my heart than lay a hand on me. . . . My
father would never dare when I was little.' Wozzeck repeats her
words in a dazed sort of way as she goes into the house.

Scene iv takes us to a beer-garden, where dancing is in progress
to a slow Ländler played on the stage by a Heurige orchestra
(2–4 fiddles tuned a tone high, clarinet in C, accordeon, several
guitars, a Bombardon in F (Bass Tuba). There is general dancing,
and a couple of exceedingly drunk workmen sing in a maudlin
way of the effect of brandy on the soul. Wozzeck comes in and
sees Marie dancing with the Drum-major; his jealousy grows
until he is about to rush on to the dance floor and separate them,
when the dance stops. The soldiers, with Andres as soloist, begin
a lusty hunting song, ending on a sustained C for the soloist. The
first workman climbs on to a table and starts a most effective
example of one of those wholly logical, wholly nonsensical dis-
courses traditionally associated with the very drunk. It is entirely
conducted in *sprechstimme*, and shows how effective and expressive a medium that can be.

A snatch of the male chorus succeeds the sermon, after which
the Fool appears on the scene, wanders over to where Wozzeck
is sitting, and observes 'Lustig, lustig . . . aber es riecht . . . ich
riech Blut' (Joyful, joyful . . . and yet it reeks . . . it reeks . . . of
blood). The whole rôle contains only thirteen notes, and yet the

tiny scene in which the Fool appears, to a mainly accordeon accompaniment, has an extraordinary and macabre fascination and significance. The dancing begins again and Wozzeck's imagination is obsessed with the idea of blood.

Scene v takes place in Wozzeck's barrack room at night. Before the curtain goes up, the sound of snoring can be heard from the sleeping occupants of the room (the chorus in five parts hum wordlessly with half-open mouths), and as soon as the stage can be seen, Wozzeck is heard complaining to Andres that he cannot sleep for memories of the dance hall. The Drum-major staggers into the room, proclaiming his conquest at the top of his voice and demanding that Wozzeck drink with him. The latter turns away and whistles to himself, whereupon the Drum-major yanks him from where he stands; they fight for a moment, Wozzeck is knocked to the ground, and the Drum-major shakes him and threatens to knock all the breath out of his body. He goes out, leaving Wozzeck staring in front of him. 'He bleeds,' exclaims Andres. The suggestion of blood seems to Wozzeck like fate's prompting: 'One after the other.'

Act III.    Musically, this act is particularly concentrated, and consists of six Inventions (that is Berg's name for them).

Scene i.    Marie's room at night. The solo viola gives out the theme. Marie is reading the story of Mary Magdalen in the Bible, and cannot help comparing what she reads with her own life. She ends with a cry for mercy: 'Saviour . . . as Thou hadst mercy on her, have mercy now on me, Lord!' The scene, which

is of haunting beauty, has *sprechstimme* when Marie reads from the Bible, ordinary singing when she comments on what she has read.

Scene ii.    A pond in the wood, later that night. Wozzeck appears with Marie, whom he prevents from going home as she wishes. He reflects on how long they have known each other, and, when Marie sees the moon rise, draws a knife and cuts her throat, then bends over her: 'Dead!' The interlude consists of two

long *crescendi* on B natural, beginning with a *ppp* solo horn, and
continuing through the whole orchestra until, after a percussive
rhythm, the second *crescendo* takes in the percussion as well.
Straight away the curtain rises on Scene iii, with the hammering
out of a quick polka on an out-of-tune piano. The scene represents an inn. Wozzeck is amongst the dancers. He takes Margret
for partner, and leads her to a table, where he tries to make love
to her. She sings a short song, but stops when she sees blood on
Wozzeck's hand. He makes some attempt to explain it away by
saying he cut his arm, then pushes through the dancers who have
by now crowded round him, and rushes from the room.

Scene iv is laid, once again, at the pond. Wozzeck searches for
the knife, which he dropped after the murder and which would
incriminate him if found. He finds it, pauses for a moment to
look at the body of Marie, then throws the knife into the water,
into which he watches it sink. The whole world seems to him
bathed in blood; he sees spots on his hands and his clothes, and
walks hopelessly into the water to wash it off. It rises to his neck,
but still he walks further, until he has disappeared from sight.
As the Doctor and the Captain come into view and comment on
the sound they hear—the sound of a man drowning, hazards the
Doctor—the orchestra suggests the waters closing over Wozzeck's
head in rising chromatic scales.

The great D minor interlude forms the climax of the opera,

and at the same time a lament for Wozzeck himself, the opera's
hero. Reference is made to music from earlier scenes, and the
themes most closely connected with Wozzeck himself are heard
in ennobled form. 'In this interlude,' says Erwin Stein, 'Berg does
not speak through the medium of the drama, but addresses us
directly. The change of accent is striking and its sincerity makes
us realise why we love Berg's music.'

Scene v takes place in the street outside Marie's house. Children are playing. Apart and playing by himself is Marie's child. Other children come running in, and one of them says that Marie has been found dead. The child cannot take in what it is being told, and goes on playing its game: 'Hopp-hopp, hopp-hopp, hopp-hopp.' The curtain drops slowly.

Wozzeck may not be an exact representation of the 'common man' but he is an artistic projection of one side of his make-up —the side which leads in logical progression from everyday circumstances to the violent consequences which are potentially their outcome. This progression in *Wozzeck* is described in musical language of such potency, in orchestral invention of such overwhelming beauty, and culminates (in the last interlude) in a passage of such compassionate humanity that it is perhaps even now not too early to acclaim the opera as a classic.       H.

# LULU

Opera in three acts by Alban Berg; text adapted by the composer from Wedekind's *Erdgeist* and *Die Büchse der Pandora*. Première in the unfinished form in which it was left by the composer at the time of his death at Zürich, June 2, 1937, with Nuri Hadzic as Lulu, Aster Stig (Dr. Schön), Emmerich (Athlete), Peter Baxeranos (Alwa), Maria Bernhard (Geschwitz), Feichtinger (Gymnasiast), Paul Feher (Painter), Honisch (Schigolch), conductor Denzler. First performed Venice, 1949, with Styx, Rehfuss, Demetz, Zareska, conductor Sanzogno ; Essen, 1953, with Spletter, Jüllich, Peter Walter, Offermanns, conductor König; Hamburg, 1957, with Pilarczyk, Blankenheim, Ruesche, Litz, cond. Ludwig, producer Rennert.

## CHARACTERS

Lulu ....................................High Soprano
Gräfin Geschwitz ..............Dramatic Mezzo-Soprano
A Wardrobe-mistress (Act I) ⎫
A Schoolboy (Gymnasiast) (Act II) ⎬ ..........Contralto
The Doctor ..............................Speaking Part
The Painter ..............................Lyric Tenor
Dr. Schön, *an editor* ...................Heroic Baritone
Alwa, *Dr. Schön's son, a writer* ......Young Heroic Tenor
An Animal-tamer (Prologue) ⎫
Rodrig, *an athlete* (Act II) ⎬ ....................Bass
Schigolch, *an old man* ..............High Character Bass
The Prince, *a traveller in Africa* ..................Tenor
The Theatre Director .......................Buffo Bass

*Lulu*, Berg's second and last opera, is written throughout in the Dodecaphonic system. When the composer died, he had finished Acts I and II, and part of Act III, i.e. part of the big ensemble in the opening scene. In addition, he had sketched, in more or less elaborate form, the whole of the rest of the work, which is to say that, except for some lines in the ensemble, all the words had been set. Some of the music of this Act was included amongst the five Symphonic Pieces from the opera, which he completed beforehand. The Symphonic suite (which requires a singer for performance) consists of (1) *Rondo* (duet Lulu-Alwa, II, i, and end of II, ii), (2) *Ostinato* (Interlude II, i–ii), (3) *Song of Lulu* (II, i), (4) *Variations* (Interlude III, i–ii), (5) *Adagio* (Interlude I, ii–iii, and end of opera, including arietta of Geschwitz).

Prologue. An animal-tamer, accompanied by the clown from his circus, steps in front of the curtain and introduces his troupe, amongst whom is Lulu, dressed in Pierrot's costume.

The curtain goes up on scene i of Act I to reveal a painter's studio, where Lulu, dressed as Pierrot, is being painted. Dr. Schön, a newspaper editor, watches the proceedings. Schön's son, Alwa, enters and is surprised to find Lulu there without her husband. She explains that she expects him at any moment, and Alwa, who works in the theatre, takes his father off to his dress rehearsal, leaving Lulu and the Painter alone. The latter admits he cannot give his mind to his work, and tries to embrace Lulu. He chases her vigorously round the room—the two voices are in canon and begin with Lulu's motif (heard first in the Prologue) and kisses

her hands just before the sound of her husband's furious knocking at the door is heard.

He succeeds in forcing it open, only to collapse at their feet with the shock of finding them in a compromising position. They gradually come to realise he is dead and Lulu comments, with more interest than regret, on his death (*Canzonetta* introduced by saxophone solo). There is a duet for Lulu and the Painter, in which his questions about her beliefs receive the unvaried answer 'I don't know', and the Painter sings an *arioso* when Lulu leaves him alone while she goes to change her clothes.

An interlude leads to scene ii, which takes place in an elegant room in which hangs Lulu's portrait as Pierrot. The Painter, who is now her husband, comes in with the mail, and Lulu reads with amazement a notice of the engagement of Dr. Schön. There follows a light-hearted *Duettino* between her and the Painter, at the end of which the studio bell rings. The Painter looks out and says it is a beggar. He goes off to his studio to work, and Lulu lets in the 'beggar', who turns out to be Schigolch, who is supposed to be her father. He expresses admiration of her present surroundings; she has gone a long way since he last saw her.

As he leaves, Schön enters (Sonata movement begins), recognises Schigolch with some surprise, and then proceeds to tell Lulu that she must stop coming to see him now that he is engaged. She retorts that she belongs to him (the slow beginning of the coda of the sonata's exposition has something of the significance of a love theme); he rescued her from the streets as a child, and anyhow her husband is blind to anything she does, and does not think of her as a person but as his 'little darling', and his 'birdy'.

The Painter enters, Lulu leaves, and Schön first urges him to watch Lulu more carefully, then, as the music gains in urgency, gradually reveals something of her past to him. He himself introduced her to Dr. Goll, her previous husband; it was just after the death of his (Schön's) own wife, and Lulu was doing her utmost to take her place. She has been known by a different name to each of her lovers; Schön calls her Mignon, Dr. Goll called her Nelly, and the Painter refers to her as Eva. The Painter makes as if to go out and talk to Lulu, but presently groans are heard and Lulu and Dr. Schön force open a locked door (rhythmical canon of percussion) to find the Painter lying dead.

The bell rings and Alwa comes in full of excitement at the news that revolution has broken out in Paris. Schön fears that the scandal which will inevitably follow discovery of the Painter's suicide will endanger his own engagement, but, editor-wise, hopes the sensation of the news from France may serve to cover it up. The curtain falls to Lulu's words, sung to her motive: 'You will marry me after all.'

An extended Interlude, in which the love theme is developed, leads to the third scene, which takes place in Lulu's dressing-room behind the scenes in a theatre. Alwa waits for Lulu to come off the stage, and reminds her how, as a young man, he wanted to induce his father to marry her after his mother's death. Lulu replies that she knows perfectly well that Dr. Schön put her on the stage so that somebody rich should fall in love with her and take her off his hands.

She goes out for the next part of her act, and Alwa observes that her life history would make a splendid story for an opera. A Prince, who intends to marry her, enters and launches into extravagant praise of Lulu. There is a noise off-stage, and Lulu is carried in after fainting during her act—an accident caused, Lulu explicitly says, by her having had to dance in front of Schön's prospective bride.

Lulu and Schön are left alone (development section of the Sonata) and a scene ensues between them, Lulu taunting him for not having already married his innocent bride, and for his un-availing attempts to free himself from her domination. In despair, he tries to tear himself away, but she shows herself the stronger (recapitulation of the Sonata) and forces him to write, word by word to her dictation, a letter to his fiancée, breaking off the engagement. The curtain falls as Schön exclaims 'Now comes my execution' (love music). Lulu prepares to continue the act which was interrupted by her fainting fit.

Act II, scene i, takes place in a palatial hall decorated in the German Renaissance style. Gräfin Geschwitz, dressed in clothes of distinctly masculine cut, is paying a call on Lulu, to whom she is obviously very much attracted. Schön, who is now Lulu's husband, is present, and when Lulu has left with Geschwitz, he shows that jealousy has brought him to the verge of madness. He looks behind the curtains, a loaded revolver in his hand, as if he expected to find some lover there. Lulu returns and she and Schön leave the stage together.

No sooner have they gone than Geschwitz sneaks back into the room and conceals herself, just before Schigolch, an Athlete and a Schoolboy come in (the last-named a 'Hosenrolle', or travesty part). The boy is in love with Lulu and Schigolch has acted as go-between in arranging a meeting. They are drinking and smoking when Lulu comes in, but all hide when Alwa is announced. Alwa with rising excitement declares his love for Lulu. She counters that it was she who was responsible years ago for poisoning his mother. Dr. Schön watches the scene from a hiding-place, and catches sight of the Athlete, who is also hiding. Schön leads Alwa, who is no longer in control of himself, from the room, and returns to launch a tirade against Lulu, offering her the revolver, with which he has been pursuing the Athlete, and telling her to use it against herself.

Next he finds Geschwitz and drags her from the room, all the time continuing to urge Lulu to commit suicide. Here follows Lulu's song (it is dedicated by the composer to Anton von Webern); in it, she justifies herself and says she has never tried to seem other than she is. Schön makes another attempt to force the revolver against Lulu, there is a cry for help from the boy, and Lulu fires five shots into Schön's body. The entire scene between Schön and Lulu is built up on an aria of five verses for Schön, the different episodes coming as interruption between the verses.

Lulu is horrified by what she has done; Schön was the only man she has ever loved. Alwa returns, and Schön's last words to him are in the nature of a demand for vengeance. Lulu in an arietta pleads to Alwa for mercy, but the curtain falls as the police appear.

The exciting Interlude between the scenes is designed to accompany a silent and largely symbolical film, showing what happens to Lulu in the time which intervenes. It shows a court scene, during whose course Lulu is condemned for the murder of Schön; her entry into hospital after she has contracted cholera; and the means of escape (about which more later) through the intervention of Geschwitz.

Scene ii takes place in the same set as scene i, the room however looking dirty and ill-kept. Geschwitz, Alwa and the Athlete (dressed as a footman) are together, and from the conversation we gather that Lulu has had cholera, from which Geschwitz has also only just recovered, that Lulu is to be rescued from the prison hospital where Geschwitz will take her place, and that Lulu is going to marry the Athlete. Schigolch takes Geschwitz off to put the plan into execution—we hear that Geschwitz in her passion for Lulu purposely contracted cholera to make the plan of escape possible.

No sooner are Alwa and the Athlete alone than the Schoolboy appears with a plan for Lulu's escape. They try to convince him that she is dead, and hustle him out of the room just before she comes in, supported by Schigolch. The Athlete is so put out when he sees her looking pale and emaciated that he shouts abuse at her, and leaves the room. Schigolch goes off to collect the tickets for Paris, and Alwa and Lulu are alone. After a passionate love duet, they leave together for Paris.

Act III, scene i. An elegant house in Paris, obviously frequented by characters of the demi-monde. The scene is one of activity. Casti Piani, an elegant white-slave trafficker, who knows of Lulu's past, suggests that she should enter a brothel; he threatens to expose her to the police if she declines his suggestion. She refuses and prepares to escape. She dresses up a manservant in some of her clothes and herself puts on boy's clothes and escapes. The police arrive to find only the servant.

Scene ii. An attic in a London slum. Lulu is now on the streets, and with her earnings keeps Alwa and Schigolch. Geschwitz appears from Paris. She has saved Lulu's Pierrot portrait and shows it to them. Several male visitors are brought to the room (one of them takes fright when he sees Geschwitz). Lulu's last pick-up is Jack the Ripper. He murders her and, when Geschwitz tries to come to her aid, kills her as well.

After the first public hearing of the work, Erwin Stein wrote as follows: 'The music itself shows Berg at the height of his musical achievement. It enriches the picture we had already gained of the composer through his very original and important achievements and is another confirmation of the fact that twelve-tone compositions are capable of the greatest variety of expression.

'The lyrical passages . . . are some of the most beautiful things Berg ever wrote. They belong for the most part to the character of Alwa, the contemplative artist who represents the opposite pole to the impulsive Lulu. Not less effective is the drawing of the other characters. The music surrounds every figure with a special atmosphere, showing up the features and giving weight to their miming and gestures. The comic element, represented by Schigolch and the Athlete, is also depicted with incisive humour. Yet the whole is enveloped in sound of a unique character. And in spite of occasional powerful *crescendos*, the orchestration of *Lulu* shows a preference for the delicate, gracious colours befitting the heroine.'                                                H.

# PAUL HINDEMITH
(born 1895)

## MATHIS DER MALER
### Mathias the Painter

OPERA in seven scenes by Paul Hindemith; text by the composer. Première May 28, 1938, Zürich Stadttheater, with Hellwig, Funk, Stig, Baxevanos, Mossbacher, Honisch, Rothmüller, Emmerich, conductor Denzler. First performed Amsterdam, 1939; London, Queen's Hall (concert version), 1939, with Stiles-Allen, Eadie, Noble, Fullard, Parry Jones, Francis Russell, conductor Raybould; Stuttgart (first performance in Germany), 1946, with Wissmann, Stoll, Czubok, Windgassen, von Rohr, conductor Leitner; Munich, 1948, with Schech, Sommerschuh, Reinmar, Klarwein, Kusche, Kuen, Dalberg, Fehenberger, conductor Solti; Berlin Staatsoper, 1948, with Klein, Beilke, Gonzar, Witte, conductor Schuler; Rome, 1951, by company from Stuttgart; Hamburg, 1952, with Wasserthal, Rothenberger, Ahlersmeyer, Melchert, Theo Herrmann, Bensing, conductor Ludwig; Edinburgh Festival, 1952, by Hamburg ensemble (producer Rennert).

### CHARACTERS

Albrecht von Brandenburg, *Cardinal, Archbishop of Mainz* .................................... Tenor
Mathis, *painter in his employment* ............... Baritone
Lorenz von Pommersfelden, *Dean of Mainz* ......... Bass
Wolfgang Capito, *the Cardinal's counsellor* ........ Tenor
Riedinger, *a rich citizen of Mainz: a Lutheran* ....... Bass
Hans Schwalb, *leader of the peasants' army* ........ Tenor
Truchsess von Waldburg, *leader of the Confederate army* ........................................... Bass
Sylvester von Schaumberg, *one of his officers* ....... Tenor
Graf von Helfenstein ........................... Mute
Gräfin von Helfenstein, *his wife* ............... Contralto
Ursula, *Riedinger's daughter* ................... Soprano
Regina, *Schwalb's daughter* .................... Soprano

*Time:* The Peasants' War, about 1525  *Place:* In, and, near, Mainz

Hindemith was a native of Mainz, and for his fifth opera he took as his central figure the early sixteenth-century painter, Mathias Grünewald, who spent much of his life in the service of the Archbishop of Mainz, and who is famous for the great altarpiece of Isenheim. He worked on the opera during the early period of the Nazi regime in Germany, and it is not hard to trace a direct relationship between the political circumstances of Germany at that time and the happenings of the opera, whose philosophical argument had to Hindemith as to Mathis a significance that was practical as well as theoretical.

The story takes place against a background of the Reformation and of the Peasants' War in Germany. It is divided into seven scenes, which are not continuous, and it is customary to have an interval after the fourth scene, by which time the opera has already lasted nearer two hours than one.

The prelude to the opera bears the sub-title of 'Engelkonzert' (Concert of Angels) and is inspired by part of the Isenheim poliptich. It is well known in the concert hall from its position as the first movement of the symphony Hindemith arranged from the music of his opera, and its contrapuntal character is typical of the composer's method in this opera as in so many of his other works.

Scene i takes place in the courtyard of St. Anthony's monastery at Mainz, where Mathis is painting a fresco. The seriousness of purpose which distinguishes the opera is immediately shown in Mathis's introspective monologue, in which his rejoicing at the coming of spring cannot be separated from his doubts as to whether he is worthily fulfilling his mission as a painter. His thoughts are interrupted by the breathless arrival of Schwalb and his daughter Regina, who are seeking sanctuary from the pursuing troops of the Fürstenbund. Mathis extends his help to them, and takes pity on Regina, who, in the midst of her misery, sings a sad little folk-song. Mathis gives her a ribbon with which she binds her hair, but their conversation is interrupted by the return of Schwalb, refreshed and with his wounds bound up. He expresses astonishment that Mathis is content to occupy himself with painting instead of taking part in the struggle for freedom. The painter appears convinced by his argument, and their voices join in an expression of conviction in the importance of the peasants' cause.

Regina rushes in to warn her father that their pursuers are in sight, and Mathis gives them his horse, telling Schwalb that he can in future count on his help. The scene ends after Mathis has admitted to Sylvester that he has helped the rebel leader to escape, and has claimed his right to answer for his actions to no one but the Cardinal.

Scene ii.    The hall in the Martinsburg, the Archbishop's palace in Mainz. The rival factions of Papists and Lutherans dispute while waiting for the arrival of the Archbishop. Pommersfelden stands with the Papists, Capito with the Lutherans, amongst whom can be seen Riedinger and his daughter, Ursula. Peace comes momentarily with the Archbishop's entrance, and all leave the hall except Pommersfelden, Capito, Riedinger and his daughter. Mathis comes in after his year of absence to be greeted with an expansive phrase from Ursula, who is in love with him. A quartet ensues in which Mathis and Ursula talk of their pleasure in seeing each other again, while the Cardinal promises Riedinger that the order to burn Lutheran books shall not be executed in Mainz. Pommersfelden objects that the order is from Rome itself, and the Cardinal reluctantly agrees that it must be carried out.

There is some dispute about the suitability or otherwise of Mathis's representation of the saints in his pictures, which turns before long to a discussion of the empty state of the Cardinal's treasury. Sylvester enters and accuses Mathis before the Cardinal of having helped Schwalb's escape. Mathis admits the accusation but pleads strongly for the peasants' cause, and begs the Cardinal not to furnish the Fürstenbund with the money they have just asked for, but instead to support the juster cause of the rebels; in return, he will serve his patron without payment for the rest of his life. The Cardinal replies that his official conduct is bound by treaties; only where art is concerned has he a free hand. Let Mathis not interfere with what he does not understand. Mathis defies his patron and his prince, and the differing points of view of the Cardinal, Mathis, Pommersfelden, Capito, and the warlike Sylvester are combined in a noble quintet. The scene ends with Mathis receiving permission to withdraw from the Cardinal's service.

Scene iii.    A room in Riedinger's house; in the background can be seen the preparations for the public burning of the Lutheran books. Riedinger and his friends attempt to hide their treasured possessions, but soldiers assisted by Capito carry them off. Capito appeases the wrath of the Lutherans by showing them a letter purporting to have come from Luther to the Cardinal in which he urges him strongly to give a lead to the clergy by renouncing his celibacy. Capito's scheme is to persuade the Cardinal, who is in urgent need of money, to make a rich marriage—and with whom more suitable than Riedinger's daughter, Ursula, who at that moment comes into the room. Riedinger himself hints at what is planned for her before he leaves Ursula, to join his fellow-Lutherans as their books are burnt in the market-place, a scene that is suggested by the chorus in the background.

Mathis appears to bid Ursula farewell. She welcomes him exultantly, and tells him how much she has missed him during his year of leave from the Cardinal's service. He answers that his spirit is sick within him and he must leave her and his work to join in the struggle for freedom; only through contact with misery can he recover his own soul. They protest their undying love for each other, but their duet ends with the cry: 'The love, the unity in which we have lived, gives way to suffering.' Mathis embraces Ursula and goes out.

When Riedinger asks her how she can preserve her calm during the calamity which has befallen those who share her religious beliefs, Ursula says she has made up her mind to accept the sacrifice demanded of her by her faith. Riedinger rejoices and proclaims that the fire lit by their enemies has signalled the beginning of a new period of determination which shall end in victory.

Scene iv.    The rebellious peasants have seized a war-ravaged village and are terrorising the local nobility. They drag in Count Helfenstein and his wife, and kill the Count almost before her eyes. Mathis protests against this betrayal of the principles for which they are fighting, and tries to defend the Countess from their molestations, but he is knocked down. Only the advent of Schwalb saves him from further injury. The peasants' leader calls them all to arms to fight the Fürstenbund army, which is even now entering the village. But they are already downhearted at the prospect of meeting trained troops, and soon come back in disorder. Schwalb himself is trapped and falls before the lances of his enemies, who come through the village to the sound of a march. Mathis only escapes with his life through the Countess's intervention, and he comes to understand his own complete failure as a man of action; his lofty ambitions, his efforts to better the lot of the peasants have ended in this. He sees Regina,

overcome with horror at her father's death, and takes her away
with him to look for shelter.

Act II. Scene v.    The Cardinal's study in the Martinsburg in
Mainz. Capito has been trying to persuade the Cardinal to renounce his oath of celibacy and to adopt the course Luther
advocates, and marry. His most cogent argument is that a rich
wife would solve the Cardinal's very considerable financial difficulties; but Albrecht resents Capito's attempt to interfere with
his conscience, and to treat him as if he were not capable of
making up his own mind. Capito tries flattery, and then introduces Ursula as the prospective bride. The Cardinal is astonished
to see her. In music of ever increasing fervour she explains to
him that only her abiding faith in Lutheranism would have driven
her to the position in which she now finds herself. Love has grown
cold within her, but she is willing to submit to marriage for the
sake of the cause she loves.

The Cardinal calls Capito and Riedinger into the room and
tells them that he is convinced by Ursula's show of faith: her
example has shown him that he too must stand by what he has
been taught. He dismisses Capito from his post as adviser, saying
he will lead a simpler life in the future; and he gives permission
to the Lutherans to declare themselves openly. There is an impressive quartet between the Cardinal, Ursula, Capito, and
Riedinger, and at its end Ursula asks the Cardinal to bless her
before she goes out again into the world. He consents to do this,
and Ursula departs, leaving behind her a man whom she has
enobled by teaching him at one and the same time the meaning
of Faith and of Tolerance.

Scene vi.    In the Odenwald, Mathis and Regina pause during
their flight. Regina says she still dreams she is pursued by the
image of her dead father. Mathis tries to calm her by describing
to her his vision of the Concert of Angels, accompanied in the
orchestra by the music we originally heard in the prelude. Together they sing the chorale ('Es sungen drei Engel'), also heard
in the prelude, until Regina falls asleep and Mathis despairingly
contrasts his present spiritual misery with the comparative state
of grace in which he painted the picture he has just described.

In the manner of the Temptation of St. Anthony, Mathis is
tempted by Luxury, wearing the face of the Countess; by wealth
(Pommersfelden); a beggar, a courtesan, and a martyr (Ursula);

scholarship (Capito); and a knight in shining armour (Schwalb). They enter successively, Mathis answers each in turn, and the music works up to a climax when the demons appear to torment the Saint. There is a great ensemble, at whose end the Cardinal, in the guise of St. Paul, comes to comfort and advise St. Anthony (part of the Isenheim altar depicts the Conversation between St. Paul and St. Anthony). St. Anthony asks what he has done that he should have reached his present state of uncertainty. St. Paul tells him that he has been untrue to himself. In throwing in his lot with the people, he has denied the gifts he had from God, and has in fact withdrawn from the people he tried to help. Let him return to his art, denying himself but dedicating his work to God. In so doing he will become part of the people. The tree knows nothing of its fruits. At the end of the vision, in which the composer speaks his mind on the subject of the artist, the two voices join together in a paean of praise, ending with a magnificent 'Alleluiah'.

It is the crucial scene of the opera (Hindemith has used the themes from it as a basis for the last movement of his Symphony), and it was presumably from the Temptation section of the Isenheim altar and the Conversation of St. Anthony and St. Paul that Hindemith initially drew inspiration for his theme and his central figure.

Scene vii.     Mathis's studio in Mainz. Mathis is lying asleep, exhausted with his work, and Ursula watches alone by the side of the dying Regina. Ursula reflects on the meaning of their lives, and on Mathis's unprecedented inspiration since his return to Mainz and to art. Regina wakes and raves about the memory of her dead father, whose face she can see in Mathis's painting of the Crucifixion. She asks Ursula to give Mathis the ribbon which she originally received from him at their first meeting, and Ursula recognises it as one she herself had given Mathis. Regina sings a couple of sentences of the chorale, before dying with Mathis by her side.

The interlude, marked 'Very slowly', is entitled 'Entombment', and serves as the slow movement of the symphony. At its end, the curtain rises to show the studio empty except for a table, on which lie several objects. The Cardinal comes to say farewell to Mathis, embracing him for the last time. Mathis himself takes a case and puts away materially and symbolically the things which have represented the main efforts of his life. It is in this spirit of utter humility that the opera ends.

Hindemith's concentration on the issues at stake has never blinded him to the necessity for putting them forward dramatically within the framework he has chosen; he makes no concessions, but he works in terms of opera as a medium. One may feel that the text is inordinately long and therefore often set without much regard for expression; that Hindemith cannot get rid of his tendency to settle down to a busy contrapuntal style the moment he is at a loss for an idea; that some of his themes seem rather slight for the weight they are asked to carry—even if all this is true, no listener who is seriously interested in opera can come away from a performance of the work without having been impressed by Hindemith's lofty conception of the artist's responsibility, and his equally lofty view of what opera can and must accomplish. Intense seriousness of purpose does not by itself secure artistic results, but integrity shines through *Mathis*, and the opera is perhaps strongest in the composer's conviction in his theme and its expression.                                    H.

# CHAPTER 15

# Italian Opera in the Twentieth Century

# ERMANNO WOLF-FERRARI
## (1876-1948)

### I QUATTRO RUSTEGHI
### The School for Fathers

OPERA in four acts by Ermanno Wolf-Ferrari; text by G. Pizzola from Goldoni; German text by H. Teibler. Première Munich, March 19, 1906. First performed Teatro Lirico, Milan, 1914; la Scala, Milan, 1922, with Labia, Soster, Fabbri, Azzolini, Scattola, conductor Panizza; Bueno Aires, 1927, with Cobelli, Cravcenco, Marengo, Azzolini, Vanelli, conductor Panizza; Berlin, 1937, with Berger, Heidersbach, Marherr, Spletter, Prohaska, Neumann, Helgers, Fleischer; Sadler's Wells, London, 1946, with Gruhn, Jackson, Hill, Iacopi, Glynne, Franklin, conductor Robertson; New York City Centre, 1951, with Faull, Yeend, Mayer, Russell, Pease, Scott, conductor Halasz.

#### CHARACTERS

Lunardo, *Venetian merchant* (Mr. Crusty) ...........Bass
Margarita, *his second wife* (Margery) ......Mezzo-Soprano
Lucieta, *his daughter by his first wife* (Lucinda) ....Soprano
Maurizio, *merchant* (Mr. Hardstone)..Bass or Bass-Baritone
Filipeto, *his son* (Peter) .........................Tenor
Marina, *aunt to Filipeto* (Maria) ................Soprano
Simon, *her husband* (Mr. Gruff).............Bass-Baritone
Canciano, *a wealthy merchant* (Sir James Pinchbeck)...Bass
Felice, *his wife* (Felicia)....................... Soprano
Count Riccardo Arcolai, *a visitor to Venice* .........Tenor
A Young Maid

Time: End of the eighteenth century        Place: Venice
(The names given in brackets were those used for the successful Sadler's Wells production, in Professor Dent's translation, when the scene was transferred from Venice to London.)

Ermanno Wolf-Ferrari has set to music more than one of Goldoni's Venetian comedies, which, written mostly in dialect, have a somewhat limited appeal. *I Quattro Rusteghi* is probably the finest of them all. The character-drawing is finished and the action moves quickly to its climax. The provincial colours of the picture have militated against rapid and wide acceptance of the opera, as of the comedy. But Germany has given it a welcome and the London production, whose translator, Professor Dent, transferred the action from Venice to London, has met with success.

The 'rusteghi' (in no sense 'rustics') are the honest, plain-speaking, conservative, domestic tyrants who, believing that woman's place is the home, forbid anything that might enliven the tedium of domestic work. It is on this conflict between old prejudices and a more generous understanding of woman's function in life that the plot of the comedy rests. It has been called a comedy of bad manners.

Act I.     Lunardo's wife, Margarita, and her step-daughter, Lucieta, are sitting knitting and embroidering. It is carnival and their thoughts turn to the amusements and gaiety of more fortunate people. Margarita remembers that before marrying Lunardo there were parties at home and occasional visits to the theatre. Lucieta is of marrying age and hopes for a husband and better times. Lunardo enters silently, desiring to speak with his wife yet unwilling to interrupt her occupation. When the two are finally alone he tells her as an important secret that he and his friend Maurizio have arranged to wed Lucieta to Maurizio's son, Filipeto. The fact that the young people have never seen each other is, to them, immaterial. Margarita's very reasonable objections are rudely ignored. Lunardo's will is law. He answers Margarita's arguments with: 'I am the master.' Maurizio is announced and Margarita retires. The two 'rusteghi' now discuss the details of the contract—Lucieta's dowry, her clothes (no silk but good, honest home-spun), jewels which must not be re-set as the fashionable people do who thus pay twice for the gems. The dour, rigid character of the domestic bears is well described in this scene.

The second part of the act takes us to the house of Marina and her husband—even more of a 'rustego' than Lunardo. Marina is singing the tune familiar to everyone from its use as an interlude before Act II. Filipeto enters and begins by asking whether his uncle is in. He is in great dread of his uncle and means to avoid him. The purpose of his visit is to enquire whether his aunt has heard anything about his own wedding. His father has informed him abruptly that he intends to give him a wife and the homely youth is flustered, yet determined not to marry a girl he does not like; he begs his aunt to help him. If having seen the girl he does not like her, he will run away rather than marry her: ('Lucieta! xe un bel nome'; 'Lucinda! her name at least is pretty'). Simon arrives and unceremoniously dismisses Filipeto. Marina has another caller, the talkative Felice, accompanied by her husband and her 'cavalier servente', Count Riccardo. The husband, Canciano, stands mute and disapproving. The two women put their heads together determined that the men shall not be allowed to have it all their own way.

Act II.    The act is preceded by the famous intermezzo, which serves admirably as an example of the composer's light, graceful style:

When the curtain rises, we are back in Lunardo's house. Lucieta has persuaded Margarita to lend her a few trinkets but Lunardo arrives on the scene and orders the girl to take off her borrowed finery. They are joined by Marina and Simon. When the women retire the men rail at them and lament the passing of the good old days when women were women and did as they were told: ('What has become of the old sort of women?'). The appearance of Felice is the signal for their departure. The other women join her, and Lucieta is congratulated on her betrothal. 'Shall I see my future husband?' she asks and hears that Felice and her friends have found a way to bring the young people together. It is carnival and Filipeto, escorted by Riccardo, plans to arrive disguised as a girl. If they should be discovered they will pass him off as a distant female relative. He soon arrives, and in a very charming little scene Marina persuades him to take off the mask. Meanwhile the men have settled their business and Filipeto's father, Maurizio, has gone off to bring the youth to the betrothal. Now Lunardo surprises the women who have just time to hide Filipeto in a closet and Riccardo in another. The situation is tense. Maurizio returns very angry with the news that Filipeto is not to be found anywhere. All that is known is that he left the house with Riccardo. Canciano then begins to show himself in his true colours. He dislikes Riccardo; he will have no dealings with him; he must be an imposter. But Riccardo is a man of spirit and hearing all that Canciano is saying comes out of hiding and challenges him. Filipeto is found, the whole conspiracy discovered, and a very angry Lunardo orders the callers to leave his house. There will be no wedding for Lucieta.

Act III.    The act begins with Lunardo, Simon, and Canciano considering in gloom the wickedness of the women's conduct. What is the next step to be? Lucieta can be sent away to the country but how can the other women be punished? The plain truth is that the women are necessary to their own comfort and, if they were sent away, the men themselves would suffer. This homely commination is interrupted by the arrival of Felice. She is received with hostility at first, for she is the arch-plotter. But her arguments are unanswerable, and, delivered with the speed and accuracy of aim which she commands, irresistible. What harm has been done? Would it not have been much worse if the young people had *not* liked each other's looks? Slowly, slowly the men begin to relent and finally and not very graciously are won over. The opera ends like a fairy story with wedding bells.

At the time of the first performance of the opera at Sadler's Wells (1945), *The Times* wrote as follows of the music: 'It flows spontaneously; it has a touch of distinction which saves it from the obvious; it is technically modern yet picks up the *opera buffa* tradition of the eighteenth century with the utmost grace and learning; it has a vein of lyrical melody and excels in ensemble.'

F.B.

# IL SEGRETO DI SUSANNA
## (Susanna's Secret)

Opera in one act by Ermanno Wolf-Ferrari; text by Enrico Golisciani (German version by Kalbeck). Première, Munich, December 4, 1909 (in German), conductor Mottl. First performed New York (by Chicago company), 1911, with Carolina White and Sammarco; Rome, 1911; Covent Garden, 1911, with Lipkowska, Sammarco; Metropolitan, 1912, with Farrar, Scotti, conductor Polacco. Revived la Scala, Milan, 1917, with Vallin, Parvis, conductor Panizza; Covent Garden, 1919, with Borghi-Zerni, Sammarco, conductor Coates; Metropolitan, 1921, with Bori, Scotti; la Scala, 1934, with Oltrabella, Biasini; London Opera Club, 1950, with Dyer, Noble. The little opera is a direct descendant of the eighteenth-century *Intermezzo*.

## CHARACTERS

Count Gil, *aged thirty* ........................Baritone
Countess Susanna, *his wife, aged twenty* ..........Soprano
Sante, *their servant, aged fifty* .....................Mute

*Time:* The present                                    *Scene:* Piedmont

After a short overture, suitably labelled *vivacissimo*, the curtain
rises to show a handsome apartment in the Count's house. Gil in
walking clothes enters hurriedly: 'The light grey cloak, pink hat
and feather . . . could I be mistaken?' He goes out quickly, and
a moment later Susanna comes in wearing a grey cloak, and a
pink hat. She gives her coat and hat and a parcel to the servant,
and goes out again, having first made sure that her husband is in
his room. No sooner has she gone than Gil reappears, and listens
at the door of *her* room, seeming relieved to find that she is there.
He must be mistaken—and yet: he has distinctly caught a smell
of tobacco in his house—and he is a non-smoker. He catches himself out being unmistakably jealous. He questions Sante whether
he is a smoker . . . or his mistress? The old servant shakes his
head at each question. Who can it be then?

Gil is in even more of a state by the time Susanna comes into
the room. He greets her, and comments on having seen someone
just like her while he was out walking; it could not be her because
he has forbidden her to go out alone. But why does she blush?
Only because he is unkind for the first time. Rapturously, Gil
assures her of his undying, unswerving devotion: 'Il dolce idillio';
a love duet follows, and at its end Gil is about to embrace his
wife, when he smells the hated tobacco smell. She is horrified that
he should notice—she knows how much he hates the smell—and
he thinks he has turned suspicion that she is visited by an admirer
into certainty. In a moment they are at cross purposes: Susanna
suspects he knows her secret—'If I'm left at home and you're late
at the club, the time goes quicker. . . . Do like other husbands,
and shut one eye discreetly to my little secret'; but Gil suspects
something quite different, and smashes the vases in his fury.
Susanna escapes to her room ('to have a good cry'), and Gil
throws himself into a chair in a paroxysm of grief. Sante surveys
the room in comic dismay, and proceeds to tidy up the mess.

After an intermezzo, during which Sante gets the room straight
again, Susanna comes out and brings Gil his gloves, hat, and

umbrella; she is sure he must want to go out. Just before he goes, she sings sweetly to him; will he not give her a word of love, one tender look, before he goes ('Via, cosi non mi lasciate')? He relents to the extent of kissing her on the forehead, and departs.

Susanna, alone, relaxes and Sante brings her the cigarettes she has been out to buy. No sooner has she lit one than Gil is heard knocking at the door. He hunts everywhere but finds no one, only the smell of tobacco. Beside himself with rage, he goes out again. This time, Susanna has time to sing an aria to the cigarette for whose refreshing perfume she so yearns: 'O gioija, la nube leggiera.' But she is not undisturbed for long. Gil suddenly appears through the window, and confronts his wife. She puts her hand behind her back, he snatches to see what she is hiding, and burns himself. The secret is out: she smokes. All is forgiven, and they each light a cigarette, dancing round each other with joy.

H.

# I GIOJELLI DELLA MADONNA
## The Jewels of the Madonna

Opera in three acts by Ermanno Wolf-Ferrari; text by Golisciani and Zangarini; German version by H. Liebstöckl. Première Berlin, December 2, 1911; Chicago and New York, 1912, with White, Bassi, Sammarco; Covent Garden, 1912, with Edvina, Martinelli, Sammarco; Metropolitan, New York, 1926, with Jeritza, Martinelli, Danise, conductor Papi. Revived Covent Garden, 1925, with Jeritza, Merli, Noto, conductor Bellezza; Chicago, 1940, with Giannini, Jagel, Czaplicki, conductor d'Abravanel.

### CHARACTERS

Gennaro, *a blacksmith* . . . . . . . . . . . . . . . . . . . . . . . . . . Tenor
Maliella, *adopted daughter of Carmela* . . . . . . . . . . . Soprano
Rafaele, *leader of the Camorrists* . . . . . . . . . . . . . . . . Baritone
Carmela, *Gennaro's mother* . . . . . . . . . . . . . . . . Mezzo-Soprano
Biaso, *a scribe* . . . . . . . . . . . . . . . . . . . . . . . . . . . . . . . . . Tenor
Cicillo, *a Camorrist* . . . . . . . . . . . . . . . . . . . . . . . . . . . . . Tenor
Stella . . . . . . . . . . . . . Soprano
Concetta . . . *friends of Camorrists* . . . . . . . . . . . . . . Soprano
Serena . . . . . . . . . . . . . Contralto
Rocco, *a Camorrist* . . . . . . . . . . . . . . . . . . . . . . . . . . . . . . Bass

Grazia, a dancer; Vendors, Monks, Populace

*Time:* The present                              *Place:* Naples

Act I.    A small square in Naples, near the sea. Carmela's house, Gennaro's smithy, an inn, and the little hut of Biaso, the

PLATE XXXV. *Wozzeck* at Covent Garden 1952. (above) The inn scene, with Marko Rothmüller as Wozzeck.

(below) After the murder of Marie; Rothmüller and Goltz.

PLATE XXXVI. Strawinsky's *The Rake's Progress*, Stuttgart 1951; producer Kurt Puhlmann, designer Leni Bauer Ecsy. (above) Tom Rakewell at Mother Goose's establishment.

(below) The scene in the grave-yard; Richard Holm as Tom Rakewell, Gustav Neidlinger as Nick.

scribe, among many other details. 'It is the gorgeous afternoon of the festival of the Madonna, and the square swarms with a noisy crowd, rejoicing and celebrating the event with that strange mixture of carnival and superstition so characteristic of Southern Italy.' This describes most aptly the gay, crowded scene, and the character of the music with which the opera opens. It is quite kaleidoscopic in its constant shifting of interest. At last many in the crowd follow a band, which has crossed the square.

Gennaro in his blacksmith's shop is seen giving the finishing touches to a candelabra on which he has been working. He places it on the anvil, as on an altar, kneels before it, and sings a prayer to the Madonna—'Madonna, con sospiri' (Madonna, tears and sighing).

Maliella rushes out of the house pursued by Carmela. She is a restless, wilful girl, possessed of the desire to get away from the restraint of the household and throw herself into the life of the city, however evil—a potential Carmen, from whom opportunity has as yet been withheld. Striking an attitude of bravado, and in spite of Gennaro's protests, she voices her rebellious thoughts in the 'Canzone di Cannetella',—'Diceva Cannetella vedendosi inserata' (Thus sang poor Cannetella, who yearned and sighed for her freedom).

A crowd gathers to hear her. From the direction of the sea comes the chorus of the approaching Camorrists. Maliella and the crowd dance wildly. When Carmela reappears with a pitcher of water on her head, Maliella is dashing along the quay screaming and laughing.

Carmela tells her son the brief story of Maliella. Once when he was ill as a baby, she vowed to the Madonna that she would adopt a baby girl and treat her as her own daughter if only her beloved son were allowed to recover. There is a touching duet for mother and son ('T'eri un giorno ammalato bambino'), in which Carmela bids him go and pray to the Madonna, and Gennaro asks for her blessing before he leaves to do so. Carmela then goes into the house.

Maliella runs in. The Camorrists, Rafaele in the van, are in pursuit of her. Rafaele, the leader of the band, is a handsome, flashy blackguard. When he advances to seize and kiss her, she draws a dagger-like hat pin. Laughing, he throws off his coat, like a duellist, grasps and holds her tightly. She stabs his hand, making it bleed, then throws away the skewer. Angry at first, he laughs disdainfully, then passionately kisses the wound. While the other Camorrists buy flowers from a passing flower girl and make a carpet of them, Rafaele picks up the hat pin, kneels before Maliella, and hands it to her. Maliella slowly replaces it in her hair, and then Rafaele, her arms being uplifted, sticks a flower she had previously refused, on her breast, where she permits it to remain. A few moments later she plucks it out and throws it away. Rafaele picks it up, and carefully replaces it in his buttonhole. A little later he goes to the inn, looks in her direction, and raises his filled glass to her, just at the moment when, although her back is toward him, a subtle influence compels her to turn and look at him.

Tolling of bells, discharge of mortars, cheers of populace, announce the approach of the procession of the Madonna. While hymns to the Virgin are chanted, Rafaele pours words of passion into Maliella's ears. The image of the Virgin, bedecked with sparkling jewels—the jewels of the Madonna—is borne past. Rafaele asseverates that for the love of Maliella he would even rob the sacred image of the jewels and bedeck her with them. The superstitious girl is terrified.

Gennaro, who returns at that moment, warns her against Rafaele as 'the most notorious blackguard in this quarter'; at the same time he orders her into the house. Rafaele's mocking laugh infuriates him. The men seem about to fight. Just then the procession returns, and they are obliged to kneel. Rafaele's looks, however, follow Maliella, who is very deliberately moving toward the house, her eyes constantly turning in the Camorrist's direction. He tosses her the flower she has previously despised. She picks it up, puts it between her lips, and flies indoors.

Act II.    The garden of Carmela's house. On the left wall a wooden staircase. Under this is a gap in the back wall shut in by a railing. It is late evening.

Carmela, having cleared the table, goes into the house. Gennaro starts in to warn Maliella. She says she will have freedom, rushes up the staircase to her room, where she is seen putting her things together, while she hums, 'E 'ndringhete, 'ndranghete' (I long for mirth and folly).

She descends with her bundle and is ready to leave. Gennaro pleads with her. As if lost in a reverie, with eyes half-closed, she recalls how Rafaele offered to steal the jewels of the Madonna for her. Gennaro, at first shocked at the sacrilege in the mere suggestion, appears to yield gradually to a desperate intention. He bars the way to Maliella, locks the gate, and stands facing her. Laughing derisively, she reascends the stairs.

Her laugh still ringing in his ears, no longer master of himself, he goes to a cupboard under the stairs, takes out a box, opens it by the light of the lamp at the table, selects from its contents several skeleton keys and files, wraps them in a piece of leather, which he hides under his coat, takes a look at Maliella's window, crosses himself, and sneaks out.

From the direction of the sea a chorus of men's voices is heard. Rafaele appears at the gate with his Camorrist friends. To the accompaniment of their mandolins and guitars he sings to Maliella a lively waltz-like serenade: 'Aprila, o bella, la fenestrella.' The girl, in a white wrapper, a light scarlet shawl over her shoulders, descends to the garden. There is a love duet: she promises that on the morrow she will join him. Then Rafaele's comrades signal that someone approaches.

Left to herself, she sees in the moonlight Gennaro's open tool box. As if in answer to her presentiment of what it signifies, he appears with a bundle wrapped in red damask. He is too distracted by his purpose to question her presence in the garden at so late an hour and so lightly clad. Throwing back the folds of the damask, he spreads out on the table, for Maliella, the jewels of the Madonna.

Maliella—in an ecstasy, half mystic, half sensual, and apparently seeing in Gennaro the image of the man who promised her the jewels, Rafaele, who has set every chord of passion in her nature vibrating—no longer repulses Gennaro, but, when at the foot of a blossoming orange tree he seizes her, yields herself to his embrace. The scene is described in the libretto with a realism that leaves no doubt as to its meaning.

Act III.    A haunt of the Camorrists on the outskirts of Naples. On the left wall is a rough fresco of the Madonna, whose image was borne in procession the previous day. In front of it is a sort of altar.

The Camorrists gather. They are men and women, all the latter of doubtful character. There is singing with dancing—the 'Apache', the 'Tarantelle'. Stella, Concetta, Serena, and Grazia the dancer, are the principal women. They do not anticipate Maliella's expected arrival with much pleasure. When Rafaele comes in, they ask him what he admires in her. In his answer, 'Non sapete . . . di Maliella la preziosa qualita' (Know you not of Maliella), he tells them her chief charm is that he will be the first man to whom she has yielded herself.

In the midst of an uproar of shouting and dancing, while Rafaele, standing on a table, cracks a whip, Maliella rushes in. In an agony she cries out that, in a trance, she gave herself up to Gennaro. The women laugh derisively at Rafaele, who has just sung of her as being inviolable to all but himself. There is not a touch of mysticism about Rafaele. That she should have confused Gennaro with him, and so have yielded herself to the young blacksmith, does not appeal to him at all. For him she is a plucked rose to be left to wither. Furiously he rejects her, flings her to the ground. The jewels of the Madonna fall from her cloak. They are readily recognised, for they are depicted in the rough fresco on the wall.

Gennaro, who has followed her to the haunt of the Camorrists, enters. He is half mad. Maliella, laughing hysterically, flings the jewels at his feet, shrieking that he stole them for her. The crowd, as superstitious as it is criminal, recoils from both intruders. The women fall to their knees. Rafaele curses the girl. At his command, the band disperses. Maliella goes out to drown herself in the sea. 'Madonna dei dolor! Miserere!' prays Gennaro. His thoughts revert to his mother: among the débris he finds a knife and plunges it into his heart.                    K.

# ITALO MONTEMEZZI
## (1875-1952)

### L'AMORE DEI TRE RE
#### The Love of Three Kings

OPERA in three acts by Italo Montemezzi; text by Sem Benelli, from his play of the same name. Première la Scala, Milan, April 10, 1913, with Villani, Ferrari-Fontana, Galeffi, de Angelis, conductor Toscanini. First performed Metropolitan, New York, 1914, with Bori, Ferrari-Fontana, Amato, Didur, conductor Toscanini; Covent Garden, 1914, with Edvina, Crimi, Cigada, Didur, conductor Moranzoni. Revivals include Metropolitan, 1926, with Ponselle, Gigli, Danise, Didur, conductor Serafin; 1939, with Jepson, Tokatyan, Bonelli, Pinza, conductor Papi; 1949, with Kirsten, Kullman, Weede, Lazzari; la Scala, 1926, with Cobelli, Lo Giudice, Morelli, de Angelis, conductor Toscanini; 1932, with dalla Rizza, Piccaluga, Morelli, Lazzari, conductor de Sabata; 1937, with Scuderi, Marcato, Tagliabue, Pasero, conductor Marinuzzi; 1948, with Petrella, Francesco Albanese, Guarrera, Rossi-Lemeni, conductor Capuana; Covent Garden, 1930, with Ponselle, Merli, Inghilleri, Autori (later Pinza), conductor Bellezza; Buenos Aires, 1938, with Rethberg, Jagel, Galeffi, Pinza, conductor Serafin; San Francisco, 1941, with Moore, Kullman, Weede, Pinza, conductor Montemezzi.

### CHARACTERS

Archibaldo, *King of Altura* ........................Bass
Manfredo, *son of Archibaldo* ...................Baritone
Avito, *a former prince of Altura* ..................Tenor
Flaminio, *a castle guard* ........................Tenor
Fiora, *wife of Manfredo* .......................Soprano
A youth, a boy child (voice behind the scenes), a voice behind the scenes, a handmaiden, a young girl, an old woman, other people of Altura.

*Time:* The Tenth Century     *Place:* A remote castle of Italy, forty years after a Barbarian invasion, led by Archibaldo

This opera is one of the most successful products of modern Italian genius, more popular, it must be admitted, in America, where it has been frequently performed, than in its native Italy. Based upon a powerful tragedy by Sem Benelli, one of the foremost of Italian playwrights, it is a combination of terse, swiftly moving drama with a score which vividly depicts events progressing fatefully toward an inevitable human cataclysm. While there are few set-pieces in Montemezzi's score, nevertheless it is melodious—a succession of musical phrases that clothe the words, the thought behind them, their significance, their most subtle suggestion, in the weft and woof of expressive music. It is a medieval tapestry, the colours of which have not faded, but still glow with their original depth and opulence.

Act I.    The scene is a spacious hall open to a terrace. A lantern employed as a signal sheds its reddish light dimly through the gloom before dawn.

From the left enters Archibaldo. He is old with flowing white hair and beard, and he is blind. He is led in by his guide Flaminio, who is in the dress of the castle guard. As if he saw, the old blind king points to the door of a chamber across the hall and bids Flaminio look and tell him if it is quite shut. It is slightly open. Archibaldo in a low voice orders him to shut it, but make no noise, then, hastily changing his mind, to leave it as it is.

In the setting of the scene, in the gloom penetrated only by the glow of the red lantern, in the costumes of the men, in the actions of the old king, who cannot see but whose sense of hearing is weirdly acute, and in the subtle suggestion of suspicion that all is not well, indicated in his restlessness, the very opening of this opera immediately casts a spell of the uncanny over the hearer. This is enhanced by the groping character of the theme which accompanies the entrance of Archibaldo with his guide, depicting the searching footsteps of the blind old man.

There is mention of Fiora, the wife of Archibaldo's son, Manfredo, who is in the north, laying siege to an enemy stronghold. There also is mention of Avito, a prince of Altura, to whom Fiora was betrothed before Archibaldo humbled Italy, but whose marriage to Manfredo, notwithstanding her previous betrothal, was one of the conditions of peace. Presumably—as is to be gathered from the brief colloquy—Archibaldo has come into the hall to

watch with Flaminio for the possible return of Manfredo, but the
restlessness of the old king, his commands regarding the door
opposite, and even certain inferences to be drawn from what he
says, lead to the conclusion that he suspects his son's wife and
Avito. It is also clear—subtly conveyed, without being stated in
so many words—that Flaminio, though in the service of Archibaldo, is faithful to Avito, like himself a native of the country
which Archibaldo has conquered.

When Flaminio reminds Archibaldo that Avito was to have
wedded Fiora, the blind king bids his guide look out into the
valley for any sign of Manfredo's approach. 'Nessuno, mio
signore! Tutto è pace!' is Flaminio's reply. (No one, my lord!
All is quiet!)

Archibaldo, recalling his younger years, tells eloquently of his
conquest of Italy, apostrophising the ravishing beauty of the
country, when it first met his gaze, before he descended the mountains from which he beheld it. He then bids Flaminio put out the
lantern, since Manfredo comes not. Flaminio obeys; then, as there
is heard in the distance the sound of a rustic flute, he urges upon
Archibaldo that they go. It is nearly dawn, the flute appears to
have been a signal which Flaminio understands. He is obviously
uneasy, as he leads Archibaldo out of the hall.

Avito and Fiora come out of her room. The woman's hair
hangs in disorder around her face, her slender figure is draped in
a very fine ivory-white garment. The very quiet that prevails fills
Avito with apprehension. It is the woman, confident through
love, that seeks to reassure him.

For the moment Avito is reassured. There is a brief but passionate love scene. Then Avito perceives that the lantern has been extinguished. He is sure someone has been there, and they are spied upon. Once more Fiora tries to give him confidence. Then she herself hears someone approaching. Avito escapes from the terrace into the dim daylight. The door on the left opens and Archibaldo appears alone. He calls 'Fiora! Fiora! Fiora!'

Concealing every movement from the old man's ears, she endeavours to glide back to her chamber. But he hears her.

'I hear thee breathing! Thou'rt breathless and excited! O Fiora, say, with whom hast thou been speaking?'

Deliberately she lies to him. She has been speaking to no one. His keen sense tells him that she lies. For when she sought to escape from him, he heard her 'gliding thro' the shadows like a snowy wing'.

Flaminio comes hurrying in. The gleam of armoured men has been seen in the distance. Manfredo is returning. His trumpet is sounded. Even now he is upon the battlement and embraced by his father. Longing for his wife, Fiora, has led him for a time to forsake the siege. Fiora greets him, but with no more than a semblance of kindness. With cunning, she taunts Archibaldo by telling Manfredo that she had come out upon the terrace at dawn to watch for him, the truth of which assertion Archibaldo can affirm, for he found her there. As they go to their chamber, the old man, troubled, suspecting, fearing, thanks God that he is blind.

Act II.     The scene is a circular terrace on the high castle walls. A single staircase leads up to the battlements. It is afternoon. The sky is covered with changing, fleeting clouds. Trumpet blasts are heard from the valley. From the left comes Manfredo with his arms around Fiora. He pleads with her for her love. As a last boon before he departs he asks her that she will mount the stairway and, as he departs down the valley, wave to him with her scarf. Sincerely moved to pity by his plea, a request so simple and yet seemingly meaning so much to him, she promises that this shall be done. He bids her farewell, kisses her, and rushes off to lead his men back to the siege.

Fiora tries to shake off the sensation of her husband's embrace. She ascends to the battlemented wall. A handmaid brings her an inlaid casket, from which she draws forth a long white scarf. The orchestra graphically depicts the departure of Manfredo at the head of his cavalcade.

Fiora sees the horsemen disappear in the valley. As she waves the veil, her hand drops wearily each time. Avito comes. He tells her it is to say farewell. At first, still touched by the pity which she has felt for her husband, Fiora restrains her passionate longing for her lover, once or twice waves the scarf, tries to do so again, lets her arms drop, her head droop, then, coming down the steps, falls into his arms open to receive her, and they kiss each other as if dying of love. 'Come tremi, diletto' (How thou art trembling, beloved!) whispers Fiora.

'Guarda in su! Siamo in cielo!' (Look up! We are in heaven!) responds Avito.

But the avenger is nigh. He is old, he is blind, but he knows. Avito is about to throw himself upon him with his drawn dagger, but is stopped by a gesture from Flaminio, who has followed the king. Avito goes. But Archibaldo has heard his footsteps. The king orders Flaminio to leave him with Fiora. Flaminio bids him listen to the sound of horses' hoofs in the valley. Manfredo is returning. Fiora senses that her husband has suddenly missed the waving of the scarf. Archibaldo orders Flaminio to go meet the prince.

The old king bluntly accuses Fiora of having been with her lover. Cowering on a stone bench that runs around the wall, she denies it. Archibaldo seizes her. Rearing like a serpent, Fiora, losing all fear, in the virtual certainty of death at the hands of the powerful old man who holds her, boldly vaunts her lover to

him. Archibaldo demands his name, that he and his son may be
avenged upon him. She refuses to divulge it. He seizes her by
the throat, again demands the name, and when she still refuses
to betray her lover, throttles her to death. Manfredo arrives.
Briefly the old man tells him of Fiora's guilt. Yet Manfredo cannot hate her. He is moved to pity by the great love of which her
heart was capable, though it was not for him. He goes out slowly,
while Archibaldo hoists the slender body of the dead woman
across his chest, and follows him.

Act III.    The crypt of the castle, where Fiora lies upon her
bier with white flowers all about her, and tapers at her head and
feet. Around her, people of her country, young and old, make
their moan, while from within the chapel voices of a choir are
heard.

Out of the darkness comes Avito. The others depart in order
that he may be alone with his beloved dead, for he too is of their
country, and they know. 'Fiora! Fiora!—È silenzio!' (Fiora!
Fiora!—Silence surrounds us) are his first words, as he gazes
upon her.

Then, desperately, he throws himself beside her and presses his
lips on hers. A sudden chill, as of approaching death, passes
through him. He rises, takes a few tottering steps toward the door.

Like a shadow, Manfredo approaches. He has come to seize
his wife's lover, whose name his father could not wring from her,
but whom at last they have caught. He recognises Avito. Then
it was he whom she adored.

'What do you want?' asks Avito. 'Can you not see that I can
scarcely speak?'

Scarcely speak? He might as well be dead. Upon Fiora's lips
Archibaldo has spread a virulent poison, knowing well that her
lover would come into the crypt to kiss her, and in that very act
would drain the poison from her lips and die. Thus would they
track him.

With his last breath, Avito tells that she loved him as the life that they took from her, aye, even more. Despite the avowal, Manfredo cannot hate him; but rather is he again disposed to wonder at the vast love Fiora was capable of bestowing, yet not upon himself.

Avito is dead. Manfredo, too, throws himself upon Fiora's corpse, and from her lips draws in what remains of the poison, quivers, while death slowly creeps through his veins, then enters eternal darkness, as Archibaldo gropes his way into the crypt. The blind king approaches the bier, feels a body lying by it, believes he has caught Fiora's lover, only to find that the corpse is that of his son.

Such is the love of three kings; of Archibaldo for his son, of Avito for the woman who loved him, of Manfredo for the woman who loved him not.

Or, if deeper meaning is looked for in Sem Benelli's powerful tragedy, the three kings are in love with Italy, represented by Fiora, who hates and scorns the conqueror of her country, Archibaldo; coldly turns aside from Manfredo, his son and heir apparent with whose hand he sought to bribe her; hotly loves, and dies for a prince of her own people, Avito. Tragic is the outcome of the conqueror's effort to win and rule over an unwilling people. Truly, he is blind.                                                  K.

# FERRUCCIO BUSONI

## (1866–1924)

### TURANDOT

A Chinese fable in two acts, after Gozzi; music by Ferruccio Busoni, text by the composer. The music was developed from incidental pieces written for Reinhardt's production of Gozzi's play in Berlin, 1911. Première Zürich, May 11, 1917. First performed Frankfurt, 1918; Berlin, 1921, with Lola Artot de Padilla, Ober, conductor Blech. Revived Venice Festival, 1940, with Carbone, Limberti, Ziliani, Colella, conductor Previtali; Hamburg, 1948, with Werth, Melchert, conductor Grüber.

### CHARACTERS

| | |
|---|---|
| The Emperor Altoum | Bass |
| Turandot, *his daughter* | Soprano |
| Adelma, *her confidante* | Mezzo-Soprano |
| Calaf, *a young, unknown prince* | Tenor |
| Barak, *his faithful servant* | Baritone |
| The Queen Mother of Samarkand, *a negress* | Soprano |
| Truffaldino, *chief eunuch* | High Tenor |
| Tartaglia ⎱ *Altoum's ministers* ⎰ | Bass |
| Pantalone ⎰ | Bass |
| Eight Doctors | Tenor, Bass |
| A Singer | Mezzo-Soprano |

Slaves, Weeping Women, Eunuchs, Soldiers, a Priest, Dancers

*Time:* Antiquity                    *Place:* The Far East

The action follows in the main the course which has become familiar to opera-goers through Puccini's opera of the same name.

Act I.    An introduction in march rhythm leads to the first scene. The stage is empty when the curtain rises, but Calaf dashes through the gates and rapturously greets the city of Peking. His old servant Barak recognises him; not having seen him for so long, he had thought he was dead. Calaf tells him that his father, Timur, is also alive, and that he himself is looking for fortune in Peking. Barak tells him the story of Turandot and the riddles, whereupon Calaf laughs and seems unable to take the riddles too seriously, even though he catches sight of some heads impaled on spears at Turandot's order. Barak points to the procession which is at that moment going by, mourning the Prince of Samarkand, who has been put to death that very day. The lament is led by the Prince's mother, an aged negress. At its end, she curses Turandot, and throws the portrait of the princess from her. Barak comments that even the portrait of Turandot is said to enslave those who gaze upon it. Calaf picks it up, looks at it, and in an arioso piece proclaims his love for its subject. He determines to try his luck.

Scene ii.     Truffaldino comes in front of the curtain and, in a high piping tenor, summons some slaves.

Slow, solemn music heralds the appearance of the Emperor Altoum, Turandot's father, who is preceded by wise doctors and attendants. The Emperor complains about his daughter's cruel behaviour, while his two comic advisers, Pantalone and the stuttering Tartaglia, gather about to flatter him. In a short aria, the Emperor prays to Confucius that he may at long last win a son in the coming trial between the stranger and Turandot. He commands that the unknown suitor be brought before him. Trumpets sound, and Calaf throws himself at the Emperor's feet. The old man is immediately impressed by the stranger's looks; who is he? Calaf answers that he is a prince, but his name must remain unknown for the present. The Emperor bids him retire now if he wants to withdraw from what is likely to prove an unequal contest, but Calaf's reply is that he desires only death or Turandot; for him there can be no third alternative. Altoum offers him honours and riches if he will renounce the trial. Pantalone and Tartaglia add their voices in an effort to dissuade Calaf, but he is adamant. The brilliant quartet ends as Calaf reaffirms his determination on a series of top A's.

Turandot enters, veiled. She demands to know who dares to match his wisdom with hers, but, when she catches sight of the stranger, admits to herself that she is moved by the sight of him. The chorus softly agrees that he is different from the other suitors, and Adelma, Turandot's confidante, in an aside recognises the prince as the young man she once fell in love with when she was a girl. Calaf again denies that there is any possibility for him but Turandot or death; Turandot's rejoinder is that his death will be her death.

The Emperor suggests that Turandot ask three easy riddles, so that the form of the trial may be honoured; after that the wedding between her and her unknown suitor can take place. Turandot refuses; the riddles are laid down by law. Truffaldino rings a bell and announces each riddle in turn. They are on a more metaphysical plane than those in Puccini's opera (see p. 657), and the answers are respectively Human Understanding, Morals, Art. After Calaf has guessed the second, Turandot offers to let her suitor free and to forego the last question. He refuses, but when Turandot unveils herself as she asks the third question, it looks as though he is lost. However, he pulls himself together and answers the third as he has the first two.

The Emperor and his entourage are delighted with Calaf's success; he calls for music, and the rejoicing is general. Turandot admits she has lost, but says the shame is more than she can bear; at the altar she will kill herself. Calaf admits that his victory is hollow if she still hates him. He offers her a fourth chance; he will himself ask her a riddle. What is his name? Calaf reflects that he who reaches his peak of happiness is fuller of sorrow than he was before.

Act II.    The chorus and its leader sing before the curtain goes up showing Turandot's room. Slaves dance and sing for the entertainment of Turandot and Adelma, but Turandot stops them abruptly and sends them away. She cannot make out her own feelings: does she love the victorious stranger after all? She knows that if she were to give way she would soon regret it. Turandot shall die untouched, is her decision. Her big aria is highly dramatic and, in spite of its greater economy, almost as taxing for the singer as the music Puccini wrote for his heroine.

Truffaldino comes in. He had headed the band of Turandot's followers whose duty it was to discover the stranger's name. His aria is exactly calculated for the high, thin voice which has characterised him throughout the opera. When he asked the stranger his name, he says, he got the answer 'Death or Turandot'.

The Emperor comes to see his daughter. He tells her he knows the stranger's name, but nothing will make him tell her; the stranger is too good for her, and he is glad that she will be humiliated in front of the whole world. Turandot faces him bitterly—he will be sorry for his unjust words to her when she faces the stranger on the following day. She turns in her misery to Adelma. Adelma says the Emperor is not alone in knowing the prince's name. In a pathetic, proud tune, Adelma says that the princess has just addressed her as 'friend', and yet keeps her a slave, in spite of her royal birth; if she will give her her freedom she will in return reveal the stranger's name which she knows. Turandot starts to protest, but Adelma says that the prince once laughed at her when she was a girl, and she wants revenge more than anything in the world. Turandot greets her as sister, and Adelma whispers into her ear as the curtain falls.

An intermezzo leads to the last scene, which takes place in the throne-room. Drums beat the rhythm of a funeral march, during which Tartaglia and Pantalone lament, asking themselves the while what the sound of mourning can be about. They are answered by the Emperor; it is for Turandot, no one else. Turandot at first agrees that it is for her, and Calaf admits that he is deeply grieved at the misery which his success induces in her. The Emperor thereupon orders gay music, but suddenly Turandot rounds on them and admits that the funeral music was part of her scheme to make her revenge the sweeter. She knows the stranger's name: Calaf! She dismisses Calaf, to the Emperor's obvious sorrow, and her suitor turns to go, saying that he will easily find death in the wars. As he turns to go, however, Turandot herself calls him back by name. She welcomes him as her husband, and the general lamentation is instantly turned to rejoicing, not least for the Emperor, for whom this means an end of sorrow.

H.

# ARLECCHINO

Opera in one act by Ferruccio Busoni, text by the composer. Première Zürich, May 11, 1917, with Alexander Moissi as Arlecchino. First performed Frankfurt, 1918; Berlin, 1921, conducted by Blech; Vienna, 1926; London (B.B.C.), 1939; Venice Festival, 1940, with Tellini, Mazziotti, Gelli, conductor Gui; Glyndebourne, 1954, with Malbin, Dickie, conductor Pritchard. Revived Berlin Staatsoper, 1946, with Beilke, Witte, conductor Schüler.

## CHARACTERS

Ser Matteo del Sarto, *a tailor* . . . . . . . . . . . . . . . . . . . Baritone

Abbate Cospicuo . . . . . . . . . . . . . . . . . . . . . . . . . . . . Baritone

Dottor Bombasto . . . . . . . . . . . . . . . . . . . . . . . . . . . . . . . Bass

Harlequin . . . . . . . . . . . . . . . . . . . . . . . . . . . Speaking Rôle

Leandro . . . . . . . . . . . . . . . . . . . . . . . . . . . . . . . . . . . . Tenor

Annunziata, *Matteo's wife* . . . . . . . . . . . . . . . . . . . . . . . Silent

Columbine, *Arlecchino's wife* . . . . . . . . . . . . . Mezzo-Soprano

*Time:* Nineteenth Century                    *Place:* Bergamo

Busoni called *Arlecchino* 'ein theatralisches Capriccio' (a theatrical caprice), and Professor Dent in his biography of the composer has suggested that it is in the nature of a play for puppets. As if to emphasise this, Harlequin speaks a prologue in which he warns the audience not to take the play too literally; it is all in the spirit of a proverb.

The work is in four parts, each corresponding to an aspect of Harlequin; we see him as rogue, as soldier, as husband, and as conqueror. A quick, lively introduction leads to the first scene. Matteo is sitting in front of his house, sewing at his leather and reading Dante to himself. In a window upstairs, Harlequin can be seen making love to Matteo's wife. Matteo comments on his reading, which reminds him, he says, of opera (the orchestra plays a bit of 'Fin ch'han dal vino' from *Don Giovanni*). Harlequin wonders how he is to get away. In the end he jumps blatantly out of the window, and, when Matteo seems surprised to see him, says to him in an agitated way, 'Don't you know the barbarians are surrounding the town?', which frightens and upsets the good man to such an extent that he forgets where Harlequin came from. In his confusion, Matteo drops the key to his front door, and Harlequin picks it up and locks the door from outside, putting the key into his pocket when he has finished. Harlequin can be heard singing gaily from behind the scenes as he goes off.

The doctor and the abbé come into sight, arguing together rather in the manner of the doctor and the captain in *Wozzeck*. The abbé sings a song in praise of Tuscany and its wine. Their slanging match abates, and they knock up Matteo, who is absent, they notice, from his usual place in front of his house. In a trio in which a march theme is prominent, he explains about the barbarians who are surrounding the town—all their daughters will be ravished and their friends killed—and asks why they have not taken refuge themselves. They say they will go off and consult the Burgomaster about the invasion, and they disappear laughing in the direction of the tavern.

Harlequin reappears dressed as a recruiting sergeant, with two supporters behind him. The music is a parodistic reference to the march from *La Figlia del Reggimento*. He tells Matteo he is wanted immediately for the army; there can be no discussion. Matteo asks for permission to take his Dante with him, and then, to the sound of a funeral march, he is marched away by the two stooges.

A minuet starts in the orchestra as Harlequin tries the key he has had copied from Matteo's; it fits, but at that moment he is spoken to from behind. He turns to find it is no other than his own wife, Columbine. Why, she demands in an aria, is he so cruel and unfaithful to her? She starts to flatter him—she would do everything for him, if he would only let her—but it is no use, and, distracting her attention for a moment, Harlequin disappears.

Columbine is determined to find out what Harlequin was after in this particular house, but at that moment she hears the tenor voice of Leandro singing a romance, and she is quite unable to resist it. Leandro hears her version of her story, and immediately offers to revenge her honour. His first song is a parody of romantic German song, his second of a classical Italian equivalent. There is a flowery love scene for the two, which is almost too much for Columbine. At any rate, she enquires whether Leandro is not being just the least little bit sloppy in the aria he is singing; let her wait for the *stretta*, is his answer. Harlequin comes on the scene, announces that Columbine is his wife, leads her off into the tavern, and draws his wooden sword to fight Leandro. He knocks him out with the flat of his sword, and, shouting 'murder' at the top of his voice, disappears into the house of Matteo.

Columbine emerges from the tavern, together with the abbé and the doctor, who are both by now very drunk. They remember that they have to see the Burgomaster about the barbarians who are invading the town, but the subject does not appear to be entirely clear in their minds. Suddenly, the doctor stumbles over the body of Leandro. With a shriek, Columbine recognises it. The other two start to wonder what they are to do at this hour of night with the body of a dead man. On further investigation, Columbine decides he is not dead after all, which suggestion at first causes consternation in the minds of the other two. However, they eventually come round to her way of thinking, and try to enlist the help of the neighbours; heads appear at the windows, but are immediately withdrawn when it becomes known what is wanted of them. The doctor and the abbé are sad but philosophical about the whole affair. Suddenly a donkey appears hitched to a cart. It is the work of providence, is the comment.

In a quartet, the abbé prays, Leandro returns to consciousness, the doctor comments on the medico-philosophical aspects of the affair, and Columbine pours scorn on all men impartially. In the end, all get into the donkey cart, and drive off.

Harlequin looks down from the window of Matteo's house and waves to them as they go, rejoicing in his freedom. He comes out, bringing Matteo's wife with him and they go off together. Matteo is seen coming towards his house. He has been deserted by his companions, presumes that peace has been concluded, and has returned home. He finds his wife has left the house, and so philosophically gets out his Dante and his sewing as before, and starts to read where he left off. The passage has to do with infidelity. . . .

A drop-curtain falls. In pairs, the various characters, including the donkey and his driver, come to make their bows to the audience. Last comes Harlequin and Annunziata, Matteo's wife; Harlequin speaks an epilogue: he introduces Annunziata to them —they have not been lucky enough to see much of her during the evening—and then asks what the moral of the story is to be. Everything is new, everything goes on as before, is his conclusion; but his advice to the audience is that they should make up their own minds.

The stage directions suggest that if a second curtain call is needed, the drop should be raised to reveal Matteo still sitting and sewing and reading and waiting.

'Few of Busoni's compositions gave him so much satisfaction as *Arlecchino*,' says Professor Dent in his biography (O.U.P. 1933). 'Both from a literary and musical point of view he regarded it as his most individual and personal work. One reason for its lack of popularity up to the present is that it demands an unusual alertness of mind on the part of the spectator. The libretto is extremely terse in style, and was considerably reduced in the process of setting it to music, for Busoni was always determined to make the musical form the deciding factor in his works for the stage. With the older composers this principle led to the expansion of the libretto by frequent repetition of the words; with Busoni it led to compression.'    H.

## DOKTOR FAUST

Opera in six tableaux (two prologues, one scenic interlude, and three scenes); text by the composer. The opera was not quite complete at the composer's death, and the last scene was finished by his pupil Philipp Jarnach. Première Dresden, May 21, 1925, with Meta Seinemeyer, Theo Strack, Robert Burg, conductor Fritz Busch. First performed Berlin, 1927, with Leider, Schorr, Soot; London, Queen's Hall (concert), in English translation by E. J. Dent, 1937, conducted by Boult, with Blyth, Parry Jones, Noble, Wendon; Florence Festival, 1942, with Oltrabella, Renato Gigli, Manacchini, conductor Previtali; Berlin 1954, with Fischer-Dieskau.

### CHARACTERS

| | |
|---|---|
| Doktor Faust | Baritone |
| Wagner, *his famulus, later Rector of Wittenberg University* | Baritone |
| A Man Dressed in Black | |
| A Monk | |
| A Herald | *Mephistopheles in his various disguises* |
| A Chaplain | Tenor |
| A Courier | |
| A Night-watchman | |
| The Duke of Parma | Tenor |
| The Duchess of Parma | Soprano |
| The Master of Ceremonies | Bass |
| The Girl's Brother, *a soldier* | Baritone |
| A Lieutenant | Tenor |
| Three Students from Cracau | Tenor, Two Basses |
| A Theologian | Bass |
| A Jurist | Bass |
| A Doctor of Natural History | Baritone |
| Four Students from Wittenberg | Four Tenors |
| Gravis | Bass |
| Levis | Bass |
| Asmodus | *spirit voices* Baritone |
| Beelzebub | Tenor |
| Megärus | Tenor |
| Sixth Voice (Mephistopheles) | Tenor |

Church-goers, Soldiers, Courtiers, Hunters, Catholic and Lutheran Students, Countrypeople

Busoni drew his text from the old puppet-play of *Faust*, and he is indebted to Goethe only for the richness and nobility of the language in which he has expressed his conception—he was, of course, a life-long student and devotee of Goethe. *Doctor Faust* represents the summing-up of his life's work.

The orchestral prelude is in the nature of an 'impressionistic study of distant bells'.[1] Towards the end of the prelude the chorus behind the scenes can be made out singing the single word 'Pax' (Professor Dent has pointed out that this part of the work was written at Zürich in 1917). The curtain goes up and an actor steps out in front of a drop-curtain to recite the verse prologue, in which Busoni explains how the subject came to be chosen.

He disappears and the first scene is revealed: Faust's study in Wittenberg, where he is superintending some alchemical process. Wagner tells him that three students are asking to see him, and, when Faust seems reluctant to receive them, explains that they have with them a remarkable book, called 'Clavis Astartis Magica'. Faust is excited; this is perhaps the book which will give him the magic power he has so long sought. The three young men, dressed in black, enter Faust's room, and announce themselves as students from Cracau. Faust is reminded of his youth, with its hopes and its dreams and its plans. The students give him the book, a key with which to unlock it, and a letter which makes it his property. He offers them hospitality, but they decline it, and take their leave. Will he see them again? 'Perhaps' is their only answer. Wagner returns, and Faust wonders why he does not show the visitors out. He saw no one, says Wagner, and Faust begins to understand the identity of the strangers. The pots on the hearth begin to hiss and crackle.

When the curtain rises on the second prologue, the scene is unchanged. It is night. With the key in hand which the students have given him, Faust loosens his girdle and with it draws a magic circle. Standing inside it, he calls upon Lucifer to send down his servant. Six tongues of flame appear hovering in the air. Each of them represents one of Lucifer's intimates; Faust questions the first five—how fast is each?—and dismisses each with contempt at the answer he gets. He steps out of the circle and seems reluctant to question the last spirit in case it too should disappoint him. A voice addresses him by name, and proclaims that it is as fast as human thought. 'The scene with the six flames,' says Professor Dent, 'is conceived musically as a set of variations on a theme; the first spirit is a deep bass, and the voices rise

[1] E. J. Dent, *Ferruccio Busoni* (O.U.P.).

progressively, so that the last—Mephistopheles—is a high tenor'. Mephistopheles's musical entrance is wickedly exacting, as he is asked to sustain successively a high A natural, a B flat, and a B natural, and the phrase in which he boasts of the speed ends on a sustained C natural.

Faust appears satisfied by the answer of the sixth voice, and he summons him to appear in physical shape. Of Mephistopheles, Faust makes an unusual demand: 'Give me for the rest of my life the unconditional fulfilment of every wish; let me embrace the world, the East and the South that call me; let me understand the actions of mankind and extend them; give me Genius! give me its pain too, that I may be happy like no other—make me *free*.'[1] But Faust has stepped outside the magic circle, and Mephistopheles will only agree to serve him at a price: after he has done Faust's bidding, Faust must agree to serve him for ever. Faust says he will serve no one, and is about to dismiss him like the others, when Mephistopheles reminds him that his creditors are at the door, that the brother of the girl he has deceived is searching for him to kill him, and that no help but the devil's will suffice to extricate him from his predicament.

Faust reluctantly agrees to Mephistopheles's bargain, and the scene ends as he signs the agreement. During the later part of the scene, an unseen chorus sings the 'Credo' and the 'Gloria' and the curtain falls as an 'Alleluiah' is heard.

The Intermezzo takes place in the Romanesque side-chapel of a great cathedral. The whole scene is dominated by the sound of the organ—Professor Dent says that Busoni 'wanted the organ to be no mere background; it was to fill the whole theatre with its reverberation. Unfortunately there are few theatres which possess organs of sufficient power to carry out the composer's design.' A soldier, described as the 'girl's brother', is praying that he may be enabled to avenge her seduction. Mephistopheles points him out to Faust and then sets about the task of removing him. He takes on the aspect of a monk and kneels beside the soldier, who does his best to get rid of him. Suddenly, soldiers appear in the doorway and point out the soldier as the man who killed their captain. They fall upon him and kill him, leaving Mephistopheles triumphant; sacrilege and murder—and both laid to Faust's account—seems pretty good going for one day.

[1] E. J. Dent, *Ferruccio Busoni* (O.U.P.).

The main part of the action now begins. The scene is laid at the court of the Duke of Parma who has just married a beautiful wife. The celebrations are suggested by the orchestral Cortège with which the scene starts (this in an extended form constitutes the second part of the 'Sarabande and Cortège from *Dr. Faust*', which is sometimes heard in the concert hall). Having regard to the end of this scene (when Faust elopes with the Duchess), it is hardly surprising that the music for all its brilliance has a sinister tang to it. The pageant and ballet which introduces the rejoicing also makes use of Busoni's *Tanzwalzer*, a composition dating from 1920 and dedicated to the memory of Johann Strauss; in this respect, it is unlike the Sarabande and Cortège which date from the same year, but were always intended as sketches for *Dr. Faust*.

The master of ceremonies proposes that the Duke and his newly wed Duchess shall receive Faust, by now famous throughout the world for his learning, and reputedly a man of sinister reputation. Mephistopheles is on hand as Faust's herald, and he announces his master, who makes a distinguished appearance, with (according to the stage directions) either black boys or monkeys carrying his train. The chorus welcomes him and expresses open admiration; the Duchess whole-heartedly concurs with such sentiments but the Duke has misgivings lest the rumours about him prove true.

Faust is greeted by the Duke, and proceeds to show his powers by turning light into darkness. He asks the Duchess what he shall do for her delectation; ask for something impossible, suggests the Duke. She would like to see Solomon, she declares; in a moment he appears before them, with the Queen of Sheba at his side. The Duke is quick to notice that the Queen has a look of the Duchess about her, and that Solomon closely resembles Faust. For her next wish, the Duchess insists that Faust shall not only perform it but divine beforehand what it is. Samson and Delilah appear; under Delilah's bed hides a black slave holding the fatal shears ready to her mistress's hand. Once again the visions wear the features of the Duchess and Faust. The third apparition is conjured up by Faust of his own accord; Salome and John the Baptist stand before the court, and near them the executioner. Again, the protagonists seem to have borrowed the masks of Faust and his noble hostess, and this time the executioner resembles the Duke. 'At a word from Salome, his head falls,' comments Faust. 'He must not die,' answers the Duchess eagerly. Faust is confident that the Duchess loves him.

The Duke makes an end of the performance by inviting Faust to the ducal table, but Mephistopheles dissuades his master, warning him that the food is poisoned, and together they leave the stage. For a moment, no one is visible, but presently the Duchess comes into sight once more, convinced that Faust is calling her. She sings rapturously of her love for him, then goes slowly out. Her voice can be heard calling off-stage.

It is suddenly daylight. The Duke of Parma is in excited conversation with his Chaplain, who tells him that the Duchess has eloped with Faust; he saw them disappear together on winged horses. It would be best to hush everything up and marry the sister of the Duke of Ferrara, who otherwise threatens war. The Duke accepts his Chaplain's counsel, and as the curtain falls, we see the hand raised in blessing turn to a claw as it emerges from his sleeve. The Chaplain was Mephistopheles in disguise.

The Sarabande, an extended and solemn orchestral piece described as a symphonic intermezzo, ushers in the last act. The scene is an inn at Wittenberg, where Faust sits drinking and discussing philosophy with his students. The discussion soon approaches a quarrel, and Faust does his best to calm things down: nothing can be proved, he says; let them follow Luther's example. ... He has not even time to get out Luther's name when the company divides into Catholics and Protestants, and a Latin *Te Deum* is heard in violent opposition to *Ein' feste Burg*.

Faust sits pensively aside until one of the students asks him to tell them of his amorous adventures with women. The orchestra *sotto voce* remembers the Cortège, and Faust starts to tell them of the most beautiful woman he ever loved, a Duchess, on her wedding day, only a year ago. Does she ever think of him now, he wonders. At that moment, in comes Mephistopheles in the guise of a messenger. The Duchess of Parma, who has just died, sends something to Faust for a remembrance. At Faust's feet he places the corpse of a new-born baby, to the general horror of the company. He proceeds to tell Faust's story in unromantic terms, and caps it by setting fire to the bundle, which was only straw. From the smoke he summons Helen of Troy.

At this point Mephistopheles leaves Faust alone. Faust raves of his dream of beauty but, just as he seems about to grasp the vision, it disappears into nothing, and he is alone once more. He turns to see three dark figures standing in the shadow, and demanding the return of the book, the key and the letter which went with them. Faust motions them away: he has destroyed what they are demanding from him. They tell him his hour has come, but he has nothing but contempt for them, and welcomes the end of his life.

The scene changes to a street in Wittenberg. It is winter, snow is on the ground, the Night-watchman's voice informs the citizens that ten has struck (it is Mephistopheles in the last of his disguises). Students congratulate Wagner on his opening speech as Rector of the University, where he has succeeded Faust.

Faust comes in, recognises Wagner's house as once his, listens as the *Dies Irae* is sung in the church, and sees a beggar woman opposite, a child in her arms. He gives her some money, but, as soon as he sees her, knows her as the Duchess. She gives him the child, saying that she has already tried twice to do so. It is dead. She disappears. Faust tries to get into the church to pray, but his way is barred by the soldier who was killed in the Romanesque church. Faust removes him—his power still extends to spirits—and tries to pray before a crucifix at the side of the church door. But he cannot find words, and, when the light from the Night-watchman's lantern shines on the crucifix, he sees the form of Helen of Troy upon it.

With a cry of horror he turns away, then masters himself for a supreme trial of strength. (At this point Busoni's score ends; the rest of the opera is finished by Jarnach.[1]) Faust lays the dead body of the child on the ground and covers it with his cloak. He throws his girdle on the ground, and steps within the circle. He exerts his will in a final effort to project his personality into the body of the child. May his faults be rectified in this child, and may it accomplish what he has failed to do. He dies, and as the Watchman announces midnight, a naked youth with arms uplifted and bearing a green twig in his hand, rises from Faust's body and walks unconcernedly through the snow. The Night-watchman lifts his lamp and looks down at the dead body. Has this man had an accident, he asks?                    H.

[1] At one time, there was talk of asking Schoenberg to undertake the completion.

# RICCARDO ZANDONAI

## (1883–1944)

### FRANCESCA DA RIMINI

OPERA in four acts by Riccardo Zandonai; text by Tito Ricordi after d'Annunzio's play of the same name. Première Teatro Regio, Turin, February 19, 1914. First performed Covent Garden, 1914, with Edvina, Martinelli, Cigada, conductor Panizza; la Scala, Milan, 1916, with Raisa, Pertile, Danise; Metropolitan, 1916, with Alda, Martinelli, Amato, conductor Polacco; Chicago, 1917, with Raisa, Crimi, Rimini. Revived la Scala, 1929, with dalla Rizza, Pertile, Maugeri, conductor Panizza; 1937, with Cigna, Parmeggiani, Maugeri, conductor Zandonai; 1942, with Somigli, Ziliani, Maugeri, conductor Guarnieri; 1946, with Carbone, Ziliani, Stabile, conductor Guarnieri; 1950, with Caniglia, Prandelli, Biasini, conductor Capuana.

### CHARACTERS

| | | |
|---|---|---|
| Francesca | ⎫ *the son and daughters of Guido* | Soprano |
| Samaritana | ⎬ *Minore of Polenta* | Soprano |
| Ostasio | ⎭ | Baritone |
| Giovanni lo Sciancato (the lame) | ⎫ | Baritone |
| Paolo il Bello (the handsome) | ⎬ *sons of Mala-testa of Ver-rucchio* | Tenor |
| Malatestino dall'occhio (the one-eyed) | ⎭ | Tenor |
| Biancofiore | ⎫ | ............Soprano |
| Garsenda | ⎬ | ............Soprano |
| Altichiara | ⎬ *Francesca's women* | ......Mezzo-Soprano |
| Donella | ⎬ | ......Mezzo-Soprano |
| The Slave | ⎭ | ............Contralto |
| Ser Toldo Berardengo, *a lawyer* | | ...................Tenor |
| A Jester | | .........................Bass |
| An Archer | | ...................Tenor |
| A Torchbearer | | ................Baritone |

Archers, Torchbearers, Musicians

*Time:* End of Thirteenth Century

*Place:* Ravenna, the house of the Polentani; Rimini, the house of the Malatesti

Act I. The scene is a court in the house of the Polentani, in Ravenna, adjacent to a garden, whose bright colours are seen through a pierced marble screen. A colloquy between Francesca's brother Ostasio and the notary Ser Toldo Berardengo informs us that for reasons of state Francesca is to be married to that one of the three sons of Malatesta da Verrucchio, who, although named Giovanni, is known as Gianciotti, the Lamester, because of his deformity and ugliness. As Francesca surely would refuse to marry Gianciotti, a plot has been formed by which she is introduced to his handsome younger brother Paolo, with whom, under the impression that he is her destined bridegroom, she falls deeply in love at first sight, a passion that is fully reciprocated by him, although they have only beheld each other, and not yet exchanged a word.

Act II. The scene is the interior of a round tower in the fortified castle of the Malatestas. The summit of the tower is crowned with engines of war and arms. There are heavy crossbows, ballistas, a catapult, and other medieval machinery of battle. The castle is a stronghold of the Guelfs. In the distance, beyond the city of Rimini, are seen the battlements of the highest Ghibelline Tower. A narrow fortified window looks out on the Adriatic.

Soon after the act opens, an attack takes place. The battle rages. Amid all this distracting, and therefore futile tumult, occurs the first meeting between Francesca and Paolo, since the marriage into which she was tricked. Their love is obvious enough. Paolo despairingly seeks death, to which Francesca also exposes herself by remaining on the platform of the tower during the combat.

The Malatestas are victorious. The attacking foes are driven off. Gianciotti comes upon the platform and brings news to Paolo of his election as Captain of the people and Commune of Florence, for which city Paolo presently departs. Malatestino is carried in wounded (he has lost the sight of an eye), but he exhibits great courage and wishes to continue the fight.

Act III. The scene is the beautiful apartment of Francesca, where, from an old tome, she is reading to her women the story of Lancelot and Guenevere.

The women dance and sing until, on a whispered word from her slave, Francesca dismisses them. Paolo has returned. The greeting from her to him is simple enough: 'Benvenuto, signore mio cognato' (Welcome my lord and kinsman), but the music is charged with deeper significance.

Even more pronounced is the meaning in the musical phrase at Francesca's words, 'Paolo, datemi pace' (Paolo, give me peace).

Together they read the story which Francesca had begun reading to her women. Their heads come close together over the book. Their white faces bend over it until their cheeks almost touch; and when, in the ancient love tale, the queen and her lover kiss, Francesca's and Paolo's lips meet and linger in an ecstasy of passion.

Act IV.    This act is divided into two parts. The scene of the first part is an octagonal hall of grey stone. A grated door leads to a subterranean prison.

Malatestino is desperately in love with Francesca, and even hints that he would go to the length of poisoning Gianciotti. Francesca repulses him. Cries of a prisoner from the dungeon have disturbed Francesca. When she complains of this to Malatestino, he goes down into the prison and kills the captive.

Gianciotti enters the room and Francesca complains to him of Malatestino's cruelty and of his attitude towards her—what it is she does not specify. Francesca has prepared food for her husband before his journey, and he removes his sword and helmet before eating. Suddenly there is a terrible cry from the dungeon; it is evident that Malatestino has carried out his intention of beheading the prisoner. A moment later, knocking is heard at the door through which Malatestino went down to the dungeon; Francesca quickly goes out so as not to have to see him again.

Out of revenge for his slighted passion, Malatestino excites the jealousy of Gianciotti by arousing his suspicions of Paolo and Francesca, pointing out especially that Paolo has returned from Florence much sooner than his duties there would justify him in doing. Gianciotti works himself up into a passion and demands to be shown proof of the accusation. Malatestino bids him wait only until nightfall and he shall have it.

The scene of part two is laid in Francesca's chamber. It is night. Four waxen torches burn in iron candlesticks. Francesca is lying on the bed. From her sleep she is roused by a wild dream that harm has come to Paolo. Her women try to comfort her. After an exchange of gentle and affectionate phrases, she dismisses them.

A light knocking at the door, and Paolo's voice calling, 'Francesca!' She flings open the door and throws herself into the arms of her lover. There is an interchange of impassioned phrases. Then a violent shock is heard at the door, followed by the voice of Gianciotti, demanding admission. Paolo spies a trap-door in the floor of the apartment, pulls the bolt, and bids Francesca open the door of the room for her husband, while he escapes.

Gianciotti rushes into the room. Paolo's cloak has caught in the bolt of the trap-door. He is still standing head and shoulders above the level of the floor. Seizing him by the hair, the Lamester forces him to come up. Paolo unsheathes his dagger. Gianciotti draws his sword, thrusts at Paolo. Francesca throws herself between the two men, receives the thrust of her husband's sword full in the breast, and falls into Paolo's arms. Mad with rage, her deformed husband with another deadly thrust pierces his brother's side. Paolo and Francesca fall at full length to the floor. With a painful effort, Gianciotti breaks his blood-stained sword over his knee.                                                                K.

# ILDEBRANDO PIZZETTI
## (born 1880)

### DEBORA E JAELE

OPERA in three acts by Ildebrando Pizzetti; text by the composer Première la Scala, Milan, December 16, 1922, with Tess, Casazza, John Sample, Pinza, conductor Toscanini. First performed Buenos Aires, 1923, with Spani, Perini, Folco, Bottani. Revived la Scala, 1936,with Carbone, Casazza, Parmeggiani, Bettoni, conductor Pizzetti; 1952, with Petrella, Elmo, Penno, Cassinelli, conductor Votto.

### CHARACTERS

| | |
|---|---|
| Deborah, *the prophetess* | Mezzo-Soprano |
| Jaele, *wife of Hever, the Kenite* | Soprano |
| Mara | Mezzo-Soprano |
| Hever, *the Kenite* | Baritone |
| Nabi, *a prince of Nephthali* | Baritone |
| Barak, *commander of the Jewish forces* | Bass |
| Azriel | Tenor |
| Shillem | Tenor |
| Jesser | Baritone |
| King Sisera | Tenor |
| Adonisedek | Bass-Baritone |
| Piram | Baritone |
| Jafia | Tenor |
| The Blind Enan | Bass |

Act I. The whole of the first act describes the situation in a series of scenes in which the principal actor is the Jewish nation. Sisera, the captain and king of Canaan, has attacked and beaten the Jewish forces, and the people, gathered in the square of Nephthali, have come to consult the prophetess, Deborah, in the hope of averting utter ruin. They tell stories of Sisera's cruelty, of atrocities perpetrated, of slain children and women. While one weeps his dead brothers, another bemoans her husband and her murdered children. The bolder spirits demand immediate action, but the spy, Hever, the Kenite, cools the warlike ardour by telling them how mighty Sisera is with his 'nine hundred chariots of iron'. The entrance of Jaele, Hever's wife, is greeted with execrations, for she is suspected of having been loved by Sisera. Jaele protests that she is pure and demands to be put to the test of 'the bitter water', which, if drunk by a sinner, was supposed to swell her body and cause her death. Her beauty wins the sympathy of the younger men. All join in an ardent prayer to Deborah to show herself and help them in their dire need. Deborah appears and takes side with Jaele against her accusers. Then she upbraids Israel for sins which deserve the punishment sent by Heaven. She prays for victory and tells the people that the hour is not far when 'that tower of pride and arrogance', Sisera, will be brought so low that a woman will secure his arms in chains.

The war hymn is interrupted by the commander of the Jewish army, Barak, who is quite willing to fight, but objects that the disparity between his army and Sisera's is great and victory, therefore, difficult, if not impossible. Deborah answers him that there is a power greater than Sisera's. Barak must lead his men to the slopes of Mount Tabor whence he can fall on Sisera's army. But because he had little faith and because he doubted, the glory of destroying the rival captain will not be his.

The people go to collect their weapons. Deborah tells Jaele that she has a special part to play. She must go once more to Sisera and persuade him to lead his forces out of the city into the open, where Barak and his warriors will destroy them.

Act II.   The second act takes place in the palace of Sisera at Harosceth. The captains of his army have been feasting, and tell stories of their deeds in war and in the sack of cities. Sisera, however, is not the cruel being described by the frightened Jews in Act I. Hearing a servant of his captain, Adonisedek, boast of his horrible brutality, he immediately orders the perpetrator to be punished in spite of the objections of his captains, who urge that the punishment of one of Sisera's soldiers will encourage his enemies.

Sisera is approached by the spy, Hever, who proposes to reveal the Jewish plan to him. Instead of praising him, Sisera upbraids him for betraying his own brethren and vows that when war is over Hever will be handed over to the people whom he betrayed. A slave announces the arrival of a lady who will not disclose her identity but offers such tokens that Sisera knows her to be Jaele. He sends away his captains and his dancing girls to receive her alone. Jaele has come to discharge the duty imposed upon her by

Deborah. Knowing Sisera's love for her, she tries to persuade him that when she rejected him before, she did not know her own mind. Sisera, too willing to believe, listens and is ready to accept her word when she tells him that the Jewish army is small and can be easily beaten in the open. A messenger arrives who gives a very different account of Sisera's opponents. They are not a few hundreds but many thousands, well armed and led. As soon as the messenger departs, Jaele asks to be at once punished for her treachery, which she freely admits. Sisera refuses to punish the woman he loves, and suddenly Jaele, who had drawn a dagger to kill him, realises that she, too, loves the foreign captain. She is on the point of yielding when a voice is heard singing a sweet lullaby. It is Mara, whose children have been murdered by soldiers and who has lost her reason.

'That is the voice which recalls me to my duty,' says Jaele, and Sisera gives her freedom to return to Israel.

Act III. The Jewish forces are victorious; 'all the host of Sisera fell upon the edge of the sword, and there was not a man left.' The act follows the narrative in Judges: 'Howbeit Sisera fled away on his feet to the tent of Jael, the wife of Heber, the Kenite . . . and Jael went out to meet Sisera and said unto him, Turn in, my lord, turn in to me; fear not. And he said unto her, Give me, I pray thee, a little water to drink, for I am thirsty. . . .' The Pizzettian text differs from the biblical narrative in the last scene. Sisera loved Jaele and would have made her his queen had victory been vouchsafed to him. Broken and weary, he retires to rest in Jaele's tent. The sound is heard of armed men approaching, and it is to prevent him from falling alive into the hands of his enemies that Jaele slays him.                                          F. B.

## CHAPTER 16

*French Opera in the Twentieth Century*

# GUSTAVE CHARPENTIER

## (born 1860)

### LOUISE

OPERA in four acts by Gustave Charpentier; text by the composer. Première Opéra-Comique, Paris, February 2, 1900, with Marthe Rioton, Deschamps-Jéhin, Maréchal, Fugère, conductor Messager. First performed Berlin, 1903, with Destinn, Goetze, Philipp, Baptist Hoffmann; Vienna, 1903, with Gutheil-Schoder, Slezak, Demuth, conductor Mahler; New York, Manhattan Opera House, 1908, with Garden, Bressler-Gianoli, Dalmorès, Gilibert, conductor Campanini; Covent Garden, 1909, with Edvina, Bérat, Dalmorès, Gilibert, conductor Frigara; Metropolitan, 1921, with Farrar, Bérat, Harrold, Whitehill. Revivals include Covent Garden, 1919, with Edvina, Ansseau, Cotreuil, conductor Coates; 1928, with Heldy, Kaisin, Journet; 1936, with Delprat, Verdière (later Maison), Bouilliez, conductor Sargent; Metropolitan, 1930, with Bori, Trantoul, Rothier; 1939, with Moore, Maison, Pinza; la Scala, Milan, 1923, with Heldy, Casazza, Pertile, Journet, conductor Toscanini; 1929 with dalla Rizza; 1934, with Favero, Casazza, Ziliani, Stabile.

### CHARACTERS

Louise .......................................... Soprano
Her Mother ................................... Contralto
Irma ........................................... Soprano
Camille ........................................ Soprano
Gertrude ...................................... Contralto
An Errand Girl ............................... Soprano
Elise .......................................... Soprano
Blanche ....................................... Soprano
Suzanne........................................ Contralto
A Street-sweeper........................ Mezzo-Soprano
A Young Rag-picker ..................... Mezzo-Soprano
A Forewoman .......................... Mezzo-Soprano
A Milk Woman ............................... Soprano
A Newspaper-girl ............................ Soprano
A Coal-gatherer ........................ Mezzo-Soprano
Marguérite .................................... Soprano
Madeleine .................................... Contralto
A Dancer
Julien, *a young artist* ........................... Tenor
Louise's Father ................................ Bass

A Noctambulist ................................. Tenor
A Ragman......................................... Bass
An Old Bohemian .......................... Baritone
A Song Writer............................... Baritone
A Junkman ....................................... Bass
A Painter ........................................ Bass
Two Philosophers ......................... Tenor, Bass
A Young Poet ................................ Baritone
A Student ....................................... Tenor
Two Policemen .............................. Baritone
A Street Arab ..... ......................... Soprano
A Sculptor .......... . .................... Baritone
An Old Clothes Man ... . .................... Tenor
An Apprentice ............................. Baritone
The King of Fools ........................ ........ Tenor

Street Pedlars, Workmen, etc.

*Time:* The present                              *Scene:* Paris

The part of Louise was created by Mlle Rioton, who then sang
for the first time in an opera house; her fragile appearance and
beautiful singing are said to have been ideally suited to the opera.

She was succeeded in the title rôle by Mary Garden, who was
to make Louise into one of her greatest successes.

There is a short prelude, which reiterates a figure used extensively in the course of the opera:

It is associated rather with the call of freedom, which, to
Louise, is inextricably bound up with Julien, than with Julien himself. Three bars before the end of the prelude is heard a motif
which refers to Louise's father.

A room in a working man's tenement. Through a large open
window can be seen a terrace belonging to an artist's studio,
which is situated opposite the building in which Louise's parents
live. As the curtain goes up, Julien can be heard and seen serenading Louise: ('O cœur ami! O cœur promis!') to No. 1. Louise
comes into the room in answer to his summons, and a conversation

ensues between them. It appears that Louise has suggested Julien should write formally to her parents asking for her hand in marriage; if they refuse permission, she will run away with him. But this, she insists, must be a last resort, as she loves her parents and hates the thought of parting with them on bad terms.

Louise asks Julien to tell her again how he first fell in love with her. He goes over it in detail—not for the first time we may imagine—from a description of his dreams (he is a poet) to the meeting of their realisation—herself—on the staircase: 'Depuis longtemps j'habitais cette chambre.' He becomes lyrical in his description of his beloved, but, as he reaches his climax, in comes Louise's Mother. She does not immediately make her presence known (except in the orchestra), but hides to listen to what is being said. The tender conversation continues, and is not without its disparaging reference to the Mother, who finally puts an end to it by dragging Louise away and shutting her in the kitchen, returning to shout to Julien that if he does not shut up she will come and pull his ears for him. Louise sneaks in for just long enough to see the letter to her parents that Julien holds up to her, and then goes back to the kitchen.

The Mother reappears and shuts the window. Louise makes an effort to keep up appearances and arranges the supper, but her Mother does not mean to leave her in peace. She imitates the tone of the conversation she has overheard, and mocks Louise's love for Julien. Only the sound of the Father coming up the stairs from work stops her laying her hands on her unfortunate daughter. The Father comes in, asks whether supper is nearly ready, and proceeds to open the letter which Julien has left for him. Louise and her Father embrace—they are obviously very fond of one another—and the family sits down to table.

Louise takes the letter over to her Father, who has left it by his plate, then goes to the kitchen to help wash up. The Father re-reads the letter, and appears to want to give the whole matter his consideration. But the Mother is furious, and, when Louise contradicts a particularly vicious insinuation about Julien, she slaps her face, to the Father's obvious displeasure. The Father asks Louise to read the paper to him. She starts, but mention of spring in Paris is too much for her, and she dissolves in tears as the curtain comes down.

Act II.   The prelude is called 'Paris s'éveille'. The scene shows a street at the foot of the hill of Montmartre. Five o'clock in the morning in April. The house where Louise works as a dressmaker is seen on one side of the stage. Various derelict citizens of Paris go about their business, whether it be the setting up of a stall from which to sell milk, or the search for something worth while amongst the rags and refuse of the city. One of the figures in this scene is the Noctambulist. He is represented as a late reveller returning home, but he is also intended to symbolise the 'Plaisirs de Paris' for which Louise and those like her long so ardently. In his symbolism, Charpentier has made use of a pun on the word 'Plaisir', which is also a kind of wafer, and whose street-seller's cry is associated musically with the Noctambulist.

Julien, accompanied by some Bohemian friends, comes to wait for Louise, in order to find out what the answer to his letter is likely to be. Street cries are heard. The girls who work at the dressmaker's begin to arrive, and they are soon followed by Louise and her Mother. The Mother goes, Louise enters the house, but is soon dragged out of it by Julien, who questions her about the answer to the letter. He is furious at the lack of rebellion in her attitude towards her parents; will she go back on her promise to come away with him?

The scene changes to the work room of the dressmaker's establishment. The girls are sitting round the tables, sewing and chattering. All is bustle and gossip. They notice that Louise has been crying, and suggest that she is in love. She denies it furiously, but Irma launches into a song on the subject of love, and soon the sound of a polka is heard from down below, immediately followed by the voice of Julien serenading Louise: 'Dans la cité lointaine.' The girls are at first pleased, but seeing that his song is addressed apparently to none of them they begin to find it a bore. Louise can bear the situation no longer, and puts on her outdoor things; asking them to explain that she has had to go home, she dashes out, and is later seen going arm in arm with Julien down the street. Peels of laughter from the girls.

Act III.   A little garden on the side of Montmartre. A small, one-storeyed house on one side. Panorama of Paris. Almost twilight. As the curtain rises, Louise sings her celebrated romance, 'Depuis le jour où je me suis donnée'. Life has changed for her since she came to live with Julien, and a new happiness has come into her existence: 'Ah, je suis heureuse!' 'Depuis le jour' has become a favourite aria, and its soaring lyricism has sufficient fervour to enable it to make a considerable impression even when heard out of its context.

Louise explains that in her workshop no one took trouble about her or appeared to like her; even her father, who loves her, always treated her as a little girl, and her mother beat and scolded her ('Qui aime bien, châtie bien'). Together she and Julien rejoice at the sight of the lights of Paris coming up one after another, together they sing of their freedom: 'Libres!'.

There follows the curious episode of the 'Couronnement de la Muse'.[1] Into the garden come Bohemians, who proceed to decorate the front of the house with paper lanterns and streamers. They are followed by a crowd and a procession whose centre-piece turns out to be none other than the Noctambulist of Act II, now dressed up as the King of the Fools. Louise is crowned Queen of Bohemia and Muse of Montmartre. But the jollity is suddenly interrupted when a sad figure is seen standing apart. It is Louise's Mother, who seems a very different person from the fire-eater of Act I. She comes to say that Louise's Father is very ill and desperately anxious to see her again. For a time, they had kept up the pretence that she was dead, but she had found him creeping along to Louise's room at night, and crying out her name. Julien is at first suspicious, but he eventually agrees that Louise may go home, the Mother having promised that she shall return to him as soon as she wishes.

Act IV. The scene is the same as that of the first act. Julien's terrace is no longer visible. Louise is still with her family, which has broken the promise to allow her to return to Julien. Her father is just recovering from the illness which has kept him from work, but he has changed a good deal since we last saw him, and the contented and resourceful man of the first act has become a grumbler: 'Les pauvres gens peuvent-ils être heureux?'. Every-thing is against him now, and he complains of the ingratitude of children, who would throw off the authority of those who love them and are prepared to die for them.

---

[1] The music is drawn from a composition of Charpentier's specially written for just such a ceremony in 1897. The Muse of Montmartre, chosen by popular vote, was to be publicly crowned, but owing to the appalling weather the function had to be put off until two years later.

The significance of what he says is not lost on Louise. But she looks longingly through the window at Paris, and when her mother says that they cannot think of letting her go back to Julien, in spite of their promise, she says wanly that he who laughs last, laughs best. She goes to say good night to her father, who kisses her lovingly and long and takes her in his arms. She draws away unresponsively, but he calls her to him, puts her on his knee as if she were still a child, and sings a 'Berceuse' to her: 'Reste . . . repose-toi . . . comme jadis toute petite'. There is real feeling in this music, and for a moment the father's self-pity can be forgotten.

But Louise's distress is too poignant to be ignored for long—and it is just that that her parents seem to be successfully doing. Louise reminds them of their promise, and then quietly but feelingly asserts her right to be free: 'Tout être a le droit d'être libre.' The sound of a waltz she heard during her brief period of freedom —the voice of Paris herself—calls to Louise. She responds passionately and invokes the name of the city to set her free. All the efforts of her Father are not enough to stifle the feeling which is growing within her. At last her Father loses his temper completely, orders her from the house, and even chases her round the room, until she runs out of the door. His anger spent, the father calls pitiably for Louise. Then he shakes his fist at the city, and the curtain falls on his cry: 'O Paris.' H.

# CLAUDE DEBUSSY

## (1862–1918)

### PELLÉAS ET MÉLISANDE

OPERA in five acts by Claude Debussy; text from Maeterlinck's play of the same name. Première Opéra-Comique, Paris, April 30, 1902, with Garden, Gerville-Réache, Périer, Dufranne, Vieuille, conductor Messager. First performed New York, Manhattan Opera House, 1908, with Garden, Gerville-Réache, Périer, Dufranne, Arimondi, Crabbé, conductor Campanini; Covent Garden, 1909, with Féart, Bourgeois, Warnéry, Vanni Marcoux, Bourbon, Crabbé, conductor Campanini; la Scala, Milan, 1908, with Ferrari, Giraud, Amato, Cirino, conductor Toscanini; Metropolitan, New York, 1925, with Bori, Johnson, Whitehill, Rothier. Revivals include Covent Garden, 1920, with Edvina, Maguénat, Huberdeau, Cotreuil, conductor Pitt; 1930, with Teyte, Bourdin, Brownlee, Autori; 1937, with Perli, Gaudin, Bernasconi, Vanni Marcoux; 1949, with Joachim, Jansen, Etcheverry, conductor Désormière; la Scala 1925, with Heldy, Bertana, Legrand, Journet, conductor Toscanini; 1949, with Boué, Bourdin, Etcheverry, Médus, conductor de Sabata; Metropolitan, 1940, with Jepson, Cathelat; 1943, with Sayao, Singher; 1949, with Dosia, Jansen.

### CHARACTERS

Arkel, *King of Allemonde* .......................... Bass
Geneviève, *mother of Pelléas and Golaud* ............. Alto
Pelléas ⎱ *King Arkel's grandsons* ⎰ .................. Tenor
Golaud ⎰                          ⎱ .............. Baritone
Mélisande .................................... Soprano
Yniold, *Golaud's son by his first marriage* ........ Soprano
A Physician ..................................... Bass

Some works of art sum up the past, some presage the future—amongst operas, one thinks of Mozart's in the first category, of *Tristan* or *Falstaff* in the second. *Pelléas* seems to do neither. Obviously Debussy was anything but a composer insulated from outside influences, but *Pelléas* belongs to no line and (unlike Debussy's piano and orchestral works) has few imitators. However, if the work is something of a dead end, it is anything but sterile; in fact, every time one hears it, one is more convinced than ever that it is a work of outstanding, uncanny beauty, of incredibly perceptive imagination, and its very lack of followers is some indication that what it has to say has been said once and for all.

So much has been written about the tenuous nature of *Pelléas* that it is perhaps worth while emphasising that such a description applies only to the dramatic side of the work. The characters do not reveal the full extent of their feelings in their every utterance —to that limited extent *Pelléas* is a 'realistic' opera—and they prefer to deal in indefinite, non-committal phrases rather than in a grandiose flaunting of their feelings. But there is no under-emphasis in the ordinary sense of that term; what Debussy was after was surely the exact opposite—a precise, unexaggerated musical statement of the sentiments which are expressed, and an equally precise indication of what the characters concerned clearly feel to lie behind those sentiments. It is sometimes difficult not to believe that, from the point of view of public acceptance of the work, more harm than good has been done by frequent quotation of the climax of the love duet in Act IV:

It was not understatement that Debussy was after—as must be clear from the passion of many other moments of the score; it was not even simplification. Gallic precision demanded that a subtle situation should be uncomplicated by formula or convention. And that of course meant that what Debussy wrote was worryingly 'different' for its original audiences.

Each scene is connected to its predecessor by an orchestral interlude, and the acts are thus musically continuous.

Act I. Scene i.   In a forest. Golaud while hunting has lost his way following a wild boar and come to a place unknown to him. There he sees a woman sitting by a spring. She acts like a figure in a fairy tale and behaves like a person strange to and isolated from the world. Finally Golaud succeeds in inducing Mélisande—she at last tells him her name after repeated urging—to follow him out of the dark woods.

Scene ii. A room in the castle. Geneviève is reading to the aged, almost blind King Arkel a letter which Golaud has written to his half-brother Pelléas: 'Voici ce qu'il écrit à son frère Pelléas'. From this letter we learn that Golaud has already been married six months to the mysterious Mélisande. He has great love for his wife, about whom, however, he knows no more to-day than he did at first in the woods. So he fears that his grandfather, the King, may not forgive him for this union and asks Pelléas to give him a sign in case the King is ready 'to honour the stranger as his daughter'. Otherwise he will steer his ship to a remote land and return home no more. King Arkel has arrived at that time of life when the wisdom of experience tends to make one forgiving toward everything that happens. So he pardons Golaud and commissions his grandson Pelléas, who has entered the room, to give his brother the sign agreed upon. Pelléas has asked him if he may leave to say farewell to a dying friend, who has written to him; but Arkel reminds him that his duty is to await his brother's return, and to tend his father who lies sick above them.

Scene iii. Before the castle. The old queen Geneviève seeks to calm Mélisande's distress at the gloominess of the world into which she has wandered. Pelléas too is there. Together they watch a ship sail away out to sea, accompanied by the sound of an invisible chorus.

Act II. Scene i. A fountain in the park. Pelléas and Mélisande go together to this thickly shaded spot in the heat of the day. Is Mélisande a Melusine-like creature? Water attracts her wonderfully. Pelléas bids her take care: 'Prenez garde de glisser.' She bends over her reflection and her hair falls into the water. Because she cannot reach the water, she is tempted to play with the ring that Golaud sent her. It slips from her hand to the sound of a harp *glissando*, and sinks.

Scene ii. There must have been some peculiar condition attached to the ring. At the same hour that it fell in the fountain Golaud's horse shied while hunting so that he was hurt and now lies injured in bed. Mélisande is taking care of him. She tells Golaud that she does not feel well here. She is oppressed by a certain foreboding, she does not know what it is. Golaud tries to comfort her; he seizes her hands and sees that the ring is missing. Then he drives her out into the night to look for it. 'Sooner would

I give away everything I have, my fortune and goods, rather than have lost the precious ring.' Pelléas will help her find it.

Scene iii.    Before a grotto in the rocks. Mélisande has deceived Golaud by telling him that the ring has slipped from her hand into the sea. So Pelléas must now lead her to this grotto in order that she may know at least the place in which she can claim that she lost the ring—a dreadful place in which the shadow of death stalks. There they see three mysterious bearded beggars, sleeping in what shelter they can find.

Act III. Scene i.    A tower in the castle. At the window of the tower Mélisande is standing combing her hair that she has let down: 'Mes longs cheveux.' Then Pelléas comes along the road

Mes longs che-veux des-cen-dent jusqu'au seuil de la    tour

that winds around under her window. He is coming to say farewell; early the next morning he is going away. So Mélisande will at least once more reach out her hand to him that he may press it to his lips. Love weaves a web about the twain with an ever thicker netting without their noticing it. Their hands do not touch but as Mélisande leans forward so far her long hair falls over Pelléas's head and fills the youth with passionate feelings. Their words become warmer—then Golaud comes near and reproves their 'childishness'. He goes off with Pelléas.

The whole scene, from the ravishing harp sound of the opening until the appearance of Golaud, is no more and no less than an operatic love scene (although no word of love is spoken)—but with what sensitivity has Debussy set it!

Scene ii.    In the vault under the castle. Like a gloomy menace Golaud leads Pelléas into these underground rooms where the breeze of death blows. Seized with shuddering they go out.

Scene iii.    On the terrace at the entrance to the vault Golaud in earnest words warns Pelléas to keep away from Mélisande and to refrain from confidential conversations with her.

Scene iv.    Before the castle. In vain Golaud has sought to quiet himself by saying that it was all nothing but childishness. Jealousy devours his heart. So now he lifts up his little son Yniold, offspring of his first marriage, to spy through a window on the intimacy of Pelléas and Mélisande. The child cannot tell him of anything improper yet Golaud senses that there is something between the couple. And he feels that he himself is old, much older than Pelléas and Mélisande. Dramatically, this is one of the tensest scenes of the whole score, and Golaud's agony and impotence are made more apparent by the innocence and fright of Yniold as he reports what he sees.

Act IV. Scene i.    In a room in the castle Pelléas and Mélisande meet. This evening he must see her. She promises to go to the old fountain in the park where she formerly lost the ring. It will be their last meeting. Even now Mélisande does not understand what is driving the youth away.

Scene ii.    The old King Arkel enters the room. The aged man has taken Mélisande to his heart. He feels that the young wife is unhappy. Now Golaud also enters. He can scarcely remain master of his inner commotion. The sight of his wife, who appears the picture of innocence, irritates him so much ('Une grande innocence') that he finally in a mad rage throws her on her knees and drags her across the room by her hair. Only Arkel understands and pities:

Si j'é-tais Dieu    j'au-rais pi-tié du cœurs des hom-mes

Scene iii.    By the old spring in the park. There is an oppressive feeling of disaster in the air. Only little Yniold does not suffer this gripping burden. He has dropped something behind a stone and is looking for it. Then he catches sight of some sheep being driven past and listens to them as they go. (This scene is usually omitted in performance.)

Scene iv.    It is already growing dark when Mélisande goes to Pelléas. And yet in their farewell, perhaps also on account of Golaud's outburst of anger, the couple clearly see what has caused their condition, and there comes over them something like the affirmation of death and the joy of dying. Fate shuts the gates of the castle upon them; like fate they see Golaud coming. They rejoice in the idea of death. Pelléas falls by Golaud's sword, Mélisande flees from her husband's pursuit into the night.

Act V. A room in the castle. Mélisande lies stretched out in bed. Arkel, Golaud, and the physician are conversing softly in the room. No; Mélisande is not dying from the insignificant wound Golaud has given her. Perhaps her life will be saved. But Golaud's bitter remorse at what he has done cannot be calmed; 'J'ai tué sans raison! . . . Ils s'étaient embrassés comme des petits enfants. . . . Je l'ai fait malgré moi.' Mélisande awakes as if from dreaming. Everything that has happened is like a dream to her. Desperately Golaud rushes to her couch, begs her pardon, and asks her for the truth. He is willing to die too, but before his death he wants to know whether she had betrayed him with Pelléas. She denies it. Golaud presses her so forcibly and makes her suffer so that she is near death. Then earthly things fall away from her as if her soul were already free. It is not possible to bring her back now. The aged Arkel brings the child she has born to her and offers the last services for the dying woman, to make the way free for her soul escaping from earthly pain and the burden of the tears of persons left behind.     K. W., H.

# PAUL DUKAS
## (1865–1935)

### ARIANE ET BARBE BLEU
#### Ariadne and Blue Beard

OPERA in three acts by Paul Dukas; text after Maeterlinck's play of the same name. Première Opéra-Comique, Paris, May 10, 1907, with Georgette Leblanc (Maeterlinck's wife), Brohly, Vieuille. First performed Metropolitan, New York, 1911, with Farrar, Rothier, conductor Toscanini; la Scala, Milan, 1911, with Pierich, Ludikar, conductor Serafin; Buenos Aires, 1934, with Bunlet, Romito, conductor Panizza; Covent Garden, 1937, with Lubin, Etcheverry, conductor Gaubert; Naples, 1950, with Varenne, Chalude, conductor Wolff.

#### CHARACTERS

Barbe-Bleu .................................... Bass
Ariane ................................. Mezzo-Soprano
La Nourrice ................................. Contralto
Sélysette ............................. Mezzo-Soprano
Ygraine ...................................... Soprano
Mélisande .................................... Soprano
Bellangère ................................... Soprano
Alladine ....................................... Mime
An Old Peasant ................................ Bass
Second Peasant ............................... Tenor
Third Peasant ................................. Bass

Peasants, Crowd

*Place:* Blue Beard's castle

Act I.    A vast and sumptuous hall of semi-circular form in Blue Beard's castle. At the back a large door, on either side of which are three small ebony doors. Through the open window, can be heard the sound of an angry crowd. They believe that Blue Beard has murdered his wives one by one, and that the beautiful Ariane is to be the next victim. Can she not be saved? They comment on the arrival of the carriage; is it true that she already knows all that there is to know about the castle? Is it true that the previous five wives are *not* dead, but still alive in a dungeon —voices are said to have been heard.

The windows of the hall shut, the roar of the crowd recedes to a murmur, and Ariane and her nurse come in by a side door. The nurse starts to lament their fate; they are as good as dead already —the crowd was trying to warn them—he is mad and has already killed five wives. Ariane is calmer; she is convinced that Blue Beard loves her, and that she must win his secret to save them all. He has given her seven keys, six of silver, one of gold; those of silver she may use to open any door she likes, that of gold she must not touch. It must be that one then that guards his secret; she will have nothing to do with the silver keys, only the gold will answer her purpose. Suiting the action to the word, she throws down the silver keys, but the nurse hastens to pick them up; they will unlock his treasure, he told them.

Taking the keys, the nurse unlocks the six doors. They slide open as she turns the keys, and from them in succession pour cascades of amethysts, sapphires, pearls, emeralds, rubies, and diamonds. Ariane is not looking for treasures, but she cannot resist the sight of the diamonds: 'O mes clairs diamants!' she sings, in a great lyrical outburst, whose high tessitura makes one wonder whether any mezzo-soprano ever negotiated the title rôle successfully.

Ariane is intent on discovering what is behind the seventh forbidden door. She bids her nurse hide herself, and puts the key into the lock. Nothing can be seen when the doors open, but a sad, subdued sound is heard; it is the sound of the other five wives, says Ariane. The chant grows stronger, and as Ariane is about to enter the vault, Blue Beard himself comes into the hall. He reproaches Ariane for her faithlessness, but she demands to know the truth. He takes her by the arm and bids her follow him. She struggles to free herself, the nurse joins in to help, and the sounds of the quarrel penetrate to the crowd waiting outside. A stone is thrown through the windows, and the nurse runs to unbolt the door, through which streams a crowd of peasants. Blue Beard prepares to defend himself, but Ariane goes gently but firmly to the people and assures them that she has not been hurt. She closes the gate.

Act II.    A vast subterranean hall. It is nearly dark. Ariane and the nurse appear, the former holding a lamp. Ariane stumbles on the other wives, lying huddled in the middle of the vaulted hall. In her joy that they are alive, she rushes to them and embraces them: 'Ah! Je vous ai trouvées!' When the nurse brings the light, she sees that the captives are ill-clothed, and that their dungeon is unprepossessing; they look dazed and frightened at the unaccustomed light. One by one Ariane calls them to her[1] and reassures them; she has not come to join them as a captive but to free them, has in fact obeyed a higher law than Blue Beard's. Outside the birds are singing and the sun is shining. A drop of water extinguishes Ariane's light, but she shows no signs of fear. The others, who are used to the dark, lead her to the light—they say there is some light in the corner of the dungeon. When she gets there, Ariane finds that there are bars and bolts, which, say the other wives, they have never tried to open. It is the sea which is behind the wall, and to open it would let in the waves. But Ariane throws herself against it, and opens it, like a door, to admit light through what appears to be a great window: 'Ah, ce n'est pas encore la clarté véritable.' She takes a stone and smashes this, and immediately the whole chamber is bathed in brilliant, blinding light, so that Ariane herself can hardly bear its brightness, and the others have to protect themselves as if against fire. Ariane encourages them to look out at the world from which they have been cut off, and she leads them off to freedom, singing joyfully as they go.

Act III.    The scene is the same as that of Act I. All the wives are adorning themselves with the jewels which Ariane found with the aid of her six silver keys. They were unable to escape from the castle, since the drawbridges rose when they approached them, the moats filled magically with water. They speculate as to where Blue Beard has gone, but Ariane bids them concentrate on adorning themselves for the freedom which will surely be theirs.

The nurse comes in hurriedly to say that Blue Beard has returned. Soon his carriage can be seen approaching. He descends from it and is attacked by the villagers, who are determined to end what they consider his tyranny. His bodyguard deserts and Blue Beard himself is wounded. The peasants bind him and are about to drown him in the moat. Others crowd into the castle, and Ariane having opened the great doors of the hall, they appear on the threshold, carrying Blue Beard. They offer him to the wives; let them take what revenge they like—he is securely bound.

[1] When Mélisande's name is mentioned, the theme from Debussy's Act I, scene iii, is heard.

Ariane thanks them and bids them go to their homes to tend their wounds.

When they have left the castle, the women all crowd round Blue Beard to see what can be done for his wounds. They are found not to be serious, but the bonds with which he is secured are so tight as to risk strangling him. Ariane cuts them with a dagger, and he is able to get up. She herself departs, although Blue Beard makes a movement as if he wished her to remain. But when she in turn asks the five wives to go with her, they decline and she leaves them with Blue Beard in the castle.        H.

# HENRI RABAUD

## (1875–1949)

### MAROUF

OPERA in five acts by Henri Rabaud; text by Lucien Népoty. Première at Opéra-Comique, Paris, May 15, 1914, with Davelli, Périer, Vieuille, conductor Ruhlmann. First performed at la Scala, Milan, 1917, with Vallin, Macnez, conductor Panizza; 1939, with Favero, Malipiero, Poli, Baccaloni, conductor Marinuzzi; Metropolitan, New York, 1917, with Alda, de Luca, Rothier, conductor Monteux; 1937, with Chamlee; Buenos Aires, 1917, with Vallin, Crabbé; 1923, with similar cast; 1935, with Bovy, Gaudin; 1942, with Denya, Singher; 1946, with Mazella, Jansen; San Francisco, 1931, with Gall, Chamlee. Revived Opéra-Comique, 1949, with Géori Boué Bourdin, Pernet, conductor Fourestier.

### CHARACTERS

| | |
|---|---|
| Princess Saamcheddine | Soprano |
| Fatimah, *wife of Marouf* | Soprano |
| Marouf, *cobbler of Cairo* | Tenor (or Baritone) |
| The Sultan of Khaitan | Bass |
| The Vizier | Baritone |
| Ali | Baritone |
| The Fellah | Tenor |
| Two Merchants | Tenor, Bass |
| Chief of the Sailors | Tenor |
| Two Muezzins | Tenor |
| The Pastry-cook Ahmad | Bass |
| The Cadi | Bass |
| Two Mamalik | Bass |

*Time:* Legendary          *Place:* Cairo, Khaitan, the desert

Act I.    Cairo. Marouf is unhappy at home. His wife, Fatimah, is ugly and has a bad disposition. When she asks for rice cake, sweetened with honey, and, thanks to his friend the pastry-cook, Marouf brings her cake sweetened with cane sugar instead, she flies into a rage and runs to tell the Cadi that her husband beats her. The credulous Cadi orders the Cobbler thrashed by the police in spite of protesting neighbours. Marouf, disgusted, decides to disappear. He joins a party of passing sailors.

Act II.    A tempest wrecks the ship, and Marouf alone is

saved. Ali, his friend, whom he has not seen for twenty years and who has become rich in the meantime, picks him up on the shore and takes him to the great city of Khaitan, 'somewhere between China and Morocco'. Marouf is presented to the townspeople as the richest merchant in the world who has a wonderful caravan on the way. He is accepted everywhere and in spite of the doubting Vizier the Sultan invites him to his palace.

Act III.    Arrived there, he offers him his beautiful daughter as a bride, in spite of the warnings of the Vizier, who advises him that it would be more prudent to await the arrival of the caravan, before taking any irrevocable step.

Act IV.    For forty days Marouf lives in luxury with the Princess. He empties the treasury of the Sultan who consoles himself with thoughts of the promised caravan which must soon arrive. At last the Princess questions Marouf who tells the truth. They decide upon flight, and the Princess disguises herself as a boy.

Act V.    At an oasis in the desert they are sheltered by a poor peasant. Marouf seeks to repay his hospitality by a turn at his plough. The implement strikes an iron ring attached to the covering of a subterranean chamber. The ring also has magic power. When the Princess rubs it the poor peasant is transformed into a genie, who offers his services, and discloses a hidden treasure. When the Sultan and his guards, in pursuit of the fugitives, appear upon the scene the sounds of an approaching caravan are also heard in the distance. The Sultan apologises. Marouf and the Princess triumph. The doubting Vizier is punished with a hundred lashes.

The music of *Marouf* is attractive, if 'obvious' in character. It is based on the sort of Eastern *pastiche* which has served its turn in everything from *Turandot* and *Hassan* to *Chu Chin Chow*; the difference is that Rabaud has mixed it more skilfully than many of his predecessors and successors. As well as the dances and court episodes, *Marouf* contains a number of effective solos: Marouf's lament ('Il est des Musulmans'), which begins the whole opera and is heard again at intervals throughout the first act, has a haunting melancholy about it; in Act II he boasts the riches of his mythical caravan in an extended aria ('A travers le désert'); in Act III he reflects in a delicious little air, imitated, says the composer, from an oriental song ('Dans le jardin fleurie').

K. W., H.

# MAURICE RAVEL
## (1875–1937)

### L'HEURE ESPAGNOLE
### The Spanish Hour

OPERA in one act by Maurice Ravel; text by Franc Nohain. Première Opéra-Comique, Paris, May 19, 1911, with Vix, Périer. First performed at Covent Garden, 1919, with Donalda, André Gilly, Dua, Maguénat, Cotreuil, conductor Pitt; Chicago and New York, 1920, with Gall, Maguénat, Defrère, Warnéry, Cotreuil, conductor Hasselmans; Metropolitan, 1925, with Bori, Errolle, Bada, Tibbett, Didur, conductor Hasselmans; la Scala, Milan, 1929, with Supervia, Menescaldi, Damiani, Baccaloni, conductor Santini. Revived Covent Garden, 1924, with di Lima, Warnéry, Couzinou; 1926, with Heldy; San Francisco, 1945, with Albanese, Garris, de Paolis, Harrell, Baccaloni, conductor Merola; Netherlands Opera, 1950, with van der Veen, Vroons, Baylé, conductor Monteux; Opéra-Comique, Paris, 1951, with Duval, Giraudeau, Vieuille, conductor Cluytens; Naples, 1952, with Marthe Luccioni, conductor Cluytens.

### CHARACTERS

Concepcion, *wife of Torquemada* ................ Soprano
Gonzalve, *a poet* ............................... Tenor
Torquemada, *clock-maker* ....................... Tenor
Ramiro, *a muleteer* .................... Baritone-Martin
Don Inigo Gomez, *a banker* ...................... Bass

*Time:* Eighteenth Century          *Place:* Toledo

The action passes in the shop of Torquemada, an absent-minded clock-maker of Toledo, in the eighteenth century. It is his day for attending the public clocks in various parts of the town. It is also the one day that his wife Concepcion can enjoy her love affairs with complete freedom. As the clock-maker leaves his house, Ramiro, a muleteer, arrives to have his watch fixed. It is a family heirloom and most important to him. Much to Concepcion's annoyance, Torquemada invites the customer to await his return. In despair Concepcion wonders what to do with the unwelcome visitor. Equally embarrassed, he offers to carry to her room one of the large clocks which her husband has declared too heavy for him to lift.

While he takes the clock to the other room Concepcion's lover

Gonzalve appears. During the muleteer's absence he is hidden in a large grandfather clock. There follows an interchange of clocks, and the unsuspecting muleteer carries Gonzalve inside a clock to Concepcion's room. Inigo, a banker, who is another admirer of Concepcion's, enters. He in his turn is hidden in a clock. Another switching of timepieces effects a change in lovers. But neither turns out to be satisfactory, the one perpetually indulging in flights of poetic fancy, the other proving simply ridiculous, and it is the muleteer who by his prowess and strength wins Concepcion's admiration; she transfers her temporary affections to him and takes him up to her room. While they are away, Torquemada returns. He finds two dejected philanderers hidden in his clocks and takes the opportunity of selling one to each of them. Concepcion and Ramiro re-enter. The husband, however, probably believes that there is safety in numbers and the opera ends with a sparkling quintet, whose moral, say the characters, comes from Boccaccio:

> Entre tous les amants, seul amant efficace,
> Il arrive un moment, dans les déduits d'amour,
> Où le muletier a son tour!

From the delightful clock noises of the opening to the Habanera quintet of the end, *L'Heure Espagnole* is full of charming music. One should however mention that it is music designed to point up the witty stage action, and that there are hardly any 'numbers' (Concepcion's exasperated 'Ah, la pitoyable aventure' is the nearest) in the accepted sense—as one might well expect from Ravel's injunction to his singers: '*dire* plutôt que *chanter*.' Gonzalve is the only exception to this rule, and he waxes positively lyrical at times (e.g. his characteristically Spanish opening song). It is all very light, and, since everyone seems to be agreed that the opera will not bear translation, we may for once legitimately call it very French as well.          K. W., H.

## L'ENFANT ET LES SORTILEGES

Opera in two parts by Maurice Ravel; text by Colette. Première Monte Carlo, March 21, 1925, with Gauley, Warnéry, Lafont, conductor de Sabata. First performed Opéra-Comique, Paris, 1926, with Féraldy, Calvet, Sibille, Bourdin, Herent, Guénot, conductor Wolff; San Francisco, 1930, with Queena Mario conductor Merola; Florence Festival, 1939, by company from

Opéra, Paris (where the work was revived that year), with Micheau, Branèze, Cernay, conductor Previtali; Buenos Aires, 1944, with Oyuela, Kindermann, Negroni, Cesari, conductor Wolff; la Scala, Milan, 1948, with Branèze, Danco, Schenneberg, Gianotti, conductor de Sabata. Revived Opéra-Comique, Paris, 1951, with Angelici, Turba-Rabier, Jourfier, conductor Cluytens.

## CHARACTERS

The Child ............................... Mezzo-Soprano
His Mother................................ Contralto
The Louis XV Chair (La Bergère) ............... Soprano
The Chinese Cup ...................... Mezzo-Contralto
[1] The Fire ............................... Soprano Léger
[1] The Princess ........................... Soprano Léger
The Cat ................................. Mezzo-Soprano
The Dragonfly (La Libellule) ............. Mezzo-Soprano
[1] The Nightingale (Le Rossignol) ........... Soprano Léger
The Bat (La Chauve-Souris) ..................... Soprano
The Little Owl (La Chouette) ................... Soprano
The Squirrel (L'Ecureuil) ................ Mezzo-Soprano
A Shepherd Girl (Une Pastourelle) ............. Soprano
A Shepherd (Un Pâtre) ....................... Contralto
The Armchair (Le Fauteuil) ............. Basse Chantante
The Grandfather Clock (L'Horloge Comtoise) .... Baritone
The Tea Pot (La Théière) ....................... Tenor
[2] The Little Old Man (Arithmetic) .................. Tenor
The Tom Cat ................................. Baritone
A Tree ........................................ Bass
[2] The Frog (La Rainette) .......................... Tenor
Settle (Le Banc), Sofa (Le Canapé),
    Ottoman (Le Pouf), Wicker Chair..... Children's Chorus
Numbers (Les Chiffres) ................ Children's Chorus
Shepherds, Frogs, Animals, Trees ................ Chorus

Colette's libretto originally began as a scenario for a ballet, which she sent to the director of the Opéra in Paris, who in turn sent it on to Ravel, who was then serving with the French Army at the front. It was not until the summer of 1920 that the composer started work in earnest, by which time the ballet scenario had become an operatic libretto. Ravel interrupted his work more than once in favour of other things, but it was finished towards the end of 1924.

[1], [2] These rôles *must* (according to the score) be sung by the same singer.

The scene is laid in a room in an old Norman country house, giving on to a garden. Big armchairs, a grandfather clock, wall-paper with shepherds and shepherdesses on it. A round cage with a squirrel in it hangs near the window. Remains of a fire in the grate, kettle singing. The cat also singing. It is afternoon. The Child, aged six or seven, is sitting at his lessons, at the height of a fit of laziness. He bites his penholder, scratches his head and mutters under his breath. Work exasperates him and he only wants to do the things he is not allowed to do.

His mother comes in with his tea, asks him how he is getting on, and is vexed to see that he has done nothing but make a blot on the table-cloth. When she asks him to promise to work, the Child puts out his tongue at her. She leaves him saying he will be left alone in the room until supper-time as a punishment. The Child suddenly loses control, and dashes about the room in-dulging in an orgy of destruction. He smashes the cup and teapot, pricks the squirrel with his pen, pulls the cat's tail, flourishes the poker, stirs up the fire, and upsets the kettle into it to produce clouds of steam and ashes. Then, brandishing the poker like a sword, he swoops on the wall-paper and pulls great strips of it off the wall. He opens the grandfather clock, swings on the pendu-lum and pulls it off, and finally makes a dash at his books and tears them up with a scream of delight. All this takes place in a few seconds and to the accompaniment of suitably vivacious music.

From now until the end of the opera, the child is going to realise the consequences of his destructive actions, and in a way that is likely to astonish him more than any other—from the objects of his temper themselves. He sinks into a chair, but, to his infinite surprise, it moves slowly away from him, to the creaking sound of a double-bassoon, and, bowing gravely to a Louis XV chair, leads her in a stately but grotesque dance. Their conversation, to which the Child listens in amazed silence, is to the effect that they will never again have to put up with the weight and the pranks of the naughty child they have had to stand for so long. They are joined in vigorous expression of this sentiment by Settle, Sofa, Ottoman, and Wicker Chair.

Next comes the mutilated clock, striking uncontrollably and complaining bitterly of the treatment which has deprived him, literally, of his balance. To hide his shame, he goes to the end of

the room and stands with his face to the wall. From the floor
come the voices of the Chinese cup and teapot ('Wedgwood
noir' says the score): 'How's your mug? Rotten . . . better had
. . . come on! . . . I punch Sir, I punch your nose. . . . I boxe you,
I marm'lad you.' The words are nonsense, compounded from
English, and the more nebulous orientalisms such as 'Mah-jong',
'kong-kong', 'Harakiri' and even 'Caskara'; the music is a
brilliant parody of the foxtrot of American jazz (1920's style),
and the nostalgic tune is sustained now by the voices, now by the

first trombone, who is ordered to 'vibrer avec la coulisse'. The
foxtrot is justly one of the most famous moments of the score,
but it evoked more hostility at the first performances than almost
any other passage.

The Child suddenly feels very much alone and goes towards the
fire, which however spits in his face and announces to coloratura
music that warmth is only for those who are good; bad children
will be burnt. The fire pursues the Child round the room until it
succumbs quietly to the ashes, which dance with it for a moment
and then extinguish it altogether. There is a procession, half comic,
half pathetic, of the shepherds and shepherdesses from the torn
wall-paper, after which the Fairy Princess rises out of the torn
picture book, on which the Child has rested his head. He was half-
way through her story, but now that the book is torn he will
never know how it will all turn out. The Child tries to hold her
back as she sinks through the floor, and his lyrical phrases after
she has gone are really moving in their mixture of simplicity and
intensity.

There is just a chance that the end of the story may be amongst
the pages which lie round his feet, and he looks for it, but in
vain. All he can find are the torn sheets of an arithmetic book,
from which emerges an old man covered with arithmetical
symbols and crowned with a Pi. Without even pausing to look
round him, the little old man starts to reel off problems of the
sort which begin 'If two taps fill a bath in . . .'. He and the Child
catch sight of one another at the same moment, and immediately

he and his platoon of figures start to torment the Child with quick-fire arithmetical nonsense. The Child is whirled into the dance, and sinks down exhausted holding his head.

He does not notice the black cat come out from under the arm-chair, yawn, and start to wash itself. It is playing with a ball when the Child notices it, and says wearily that he supposes it too has acquired the habit of speech. The cat signs that it has not, and spits at him, before going off to the window, where a white cat has appeared. Now comes the famous Cats' love duet, which caused such a storm at the first performance. No word is spoken, but the 'Mi-inhou' and 'Mornaou', which Colette has chosen to represent cats' speech, are set to exact notes and marked 'nasal'.

The result is brilliantly real, and the animals work themselves up to a frenzy of excitement before bounding out of the window into the garden.

The Child follows them hesitatingly, and at this point the stage directions require that the room walls fall away, the ceiling disappear, and the Child with the two cats be transported into the garden, which is flooded with moonlight and lit by the last rays of the setting sun. The short and very beautiful orchestral interlude is for strings; piccolo and Swannee whistle imitate bird noises and the whole atmosphere is one of pure moonlight and magic. A chorus of frogs can be heard from behind the scenes, and the Child is delighted to be out in the garden he loves so well.

But even here he is not to escape the accusing voices which have haunted him indoors. The tree complains about the cuts made in his flanks the day before, and the Child leans his cheek against the tree in sympathy. A dragonfly flashes across the scene calling for the mate she has lost, and who is now pinned to the wall in the Child's room. A nightingale is heard against the background of the frogs' chorus (the music soars to a top F), and a bat complains that his mate was killed by the Child, leaving the family helpless. Frogs come out of the water and sit round the edge until the pool is completely ringed with them. They dance. One lays its head on the Child's knee, and is immediately admonished by a squirrel for taking such a risk with so dangerous a creature. She herself was able to escape, but another squirrel was caught and now languishes in a cage in the Child's room. The Child tries to explain that it was so as to be able to gaze for ever into the squirrel's beautiful eyes that he took her captive, but this answer proves anything but satisfactory to the squirrel, who makes a moving plea for the freedom she and her kind love above everything else.

The Child realises that the animals are happy all round him, and begins to feel lonely with no one paying any attention to him. Suddenly he cries out 'Maman'. Immediately the atmosphere of peace is broken. Some animals disappear, but those who stay behind form a menacing chorus, with the Child as the object of their dislike. Each one has a grudge to pay off, and together they rush at the Child, catch hold of him, buffet him, turn him round, shove him, and then forget all about him as, in their anxiety to be the first to down him, they become excited at the battle and turn on each other.

The Child is pushed over into a corner of the stage, when all of a sudden a little squirrel who has been wounded limps over towards him. The Child takes a ribbon and binds up the squirrel's paw, watched by the other animals. Their animosity turns to something quite different as they exclaim in amazement at the Child's kindly action. 'He has stifled the bleeding, he has bound up the wound.' What can they do to help him, now that he looks so helpless and lonely all by himself in the garden? Just now he cried out; what was the word? They try to call 'Maman', thinking that will help the Child, whom they now know to be good and kind. The animals help him up and start to lead him towards the house, whose windows have just been lit up. The opera ends as the Child calls simply and confidently 'Maman'.

One can only imagine that the neglect of Ravel's operatic masterpiece is due to the twin difficulties of translation and of fulfilling the exacting stage directions. There can be no other reason, as the music is in many ways the best and most complete that he ever wrote. He is at the very height of his powers, and working well within them to produce a work whose inventiveness appears to be equal to every facet of the situations he has under-taken. Above all the subject is one that exactly suits his peculiar type of genius; the work brilliantly switches from parody to the most moving lyricism, to onomatopoeic representation of the story. It is hard to imagine the listener who would not be en-chanted by its fancy and fantasy, particularly now that the opera is anything but the rarity it used to be, since the gramo-phone recording is perhaps the best ever made of an opera.

H.

# DARIUS MILHAUD
(born 1892)

## LE PAUVRE MATELOT
### The Poor Sailor

OPERA in three acts by Darius Milhaud; text by Jean Cocteau. Première December 16, 1927, at Opéra-Comique, Paris, with Madeleine Sibille, Legrand, Vieuille, Musy, conductor Lauweryns. First performed Berlin, 1929, with Novotna, conductor Zemlinsky. Revived with new orchestration Geneva, 1934; Philadelphia, 1937, with Anna Leskaya, Fritz Kreuger; Vienna, 1937; Opéra-Comique, 1938; Berlin, 1947, with Enk, Schuffler, Heinz Nissen, Schirp; Düsseldorf, 1948, with Teschemacher, Ostertag, conductor Hollreiser; London Opera Club, 1950, with Vyvyan, Servant, Loring, Wallace, conductor Renton; la Scala, Milan, 1950, with Favero, Malipiero, Inghilleri, Beuf, conductor Sanzogno; Hamburg, 1951.

### CHARACTERS

The Wife ....................................Soprano
The Sailor ....................................Tenor
His Father-in-law ................................Bass
His Friend ....................................Baritone

*Time:* The present                    *Place:* A sea-port

The opera, which is dedicated to Henri Sauguet, is divided into three acts, but is played without intervals and in all lasts only some thirty-five minutes. The action takes place in and near a bar kept by the Wife. Also visible are the street and a wine shop kept by the Friend. The Wife and the Friend are dancing. She has waited fifteen years for the return of her husband from abroad, and has steadfastly refused to give up hope of his return, in spite of his long absence. The Friend is disposed to encourage her to hope, and he expresses admiration for the way she has remained faithful; a port like this, he says, is not the sort of place where one would expect to find *that*. She is perfectly candid; she might have deceived her husband if he had been there, but with him away and his photograph still hanging over the bed, how could she do such a thing? Besides, no other man has yet caught her fancy.

Her Father takes a very different view of this chastity of his daughter's; why can't she find herself a man, who could take over the bar and run it properly? The Friend says that he himself has proposed to her, but she has always turned him down. She makes the obvious retort; supposing they did get married, and one day the bell rang and in walked her husband—his friend? Her Father still refuses to take the same view, even when optimistically she imagines him coming back as rich as Crœsus. If he is poor, there is no crime she would not commit to set him up again properly.

The Friend goes back to his shop. The Father repeats his suggestion that they would make a fine pair, but the Wife gives lyrical expression to her resolve to remain true to the husband she still believes will return to her. Her Father reminds her that she was twenty-five when he left, and is now forty. While they are arguing and before they leave the stage, the Sailor himself appears unobserved in the street, hesitates in front of their door, and then decides not to open it. What if his own wife does not recognise him—nobody has so far. Would it not be best to see first what effect his appearance has on his Friend? He knocks, and is at first rejected as a drunkard, until he mentions that he has a wife opposite. Then his Friend recognises him. The Sailor congratulates himself that he did not risk going home unannounced. He has changed, he knows; in the fierce climates he has known, who would not have done? He asks after his wife, and is reassured that she is waiting for him. He has money enough to end all her troubles.

The Friend is for going over straight away, but the Sailor suggests he sleeps in his Friend's house for the night. He would like to meet his wife as a stranger; his travels have given him a taste for adventure and this shall be his last.

Act II.     Next day, the Sailor bids his Friend good-bye, and goes, not without some misgivings, to see what his reception will be like at the bar. He tells his Wife that he brings her news of her husband; he has returned, but dare not come to her until nightfall, as he is pursued by creditors. She says they cannot help him; they are penniless themselves. The Sailor is sceptical; since when has a pretty woman gone short of money? His Father-in-law sneers at the Wife, but she takes no notice, and leads a short ensemble of strong rhythmical impulse: 'Cher époux!' She is filled with delight that her husband is likely to be restored to her, and quite undismayed to learn that had he accepted the love of a cannibal queen he might have come home with the treasures which in point of fact devolved upon his shipmate. The Sailor shows her the pearls which were his reward, he says, for taking her husband's place as the queen's lover.

The Sailor asks if he may stay the night with them, and is told that no one who brings such good news could be refused so small a request. The Friend is full of curiosity to know what has happened, and he thinks of the excuse of returning the heavy hammer he borrowed the previous day from the Wife. She does not tell him that she has had news of her husband, but, as she locks up, she is struck with the resemblance which the weary Sailor, stretched out on a bench, bears to her husband.

Act III.　　The Sailor lies asleep. The Wife comes in with the hammer in her hand, looks at him for a moment, raises it, then apparently thinks better of her plan. She coughs, but he does not stir. She raises the hammer again and strikes him on the head with it. When he moves convulsively, she strikes him again, then drops the hammer, and rifles his pockets quickly, removing the pearls. The noise arouses her father, whom she instructs to help her carry the body. They will dump it in the rain-water tank, and tell the neighbour that their visitor had to leave early in the morning. There is a knock at the door, but they stay quiet, and their neighbour leaves them undisturbed. They prepare to carry the body away, as the Wife sings lyrically of her husband's impending return.　　　　　　　　　　　　　　　　　　　　H.

# OPERAS-MINUTES

Three one-act operas, lasting about eight minutes each, by Darius Milhaud; text by Henri Hoppenot. *L'Enlèvement d'Europe* was first given at Baden-Baden, July 17, 1927, in conjunction with Toch's *Die Prinzessin auf der Erbse*, Hindemith's *Hin und Zurück*, and Weill's *Mahagonny* The same work was performed for the first time with the other two Opéras-Minutes (*La Délivrance de Thésée* and *L'Abandon d'Ariane*) at Wiesbaden, April 20, 1928. First performed Budapest, 1932, in Hungarian.

These miniature but highly entertaining operas are nothing if not satirical in object. Mythology in general, and more particularly the classical French interpretation of it, are spoofed to the limit, alike by librettist (who, like Claudel, has represented his country as ambassador) and composer. Milhaud's *Phèdre* bears the same relationship to Racine's as Offenbach's *Orphée* does to Gluck's. The music itself, spiced with South American rhythms, is very attractive, and Milhaud's quick-fire inventiveness seems peculiarly well suited to the original form he has invented.

## L'ENLÈVEMENT D'EUROPE

### CHARACTERS

Agénor .......................................... Bass
Pergamon, *Europe's suitor* ..................... Baritone
Jupiter, *in the guise of a bull* ..................... Tenor
Europe, *Agénor's daughter* ..................... Soprano

Chorus of 'maîtresses-servantes' ......... { One Soprano / One Mezzo / One Contralto

Chorus of Soldier-Labourers ............ { One Tenor / One Baritone / One Bass

The set represents the front of the palace of King Agénor of Thebes. The chorus of women is hanging about near a well, and that of the men near a field. The Chorus reiterates the name of 'Europe', in alternate rising 7ths and 9ths. Pergamon emerges from the palace, and gives vent to his wrath at the discovery that Europe prefers the society of bulls and cows to that of a hero like himself. Agénor agrees that his daughter has never shown much taste for the company of men of war-like accomplishments. She appears with the bull to which she has taken so evident a fancy, and the chorus makes scornful reference to her passion for its bellowings.

Jupiter explains his love for Europe, and pleads passionately for satisfaction of 'cette double ardeur du taureau dans mes reins et du Dieu dans mon cœur'. The chorus mocks the beast, and Pergamon, beside himself, draws his bow and looses an arrow at his rival, much to the consternation of the bystanders. The arrow strikes home, but the bull shakes itself free and the missile speeds back to him who dispatched it, and transfixes him. After Pergamon's death, the chorus sings a valediction, in which the 7ths and 9ths of the beginning are prominent. Europe rides away into the distance with the bull.

H.

## L'ABANDON D'ARIANE

### CHARACTERS

Ariane ......................................... Soprano
Phèdre, *her sister* ............................. Soprano

Thésée .........................................Tenor

Dionysos, *the god, in disguise* ...................Baritone

Chorus of Shipwrecked Mariners ........ {
One Tenor
One Baritone
One Bass

Chorus of Gypsy Bacchants............. {
One Soprano
One Mezzo
One Contralto

The scene represents part of the island of Naxos; rocks visible in the background. During the piece, darkness falls, and it is almost night at the end. As the curtain rises, the stranded mariners are grouped left, playing dice, the Bacchants are sitting around a cooking pot, looking like gypsies; Dionysos is amongst the Bacchants, dressed as a beggar. Like a Greek chorus, the two groups join to convey the information that it is Ariane's custom to come to that part of the island every night in order to escape the attentions of Thésée, whom she cannot abide. Phèdre meanwhile longs unavailingly for his caresses.

Before long, the two sisters, dressed exactly alike, come into view, and each gives vivid utterance to the sentiment ascribed to her by the chorus, which for its part prays to Dionysos to help each in her different affliction. Dionysos, in his capacity as a beggar, laments his blindness and begs for charity. Each sister gives him money. When the sailors announce that Thésée can be seen coming that way, Ariane says she will hurry away, while Phèdre rejoices at the prospect of seeing her beloved.

Thésée cries aloud the name of Ariane, and tenderly asks if no one can give him information as to her whereabouts. Dionysos offers him a cup of precious wine for which he returns thanks in an exultant musical sentence ending resoundingly on a high B flat. The wine has the effect of making him see double, and when Phèdre comes from her place of concealment he thinks she is the two sisters and goes out with her. The chorus comments in Tango rhythm, and Dionysos informs Ariane that Thésée will in future regard Phèdre as his consort. She thanks him for his kindness towards her, and a moment later Dionysos and the Bacchants shed their beggar's clothes and are revealed in dazzling white. Ariane and her sister gave alms to a god and his reward is to grant their joint wishes. She has one more request; may she finish her days with Diana in the firmament on high? It becomes darker and Dionysos leads her up the rocks; behind her appears the constellation of Ariadne. The chorus rejoices; the opening chorus is repeated in a different rhythm (alternating 6/8 and 5/8 in a bar), and sung over an instrumental accompaniment that has the flavour of a modernised version of a *toccata* from one of Monteverdi's operas.                                                H.

# LA DÉLIVRANCE DE THÉSÉE

## CHARACTERS

| | |
|---|---|
| Aricie . . . . . . . . . . . . . . . . . . . . . . . . . . . . . . . . . . . . | Mezzo-Soprano |
| Phèdre, *her sister* . . . . . . . . . . . . . . . . . . . . . . . . . . . . | Soprano |
| Hippolyte, *son of Phèdre* . . . . . . . . . . . . . . . . . . . . . . . | Baritone |
| Théramène, *Hippolyte's friend* . . . . . . . . . . . . . . . . . . | Baritone |
| Thésée, *husband of Phèdre* . . . . . . . . . . . . . . . . . . . . . . | Tenor |
| Chorus of Distant Voices . . . . . . . . . . . . | Mixed Vocal Quartet |

A great hall in the palace of Thésée; a throne in the middle. Hippolyte complains to his friend Théramène of the unwelcome attentions of his mother, Phèdre; he is in love with Aricie, to whom he presently pours out his heart, only to be told that Aricie cannot make a decision either way without the consent of Thésée, Hippolyte's father. Enter Phèdre, whose presence causes Aricie and Théramène to withdraw respectfully. She is overjoyed to find Hippolyte alone, but he repulses her, and the trumpets announce the return of Thésée from yet another successful and hazardous exploit. When Thésée appears, Phèdre turns the tables and asks for his protection against her incestuous son. Thésée promptly banishes him and orders him to go out to do battle with the monster which even now threatens the walls of the city.

The chorus takes up the very attractive rhythm of the *Beguine*, which started as Hippolyte left the stage with Théramène; the words are 'Oui, c'est lui! C'est bien lui!'. With the chorus as background, Thésée gives an account of his adventure:

J'arrivai: Ils tremblèrent;
J'avançai: Ils reculèrent;
Je dégainai: Ils décampèrent;
Je les tuai: Ils expirèrent!

Thésée being a tenor, they 'decamp' on a top C, but, by the time his miniature aria has come to an end, the chorus is exclaiming

at some new misfortune: 'O douleur! O tristesse!' In spite of the
pleas of Phèdre and Aricie, they make no attempt to explain what
causes their distress and alarm, but in no time Théramène, who
has witnessed all, returns. He takes up his position for 'Le Récit'
(a reference to Racine's *Phèdre*) and begins: 'A peine nous
sortions,' only to be interrupted by the omniscient Thésée: 'Je
connais . . . finis vite.' There is nothing left for Théramène to do
(he makes this quite clear) but to revenge the death of Hippolyte.
He takes out his sword and stabs Phèdre to the heart, whereupon
Thésée orders the guards to hang him from the nearest tree.

Aricie aided by the wordless chorus laments the series of
disasters which have befallen them in a single day, but consolation
for the two survivors is close at hand. Thésée puts his arm round
Aricie, and in phrases of exaggeratedly lyrical character invites
her to console herself with him. Poor Aricie, who has earlier been
referred to as 'craintive' and 'pudique', seems to be the only one
of the characters to benefit from the catastrophes, and by the end we
find Thésée addressing her more optimistically as 'la timide Aricie'.

H.

# CHRISTOPHE COLOMB
## Christopher Columbus

Opera in two parts and twenty-seven scenes by Darius Milhaud; text by
Paul Claudel. Première Berlin, May 5, 1930, with Reinhardt, Scheidl, conductor Kleiber. Given in concert form in Paris 1936, London 1937, Antwerp
1940, New York 1952, with Dow, David Lloyd, Harrell, Brownlee, Normar
Scott, conductor Mitropoulos.

### CHARACTERS

| | |
|---|---|
| Isabella, *Queen of Spain* | Soprano |
| Christopher Columbus I | Baritone |
| Christopher Columbus II | Baritone |
| The Narrator | Speaker |
| The Counsel for the Prosecution | Speaker |
| The Representative of the Sailors | Speaker |
| The Major-domo | Tenor |
| The Master of Ceremonies | Tenor |
| The Cook | Tenor |
| The King of Spain | Bass |
| The Commandant | Bass |
| The Messenger | Baritone |
| The Sultan Miramolin | Tenor |

Chorus, officer, counsel, creditors etc., etc.

*Christophe Colomb* is in the tradition of French operas built on the largest possible scale, a tradition which was carried forward from Lully by Rameau, Spontini, Berlioz, Meyerbeer. Milhaud and Claudel have however rejected the quasi-realistic treatment of their subjects which was adopted by at any rate the more recent of their predecessors (if the word realistic has any validity when applied to stage works), and have concentrated on the symbolical aspects of the story of Columbus. The resulting opera is thus not only highly exacting to stage—it involves a vast apparatus—but anything but easy for the audience to understand. It belongs in fact, as Professor Dent has said in his Pelican *Opera*, to the category of works which one expects to see only once in a lifetime.

Act I.　(1) The Narrator and Chorus come on in procession, after which (2) the Narrator announces: 'The Book of the Life and Voyages of Christopher Columbus, who discovered America. In the name of the Father, and of the Son, and of the Holy Ghost.' (3) With the Chorus murmuring in the background, and supported by the percussion, the Narrator prays for light and strength in his endeavour to explain the book. (4) On a cinematic screen at the back of the stage, a globe can be seen spinning round; above it can be made out a dove, glowing with light.

(5) A humble inn at Valladolid. Columbus is seen as an old, broken man, his only possession a mule. (6) Narrator and Chorus call on him to join with posterity in looking at his past life and the results of his actions. The Counsel for the Prosecution signifies his presence. (7) The Narrator refers to the court of Spain, and the embodiments of Envy, Ignorance, Vanity, and Avarice put in an appearance to the accompaniment of Spanish dance rhythms. Prosecution and Defence argue over the behaviour of the King of Spain towards Columbus, and Columbus himself is eventually stung into entering the discussion. He is accused of lying and exaggeration, but defends himself.

(8) An orchestral passage accompanies the clearing of the stage, which is effected by a cloud of doves ('Colombes' in French). (9) The Court of Isabella the Catholic. The Queen is shown as a child surrounded by a childish court. She receives Sultan Miramolin (also represented by a child), who gives her a dove in a cage. She accepts the gift, puts a ring on its foot, and releases it. The scene is accompanied by a wordless chorus.

(10) The dove over the sea. (11) The Narrator continues the story of Columbus. As a boy he read the story of Marco Polo; the screen shows a jumble of incidents in the tale, and when Columbus's mother or his sister comes to look over his shoulder at what he is reading and so enters into his consciousness, she also appears on the screen. There is conflict between the views of the Man at the Window, who urges him to seek adventure, and the Chorus, which tries to prevent him leaving his family. His second self bids him follow the call of adventure, in the name of God. As the scene ends, a dove flies in through the window, with a ring on its foot.

(12) Columbus leaving Genoa says good-bye to his family, and sets out over the seas. He interrogates a dying sailor as to what he has seen in the West. (13) Columbus and his creditors. He glories in the sea he has conquered, but the cries of his creditors will not be silenced; three guitarists add their voices, but the creditors agree that a last voyage, however desperate an undertaking, represents their only chance of payment. (14) Columbus goes to the court of the King of Spain, and tells the Major-domo that he has not come to ask anything of the King, but rather to give him something. He is mocked for his opinions and his pretensions, and the Major-domo tells him to come back to-morrow, taking care however to ask on the sly whether he has gold to offer.

(15) Queen Isabella is seen at prayer. On the screen appear representations of the crowds, the processions, battles which have led to the capture of Granada and the unification of Spain. A wordless chorus accompanies her prayer to God. She has played her part in the unification of Spain by bringing Aragon to Castile; may she not now lay down her life, her duty accomplished? She sees a mystical vision and hears the voice of Saint James, demanding that she look beyond the seas. Had she not another ring beside that she gave her husband? Yes, she put it on a dove's foot and she saw it again on Christopher Columbus's hand.

(16) Cadiz. Recruiting is going on for the three vessels which are to form Columbus's expedition of discovery. (17) The Master of Ceremonies calls the roll of the demon gods of America. They make reference to the plagues they will inflict on Columbus and his crew. (18) Columbus receives representatives of the crew, who come with complaints that food is short. The men wish to return and give up the expedition which they think is condemned by God

from above. Columbus consults his senior officers and men, and all advise him that the expedition is doomed unless he turns back at once. He refuses and the situation becomes ugly with the threat of mutiny. Columbus speaks up bravely to defend his policy, and is so convinced that he is right in his calculations that he bids the sailors drink the water they have with them and eat the food; sufficient will still remain for their needs. No sooner are the words out of his mouth than a bird appears, and the scene ends with a cry of 'Land!' from the look-out.

(19) America. The ships can be seen approaching, and from them is heard the sound of a 'Te Deum'. The first part ends with the large-scale setting of the 'Sanctus'.

Act II. An interlude shows the effect Columbus's discovery has on the whole world; nobody talks of anything else, but whether the earth is round and the New World possible. The Narrator tells of the difficulties which follow the discovery of America; the cruel treatment of the natives leads to revolt and further repression; the New World does not bring the profit expected of it, and Columbus's enemies are busy in Spain. (1) The King summons three wise men to give him counsel. They give their advice in oblique form, but warn the King against his subject Columbus: 'you must honour him—you must watch him —you must bury him.' (2) Controversy. The orchestra plays quietly while the different groups engage in argument among themselves.

(3) On his fourth voyage, Columbus was put in chains by the man appointed by the King to take over his command; he is seen lying bound in the hold of the ship, where he is visited by his successor and exhorted to put forth his influence in saving the ship, which has run into dangerous waters. The Commandant is accompanied by the Cook, who begs Columbus to act like Samson pulling the Temple of Dagon about the ears of the Philistines, and destroy the ship. But Columbus prays and three times the ship weathers the crises which come upon it.

(4) Christopher Columbus's conscience. The Cook acts as guide while Columbus looks back at his past actions and their consequences. He sees the inhabitants of America, on whom his discovery of the new continent has brought ruin and destruction; the slaves he sold to pay his debts; the wife and mother he abandoned; himself as he was contented at Genoa, and at Lisbon; and

his own ghost. The Cook reminds him that there are other unknown seas beyond the one he has discovered, and tells him that
the New World will not be named after him but after an obscure
member of his own crew, Amerigo Vespucci, whom he can
scarcely remember.

(5) The boat arrives safely, and the scene changes to Spain. A
Messenger comes from Queen Isabella. On her bed of suffering,
she thought of Columbus and his expedition, and now sends
words of comfort to him on his return to Spain. Her funeral procession can be seen crossing the stage. (6) The book is almost
finished, says the Narrator. The servant at the inn comes in to
demand payment of Columbus's bill. Will the innkeeper not wait
three days, asks Columbus; he once asked his sailors to wait three
days before killing him, and in those days he discovered a New
World. Will the innkeeper not do the same? That worthy answers
that he will take the mule unless he is paid by to-morrow, and
goes out, leaving Columbus in despair, and praying for help.

(7) The Paradise of the Idea. The scene takes on a resemblance
to that of Act I, scene ix, the court of Isabella in Majorca. But it
has changed, and everything has become the colour of silver. It
is paradise. Isabella greets her friends, and is welcomed by the
ladies of her court—all children, as in the previous scene in these
surroundings. Sultan Miramolin comes to bring her gifts, and she
remembers when he gave a dove long ago, and she put her ring
on its foot. How can she enter into the kingdom of heaven without her friend Christopher Columbus, she asks? Let him be
fetched. No one has been able to find him, she is told; he is not
to be found in any of the palaces of Spain. But Isabella can see
him in the inn at Valladolid, and she is told that he is dying on a
bed of straw. She is further told that he does not wish to come
at her command, but intends to fulfil his destiny, with her ring on
his finger. She may have his mule.

(8) The scene disappears. The image of Saint James appears
on the screen; he it was who guided the Queen safely to heaven.
Isabella leads a prayer for Columbus. At the final Alleluiah, a
dove flies from the globe.                                    H.

# CHAPTER 17

# Russian Opera in the Twentieth Century

# IGOR STRAWINSKY

## (born 1882)

## LE ROSSIGNOL
### The Nightingale

OPERA in three acts by Igor Strawinsky; text by the composer and S. Mitousoff after Hans Andersen's fairy tale. Première Paris, Opéra, May 26, 1914; first performed Drury Lane, London, 1914, with Dobrovolska, Petrenko, Brian, Andreef, Warfolomeiev, conductor Cooper; Covent Garden, 1919 (in English), with Nelis, Clegg, Moore, D'Oisly, Richardson, Austin, conductor E. Goossens (snr.); New York, Metropolitan, 1926, with Talley, Bourskaya, Wakefield, Errolle, Schützendorf, Didur, conductor Serafin; la Scala, Milan, 1926, with Pasini, conductor Strawinsky; Buenos Aires, 1927, with dal Monte, Tedeschi, conductor Calusio; Berlin (as ballet), 1929; revived Trieste, 1935, with Menotti, conductor Salfi; Genoa, 1937, with Pagliughi, Fort, conductor Gui; Palermo, 1950, with Grani, conductor Questa; Holland, 1952, with Dobbs, conductor Bruck.

### CHARACTERS

The Fisherman ................................. Tenor
The Nightingale ............................. Soprano
The Cook ........................... Mezzo-Soprano
The Chamberlain ............................. Bass
The Bonze ..................................... Bass
1st Japanese Envoy ........................... Tenor
2nd Japanese Envoy .......................... Baritone
3rd Japanese Envoy............................ Tenor
The Emperor of China ....................... Baritone
Death ........................................ Alto

Chorus of Courtiers and Ghosts

Act I.    A forest on the seashore at night. At the back of the stage a Fisherman in his boat. He is waiting to hear the Nightingale which delights him every night causing him to forget his fishing. And after a while the Nightingale begins to sing. Presently other interested spectators arrive—the King's Chamberlain, a Bonze (priest) and the King's Cook, the latter bringing her confederates and other courtiers to give the Nightingale a formal invitation to court to sing before the Emperor. The Nightingale remarks that her voice is far sweeter in the forest than in the palace. Since, however, the Emperor wills it otherwise, the Emperor shall be obeyed.

The bird alights on the hand of the Cook, who takes it to the palace while the Fisherman continues to sing the praises of the bird.

Act II.    The act opens with an entr'acte (with chorus) during which the stage is hidden by veils. The chorus inquires of the Cook (who has been appointed 'Grand Cordon Bleu') about the Nightingale. The Cook describes the little bird whose songs fill the eye with tears. As the curtain rises the Chamberlain announces the Emperor, who arrives in great state with the Nightingale. At a sign from the Emperor the Nightingale begins to sing and the Emperor is so charmed that he offers the Nightingale the order of the Golden Slipper. But the bird requires no other honour than that of having charmed the great monarch. Three envoys from the King of Japan offer the Emperor a mechanical bird which also sings. As soon as the mechanical nightingale's song begins the real one flies away. The Emperor, affronted, condemns it to perpetual banishment. The voice of the Fisherman is heard again as the curtain descends.

Act III.    The Emperor is ill and Death sits at the foot of his bed wearing the imperial crown and grasping his standard. The ghosts of his good and his bad deeds crowd round the bed. The Emperor calls for his musicians. The Nightingale answers the call. It has come to banish ghosts and to sing of the coming dawn. Even Death is persuaded by the loveliness of the song to give back the crown and the standard. The Nightingale's charm has conquered disease, and as the courtiers arrive in solemn procession to salute the ruler whom they expect to find dead, the sun floods the room with light, Death disappears and the Emperor rises from his bed and wishes his courtiers a good morning. The Fisherman bids all acknowledge in the song of the Nightingale the voice of heaven.                                          F. B.

Le Rossignol was begun in 1908 just before the death of Strawinsky's teacher, Rimsky-Korsakov, but interrupted after the completion of the first act by the commissioning by Diaghilev of The Fire Bird. A request from the newly founded Free Theatre of Moscow to complete the opera led, in 1913, to a resumption of work, but now, of course, by a much maturer composer than the comparative beginner of 1908. The styles of Act I and Acts II and III are, however, not so sharply contrasted that unity is ruled out, particularly taking into account the fact that Act I is little more than a lyrical prologue to the action of the two succeeding Acts; but some critics have found a discrepancy. As it is, the opera is not too well adapted to the needs of the stage, and, in spite of the charm of much of the music and the colourful orchestration, there is little dramatic impetus behind it all.

The delightful melody of the Fisherman's song, which is used

to frame each act, the pageantry of the Chinese March, the delicate, expressive filigree of the Nightingale's exacting coloratura

music—these elements do not in themselves form a substitute for the type of dramatic expression which is so immediately recognisable, for all that it is accompanied by precious little action, in *Oedipus Rex*. All the same the opera, which lasts about fifty minutes, has a lyrical charm of its own, which entitles it to more frequent revival than it has recently had.          H.

## OEDIPUS REX

Opera-oratorio in two acts by Igor Strawinsky; text by Jean Cocteau after Sophocles, translated into Latin by J. Danielou. Première Théâtre Sarah Bernhardt, Paris, May 30, 1927 (as an oratorio), conducted by Strawinsky. First performed on the stage in Vienna, 1928; Berlin, 1928, conductor Klemperer; New York (concert), 1928; New York (stage), 1931, conductor Stokowski; Buenos Aires, 1931; London, Queen's Hall (concert), 1936, with Slobodskaya, Widdop, Harold Williams, Norman Walker, conductor Ansermet; Florence Festival, 1937, with Alfano, Malipiero, conductor Molinari; la Scala, Milan, 1948, with Danco, Demetz, conductor Sanzogno; Berlin, 1951, with Ilosvay, Krebs, Frick, conductor Fricsay; Cologne, 1951, with Mödl, Pears, Rehfuss, conductor Strawinsky (concert); Paris, 1952, with Zareska, Simoneau, conductor Strawinsky (staged by Cocteau); Holland Festival, 1952, with Bouvier, Vroons, conductor Bruck; Edinburgh 1956 by Hamburg Company, with Ilosvay, Melchert.

### CHARACTERS

Oedipus, *King of Thebes* ........................Tenor
Jocasta, *his wife* ......................Mezzo-Soprano

¹ Creon, *Jocasta's brother* ....................Bass-Baritone

Tiresias, *a soothsayer* ...........................Bass

The Shepherd .................................Tenor

¹ The Messenger ........................Bass-Baritone

Chorus (Tenors and Basses)

The action is continuous, although divided into two acts. It is put forward in the shape of six tableaux, with a minimum of action (the characters are directed to give the impression of living statues), and that explained beforehand in the language of the audience by a narrator. The text is in Latin.

Act I.    1. The Narrator sets the scene for the audience; of Oedipus he says: 'At the moment of his birth a snare was laid for him—and you will see the snare closing'. In the opening chorus, 'Kaedit nos pestis',² the men of Thebes lament the plague which is destroying the inhabitants of the town. They beg their king, Oedipus, to help them in their affliction. This he promises to do: 'Liberi, vos liberabo.'

Li _ _ _ be-ri, vos      li _ - be-ra-bo

2. Creon, who has been sent to Delphi to consult the oracle, returns. In an aria, 'Respondit deus', he reports that the god has revealed that Laius's murderer still lives on in Thebes, undetected and unpunished. He must be discovered. Oedipus answers that he himself, with his skill in solving riddles, will track down the murderer: 'Non reperias vetus skelus.'

3. The chorus prays to Minerva, Diana and Phoebus (or Athene, Artemis, and Apollo, as they would be in Greek), and welcomes Tiresias, whom Oedipus has decided to consult. Tiresias is blind, and referred to by the Narrator as 'the fountain of truth', but at first he refuses to answer the King's questions. Oedipus taunts him, and he makes it clear that he will hold nothing more back: the King's assassin is a king! ('Dikere non possum'). Oedipus is furious at the implication behind the words, and suggests that Creon and Tiresias are in league to oust him from the throne: 'Stipendarius es' he snarls at Tiresias. The aria ('Invidia

---

¹ These rôles may be taken by the same singer.

² The spelling used is often onomatopoeic, to ensure uniform pronunciation.

fortunam odit') dies away in silence, and is succeeded by a magnificent chorus of greeting and praise to Queen Jocasta: 'Gloria!' This is the end of the first act.

Act II begins with a reprise of the sonorous 'Gloria' chorus.

4. Jocasta is now seen on the stage. She has come, says the Narrator, attracted by the dispute of her husband and her brother. How can they raise their voices thus in anger in the stricken city ('Nonn' erubeskite, reges')? Oracles, she says, are accustomed to deceive those who consult them ('Mentita sunt oracula'); did they

O - ra - cu - la, o - ra - cu - la,  .. men - ti - ta sunt o - ra - cu - la.

not predict that her former husband, Laius, would be killed by his own son, and was he not in fact murdered by robbers at the cross-roads ('trivium') between Daulia and Delphi? The chorus takes up the word 'trivium', but its repetition has the effect of filling Oedipus with horror. In a duet with Jocasta ('Pavesco subito, Jocasta') he explains that on his way from Corinth to Thebes he himself killed a stranger at that very cross-roads. Jocasta makes an attempt to reassure him ('Oracula mentiuntur'), but it is of little avail.

5. The messenger steps forward to inform Oedipus that King Polybus is dead, and that Oedipus, so far from being his son, was only adopted by him. The messenger goes on to tell how Oedipus as a baby was rescued by a shepherd after he had been abandoned on the mountain side and then handed over to King Polybus ('Reppereram in monte puerum Oedipoda'). The shepherd corroborates his evidence, and his words so overwhelm the Queen that she disappears from the scene, convinced and horror-stricken by what she has heard. Oedipus, however, thinks she is merely ashamed of his apparently lowly birth ('Nonne monstrum reskituri'), and it is only after the messenger and the shepherd unite to accuse him of parricide and incest that he is conscious of his crime and its enormity. The chorus repeats the words of the King's accusers, after which shepherd and messenger withdraw. With a quiet dignity that has not been in evidence in his previous utterances, Oedipus resigns himself to acknowledging the truth. On the words 'Lux facta est', he disappears.[1]

[1] By means of a trap-door, according to the original stage directions.

6. The messenger reappears, and the Narrator explains that the audience is about to hear the monologue: 'The divine Jocasta is dead'; he describes how she has hanged herself and how Oedipus has pierced his eyeballs with the golden pin Jocasta wore. He bids farewell to Oedipus—Oedipus whom his people loved.

The great scene in which the messenger and the chorus bewail Jocasta's suicide ('Divum Jocastae caput mortuum!') brings the

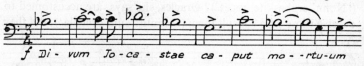

work to its emotional climax. As the messenger disappears, and Oedipus is seen with his pierced eyes, the chorus comments gently on his broken condition and bids him a last farewell.

The work is short (it lasts about an hour), and from the opening chorus the expression is direct and, whether Strawinsky likes it or not, emotional. Oedipus himself is a fascinating character study, passing as he does from the heights of power and self-confidence, through arrogance (in his attitude to Creon and Tiresias) and self-pity ('Amiki, amiki' in the aria 'Invidia fortunam odit'), until he reaches a condition of understanding and horror at his position. It is interesting to note that he uses a musical language that is, in its vocal line, curiously like that of Monteverdi's *Orfeo*, particularly in its expressive use of coloratura (e.g. Ex. 1). Oedipus is the central figure, but the climaxes are often associated with his surroundings. Successive heights of intensity are reached with the magnificent 'Gloria' chorus which closes the first act and begins the second, the aria for Jocasta and her duet with Oedipus, and the very powerful section in which the Messenger and the chorus lament the suicide of Jocasta. The form of the work may seem anti-operatic to those who have not heard it; but the music expresses drama and character in every bar, and even if stylisation had been avoided and movement added at every possible moment, nothing would have been added to the total effect, which, as far as I am concerned, is shattering.     H.

# THE RAKE'S PROGRESS

Opera in three acts and an epilogue by Igor Strawinsky; text by W. H. Auden and Chester Kallman. Première Venice Festival, September 11, 1951, with Schwarzkopf, Tourel, Tangeman, Rounseville, Otakar Kraus, Cuénod,

Arié, conductor Strawinsky. First performed Zürich, 1951, with Harvey, Malaniuk, Lichtegg, Wolff, conductor Reinshagen; Stuttgart, 1951, with Wissmann, Marta Fuchs, Holm, Neidlinger, conductor Leitner; la Scala, Milan, 1951, with Schwarzkopf, Elmo, Picchi, Kraus, Cuénod, conductor Leitner; Vienna, 1952, with Berger, Höngen, Schock, Jerger, conductor Hollreiser; London (B.B.C. broadcast), 1953, with Catley, Pollak, Young, Kraus, conductor Sacher; Metropolitan, New York, 1953, with Güden, Thebom, Conley, Harrell, conductor Reiner; Edinburgh Festival (Glyndebourne Company), 1953, with Elsie Morison, Merriman, Richard Lewis, Hines, conductor Wallenstein.

## CHARACTERS

Trulove............................................Bass

Anne, *his daughter* ............................Soprano

Tom Rakewell, *her sweetheart* ....................Tenor

Nick Shadow ................................Baritone

Mother Goose, *a brothel-keeper* ..........Mezzo-Soprano

Baba the Turk, *bearded lady in a circus* ....Mezzo-Soprano

Sellem, *the auctioneer* ............................Tenor

Keeper of the Madhouse ..........................Bass

Whores and Roaring Boys, Servants, Citizens, Madmen

*Time:* Eighteenth Century          *Place:* England

Act I.    After a very short prelude, the scene opens to show the garden of Trulove's house in the country. It is spring. In an arbour, Anne and Tom are seated. A trio develops, Anne and Tom rejoicing in the season which seems made for their love ('The woods are green'), and Trulove in the background expressing the hope that his fears about Tom's future may prove unfounded. Anne goes indoors and Mr. Trulove tells Tom that he has secured for him the offer of a city position. When Tom declines, he comments that his daughter may choose a poor husband, but he will see to it she does not marry a lazy one.

Tom alone is scornful of his prospective father-in-law's attitude; why should he waste his time in an office? He has other plans, and proposes to rely primarily on the goddess of fortune. 'Since it is not by merit we rise or we fall,' is the burden of his

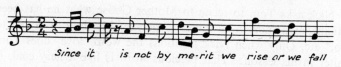

Since it    is not by me-rit we    rise or we fall

aria, whose vigorous expression suggests that Tom underestimates his own energies. He breaks off: 'I wish I had money.' Immediately a figure appears at the garden gate, and asks for Tom Rakewell. It is Nick Shadow, the bearer, so he says, of good tidings for Tom and anyone else who wishes him well. Tom calls into the house for Anne and Trulove, and Nick tells all three that Tom has been left a fortune by an uncle he never knew.

Tom rejoices in his good luck ('I wished but once, I knew that surely my wish would come true'), and thanks Nick for his tidings. Nick in his turn thanks him that he has found a new master, and Anne and Trulove thank God for the turn in Tom's fortunes. The words 'Be thanked' for each character are set to a dropping minor ninth. For a moment, Tom and Anne sing happily to one another ('O clement love'), but Nick interrupts to say that the inheritance of a fortune entails certain business transactions; they must go up to London immediately. Anne starts to say good-bye to Tom, Nick returns to say that the carriage waits, and Tom agrees to reckon up what his services have been worth a year and day after his engagement. A further farewell, a further warning on the part of Trulove that fortune so easily come by may prove an inducement to idleness, and the stage is clear. Nick turns to the audience: 'The Progress of a Rake begins.'

Scene ii is set in Mother Goose's brothel. It opens with a brilliant introduction and chorus for Whores and Roaring Boys:

Roaring Boys: With air commanding and weapon handy
We rove in a band through the streets at night,
Our only notion to make commotion
And find occasion to provoke a fight.

Whores: With darting glances and bold advances
We open fire upon young and old;
Surprised by rapture, their hearts are captured,
And into our laps they pour their gold.

Nick asks Tom to recite to Mother Goose what he has been taught: 'One aim in all things to pursue: My duty to myself to do,' etc. Only when Nick mentions the word 'love' does Tom falter in his lesson: 'That precious word is like a fiery coal, it burns my lips.' Nick introduces Tom to the company as 'a stranger to our rites', and according to custom, Tom is asked to sing. 'Love, too frequently betrayed' is the theme of his beautiful cavatina, with its rippling clarinet accompaniment.

'How sad a song,' comment the habitués of the brothel; but sorrow is quickly forgotten in such surroundings. Mother Goose claims Tom as hers for the night, the chorus form a lane with the men on one side and the women on the other, as in a children's game, and Mother Goose and Tom walk slowly between them to a door back-stage. The chorus sings away merrily (in a manner not far removed from 'Oranges and Lemons') and their refrain, 'Lanterloo', brings the scene to an end.

The third scene has the same setting as the first. Anne is sad that no word has come from Tom since he left for London. 'Quietly night, O find him and caress' she sings in a full-scale aria. There is an interruption as Trulove calls from the house, and Anne makes up her mind that Tom needs her more than her father does. This gives the cue for the cabaletta (Strawinsky actually uses the word in the score—perhaps the only time a composer has ever done this); it is a lively tune punctuated by a brilliant little orchestral *ritornello:* 'I go to him. Love cannot falter.'

Act II, scene i. Morning room of Tom's house in London. Tom is at breakfast. He has not found happiness in London, and he sings of the city's disillusion, which he contrasts with life at the side of the one true person he knows and of whom now he dare not even think. The music is in the form of an extended, loosely knit *scena:* 'Vary the song, O London, change!'

At Tom's words 'I wish I were happy', Nick appears and shows his master an advertisement for a circus, in which is featured Baba the Turk, the bearded lady. Let him advise his master: marry Baba! If he wants to be free and happy, he must be unlike the 'giddy multitude . . . driven by the unpredictable Must of their pleasures and the sober few . . . bound by the inflexible Ought of their Duty'; he must 'learn to ignore those twin tyrants of appetite and conscience'. How better than by marrying Baba? The music of Nick's aria, 'That man alone his fate fulfils', for the first time suggests the sinister purpose behind the façade of bonhomie. Tom looks up from the broadsheet and begins to laugh: 'My tale shall be told, Both by young and by old.' It is agreed that he shall marry Baba the Turk.

Scene ii.    Outside Tom's house in London. Anne is waiting
apprehensively for him to return home. A procession of servants
carries parcels into the house, and Anne wonders what their
significance can be. A sedan chair is borne in. Tom gets out of it
and comes quickly up to Anne. She must leave London, where
'Virtue is a day coquette', and forget him; he is not worthy of
her. At that moment a head is poked out of the sedan chair; it is
Baba, heavily veiled, demanding to know how much longer she
is to be kept waiting. Tom admits she is his wife. There is a trio
in which Anne and Tom sing of their might-have-beens, and
Baba expresses her extreme dislike of being kept waiting. Anne
leaves, Tom helps Baba from the chair, and, to the acclamations
of a crowd which has gathered to welcome her, she enters the
house. As a climax to the scene, she unveils and reveals her beard.

Scene iii.    The same room as Act II, scene i, except that it is
now cluttered up with every conceivable kind of object: stuffed
animals and birds, cases of minerals, china, glass, etc. Tom and
Baba are at breakfast. Tom sulks, but Baba chatters on breathlessly and appears to be in the middle of a detailed inventory of
her possessions, which she has picked up all over the world in
the course of her colourful career. After a bit she becomes conscious that Tom has not spoken, and turns lovingly to him. He
repulses her, and, losing her temper, she paces furiously about
the room, smashing the more fragile but less valuable parts of
her collection, and proclaiming angrily that Tom must be in love
with the girl he met when they first came to the house. She embarks on a florid phrase, but Tom, throwing patience to the
winds, seizes his wig which is standing nearby, and shoves it
over her face back to front so that she is cut off in mid-note.

His misery is complete, and there is only one remedy: sleep.
While he is asleep, Nick comes in, wheeling an object covered
with a dust sheet. He removes it and discloses a fantastic baroque
machine, into which he puts first a loaf of bread, and then above
it a piece of broken china. He turns the handle, out comes the
loaf. Tom wakes up with the words 'I wish it were true', and
explains to Nick that he has had a dream in which he invented
a machine which turned stones to bread, and so relieved the
sufferings of mankind. Nick asks him if it was anything like what
he sees beside him, and Tom demonstrates it to his own complete
satisfaction. Nick encourages Tom to think he may make his

fortune with this invention, then suggests he ought to tell his wife. 'My wife?' says Tom with a gesture in her direction, 'I have no wife. I've buried her.'

Act III. The first scene is laid in Tom's room, as for Act II, scene iii, except that now everything is covered in dust and cobwebs. Baba is still sitting motionless at the table, where she was left with the wig over her face. An auction is about to take place, and the citizens are examining the objects up for sale. From time to time, they comment on the extravagance and false promises which have brought ruin to so many and which have caused this sale. Anne comes in, searching for Tom, but no one can give her any definite news of him. She decides to look for him in the house.

The door is flung open and in comes Sellem, preceded by servants carrying an auctioneer's apparatus. He gets down to business straight away, and his patter is as resourceful (and as meaningless) as one would expect. It is all carried off with great style, and the waltz tune as Sellem puts up the various items is positively elegant in its inconsequentiality (as anyone will know who heard the incomparable performance of Hugues Cuénod at the première). Finally he comes to Baba, whom he introduces in an awe-struck whisper:

> An unknown object draws us, draws us near.
> A cake? An organ? Golden Apple Tree?

The bidding rises higher and higher, and Sellem, to calm the crowd, snatches off the wig. Baba finishes her phrase, and turns to strike consternation into the bystanders. Each knows her, and she dominates all. Even the sound of the voices of Tom and Nick off-stage (singing a ballad tune which resembles 'Lillibullero') in no way disconcerts her: 'The pigs of plunder' is her only comment. She comforts Anne: 'You love him, seek to set him right: He's but a shuttle-headed lad'; then, with the greatest dignity announces her intention of returning to the stage and her interrupted career.

Again, the voices of Tom and Nick are heard below, and Anne leads the stretto-finale: 'I go to him, I go, I go, I go, I go to him.' Baba tells Sellem to fetch her carriage, and orders the crowd out of her way: 'The next time you see Baba, you shall pay.'

The scene changes to a churchyard. The smell of death is in the music, and Tom's utterances have a new sense of seriousness:

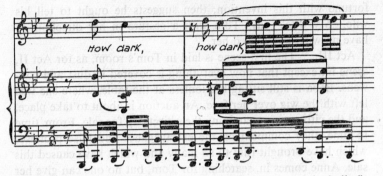

Nick reveals himself in his true colours (to the tune of the ballad):

> A year and a day have passed away
> Since first to you I came. . . .

> 'Tis not your money but your soul
> Which I this night require.

The vocal writing for Tom, caught in the trap of his own devising, in some respects recalls that for Oedipus in a similar situation; it is Strawinsky at his most expressive and his most powerful, and the crucial scene of the opera. Nick relents to the extent of inviting Tom to play cards in a last effort to save himself from hell. Tom wins the game, but in his rage Nick condemns him to insanity.

Nick sinks into a nearby grave and the stage remains dark for a moment. When the lights come up again, Tom is sitting on a green mound, putting grass in his hair and singing in a child-like voice: 'With roses crowned, I sit on ground, Adonis is my name' (the ballad-tune again). The scene is very short, but the musical suggestion of madness is achieved with economy of means but extremely moving results.

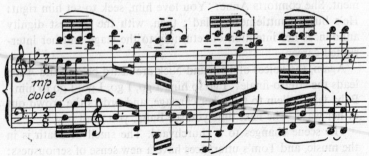

The scene changes to Bedlam. Tom is surrounded by madmen. In his own mind he is still Adonis, and he exhorts the company to prepare for his wedding with Venus. The sound of a key turning in the lock is heard, and the chorus's reaction is swift:

> Hark! Minos comes who cruel is and strong:
> Beware! Away! His whip is keen and long.

But it is the gaoler bringing with him Anne, who has come to visit Tom. Anne addresses Tom as Adonis, and in a moment he is happy not only that she has come, but that he is proved right in the sight of his fellow madmen, who predicted that no Venus would answer his call. There is a love duet, and at its end Anne helps the exhausted Tom on to the straw pallet, which lies in the middle of the room. She rocks him to sleep with a Lullaby.

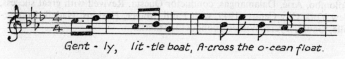

Gent - ly, lit - tle boat, A-cross the o-cean float.

The gaoler brings in her father, who leads her gently away.

When she has gone, Tom wakes and raves of his Venus, who was with him and has disappeared. The others will not believe that she was ever there, and he sinks back dead on the mattress.

> Mourn for Adonis, ever young, the dear
> Of Venus: weep, tread softly round his bier.

The curtain descends and in front of it step the five principal characters, Anne, Baba, Tom, Nick, and Trulove, to sing an epilogue. The moral:

> For idle hands
> And hearts and minds
> The Devil finds
> A work to do.

H.

# SERGEI PROKOVIEV
## (1891–1953)

### THE LOVE FOR THREE ORANGES
#### Lyubov k trem Apelsinam

OPERA in a prologue and four acts by Sergei Prokoviev; text by the composer after the comedy of Carlo Gozzi. Première Chicago, December 30, 1921, with Koshetz, Pavlovska, Falco, Dusseau, Mojica, Dua, Defrère, Cotreuil, Dufranne, conductor Prokoviev. First performed New York (Manhattan Opera House), 1922, with Chicago cast; Cologne, 1925, with Elsa Foerster, conductor Szenkar; Berlin, 1926; Leningrad, 1927; la Scala, Milan, 1947, with Gatta, Madonna, Ticozzi, del Signore, Nessi, Colombo, Arié, Dalamangas, conductor Questa. Revived with great success, New York City Centre, 1949, with Faull, Mayer, Haskins, Nadell, Rounseville, Gauld, Tyers, Winters, conductor Halasz.

### CHARACTERS

The King of Clubs, *ruler of an imaginary kingdom,*
  *whose inhabitants are clothed as playing cards* . . . . . . . Bass
The Prince, *his son* . . . . . . . . . . . . . . . . . . . . . . . . . . . . . Tenor
Princess Clarissa, *niece of the King* . . . . . . . . . . . . . Contralto
Leandro, *his prime minister, dressed as King of*
  *Spades* . . . . . . . . . . . . . . . . . . . . . . . . . . . . . . . . . . . . Baritone
Truffaldino, *jester* . . . . . . . . . . . . . . . . . . . . . . . . . . . . . Tenor
Pantaloon, *friend and adviser of the King* . . . . . . . . Baritone
The Magician Celio, *protector of the King* . . . . . . . . . . . . Bass
Fata Morgana, *a witch, protectress of Leandro* . . . . . Soprano
Linetta ⎤ *the Princesses hidden* ⎧ . . . . . . . . . . . . Contralto
Nicoletta ⎬ *in oranges* ⎨ . . . . . . . . Mezzo-Soprano
Ninetta ⎦ ⎩ . . . . . . . . . . . . . Soprano
The Cook . . . . . . . . . . . . . . . . . . . . . . . . . . . . . . . . . . . . . Bass
Farfarello, *a devil* . . . . . . . . . . . . . . . . . . . . . . . . . . . . . . . Bass
Smeraldina, *Fata Morgana's black servant* . . Mezzo-Soprano
The Master of Ceremonies . . . . . . . . . . . . . . . . . . . . . . . Tenor
The Herald . . . . . . . . . . . . . . . . . . . . . . . . . . . . . . . . . . . . Bass
The Trumpeter . . . . . . . . . . . . . . . . . . . . . . . . Bass Trombone
Ten Reasonable Spectators . . . . . . . Five Tenors, Five Basses

Monsters, Drunkards, Gluttons, Guards, Servants, Soldiers, Jokers, Highbrows, Wits, Romantics, Lowbrows, Little Devils, Doctors, Courtiers

The opera is a farcical but entertaining re-working of the *commedia dell'arte* atmosphere (itself partly parody) of Gozzi's play. The prologue shows the dispute between the protagonists of the various forms of theatrical entertainment. Each faction insists that nothing other than their favourite shall be played, but all are put to confusion when ten masked announcers appear to inform them that, whatever they say, they are going to see something quite different from what they are used to, 'The Love for Three Oranges'! The curtain parts to allow a 'trumpeter' (playing a bass trombone) to announce the appearance of a herald, who in his turn announces that the burden of the story is the apparently incurable hypochondria of the son of the King of Clubs.

Act I, scene i.    The King's palace. The doctors inform the King that his son cannot be cured of his illness, and the King immediately goes into paroxysms of grief; who will succeed him if his son is removed from him? His odious niece, Clarissa, presumably. Here there is some anxiety amongst the spectators on the stage in case the King should lose his dignity. The King makes up his mind that the boy must be made to laugh, as the physicians allowed that there was a chance of curing him if that could be achieved. Pantaloon suggests that the most likely way of doing it would be through feasts and theatrical performances. He shouts for Truffaldino, who undertakes to arrange everything, and disappears.

The King sends for Leandro and orders that plans for feasts and spectacles be put in train. Leandro, who is not at all anxious for the Prince's recovery, tries to raise objections to the scheme, and the scene ends with Leandro and Pantaloon shouting abuse at each other.

The stage darkens, a curtain covered with cabalistic signs descends, and Celio and Fata Morgana, surrounded by a chorus of little devils, proceed to play against each other with gigantic cards. Behind their chairs, the representations of the King of Clubs and the King of Spades respectively show that the game is in effect that of the King's protector against Leandro's. Celio loses. The music occurs in the suite as 'Scène infernale'.

The scene returns to the King's palace, where Leandro and the wicked Clarissa have reached an understanding, whereby the Princess undertakes to marry Leandro, who must encompass the Prince's death and so clear the way for her accession. She is not satisfied with the progress so far made, but Leandro is confident that his method—to fill the Prince full of tragic prose and boring verse—will yet prove lethal. There is an interruption as the spectators in the boxes get out of hand and invade the stage. When Clarissa demands action, Leandro discovers the negress Smeraldina is eavesdropping. They threaten to kill her, but she reveals that Celio protects the Prince and may yet succeed in his stratagems to make him laugh. Only through the intervention of Fata Morgana, her mistress, can this be avoided. If she comes to the festivity, all will yet be well. The three voices are raised, calling for Fata Morgana.

Act II.    The Prince's room. He is surrounded with medicines of all sorts and on his head is a compress. He is ill and bored, and none of Truffaldino's antics suffices to make him laugh. In the end, Truffaldino persuades him to dress and watch the diversions which have been planned for his benefit. The well-known march

begins in the orchestra, and continues as an interlude to the second scene, which takes place in the great hall of the palace. The King is there with Clarissa, and also in evidence are Leandro and Pantaloon. The Prince is dressed in a thick coat and covered in furs lest he catch cold.

Truffaldino stages a comic battle between 'monsters', and later turns loose a crowd of drunkards and gluttons to fight for food and drink; all to no avail—the Prince does not laugh. In despair, he looks round him and catches sight of the witch Fata Morgana. He is horrified that such an old hag should intrude and tries to eject her. In their struggle, she loses her balance, does an involuntary somersault, and achieves the apparently impossible: the Prince starts to laugh. The whole court, and even the spectators, join in, and in their delight, everyone starts to dance—everyone, that is to say, apart from Leandro and Clarissa who are anything but pleased at the turn events have taken.

But Fata Morgana is not long in recovering from her discomfiture. She curses the Prince and, surrounded by her troop of little devils, pronounces his fate; he will fall in love with three oranges, and will pursue them to the ends of the earth. Immediately, the Prince starts to cry out that he will depart forthwith on his journey, accompanied by Truffaldino. Amidst general lamentation, the little devil Farfarello appears and with a pair of bellows wafts the wanderers on their way.

Act III.   The desert. Celio makes a vain attempt to restrain Farfarello from wafting the Prince and his companion to perdition, but Farfarello tells him that his loss at cards has rendered his magic powers inoperative—and he proves as much by disobeying him. The Prince and Truffaldino appear, and the Magician, having discovered they are seeking the three oranges, advises them, if they ever find them, to cut them open only near water. He also warns them that they are in the keeping of the terrible Creonte, who takes the form of a gigantic cook. In case it may help, he gives Truffaldino a magic ribbon, hoping it may distract the cook's attention while they filch the oranges.

Farfarello appears again with his bellows and like lightning the Prince and Truffaldino are transported towards their destination. This is the *scherzo* of the suite, which, with the March, has become the most popular section of the work.

The two adventurers stand in front of the castle, and are filled with fright at what lies before them. They are about to go into the kitchen, when from it emerges the colossal cook. Both hide, but Truffaldino is quickly discovered, and saved from the cook's wrath only because the latter sees and falls hopelessly for the ribbon round his neck. Meanwhile the Prince creeps silently into the kitchen, and emerges a moment later with the three oranges, which are of a calibre that befits their vast guardian. The cook asks for the ribbon, is given it as a present, and capers with delight, while, to the music of the *scherzo*, the Prince and Truffaldino make their escape.

We meet them again in the desert, where the oranges they have been carrying have grown to really huge dimensions, big enough one might think to contain a human being. The Prince falls asleep, but Truffaldino is so thirsty he cannot resist cutting open one of the oranges, which, in spite of Celio's warning, he hopes may assuage his thirst. He cuts the skin and out steps Princess Linetta. She says that she will die of thirst if she is not immediately given some water, and, when none is forthcoming, demonstrates that she can be as good as her word. The same happens when Princess Nicolette comes from the second orange. Truffaldino, at his wit's end and unable to wake the Prince, rushes despairingly off into the desert.

The Prince awakes, appears in no way disconcerted by the sight of the two dead girls but orders four soldiers who conveniently appear to bury them with all due honour. Then he addresses himself to the third orange, which, he is sure, contains all that he has ever dreamed of. He cuts it open with his sword, and a third girl appears, more beautiful than the others; he immediately recognises her as the one being he has waited for since birth. She expresses sentiments that are in no way dissimilar, except that she adds to them a request for water that is no less urgent than that of the other princesses. She sinks into the Prince's arms, and it looks as though she will follow the other ladies to the grave. The spectators, however, rouse themselves to save what looks likely to develop into an impossible situation. A bucket of water is produced from one of the boxes, and the Princess's life is saved. The Prince and his prospective bride enthuse over each other (and are nearly interrupted from the boxes), but, when the Prince says they must return to his father's palace, she demurs: he must fetch her a suitable dress before she can think of meeting his father.

Princess Ninetta is alone. Towards her glides the figure of Smeraldina, behind whom looms the shadow of Fata Morgana. The occupants of the boxes are in a fever-heat of anxiety, which turns out to be fully justified when Smeraldina sticks a long magical pin into Ninetta's head. She groans long and sadly, and is seen to have been turned into a rat. The spectators quickly regain the boxes they have left, and Fata Morgana tells Smeraldina that she must take Ninetta's place when she meets the King.

The sound of the March is heard, and a procession appears, with the King and the Prince at its head. They come up to Smeraldina, who proclaims herself the princess, much to the Prince's dismay. He refuses to marry her, saying this negress is by no means the girl he left; but his father objects, and he is forced to give her his arm and lead her back to the palace.

Act IV. When the curtain rises, the cabalistic curtain of Act I, scene ii, is seen again. Fata Morgana and Celio are at it again, abusing one another like pickpockets, and making accusations of everything from lack of imagination to being a fake. Fata Morgana seems to be having the better of the argument, when the spectators get out of their boxes, surround her, and shove her into a section of the structure from which they have come, shutting the door firmly behind her. Smoke and fire can be seen, and for the moment Celio is triumphant.

Scene ii. The royal throne-room. Leandro and the master of ceremonies make last-minute adjustments, but it is not long before the procession is upon them. When the curtains round the throne are drawn aside, in the Princess's place can be seen sitting a large rat—Princess Ninetta in her metamorphosed state. All are aghast, the King sends for his guards, but Celio does his best to transform the rat into the princess he knows it to be. All of a sudden his efforts work, and Princess Ninetta stands before them. The Prince is beside himself with joy, and Smeraldina's discomfiture is complete. She is recognised as an accomplice of Leandro, and is accused with him and Clarissa of treason. For a moment the court watches the King go through the agonising process of making up his mind; then he turns to them full of resolve: all the culprits shall be hanged. In vain does Truffaldino plead for mercy; the King will grant none.

As the guards move towards them, the guilty crew takes flight, and soon the scene is covered with parties chasing each other, all of a dither in case the traitors get away, but none knowing which way they have gone. Suddenly, Fata Morgana appears in the middle of the stage, a trap-door opens, and her followers disappear down it to safety. The courtiers arrive too late, and there is nothing to do but cry 'God save the King' which the King immediately amends to 'God save the Prince and Princess'. (At the City Centre, there were one or two changes of detail. The last scene took place in the kitchen of the royal palace, where Truffaldino had fallen asleep and burnt the toast. The Princess, changed into a white pigeon, not a rat, suddenly flutters down into the kitchen, and is disenchanted by Celio. The traitors are condemned to sweep the kitchen, not to die, but are saved from this fate-worse-than-death by Fata Morgana. The opera ends with a repetition of the March.)        **H.**

CHAPTER 18

*English Opera in the Twentieth Century*

# FREDERICK DELIUS

## (1862–1934)

### A VILLAGE ROMEO AND JULIET

OPERA in a prologue and three acts by Frederick Delius; text by the composer, based on a story by Gottfried Keller. Première Berlin, February 21, 1907. First performed Covent Garden, 1910, with Ruth Vincent, Hyde, Dearth, Maitland, conductor Beecham. Revived 1920 with Licette, Hyde, Heming, Michael, conductor Beecham; Royal College of Music, 1934, conductor Beecham.

### CHARACTERS

| | | |
|---|---|---|
| Manz } rich farmers { | ........................ | Baritone |
| Marti } | ........................ | Baritone |
| Sali, *son of Manz* { as a child | .................. | Soprano |
| { as a man | ..................... | Tenor |
| Vreli, *daughter of Marti* | ....................... | Soprano |
| The Dark Fiddler, *rightful heir to the wood* | ....... | Baritone |
| Two Peasants | ................................ | Baritone |
| Three Women | ................ | Soprano, Mezzo-Soprano |
| Gingerbread Woman | ......................... | Soprano |
| Wheel-of-Fortune Woman | .................... | Soprano |
| Cheap Jewellery Woman | ................ | Mezzo-Soprano |
| Showman | ................................. | Tenor |
| Merry-go-Round Man | ....................... | Baritone |
| The Slim Girl | .............................. | Soprano |
| The Wild Girl | ........................ | Mezzo-Soprano |
| The Poor Horn-player | ........................... | Tenor |
| The Hunch-backed Bass Fiddler | ................... | Bass |

*Time:* Mid-Nineteenth Century. Six years elapse between the first and second scenes

*Place:* Seldwyla, Switzerland

Professor Arthur Hutchings, author of the most recent book on Delius, admonishes the listener: 'Opera-goers who require the stage properties and dramatic interruptions of Italian opera, the pageantry and ballet of Russian opera, the discrimination of character and emotional versatility of Mozartian opera, cannot fail to be disappointed in *A Village Romeo and Juliet*. No opera is more musical, because in no opera has the composer been more certain that by music he would tell the tale; Cecil Gray has called it "a symphonic poem with the implicit programme made explicit upon the stage." ... In this work the opera-goer must expect only music, and music chiefly of the same kind—sustained, dreamy beauty, slightly off-set by the sinister strains of the Dark Fiddler or the litigious quarrels of the farmers.'

Scene i.    September. A piece of land luxuriously overgrown on a hill, the broad fields of Manz and Marti lie on either side, only a small piece of either field being visible. Manz and Marti are rivals for the strip of wild land which lies between their fields. They are both ploughing when the action begins, and each, when the other is not looking, takes an extra furrow out of the waste land.

Sali and Vreli bring their parents' midday meals, then go off to play together in the woods. Manz and Marti reappear to eat their dinners together. The children come out of the wood at the same time as the Dark Fiddler can be heard in the distance. Marti recognises him, and knows that the land should be his, but that, being a bastard, he has no legal right to it. The Fiddler disappears, watched by the children. Their parents are no less baffled by his appearance than they are. They start to discuss the prospective sale of the land, each criticising the way the other has stolen a furrow here and there. They quarrel furiously, and forbid their respective children ever again to play with each other.

Scene ii.    Six years later. Outside Marti's house, which has a neglected air about it. The children are now grown up, and ever more closely drawn towards one another. Sali comes towards the house, from which Vreli presently looks out longingly. They patch up a quarrel, caused one imagines by the lawsuit in which their parents have been frittering away their heritages. They are pessimistic about the situation, but Sali hopes all may yet come right if they stick together. They make an appointment for the evening, in the fields.

Scene iii.    The wild land, overgrown with poppies. Sali waits for Vreli, who comes in and calls him, then hides until he finds her. Their delight in each other's company is obvious. The sound of the Dark Fiddler's playing is heard, and he reminds them that they have played on his land. Now that they are all beggars, he feels they are equal. Why do they not come with him and share his vagabond's existence? He does not seem to expect an answer, but is confident they will meet again. Vreli remembers that the last time they saw him was on the dread day when their fathers quarrelled. Sali reassures her, and they talk happily of their childhood days. They embrace.

Marti can be seen looking for Vreli. He spies them, and is dragging Vreli away when Sali fells him with a blow.

Scene iv.  A slow introduction leads to a new scene, the interior of Marti's house, now quite bare, apart from a bed and a bench. Vreli is sitting in front of the fire, reminding herself sadly that this is her last night in her old home. Sali comes in, and after an ecstatic greeting, they sing of their love, and pledge their word never to leave each other again. Vreli tells Sali that she has just taken her father away, as he has lost his mind as a result of Sali's blow. She will have to leave as the house has been sold. They sit down together in front of the fire, and fall asleep in each other's arms. The stage grows dark, and their dream is represented in music. They dream they are being married in the old church of Seldwyla. Church bells ring, the organ plays, a hymn is sung, and finally the bells ring again merrily.

Dawn breaks, and the lovers awake to understand that it was all a dream. Can they not have a whole day together, asks Vreli, in which to wander through the woods, and dance? 'To Berghald,' exclaims Sali. The sound of yodelling can be heard in the distance, and together they leave the house.

Scene v.  The Fair. The whole apparatus of a fair, from merry-go-rounds to shooting galleries, is visible. The various sellers cry their wares, and the showman leads some of the crowd into a tent. Enter Sali and Vreli. They look happy, and join in the gaiety of the fair until they are recognised by a woman from Seldwyla, with her companions. They buy everything that attracts them, but suddenly notice that they are being watched curiously by the crowd. Self-consciously they leave the fair, and make for the Paradise Garden, another dancing place.

The interlude during the change of scene is the famous walk to the Paradise Garden (composed five years later than the rest of the opera to themes from it). In the middle of the interlude, the stage directions indicate that Sali and Vreli should be seen resting on their journey.

Scene vi.  The vagabonds are heard in the distance before the curtain rises. When it does, it is to reveal a dilapidated country house, now used as an inn. The river flows nearby, and a barge full of hay is moored on it. The Dark Fiddler and his companions the vagabonds sit round a table. It is evening. The Dark Fiddler is evidently telling his friends the story of the strife between Manz and Marti and its origin.

As he reaches the inconclusive end of his story, Sali and Vreli come into the garden. The Dark Fiddler strongly advises them to take to the road and join him and his friends. The Dark Fiddler plays while they dance. All join him in trying to persuade the two young lovers to join them, but they fear they are too respectable for a vagabond's life. Sali and Vreli agree that they could never take to the new life that is suggested to them. Bargemen are heard singing in the distance, and gradually it dawns on Sali and Vreli that the only way out for them is to 'drift down the river' like the bargemen, but with a difference; they can never return.

Watched by the Dark Fiddler and the vagabonds, they get into the barge. Vreli throws her nosegay into the river, and Sali draws the plug from the bottom of the boat and throws it in too. As the boat moves out into the middle of the stream, Sali and Vreli fall into each other's arms on the bed of hay. Boatmen can be heard in the distance singing 'Ho, travellers we a-passing by'. Of the end, Professor Hutchings has written: 'The orchestra alone then concludes the work with a perfection unattainable by words; the music can suggest the deep and enfolding waters. However much the pathetic emotions have been stirred, we are satisfied and comforted almost as by the "happy ending" of comedy.'

H.

# ETHEL SMYTH
## (1858–1944)

### THE WRECKERS
#### Standrecht

OPERA in three acts by Dame Ethel Smyth; text by Henry Brewster (in French) from his Cornish drama, *Les Naufrageurs*. Première Leipzig, November 11, 1906. First performed London (Queen's Hall concert), 1908, conductor Nikisch; His Majesty's Theatre, 1909, conductor Beecham; Covent Garden, 1910, with Edyth Walker, Edith Evans, Booker, Koubitzky, Weidemann, Ranalow, conductor Walter; Sadler's Wells, 1939, with Coates, Gruhn, Wright, Roderick Lloyd, Hargreaves, conductor Braithwaite.

### CHARACTERS

Pascoe, *headman of the village and local preacher*
   *aged fifty-five* ........................ Bass (Baritone)
Lawrence, *keeper of the lighthouse* .............. Baritone
Harvey, *Lawrence's brother-in-law* ................. Bass
Tallan, *landlord of the tavern* ..................... Tenor
Jack, *son of Tallan, aged fifteen* ........... Mezzo-Soprano
Mark, *a young fisherman* ........................ Tenor
Thirza, *wife of Pascoe, aged twenty-two* .... Mezzo-Soprano
Avis, *daughter of Lawrence, aged seventeen* ....... Soprano
A Preacher, Fishermen, Shepherds, Miners, and their Women; also Wreckers and Pietists

The drama unfolds itself on the Cornish coast, in the second half of the eighteenth century, at the time of the Wesleyan Revival. The Cornish village in which the action takes place is inhabited by a fierce people who believe that wrecks on their coasts are a direct gift from Providence. For a long time ships have passed the dangerous coast in safety and the inhabitants are on the verge of famine. Believing this to be a punishment for their sins, they implore Heaven to deliver into their hands mariners to murder and ships to rob.

Act I.  The chapel bells are calling the congregation to prayer, and as the curtain rises a number of people are seen on the way to church singing a hymn. Tallan and Jack, coming from the tavern, profess to believe in wine rather than prayer. A gust of wind, however, is enough to drive all other concerns from their minds. For wind means a bad sea and a bad sea may bring a wreck to their coast. The sight of Pascoe, their chief man and preacher, causes the merry-makers to put down their glasses hastily. Pascoe reproves them, but as soon as he is gone Avis boldly challenges their belief in Pascoe. It is not because of their sins that ships go in safety, she says, but because some traitor has been lighting a beacon to warn sailors off the coast. Her father, Lawrence, keeper of the lighthouse, has himself seen the beacon when on stormy nights he put out the lamp of the lighthouse to lure ships to destruction. Pascoe's wife, Thirza, enters, and while some avoid her, others ask her to join them in prayer. Thirza returns a disdainful answer, and, turning her back on the wreckers, enters her cottage.

As soon as she has gone the others go to chapel, leaving Avis alone. She hides and sees Mark passing and throwing flowers through the window of Thirza's cottage. Avis, who is herself in love with Mark, comes forward and accuses him of neglecting her for Thirza. Mark makes light of Avis's jealousy, and, declaring that she is but a child whose fancies are not to be taken seriously, joins the worshippers in the chapel. Seeing Thirza enter with Mark's flower on her breast, Avis hints at her knowledge that Thirza, enamoured of Mark, has betrayed her husband. Pascoe, returning, sends Avis to chapel, then gently rebukes Thirza for not going there. Thirza answers that to pray for the destruction of ships and sailors in order to enrich the villagers is revolting to her. She abhors the wreckers. Pascoe defends them, pleading ancient customs, but Thirza will not listen. She recalls with horror the awful scenes she has witnessed; Pascoe himself has become hateful in her sight. As she runs away, the people issue from the chapel praising the preacher who 'shouted and thundered' till 'all felt convicted of sin'. After they are gone, Lawrence, Harvey, Tallan, and Jack consult about the steps to be taken to discover who signals to the ships. They decide to watch various parts of the cliffs, and the act ends as the people prepare to attack a barque which has been seen driving on the rocks.

Act II.    The act is ushered in by a prelude describing the 'Cliffs of Cornwall', which has had considerable success as a concert piece. The scene represents a desolate part of the seashore where Avis and Jack are watching for the 'traitor'. Avis at first is very scornful of Jack's efforts, then, thinking that Jack's friendship may be of use to her, allows him to kiss her. As they go to watch elsewhere, Mark enters determined once more to warn ships off that fateful strand. He collects wood for his bonfire and is about to light it when Thirza enters and begs him not to do it as the beach is watched, and should he be discovered he would be killed as a traitor. In a great love scene, the two decide to go to some distant country together, and forgetting all prudent counsel, Thirza herself applies the torch to the fire. It will be their farewell to Cornwall. Pascoe is led thither by the light of its flame and discovers Thirza in the arms of Mark. The latter escapes, but Thirza proudly boasts of having lit the fire, and tells Pascoe that she loves another. Pascoe falls senseless while the crowd gathers around them. He will be taken to the cave where 'traitors' are judged and, if found guilty, condemned to death.

Act III.    The crowd assembles in the cave which opens on the sea through a narrow archway. A path leading to the top of the cliff can be barred by an iron gate. Amongst the crowd are Thirza, Avis, and Jack. A little later Harvey, Tallan, Pascoe, and Lawrence join them. Still later, Mark appears. It is dawn, but torches are necessary to light the dark cave. Lawrence is the accuser. He relates how he and the others saw the fire and, going to it, found Pascoe in a swoon close by the beacon. Pascoe refuses to say whether he himself lit the fire, whereupon Avis, pointing to Thirza, accuses her of having bewitched her husband. Thirza answers contemptuously, but if Pascoe cannot or will not deny the accusation, he must die. Then Mark comes forward and owns that it was he who lit the warning light, at the bidding of 'a voice that we needs must follow'. He demands to be condemned. Thirza then says that if it was Mark who betrayed them, hers was the real guilt. Avis seeks to save Mark by asserting that he passed the night with her, but her stratagem fails. Thirza and Mark are both condemned to death and left in the cave, where the rising tide must drown them. The crowd leaves, locking the gate that leads to the top of the cliff. Their voices outside singing the psalm for the passing of souls mingle with the last song of the lovers as the waves invade the cave.                          F. B.

# THE BOATSWAIN'S MATE

Comedy in one act and two parts. After W. W. Jacob's story of that name. Dramatised for music and composed by Ethel Smyth. Accepted for performance in Germany, the production was prevented by the outbreak of war in 1914. First performed in London in 1916 at Shaftesbury Theatre, with Townsend, Pounds, Ranalow, conductor Goossens. First performed Old Vic, 1922; Covent Garden, 1923, with Buckman, Sidney Russell, Michael, Allin, conductor Goossens; Sadler's Wells, 1933, with Naylor, Cox, Austin, Brindle, conductor Beecham.

## CHARACTERS

Harry Benn, *ex-boatswain* ........................Tenor
Ned Travers, *ex-soldier*........................Baritone
Mrs. Waters, *landlady of 'The beehive'* ..........Soprano
Mary Ann, *a servant girl* ..............Burlesque Actress: need not sing
Policeman .......................................Bass
Chorus of Agricultural Labourers. Two Cats (behind the scenes)

*Time:* Twentieth Century          *Place:* England

N.B.—The opera may be played either with a pause between Parts I and II, or straight through. Part I consists of spoken dialogue and music; Part II is wholly music.

Part I.   The scene represents the outside of a country inn, 'The Beehive', kept by a buxom widow, Mrs. Waters. The exboatswain, Harry Benn, drinks his beer and hopes to put an end to his loneliness by marrying Mrs. Waters. As 'The Beehive' stands alone in a country road he believes that the security afforded by the presence of a man on the premises must be a cogent argument in his favour. That very night the maid, Mary Ann, will be away, and Benn urges his suit. But Mrs. Waters will have none of him. Having tried marriage once, she is of opinion that 'once bitten, twice shy' is a good saying. She has to go to the post office, and she asks Benn to look after any customer who might turn up. Left to himself, Benn recalls his wanderings over the world and the visions which haunted them—visions of 'piling up dollars and choosing a wife'. His reminiscences are cut short by the arrival of the ex-soldier Ned Travers, who mistakes him for the landlord. Benn explains that without being the landlord he is in charge because of the great friendship existing between himself and the landlady. Travers winks knowingly, and the pair get on famously together, Benn promising Travers a job as soon as Mrs. Waters (who has refused him five times in the last fortnight) changes her mind. While Travers sings of his adventures when he was in the Army, Benn has matured a plan in his mind to bring matters to a head and make Mrs. Waters look upon him with a more favourable eye. And this he tactfully suggests to his new friend, whose help is indispensable. In the middle of the night Travers is to effect an entrance in to 'The Beehive' and frighten the landlady. When she cries out Benn will rush in, tackle the supposed burglar, win her gratitude and her hand. Travers demurs at first, but two good sovereigns persuade him to undertake the job. To be quite safe he obtains from Benn a written declaration dictated in the style of grand opera recitative to the effect that Travers only pretends to be a burglar and that 'all is above board and ship-shape'. This declaration Benn signs and gives to Travers.

Part II.    The interior of 'The Beehive' at night. The moon shines outside. Benn and Travers appear at the window. They force the catch and Travers enters. After exchanging a few final remarks with Benn he is left alone to fulfil his mission. He takes off his boots, and humming a song, begins to ascend the stairs leading to Mrs. Waters' room. It is not easy to climb in the dark without making a noise. He stumbles, and a light from above announces that the noise has been heard. Mrs. Waters appears, a light in one hand, a gun in the other. Travers hastily hides in a cupboard. Mrs. Waters follows and turns the key, locking him in. Having secured her supposed burglar, she is on the point of rousing the neighbours when Travers begs her to desist, assuring her he is no burglar and giving her Benn's declaration. Mrs. Waters is amazed, but she opens the door of the cupboard on condition that Travers will do exactly as she tells him. A charming duet, 'O dear, if I had known he was quite a young man, I'd have put on more clothes!' hints at future developments. But Mrs. Waters means to give Benn a lesson. She will fire the gun at a mat and pretend she has killed the burglar. No sooner said than done. Travers hides while Mrs. Waters fires and then calls out 'murder'. The expectant Benn rushes in to find a very different situation from the one he had planned. He is staggered by the new turn of events and horrified when the landlady sings a valse tune to 'The first thing to do is get rid of the body'. He is sent to dig the grave, haunted by the fear of ghosts, but soon returns with a

policeman to whom he has given himself up for the murder of
Travers at 'The Beehive'. The arrival of the policeman is heralded
by the fate-motif of Beethoven's C minor symphony. A very lively
quartet ensues, for Mrs. Waters has to produce Travers and convince the representative of the law that there has been no murder.
Finally the policeman and Benn are driven out of doors by
Travers and Mrs. Waters. Travers improves the situation by
making love to Mrs. Waters, who at first appears indignant, then
softens and finally permits him to return to enquire as to new
possible developments. It would be the best joke of all if Benn
should find Travers installed as the landlord of 'The Beehive'.
Mrs. Waters takes down the handglass and looks at herself with
evident satisfaction, while Mary Ann returns to find that 'the
missus can kick 'er 'eels' in her delight at the unexpected outcome
of the adventure.                                              F. B.

# FÊTE GALANTE

A dance-dream in one act (after Maurice Baring's story of that name),
dramatised and composed by Ethel Smyth. Poetic version by Edward Shanks.
First performed at Birmingham in 1923, and later that year at Covent Garden,
with Doris Lemon, Cruickshank, Tudor Davies, Mummery, Ellis, conductor
Pitt.

## CHARACTERS

The King .............................. Bass-Baritone
The Lover ..................................... Tenor
Pierrot ................................. Light Baritone
Harlequin .............................. Light Tenor
The Queen ........................... Mezzo-Soprano
Columbine ............................ Light Soprano
Pantaloon
Four Puppets ........................... Mixed Voices
                Courtiers, Guests, Satyrs, Bacchantes, etc.

While the orchestra plays a sarabande the curtain rises on a
Watteau garden filled with the crowd of guests dressed in the
gorgeous costumes of the period, some of them masked. The King
and Queen are amongst them. While a soft chorus sings about
the beauty of the night and dancers perform languid, slow dances,
the Queen drops her handkerchief which is picked up by a tall
man in a domino whom the Queen recognises. The incident passes

unnoticed and the festivities proceed. A puppet drama is produced and explained to the guests by a quartet of singers. At the end Columbine dances alone and receives the thanks of the King, who claims her for the second dance. Columbine protests that she does not deserve such honour and escapes. She has other plans. As soon as the King and Queen have left with their guests she returns to ask Pierrot to dance with her. But Pierrot is moon-struck, sad, and weary; he turns a deaf ear to her protestations of love. Harlequin comes to invite Columbine to dance. Colum-bine, hurt at Pierrot's coldness, accepts. They go, and Pierrot, left alone, apparently concludes with Andrew Marvell that 'two paradises 'twere in one to be in paradise alone'. As he lies down under the bushes a madrigal is heard in the distance. The peaceful scene is interrupted by the arrival of the Queen and the Lover. Pierrot sees them but does not recognise them at first. They re-move their masks and the Lover takes off his domino, revealing a Pierrot costume. A beam of moonlight strikes the lovers and Pierrot recognises the Queen. Alarmed at what he has seen, he attempts to crawl away. Unfortunately Columbine appears on the scene, and mistaking the Lover (in Pierrot costume) for Pierrot, goes to tell the King. Pierrot attempts to warn the Queen, and the Lover has just time to put on his mask and disappear when the King arrives with Columbine. He walks up ceremoniously to the Queen and begs her to accompany him to where the guests are assembled. They go and Columbine accuses Pierrot of having abandoned her for the Queen. Pierrot refuses to answer the accu-sation. The King returns, and although he is aware that Pierrot is not the Queen's lover, he demands to know what Pierrot has seen. Again Pierrot refuses to answer. The King threatens and implores. Pierrot is adamant and talks in the style of the puppet play. The King loses his patience and motions to the guards who seize Pierrot. The guests return. A wild dance is started, the dancers moving gradually off the stage. Only the King and Queen, Pierrot and his guards remain. The stage darkens slowly. A piercing scream is heard and light returns to show Pierrot hanging from a beam. In the distance the opening chorus is heard again.

F. B.

# GUSTAV HOLST

## (1874–1934)

### SĀVITRI

AN episode from the Mahā Bharata. Words and music by Gustav Holst. Première Wellington Hall, November 5, 1916. First performed Lyric Theatre, 1921; Covent Garden, 1923, with Dorothy Silk, Heseltine, Farrington, conductor Pitt; Sadler's Wells, 1935, with Vowles, D. M. Jones, Roderick Lloyd, conductor Corbett; Oxford, 1937; Cincinnati, 1939; St. Pancras Town Hall, 1952, with Cantelo, Young, Hemsley, conductor Davis.

### CHARACTERS

Satyavān, *a woodman* ............................Tenor
Sāvitri, *his wife*.................................Soprano
Death ...........................................Bass

*Scene:* A wood at evening

The following note has been added to the score by the composer by way of preface: 'The piece is intended for performance in the open air or in a small building. When performed out of doors there should be a long avenue or path through a wood in the centre of the scene. When a curtain is used, it should be raised before the voice of Death is heard. No curtain, however, is necessary.' The orchestra consists of two string quartets, a contra-bass, two flutes and an English horn. There is also a hidden chorus of female voices.

The play opens on an empty stage. A voice is heard calling to Sāvitri. Death, the Summoner, whose path may not be turned, draws near to carry Satyavān, Sāvitri's husband, through the dark gates that sooner or later open for all. Sāvitri enters, distracted by the awful cry she has heard, unable to realise how or why Satyavān, young, strong, and fearless, should be taken from her. His voice is heard as he approaches on the homeward way after the day's labour, singing of Sāvitri's loveliness. He finds her sick with fear and trembling. The distant voices of the chorus give an eerie colour to the scene while Sāvitri laments the vanity of all things. Trees and shrubs and all that walks and creeps are unreal. The only reality is Death. It is Sāvitri who feels the coming doom, and her senses, sharpened by poignant grief, hear and see things that are hidden from her husband. Hearing her cry out wildly, 'He comes', Satyavān picks up his axe and boldly challenges the stranger. The brave words die on his lips, the axe falls from his hand, and after an appeal to Sāvitri he sinks to the ground while Death slowly approaches to claim him as his own. Sāvitri gathers the body in her arms and sings softly to weave a spell so that no evil thing may come near. When Death is quite close she is herself overcome for a moment, but conquering her fears, she finds the strength to welcome the 'Just One'. 'I myself,' she sings, 'can almost see the gentle faces and hear the voices of those that are in Death's Abode where the air is holy,' and she asks Death to be taken there together with Satyavān. That may not be, answers Death, but, since Sāvitri, far from shrinking, gave him welcome, he will grant her a boon which, however, must not be Satyavān's life. 'Well then,' says Sāvitri after a while, 'grant me life.' 'But thou hast life now,' objects Death. 'If thou art not a blind spirit,' retorts Sāvitri, 'thou must understand that, for a woman, Life means stalwart sons and bright-eyed daughters: Life is a communion and eternal.' Her passionate pleading succeeds. Death grants her the boon—Satyavān's life, because if Satyavān dies Sāvitri's voice must become mute and she herself but 'an image floating on the waters of memory'. True to his word, Death goes away and Satyavān comes to life again. The opera ends with Sāvitri singing gently to Satyavān as she sang when she held him lifeless in her embrace.

*Sāvitri* occupies in the works of its composer the place which *The Prodigal Son* occupies amongst the works of Debussy. If in some respects it is not quite a mature product, it contains nevertheless seeds which later came to ripeness in the remarkable later works. In the handling of chorus and orchestra there is already ample evidence of a strong individual bent and the employment of free rhythms is also very characteristic. The chorus is used throughout as part of the orchestra, singing not words but the sound of the vowel 'u' in 'sun'. In this way Holst obtains some novel and very beautiful effects. F. B.

# RUTLAND BOUGHTON

(born 1878)

## THE IMMORTAL HOUR

OPERA in two acts by Rutland Boughton, the libretto being adapted from the play and poems of Fiona Macleod.

On August 26, 1914, *The Immortal Hour* was performed at Glastonbury. It was an immediate success, and Elgar pronounced it a work of genius. The chief interpreters on that occasion were Irene Lemon (Etain), Frederic Austin (Eochaidh), Muriel Boughton (Spirit Voice), Neville Strutt (Manus), Agnes Thomas (Maive), Arthur Trowbridge (Old Bard), Arthur Jordan (Midir), and the composer himself sang the part of Dalua. The war delayed its production in London, and it was only in 1920 that it was given there at the Old Vic Theatre. In 1922 the Birmingham Players brought it to London, where it played at the Regent Theatre for 216 performances, with Gwen Ffrangcon Davies as Etain; Kingsway Theatre, London, 1926; New York, 1926; Royal Academy of Music, 1939; Sadler's Wells, 1953, with Patricia Howard, Lanigan, Hargreaves, Clarkson, conductor Robertson.

### CHARACTERS

Dalua ..................................... Baritone
Etain ..................................... Soprano
Eochaidh.................................. Baritone
Spirit Voice ......................... Mezzo-Soprano
Manus .................................... Bass
Maive .................................... Contralto
Old Bard ................................. Bass
Midir .................................... Tenor

Chorus of Druids and Warriors

Act I, scene i. A forest. A pool in the background.

Dalua, the Lord of Shadow, a creature of the fairy world, passes wearily through the forest. The spirits of the trees dance around him in the darkness while a ghostly chorus mocks him. Sternly he tells them to be still for he hears the voice of another wanderer in the darkness. The spirits disappear. Dalua hides behind a tree while Etain comes haltingly forward. She comes from the land of the young, where death is only a passing shadow, and there she would return even though she finds fair the moonlight and the woods. Dalua recognises her and, stepping forward, salutes her, 'daughter of Kings and Star among the dreams that are lives and souls'. She does not know him; she has forgotten the fairy world to which she belongs and which Dalua seeks to recall to her. She does not know why she is in the wood. But Dalua knows. A King of men has wooed the 'Immortal Hour'. He felt in his heart such a love that the earth could not appease and has called upon the gods to send him one fairer than any mortal maid and the gods sent Etain. Who is this King? asks Etain. He is coming hither now—answers Dalua—and he shall have the madness he desires and think it wisdom. Etain goes out slowly while the sound of the horn heralds the coming of Eochaidh, the King. Dalua salutes him and the King recognises in him one whom he has known in dreams—why is he in this lonely wood? 'I am here,' says Dalua, 'to drink at the fountain of all dreams.' The scene ends and the voices of Dalua and Eochaidh are heard receding in the distance.

Scene ii.    The hut of Manus and Maive. Manus sits before the pine-log fire. His wife stands at the back, plucking feathers from a dead cockerel. In a sheltered recess sits Etain.

Manus and Maive are discussing the stranger who has just visited them and given them three pieces of gold—one for Etain, one for any stranger who might come, and one for keeping silence. Etain laments the beauty of her world, lost to her, and asks the peasants if they know of it. But Manus is afraid to answer. Just then the horn is heard outside. It is Eochaidh calling to the people in the hut. He is told to enter and, exchanging a greeting with his humble host, the King sees Etain. Manus and Maive retire in the shadow while Eochaidh and Etain are left to sing their love. The whole scene is dominated by the beautiful phrase

The King makes himself known to Etain who can only tell him her name because she is still bewildered by a strange darkness on her mind. The course of true love runs smooth enough until voices are heard singing the praise of the lordly ones 'who dwell in the hills'. The theme has haunting charm:

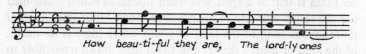

How beau-ti-ful they are, The lord-ly ones

The curtain descends with Eochaidh kneeling by the side of Etain, who listens spellbound as the voices outside slowly melt away in the distance.

Act II.   A year has passed and Druids are celebrating the anniversary of the meeting of their King Eochaidh and his bride. Etain would like to speak to them and thank them for their welcome when she is suddenly assailed by strange thoughts and longings. Wearily she bids them farewell and would retire, when Eochaidh begs her to remain and not leave him alone this night. He is full of forebodings, having heard strange laughter and seen in the gloom ghostly shapes. Surely Dalua has bewitched his eyes. Etain too has heard the magic music; she must go. Slowly she descends from her throne and goes out. The King sends away the bards and the warriors. As they move to go they are confronted by a stranger, Midir, who comes to claim a boon. He is himself a King's son. He wishes the King well; may he obtain his heart's desire. Eochaidh grants the boon and requests the bards and druids to leave him alone with the stranger. As soon as they are gone the King turns eagerly to Midir, whose power he feels to be more than mortal, and asks: 'Give me my heart's desire. Tell me there is to be no twilight upon my joy.' Midir answers him by throwing off his cloak and, clad in pure gold, tells the story of Aedh the shining god and of Dana; how they loved and how Oengus was born of their union. Murmuring 'dreams, dreams', Eochaidh turns to the subject of Midir's request for a boon. Midir asks to be allowed to kiss the Queen's hand. Eochaidh has promised, and although he grieves at the thought of waking the Queen weary with sadness and dreams, he sends for her. While they are waiting for Etain an old bard sings of things that have come and gone and of dreams that have passed silent and swift like shadows. Etain appears in the doorway dressed as she was when Eochaidh first saw her in green with the mystic mistletoe in her hair. She does not recognise Midir but readily allows him, at the King's request, to kiss her hand and to sing a song he has made. The song is the one that has been heard at the close of the first act, exalting the 'lordly ones in the hollow hills'. Its effect on Etain is that of a spell, and when Eochaidh would come near her she seems unaware of his presence. Then Midir sings another more joyous song of the land of youth where there is no death, of the land of heart's desire, and Etain feels drawn irresistibly to him. In a strained voice Eochaidh implores Etain to stay but Etain no longer hears him. An unseen chorus now takes up the haunting melody and Etain slowly follows Midir as in a trance. The stage grows dark; only a light shines where Midir stands. As he passes out of sight complete darkness falls on the stage. Dalua enters, and rapidly touches Eochaidh, who falls inert to the ground.                                                                         F. B.

# RALPH
# VAUGHAN WILLIAMS
## (born 1872)

### HUGH THE DROVER

OPERA in two acts by Ralph Vaughan Williams, text by Harold Child. Première Royal College of Music, London, July 4, 1924. First performed His Majesty's Theatre, 1924, with Mary Lewis, Tudor Davies, Collier, conductor Sargent; Toronto, 1932; R.C.M., 1933; Sadler's Wells, 1937, with Cross, Tudor Davies, Llewelyn, conductor Collingwood; New York, 1952. Revived Sadler's Wells, 1950, with Gartside, Johnston, Roderick Jones, conductor Robertson.

### CHARACTERS

A Showman ........................... High Baritone
Mary, *the constable's daughter* .................. Soprano
Aunt Jane, *the constable's sister* ................ Contralto
The Turnkey ................................... Tenor
The Constable ................................... Bass
John the Butcher ....................... Bass-Baritone
Hugh the Drover ............................... Tenor
A Cheap-Jack ................................ Baritone
A Shell-fish Seller ............................. Bass
A Primrose-seller ........................... Contralto
A Ballad-seller ................................ Tenor
Susan ...................................... Soprano
Nancy ........................................ Alto
William ...................................... Tenor
Robert ........................................ Bass
A Fool ........................................ Bass
An Innkeeper ................................. Bass
A Sergeant ................................. Baritone

Townspeople, Toy-sellers, Boys, Soldiers, Stall-keeper,
Juggler, Dancing-girl, Trumpeter, etc.

*Time:* About 1812        *Place:* A small town in the Cotswolds

The composer of *Hugh the Drover* has made extensive use of English folk songs in his score, giving the music a peculiar flavour and affecting also the treatment of the story, which bears a distinctly original stamp. Although all the melodies seem to bear some resemblance to folk songs, five authentic traditional tunes ('Cockles', 'Toy Lambs', 'Primroses', 'Maria Martin', and 'Tuesday Morning') are used in the first act and one (the psalm-tune 'York') in the second.

The action takes place in a small town in the Cotswolds; the time is the early nineteenth century.

Act I.   The scene represents a fair with booths and stalls amongst which the crowd of sightseers moves slowly, admiring, laughing, jesting with showmen, ballad singers and Cheap-Jacks. The Showman has a dummy of Napoleon 'Boneyparty', which is to be set on fire to delight the patriots of Cotsall. The voice of Mary is heard singing 'I'm to be married on Tuesday morning'. Mary is to marry on the morrow John the Butcher; but the thought of the wedding gives her no joy; she does not love John, the strongest and richest man in the town. Her Aunt Jane persuades her to accept her fate, when a stranger, Hugh the Drover, comes by; it is love at first sight with both Hugh and Mary. 'Sweet little linnet' he calls her, and instead of riches he offers her a roaming life of toil. Hugh's rousing song of the open road stirs Mary's fancy; she is not afraid; with him and with him alone can she find peace.

John enters with the crowd and eagerly embraces the proposal to fight Hugh for Mary. The crowd make a ring for the two champions; they fight, and John does not fight fair. Hugh, undismayed, continues the fight and, in the end, beats John. But John, rather than resign his claims to Mary, accuses Hugh of being a French spy. Mary is sure that Hugh cannot be a traitor; the crowd is not as faithful, and now acclaims the Constable (Mary's father), who will put Hugh in the stocks. Hugh is dragged off while the crowd jeers at the 'French spy'.

Act II, scene i.   The market-place of the town. Afternoon. (The composer directs that this scene may be omitted if the opera is found to be too long; the act then starts with scene ii.) Hugh, guarded by John and four other men, is brought in and about to be put in the stocks. The Constable asks John whether it might not be more prudent to let Hugh go; how can they prove he is a spy? John shows him money; *that* can prove anything.

Mary comes in, asks her father's pardon, and says she is now willing to marry John. The Constable is for taking her at her word, but John is still suspicious, the more so when she asks for Hugh to be freed since it is on her account that he is in the stocks. The Constable suggests they let him go—they have no evidence against him—but John sees through Mary's stratagem, and urges them to bind Hugh fast lest he should escape. Mary and Aunt Jane lament the failure of their scheme, and they leave Hugh alone in the stocks.

Scene ii.    The church bells play the psalm-tune 'York'. Early morning the next day. Hugh is in the stocks.

John and his friends have made a night of it. In passing they come to taunt and hit Hugh who, of course, cannot retort. As soon as they go Mary comes to set Hugh free, having taken the key of the stocks from her father. The lovers are on the point of running away when voices are heard. A woman has caught sight of Hugh and Mary and gives the alarm. Hugh goes back to the stocks and hides Mary under his cloak. The Turnkey and the Constable are pacified at the sight of him, but no sooner have they gone when other sounds of May festivities come to the lovers' ears. It is John, who comes to wake up Mary, bringing a spray of mayflowers. Mary cannot be found. The Constable, Aunt Jane, and the Turnkey, coming to inquire into the new mystery, discover Mary sitting in the stocks side by side with Hugh. Many would set Mary free; she refuses to go. The Constable disowns her; John declares that a trollop from the stocks is not a fit wife for him, but the crowd sympathises with the generous girl. There is every likelihood of a fight between the friends of John and the friends of Mary and Hugh when the arrival of soldiers called to take away Hugh puts an end to the dispute.

John is very anxious that Hugh should be instantly arrested and tried. As soon, however, as the sergeant looks at Hugh he discovers an old comrade; His Majesty has no better friend in England than Hugh the Drover. Annoyed at having come on a wild-goose-chase he refuses to go away empty-handed. He takes John and promises to make a soldier of him. The Constable apologises to Hugh; their friends beg them to stay. In a final homily Hugh tells them that he does not love the smooth, sleek life of the town, and prefers 'the windy wolds of life', where man has to do and dare or die. It is a call that he and Mary must obey. They go, followed by the farewells of their friends.

F. B.

# THE POISONED KISS

Opera in three acts. Music by Ralph Vaughan Williams. The libretto of the opera, by Evelyn Sharpe, is derived partly from a tale of Richard Garnett and partly from Nathaniel Hawthorne's story of Rapaccini's daughter. *The Poisoned Kiss*, composed during 1927–8, was first presented at Cambridge on May 12, 1936, and later the same year at Sadler's Wells theatre, London.

## CHARACTERS

Hob ⎫
Gob ⎬ *assistants to Dipsacus*
Lob ⎭

Dipsacus, *a professional magician* ................... Bass
Tormentilla, *his daughter* ...................... Soprano
Angelica, *her maid* ........................... Soprano
Amaryllus, *son of the Empress of Golden Town* ...... Tenor
Gallanthus, *his jester* ........................ Baritone

1st Medium ⎫
2nd Medium ⎬ *assistants to the Empress*
3rd Medium ⎭

The Empress Persicaria ..................... Contralto

Described as a romantic extravaganza, the opera is really a fairy tale set to characteristic and very charming music, and with spoken dialogue to help along the action.

The overture, compounded of tunes later heard in the opera, is directed to be played with the house lights up.

The first act is set near the house of Dipsacus on the edge of a forest where no man dwells. After the rise of the curtain rival choirs, representing the powers of good and evil, sing of the beauty of day and night respectively, but as soon as they have gone Angelica is left to lament the fate of an attractive young girl whose life passes in complete seclusion. All unknown to her, however, the prince and his jester have been roving in the forest and now the jester, Gallanthus, arrives. Angelica, who has never seen a young man before, falls in love with him; Gallanthus falls in love with her. Their billing and cooing is interrupted by the coming of Dipsacus who is aware that strangers have entered what he considers his own province, and he means to expel them by magic. The stage is emptied, but now Tormentilla arrives followed by Amaryllus. He met her in the forest nursing a cobra and, fearing for her life, has struck the snake a blow with his cane. Tormentilla does not fear snakes. She has been fed on poisons by Dipsacus, who has his own reasons for the strange diet. But Amaryllus does not know it and cannot understand why Tormentilla instead of thanking him weeps over her pet that has been hurt. An understanding is, however, soon reached when youth calls to youth; in their love duet, Amaryllus sings 'Blue larkspur in a garden, White clouds in summer skies', while Tormentilla, reared on poisons, uses the same tune for 'Black henbane in a thicket, Slime of the serpent's trail'. The two are about to go roving in the forest when Dipsacus intervenes. After some questioning Tormentilla whispers the word Love, upon which Dipsacus tells her his plans. When he was young he was scorned by the Empress of Golden Town and he has vowed to be revenged. He has fed Tormentilla on poisons solely in order that her kiss should be death to any lover. She will have to meet the Empress's son, make him kiss her and thus kill him. That is Dipsacus's design. But Tormentilla refuses to be a party to such a murderous plot and the angry magician instantly banishes her and her maid. They, for their part, are not unwilling to go, especially as Angelica has abstracted a piece of the philosopher's stone which has the same virtue as Aladdin's lamp. They rub the stone, express a wish and the stage is filled with a host of milliners and dressmakers with their latest creations. As they go, the curtain falls.

Act II.    Tormentilla's apartments in Golden Town. The room is filled with flowers sent by Tormentilla's admirers. Her beauty has excited such interest that when abroad she must wear a veil to avoid the unwelcome attentions of Golden Town gallants. She loves the prince whom she believes to be a shepherd boy, for the cunning son of the Empress, wanting to be loved for himself alone, has concealed his identity. Part of the act is taken up with the plots of three assistants of the Empress and counterplots of three assistants of the magician. The assistants of the Empress have been instructed to poison Tormentilla, for that is the way in which the jealous mother gets rid of any young woman likely to steal her son's affections; the assistants of the magician on the other hand plot to bring the young lovers together so that the prince should kiss Tormentilla and die. The assistants of the Empress fail in their purpose. They present Tormentilla with a box of poisoned chocolates. but she, having been made immune, eats them with relish and without the least harm. The assistants of the magician are more successful. They bring the prince to Tormentilla's apartment; the lovers meet and kiss and the prince falls, apparently dead.

Act III. We are now in the palace of the Empress. The prince is not dead, having been fed on antidotes since childhood, but he is ailing. The doctor, seriously alarmed, bluntly tells the Empress that the only way to cure him is to bring to his side the woman whose name is ever on his lips. The Empress is very angry, but if neither her spells nor the art of the physician will serve, Tormentilla will have to come and stay till the prince is restored to health.

Meanwhile Dipsacus, who knows all that has happened, comes to gloat over the distracted woman who once jilted him. He boldly tells the Empress that he and his magic alone are responsible for the prince's illness. They quarrel at first; but the thoughts of the past crowd on them; the old love is not dead; they grow sentimental and fall into each other's arms. They are found in this position by the prince and Tormentilla. Marriages are arranged—not excluding the marriage of Gallanthus and Angelica. The act which began with a waltz and a tango (the composer's touch is ever light) ends in a glorious hornpipe dance. No magic has power against true love, and love has conquered once more.

F. B.

## THE PILGRIM'S PROGRESS

A morality in a prologue, four acts and an epilogue, founded on Bunyan's Allegory of the same name; music by Ralph Vaughan Williams. Première Covent Garden, April 26, 1951, with Arnold Matters, Inia Te Wiata, Norman Walker, Edgar Evans, conductor Leonard Hancock.

### CHARACTERS

John Bunyan, *the writer* .................. Bass-Baritone
The Pilgrim ................................. Baritone
Evangelist ................................... Bass
The Four Neighbours:
Pliable ...................................... Tenor
Obstinate .................................... Bass
Mistrust ..................................... Baritone
Timorous ..................................... Tenor

| | | |
|---|---|---|
| Three Shining Ones | in the House | Soprano, Mezzo, |
| The Interpreter | Beautiful | Contralto, Tenor |
| Watchful, *the Porter* | ...................... | High Baritone |
| A Herald | ........................... | High Baritone |
| Apollyon | in the Valley of | ............ Bass |
| Two Heavenly | Humiliation | |
| Beings | | Soprano, Contralto |
| Lord Lechery | | Buffo Tenor |
| A Jester | | Dancer |
| Demas | | Baritone |
| Judas Iscariot | | Baritone |
| Simon Magus | | Bass |
| Worldly Glory | | High Baritone |
| Madam Wanton | | Soprano |
| Madam Bubble | *in Vanity Fair* | Mezzo-Soprano |
| Pontius Pilate | | Bass |
| Usher | | Buffo Tenor |
| Lord Hate-Good | | Bass |
| Malice | | Soprano |
| Pickthank | | Contralto |
| Superstition | | Tenor |
| Envy | | Bass |
| A Wood-cutter's Boy | ................. | Soprano or Treble |
| Mister By-Ends | ........................... | Buffo Tenor |
| Madam By-Ends | .......................... | Contralto |
| Three Shepherds | ................. | Tenor, Baritone, Bass |
| The Voice of a Bird | ......................... | Soprano |
| A Celestial Messenger | ......................... | Tenor |

Chorus of the Men and Women of the House Beautiful, of 'Certain persons clothed in gold', of Doleful Creatures, of Traders in Vanity Fair, of Angels in the Celestial City.

Act I. Prologue. 'Bunyan is sitting in Bedford Gaol and is writing the last words of *The Pilgrim's Progress*, "So I awoke, and behold it was a dream." Then he stands and, turning to his hearers, reads from the beginning. As he reads there appears a vision of the Pilgrim with a burden on his back, with his lamentable cry "What shall I do?" A curtain falls hiding Bunyan, and the Pilgrim is left alone reading his book and lamenting'—thus the synopsis printed as an introduction to the piano score.

The Evangelist appears and directs Pilgrim to the Wicket Gate, encouraging him to bear his burden until he comes 'to the place of deliverance'. Pilgrim is about to go when four neighbours, Pliable, Obstinate, Mistrust, and Timorous, attempt to dissuade him from his perilous undertaking. At the behest of the Evangelist, he starts again in quest of 'Life, eternal life!'

The Wicket Gate: behind it, the House Beautiful. Pilgrim stumbles in and kneels in front of the Cross. He hears the voices of Three Shining Ones, who presently appear, take the burden off his back and lay it on the Sepulchre, then raise him to his feet and lead him to the gate. An Interpreter receives him, and a chorus of men and women welcome him to the house. Pilgrim kneels while the Interpreter places the mark of the seal on his forehead. A procession appears, carrying a white robe, which the Three Shining Ones place on Pilgrim's shoulders. The Interpreter slowly leads Pilgrim into the house.

A Nocturne interlude leads straight to Act II (and should only, says the composer, be included if it is wished to perform Acts I and II without a break). Watchful, the porter of the house, goes his rounds and prays for the blessing of sleep on all that rest within.

An open road stretches out straight from the back of the stage. A Herald steps forward: 'This is the King's highway. . . . It is straight as a rule can make it. Who will go on that way?' Pilgrim asks for his name to be set down in the book, and while the scribe enters it and Pilgrim is provided with armour, the chorus sings Bunyan's hymn, 'Who would true valour see, Let him come hither.'

The Valley of Humiliation, a narrow gorge, shut in at the back by a bare grey hill. A Chorus of Doleful Creatures is howling when Pilgrim appears. He is hailed by Apollyon, who proclaims that he is King of the region wherein Pilgrim was born and challenges him to fight for his soul. Pilgrim is victorious in the combat, but sinks down weak with his wounds until revived by two Heavenly Beings, bearing a branch of the Tree of Life and a cup of the Water of Life. The Evangelist appears and announces new trials for Pilgrim; he shall pass through Vanity Fair, where he will be ill-treated by the inhabitants: 'Be thou faithful unto death, and the King shall give thee the Crown of Life.' Pilgrim is invested with the Staff of Salvation, the Roll of the Word and the Key of Promise.

Act III. Vanity Fair. Booths are up against the house walls on each side of the stage. A lane runs up stage between the booths. The Chorus stands round the booths dressed in fantastic dresses of all periods. 'All that the world can provide is for sale. Every age and every nation is represented and among them Lord Lechery offers his particular brand of merchandise. The Pilgrim enters and the crowd surrounds him. "What will ye buy?" But the Pilgrim prays to keep his eyes from vanity. A procession enters of various well-known characters who succumbed to the lure of gold or power, Demas, Judas Iscariot, Simon Magus, Worldly Glory, and Pontius Pilate. Then the mood changes, Madam Bubble, Madam Wanton, and Lord Lechery offer him the lust of the flesh and the pride of life, but the Pilgrim waves them away. "I buy the truth." He defies their Prince Beelzebub, the father of lies. At this moment appears the Lord Hate-Good, who, after hearing the witnesses against the Pilgrim, condemns him to prison and death' (so is the scene described in the synopsis to the score).

The Pilgrim in prison laments his condition. Why has God forsaken him? Suddenly he remembers the Key of Promise which has been entrusted to him. He puts it into the lock and the gates fly open. The moon gradually illuminates the landscape and reveals the Pilgrim's Way, up which Pilgrim strides.

Act IV. The edge of a wood. The Pilgrim's Way is seen stretching out into the distance with the Delectable Mountains far off. When the curtain rises, a Woodcutter's Boy is sitting and chopping firewood. He sings gaily as he works. Pilgrim asks him how far he still has to go before he reaches the Celestial City. He is told that it is not far from the Delectable Mountains which are visible from where they stand. Enter Mister and Madam By-Ends. They are full of talk, but admit that though some 'are for religion in rags and contempt', they themselves 'are for him when he walks in his golden slippers in the sunshine and with applause'. They refuse to accompany Pilgrim on the terms he proposes, preferring their old principles, 'since they are harmless and profitable'. Pilgrim goes on, leaving the boy alone.

The Delectable Mountains, near the Heavenly City. This is the episode known as *The Shepherds of the Delectable Mountains* and performed separately under that title as early as 1922 and frequently revived since then (though it lasts little more than quarter of an hour, it stands well by itself and achieved considerable popularity in the nineteen years between its first performance and its incorporation in the longer work). Three shepherds are kneeling in prayer just before sunset. Pilgrim enters and asks them if he is in the way to the Celestial City. They reassure him and ask him to stay with them for a while, to solace himself with the good of the Delectable Mountains. The voice of a bird is heard singing, and the shepherds join in the hymn. But a Celestial Messenger appears to summon Pilgrim to the Celestial City, and, as a symbol of his mission, ceremonially pierces Pilgrim's heart with an arrow. He leads Pilgrim off, and points the way forward. As Pilgrim is seen entering the River of Death, the shepherds raise their voices in song, being joined before the end of the scene by the sound of an invisible chorus.

The stage is quite dark. A distant trumpet sounds, and the voices from the Celestial City are heard a long way off but gradually getting nearer. Men and women on earth join in with them. Darkness gradually gives way to light, and Pilgrim is seen climbing the stairs to the Gates of the City. They open and he is welcomed by angels. His Pilgrimage is over.

Epilogue. The vision fades. Bunyan addresses his hearers and shows them his book. 'O come hither, and lay my book, thy head and heart together.'

It has been rightly said that the key to the work lies in its title: it is a Morality, not an Opera. The composer has been more interested in evoking a half-mystical, half-pastoral atmosphere than in creating dramatic tension through concentration on character and situation. But, even if *The Pilgrim's Progress* eventually attains more success as an oratorio than as an opera, as many people suggested at the time of its first performance, it stands as a monument to the composer's life-long seriousness of purpose (he was seventy-eight when it was first given) and equally long preoccupation with the subject of Bunyan's allegory. In his score, he has not only incorporated the episode of *The Shepherds of the Delectable Mountains* but has also drawn extensively upon material already familiar from the fifth symphony (at the time this work was first performed, it was explicitly stated that the composer had used themes from his then unfinished opera).

H.

# BENJAMIN BRITTEN

(born 1913)

## PETER GRIMES

OPERA in a prologue, an epilogue, and three acts by Benjamin Britten; text by Montagu Slater, after the poem by George Crabbe. Première Sadler's Wells, London, June 7, 1945, with Joan Cross, Coates, Iacopi, Turner, Bower, Pears, Roderick Jones, Donlevy, Brannigan, Morgan Jones, Culbert, conductor Goodall. First performed Stockholm, 1945, with Sundström, Svanholm, Sigurd Björling, Jacobsson, Wirén, Gösta Björling, conductor Sandberg; Berkshire Festival, U.S.A., 1946, with Manning, Horne, Pease, conductor Bernstein; Zürich, 1946, with Cross, Cordy, von Sieben, della Casa, Moor, Pears, Andreas Boehm, Rehfuss, Vichegonov, Libero de Luca, conductor Denzler; Basle, 1946, with Annie Weber, Wosniak, Roth müller, Preger, Ollendorf, conductor Krannhals; Hamburg, 1947, with Schlüter, Gura, Rothenberger, de Freitas, Markwort, Broecheler, Pfeifle, Roth, Göllnitz, conductor Hollreiser; Berlin, 1947, with Grümmer, Witte-Heinz Nissen, Schirp, conductor Heger; Covent Garden, 1947, with Cross, Coates, Pears, Tom Williams, Brannigan, Norville, conductor Rankl; la Scala, Milan, 1947, with Danco, Ticozzi, Prandelli, Colombo, Borriello, Campi, del Signore, Savarese, Nardi, conductor Serafin; Metropolitan, New York, 1948, with Resnik (later Stoska), Jagel (later Sullivan), Brownlee, Hines, Garris, conductor Emil Cooper.

### CHARACTERS

Peter Grimes, *a fisherman*........................Tenor
John, *his apprentice* .............................Silent
Ellen Orford, *a widow, schoolmistress of the*
    *Borough*.....................................Soprano
Captain Balstrode, *retired merchant skipper* .......Baritone
Auntie, *landlady of 'The Boar'* .................Contralto
Her two 'Nieces', *main attractions of 'The Boar'*...Soprano
Bob Boles, *fisherman and Methodist* ................Tenor
Swallow, *a lawyer* ..............................Bass
Mrs. (Nabob) Sedley, *a rentier widow of an*
    *East India Company's factor* ............Mezzo-Soprano
Rev. Horace Adams, *the rector* ...................Tenor
Ned Keene, *apothecary and quack* ...............Baritone
Dr. Thorp .......................................Silent
Hobson, *the carrier* .............................Bass

Chorus of Townspeople and Fisherfolk

*Time:* Towards 1830

*Scene:* The Borough, a small fishing town on the East Coast

The idea of *Peter Grimes* came to Britten in America in 1941 after reading an article by E. M. Forster on the subject of George Crabbe, the poet of England and more particularly of East Anglia. Shortly afterwards, Koussevitzky, the conductor, offered to commission him to write an opera, and, immediately on his return to England (in the spring of 1942), he set to work with Montagu Slater to hammer out the libretto.

This is freely adapted from Crabbe's story, which forms a part of his long poem, *The Borough*. The venue remains Aldeburgh, where Crabbe was born and where Britten, shortly after the première of *Peter Grimes*, made his home, but the character of Peter Grimes is to some extent softened; he is no longer the uncomplicated sadist of Crabbe's poem, but a proud, self-willed misfit, whose uncompromising independence and unwillingness to accept help brings him in the end to disaster.

Prologue. The Moot Hall of the Borough, where the inquest is being held on Grimes's apprentice who died at sea. As the curtain goes up, we hear in the wood-wind a theme which is associated with Swallow, the Borough lawyer and Coroner (No. 1).

The people of the Borough, who crowd the hall, suspect Grimes of having caused the boy's death, and feeling runs high. When asked to give evidence, Grimes repeats the oath after Swallow in notes an octave higher and of double the time value. He tells a story of distress at sea, how he and the boy, when out fishing, were driven from their course by a change of wind, how they were three days without water, and how the boy died of exposure.

When it comes to confirming the details of what occurred when Grimes landed his boat, Swallow and Grimes refer in turn to Ned Keene, the Rector, Bob Boles, Auntie, Mrs. Sedley, and Ellen Orford, who corroborate the evidence as their names are called. (This device is entirely plausible from the point of view of the drama, and allows in the shortest possible time an exposition of the characters of all the main figures of the opera.) There is some interruption from the onlookers, and at the end the Coroner gives his verdict: '. . . your apprentice died in accidental circumstances. But that's the kind of thing people are apt to remember', and at the same time advises Grimes to get a grown-up, not a boy, to help him in future. Grimes tries to make himself heard above the growing uproar in the court, but it is impossible, and Hobson, after vainly shouting for silence, clears the court.

Grimes and Ellen Orford are left alone, and Ellen tries to give what comfort she can. Their duet begins with Ellen singing in E major, Peter in F minor, but as Peter gradually warms to her quiet confidence in his future, he takes up her key and they finish together: 'here is a friend.'

Britten begins each of his three acts with a so-called Interlude, and also connects the two scenes of each of them with a similar orchestral piece. Prologue and Act I (which takes place on the beach, showing the Moot Hall, Boar Inn, and the porch of the church) are joined by the first of these Interludes (2A):

This calm piece seems to express the typical movement of waves and water (No. 2B):

which so often heralds a new day for the fishermen of the Borough.

The first part of the scene is in the form of an extended chorus (No. 3) with interruptions from Auntie, who opens up for the

day; Boles, who protests at anything which comes into the category of fun; Balstrode, who is concerned with what the weather has in store; the Rector and Mrs. Sedley, who wish each other 'Good morning'; and Ned Keene, who says he is anxious for an assignation with one of Auntie's 'Nieces' that night.

In the meanwhile, the fishermen and their womenfolk go about their daily business, mending nets and preparing for the day's work. Grimes's voice is heard off, calling for help with his boat, which is refused him until Balstrode and Keene decide to give him a hand.

Keene tells Grimes that he has found him another apprentice whom he has only to fetch from the workhouse. When Keene asks him, Carter Hobson refuses to have anything to do with the transaction: the cart's full. 'I have to go from pub to pub,' sings Hobson, in what Britten describes as a 'half number'. The chorus supports Hobson's refusal, but Ellen Orford takes up his tune and offers to help him mind the boy if he will agree to bring him back. The chorus's protest rises in vigour until Ellen takes her stand firmly against them: 'Let her among you without fault cast the first stone.' Her D minor *arioso* is the first extended solo writing of the opera, and its mixture of determination not to give way to the weight of opinion, and of tenderness, well illustrates the character of her music throughout the opera. Hobson yields to her pleading, and Mrs. Sedley asks Keene if he yet has her pills, her laudanum. He says he will not get them until that night; let her meet him in the pub and collect them.

Balstrode sees through his glasses that the storm cone has been hoisted, and he leads a great fugal ensemble, in which join the voices of Keene, Auntie, the two Nieces, Bob Boles, the chorus and orchestra (one of the characteristics of the Nieces is that they nearly—but not quite—always sing together in unison). Bob Boles calls on the Borough to repent, and the passage ends with the fervent prayer: 'O tide that waits for no man, spare our coasts.' The storm music is now firmly established, and it dominates the rest of the act.

Balstrode comments on Grimes's apparently convinced isolation—even now, he stays out in the storm, instead of coming into the pub—and suggests that he would be better off working on a merchantman, away from the gossip of the Borough. He is 'native, rooted here', replies Grimes: ' By familiar fields Marsh and sand.' Touched however by the old captain's kindliness, he tells him in an *arioso* passage the story of his awful experience when alone at sea with only the corpse of the dead boy to keep him company in the boat. He plans to stop the gossips with the only thing they listen to—money (a rapid *scherzando* passage). The duet grows in intensity as he refuses to listen to Balstrode's advice. Left alone, he reflects passionately on the peace which could be his were Ellen to become his wife.

The interval of the ninth has been thought to characterise Grimes's maladjustment, and we hear it in its minor form at the beginning of the scene with Balstrode (No. 4A)

We strained    in - to    the    wind

and resolved into the major when he thinks of Ellen and his possible salvation (No. 4B).

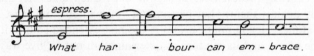

What    har - - bour    can    em - brace.

With the fall of the curtain, we hear for the first time the full force of the storm in the orchestral interlude which follows, and which is developed from the storm themes already heard, with a reference in the middle to No. 4B.

Scene ii is placed in the interior of The Boar, where warmth and calm contrasts with the storm which enters each time one or other of the characters opens the door to come in. Mrs. Sedley is an unexpected visitor, but she explains that she is waiting there for Ned Keene.

Two episodes characterise the music: Balstrode complains about the noise the frightened 'Nieces' make, and is rebuked by Auntie in a half-humorous piece; Bob Boles makes drunken advances to one of the Nieces, tries to hit Balstrode, who overpowers him and leads the company in 'We live and let live, and look we keep our hands to ourselves.'

Grimes comes in, and Mrs. Sedley promptly faints. Grimes takes little notice of what has been or is going on inside The Boar but sings introspectively of the mystery of the skies and human destiny: 'Now the Great Bear and Pleiades.' The melody is in the orchestra and in canon, but the effective words, the contrasting *molto animato* in the middle, and the suggestive and reiterated 'Who, who, who, who, who can turn skies back and begin again' make this into a *scena* of haunting beauty.

The reaction to Grimes's mood is, not unnaturally, one of consternation, and Ned Keene saves the situation by starting off a round: 'Old Joe has gone fishing.' Three distinct tunes are used and combined in the metre of 7/4 (No. 5).

The storm is heard again, and Hobson the carter comes in with Ellen and Grimes's new apprentice. The bridge is down, they almost had to swim, and everyone is chilled to the bone. Auntie offers refreshment, but Grimes wants to be off, taking the boy with him. Ellen tells him gently: 'Peter will take you home,' upon which the chorus comments derisively 'Home! do you call that home!'

Act II opens with a prelude in complete contrast to what has gone before. It is Sunday morning, and the sunlight is reflected off the waves as everyone goes to church. The interlude is made up of a lively and brilliant *toccata* (No. 6) which contrasts with

a broad, appealing lyrical tune, heard first on the violas and 'cellos (in unison) and again, immediately on the rise of the curtain, sung by Ellen who comes in with John, the new apprentice (No. 7):

con espansione

*f* Glit-ter of waves and glit-ter of sun-light

Bid us re-joice and lift our hearts on high

The scene which follows takes place within a frame provided by the music of the church service which is heard from time to time off-stage. During the hymn (*maestoso*) Ellen talks to the boy about his life at the workhouse, and her own love of her teacher's life and determination that the new apprentice's life should be different from that of the old, ending 'Every day I pray it may be so.' The beginning of the confession and responses (*Recitativo agitato*) coincides with Ellen's discovery that the boy has a torn coat and—worse—a bruise on his neck. With the Gloria (*Andante con moto*) she tries, in music of aria-like stature, to provide comfort for herself almost as much as for the boy. Peter Grimes comes in quickly as the chorus begins the Benedicite (*Allegro agitato*), and tells the boy they are off to work, answering Ellen roughly when she reminds him that it is Sunday, a day of rest. The chorus starts the Creed (*Adagio*) as Ellen pleads with Peter to adjust his ways to the boy's tender years. 'Were we mistaken when we schemed to solve your life by lonely toil?' she asks him, and concludes: 'Peter! we've failed'—and he cries out in agony and strikes her, matching the chorus's 'Amen' with his own *fortissimo* 'So be it, and God have mercy upon me!' (No. 8).

largamente

*ff* So be it And God have mer-cy upon me

Grimes drives the boy off in front of him, and leaves Ellen to make her way weepingly home.

Auntie, Bob Boles, and Ned Keene sing a brisk trio based on Grimes's example 8: 'Grimes is at his exercise', and the service comes to an end, spilling its congregation on to the beach. Some of them, Mrs. Sedley naturally amongst them, have heard the noise of the quarrel during the service, and the chorus murmurs in indignation at what it only half understands. Balstrode tries to exert a calming influence, Swallow chips in with a sitting-on-the-fence platitude, but Bob Boles inflames popular sentiment and calls on Ellen Orford, who has come back to collect her things, to tell them what was going on.

She attempts to explain in terms of what they tried to do, but the weight of opinion is too solidly against her—she is now firmly associated in their minds with Grimes and his misdeeds—and though her voice rises higher and higher in her efforts to make herself understood, the ensemble and the chorus cap her efforts, on which they have commented derisively all the time, with a cry of 'Murder!' In spite of Balstrode's protest that they are wasting their time, the Rector and Swallow organise a party to investigate what is going on at Grimes's hut, Carter Hobson beats his drum to call the men together in the emergency, and they march off together to the tune of a vindictive chorus, whose last words are 'Bring the branding iron and knife, what's done now is done for life.'

As their voices die away in the distance, two flutes in seconds introduce a 6/8 'trio' for the two Nieces, Auntie, and Ellen (except in the first phrase the Nieces sing in unison), whose calm beauty provides a contemplative ending to a scene which has otherwise been dramatic and even violent. The women reflect on their relationship with men; 'Do we smile or do we weep, Or wait quietly till they sleep?'.

The interlude joining the first scene of Act II to the second is a Passacaglia, which is the centre-piece of the whole opera. It is built up on example 8, and through it runs a desolate viola solo, which represents the fate of the apprentice caught up in Grimes's destiny.

The curtain rises on scene ii in Grimes's hut, an upturned boat boarded in to afford shelter from the weather, and full of ropes and fisherman's tackle. Until the sound of the chorus off-stage just before its end, the scene consists of an extended monologue for Grimes, the boy's part being confided to a single scream.

The music settles down to an aria, in which Grimes seeks to contrast what he is in reality with what he has always dreamed and planned, with Ellen's help, to be. The florid cast of the music and the idyllic nature of the words eventually gives place to a feverish description of that awful vigil with the dying apprentice in the boat. With the words 'in harbour still and deep' the aria comes to an end, and in the next bar the sound of the investigation procession from the village can be heard. Grimes reacts violently to it, thinks the boy is the cause of its coming to his hut, and shouts his defiance of what it can do to him. With an admonition to be careful, Grimes hustles the boy down the cliff, turns as he hears the unwelcome visitors nearing his door, and hears the boy scream as he falls down the cliff to his death. Grimes climbs quickly after him. With the scream, the orchestral sound cuts off suddenly and leaves only an eerie echo on the celesta.

The Rector puts his head round the door, and is followed by Swallow, Keene, and Balstrode. They find nothing, but comment on the open door with the precipice almost directly beyond it, and the neatness of the hut, and Swallow sums up the feelings of all when he says that the whole episode seems to have ended by quieting village gossip once and for all.

Act III opens with a Moonlight prelude of great simplicity and beauty, whose rising theme is punctuated now and then by a little figure for flute and harp.

The curtain rises to reveal the same scene as the first of Act I (the Borough street and beach), this time at night. A dance is in progress in the Moot Hall, and there is a steady procession between there and The Boar. The off-stage band plays a rustic jig, and Swallow appears, all dignity discarded, chasing one of the Nieces and singing a raffish tune. The first Niece is presently joined by the second—they find safety in numbers—and together they elude Swallow, who angrily goes into The Boar, leaving the orchestra to enjoy his tune. Ned Keene, with intentions that are in no way dissimilar from Swallow's, starts off for the place where the Nieces have gone into hiding, but is waylaid by Mrs. Sedley, who, to the accompaniment of a *Ländler* from the off-stage orchestra, and much to his disgust, tries to enlist his interest in proving Peter Grimes a murderer.

While the orchestra starts up a hornpipe, the older members of the community bid each other good night, the Rector outdoing everyone in affability. Mrs. Sedley, hardly visible, broods in the darkness: 'Crime which my hobby is sweetens my thinking.' She is still in concealment when Ellen and Balstrode walk up from the beach, the latter revealing that Grimes's boat is in, but he is nowhere to be found, the former overcome by recognising the boy's jersey, which she herself had made him, and which Balstrode has found washed up by the tide.

Ellen's aria, 'Embroidery in childhood was a luxury of idleness'

Andante con moto tranquillo — cresc

pp Em- broi - -de-ry in child - -hood was a lu- - -xu -ry of i-dle-ness

(No. 9), is, like the trio at the end of the first scene of the previous act, a moment of stillness in the drama, which has been advanced in one way or another by every other section of the music, but which is here commented upon in music that is florid and exacting, but whose effect is one of tranquillity and resignation. It is the most extended aria of the opera, and also one of its most affecting passages.

Ellen is in despair, but Balstrode says there may yet be something they can do for him, in his hour of 'unearthly torment'. Mrs. Sedley now has the clue she needs, and she goes officiously towards the door of The Boar, and calls for Mr. Swallow. Auntie protests that her customers come to her for quiet and peace, but Mrs. Sedley is not to be gainsaid, and Swallow eventually comes out to find out what all the noise is about. When he hears that Grimes's boat is back he orders, as mayor of the Borough, that Hobson take a posse of men and find Grimes. Hobson summons the men to help him, and in an atmosphere of hysteria and brutality, which is horrifyingly reflected in the big ensemble, 'him who despises us we'll destroy', the inhabitants set out to hunt down the fellow-citizen they cannot understand. The scene ends with *fortissimo* cries of 'Peter Grimes' before the curtain comes down.

The sixth interlude, a short one, has been described by Sack-ville-West as 'one of the strangest and most imaginative passages in the opera.... The music, which transfers us from the one-track hysteria of the crowd to the echoing limbo of Grimes's mind, is ... bound together by a single chord, a dominant seventh on D—held, *ppp*, throughout the interlude by three muted horns. Figures of nightmare sea-birds fly through the fog uttering fragments of themes which Grimes has sung earlier in the opera. . . .'

As the curtain rises, the search-party can be heard crying 'Peter Grimes', and at the same time a fog-horn (tuba off-stage on E flat followed by an appoggiatura D natural) makes itself heard. Grimes drags himself in, and has a long mad scene to himself, accompanied only by the off-stage chorus and the fog-horn against the background of the horn chord. He babbles of home, and sings snatches that remind him of the various stages of his tragic story. Ellen comes in with Balstrode and tells him they have come to take him home, but he appears not to recognise her until he sings a reminiscence of example 4B, which represents his aspirations and is now associated with what he has failed to obtain. Balstrode drops into ordinary speech (the chorus and the unvarying fog-horn have, for the first time since the interlude, ceased to make themselves heard) to tell Peter to take his boat out to sea and sink her there. He goes off to help Peter with the boat, then returns and leads Ellen away.

Very quietly, three violins begin to play the music of the prelude to Act I (No. 2A), as the stragglers return from the unsuccessful chase. It is morning, and the chorus sings the same tune as at the beginning of Act I. Swallow looks through his glasses to confirm the coastguard's report that a boat has been seen sinking out at sea, but no one is interested. The Borough has forgotten its manhunt and prepares to get on with another day (No. 3).

H.

# THE RAPE OF LUCRETIA

Opera in two acts by Benjamin Britten; text by Ronald Duncan, based on André Obey's play, *Le Viol de Lucrèce*. Première at Glyndebourne, July 12, 1946; the work was later toured throughout England with a double cast, the first-named singer in each case having sung at the première: Cross (Nielsen), Ferrier (Evans), Ritchie (Duff), Pollak (Lawson), Pears (Schiøtz), Kraus (Rogier), Donlevy (Sharp), Brannigan (Walker), conductor Ansermet (Goodall). First performed Basle, 1947, with Lorand, von Sieben, Wosniak, Gschwend, conductor Krannhals; Chicago, 1947, with Resnik, Kibler, Kane, Rogier, conductor Breisach; Mulhouse, 1948, with Sabatier, von Sieben, Bécour, Clément, conductor Krannhals; Paris, 1948, with Mulhouse company; New York, 1949, with Lewis, Kitty Carlisle, Kane, conductor Breisach; Rome, 1949, with Vitali-Marini, Gardino, Manuritta, Franci, conductor Santini; Salzburg Festival, 1950, with Kupper, Höngen, Güden, Dagmar Hermann, Patzak, Uhde, Poell, Böhme, conductor Krips; Munich, 1951, with Schech, Barth. Klarwein, Uhde, conductor Heger.

## CHARACTERS

Male Chorus....................................Tenor
Female Chorus...............................Soprano
Lucretia.....................................Contralto
Collatinus, *her husband* ...........................Bass
Lucia, *her attendant*...........................Soprano
Bianca, *her nurse* ...........................Contralto
Tarquinius, *Prince of Rome* ...................Baritone
Junius, *a Roman general* ......................Baritone

*Time:* 500 B.C.                    *Place:* In or near Rome

Although *The Rape of Lucretia* is to date the most lyrical of Britten's operas, its actual organisation is more formal than for instance that of *Peter Grimes*. The two acts, which are divided into two scenes each, take place within a musical and dramatic frame provided by a Male and a Female Chorus. These two commentators assume, together with the orchestra, the duties of preparation, comment, heightening of the tension, and summing-up which, in *Grimes*, were allotted to the orchestra alone, and in fact the interludes in the middle of each act are vocal as opposed to the purely instrumental equivalents in the earlier opera. The function of the Choruses is not only to act as a link between the authors and the audience, but also to give expression to the reactions of both these elements to the story which is being enacted on the stage, and which has evidently assumed a mystical significance to musicians and poet. The opera is scored for chamber orchestra.

Act I.    The Male and Female Choruses are discovered sitting on thrones, one on either side of the stage. They move about hardly at all during the course of the opera, and they are at times (e.g. during the interludes) cut off from the main part of the stage by a back-cloth.

We are *in medias res* straight away as the Male Chorus announces *con forza* in the third bar: 'Rome is now ruled by the Etruscan upstart, Tarquinius Superbus.' In a nervous half arioso, half recitative style, he introduces the story by sketching in the historical background against which it is set. The particular situation—the war against Greece—is indicated by the Female Chorus before the two voices join in a lyric statement of their own position (No. 1):

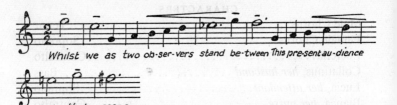

Whilst we as two ob-ser-vers stand be-tween This pre-sent au-dience and that scene.

The front-cloth rises, as the orchestra (muted strings and harp) suggests an atmosphere of oppressive heat, a night alive with the noise of crickets and bull-frogs. The scene is a camp outside Rome, with the generals' tent in the foreground. The Male Chorus and the orchestra are interrupted in their description of the lights of distant Rome by an explosive type of drinking song for the officers.

The officers discuss the outcome of their bet the night before, when they rode home unannounced to see what their wives were doing in their absence. Only Lucretia, Collatinus's wife, was at home, and the others, not excluding Junius's Patricia, were all found in one compromising situation or another. 'And Collatinus has won the bet', shouts Tarquinius, 'And Junius is a cuckold, a cuckold's a cock without a crow. . . .' Tarquinius's motif is heard for the first time at the words 'You forget I am the *Prince of Rome*' (the four descending notes C, B, A, and G sharp).

Tarquinius and Junius quarrel and start to fight but are separated by Collatinus, who suggests they drink a toast together. Tarquinius immediately proposes it (No. 2):

To the chaste Lu - cre - tia!

and all join in This is the Lucretia motif.

At its end, Junius rushes angrily from the tent, pulling the flaps shut behind him; he is furiously jealous of Lucretia's chastity, and repeats her name again and again, easing his agony by abusing her. His aria is developed to a point at which the idea of revenge fills his mind, when for the second time the Male Chorus takes over from him. What Junius might have said aloud, or at any rate what he would have admitted to feeling, is sung by him; the jealousy which causes his anger and the thoughts it suggests to him—things he would *not* have admitted to feeling—are described by the Male Chorus in music of insinuating character (No. 3).

Junius ends his aria with a final, explosive 'Lucretia!' (example 2), and Collatinus walks out to him to reason with him and persuade him to take a less directly personal view of the situation. Collatinus's aria, 'Those who love create', replaces one written for the first version of the opera, which had the dramatic disadvantage of involving Collatinus in not understanding that Junius's driving motive is jealousy. The change was made in order to reduce the risk that Collatinus might appear too soft a character to be pitted against Tarquinius—one of nature's cuckolds in fact. Collatinus goes off to bed, leaving Tarquinius and Junius to resolve their differences in a striking duet, which finishes with a canon at the half bar; as they put it,

Junius: It seems we agree.

Tarquinius: But are not of the same opinion!

Junius leaves Tarquinius alone, after suggesting that to prove Lucretia chaste is something even the Prince will not dare to attempt. The Male Chorus to the orchestral accompaniment of the opening of the scene comments on Tarquinius's indecision, until his cry of 'My horse! My horse!' reveals that his mind is now all too firmly made up.

The curtain falls rapidly and immediately the Male Chorus begins a graphic description of Tarquinius's Ride to Rome.

The music's energy mounts until the Ride is brought to a temporary halt by the River Tiber. Tarquinius and his horse take to the water, and the Chorus describes their crossing (No. 3). The slow *crescendo* from the solo flute's *ppp* to the full orchestra's *ff* is extraordinarily evocative, and the Ride culminates in the Chorus's *ff* 'Lucretia' as the curtain goes up to reveal the hall of Lucretia's house.

In Lucretia's house, all is peace. She and her two female companions are spinning, and the Female Chorus's beautiful spinning song, with its flute and harp accompaniment, not only sets the mood but also frames the three solo verses, each with its 'nostalgic ninth', which Lucretia, Bianca, and Lucia sing in turn. Lucretia thinks she hears a knock, but finding it is not Collatinus or his messenger, as she had hoped, sings an arioso, 'How cruel men are to teach us love'. The women prepare for bed, and a trio develops between Lucia and Bianca, who vocalise on 'Ah' while folding up the linen, and the Female Chorus who comments on this ubiquitous and calming feminine action.

'How quiet it is to-night', reflects Lucretia; '. . . it must be men who make the noise', retorts Bianca, and immediately we hear a suggestion of Tarquinius's Ride in the orchestra. Lucia continues to muse in the strains of the Linen trio, Male and Female Choruses point to the contrast between the peace within and the man who is coming so fast to disturb it, and a loud knocking announces that Tarquinius has arrived. The rest of the scene is carried on in pantomime, to the expressive comment of the two Choruses, until Lucretia's two companions remark on the strangeness of a visit so late from the Prince whose palace lies only just across the city, but who is asking for Lucretia's hospitality. She cannot refuse it, and there starts a chain of 'Good nights', each one based on Tarquinius's motif but subtly different from the next, and each introduced by one or other of the Choruses. The act ends when all have done suitable obeisance to the Prince.

Act II.     As before, the two Choruses introduce the act.

The curtain rises to show Lucretia asleep in bed as the bass flute, muted horn, and bass clarinet introduce the Female Chorus's Lullaby, a tune of exquisite sensitivity. It is marked

*piano* throughout, and by the end the composer writes *ppppp* over the score. The hushed atmosphere is continued in the next section, in which the Male Chorus, speaking in a mysterious voice accompanied only by percussion, describes Tarquinius's approach to Lucretia's room. As Tarquinius reaches the head of the bed, the first phrase of the Female Chorus's Lullaby is heard again. In an extended and impressive aria, Tarquinius sings of his feelings for Lucretia; the middle section is heard against the Female Chorus's Lullaby, and at the end of the aria Tarquinius bends over Lucretia to wake her, as he has planned, with a kiss.

Lucretia wakes (to the sound of the 'whip'—a little used orchestral instrument) and is confronted with the sight of Tarquinius. Immediately the character of the music changes. Lucretia pleads for mercy in music of rapidly rising tension, and Tarquinius does his best to establish that her resistance is diminishing: 'Can you deny your blood's dumb pleading?' The Choruses take Lucretia's part in the quartet which ensues: 'Go, Tarquinius, whilst passion is still proud and before your lust is spent', but it is too late, and Tarquinius pulls the cover from the bed and threatens Lucretia with his sword. The scene ends with a statement by the quartet *a capella* of the music heard originally in Junius's soliloquy (No. 3), and Tarquinius beats out the candle with his sword as the curtain falls rapidly.

The Interlude takes the form of a figured chorale sung by the two commentators, in which they interpret the scene they have just witnessed in Christian terms. The Interlude dies away and the front-drop goes up to show the hall of Lucretia's house as in the second scene of Act I. Everything is flooded with light, and Lucia and Bianca exult in the beauty of the day. Their *aubade* gives them plenty of opportunity for coloratura display, before they discuss whether it was Tarquinius they heard gallop out of the courtyard earlier in the morning. Lucia sings a little arietta, 'I often wonder whether Lucretia's love is the flower of her beauty,' before Lucretia is seen coming into the hall.

She is obviously full of foreboding, and her initially quiet behaviour gives way to something like hysteria when she is offered the orchids to arrange: 'How hideous! Take them away!' She bursts into wild activity and orders Lucia to send a messenger to Collatinus, telling him to come home. She laughs hysterically but calms sufficiently to arrange the rest of the flowers, which she she does while sings an aria, a miniature of beauty and pathos and one of the major inspirations of the score. Bianca's aria is in complete contrast; she remembers when life was still sweet and fresh for all of them before the fatal yesterday.

There is a short interchange between Bianca and Lucia (Lucretia has left the stage) in which the former bids the latter prevent the messenger reaching Collatinus; but it is too late, and in a moment Collatinus and Junius are with them, demanding to know where Lucretia is.

Lucretia herself comes in, dressed in purple mourning, and in eleven bars of orchestral music (cor anglais and strings) the essence of her tragedy is conveyed. It is a passage of incomparable beauty and poignancy. Collatinus addresses his wife in words and music that are calculated to comfort and sustain her, affirming that they must never again be parted. Their voices blend before Lucretia makes her confession to Collatinus, the orchestra punctuating what she has to say with *sotto voce* memories of the music which went with what she is describing. Finally, she sings a modified version of No. 3 ending, 'For me this shame, for you this sorrow'. Collatinus attempts to forgive her, but she is overcome by what has happened to her, and stabs herself, dying in Collatinus's arms.

Her funeral march (marked *alla marcia grave*) takes the form of an extended *chaconne*. It is sung by all the characters in tableau, Collatinus and Junius first, then Bianca and Lucia, and finally the two commentators joining their voices in the magnificent ensemble. The protagonists in the drama kneel round the body of Lucretia, while the commentators continue to discuss the tragedy. The Female Chorus cannot accept the finality with which the story has closed, and ends incredulously 'Is this it all?' to which she receives conclusive answer from her male companion: 'It is not all . . . For now He bears our sin and does not fall . . . In His passion is our hope, Jesus Christ, Saviour, He is all, He is all.' The Christian ethic has been allowed to draw its moral from the pagan story. The opera ends with a final statement of the lyrical passage heard at the end of the prologue (No. 1).

H.

# ALBERT HERRING

Opera in three acts by Benjamin Britten; text by Eric Crozier, adapted from Maupassant's story *Le Rosier de Madame Husson*. Première Glyndebourne,

June 20, 1947, with Joan Cross, Ritchie, Evans, de la Porte, Parr, Pears, Sharp, Parsons, Lumsden, Roy Ashton, conductor Britten. First performed Hanover, 1950, conductor Schüler; Berlin, 1950, with Losch, Krebs, Brauer, Heinz Nissen, conductor Ludwig; New York, 1952, by Opera Futures Workshop, conductor Shaynen.

## CHARACTERS

Lady Billows, *an elderly autocrat* ................Soprano
Florence Pike, *her housekeeper* .................Contralto
Miss Wordsworth, *head teacher at the Church*
    *School* .......................................Soprano
Mr. Gedge, *the Vicar* .........................Baritone
Mr. Upfold, *the Mayor*..........................Tenor
Superintendent Budd ..............................Bass
Sid, *a butcher's assistant* ......................Baritone
Albert Herring, *from the greengrocer's* .............Tenor
Nancy, *from the bakery* ..................Mezzo-Soprano
Mrs. Herring, *Albert's mother* ............Mezzo-Soprano
Emmie ⎫          ⎧ ....................Soprano
Cis  ⎬ *village children* ⎨ ...................Soprano
Harry ⎭          ⎩ ....................Treble

*Time:* April and May of 1900     *Place:* Loxford, a small
                                   market-town in East
                                   Suffolk

**Act I.** The curtain rises after two bars of the busy prelude to show the breakfast room of Lady Billows's house, where Florence, her housekeeper and devoted assistant, is tidying up the room. Lady Billows is half heard calling instructions from her room (off-stage), and Florence checks off in her notebook what she has to see to that morning; sample: 'Advert in chemist's window ... indecent ... tear it up!'. Florence seems about to favour us with some revelation of her private aspirations, when a knock is heard at the door, which Florence opens to admit in succession Miss Wordsworth, the Vicar, the Mayor, and Superintendent Budd, who together form the committee which is to decide between the rival candidates for the position of Queen of the May.

An *alla marcia* introduces her Ladyship, who seems at one moment in danger of not noticing her visitors, except to complain that the room stinks of tobacco. But the situation is saved, and, while she greets the committee, the orchestra begins the fugal tune which develops after a bit into a full-blooded quintet: 'We've made our own investigations and bring you our nominees.'

They sit down. Lady Billows rhapsodises on the subject of the position of May Queen, her first four notes constituting a 'Festival motif' (example 1), and grows eloquent as she considers the

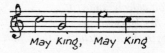
May King, May King

'state of complete moral chaos' from which it is expected to retrieve the town. In a scene accompanied sometimes by the piano, sometimes by the orchestra, the names are put forward *quasi ballata* by each member of the committee and vetoed with uncommon gusto by Florence, who does not hide the relish with which she chalks up a black mark against each successive name. A short quartet, beginning with the Vicar's 'Oh, bitter, bitter is the fruit' and ending with Budd's pregnant 'and darkness has its uses', leads to a furious aria for Lady Billows. She denounces the town as a 'spawning-ground of horror', and Florence takes particular pleasure in repeating her last words—'sty the female sex has soiled'.

It is the moment for a brain-wave, and Superintendent Budd has it: why not a *King* of the May? He launches headlong into an aria: 'Albert Herring's clean as new-mown hay', but the other members hint delicately that he is perhaps an unnecessarily backward boy, and Lady Billows snubs the suggestion as firmly as she can. She calls helplessly on the Vicar for some comfort in an awkward situation; there *are* apparently no virgins in Loxford. The Vicar rises to the occasion with a string of persuasive platitudes and a big *cantabile* tune ('Is Albert virtuous, yes or no?') which is taken up by the others, and eventually repeated drowsily by Lady Billows.

'Right! We'll have him! May King! That'll teach the girls a lesson!' she says, and leads off the fugal finale (No. 1). She leaves the room for a moment and returns to transform the finale into a florid, Purcell-like choral ode, with which the scene ends.

The interlude prepares us for the village children whom we are to meet in the next scene. The rhythm of their song (or rather of the game they are playing) is announced by the percussion, and the curtain goes up to show the interior of Mrs. Herring's grocer's shop, outside which can be seen playing Emmie, Cis, and Harry: 'Bounce me high, bounce me low'. The ball bounces into the shop, and Harry goes in after it, taking the opportunity to pinch some apples for himself and the others. They are interrupted by Sid, who empties Harry's pockets, and, pausing to take an apple for himself, shouts for Albert.

The hero makes his entrance backwards, through the door, and carrying a hundredweight of turnips (or so he tells us). Sid gives his order and offers to toss Albert for it, double or quits. But gambling is not in Albert's line: 'Mum wouldn't like it.' Sid tempts him to break the apron strings with a recital of the pleasures of independence: 'Tickling a trout, poaching a hare.' Albert tries not to listen, and Sid is just off, when Nancy, his girl friend, the baker's daughter, comes in, obviously in the middle of her shopping.

Sid buys Nancy a couple of peaches (from the firm's petty cash, he says), and tells her to bring them that night and meet him at quarter past eight for a walk together in the moonlight; if she is late, he will whistle under her window. Albert comments on their duet, which thus becomes a trio, moreover, of true lyrical beauty. Sid and Nancy go off together, Sid of course forgetting to pay for his herbs, and Albert is left alone to think about what he has seen and heard. His monologue begins with a rapid passage marked *Risoluto*, in which he wonders if his mother's strictness really leads to anything valuable, and continues with flowing phrases as he reflects on what he misses. It is interrupted by another customer—Emmie come to buy herbs for a stew—but ends with a half-defiant 'Golly, it's about time!'.

Florence comes into the shop and sends for Mrs. Herring, to tell her that the Festival Committee is about to pay her a visit. There is no time for further explanation before Lady Billows is upon them, announcing (No. 2).

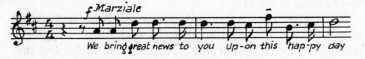

It is a forthright tune, and in its course she conveys, amongst other things, the information that the prize consists of twenty-five golden sovereigns.

The visiting party makes its way home, and the winner is left alone with the jubilant Mrs. Herring, who is only momentarily put out when Albert says firmly that he intends to refuse the prize. Mum's firmness is very much to the fore as she sends him upstairs to repent his abortive rebellion, to delighted cries of 'Albert's Mum took a stick, Whacked him on the thingmijig' from the children, who have watched the scene through the window.

Act II.    Horn calls on the Festival motif (No. 1) run through the short prelude, before the curtain goes up on the inside of a marquee set up in the vicarage garden. 'There is a long trestle table loaded with cakes, jellies, and other good things. Nancy is bringing in plates of sandwiches.'

Sid tells Nancy what has been going on down at the church, in an aria that is richly ironical. What of Albert? 'The poor kid looks on tenterhooks. He's in the mood to escape if he could.' 'You've got some scheme,' says Nancy, and Sid takes her outside to tell her what it is.

With the flute twittering away *presto* above the strings (No. 3),

Miss Wordsworth brings in the children to run through the anthem they are going to sing in celebration of Albert's coronation as King of the May.

The children are much excited at the prospect of the feast, but at last, in spite of difficulties of pitch, enunciation, and general restlessness, the rehearsal comes to an end, and teacher and children leave the tent just as Nancy and Sid return to it, the plot having been revealed. Sid pours rum into the lemonade glass in Albert's place (to the accompaniment of the *Tristan* chord) and all is ready for the reception of the official procession.

Miss Wordsworth hurries the children back, and Superintendent Budd, Mrs. Herring, the Mayor, Florence, the Vicar, and Lady Billows come in successively, each singing characteristic music. The anthem goes off quite well ('Rather modern, wasn't it?' and 'Crikey! What an awful noise' are the comments of Lady Billows and Sid respectively), flowers are presented to Lady Billows, Albert and Mrs. Herring and Miss Wordsworth and the children are thanked for their contribution to the feast. All take their places to a confused burble of conversation (as highly organised as the rest of the music), and the Vicar rises to introduce the first speaker.

This, of course, is Lady Billows, who begins with phrases of an ambitious range that rivals even Fiordiligi's. She loses her notes, but general applause covers the gap and she presents Albert with his prize of twenty-five sovereigns. In turn, and each introduced by the Vicar, come speeches from the Mayor, Miss Wordsworth and Mr. Budd, and finally Albert is called on to make some sort of reply. He can get no further than 'Er. . . er. . . thank you . . . very much', but rejoicing is general, and the Vicar leads off a congratulatory ensemble: 'Albert the Good! Long may he reign!' (No. 4), before the end of which Albert manages to call for three cheers for her Ladyship:

Albert drinks to the toast, enormously likes what he tastes, and comes round to Nancy for more, reaching her with a resounding Hiccup (on a top C flat). He is cured, by drinking from the wrong side of a glass, and the curtain goes down as the feast gets under way, and a fugue starts on the melody of 'Albert the Good'.

The interlude continues with the noise of the feast for a bit, then changes character as May Day turns into May Night and becomes a nocturne. Scene ii takes place inside Mrs. Herring's shop a little later that night. Albert comes back from the feast, enters gaily, and sings exuberant reminiscences of his triumph, punctuating his song by banging the shop door and ringing the bell. In his *scena*, he runs through a variety of subjects, from the necessity of finding some matches, to the charms of Nancy —and at mention of her, Sid's whistle can be heard outside in the street as he attempts to hurry up the keeping of their rendezvous. Outside, Nancy comments sympathetically on Albert's plight and shyness, they sing a short but forceful duet, kiss, and are off, leaving behind a much shaken, even an excited Albert.

Gone are most of Albert's inhibitions, and for the first time he sees himself as others see him, a shy, gawky, mother-ridden boy. He remembers the money in his pocket and decides to toss for it, whether he shall go off on the bust ... or not. It comes down heads 'for yes', he hears Sid's whistle far off, imitates it, seizes his hat and mackintosh, and starts off to find out what he has been missing all this time.

Act III.    The *prestissimo* prelude immediately suggests the atmosphere of the man-hunt which follows the discovery of Albert's disappearance. Nancy sings three verses of an aria which has been aptly described as Mahlerian in feeling, before Sid comes wearily into the shop, complaining that one can hear nothing but Albert's name everywhere.

Superintendent Budd asks for Mrs. Herring, and observes to Sid that murder, arson, robbery, rape (*Lucretia* motif) he can deal with, but 'God preserve me from these disappearing cases'. Mrs. Herring comes down, a picture of inconsolable grief. She has only one photograph of Albert, but the Superintendent is welcome to that for identification purposes; 'it was took on the pier at Felixstowe, when his Dad was alive, in a studio' she says, to realsounding barrel-organ accompaniment. Mrs. Herring begins the quartet (*come un lamento*) which ensues; Nancy, and later Miss Wordsworth and the Vicar, join her.

Harry complicates matters with his shouted: 'There's a Big White Something in Mrs. Williams' well', and Mrs. Herring collapses, just as Lady Billows, preceded by characteristic music, comes to join in the practical side of the hunt. She and Florence comment on the inadequacy of the steps which have so far been taken to find Albert, but a procession appears escorting the Mayor, who carries a tray, on which is Albert's orange wreath— 'Found on the road to Campsey Ash, crushed by a cart'.

There ensues the Threnody (No. 5), a great ensemble for nine voices, on an *ostinato*. Each individual has a characteristic verse to himself, the others meanwhile continuing the lament.

The shop bell rings, and Albert pokes his head round the door. 'What's going on?' he asks, and immediately a storm of re-crimination and questioning breaks around his head. He must explain everything at once, and only Sid and Nancy take his part and protest against 'prying and poking and probing at him, with your pious old faces delighting in sin'. All the same, Albert starts to tell them a story in which more is hinted at than actually described. All are horrified, and their horror is not diminished when Albert blames it all on the life of repression and molly-coddling he has been forced to lead. At the end of his recital of his doings, Albert sings a tune (No. 6) which is at the same time

ridiculously mild and inoffensive, and also warm and curiously full of understanding, even wisdom. Its effect on everyone is electrical; they have met their match and can no longer patronise their innocent May King.

'I didn't lay it on *too* thick, did I?' Albert asks Sid and Nancy; then, seeing the children mocking him from the window, he invites them inside to sample what the shop can offer in the way of fruit. The opera concludes as they all sing example 2, and Albert throws his orange-blossom wreath into the audience.      H.

## LET'S MAKE AN OPERA!

An entertainment for young people, in two parts (and three acts); text by Eric Crozier, music by Benjamin Britten. Première at the Aldeburgh Festival, June 1949, with Gladys Parr, Anne Sharp, Elizabeth

Parry, Max Worthley, Norman Lumsden, John Moules, conducted by Norman Del Mar. During 1949, given by the English Opera Group at the Wolverhampton and Cheltenham Festivals, and at the Lyric, Hammersmith, during November, December 1949 and January 1950. The opera was broadcast in September 1949 and televised in February 1950, and has been frequently produced abroad.

## CHARACTERS

| *Of the Play* | *Of the Opera* | |
|---|---|---|
| Gladys Parworthy | Miss Baggott, *the housekeeper* | ...Contralto |
| Norman Chaffinch, *a composer* | Black Bob, *the sweep-master*, and Tom, *the coachman* | ...Bass |
| Max Westleton | Clem, *Black Bob's assistant*, and Alfred, *the gardener* | ...Tenor |
| Pamela Wilton | Rowan, *the nursery-maid* | ...Soprano |
| Anne Dougall | Juliet Brook (aged fourteen) | ...Soprano |
| Mr. Harper | The conductor of the Opera | |
| John | Sam, *the new sweepboy* (eight) | ...Treble |
| Bruce | Gay Brook (thirteen) | ...Treble |
| Monica | Sophie Brook (ten) | ...Soprano |
| Peter | John Crome (fifteen) | ...Treble |
| Mavis | Tina Crome (eight) | ...Soprano |
| Ralph | Hugh Crome (eight) | ...Treble |

*Time:* 1810  *Place:* Children's nursery of Iken Hall, Suffolk

It is suggested that the names of the actual performers be used for the characters of the play. The accompaniment is for solo string quartet, piano duet (four hands on one piano), and percussion (one player is enough). For the grown-ups, professionals or gifted amateurs are needed, but the children (apart from Juliet) should be played by children. The composer characteristically adds a note to the effect that the boys should not be scared of using their chest voices.

The first two acts of *Let's Make an Opera!* are in the form of a play and illustrate the preparation and rehearsal of *The Little Sweep*, a children's opera which is performed in Act III.

Act I.   The drawing-room of Mrs. Parworthy's house. A piano, arm-chairs, standard-lamps are visible. When the play begins, the various characters are grouped round Mrs. Parworthy as she tells them a story handed down to her by her own grandmother, the Juliet Brook of the opera. The children, and also the grown-ups, comment on the story as it unfolds, and there is a discussion as to whether it would be better to do it as an opera or as a play, but the decision is never really in doubt, and the main question is whether the opera can be written and rehearsed in time for performance during the Christmas holidays.

The second scene is concerned with some early stages of rehearsal and the successful auditioning of Max Westleton, of the local building office. Snatches of the music which is later to be heard in the opera are introduced here, sometimes played on the piano by Norman Chaffinch, who is supposed to be the composer, or else sung by one or other of the characters, including of course the children.

Act II represents the stage of the hall or theatre just before the dress rehearsal of *The Little Sweep*. The set is nearly, but not quite, complete, and more rehearsal takes place. The conductor takes the opportunity of rehearsing the audience in the four songs it is required to sing, first with piano and then with orchestra. This section of the play is cunningly devised so that there is some talk on the stage and even some music in between two of the four audience songs; after the curtain comes down, there are only two to rehearse without benefit of stage diversion—apart that is to say from what the ingenuity of the conductor can devise.

*The Little Sweep* has no overture but opens with the first of the four songs which require the participation of the audience, the 'Sweep Song'. This song, which is sung with the curtain down, incidentally introduces its performers to the intricacies of 5-in-a-bar. When the curtain rises, the nursery can be seen in all its prettiness, and Clem and Black Bob in their turn are heard singing the 'Sweep Song' as they drag in little Sammy, their apprentice. One of the things attempted earlier in the play is an explanation of 'ensemble'—one of the children wonders in what way it differs from a chorus, and is told each person has his or her own musical line. An ensemble of exactly this type is the second number of the opera, and the definition is made doubly clear, since each character sings his own line as a solo before joining in with it in the ensemble. 'Sweep this chimney' admonishes the crotchety old Miss Baggott; 'Small and white and stained with tears' begins Rowan's attempt to comfort Sammy; 'Chimbley-sweepers must 'ave boys' runs the mock apology of Clem and Black Bob.

Miss Baggott takes Rowan next door to cover everything up with dust-sheets, leaving the two sweeps to get on with the job.

With horrid relish, they pull Sammy's clothes off, tie a rope round his waist and send him up the chimney, with the unambiguous instruction: 'Scrape that flue clean, or I'll roast you alive.'

For a moment the nursery is empty, but the children can be heard off-stage organising a game of hide-and-seek. Juliet runs in, hides under a dust-sheet and is discovered by Johnny, who promptly hides with her. Before the others arrive, they hear sounds from the chimney: 'Help! I'm stuck.' They call the others (in this section the dialogue is spoken) and together all take hold of the rope and start to pull, at first gently, then more vigorously when Sammy seems to be very firmly stuck indeed: 'Pull the rope

gently until he is free.' Of this section of the opera, Imogen Holst has written[1]: 'distant cries of "Where are you?" bridge the narrow gap between speech and song. The rescue of Sammy . . . bridges the still narrower gap between singing and dancing, for the children's 12/8 tune . . . brings its own action with it.'

Sammy comes tumbling out of the chimney, there is a moment of gasped astonishment, and then 'Is he wounded?' is the question to which all want an answer. The best Sammy can do is repeat pathetically 'Please don't send me up again'. The vocal line is passed from one child to the next, the twins, Hugh and Tina, usually singing together. The children quickly decide that they must hide Sammy from the frightful sweeps, and, taking him by the hand, lead him across the dust-sheets towards the window; 'Sooty tracks upon the sheet' they sing in unison as they lay the false trail. Footsteps can be heard, and the children bundle Sammy into their toy-cupboard, hide his clothes, and then themselves disappear under the dust-sheets. When Miss Baggott and the sweeps come into the room it is apparently empty. Straight away they notice the tell-tale footsteps, and their reaction is expressed in a flabbergasted, breathless version of

[1] In her chapter on 'Britten and the Young' in the symposium on the composer, edited by Donald Mitchell and Hans Keller and published by Rockliff.

'Sooty tracks'. Clem and Black Bob yell for Sam; there is no answer, and, with Miss Baggott, they launch into a ferocious vengeance trio ('Wait until we catch him'), at the end of which the sweeps disappear to look for their apprentice, leaving Miss Baggott shouting impotently after them: 'Come back.'

Rowan is left in the room, which is still apparently empty, and she has an agitated recitative, followed by a smooth *cantilena* in which she gives fervent expression to her hope that Sammy will evade his masters. She is interrupted in full song by the sight of the children's heads emerging from under the sheets. They enlist her help, and decide that the first thing to do is to give Sammy a bath. That obviously cannot be done in full view of the audience, so the curtain comes down and Sammy's ablutions are described in the second audience song, 'Sammy's Bath', a syncopated tune in 3/4 time of vigorous character, to whose third verse the fiddles provide a markedly chromatic accompaniment.

The curtain goes up again and Rowan and the children, still to the tune of 'Sammy's Bath' and (our eyes tell us) with complete justification, sing: 'O Sammy is whiter than swans as they fly.' Sammy thanks them, and they ask him how he came to be mixed up with his blackguardly employers. Sammy explains that his father broke his hip and had to sell him to find money to support the family—but the explanation shocks his listeners, the more so when Sammy adds deprecatingly that he is, after all, nine next birthday. There is a slow, sad ensemble in which Rowan and the children try to offer Sammy comfort ('O why do you

weep through the working day?'), only to receive the unvarying reply from the object of their sympathies: 'How shall I laugh and play?' Johnny suggests that they should take Sammy away with them when they leave next day, and, after some persuasion, Rowan agrees to leave a space in the top of a trunk.

Suddenly, Miss Baggott is heard coming along the passage. To the accompaniment of music marked *presto furioso* Sammy is hidden in the toy-cupboard, the bath and utensils removed, and the toys produced as if by magic. When the tyrannical old house-keeper appears, the children have formed 'a sedate tableau around the fire' (as the libretto has it), and there seems to be no cause for suspicion. Miss Baggott is all in, and punctuates her imprecations against the sweeps with frequent references to her extreme fatigue: 'Oh! my poor feet!' The children smother her with compassion, but it is not long before Miss Baggott is at her old games again, criticising the way Rowan has done the room ('Curtains crooked') and expecting to find that the toys have not been properly tidied in the cupboard. She goes towards it to make certain, and is just about to open the door when Juliet saves the situation by collapsing dramatically, with a loud scream. 'Help, help! She's collapsed'; Miss Baggott fusses round her, sends for feathers and tapers and arranges for her to be put to bed. The children meanwhile group themselves near by and moan reverently, and, when action seems called for, help to carry Juliet from the room, then return to rejoice at the complete success of Juliet's stratagem.

There is another interlude (with the curtain down), and the audience sings 'The Night Song', whose delicious tune well lives

*The owl wide winging thro' the sky In search of mice and lesser fry*

up to its description of *andante tenebroso*. The audience divides into four sections to describe the nocturnal habits of owl, heron, turtle-dove and chaffinch (with suitable bird noises at the ends of verses), and all combine for the last two verses. The last scene takes place the following morning. Juliet brings Sammy his breakfast, and sings an aria to him: 'Soon the coach will carry you away.' She gives him three half-crowns, a parting gift from her brother and sister and herself, and then the others come in to say good morning to their departing visitor. To each of them the seemingly imperturbable Sammy makes the same brief, but in the circumstances singularly appropriate, reply:"Morning! 'Morning!' After kisses all round, he is packed into the trunk, and the lid fastened down.

Tom, red-faced and permanently short of breath, with the assistance of Alfred, laid low by chronic lumbago, comes to take the trunk downstairs. With a maximum of delay and comic business, they take hold of it, but it won't shift. Miss Baggott makes a great deal of fuss, but Tom and Alfred are adamant: 'Either that there box is unpacked or we leave her where she lies.' Finally a solution is found when Rowan and the children offer to lend a hand, and the trunk is triumphantly transported from the room, Miss Baggott following it with her habitual grumble: 'Don't drop it!'

There remains only the finale—the *envoi* it might be called, Johnny, the Twins and Rowan rush in to say good-bye, Juliet. Gay, and Sophie wave from the window and describe the progress of the carriage down the drive. The percussion imitates the horse's hooves, and the entire cast returns to the stage and sings the verses, with the audience supplying the refrain:

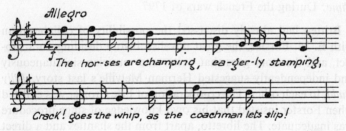

H.

## BILLY BUDD

Opera in four acts by Benjamin Britten; words by E. M. Forster and Eric Crozier, based on the story by Herman Melville. Première Covent Garden, December 1, 1951, with Pears, Uppman, Dalberg, Alan, Geraint Evans, Langdon, Marlowe, Te Wiata, McAlpine, conductor Britten. First performed Wiesbaden, 1952, with Liebl, Gschwend, Stern, Kronenberg, Böhmer, conductor Elmendorff; Paris, 1952, with London cast.

## CHARACTERS

Captain Vere, *in command of H.M.S. 'Indomitable'* . . Tenor
Billy Budd . . . . . . . . . . . . . . . . . . . . . . . . . . . . . . . . . . . . Baritone
Claggart, *master-at-arms* . . . . . . . . . . . . . . . . . . . . . . . . . Bass
Mr. Redburn, *First Lieutenant* . . . . . . . . . . . . . . . . . . Baritone
Mr. Flint, *Sailing Master* . . . . . . . . . . . . . . . . . . Baritone
Lieutenant Ratcliffe . . . . . . . . . . . . . . . . . . . . . . . . . . . . . Bass
Red Whiskers, *an impressed man* . . . . . . . . . . . . . . . . . Tenor
Donald, *a member of the crew* . . . . . . . . . . . . . . . . . . Baritone
Dansker, *an old seaman* . . . . . . . . . . . . . . . . . . . . . . . . Bass
Novice . . . . . . . . . . . . . . . . . . . . . . . . . . . . . . . . . . . . . . . Tenor
Squeak, *ship's corporal* . . . . . . . . . . . . . . . . . . . . . . . . . Tenor
Bosun . . . . . . . . . . . . . . . . . . . . . . . . . . . . . . . . . . . . . . Baritone
First and Second Mates . . . . . . . . . . . . . . . . . . . . . . . Baritones
Maintop . . . . . .      . . . . . . . . . . . . . . . . . . . . . . . . . . . . Tenor
The Novice's Friend . . . . . . . . . . . . . . . . . . . . . . . . . . . Baritone
Arthur Jones, *an impressed man* . . . . . . . . . . . . . . . . . Baritone
Four Midshipmen . . . . . . . . . . . . . . . . . . . . . . . . Boys' Voices
Cabin Boy . . . . . . . . . . . . . . . . . . . . . . . . . . . . . . . . . . . Spoken
    Officers, Sailors, Powder Monkeys, Drummers, Marines
*Place:* On board H.M.S. *Indomitable*, a seventy-four
*Time:* During the French wars of 1797

Britten had already discussed the possibility of collaboration
with E. M. Forster, the great novelist, before deciding on a subject, and the story goes that writer and musician simultaneously
and independently suggested Herman Melville's last story, *Billy
Budd*, to each other. The co-operation of Eric Crozier was enlisted
when Forster insisted that his own knowledge of stage procedure
was inadequate. The libretto, apart from the shanties and a direct
quotation from Melville's own ballad, 'Billy in the Darbies', is
in prose, and there are no women in the cast.

The background to the story is to be found in the ideas which
were aroused by the philosophical implications of the French
Revolution, and in conditions in the British Navy at that time.
The action is set in 1797, just after the mutinies at Spithead and
the Nore, when memories of 'the floating Republic' were still
very much in people's minds. Fear of mutiny, and in fact of anything which might be a conceivable prelude to mutiny, dominated

the reactions of the officers—this must be remembered in *Billy Budd*—and conditions on board ship in 1797 were such as to form an atmosphere which would be, to say the least of it, conducive to unrest and disaffection.

Act I.     For the Prologue, Captain Vere is shown as an old man. Years after his retirement, he meditates on his career and what it has taught him, on the mystery of good and evil, and on the unfathomable ways of Providence which provides a flaw in every attempt at good. Doubt, expressed musically by an ambiguity between the keys of B flat major and B minor, provides the emotional key to the scene. We hear for the first time the music later associated with Billy's stammer when Vere refers to 'some imperfection in the divine image'. The Prologue, which is played with Vere standing in isolation but with the stage in darkness apart from a spotlight on him, comes to an end as Vere's mind goes back to the year 1797.

The lights go up on the first scene, which shows the main deck and quarter-deck of H.M.S. *Indomitable*. An area of the main deck is being 'holy-stoned' by some sailors, who are urged on in their work by the first mate. The music suggests the ship's calls. At intervals the men sing while they work, and their music has a double significance: it combines the half-contented, half-dangerous swell of the sea in its motion, and derivations from it are used throughout the opera to suggest the idea of mutiny. In the last scene of the opera, it returns with increased emotional effect (No. 1):

Mr. Flint, the Sailing Master, watches the work, pulls a man up for not taking his full share in it, and gives orders to the Bosun; a party of young Midshipmen (trebles) try to show their authority by giving orders in their turn and are mocked by Donald as they cross the decks; and all the while the working song continues. One of the men, the Novice, collides accidentally with the Bosun and is threatened with the cat; the Bosun organises a working party to hoist a sail. The Novice slips as he runs off and the Bosun turns savagely on him and has Squeak, the ship's corporal, list him for twenty strokes.

To the sound of the working song, the stage empties, leaving Mr. Flint alone on the quarter-deck. The look-out spots the guard-boat returning from a press-ganging expedition, Mr. Redburn comes up on deck, Claggart is sent for, and preparations are made for the reception of the recruits, while Mr. Flint grumbles away in a short aria about the inadequacy of the recruits who come to join the ship's company: 'We seem to have the devil's own luck.' Mr. Ratcliffe, who has led the party which boarded the merchant-man, *Rights o' Man*, reports that he has returned with three recruits. As Claggart steps forward to take charge of questioning them, he is announced by the tuba and timpani (as already adumbrated during Flint's aria), and his first utterance (2A) con-stitutes his motif (No. 2):

Red Whiskers does his best to protest against his enforced enlistment (in music that is all semi-quavers), Arthur Jones replies meekly enough, and finally Billy Budd answers confidently and enthusiastically that the sea is his life and his trade is 'Able Sea-man'. When asked about his parents, he is undismayed: 'Haven't any. They say I was a . . . was a . . .'—and the stammer music is heard as he tries to get out the word 'foundling'. The officers are delighted with their new recruit—'He is a king's bargain' is Clag-gart's sardonic comment—and place him in the foretop watch. In an exhilarating passage marked *very lively*, Billy rejoices in his new life: 'Billy Budd, king of the birds!' He ends with a farewell to what is past, and to the ship on which he served: 'Farewell to you, old comrades, farewell to you for ever. . . . Farewell, *Rights o' Man*' (No. 1). This brings an immediate reaction from the officers, who jump to the conclusion (as in Melville) that it has a political significance.

The decks are cleared, and Mr. Redburn instructs Claggart to keep a watch on the new recruit. Claggart waits until the First Lieutenant has gone below, then vents his spleen: 'Do they think I am deaf. . . . These officers! They are naught but dust in the wind.' He summons Squeak, who thinks at first it is Red Whiskers he is to watch, but is told to keep an eye on Billy Budd, and to provoke him by petty thefts from his kit-bag. Claggart continues to express his hatred of the life in which he finds himself, but is interrupted by the arrival of the Novice's friend to report that the flogging has taken place, and that the offender has collapsed as a result of it; he cannot walk. 'Let him crawl' is Claggart's cynical reaction; he turns on his heel and leaves as a sad little procession comes in to a pathetic tune on the saxophone (the particular colour of this instrument is associated with the Novice). The Novice is half-dragged, half-carried in by a little band of men, amongst them the Novice's friend. In the subdued ensemble which follows (a trio, as the semi-chorus sings in unison), the Novice expresses utter despair—his heart is broken as well as his body—and the others try to comfort him, in spite of their conviction 'We're all of us lost for ever on the endless sea' (No. 3):

As they go out, Billy and Dansker, followed by Donald and Red Whiskers, emerge from the shadows where they have been watching. Their *scherzando* quartet is in complete contrast to what has gone before. The old hands make fun of Red Whiskers and assure him and Billy that it will be their turn next. Dansker dubs Billy 'Baby Budd', and Donald catches hold of Red Whiskers's beard and pulls him around. The horse-play comes to a sudden end as Claggart appears on deck, and a moment later Captain's Muster is heard (on the flutes). Donald has just time to refer to the Captain as 'Starry Vere' (it is Vere's motif, the inversion of the lament, No. 3)

No. 4

before the ship's company comes quickly on deck, and is ordered
by Claggart to fall in without delay.

The officers begin to make their way on to the quarter-deck,
and as the music reaches a climax, Vere himself appears. In
language and music that is quite free from bombast, he addresses
the ship's company and informs them that they are nearing action.
He will do everything he can for them when it comes to battle,
and the victory must come from their combined efforts. The men
are enthusiastic about what he has to say, and Billy leads a chorus
of praise for Vere as the act comes to an end.

Act II.    Evening, a week later. Vere, alone in his cabin, sends
his cabin boy to ask his officers to take a glass of wine with him.
He is reading, but looks up from his book, and in a few beautiful
arioso phrases prays that he and his company may be allowed
grace to emulate the virtues and the courage of the people of
ancient times: 'O God, grant me light, light to guide us all.'

No. 5

Mr. Redburn and Mr. Flint are announced, and together they and
Vere drink the King's health, then fall to discussing the prospect
of action, which they all think is imminent. Flint takes a bluff
seaman's view of the war, and starts a *scherzando* duet, 'Don't
like the French', in which Redburn joins with some relish. Vere
smiles and admits he shares their sentiments; another toast—
'The French, down with them!'

The word 'mutiny' creeps into the conversation, and immediately casts its shadow over the officers' thoughts. In a short aria,
marked *pp* and *cantabile*, Redburn takes up Flint's reference to
'Spithead, the Nore, the floating republic' (No. 1). He was there,
and he knows what mutiny of that sort can mean. 'O God, preserve us from the Nore' is his prayer. Vere's comment is even
firmer, as he denounces the ideas, French in their origin, which

gave rise to the scandal of the Nore. 'We must be on our guard' is his conclusion. The others remember 'that young chap who shouted out "Rights o' Man"', but Vere is of the opinion that there is nothing to fear from that quarter. The sound of singing can be heard from below, and Vere makes a kindly reference to the loyalty of their crew, before Mr. Redburn knocks briskly on the door and announces, 'Land on the port bow. . . . Enemy waters'. The two officers leave Vere to go to their stations and the Captain is left alone, first reading, then listening more and more intently to the sound of the shanty which wells up from the berth-deck.

One of the happiest moments in the opera comes with the first sound of the singing of the crew, when Vere's comments seem to radiate confidence and a sympathetic understanding of the comradeship and mutual trust which go to make a happy and efficient ship.

Scene ii takes place in the berth-deck. It is preceded by an orchestral interlude, making use of the shanty which has already been hinted at in the cabin scene ('Blow her to Hilo'), going on to a second ('Over the water'), and then returning to the first to land with overwhelming effect on a great golden chord of E flat major (chorus and orchestra) as the curtain rises. The scene is animated and yet contented. The first shanty drifts slowly to an end and Donald starts another in a brisker tempo: 'We're off to Samoa, by way of Genoa.' Red Whiskers and Billy add verses of their own, and the whole thing works up to an exuberant climax for full orchestra and chorus.

Billy and Red Whiskers try to persuade Dansker to join in the fun, but he pleads age and indifference: 'There's only one thing in the world that I want and I ain't got it.' Billy offers to lend him the tobacco he wants and goes off to get it from his kit-bag. The sound of his stammer is heard, and a moment later he drags Squeak out into the open, protesting that he has not been at Billy's kit-bag as Billy seems to think. But Squeak spoils his case by drawing a knife, and a fight begins between the two, with everyone taking Billy's side. Billy floors him in an instant, and next thing Claggart is among them, demanding to know how the whole thing started. He turns to Dansker for an explanation, and gets it in the simplest terms imaginable. Squeak is arrested, clapped in irons, and, when he threatens to blow the gaff about

Claggart's advice to him, gagged as well. 'As for you . . .', says Claggart, turning to Billy (2A), 'Handsomely done, my lad. And handsome is as handsome did it, too' (the words are Melville's).

The sound of 'Over the water' is heard off-stage, and Claggart remains motionless, muttering 'Handsomely done, my lad' to himself. When the lights have receded from the hammocks and all other noise is stilled, he permits himself to give expression to the thoughts which govern his heart: 'O beauty, O handsomeness, goodness, would that I never encountered you!'. Claggart recognises in Billy what Iago found in Cassio:

> He hath a daily beauty in his life
> That makes me ugly,

or, as Claggart himself puts it, 'The light shines in the darkness, and the darkness comprehends it and suffers'. His musical denunciation of the power of good with which he finds his own evil face to face is accompanied by a trombone solo, and the sinister power of the aria reaches a climax with its ending: 'I, John Claggart, Master-at-arms upon the *Indomitable*, have you in my power, and I will destroy you.'

Claggart's revelation of his evil purpose is immediately followed by the entrance of the Novice (No. 3). Two curious scenes ensue, both nocturnal in character and marked *pianissimo*. The first is between Claggart and the Novice, whom he has sent for with a view to forcing him, through his fear of future punishment, to obtain evidence against Billy. The Novice, after a moment of revulsion against the scheme, accepts the guineas which Claggart gives him to pass on to Billy. His agonised remorse at the part he is forced to play ('It's fate, I've no choice, everything's fate') nevertheless leads him straight to where Billy lies asleep.

The second nocturne-like scene is between Billy and the Novice, and it is introduced by a tune of uncanny peace, on a solo 'cello over two bass clarinets (the tune is heard again in a far more extended form at the beginning of Act IV) (No. 6):

PLATE XXXVII. Peter Pears and Joan Cross in *Peter Grimes*, Zürich
1946.

PLATE XXXVIII. *The Rape of Lucretia*, 1946. *L. to r.* Flora Nielsen (Female Chorus), Kathleen Ferrier (Lucretia), Frank Rogier (Tarquinius), Aksel Schiøtz (Male Chorus). Producer Eric Crozier, designer John Piper.

Billy takes time to wake up, and even longer before he understands the import of what the Novice is driving at, with his talk of pressing and gangs and whether Billy won't lead them. When he tumbles to it, the Novice scampers off as Billy is seized with another fit of stammering, which resolves itself when Dansker appears on the scene, roused by the unusual noise. Billy's nervousness betrays itself in some agitated phrases as he tries to tell Dansker what the fuss is about. But Dansker understands all too well when he hears what Billy has to say about guineas and mutiny. The act ends with a big-scale duet for Billy and Dansker, which is cast in the form of a passacaglia. Dansker enunciates its theme with a variation of Claggart's motif (No. 7):

Billy puts forward the argument that Claggart likes him, that he himself likes the life on board where his ship-mates are his friends, that he is rumoured as a candidate for promotion. Dansker's rejoinder is unvarying: 'Jemmy-legs is down on you'.

Act III brings the action with the French to an abortive climax, and sees the conclusion of Claggart's efforts to pull down the power for good which he has detected in the ship's company.

The first scene shows the main- and quarter-decks (as for Act I) some days later. Before the curtain goes up, the music is already dominated by the *ostinato* rhythm which is used for the battle. Vere and Redburn are worried by the look of the rapidly increasing mist, but further conversation is prevented by the appearance of the Master-at-arms, who removes his cap as a sign that he wishes to speak to the Captain. Vere's thoughts are still concerned with the effect the weather is likely to have on the prospect of action, but consents to see Claggart. The latter, with frequent reference to his own long and faithful service, starts to formulate a charge against some sailor as yet unnamed, who, he says, is likely to endanger the safety of the ship. Vere grows impatient at Claggart's circumlocution, but the interview is cut short by a yell from the main-top: 'Enemy sail on starboard bow!'

At the same moment the mist lifts and instantly the stage (like the music) hums with activity. Sail is crowded on, Vere orders action stations, and the heartfelt relief of the crew at the prospect of a reward for the weeks of waiting is expressed in Example 8:

Gunners run to their guns and start loading, seamen go to the nettings with lashed hammocks and stow them as a rough screen against shot, sand is scattered on deck, water-tubs and matches are made ready, powder monkeys with a high-pitched and continuous yell scramble to their stations, and finally the marines march into position. A call for volunteers for a boarding party is answered by Donald, Red Whiskers, Dansker, and (from high up in the rigging) Billy. All is ready and excitement reaches fever-heat, but the enemy is still out of range. There is a general prayer for wind to fill the sails, a moment when it looks as though anticipation will be realised, the climax when a shot is fired, and then frustration which amounts almost to despair when the mist returns to render further pursuit impossible (the music associated with the mist is used again later). Orders are given to dismiss, and the officers are depressed about the effect this set-back may have on discipline.

Claggart is again seen standing cap in hand waiting to be noticed by the Captain. He seems about to re-open his preamble ('. . . nothing but my duty could bring me back . . .') but this time Vere makes no attempt to hide his impatience at the turn events have taken ('Now be brief, man, for God's sake'), and at the evasive way in which Claggart starts out to tell his story ('Mutiny? I'm not to be scared by words'). The Master-at-arms shows the Captain the gold which was used, he says, by a common seaman to bribe a comrade. Vere is sceptical; how would a sailor have gold in his possession? When Claggart brings out the name of Billy Budd, Vere is frankly incredulous: 'Nay, you're mistaken.

... Don't come to me with so foggy a tale.' The Master-at-arms persists in his story, and Vere flares up at him: 'Claggart! Take heed what you say. There's a yard-arm for a false witness.' He sends a boy for Billy and tells Claggart to follow the accused into his room and there confront him with his charge.

As the officers come forward towards Vere, he exclaims vehemently: 'O this cursed mist.' There is a short quartet, one of those moments of tenderness in which the score abounds, and which seems to express a sympathy with the aspirations of the crew, as well as (from Vere's point of view) a determination to clear up a mystery which was rapidly becoming inextricably connected with the physical phenomenon of the mist. In the Interlude which follows, the music of the mist surrounds chorale-like statements of No. 5, and the conflict is clearly that going on in the mind of Vere, who is faced with discovering the truth or otherwise of an accusation which, if substantiated, carries the supreme penalty with it.

Fanfares, associated with Billy, bring the interlude to an end, and the curtain goes up to reveal Vere with the mists cleared and his mind made up, as is apparent from his first words: 'Claggart! John Claggart, beware! I'm not so easily deceived . . . .' Billy himself comes in, full of confidence that he has been summoned to hear that he has been promoted, and unable to keep the words off his lips. Vere encourages Billy to talk, which he does enthusiastically, while, to a lyrical tune, Vere reflects 'this is the man I'm told is dangerous'.

Claggart is admitted, and, after Vere has cautioned both men to speak only the truth, proceeds immediately to charge Billy with mutiny (derivation of mutiny motif). Vere orders Billy to make answer to his accuser. He is seized with stammering and suddenly hits out at Claggart, striking him a blow in the middle of the forehead. Claggart falls, and, after a couple of gasps, lies motionless. Vere kneels down by him, and quickly realises he is dead. He sends Billy, who has remained motionless since Claggart fell, into his stateroom, and shuts the door after him, then orders his cabin boy to fetch the officers.

Vere is in no doubt as to the predicament he is in. Claggart's evil purpose is clear enough, and yet his innocent victim by his own action has doomed himself, and there is no way of averting the penalty which hangs over his head. Vere's agony is made very apparent in a monologue. The officers enter the cabin and are immediately told the facts. Each reacts differently: Redburn: 'What is the truth? Justice is our duty'; Flint: 'What unheard-of brutality . . . revenge . . .'; Ratcliffe: 'The boy has been pro-voked . . . let us be merciful.'

Vere summons a drumhead court, which he will attend as witness and over which Redburn will preside. Billy is brought in, the charge read to him, and Vere states the bare facts. Billy agrees that they are true, and can plead nothing but his innocence of what Claggart charged him with. Vere declines to add supposition and opinion to the facts as he has stated them, and, in spite of Billy's agonised 'Captain Vere, save me', he is told to wait in the inner room. The three officers consider their verdict. The penalty Billy's action has made inevitable is clearly laid down in the Mutiny Act, the Articles of War, King's Regulations; there is nothing to discuss. They appeal for guidance to Vere, but he refuses to interfere. Their verdict is 'Guilty', and they pronounce the penalty: 'Death. Hanging from the yard-arm.' Vere accepts the verdict, and orders that it be carried out next morning; the Master-at-arms to be buried with full naval honours.

In *Billy Budd*, the tragedy is seen as it were through the eyes of Vere, and poignant expression of it comes at the end of this act, first in an arioso for Vere himself, and then in the extra-ordinary ending when, after Vere has gone to inform Billy of the verdict and the stage is left empty, Britten writes a succession of thirty-five common chords, whose different dynamics and scoring convey the changes of emotion with which the message is given and received. It is in effect a great cadence in F major, and in the last half a dozen bars recurs a suggestion of the 6/8 tune heard when Billy was woken up by the Novice in Act II (No. 6).

The first scene of Act IV shows a bay of the gun deck, shortly before dawn the next morning. Billy is in irons between two cannon. The music continues where Act III left off, and above the gently swaying accompaniment Billy sings a slow, pathetic tune of resignation and farewell (No. 6). The words are Melville's, taken from the poem which he describes as composed by a ship-mate after the execution and put posthumously into the mouth of Billy himself ('Billy in the Darbies').

Billy's introspection comes to an end when Dansker steals in, ignoring the rule which forbids the prisoner to talk to members of the crew while awaiting execution, and brings him a mug of grog. 'All's trouble' he says, 'Some reckon to rescue you . . . they swear you shan't swing.' The idea that his death may precipitate the mutiny whose idea he abhors, fills Billy with new courage. He is vigorous in denunciation of any plan to set him free, and says Dansker's news has jolted him out of 'thinking on what's no use'. What has happened and is going to happen to him he ascribes to the workings of fate: he had to 'strike down that Jemmy-legs', and 'Captain Vere has had to strike me down, fate.' He says good-bye to Dansker, and his new courage finds expression in an ecstatic ballad tune, which is as simple as it is moving (No. 9). The chords with which the previous act ended recur again in the accompaniment.

The interlude is made up from the calls associated with the ship's routine and the music of the verdict, and the curtain goes up to show the main deck and quarter-deck at four o'clock the next morning. Daylight is just beginning to show, and the ship's crew assembles to the sound of a funeral march, which can be described as a fugue on a rhythm of timpani and drums, on which is imposed music characteristic of each group as it enters to watch the grim pageantry of the execution. Vere takes his place and straight away Billy is led in between a guard of marines. Mr. Redburn reads the sentence, Billy turns to Vere and shouts to him 'Starry Vere, God bless you', and his cry is taken up by the crew. Then he turns about with his escort, and marches smartly out. Vere removes his hat and all eyes turn to follow Billy as he ascends the mast.

The men on the main deck suffer an immediate revulsion of feeling, and turn in rebellion to the quarter-deck. This is the moment described in Melville: 'Whoever has heard the freshet-wave of a torrent suddenly swelled by pouring showers in tropical mountains, showers not shared by the plain; whoever has heard the first muffled murmur of its sloping advance through precipitous woods, may form some conception of the sound now heard.'

Britten writes a *presto* fugue on a variation of the mutiny theme (to the sound of 'ur' in 'purple'), but this savage incoherence gradually changes to a passionate echo of the swelling music associated with the routine work in the first act (No. 2). This ending to the drama seems to indicate that this is no theme of disillusionment, but rather carries a message of confidence, if not in Good itself, at least in Man's capacity to understand and be influenced by Good.

The light fades and presently Vere is seen standing alone, an old man as in the Prologue. For a moment it looks as though he finds the memory of what he might have prevented too much for him ('I could have saved him . . . O what have I done?'), but he takes strength from Billy's ballad (No. 9) and this is combined with the 'cadence of comfort' from the end of Act III. The Epilogue comes quietly to an end as the orchestra stops playing, the lights fade, and only Vere's voice is heard rounding out the story to which he has introduced us.                H.

# GLORIANA

Opera in three acts by Benjamin Britten, words by William Plomer. First performed Covent Garden at Gala in connection with Coronation of Queen Elizabeth II, June 8, 1953, with Cross, Vyvyan, Sinclair, Leigh, Pears, Geraint Evans, Matters, Dalberg, Te Wiata, conductor Pritchard.

## CHARACTERS

Queen Elizabeth the First ......................Soprano
Robert Devereux, Earl of Essex ...................Tenor
Frances, Countess of Essex ..............Mezzo-Soprano
Charles Blount, Lord Mountjoy ...............Baritone
Penelope (Lady Rich), *sister to Essex* ............Soprano
Sir Robert Cecil, *Secretary of the Council*.........Baritone
Sir Walter Raleigh, *Captain of the Guard* ............Bass
Henry Cuffe, *a satellite of Essex* ................Baritone
A Lady-in-Waiting ............................Soprano
A Blind Ballad-Singer .............................Bass
The Recorder of Norwich ........................Bass
A Housewife .........................Mezzo-Soprano
The Spirit of the Masque ........................Tenor
The Master of Ceremonies ........................Tenor

The City Crier . . . . . . . . . . . . . . . . . . . . . . . . . . . . . . . . Baritone
Chorus, Dancers, Actors, Musicians
*Scene:* England in the time of Queen Elizabeth I
*Time:* The later years of her reign, which lasted from 1558 to 1603

Act I, scene i.    The prelude is marked 'very lively', and the
rhythm of the brass calls anticipates the chorus's commentary on
the events of scene i, which take place outside a tilting ground.
A tournament is in progress inside. Cuffe looks through an opening in the wall and reports to Essex that Mountjoy has accepted
a challenge, and that the crowd acclaims its favourite: 'Our joy
mounts up, our hope Mountjoy'. Essex is furiously jealous, when,
to the evident delight of the crowd, Mountjoy is victorious, and
receives his prize—a golden chessman—from the Queen herself.

At this point the bustle and excitement of the tournament give
way to a hymn-like tune sung by the crowd in praise of the
Queen (No. 1):

> 'Green leaves are we, Red rose our golden Queen,
> O crowned rose among the leaves so green.'

The music later symbolises the affectionate relationship between
the Queen and her subjects, and is one of the opera's dominant
themes.

Mountjoy appears and bids his page bind his prize upon his
arm. Essex accuses him of arrogance and provokes him to fight.
A trumpet fanfare off-stage causes Essex to drop his guard for a
moment, and he is slightly wounded in the arm. The trumpets
draw nearer, and the Queen emerges from the tilting ground,
surrounded by her court and followed by the crowd. She wastes
no time in summing up the situation, and upbraids both lords
for offending against the rule that no duel may be fought at
court. She turns to Raleigh for his view, and he gives it—as one
'of riper age'. In an aside, both Essex and Mountjoy make quite
clear that they bitterly resent what they regard as Raleigh's

insolence—he is older and more experienced than they are but of far less exalted origin, and they resent it the more for that.

The Queen summons the two late combatants to her, and tells them she has need of them both; let them come to court, but as friends, not as enemies, and they can count on her support and protection. There is an ensemble, in which the Queen, Essex, Mountjoy, Cuffe, Raleigh and the chorus join, and a trumpet march brings the scene to an end (No. 1.).

Scene ii.    The Queen's ante-room in Nonesuch Palace. The Queen is closeted alone with Cecil. She refers to the recent duel between the two young lords, and asks Cecil whether he has had news of the reaction of Lady Rich to the fight—'the dark Penelope' who is sister to Essex, mistress to Mountjoy.[1] When she admits her liking for Essex, 'the lordly boy', Cecil (whom she calls by his historical nickname of 'pygmy elf') warns her to be on her guard. In a short lyrical passage the Queen reminds Cecil that she has wedded herself to the realm; she seeks no husband and is content if her people are happy (No. 1)—she has learned from her preceptor, Ascham, that Love is better than Fear. Cecil reminds her of his father's ancient counsel to the sovereign whom he loved and served so long:

> 'There comes a moment when to rule
> Is to be swift and bold:
> Know at last the time to strike:
> It may be when the iron is cold!'

As the Queen and her counsellor turn to affairs of state, a theme is heard which is associated throughout the opera with the cares of government, and often, because his presence betokens preoccupation with them, with Cecil as well (No. 2):

Its optimistic rise in the major and measured fall in the minor is characteristic. At mention of the possibility of a new Armada

---

[1] Whom she married after the death of her husband, Lord Rich.

from Spain, the Queen laments the certain waste of life and money: 'We can but watch and wait' (No. 2).

Essex is announced and Cecil withdraws. Essex's greeting to his sovereign and his cousin[1] is exuberant (No. 3):

and the Queen asks her Robin—as she calls him—to soothe her worries by singing and playing to her. Suiting the tune to the words and accompanying himself on the lute, Essex sings 'Quick music's best when the heart is oppressed', a little lyric whose enchanting, quicksilver grace is too remote from the Queen's mood to afford her the comfort she seeks. Essex sings again, this time quietly, slowly, and with a depth of feeling and sensitivity that affords a complete musical recreation of that quality which one may suppose caused the Queen to pin her faith for the future to her brilliant but unpredictable cousin (No. 4):

The music has a far-reaching significance in the opera and epitomises their relationship. For Essex it stands for the trust and affection which he can give as well as receive in his most intimate moments with his sovereign; for Queen Elizabeth it symbolises the one link with youth and brilliance which is left her in her old age—a link that is as much practical as sentimental, since Essex's prowess is in her mind as intimately linked with the

[1] His mother, Leicester's widow, was niece to Ann Boleyn, Queen Elizabeth's mother.

fortunes of England as with those of England's Queen. The words of the poem Britten has set are by Essex himself.

There is an affectionate duet between the two, which is interrupted when Elizabeth points to the silhouette of Raleigh, which can be seen at the entrance. Essex refers to Raleigh as 'the jackal', and denounces him as his enemy who is, with Cecil, determined to prevent him going to Ireland, there to overthrow the Queen's enemy, Tyrone. At this point occurs a phrase associated with Essex's fatal ambitions, which plays a prominent part in the opera (No. 5):

The Queen dismisses Essex and is alone.

The Queen's thoughts run to duty and to love—the claims of one, the solace of the other, and their mutual incompatibility. Her soliloquy begins with a *forte* statement on the trombones of No. 1, which dominates it. After a triumphant resolution,

> 'I live and reign a virgin,
> Will die in honour,
> Leave a refulgent crown',

the Queen kneels and prays to God for strength and grace to fulfil the high office to which she has been called. The accompaniment is based on a fourteenth-century setting of the 'Gloria'.

Act II, scene i.     The Guildhall at Norwich. It was Queen Elizabeth's custom to make periodic tours of England—during which time she was said to be 'On Progress'—and, when the curtain rises (the town bells peal in the orchestra), she is attended by her court, Essex, Cecil, Raleigh, and Mountjoy amongst them, and the Recorder of the City of Norwich is coming to the end of his address of welcome. The Queen thanks him and the citizens for their greetings, is cheered by the assembled populace, and, when the Recorder comes to kneel in homage and stumbles, helps him solicitously to his feet: 'Good sir, your homage hath nearly proved your undoing.' The Recorder asks her if she will see the Masque they have prepared in her honour, an invitation to which the Queen signifies her assent but which provokes an impatient aside from Essex, chafing at the enforced inactivity (No. 5). Ireland is again uppermost in his mind.

The Masque begins. A chorus is grouped round a fanciful leafy bower, with the Spirit of the Masque in the centre. After a salute to Gloriana, Time and Concord, represented by male and female solo dancers, appear and dance together. They are followed by troupes of country maidens and rustic swains, and finally all unite in homage to Gloriana. The music is a set of six contrasted dances, introduced by the Spirit of the Masque and set for unaccompanied voices. The Queen graciously returns thanks to the citizens of Norwich, and the finale makes great use of No. 1.

The second scene is laid in the garden of Essex's house. It is evening. The fresh, lyrical atmosphere of the early part of the scene is immediately established by an introduction for flutes, celesta, and muted strings *pizzicato*. Mountjoy sings of his love for Penelope Rich, who presently appears and greets him rapturously. Their duet has not run its course before it is interrupted by the voices of Essex and Lady Essex, who do not see them and are discussing the Queen's continued refusal to advance Essex to the position of Lord Deputy in Ireland, which he considers his due. Mountjoy and Penelope comment on Essex's displeasure (No. 5), then resume their colloquy. But Essex's anger mounts— 'In time, I'll break her will, I'll have my way'—and his sister and his friend break off to warn him against talk which others might consider treasonable. A quartet develops, in which Essex's impatience overflows, Lady Essex urges caution, and first Penelope, later even Mountjoy, encourage him to hope for preferment as time reduces the Queen's grasp on power: 'Ours to decide what other head will wear the crown. . . . Ourselves to rule the land.'

The third scene of Act II takes place in the great room in the Palace of Whitehall during the course of a Ball given by the Queen. The whole scene is built up on a series of dances in the Elizabethan style, which are used to frame a considerable development of the dramatic situation. A majestic pavane is taken up by the stage band as soon as the curtain rises; the court is dancing. A buzz of conversation follows but quietens when the Queen's lady-in-waiting comments admiringly on the splendour of Lady Essex's dress. 'Will the Queen approve?' is Frances's less confident reply as the Master of Ceremonies announces a Galliard, a quick dance to slow music (it is marked *gently flowing*).

The Queen enters (No. 1), catches sight of Lady Essex and looks her up and down, then orders that 'La Volta' be played. This is a brilliant piece in 6/4 time; its salient feature was the tossing of the ladies in the air by their partners (a famous picture of Queen Elizabeth dancing 'La Volta' exists at Penshurst to the present day). The vigorous nature of the dance exhausts even the apparently inexhaustible Queen, and she commands that the ladies go to change their linen, as was the custom of the day, while a tiny Morris dancer performs for the entertainment of those who remain. At the end of his dance, Lady Essex hurries in, breathlessly complaining that her new dress has disappeared while she was changing. The reason is not far to seek, for the Queen suddenly returns, wearing the missing dress. It is much too short for her, and she looks grotesque. For a moment she stalks round, while the court looks on in amazement, then turns to Lady Essex:

'If being too short it becometh not me
I have it in mind it can n'er become thee.' [1]

The Queen leaves, and in an ensemble Essex, Mountjoy, and Penelope attempt to comfort the stricken Frances Essex, who for her part is more concerned with the inflammatory effect the episode may have on her husband than with the insult offered to herself. Her anxiety is not without foundation; to her own conciliatory 'And as the Queen hath her conditions, Robert, take care!' Essex retorts 'Conditions! Her conditions are as crooked as her carcase!'. So unguarded and extreme an utterance dismays even Penelope, but as usual the Queen turns out to be unpredictable. She caps her insult to Essex's wife by returning to the stage with her Councillors to proclaim formally that Essex is appointed Lord Deputy in Ireland and charged to subdue the rebellious Tyrone (No. 5). The chorus salutes the 'Victor of Cadiz' and implores him to overcome the foreign threat, while the Queen and the other principal characters react to the appointment in their different ways, whether jealous, ambitious, or loving. Essex himself sings of the charge entrusted to him (No. 5), and the scene comes to an end when the Queen commands a 'Coranto', which is danced by the entire court as the curtain comes down.

[1] The episode may at first strike a modern audience as too extraordinary to be credible, but it is based on an authenticated incident, when the Queen humiliated a lady of the court suspected of being Essex's mistress.

Act III.    The tragedy of *Gloriana* is first of all that which almost inevitably, in some way or other, attends a ruling prince, and only secondly that of Essex, the individual in whose fate the sovereign's hopes for the future of the country are epitomised. The catastrophe which is to bring about the fall of Essex—the failure in Ireland—has already taken place when Act III begins; and it is the Queen we see take the 'tragic' decision, not Essex. The working out of his destiny involves the tragedy of the Queen whose trust he held.

The prelude is marked *quick and agitated*. When the curtain goes up we are in the Queen's ante-room at Nonesuch. It is early morning and the maids of honour are in conversation. The subject is Ireland. The news is of delay, and instead of the defeat of Tyrone, it looks as though they will soon be talking of the fall of Essex. Suddenly another lady-in-waiting enters in great perturbation to ask if the Queen is yet dressed. There is a great stir below. . . . She need go no further, for Essex himself bursts into the room, demanding to see the Queen. When told she is not yet ready, he sweeps back the curtain behind which she can be seen without her wig at her dressing-table.

She dismisses her attendants, and turns to him (No. 3). At first the interview is quiet: 'But what must I forgive? Because you catch an ageing woman unadorned,' asks the Queen. There is a moment of sadness ('You see me as I am'), which leads to a tender duet ('Because you're here where larks alone have right of audience'), and it is not until Essex mentions the foes which 'beset me now here in England, at home' (No. 5) that the Queen rounds on him and puts her as yet unspoken accusations into words. He has failed in his trust; he.is not only unfit but untrue. Essex pleads his devotion to her (No. 3), and her anger quickly changes to sorrow, until he is reduced to memories: 'O put back the clock to the birth of our hope!' The scene grows in intensity as the music gets slower and softer until Essex and the Queen together recall the song which has symbolised their relationship (No. 4). 'Go, Robin, Go! Go!' (No. 2).

The Queen is quickly joined by a lady-in-waiting, who in her turn is followed by the others. As the tiring-maids finish the Queen's toilet, the maids-of-honour, led by the lady-in-waiting, sing gently and comfortingly to their mistress. When Cecil arrives, the Queen is majestically arrayed (No. 1). He tells her that Tyrone is still unsubdued, and that Essex has not only failed in his mission but has brought with him a horde of his unruly followers. The Queen makes up her mind without delay and gives orders that Essex be kept under supervision. With the music dominated by No. 5, she comments: 'I have failed to tame my thoroughbred.'

Scene ii is laid in a street in the City of London. The short orchestral prelude is based on No. 6. A blind Ballad-Singer[1] sits outside a tavern surrounded by old men, and relays what he hears to his listeners. He is the medium through which we hear of the progress of Essex's rebellion, from the moment when it is first discovered that the Earl is free, until Essex is publicly proclaimed a traitor by the City Crier. There are interruptions between the Ballad-Singer's verses from a rabble of boys, led by a couple of armed followers of Essex; from Cuffe, who tries to recruit support for his master, and is routed with the aid of a bowl of slops by an angry housewife; and from the City Crier with his dread proclamation. The scene is built up on the Ballad-Singer's tune (No. 6) which is marked *very freely*, and which has a curious, camp-fire, popular quality about it that is peculiarly appropriate to its position in the opera:

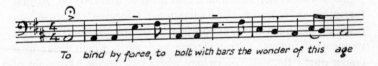

To bind by force, to bolt with bars the wonder of this age

Scene iii. A room in the Palace of Whitehall. The orchestra preludes on No. 7, and the curtain goes up to show Cecil, Raleigh, and other members of the Council waiting to acquaint the Queen with their decision in the case of the Earl of Essex. They are

No. 7

Es-sex is guil-ty and con-demned to die

unanimously agreed that he is guilty, but Cecil warns them that

---

[1] In Elizabethan times, ballad-singers were accustomed to convey the news of the day in their impromptu ballads, which they sang accompanying themselves on the Gittern, a stringed instrument; they were thus a sort of cross between newspaper-seller, news-commentator, and calypso singer.

the Queen may yet hesitate to make up her mind, may even pardon him. When she enters they inform her of the verdict and, when Cecil tries to press her to make a quick decision lest the people should doubt Essex's guilt, she forbids him to prate to her of her duty.

She is alone and her dilemma is forcefully portrayed until Raleigh steps in and announces that Lady Essex, Penelope Rich, and Mountjoy have come to intercede for the fallen Essex. After an ensemble, Lady Essex is promised (No. 1) that, whatever happens to her husband, her children will not suffer. It is the turn of Penelope to make her plea, which she does in terms which can only be described as feudal: it is not only Essex's service to his Queen but his rank which entitles him to a pardon. The Queen is roused to fury by her words, and sends for the warrant to sign it in the presence of the woman who has thus opened her eyes to danger. Penelope shrieks with anguish as the orchestra has a *fff* statement of No. 4, which is to dominate the rest of the opera.

From the departure of Essex's three supporters, the stage darkens and the action becomes unrealistic—as if to emphasise this, the dialogue is mostly spoken against an orchestral background of No. 4. Various episodes of the end of Queen Elizabeth's life are recalled. Her godson Harrington reminds her that he knew Essex in Ireland, Cecil pleads to be allowed to approach James VI of Scotland about his succession, the French Ambassador presents his credentials, the Queen makes her so-called Golden Speech to the House of Commons ('I have ever used to set the last Judgment day before mine eyes'), the lady-in-waiting goes to fetch some nourishment, and then thinks she has seen the ghost of her mistress. Cecil appears again in an effort to get the Queen to go to bed, and the Archbishop of Canterbury is seen kneeling in prayer. As the Queen's life draws to its close, from behind the scenes can be heard the chorus singing softly to the tune of No. 1.                                                        H.

CHAPTER 19

# Czech Opera in the Twentieth Century

# LEOŠ JANÁČEK
## (1854–1928)

### JEJÍ PASTORKYŇA
### JENUFA
#### (Her Foster-daughter)

OPERA in three acts by Leoš Janáček, text by the composer founded on a story by Gabriella Preissová. Première Brno, January 21, 1904, with Marie Kabelacova, Leopolda Svobodova, Stanek-Doubravsky, Prochazka; it was Janáček's first performed opera and scored a considerable local success. First performed Prague, 1916, with Ungrova, Horvatova, Schütz, Lebeda, when it immediately became a popular favourite. Translated into German by Max Brod (from whose version most other translations have been taken), and performed Vienna, 1918; Cologne, 1918; Berlin, 1924, with Jurjewskaya, Ober, Soot, Jöken, conductor Kleiber; Metropolitan, New York, 1924, with Jeritza, Matzenauer, Oehmann, Laubenthal, conductor Bodanzky; revived Venice, 1941; Stockholm, 1941, with Herzberg, Wettergren, Beyron, Svanholm; Berlin, 1942, with Müller, Marta Fuchs, Argyris, Anders; Vienna, 1948, with Welitsch, Helena Braun, Patzak, Treptow; Holland Festival, 1951, with Brouwenstijn, Vroons; Buenos Aires, 1951, with Lemnitz, Fischer, Ludwig, Fehenberger; Rome, 1952, with Caleva, Pederzini, Sinimberghi, Bergonzi; London, Covent Garden, 1957, with Shuard, Fisher, cond. Kubelik.

### CHARACTERS

Grandmother Buryja, *owner of the mill* .........Contralto

Laca Klemen    { *stepbrothers, grandsons of*    } .....Tenors
Stewa Buryja    {    *Grandmother Buryja*    }

Kostelnicka Buryjovka, *daughter-in-law of Grandmother Buryja* ('*Kostelnicka*' *means* '*wife of the sexton*'); *a widow*........................Soprano

Jenufa, *her foster-daughter* ....................Soprano

Foreman at the Mill ...........................Baritone

Mayor of the Village .............................Bass

His Wife.............................Mezzo-Soprano

Karolka, *their daughter* ..................Mezzo-Soprano

A Maid ............................Mezzo-Soprano

Barena, *servant at the mill* .....................Soprano

Jano, *shepherd boy*............................Soprano

Aunt .........................................Contralto

Musicians, Village People

Act I.     A lonely mill in the mountains. Jenufa, a pot of rosemary in her arms, stands by the stream looking into the distance.
Old Grandmother Buryja sits in front of the mill peeling potatoes.
Laca is near her, shaping a whip-handle with his knife. It is late
afternoon. The prelude (in 6/4 time) has running through it the
tinkling sound of the mill at work (xylophone). Jenufa laments
that Stewa has not yet returned, and wonders despairingly
whether he has been taken as a soldier by the recruiting officer.
She is in love with him—in fact, carries his child within her—
and her heart will break if he leaves her.

Laca makes sarcastic reference to his place in the household;
he is only worth his food and lodging in return for the work he
can do, and Stewa has always been the idol of old Grandmother
Buryja. At this point the orchestra shows the pity for the foibles
and misfortunes of his characters which is one of Janaček's
strongest and most lovable qualities and which pervades his operas,
but Laca's vocal line remains uncompromisingly bitter, and
Jenufa reproaches him for the way in which he speaks to the old
woman. Grandmother Buryja affirms that she is mistress in her
own house without respect of kinship, but Laca wonders aloud
what would be Jenufa's reaction if Stewa were taken for the
army. She is dismayed at how he seems able to read her feelings,
and tries to cover up her embarrassment by assuring her grandmother she will finish the house work. Superstitiously, she is
concerned with keeping her rosemary plant alive and fresh; if it
withers it is a sign that bad luck will quickly follow.

Jano, the shepherd boy, is heard calling happily from the mill.
A new sense of joy comes into the music as he announces that
he really can read now. Jenufa seems as pleased as he, and, after
he has run off, Grandmother Buryja observes that Jenufa is as
much the teacher at heart as her foster-mother. Jenufa responds
sadly to her compliments.

The foreman of the mill comes on to the scene, and asks Laca
what he is working at. A whip-handle—but his knife is blunt,
says Laca, and gives it to be ground (the xylophone is heard
again in the orchestra). Laca and Jenufa quarrel for a moment,
and Laca taunts her with her love for Stewa. She goes off, and
Laca remarks bitterly to the foreman that she will make a splendid
sister-in-law with those sweet ways of hers. The foreman, however, is not deceived and pays a compliment to Jenufa's beauty,

commenting that this is anyhow not news to Luca, who has certainly noticed it himself. Laca mocks at love, and says he put worms round Jenufa's rosemary so that it might die, and bring bad luck to her prospect of marriage to Stewa. The foreman is distressed to hear what Laca has to tell him, and warns him about his behaviour towards Jenufa. What if Stewa be taken for a soldier, says Laca; but the foreman has heard that he has been passed over and is free. Jenufa and Grandmother Buryja are delighted at his words, which they overhear, but Laca cannot conceal his jealousy that Stewa's luck should serve him even in this. Kostelnicka appears and goes into the mill, and Grandmother Buryja suggests they follow her. Jenufa, however, begs to be left alone to meet Stewa when he returns.

The jaunty song of the approaching recruits can be heard in the distance, and they are followed by Stewa, who is extremely drunk. With an almost hysterical cry, Jenufa tries to bring Stewa to his senses, but he answers crossly, boasting of his prowess with the girls —look at the flowers he has had from one of them—and throwing money to his companions, whom he orders to sing and dance for the entertainment of him and his Jenufa. They start up a song, in which Stewa joins, and in between the verses the orchestra plays for the dance, into which Stewa drags the unwilling Jenufa.

On the surface the scene is as gay as the dances in *The Bartered Bride*, but Kostelnicka interrupts it imperiously. She is a formidable and authoritative—almost authoritarian—character, and when she reads the company a lecture and makes it apply particularly and unmistakably to her rich nephew Stewa, there is no gainsaying her. Until he can prove that he has stopped drinking by a year of sobriety, there is to be no more talk of a wedding with Jenufa. Nobody tries to contradict her, although the chorus comments that she is a bit too severe, an opinion with which Grandmother Buryja concurs, at least in so far as it concerns her favourite Stewa (Laca has cause for another ironical aside).

Grandmother Buryja sends the musicians packing, and tells Stewa to go and sleep off his drunken condition. It is partly the fault of his companions that he is so drunk, she says—this causes a sarcastic comment from the said companions. The scene comes to an end with a short *fugato* in which Grandmother Buryja warns Jenufa that life is full of sorrow, which must be borne. In turn, she is joined by the foreman, Laca, the chorus and finally Jenufa herself, whose line soars up to C flat. The xylophone makes a practical comment on the words that have just been heard: there is a background to life, in this case the mill, which goes on regardless of the emotions of the men and women in front of it.

Jenufa and Stewa are left alone, and Jenufa pleads her love for him and her fear that her secret should be found out. Her music at this point is dominated by a recurrent figure:

The short phrase seems perfectly to characterise the situation: Jenufa's confession of love and anxiety is dragged out of her, almost in spite of herself, with long pauses between phrases, yet the music never fails to convey the warmth of her nature. Stewa answers crossly, and practically accuses Jenufa and her foster-mother of nagging at him, so that Jenufa loses her patience and shakes him vigorously. Even when he partially pulls himself together, his answers have a conventional gallantry, which in no way reassures Jenufa. When Laca returns Jenufa is alone in her misery; he makes derisive reference to Stewa's hang-dog look just now when he felt the rough side of Kostelnicka's tongue, but this only provokes Jenufa to take Stewa's side even more firmly than before. In a final effort to provoke some revulsion of feeling towards the lover he considers unworthy of her, Laca picks up the flowers which Stewa has dropped and which were given him by some female admirer; let her pin *them* on her dress! Even this attempted insult Jenufa accepts defiantly, for Stewa's sake. Laca's comment is that Stewa only looks at her because of her rosy-apple cheeks. He makes as if to embrace Jenufa and slashes her across the cheek with the knife.

She runs into the house screaming, while Laca laments the horrible thing he has done. The servant Barena suggests that it happened accidentally, but, after Grandmother Buryja has gone to help Jenufa, the foreman accuses Laca of having, for all his present remorse, committed the crime on purpose.

Act II is set in the living-room of Kostelnicka's house. In it can be seen a big peasant stove, a bed, and furniture, and on the walls are holy pictures. A tense atmosphere is established in the music straight away, and the curtain goes up to show Kostelnicka and Jenufa sewing, the latter's wound still visible. They are talking about Jenufa's secret; the baby has been born, but Jenufa has not seen his father for weeks now. Kostelnicka is worried in case she has been too severe; but, whatever her feelings for Jenufa, she cannot find it in her heart to forgive Stewa for his behaviour. Jenufa thinks she hears her baby call, but she returns a moment later; he is sleeping peacefully. Every utterance of Jenufa's shows her joy in her child, every one of Kostelnicka's, the pride which has been so cruelly hurt by the shame which has come to her beloved foster-child and which has become an obsession with her. Kostelnicka gives Jenufa a drink, with a narcotic in it to make her sleep, and Jenufa goes into the inner room.

Kostelnicka has sent for Stewa. She admits to herself that she has prayed that the child might die, but that, her prayers being unanswered, she must steel herself to the thought of a marriage between Jenufa and Stewa. When Stewa comes, she reproaches him for not having been to see them before; he admits he did not even know that the child had been born. He shrinks from going in to see Jenufa and his son, and seems half remorseful for what he has done to her, half resentful that her beauty has been spoilt —for that at least he cannot be blamed although it means the end of his love for her. He will not grudge the child money—but no one must know that it is his.

Kostelnicka pleads with him; at least he must see his child. As Stewa says, her pleas would melt the heart of a stone:

They grow in intensity when Stewa breaks down, but he still persists in his refusal to marry Jenufa, and eventually admits that he is contracted to marry Karolka, the mayor's daughter. Stewa runs out and, as Kostelnicka screams in horror, Jenufa's voice is heard coming from the inner room, calling in her sleep. For a moment Kostelnicka is afraid she has woken up, but there is no further sound and she continues to brood on the problem which seems now to be left to her, and her alone, to solve, if solution be possible.

Laca comes in, angry that Stewa was there, but still anxious above all things to win the love of Jenufa. He asks Kostelnicka if Jenufa is yet back from Vienna—it was given out that she went away—and is delighted to hear that she has returned. But Kostelnicka has not the heart to hide the truth from him any longer, and she tells him about the child. He is horrified at the idea that marriage with Jenufa involves taking Stewa's baby, and Kostelnicka, who sees Jenufa's last chance slipping away from her, makes her decision and tells him that the baby is dead. She sends him out to make enquiries about the wedding of Stewa and Karolka, and is left alone, face to face with the facts as they are and the facts as she has represented them. For a moment she wonders whether she can hide the baby. No, he would always bring bad luck on Jenufa; he is a true child of Stewa. There is no other way but to kill him. The music represents her agony and indecision, and the scene is one of terrible power, particularly towards its end, when Kostelnicka yells her own name in horrible reproach at her shadow. She goes into the bedroom and brings the child out, wrapped in her shawl.

Jenufa wakes, and calls for Kostelnicka, tenderly at first, then more urgently as she begins to realise, half-drugged by the sleeping draught as she is, that Kostelnicka is not there. She draws the curtains and looks out at the stars, then suddenly realises that her baby has gone too; Kostelnicka must have taken him to the mill to show to Stewa, is her explanation. She prays for his future, and the music is suffused with sadness and tenderness, which is dispelled for a moment when Kostelnicka comes back in a state of extreme agitation, but returns after Jenufa has been told that her child is dead and buried (Kostelnicka explains this by saying that Jenufa has been unconscious and delirious for two days, during which time his death and burial occurred).

Kostelnicka tells Jenufa that Stewa has been there, and has offered to give the child money, but steadfastly refused to marry her, even admitting that he was engaged to Karolka. Jenufa must cast his memory from her mind. When Laca comes in, his joy at seeing Jenufa again is touching in its sincerity. In response to Kostelnicka's urgings, he asks Jenufa if they cannot finish their lives together. Jenufa is at first dignified and reserved, but she cannot hide her tender feelings for Laca, and Kostelnicka exclaims to herself that her action has put everything right. Just then, the window blows open, and the icy blast brings a horrible sense of foreboding and disaster to Kostelnicka who cries out in alarm, and clings desperately to Jenufa and Laca.

Act III.    The scene is the same as in Act II. Jenufa, now looking much better, is preparing for the wedding, and Laca sits by her side. Near them is old Grandmother Buryja. Kostelnicka, looking haggard and worn, paces up and down the room. The maid prattles away, but Kostelnicka is obviously in a state of nervous exhaustion, and, when there is a knock at the door, she startles them all with her agitated reaction. It turns out to be only the mayor come to offer his congratulations, but even his equanimity cannot restore Kostelnicka to calm. Eventually, she takes them all in to see the trousseau she has made for Jenufa, and bride and bridegroom are left alone. Jenufa is unhappy that her decision not to wear the customary wedding garland should have occasioned comment from the mayor's wife, but Laca gives her the flowers he has brought her, and she pins them to her dress. He cannot stop reproaching himself for what he has done to her; all his life must be spent making her amends, if that is ever possible. It transpires that it is at Jenufa's insistence that Laca has been reconciled to Stewa, even to the extent of asking him to the wedding, with his bride-to-be.

Karolka comes in with Stewa to congratulate the happy couple. The visit looks likely to be completed without a word from Stewa, but Laca asks him whether his own wedding-day is yet fixed. In two weeks' time, says Stewa; but Karolka is determined to play the minx, and says she may yet change her mind. Stewa is indignant at the idea that he might be jilted, but relapses into silence when Jenufa expresses the hope that true love will never hurt him. The others return, and outside gathers a group of girls, headed by Barena and bringing flowers to offer to Jenufa. They sing a little wedding song, and then bride and bridegroom are blessed by Grandmother Buryja.

Suddenly, cries are heard outside. The body of the murdered baby has been discovered in the mill-stream now that the ice has melted. Jano rushes in screaming out the news and goes out, taking the mayor with him, followed by the others except Stewa, Kostelnicka and Grandmother Buryja. Kostelnicka becomes hysterical, but attention shifts from her when the voice of Jenufa can be heard from outside crying that she recognises the baby as hers. In spite of Laca's efforts, she continues to ask why the baby was not properly buried, and feeling against her rises until the mob is ready to stone her for what they cannot but think is her crime. Laca is prepared to defend her, but silence falls on them all when Kostelnicka raises her arms and tells them quite quietly that the guilt is hers. She tells the story, and for a moment Jenufa turns from her in revulsion. But it is only too clear that her crime has been committed in an effort to do good, and Jenufa's great act of forgiveness towards Kostelnicka somehow redeems the crime from its sordid implications. For a moment it looks as though Kostelnicka will kill herself, then she remembers she will be needed as a witness if Jenufa is not to suffer for something of which she is guiltless, and she goes quietly away with the mayor.

The others go, but Jenufa and Laca remain behind. Sadly Jenufa tells him to follow them. She must live out her life alone, though she is grateful to him for his greatness of spirit, and readily forgives him for the injury he did her; love for her was at the back of it, just as love was the cause of her own sin. Laca begs to be allowed to remain at her side, and his reward is Jenufa's great cry of exultation as she understands that their sufferings have brought them a greater love than she has ever known before. This is not just a conventional happy ending. The music has a freshness of its own, and the quality of Laca's devotion is pointed up by situation and music alike.     H.

# KATYA KABANOVA

Opera in three acts by Leoš Janaček, text by Cervinka, founded on Ostrovsky's *The Storm*. Première Brno, October 23, 1921, with Marie

Vesela, Karel Zavrel, conductor Neumann. First performed in Prague, 1922, conductor Ostrcil; in German, translated by Max Brod, at Cologne, 1922, with Rose Pauly, Schröder, conductor Klemperer; Berlin, 1926. Revived Munich, 1948, with Schech, Klarwein; Dresden, 1949, with Trötschel, Schindler. First performed in England, Sadler's Wells, 1951, with Shuard, Rowland Jones, conductor MacKerras.

## CHARACTERS

Vanya Kudrjas, *clerk to Dikoy* .................... Tenor
Glasha, *a servant* ...................... Mezzo-Soprano
Dikoy, *a rich merchant* ........................... Bass
Boris Grigorievitch, *his nephew* .................... Tenor
Feklusha, *a servant* .................... Mezzo-Soprano
Marfa Kabanova, *a rich merchant's widow*
   (Kabanicha) .............................. Contralto
Tichon Ivanitsch Kabanov, *her son* ................ Tenor
Barbara, *foster-child in the Kabanov household*
                                     Mezzo-Soprano
Katerina Kabanova (Katya), *Tichon's wife* ....... Soprano
Kuligin, *friend of Vanya* ...................... Baritone

*Time:* About 1860.     *Place:* The little town of Kalinov on the
                                     banks of the Volga

In *Katya Kabanova*, Janaček contrasts the old and the new, the ancient Slavonic matriarchy (symbolised in Kabanicha) and the independent, enlightened modern generation (symbolised by Barbara and Vanya Kudrjas). In between these two conflicting forces are found the unemancipated Katya and Boris; Katya is oppressed by Kabanicha and Boris by his brutish uncle, Dikoy.

The prelude, with its *pp* B flat minor chords and its fateful drum figure against muted trombones, is concerned with setting the atmosphere which is to prevail throughout the opera, but at the same time it serves as an exposition of leading motives. We are made acquainted soon after the opening with an agonised figure of three (later four) adjacent chromatic notes which, it had been suggested, symbolises the painful friction of people living too closely together; the first *allegro* passage has an important theme in the oboe (much used later in the opera) against a background of flute and sleigh-bells (Tichon's departure); but most important of all is the tender

which dominates the prelude, and is heard, with its derivations, very frequently in the course of the opera.

The curtain rises to show the outside of the Kabanovs' house, which stands on the banks of the Volga and from which a broad view of the river can be seen. Kudrjas is sitting on a bench exclaiming at the beauty of the river—a point of view with which Glasha, who works for Kabanicha, cannot sympathise. In the distance can be seen Dikoy, waving his arms about angrily as is his custom; Kudrjas and Glasha retire out of sight, in case he takes it into his head to give them a piece of his mind. Dikoy comes in, complaining at his nephew Boris's laziness—though what he is expected to work at on a Sunday morning Boris himself is unable to guess, nor does his uncle seem disposed to enlighten him. Dikoy makes no secret of his dislike of Boris, but he goes away when he has learned from Glasha that Kabanicha is still in church.

Kudrjas listens sympathetically while Boris explains that he only stays with his tyrannical, loud-mouthed relation because of the terms of his grandmother's will; the money is to go to him and his sister when they come of age, provided they do what their uncle tells them. His sister has so far been kept away from Dikoy by their mother's family in Moscow, and if it were not for her, Boris himself would long ago have left Dikoy and given up his inheritance.

At that moment, the people are seen coming back from church, and Kudrjas has to be restrained from going by the overwrought Boris. As Boris laments his rapidly-departing youth, Katya's theme is stated *dolce* and for the first time by the oboe.

At the same time, Glasha tells Feklusha that her employer, Kabanicha, is a hypocritical old tyrant. Boris gazes into the distance and his rapturous phrases tell the listener as plainly as his words that he is in love. To the accompaniment of repeated statements of Katya's theme, he admits to Kudrjas that Katya

is the object of his adoration—a married woman! The theme is
heard in its most characteristic form as Katya comes into sight:

Kabanicha leads her little family party back from church. She
pauses in front of the house to urge Tichon, if he wants to please
his mother, to go that very day to the market at Kazan. He
immediately agrees, but Kabanicha makes a sneering reference
to his wife Katya, and suggests that since his marriage he has
paid his mother less than the respect and deference due to her.
Tichon hotly protests that he loves both, but when Katya also
gently claims to love her mother-in-law, Kabanicha turns on her
and insults her; who asked her opinion? Barbara is sarcastic:
'Oh, what a place to choose for a sermon!'[1] Katya goes into the
house, and Kabanicha continues her abuse; Tichon is too soft
with Katya, and would make no protest even if she were to take
a lover. Kabanicha goes, and Barbara vehemently abuses Tichon
for not taking Katya's part more firmly; she knows exactly what
he will do now—drink to forget the scene. Barbara is alone as
the curtain falls; 'Oh, how could anyone not love her?' is her
comment on Katya's unhappiness.

The second scene is set inside the Kabanovs' house. Katya and
Barbara are in conversation, and the former gradually pours out
her heart to Barbara. She is unhappy in her present surroundings
—a fact Barbara knows well. When she was young and unmarried,
she was as free as the birds, and like them she wandered
unhindered wherever she wished. She describes her girlhood.
Even then, her mother treated her as a child and knew nothing
of her fancies and longings. The music grows in intensity as she
describes going to church alone; 'I felt as if I was entering
Paradise,' she says. She saw visions of angels, lofty golden
cathedrals high in the sky; she felt as if she were flying over the
mountains and forests, surrounded by invisible choirs. For a
moment she loses control of herself and reveals that strange desires
fill her being, she is tempted to sin.

[1] Translation by Norman Tucker.

Barbara encourages her to describe her dreams. She says she feels that a voice is whispering in her ear, someone is embracing her and urging her to go with him—and she yields to his persuasion. Katya breaks off; how can Barbara, a child, understand what she means? But Barbara protests that she is not as innocent as Katya thinks; she has sins on her own conscience. Katya says that no sin can be worse than that of loving some other man than one's own husband, but Barbara asks why that should seem so dreadful; perhaps when Tichon has gone, Katya will see this other man.

Katya protests vehemently, and at this moment Tichon appears saying that he must leave immediately for Kazan, as his mother wishes him to. In spite of Katya's protests, he can neither remain nor take her with him. Katya asks him to make her swear a dreadful oath not to see or speak to a stranger while he is away, but he refuses to ask her to do such a thing. Katya starts to formulate an oath, but Kabanicha comes in and bids her son prepare for the journey. Before he leaves, he must give his orders to his wife—and in the presence of his mother, so that she may hear exactly what he says. He repeats in a milder form the injunctions of Kabanicha, and, in spite of his protests, they include a prohibition against seeing other men. It looks as though Katya will break down as she kisses her husband good-bye—Kabanicha's grim comment is 'Shameless girl! Is he your lover?'

Act II.    Living-room of the Kabanovs' house, later the same day. When the curtain rises, Kabanicha is obviously in the middle of a spate of nagging at Katya. Why can't she be like other wives —those that love their husbands, that's to say—and stay weeping in her room for the rest of the day when he goes away? She might at least pretend to weep; that would show people her word is to be trusted! Having vented some of her spite, Kabanicha leaves the room.

Barbara says she feels hot; she will go into the garden, using the key which Kabanicha *thinks* she has hidden, but for which Barbara has substituted another key so that she will not know it has gone. If she should see 'him', says Barbara cryptically, she will tell him that Katya is waiting by the gate of the garden. Barbara goes out leaving the key. For a while Katya wrestles with temptation; she has the key to hand, should she use it? Suddenly, she can hear the voice of Kabanicha. She hides the

key, but the danger passes, and the flood of relief which succeeds
it tells her more certainly than could anything else that her love
for Boris is too strong for her. Nothing could be more psycho-
logically right than the musical portrayal of this sudden and
involuntary crumbling away of resistance.

Katya goes out, to be succeeded by Kabanicha, who is followed
by Dikoy. Straight away he admits that he is a bit drunk, but he
protests that he does not want to go home. 'Speak to me harshly'
is the request he has come to ask of Kabanicha—she alone dares
do such a thing. Money is the thing that causes him to sin. The
other day, just after confession, a peasant asked him to pay some
money he owed; he cursed him, all but thrashed him, and then
went down on his knees to beg forgiveness. 'You should learn
better manners' is Kabanicha's retort.

The scene changes to the garden below the house. The summer
night is hot. Kudrjas arrives first and sings a care-free peasant
song to balalaika accompaniment. He is waiting for Barbara,
and is surprised to see Boris, who explains that someone he passed
in the dark told him to come there, and he felt that he should not
ignore the suggestion. Kudrjas tries to warn him, but Boris is
plainly too much in love to benefit from warnings. Barbara
signals her arrival by singing another snatch of folk-like melody,
to which Kudrjas makes appropriate answer. As she passes Boris,
she tells him that Katya will not be long. He waits impatiently
and with growing excitement as Katya comes into sight. In spite
of herself, Katya admits her love for him and falls into his arms.
There is apprehension as well as poignancy and yearning in their
duet. The whole scene is saturated with the magic of the summer
night, and a unique effect is produced by the blend and contrast
of the characteristics of the two pairs of lovers, the one passionate
and care-free, the other rapturous but guilty. The singing ends
with a little folk-like duet for Barbara and Kudrjas, but the
shattering emotional climax comes in the orchestra, when Katya
and Boris return to the stage and their pent-up feelings are expressed in three highly charged orchestral phrases, which are
more revealing than might be a vocal section of ten times the
length.

Act III.    Ten days later. The scene is laid in a tumble-down
summer house on a terrace by the Volga. Kudrjas and Kuligin,
his friend, take shelter from the storm which threatens, and which

bursts upon them with considerable violence. They look at the pictures on the walls; there is one of Ivan the Terrible, which elicits the sarcastic comment that Russia has never wanted for tyrants—there is one in every family. As if to match the words, Dikoy comes in, pushing everyone out of his way, and complaining that he sees far too much of Kudrjas every day to want to see him again. Kudrjas suggests that the frequent storms indicate the village should have lightning-conductors; he tries to explain what they are, but meets short shrift from the superstitious Dikoy, who takes each storm to be a warning from God to sinful mankind.

The rain stops and all leave the shelter, except Boris and Kudrjas. Barbara appears, and whispers to Boris that Tichon is back, and his return has driven Katya quite out of her senses, so that she seems ill with worry. Boris hides as Katya comes in, supported by her husband and preceded by Kabanicha. Thunder can be heard in the distance and the storm starts all over again at just the moment when Katya catches sight of Boris. In spite of the efforts of Barbara, who tries to restrain her, she calls to Tichon and Kabanicha at the top of her voice, and confesses not only her adultery but names the man with whom she has sinned. The scene has an added horror in that it builds up with incredible rapidity from comparative calm to climax and catastrophe. Tichon at first does not want to listen to Katya's confession, and is beside himself with unhappiness, but Kabanicha's comment is one of self-justification: 'Son, your mother warned you!'

The second scene re-introduces the great unifying influence of the story, taking place as it does on the banks of the Volga. Katya has fled from her family after her confession, and they are looking for her. It is night, and Tichon's remarks to Glasha reveal that his mind is a turmoil of doubt; women like that should not just be killed, he says, but buried alive—and yet he still loves Katya, and how could he harm her? He and Glasha continue their search, and Barbara and Kudrjas run in, the former explaining the behaviour of Kabanicha. They agree that there is nothing for it but to run away together, and their careless decision accords well with what the music has told us about them during the rest of the opera.

The voices of Tichon and Glasha can be heard calling in the distance. Katya comes slowly on to the empty stage, hoping sadly

PLATE XXXIX. Lidy van der Veen (Kostelnicka) and Gré Brouwenstijn (Jenufa) in *Jenufa*, Amsterdam 1951.

PLATE XL. *Porgy and Bess*: the crap game, London 1952.

to see Boris once again. Her experience has obviously affected her very strongly, and she cannot think coherently. How would Boris speak to her now? The thought of the night overwhelms her with horror, but she reflects that she will never see another night. Suddenly, remembrance of her love fills her heart with longing; she calls for Boris, and, as if in answer to her cry, he appears. Perhaps nothing in the opera is sadder than the quiet way in which the two lovers accept one another and each finds consolation in the presence of the other. Boris tries to comfort her, but her mind wanders and she cannot remember what she wants to say to him. At first she wants to go away with him, then changes her mind. Suicide is forgotten, and she pictures her future life, perpetually tortured by Kabanicha. Sadly she asks him to give alms to all the beggars he meets, with the request that they pray for her. They say good-bye.

Katya is alone, and goes towards the bank of the river. She thinks of the birds and the flowers which have comforted her in life and will be with her in death, 'so peaceful, so lovely . . . and I must die'. She throws herself into the river. The voices of one or two men who have seen her fall are heard; Tichon and Kabanicha rush to the spot, the latter restraining her son, Tichon protesting that it is Kabanicha who has killed Katya. Her body is carried up on to the bank by Dikoy, and the last words of the opera are sardonically given to Kabanicha: 'Let me thank you, friends and neighbours, for your kindness.'

*Katya* is the logical development of *Jenufa*. The extraordinarily tense atmosphere of the story is matched by a similar quality in the music, which has an economical, compressed quality that is hardly to be found to quite the same degree in other operas. It is from this very close juxtaposition of the broadest of lyrical themes with the most insistent of dramatic, that Janaček derives his unusual power, and the concentrated nature of both music and drama in *Katya* makes it particularly in evidence in this work—which, to the present writer, seems one of the most remarkable of the twentieth century.                                        H.

# JAROMIR WEINBERGER
(born 1896)

## SCHWANDA THE BAGPIPER
(Švanda Dudák)

OPERA in two acts by Jaromir Weinberger; text by M. Kares. Première Prague, April 27, 1927, conductor Ostrcil. First performed Breslau, 1929; Berlin, 1929, with Müller, Branzell, Soot, Scheidl, Schützendorf, Helgers, conductor Kleiber; Vienna, 1930, with Angerer, Rünger, Piccaver, Hammes, Mayr, conductor Krauss; Metropolitan, New York, 1931, with Müller, Branzell, Laubenthal, Schorr, Andresen, Schützendorf, conductor Bodanzky; Covent Garden, 1934, with Ursuleac, Rünger, Kullmann, Schoeffler, Kipnis, Sterneck, conductor Krauss; Buenos Aires, 1935, with Fleischer, Kovaceva, Pataky, Gaudin, Baccaloni, conductor Panizza. Revived Düsseldorf, 1949, with Spletter, Gester; Sadler's Wells, 1948, with Shires, Gerald Davies, Roderick Jones, Glynne, conductor Robertson.

### CHARACTERS

| | |
|---|---|
| Schwanda the Bagpiper | Baritone |
| Dorotka, *his wife* | Soprano |
| Babinsky, *a romantic robber* | Tenor |
| The Queen | Mezzo-Soprano |
| The Magician | Bass |
| The Judge | Tenor |
| The Executioner | Tenor |
| The Devil | Bass |
| The Devil's Familiar Spirit | Tenor |
| The Captain of Hell's Guard | Tenor |
| Two Forest Rangers | Tenor, Bass |

**Act I.** Close to a forest is the cottage where Schwanda, the piper of Strakonitz, dwells with his young wife, Dorotka. As the curtain rises, two armed foresters hasten to the cottage to enquire whether a suspicious stranger has been seen in the neighbourhood. They are after the robber, Babinsky. Dorotka, however, cannot help them; she has seen no one and the foresters depart to try their luck elsewhere.

No sooner have they gone than Babinsky, who has been hiding in the high branches of a tree, drops to the ground before the

astonished Dorotka. She questions Babinsky and her astonishment grows when she learns that Babinsky has never heard of
her famous husband, Schwanda, the bagpiper of Strakonitz. Why,
the devil himself envies Schwanda his gift. 'Are you the Devil?'
asks the gentle Dorotka. Babinsky, who obviously is struck by
Dorotka's beauty, is rather hurt. But Schwanda arrives from the
fields where he has been working, and courteously asks his unknown guest to share their meal. In the course of the conversation Babinsky tells the story of the great robber Babinsky, the
friend of the poor, the hero of a thousand adventures. The story
makes an impression on Schwanda, who would willingly go and
see the great world.

'A man gifted as you are,' replies Babinsky, 'could easily make
his way.' He tells of people who are wealthy and bored and of
the Queen whose heart is ice and who waits and waits for someone who can melt it. Schwanda's ambition is on fire. Dorotka
would hold him back but, while she is out of sight, Schwanda
departs with Babinsky.

The second scene shows the chamber of Queen Iceheart, who
vainly hopes to find a cure in the tricks of the court magician.
Then, to the tune of the now famous polka, Schwanda enters.
His music is simply irresistible; the Queen's maids-of-honour and
pages dance. 'Who art thou, bringer of jollity?' asks the Queen.
'I am Schwanda,' replies the piper in a jovial aria, in which the
chorus joins; 'I go where there is bitterness and sorrow; I blow

on my pipe and at once the clouds melt and the whole world
rejoices.' The Queen is so much enamoured of the music that she
decides to wed the musician forthwith. Schwanda, fascinated by
the prospect of sharing a throne, agrees and kisses the Queen.

But if Schwanda can forget the faithful Dorotka, Dorotka, far
from forgetting Schwanda, has followed him, and now overtakes
him to tax him with infidelity. Schwanda's forgetfulness, however, was but a moment's aberration. The Queen, learning this,

orders both to appear before the judge, who will condemn them to death.

In the third scene we see the scene of judgment when sentence is passed on Schwanda and Dorotka. They are to suffer the extreme penalty. But just as the execution is about to take place, the executioner discovers that his axe has been stolen. It is Babinsky who comes to the rescue of his friend, and now hands him the pipes. Schwanda plays and the court and public are helpless; they *must* dance while Schwanda and his friends move slowly towards the gate and go out of the town (Furiant).

Once they are well away Dorotka turns on him and taunts her errant husband. Schwanda denies everything. 'If I have given the Queen a single kiss may the Devil take me,' he exclaims. The Devil does; and Schwanda disappears.

Act II.     The scene represents hell. The Devil is playing cards by himself; no one trusts his card-playing, and thus he is reduced to a lonely game of Patience. Schwanda is there too. But Schwanda need not obey the Devil, since he has not been sent there but came of his own free will, and the rules of hell do not apply to him. The Devil is very bored, and begs Schwanda again and again to play for him. His requests meet with a blank refusal: Schwanda will not play to the Devil. The Father of Lies is at a loss for arguments, but he overhears Schwanda's lament for his lost earthly joys, above all for Dorotka, who made life pleasing to him. Here is his opportunity. He shows Schwanda the spectre of Dorotka and tells him he has but to sign a paper to get her. Schwanda signs quickly the paper giving away his soul. But instead of producing Dorotka, the Devil tells him that now, as his subject, he is bound to obey and, to begin with, he must play on his pipes.

The timely arrival of Babinsky saves Schwanda for the moment. The robber is, of course, well known to the Devil, who respects Babinsky's well-known skill. Moreover, he is only too pleased to welcome a man who is not afraid of having a game of cards with him. They gamble desperately, and in the end the Devil loses everything. The Devil is now a poor devil indeed. 'Be a man,' he is told, 'and bear your loss with courage.' He is sad; nothing is left him; he has gambled away his kingdom, his treasure, the soul of Schwanda, the insignia of his office; 'What sort of a devil am I now?' he asks, full of self-pity.

Babinsky, however, is generous. He will leave the Devil his kingdom and his insignia; only Schwanda must be free to go with him. The servants of hell cheer Babinsky, while the Devil thanks him and promises that should he ever return he will be welcomed as 'a son of the house'. To crown it all the piper will play them a tune so that they may learn what the playing of the great master Schwanda of Strakonitz is like. This is the ingenious fugue, which has become popular in the concert hall where it is played in conjunction with the polka.

The fifth and last scene takes us back to Schwanda's cottage. Babinsky makes a last attempt to divide the lovers. He tells Schwanda that, although he may not have known it, he has lived twenty years in hell; that Dorotka is now an old peasant woman who, most likely, will not know him again, and invites him to go back to the great world where young queens and princesses live.

Schwanda has learnt his lesson. Never again will he depart from his beloved. 'Dorotka! Dorotka!' he calls at the door of the cottage, and Dorotka comes to him as young and beautiful as ever. Babinsky retires discomfited. Peasants passing see Schwanda and rush to congratulate him on his return.                    F. B.

CHAPTER 20

*Hungarian Opera in the Twentieth Century*

# BELA BARTOK
## (1881–1945)

### DUKE BLUEBEARD'S CASTLE
#### (A kékszakállú Herceg Vára)

OPERA in one act by Bela Bartok, text by B. Balázs. Première Budapest, May 24, 1918. First performed Frankfort, 1922; Berlin, 1929. Revived Budapest, 1937; Florence Festival, 1938 (by Budapest company); Zürich, 1948, with Malaniuk, Pernerstorfer; Berlin, 1951, with Ilosvay, Hoffmann, conductor Fricsay; Naples, 1951, with Malaniuk, Petri, conductor Fricsay; New York City Centre, 1952, with Ayars, Pease, conductor Rosenstock; B.B.C., London, 1953, with Cross, Matters; Sadler's Wells 1954, with Elliott, Ward.

### CHARACTERS

Duke Bluebeard ................................. Bass
Judith, *his wife* ........................ Mezzo-Soprano

Bartok's short opera (it lasts less than an hour) is one of the most impressive of his early works. Whatever it may owe in its conception to Debussy and to Maeterlinck, the music is characteristic of its composer. The piece has almost no action, and yet the music is essentially dramatic, just as the orchestral colour retains life and vigour even in its most sombre moments. It is probably due to its serious character and the static nature of the drama more than to the difficulty of fitting other than Hungarian words to the Hungarian music that the opera owes its infrequent performance.

A bard appears before the curtain to establish that the action of the opera is legendary in character. When the curtain rises, it reveals a large round room, gothic in style. On the left, a staircase leads up to a little iron door. To the right of this staircase can be seen seven larger doors. There are no windows or ornaments of any kind. The room is like a great, empty cavern. It is dark.

Bluebeard enters, leading Judith by the hand. She has left her parents and her home to follow him, and is only just regaining her courage. She sees the doors and wants to open them to let light and air into the castle. She knocks at the first door, and hears a long sigh like that of the wind. With the key that Bluebeard gives her, she opens the door, from which immediately streams red light (violins *tremolo*, flutes *arpeggio*). It is the torture chamber, and Judith exclaims that the walls are wet with blood; but she is not afraid.

In succession she opens four more doors. A shaft of bronze-coloured light (solo trumpet, woodwind trills) comes from the Armoury; golden light (violin solo, three trumpets) pours from the Treasury, from which she takes a jewelled cloak and a crown; bluish light (harp *glissando*, strings *tremolo*, solo horn) comes from behind the door which conceals the garden; and a dazzling white light (full orchestra, organ) blinds her as she opens the door which gives on to Bluebeard's kingdom. Each time Judith sees signs of blood: on the weapons in the armoury, on the jewels and robes in the treasury, on the flowers in the garden, even in the colour of the cloud over the kingdom itself.

Judith will not heed Bluebeard's warning, but opens the sixth door (harp, clarinet *arpeggios*). When she asks Bluebeard what is the significance of the water behind it, he answers 'Tears'. He tries to turn her from completing her purpose and takes her lovingly in his arms. She asks him if he has loved other women, and, when he tries to evade the question, demands that he give her the seventh key so that she may find out what the door conceals. As he gives it her, he tells her that it will show her all his former wives.

She opens the seventh door and immediately the sixth and fifth doors close; at the same time the light in the hall begins to grow dimmer. Three beautiful women emerge. Bluebeard kneels before them and assures them that they are not forgotten, and even Judith is filled with awe at their beauty. In his first wife Bluebeard sees the embodiment of the morning of his existence, in the second of his noonday, in the third of evening. One by one they disappear through the door, and the fourth door closes. Then he addresses Judith. She is the most beautiful of all, and her he met in the night; after her is eternal darkness. He goes slowly to fetch the crown and robe from the third door, which closes after him, and adorns Judith with them. For a moment she pleads with him, then turns and goes through the seventh door which shuts after her. Bluebeard is alone once more.                    H.

# ZOLTAN KODALY

### (born 1882)

## HARY JANOS

FABLE in three acts, text by Bela Paulini and Zsolt Harsanyi, music by Zoltan Kodaly. Première Budapest, October 16, 1926. First performed Cologne, 1931; Zürich, 1950, with Malaniuk, Boehm, conductor Reinshagen. New production Budapest, 1952, with Maria Matyas, Imre Pallo. Very successful in Hungary.

### CHARACTERS

Hary Janos ................................. Baritone
Ilka (Orzse), *his fiancée* ...................... Soprano
Empress of Austria .......................... Soprano
Emperor Napoleon ......................... Baritone
Marie-Louise, *his Austrian wife* .......... Mezzo-Soprano
Old Marzci, *Marie-Louise's coachman* .......... Baritone
Ritter von Ebelasztin, *Chamberlain to Empress*
   *Marie-Louise* ................................. Tenor

Kaiser Franz of Austria ................. ⎤
Countess Melusine ⎱ *Ladies-in-waiting* ...... ⎥
Countess Estrella ⎰ *to Marie-Louise* ...... ⎥
Hungarian Sentry ...................... ⎥
Russian Sentry ........................ ⎥
General Blood-and-Thunder .............. ⎥
General Dufla ......................... ⎬ Speaking rôles
First and Second Hussars ............... ⎥
First and Second Artillerymen ........... ⎥
Village Elder ......................... ⎥
A Student ............................ ⎥
Abraham, *an innkeeper* ................. ⎥
First and Second Peasants .............. ⎦

Generals, Hungarian and French Soldiers, Peasant Women, Court Servants, People

*Time:* Beginning of nineteenth century     *Place:* Hungary

*Hary Janos* is less in the nature of a true opera than of a play with a quantity of incidental music. Nevertheless its home in Hungary is in the opera house, and it has been successfully played abroad, notably in Switzerland. Only a few of the large number of characters actually sing, but there are no fewer than thirty musical numbers in the score, varying from a full-dress operatic finale to a few bars of incidental, atmospheric music. The play is conceived as a fantastic adventure told to his cronies by an ignorant but imaginative Hungarian peasant, and nothing that happens in it bears any relation to reality, being based exclusively on what Hary would expect it to be like. Kodaly has clothed the story in music of great charm and individuality, as will be readily admitted by anyone who knows the attractive orchestral suite drawn from the opera.

Prologue.   The prelude (called *The story begins* in the suite) aptly sets the 'once upon a time' atmosphere. The scene is an Inn, on one of whose walls hangs a crude picture of Napoleon. What sort of story is Hary Janos likely to tell to-day, asks the village elder. When Hary appears, a student points to the picture of Napoleon: that was a great hero. I once took him prisoner with my own hands, is Hary's rejoinder!

First adventure.   The scene is the border of Galicia and Russia. On the Russian side, it is deep winter; the sentry is muffled in furs and stamps about, blowing on his hands, and snow covers the scene. On the Hungarian side, the sun is shining, the flowers are out, and the Hussar drips with sweat and from time to time mops his forehead. They comment on the weather. One's drink is too hot, the other's is frozen; they exchange. As the curtain goes up and during the early part of the conversation, a flute solo gives out the tune of the big duet, which occurs later in the scene. A woman who tries to cross from Hungary into Russia (she has a bit of music to herself) is turned back and departs disconsolate. A Jewish family, also introduced musically, comes from the Russian side but is not allowed to leave.

Ilka appears, singing a little unaccompanied song. When the sentry makes eyes at her, she warns him that she will set Hary Janos on him if he does not stop immediately. She goes out. Female voices are heard singing, and the Hungarian sentry says that they are girls of the village; where they are, Hary cannot be far away. He is right. Hary appears, asks for Ilka, is told which way she went, and, shooing away his female companions, goes off to find her.

Herr von Ebelasztin, Chamberlain at the French court, puts

his head out of the Russian side of the guardroom and complains that his Empress has not been allowed to pass the frontier. Hary and Ilka return and are soon in conversation with Marczi, the Hungarian coachman employed at the French court. Nothing will suit the French, he says, but to de-Hungarianise him, a process he is strenuously resisting. When he tells Hary that the Empress is being kept in the Russian guardroom, Hary demands of the guard that she be let through. 'No one in, no one out' is the Russian's answer. There seems no solution until Hary takes hold of the guardroom and pulls it bodily into Hungarian territory, where-upon the ice and snow immediately begin to melt, and the flowers to bloom.

Marczi compliments Hary and Ilka on their mutual suitability, and, when he goes back into the house, they sing a beautiful duet: Tiszán innen, Dunán túl' (Rivers shining, rivers twain, There's a drover with his horses on the plain[1]). The tune, of haunting, nostalgic beauty, occurs as the third item in the orchestral suite.

Marczi returns and toasts the lovers in an attractive drinking song, but Ebelasztin complains of the noise and they are all ashamed at the thought that they may have disturbed the Empress's rest. She, however, emerges and asks who it was who sang so attractively. When told it was Hary, she asks him to come to Vienna with her, and offers to grant him three wishes. He asks for double rations for his horse; for a nice Hungarian livery for Marczi, and for permission for him to retain his moustache; and to be allowed to take Ilka to Vienna with him. All are granted.

The Russian re-appears, full of apprehension that he will be hanged if the guardroom's altered position is found. Ebelasztin tries to push it back but cannot, and it is not until Hary consents to do it that any progress is made. Back in Russian territory, it immediately starts to freeze again.

Second adventure. This section is introduced by the famous Intermezzo with its intoxicating rhythms. The scene is the park of the Imperial Palace in Vienna, viewed strictly through the eyes of Hary's imagination, i.e. the bushes have blossoms in the shape of an Imperial crown, the trees are of gold, the dove-cot is inhabited by a two-headed eagle. In the course of a conversation between Hary and Marczi, it appears that all are conscious of the animosity with which Ebelasztin regards Hary, although they are

[1] English translation by Professor Dent and Dennis Arundell.

somewhat reassured when, a moment later, the Empress Marie-Louise appears and tells Hary to call on her for help if he is ever in need. Ebelasztin sends Hary off to the riding-school, where—so Ilka tells us a short time later—he is put on to the fiercest horse in the stable, which immediately dashes on to the roof. But Hary returns quite unconcerned, having put Lucifer quietly away in his stall. Marie-Louise gives Hary a violet she has picked, much to the rage of Ebelasztin, who has asked for it for himself.

The Austrian Empress joins the group (she is knitting a golden stocking), and Marie-Louise blushingly points out the mighty Hary to her. Hary has an opportunity of advising the Empress on an old recipe which he recommends for the Emperor, who, he is told, is unwell. Ilka appears from the kitchen with a dish of sweet-corn, whose seeds (of real gold) she proceeds to feed to the two-headed eagle. Ebelasztin joins her, and says he carries in his bag Napoleon's declaration of war on Austria, to use when he thinks fit. Marie-Louise's gift of the violet to a peasant bumpkin is quite sufficient provocation, and he will use it forthwith. A moment later, military noises are heard from the palace, and everyone rushes in saying that war has been declared by France. Hary, by now promoted Captain by the Emperor, kisses Ilka good-bye, and the curtain falls as General Dufla wheels on an enormous cannon.

Following the Intermezzo, the music of the Second Adventure consists of three songs and an extended orchestral incident depicting the palace clocks striking midday, much to the delight of the astonished Hary (this is included in the suite). Marie-Louise sings a little song about a cuckoo as she picks the violet which is to cause the ructions between Ebelasztin and Hary and so to lead indirectly to the declaration of war. Ilka has two songs, one brief and almost pathetic in character as she reflects on the danger Hary ran when he rode the wild Lucifer, the other brisk and lively as she feeds the Imperial fowls; this is one of the most charming pieces in the score.

Third Adventure. The battlefield; in the background is the fortress of Milan, and behind that the mountains. Cannon are in evidence, and hussars stand about, amongst them Hary, by now promoted Colonel. A chorus of soldiers can be heard, at first melancholy but gradually growing more animated as they contrast the wonders of what they can now see with the village life they knew back at home; there are even dragons in the mountains here, says Hary. In richly comic terms, the hussars discuss the military situation with General Blood-and-Thunder; shots are heard, and the General's immediate reaction is to give the order: 'Withdraw according to plan.' French soldiers appear, Hary draws his sabre and, by the mere act of doing so, creates a draught which fells his opponents to the ground. The music of the battle (included in the suite) is in three distinct stages. First of all, the French band can be heard off; when it comes on, Hary is laying low the army with the wind of his sword, with the result that the playing of the band becomes more and more confused. Very soft percussion heralds the entry of Napoleon—in atmosphere it is rather like the accompaniment that would be given to an ogre in an English pantomime—but soon the brass enters *fortissimo*, with a hint of the 'Marseillaise' somewhere in the music. Napoleon falls on his knees and is taken prisoner by Hary, who declares the war over. There is a funeral march, dominated by a moaning little tune on the saxophone.

Marie-Louise comes on the scene and is contemptuous of the beaten Napoleon, who has a little song to the tune of the funeral march. Everyone congratulates Hary—he ought to be a General, says Blood-and-Thunder—and, to the accompaniment of gypsy music, a feast is prepared, Hary and Marie-Louise taking the opportunity of dancing together. Ebelasztin and Ilka come in, the latter admitting that the former's warnings seem to have had something behind them when she sees how Hary is behaving—is this war's hardship, she asks bitterly.

There is an acrimonious exchange between Ilka and Marie-Louise, when the former dances with Hary—they are obviously very much in love. Marie-Louise announces she is going to marry Hary, and when the latter demurs, she rushes off threatening to commit suicide. Hary naturally manages to save the situation, and he leads a big marching ensemble as the episode comes to an end.

Fourth Adventure. Hary's elaborately furnished room in Vienna (the style is not at all Hungarian). The Empress and Marie-Louise sing a duet to the accompaniment of a chorus of attendants, Marie-Louise wondering which of her ten suitors she shall marry, her mother plumping for Hary. Marie-Louise's only doubts on the score are because she has already discovered that Hary will not always do as he is told; for instance, he has never yet kissed her.

To the accompaniment of outrageously noisy music, the Emperor leads in a procession in honour of Hary, who will in future, he announces, be endowed with half the Empire and half the Imperial Palace. At the feast Hary is not himself and will eat nothing; he is even cross when told the double-headed chickens are normal fare for the Imperial table. The Emperor toasts Hary in a speech, and then, to a march, in come the little archdukes to shake hands with the hero of the day.

Hary admits that he cannot marry Marie-Louise, not least because he has a sweetheart of his own—Ilka. If he is to have a reward, says Hary, may he be let off half his military service, so that he can go home and get married. The Emperor grants his request, and Hary hands back his baton to General Blood-and-Thunder. Ilka comes in, knowing nothing of what has happened, and sings a melancholy and very beautiful song—perhaps, with the duet of the first adventure, the best sustained lyrical passage of the opera. Hary, now dressed as an infantryman, returns (for a hussar, infantry uniform is practically the same as civilian clothes, he observes), and swears allegiance to the Emperor, whether he serves him as soldier or as farmer. There is only one more complication to clear up. Ebelasztin is sent in chains to Hary by the Emperor Napoleon, but Hary magnanimously pardons him and leads him over to his beloved Marie-Louise. The finale, for Hary, Ilka, and the chorus, makes use of material already used in the opera, notably the love duet and the intermezzo.

There is an epilogue, set in the same inn as the prologue. Hary Janos finishes his story: he and Ilka walked home and were married. Now, Ilka having died, there is no one to witness his story but he.                                         H.

CHAPTER 21

*Spanish Opera in the Twentieth Century*

# MANUEL DE FALLA
## (1876–1946)

### LA VIDA BREVE
### The Brief Life

OPERA in two acts by Manuel de Falla, text by C. Fernandez Shaw; French version by P. Milliet. Première Nice, April 1, 1913, with Lillian Grenville, David Devries, Cotreuil, conductor Miranne. First performed Opéra-Comique, Paris, 1914, with Carré, Brohly, Francell, Vieuille, conductor Ruhlmann; Madrid, 1914; Buenos Aires, 1923; Metropolitan, 1926, with Bori, Tokatyan, d'Angelo, conductor Serafin; la Scala, Milan, 1934, with dalla Rizza, Castagna, Masini, Romito, conductor Votto. Revived Buenos Aires, 1946; San Carlo, Naples, 1951, with Arzimendi, Sinimberghi, conductor Fricsay; la Scala, Milan, 1952, with Araujo, Francesco Albanese, Beuf, conductor Giulini; Holland Festival, 1953, with de los Angeles, Vroons.

### CHARACTERS

| | |
|---|---|
| Salud, *a gypsy* | Soprano |
| Her grandmother | Mezzo-Soprano |
| Carmela, *a young girl* | Mezzo-Soprano |
| Paco | Tenor |
| Uncle Sarvaor | Bass |
| A Singer | Baritone |
| Manuel, *Carmela's brother* | Baritone |
| A Voice in the Forge ⎫ | |
| Voice of a Street-seller ⎬ | Tenor |
| A Distant Voice ⎭ | |

*Time:* The present                              *Place:* Granada

*La Vida Breve* is the earliest of Falla's works which is still generally performed. It was written in 1904–5 and won a prize in Madrid, but was not immediately mounted on the stage. When Falla first went to Paris, he took the score with him, and the work was finally performed in 1913.

Act I. The curtain rises after a dozen bars of introduction. Courtyard of a gypsy habitation. On one side of the stage, the house where the gypsies live, on the other the entrance to a smithy, from which can be heard a mysterious sound of singing. Salud's old grandmother is feeding some birds in a cage. One is going to die, she thinks—perhaps of love, like Salud. The voices of street-sellers (off-stage, like that of the soloist in the smithy) can be heard.

Salud comes in from the street, looking unhappy. Her grandmother tries to reassure her; of course Paco will come. Salud is fearful that she may lose one of the two things she most values: the loves of Paco and of her grandmother. Alone Salud listens to the voices from the forge, and then sings a song with a sad philosophy—long live those who laugh, short life to those who cry: 'Vivan los que rien!' The poignant beauty of the music is like that of a folk-song, and indeed it is founded on the Andalusian style.

But her grandmother comes to tell Salud that Paco is coming. Her joy is complete, and in their duet her sincerity and innocence contrasts with his more conventional utterances—Professor J. B. Trend, in his book on Falla, has suggested that the Massenet-like cast of Paco's music is intended to contrast with the characteristic folk style of Salud's. Salud's grandmother and her uncle observe the scene, and he mutters that he would gladly take revenge on Paco, whom he knows to be going to marry another girl the very next day. He is only playing with Salud.

The second scene is in the form of an intermezzo. A view of Granada from Sacro Monte can be seen.

Act II.    A small street in Granada. Through the open railings can be seen the courtyard in which is being celebrated the betrothal of Paco and Carmela with song and dance. A professional singer has been engaged to entertain the company. He sings an Andalusian song, which is followed by a dance, made famous all over the world by generations of fiddlers who have appropriated it as an encore piece.

Just before the dance finishes, Salud appears and rushes to see what is going on. She is in despair when she finds her worst fears realised, and Paco laughing and talking with the girl who is separating him from her for ever. Her grief spills over in a terrible lament, and she longs for death. Her grandmother and uncle arrive, and the latter tries to relieve the situation by cursing Paco and everything to do with him. Salud hears Paco's voice and makes up her mind to speak to him once again. She repeats the sad song of the forge: 'The man that's born of a woman, is born in an evil day.' Salud is determined to enter.

During an interlude the scene changes to the courtyard of the house. The guests are well dressed. Immediately the curtain rises there is a dance, hardly less well known than the previous one. Paco is ill-at-ease, having heard the voice of Salud. Manuel makes a speech to congratulate the happy pair, but Paco becomes more and more uncomfortable as Uncle Sarvaor comes into the patio, followed by Salud. Sarvaor offers their services to entertain the company, but Salud denounces Paco's treachery towards her in tones that would almost appear calm did they not so obviously conceal deep feeling. She falls dead of shock at Paco's feet, and her grandmother and Uncle Sarvaor curse Paco as the curtain falls.                                                                    H.

# ENRIQUE GRANADOS

## (1867–1916)

### GOYESCAS

OPERA in three scenes (one act) by Enrique Granados, text by Fernando Periquet. Première Metropolitan, New York, January 28, 1916, with Fitziu, Perini, Martinelli, de Luca, conductor Bavagnoli (in Spanish). First performed Opéra, Paris, 1919; Buenos Aires, 1929; la Scala, Milan, 1937, with Carbone, Elmo, Civil, Poli, conductor Capuana; Royal College of Music, London, 1951.

#### CHARACTERS

Rosario, *a highborn young lady* . . . . . . . . . . . . . . . . . Soprano
Fernando, *a young officer, her lover* . . . . . . . . . . . . . . . Tenor
Paquiro, *a toreador* . . . . . . . . . . . . . . . . . . . . . . . . . . Baritone
Pepa, *a young girl of the people, Paquiro's*
    *sweetheart* . . . . . . . . . . . . . . . . . . . . . . . . . . . Mezzo-Soprano

Majas and Majos

*Time:* About 1800                    *Place:* Spain

The characters and setting of the opera are suggested by the work of the great Spanish painter Goya. The opera opens with a crowd of majas and majos enjoying a holiday on the outskirts of Madrid. Some of the majas are engaged in the popular pastime of tossing the *pelele* (a man of straw) in a blanket. Paquiro the toreador is paying compliments to the women. Pepa, his sweetheart of the day, arrives in her dogcart. Popular, she is warmly welcomed. Soon Rosario, a lady of rank, arrives in her sedanchair to keep a tryst with her lover, Fernando, a captain in the Royal Spanish Guards. Paquiro reminds her of a *baile de candil* (a ball given in a room lit by candlelight) which she once attended. He invites her to go again. Fernando overhears his remarks, and his jealousy is aroused. He informs Paquiro that Rosario shall go to the ball, but that he, Fernando, will escort her. He extracts Rosario's promise to go with him, while Pepa, enraged by Paquiro's neglect, vows vengeance upon her.

The second tableau shows the scene at the ball. Fernando appears with Rosario. His haughty bearing and disdainful speech anger all present. The two men arrange for a duel that evening, and when Rosario recovers from a swoon, Fernando takes her away.

The third tableau reveals Rosario's garden. She is discovered sitting by herself on a stone bench listening in pensive mood to the song of the nightingale. This is the famous aria called 'The Lover and the Nightingale' (La Maja y el Ruiseñor), one of the most beautiful and luxuriant nocturnes ever written for voice and orchestra.

Fernando visits Rosario before keeping his appointment with Paquiro. When a bell strikes the fatal hour, Fernando tears himself away. He is followed hesitatingly by Rosario. Soon the silence is broken by a cry from Fernando, followed by a shriek from Rosario. The lovers reappear. Rosario supports Fernando to a stone bench where he dies in her arms.

Enrique Granados, perhaps the first important composer from Spain to visit North America, was born July 27, 1867, at Lerida, Catalonia. He died March 24, 1916, a passenger on the *Sussex*, torpedoed in the English Channel. The music of *Goyescas* is drawn from his suite of piano pieces of the same name.

K.

# CHAPTER 22

## *American Opera in the Twentieth Century*

# VIRGIL THOMSON
## (born 1896)

### FOUR SAINTS IN THREE ACTS

OPERA in four acts, text by Gertrude Stein (*an opera to be sung*). First given in concert form, Ann Arbor, Michigan, May 20, 1933; on the stage, at Hartford, Connecticut, February 8, 1934, by the Society of Friends and Enemies of Modern Music, conducted by Alexander Smallens, staged by Frederick Ashton, scenery and costumes by Florine Stettheimer. The opera was sung by negroes, including Edward Matthews as Saint Ignatius, Beatrice Robinson Wayne, and Bruce Howard as Saint Teresa I and II, Embry Bonner as Saint Chavez, Bertha Fitzhugh Baker as Saint Settlement, and Abner Dorsey and Altonell Hines as Compère and Commère. First performance in New York, 44th Street Theatre, February 20, 1934. The work has since been heard in both concert and radio performances, and in May 1952 was presented by a negro company in Paris during the Festival of Twentieth Century Art, with Inez Matthews, Edward Matthews, conductor Virgil Thomson.

### CHARACTERS

| | |
|---|---|
| Compère | Bass |
| Commère | Mezzo-Soprano |
| Saint Teresa I | Soprano |
| Saint Teresa II | Contralto |
| Saint Ignatius Loyola | Baritone |
| Saint Chavez | Tenor |
| Saint Settlement | Soprano |

Double chorus of named and unnamed saints; six dancers

Gertrude Stein's text is partly evocative, partly satirical, and at no time lays any particular stress on meaning. Virgil Thomson, one of the best-known of American music critics, has written music for it which is the reverse of pretentious; he does not scorn the trivial (the work has been described as 'the opposite of epochal') and yet the relationship of un-meaning words and simple tunes is curiously rational. The straightforward tunes are simply harmonised—Thomson himself has said that 'the lack of the expected dissonance is the most striking characteristic of the score' (quoted in *American Opera* by Edward Ellsworth Hipsher) —and the music is always singable, and by no means devoid of that quality which makes it stick in the memory. The composer decided on the negro cast because of the clarity of their diction and because of their natural approach to religious subjects. A note in the score tells us that 'the precedent need not be considered binding'.

The surrealist nature of the work is emphasised by the fact that the scenario used for the original production was written (by Maurice Grosser) *after* the words and music had been completed. The original act headings (which are the only indications of 'story' the libretto contains) are given in italics in the following synopsis.

Prelude.    *A narrative of Prepare for Saints.* The choral overture in waltz time on the following words:

> To know to know to love her so.
> Four saints prepare for Saints,
> Four saints make it well fish.
> Four saints prepare for saints it makes it well fish
>     it makes it well fish prepare for saints

leads to some conversation between the chorus, Compère, Commère, and various saints, and ends with the Commère and Compère reading out a lengthy list of saints, many of whom are not mentioned at any other point in the opera.

Act I.    *Saint Teresa half indoors and half out of doors.* The scene is the steps of the Cathedral at Avila. Saint Teresa enacts for the instruction of saints and visitors seven scenes from her own life. The first has the Compère and Commère and two choruses singing antiphonally, then an aria for Saint Teresa with choral interjections. Saint Ignatius joins the guests just before the end of the first tableau, which gives way to the second, in which Saint Teresa, holding a dove in her hand, is photographed by Saint Settlement. In the third and fourth tableaux Saint Ignatius serenades Saint Teresa, and then offers her flowers. In tableau five Saint Ignatius and Saint Teresa II admire the model of a Heavenly Mansion. In tableaux six and seven, Saint Teresa II is shown in an attitude of ecstasy, and rocking an unseen child.

Act II.    *Might it be mountains if it were not Barcelona.* The scene is a garden party near Barcelona. The Compère and Commère sit at the side in an opera box from which they can watch the proceedings and where they are presently joined by both Saint Teresas and Saint Ignatius. A Dance of Angels is performed for their pleasure and there is a party game, after which everyone goes out except the Compère and Commère. There is a love scene between them, and the two Saint Teresas return in time to see it, and are pleased at what they see. A telescope is brought in and as the two Saint Teresas look through it a vision of a heavenly mansion appears. 'How many doors how many floors and how many windows are there in it?' ask the saints.

Act III. *Saint Ignatius and one of two literally.* The scene is a garden of a monastery on the sea coast. The men saints are mending a fish net. The introductory *allegro moderato* for the orchestra alone leads to a conversation about monastic life between Saint Ignatius, the two Saint Teresas and Saint Settlement, but the men stop their work and listen as Saint Ignatius describes to them his vision of the Holy Ghost. This is his well-known aria, 'Pigeons on the grass alas'; the vocal line is occasionally taken over by the chorus or the Compère, and there is an off-stage heavenly chorus to sing the words 'Let Lucy Lily Lily Lucy Lucy let Lucy Lucy Lily Lily Lily Lily Lily let Lily Lucy Lucy let Lily. Let Lucy Lily'. Saint Chavez lectures to the men, there is a dance in the Spanish style, a storm is quieted by Saint Ignatius, and Saint Ignatius predicts the Last Judgment. It grows dark, there is a devotional procession, and the Intermezzo recalls the opening of the prologue.

Act IV. *The sisters and saints reassembled and re-enacting why they went away to stay.* The Compère and Commère discuss whether there shall be a fourth act, and when they have made up their minds, the curtain rises to show all the saints in heaven. They join in a hymn of communion 'When this you see remember me', the Compère announces 'Last Act', and the chorus and principals reply *fortissimo* 'Which is a fact'.                    H.

# GEORGE GERSHWIN
## (1898–1937)

### PORGY AND BESS

O PERA in three acts by George Gershwin; text by du Bose Heyward and Ira Gershwin. Première Boston, September 30, 1935, with Todd Duncan (Porgy), Anne Brown (Bess), Warren Coleman (Crown), Eddie Matthews (Jake), Abbie Mitchell (Clara), Bubbles (Sporting Life), Eva Jessye Choir, produced by Rouben Mamoulian, conductor Alexander Smallens. First performed Zürich, 1945, with Cordy, Eftimiades, Kovacs, Boehm, Chabay, conductor Reinshagen; 1950, with Funk, Malaniuk, Jungwirth, Boehm, Wosniak, conductor Ackermann; Copenhagen, 1946, with Anne Brown and Einar Nørby. In 1952, an all-negro company set out from the States and toured with the opera through the capitals of Europe (notably Berlin and Vienna), ending up in London in the autumn at the Stoll Theatre, where they stayed until February 10, 1953, playing to packed houses. The cast included Pryce, Thigpen, Warfield, Cab Calloway, conductor Smallens.

### CHARACTERS

Porgy, *a cripple*............................Bass-Baritone
Bess, *Crown's girl* ............................Soprano
Crown, *a tough stevedore* ......................Baritone
Serena, *Robbins's wife*........................Soprano
Clara, *Jake's wife* ............................Soprano
Maria, *keeper of the cook-shop* .................Contralto
Jake, *a fisherman* .............................Baritone
Sporting Life, *a dope pedlar* .....................Tenor
Mingo ..........................................Tenor
Robbins, *an inhabitant of Catfish Row* ..............Tenor
Peter, *the honeyman* ...........................Tenor
Frazier, *a negro 'lawyer'* ......................Baritone
Annie ..................................Mezzo-Soprano
Lily, *Peter's wife, strawberry woman* ...... Mezzo-Soprano
Jim, *a cotton picker* ....................Baritone
Undertaker...............................Baritone
Nelson .........................................Tenor
Crab man ......................................Tenor
Mr. Archdale, *a white man* ⎫
Detective ⎬ ............Speaking Parts
Policeman ⎭

Coroner
Scipio, *a small boy* } . . . . . . . . . . . .Speaking Parts

*Time:* Recent past    *Place:* Charleston, South Carolina, U.S.A.

The scene is laid in Catfish Row, which is, according to the synopsis in the published score, 'a former mansion of the aristocracy, but now a negro tenement on the water front of Charleston, South Carolina'.

Act I, scene i, shows the inside of the court. After a short *allegro con brio* introduction, we are introduced to the variegated night life of the court. There is singing and dancing and presently a lazy Lullaby can be heard, sung by Clara, who nurses her baby. It is 'Summer time, an' the livin' is easy', and the song's lyric beauty has made it one of the most famous in the opera, and in fact of all Gershwin's songs. The lights fade from one group and come up on another where a crap game is seen to be in progress. The episodic music reflects the varied nature of the stage action, and the Lullaby is heard again as background to the game. Jake says he will take it on himself to send his and Clara's baby to sleep, and he sings 'A woman is a sometime thing', the bystanders joining in the refrain. A caterwaul from the baby brings this episode to an end.

The honeyman's call is heard before Porgy is spied coming towards the court. He is a cripple who cannot stand upright, and he gets about in a little goatcart. Everybody seems pleased to see him, and they twit him about Bess—'I think he's soft on Crown's Bess,' says Jake. Porgy defends Bess's reputation when it is attacked, and blames her present degradation on 'the Gawd fearin' ladies an' the Gawd damnin' men'. Porgy laments his crippled, lonely state, particularly with reference to women, but attention is diverted from him when Crown comes in with Bess, calling loudly for drink and going unsteadily to join the crap school. The play goes on, although Crown finds difficulty in reading the dice, a fact that does not escape the comment of the bystanders. Crown objects to losing his money when Robbins beats him in the game. He throws Robbins to the ground, attacking him with a cotton hook and killing him, to the horror of the inhabitants of Catfish Row. Bess gives Crown money and urges him to be off out of the way of the police; he says firmly that he will be back; any arrangement she may care to make in the meanwhile with another man will be with his permission—but strictly temporary.

Sporting Life approaches Bess and offers to take her to New York with him, but she spurns his offer, and tries to find shelter from someone in the court—unsuccessfully, until Porgy opens his door and lets her in, just as the police whistles can be heard blowing outside.

The scene changes to Serena's room, where Robbins's body lies on the bed, a saucer on its chest to receive any contributions which may be forthcoming against the expense of his burial. A large number of people are watching by the body, singing a spiritual as they mourn. Porgy and Bess enter and put money in the saucer, and the mourners exhort each other to follow their example. Porgy leads a rhythmic spiritual before a detective puts his head round the door and comes in. By accusing Peter of the murder, he gets the others to say that Crown did it—but he hauls off the protesting and inoffensive Peter (who is half deaf) as a 'material witness'.

Porgy reflects on the injustice of taking off an old man who never did anyone any harm, while a criminal like Crown wanders about scot-free, waiting to duplicate his crime. The wake goes on, and Serena, swaying to her words, begins a big lament, 'My man's gone now' in which the chorus supports her. The undertaker comes to see Serena and agrees to bury Robbins for the $15 which is all that is in the saucer. Bess leads the last of the spirituals, 'Oh, we're leavin' for the Promise' Land', and the scene comes to its end.

Act II takes place a month later. Jake and the fishermen are repairing their nets and preparing to put to sea, singing as they do so, 'It take a long pull to get there'. In spite of the warning that the time of year is coming round for the September storms, Jake and his friends are determined to set out. Porgy appears at his window, laughing and singing his Banjo song, 'Oh, I got plenty o' nuttin'', an infectious and brilliant piece which causes the chorus to comment on the change for the better which has come over him since Bess has been living with him.

Sporting Life is sauntering around the court when Maria the cook sees that he has some dope with him. She gives him a piece of her mind, and when he suggests that they should be friends, catches him by the throat, bends him back over the table, and treats him to a lecture on what he has got coming to him from her. She only releases him when Lawyer Frazier comes in, looking for Porgy, to whom he sells a 'divorce' for Bess, clinching the bargain when he points out that it is naturally much more difficult (and expensive) to divorce somebody who has never even been married. The scene takes place to the accompaniment of choral comment on her age, and all the other details which Frazier asks her for.

There is another visitor, when Mr. Archdale appears, also asking for Porgy. At first everybody is too suspicious to tell him, but he wins them over, and informs Porgy that he will go bond for his friend Peter now in gaol. As he turns to leave, Porgy exclaims in horror at the sight of a buzzard flying over the court. If it alights, he explains to Mr. Archdale, it brings bad luck to everyone living in the house. Porgy's Buzzard song, with the chorus, is sometimes omitted,[1] seemingly at the suggestion of Gershwin himself, who thought the rôle of Porgy needed shortening if the singer were going to stand the strain of eight performances a week for a long run (one may be forgiven, too, if one thinks of it as only partially a loss; it is a long way from being the best number in the opera).

Sporting Life sidles up to Bess and again suggests they should team up and go off to New York, but she tells him she hates the sight of him—and she will have nothing more to do with the 'happy dust' he offers her. Porgy twigs what is going on and reaches round his door to catch hold of Sporting Life's wrist, making him cry out with the strength of his grip. He warns him to keep away from Bess.

It is the day of the organised picnic, and everybody disappears to get themselves ready, leaving Porgy alone with Bess, who tells him she does not want to go since he cannot. There is an extended love duet for the two of them, 'Bess, you is my woman now', at whose end the stage fills with life, a military band strikes up a 'Tempo di Marcia giocoso', and with a maximum of noise the picnickers start on their way. Maria persuades Bess that she must come along after all, and she takes a fond farewell of Porgy, who is left singing happily 'I got plenty o' nuttin.''

Scene ii is on Kittiwah Island, the evening of the same day. The picnickers dance riotously and Sporting Life treats them to a

[1] In the 1952 London production it was transferred to the last act.

sermon in praise of the virtues of scepticism, 'It ain't necessarily so', whose jaunty tune and brilliant lyrics have made it one of the most popular and also one of the best numbers of the score. Two samples of its outrageous rhymes:

> It ain't necessarily so,
> De t'ings dat yo' li'ble
> To read in de Bible,
> It ain't necessarily so;

and

> Oh, Jonah, he lived in de whale,
> Fo' he made his home in
> Dat fish's abdomen,
> Oh, Jonah, he lived in de whale.

Serena comes on the scene, sees the dancing, and denounces the whole pack of them for sinners, also reminding them, more prosaically, that the boat is leaving soon and that they must hurry to get on board.

Bess waits behind a moment, and Crown appears in front of her. He tells her that he will be back for her soon, but she pleads to be allowed to stay in peace with Porgy, who has taught her to live decently. Crown laughs at what she says, and says he regards her living with Porgy as a temporary (but permissible) arrangement, which will cease the moment he comes back. Bess suggests he find some other woman ('Oh, what you want wid Bess?'), but she cannot resist Crown's old fascination, and when he takes her in his arms, she is too weak to deny him anything. She stays behind with him and the boat goes off without her.

Scene iii.     Jake and the fishermen prepare to go off fishing, singing a snatch of 'It take a long pull to get there'. Peter is back from prison, and the sound of Bess's voice coming in a delirium from Porgy's room indicates that she too has returned from Kittiwah Island. She was lost for two days and was incoherent when she finally got home. Serena prays for her to get well, and at the end tells Porgy: 'Alright now, Porgy. Doctor Jesus done take de case.' The cries of respectively the strawberry woman, the honeyman, and the crab man are heard, before Bess calls from off-stage, evidently well on the way to recovery. She talks to Porgy, who says that he knows she has been with Crown, but that it makes no difference to his love for her. She admits that she told Crown she would go with him when he comes for her, but pleads with Porgy to keep her for himself; she wants to stay but is afraid of the effect Crown's presence may have on her: 'I loves you, Porgy.' Porgy tells her he will take good care of Crown if he returns.

Clara is anxiously watching the sea, and presently her apprehension is confirmed, and the sound of the hurricane bell can be heard before the scene comes to an end.

The curtain for scene iv rises on Serena's room. Outside there is a terrific storm; inside the negroes are huddled in groups and sing. Every face is filled with fear as all pray for the danger, which threatens them and those they love, to be averted. 'I hear death knockin' at de do,'' sings Peter—and almost immediately a real knock comes, and is answered with a hysterical rush to hold the door against whoever is trying to come in by it. It turns out to be Crown. The prayer stops with his entrance, and he orders Bess to him, throwing down Porgy who makes a move to come between them. Serena warns him against violent behaviour; at any moment, the storm may get him. 'If God want to kill me,' he sings, 'He had plenty of chance 'tween here an' Kittiwah Island.'

The keening seems likely to go on indefinitely, but Crown stops it with his violent opposition, and in his turn he strikes up a cheerful jazz number, 'A red-headed woman makes a chow-chow jump its track'. Suddenly, Clara sees the boat, in which Jake put out to do his fishing, floating upside down in the river. She deposits her baby in Bess's arms while she goes off despairingly to learn the worst. Bess urges some man to follow her, but only Crown will venture out, which he does, with the promise that he is coming back to get Bess. The act ends with a renewal of the prayer for mercy.

Act III, scene i, takes place inside the courtyard. The inhabitants are mourning Clara, Jake, and Crown, all of whom they think lost in the storm. When they reach the point of praying for Crown, they are interrupted by laughter from Sporting Life. His levity is promptly scolded by Maria, but he hints that he knows Crown is not dead, and he slyly wonders what will be the upshot of the rivalry between Crown and Porgy over Bess. Bess is heard singing Clara's Lullaby to the baby she left behind her when she rushed off into the storm, and the inhabitants of the court drift off to bed, leaving it empty.

Suddenly, Crown can be seen at the gate. He picks his way stealthily across the court, then crawls towards Porgy's door. As he passes the window, the shutter opens silently and an arm is extended, grasping a long knife, which it plunges into Crown's back. Crown staggers into an upright position, and is seized round the neck in Porgy's iron grip and slowly throttled. Porgy exclaims: 'Bess, you got a man now, you got Porgy.'

Scene ii. Next afternoon. The police come to clear up the mystery of Crown's death. They question Serena, who it appears has been ill, and knows nothing of the death of the man who— every inhabitant of Catfish Row is prepared to swear—was responsible for killing her husband, Robbins. Porgy is roped in to identify Crown's body, and is dragged away protesting that he won't have anything to do with Crown, his reluctance having been increased by Sporting Life's helpful suggestion that Crown's wound will begin to bleed the moment the man that killed him comes into the presence of his body.

Bess is left alone, and Sporting Life seizes the opportunity to offer her some 'happy dust' to tide over her nerves at the prospect of losing Porgy. She tries to refuse, but cannot resist it, and Sporting Life sings a persuasive *Blues*, 'There's a boat dat's leavin' soon for New York', with the object of tempting her to come away with him. He goes out, leaving a second packet of dope behind him, and, after he is gone, Bess sneaks out of her room, and takes it inside with her.

The third scene plays again in Catfish Row, a week later. Normal life is going on, everyone says 'good morning' to everyone else, the children dance and sing, and Porgy is welcomed home after his week away—he would not look at Crown and was gaoled for contempt of court. Everyone is disconcerted by Porgy's arrival, but he distributes the presents he has bought them all (as a result of some successful crap-shooting in prison), and does not begin to notice that anything is wrong until he looks for Bess, whose present is the last and best. She is nowhere to be found, and he sees Serena looking after Clara's baby, which had been left in Bess's charge. 'Oh, Bess, oh where's my Bess?' he sings; Serena and Maria join in his song with explanations, the one excusing, the other condemning Bess for what she has done. Porgy's longing is admirably expressed in this trio, and in the final 'Oh Lord, I'm on my way', a spiritual with chorus, which

Porgy sings as he starts off to follow Bess to New York, where he is told she has gone. He drives out of Catfish Row in his goat-cart with his mind made up that, wherever she is, he will find her and bring her back.

*Porgy and Bess* is the first American opera to make a genuine success. It is also perhaps the only opera founded on the jazz of the nineteen-twenties and -thirties to survive the war which put an end to the period—which is perhaps partly due to the fact that most European composers (e.g. Krenek in *Johnny spielt auf*) used the medium satirically, and Gershwin was employing it as a folk basis for a story concerned with a community to whom jazz was a natural means of expression. H.

# GIAN-CARLO MENOTTI

## (born 1911)

### THE MEDIUM

OPERA in two acts by Gian-Carlo Menotti, text by the composer. Première Brander Matthews Theatre, Columbia University, May 8, 1946, with Evelyn Keller, Claramae Turner, conductor Luening. First performed New York (revised, and sponsored by Ballet Society), 1947, with Keller, Powers, conducted by Barzin; London, Aldwych Theatre, 1948, with Powers, conductor Balaban; Genoa, 1950, with Pederzini, conductor Sanzogno; Venice, Bari, Palermo, Turin, 1951–2, each time with Pederzini.

### CHARACTERS

Monica, *daughter of Madame Flora* .............. Soprano
Toby, *a mute* ................................. Dancer
Madame Flora (Baba), *a medium*............... Contralto
Mrs. Gobineau ⎫ ⎧ ................. Soprano
Mr. Gobineau ⎬ *her clients* ⎨ ................. Baritone
Mrs. Nolan ⎭ ⎩ ......... Mezzo-Soprano

*Time:* The present        *Place:* U.S.A.

Of *The Medium*, the composer himself has written (in notes to a complete gramophone recording published by Columbia Records in America): 'Despite its eerie setting and gruesome conclusions, *The Medium* is actually a play of ideas. It describes the tragedy of a woman caught between two worlds, a world of reality which she cannot wholly comprehend, and a supernatural world in which she cannot believe. Baba, the Medium, has no scruples in cheating her clients . . . until something happens which she herself has not prepared. This insignificant incident . . . shatters her self-assurance, and drives her almost insane with rage.' He goes on to explain that the idea for the opera came to him in 1936 when, staying near Salzburg, he was asked to go to a séance by some friends. It was not so much his own scepticism that struck him as the way his friends were pathetically anxious to believe that the spirit of their dead daughter was talking to them through the medium.

Act I.     Madame Flora's parlour. A puppet-theatre in one corner of the room. In a corner a tiny statue of the Virgin. No windows; the time of day is ambiguous throughout the play. When the curtain rises Toby is kneeling near a trunk from which he takes out bits of stuff and improvises a costume. Monica combs her hair and sings to herself. She tells him he is the King of Babylon, and they bow to each other. Then the sound of the door slamming down below frightens them, and they stand rigidly still. Madame Flora enters: 'How many times I've told you not to touch my things. . . . Is anything ready? Of course not.' Monica calms her mother, and they prepare for the séance, Monica putting on a white dress and veil, and Toby testing the various devices hidden in the puppet-theatre.

The clients arrive. One of them has not been before, but the others, who have been coming for two years, tell her how wonderful Madame Flora is. Mrs. Gobineau talks about their little child who was drowned in a fountain in their garden in France. The séance begins. All the lights, except the candle in front of the Madonna, are put out, and they sit round the table, their hands touching. Baba moans, and Monica slowly appears in a faint blue light, singing 'Mother, mother, are you there?' Mrs. Nolan is convinced it is her daughter, and she asks her various simple questions, which are answered to her satisfaction. Monica asks her about a gold locket, but it appears she has never had one, and immediately the apparition starts to disappear; Mrs. Nolan dashes towards the place where the figure appeared, but is restrained by the others.

Monica next imitates the sound of a child laughing for the benefit of the Gobineaus. Suddenly, Baba shouts hysterically, and turns on the light. 'Who touched me?' They try to reassure her —Mr. Gobineau even says such things have often happened to him at her séances—but she sends them away. As they go they sing a trio: 'But why be afraid of our dead?'

Baba is in a paroxysm of fear, and she seizes Toby from the puppet-theatre, and tries to blame the whole phenomenon on him. Monica takes her away and soothes her with an extended melody, which Toby accompanies on a tambourine: 'O black swan, where oh where is my lover gone?' Baba suddenly thinks she can hear voices, and sends Toby round to see what is there; when he comes back to indicate there was nothing there, she falls on her knees and prays. Monica repeats a few phrases of the cradle song.

Act II takes place in the same setting as Act I; it is evening a few days later. Monica sits in front of the puppet-theatre watching a performance which Toby is giving. She applauds, and then sings while he dances barefoot round the room. The dance becomes a sort of love duet, in which Monica sings for both and Toby mimes his part. She has guessed his love for her, and tries to divert it into play-acting, which she knows he enjoys.

Baba drags herself up the stairs, and Toby retreats into a corner before she gets into the room, Monica having already left to go to her own room. Baba questions Toby about the incident of a few days back; did he touch her throat? Was he the one? She cannot get him to admit it, tries to keep her temper, then loses it hopelessly, seizes a whip and beats the unfortunate boy unmercifully. The doorbell rings, and the Gobineaus and Mrs. Nolan enter. Is it not the night of the séance? Yes, she says; but there will be no more—they were all frauds. She wants to give them their money back, but they will not admit they have been cheated; it has all been too real. Even the sight of the stage props and the sound of Monica imitating the children's voices does not convince them; those were not the voices they heard. Nothing will convince them, and they beg for another séance, until Madame Flora loses her temper suddenly and yells to them to get out. She tries to send Toby too, but Monica pleads for him, helpless as he is. Baba however is insistent, and Monica has only just time to say good-bye to Toby before he has run down the stairs and out into the street.

The voices come back to Baba. In desperation she goes to the cupboard and pours herself several drinks. She sits down at the table with the bottle in front of her. 'Afraid? Am I afraid?' she asks herself. She passes her life in review, and thinks of the horrible things she has known; then tries to comfort herself with the song of the black swan. Her scene dies away in hysterical laughter. For a moment she prays for forgiveness; then falls asleep, exhausted.

Toby comes up the stairwell, tiptoes across to Monica's room, finds the door locked, and hides behind the sofa when Baba stirring in her sleep knocks the bottle over. He starts to look in the trunk, but the lid falls with a bang, Baba wakes up with a start, and Toby hides behind the puppet-theatre. She yells 'Who's there?' but gets no answer, and taking out a revolver from a drawer shoots hysterically at the curtain. There is a moment of stillness, then a spot of blood appears on the white curtain. 'I've killed the ghost,' says Baba. Toby's hands clutch the side of the screen, which collapses with his weight, and he falls dead into the room. 'I've killed the ghost,' says Baba, as Monica pounds on the door and asks to be let in: 'I've killed the ghost.'   H.

## THE TELEPHONE

Opera buffa in one act by Gian-Carlo Menotti, text by the composer. Première Heckscher Theatre, New York, February 18, 1947, with Marilyn Cotlow, Paul Kwartin, conductor Barzin. First performed Ethel Barrymore Theatre, New York, 1947, with Cotlow, Rogier, conductor Balaban; London, Aldwych Theatre, 1948, conductor Balaban; Zürich, 1949, with Oravez, Rehfuss; Hamburg, 1952, with Rothenberger, Günther; London, St. Pancras Town Hall, 1952, with Cantelo, Hemsley.

### CHARACTERS

Lucy........................................Soprano
Ben ........................................Baritone
*Time:* The present                    *Place:* U.S.A.

Most performances of *The Medium*, at any rate those in English, have been preceded by performances of *The Telephone*, the little comedy Menotti wrote for the Ballet Society's first New York presentation of *The Medium*. But *The Telephone* would appear to have a life of its own, and it makes a capital curtain-raiser, a modern *intermezzo* as it were, in the style of Wolf-Ferrari's *Il Segreto di Susanna*.

The scene is Lucy's apartment. The opening music clearly indicates the *opera buffa* nature of the ensuing work. Lucy is busy opening a parcel which Ben has just handed her; 'Oh, just what I wanted,' she exclaims, as she unwraps a piece of abstract sculpture. Ben has something to tell her, he says, before his train goes in an hour's time. He seems to be reaching the point, when the telephone rings. Lucy answers it in a little *arietta* which seems to comprise all the things she always says to all her friends on the telephone. At one point in the conversation she dispenses with words altogether, then, much to Ben's dismay, seems to be about to go through the entire list of enquiries she has already made; but in the end she rings off.

Ben is about to start again, is again interrupted, but this time fortunately by a wrong number. An unfortunate mention of the time prompts Lucy to dial TIM, to discover that it is 'four-fifteen and three and a half seconds'. Another attempt is frustrated by another peal of the telephone bell. This time the conversation is fast and furious, and Lucy seems to quarrel with a boy friend. Ben comforts her, but she goes off to her bedroom to get a handkerchief. Ben thinks wrily of the impossible rival he has to face in the telephone, with its 'hundreds of lives and miles of umbilical cord'. He is about to cut the line when the telephone rings loudly and desperately ('Like a child crying for help,' says the libretto), and Lucy comes in and takes it protectively in her arms.

Lucy must make a call to tell her friend Pamela about the quarrel with George. Again the conversation makes an *arietta*, but this time Ben's voice joins in underneath Lucy's, complaining that he will never get the chance to say what he wants to say. He goes out, much to Lucy's surprise ('I have a feeling he had something on his mind'). At one side of the stage Ben now becomes visible dialling in a telephone box. Presently Lucy's bell rings, and she is confident it must be him. This time he makes no mistake about it and gets the proposal in early, and is immediately accepted. Lucy demands only one thing: that he shall not forget. . . . What? asks Ben; her hands, her eyes, her lips? No, her number, exclaims Lucy, and the opera ends in a skittish waltz tune, in which Ben promises never to forget her number. She dictates it to him. . . .                                                              H.

## THE CONSUL

Opera in three acts by Gian-Carlo Menotti; text by the composer. Première Philadelphia, March 1, 1950, with Neway, Powers, Lane, Marlo, MacNeil, Lishner, McKinley, Jongeyans, conductor Lehman Engel. First performed New York, 1951, by same cast; Cambridge Theatre, London, 1951, with Neway, Powers, Lane, Lishner, Kelley, conductor Schippers; Hamburg, 1951, with Mödl, Koegel, Wasserthal, Ilosvay, Marschner, Meyer-Bremen; Zürich, 1951, with Schulz, Malaniuk, conductor Reinshagen; la Scala, Milan, 1951, with Petrella, Powers, Gardino, Guelfi, Campi, MacKinley, Modesti Cassinelli, conductor Sanzogno; Vienna, 1951, with Zadek, Schürhoff, Rohs, Braun, Jerger, Szemere, Rus, conductor Zallinger; Berlin, 1951, and Munich, 1952, with Borkh; Sadler's Wells, 1954, with Shuard.

### CHARACTERS

John Sorel .................................... Baritone
Magda Sorel, *his wife* ........................ Soprano
The Mother .................................... Contralto

Secret Police Agent ............................. Bass
First and Second Plain-clothes Men ............... Silent
The Secretary ......................... Mezzo-Soprano
Mr. Kofner ......... Bass-Baritone
The Foreign Woman | *waiting* | .......... Soprano
Anna Gomez | *in the* | .......... Soprano
Vera Boronel | *Consul's* | ......... Contralto
The Magician (Nika | *office* |
Magadoff) ............... Tenor
Assan, *friend of John Sorel* .................... Baritone
Voice on the Record ......................... Soprano

*Time:* After World War II          *Place:* Somewhere in Europe

Menotti's first full-length opera deals with a subject which was
familiar to every member of every one of its early non-English-
speaking audiences. Its immediate success was perhaps due in
greater measure to the grippingly theatrical—not to say realistic
—nature of its story than to a comparable power in its music.

The country in which the action takes place is not identified,
any more than is the consulate whose secretary is the embodiment
of every form-ridden bureaucrat in every big city in the world.

Act I.    The first scene takes place in the home of John Sorel.
It is early morning, and the room is empty and dark. The sound
of a gramophone record is heard as the curtain rises, coming from
a café across the street: 'Tu reviendras. . . .' Suddenly the door
is flung open and Sorel staggers into the room, and throws himself into a chair. Magda hears the noise and runs to him, and
immediately starts to bandage the wound which she sees in his
leg. He tells her and the Mother, who has followed her into the
room, the usual story: there was a secret meeting, the police had
been tipped off about it and shot at them as they made their
escape across the roofs, wounding him and killing another.
Magda looks out of the window, and sees the police. John is
helped towards the window, and goes to what is obviously an
agreed hiding-place, leaving his wife and mother to tidy up the
room in preparation for the questioning which must inevitably
follow in a few seconds.

As the secret police agents enter, the Mother is rocking the
cradle, in which lies the little child of Magda and John. She sings
a mournful song of lament for the peace which has vanished from

their lives: 'Shall we ever see the end of all this?' The agent starts to question Magda, who answers non-committally. His threats are not just those of a bully, but carry potential danger in them: 'Courage is often a lack of imagination. We have strange ways to make people talk. Oh, not at all the way you may think. . . . People like you can defy strength, but not the beat of your own heart.'

The agents leave, and Magda and the Mother watch as they arrest somebody opposite and drag him away. John comes down from his hiding-place; he must get away. He tells them that the signal which shall tell them that there is a message from him shall be the breaking of their window by a stone. When this happens, they are to send for Assan, the glass-cutter, who will bring them news. Magda and John bid each other farewell ('Now, O lips, say good-bye'), and their duet becomes a trio when the Mother joins her voice with theirs before the end of the scene.

Scene ii.　The cheerless waiting-room of the Consulate, in one corner of which is the Secretary's desk, and behind it a door leading to the Consul's room. Mr. Kofner comes forward to renew his application for a visa; he has everything now . . . but the photographs turn out to be the wrong size. A 6/8 *allegretto* movement suggests the monotonous, automatic nature of the dealings between applicant and Secretary. As he moves away, the Foreign Woman comes up to the railing which separates the Secretary's desk from the rest of the room, and starts to make an enquiry. She does not know the Secretary's language, and another complication seems to have been introduced, but Mr. Kofner volunteers to act as interpreter. It appears that her daughter ran away with a soldier, who has now left her with a three-months-old baby. The daughter is ill and needs her mother's help; can she have a visa to visit her? Yes, says the Secretary; if she fills out the forms and her application is accepted, she may be able to leave in a couple of months' time. She is stunned by this information, but Mr. Kofner leads her away to fill in the forms.

More people come into the waiting-room, and Magda advances to the desk. The dialogue between her and the Secretary is typical of Menotti's style:

Magda: May I speak to the Consul?

Secretary: No one is allowed to speak to the Consul, the Consul is busy.

Magda: Tell him my name.

Secretary: Your name is a number.

Magda: But my name is Sorel, Magda Sorel. The wife of Sorel, the lover of freedom.

Secretary: Sorel is a name and a name is a number.

Magda: May I speak to the Consul?

Secretary: No one is allowed to speak to the Consul, the Consul is busy.

The duet gains in intensity: 'Explain to the Consul, explain . . . that the web of my life has worn down to one single thread . . . ' But it is still a question of filling in forms and making applications in the customary manner, and Magda is handed a batch of forms as Nika Magadoff comes forward. He starts to do some simple conjuring tricks in an effort to impress the Secretary with his bona fides, but a slow ensemble begins ('In endless waiting-rooms'), and he joins in it. As the curtain falls, it has become a quintet in which Magda, Anna Gomez, Vera Boronel, the Magician and Mr. Kofner express the agony of frustration which their daily attendance at the Consulate entails.

Act II, scene i.     Sorel's house, a month later. The same record is being played in the café opposite. Magda and her Mother are discussing the possibility of getting a visa. When Magda goes out, her Mother tries to cheer up the little baby. She sings him a lullaby, 'I shall find for you shells and stars,' and, after Magda has returned to the room and fallen asleep in a chair, goes out in her turn. Magda stirs in her sleep, and in her nightmare she sees John and the Secretary, whom he introduces to her as his sister. Magda is terrified of her, more particularly since John seems drawn to her. The nightmare comes to an end with a horrible vision of a dead child.

Magda wakes up with a scream, and is comforted by her mother. Suddenly, a stone shatters the glass of the window, and Magda rushes to the telephone to carry out John's instructions. She has no sooner finished talking to Assan than there is a knock at the door, which opens to reveal the Secret Police Agent. He starts to insinuate that there would be no obstacle to her joining her husband if she would only give him the little information about her husband's friends which he wants. She loses control and yells at him to get out, and threatens to kill him if he returns. He is by the door when Assan arrives to mend the window.

Assan tells Magda that John is still hiding in the mountains, and will not leave the country until he knows that his wife has a visa and can follow him. She says that he must be told that arrangements are complete; it is not true, but there is no other way of compelling him to save his own life. Assan agrees to do as he is asked, and leaves the room.

During the scene between Magda and Assan, the Mother suddenly realises that the little half-starved child has died quietly in his sleep. She gives no sign to Magda, but remains quite still by the cradle, not rocking it, not singing to the child. As soon as she looks at her, Magda knows what has happened. She stops her mother weeping ('It is too soon to cry'), but the Mother says she is thinking of John, 'Who will never see his baby again'.

An interlude takes us to scene ii, in the Consulate, a few days later. The Secretary is standing by the filing-cabinet, looking for something; Anna Gomez is by the railing, and the Magician, Vera Boronel, Mr. Kofner, and the Foreign Woman are waiting in the room. The Secretary finds the card and reads: 'Three years in concentration camp. Husband, prisoner; whereabouts, unknown. No documents. I don't see what we can do for you.' It is only one case among many, and there is nothing to do but fill in forms, and try above all to avoid despair.

Magda comes in and asks to jump the queue, but the Magician explains in a kindly but firm way that he has been seven times to the Consulate, and always when his turn came it was time for the Consulate to close; he *must* take his turn now. There is a fairly long scene in which he again demonstrates his professional powers of conjuring and of hypnotism, much to the Secretary's dismay. He puts all the occupants of the waiting-room into a trance, and then makes them dance happily together, until the Secretary becomes quite desperate over the unaccustomed turn events have taken. She begs Magadoff to return everyone to normal, which done he leaves the room.

The others allow Magda to go ahead of them. The Secretary does not remember her until she has looked her up in the card-index, and Magda is frantic with worry and near to despair. She demands to see the Consul but is again refused. Finally, she can bear it no more, and throws self-control to the winds, launching out into a denunciation of the bureaucratic system and the injustice it leads to. The rest of the act is given up to a *scena* for

Magda, with interruptions from the Secretary and the others waiting at the Consulate: 'To this we've come: that men withhold the world from men.' Her outburst is at first directed at the useless questions upon which lives depend: 'What is your name? . . . My name is woman. Age: Still young. Colour of hair: Grey. Colour of eyes: The colour of tears. Occupation: Waiting.' Her passionate indignation is finally summed up in a brave phrase: 'Oh, the day will come, I know, when our hearts aflame will burn your paper chains. Warn the Consul, Secretary . . . .'

The Secretary cannot conceal her own feelings, although she does her best: 'You're being very unreasonable, Mrs. Sorel.' She goes into the Consul's office, saying that she will ask if he can see her just a minute. The improbable happens when she comes out and informs Magda that she may go in when the important visitor who is with him has left. Anticipation rises as two shadows are seen on the glass panel of the door. The visitor shakes hands, but, when he turns into the room, he is seen to be the Secret Police Agent. Magda faints.

Act III, scene i.    The Consulate. Magda is waiting to see the Consul, in spite of the Secretary's warning that the place will be closed in ten minutes' time. Vera Boronel comes in, states her name, and is greeted with something like pleasure by the Secretary; at last there is somebody to whom she can give good news —her papers are through! Again there is an *allegretto* for the mechanical, trivial business of signing papers—even papers that represent the prospect of such happiness as these—and the two women sing happily together: 'All the documents must be signed.'

Assan hurries in, looking for Magda, whom he tells that the news about John is bad; he has heard that his child and his mother are dead, and intends to come back over the frontier to fetch his wife. While the Secretary and Vera Boronel go on signing papers, Magda and Assan try to think of a way of convincing him that he must not come back. Magda thinks she knows one, and writes a note which she confides to Assan, refusing however to tell him what she has written.

Everyone leaves, and presently the Secretary too is ready to go. For a moment she seems to see the faces which have confronted her all day long on the benches in the waiting-room. 'One must not think,' she says. 'Why must there be so many names? Their cases are all alike.' She is about to leave when John rushes into the room, looking behind him to see that he is not being followed. He asks if Magda has been there, and is told he may still catch up with her if he hurries after her. But that he cannot do, he protests, since he was followed to the Consulate by the police, who will not allow him to leave. At that moment, a confused noise is heard outside, and as John pulls out his gun, the Secret Police Agent comes in, followed by two plain-clothes men. John's gun is knocked out of his hand, and, when the Secretary protests that no arrest can be made in the Consulate, the Secret Agent says that Sorel will be coming with them of his own free will, not as an arrested man.

As they leave, the Secretary dials furiously, and when the curtain goes up again on scene ii, after an interlude based on a march rhythm, the telephone can be heard ringing in Mrs. Sorel's room, which she presently enters, though only after the bell is silent. She makes preparations to commit suicide, and turns on the gas.

As she bends over towards the stove with a shawl over her head, the walls dissolve and the figures from the Consulate appear, looking exactly as Magda has known them there. Behind them are John and the Mother, the former in dark clothes, the latter in an old-fashioned wedding-dress. Magda talks to them, and the ghostly chorus sings the march tune of the interlude. Gradually the figures disappear and the music which has gone with them, and all that can be heard is the sound of Magda's deep breathing. Suddenly the telephone begins to ring. Magda stretches out her hand as if to answer it, but her reaction is feeble, and she falls inert over the chair, while the telephone bell continues to ring. The curtain falls as the orchestra gives out the tune associated with Magda's protest at the end of Act II.          H.

# INDEX

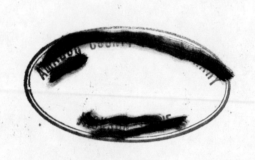